The Greek Empire of Marseille

The Greek Empire of Marseille: Discoverer of Britain, Saviour of Rome

by
Christopher Gunstone

*BA (Hons) History and Archaeology,
ACIM*

Copyright © 2013 by Christopher Gunstone
Published by Silver Shields
www.silvershields.co.uk

All rights reserved. This book or any portion thereof may not be reproduced or used in any manner whatsoever without the express permission of the publisher except for the use of brief quotations embodied in critical reviews and certain other non-commercial uses permitted by copyright law.

Printed by CreateSpace.

First edition July 2013.
Second edition December 2013.

Gunstone. C, *The Greek Empire of Marseille: Discoverer of Britain, Saviour of Rome*, 2nd edition, Silver Shields, 2013.

Subjects:
History > Ancient > General
History / General
History / Greece / Rome / Britain / France / Spain / Iceland / Asia Minor
Social Science / Archaeology
Natural Science / Geography
Natural Science / Astronomy
Natural Science / Earth and Planetary

Includes Bibliography, Biographies, Chronology, Endnotes, References and Index.
579 pages, 106 Illustrations, Maps and Table.

ISBN-10:148123966X

ISBN-13:978-1481239660

૱ ૱

To my Mother and Father for their encouragement and support.

To the explorer in all of us and the excitement of discovering something we did not know.

૱ ૱

Acknowledgements:

Professor Barry Cunliffe's fascinating lecture in London 2003 on the explorer Pytheas: Eleftheria and Parikiaki newspapers for publishing my article of it, which eventually led to this present book.

The cooperation and efficient response from all the numismatic website owners featured in this book is much appreciated.

Professor A. Trevor Hodge for clarification on Apollonides of Massalia during the siege by Julius Caesar and also the permanent gnomon made of masonry in ancient Massalia (Marseille).

Conservateur en chef du patrimoine, Odile Bérard-Azzouz, Musée de L'Éphèbe at Le Cap d'Agde, France for permission to take photographs of the bronze statue L'Éphèbe.

Conservateur en chef, Jean-Louis Coudrot, Musée du Pays Chatillonais for the photographs of the Vix Krator.

Professor Ö. Özyğit, Director of excavations at Phokaia (Foça, Turkey) for a photograph of the ancient city wall.

Dr J. Braybrook, Birkbeck, University of London for an English translation from French on the Greeks at Arles.

Archaeologists: Marta Santos Retolaza, Director, and Elisa Hernández, Emporion site, Ampurias, Spain for their time and up to date information.

Archaeologist Maria Anne Puig Griessenberger, Projecte Museològic, Museu De La Ciudadela de Roses, Rhodus site (Roses), Spain for her time and up to date information.

Dr Philip de Jersey, Guernsey Museum and Art Gallery clarifying references for Massalia coin hoard on Jersey, Channel Islands found in 1875.

Kostas Markos, Grafis, Thessaloniki, Greece.

Anastasia and Heleni, Librarians, Municipal Library (Ethniki Bibliothiki), Thessaloniki, Greece.

Intercollegiate programmes Birkbeck and Kings College London (KCL): Birkbeck Archaeological Society and KCL Classics Society.

Maria Gunstone for a computer.

Sue, Rosina, Paul and Mike, Librarians, Institute of Classical Studies Library, Senate House, University of London.

John Mathews, IT Services, Birkbeck, University of London, for help with Microsoft programmes.

CONTENTS

Acknowledgements ... i

List of Illustrations ... v

Introduction ... 1

Chapter 1 Real History is Reading between the Lines ... 1

Chapter 2 Massalia ... 13
    Greek Cities in the Western Mediterranean ... 74
    Cities Founded by Massalia ... 87
    Massalia's Political Constitution ... 137
    Massalia's Explorers ... 139

Chapter 3 The Greek Phocaeans, Founders of Massalia (Marseille in France) ... 153
    Greeks, Phoenicians and Carthage ... 165

Chapter 4 Pytheas of Massalia the Astronomer and Explorer ... 171
    Massalia–First Measurement ... 172
    The Tregor–Second Measurement ... 175

Chapter 5 Britain is Discovered and Named by Pytheas ... 179
    Pytheas Gives Britain its Name ... 181
    Isle of Man–Third Measurement ... 182
    Isle of Lewis–Fourth Measurement ... 183
    Orcas ... 186

Chapter 6 Shetland Islands to the Frozen Sea ... 189
    Shetland Islands-Fifth Measurement ... 189
    The Island of Thule ... 190
    The North Pole ... 192

Chapter 7 Abalus the Amber Island ... 195

Chapter 8 Pytheas Writes His Book *On the Ocean* ... 199

Chapter 9 Alexander the Great, Carthage and the Pillars of Hercules ... 203
    Mediterranean Campaign ... 206

Chapter 10 Pytheas of Massalia: Overlooked and Revalue ... 211
    Polybius ... 211
    Strabo ... 214
    The Sources ... 217

Chapter 11   The Return Journey to Massalia   219
   Pytheas's Crew   220
   Ship   220
   Local Boats   221
   Length of Voyage   222
   Latitude   223

Chapter 12   Massalia Ally of Rome   225
   First Treaty between Rome and Carthage 509 B.C.   226
   Hannibal   231
   Battle of the Ebro, Spain   233

Chapter 13   Massalia Capitulates 49 B.C.   251
   Siege by Julius Caesar   254
   Naval Battles   255
   Massalia Attempts to Reclaim its Territories   266

Chapter 14   Julius Caesar, Britain and Pytheas of Massalia   273

Chapter 15   Continuity within Change   277
   Greek Language in Massalia   292
   Attack by Greeks on Massalia A.D. 848   301
   Eleventh Century A.D. Greeks at Marseille and Arles   304
   Greeks at Marseille (Massalia) in the Nineteenth Century A.D.   317

APPENDIX   325
   Massalia and Agricola the Roman Governor of Britain   325
   Island of Thoule (Iceland)   325
   Casserterides–the Tin Islands   327
   Founding a Greek Colony   327
   Oracles   329
   Distances   331
   Sailing Times   332
   Early Explorers of the Atlantic   333
   Pillars of Hercules (Herakles)   335
   The Great Library of Alexandria and Pergamum Library   336

Chronology and Biography   339

Notes   352

Bibliography   511

Index   551

List of Illustrations

Figures and Credits.

Front Cover
'Captains' by artist Andreas Müller in Braun and Schneider, *Historic Costumes in Pictures*, Plate 3 Ancient Greece, series 1861-90, reissued by Dover Publications, 1975. ISBN 0-486-23150-X. By permission of Dover Publications, <www.doverpublications.com>. Cover design by Createspace.

Back Cover
Massalia silver drachma (so-called heavy drachma), c. 390 B.C. Obverse: head of Artemis facing right, hair adorned with sprigs of olive, earring and necklace from the museum Cabinet des Medallions, Bibliothèque nationale de France (BNF), Paris, France. By permission of photographer Marie-Lan Nguyen, <jastrow@pip.pip.org> ©Marie-Lan Nguyen/Wikipedia Commons, under Creative Commons Attribution-2.5 Generic (CC BY 2.5). Cover design by CreateSpace.

Figure 1.
Map of the Greek and Phoenician settlements from Spain to the Black Sea around 550 B.C.
1 = Ionian Greeks, 2 = Doric Greeks, 3 = Other Greeks, 4 = Phoenicians.

Figure 2.
A model of the ancient Greek city of Massalia (Marseille) in the Musée d'Histoire Marseille.

Figure 3.
From one of the three large temples this Ionic capital, end of sixth century B.C. was found in Massalia (Marseille) and is 1.80 m wide. The temple would have been of considerable size when compared to a capital on the Propylaia at Athens that is 1.65 metres wide. Photographed at the Musée d'Histoire de Marseille.

Figure 4.
Amphitheatre, Marseille (Massalia). Excavated in 1945, four rows of stone seating from the Roman era that probably replaced a Greek amphitheatre made of wood. From Woodhouse, A. G. *The Greeks of the West*, Thames & Hudson, 1962, Plate 30, photograph by Professor F. Benoit. By permission of Thames & Hudson.

Figure 5.
Massalia's Treasury at Delphi is the first building after the round Tholos on the left and the second building after is the Doric Treasury.

Photograph 'View of the Tholos' by Francis E. Luisier. Wikipedia, Creative Commons Attribution 2.0 Generic (CC BY 2.0) licence.

Figure 6.
The entrance to Vieux-Port Marseille from the sea, previously called the Harbour of Lacydon of the ancient Greek city of Massalia.

Figure 7.
Growth of Massalia from 600 B.C.–100 B.C. Based on illustrations of Dessin d'Henri Treziny and Marc Bourion in Bizot, B. et al, *Marseille Antique,* Éditions du Patrimonie, 2007.

Figure 8.
Base of a Greek tower overlooking the end of the Horn of Lacydon clearly outlined by new harbour walls constructed first century A.D. ending on the left where the main road from Italy into the city passed through a double gate-house of the second century B.C.

Figure 9.
Marseille, side view of a Greek tower. On the right is the line of harbour wall ending with road from Italy, right to left, going into the city. On the left the remains of the Greek city wall fortifications second century B.C. and an outer Roman wall fifth century A.D.

Figure 10.
Facing the ancient city of Massalia. In the foreground are the harbours walls of the Horn of Lacydon.

Figure 11.
Carved stone from an earlier building reused into the first century A.D. harbour wall of the Horn of Lacydon.

Figure 12.
A seagull on the ancient city wall of Massalia by the Horn of Lacydon.

Figure 13.
Marseille panorama, on the left is the Gulf of Lion; middle Vieux-Port (Harbour of Lacydon). The darker roofs shows the old city's triangular shape. The Horn was to the right of the harbour, filled in and built upon in the seventh century A.D.

Figure 14.
Amphora Massaliote late fifth–early fourth century B.C. photographed at the Musée des Docks Romains, Marseille.

Figure 15.
Ionian bowls sixth century B.C. black type A (Villard and Vallet) and Ceramic bowl light colour with handles. Photographed at the Musée des Docks Romains, Marseille.

Figure 16.
Attic Black figure pottery on red background second half of the fifth century B.C. photographed at the Musée des Docks Romains, Marseille.

Figure 17.
Small Kantharos of the early Hellenistic period: Greek graffito says 'tes Hygies' which means 'of Health' (Hygieia being the Greek goddess of healing), photographed at the Musée des Docks Romains, Marseille.

Figure 18.
Vix Krater c. 530 B.C. found in a burial mound at the cemetery of Mt. Laissos. The largest and finest Greek Krater found so far. Photograph from and by permission of the Musée Chatillon-sur-Seine. <http://www.musee-vix.fr/fr/>, viewed on 11 November 2010.

Figure 19.
Vix Krater c. 530 B.C. Musée Chatillon-sur-Seine in Burgundy, France. The Krater held 1,100 litres of wine the equivalent today of 1,466 bottles of wine at 75cl each. Photograph from and by permission of the Musée Chatillon-sur-Seine. <http://www.musee-vix.fr/fr>, viewed on 11 November 2010.

Figure 20.
Map of the Celtic tribes around Massalia (Marseille) c. first century B.C.

Figure 21.
'Auriol type' coins found at Auriol near Massalia (Marseille). Auriol types may have been minted in Gaul or Asia Minor. They were divisions of the Phocaean drachma. Hemiobol, Milesian type c. 475-465 B.C. Obverse: head of Apollo facing left, pronounced hair pattern on head and on back of the neck/reverse: crab. Weight 0.75 g. By permission of ogn-numismatique Ref. 3187.

<http://www.muenzauktion.com/crinon/item.php5?id=2822&lang=jp&psid=592bd763ea12c81ab39188fdc8df27e3>, viewed on 13 October 2010.

Figure 22.
'Auriol type' hemiobol, Milesian type. 475–465 B.C. Obverse: head of Aphrodite facing left/reverse: incuse-hollow square. Weight 1.11 g. By permission of ogn-numismatique Ref. 3185.
<http://www.ogn-numismatique.com/article.asp?langue=fr&article=3185>, viewed on 13 October 2010.

Figure 23.
Obol c. 475–465 B.C. Obverse: head of Athena, with Corinthian helmet, facing left/reverse: incuse irregular hollow square. Weight 0.90g. By permission of Joseph Sermarini, Forum Ancient Coins, <http://www.forumancientcoins.com/gallery/displayimage.php?album=4094&pos=38>, viewed on 1 February 2013.

Figure 24.
'Auriol type' tritemorion, Phocaean type 470–460 B.C. Obverse: ram's head facing right/reverse: cross recessed, full of cross points. Weight 0.23 g. By permission of ogn-numismatique,
<http://www.muenzauktion.com/crinon/item.php5?id=2822&lang=jp&psid=592bd763ea12c81ab39188fdc8df27e3>, viewed on 15 November 2010.

Figure 25.
Massalia 450–400 B.C. Obverse: helmeted head facing right, with circle and four rays emblem/reverse: wheel of 4 spokes. Weight 0.94 g. By permission of KUNKER Coins owned by Fritz Rudolf Kuenker GmbH & Co. KG. Website <www.kuenker.de> viewed on 19 October 2010, Lot 7037 Auction 168, <http://www.acsearch.info/record.html?id=382105>, viewed on 19 October 2010.

Figure 26.
Massalia AR obol *circa* fourth century B.C. Obverse: youthful head of Apollo facing left/reverse: wheel of four spokes with letters MA. Weight 0.66 gm.

By permission of Classical Numismatic Group Inc. <www.cngcoins.com>; <www.historicalcoins.com>; <www.wildwinds.com>, viewed on 5 November 2010.

Figure 27.
Massalia AR obol, 350–215 B.C. Obverse: Apollo facing right/reverse: wheel of 4 spokes with letters MA. Weight 0.60g. By permission of KUNKER Coins owned by Fritz Rudolf Kuenker GmbH & Co. KG. Website <www.kuenker.de>, viewed on 19 October 2010.

Figure 28.
Massalia obol, fourth century B.C. Head of the God Lacydon (source of the water for the Harbour of Lacydon) facing right with letters MASSALIATAN, and letters on left/reverse: wheel of four spokes, with letter M. Weight 0.80g. In this specimen the legend is practically complete with the name of the city. Ref. 83195.

By permission of Alain Poinsignon <www.poinsignon-numismatique.com>, viewed on 15 November 2010.

Figure 29.
Massalia silver heavy drachma early fourth century B.C. Obverse: head of Artemis facing right, hair adorned with sprigs of olive, earring and necklace/reverse: prowling lion facing right, with letters above ΜΑΣΣΑ (MASSA) for Massalia (Marseille) from the museum Cabinet des Medallions, BNF, Paris, France.

By permission of photographer Marie-Lan Nguyen, <jastrow@pip.pip.org> ©Marie-Lan Nguyen/Wikipedia Commons, under Creative Commons Attribution-2.5 Generic (CC BY 2.5).

Figure 30.
Massalia, heavy bronze c. 220–215 B.C. Obverse: helmeted head of Athena facing right/reverse: tripod in front and head of Apollo behind facing left with letters on right ΜΑΣ (MAS). Weight 7.97.g. By permission of Anthony Moi, *D'aqua-sextius a Massalia,* <http://massaliote.blog-4ever.com>, viewed on 24 November 2009.

Figure 31
Massalia, AR drachma, second century B.C. Obverse: head of Artemis diademed and draped facing right, bow and quiver at shoulder/reverse: lion prowling facing right, ΜΑΣΣΑ (MASSA) at top, monogram and K below, ΛΙΗΤΩΝ (LIHTON) in exergue. Weight 2.62 gm.

By permission of Classical Numismatic Group Inc. <www.cngcoins.com>, viewed on 19 October 2010. <http://www.wildwinds.com/coins/greece/gaul/massalia/Depeyrot_31.txt>.

Figure 32.
Massalia c. 200-150 B.C. drachma, silver, 2.69 g 12. Head of Artemis facing right, wearing olive wreath, pendant earring and necklace, behind neck bow and quiver/reverse: lion walking to right with head slightly lowered, letters ΜΑΣΣΑ (MASSA) at top, in exergue H H.

By permission of Nomosag.com <http://www.acsearch.info/search.html?search=similar%3A172152#8>, viewed on 1 February 2013.

Figure 33.
Massalia, large bronze with bull, 200–49 B.C. Group 1, series 3, LT.1515 variant. Obverse: Apollo facing left/reverse: butting bull facing right, below letters ΜΑΣΣΑΛΙΗΤ (MASSALIT), above object. 11.90gm.

By permission of Thierry Dumez Numismatique, MA Shops, <http://www.ma-shop.com/dumez/item.php5?id=1720&lang=en&PHPSESSID=e150e177ea4492b978555b4 4a79b36c9>, viewed on 14 November 2010.

Figure 34.
Massalia, AR brockage drachma, second to first century B.C. Obverse: lion standing facing right, letter T below. APP in exergue/reverse: incuse of obverse. Weight 2.44 gm. By permission of CNG Classical Numismatics Group Inc. <www.cngcoins.com>, viewed on 19 October 2010.

Figure 35.
Massalia, silver AR tetrobol, 130–121 B.C. Artemis facing right bow and quiver over shoulder/reverse: lion walking left, above letters MASSA and below ΑΛ (AL) in exergue. Weight 2.61 gm. By permission of <www.wildwinds.com>, viewed on 19 October 2010.

Figure 36.
Massalia, silver MA obol, c. 121–82 B.C. Anepigraphic head of juvenile facing left (river god Lacydon?) horned, wavy hair drawn back. Reverse: letters M in 3rd and A in 4th quarter in wheel of 4 spokes with central hub, weight 0.67 g. <http://www.ma-shops.com/cgb/item.php5?id=18158&lang=en>, viewed on 9 May 2013.

Figure 37.
Massalia. AE coin after 49 B.C. Obverse: helmeted head of Athena facing right with letters MA/reverse: Athena standing facing left with spear raised and shield. Weight 2.96 g 8 h. Size 11 mm. By permission of <www.coinarchive.com>, viewed on 7 September 2009.

Figure 38.
Massalia 'AI' AE13, bronze, after 49 B.C. Obverse: Athena in a Corinthian helmet facing right/reverse: eagle, head facing right. Weight 2.6 grams, size 13 mm. By permission of CNG Classical Numismatic Group Inc., <www.cngcoins.com>, <http://wildwinds.com/coins/greece/gaul/massalia/i.html>, viewed 5 November 2010.

Figure 39.
Massalia. AE after 49 B.C. Obverse: helmeted head of Athena facing right, with letter M/reverse: lion facing left, Letters D above and P below. Weight 3.02 g, 6 h. Size 12 mm. By permission of CNG Classical Numismatic Group Inc., <www.cngcoins.com>. <http://www.coinarchives.com/a/lotviewer.php?LotID=313594&AucID=563&Lot=22>, viewed 7 September 2009.

Figure 40.
Massalia. AE coin issued after 49 B.C. Obverse: helmeted head of Athena facing left/reverse: galley facing right. Weight 1.92 g 9 h. Size 12 mm. By permission of CNG Classical Numismatic Group Inc. <www.cngcoins.com>. <http://www.coinarchives.com/a/lotviewer.php?LotID=313594&AucID=563&Lot=25>, viewed on 7 September 2009.

Figure 41.
Map of Phocaean/Massaliote cities in Spain, France and Monaco.

Figure 42.
Corinthian helmet 650–625 B.C. dredged up from the Guadalette River in Spain in 1938. Permission and photograph from the Museo Arqueológico Municipal de Jerez de la Frontera.

Figure 43.
Aouenion (Avignon) drachma, second to first century B.C. Obverse: head facing left/reverse: boar facing left with letters above AYOE. Aouenion produced silver drachma, mite, and small bronze coins. By permission of Sebestian Arcas. <http://monnaiesdemarseille.blog4ever.com>, viewed on 5 November 2009).

Figure 44.
Aouenion (Avignon) obol, second to first century B.C. silver coin. Obverse: head of Apollo wearing laurels facing left/reverse: wheel 4 spokes, in each quarter one letter A, O, Y, E for Aouenion (Avignon). Aouenion produced silver drachma, mite, and small bronze coins. By permission of Sebestian Arcas. <http://monnaiesdemarseille.blog4ever.com>, viewed on 5 November 2009.

Figure 45.
Monaco (Heracles Monoikos). Either Phocaea or Massalia founded a colony here in the sixth century B.C. On lower right, the square, on the promontory begins with the royal palace of the Prince of Monaco. The Greek acropolis is under the palace area. At either side are the favoured position of two harbours on the right is the Port Fontvieille and on the left the larger Port Hercule (Hercules). Photograph by George Dick. Image from <http://en.wikipedia.org/wiki/File:MonacoLibreDroits.jpg> under 'GNU Free Documentation licence 1.2 version or later' and 'Creative Commons Attribution Share-Alike 3.0 Unported'.

Figure 46.
Greek bronze statue L'Éphèbe d'Agde second century B.C found in the River Hérault in front of the Cathedral Saint Etienne in Agde, France. Characteristic style of the sculptor Lysippus thought to be Alexander the Great when he was about sixteen and Regent of Macedonia. Displayed in the museum of underwater archaeology Musée de L'Éphèbe at Le Cap d'Agde in France. Photographed by permission of the Musée de L'Éphèbe. <http://www.capdagde.com/le_musee_de_l_ephebe-modele01-1678-FR-DECOUVRIR.html>.

Figure 47.
Greek bronze statue L'Éphèbe d'Agde second century B.C. back view on display at the museum of underwater archaeology Musée de L'Éphèbe at Le Cap d'Agde, France. Photographed by permission of the Musée de L'Éphèbe. <http://www.capdagde.com/le_musee_de_l_ephebe-modele01-1678-FR-DECOUVRIR.html>.

Figure 48.
Greek bronze statue L'Éphèbe d'Agde second century B.C. side view showing diadem around head and Macedonian style of holding clock around left shoulder and arm on display at the museum of underwater archaeology Musée de L'Éphèbe at Le Cap d'Agde, France. Photographed by permission of the Musée de L'Éphèbe. <http://www.capdagde.com/le_musee_de_l_ephebe-modele01-1678-FR-DECOUVRIR.html>.

Figure 49.
Greek bronze statue L'Éphèbe d'Agde second century B.C. Front view: with the Macedonian style of holding a cloak around the left shoulder and arm on display at the museum of underwater archaeology Musée de L'Éphèbe at Le Cap d'Agde, France. Photographed by permission of the Musée de L'Éphèbe. <http://www.capdagde.com/le_musee_de_l_ephebemodele01-1678-FR-DECOUVRIR.html>.

Figure 50.
Agde (Agathe Tyche), aerial view. The ancient Greek city was along the riverside, left of the bridge follow the green tree line to right then before the end, take the road straight back to the river. The L'Éphèbe d'Agde Greek bronze statue was found in the river in front of the riverside Cathedral (right of bridge). Upper right is the extinct volcano Mont St. Loup and beyond the Mediterranean.

Figure 51.
Part of the medieval city wall of Agde (Agathe Tyche) above the Greek walls.

Figure 52.
Sant Marti d'Empúries, Spain (paleopolis the first Greek city of Emporion). City wall next to the church with Roman large cut stones at base fitted together with no mortar, next to the supposed site of an earlier Greek temple Artemis of Ephesus.

Figure 53.
Saint Marti d'Empúries, Spain (paleopolis first Geek city of Emporion), medieval city wall and well.

Figure 54.
Saint Marti d'Empúries (paleopolis the first Geek city of Emporion), Spain: the medieval well with a reused white marble stone from an earlier period?

Figure 55.
Emporion, Spain c. 450–425 B.C. AR trihemiobol. Obverse: two confronted Sphinxes their heads joined in janiform style/reverse: rough incuse. Weight 0.89 g. By permission of CNG Classical Numismatic Group Inc., Ref: 770313 <http://cngcoins.com/Coin.aspx?CoinID=100887>, viewed on 20 November 2010.

Figure 56.
Emporion, Spain, silver trihemiobol c. 450–425 B.C. Obverse: man-headed bull facing left/reverse: rough incuse. Weight 1.09 g. By permission of CNG Classical Numismatic Group Inc., <www.cngcoins.com>, <http://www.acsearch.info/record.html?id=38567>, viewed on 20 November 2010.

Figure 57.
Emporion, AR mint, drachma, third century B.C. Persephone facing left, city name ΕΜΠΟΡΙΤΩΝ (EMPORITON). Reverse: horse standing facing right, above Nike (Victory); Die Axis in numbers:7 Diameter:40 Weight: 4.83 gm. ID: SNGuk_0902_0013. SNG Vol: IX British Museum, Part II, Mint: Emporion, <http://www.sylloge-nummorum-graecorum.org>, viewed on 2 February 2013

Figure 58.
Emporion, Spain c. 241 B.C. AR drachma. Head of Arethusa facing right with three dolphins around/reverse: Pegasus flying right, with city name ΕΜΠΟΡΙΤΩΝ (EMPORITON). Weight 4.54 g. By permission of KUNKER Coins owned by Fritz Rudolf Kuenker GmbH & Co. KG.
Website: <www.kuenker.de>. Lot 8095, auction 153, viewed on 20 October 2010.
http://www.acsearch.info/record.html?id=204227

Figure 59.
Emporion, Spain. Attic black figure libation and perfume vases, terracotta dove (symbol of life) from tomb 164 Bonjoan necropolis sixth century B.C.

Figure 60.
Emporion, Spain. Red figure krater for mixing wine and water fifth to fourth century B.C.

Figure 61.
Emporion, Spain. Hellenistic Breakwater constructed in the second century B.C. for the ancient Greek harbour. A length of 80 metres still survives.

Figure 62.
Emporion, Spain: walls with cyclopean masonry. The base of south gate tower built in the second century B.C. The previous earlier fourth century B.C. southern wall was dismantled and extended 25 metres forwards reusing the stones.

Figure 63.
Emporion, Spain. Greek mosaic second to first century B.C with the word ΗΔΥΚΟΙΤΟΣ (how sweet it is to be reclined) and was likely to have been a small banqueting hall for *symposia*.

Figure 64.
Emporion, Spain. Temple and statue of Asclepius, god of medicine, on a white tesserae floor as viewed from the acropolis. In front on the left are cisterns for the ritual cleaning of people that came to be healed. The temple underwent dismantling and remodelling in fourth and second century B.C.

Figure 65.
Emporion, Spain, three cities: 1. Original Greek paleopolis on an island: 2. Greek neapolis on the mainland: 3. Hellenistic Breakwater (remains) originally longer and opposite another extending out from the paleopolis: 4. Harbour: 5. Roman city: 6. Present day coastline: 7. River Fluvia.

Figure 66.
Greek city of Rhodus, Iberia (Spain). The new city wall made of granite constructed during the Second Punic War 218–201 B.C.

Figure 67.
Greek city of Rhodus, Iberia (Spain). New commercial district 'Barri Hel-lenistic' third century to 195 B.C. built opposite and west of the old city across the River Rec Fondo and connected by a bridge.

Figure 68.
Greek city of Rhodus, Iberia (Spain) 375–195 B.C. Posts mark out the coastline at that period: the medieval monastery is on the hill of Turó de Santa Maria on top of the original city: to the right is the excavation spoil heap next to a second century B.C. city wall.

Figure 69.
The Greek city of Rhodus (Rhode now Roses in Spain) starting minting silver coins c. 250 B.C. Obverse: a head of Persephone facing left, letters on left/reverse: a rose in full bloom. From Cabinet des Medallions, BNF, Paris, France. Photograph by PHGCOM, Creative Commons Attributions-Share 3.0 Unported license.

Figure 70.
Map of Greek city of Olbia, Gaul (France) 350 B.C.

Figure 71.
Remains of the Main Gate guarded by zigzag wall and two towers, north-western section of the wall, Greek city of Olbia, Gaul (France) 350 B.C.

Figure 72.
City Wall south-western section of the Greek city of Olbia, Gaul (France) 350 B.C.

Figure 73.
Some of the 36 blocks of houses in the Hippodamian grid-iron layout but unusually within a square city plan. Greek city of Olbia, Gaul (France) 350 B.C.

Figure 74.
The city well and main street of the Greek city of Olbia, Gaul (France) 350 B.C.

Figure 75.
Temple of Artemis by the north-eastern wall, Greek city of Olbia, Gaul (France) 350 B.C.

Figure 76.
Coin of Antipolis (Antibes), c. 44–43 B.C. small bronze. Obverse Clerc gives Aphrodite while Maurel is definite with head of Apollo facing right/reverse: Nike (Victory) standing crowning a trophy to the right with the inscriptions ANTIP(OLITON) and LEPI(DOS) also written in Greek. Website <www.dumez-numismatique.com> Ref.1495, viewed on 14 December 2009.

Figure 77.
Antibes, France founded by the Phocaean Greeks c. sixth century B.C. as Antipolis.

Figure 78.
Stone blocks of the Greek city sea wall visible at the bottom. Antibes, France originally the Phocaean Greek city of Antipolis founded c. sixth century B.C.

Figure 79.
Stone blocks from the Greek period at the bottom corner section of the sea wall. Antibes, France originally the Phocaean Greek city of Antipolis founded c. sixth century B.C.

Figure 80.
Nicaea (Nice, France) Phocaean Greeks founded the city c. sixth century B.C. beside and/or on top of the promontory. Their harbour could have been on either side.

Figure 81.
Port de Nice Harbour by the side of the Greek acropolis of Nicaea (Nice, France).

Figure 82.
The acropolis of Nicaea (Nice) with a medieval cathedral ruin tenth century A.D. possibly on top of the earlier Greek settlement. The acropolis remained a strategic fort until dismantled in A.D. 1706.

Figure 83.
Kylix, depicting a 'round-built merchant-ship' and pentaconter, the size is 8 inches diameter and 3.5 inches high. This drinking cup was Attic made 520-500 B.C. and found in a tomb in Vulci Italy. Now on display at the British Museum vase number B436.
<http://www.britishmuseum.org/research/search_the_collection_database/search_object_details.aspx?objecti d=399714&partid=1&searchText=ancient+greek+pottery+ships+pirate+merchant&fromADB.C.=ad&toADB .C.=ad&numpages=10&orig=%2fresearch%2fsearch_the_collection_database.aspx&currentPage=1>, viewed on 29 October 2010.

Figure 84.
Phocaean coin Electrum (amalgam of gold and silver). Phocaea was one of the first states to use coins after its attributed invention in Lydia in the seventh century B.C. The earliest Electrum coin hoard of 19 in a pot was found by the British Museum excavators in Ephesus next to 74 other coins buried in the foundation of the Temple of Artemis c. 600 B.C. Lydia between 560–547 B.C. changed to separate gold and silver coins. Silver coins spread from Lydia and Ionia to other parts of Asia Minor.
<http://www.britishmuseum.org/explore/themes/money/the_origins_of_coinage.aspx>, viewed on 21 November 2010. Obverse: seal (pun on the name of Phocaea φωκη=Seal) swimming facing left, and catching an octopus. Around the seal are two rectangles and another object/reverse: incuse with an emblem/map of Phocaea? By permission of Jean-Albert Chevillon, <http://numis-ext-occ.monsite.orange.fr>.

Figure 85.
The ancient city walls of Phokaia (Phocaea) 590–580 B.C. Permission and photograph by Professor Ö. Özyğit, Director of excavations at Phokaia (Foça, Turkey).

Figure 86.
Broken stone base of an honorary statue upside down. Photographed on 18 June 2011, a Greek inscription for Lucius Vibius Eumenes, c. first century B.C. to second century A.D. Phokaia (Phocaea).

Figure 87.
Close up of partial Greek inscription for Lucius Vibius Eumenes, c. first century B.C. to second century A.D. Phokaia (Phocaea).

Figure 88.
Temple of Athena western podium walls, first quarter sixth century B.C. Phokaia (Phocaea).

Figure 89.
Excavated walls at the side of the acropolis of Phokaia (Phocaea): the stone blocks are similar and finely made as those of the city wall.

Figure 90.
A finely carved stone, Phokaia (Phocaea).

Figure 91.
The city wall of ancient Phokaia (Phocaea) peninsula: beneath the acropolis facing the sea, on below right are niches for the goddess Cybele.

Figure 92.
Map of the known world in fourth century B.C. reconstructed from details in the fragments of the geography *Ges Peridos* by Hecataeus of Miletus. Some versions include the Tin Islands somewhere in the North Atlantic. By permission of Martin, Geoffrey. J. *All Possible Worlds: A History of Geographical Ideas*, Oxford, 2005, Fig. 2.

Figure 93.
Map of Pytheas of Massalia's voyage of discovery c. 320s B.C. Various routes are available, up the River Rhône, or Narbo along the river to Bordeaux on the Atlantic coast, or through the Straits of Gibraltar (The Pillars of Hercules) to where Pytheas took measurements and observations. 1= Massalia (Marseille), 2=Tregor, Brittany, 3 = Isle of Man, 4 = Isle of Lewis, 5 = Shetland Islands, 6 = Island of Thule (Iceland).
Map outline based on Philip & Son, Octopus Publishing.

Figure 94.
Massalia minted this coin for the imperator and Roman Consul Gaius Valerius Flaccus in 85 B.C. By permission of <www.wildwinds.com>.

Figure 95.
'Captains' by artist Andreas Müller in Braun and Schneider, *Historic Costumes in Pictures*, Plate 3 Ancient Greece, series 1861-90, reissued by Dover Publications, 1975. ISBN 0-486-23150-X. By permission of Dover Publications, <www.doverpublications.com>.

Figure 96.
The siege of Massalia 49 B.C. The sea, marshes, ravines, high walls and towers protected Massalia. Arrows indicate the main areas of attack by the Romans. In addition thirty mines were tunnelled to the city walls. Based on illustrations from Hermary, A. Hesnard, A. and Tréziny, H. *Marseille Grecque: La cite phocéenne (600–49 av. J-C)*, Editions Errance, 1999, and also Dodge, Lieutenant Colonel. T. A. *Caesar*, Greenhill Books, 1995, p. 475.

Figure 97.
The siege of Massalia as described by Vitruvius. Roman strategies and Greek counter measures. Based on Rowland, I. D. *Vitruvius: Ten Books on Architecture*, Cambridge University Press, 1999.

Figure 98.
Silver Denarius coin issued in Rome by Julius Caesar's moneyer L. Hostilius Saserna in 48 B.C. is thought to commemorate Julius Caesar's victory in Gaul and Massalia in 49 B.C. Obverse: head of Gallia facing right and Carnyx behind/reverse: goddess Ephesian Artemis standing holding spear and leaping stag. Name on left SASERNA (clockwise upwards) and vertically downwards on right L.HOSTILIVS. Weight 3.66 gm. By permission of <www.coinarchives.com>, viewed on 7 September 2009. Also found as Example 15 <www.wildwinds.com/coins/sear5/s0419.html>, viewed on 26 May 2013.

Figure 99.
Massalia mint 44–43 B.C. AR silver Denarius with Pompey the Great facing right inscription NEPTVNI (Neptune), trident on right and dolphin below head facing right/reverse: inscription Q. NASIDIVS, 'ornate galley, advancing right with bank of rowers under full sail; on the prow stands the hortator, and in the stern is seated a man guiding the rudder; six rayed star in upper left field', made and issued in Massalia by Pompey's son Pompeius Sextus. Weight 3.73 g, 6 h. 'Coins of this issue do not bear the title *praefectus classis et orae maritimae* (commander-in-chief of the fleet and of the sea coasts) awarded to Sextus by the Senate in April 43 B.C. indicating a prior striking date'. Sextus was in Massalia keeping a safe distance while watching the

volatile political events in Rome. By permission of CNG Classical Numismatic Group <www.cngcoins.com/Coin.aspx?CoinID=115032>, viewed on 4 September 2010.

Figure 100.
Engraving Marseille 1575, Braun and Hogenberg, *Civitas Orbis Terrarum*, vol. II–12. admitted to Sebastian Munster and first published in the 1575 edition of Munster's *Cosmographia*. The city wall extends beyond the Horn, which had been filled in during the seventh century A.D. By permission from Map copyright of The National Library of Israel, Eran Laor Cartographic Collection, 'Shapell Family Digitization Project and the Hebrew University of Jerusalem', Department of Geography-Historic Cities Research Project. <http://historic-cities.huji.ac.il/> *Cities in the World* site.

Figure 101.
Both spellings of Marseille in Greek and Italian, Massalia and Marsiglia, appear on the Greek label of Formil washing machine liquid detergent with special fragrance from the soap SAVONNERIE MARSELLA.

Figure 102.
A beautifully decorated small café **'En Suisse Le Palais du Roi'**, 1 Arr. Rue des Feuillants corner of Rue Canébiere, Marseille. According to the chef decorated in 1889 with tiles illustrating the arrival of the Phocaean ships and the legend of the foundation of Marseille with King Nannus, Glyptis and Protis complete with columns and Pan-Athenaia surround at top. The manufacturer's name on the tiles was Gilardon i Fils & Cie Ceramistes, Choisy-le-roi, J. B. Pons & Cie agents Marseille. Photographed 17 July 2009.

Postscript
The following four figures are a must and in the only space available for this second edition.

Figure 103, page 548.
Massalia AE bronze coins found in Kent at Tilmanstone: Apollo/bull, Greek letters above MA[Σ]: and at Minster-in-Thanet, Apollo/bull, with Greek letters above MAΣ. By permission of David Holman.

Figure 104, page 548.
Sixth century B.C. Greek Corinthian helmets dredged up from the: Guadalquivir estuary Huelva, Spain, permission from Museo Arqueológico Nacional, Madrid, Spain. <http://ceres.mcu.es/pages/Main> viewed 27 Nov 2013 copyright <fotografia.man@mcu.es>: and from the Ria Huelva, Academia de la Historia-Collecion Madrid, copyright <www.superstock.co.uk>.

Figure 105, page 549.
A sixth century B.C. bronze Greek Corinthian helmet uncovered in Baux-de-Provence, France. By permission of Dominique Garcia.< https://www.academia.edu/4457711/Le_casque_corinthien_des_Baux-de-Provence> viewed 25 November 2013.

Figure 106, page 555.
Cast bronze coin found in Kent, second century BC, prototype for British potin coins. Apollo/bull with Greek letters above MAΣΣAΛ[I] for Massalia. By permission of Rod Blunt and finder Mike Jameson. <http://www.ukdfd.co.uk/ukdfddata/showrecords.php?product=20157&cat=52> viewed 29 November 2013.

Table 1, (in Chapter 11, section Latitude). Measurements taken by Pytheas of Massalia on his Atlantic voyage in the fourth century B.C. and converted into latitudes by the mathematical astronomer Hipparkhos of Nikaia (Hipparchus of Nicaea, Bithynia, now Iznik in Turkey) second century B.C.

Introduction

'The sea frequented by the Greeks, that beyond the Pillars of Hercules, which is called the Atlantic' (Herodotus, *Histories*, Bk. I. 203)

The Greek city of Massalia (Marseille) founded several Greek cities in France, Monaco, Spain and Corsica. Among those from its empire still surviving today are:

Le Brusc, Agde, Antibes, Nice, Monaco, Sant Marti d'Empúries, Roses, Benidorm, Alicante and Aléria (Corsica).

From its earliest foundations Greek Massalia (Marseille) became a loyal ally of a then small state called Rome when it was still ruled by kings, assisting them to grow in many wars and crucially so against the formidable Celts and arch-rival Carthage. Massalia rescued the Roman Republic from starvation and extinction by raising and adding to the ransom for the Gauls to leave Rome under siege in 390 B.C.

The story of Massalia has been overlooked as most attention focuses on easily available sources for events in mainland Greece with Athens and Sparta, and Alexander the Great's spectacular conquests and explorations in the East. Massalia had an impact on civilising the barbaric southern Gauls (Celts) from fierce warring nations to living in walled cities, farming, and the rule of law to settle disputes. The Greek legacy on their economy is still crucial to France and Spain today having introduced the cultivation of olive trees and the grapevine for wine.

Greek culture laid the foundations of our own, but little did we know that it also discovered, explored and gave Britain its name quite literally putting us on the map. In Marseille there is a modern bronze plaque set into the promenade with the inscription 'Here c. 600 B.C. landed Greek sailors from Phocaea, a Greek city of Asia Minor. They founded Marseille, and from there Civilisation spread through to the West'.

Πυθέας ὁ Μασσαλιώτη Pytheas of Massalia (Marseille)

Pytheas of Massalia was a Greek astronomer, scientist and explorer. He made a dramatic voyage of discovery into the Atlantic during the fourth century B.C. The story became overlooked for centuries until the President of the Royal Geographical Society Sir Clements Markham's article in 1898. [1] Growing interest from scholars like Christina Horst Roseman, Emerita Professor of Classics and Art History at Seattle Pacific University, who carefully drew together all the known fragments from 18 ancient writers that had quoted from Pytheas's lost book *On the Ocean* Περὶ τοῦ Ὠκεανοῦ and a decade of recent archaeological work by Sir Barry Cunliffe, Emeritus Professor of European Archaeology at Oxford University, they uncovered a remarkable story of exploration.

Fortunately the astronomer Pytheas took measurements at five points on his journey that have survived. In the light of recent scholars' work they have proved his calculations correct and that Pytheas of Massalia (Marseille) in the fourth century B.C. made an incredible journey into the unknown Atlantic discovering Britain 265 years before the Romans.

Pytheas of Massalia was the first to give the name Britain, circumnavigate it and recorded the name of its people. He calculated Britain's landmass to within 2.5 per cent accuracy and the length of its coastline: described how the people lived: and found the origin of the valuable tin and amber trade. Pytheas went on to discover the island of Thule (Iceland), the frozen sea and the Arctic Circle; saw a 22-hour day and calculated correctly the position of the North Pole. He developed theories of the tides being affected by the moon and that the earth was a sphere. Pytheas located Abalus the Amber Island near Denmark, and identified two Germanic tribes on the mainland before returning home to his starting point the city of Massalia (Marseille) on the Mediterranean coast of France.

Today we still use his calculations that formed the system of parallels of latitude to map the earth. After 2,300 years Pytheas of Massalia's remarkable achievements deserves every recognition as one of the great explorers who faced experiences far beyond his everyday world and extended the knowledge of the world we live in.

With only inscriptions on stone there are as yet no surviving documents from the Greek city of Massalia (Marseille) and its colonies in France, Monaco, Spain and Corsica. References are found amongst several ancient writers. Full quotations are given to experience the words of the time and these primary sources have been compiled together with archaeological evidence to give you this insight into a remarkable and little known part of our history.

Chapter 1

Real History is Reading between the Lines

The Greek historian Polybius wrote a history to explain the rise of Roman power in forty volumes. [2] He tells us that at the approach to the Battle of the Ebro 217 B.C. the Roman fleet of thirty-five ships had first anchored eighty stades distance from the enemy. Gnaeus Cornelius Scipio the Roman consul sent

> two swift Massaliot ships [from the Greek city of Massalia, Marseille in France] to reconnoitre, for these used to head the line both in sailing and in battle, and there was absolutely no service they were not ready to render. Indeed if any people have given generous support to the Romans it is the people of Marseilles [Massalia] both on many subsequent occasions and especially in the Hannabalic War. [3]

How is it that the Greek city of Massalia though it is recorded also by Justin [4] and Lucan [5] as Rome's ally since c. 600 B.C. faithfully supported Rome in all their wars that we have few reports of this other than Polybius [6] and Cicero regarding their vital help against the Celts in Transalpine Gaul? Strabo states that having acquired the Romans as friends they had many times 'rendered useful service to the Romans'.[7] Ammianus Marcellinus also confirms 'Massalia, by the alliance with and power of which we read that Rome itself was more than once supported in moments of danger' was still known in the fourth century A.D. [8] Massalia's effect on the Roman people was high in their memory [9] yet so little written evidence seems to have survived.

We are taught to question our sources and to be aware of bias and inaccuracy. We can illustrate this in modern times by the popular medium of films. During World War 2 (WW2) mainly British forces conducted the campaign in Burma. In 1945 their American allies made 'Objective Burma' a film starring Errol Flynn, and actors playing American troops conducting all the action. The Turner Classic Movie review records that Burma was 'a theatre of operations the Brits always claimed as their own'. [10] (The Americans did play a vital part in North Burma capturing the town of Myitkyina enduring tremendous losses in 1944 together with Chinese forces and Kachin Guerrillas and opened the Burma Road). [11] Though the film had good reviews and was a big box office hit in America there was much public protest in Britain and the film was banned here before general release. Due to the scriptwriters/editors overlooking to mention their allies adequately, history had in effect been rewritten inadvertently and while events were current. As millions more would see the film and not a history book we can see how easy it is in the popular record to give an entirely different impression than what actually happened. The producers Warner Brothers Film Company made a 'conciliatory prologue of newsreel footage of the British in combat at Burma' to accompany the film when it was finally shown in Britain seven years later in 1952. [12] By complete contrast the film about the Myitkyina campaign 'Merrill's Marauders' directed by Sam Fuller in 1962 for Warner Brothers starts the film with a prologue explaining the conflict in Burma and giving credit to the allied efforts, but missed out their Chinese allies. [13]

The D-Day landings on Normandy beaches consisted of 5,000 ships, the greatest armada ever seen involving the allied forces. A film produced in 1962 called 'The Longest Day' that included John Wayne, Robert Mitchum, Richard Burton and a host of other film stars from Britain and Germany show vividly the British and American forces and their struggles of the 6 June 1944. However the Canadian Army is only briefly mentioned twice.

In reality the Canadian Army, the third-largest force, were given Juno Beach and town of Caen as their objectives and to link up with the British on Sword Beach and the Americans on Utah Beach. Lancaster bombers and Spitfires from the Royal Canadian Air force supported the invasion; 450 Canadian paratroopers were landed behind enemy lines; the Royal Canadian Navy supplied 110 ships and approximately 10,000 sailors, and 14,000 Canadians soldiers were landed.[14] The Canadians; always modest, faithful and there when you need them. Rather than trust to fading memory, the Juno Beach Centre organization with its president Garth Webb a D-Day veteran set about building a museum. On 6 June 2003 the Canadians opened in Normandy the Juno Beach Centre to commemorate the Canadian efforts in World War 2.[15]

The brief mention of the Canadian Army at the Normandy landings, including them in general under one name of 'allies' though the third-largest force is not deliberate in the popular records and it seems that in history some events always get generally overlooked or recorded with a bias towards the majority that took part. American popular histories like the Roman annalists mainly recorded their own actions and their own point of view from the considerable effort, vital contribution and terrible sacrifice they undeniably made. In the more detailed American history volumes the allies are properly and accurately included.

The total numbers of troops landed at Normandy on D-Day 6 June 1944 were:[16]

- Americans   73,000
- British and other allies   61,715
- Canadians   14,000 [17]

In the 'Battle of Britain' the general written history does not mention the vital contribution of the Canadian pilots. Fortunately the film of the same name released in 1969 did feature a Canadian Officer (played by Christopher Plummer) prominently as well as Polish and French pilots serving in the R.A.F. A list of other nationalities that fought was given at the end of the film produced by Benjamin Fisz and Harry Saltzman.[18] Fisz, who had flown for the R.A.F. in the battle, wanted to make a film to remind the younger generation of British of the past and draw them into the cinema to see a British film rather than an American one. Negotiations with Rank broke down over profit-sharing. Then Paramount pulled out of financing the film when Harry Saltzman refused to 'add more American content'.[19] United Artists eventually financed the film. Made at a time when there were still many alive who took part and had suffered in the Blitz. Director Guy Hamilton ensured the film was a more accurate representation [20] of what happened.

On entering World War 2 in December 1941 the Americans needing to lift their own morale against Nazi propaganda answered in their typical show business expertise by using a theatrical family The Four Cohan's life story growing together as the United States enlarged from the 1870s. This very entertaining hit musical film released in 1942 was called 'Yankee Doodle Dandy'.[21] George M. Cohan (played by the superb James Cagney and awarded an Oscar) wrote a new 'battle hymn of the republic' in World War One called 'Over There', which became a popular song.[22] The film covers in a minute the American entry into the war, men training, boarding ships, the Eiffel Tower, two explosions, Armistice declared, victory march back home, with Cohan saying 'We had won the World War. Manhattan went wild'. Unfortunately there was no actual mention of the allies. This was a patriotic film trying to give some confidence by past deeds to combat the real fears of life and death at that present time.

Nazi Germany thought the rivalry between the allies, political and cultural [23] would eventually split them up as they did after World War One. [24] Arguments between families are just that and though there are always exceptions e.g. Suez Crisis 1956, [25] generally families close ranks and unites against an outside threat. A few generations on with British imperialist and American republican antagonisms now long gone, just echoes of friendly cultural rivalry still continues to the modern time and evident in the popular U.S.A comedy series 'Friends'. Accessed from Freeview TV channels, a modern day Elysium Fields, where an actor never grows old in endless back to back re-runs of serials! Here at the meeting of the prospective in-laws of Ross (American) and Emily (British) they argue about the wedding payments and Ross's father retorts, if it was not for us you would be speaking German! Perhaps if there had been a Briton on the comedy writing team there could have been a reply to the New Yorker, and if it was not for the British you would all be speaking Dutch! (The Dutch represented by the character café manager Gunther [26] also in love with Rachel, symbolising mid-America, who he/they can never have). In the early and later series on the wall of Gunther's café 'Central Perk' behind the chair on the right is the British monarch's coat of arms of Lions and Fleur-de-Lis and later changed to the three lions. Both significant symbols because the British took over the Dutch colony of New Amsterdam in America and renamed it New York. [27]

Again in popular books Wellington and the British defeated Napoleon and the French at Waterloo in 1815. Similar to the Americans mentioned above, here we have the British referring to only their own efforts (as the largest contingent) with little if any acknowledgement given to their allies who also played a crucial part.

The Anglo-Allied Army at Waterloo commanded by Wellington was 73,200 soldiers and cavalry.

Percentage of the total:
- British 36%
- King's German Legion 10%
- Nassau 10%
- Brunswick 8%
- Hanoverian 17%
- Dutch 13%
- Belgian 6%

This would have meant that 45% of the Anglo-Allied Army spoke German as their first language.[28]

Barbero gives the figures at around 67,000: British 24,000: King's German Legion 6,000: Brunswick 6,000: Hanoverian 11,000: The army of the Netherlands comprised of: Dutch 9,000: Belgian 4,000: Nassau nearly 3,000 (German). [29]

However when one looks at the more detailed history books we find that Wellington was very nearly defeated only because he tenaciously clung to the ridge near Waterloo specifically waiting to join forces with Marshal Blücher and the Prussian Army, [30] who made victory possible with his arrival late in the day [31] together with General Friedeich von Bülow's action at Plancenoit and Frischermont on Napoleon's flank. [32]

As vital as the Prussians expected arrival was they could not have beaten Napoleon alone without Wellington's holding action for the whole day at great cost and his tactical skills in; deployment on a narrow front that allowed him to have much more fresh allied troops in reserve out of sight beyond the ridge [33] (that later played a crucial part [34] together with Maitland's rapid fire [35] in breaking Napoleon's 'Old Guard' final assault): [36] and in holding the allied army together. The armies of Wellington and Napoleon were similar in total but the Prussian Army was greatly outnumbered by the French.

Total of Armies 18 June 1815 at Waterloo

Though sources differ in totals they at least agree that Napoleon and Wellington's armies were very close in numbers Napoleon had been mistaken to think Wellington had more on the day.[37]

French Army   77,500 [38]

From his total army available of 105,500 Napoleon ordered Grouchy and 30,000 French on the 17 June to pursue and keep the Prussians separated from joining Wellington. [39] Two thousand lightly wounded French joined Napoleon bringing his total to 77,500 at Waterloo 18 June 1815.

Anglo-Allied Army   73,200 [40]

Prussian Army   49,000 [41]

Wellington and Blücher needed each other. For the Anglo-Allied Army it was a costly Pyrrhic victory and one that prompted Wellington to say 'Next to a battle lost, the saddest thing is a battle won'. The film 'Waterloo' with Christopher Plummer as Wellington, Rod Steiger as Napoleon and Serghi Zakhariadze as Marshal Blücher at least shows one ally and the others are mentioned once by Marshal Ney. Produced in 1970 by the Soviet film director Sergei Bundurchuk who was ironically perhaps freer, (than the usual Soviet bias and propaganda while the Soviet Army provided most of the film's army extras along with the British Army First Battalion Gordon Highlanders), to give an objective view, as his own country Russia was not involved at the Battle of Waterloo and the film was a co-production between Dino De Laurentis Cinematografica Rome and Mosfilm Moscow?

History tends to get précised and shortened. For example we were taught at school that the Roman Empire ended in A.D. 476. It was with some surprise to discover many years later that this was only the West Roman Empire. In fact the East Roman Empire (Byzantine) with its capital at Constantinople (Istanbul) continued until conquered in 1453 and in Trebizond 1461. [42]

Mainstream films and books have limited space and cannot fit everything in that happens. Much film ends up cut out on the editing floor; main facts of the story take priority over others facts discovered no matter how interesting. Costs of production and artistic licence are given as excuses for fanciful interpretation of events. The excellent recent film 'Troy' with Brad Pitt as Achilles is unfortunately not entirely accurate i.e. Agamemnon was not killed in Troy but on his return to Mycenae at home by his wife. [43] In 'Alexander' the film produced by Oliver Stone starring Colin Farrell, we see Cassander several times in the battles but in reality he only met up with Alexander the Great much later at Babylon shortly before Alexander died either from either a mosquito bite infection *falciparum malaria*,[44] poison[45] or excessive alcohol and fever.[46] The overall story is compressed to fit into limited space of film time.

In World War 2 much of the Canadian contribution is mentioned in military and specialist books, documentary films, and of course by the people who were there. As time goes by that generation and their children who are told the stories by their fathers and families pass away, and if the oral record dies with them, there only remains what was written. Many books were lost with the passing of the Roman Empire and what we have left of the ancient world tells us only part of what really happened.

The stories written by the old Roman annalists naturally emphasised the glory of Rome and their legions but later historians thought that not all the stories were true.[47] Certainly events happened and the Romans were generous in sharing the spoils of war in gratitude with their allies.[48] After the war against Antiochus the envoys of Rhodes made a speech at the Senate in Rome:

> It is open for you to enrich your allies with the prizes of war, and at the same time to avoid any departure from your settled policy . . . You fought for the honour of your commonwealth and the renown which you enjoy throughout the whole race of man, who have long looked upon your sovereignty and your name as only second to the immortal gods.[49]

Praise for their allies there may have been orally but in the popular written record the Romans claimed all the honour and glory. Then as now some stories however survived in more specialist or military books and others written by foreign writers like the Greeks Polybius, Posidonius, Strabo, and Pompeius Trogus a Latin historian and Roman citizen whose ancestors were Celts from Gallia Narbonensis (neighbours of Massalia). It is written that when the Greek city-state of Massalia (Marseille) asked for Roman help against the Celts that the land captured was not kept by the Romans, as they gave it to their ally Massalia. This was repeated by Roman Consuls, Quintus Opimius (155 B.C.), Giaus Sextus Calvinus (123–122 B.C.), and Marius (102 B.C.). These bear out that the Republic before it became corrupted by power and wealth did indeed fight for honour[50] and Roman justice was known and appealed to by many foreign powers as Cicero the prolific Roman orator stated later:

> That as long as the empire of the Roman people maintained itself by acts of service, not of oppression; wars were waged in the interest of our allies or to safeguard our supremacy; the end of our wars was marked by acts of clemency or by only a necessary degree of severity; the senate was a haven of refuge for kings, tribes, and nations; and the highest ambition of our magistrates and generals was to defend our provinces and allies with justice and honour. And so our government could be called more accurately a protectorate of the world than a dominion.[51]

The Romans did not occupy Sardinia when asked by the rebels or accept the surrender of Utica, which would have been to their gain 'but held to their Treaty engagements'.[52]

Wallbank mentions two different viewpoints, 'Roman προαιρεσις (praresis) which sought, from the time of Fabius Pictor, to interpret all Roman expansion as defensive actions' in contrast to Polybius's view that 'the Pyrrhic War led Romans to envisage conquest of all Italy' and the Hannibal War led to conquest of whole world.[53]

Though the political climate was changing we still have before the Roman civil war Pompey the Great and Julius Caesar both giving in turn conquered land in Gaul and the revenue from them to their ally the Greek city-state of Massalia (Marseille). [54]

Even today many popular books on ancient Greece have maps to illustrate the spread of ancient Greek colonies/settlements. They usually just show those of the central and East Mediterranean and that gives us an incomplete picture. The maps stop at Sicily where the Athenians were defeated by the Greek city of Syracuse 415–413 B.C. [55] Only in the more detailed books are the many Black Sea and Western Mediterranean colonies/settlements in Spain, France, Monaco and Corsica included.

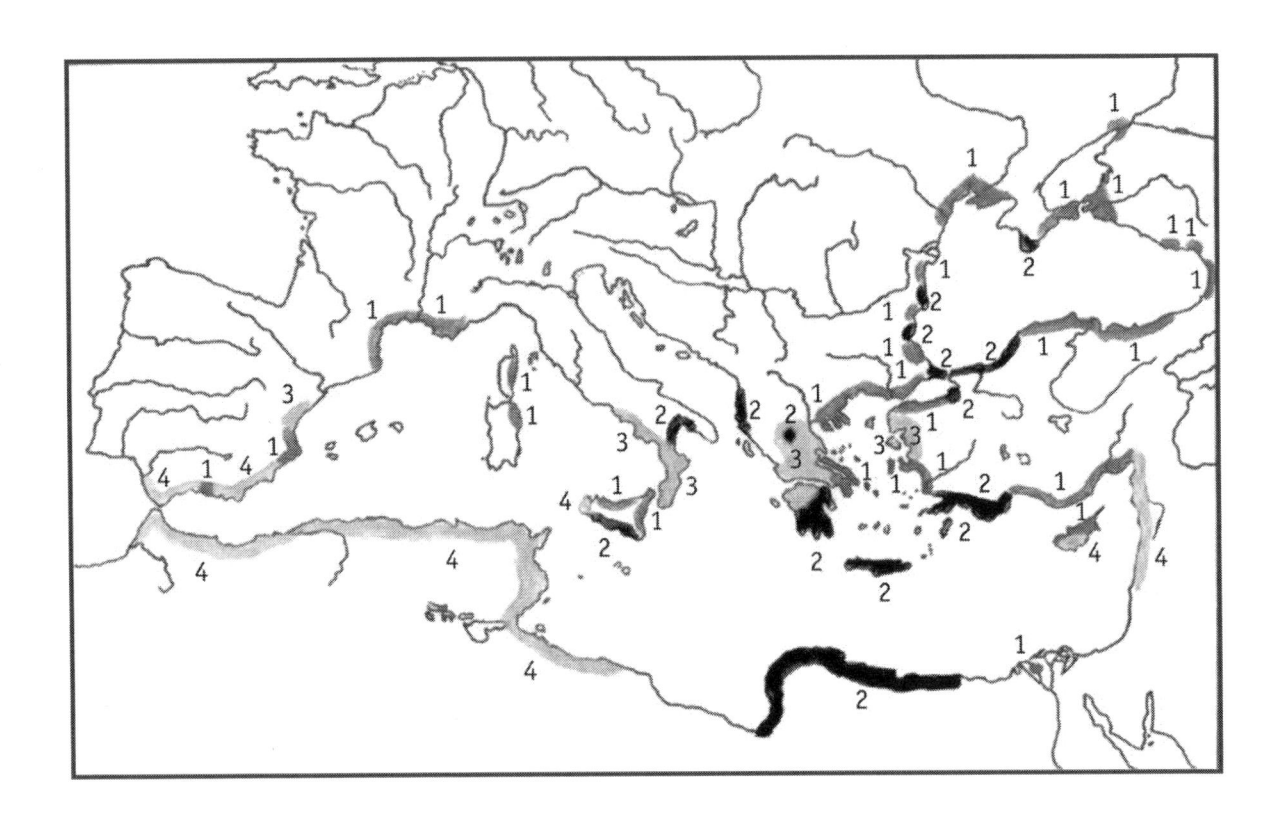

Figure 1. Map of the Greek and Phoenician settlements from Spain to the Black Sea around 550 B.C.
1 = Ionian Greeks, 2 = Doric Greeks, 3 = Other Greeks, 4 = Phoenicians.

We have a deep affection and admiration for the Ghurkhas at first allies and subsequently in the regiments of the British Army. [56] As Massalia may have been to Rome they have a most loyal and somewhat legendary status in their military skill and exploits. Yet when there is a military engagement little is written about them. The British soldiers who were with the Ghurkhas know what they did and spread the stories back home becoming part of the oral folklore. There are of course military books where the Ghurkhas appear. In mainstream books they rarely get a mention but their reputation is still well known in the hearts of the British people. Perhaps this is how the Greek city-state of Massalia (Marseille) gets little mention, but was deeply embedded in the hearts of even the ordinary Romans as Cicero stated in more than four different speeches.

Julius Caesar's 12-day Triumph into Rome September 46 B.C.

After being so long away Julius Caesar could at last celebrate in Rome his many conquests. His conquests were displayed as over four continents as if he had virtually conquered the world. Each 'continent' was given a Triumph lasting four days of celebrations and twelve days in all spread over a month, showing his conquests in Gaul (France), Africa, Egypt, and Pontus (by the Black Sea, Asia Minor). [57]

Roman Generals also used large paintings to illustrate scenes of their conquests. Similar large paintings/portraits etc. were often a part of Communist parades in the twentieth century and even now. During a triumph Roman citizens would be paid something from the General as part of the spoils of war such as corn, oil and money. [58] Appian writes that to each member of the Plebs (Plebeian = freeborn Roman citizens of the lower class) Caesar had given 100 denarii. [59] Dio reports 'Rioting broke out amongst the veterans who were resentful of the citizen's share of the spoils'. [60] Though he was careful not to label anything a Triumph that concerned the Romans as the civil war was 'discreditable' Caesar still displayed twenty varied pictures showing all the events. Appian wrote, 'The crowd though they felt intimidated, groaned at the disasters to their own people'. [61] Even though the Plebs had been paid Cicero stated the debt they owed to their ancient ally Massalia, and the shame and disapproval of the Roman people during Caesar's triumph into Rome when they saw displayed amongst his victories a model of Massilia, (Massalia, Marseille in France) the city he captured during the civil war against Pompey the Great:

> When you are so bitter, O Quintus Fufius, against the people of Marseilles [Massilia], I can not listen to you with calmness. For how long are you going to attack Marseilles? Does not even a triumph put an end to the war in which was carried an image of that city, without whose assistance our forefathers never triumphed over the Transalpine nations? Then, indeed, did the Roman people groan. Although they had their own private griefs because of their own affairs, still there was no citizen who thought the miseries of this most loyal city unconnected with himself. Caesar himself, who had been the most angry of all men with them, still, on account of the unusually high character and loyalty of that city, was every day relaxing something of his displeasure. And is there no extent of calamity by which so faithful a city can satiate you? Again, perhaps, you will say that I am losing my temper. But I am speaking without passion, as I always do, though not without great indignation. I think that no man can be an enemy to that city, who is a friend to this one.[62]

Cicero mentions in *De Officiis* Massalia's special status when comparing Julius Caesar to the dictator Sulla:

> And so, when foreign nations had been oppressed and ruined, we have seen a model of Marseilles [Massilia] carried in a triumphal procession, to serve as proof to the world that the supremacy of the people had been forfeited; and that triumph we saw celebrated over a city without whose help our generals have never gained a triumph for their wars beyond the Alps. I might mention many other outrages against our allies, if the sun had ever beheld anything more infamous than this particular one. Justly, therefore, are we being punished. For if we had not allowed the crimes of many to go unpunished, so great licence would never have centred in one individual . . . one would realise that, if such rewards are offered, civil wars will never cease to be . . . And so in Rome only the walls of her houses remain standing—and even they wait now in fear of the most unspeakable crimes—but our republic we have lost for ever. [63]

In his *Philippic* speech against Mark Antony, Cicero states,

> For who ever was a more bitter enemy to another than Caesar was to Deiotarus [king of Galatia]? He was as hostile to him as he was to this order, to the equestrian order, to the people of Massilia, and to all men whom he knew to look on the republic of the Roman people with attachment. [64]

Massalia's Strategic Position

Grant assesses that during the Roman Civil War Massalia's defiance was a major obstacle to Julius Caesar, because it could cut his communications to Spain. If it was an active opponent, 'the communities of Spain, in the Further province, where two tenures of office had left him many dependants, were unlikely to come out openly in his favour'. [65]

Public opinion at Rome was highly sensitive at successive developments. After losing his two pontoon bridges, which seemingly left Caesar trapped in Spain several Senators went over to Cicero and joined Pompey now in Greece. Caesar crossed one of the rivers by constructing coracles he learned from Britain, escaping the trap. This plus his naval victory at Massalia brought several Spanish towns north of the River Ebro including Osca over to him. [66]

Cicero in his defence speech of Fonteius reveals the strategic position, destiny and responsibility of Massalia to that of Rome:

> Help comes to this unhappy and innocent gentleman in the shape of the entire community of Massilia, which not only strives to exhibit due gratitude to my client to whom it owes its preservation, but also believes that the obligation and the destiny imposed upon by its geographical situation is to protect our fellow-countrymen from molestation at the hand of those tribes [Celts]. [67]

Pompey the Great had fought and defeated tribes in the Alps who he described as 'enemies at the throat of Italy.' [68] He also gave to Massalia 'the lands of the Volcae Arecomici, and Helvii' to keep under their control. [69]

The Romans owed a lot to their Italian Allies *socii* [70] as they supplied at least half of the Roman Army with soldiers and three quarters of their cavalry for the military campaigns [71] but their exploits rarely get mentioned in Roman victories or recorded in Roman history. No matter what size the Roman contribution was they had led the war and so claimed all the credit and honour in the written record. We hear most about the Italian allies when they wanted equality with Roman citizenship. This was denied several times to the allies (*socii*), who eventually caused the Social Wars ('wars of the allies') [72] between them and Rome in 91–88 B.C. [73]

When those generations pass and the oral memory gone too, later generations only have the written record. Sometimes events are known to have happened yet little is written on them because they were so well known at the time and people do not need to write what is so obvious and common knowledge. When those generations pass away the knowledge goes with them. This unfortunately leaves a puzzle for later generations when we no longer have the verbal context.

By reading between the lines of what is left we may get a better idea of what really happened. On the one hand we have the Treaty [74] and special privileges decreed by Rome to the independent Greek city-state of Massalia (Marseille) for raising and helping to pay the ransom of gold for besieged Rome in its darkest hour 390 B.C. [75] Also the city of Caere attacked the Gauls when they left Rome taking their booty, and had 'saved all who fled to them for refuge from Rome' and returned the sacred flame and the Vestal Virgins. In gratitude the Romans gave the Caeretani the right of Roman Citizenship but 'on account of the bad managers which the city had at that time' [76] did not enrol them among the citizens, relegating them with the others who had no share in equal rights to the 'Tablets of the Caeretani' (*Tabulae Caeritum*). [77]

On the other hand we have the surviving popular stories that only Roman valour redeemed Roman humiliation with their Dictator Camillus rallying the Romans into an army who arrived just in time to stop the ransom of gold the Romans had raised being paid to the Gauls. Camillus also destroys the Gauls outside of Rome capturing their leader Brennus. 'However this tale is an invention of Roman vanity'.[78] Other sources tell us why the Gauls left Rome after a seven-month occupation and siege of Capitoline Hill. As the Gauls' settlements in the north were being attacked 'by the Veneti' they made a treaty with the Romans [79] and having been paid the ransom of gold [80] they left Rome. The story of Camillus arriving to stop the ransom being paid could well have been propaganda. [81] Grant mentions in an Etruscan version the ransom was paid to the Sennonian Celts by Caerae. [82] Strabo also records the Galatae (Celts) left Rome 'with what the Romans had willingly given them'. [83]

Langhorne adds that there was reason to question the last part of the story concerning the withdrawal of the Gauls (Galatae, Celts) from Rome in 390 B.C. Plutarch copied this from Livy but Livy writes later in vol. 4. X.16 that the Gauls 'feeling of enmity to the Roman people, whose defeat at their hands and ransom for gold, they were wont to relate with no idle boast'. Polybius, Justin and Suetonius also write that they received a ransom of gold and returned safely to their own country. [84] Suetonius actually points out in his story of Drusus recovering the ransom of gold in Gaul, where he was a 'governor of praetorian rank', contradicts that of Camillus who had allegedly redeemed it centuries before. [85]

What could be the reason for any propaganda? [86] Rome had lost most of her subjects and territories being reduced to nearly its original limits. The Latins and the Hernicans dissolved the League with the Romans and wars broke out on all sides. [87] Rome could not afford to be seen any weaker and the propaganda of not being defeated even when all seemed lost was necessary? As Polybius records the Romans

> after making a truce on conditions satisfactory to the Gauls and being thus contrary to their expectation reinstated in their home and as it were now started on the road to aggrandizement, continued in the following years to wage war on their neighbours. [88]

Remarkably it is true that Camillus and the army from this low point were able to reorganise themselves and recover Roman power within a few years.

Yet in spite of propaganda the story of the ransom persisted. Several centuries later the story was still known as King Mithridates VI (134 B.C.-64 B.C.) in a speech to his troops showing the Romans had been defeated before refers to the capture of Rome by the Gauls 'removed not by warfare but by a payment of a ransom'.[89] Also the Greek Aetolians taunted a Roman embassy that they 'had been unable to protect their own city against the Gauls and, when it was captured, had not defended it with cold steel but paid a ransom for it in gold'. [90]

From Cicero we learn that without the help of their Massalian ally Rome would never have succeeded outside the Italian peninsula past the Alps to deal with the constant Celtic threat. Polybius, Lucan, Justin, Strabo and Ammianus Marcellinus relate the loyalty and help Massalia gave to Rome. Though 90 per cent of Massalia's empire was confiscated by Julius Caesar he respected the city's independence because of its 'fame and antiquity'.[91] The Sennonian Gauls had once captured Rome except for the small area of the Capitoline Hill [92] under siege for seven months until Massalia raised and added to the ransom for them to leave. [93] But for the crucial naval Battle of the Ebro would Rome have survived Hannibal? From Sosylus of Sparta we learn it was the tactics of the Massalian Navy that won the battle where Carthaginian Hasdrubal was defeated [94] while Livy only mentions the Roman effort. [95] This defeat prevented Hasdrubal sending men and supplies to his brother Hannibal fighting the Romans in Italy. Appian records Carthage 'sent neither soldiers nor money' [96] to Hannibal. Without Massalia's military, naval and financial help at crucial times would Rome have survived to become a world power?

Chapter 2

Massalia

In Modern Greek the city of Marseille is still called by its ancient name Massalia. The French pronounce this as Marsej:e (Marseille) and its people Marseje,-e:z (Marseillais). [97] The national anthem of France is named La Marseillaise after them who had made it a popular song during the French Revolution. In 2013 Marseille as the European City of Culture had an awarded budget of over 90 million Euros to be spent on events. Today it is the second-largest city in France in size and the third largest in population with 1,601,095 people recorded in the census of 2006, [98] but what was it like in ancient times? Why did the ancient Greeks choose to build a city there on the coast of France?

We know from Herodotus and Appian that the ancient Greek Phocaeans already had firm trading contacts with Tartessos in Spain.[99] Strabo states that Maenaca (Mainake) in Spain 'lies farthest of the Phocaean cities in the west is farther away than Calpe, and is now in ruins (though it still preserves the traces of a Greek city)'.[100] Maenaca (Mainake, between Almunecar and Malaga) was possibly the Phocaeans' oldest colony in the West founded c. 625–600 B.C. to c. 530 B.C. Aubert suggests it could have been Phoenician and abandoned c. 600-570 B.C.[101] The need to establish colonies/settlements/trading posts where ships could safely stop at night and also protect trade routes were logical.[102] Even without Maenaca the discovery of the Harbour of Lacydon (Vieux-Port, Marseille) near the River Rhône and trade to the interior of Gaul by ship was a commercial opportunity needing to be exploited? Rivet suggests that Massalia (Marseille) was founded primarily as a 'staging post' for their silver trade with Tartessos, as the River Rhône delta at 43 km distance[103] was nearly a day's sail from Massalia.[104] It was only when the Carthaginians destroyed Tartessos and Maenaca [105] that the Massaliotes turned their attention to Gaul (France) via the River Rhône. [106]

Excavations have shown the harbour at Marseille was occupied around 3400–3000 B.C. Middle Bronze Age [107] though it seems empty when the Greeks from Phocaea arrived. Blakeway's article illustrates a Greek vase found at Marseille dating from the eighth century B.C. and thought to be Cycladic Geometric while another was thought to be East Greek Geometric in style. [108] Though this is evidence of Greek goods they may have been carried there by Greek, Etruscan or Phoenician traders?

Massalia (Marseille) was founded in France c. 600 B.C. by Greeks from Phokaia, Phocaea. Phocaea was a Greek city near Smyrna in Ionia Asia Minor (now called Foça, near present day Izmir in Turkey). Thucydides [109] writes that the Phocaeans founded Massalia after a naval victory over the Carthaginians though he may have been referring to the reinforcement of Massalia when nearly half of the Phocaeans left Ionia from the Persian invasion in 546 B.C. [110]

There are several foundation stories from Aristotle, Plutarch, Strabo, Livy, and Justin. Most have the same elements and characters though some changes as you would expect from spoken stories passed on to person to person until that version is written down.

We have written evidence but do these stories have any basis in fact? We know that colonies not only from folklore but also because of religious duty would have kept alive the age of their foundation, the origin of the colony and the name of the founder [111] in which worship of the Oikistes kept those memories current. Though presently some scholars argue that several cities in the fourth century B.C. may have invented their own foundation stories this does not take away that others may have survived from an earlier time [112] or that some of the stories may well be true. [113] Invented foundation stories are attempts to create a pedigree and imitate an original that someone else already has.

While Aristotle writes that the Phocaeans founded Massalia with Euxenus marrying the king's daughter and later their son Protis also married a daughter of the king, we have in the version by Justin that Protis was a leader who married the king's daughter. Euxenus's wife is called Petta while Protis's wife is called Gyptus and in both versions the wives change their names to Aristoxena. Plutarch writes of Protis as a merchant who won the friendship of the king and founded Massalia. [114]

One story Aristotle wrote in his book *Constitution of Massalia*. Though the book is now lost we have this from Athenaeus who had quoted Aristotle. 'The people of Phocaea, in Ionia, devoted as they were to commerce, founded Massalia. Euxenus was a friend of King Nannus'. On a day celebrating his daughter Petta's nuptials, Euxenus arrived. After dinner Petta was to give a drink to the person she chose to marry, she chose Euxenus and changed her name to Aristoxene. 'And there is a clan in Massilia to this day descended from the woman and called Protiadae; for Protis was the son of Euxenus and Aristoxene'. [115]

Here we have a clan named after their leader Protis would by its very existence keep his memory alive and they were still active in Massalia at the time when Aristotle was writing in the fourth century B.C.

In Justin there is the detail of the Harbour of Lacydon (Vieux-Port, Marseille). Justin [116] uses as his source a local writer Trogus Pompeius a Latin historian writing in 10 B.C. Trogus Pompeius's forefathers were of Vocontian origin (Celtic) in Gallia Narbonensis and neighbours to Massalia. [117] He recorded that the Phocaeans were given the site on the coast of France when Protis the Phocaean leader married Gyptus, the daughter of King Nannus of the Segobriges, a Ligurian tribe. The king gave the Harbour of Lacydon to Protis and Gyptus as wedding present. The Phocaeans built the city of Massalia there:

> The Phocaeans, constricted by territory which was limited and barren, had in fact turned their attention more to the sea than the land, and had been making their living from fishing, trading and often even from piracy, which in those days was considered a noble occupation. [118]

Justin continues,

> In the time of King Tarquin some young Phocaeans sailed from Asia into the mouth of the Tiber and made an alliance with the Romans, after which they set off in their ships for the most remote inlets of Gaul, founding Massilia between the Ligurians and the wild Gallic tribes. Their exploits were impressive, as they defended themselves against the barbarous Gauls or themselves went on the attack against those by whom they had been attacked. [119]

Some scholars think that Justin's story had projected back in time the treaty made between the Punic Wars in the third century B.C. into an earlier formal alliance. Thiel while agreeing this is so is definite that at least the friendship between Massalia and Rome went back centuries before. He also points out that 'friendship' could be substantial in commitment as later the island city-state of Rhodes, a great naval power, assisted Rome in the Second Macedonian War and the Syrian War long before any formal treaty between them. [120]

King of Rome-the Greek Connection

King Lucius Tarquinius Priscus 616–578 B.C. was the fifth king of Rome. He was Etruscan by birth but half Greek by descent. His father was Demaratus, a wealthy citizen of Corinth who was driven from his country by a revolution [121] and had settled in the Etruscan city of Tarquinii [122] marrying a native woman.[123]

Murray relates a story from Dionysius that 'the Bacchiad Damaratos, who was engaged in the trade with Etruria, and, when the tyranny came, settled in exile at Etruscan Tarquinia with a number of Corinthian artists, introduced pottery and terracotta sculptures to Italy, and fathered Tarquin king of Rome'. [124] Dionysius mentions the tyrant at Corinth was Kypselos. [125]

Though based on the Greek alphabet writing appears in Etruria at the end of eighth century B.C. and Latium shortly afterwards. The Roman historian Tacitus mentions that this was due to Demaratus who taught them the alphabet. [126]

Strabo writes,

> . . . Demaratus arrived, bringing with him a host of people from Corinth; and, since he was received by the Tarquinians, he married a native woman, by whom he begot Lucumo. And since Lucumo had proved a friend to Ancus Marcius, the king of the Romans, he was made king, and his name was changed to Lucius Tarquinius Priscus. [127]

Demaratus having been 'one of the men who had been in power at Corinth, fleeing from the seditions there carried with him so much wealth from his home to Tyrrhenia that not only he himself became the ruler of the city that admitted him, but his son was made king of the Romans'. [128]

Demaratus's son married Tanaquil from a noble Etruscan family and Lucius became a Lucomo (noble) in their state. [129] Tanaquil was ambitious for her husband and persuaded him that they would advance more quickly if they moved to Rome. [130] When Demaratus died Lucomo inherited all his wealth. This was heightened by his marriage to a highborn Etruscan Tanaquil. But the Etruscans still looked upon him 'as a son of a banished man and a stranger'. Her idea was to move to Rome 'where all rank was of sudden growth and founded on worth'. [131]

Proving to be a good friend to Ancus Marcius, king of Rome he followed him to become the next king. [132] Many kings of Rome were outsiders and not from the patrician class.[133] In the legendary history of Rome, Lucomo was made king by the Senate and people in 615 B.C. [134] and changed his name to Lucius Tarquinius Priscus. [135] However, Livy says Lucomo had already changed his name and was appointed guardian by King Ancus of his children in his will. [136] When Ancus died Lucomo sent the children out for the day. He then made a speech saying that he would be the third outsider to aim at sovereignty and the people voted him king. It seems the senate may have opposed him as once in power he created a hundred new senators to add to the senate, who were loyal to him. [137] Cornell points out that King Marcus Ancus had been a patron of the Plebs. King Tarquinius Lucius Priscus canvassed the people and his reforms angered the aristocrats.[138] Perhaps that is why King Tarquin created 100 new senators loyal to himself?

Demaratus adorned Tyrrhenia 'by goodly supply of artisans who had accompanied him from home' [Corinth] [139] and his son did the same by 'means of the resources supplied by Rome'. [140] Such was their closeness that Strabo writes 'it is further said that the triumphal, and consular, adornment, and, in a word, that of all the rulers, was transferred to Rome from Tarquinii, as also the fasces, axes, trumpets, sacrificial rites, divination, and all music publicly used by the Romans.' [141]

Perhaps there is a real link to give the story a basis in fact. 'Corinth is called wealthy because of its commerce' [142] and was 'master of two harbours, of which the one leads straight to Asia, and the other to Italy; and it makes easy the exchange of merchandise from both countries that are so far distant from each other'.[143] This was a mid-point from west to east and vice versa. Cargoes could be reloaded onto other ships to continue their journey and thereby avoid the seas beyond Meleae and its 'contrary winds'. The Phocaeans were foremost traders and it is likely they had commercial contacts with Corinth [144] and Demaratus one of its leaders. [145] It is within the realms of possibility that the Phocaeans had previous contacts with Demaratus, and it made good commercial sense to renew those contacts. As mentioned by Justin they 'made alliance with the Romans' and therefore must have seen the king of Rome to secure it? The foundation of Massalia is established at c. 600 B.C. [146] Livy says the Phocaeans arrived in Gaul during the reign of the king of Rome Lucius Tarquinius Priscus 616–578 B.C. While the traditional dates of the monarchy are not accurate [147] kings Ancus and Priscus are more historical figures with some leeway on their dates. [148] For the founding fathers of Massalia, so far away from Phocaea, making trade links and acquiring an ally nearer to themselves in the Western Mediterranean was good policy.

Archaeological Evidence

History records something of what happened and archaeology is material evidence. There were trading links between Italy and Greece from 1600–1200 B.C. until the Dark Ages. A second phase resumed between the Greeks and Etruria during the first half of the eighth century B.C. by Euboeans. Two areas of contact were particularly rich in metal deposits: 'the Tolfa Mountains between Caere and Tarquinia and in North Etruria, Elba and Populonia'. [149]

There is archaeological evidence of Corinthian influence on Etruscan civilization during 650–600 B.C. [150] that would be within the period for Demaratus as ruler of Tarquinii.

Archaeological evidence was also found of an Ionian trading post at Gravisca a harbour for Tarquinia in Etruria and trading from around 600 until 480 B.C.[151] Morel mentions that a Phocaean presence had been doubted previously but since the discovery at Gravisca in 1969 it 'now appears probable' and 'they are even considered to have "opened" the trading post'. [152] The harbour site, 8 km from Tarquinia, was a commercial settlement with a small shrine dedicated to Aphrodite and pottery inscribed to her as well as Hera (with more than half of the fifty found), Apollo and Demeter. The onomastic evidence showed that these Greeks were Ionians from the area of Miletus, Samos and Ephesus and were settled there. Also found were two wells, a few post holes of fences, wattle and daub huts. More than five thousand Greek and locally made lamps were found, which was an 'important feature in the worship of Demeter'. The bronze cauldrons, ivory boxes, several bronze statuettes of 'good Greek manufacture, fine cups of renowned potters' all indicate visits by wealthy dealers. An Aegintean Sostratus [153] who was known for his wealth by Herodotus set up an inscribed anchor in the sanctuary. [154] There were thousands of poorer gifts of lamps and small libation vessels of Greek and local production indicating that most visitors were of 'lower social position'. Gravisca was a 'spiritual and physical centre for hundreds of Ionian refugees' that had abandoned their land from 540 to 480 B.C. for a better life. Unlike Massalia that could expand amongst the Segobriges into a city, the trading post at Gravisca could not due the presence of the powerful Etruscans on the rest of the site. [155] Massalia extended its city wall twice during 600 to 500 B.C. doubling in size and indicating an increase of population (see Figure 7).

There is a sudden end to Greek remains at Gravisca after 480 B.C. Professor Torelli explains this phenomenon by: wars of Hellenes against Persia and Carthage: movements of Sabellian tribes in Italy: decline of Etruscan power in Latium and Campania: social disturbances in the main *poleis* (cities) of Latium and South Etruria. This coincides with a sudden decline and quality in artistic production in Etruria for example painted tombs. [156]

Justin continues that the Phocaeans after seeing the gulf around the River Rhône 'were captivated by the beauty of the spot' [157] they returned home and persuaded others to join them. The leaders of the fleet were Simos and Protis. They visited King Nannus of the Segobrigii requesting an alliance. On that day the king's daughter was to be married and at the feast she saw Protis and chose him as her husband. The king gave them a remote bay, the natural Harbour of Lacydon, as a wedding present to build their city of Massalia. The Ligurians kept a jealous eye on the development of Massalia and attacked it a few times. The Greeks not only fought successfully but also built more colonies in the territory they captured. [158]

When Nannus died his son Comanus became king and a chief persuaded him that Massalia should be crushed now before it was any stronger and one day might overwhelm Comanus. The Massalians had a festival called Floralia [159] and the king set a trap for that day by sending in warriors hidden in carts. They were to open the city gates at night while Massalia was 'buried in sleep and wine', and let in Comanus and his army who were hiding in the hills. A woman who was a relative of the king was in love with a young Greek and told him of the plot. He reported the danger to the magistrates and all the Ligurians in the city and those in the carts were arrested and killed. The Massaliotes then laid a trap for Comanus. He and seven thousand were killed. 'From that day forward the people of Massalia have kept their gates shut on feast days' [160] with guards patrolling the walls, maintaining their security even in times of peace.

The many wars the Greeks fought with the Ligurians and the Gauls 'made the valour of the Greeks celebrated among their neighbours'. They routed Carthaginian forces on many occasions, formed an alliance with the Spaniards, and were 'loyal to the treaty made with Romans almost at the foundation of Massalia, energetically supporting their allies in all their wars.' [161]

In Lucan's epic poem *Pharsalia* he writes a speech by the Massaliotes to Julius Caesar 'That Massalia has always shared your people's fates in foreign wars is attested by every age included in the Latin annals'. [162] Though one allows for poetic licence Lucan refers to something that was known to Romans and he had original sources available.

Plutarch writes,

> In those times, as Hesiod tells us, "work was no disgrace", no trade carried with it any mark of inferiority and commerce could even win a man prestige, because it gave the merchant familiarity with barbarous countries and gained him the friendship of foreign rulers and a wide experience of affairs. Some merchants even became founders of great cities, such as Protis, for example, who won the friendship of the Gauls living along the Rhône [Rhodanus] and founded Marseille [Massalia]. It is said that both Thales and Hippocrates the mathematician engaged in trade, and Plato paid for the expenses of his stay in Egypt by selling oil. [163]

Is Plutarch making a point here in contrast to his own time? Was this in general, either Greeks and/or Romans? Was there now a difference in that the elite were narrow in thinking that creating wealth only from owning land as being of merit? Inherent land owning, with its rank and privilege for the few, increased snobbery and divisions of class with rich and poor that still prevails in modern times. Even in fourth century Athens trade was mainly handled by metics, resident immigrant Greeks from the Black Sea colonies, Greek islands and Massalia who had some privileges but not the right to vote in Athens. [164] But it may be that, as Metics could not own land most of them would be a majority working in Trade as well as Athenians. Osborne says there is evidence that Athenians worked in trade and nothing to stop them from doing so. [165]

The Celts had their problems with overpopulation. Another story by Livy records that during the reign of King Tarquinius Priscus (616–578 B.C.) in Rome; Ambitgatus was the Celtic king of the Bituriges and head of three Gallic tribes. Under him Gaul had become 'rich and populous'. He appointed his nephews Segovesus and Boellovesus to take the excess population and find 'such new homes as the gods by signs from heaven might point out the way to'. After consulting the gods Segovesus went to South Germany and Bellovesus to Italy. Bellovesus collected the 'surplus population—Bituriges, Arverni, Senones, Aedui, Ambarri, Carnutes, Aulerci' and stopped at Triscastini by the 'towering wall of the Alps'. They did not know of any path over this mountainous barrier:

> Another consideration delayed them, for they heard that a strange people–actually the Massilienses, [Massaliotes] who had sailed from Phocaea–were seeking for somewhere to settle and were in conflict with the Salui. The superstitious Gauls took this as an omen of their own success and helped the strangers to such effect that they were enabled to establish themselves, without serious opposition, at the spot where they had disembarked. [166]

The Gauls then crossed the Alps by the Taurine and Duria Passes. They defeated the Etruscans near the River Ticinus. 'Finding they were in the territory of the Insubres, the same name as one of the cantons of the Aedui, took it as another favourable omen and founded the town of Mediolanium' (Milan). Only in Livy is there mention of any conflict at the arrival of the Phocaeans.

Ammianus Marcellinus writing in fourth century A.D. in the section on 'The Origins of the Gauls' includes,

> But in fact a people of Asia from Phocaea, to avoid the severity of Harpalus, prefect of king Cyrus, set sail for Italy. A part of them founded Velia in Lucania, the rest, Massilia [Marseille] in the region of Vienne. Then in subsequent ages, they established no small number of towns, as their strength and resources increased. [167]

In summary of the surviving foundation stories we have:

- An oracle tells the Phocaeans to go to Ephesus where they collect a Xoanon (wooden sacred image of Artemis) and Aristarcha who becomes their priestess on establishing the colony. (Strabo) [168]
- The Phocaeans sail up the Tiber to seek an alliance with the Romans in the time of King Tarquin. (Justin)
- The Phocaeans landed in Gaul when Lucius Tarquinius Priscus was king of Rome and were in conflict with the Salui. Bellovesus a chief of the Gauls helped the Phocaeans to be able to settle without serious opposition where they had originally landed. (Livy)
- Euxenos becomes friends with Nannus, king of the Segobriges and marries his daughter Petta who selects him at a feast where she could choose a husband. They have a son called Protis. (Aristotle, from Athenaeus)
- Protis a merchant wins the friendship of King Nannus and founds Massalia. (Plutarch)
- Protis and Simos leaders of a Phocaean fleet arrive seeking an alliance with King Nannus. They arrive when the king's daughter was to choose a husband at a feast. Protis marries Gyptis a daughter of King Nannus who chose him and the king gives them a 'remote bay' the Harbour of Lacydon as a wedding present. (Justin)
- They established Velia, Massilia, and several towns over the centuries. (Am. Marcellinus).

From these elements we can draw a hypothesis that perhaps as traders:

Euxenos and the Phocaeans established trading links on the coast of Gaul. Euxenos becomes friends of King Nannus of the Segobriges. Arriving on a day the king's daughter Petta was to celebrate getting married by their custom she could choose a husband by offering him a drink. Petta chooses Euxenos. She changes her name to Aristoxene. They have a son called Protis. The Phocaeans decide on a colony nearby to secure and protect their trade route primarily to Spain and later up the River Rhodanus (Rhône). Simos and Protis persuade other Phocaeans to return with them. A fleet is gathered at Phocaea led by Simos, and Protis (a merchant and the grandson of King Nannus). An oracle provides a guide Aristarcha and a sacred image from the Ephesian Artemis. The young Phocaeans sail up the Tiber to make an alliance with the Romans. They land in Gaul when Tarquinius Lucius Priscus was king of Rome. He is the son of the Bachiadeae Demaratus of Corinth, a very wealthy Greek merchant trader who became the ruler of neighbouring Tarquinii.

The Phocaeans sail on to seek another alliance this time with King Nannus. On landing they are in conflict with the Salui and Belovesus a Chief of the Gauls also seeking a new home, helps them establish themselves where they had disembarked. Protis arrives on the day another of King Nannus's daughters Gyptis is to be married (Nannus had probably married again for 20 years to have passed to have another daughter of marriageable age and young enough for Protis or he was another having the same name or title King Nannus i.e. Nannus II or III etc.?). Gyptis follows the same custom of choosing a husband and she chooses Protis by offering him a drink. Gyptis changes her name to Aristoxene. Cementing family ties and an alliance with marriage King Nannus gives them a 'remote bay' the natural Harbour of Lacydon as a wedding present. Protis founds the city of Massalia there. Family came first but not to the approval of all the other Ligurians. A trading post is one thing but a growing city quite another. When Nannus died his son Comanus became king. One chief advises King Comanus to destroy Massalia before it becomes too large and overwhelms them. Massalia defeats Comanus and 7,000 Ligurians and continues to grow forming its own colonies along the coast and inland. The Massaliotes 'routed Carthaginians forces on many occasions and made an alliance with Spaniards'. They were 'loyal to the treaty made with the Romans almost at the foundation of Massalia, energetically supporting their allies in all their wars'. [169]

Could there be any significance in the mention of a 'remote' bay 'between the Ligurian and the wild Gallic tribes'? Why emphasise 'remote'? Firstly the Celts may have occupied a territory but the coast was not used? The land around the future Massalia was poor and the arable land much further inland. Presumably the area was therefore empty up to the Oppidum of Baou de Saint-Marcel. [170] The land's ownership may be in a disputed area not a defined border as it was 'between the Ligurians and the wild Gallic tribes'? Secondly the Celts here in Provence were not sea going sailors at this time? Much later the Ligurians were. [171]

In the seventh century B.C. at the time of Protis the coastal land could have been empty with the Celts and Ligurians preferring to live inland. The coast is not of great value to them. Therefore the coast is considered 'remote' though being within a territory of the tribes. The Salui objected to the incomers. Belovesus intervenes and either arbitrates and/or forces the Salui to stop opposition. King Nannus overall in charge of the area gives a 'remote bay' to Protis at the marriage to his daughter Gyptis as a wedding present. The Phocaeans expanded and establish more towns over the centuries.

The City of Massalia (Marseille)

Strabo writing in the first century B.C. recorded that the harbour of Massalia lies at the foot of a rock facing south and well-fortified 'as is the rest of the city though it is of considerable size'. On the headland were the Ephesium and a temple of the Delphinian Apollo 'the latter shared in common with all Ionians'. It seems this referred not to Delphi the place but a dolphin Delphini, a sea god in the guise 'of a dolphin, guiding ships safely across the oceans.' [172]

Figure 2. A model of the ancient Greek city of Massalia (Marseille) in the Musée d'Histoire Marseille.

The Ephesium was solely dedicated to the Ephesian Artemis. An oracle had told the Phocaeans when they were setting sail to take 'a guide received from the Ephesian Artemis'. On reaching the city of Ephesus the goddess commanded a woman called Aristarcha to sail with the Phocaeans taking a Xoanon, a reproduction of wooden sacred image, with her. Once Massalia was established and a temple built the Phocaeans appointed Aristarcha priestess. Strabo recorded that in all the cities Massalia founded the people gave this 'goddess honours of the first rank and they preserve the artistic design of the "xoanon" the same, and all the other usages precisely the same as is customary in the mother-city'. [173]

A find of an Ionic capital in a church Fouille rue de la Cathedral Marseille was dated to sixth century 525-510 B.C. The capital is 1.80 m wide and the scale of the temple would have been of considerable size. By comparison the width of the Ionic capitals on the Propylaia at Athens is 1.65 metres approximately. [174]

Figure 3. Ionic capital 1.80 metres wide, 520-510 B.C. found in Massalia (Marseille) and on display at the Musée d'Histoire Marseille.

Around 650 B.C the Cimmerians had destroyed the shrine of Artemis outside the walls of Ephesus in Ionia, Asia Minor. During the reign of Croesus 564–546 B.C. there was a big scale of restoration and a famous sculptor Endoios carved a new statue of the Goddess in hardwood.

Theophrastus, the botanist, mentions palm wood as popular for making images, as it was both tough and easy to carve. [175] The Phocaeans also worshipped the goddess Athena and had a temple to her in Massalia. In the mother-city of Phocaea there was a famed sixth-century temple to Athena. [176]

Stephanus of Byzantium (Massalia F 72) quoting Timaeus, the fourth-century B.C. historian of the western states, wrote that

> The captain <of the Phocaean colonists> approaching by sea and seeing fish (*haliea*) <there> ordered the mooring cable to be tied *(massai)* — for they say *massai* "to tie" in the Aeolic dialect; thus (*Massalia*) "received its name from the fish and the tieing"'.[177]

The ancient city of Massalia had the similar elements of other Greek cities, temples, amphitheatre, Agora (market place), Prytaneion (town hall), gymnasium and stadium. Though we have an exception recorded by Pausanias who described Panopeus near Chaironeia in Greece as a city though it had none of the civic buildings 'They also sent two delegates to the Phokian [Phocis] assembly'. [178] He records Panopeus did have hereditary boundary stones and from this it would seem a Greek city was one that also had 'boundary stones'. Such stones were usually hereditary and had a religious significance.

The Agora is situated as in the Place de Lenche. Water storage was increased in the second century B.C. with seven chambers 5 x 10.4 m each, side by side individually roofed by barrel vaults found at the St. Sauveur convent, Place de Lenche. [179]

In Massalia a reused stone for a tomb had been carved with a Christian cross but on the other side in Greek Clerc records as T] ΟΣΤΑΔΙΟΝ The Stadium [180] date 2nd century A.D. This stone was found in 1852 when building the La Major cathedral in the south of the city. Probably the stadium was nearby though Clerc suggests it could also have been north just outside the Greek city at Canebière [181] or east by the Butte des Carmes and the *Via Aquensis*.[182] He thought this stadium was more for athletics and gymnastics rather than horses and chariots.

There is also a Hellenistic bathhouse found in the rue Leca dating to between fourth to third century B.C. [183] Also discovered were some rectangular buildings by la rue Sainte-Elisabeth/rue Trigance from late fourth to early third century B.C. including one 9 m by 5.50 m that had an inscription formed of black, grey and white tesserae spelling out in Greek XAIPE (welcome) and a quantity of vases. [184]

Four rows of stone seating have been found at Rue des Martégales at the place called 'Théâtre Grec'. The amphitheatre was probably made of wood being replaced by stone in the Roman era [185] around the first century A.D. However, it was still Greek in design with 'circular marbled orchestra and no vomitoria'. There was a lip carved into the seats to stop feet sliding into the backs of anyone sitting in front, which was a feature of seats in Greek theatres in Sicily and the East Mediterranean.[186]

Figure 4. Part of the amphitheatre of Massalia (Marseille) excavated in 1945.

On the southern shore of Lacydon opposite Massalia by the Bassin de Carénage was an ancient Greek cemetery.[187] There were others north and outside the city wall at Sainte-Lazare,[188] Sainte-Barbe,[189] Saint-Mauront[190] and at Lazaret d'Arenc.[191]

On the northern shore of Lacydon (Vieux-Port) was the dock for commercial use and a separate naval base with accompanying ship sheds.

The Phocaeans who went to Massalia also took with them grapevines and olive trees, which became very important to the economy of France into the present day as enormous producers of wine, olives and olive oil. Though there were grapevines growing wild it was the wine cultivation by the Greeks that was the innovation and a lasting legacy.[192]

Here the olive tree became the special tree of Artemis and not the palm tree as in Ephesus and Syracuse. Fourth century B.C. coins of Massalia show the goddess as a young girl with an olive crowned head similar to those from Syracuse.[193] A coin workshop dating back to the Hellenistic period has been excavated in Marseille (Massalia). The location was unusual compared to Athens and Pella instead of being near the Agora (market) the Massaliotes' coin workshop was next to the port.[194]

The Greeks city-states though stubbornly independent had overwhelming ties in common of family, language, culture and religion.[195] Massalia with their goddess Artemis of Ephesus and god Delphinian Apollo continued relations with the sanctuaries of these cities. As with the other Greeks city-states, 'Massalia maintained its own treasury at Delphi in Greece'.[196] They built their own treasury to the god at Delphi in Greece c. 540–530 B.C. in thanks for a Massaliote victory at the sea Battle of Alalia.[197] The Treasury of Massalia is in the Sanctuary of Athena Pronaia between the Doric treasury and The Tholos. The columns had palm capitals rather than Ionic volutes.[198] The feature of leaf capitals may indicate this was a characteristic of North Ionia.[199] The treasury was 28 feet by 20 feet, with an 'Ionic order of base-mouldings round the walls, consoles, the continuous sculptured frieze, and the profusion of carved ornaments'. Large convex mouldings, with horizontal grooving, exactly like the top of an Asiatic Ionic base'. There were 'typical Asiatic bases of the Ephesian type'.[200] Some fragments of the decorations and statues in Massalia's Treasury survive and are on display in Room IX of the Delphi Museum.[201]

Figure 5. Massalia's Treasury at Delphi is the first rectangular building to the left of the round Tholos with columns. The second building after is the Doric Treasury.

Massalia assisted with the Phocaean foundation of Alalia (Aléria) in Cyrnus (Corsica) following 'a direction of an oracle'. In 546 B.C. the Persians devastated Phocaea and refugees fled to Alalia.[202] Bias of Priene (one of the seven sages of Greece) had been consulted and he advised the Phocaeans to migrate en masse to Sardinia, while much earlier Thales of Miletus had advised them to 'establish a single seat of government' at Teos in the centre of Ionia.[203] Harpagus was appointed by Cyrus the Persian king to 'conduct the war in these parts, he entered Ionia' and 'Phocaea was the city against which he directed his first attack'.[204]

The people of Phocaea, when besieged by the Persian general Harpagus, asked the Persians to withdraw for a 'single day to deliberate on the answer they should return' to the terms given to them by him. Harpagus told them he knew what they were up to but granted a temporary withdrawal anyway! After they withdrew the Phocaeans embarked on their ships with their families, household goods, religious images and 'votive offerings from the fanes' then sailed away to Chios [205] at night under Creontiades leadership and subsequently onto Cyrnus [Corsica] and Massalia. [206] Popper suggests that the philosopher Xenophanes was likely amongst those who went to Cyrnus; together with his mention of Elea he was possibly the source for Herodotus on this Phocaean section. [207] Herodotus records they took with them everything but 'paintings and the works of stone or brass'.[208] He has the departure during the day but Strabo has it at night. Strabo is citing as his source Antiochus of Syracuse. 'The Persians, on their return, took possession of an empty town.' [209]

Strabo's sources, Antiochos of Syracuse (second half of the fifth century B.C.) [210] and Aristoxenus of Tarentum (fourth century B.C.) [211] both mention that after the siege by Harpagus, the Phocaeans left Phocaea and inhabited Massalia. The following is written by Aristoxenus, [212]

Φ΄ γὰρ καὶ ιδ ἔτη ἔγγιστα ἀπὸ τῶν Τρωϊκῶν ἱστορεῖται μέχρι Ξενοφάνους τοῦ φυσικοῦ καὶ τῶν Ἀνακρέοντός τε καὶ Πολυκράτους χρόνων καὶ τῆς ὑπὸ Ἁρπάγου τοῦ Μήδου Ἰώνων πολιορκίας καὶ ἀναστάσεως ἣν Φωκαεῖς Φυγόντες Μασσαλίαν ᾤκησαν.

Approximately 514 years after the Trojan War and the times of the physical philosopher Xenophanes, of Anacreon and Polycrates, and of the blockade of Ionia by Harpagus the Persian and the migration of the Phocaeans to Marseille [Massalia] to escape it.

Herodotus mentions the Phocaean refugees first went to Chios and offered to buy some islands to settle in but the Chians refused fearing they would 'establish a factory there, and exclude their merchants from commerce of those seas'. [213] With Arganthonius dead and with it the offer to settle in Tartessos the Phocaeans determined to settle in their other colony of Alalia in Cyrnus (Aléria, Corsica). Briefly they returned to Phocaea overcoming the Persian garrison but decided to leave. However more than half changed their minds being 'seized with such sadness and so great a longing to see once more their city and ancient homes' breaking an oath never to return until a heavy mass of iron they had sunk 'reappeared on the surface' and decided to sail back to Phocaea while the rest sailed for Cyrnus (Corsica). [214]

Having arrived at Cyrnus, the Phocaeans 'established themselves along with their earlier settlers at Alalia and built temples'. [215] The Massaliotes lost their strategic position in Corsica (Cyrnus) after the Battle of Alalia c. 540–535 B.C. This was because of an alliance between Carthage and Etruscan Caere. As Herodotus tells us [216] 'For five years they [the Phocaeans] annoyed their neighbours by plundering and pillaging on all sides, until at length the Carthaginians and Tyrrhenians [Etruscans],[217] leagued against them, and sent a fleet of sixty ships each to attack the town'. Massalia had used its fleet before against Carthage but still maintained its trading associations with the Etruscan city-states of Etruria. [218] Although outnumbered two to one, the Phocaeans showed their superior naval skills by beating a combined fleet of 120 ships. The Phocaeans at Alalia lost forty out of their own sixty ships and the ramming beaks of the remaining twenty 'were no longer serviceable'. This was a Cadmeian or Pyrrhic victory. Another 'victory' like this would be too costly in ships and manpower so they wisely decided to leave Alalia. Those captured Phocaean crews from the forty ships were taken to the coast of Agylla and stoned to death. Herodotus mentions that whenever livestock or people passed the spot where the Phocaeans were murdered they suffered palsy or distortions of the body, or lost use of some of their limbs. The people of Agylla consulted the oracle of Delphi on 'how to expiate their sin'. The Pythoness instructed them to honour the Phocaean dead by 'magnificent funeral rites, and solemn games, both gymnic and equestrian', which they still observed.

According to the historian Antiochus Syracusanus the Phocaeans after leaving Phocaea under the leadership of Creontiades 'sailed first to Cyrnus and Massalia, but when they were beaten off from those places founded Elea'. [219] We know from Herodotus that at Cyrnus they were 'beaten off' by the Tyrrhenians and Carthaginians. But who beat them off at Massalia? Could it have been the Massaliotes? Were they upset at Alalia's Phocaeans 'plundering and pillaging on all sides' and making trade difficult with one of their main markets the Tyrrhenians (Etruscans) [220] on who they relied heavily for supplies of wine for themselves and to sell on in Keltike (Gaul) at that period or could other pirates or Carthaginians have intercepted them before reaching Massalia? This may suggest two waves of immigration at Massalia after its foundation c. 600 B.C.

1. After the Persian invasion of Phocaea c. 545 B.C. that increased the population. Aristoxenus of Tarentum only mentions they went to Massalia and nothing about Cyrnus.[221]
2. Second wave, after the Battle of Alalia c. 540 B.C. that was 'beaten off'. [222]

Herodotus records that the surviving Phocaeans in the twenty ships collected their families in Alalia and with the 'goods and chattels that the vessels could bear' sailed to a Greek city in South Italy called Rhegium (Reggio de Calabria) [223] who was their ally. [224]

On showing the Phocaeans a new site it was a 'man from Posidonia who suggested that the oracle [given to the Phocaeans twenty-five years before] had not meant to bid them set up a town in Cyrnus the island, but to set up the worship of Cyrnus the hero' (Crynus a son of Hercules). [225] The Phocaeans left Rhegium and founded the city, which they called Hyele (Elea, Velia) c. 540 B.C. [226] (Castellammare di Brucia, now Castellammare di Velia) in South-West Italy where their new colony prospered. Through Parmenides (born c. 515 B.C.) the city of Elea achieved a big reputation for philosophy. Aristotle regarded him as one of the principal founders of metaphysics and Plato used his analysis in support of his own doctrine of Forms (Ideas). [227] Parmenides and Zeno were famous Pythagorean philosophers at Elea. [228] Zeno was the reputed founder of 'dialectic' and the 'originator of the famous paradoxes'. [229]

Pausanias writing about Delphi records,

> . . . the fourth is called the temple of Athena Forethought. Of its two images the one in the fore-temple is a votive offering of the Massaliots, and is larger than the one inside the temple. The Massaliots are a colony of Phocaea in Ionia, and their city was founded by some of those who ran away from Phocaea [this was actually the second wave c. 545 B.C.] when attacked by Harpagus and the Persians. They proved superior to the Carthaginians in a sea war, acquired the territory they now hold, and reached great prosperity. The votive offering of the Massaliotes is of bronze. [230]

Pausanias continues 'The Apollo, very near to that lion [bronze from Phocis] was dedicated by the Massaliotes as first fruits of their victory over the Carthaginians'. [231]

In the small rowing boats as you can see in the annual Oxford and Cambridge boat race a Cox (coxswain) is needed, someone who coordinates the rowers to move their oars at the same time shouting 'In, Out, In, Out' so they do not get tangled and to alter speed together. On the larger and longer Greek ships with many oars, men at the front would not be able to hear voice commands, so to keep the oars in time and to vary speed they used the Aulos.

The Aulos was a wind instrument and very much part of ancient Greek life. The sound of the Aulos was like a reed sounding oboe, usually two pipes played together [232] that 'provided rhythms for theatre plays, tragedy, comedy, dithyramb, marching armies, rowers, sacrificers and symposia, demolishers of walls and women as they worked.' [233]

An Aulos was always used in rowing ships by a 'trieraules' (pipe player). In Hollywood films (pictures, 'flicks', movies) scenes of ancient ships usually show a man with big wooden hammers beating out rhythm for the rowers. This was not used in Greek ships because the low bass sound would blend in and get lost with the similar noises of a battle. Whereas the sound of the Aulos, a reed instrument, is higher in range, distinct and can carry over a long distance. A modern proof of this is the Scottish Highland bagpipes (also known as the war-pipes) used by the British Army Scottish regiments in battle. The boatswain κελευστής shouted the stroke rhythmically and the aulos piped the time. [234] In smaller boats two swords could be clashed together or hands clapped to keep time and rhythm.

The Phocaeans had established Massalia within a circuit of a mile and a half on three low hills. It occupied a steep limestone peninsula beside the natural Harbour of Lacydon (Vieux–Port). Archaeological evidence of earliest foundations with Rhodian, Ionian, Corinthian and Attic pottery in stratified layers has been found at Eglise de la Mare and Fort St. Jean. [235]

Massalia was protected by a marsh and flanked by streams to the east landward side and by sea for the rest. The marshes were drained and filled-in during the late fifth century B.C. and a road constructed to the east of the city.[236] The headland gave the city shelter from the cold dry mistral wind in winter and spring. Placed over 40 km from the mouth of the River Rhône the main harbour avoided any silting up.

The coastline around Massalia has several bays and coves (anse) and the many calanques (fjords) towards Cassis, which can give the Greek ships shelter overnight. Sailing along the coast from a distance to the shore one could easily miss the natural Harbour of Lacydon (Vieux-Port), as the entrance is at an angle and the land looks continuous. Just past the Pharo headland there is a little cove and beach at Roucas Blanc where a Greek ship could pull in and onto the beach overnight but you would not see Lacydon Harbour (Vieux–Port) behind due to the hills. However sailing from the west closer to the shore just before Pharo at the headland at Fort St-Jean the ancient Greek sailors would have seen an inlet wide enough for their ship. Proceeding along Le Goulet (the gullet) rowing for a few minutes it still seems like an inlet or narrows than the channel turns left and astonishingly opens out into the large natural Harbour of Lacydon (Vieux–Port). At the far end on the left was a creek where the Greeks discovered fresh water springs. Beyond this were marshes. The creek was deepened into the Horn of Lacydon Harbour. A causeway at the top became the primary entry into the city [237] through the double gatehouse.

Figure 6. The entrance to Vieux-Port of present day Marseille previously called the Harbour of Lacydon of the ancient Greek city of Massalia.

Between the two headlands the promontory on the left was a better place to build a city as it was protected on two sides by the sea and one side only facing the land beyond, just like Byzantium (Constantinople-Istanbul). There were also three hills on which to have an acropolis and situate temples to Artemis and Apollo. Strabo [238] and Justin [239] also mention a Temple of Athena. The three hills were the Butte Saint-Laurent, Butte des Moulins and Butte de la Roquett. By 500 B.C. the city extended again to include another hill the Butte des Carmes and down to the Horn of Lacydon. [240]

The temples would overlook and protect the city and be a welcome sight and landmark to sailors out to sea. Also Massalia was far enough away from the River Rhône to avoid silting up. [241] Inside the Byzantine style and beautifully decorated church at Notre dame-de-la-Garde built in 1853 [242] opposite the ancient city are three domes on the ceiling. The first near the altar is circled at the bottom with Latin and Greek words. The other two domes are circled in Greek words. Above the altar is a mosaic of a sailing ship, so much a part of the maritime history of Marseille. The church dominates the present skyline overlooking ancient and modern Marseille and is a welcome site for those far out to sea. It is the best place to see an overview of the city, harbour and islands.

Justin wrote that the Phocaeans after seeing the gulf around the River Rhône 'were captivated by the beauty of the spot'.[243] The excitement the Greeks must have felt with the discovery of Lacydon would have been great as to have persuaded so many of their fellow Phocaeans to come and make a settlement there. It still has that excitement today when you sail through the two headlands and into the harbour. The coastline has the same look as that of Greece with grey rock and shrubs. Whereas Phocaea is hemmed in by their yellow/brown steep hills covered with shrub and cannot expand,[244] Massalia's coast extends at least 7 km inland before the hills rise to the mountains. Though the soil was poor, unlike other Greeks this is what the Phocaeans were used to. The Phocaeans not only proved skilful in astronomy and navigation but tough in surviving and resourceful to be able to make a living in their settlements.

Walking along the present city of Massalia (Marseille) in the summer heat, along the promenade in the evening so much a feature of Greek life as it is too hot to be indoors, the colour of the blue sky and close to the sea it felt so familiar. Also the Frioul Islands just off shore was like the entrance to Phocaea.[245] No wonder that the Greek Phocaeans founded Massalia there; it was a home from home an Apoikia.

Growth of Massalia

Massalia grew faster than first planned for within sixty years the original city wall was enlarged due to the refugees from the Persian invasion of their mother-city of Phocaea 545 B.C. Many went to Alalia (Aléria) in Corsica but some would have gone to their families, friends or employers[246] at Massalia. Also we have Antiochos of Syracuse[247] who states the refugees went to live in Massalia and Cyrnus, and founded Elea (Hyele, Velia), as well as Aristoxenus of Tarentum who wrote that they went to Massalia.[248]

From the original foundation in 600 B.C. Massalia had enlarged three times by 100 B.C. Please note that the original shoreline of the harbour was different (see Figure 7). The present city has extended out into the harbour.

There were artificial terraces that changed shape several times as the city grew. Houses were constructed 'in terrace-form on the slopes of the hills and in regular blocks in the lower areas, using stone, wood, and unbaked brick'.[249] Vitruvius mentions roofs 'without tiles made of mud, mixed with earth and straw'.[250] White limestone for the buildings came mainly from the nearby hill of Sainte-Victor south of Lacydon (Vieux-Port). The pink limestone from the La Couronne quarry became more popular in use particularly from the second century B.C.[251] The Greek city walls excavated so far in the Jardin des Vestiges are from the second century B.C. and seem on top of an earlier wall following the same line. There is a double gatehouse with the main road to Italy, which is paved, running through it. The late Roman surface of the well-constructed road consists of limestone slabs from Cassis with transverse grooves to stop horses slipping. A milestone dedicated to Constantine II A.D. 337–340 was situated 30 metres east of the gate.[252] The excavated wall is built from the stone quarries of La Couronne 40 km away and constructed in the '*emplekton* technique', three metres thick, and joined without cement or metal brackets. A herringbone pattern is carved on the facing stones the same as at Saint Blaise.[253]

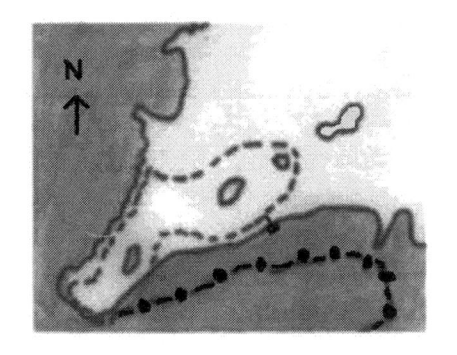

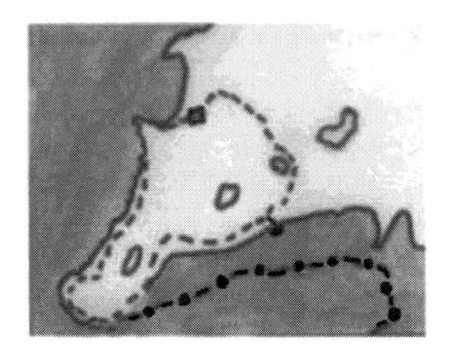

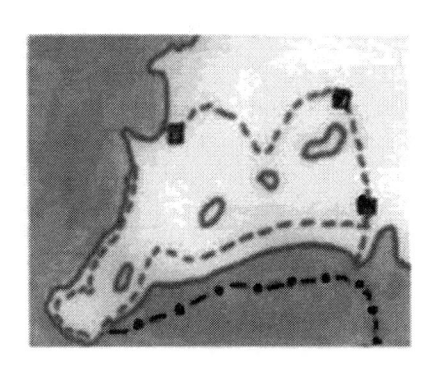

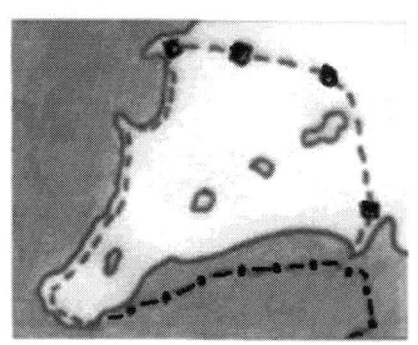

Figure 7. Growth of the Greek city-state of Massalia (Marseille) from 600 B.C.–100 B.C. Walls — — —. Gates ■. Present harbour •—•—•.

Winds

Seeing a sailing boat with two sails approaching the Le Goulet entrance into Marseille's harbour in the early evening in July with the breeze filling both sails, suddenly not filling the first sail and picking up to full sail must be tricky to turn and enter. The sails were then lowered and the boat's engines gave the power needed to turn into the harbour. For the Greek Pentoconters and Triremes they had the power of their oars to get through this stretch of water. Waiting a few days for the strong breezes to drop I went on one of the many tour boats with a powerful engine at 11.30 am around the bay and the Islands of Chateau d'If and Frioul. Vieux-Port (Lacydon Harbour) and Le Goulet was as calm as a mill-pond yet shortly out from the entrance it was very bouncy as the currents and wind were quite strong where the sailing boat the other evening seem to lose full sail power trying to turn due to the direction of the wind.

In the Braun and Hogenberg map of A.D. 1575 [254] (Figure 100) in the top right of the city we see at the beginning of Moulins (windmills) there was a tower 'Tour de Horolog'. Whether this may have been placed on the site of the masonry gnomon of Pytheas to fix the latitude of the ancient Greek city of Massalia is going by the name alone as a tentative clue. Pliny the Elder explains the Horologian or Dial,

'The understanding of Shadows, and what is named Gnonomice, Anaximenes the Milesian the disciple of Anaximander above-named discovered: and he was the first also that showed in Lacedaemon the Horologue (or Dial) which they called Sciotericon'. [255]

The ancient Greek market place (Agora) has been identified at Place de Lenche. [256] From west to east (left to right in the photograph Figure 2) Temple, Amphitheatre, Agora, and Temple. The Greek Theatre, Roman Docks and the Greek Ionic capital of a temple were discovered in the post-war reconstruction. The area around City Hall had been proposed for demolition by the architect Beaudoin, commissioned by the council of Marseille in 1940 but the Second World War intervened. In January 1943 five acres of the old city next to the Harbour of Lacydon (Vieux-Port) were dynamited by German engineers.[257] Hitler had called Marseille a nest of spies. [258] Twenty thousand Marseillais had been ordered to evacuate their homes by Nazi SS troops and French Vichy police officers. During the post-war reconstruction the slopes to the north of the site were all flattened changing the topography.[259] Archaeological excavations for Marseille were directed by Professor Fernand Benoit Chief Archaeologist for Provence who did much to find and save some of Marseille's ancient past in spite of the prevalent desire to speedily eradicate the recent damage and memories of the war.

Figure 8. Behind the base of a Greek Tower overlooking the end of the Horn of Lacydon clearly outlined by new harbour walls constructed first century A.D. ending on the left where the main road from Italy into the city passed through a double gatehouse of the second century B.C.

Figure 9. Side view of the base of a Greek tower: on the right the first century A.D. new harbour walls of the Horn of Lacydon clearly ending with the ancient main road from Italy right to left going into the city through a Greek double gatehouse second century B.C.

Figure 10. Foreground, the line of the harbour wall of the Horn facing the ancient Greek city with a tower on the left and the city walls on the right. The Horn ends a few yards to the right and next to the main road to the city through a double gatehouse.

Figure 11. Carved stone from an earlier building reused into Massalia's Horn of Lacydon Harbour wall.

Figure 12. A seagull on the city wall of Massalia (Marseille) by the ancient Horn of Lacydon docks.

Figure 13. Marseille panorama, on the left is the Gulf of Lion; middle Vieux-Port Harbour (Lacydon). The darker roofs in the middle show a triangular shape of the old city. The Horn was to the right of the harbour, filled in and built upon in the seventh century A.D.

The present city has over the centuries built into Lacydon Harbour with houses, jetties and promenades. On the north side the original coastline of the ancient Greek city is along the line of the Museum of the Roman Docks by Rue du Lacydon and Rue des Olives. In Place Vivaux the Roman docks installations can still be seen in situ as well as artefacts from sixth century B.C. to fourth century A.D. On the east side by The Bourse, the roads and promenade are all where the Horn and the bottom end of Lacydon used to be. The Horn of Lacydon was 180 metres long and 3 metres deep.[260]

The Bourse Centre

The site behind the Stock Exchange (le Bourse) was cleared in 1967 to make a shopping centre. The Horn of Lacydon was discovered, with remains of houses: a Greek city gate with two towers, a section of the substantial city walls, the masonry outline of the Hellenistic and later Roman docks, tryglyphes and metopes Doric in style 9 m by 13 m enclosing an area for cremations,[261] a reservoir with evidence of a water wheel, and the large paved main road from the city gate towards Rome. The road also formed a straight line into the city along the present Rue Henri Foccai and Grande Rue. The basement of the Centre Bourse is the Musée d'Histoire de Marseille that leads out onto the Horn of Lacydon and contains the excavated Greek walls that zigzag and a double gatehouse of the city gate second century B.C. with the paved roadway. The tower on the gate had two arrow slits (though these became known the 'Walls of Crinas' his rebuilding work took place during the first century A.D.), in front is a fifth century A.D. Roman outer wall [262] and the built up harbour in Hellenistic and Roman times now in the Jardin des Vestiges. The main lawn was placed at the same level as where the blue water in the harbour would have been and is now an equally restful 'sea' of green. Several cats reside in the garden fed by the voluntary beneficence of an elderly French lady. Large seagulls confidently stroll at leisure amongst the cats undisturbed along the ancient docks now void of water yet still looking for a meal, perhaps sensing the presence of water in the subterranean marsh extending as far back as Cours Belsunce. [263]

In the Museum d'Histoire de Marseille the display states the three main gods worshipped at Massalia were Ephesian Artemis, Apollo Delphinian and Athena. There was also Dionysius, god of wine, Leucothea *la déesse blanche* (white goddess) *salvatrice des naufrages*, Aphrodite, Hercules and Lacydon young god of the Horn (*Lacydon le jeune dieu cornu*). Among 50 seated Cybele *naiskos stelai* of local limestone shaped like a miniature temple found in Marseille [264] was displayed a small statue of Asiatic goddess Cybele of the sixth century B.C. found in les fouilles de la Place Villeneuve-Bargemon. The museum was closed in 2011 to undergo a complete refurbishment in time for the European City of Culture events of 2013. [265]

Morel points out with interest the cult of 'Leucothea, the white goddess' helpful to navigators, that showed affinities with the people of Lampsacos, Hyele [Elea] and Euboeans as something significant with the 'Phocaean Tyrrhenian emporia'. [266]

Due to the poor quality of the surrounding land for producing wheat/cereals, Massalia was founded for trade [267] and subsequently controlled the route up the River Rhône into Gaul. Strabo comparing the Greek and Roman ways of founding cities wrote, 'for if the Greeks had the repute of aiming most happily in the founding of cities, in that they aimed at beauty, strength of position, harbours and productive soil'. [268] But for the Phocaean founders the rugged soil was just like that of Phocaea and the poor land that may have deterred other Greeks was what the Phocaeans were used to as they successfully made the cities of Elea and Massalia. [269] The Massaliotes were able to plant olive trees and grapevines. [270] Olives are also suited to 'poor soils and also steep slopes' up to 650 metres while grapevines can produce at 750 metres. [271] Archaeological evidence of a vineyard from the Hellenistic period was found close by Massalia at Saint-Jean du Désert. Another from the beginning of the third century B.C. was found while excavating the Alcazar 'not far from the surrounding wall' of Massalia. [272] They traded wine and pottery for corn and amber.

What could have led the Massaliotes into the interior? Tin was also available from the Lower Loire. Greek vases from the sixth and fifth century B.C. and Massaliote amphorae have been found at Bourges and elsewhere. Other attractions may have been 'copper in the southern foothills of the Massif Central, iron from the interior of the country, and Gallic gold', as well as wheat, 'salted meats of Franche-Comté' a 'region with a concentration of Phocaean imports'. [273] Egypt under Ptolemy Philadelphus during the third century B.C. obtained supplies of iron from Massalia and Etruria. [274]

From their own coastal area Massalia could access 'fish products, salt, coral, purple, trachyte, resin, cork, soda, aromatic and medicinal plants'. [275] Quantities of Massaliote amphorae (pottery made vessels for transporting the wine, oil etc.), fine figured pottery, bronze flagons and wine drinking vessels have been found in 'southern Gaul and as far north as the upper Danube'. [276] Athenaeus comparing wines wrote 'The wine from Massalia good; but it is uncommon, rich, and full-bodied'. [277] Athenaeus mentions various drinking containers such as the Phialai 'the vessel that is set both its stems and its brim; and this mode of setting the Phialai is Ionic and ancient. At any rate the people of Massalia to this very day place the Phialai face down'. [278]

Among important markets for the Massaliotes were the Etruscans. Over 80 per cent of the amphorae found in the old port excavations at Massalia dated 600-530 B.C. was Etruscan. There is a suggestion that Etruscan 'metics' lived in Massalia from the inscriptions they left there and in the cities of Saint Blaise and Lattes. Massalia begins to dominate the wine market in the region by late fifth century and by the fourth century Etruscan commerce has reduced considerably.[279] Perhaps it may be that as Massalia extended its possession of land of the 'surrounding plains'[280] it would take some years for grapevines to be established to the point where they had a surplus of their own produced wine to sell and trade. In the meantime wine was readily available from the Etruscans in Italy that can account for the evidence of its amphorae found at Massalia.

For the Etruscans it was good business selling to the Massaliotes back home, even if a rival trader this was a sure customer, as well as those they had in Gaul at a greater distance. Wine was a consumable product with demand greater than supply. If we use the measure of the wine imports from Etruria it would seem that it took Massalia around seventy years from its foundation in 600 B.C. to have extended and control enough of the surrounding land to have established a sufficient quantity of its own grapevines for wine production to export. Though we must take into account that wines were also imported from Ionian cities like Thasos, Cos, Cnidos and also Rhodes in particular.[281] Depending on the quantity this may have affected the drop in imports from Etruria?

Massalia's Chora (Territory)

How far inland was the Massalia Chora (territory)? Various arguments have been put forward that up to the late third century B.C. expansion was limited to 10 km in the Huveaune Valley hemmed in by mountains, hills and native hillforts. Buried Massaliote coin hoards suggest a large area of commerce dating from: **mid-3rd century B.C.** in Lattes and late **3rd** in Marseille: **3rd to 2nd century B.C.** Agde, Apt, Avignon, Beaumes-de-Venise, Bougé-Chambalud 50 km S of Lyon (2,000 AR obols), Bourges 60 km NE of Lyon (1,000+ AR obols), Fontes, Saint-Gervais (7,000 AR obols), Saint-Romans 35 km W of Grenoble (3,000 AR obols), Tourves, and Vitrolles: **2nd century B.C.** in Entremont, Ansouis, Cadenet 30 km N of Aix (1,800 AR drachma), Tourdan, Valence, Aix, and Bouches-du-Rhône: **2nd to 1st century B.C.** in Le Brusc, Charbuy, Tournoux near Barcelonnette, Tourves, and Marsillargues: **1st century B.C.** in Glanum, Castlet de Fontvielle, and Cavaillon.[282]

The size of Massalia and its population was no smaller than some of the other cities of Magna Graecia but without the fertile land. Massalia was able to maintain this level of population from transporting grain via the sea, as did Athens. The expansion of the Romans in France actually benefited the Massaliotes with an increase in territory.[283] Nevertheless we should take into account that before the Romans entered the region permanently we do have mention from Plutarch that after the Battle of Aquae Sextiae (Aix-en-Provence) at Mont St. Victoire due to the huge number of slain Ambrones and Toygeni that the Massaliotes 'fenced their vineyards round with the bones of the fallen'.[284] If the Massaliotes had grapevines planted here at a distance of over 33 km from Massalia this would indicate a larger territory under their control around 102 B.C. Baux-de-Provence is 83 km from Massalia where a sixth century B.C. bronze Corinthian helmet was found[285] (see Figure 105).

Even if it was only 10 km of this suggested small development of territory and a large gap i.e. not having a continuous territory before reaching the next Massaliote city, one could put forward the argument that Massalia did not have an empire in the grand sense as 'a political unit having an extensive territory' but it could also be made up of a 'number of territories or nations' and either type ruled by a 'single supreme authority', or in an example given for a publishing empire 'an extensive enterprise under a unified authority'.[286] Phocaea founded cities in the Western Mediterranean and Massalia did the same is proved archaeologically. The Delian League with its member city-states spread far and wide over the Aegean Sea is often described as becoming the 'Athenian Empire'[287] in that one city led politically and militarily enforced its decrees on the others.

Pausanias described Panopeus near Chaironeia, as a Greek 'city' even though he notes it did not have any civic buildings.[288] Massalia had a government system that was highly praised by Aristotle, Strabo and Cicero: civic buildings: and was definitely the leading city of its colonies. But what as: an empire, a commercial network or a commonwealth? Massalia consisted of elements from all these. A flexible system allowing some autonomy is possibly indicated by Emporion and Rhodus's coin minting? We have evidence of direct rule of at least two of their cities [289] and therefore Massalia could also qualify as an empire with its army and navy that enforced and maintained its independence for over five centuries. Massalia the city founded by merchants could be described, given another definition of an empire, as 'an extensive enterprise under a unified authority'.[290]

Amphorae and Dolia: Transporting Goods

Amphorae were needed to store and transport goods and were made of two types. One was of light clay called 'feldspathiques' around 550/540-500 B.C. The other type 520/510 B.C.[291] used a mica temper was added to local clay to produce amphorae made in Massalia. The mica temper came from the coast of the Maura Mountains 90 km east of the city.[292] A few of these amphorae have been found at late Halstatt and early La Tene sites that were phases of Celtic culture.

From its foundation c. 600 B.C. Massalia imported Etruscan wine then exported it to Gaul until they were able to produce a surplus from their own grapevines, as is evident from the widespread remains of Massaliote amphorae after 530 B.C.[293] However this may not be exclusively carrying Massaliote wine if wine was still imported in ships with large dolia. The dolia being fixed and inbuilt into the ship the wine would have to be emptied into smaller containers to transfer it from ship to shore and beyond? Logically they would be using their own locally made amphorae. What the Massaliote amphorae remains can indicate is the reach of their trade. There seems to be a lack of Massaliote wine amphora 225–200 B.C. while their merchants traded in Italian wines?[294] The remains of Italian amphorae after 125 B.C. show a ten-fold increase in Gaul and by 100 B.C. Italian wines had replaced those of Massalia for export.[295] Bats mentions a new type of Massaliote flat-bottomed amphorae appears in the later first century B.C. (found at the Butte des Carmes, Massalia) suggesting an increase in trade of their own wine and not just those they imported?

Shipwrecks

There have been few ancient shipwrecks found off Spain, Languedoc and Rousillion. But on the rocky Provencal coast particularly the bay of Massalia twenty-seven have been found from the sixth to mid-first century B.C. These ships show evidence of mixed cargoes from different areas e.g. fifth century B.C. shipwreck 'Plane 2 near Massalia (Marseille) had around fifty mixed Italo-Greek, Massaliote, and Punic amphorae, an assortment of Attic fine ware ceramics and at least sixty copper ingots'.[296]

A ship discovered in 1970 and given the name La Madrague de Giens was 130 foot long (40 m) and weighed approximately 400 tons. The ship had been loaded with 600 amphorae. Another ship given the name La Cavaiere found in the bay was smaller around 20 tons and used to distribute the cargo from the larger ships. At Massalia there were thirteen Phocaean shipwrecks, only two of them were 26 feet long, and their capacity of cargo would be around thirty amphorae. The length of these boats was 130 feet, 65 feet and 26 feet. Luc Long head cultural preservationist at DRASSM describes the trade was at all levels.[297] There was the 'vin de table' the basic everyday day wine transported in bulk as people drank a lot. This was transported in huge jars called 'dolia' and vintage wines travelled in amphorae.

Figure 14. Amphora Massaliote, late fifth to early fourth century B.C. Musée des Docks Romains, Marseille.

Several dolia were discovered as part of the 'Docks Romains' in Massalia next to the ancient shoreline of the Harbour of Lacydon (Vieux-Port) in 1947.[298] The later Roman docks (Docks Romains) in Massalia were built c. A.D. 40-50 and in use until the fourth century A.D. when it was destroyed by a fire. Benoit who oversaw the excavation found remains of a second floor giving access straight onto the main east-west road.[299] We know from Martial (first century A.D.) that Massalia exported their wine to Rome.[300]

Dolias were made of baked clay and could hold as much as 2,500 litres of wine and were as tall as five and a half feet (1.7 m). Dolias were wedged and fixed into the centre of the ship's hull while the ship was being built, before the cross beams and bridge was fitted. Some ships carried fifteen of them. They were like the tankers of their day. There were risks for sailors, as Dolias did not have a consistent strength.

Robert Roman an ancient shipbuilder researcher at MMSH humanities research centre in Aix-en-Provence thought this system was given up in under two centuries for safety reasons.[301] It was crucial for the ship's stability to stack the amphorae expertly so as not to break in a storm or rough seas. The amphorae could be stacked three or four rows high. Fenders were slipped in between the gaps for extra stability. A dolia breaking and releasing 2,500 litres of wine sloshing about beneath deck would be disastrous for the ship's balance. There is evidence that dolias were carefully maintained and many have been found with cracks that have been repaired with lead seals.[302]

At first Massalia imported fine ceramic from Athens for home consumption and some was traded to natives between sixth to fourth century B.C. By third century B.C. Campania wares took over from Attica as main import. Within a generation of Massalia's founding they started producing their own ceramic fine ware of two wheel-made types 'Ceramique clarie' (Pseudo Ionian) and 'Gray-Monochrome'. The former was popular down to the second century B.C. while the latter lasted to the end of the fifth century B.C. Massalia and its colonies used them and to trade with the natives.[303] 'Ceramique clarie' was popular taking its forms in turn from Ionian, Attic and the Campanian.

Designs from the natives such as a 'carenated bowl' popular with the Celts in the Rhône basin were featured in Gray-Monochrome made at Massalia. This showed they were producing for the local markets.

At Carpentras 20 km north-east of Avignon, excavations 2 km east from here uncovered the site of the Memnini tribe who were neighbours of the Cavares and Voconces. Various pottery fragments found included Phocaean grey bowls with wavy decorations, local products with the same decoration imitating Phocaean vases. Urns, basins from rough clay and Campanian pottery are represented. Also some bronze coins with the bull of Massalia.[304]

Massalia cooking ware seems to have been produced by local workshops in the area surrounding Massalia between second and first century B.C. As to where this was done before it is assumed in Massalia itself. A 'large amphorae kiln' was found north of Moulins Hill in Massalia dating to the fifth century B.C.[305] and for a short period (425–325 B.C.) Massalia made 'a series imitating Attic black gloss ceramics'. Further evidence of pottery production is found in Marseille (Massalia) with kilns/kiln wasters at 'rue Negrel, the rue Leca, the Centre Bourse, and the Butte des Carmes'.[306]

Figure 15. Ionian bowls sixth century B.C. black type A (Villard and Vallet) and ceramic bowl light colour with handles on display at the Musée des Docks Romains Marseille.

Figure 16. Attic black figure pottery from the second half of the fifth century B.C. displayed at the Musée des Docks Romains Marseille.

Figure 17. Kantharos early Hellenistic period: Greek graffito says 'tes Hygies' which means 'of Health' (Hygieia being the Greek goddess of healing) in the Musée des Docks Romains Marseille.

In the old Iberian settlement of Pech-Maho near Narbonne in Languedoc an Etruscan lead letter tablet was discovered dating between 575–550 B.C. This was also used by a Greek to record a contract of a boat at Emporion, Spain (a colony of Massalia) by two Greek merchants Kypros and Heron of Ios. The witnesses had Spanish names of Basigerros and Bleruas. The Greek wrote over the soft lead that contained another earlier contract made by Etruscans. The original writing of Etruscan with two names of Venel and Utavo describes a business deal at Matalai (Massalia).[307] There was writing in Greek on one side and on the reverse Etruscan. The size was that it could be held in the palm of your hand rather than a stone or bronze tablet and being lead could be reused.[308] The writing states that 'a Greek called Heronoiios has a half share to the value of "two eights and a half", of which "two sixes and a half" have already been paid "on the river . . . where the barges are usually moored"'. The lead document is drawn up in the 'usual Greek practice but the witnesses have strange Iberian names, Basigerros, Bleraus, Golobiur and Sedegon' and going on other documents Murray suggests this one refers to the wine trade.[309]

Gradually Massalia spread their cultural influence along the lower Rhône valley. Greek goods made their way up the River Rhône and remains of Greek pottery at Mt. Lassois were found just over a hundred miles south-east of Paris overlooking the Seine. At Vix, the cemetery of Mt. Lassois, in the burial mound of a woman thirty-five years old described as the 'Vix princess' the largest and finest Greek bronze krater was discovered in 1953 and now on display at Chatillon-sur-seine. Made c. 530 B.C. in South Italy (Magna Graecia)[310] the neck decorated with warriors and chariots and its handles with gorgons, standing 1.64 metres high. The huge Krater could hold 1,100 litres of wine. That is the equivalent today of 1,466 bottles of wine.[311]

Figure 18. Vix Krater c. 530 B.C. found in a burial mound at the cemetery of Mt. Laissos, France. At 1.64 metres high it is the largest and finest Greek Krater found so far.

Figure 19. Vix Krater c. 530 B.C. being positioned at the Musée Chatillon-sur-Seine in Burgundy, France. The Krater held 1,100 litres of wine the equivalent of 1,466 bottles of wine at 75cl each.

The Vix Krater was found together with an Etruscan bronze flagon [312] and three basins [313] and two Athenian clay cups, one from c. 525 B.C. black figure by the 'Wraith Painter' diameter 18 cm,[314] which dated the burial to the end of the sixth century B.C. [315] The Greek and Etruscan wine-drinking kit indicates a role of feasting and imported wine in that Celtic society as well as the high status of a woman. [316] A Greek bronze cauldron was found in a tumulus two miles away with four griffin protomes below its rim complete with its tripod stand. [317]

Another bronze griffin from a bronze cauldron was found in the Loire near Angers that is a possible tin route from the Channel, Brittany, and River Loire to the River Rhône. Greek vases of the sixth to fifth century and Massaliote amphorae were found at Bourges and other sites.[318] Nimes was trading with Massalia from the fifth century B.C. [319] Greek objects were traded as far as: Switzerland: Germany (Greek ivory sphinxes found in a Halstatt grave at Asperg, Stuttgart): a cauldron found near Stockholm in Sweden: and Greek pottery discovered at the Heuneberg fortress town in South Germany.

Unlike Mt. Lassois getting to the fortress town of Heuneburg overlooking the Schwabian Danube south-west of Munich needed several changes of transport. A large section of the wall is 'mud brick on a stone sockle with projecting rectangular bastions at intervals' built c. 550 B.C. and suggests a Greek specialist in charge of construction at Heuneburg.[320] The Mediterranean building material is unsuited to the central European climate and seems to be built for ostentation.[321] Boardman (1999) also mentions some later sixth century B.C. Greek pottery has been found there.

At Hochdorf near Asperg there was found a bronze beam of a pair of fine Greek scales used for measuring level of payment for traded goods against Greek precious metals coins, a form of transaction used in the sixth century B.C.[322] At Hochdorf a Halstatt grave revealed a bronze cauldron 'with tree loop handles and lions on the shoulder' they included other works thought to be made in Italy and Etruria.[323] There was also a silver goblet (now lost) with a Gallic inscription in Greek letters 'mead of a kinsman'.[324] Also a Halstatt burial at Asperg has a bronze tripod stand and Greek ivory sphinxes with amber faces 'from Italy'. A fine Spartan bronze vase 64 cm high made c. 600 B.C. was found at Grachwyl, Switzerland.[325]

Mount Lassois is situated above the River Seine: Heuneberg on the Upper Danube: Britzgyberg at the Burgundian Gate dominated the River Ill flowing into the River Rhine: and Asperg commanded traffic on the River Neckar. All these towns were Princely seats commanding strategic positions. Archaeology can show Greek goods went into France, Spain, Germany, Switzerland, Austria, and up to Sweden but not who carried them. Nevertheless a definite Greek presence from Massalia is suggested; in Mount Lassois with the craftsmen needed to assemble the huge bronze krater for mixing wine and water and holding up to 1100 litres found in Vix; the Mediterranean style of construction of mud brick city wall at Heuneberg; and the bronze scales dating from 550 B.C. used for trading goods against Greek precious metal coins found at Hochdorf, Asperg.[326]

The abandonment of the Halstatt fortress towns saw wealth and power of the barbarians move to the east and north. The lack of trade saw Mt. Lassois abandoned to. With the evidence available by 1980 Boardman thought Massalia's imports of fine pottery declined as the market seemed to have dried up by 500 B.C. marking 'the transition between the cultures of Halstatt and La Tene'.[327] However the view that there was a 'recession' in the fifth century B. C. and in one generation Massalia had lost their trade routes to the Atlantic and through France will need to take into account recent finds. Greek pottery imported at Bourges was at its highest between 530 and 420 B.C.[328] with Bragny and Lyon-Vaise c. 400 B.C. also showing an active market penetration of Greek goods.

Around the Gulf of Lion there were a mass of imports during the fifth century B.C. of Attic red figure cups, rarer kraters, and containers including lekanides found in Theline (Arelate, Arles), La Monédière near Bessan not far from Agde (Agathe Tyche), Béziers, Enséurune, Mailhac; Montlaurès and Pech-Maho near Narbonne, and Ruscino near Perpignan.[329]

Massalia and its colonies in the Western Mediterranean were strong enough to survive a recession if indeed there had been one. Boardman had noted further inland the imported bronzes and pottery of this time were shown from archaeology to be Etruscan.[330] Therefore he suggested that new routes to the Celts through Italy had been created. Other Greeks colonies had started to appear along the Adriatic. Corcyra and Cnidians from East Greece founded a colony on an island 'Black Corcyra' (Korčula) to supply the new routes in North Italy. Boardman says the settlement took place early sixth century B.C.[331] In the fourth century B.C. the Issaians also sent settlers to Black Corcyra.[332]

Corcyra (Corfu) was originally founded for the western trade route. Corcyra and Corinth had founded Epidamnus (Dyrrachium, now Durazzo, Albania) in 627 B.C. Corinth founded Apollonia (near Pojani, Albania) further south by 600 B.C. [333]

There were Greek trading posts in Etruscan cities. Though it is not clear whether founded by Greeks or Etruscan, Spina contained so many Greeks that they themselves called it a Greek city and in the ancient cemetery, archaeologists have discovered the largest quantity (4,000) of Athenian vases ever found. [334] By Strabo's time

> Spina, which though now only a small village, long ago was a Greek city of repute. At any rate, a treasury of the Spinitae is to be seen at Delphi; and everything else that history tells about them shows that they were once masters of the sea. Moreover, it is said that Spina was once situated by the sea; although at the present time the place is in the interior, about ninety stadia distant from the sea. [335]

During the fifth and fourth century B.C. the city of Massalia expanded with the city walls being extended particularly the northern section.[336] No foreigner was allowed to carry weapons in the city. Women were not allowed to drink wine. 'There was a law, as in Miletus compelling women to drink water.' [337] Massalia's Phocaean identity and cultural traditions were strong and showed continuity across the ages. This is recorded by Cicero, [338] Livy, Strabo and Valerius Maximus.[339] Silius Italicus writing in the first century A.D. stated 'The settlers from Phocaea though surrounded by arrogant tribes and kept in awe by their savage rites of their barbarian neighbours, still retain the manners and dress of their ancient home among warlike populations.' [340]

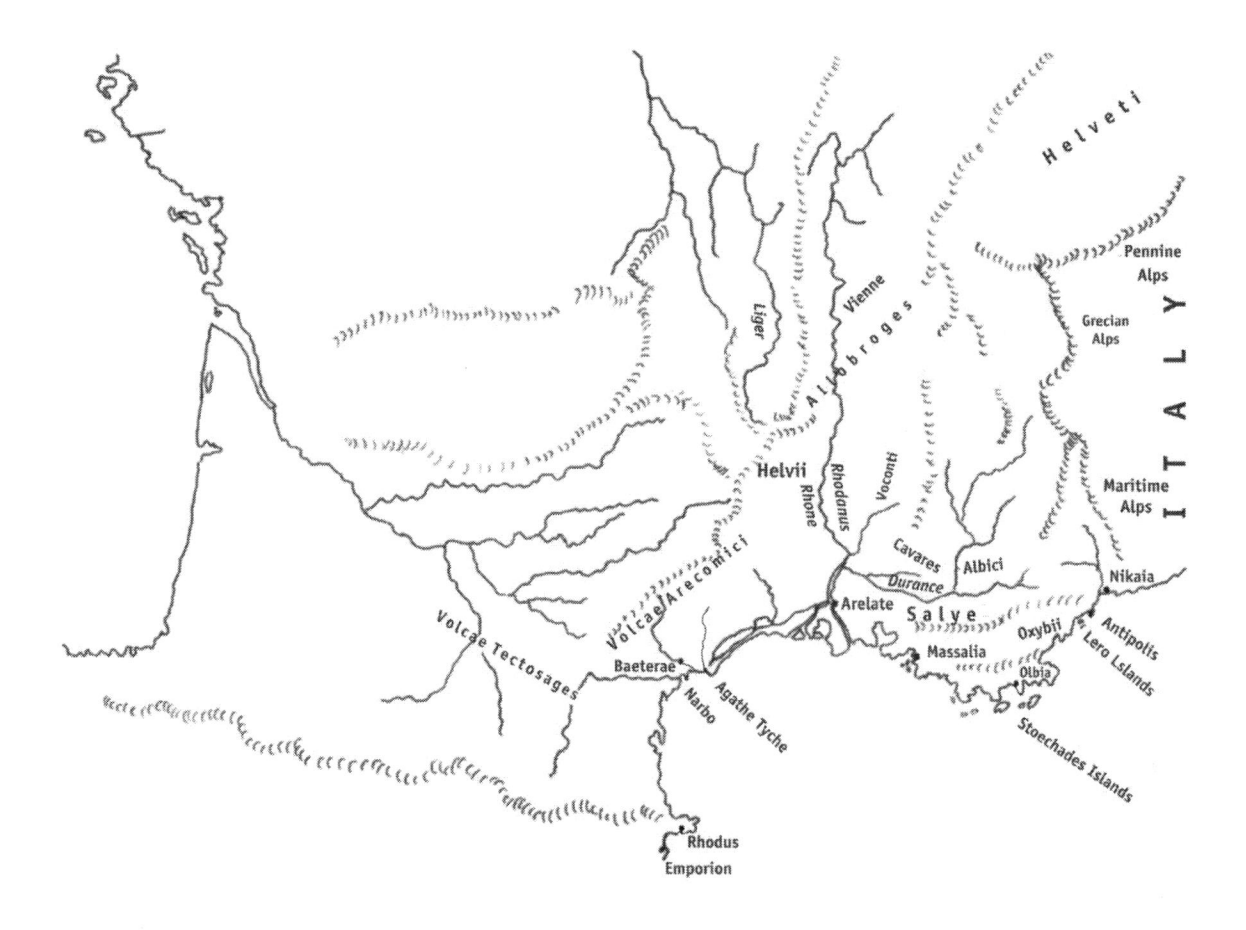

Figure 20. Map of the Celtic tribes around Massalia c. first century B.C.

Events Connected to Massalia (Marseille)

Invasions around the mother-city Phocaea in Asia Minor caused a number of Ionians to leave and come to the Western Mediterranean cities of Magna Graecia in South Italy, [341] Alalia (Aléria) in Corsica [342] and Massalia (Marseille) in France. [343]

600 B.C. Massalia (Marseille) founded in Gaul (France) by settlers from the Greek city of Phocaea in Ionia, Asia Minor. [344]

565 B.C. Phocaea together with Massalia establish their colony of Alalia (Aléria in Corsica). [345]

546 B.C. Following the conquest of Lydia by King Cyrus and the Persians, [346] ambassadors from the Greeks of Aeolia and Ionia went to see Cyrus at Sardis.[347] He refused their offers. The Ionians set about fortifying their cities. All except the Milesians who had a separate treaty with Cyrus attended subsequent meetings in Panionium. The Ionians all agreed to 'send ambassadors to Sparta to implore assistance'.[348] Deputies from the Aeolians and Ionians were sent 'with all speed to Sparta'. [349] In Sparta they chose Pythermus from Phocaea to be their spokesman. After a long speech the Spartans 'were not to be persuaded, and voted against sending any succour'. [350] However, the Spartans sent a Penteconter (fifty-oared warship) to assess the situation and arrived at Phocaea 'the most powerful of the remaining Ionian states'. [351] They 'sent to Sardis Lacrines, the most distinguished of their number to prohibit Cyrus, in the name of the Lacedaemonians, from offering molestation to any city of Greece, since they would not allow it'.[352]

545 B.C. [353] Herodotus recorded that after fleeing Harpagus and the Persian invasion the Phocaeans sailed to Chios [354] having made an oath never to return to Phocaea. However 'more than half their number' could not bear to leave and returned to Phocaea [355] while the rest sailed to their colonies in Alalia (Aléria in Corsica) and Massalia (Marseille in France). Most Phocaeans from Alalia departed five years later to found Hyele (Elea, Velia, modern Castellammare di Brucia) in South Italy [356] following the naval Battle of Alalia against the combined fleets of Carthaginians and Tyrrhenians c. 540 B.C.[357]

540–530 B.C. Theline (Arelate, Arles) this was originally a native settlement of the seventh century B.C. as revealed by the excavations of the Winter Gardens/Jardin d'Hiver. Other objects found shows that Greeks settled alongside the local town from 540–530 B.C. The thousands of fragments of Massaliote amphorae and some pottery found in the Vaise quarter of Lyon confirm the importance of this route for trading 'from at least 540 B.C.' [358] Lyon and Arles are connected via the River Rhône; the River Saône joins the River Rhône at Lyon: and part of Massalia's trade route.

535 B.C. Theline (The Provider) later grew into Arelate (Town-in-the marsh), Arles.[359] The first Phocaean settlement was destroyed by the Ligurians c. 535 B.C.[360] Theline[361] is mentioned by Avienus along with Rhodonusia as Greek cities in Gaul, [362] *Arelatus illic civitas attollitur / Theline vocata sub priore saeculo / Graio incolente. multa nos Rhodano super /. . .* [363]

c. 540 B.C. Massalia minted coins from 540 B.C. 'in which small silver coins of Phocaea circulated in Provence'. A treasure of 2,130 coins dating to 525–470 B.C. was found in the village of 'Auriol' near Marseille (Massalia). This 'Auriol type' 'was silver anepigraphic coins (first of all obols, their multiples and divisions) of the Phocaean and, later, Milesian standard usually bearing on the reverse a hollow square.' [364] Some of the earliest depictions of black Africans appear on twenty-four of the half obol coins 490–470 B.C. that Picard has under 'religious' or in connection with Odysseus's travels: [365] perhaps even from Euthymenes of Massalia's exploration of West Africa? After c. 480 B.C. small denominations continue but with double relief. Massalia minted various issues of silver drachma and bronze obols with obverse: head of Apollo/reverse: wheel. Helmeted male head with wheel emblem/wheel: Artemis/lion: Athena/tripod: Athena/Eagle: Lacydon/wheel: Lacydon/lion and others. The name of the city either as M, MA, Massa, Massali, and Massaliton appears and coin minting continued even after the capitulation to Julius Caesar 49 B.C. [366]

Fifth Century B.C.

494 B.C. Ionian Revolt from Persia

Battle of Lade

The Ionian states assemble a fleet of 353 triremes at Lade [367] with 70,000 allied Greek troops against the 600 mostly Phoenician vessels [368] and are persuaded by Dionysius of Phocaea to give him the naval command. Though he only had brought three ships [369] the naval skills of the Phocaeans were known. Sailing out and fighting was not enough. Tactics and complex manoeuvres were needed and that took practice. He vigorously trained the Ionians who after a week morning till night had had enough of the hard training and refused any more or to take orders 'of this Phocaean braggart'. [370]

Seeing 'that all was disorder among the Ionians' the Samians made a deal with the Persians. During the following Battle of Lade with the Phoenician fleet of the Persian's the Samians withdrew, the Lesbian fleet followed 'and the example once set was followed by the greater number of the Ionians'. Eleven of the Samian ships refused to withdraw and fought. Also the Chians with their 100 ships took on the Persian's Phoenician fleet but lost.

Dionysius having captured three ships saw the battle was eventually lost and knew the Persians would now be free to take Phocaea and the rest of Ionia. He sailed off to Phoenicia sinking many merchantmen and 'gained a great booty'. Then Dionysius went to Sicily where he 'established himself as a corsair, and plundered the Carthaginians and Tyrrhenians, but did no harm to the Greeks'. [371]

480 B.C. Xerxes I, king of Persia plans the invasion of mainland Greece. He 'commanded all his admirals to assemble the ships at Cyme and Phocaea, and he himself collected the foot and cavalry forces from all the satrapies and advanced from Susa'. [372]

406 B.C. The greatest sea battle of Greeks between Greeks took place at the Arginusae Islands. The Athenian fleet led by Callicratidas lost twenty-five ships and the Peloponnesians lost seventy-seven. From the following storm the coast of Cyme and Phocaea were 'strewn with wreckage and bodies'. [373]

A Woman from Phocaea Captivates the Persian King

401 B.C. Xenophon in his book the *Anabasis* talks of a Phocaean woman of 'great sense and beauty'. Spelman illuminates that she was the daughter of Hermotymus and called Milto. With other women she was taken away from her family by the local satrap and sent to Cyrus. She became the mistress of Cyrus and called by him Aspasia. Their attachment to each other became famous in Ionia and Greece. On Cyrus being killed during his revolt his brother King Artaxerxes captured her. Aspasia became his favourite and nearly caused a revolution as she switched her affection to his eldest son Darius, subversion in the twinkle of an eye. As was the custom King Artaxerxes could grant one favour to his acknowledged successor and Darius asked for Aspasia. Artaxerxes was disappointed but granted this request. This must have rankled and he could not get over it, as Artaxerxes eventually had Aspasia removed to become a priestess of Artemis of Ecbatana.[374] Darius, unhappy with the turn of events, then plotted to have his father killed but on being discovered it ended in his own destruction.[375]

Western Mediterranean

Nimes in France was trading with Massalia (Marseille) from the fifth century B.C.[376] Massalia's influence is evident in the imported ceramics, money, sculptures, inscriptions, and writing in the later Gallo-Greek script (Greek writing with Gallic language). A stone torso of a warrior with a cowl like helmet, torc, breastplate and belt with hooked buckle was found in the Grézane quarter of Nimes dating to the fourth century B.C.[377]

Greek pottery imports to Bourges 60 km NE of Lyon were at its highest between 530 and 420 B.C.[378] A hoard of 1000+ Massalia AR obol coins buried 3rd-2nd century B.C. was found here.[379]

400 B.C. Greeks drew away from centre of lower Rhône valley to the Massaliote colony of Theline (Arelate, Arles). The city had a mixed population.[380]

Circa **400 B.C.** Celtic penetration reached the Ligurians and they formed the Celto-Ligurian League under a single ruler who led them against Massalia.[381]

Strabo writes 'The Ligurians were not Celtic. But in mode of life they were similar to the Celts'[382] and 'Because they use bronze shields some infer that they are Greeks'.[383]

Justin records this story, that around c. 400 B.C. Massalia was under siege from the Ligurians led by Catumandus. 'He was terrified by a dream of a fierce-looking woman who said she was a goddess'.[384] He broke off the siege and asked the Massaliotes permission to enter and to pay his respects to the gods. 'When he came to the acropolis of Minerva [Athena]' there on seeing the statue of the goddess recognised her as the same he had seen in his dream 'He congratulated the people of Massalia on the protection which he could see the immortal gods afforded them, presented a golden necklace to the goddess and made a permanent treaty with the people of Massalia'.

Strabo writes 'There are to be seen many of the ancient wooden images of Athena in sitting posture, as for example, in Phocaea, Massalia, Rome, Chios and several other places'.[385]

Fourth Century B.C.

Circa **390 B.C.** (Varronian Chronology) the Massaliotes were returning from Delphi after giving thanks from being delivered from the Ligurians. They heard that Rome was under siege from the Gauls, the news was 'met with public mourning' in Massalia. Because of their early ties of friendship, Massalia collected gold and silver 'from public and private sources'[386] to add to the ransom the Gauls were asking to leave Rome.[387] In gratitude Rome made a decree where Massalia would be 'exempted from taxation'[388] and 'granted seats amongst the senators for public shows and given a treaty putting them on equal footing with Romans'.[389]

Several centuries later the story of the ransom was still known as King Mithridates in a speech to his troops showing the Romans had been defeated before refers to the capture of Rome by the Gauls 'removed not by warfare but by a payment of a ransom'.[390] Also the Aetolians Greeks taunted a Roman embassy that they had lost Rome and 'had not defended it with cold steel but paid a ransom for it in gold'.[391]

ATHENS

Sailors had a low status and were classed as 'thetes' and the captain was of the class of the 'zeugitae'. Meijer writes that few merchants were actually Athenian citizens [392] while Osborne says there is evidence of Athenians taking part in trade themselves.[393] One old oligarch complained that it was impossible from their clothes to tell a citizen and metic apart.[394] The port of Athens was Piraeus clearly marked by boundary stones. At some point Piraeus saw introduced the *dikai emporikai* and ten elected magistrates *epimeltai tou emporiou* to supervise corn imports.[395] Immigrants from Megara, Syracuse, Black Sea and Massalia did much of the work of trading. The Athenians gave them the status of 'metics' and unlike other foreigners they could attend cults and religious festivals (metics featured in the Panathenaia Parthenon North Frieze V.13. British Museum), and had protection under the law. For this status they had financial and military obligations.[396] Metics had to pay a special tax the *metoikion*.[397] Apart from rare occasions metics generally were not given Athenian citizenship and could not vote, own land or houses. However, many made a wealthy life through trade and manufacture in Athens.[398]

Demosthenes against Zenothemis

The price of wheat in Athens was reduced in the fourth century by the arrival of wheat from Sicily, which competed with that from Egypt.[399]

Demosthenes the famous Athenian orator made a speech in court against Zenothemis in Athens regarding his loan of money and a cargo of grain on a Massaliote ship manned by Massaliote sailors.[400] The ship brought its cargo from Syracuse in Sicily. During the voyage Hegestratus tried to make a hole in the bottom of the ship. For he knew once the ship sank he could claim it was lost at sea and by Greek law not have to pay any loan of money back. In this case it was Demosthenes who had loaned the money. As Hegestratus was discovered early in the act, he escaped, jumped overboard and drowned. The ship was not damaged.

Demosthenes's agent was on board and 'persuaded the sailors [Massaliotes] with rewards if they brought the ship to port.' They safely docked at Cephallenia where the magistrate there decided the vessel should return to Athens, from which port she had set sail. Zenothemis then 'schemed together with the Massaliotes, the fellow countrymen of Hegestratus, to prevent the vessel from completing their voyage to Athens, saying he himself was from Massalia; that the money came from thence; and the ship owner and leaders were Massaliotes.' [401] Despite these plots they arrived safely in Athens.

Demosthenes protested in court that Zenothemis with great cheek had 'brought suit against me' and 'actually laid claim' to the cargo of his grain 'honestly purchased in Sicily!' We do not know who won the case, as the fragment is not complete.[402]

Demosthenes against Boeotus

In another case *Against Boeotus* 2, Demosthenes had received the sum of 300 'Phocaic staters from Apollonides.[403] A stater from Phocaea was a little heavier than one from Cyzicus that were made of Electrum, ¾ gold and ¼ silver; twice as heavy as an ordinary gold stater and worth 28 Attic Drachmae.[404] Thucydides (iv.52) records that Mitylenian and Lesbian exiles with mercenaries capture Rhoetum in 424 B.C. and restored it 'without injury' on payment of 2,000 Phocaean staters.

Isocrates

Isocrates, once a student of Gorgias, opened his own famous Literary School of which Aristotle became one of his students before joining Plato's Academy. Isocrates actively promoted the belief in a Pan-Hellenic unity of independent states joining together of their own free will. He uses Massalia as an example to the Athenians to win back the honours they had:

> Even more should we deserve the ridicule of men if, having before us the example of the Phocaeans who, to escape the tyranny of the Great King, left Asia and founded a new settlement at Massilia, we should sink into such abjectness of spirit as to submit to the dictates of those whose masters we have always been throughout our history.[405]

Pytheas of Massalia's Gnomon

Pytheas of Massalia, an astronomer and explorer, had used a gnomon to show the length of the sun's shadow and determine position of latitude. To commemorate Pytheas a permanent gnomon was erected in Massalia (Marseille) as he had set the latitude of his city at 43°3'25"N (by adding the semi-diameter of the sun of 14 minutes we have the present figure of 43°17'4"N).

Hodge quotes Clerc, *une véritable célébrité s'etait attachée au gnomon qu'il avait fait construire á Marseille, afin de déterminer la latitude exacte de celle ville,* this was a permanent gnomon built of masonry.[406]

The discoveries of Pytheas in the North Atlantic are discussed in the following chapters.

Travel in the Greek World

Festivals
The English Derby Cup horse race is world famous and was in the far-flung corners of the British Empire. Such events are well known and interest in them high and maintained. Events like travelling to Mecca for Muslims and Jerusalem for Hebrews, Christians and Muslims for many centuries made religious journeys to these centres that involved travel across land and sea. Today travel to music and sporting festivals attracts hundreds of thousands.

Games and festivals in ancient Greece involved travel from all the colonies. As there was no consistent calendar among the Greek states the Pythian Games at Delphi sent out nine citizens, *Theoroi*, to declare the date of the festival and the start of the sacred truce 'to all Greek cities, from the Crimea to Marseille [Massalia] and from Cyrencia to Asia Minor, asking them to send athletes'.⁴⁰⁷ The popularity of these festivals is evident from a list of *Theorodokoi* (those citizens who received the *Theoroi)* representing over 500 cities for the Games at Delphi during the late third century B.C. ⁴⁰⁸ (See Chapter 2, section 'Inscriptions found, Delphi').

Theoroi began their journey six months before the month of Boukation (mid-August to mid-September when the Amphyctyonic League met and who were in charge of the festival). The routes the nine *Theoroi* would take are known from inscriptions found at Delphi. Also inscriptions were found in the cities with names of *Theorodokoi* who were citizens that had looked after and helped the *Theoroi* fulfil their duties. The Pythia commenced in the third year of the Olympic cycle and the sacred truce *heiromenia* lasted one year.⁴⁰⁹

The festivals were prestigious events and cities taking part sent their 'official mission, The*oria*, consisting of the athletes, officials and elite citizens, who often supported the mission by personal donations. This included offering and dedications to the gods, and the animals for the sacrifices'.⁴¹⁰ There must have been a great movement of people from the colonies to attend religious festivals and athletic Games across the Greek world. Many ships transporting, time for meetings, making business contacts, social interaction, family contacts and who was of marriageable age. Just how much movement is illustrated by the 'Judges of the Hellenes' and the Eleans (from Elis) who sent envoys inviting the philosopher Apollonius of Tyana to the Olympic Games in the first century A.D.⁴¹¹ Also in a discourse from Dio Chrysostom when he writes about Diogenes of Sinope (fourth century B.C.) at the Isthmian Games at Corinth.

Diogenes was the famous philosopher that lived in a clay barrel. He was the founder of the Cyreniac or Hedonistic school of philosophy.⁴¹² Philosophers and good generals were admired and valued by the Greeks. When Alexander the Great was in Corinth he asked Diogenes if there was anything he could do for him and was told 'Yes, stand aside; you are keeping the sun off me.' ⁴¹³ His companions were 'laughing and jesting' at Diogenes but Alexander said, 'But verily if I were not Alexander, I would be Diogenes'.⁴¹⁴ Diogenes gives a fuller version of the event in his letter to Phanomachos.⁴¹⁵

Prior to meeting Diogenes in Corinth, Alexander the Great may have seen Diogenes at the Battle of Charoneia where Diogenes of Sinope had remonstrated with King Philip II of Macedon in that he claimed 'descent from Heracles yet destroying the people [Athenians] who took up arms to defend the children of Heracles'.⁴¹⁶

Diogenes would visit the Isthmian Games at Corinth. The Corinthians did not pay Diogenes so much attention as strangers would because they were used to seeing him. Dio Chrysostom wrote 'all who came to the festival from Ionia, Sicily, and Italy, and some of those who came from Libya, Massilia [Marseille] and Borysthenes [on the Black Sea]' ⁴¹⁷ would come in particular to see Diogenes and hear him speak 'for even a short time so as to have something to tell others rather than to get improvement for themselves. For he had the reputation of having a sharp tongue and being instantly ready with an answer for his interrogators'. Dio continues:

> Whenever he discovered anyone who was foolishly puffed up and lost to all reason on account of some worthless thing; for he would humble the man a little and relieve him of some small part of his folly, even if as one pricks or punctures inflated and swollen parts. ⁴¹⁸

When he put a victor's crown made of pine on his head the Corinthians asked him to take it off, as he had won no victory in the Games. Diogenes replied,

Many and mighty antagonists have I vanquished, not like the slaves who are now wrestling here, hurling the discus and running, but more difficult in every way–I mean poverty, exile, and disrepute; yes and anger, pain, desire, fear, and the most redoubtable beast of all, treacherous and cowardly, I mean pleasure, which no Greek or barbarian can claim he fights or conquers by the strength of his soul, but all alike have succumbed to her and failed in this contest–Persians, Medes, Syrians, Macedonians, Athenians, Lacedaemonians–all, that is, save myself.[419]

The Massaliotes and the other visitors would have much to tell back in their colonies and keeping the people in touch with stories of ideas and events from far away in other parts of the Greek world. A Greek world it certainly was with colonies extending from Spain to the Black Sea. By the time of Dio Chrysostom this Greek world was one of culture, which ironically reached another golden age (called the Second Sophist) being free from warring with each other, under new political masters the Romans whose emperors,[420] particularly Hadrian, admired, adopted and promoted Greek culture.[421]

Third Century B.C.

Over the next two centuries after Pytheas, Massalia also kept the friendship of the main tribes that controlled their overland tin route through both the River Rhône or Narbo and River Aude, namely the Volcae across the River Gironde, the Nitiobries at Agen, the Vivisci around the Gironde[422] and the Albici who lived in the mountains overhanging Massalia.[423] Whereas they had periodic conflicts with not only the Saluvi (Sallyes), who had their territory from around Entremont to the River Durance and along the 'seaboard as far as the Ligures',[424] but also with the Ligurians situated between themselves and Italy.

Massalia reinforced its commercial route against attacks by Celto-Ligurians with the foundation of Tauroention (Le Brusc, near Toulon) on the coast c. 300 B.C.[425]

Athenaeus writes,

As for the Iberians, though they go forth in stately embroidered robes and wear tunics reaching to the feet, they are not at all impeded in the strength they display in war. But the people of Massilia, who wore the same fashion of dress as the Iberians, became effeminate. At any rate their behaviour is indecent on account of the weakness of their souls, and are effeminate through luxury; whence also a proverb has become current, "May you sail to Massilia!".[426]

Plutarch also mentioned they wore their hair long and reeking with perfume.[427] This may have been a fashion or stage of a few people or more that did not last as we have in contrast views by Silius Italicus, Valerius Maximus, Livy and Strabo.

Does Athenaeus mean all the people or does he use the description as one might today 'everybody does it' when in fact it is only the circle of people you know and not the majority of people. Can we determine the behaviour of all from a few? The actions of a few are not necessarily the actions of the many. Publicity given to a minority of people's activities can give a false view of the majority who do not do the same things or behave in the same way. Here we have other views in contrast.

Silius Italicus, writing in the first century A.D. stated that they still wore the same fashion as Ionian style and were resistant to the surrounding cultures and customs.[428] Strabo (64 B.C.–A.D. 21) was in praise for 'The simplicity of the modes of life, and of the self-restraint, of the Massaliotes: the maximum dowry among them is a hundred gold pieces, and five for dress, and five for golden ornaments'.[429]

Funeral rituals and mourning also reflected self-restraint and archaeological evidence in and around Massalia would confirm this. Finds in burials were mainly of modest grave goods, with pottery, glass, lamps and sometimes coins. The graves were sometimes marked by a stone stele, and mostly undecorated carrying a simple inscription. There were cremations as well as burials found outside the city gates near the Bourse and also the Sainte-Barbe cemetery had over 500 graves mostly cremations from the end of the fifth century B.C. to second century A.D.[430] by the Port d'Aix.[431] The Bourse site revealed two 'funerary terraces' of the fourth century B.C. that had 'aristocratic cremation burials' and one wall was decorated with 'low triglyphs'.[432] Lomas also mentions one retaining wall was decorated with triglyphs and cremations were in bronze, lead or ceramic urns accompanied by modest grave goods dating from fourth to second century B.C.[433]

The Greek necropolis following the usual custom was placed outside the city walls and one beyond the Butte St. Charles had 548 tombs. In 2012 another fifth to fourth century B.C. Greek cemetery has been discovered at the hill of Lazaret d'Arenc: so far six sarcophagi, urns and ashes have been revealed.[434] At a 'native environment' there is apparently a Greek necropolis dated to the second half of the fifth century to beginning of the fourth century B.C. at Saint-Mauront.[435]

Rituals, Scapegoats and Medicine

During times of great anxiety such as plague where they had no cures, the Greeks would use either of two rituals, Pharmakos (scape-goat), and Katharsia (purification) hoping to cleanse the city. Massaliotes used their own version of the ritual of Pharmakos as recorded by Servius Petronius where a 'poor man was offered pure and costly food for a year, then decked in boughs and sacred vestments, he was led around the whole town amid curses and finally chased away'.[436] There are two surviving versions. The other by Lactantius Placidus does not mention Massilia but only Gaul; it is an annual custom; and the Pharmakos is killed. The killing may have been a misunderstanding as was found in later archaeological epigraphic evidence of the same ritual performed at Abdera where it became clear that the stoning referred to expelling the Pharmakos out of the city and not stoning to death.[437]

Various versions of scape-goat appear all around the ancient world and also ended with the Pharmakos being killed.[438] The custom of a ritual expulsion of human scapegoats who were not killed as in Massalia was carried on in other Ionian cities.[439]

In a similar vein the transferring of ills to another object to get rid of the affliction was evident during a lot of flu and deaths in Thessaloniki in Greece 1946. A life size effigy of an old woman like a witch was made and put on the back of an open lorry. The ugly effigy was called 'E gripi' (the flu) and was driven around the streets on a weekday and a parade of priests, army, navy, scouts, people and music followed the lorry until they came to an empty space near the White Tower and the effigy was burnt to get rid of all the flu.[440]

There are later in the Roman period epitaphs in Gaul of Greeks who studied medicine perhaps at Massalia, as there had been very famous doctors from this city.[441] The following were in Latin script. At Arles there is recorded one Dionysius and Julius Hermes;[442] at Nimes, a female doctor Flavia Hedone.[443]

```
         FLAVIAE
         HEDONES
         MEDICAE
         EX • T •
```

At Narbonne we have Heraclides, liberated of Xanthermus and L. Pomponius Diocles;[444] and in the Vienne region M. Apronius Europus, and *medicus Asclepiadius*.[445]

Massalia's Famous Doctors Crinas and Charmis Practising in Rome

Pliny the Elder recorded,

> No actor, no driver of a three-horse chariot, was attended by greater crowds than he [Thessalius] as he walked abroad in public, when Crinas of Massalia united medicine with another art, and being of a rather careful and superstitious nature, and regulated the diet of patients by the motions of the stars according to the almanacs of the astronomers, keeping watch for the proper times, and outstripped Thessalius in influence. Recently he left ten millions, and the same sum he spent upon building the walls of his native city and other fortifications was almost as much. These men were ruling our destinies when suddenly the state was invaded by Charmis, also from Massalia, who condemned not only previous physicians but also hot baths, persuading people to bathe in cold water even during the winter frosts.[446]

Pliny continues,

> It is well known that Charmis aforesaid exchanged one sick provincial for 200,000 sesterces by a bargain with Alcon the wound-surgeon; that Charmis was condemned and fined by the Emperor Claudius the sum of 1,000,000 sesterces, yet as an exile in Gaul and on his return from banishment he amassed a like sum within a few years.[447]

Massaliotes Abroad

There is one funerary inscription found in Tharros (east coast of Sardinia) that records
Euxene daughter of Anaxilaos of Massalia [448]

Hermary suggests that a Massaliote name Kintos appear in the Greek mercenaries serving in Egypt.[449] Clerc mentions visitors Poseidonax, son of Polyxenos of Massalia' and also 'Dionysios of

Massalia' who carved their names on the wall of the tomb of 'Syringes' in the Valley of the Kings, Luxor, Egypt. [450]

Third to Second Century B.C.

Funerary inscriptions of Massaliotes abroad have also been found in Athens. Theodoros son of Leomachos, Massaliotis; [451] Hetairos, son of Leon, Massaliotis; [452] Sphairos son of Platon, Massaliotes; [453] Melisos son of Melisos, Massaliotis; [454] Acropolis daughter of Apollonios, Massalietis; [455] Cleopatra daughter of Alexandros, Massalietis.[456] (See section Inscriptions found: Athens).

Strato of Lampsacus was the third head of the Lyceum in Athens and the teacher of Ptolemy Philadelphus in Alexandria shortly before Theophrastus died. [457] The city of Lampsacus was the Phocaean colony that Massalia had interceded on its behalf with Rome 196 and again in 190 B.C.

From the mother-city, Telecles of Phocaea became Head of the Academy in Athens and was buried in Athens during the archonship of Nikosthenes (167/6 B.C.). [458]

On the island of Delos was found an inscription in honour of Massaliote, Leon son of Leon, Proxenos and Evergete of the temple of the Delians, from the Council and People of Delos [459] and a funerary inscription Philon son of Metrodoros. On the island of Rhodes: Soteridas, Thales son of Poseidermos,[460] and also a first name missing followed by 'son of Epaphrodites, and Massaliota'.

Four funerary inscriptions of Massaliotes honoured Proxenes of the city have been found at Delphi in Greece dating to the first half of the second century B.C. Theodoros son of Heronax, Kleodamos son of Kaikos, Crinas son of Pythias and Pythias son of Crinas.[461]

In the Delphi list of the Theorodokoi (receivers of the sacred envoys) of Massalia include the same names as the Proxenes.[462]

In Massalia Zenothemis was a popular name. Others found there include Protis, Apellis, Aris, Alexis, Apollonides, Herylos, Hipponikos, Leukon, Lykaithos, Mikion, Oulis, Parmenon, Xeinandros Themis, Thespis, Prexis, and Pythis.[463]

Massalia and Celts

Third-Second Century B.C.
'Gallo-Greek' Script.
Around the late third to early second century B.C. Celts living east of the River Rhône adapt the Greek script used in Massalia and its colonies in writing a Celtic language.[464]

The influence of Massalia amongst the Celts as far away as Asia Minor is illustrated by ambassadors led by Hegesias from the Phocaean city of Lampsacos who were sent to Massalia 197/196 B.C.[465] asking them to influence the Celtic Tolostoagian of Galatia in Asia Minor not to join Antiochus III of Syria in fighting Rome. However, the Tolostoagians rejected the letter Massalia sent.[466]

Celtic tribes from around the region of Milan and Ticino in north Italy made tetrabols coins. These were copies of Massaliote coins. Obverse: head of Artemis/reverse: a lion, sometimes marked ΛΛΛΣΛΛ, which was a poor copy of ΜΑΣΣΑ (Massa, short for Massalia). They were struck around 200 B.C. and in circulation for about 200 years.[467] Though these Celts lived in North Italy they continued to take their coin design not from the Romans but from the Greeks at Massalia. Just before Hannibal invaded Italy the Roman envoys travelled around Gaul to get the good will of the Celts. Livy says they were met with laughter and the retort that the Romans were being no friends to themselves and by injuring their compatriots living in North Italy.[468] British Celtic coins of the second century B.C. also show Massalia's influence in design with a head of Apollo and on the reverse a butting bull with the letters MA (for Massalia).[469]

Livy (59 B.C.–A.D. 17) recorded a similar description of Massalia to that by Cicero, *Pro Flacco* 63-64:

> The people of Massilia, whom, if inborn nature could be conquered, so to speak, by the temper of a land, so many untamed tribes around them would have long ago been barbarised, we hear are held in the same respect and deservedly paid the same honour by you as if they dwelt in the very navel of Greece. For they have kept not only the sound of their speech along with their dress and their outward appearance, but, before all, their manners and laws and character pure and free from the corruption of their neighbours.[470]

Wine

Martial wrote an epigram 'When your dole shall strike of the list a hundred citizens, you can serve them the smoky wines of Massilia'.[471] T. E. Page explains Martial's epigram 'for when you wish to repay clients for their services' and that 'Massilia had a bad reputation for exposing wines too long':[472]

> Whatever the unconscionable smoke rooms of Massilia bring together, whatever jar takes age from fire, come from you, Munna. You served your unfortunate friends dire poisons by sea and length of road, and at no easy price, but one which would content a flagon of Falerian or Setine, beloved of its cellars. Methinks the reason why it is so long since you came to Rome is to avoid drinking your own wines.[473]

Shackleton Bailey points out that Martial should perhaps have directed his criticism elsewhere as Pliny commends Massalian wine, but the other wines of Narbonensis were 'corrupted in the making by smoke and worse things'.[474]

It would seem that an unsatisfied and overcharged customer can sure hold a grudge as Martial unleashes another epigram, 'Forbear, boy, to mix Massilia's smoke with snow water, lest the water cost me more than the wine'.[475]

Speaking about trade much later between second and third century A.D. with the Celts Athenaeus says, 'The liquor drank in the houses of the rich is wine bought from Italy, and the country round Massalia, and is unmixed; though sometimes a little water is added'.[476]

The Story of Herippe-ΠΕΡΙ ΗΡΙΠΠΗΣ
Circa 257 B.C.

During the invasion of Ionia by the Gauls some had raided a temple outside of Miletus on the feast of Thesmophoria, which was celebrated by women. They carried off the women some of who were ransomed for large sums of silver and gold. Others the barbarian became attached to and one was Herippe wife of Xanthus, a noble of Miletus with whom she had a child of two years in age. Xanthus changed much of his possessions into 2,000 gold pieces and crossed over to Italy. From there he went to Massalia and into the country of the Celts where he found her living 'as the wife of one of the chief men of that nation'. He asked to be taken in and was well received by the Celts. His wife flung her arms around him. Her Celtic captor appeared and when related by her the journey her husband had made to pay a ransom he was delighted at the devotion of Xanthus and ordered a banquet of his friends and relations. He asked through an interpreter how much was Xanthus's fortune and he replied, 'It amounts to 1,000 pieces of gold'. The barbarian told him 'to divide it into 4 parts, one for himself, his wife, and his child, and the fourth to be left for the woman's ransom'. While the barbarian was asleep in his room Herippe remonstrated with Xanthus for promising what he did not have and this would put them in danger from the barbarian. Xanthus told her he actually had double that amount hidden in his servant's boots, as he had not 'hoped to find so reasonably a barbarian'.[477]

The following day Herippe went to the Celt and told him how much Xanthus really had and to put him to death adding she really preferred him 'far above both her native country and her child and as for Xanthus, that she utterly abhorred him'. Instead of pleasing the Celt he decided to punish her. He accompanied them amicably on the first part of the journey and 'at the limit of the Celt's territory' he said he wished to perform a sacrifice. He told Herippe to hold the victim 'as she had been accustomed to do on other occasions. He drew his sword and cut off her head'. He then told Xanthus of her treachery and 'not to take it in bad part' and 'gave him all the money back'.[478]

This 'love romance' is originally from the first book of the Stories of Aristodemus of Nysa. In his version he has different names of Euthymia instead of Herippe, and the Celtic chief as Cavaras. The Cavares were a people [479] south-east of Aouenion (Latin *Avennio*, French *Avignon*).

Second to First Century B.C.

Strabo records this story from Poseidonius:

> Poseidonius says that in Liguria his host, Charmolean, a man from Massalia, narrated to him how he had hired men and women to work together for ditch-digging; and how one of the women, upon being seized with the pangs of childbirth, went aside from her work to a place near by, and, after having given birth to her child, came back to her work at once in order not to lose her pay; and how he himself saw that she was doing her work painfully, but was not aware of the cause till late in the day, when he learned it and sent her away with her wages; and she carried the infant out to a little spring, bathed it, swaddled it with what she had, and brought it safely home.[480]

First Century B.C.

Vitruvius the Roman architect and engineer noted that 'Likewise in Massilia we can see roofs without tiles, made of earth mixed with straw: In Athens on the Aeropagus there is to this day a relic of antiquity with a mud roof'.[481]

Evidence of the Gallo-Greek script dates from the end of the third century B.C.[482] and by the early first century B.C. Greek script is being used in the upper Rhône valley and Burgundy.[483]

Strabo writes that the Celts had begun attending school in Massalia and the Galatae were 'fond enough of the Greeks to write even their contracts in Greek.'[484] Julius Caesar had found in the camp of the Helvetii a census of their population in Greek script.[485] The Nervii had 'six hundred senators' and could this system have been learnt from the government of Massalia?[486] Although Caesar records that the Druids never wrote anything down and memorised their knowledge, he adds 'although in almost all other matters, and in their public and private accounts, they make use of Greek letters'.[487] Again we can see a connection between Celts and Greeks through the schools at Massalia.

A later writer during the sixth century A.D. Isidore of Seville used Varro as a source from the first century B.C. who had written that Massalia was a tri-lingual city with Greek, Latin and Gallic (Celtic) spoken:

Massiliam condiderunt et ex nomine ducis nuncupaverunt. Hos Varro trilingues esse ait, quod et Graece loquantur et Latine et Gallice.[488]

Massalia and 'other Greek neighbours'
See section on Bèziers.

Strabo recorded,

> This, then is what I have to say about the people who inhabit the dominion of Narbonitis, whom the men of former times named "Celtae"; and it was from the Celtae, I think, that the Galatae as a whole were by the Greeks called "Celti"—on account of the fame of the Celtae, or it may also be that the Massaliotes, as well as other Greek neighbours, contributed to this result, on account of their proximity.[489]

> ταῦτα μὲν ὑπὲρ τῶν νεμομένων τὴν Ναρβωνῖτιν ἐπικράτειαν λέγομεν, οὓς οἱ πρότερον Κέλτας ὠνόμαζον ἀπὸ τούτων δ' οἶμαι καὶ τοὺς σύμπαντας Γαλάτας Κελτοὺς ὑπὸ τῶν Ἑλλήνων προσαγορευθῆναι, διὰ τὴν ἐπιφάνειαν ἢ καὶ προσλαβόντων πρὸς τοῦτο καὶ τῶν Μασσαλιωτῶν διὰ τὸ πλησιόχωρον.

From καὶ there is an assumption that Strabo means 'other Greek neighbours' of the Massaliotes in Gaul rather than 'other Greek neighbours' of the Celts elsewhere in the Greek world?

This section of the Greek text in the Loeb 1923 edition is the same as that in Radt's 2002 edition.[490]

Massalia's Influence on the Celts

The influence of Massalia and its cities on the surrounding cultures of the Celts in Gaul over the next few centuries was immense. Strabo (64 B.C.–A.D. 24) wrote:

> Their present state of life makes this clear; for all men of culture turn to the art of speaking and the study of philosophy; so that the city, although a short time ago it was given over as merely a training-school for the barbarians and was schooling the Galatae to be fond enough of the Greeks to write even their contracts in Greek [491]

Strabo thought it was because of the 'overmastery of the Romans' that

'the barbarians who are situated beyond the Massaliotes became more and more subdued as time went on, and instead of carrying on war have already turned to civic life and farming'. [492]

But Strabo also records the Celts going to school in Massalia and this was already going on before the Romans [493] had conquered the area 'beyond the Massaliotes'. Does Strabo mean beyond the Massaliote chora/territory/area of economic influence and trade? Though most of the Gallo-Greek inscriptions are found in or around the Roman period, a few have been dated to the third century B.C. Once learnt particularly in Transalpine Gaul the Celts carried on using their script up to mid-first century A.D. in spite of the Roman conquest.[494] From over sixty Gallo-Greek stone inscriptions found ten were discovered in Nimes and ten in Glanum.[495] Julius Caesar found documents in the camp of the Helvetii recording their census in Greek [496] and the Druids using Greek letters.[497] We also have the view of the late first century B.C historian Pompeius Trogus as a source for Justin the Roman historian in the second century A.D. who recorded that

> It was from these Greeks that the Gauls learned to live in a more civilised manner, abandoning or modifying their barbarous ways; they learned to practice agriculture and encircle their cities with walls. Then they became used to life governed by law rather than armed might, to cultivating the vine and planting the olive-tree; and so brilliantly successful was the society and its affairs that, instead of Greece emigrating to Gaul, it looked as if Gaul had been moved to Greece. [498]

Juvenal in his *Satires* sarcastically notes 'eloquent Gaul has trained the pleaders from Britain, and distant Thule talks of hiring a rhetorician'! [499] Between these views there seem to be a distinction between adopting ways of life that become your lifestyle by one's own free will and keeping the better of your own customs than those imposed by colonization of a foreign people whereby to get on within the new order one is motivated by inducement of advantages or even under duress. Sometimes only 'modifying' behaviour would apply as some local traditions are ingrained and hard to change. Justin does record that

> The Ligurians, however, kept a jealous eye on the city's [Massalia] growth and harassed the Greeks with continuous warfare, but the Greeks so distinguished themselves in repelling the dangers that they crushed their enemy and established numerous colonies in the captured territory. [500]

Coins

Weights of drachmas varied. For Athens an obol was ⅙ of a drachma, 100 drachmas = mina, 60 minas = 1 talent.[501] In coin evidence we see several southern silver groups amongst the Celts who copied coins from three Greek cities, Massalia in Gaul, Emporion and Rhodus (Massaliote colonies) in Spain. Massalia imitation coins are found with other Celtic groups found north of the Po in North Italy. Emporion types are found in the area between Dordogne and the Liger (Loire) rivers and in the south-east of the Garrone, France. In between these two groups of Emporion imitations we find copies of coins from Rhodus[502] particularly amongst the Volcae Tectosages.[503] Greeks paid the Celts for military services in Greek coins. The dominant design in Celtic copies was Philip II of Macedonia gold staters with Apollo on the obverse and a two-horse chariot on the reverse.[504]

Emporion produced anepigraphic coins from the fifth century B.C. without an inscription and from the fourth century B.C. has silver Drachmas. Varieties were copies based on South Italy and Athens designs e.g. obverse: head of Athena/reverse: owl between letters EM (for Emporion).[505] By the end of the fourth century B.C. coins of greater value were minted, obverse: head of Persephone, ear of corn in hair, word ΕΜΠΟΡΙΤΩΝ (EMPORITON)[506] and the reverse shows a horse with Victory flying over. This changed towards the end of the First Punic War to the head of Arethusa (of Syracuse) facing right, surrounded by three dolphins, and on the reverse a flying Pegasus facing right with letters ΕΜΠΟΡΙΤΩΝ (EMPORITON). Pegasus became the symbol of the city.[507] Opposite Emporion across the Gulf of Roses was Rhodus (Rhode).

Rhodus (Rhode, Roses, in Spain) starting minting silver coins c. 250 B.C.[508] with a head of Persephone facing left but on the reverse a rose in full bloom.[509] The rose may be in memory of their possible supposed original founders the island of Rhodes[510] who also had a rose on their coins and as a pun on their name? On-going archaeological excavations have not as yet found any residential remains earlier than the fourth century B.C. and the evidence so far indicates Massalia founded Rhodus (Rhode).[511]

Massalia's Coins

Massalia minted coins from 540 B.C. A treasure of 25 types of 2,130 coins (Greek imports, Celtic imitations and from Marseille) dating to 525–470 B.C. was found in the village of 'Auriol' Provence. Morel explains this 'Auriol type' that 'was silver anepigraphic coins (first of all obols, their multiples and divisions) of the Phocaean and later Milesian standard usually bearing on the reverse a hollow square'. These types were found around western Provence, and some in 'the treasure of Volterra in Etruria, and on some sites in Spain'.[512] Marseille's (Massalia) compatriot city of Hyele (Elea, Velia) had some identical designs but double the weight of Massalia; 'drachms with forepart of lion to right gnawing a bone'.[513]

Further evidence of coins made in Massalia from the fifth century is of fine silver obols with the head of Artemis and on the reverse a crab with an initial M for Massalia. Between 450–400 B.C. another design appeared on obol coins, obverse: helmeted (Pilos type)[514] head facing right, with circle and four rays emblem on the helmet/reverse: wheel of four rays/spokes. Weight 0.85 g.[515] Clerc suggests the emblems are rays representing the sun and Apollo was also the Sun God.[516] There were also coins depicting their river god Lacydon facing right with his name and legend Massaliotan or Massali. On the reverse a wheel of four rays/spokes, with or without the letter M[517] and later replaced by a lion with letters ΜΑΣ (MAS) found in 1993 at the Oppidum Saint-Marcel.[518]

Other designs feature the head of Apollo and a wheel with four rays/spokes on the reverse. During the early fourth century B.C. the Head of Apollo appears more frequently and on the reverse a wheel with four rays/spokes with letters MA for Massalia. Also appearing are the best known silver heavy drachmas (3.70g) with the head of Artemis facing right with sprigs of olive adorning her hair and on the reverse a lion with the abbreviated name of the city ΜΑΣΣΑ (MASSA). The first were struck on the 'Campanian' heavy standard as used by Elea (Velia a Phocaean colony). [519] Thereafter obols continued until 241-218 with introduction of the light drachma, Artemis/lion, 2.60-2.75 g. [520]

By the second century the obverse changes with a head of Artemis and a quiver over the shoulder. We also see on the reverse the name of the city ΜΑΣΣΑΛΙΗΤΩΝ (MASSALITON). Carson states that this issue had the same standard weight of the Roman victoriate. During the next two centuries there were several types of bronze coins issued with the head of Apollo and on the reverse a charging bull, or the head of Athena and on the reverse a tripod. [521] Carson also suggests that the imitations of Philip II of Macedonia gold staters by the Celts were more accurately imitated in Gaul as opposed to the valleys of the Rhine or Danube, which suggests they were more frequently used via 'trade through Greek settlements like Massalia' [522] than it would seem just in pay to Celts for military services abroad.

From 261 B.C. after the fall of the independent Greek city of Syracuse (in Sicily) and its coin production there seem to be an increase in the number of bronze coins Massalia issued. There was a brief revival of Greek coin production in South Italy (Magna Graecia) at the time of Hannibal in the name of his Greek allies under the Brettian League. [523] But after Hannibal's defeat Massalia was the only main producer of Greek coins in the West. Massalia's coins were the chief currency in southern Gaul. They were much imitated by the Celts in Gaul and North Italy, as well as by Iberians and copies have been found as far as Britain [524] using the same design obverse: head of Apollo/reverse: butting bull and letters MA. [525]

A bronze coin AE hemiobol with Apollo facing right/reverse: a butting bull facing right letters ΜΑΣΣΑ above, EM in exergue, weight 2.5 grams, size 15 mm was minted between 149 B.C. to 40 B.C. [526] in the same design a bronze AE 15, weight 2,300 g, maximum diameter 14.9 mm: [527] juvenile head facing left/wheel, letters MA, minted 121–82 B.C. (see Figure 36). There was an increase in 'petit-bronze' coins in the early first century B.C. with large amounts found on native sites in Provence and East Languedoc. [528] Coins made after losing most of its empire to Caesar in 49 B.C. show obverse: helmeted head of Athena/reverse: an eagle, galley, caduceus, dolphin, Athena standing with spear and shield, lion, tripod, or joined hands. [529]

Coins from Massalia have been found in the Augustan legionary fortress of Hunerberg at Nijmagen, Netherlands. This fort was not occupied again until the Flavian period. [530]

How long did Massalia continue to produce its own coins? With a lack of information in the following period Barruol points to the Romanization of the surrounding area and its use of Roman money becoming the main currency and supplanting local coins. [531] Several books give a production period up to 49 B.C. but a discovery by Michele Bats at Olbia of a small bronze 'tardif', obverse: helmeted head facing right, 'frappe hors champ', reverse: illegible, was dated to after 49 B.C. [532] There are several professional numismatic coin websites that also have listed small bronze coins 'after 49 B.C.' that shows the mint at Massalia still active within its continuing status as a independent Greek city-state and that status confirmed by Julius Caesar and Rome as a *civitas foederata*. [533] Brenot gives coins up to the end of the first century B.C. but with a question mark. [534]

Figure 21. Auriol type' coins found at Auriol near Massalia (Marseille). Auriol types may have been minted in Gaul or Asia Minor. Hemiobol, Milesian type c. 475–465 B.C. Obverse: head of Apollo facing left, pronounced hair pattern on head and on back of the neck/reverse: crab. Weight 0.75 g. They were divisions of the Phocaean drachma.

Figure 22. 'Auriol type' hemiobol, Milesian type. 475–465 B.C. Obverse: head of Aphrodite facing left/reverse: incuse-hollow square. Weight 1.11 g.

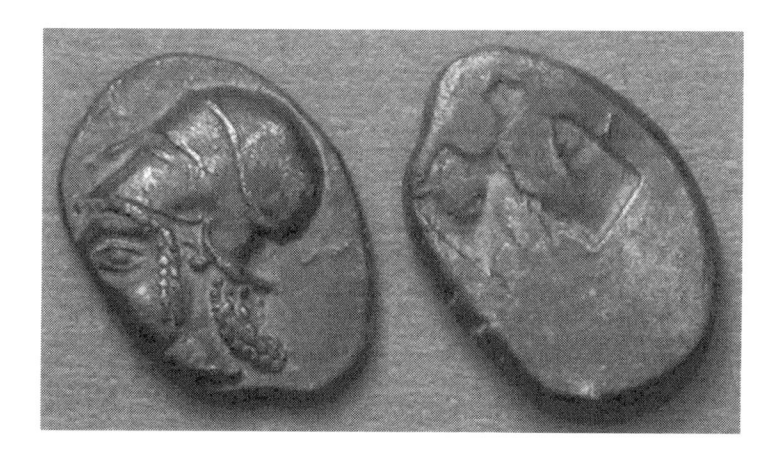

Figure 23. Obol c. 475–465 B.C. Obverse: head of Athena, with Corinthian helmet, facing left/reverse: incuse irregular hollow square. Weight 0.90g.[535]

Figure 24. Auriol type' tritemorion, Phocaean type 470–460 B.C. Obverse: ram's head facing right/reverse: cross recessed, full of cross points. Weight 0.23 g

Figure 25. Massalia 450–400 B.C. AR obol. Obverse: helmeted head facing right, with circle and four rays emblem/reverse: wheel of 4 rays/spokes. Weight 0.94 g.

Figure 26. Massalia AR obol *circa* fourth century B.C. Youthful head of Apollo facing left/reverse: wheel of 4 rays/spokes, letters MA. Weight 0.66 gm.

Figure 27. Massalia AR Obol 350–215 B.C. Obverse: Apollo facing right/reverse: wheel of four rays/spokes, letters MA. Weight 0.60 g.

Figure 28. Massalia fourth century B.C. obol. Obverse: Lacydon river god facing right with legend ΜΑΣΣΑΛΙΩΤΑΝ (MASSALIOTAN)/reverse: wheel of four rays/spokes and letter M.

Figure 29. Massalia, silver heavy drachma, early fourth century B.C. Obverse: Artemis facing right, hair adorned with sprigs of olive, wearing earring and necklace/reverse: prowling lion facing right, with letters above ΜΑΣΣΑ (MASSA) for Massalia.[536]

Figure 30. Massalia, heavy bronze c. 220–215 B.C. Obverse: helmeted head of Athena facing right/reverse: Tripod in front and head of Apollo behind facing left with letters on right ΜΑΣ (MAS). Weight 7.97 g.

Figure 31. Massalia, AR drachma, second century B.C. Obverse: head of Artemis diademed and draped facing right, bow and quiver at shoulder/reverse: lion prowling facing right, ΜΑΣΣΑ (MASSA) at top, monogram and Κ below, ΛΙΗΤΩΝ (LIHTON) in exergue. Weight 2.62 gm.

Figure 32. Massalia c. 200-150 B.C. drachma, silver, 2.69 g 12. Head of Artemis facing right, wearing olive wreath, pendant earring and necklace, behind neck bow and quiver/reverse: lion walking to right with head slightly lowered, letters ΜΑΣΣΑ (MASSA) at top, in exergue H H. This particular 'H H' group are exceptionally fine reminiscent of the best engravings of the fourth century B.C. issues of Magna Graecia.

Figure 33. Massalia, large bronze with bull, 200–49 B.C. Group 1, series 3, LT.1515 variant. Obverse: Apollo facing left/reverse: butting bull facing right, below letters ΜΑΣΣΑΛΙΗΤ (MASSALIT), above objects. 11.90 gm.

Figure 34. Massalia AR brockage drachma, second to first century B.C. Obverse: lion standing facing right, T below, ΑΠΠ (APP) in exergue/reverse: incuse of obverse.

Figure 35. Massalia, silver AR tetrobol, 130–121 B.C. Artemis facing right bow and quiver over shoulder/reverse: lion walking left, above letters MASSA and below AΛ (AL) in exergue. Weight 2.61 gm.

Figure 36. Massalia, obol MA, silver c. 121–82 B.C. Anepigraphic head of juvenile facing left (river god Lacydon?) horned, wavy hair drawn back. Reverse: letters M in 3rd and A in 4th quarter in wheel of 4 spokes with central hub, weight 0.67 g.

Figure 37. Massalia, AE, after 49 B.C. Obverse: helmeted head of Athena facing right with letters MA/reverse: Athena standing facing left with spear raised and shield. Weight 2.96 g. Size 11 mm.

Figure 38. Massalia 'AI' AE13, bronze, after 49 B.C. Obverse: Athena in a Corinthian helmet facing right/reverse: eagle, head facing right. Weight 2.6 grams, size 13 mm.

Figure 39. Massalia, AE coin after 49 B.C. Obverse helmeted head of Athena facing right, with letter M/reverse: lion facing left, Letters D above and P below. Weight 3.02 g, 6 h. Size 12 mm.

Figure 40. Massalia, AE coin after 49 B.C. Obverse: helmeted head of Athena facing left/reverse: galley facing right Weight 1.92 g, 9 h. Size 12 mm.

Massalia (Marseille)

Valerius Maximus a Roman writer of the first century A.D. wrote that the Massaliotes were quite remarkable for 'their austere way of life, their adherence to old ways, and their love for the Roman people.' A slave's freedom could be 'revoked three times', but if it was found out that the 'slave has cheated his master three times' he should not be 'helped after making a fourth mistake. It was his own fault if he loses his rights because he has exposed himself to that risk too many times'. He noted that they were 'very hospitable, and want to be kind to visitors, but they want to keep themselves safe too'. They did this by not allowing anybody with a weapon to enter Massalia. 'There was a man on the spot who takes the weapon, keeps it safe, and returns it when the owner is leaving the city'.[537] The government of 'Massalia was a keen guardian of strict morality'. Mimes were not allowed on stage as they many of them contained

> sexual activity and it did not want people to get into the habit of looking at such scenes in case they might feel they were free to imitate them. The city closes its gates against all those charlatans who try to support a lazy lifestyle by pretending to be religious. It thinks that such false and deceptive cults should be done away with.[538]

From the founding of Massalia a sword was left at the place where criminals were executed. 'The sword is eaten away with rust' and though it hardly could be used Valerius Maximus thought this was a typical example of how the Massaliotes 'preserved everything that has been handed down by ancient tradition even in the smallest details'.

Anyone who wanted to commit suicide went to the Six Hundred who kept a poison made from hemlock and gave it free of charge only if the person had a 'good reason for leaving this life'. They held an 'inquiry with manly kindness, and they do not allow anyone to end his life casually'. For others that had died there were two chests that were kept 'before the city gates'. One was for the bodies of free men and the other for slaves. The bodies were carried by wagon

> to the place of burial without any wailing and lamentation. Mourning was confined to the day of the funeral, and it ends with a sacrifice in the home and a banquet for friends and relatives: What is the point in giving in to human sorrow or resenting the gods because they do not want to share their immortality with us?[539]

Though Strabo also mentions slave burials at Massalia does this infer a slave trade as it could be locals who because of debt become slaves as in Athens?[540] Valerius Maximus writes the only other ancient surviving reference that mentions slaves in Massalia. They are mentioned later during A.D. 502-552[541] and from the medieval period to the eighteenth century the Galley-slaves of the French Navy.[542] There is recorded a *venaliciarius graecarius* (a slave-dealer Greek) *Cneus Naevis Diadumenus* on an epitaph in Nimes.[543] Though Clerc questions this by adding *Diadumenus* may have dealt through Egypt and Syria via Narbonne (a sea port in Gaul)[544] and possibly a direct trade to Romans in Gaul? Narbonne was the first permanent Roman colony outside of Italy and the single Roman port in Gaul that was founded in 118 B.C. amongst senatorial opposition.[545] Also the epitaph is in Latin script.

Diodorus Siculus wrote that Italian traders transported wine into Gaul as 'the Gauls are exceedingly addicted to the use of wine' and 'for an incredible price' were getting 'a slave in exchange for a jar of wine'.[546] How many times did this actually happen as it could have been just the once and so 'incredible' that the story stood out not only for profit but in Celtic weakness/addiction, like exploitation of American Indians by alcohol in the Wild West; despite the Celtic Nervii and the Seneca Handsome Lake movement respectively self-regulating attempts to ban alcohol?[547] However one estimate suggests that in free Gaul before the Roman conquest 15,000 slaves per year were exchanged this way.[548] Being 'Italian traders' it is most likely they worked from their base the Roman colony of Narbo and its direct trade to Rome. Perhaps having slaves did not affect the Gauls in the feeling of kinship with their compatriots as mentioned by Livy.[549]

Though some scholars have speculated, there is actually no mention of a slave trade in ancient Massalia from the few sources we have left. But Rihill suggests it was because of such a trade that native hillforts develop at the time of Massalia's settlement 600 B.C. as previously there were small settlements of forty or less people.[550] Whereas Morgan and Arafat raises the point that the trading nature of ancient Massalia so far away from the other Greek city-states would more likely have been one based on 'consensus and co-existence'[551] with the local populations that provided a substantial market for goods and produce very much like their colony Emporion's relations with the Iberians in Spain.[552] There is as we have noted the far reaching reputation of Massalia amongst the Celts that ambassadors from the Greek Phocaean city of Lampsakos (in Asia Minor) went to Massalia to ask them to influence the Celtic Tolostoagian (in Asia Minor) not to join Antiochus III of Syria in fighting Rome.[553] Could such a good reputation amongst the Celts been credible if Massalia had dealt in Celtic slaves? This is not just looking at the past with twenty-first century morals for even in the past we had the Aristonicus revolt 131 B.C. in Asia Minor[554] that promised freedom to any slave that would fight for the State;[555] two slave revolts in Sicily 135–132 B.C. and 104-100 B.C. plus the slave revolt of Spartacus 73–71 B.C in Italy.[556]

Strabo records that Massalia had

> dry-docks and an armoury . . . In earlier times they had a good supply of ships, as well as arms and instruments that are useful for the purposes of navigation and for sieges; and thanks to these they not only held out against the barbarians, but also acquired the Romans as friends, and many times not only themselves rendered useful service to the Romans, but were also aided by the Romans in their own aggrandizement.[557]

It would seem that Massalia still kept its naval security on a serious level. Strabo in describing the dockyard on the island of Rhodes wrote 'As for the roadsteads, some of them were kept hidden and forbidden to the people in general'. For any individual found spying on them the penalty was death:

> And here too, as in Massalia and Cyzicus, everything relating to the architects, the manufacture of instruments of war, and the stores of arms and everything else are objects of exceptional care, and even more so than anywhere else.[558]

Strabo continues,

> And its adornment [Cyzicus] appears to be of a type similar to that of Rhodes and Massalia and ancient Carthage. Now I am omitting most details, but I may say that there are three directors who take care of the public buildings and the engines of war, and three who have charge of the treasure-houses, one of which contains arms and another engines of war and another grain. They prevent the grain from spoiling by mixing Chalcidic earth with it.[559]

During the Hellenistic period the dry docks for Massalia's navy was at the eastern end of the Harbour of Lacydon. Next to the naval dockyard and on the left was the commercial ship area and neither of these sections was walled leaving the beach open to the city and presently marked by the l'Hotel de Ville and Place Jules-Verne. Modern day Marseille has built out a couple of hundred metres into the harbour with a road, buildings and promenade. On the opposite northern side facing the open sea was the cove (anse) of Ourse though it was walled it is not known if this was used as a harbour. However it would follows the usual favoured pattern of Greek sites to have two harbours like Syracuse and Corinth. Perhaps the Anse de l'Ourse may have been used when the winds were too strong for ships to turn into Lacydon or when leaving? The Anse de l'Ourse was just beyond the present cathedral La Major before the cove of Joliette but the anse and cove have now disappeared with the modern docks Bassin de la Grande Joliette extending out into deeper water for the visiting ocean liners. The present day metro station Joliette is by the original cove and the nineteenth-century A.D. dockside warehouses were renovated in 1991.

Second Century A.D.

Lucian, writing on friendship, was in Italy as an ambassador and a Massaliote in the street pointed out Zenothemis of Massalia, the son of Charmolaus, with his wife passing by in a chariot. Zenothemis was handsome and wealthy and his wife 'not only was she repulsive in general, but her right side was shrivelled and the eye wanting–a hideously disfigured unapproachable nightmare'. The Massaliote told Lucian how they came together. 'Menecrates, the father of the misshapen woman', was friends with Zenothemis. Both were wealthy. Menecrates had his property confiscated by judicial sentence, when he was disenfranchised by the Six Hundred for presenting an unconstitutional measure. 'That', said he 'is the punishment we Massaliotes inflict whenever anyone proposes an unconstitutional enactment'.

Menecrates was distressed 'in a moment he had become poor instead of rich and dishonoured instead of honoured'. Most of all he was worried about his daughter, who was marriageable and eighteen. Even before with his wealth 'no well-born man, though poor, would readily have agreed to accept her'. It was said that she also had the falling sickness when the moon was waxing. Zenothemis told Menecrates not to fear he would not lack what he needed and your daughter 'would find a husband worthy of her lineage'. He took Menecrates home and shared his wealth with him.

Later Zenothemis ordered a dinner prepared and invited his friends including Menecrates, to a wedding feast, pretending to have persuaded one of his comrades to promise to marry the girl. After the dinner was finished and they poured the libation to the gods, Zenothemis held out to him his cup, full of wine and said,

> "Accept, Menecrates, the loving-cup from your son-in-law, for I shall this day wed your daughter Cydimache; her dowry I received long ago, amounting to twenty-five talents". The other said: "No, no, Zenothemis, do not! May I never be so mad as to suffer you, who are young and handsome, to make a match with an ugly, disfigured girl!" But while he was saying this, Zenothemis picked up the girl bodily and went into his chamber, from which he returned presently, after having made her his wife.

From that time on he has lived with her, cherishing her beyond measure and taking her about with him everywhere, as you see. Not only is he unashamed of his marriage, but indeed seems to be proud of it, offering it as proof that he thinks little of physical beauty or ugliness and of wealth and glory, but has high regard for his friend, for Menecrates, and does not believe that the latter's worth, as regards friendship, was lessened by the vote of the Six Hundred.

Already, however, Fortune has requited him for this conduct. He has had a beautiful boy by the ugly woman; and besides, only recently, when the father took the child in his arms and brought him into the Senate-house wreathed with leaves of olive and dressed in black, in order that he might excite greater pity on behalf of his grandfather, the baby burst into laughter before the senators and clapped his two hands, whereupon the senate, softened by him, set the condemnation aside in favour of Menecrates, so that now he is in full possession of his rights and privileges through employing so tiny an advocate to present his case to the members in session.

Lucian finishes the story with the comment 'Such are the deeds which, according to the Massaliote Zenothemis performed for his friend; as you see, they are not trivial'. [560]

Greek Cities in the Western Mediterranean

Greek Colonisation/Settlements

'For they, [Greeks] especially those who had insufficient land, made expeditions against the islands' (Thucydides, I. 15.1)

There are indications from Strabo as to earlier Greek exploration of the Western Mediterranean. They may have established colonies, settlements or trading posts like those at Bèziers with a strong Greek presence from the fifth century B.C.; [561] Rhodus (in Spain) by the Rhodians (though archaeological excavations reveals nothing earlier than the fourth century B.C. and was founded by Massalia); and Saguntum by Zacynthon (Strabo, Book. III, 4.6) though these and others could have been abandoned for several years or later absorbed by Massalia?

The name Saguntum (Ζακανθαίων Zacanthaion) was assumed Greek, as it sounded so similar to Zacynthon. [562]

Livy also says of Saguntum *Oriundo a Zacyntho insula dicuntur mixtique etiam ab Ardea Rutulorum quidam generis* (Livy xxi.7.2) founded by Zacynthos with an admixture of Rutulians from Ardea; there is further mention in Pliny, *Nat. Hist.* xvi.79.216; Appian. *Hisp.*7.

Isidore of Seville records that *Saguntum Graeci ex insula Zacyntho profecti in Hispania condiderunt; quam Afri postea bello inpetitam deleverunt.* [563]

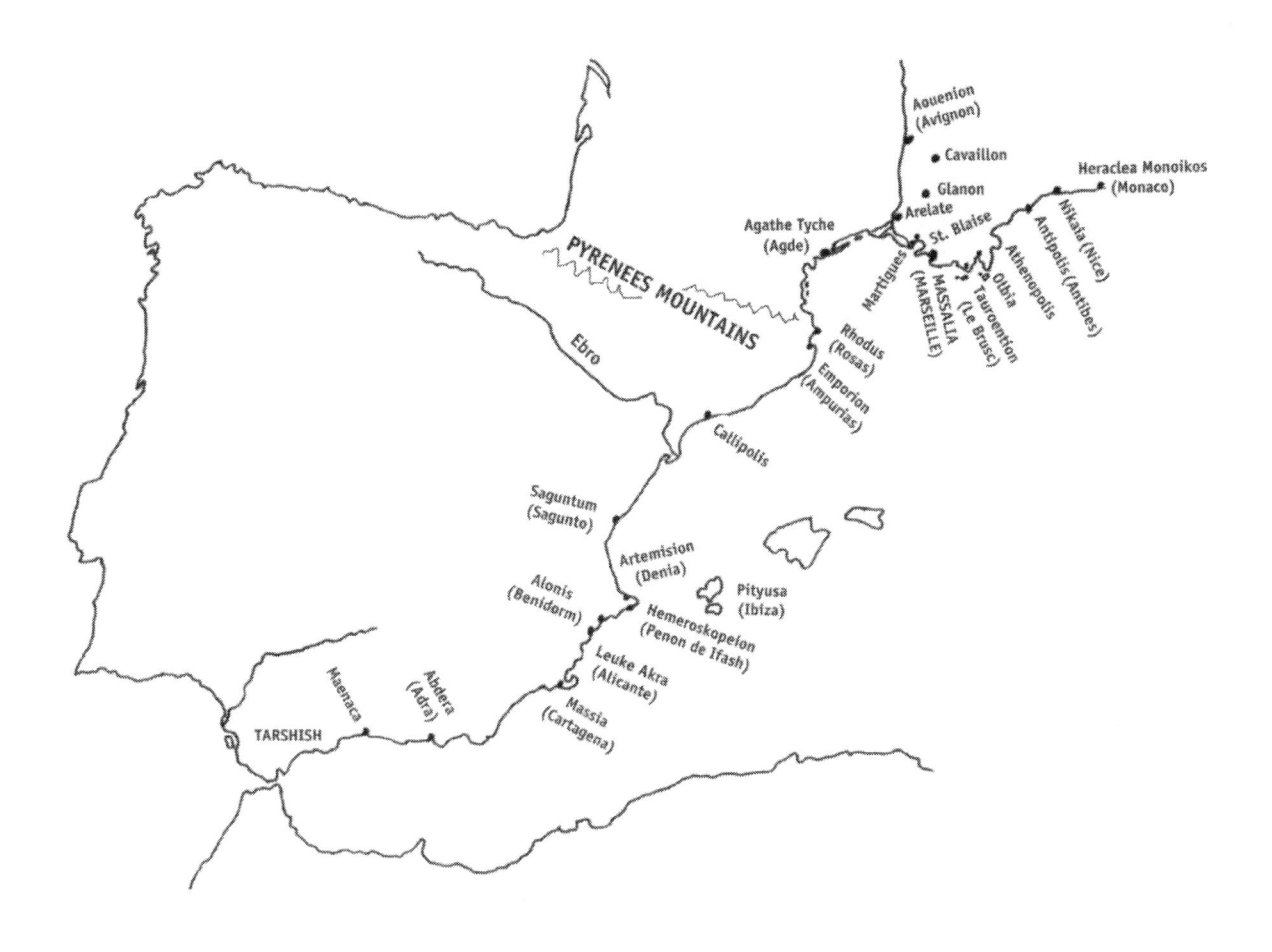

Figure 41. Phocaean/Massaliote cities in Spain, France, and Monaco (Heracles Monoikos).

Spain

A sherd of Attic geometric from mid-eighth century B.C. has been found in Huelva and East Greek pottery from the seventh century B.C. was found along the Iberian coast at Cerro de Villar and Huelva.[564] A Greek Corinthian helmet 650–625 B.C. was dredged up from the Guadalette River, Cadiz, Spain in 1938 [565] and on display in the Museo Arqueológico Municipal de Jerez de la Frontera, Spain. Height: 22 cm, width: 16.5 cm, maximum diameter: 22 cm and described as made of hammered bronze, early seventh century B.C. with nose guard broken off.[566] (See Figure 42).

A second Greek Corinthian helmet, mid-sixth century B.C. with palmette decoration around the eye slits, was found in the sea 50 miles away next to the Guadalquivir estuary near modern day Huelva[567] and is in the Museo Arqueológico Nacional, Madrid. Height: 23 cm, width: 20 cm, diameter: 30.50 cm, thickness: 0.20 cm (Figure 104, page 548): (another was found in the Ria Huelva 550-500 BC, and one in a rescue dig in Malaga 7th-6th century B.C.).[568] A seventh to sixth century B.C. ring with a 'cryptic Greek inscription' was also found at Guadalquivir.[569] Further inland from Huelva in South-West Spain an Attic black-figure cup c. 550 B.C. was discovered in a grave at Medellin within the region of silver mines.[570] The cup has an image of Zeus holding a thunderbolt.

Figure 42. Corinthian helmet 650–625 B.C. with nose guard broken off, dredged up from the Guadalette River, Cadiz, Spain and now in the Museo Arqueológico Municipal de Jerez de la Frontera.

Chronology for the Greeks in Spain
(Suggested by Rhys Carpenter). [571]

First Main Period of Greek Trade with Spain
620 B.C. to before 500 B.C.

There is Greek pottery evidence from c. 625 B.C. in Spain and massive imports in the early sixth century B.C. particularly in Malaga and Huelva. [572] Malaga to Huelva by sea is 234 nautical miles.

c. 520 B.C. Carthage bars Greek ships from Tartessos in Spain.

Events Effecting Control of the Seas
480 B.C. Carthage defeated by Greeks at Himera in Sicily led by Gelo, king of Syracuse and Theron Tyrant of Agrigentum against Carthaginian Hamilcar the Mangoib (said to have been on the same day as the Battle at Salamis where the Greek allied Navy defeated the Persian Navy of Xerxes).

475 B.C. The Etruscan Navy destroyed off Cumae, Italy by Hiero I, tyrant of the Greek city of Syracuse, Sicily.

Around c.500 B.C. the ruler of Pozo Moro (Albacete) was buried with a few Greek imports of 'clear ritual significance'. The local aristocracy of the fourth century B.C. were buried with up to sixteen Greek vases of four types 'clearly trade lots and not ritual sets'. [573]

Second Period of Greek Trade with Spain
450 B.C.–250 B.C.?

The above mentioned end date suggested by Carpenter (1966) for the second phase needs adjusting to take into account subsequent archaeological evidence of the continuation of Greek trade from Massalia's thriving colonies in Catalonia Spain, of Rhodus (Roses) fourth century B.C.–195 B.C. [574] and Emporion (Empúries) c. 600–575 B.C. until A.D. 96 (after the Flavian period). [575] Julius Caesar defeated their mother-city Massalia in 49 B.C. and placed a colony of Romans next to Emporion to ensure the city's future loyalty. Between c. 36–27 B.C the cities became the Roman Municipum of Emporiae [576] and could be used as the date when Greek political independence ended here. Greek trade in Spain would have continued into the last quarter of the first century A.D. when decline accelerated due to other commercial centres along the coast beginning to dominate trade. In the last quarter of the first century A.D. it seems depopulation started in the Neapolis first and it was abandoned. A steady depopulation also affected the Roman city, which increased in the second century to [577] the third quarter of the third century A.D. After which no indication has been found to say it was inhabited. [578] Therefore a suggested date for the second phase of Greek trade in Spain could be 450 B.C.–A.D. 96 (end of Flavian period).

Massalia had trade relations with Valencia, Murcia and Catalonia. [579] There was for a period Greek influence on indigenous sculptures, [580] which can be seen in the Archaeological Museum in Madrid. [581] They include an important statue Dama de Elche that was found near Elche (ancient Helike) dated to between 450–350 B.C. [582] Also Greek-Iberian script in the Alicante and Murcia region is dated to fourth century B.C. [583] In Contestania (approximately the Alicante region) the Greek-Iberian script has an adapted Ionic, a type of epigraphy not found elsewhere in Iberia. Hoz suggests bi-lingual writers and instructors and therefore Greeks living in South-East Spain far beyond Emporion. [584]

Trading Post in Italy

Gravisca c. 600 until 480 B.C.

There is archaeological evidence of an Ionian trading post at Gravisca, at the Harbour of Tarquinia in Etruria [585] and thought to have been trading from c. 600 until 480 B.C. [586] The site was a commercial settlement with shrines and pottery inscribed to Hera, Apollo, Aphrodite and Demeter. Amongst the finds was an inscribed anchor set up by an Aegintean Sostratus [587] who was known for his wealth by Herodotus. [588] Morel points out that a Phocaean presence had been doubted previously but since the discovery in 1969 it 'now appears probable' and 'they are even considered to have "opened" this trading post'. [589] This coincides around the date of Justin's story from Pompeius Trogus of Phocaeans on their way to found their settlement at Massalia who sailed up the Tiber during the reign of King Tarquin and 'made alliance with the Romans': and Livy who says their arrival in Gaul was in the reign of the king of Rome Lucius Tarquinius Priscus (616–578 B.C.). Tarquinius was the son of the exile Demaratus of Corinth. [590] Demaratus was also 'ruler of the city' Tarquinia [591] where Tarquinius was born.

Trading Posts in France

Bessan.
Greeks, possibly Phocaeans, establish a site at La Monédière at Bessan, 15 km from the sea up the valley of the Hérault between 533–500 B.C. This had access to the mining resources of Cévennes. Their rectangular houses had an apse and a stone foundation with mud brick walls. [592]

Rhodanousia.
Though Avienus had described Rhodanousia as a city Morel suggests this was more of a trading post and may be located at Espeyran on the Petit Rhône. There is a settlement here dating from 525-500 B.C. There are Massaliote features found here and more so from 475 B.C. with houses of mud bricks on pebble foundations, Massaliote amphorae and West Greek vases. [593]

Baetera (Bèziers).
Strabo mentions 'Baetera, a safe city' near Narbo. [594] There is a strong Greek presence here from fifth century B.C. Differences between the pottery found here and that in Massalia led excavators to suggest that the site may have been founded by other Greeks and not Phocaeans? [595]

One is reminded of the statement by Strabo,

> This, then, is what I have to say about the people who inhabit the dominion of Narbonitis, whom the men of former times named "Celtae"; and it was from the Celtae, I think, that the Galatae as a whole were by the Greeks called "Celti"—on account of the fame of the Celtae, or it may also be that the Massaliotes, as well as other Greek neighbours, contributed to this result, on account of their proximity. [596]

ταῦτα μὲν ὑπὲρ τῶν νεμομένων τὴν Ναρβωνῖτιν ἐπικράτειαν λέγομεν, οὓς οἱ πρότερον Κέλτας ὠνόμαζον ἀπὸ τούτων δ' οἶμαι καὶ τοὺς σύμπαντας Γαλάτας Κελτοὺς ὑπὸ τῶν Ἑλλήνων προσαγορευθῆναι, διὰ τὴν ἐπιφάνειαν ἢ καὶ προσλαβόντων πρὸς τοῦτο καὶ τῶν Μασσαλιωτῶν διὰ τὸ πλησιόχωρον.

From the last **καὶ** there is an assumption that Strabo means 'other Greek neighbours' of the Massaliotes in Gaul rather than 'other Greek neighbours' of the Celts elsewhere in the Greek world?[597]

Baetera (Bèziers) coins were of bronze with the inscription in Greek of the people Longostalètes. Head of Hermes on the obverse facing right and on the reverse the Caduce and the inscription ΛΟΓΓΟΣΤΑΛΗ(ΤΩΝ). [598]

Other coins were with the head of Heracles facing right and on the reverse a wild boar facing right in a field, with three points and also the head of Heracles facing right, behind the head a 'mausse', and on the reverse a lion with either one of four names Kaintolos, Amytos, Bitous or Rigantikos. A base of a funeral stele inscribed to brothers and professors Philon and Artemidorus are dated to second century A.D. [599]

Aphrodisias, (Portus Veneris–Port of Venus)
Strabo mentions the Temple of Aphrodite here at the foot of the Pyrenees on a promontory 'marks the boundary between the province Narbonitis and the Iberian country'. The temple's distance from Narbo was sixty-three miles and to Antibes (Antipolis) 277 miles. Though he mentions other authors vary between 2,600 stadia or 2,800 stadia from the 'temple of the Pyrenaean Aphrodite' to the Varus River. [600]

Phocaean Cities in the Western Mediterranean

CORSICA

Alalia c. 565 B.C. (Aléria on the east coast of Corsica) founded together with help from Massalia.[601] Dominguez estimates the colony boosted by the refugees from Phocaea fleeing the Persian invasion of 545 B.C. would have made a population of 20,000 or more and occupied a territory of 200 km².[602] Herodotus wrote that many of the Phocaeans left after the Battle of Alalia in 540 B.C. to mainland Italy and founded Elea (Hyele, Velia). [603] Archaeological evidence shows Alalia was not entirely abandoned by the Phocaeans and continuing in a smaller capacity until the Etruscans occupied it. Remains of a city wall have been found 'of the *agger* type with a broad *glacis* in front of it' (possibly sixth century B.C.) as well as sixth century B.C. dwellings of mud brick and pottery of an archaic date. [604] Archaeology has given a good indication that the Phocaean stayed on but not how long as they become overlaid by the Etruscans. Fortunately new scientific techniques are always developing and the study of genetics is a revealing addition to archaeology.

Genetic Study

A recent genetic study carried out with 323 men from across Corsica and likewise fifty-one in Provence (France) revealed a genetic marker E-V13 identical to that found within a sample of eighty-nine Greek males in Greece whose grandparents came from the Phocaea and Smyrna areas in Ionia. The results from the samples taken were East Corsica 4.6%, West Corsica 1.6%, and Provence 4 %. [605]

Kalaris (Galéria on the west coast of Corsica). Diodorus lists this as a Phokaian (Phocaean) city [606] though Oldfather thought it might be a corruption for Aleria mentioned above. [607] However, the recent genetic study confirms a Phocaean presence on this side of the island and archaeologists have identified Galéria as the site for ancient Kalaris. [608]

Dunbabin also points out the Tyrrhenian city on the island was called Nikaia, which shared the same name as the other Phocaean colony in Gaul (present day Nice), and may have been at first Phokaian (Phocaean). [609]

SARDINIA

In the fifth century B.C. the Greeks regarded Sardinia as a kind of El Dorado. [610]

Olbia near Terranova, Ikhnusa.[611] Dunbabin suggests this may have been a 'short-lived Phokaian (Phocaean) colony' on Sardinia, [612] which also shared the same name with their other colony Olbia in Gaul.

During the time of Harpagus's invasion for Cyrus, king of Persia it was Bias of Priene who advised the Ionians to set sail for Sardinia 'and there found a single Pan-Ionic city; so they would escape from slavery and rise to great fortune, being masters of the largest island in the world'. [613] Herodotus thought Sardinia was the largest island at that time. [614]

During 494 B.C. Aristogoras of Miletus made a suggestion to his 'brothers-in-arms . . . Should he go out at the head of a colony to Sardinia' to escape King Darius and the Persians? Aristogoras went to Myrcinus in Edonia instead. [615]

ITALY

Hyele (Elea–Velia) c. 540 B.C. (Castellammare di Brucia, now Castellammare di Velia) in South-West Italy was called Hyele by the Greek Phocaeans (Strabo, vol. 3. VI.1.1) and founded by them after leaving Alalia and a short stay at the Greek city of Rhegium (in South Italy), who were their allies. [616] Hyele was the last Greek city to be founded in South Italy. [617] The city wall dates from c. 520 B.C. and was reconstructed in 480–470 B.C. The wall was divided into compartments.[618]

Strabo tells us though inferior in territory and population they were victorious against the Leucani and Poseidoniate and 'compelled by the poverty of their soil, to busy themselves mostly with the sea and to establish factories for the salting of fish and other such industries'. [619] They built their acropolis on a hill 100 meters from the sea (the sea is now about 700 meters away) and the city was a major port.[620] Elea became famous for philosophy through Parmenides (born c. 515 B.C.) and Zeno (born c. 490 B.C.). Aristotle regarded Parmenides as one of the principal founders of metaphysics and Plato used his analysis in support of his own doctrine of Forms (Ideas).[621] Strabo also records that Zeno and Parmenides were famous Pythagorean philosophers at Elea.[622]

The name *Oulis* used by some of the Elean medical school appears at the sanctuary of Aristaios at l'Acapte near Olbia in Gaul as well as on a lead strip in Massalia (both Phocaean cities).[623]

Elea (Hyele, Velia) and Neapolis (Naples) were strong enough to resist the Samnites and Leucanians invasions after 420 B.C.[624] *Circa* 390 B.C. Elea joined other cities in South Italy, the Italiote League, to resist the Tyrant of Syracuse Dionysios I. By 272 B.C. Elea was allied to Rome.[625] As a naval ally (*socii navales*) it was exempt from military levy but required to provide ships from time to time.[626]

The Greek cities of Elea and Neapolis (Naples) provided priestesses of Demeter to the Romans.[627] The Eleans worshiped seafaring deities particularly Leucothea. Similar to Massalia, Phocaea and other cities in Asia Minor a *naiskos* enclosure with a seated deity has been found here. There were also cults of Zeus, Hera, Athena or Asclepius (often testifying to an Athenian influence).[628]

Elea maintained its independent status as a *civitas foederata* of Rome until 89 B.C. when it became a Roman *municipium*.[629] Documents from Elea show a continuation of Greek language and culture after the Social Wars to at least the first century A.D. while the political classes were Romanised.[630]

FRANCE

Massalia (Marseille) founded 600 B.C. by the Harbour of Lacydon (Vieux Port). Here was the birthplace of explorers Euthymenes and Pytheas. Massalia's system of government was analysed by Aristotle and Strabo. Strabo considered the city 'of all the aristocracies, theirs is the best ordered'.[631] Massalia was a centre for trade including tin from Britain and amber from around Jutland. Pottery and amphorae evidence shows Massalia trading along the Rhône valley. Greek goods have been found in central Europe and as far as Sweden. Massalia minted its own silver and bronze coins from the fifth century B.C.[632] and created several colonies of its own. The city was a centre of culture with many schools attracting Roman nobles and Celts. Massalia had a large cultural and economic influence in southern Gaul (France) and some in Iberia (Spain) where Gallo-Greek and Greek-Iberian scripts were used by the indigenous populations respectively.[633] By establishing the cultivation of olive trees and grapevines they gave these two countries a lasting and prosperous legacy.

Marseilleveyre Mountains
Offerings of Greek ceramics, vases, miniature kylix and lamps, were found in caves and grottos at Marseilleveyre Mountains 9 km south-east of Marseille dating from sixth century to second century B.C.[634]

Theline (The Provider, later called Arelate (Town-in-the marsh), Arles).[635] Theline is mentioned by Avienus along with Rhodanousia as Greek cities in Gaul.[636] Theline is possibly the old name for Arelate that grew into Arles. Excavations at Arles Winter Gardens uncovered remains of buildings that together with a quantity of previous pottery finds support a Greek presence near to the time of the foundation of Massalia c. 600 B.C.[637] The first Phocaean settlement at Arles was destroyed by the Ligurians c. 535 B.C.[638]

La Couronne was an early trading post that diminished with the growth of Massalia 40 km away. The excavated city walls of Massalia at the Horn are dated to second century B.C. and were built from the La Couronne quarries.[639] The quarries also provided building stone for the port of Massalia in the Hellenistic period, and also the new port installations and extensive building in the city during later Greek and Roman periods first to third century A.D.[640]

The following two cities it seems were already in existence.

Aouenion (Latin *Avennio*, French *Avignon*) attracted Greeks in the sixth century B.C. as a trading centre.[641] Stephanus of Byzantium wrote that it was a Massaliote Greek city but Pliny and Pomponius Mela wrote it was an oppidum (hillfort) of the Cavares.[642]

One tombstone with a Phoenician inscription was discovered there in 1897 with an estimated date as the third century B.C.[643] Nevertheless it would seem Greeks made up part of the population. Greek influence is found on the coins minted there with the city name in Greek. Also found was a hoard of 1265 Massaliote AR and fragment obol coins.[644] The excavations at St. Agricol produced large Greek block walling that could indicate Massaliote control of the city. Three parallel sections of wall were uncovered that marked the southern limit of the Roman Forum. At the deepest level there was Greek masonry.[645]

Livy mentions that some of the Volcae occupied the land east of the River Rhône. Rivet suggests this land may be the same that was handed over much later by Pompey the Great to the Massaliotes who might have controlled it from Avignon rather than Glanum.[646]

Geographically it is also the northern limit for growing olives.[647] The ancient Greeks generally seemed to prefer making permanent settlements where they could grow the olive or grape.

A find of an inscription in Arles that mentions *Iulia Augusta Avennio* establishes that a Latin colony was founded in Avennio (Avignon) after 27 B.C. during the Augustan age long before the Roman colony established by Hadrian.[648]

Cavaillon (south-east of Avignon). The local tribe of Cavares came under the rule of Massalia early on. They dominated an important crossing of the River Durance. Their oppidum (hillfort) was the Celto-Ligurian Cabellio (Colm Sainte-Jacques)[649] Stephanus of Byzantium gives Artemidorus as his source that Cavallion was a Massaliote city.[650] Cavallion minted its own coins and has grave stelai with Gallic names, both were written in Greek.[651]

Figure 43. Greek drachma of Aouenion (Avignon) second to first century B.C. Obverse: head facing left/reverse: boar facing left with letters above AYOE for Aouenion. Aouenion produced silver drachma, mite, and small bronze coins.

Figure 44. Aouenion (Avignon) obol second to first century B.C. Silver coin, obverse: head of Apollo wearing laurels facing left/reverse: wheel 4 spokes, in each quarter a letter AOYE for Aouenion. Aouenion produced silver drachma, mite, and small bronze coins.

Cities Founded by the Phocaeans on the French Riviera

Antipolis (Antibes). Archaeological finds of pottery suggest an early date c. sixth century B.C. and was founded either by Phocaea direct or by Massalia (see next section). [652]

Heracles Monoikos (Monaco) sixth century B.C. said to have been visited by Heracles (Latin *Hercules*) where he defeated the Ligurian Albion here by himself. The name Monoikos (Latin, *Monoecus*) may refer to this and can also mean solitary or lonely. [653]

Ammianus Marcellinus fourth century A.D. historian wrote of the roads,

> The first of them, near to the Maritime Alps, was made by Theban Hercules; and he it was who gave to these Alps the name of the Grecian Alps. In the same way he consecrated the citadel and port of Monoaecus to keep alive the recollection of his name forever. [654]

Ammianus had crossed the Alps himself in the winter of A.D. 355 with the young Emperor Julian and his guards. [655]

Strabo mentions the 'coastal voyages of the Massaliotes reach even as far as the Port of Monoikos. The distance from the Port of Monoikos to Antipolis is a little more than 200 stadia'. [656] He also records that there is a temple of Heracles Monoikos there.

The site had the Greek preference for a promontory, which could give shelter from the winds for their ships. In the photograph Figure 45 the royal palace (the square in the foreground on the promontory) is on top of the Greek acropolis. To the left is Port Hercules and to the right Port Fontvieille. A mid-third century B.C. buried coin hoard was found in Monaco consisting of 21 AE: 2 from Neapolis (Naples) and 19 from Carthage Sardinian mint. [657]

Monaco is divided from Nice (Nikaia) by a barrier of mountains and even in the nineteenth century A.D. they needed to be scaled as they drop perpendicular to the sea and there was no route available at their base. By foot it was four hours and by carriage six using a winding route over the mountains. Like Hercules travellers found it quicker to walk. 'Apollo has his horses; Diana her hinds; Amphitrite has her dolphins; Venus her doves; the swift Mercury his winged sandals; but Hercules, who traversed the world, receives nothing from the poets but the strength of his limbs'. [658] Approaching by boat from Nice one can see what the Phocaean sailors would have seen, a spectacular sheer curtain of mountains and in front the promontory with a foothold of land.

Until the introduction of the railway in 1868 Monaco had maintained itself with very little arable land in poverty. However the ancient Greek Phocaeans skilful and resourceful were able to make this, Elea and Massalia, all lands that deterred other Greeks due to the rugged terrain and 'poverty of their soil' [659] into prosperous and viable cities.

Figure 45. Monaco founded by the Greek Phocaeans as Heracles Monoikos. The Greek acropolis is under the royal palace first buildings on top of the promontory. To its left is Port Hercule (Hercules).

Cities Founded by the Phocaeans in Spain

Mainake, (**Maenaca** east of Malaga in Spain. [660] Strabo records Maenaca 'lies farthest of the Phocaean cities in the west is farther away than Calpe, and is now in ruins (though it still preserves the traces of a Greek city)'. [661] Aubet (2007) raises some questions on Strabo's report and that Mainake due to a lack of Greek archaeology might have been Phoenician. [662] Carpenter (1925) suggested that Mainake was first settled by Phocaea c. 620–600 B.C. and was still flourishing as late as 530 B.C. [663] Aubet says that Mainake predated Malaga and archaeology suggests it fell into ruins between 600-570 B.C. [664] From Mainake to Tartessos was two days sail. [665] An overland route of five days connected it to Tartessos.[666] Both Mainake and Tartessos were completely destroyed by Carthage and with their main ports of trade gone this possibly excluded the Greeks from the Atlantic. [667] Tartessos was destroyed so that Gades would have no rival in the area. Mainake must also have given place to Malaga. These two towns vanished so thoroughly [668] that later writers believed Tartessos was Gades, and Phocaean Mainake was confused with Phoenician Malaga, which was about twelve miles away. [669] Mainake predated Malaka (Malaga) and was surrounded by swamps. The city was on an island that was obtained by concession of the natives and had a port. [670]

While some of the other Iberian currencies are attributed to Emporion in influence, the other possible Greek Phocaean cities such as Mainake and Hemeroscopian along the east coast of Spain may have issued coins of their own?[671] We do have evidence of Rhodus (Latin *Rhode*, Spanish *Roses*) issuing coins from the third century B.C. with imitations found in France[672] and also Emporion (Empúries, Spain) issued coins from the fifth century B.C.[673]

Professor Marion gave three colonies west of Mainake:[674]

Abdera, (l'Adra in the province of Almeria).

Almunecar, east of Malaga *

Hermeroskopion, in the province of Valence.

Strabo briefly mentions Abdera as a city founded by the Phoenician[675] though this may have been taken over by Massalia?

*Apart from the suggestion by Marion (1914) regarding Almunecar there does not appear to be any evidence as Aubet (2006) writes of it as a Phoenician settlement because there were twenty-one burials over a period of 100 years (730-625 B.C.) suggesting 'the presence of two or three principal rulers per generation at the head of the colony'.[676] Braun identifies Almunecar as Sixos a Phoenician settlement 750/720 B.C.[677] It was an old idea that Maenaca was either Almunecar or Cerro de Villar.[678] See above section on Mainake, Maenaca.

Leuke Akra (Alicante). Destroyed in the third century B.C. with evidence of a burnt level. Later overbuilt by an Iberian village with evidence of Iberian and Carthaginian pottery and a Carthaginian castle was built on the hill, which inherited the name. Bosch-Gimpera suggested that Greek refugees may have gone to Artemision (the present day Dénia in Spain) 'which became important at this time'.[679] Leuke Acra is also listed by the *Cambridge Ancient History* as one of Massalia's colonies.[680] At Alt-de-Benimaquia is evidence of local wine production from the beginning of the sixth century B.C. At first under aristocratic control more quantity led to wider use.[681]

Santa Pola, twenty kilometres south of Alicante. The city may have been built by Phocaeans from Massalia or 'other Greeks'. Excavations at La Picola (Santa Pola) 'suggests a small trading centre under the control of native Iberians from the nearby settlement of Illici, with just enough Greek architectural elements to indicate a possible Greek presence on this site'. Rouillard mentions this settlement lasted c. 450 to c. 330 B.C.[682] The settlement was 2,980 m² with Greek foundations, defence systems, measurements and a grid layout site but with Iberian lifestyle that suggests a mixed population.[683] Houses were laid out as in the Greek Phocaean paleopolis of Emporion, (Spain) the same width as the streets and at right angles to the street. 'The foot is the same (29.5/30cm), and the only difference is the module: 12 feet' (in the Phocaean paleopolis of Emporion it was 10 feet).[684] Alternatively Zacher mentions Santa Pola as the port for the Greek city of Helike (Elche)[685] nine miles away.

Altea, fifty kilometres north of Alicante. At present a tenuous link only in the name as a clue from the Greek *Althaia* meaning 'I heal' and situated at the mouth of the River Algar, which means 'the river of health'.[686]

Massai and Callipolis may have been colonies of 'the other Greeks'? [687]

Massai (Mastia, later called New Carthage present day Cartegena). Carpenter has Massai as originally a Phocaean town still flourishing by 530 B.C. [688] near the time the Massaliote periplus was written c. sixth century B.C. [689] that Avienus used in his poem *Ora Maritima*, lines 449–6,

> 'there with high walls
> Above the bay's head towers MASSIA'. [690]

Massia traded lead and iron ore as well as fish products and the original people of the surrounding villages were related to the Tartessians. [691] A treaty between Rome and Carthage in 348 B.C. made Mastia the limit for Roman ships in the Western Mediterranean. [692] Carpenter suggests that the Carthaginian Hamilcar re-founded Massia (or Mastia) as Carthage Novo (New Carthage) between 228-221 B.C. [693] though Braun has this as founded by Hasdrubal in 221 B.C. Stephanus cites Hecataeus for four *poleis* (cities) of Mastianoi (in the Ionic dialect Mastienoi). [694]

Callipolis. Avienus writes in *Ora Maritima* (508–10),

> That famed Callipolis which with
> Vast Height
> Of rampant walls and lofty battlements
> Touches the sky. [695]

Carpenter gives this reference from Avienus but little else has been found since to establish this as Tarragona or in its vicinity. [696]

Cities Founded by Massalia

Agathe Tyche (Good Fortune/Luck) c. 580 B.C. is present day Agde in Languedoc, France originally at the mouth of the River Hérault (now 4 km from the mouth due to silting). Skymnos listed the city as founded by the Phocaeans. [697] Hodge writes that the city seems to have come under Massaliote control towards the end of the fifth century B.C. [698] Strabo states it was founded by the Massaliotes. [699] The Massaliotes founded their city at Agde at the end of the fifth century B.C. [700] Excavations on the city's ramparts show there was intense Massaliote activity in Agde from fourth to second century B.C. [701] According to their museum of underwater archaeology, Musée de L'Éphèbe at Le Cap d'Agde, Agathe Tyche was the second oldest Greek city founded in France [702] and therefore Massalia's first colony. (Another Greek settlement 533-500 B.C. was 15 km upriver, which might have been Phocaean or 'other Greeks' see section on Bessan).

From the end of the sixth century Agathe Tyche was around 3.5 hectares in size and extending to 4.5 hectares by second century B.C. [703] The terrain was ideal being a volcanic mound for the city and down to the riverside with a natural basalt embankment making it easy for their ships to dock. [704] Excavations down to the second century B.C. level showed they were built on earlier fourth-third century B.C. foundations. [705] An inscription now lost dated to the late second century B.C. was dedicated to the mother-goddess and the Dioscouroi [706] this had been uncovered in the foundations of l'Hôtel de Ville.

ΑΔΡΗ •ΜΗ
ΤΡΑCΙ • ΚΑΙ
ΔΙΟCΚΟΡΟΙ [707]

Two further inscriptions were found with a dedication to a god Teuchares on a cylindrical basalt third century B.C. in the Saint Sever area. The other on a damaged lead plate/plaque (*plaque en plomb*) with 250 Greek letters written in an Ionian dialect, fourth century B.C. [708]

The city had adequate surrounding land for agriculture to support 1,500 people. Its 20,000 hectares had half for grain production and arboriculture. The output was equal to the large Greek city in Italy called Metapontium. [709] Rivet (1988) points out that Agde is the only example of land in Gaul the Greeks took over to support their colonies (cadastration) possibly between the fourth and second century B. C. [710] The land was geometrically divided up (centuration) as far as the later road Via Domitia near Béziers [711] at approximately 20 km distance.

Agathe Tyche had basalt quarries for making olive presses and grindstones for domestic use and export. Several basalt-grinding stones from Agathe Tyche were found at another Massaliote colony of Olbia near Hyères, Toulon. [712]

From the mid-fourth century onwards there were lagoons for salt extraction and easy access to fishing. [713] Agathe Tyche imported wines from Massalia. [714]

Trade of the native pre-Greek city with Greeks [715] shows early seventh century B.C. rare Greek types of *sykyphoi* and cups that were excavated in the necropolis by André Nickles. [716] His excavations [717] were in the areas of La Glacière, Picherie Square, and the Peyrou Necropolis [718] that revealed 180 tombs. [719] Excavations were also conducted in 1998 and the level of the Greek city was at 4.5 metres under the present sidewalks. [720]

The Greek city was well situated being en route between Massalia and Spain by the old coastal road 'Voie Héracléenne': the river traffic of its port: and access to the deep sea. [721] From Agathe Tyche (Agde) it was 130 nautical miles to the River Aude landing at Narbo. From Narbo the overland route is 400 km to Bordeaux on the Atlantic Ocean, a journey of 7–10 days. [722] Agde was later called 'The Black Pearl of the Mediterranean Sea' as it is built from the local dark coloured volcanic stone. [723] A hoard of 135 AR Massaliote drachmas coins buried third to second century B.C. was uncovered. [724]

Found in the River Hérault in front of the Cathedral Saint Etienne in Agde, by underwater diver Jacky Fanjaud (G.R.A.S.P.A.) in 1964, was a magnificent Greek bronze statue 1.33 metres high. Part of one leg was found six months later. The feet are missing and with them would make a height of 1.40 metres. Given the name L'Éphèbe d'Agde it is displayed, after restoration in Paris, in their new museum of underwater archaeology 'Musée de L'Éphèbe' at Le Cap d'Agde. [725] The bronze statue is of a naked young man with a cloak over the left shoulder and wrapped around the left forearm and is of the Macedonian military cloak type *Chlamys*. There is also a diadem around the head that was customary of Macedonian kings. [726] The hairstyle and diadem is very similar to that used by Seleucas I Nicator one of Alexander's successors. [727]

Comparative studies made show L'Éphèbe d'Agde to be in the style of Lysippus.[728] He was the only person officially allowed by Alexander the Great to make sculptures of him though other sculptors made many. This statue was made in the second century B.C.[729] probably by the school of Lysippus and based on their portraits of Alexander. The style has the typical melancholy look; head tilted to the left, lips slightly apart, and locks of hair of Alexander the Great. Pliny the Elder writes that Lysippus 'made many studies of Alexander the Great, beginning with one in his boyhood'.[730] The museum assessed that the muscles of the statue was of a young man or adolescent and likely to be that of Alexander around the age he was Regent of Macedonia at sixteen.[731] The thought occurred to me I was standing next to a life size statue of a young Alexander. But later I read that both Cicero and Pliny mention that Lysippus said publicly 'whereas his predecessors had made men as they were, he made them as they appeared to be'. By making the head slightly smaller he increased the figure's height.[732] However, it was still an amazing experience to actually see this beautiful bronze statue for real.

A much larger replica of L'Éphèbe d'Agde has been made and put on a roundabout outside the town of Agde. This is also impressive. Why the original and other Greek remains were in the river we do not know. Recently French archaeologists using sophisticated scanning equipment on a boat have recovered several Roman sculptures from the river at Nimes.

Figure 46. Greek bronze statue L'Éphèbe d'Agde second century B.C found in the River Hérault in front of the Cathedral Saint Etienne in Agde, characteristic in the style of Lysippus and thought to be Alexander the Great when he was sixteen and Regent of Macedonia.

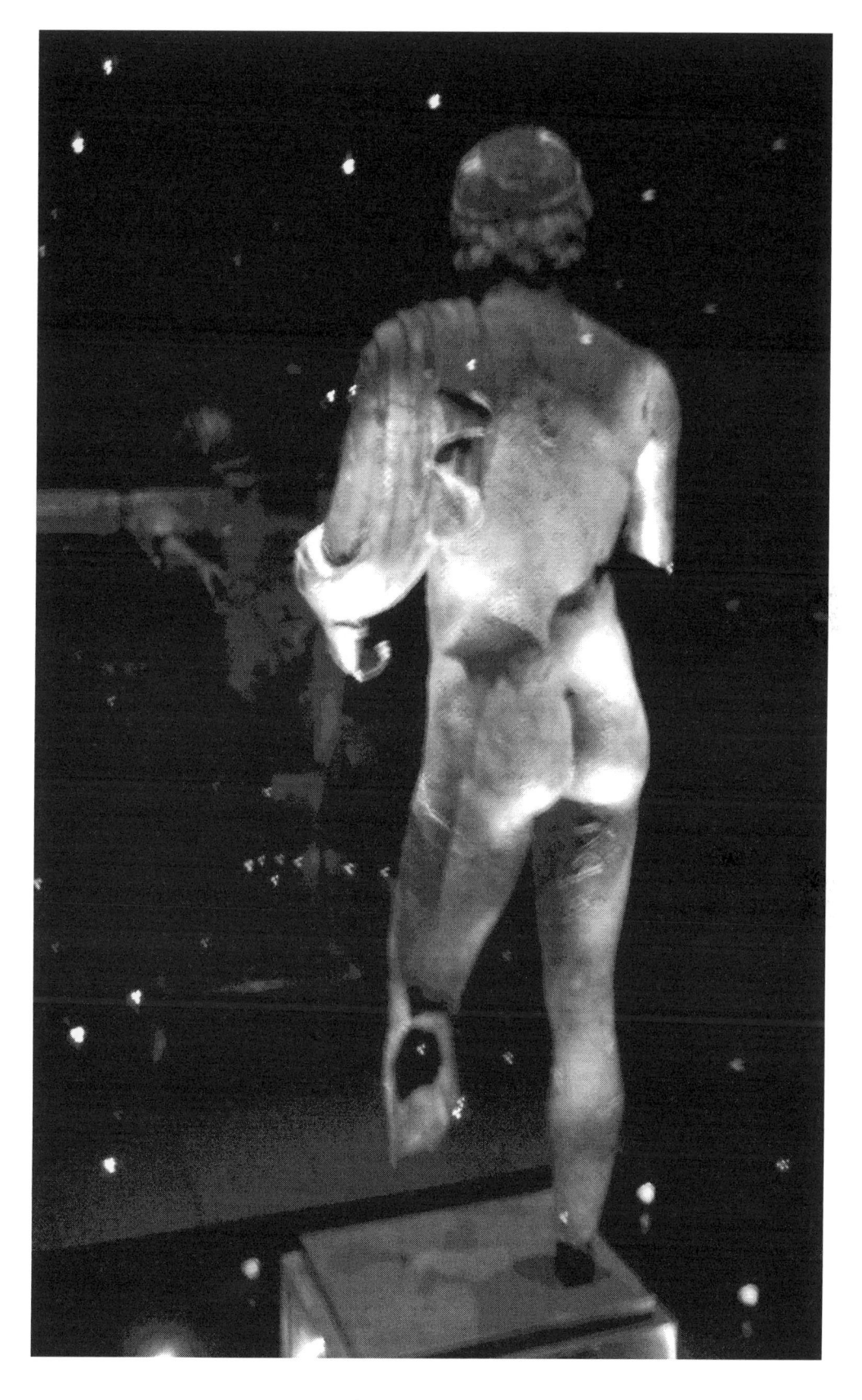

Figure 47. Greek bronze statue L'Éphèbe d'Agde second century B.C. back view.

Figure 48. Greek bronze statue L'Éphèbe d'Agde second century B.C. side view showing diadem around head and Macedonian style of holding clock around left shoulder and arm.

Figure 49. Greek bronze statue L'Éphèbe d'Agde second century B.C. front view showing the Macedonian style of holding a cloak around left shoulder and arm.

The L'Éphèbe statue in the museum alone is well worth a visit as well as the other finds. A Hellenic bronze statue of Eros 63.5 cm high, the body is very ordinary bronze with squares visible in contrast to the fine detail of the head, eyes and hair. On the back is a place for wings (missing).[733]

Another very interesting bronze is a statue 80 cm high of a boy six to seven years old found between Le Cap d'Agde and Marseillan. There were deliberately no eyes and it seems a funerary statue. He wears a short tunic that is belted. Across the top of the head from front to back is a topknot and covering it a wide ribbon decorated with a thunderbolt a symbol of Zeus. Zeus was not used for children but the successors of Alexander the Great used the thunderbolt inherited from Alexander who claimed to be the son of Zeus Ammon. The child is wearing sandals, which is unusual as they went barefoot; a snake bracelet around the right ankle and the ears pierced for earrings that eastern kings wore all suggest a royal child. Dated first century B.C. to first century A.D. the statue represents either Caesarion (47–30 B.C.)[734] son of Cleopatra VII and Julius Caesar or Ptolemy the son of Cleopatra VII and Mark Antony.

Found by Nicolas Figuerolles at the depth of six meters on the same site as the Caesarion or Ptolemy statue was a virtually intact Emblema mosaic illustrating the musical contest between Apollo and Marsyas dated first century B.C. to first century A.D. The mosaic is an intricate masterpiece of over 1,500 pieces 3–4 mm each in a portable block 7 cm thick, weighing 37.5 kg and in excellent condition.[735]

There is also a Hellenistic bronze wing of Victory/Nike with finely detailed feathers found a hundred metres from the L'Éphèbe d'Agde in the River Hérault. The rest of the statue is missing. From the scale and style this Nike would be very similar to the Victory statue second to first century B.C. in the Museum of Breccia in Italy.[736]

A few weeks before Fanjaud discovered the L'Éphèbe statute at Agde diver Andre Bouscares discovered another find from a shipwreck at Rochelongue. This shipwreck had eighty-nine kilograms of copper ingots, tin and 1,700 bronze items e.g. belt buckles, axe heads, earrings, and arrowheads dated to end of seventh to beginning of the sixth century; the mixture of objects suggests they were trading objects for recasting.[737] At La Motte a village in a lagoon a large find of over 300 various bronze objects [738] including necklaces decorated with amber pearls was dated to the end of the ninth and beginning of the eighth century B.C. A bronze workshop must have been somewhere on the strategic point on the coast at the mouth of the River Hérault probably even earlier to the Iron Age and was trading inland? Could this be the reason why Massalia founded Agathe Tyche (Good Fortune) at the entrance to the River Hérault as well as being a safe port for other Phocaean ships travelling from Tartessos, Mainake (Maenaca), Emporion and Rhodus to Massalia, Alalia, Elea and Phocaea in their own network as well as other ports of call? Agde remained the most active port in the Gulf of Lion up to the nineteenth century until silting of the river necessitated a new deeper port, the Grau d'Agde, 4 km downstream at the present mouth of the river and the sea.

A beautifully decorated bronze Etruscan Tripod 62 cm high was found at the Tour du Castellas between Marseillan and Sète dated fifth century B.C. and thought to have been made in Vulci in Italy.[739] The museum also has many Greek and Roman anchors and amphorae, dolia, part of an ancient ship, and also canons from the seventeenth to nineteenth century A.D.[740] a great place to visit.

Figure 50. Agde (Agathe Tyche), aerial view. The L'Éphèbe d'Agde Greek bronze statue was found in the river to the right of the bridge in front of the riverside Cathedral. Top right is Mont St. Loup and beyond the Mediterranean.

At Agde a remnant of the medieval wall exits by the Agathe statue and fountain and some Roman foundations are visible at the base of the wall next to the bridge. On the aerial photograph (Figure 50) to the left are the lagoons Etang du Bagnas and the Basin du Thau and at the top the Mediterranean. Looking at Agde you can still make out the area of the original Greek city above and along the river. Near the bridge the Greek city occupied the highest ground of 16 metres around the Glacière district and was built upon by the medieval city taking much of the same shape as the original. Some ceramics and three Greek inscriptions have been found.[741] The circuit walls show two phases of building first in the sixth century B.C. and repairs in the fifth century B.C.[742] Left of the bridge the road and tree line keeps the shape of the city walls from left to right: before the tree line ends (for the Greek city) turning down the street towards the river. The medieval extension is to the right of this narrow road. Together the old town section keeps a French medieval style of narrow streets and is unique in being built from the local basalt volcanic rock, as it lies within the extinct volcano (750,000 years ago) complex of Mount Saint Loup visible between Agde and Le Cap d'Agde.[743] The volcanic stones of the buildings have a dark grey appearance that from a distance seems black and particularly so when wet.

Figure 51. Agde (Agathe Tyche) the medieval city wall above the Greek walls.

The present Church of Saint Sever built in A.D. 1499 is named after a Syrian prince who came to Agde and founded a monastery in the fifth century A.D. Being close to the river area it is still known as the fisherman's church. The other ancient church is Saint Andrew and both basilicas were situated outside the Greek city walls. [744] The present Saint Andrew built in 1525 was built over the city's first church of the fifth century A.D.

The Council of Agde (*Concilium Agathense*) was held in Agde in A.D. 506 with 35 bishops under Caesarius of Arles in the beginnings of the transition of the Graeco-Roman social order to the barbarian conquerors. [745] Agde had been converted to Christianity in the fifth century A.D. and remained a powerful bishopric until 1790 with the execution of the bishop Charles François de Vermandois de Rouvroy de Sandicourt (St. Simon) in 1794 by the French Revolution and one of its last victims.

The Romanesque Cathedral St. Etienne is unique in basalt stone rebuilt in the ninth century A.D. and fortified in A.D. 1173 with a 35-metre tower and walls 2–3 metres thick. The chapel at the side is built over a Roman crypt still visible. Next to the cathedral was the large bishop's palace, now converted into the hotel/restaurant La Galiote.

The people of Agde, the Agathosie, are proud of their Greek heritage and modern made statues are found in the town to Agathe, and Amphitrite goddess of the sea. There is a pleasant promenade on both sides of the river and an active boatyard still keeping the maritime traditions of Adge alive.

The Cape of Agde's coastline is unique in France being formed from a volcanic complex now extinct. On Le Cap d'Agde there is one golden beach La Plagette and on the other side a cove Plage de la Grande Conque with a black beach of fine eroded volcanic rock on top of golden sand. This and the surrounding volcanic cliff are well worth a visit. In both directions are a total of 23 km of golden sand beaches by the Mediterranean Sea. The author Robert Louis Stevenson travelled here and remarked on the problem of mosquitoes but since the late 1970s DDT was used to spray breeding areas successfully with an on-going programme where local residents have a 0800 telephone number to alert the authorities if a mosquito is seen. [746] When the Phocaean ships from Massalia first arrived they would see the landmark Mount Saint Loup and on either side bays. The entrance to Agde (Agathe Tyche) was at the end of the River Hérault (Arauris) opening into a wide mouth on the Mediterranean Sea. Due to silting up over the centuries there may be now inland under the fields some sunken ships where the river and sea originally flowed.

Emporion (Latin *Emporiae*) founded c. 600–575 B.C. at the end of Gulf of Roses on the Costa Brava, North-Eastern Spain. Strabo writes that originally the Massaliotes settled offshore on the little isle of Medas, now called the old city, [747] near the mouth of the Ter River, they moved to the mainland promontory using the mouth of the River Cloudiness (Mega) as a harbour. Their neighbours the Indicetans had their own government but for security asked the Greeks to make a common wall to encompass both peoples and divided by a wall through the centre for the two peoples. Eventually 'the two peoples united under the same constitution, which was a mixture of Greek and Barbarian laws'. [748] Later this city gained independent status. 'As for the inland territory which they hold, one part is fertile, while the other produced the spart, of the rather useless, or rush, variety; it is called "Juncarian Plain."' [749] Strabo notes that 'The Emporitans were quite skilful in flax-working'. They also occupied some of the heights of the Pyrenees 'as far as the Trophies that were set up by Pompey, past which runs the road from Italy to what is called "Farther" Iberia, and in particular Baetica'. [750]

The paleopolis (old city), present day Sant Marti d'Empúries, was ideally placed as an island or rock on the end of a peninsula next to the River Fluvia on the northern side from which the Phocaeans could sail up and trade with the Iberians further inland. On the southern side was a bay for their ships. Within fifty years the Phocaeans established themselves on the mainland at the other end of the same bay about 1 km distance.

Today the palaiapolis (old city) on the island is joined to the mainland opposite neapolis (new city). Recent excavations in the old city have revealed Greek settlement to 575/550 B.C. including rectangular houses with stone socles and beaten floors.[751] There was an indigenous Iron Age village with rectangular mud huts c. 650/625—580 B.C. A marketplace at the end of the seventh century B.C. is suggested by evidence of West Phoenician and Etruscan amphorae and objects from East Greece. The huts were superseded c. 580–560 B.C. with new rectangular foundations standardised to 2.75 m x 2.95 m at right angles to the streets.[752] Houses are the same width as the streets, 'the foot is the same (29.5-30 cm), and the only difference is the module: 10 feet'.[753] Traces below the present church of Saint Marti d'Empúries is thought to be part of the Temple of Artemis of Ephesus goddess of the Ionian Greeks [754] but not proved as yet. Part of the wall next to the church with large blocks of cut stone at the base is Roman (see Figure 52).[755]

Figure 52. Saint Martí d'Empúries (paleopolis first Geek city of Emporion) the city wall next to the church. Large cut stones at base fitted together, Roman, next to the supposed site of a Greek temple of Artemis of Ephesus.

The medieval well at the north-east gate had two squares of white marble placed upright in between local stone and tiles. One was carved and a base belonging to something else. Looking in the well that went down some thirty feet it was made of white marble that had been shaped into smaller and uniform size stones. At the top on one side there were some stone made of white/reddish marble. It would seem the marble would have been reused from the ancient Greek or Roman buildings?

Ms. Dolu, the owner of the shop Odissa, told me there was an ancient Greek mosaic under her shop floor facing out diagonally to the left and was brown with white patterns. She also said there was a Greek carved base or top marble stone as part of the medieval well.

Figure 54. Saint Marti d'Empúries (paleopolis first Geek city of Emporion): the medieval city wall and well.

Figure 53. Saint Marti d'Empúries (paleopolis first Geek city of Emporion). A medieval well with a reused white marble carved stone from an earlier period.

Archaeologists Marta Santos Director and Elisa Hernández leading the excavations at Emporion were of the firm opinion [756] that the indigenous Iberians Untikacestan (Indiketes) here did not make their own coins in Emporion. Their own coins were produced in their capital Ullastret about 25 km from Emporion and their design clearly shows Greek influence.[757] Ullastret has been found but Indika their local town by Emporion has not.

During the fifth century B.C. Emporion according to Dominguez Monedero had an estimated population of around 2,000 and minted its own coinage using the Massaliote weight standard but with its own iconography.[758] Coins of anepigraphic minor denominations were produced in the fifth century B.C. Other coins from the fifth and fourth century B.C. were inscribed with either EM, EMΠ or EMΠOP.[759] From the fourth century Greek coins of a silver drachma featured designs from South Italy and Athens. A ceramic jar buried in the 'sub-soil of a tavern' near the entrance to the agora (market-place) around 385-375 B.C. included 897 small silver coins. Most were from the mint of Emporion and displaying the head of the goddess Athena/reverse: owl between the initial EM (for Emporion).[760] By the end of the fourth century drachmas of greater value appeared, obverse: head of Persephone, ear of corn in hair, city name EMΠOPITΩN (EMPORITON), reverse: horse standing, victory flying over. This changed toward the end of the First Punic War to obverse: the head of Arethusa (of Syracuse), surrounded by three dolphins/reverse: Pegasus, city name EMΠOPITΩN.[761] Pegasus became the symbol of the city.[762]

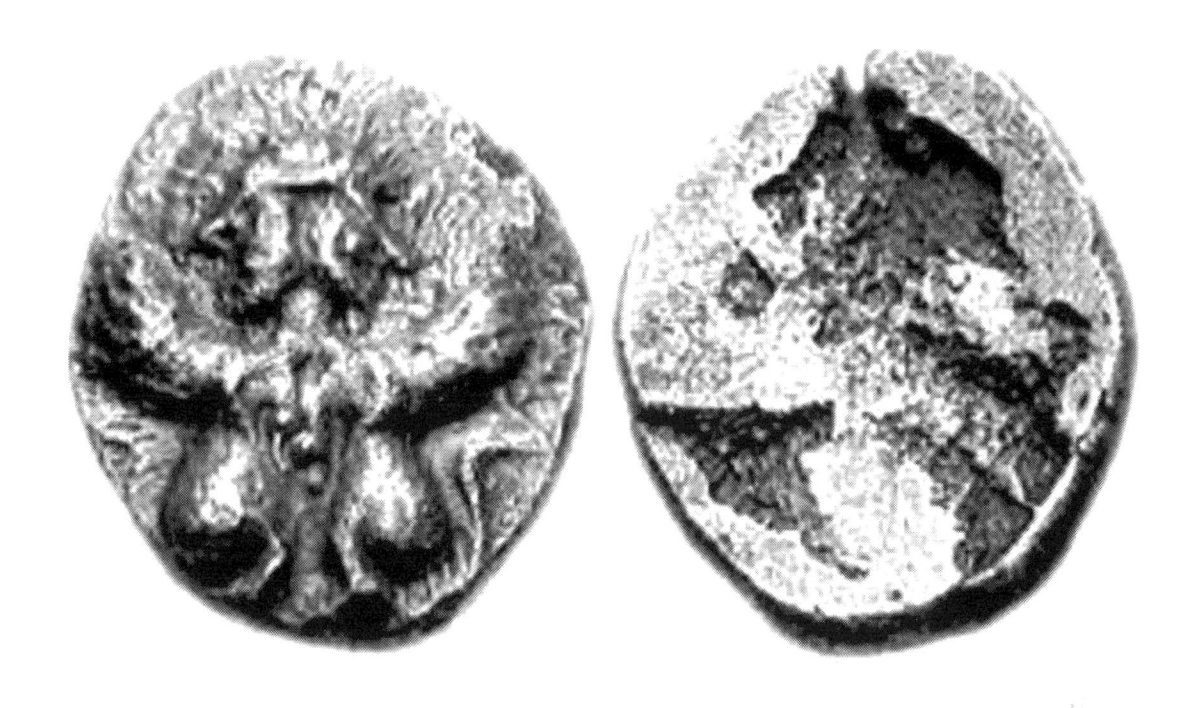

Figure 55. Emporion, Spain, c. 450–425 B.C. AR, trihemiobol. Obverse: two confronted Sphinxes their heads joined in janiform style/reverse: rough incuse. Weight 0.89 g.

Figure 56. Emporion, Spain, trihemiobol c. 450–425 B.C. Obverse: man-headed bull facing left/reverse: rough incuse. Weight 1.09 g.[763]

Figure 57. Emporion, Spain, AR Mint, drachma, third century B.C. Obverse: Persephone facing left, city name ΕΜΠΟΡΙΤΩΝ (EMPORITON)/reverse: horse standing facing right, above Nike (Victory); Die Axis in numbers:7 Diameter:40 Weight: 4.83 gm.

Figure 58. Emporion, Spain, c. 241 B.C. AR drachma, head of Arethusa facing right with three dolphins around/reverse: Pegasus flying right, with city name below ΕΜΠΟΡΙΤΩΝ (EMPORITON). Weight 4.54 g.

Figure 59. Emporion, Spain: Attic black figure libation and perfume vases, terracotta dove (symbol of life) from tomb 164 Bonjoan necropolis sixth century B.C

Figure 60. Emporion, Spain: red figure Krater for mixing wine and water fifth to forth century B.C.

There was found a letter written on thin lead. The archaeological context suggests a date at the end of the fifth century B.C. but the palaeographic and linguistic criteria suggests towards the end of the sixth century B.C. The letter contains the first recorded name of the Emporitoi (dwellers of Emporion) and instructions to the addressee to make a deal with a third person named Based(as) probably an Iberian name to a place named Saiganthe, possibly Saguntum. [764]

There was evidence of wine cultivation in the territory of Emporion and its Iberian neighbours. Grapes were cultivated there from the mid-seventh century B.C. though there is a higher level of finds after the fifth and fourth century B.C. and in the 'samples from the first half of the third century B.C. at Puig de Sant Andreu d'Ullastret and the Neapolis of Emporion'. Possibly to increase wine production and/or to introduce new varieties there was a cargo of grape-vines found in a shipwreck dated to 375 B.C. called El Sec (Calvià, Mallorca) that was making a 'voyage from Athens, Sicily to the Iberian peninsula'. [765] Quesada mentions there was wine produced in Spain before Greek colonisation. [766]

Massalia's cultivation of the olive trees affected the 'south and interior of Gaul as well as the north of the Iberian peninsula'. There were wild olive trees but they are found in thermo-Mediterranean or lower meso-Mediterranean bioclimatological areas different to the grapevine. [767]

Livy wrote that the Greek part of the town wall of the neapolis (new city) was 400 paces long and opens to the sea. The Spanish part of the wall went further back 'of 3 miles around'. 'The Greek dividing wall facing the interior was strongly fortified, with only a single gate leading in that direction and a magistrate posted as a continuous guard'. [768] The main entrance was the southern gate. The northern side faced the natural harbour. The western wall faced a slope up to a plateau.

By c. 375 B.C. the city was heavily fortified, with cyclopean masonry with double gateways, enclosing an area of 2.75 ha. The Marti cemetery contains Greek and non-Greek types of grave goods. The inscriptions as late as the fourth century B.C. are in both Greek and Iberian. [769]

Clerc illustrates one inscription found at Emporion. Dated between 3rd to 1st century B.C., with the names of Thespi, Aristoleou, of Massalia, welcome. [770]

ΘΕΣΠΙ
ΑΡΙΣΤΟΛΕΟΥ
ΜΑΣΣΑΛΙΗΤΑ
ΧΑΙΡΕ

There were two Greek Curse tablets made of lead excavated at Emporion from Hellenistic debris of the necropolis and now in their museum. [771] Tablet 1 from the fourth to third century B.C. height 10.7, width 19.5 cm was folded twice with the names Aristarchos, Aristotelis, Sosidimos, Epikoros, Parmenon, Kaustirios, Dimit[rios], and Pythogenis. [772] The names listed on Tablet 2 (also folded twice) from the third century or later are Tintiton, Posidonas, ' E´ orton, Sosipatros, Ermokaikos, and Parmenon. Only the name Tiniton is not Greek. Both Kaustirios and Ermokaikos are personal names derived from rivers near Phokaia and compare with the Massaliote name Ermokaikozanthos which adds a third the River Xanthos Ξάνθος. The first two names show Ionic onomastic continuing in Emporion and the Ionic and Phocaean character is evident in all the texts found. [773]

The name Parmenon appears on 'both tablets (I 5 and II 6)' and probably not the same person. The name was also found in Massalia and 10 more examples in their colony of Olbia (including a Parmenon and Parmenikka). [774]

The earliest finds have been in the northern part of Neapolis (New City) between 600–550 B.C. while those of the southern part date to c 500–450 B.C. Three kilns were found dating to 580–550 B.C.[775] Between 450–400 B.C. the Sanctuary was situated in the south-west area and during the next fifty years reorganised and dedicated to Asclepion. The previous temple, which seems to have been outside the city walls was dismantled and replaced with a smaller one to Asclepius and now included within the new city wall.[776] The statue of Asclepius was recovered in 1909 having been dumped in one of its cisterns situated in front of the temple used for ritual cleansing associated with the worship ritual and made of different marbles from the island of Paros and Attic Pentelic quarries at the end of the fourth century B.C. Over time it had been maintained by repairs and parts of the snake had been made from local sandstone.[777] Votive vases were excavated next to the temple. There was expansion of the city walls to the south c. 375–350 B.C. A defensive parapet (proteichisma) was erected in front of the southern city wall c. 230-200 B.C.[778] The first harbour was north of the Neapolis and at the end of the second century B.C. a breakwater was built to protect it. As trading increased new facilities were needed. A second harbour was established to the south-east in Riells-La-Clota at L'Escala also in the second century B.C.[779]

Figure 61. Emporion, Spain: Hellenistic Breakwater second century B.C. for the ancient Greek harbour. A length of 80 m still survives.

The breakwater was in two sections and projected out from the paleopolis and the other from the neapolis. The neapolis part of the Hellenistic breakwater (80 m) still exists and even with erosion it is substantial and impressive to see. The Breakwater is dated to the end of second to beginning of first century B.C. with 'a double face of blocks of calcareous stone filled with concrete'.[780] The use of concrete is recorded after the arrival of the Romans. Behind the breakwater are beautiful golden beaches, sand dunes and beyond where the harbour was is now a field right up to the embankment. On top of this embankment there is a plateau where the Roman city was situated. When the Romans joined the two cities together they did this by extending their wall to join the south-west corner of the Greek wall. The Romans still left unoccupied the space between the two cities even when under the same administration of the Municipum c. 36–27 B.C.

In the Emporion territory there were 'fields of silos' particularly in sites such as Pontós from fifth to second century B.C. that had the estimated capacity to store all the annual cereal production of the Emporion region.[781]

Appian mentions they together with the Saguntines 'and the other Greeks, both those who lived in the region of the town called Emporion and those elsewhere in Iberia, fearing for their safety, [from Hannibal and the Carthaginians] sent an embassy to Rome.' The agreement made between Carthage and Rome 'not to cross the River Ebro under arms' left the Greek cities 'autonomous and free' from Carthage.[782]

Appian gives the details that from 197 B.C., while Rome was preoccupied with Gauls on the Po and with Philip V of Macedon; the Iberians saw their opportunity to attempt a revolution. However the Romans were able to send to Spain generals Sempronius Tuditanus, Marcus Helvius and after them Minucius. Spanish resistance was strong and by 195 B.C. Cato was sent with a larger force. Cato arrived at Emporiae and the Spaniards assembled 40,000 against him. Before the fight he 'dismissed all the ships back to Massilia so the troops would have no escape and had to win'.[783]

Livy also records that by c. 195 B.C. one third of the Greeks manned the walls every night 'they posted their sentinel and sent out patrols'. No Spaniard was admitted to the city, nor did the Greeks themselves leave the city without good cause. Livy wrote, 'The Spaniards had no experience with the sea'. They enjoyed making business with the Greeks and wanted 'foreign merchandise, which they brought in their ships' and in return the Spaniards 'disposed of the products from their farms'.[784]

Emporion also had a small arsenal with artillery that was exploited by Roman generals, like Scipio Aemilianus, in their campaigns during the second century B.C.[785] Amongst a hoard of weapons found in the arsenal at the neapolis of Emporion by the south gate during 1912 was a catapult. The hoard was dated to the first half of the second century B.C. This was the first ever discovered and it had an original iron spring frame of the small arrow-shooting catapult *euthytonon* of typical Hellenistic design.[786]

Figure 62. Emporion, part of the cyclopean city wall base of south gate tower second century B.C. The previous southern wall was dismantled and extended 25 metres reusing the stones.

There is evidence of a major building programme in the second century B.C. A new market Agora with a stoa was constructed on the northern side and porticoes on the other sides.[787] Most of the present Greek city excavated so far has been down to the second century B.C. level and there is much to see. A new southern wall had been built 25 metres out and constructed from the massive stones, some are actually big boulders with a little shaping, that were taken from the dismantling of the earlier fourth century B.C. southern wall.[788] Two square towers, the lower sections of calcareous stone, protected the gates of which one was iron, and behind it another of wood with two hinges covered in lead still surviving. Another larger tower to the west protected the south-west corner. The Temple of Asclepius underwent remodelling. To the west of the Gate's entrance the extended area inside the wall allowed space for the sanctuary of Sarapion dedicated to Isis and Zeus Serapis (first century B.C.). Noumas paid for the Serapion according to a stone inscription in Greek and Latin that was found and dated to middle of the first century B.C. Noumas was of Alexandrian origin.[789]

Figure 63. Emporion. Greek mosaic second to first century B.C with the word ΗΔΥΚΟΙΤΟΣ (how sweet it is to be reclined) and likely to be a small banqueting hall for *symposia*.

Outside the museum is one small banqueting hall most likely for *symposia* (second to first century B.C.) with a mosaic floor with the word ΗΔΥΚΟΙΤΟΣ (how sweet it is to be reclined) at its entrance (see Figure 63).

A large mosaic floor was uncovered in the north-east part of the Neapolis. Outside of the main border alongside and near one corner were the words

ΧΑΙΡΕ ΑΓΑΘΟΣ
ΔΑΙΜΩΝ

Welcome, good spirit. [790]

Figure 64. Emporion. The temple and statue of Asclepius, god of medicine: statue placed on a white tesserae floor. In front of the temple were cisterns for the ritual cleaning of people that came to be healed. The temple underwent dismantling and remodelling in the fourth and second century B.C.

I was most impressed to see that the Greeks had designed a cistern under even the small houses or courtyards to channel rainwater from their roofs and floors into it.[791] This made sure they had their own personal reserve supply as well as those cisterns provided in public squares by the civil authorities. They knew the value of water over two thousand years ago. On a grander scale you can see the intriguing underground Basilica Cistern in Istanbul built by the Emperor Justinian in the fifth century A.D. 360 by 230 feet.[792] But with increasing periods of droughts even in a country once known for a wet climate like modern day Britain we would do well to make provision in our gardens and public places for the storage of rain water to allow for periods of drought and not waste precious resources. Such reserves could even be linked into a national grid? A few dams in the remoter parts of Scotland where rainfall is still high would be wise and of great benefit to Britain.

When Livy wrote about the supposed Roman foundation in third century B.C. he was confusing this with different stories of Roman involvement in the area that was relating to the Second Punic War of 218 B.C. with the landing at Emporion of a Roman Army under Gnaeus Cornelius Scipio to cut off the supplies to Hannibal. Following the revolt by some Iberian tribes in 197 B.C. Marcus Porcius Cato established a military camp on the higher plateau next to Emporion in 195 B.C.[793] The Romans started their own separate city and colony at the beginning of the first century B.C. on this plateau keeping it separate from the Greek city below, which is proved archaeologically.[794] The city of the indigenous Indeke that joined the Greek city of the neapolis of Emporion has not been found as yet but may be under the Roman city [795] or under the present car park opposite the Greek south gate? [796]

Remarkably in close proximity there were in reality three cities with Emporion's palaipolis and neapolis and the Roman *Emporiae* and there was no conflict. There must have been more than enough trade for everyone. Excavations are on-going and one sixth of the Roman city has been uncovered. Several mosaic floors of some of the villas are certainly evidence of a wealthy city, as well as a substantial Forum, and an amphitheatre outside the south wall that could seat 3,300 people.

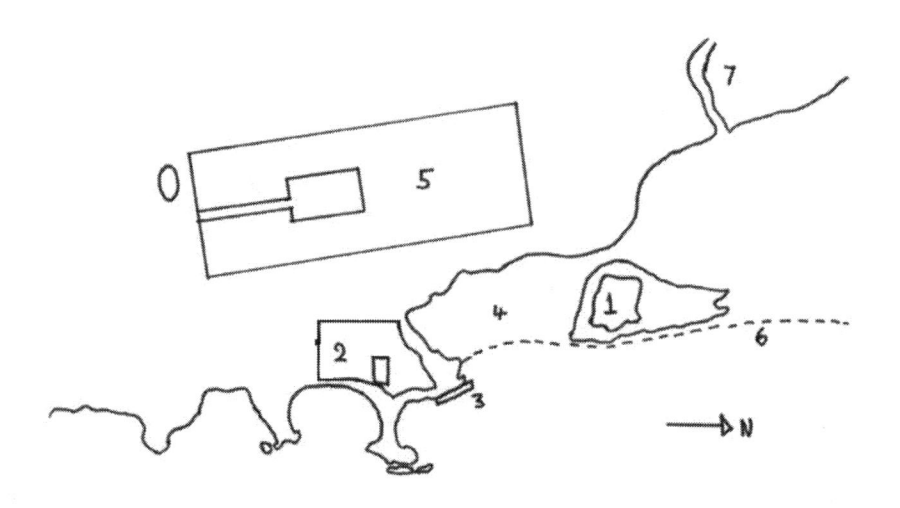

Figure 65. Emporion, three cities, first century B.C. 1. Original Greek paleopolis on an island: 2. Greek neapolis on the mainland: 3. Hellenistic Breakwater (remains) originally longer and opposite another extending out from the paleopolis: 4. Harbour: 5. Roman city: 6. Present day coastline: 7. River Fluvia.

The Romans had established their city 150 m west of the Greek neapolis c. 100 B.C. The city 22.5 hectares [797] was surrounded by a wall, lay out in an orthogonal grid, and was divided into north and south by a transverse wall. The Roman southern wall was made of stones for approximately 5 feet: above about 10 feet high was made of Roman concrete walls and roof: and the space between filled with earth and stones. On top were channels across the width of the roof at regular intervals 'for slotting in the wooden cross bars to support the plank moulding' [798] along the whole length of the southern wall. During the first century B.C. the Greek neapolis and the Roman city were united.[799] Appian [800] and Livy wrote that Julius Caesar added a Roman colony to the mixed population of Iberians and Massaliotes in the Massaliote colony of Emporion (Empúries, Spain). [801] This was after Caesar had captured Massalia in 49 B.C. AL Margo suggested that the 'Greeks of Emporiae followed the Massaliote opposition to Caesar and that Caesar showed his favour to the native inhabitants by giving them citizenship first'. [802]

Strange how history can repeat itself, reflecting the first foundation in so much as when the native Indicetans asked the Greeks to build a city with one city wall to encompass both people with another wall between them in the city [803] to keep their areas distinct from each other, the Romans now made a common wall to encompass the Greek (neapolis) and Roman city. Archaeologists have found the new wall that joined the two cities which was only from the south-west corner of the Greek wall [804] at an angle of approximately 50° degrees until it met the Roman city wall some way before the

Roman south-east corner. Coins appear in Augustus's reign with the inscription *MUNICI EMPORIA*.[805] The amalgamation of these two cities may have coincided with the creation of the Municipium Emproriae of c. 36–27 B.C.[806] Even though they amalgamated, the area between the Greek city and the Roman (on the higher plateau) was not built upon and a space kept between them. The Indicetans still existed there as Pliny the Elder records 'Amporias, one part of which is inhabited by the original natives and the other by Greeks descended from the Phocaeans'. [807]

What eventually happened to the Greeks? They continued to live in their two cities but it would seem the larger Roman city dominated trade and the Greek cities declined. The Greek neapolis was abandoned after A.D. 96.[808] By the third quarter of the third century A.D. the Roman city on the plateau was also abandoned possibly because commercial traffic was no longer as profitable. This decline may have just been local as at this time Cartagena further along the coast experienced a commercial boom.[809] However the smaller paleopolis (old city) protected by its own city wall continued and in the late Roman period was using the port facilities with evidence of goods from Africa, the Orient and the south of Gaul. Without further excavations it is difficult to know how long the Greeks or Romans stayed on in the paleopolis. However, the paleopolis did remain continuously occupied and carried on under indigenous people to the present day [810] as Sant Marti d'Empúries.

After the Neapolis was naturally covered over from a long period of abandonment there was in the fourth century A.D. a Christian church with niches and mosaic floors built behind the Hellenistic *stoa* and a cemetery with over 500 burials (in the northern part extending to the west) from the city of Empúries (that was now reduced to the area of Sant Marti d'Empúries, the original paleopolis) until the Moslem invasions c. A.D. 715.[811] This was an important ecclesiastical seat for the bishop; where one called Paulus attended the council at Tarragona in 516; and the temporal seat as the county capital for the Count of Empúries until seventh century A.D. With the transfer of the capital to Castelló d'Empúries the memory of Emporion disappeared while Sant Marti d'Empúries continued.[812] In the sixteenth century fishermen from here founded the nearby town of L'Escala.

Cities that are not maintained become overgrown with plants, shrubs and trees. Abandoned cities become buried over time also by the constant falling of stardust. The Greek neapolis and the Roman city became buried and lost until identified by the bishop of Girona Joan Margarit in the fifteenth century but was soon forgotten again.[813] Later Servite Monks built a monastery on the abandoned site of neapolis (new city) in 1606 and rediscovered both the Roman and Greek buried cities. The monastery closed in 1835 and later plundering of the site continued until 1907 when the architect Joseph Puig I Caldfach and Enric de la Riba, President of the Diputacio de Barcelona bought up the land and subsidised the Junta de Museus of Barcelona for systematic excavations.[814] The monastery buildings have now been joined up to make the museum, shop, and offices of the archaeologists. This unique site is a must to visit. Archaeology and golden beaches, what a combination! As I was told several times there 'the Greeks certainly chose the best places'.

The site of Empúries can be reached by air to Girona (the medieval city centre is worth a visit in itself) and taking a bus to L'Escala or air to Perpignan and train to Figueres Vilafant then bus. There is also a high-speed train from Paris to Figueres Vilafant (five and a half hours) that also continues to Girona and Barcelona.

Rhodus, (Latin *Rhode*, Spanish *Rosas, Roses*) belonging to Emporiae (Emporion) as recorded by Strabo 'though some say it was founded by Rhodians'.[815] The Rhodians were also thought to have named the River Rhodanus (River Rhône). Pliny the Elder mentions a 'former site of Rhoda, a colony of Rhodes, that has given its name to the Rhone' when discussing the area from Agde to the mouth of the Rhône, and the district of the Volcae Tectosages.[816] Strabo writes that the Rhodians made voyages to Spain before the first Olympiad colonizing the Balearic Islands and Parthenope on the Bay of Naples.[817] However, there is ample archaeological evidence of the Greek colony of Rhodus in Spain. While Dunbabin suggests Greek settlements by the trace of *usa* in the end of names by either Phokaians or Rhodians he is doubtful of a date of earlier than the seventh century B.C. for the island of Rhodes to found or re-found Rhodus (Rhode) in Spain.[818]

Professor Hodge (1999) tentatively raised the possibility he admits from scant literary references that the Greek Rhodus settlement in Spain may predate Cumae c. 750 B.C. settlement in Italy [819] adding that archaeological work needs to be done to prove this. In the following years speculations about the origin of Rhodus (Rhode, Roses) opposite Emporion across the Gulf of Roses have not as yet been proved as archaeological excavations since have not found any foundation earlier than the fourth century B.C.[820] There was no link of origin to the island of Rhodes and on present archaeological evidence Rhodus was founded by Massalia in the fourth century B.C. The link with the island of Rhodes may have been 'invented' during the Hellenistic period in an attempt to explain origin. Though I wonder, through the symbol of the rose on the reverse of their coins, was there a memory of the island of Rhodes that also used the Rose as a pun on their name? Then again as the city of Rhodus did not produce their own coins until c. 250 B.C. they may have used the Hellenistic story of supposed origin whether true or not in at least establishing their own identity while being part of the Massalia network particularly with Emporion just across the Gulf of Roses.

The Greeks abandoned Rhodus c. 195 B.C. however, the ships of Emporion still continued to use the port area first century B.C. to second century A.D. and it may be because of this that Strabo wrote that 'Rhode belonging to Emporion'.[821] That the coastline shifted forward in the ancient period is evident by remains of a later Roman building second to fourth century A.D. (for fish salting) in front of the previous buildings in the commercial neapolis (new city) of the Barri Hel-lenistic. The Romans in turn abandoned the site (now called by them Rhode) possibly due to commercial competition from other cities along the coast. Later the Visigoths occupied Rhode from the fourth to seventh century A.D.

Earliest finds of Attic Greek black pottery (skyphos and kylix) for Rhodus (Roses) date to the fifth century B.C. However the earliest residential remains are from the beginning of the fourth century B.C. and during the third century B.C. a new habitation area was laid out on the orthogonal street grid'.[822]

When looking at archaeological remains particularly when you only have the foundations left some of the living areas of the houses seem small. However even at the foundation stage on some of the houses featured on Channel 4 TV's Grand Designs they do not look very grand either and it is hard to imagine how good they could be once the houses are completed. Some of the Greek houses featured at Emporion (Spain) and Olbia (France) would not seem so small once a second floor was added.

Figure 66. Greek city of Rhodus, Iberia (Spain): in the foreground the new city wall made of granite during the Second Punic War 218–201 B.C.

Figure 67. Greek city of Rhodus, Iberia (Spain): new commercial district Barri Hel-lenistic third century–195 B.C. built opposite the old city and was connected by a bridge across the River Rec Fondo.

Figure 68. Greek city of Rhodus, Iberia (Spain) 375–195 B.C. Posts by the path from left to right mark out the coastline at that period: the medieval monastery is on the hill of the original city: to the right is the excavation spoil heap next to a second century B.C. city wall.

In the Treaty of the Ebro 226 B.C. the Massaliote colonies of Emporion and Rhodus were not included and free from Hasdrubal and Carthaginian control.[823] On the east side in front of the paleopolis (old city) facing the neapolis (new city) Barri Hel-lenístic and by the River Rec Fondo, now gone, excavations have uncovered the foundation of a Greek city wall made from blocks of granite stone in two lines and filled in between with smaller stones, with what appears to be a gate and tower that were constructed during the Second Punic War 218–201 B.C.[824] Emporion also made a new south wall during the mid-second century B.C.[825]

The original coastline was further in and much closer to the first Greek city of Rhodus (at the Cuitadella de Roses).[826] The ancient coastline is shown by the posts from left to right by the path in the photograph. The foundation of Rhodus was ideally placed between two rivers La Trencada and the Rec Fondo. The paleopolis (old city) 375–195 B.C. was on the hill Turó de Santa Maria facing a good natural harbour. Due to their commercial success the city was extended across the River Rec Fondo opposite the city wall and connected by a bridge. This neapolis (new city) third century to 195 B.C. was built in orthogonal square blocks. Here in the Barri Hel-lenístic were workshops and two kilns found so far. They made in particular pottery called black varnish, which was the colour of the glaze. There were wharfs and a wall parallel to the beach with breakwaters. The Greek ships would anchor in the harbour and unload onto smaller ships ferrying to the wharfs. Under the sixteenth-century A.D. parade ground in front of the ancient shoreline Hellenistic and Late Roman archaeological evidence has been found.

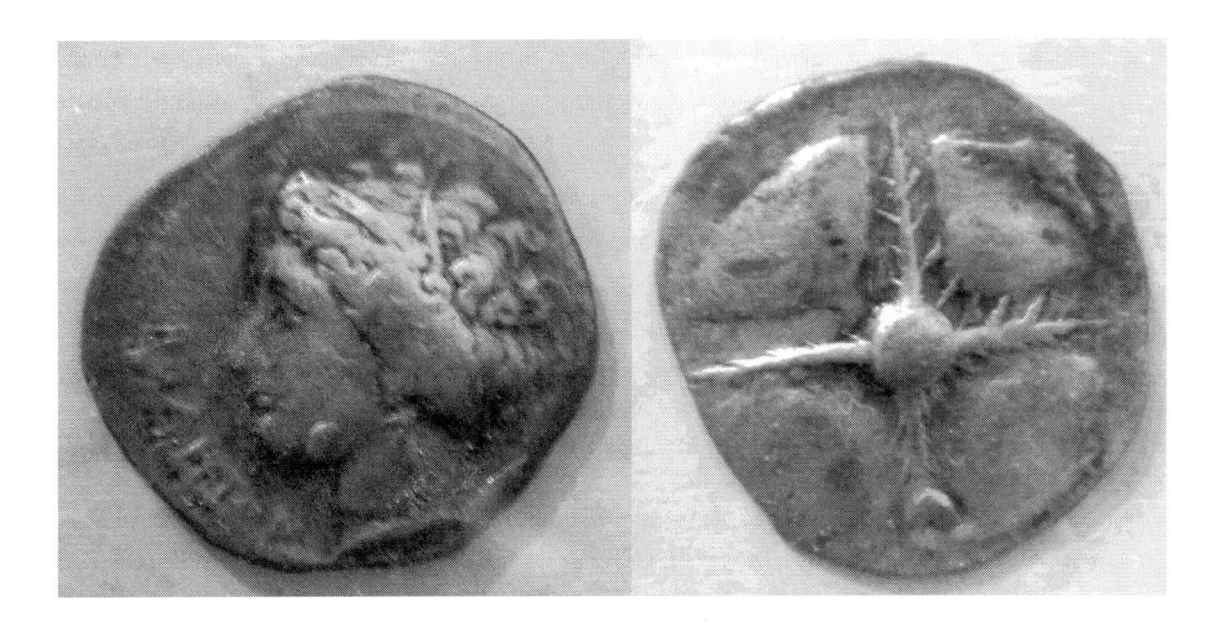

Figure 69. The Greek city of Rhodus, Iberia (Spain) started minting silver coins c. 250 B.C. Obverse: Persephone facing left, with legend/reverse: rose in full bloom.

Circa 250 B.C. Rhodus minted its own silver coins drachma, obols, and also bronze.[827] The silver coins AR drachma weighed 70–78 grains; the obverse shows the head of Persephone, city name ΡΟΔΗΤΩΝ, and on the reverse a rose the same as that from Rhodes. These and local imitations of them were widely spread in Gaul [828] particularly amongst the Volcae Tectosages.[829]

Rhodus (Rosas, Roses) was abandoned c. 195. B.C.[830] This took place by the devastation from the Roman consul Marcus Porcius Cato (Cato the Elder) who 'forcibly dislodged a garrison of Spaniards that were in that fortress' after a revolt by Rhodus (Rhode) during a major rebellion in Spain.[831]

Amongst the discoveries at Rhode found in 1938 is a fragment of a lead tablet 33 mm long and 4-5 mm wide with a Greek inscription of eight lines dated between third to second century B.C.[832] now in the archaeological museum in Girona. This was written in capitals and has been reconstructed and transcribed into miniscule script by Coupry as:

Εὐτύχη Ἀποστελῶ σοι ἐπιστολὴν περὶ τῶν σωματίων.

Salut. Je t'enverrai une letter concernant les esclaves.
(Greetings. I shall send you a letter concerning the slaves).

After the Greek, Roman, and Visigoths occupations the site, Rhode later became a small medieval town to the west side of the hill Santa Maria. On top of Santa Maria Hill was a monastery and church being enclosed by a wall and attached to the town.

Fortunately modern Rhode (Roses), a delightful town with a honeycomb of small shops and excellent beaches, has built up outside of the fortress, which left archaeologists free to excavate. A museum showing finds from the fortress and nearby from Palaeolithic, Greek, Roman and

Visigoths, and up to the nineteenth century is also on site and the substantial five-pointed shaped fort and earlier medieval ruins are well worth a visit in themselves.

There are two ways by air one can reach Roses either from Girona (Spain) or Perpignan (France). There is also a high-speed train from Paris to Figueres Vilafant five and a half hours journey. Figueres is the birthplace of the surrealist artist Salvador Dali and they have a Dali Museum there. Opposite Figueres Vilafant station is the vast pentagonal San Fernando (Sant Ferran) fortress built in 1743. [833] Take a bus or taxi from the railway station to Figueres bus station and change for Roses to see the site of ancient Rhodus. From Figueres or Girona you can also get the bus to L'Escala to visit Emporion. Make sure you have a current bus timetable from SARFA. Coming from Perpignan to Figueres Vilafant by train (30 minute journey) you will pass through a string of mountains the Pyrenees and see for yourselves the natural barrier that divided the ancient Iberians from the Celts and the frontier for the Roman Spanish and Gallic provinces. [834]

Literary Evidence

A study of 313 Greek inscriptions found in Catalonia, Spain 6th century B.C. to 10th century A.D. is in I. Canoś i Villena, *L'Epigrafia Grega a Catalunya*, including photographs. We have ancient literary references for other Greek cities in Spain but no archaeological evidence as yet except for Emporion and Rhodus. [835]

Alonis (Benidorm) Richardson and Wallbank both list this as a Massaliote city in Spain including it in the colonies that were lost to the Carthaginians in the Treaty of the Ebro 226 B.C. between Carthage and Rome. [836] Stephanus of Byzantium lists this as 'an island and city belonging to Massalia' but does not give the location. *The Cambridge Ancient History* also lists this as one of Massalia's colonies. [837] Professor Hodge places this in the Côte d'Azur in France as Benoit suggested it could have been at Saint-Mandrier at the mouth of Toulon, which was once an island.[838]

Artemision (Dénia, near Alicante, Spain). The Massaliotes built a city and temple to Ephesian Artemis on the promontory in the vicinity of Hemeroscopium (Peñon de Ifach, Calpe) at the foot of the Pyrenees. [839]

Strabo wrote, 'It is also called "Dianium," the equivalent of "Artemisium"; it has iron mines with fine deposits near by, and small islands, Planesia and Plumbaria, and above it a lagoon of salt-water four hundred stadia in circuit.' [840] The goddess Diana was the Roman equivalent of the Greek goddess Artemis.

Artemision became important in the third century B.C. and may have been reinforced by refugees from the Greek city of Leuke Akra (Alicante), which had been destroyed by the Carthaginians. [841]

The Massaliotes heard of the Phoenician Carthaginian navy's *diekplous* tactics and especially a defensive manoeuvre used at Artemision by Heracleides of Mylasa, who was 'superior to his contemporaries in intelligence' and the cause of the victory. [842] This may have been the Artemision in Spain as there is some doubt in establishing this particular engagement as the same as the famous Artemision naval battle in Greece 480 B.C. [843] But we do know from Sosylus of Sparta that the Massaliotes used the knowledge from a naval battle at Artemision. The Massaliote Navy prepared against the *diekplous* tactic themselves to win the naval Battle of the Ebro in 217 B.C. with their Roman allies against Hasdrubal (Hannibal's brother) and the Carthaginians. [844] (See Chapter 12 section Battle of the Ebro).

Could this Artemision have been some of the 'other Greeks' in Spain that Appian mentions,[845] and elsewhere as the excavations at Bèziers in France have suggested?[846]

Strabo writing on Iberia mentions:

'Now between the Sucro River and New Carthage [Cartagena], not far from the river, there are three small Massaliote cities'.[847]

Hemeroscopium ('The Lookout' by the Peñon de Ifach, Calpe)[848] in Spain. Strabo records it was

> held in very great esteem, since it has on its promontory a temple of the Ephesian Artemis; and it was used by Sertorius as a naval base. For it is a natural stronghold and adapted to piracy, and is visible at a considerable distance to the approaching sailors. It is also called "Dianium", the equivalent of "Artemisium".[849]

Carpenter (1925) suggested that Hemeroscopium was first settled by Phocaea c. 620–600 B.C.[850] Domínguez (2004) reports that there is no archaeological evidence found so far and the literary evidence may have been 'invented' in Roman times.[851]

Scombraria, (in Spain) the 'Island of Hercules' near New Carthage, named 'from the Scomba fish caught there, from which the best fish sauce is prepared'.[852]

Saguntum (in Spain). Despite a treaty between Carthage and Rome, Hannibal destroyed the city. The Romans used this as a backdated pretext to start the Second Punic War between Carthage and Rome. Strabo says that Saguntum was originally founded by the Zacynthians (from the Greek Island of Zacynthos)[853] Appian records this[854] and also Isidore of Seville.[855] The name Saguntum (Ζακανθαίων Zakanthaion) was assumed Greek, as it sounded so similar to Zacynthon.[856]

Commercial relations between Saguntum and Massalia were possibly responsible for the Roman Alliance.[857]

Three Cities

Strabo mentions three other cities near Saguntum of:[858]
- Cherronesus
- Oleastrum
- Cartalias

He gives no description of origin or ethnicity. We can only say that the first and last sound like Greek names and could be part of 'the other Greeks' in Spain who Appian mentions went with Saguntum to the Romans asking for help against Carthaginian expansion?[859]

Until there is archaeological evidence we must show caution as these names may be genuine or a mixture of foreign names that were recorded into the nearest Greek word or with Greek endings as raised by Hodge and also Aubert.[860]

Strongholds

Strabo wrote that Massalia founded the following cities as strongholds 'wishing at least to keep free the sea, since the land was controlled by the barbarians'.[861]

Tauroention, Tauroentum, Tauroeis, (Le Brusc, near Toulon) c. 300 B.C.
During 49 B.C. Massalia's fleet [862] allied with sixteen ships from Pompey the Great commanded by Lucius Nasidius were defeated by the ships of Julius Caesar commanded by Decimus Brutus during the Roman civil war.[863] Julius Caesar calls the city Tauroenta a fortified outpost of Massalia *castellum Massiliensium*.[864] Artimedorus placed the foundation at the time of the fall of Phocaea (sixth century B.C.) but Domínguez says there is general agreement on a third to second century B.C. date of a foundation.[865] A Massalia coin hoard buried second to first century B.C. included AR, AE (medium size), 1,500 AE (small) and Roman Republic AE. [866]

During the Roman era the site enlarged and there was an increase in activities as is evident by the ceramic finds in the town and port area particularly during the Flavian period. The city seems to have been abandoned in the second century A.D. while the port continued to be used by ships for shelter from storms up to the fifth century. [867]

Olbia, (Fortunate) c. 350 B.C. Situated on the coast by Saint Pierre L'Almanarre near Hyères between Giens and Toulon. Olbia's ancient Greek population was around 1,000. The site was square and surrounded by walls 160 metres each side. The harbour on the south side is now partly eroded by the sea and remains of a later Roman jetty can been seen in between the waves. Professor Hodge (1996) points out that while the city follows the gridiron Hippodamian layout, the geometrically square city plan was unusual amongst other Greek cities that followed the Hippodamian street plan. The buildings were organised into 36 blocks of traditional Greek oblong format. A block of stone was found in a monument next to the north wall written in Greek 'of Aphrodite'.[868]

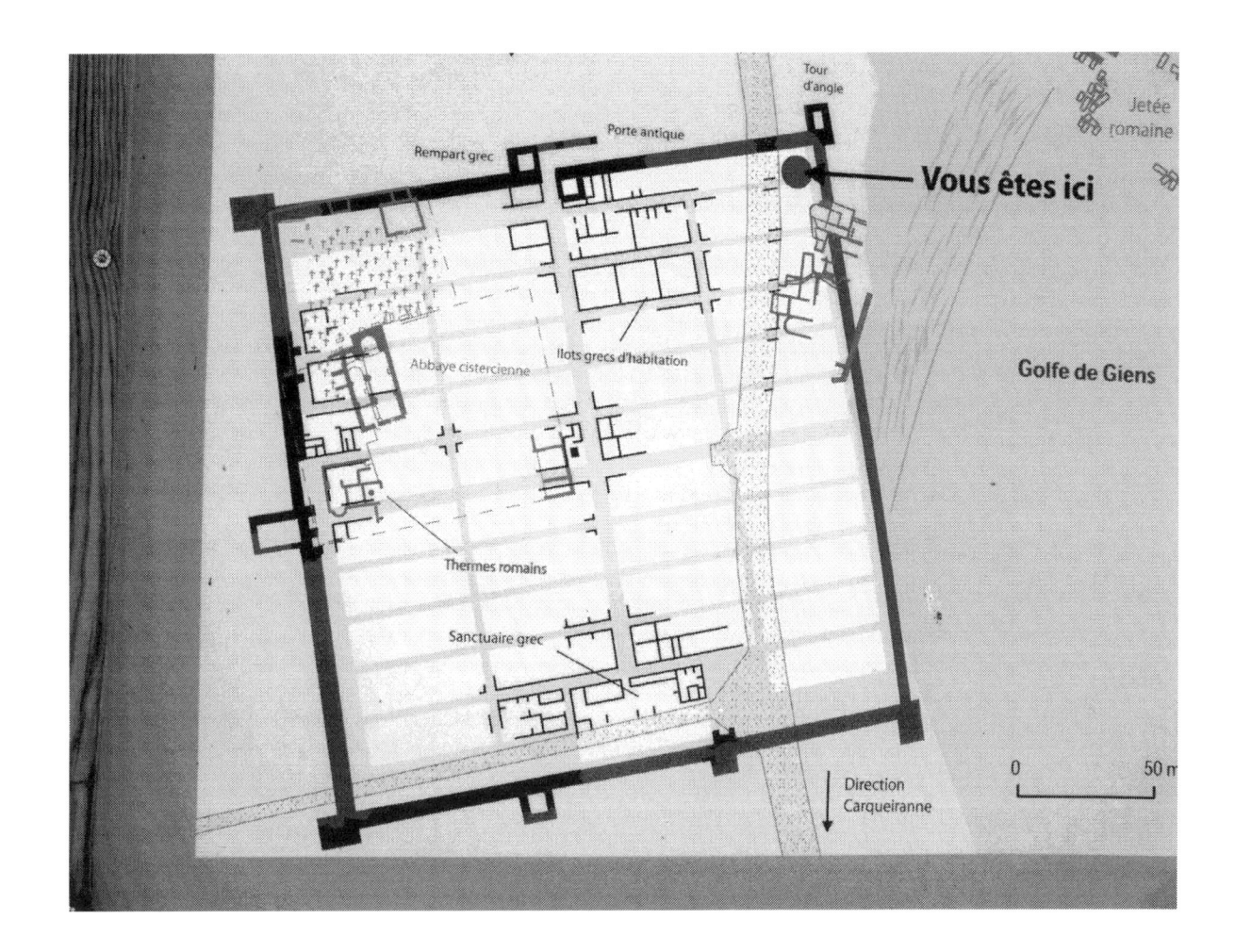

Figure 70. Map of the Massaliote colony/stronghold of Olbia in Gaul (France) founded c. 350 B.C. Excavated areas are shown. The modern main road runs through the site on the right.

There was a Ligurian fort (oppidum) at Costebelle just 2 km north of the city. Olbia may have been built to prevent Ligurian control of the coastline as Strabo does say it was built as a 'stronghold against the Sallyes and Ligures who live in the Alps'. There is a destruction level in the mid-first century B.C. and Professor Hodge surmises this may have coincided with the siege of Massalia by Julius Caesar in 49 B.C. There is a superimposed stratum of Roman occupation with Roman bath and hypocaust.[869] Bats (1996) says Olbia still belonged to Massalia after Caesar's victory in 49 B.C.

Visiting the site in early July 2011 one can see that excavations have so far revealed the Gate into the city, the first street and houses parallel to the gate; the city well by the crossroads in the city; the temple area, the later Roman baths with red painted walls, and a medieval church. The Greek sanctuary is at the end of the western road through the centre of the city. The first sanctuary, now with a palm tree growing in it, was dedicated to Artemis and the temple would have been visible from the entrance to the city. Votive objects were found here, statuettes, masks, graffiti, and inscriptions.

Figure 71. The main gate was guarded by a zigzag wall and two towers, Greek city of Olbia, Gaul (France) 350 B.C.

Figure 72. Greek city of Olbia, Gaul (France) 350 B.C., excavated south-western city wall.

Figure 73. Greek city of Olbia, Gaul (France) 350 B.C., some of the 36 blocks of houses in Hippodamian gridiron layout unusually within a square city plan.

Figure 74. Greek city of Olbia, Gaul (France) 350 B.C., main street and well in the city centre.

Figure 75. Temple of Artemis by the north-eastern wall: Greek city of Olbia, Gaul (France) 350 B.C.

Uncovered in 1964 by the sanctuary at the western ramparts was a vase of twenty-nine Massalia silver drachma and two small bronze coins in three variations: obverse: the head of Artemis/reverse a lion: and with the legend of ΜΑΣΣΑ or ΜΑΣΣΑΛΙΗΤΩΝ.[870] Other remains of a second century B.C. sanctuary were found situated against the northern ramparts to Aphrodite goddess of love and guardian of sailors. Retrieved from the same area in 1967 was a hoard of one hundred Massalia bronze coins with laurelled head of Apollo facing right and on the reverse a charging bull.[871] Other names recall secondary divinities 'etron (property) of the Mothers', chotonic deities, and another 'eros (property) of the Hero'.[872] The Greek houses so far excavated were divided into three-square blocks of 120 m².

The approach to the eastern main gate some thirty feet away is on a lower level. The sea covered this area in ancient times with a natural port for ships to anchor near the city gate. This port area has been filled in over the centuries and the coastline is now level where the city south wall faced the sea. Originally a strip of land came up to the city gate next to the port. The Massaliotes using the topography to best advantage it seems they made only one gate into the city in the eastern wall by the port. The large uncut boulders of the city wall were replaced with squared blocks in the second century B.C.[873] The gate was positioned in a zigzag with one tower and wall long enough to screen the second tower at the main wall diagonally behind that led to the main central street running the entire length of the city. The first visible four courses of stones of the city wall are substantial, carved to fit without mortar and are of a reddish brown colour. From the outer stones there was an infill of earth and smaller stones nearly twenty feet before the wall ended and faced with a line of smaller shaped stone blocks. The houses seem small but looked better in the illustrations of what they would have looked like. The imaginative illustrations on the information plaques in the site are very helpful. Olbia's main well was built of stone blocks carved to fit circular on the inside. The city went right to the coastal edge and was abandoned in the seventh century A.D. The modern day road passes over it along the coast but fortunately the rest of the city ruins is unoccupied and under excavation. There are adjacent beaches for swimming.

You can see this interesting and unique Greek city of Olbia from April to September.[874] There is a local airport Toulon-Hyères. The airport is actually nearer to Hyères of which the medieval town centre is well worth a visit. From Hyères bus station to Olbia is a 15 minute ride. The same bus continues to Toulon.

Several basalt-grinding stones for domestic use from another Massaliote colony Agathe Tyche (Agde, France) were found here in Olbia.[875]

The earliest coins found by excavations (up to 2006) led by Michel Bats date to 205–49 B.C. from Massalia. From 205–49 B.C. we see small bronze from Massalia with ΜΑΣΣΑ (MASSA) above a charging bull facing right. From 215–200 B.C. the big bronze appears. Examples show a head facing right but reverse illegible. The weights of the small bronze obols differed between 1.97 g, 1.53 g, 2.01 g, 1.21 g, 1.66 g, and 2.91 g. Why there should be this fluctuation could be related to the supply of bronze or the ups and downs of the economy. There followed 200–121 B.C. the wheel design obols (from Massalia) with a head of Apollo facing right and on the reverse MA in a wheel, weight 0.64 g. From 205-49 B.C. the middle bronze coin of bull had a head of Apollo facing left and on the reverse a bull charging to the right, weight 3.75 and another 3.19 g.[876]

With most of Massalia's colonies lost to Julius Caesar one Massaliote coin dated after 49 B.C. has been found in Olbia showing the Massaliote mint still active (coin number No.91, US 6077, excavation year 1985, Phase 6B, small bronze 'tardif', obverse: helmeted head facing right, 'frappe hors champ', reverse: illegible). Other coins found here were from Cabellio, Rome, Nimes, Vienne (in Gaul), Lyon, Siscia and Antipolis (Antibes).

The latest coin was from Constantinople dated A.D. 340–380 that was a AE4 type with a diademed bust facing right and on the reverse a soldier with lance and horseman, inscription FEL TEMO REPARATIO, weight 0.36 g.

The coins from neighbouring Antipolis (Antibes) found in Olbia are dated 40–20 B.C. A bronze coin of Victory showing; the letters N( )ΛI; head of Artemis facing right and on the reverse Victory holding a wreath, trophy illegible.[877]

The Sanctuary of Aristaios

This sanctuary is nearby Olbia on the Giens peninsula at L'Acapte. The peninsula is joined to Olbia but may have been an island during the Greek period of settlement. There may have been farming here as well as the salt-pans (still working today) that supplied the fort at Olbia? At the sanctuary a large amount of votive offerings were found from end of second century B.C. to beginning of first century A.D. Excavations revealed 35,000 sherds of pottery, from 500–600 vases, and identification of 225 names. One inscription by its donor reads 'Aristodemos, son of Dionnis, of Massalia (Massaleus)'.[878] Typical Hellenistic period names were also found Demetrios, Dion, Dionysios, as well as those from the Phocaean cities of Massalia and Hyele (Elea, Velia in Italy) 'Apollonides, Hérylos, Hipponikos, Leukon, Lykaithos, Mikion, Oulis, Parmenon and Xeinandros'.[879] One inscription (*IGF* 68-14) might indicate intermarriage 'Dionysermos, son of Keltikios and Parmenikka, to Aristaios, according to their wishes'.

Ten examples (one with the names Parmenon and Parmenikka) have been found in Olbia by J. Coupry and M. Giffault. They report that 'the Phokaian and Ionic character of the onomastics is indeed evident throughout the texts'.[880]

Antipolis (The City Facing), **Antibes**. Pottery finds suggest the city was founded c. sixth century B.C. and possibly direct from Phocaea or Massalia.[881] Though near Nicaea (Nice), the name might possibly refer to 'facing' the direction from where they came Phocaea or 'facing' Cyrnus (Corsica) where they had their colonies of Kalaris (Galéria) and Alalia (Aléria) or the sea route they used? Hodge suggests perhaps it might have been a native name that was recorded to its nearest sounding word in Greek.[882] Another possibility is that Antipolis faced a nearby oppidum of the Ligures already there founded at the beginning of the sixth century B.C and reconstructed around 575 B.C.[883]

The building of a city in close proximity to another also occurred at Olbia with the Ligurian oppidum of Costebella only 2 km away and Nikaia (Nice) with the oppidum (hillfort) of Cimiez also 2 km away. Whereas the oppidum had their control of the land the Greek cities as it were perched by the coast had the sea, which was like a motorway (sometimes slow and other times fast) used by their ships and naval skills for: supplies, trade, and reinforcement either military or settlers, or even escape.

Due to the design of the city not round or square but in a long narrow strip perhaps one possibility for the name is the sea itself? No ships could actually dock along its length and the natural harbour was at the top to the left at the Anse St. Roch. Therefore it was a city not just by the sea but virtually the whole length of it was a 'city facing' the sea?

Figure 76. A rare coin from the Greek city of Antipolis (Antibes, France), c. 44–43 B.C. Obverse: head of Apollo facing right/reverse: Nike (Victory) standing crowning a trophy to the right with the inscriptions ANTIP(OLITON) and LEPI(DOS) both written in Greek.

The city produced its own bronze coins and these are now rare. As well as those found in Olbia mentioned above,[884] see Figure 76 dated to c. 44–43 B.C. Obverse Clerc gives Aphrodite but Maurel is definite with head of Apollo/reverse: Victory crowning a trophy to the right with the inscriptions ANTIP(OLITON) and LEPI(DOS) both written in Greek.[885] The worn image becomes clearer the longer you look just like excavating. The Roman Triumvirate was Lepidus, Mark Antony and Octavian (later called Augustus Caesar). While Mark Antony had been assigned Gaul to administer, Lepidus was given 'Old Gaul' the part up to the border of the Pyrenees Mountains and Spain.[886]

Martial mentions the quality fish sauce of Antipolis 'a jar ruddy from Antipoliton tunny blood'[887] as well as Pliny who calls the sauce made from tuna *garum*.[888] *Garum* sold for 1000 sesterces for two congii (12 pints).[889] Antipolis also made an inferior pickle [890] called Muria, which was used for dysentery, sciatica and coeliac disease.[891]

Among the Greek inscriptions found in Antibes (Antipolis) is the 'Antibes stone' a 64 cm flint late fifth century B.C. with archaic East Greek script of four lines. Terpon, who is a 'servant of Holy Aphrodite', is invoking blessings to those who set up the stone.[892] The diorite stone is not found locally.[893] There may have been a temple to Aphrodite or cult at Antipolis.[894] The inscription in capital letters is recorded in the *Inscriptionum Graecarum* (IG) with a transcription in miniscule script:

ΤΕΡΠΩΝΕΙΜΙΘΕΑΣΘΕΡΑΠΩΝ
ΣΕΜΝΗΣΑΦΡΟΔΙΤΗΣ
ΤΟΙΣΔΕΚΑΤΛΣΤΗΣΑΣΙΚΥΠΡΙΣ
ΧΑΡΙᴺΑΝΤΑΠΟΔΟΙΗ

Τέρπων εἰμὶ θεᾶς θεράπων
σεμνῆς Ἀφροδίτης
τοῖς δὲ καταστήσασι Κύπρις
χάριν ἀνταποδοίη. [895]

Also in their archaeological museum were finds of fourth century B.C. Apulia ware, vases, kanthara, a krater and a perfume vase dated 370–260 B.C. Also fourth century B.C. Campanian ware and from 300–200 B.C. there were plates and vases. Etruscan wears from fourth to first century B.C. with a head, feet and pig made of clay, a Bucchero and vase. Also present were Attic red figure from the end of seventh to beginning of sixth century B.C. and Corinthian seventh century B.C. vases: including several fragments of black pottery with Greek inscriptions from second to first century B.C. A Greek lead curse has so far revealed the name Damophanes. [896]

One of the few inscriptions found from Antipolis Ἀντίπολις (Antibes) appears in the *Corpus Inscriptionum Grecarum* (CIG) with a transcription in miniscule as follows: [897]

ΑΝΤΙΠΟΛΙC . ΚΑΙ . ΟΙ . ΠΟΛΙΤΑΙ . ΤΟ
ΓΕΝΙΚΟΝ . ΜΟΝ . ΚΑΙ . ΜΑΝΓΟΝ
ΚΑΙ . ΟΥΕΛΑΡΙΟΝ . ΚΑΙ _ _ _ _

Ἀντίπολις καὶ οἱ πολῖται τὸ γενικὸν
μον[ο]μά[χω]ν καὶ οὐελαρί[ω]ν καὶ _ _ _ _ _ _

Excavations have revealed a theatre (in the part of the city extended by the Romans) that was destroyed in 1691 [898] and the site is under the present bus station.[899] A building possibly a temple and some 'notable cisterns' found close to the coast is partly under the present Cathedral and Chateau Grimaldi/Musée Picasso, and a probable Roman amphitheatre is in Rue de Fersen.[900] Greek building remains are limited to some of the oldest cut stones that are under the cathedral and possibly a few courses of ashlars at the bottom of the sea wall.[901] The original Greek city was in a long rectangle parallel to the sea including the highest part of the rock. The coastline has changed over the centuries as the top of the original city was right up to the sea and the natural harbour was to the left at the Anse St. Roch.[902]

A large forty metre high tower was built next to the cathedral in the eleventh century A.D. due to Saracen attacks and many of the large stone blocks used were from the Roman period when the city was extended. Antibes old quarter has kept its character from the medieval city. Keeping the Greek heritage of the area in the names is a modern scientific and technological park a few kilometres to the north being called Sophia-Antipolis and there is also the university Universite de Nice Sophia Antipolis.[903]

Figure 77. Antibes, France founded by the Phocaean Greeks c. sixth century B.C. as Antipolis.

Figure 78. Stone blocks of the Greek city sea wall at the bottom. Antibes, France originally the Phocaean Greeks founded city of Antipolis c. sixth century.

Figure 78. A Corner section of the sea wall: stone blocks of the Greeks at the bottom, Antibes, France originally the Phocaean Greek founded city of Antipolis c. sixth century.

Strabo records that Antipolis (Antibes) became an Italiote city after a suit against the Massaliotes becoming 'free from their orders' (an Italiote city was the description of a Greek city in Italy).[904] Pliny the Elder lists this as 'the town of Antibes with Latin rights'.[905] Rivet suggests that Antipolis must have sided with Julius Caesar during the Civil War 49 B.C. unlike the other Massaliote cities and that is why it was left independent from Roman control. Its citizens were enrolled into the Roman tribe Voltina.[906]

Nikaia, (Latin *Nicaea*), Nice c. sixth century B.C.?[907] According to Strabo was still subject to Massalia when the new Roman boundary at the River Varus between Antipolis and Nicaea placed it in Italy. 'Nicaea remains subject to the Massaliotes and belongs to the Province' (Narbonitis).[908] Also we have here the Gaius Memmius Macrinus inscription as quoted previously.[909]

Aloupes relates the story that the Ligurians were raiding Antipolis as they had taken wood from the Alpine forests. Massalia needed the wood to make big ships. Trees of eight-foot diameter were taken down the River Var. The Ligurians wanted payment as they regarded the forests as theirs. Because of a victory over the Ligurians, Massalia founded this city called Nikaia (Nice), which means victory [910] though Hodge thinks the name is a *rhabillage* from a previous native name that sounded similar but may have meant something else.[911]

A few kilometres north of the ancient city (about ten minutes on the local bus No. 22) and higher up was a Ligurian oppidum occupied by the Vediantii [912] called Cimiez (presently part of modern day Nice). Today there is a good archaeological museum leading out into the excavated later Roman town. The Roman Emperor Augustus chose Cimiez in 14 B.C. as the site for Cemelenum the capital city of the *Alpes Maritimae* province.

Cemelenum developed as a separate city to Nice. This was probably because Nikaia (Nice) and its surrounding territory, plus Olbia, the Stoechades Islands and Athenopolis continued to belong to Massalia after losing most of their Greek Empire of Marseille (Massalia) when Massalia capitulated to Julius Caesar in 49 B.C. following a six-month siege during the civil war with Pompey.[913]

Greek ceramics fragments dating to end of sixth to early fifth century B.C. have been found in Nikaia and probably were made in the workshops in Massalia as well as the amphorae fragments.[914] There are also two Kylix fragments, Attic made, end of fifth to beginning of the fourth century B.C. Pottery finds from the second century B.C. to fourth century A.D.[915] were found at the old cathedral of Nôtre-Dame-du-Château.[916] Hodge thought there was little arable land to support a colony and what was available being under control of the Ligurians only 2 km away.[917] Therefore the settlement would seem to be on the acropolis or below or both and supplied by the sea. Though one should not discount trade with the locals as that could supplement the imports of food. As we now know founding colonies in places with little arable land, that would have deterred other Greeks, was a Phocaean speciality of expertise with the exceptions of their colonies of Agathe Tyche (Agde) and its cadastration-ample land organised to support their colonies,[918] and the grain silos of Emporion.[919]

The site of Nikaia, Nicaea (Nice) has the favoured Greek location of a promontory (Parc de la Colline du Château) where the Greek acropolis was probably situated? There is a harbour Port de Nice at the side. A series of modern pebble mosaics depicting Greek mythology decorates one of the paths in memory of Nice's ancient Greek heritage. Excavations show the foundations of the tenth century medieval cathedral where perhaps some stones from earlier constructions may have been used? There is a commanding view and it was a strategic fortified rock until dismantled by the French in A.D. 1706. The port is also sheltered from the wind by Mount Alban and Mount Boron opposite and there is another bay Villefranche-sur-Mer behind them. In the next bay at Beaulieu-sur-Mer is a reconstructed second century B.C. luxurious Greek palace of Delos called Villa Kérylos, which is open to the public during parts of the summer season.[920] It would be an interesting experience to see something in its magnificent entirety instead of just a ruin.

In Nice between the River Paillon and left of the Promontory was probably the site of the Greek city if they had expanded from the acropolis? There is conjecture as to where the Greek colony of Nikaia was situated. Bromwich suggests it was probably at Vieux Nice to the west of the promontory. The River Paillon at that time had a branch joining the sea at the Promenade des Anglais and the beach was suitable for unloading small ships.[921] My own feeling looking around was that the city was here and that the promontory was a lookout that could be used a stronghold when necessary (as it is not easy to get to your ships unless there were passages within the promontory). Here between the promontory and the River Paillon the later medieval city grew and extended in size to its present boundaries, which is charming and distinct in architecture from the larger modern city. The tall houses and narrow streets provide shade in the summer heat of the Riviera.

Figure 80. Nikaia Nicaea (Nice, France), Phocaean Greeks founded the city c. 300 B.C. beside and/or on top of the promontory. Their harbour could have been on either side.

Figure 81. Port Nice Harbour by the side of the Greek acropolis of **Nikaia** Nicaea (Nice, France).

Figure 82. The acropolis of **Nikaia** Nicaea (Nice) with the 10th century A.D. medieval cathedral ruin possibly on top of the earlier Greek settlement. The acropolis remained a strategic fort until dismantled in A.D. 1706.

Strabo puts the cities of the Massaliotes in the following order in Book IV.1.5.

Cities Founded in Iberia (Spain) as Stronghold against the Iberians:
- Hemeroscopium
- Emporium
- Rhodus

Strabo records that 'They [Massaliotes] also taught the Iberians the sacred rights of the Ephesian Artemis, as practised in the fatherland, so that they sacrificed by the Greek ritual'.[922] Buxó writes that the introduction of cultivating the olive trees and grapevine made changes in the structure of native societies that based their living around traditional crops of cereals and vegetables. The introduction of wine replaces alcoholic drinks made from cereals. There is an 'adaptation of practices of indigenous societies to ceremonies of Mediterranean origin'.[923]

Strongholds Built against the Barbarians Who Lived around the Rhodanus (River Rhône)
Rhoe Agathe

Strongholds against the Sallyes and Those Ligures Who Live in the Alps:
- Tauroention
- Olbia
- Antipolis

The Stoechades Islands, (Isles d'Hyères) East of Toulon
Strabo records these were five islands off the Massalia coast and called Stoechades:

> Three of them of considerable size and quite two small. They are tilled by Massaliotes. In early times the Massaliotes had also a garrison, which they placed there to meet the onsets of the pirates, whence the islands were well supplied with harbours.[924]

Cornutus Scholiast to Lucan (III.516) records the islands belonging to Massalia 'Stoechades insulae Massiliensium'. Tacitus calls the Stoechades *Massiliensium insulas* (îsles d'Hyères).[925] During the struggle before Vespasian became Roman emperor the Stoechades Islands had been where Valens, sheltering from bad weather, was arrested by fast galleys sent by Paulinus.[926]

In *The Voyage of Argo: The Argonautica*, by Apollonius of Rhodes he mentions the Argo landing on the 'sacred Isle of Amber' and they pass 'the Ligurian Islands that are called the Stoechades'.[927]

Though some infer the name of the islands means 'in a row' Hodge points out Stoechas also refers to lavender for which Provence is still famous for producing.[928] The largest island of the îsles d'Hyères is called the Porquerolles.[929] However identification with Strabo's five islands while Pliny only mentioned three is 'oversimplified' as Rivet points out that since ancient times two former islands in the area are now joined to the mainland. Presqu'ile de St. Mandrier (south of Toulon) and the Presqu'ile de Giens (south of Hyères).[930]

La Galère, c. 100 B.C. Morel describes this as a fisherman's settlement on the eastern coast of the island of Porquerolles.[931]

500–400 B.C.
After an economic depression in the fifth century B.C.[932] Massalia expanded their territory in the fourth to third century B.C. establishing outposts at Theline and Glanon.[933]

Theline Town-in-the-Marsh (later called Arelate, and today Arles). The Greeks settled alongside the local town from 540–530 B.C.[934] and their first Phocaean settlement was destroyed by the Ligurians c. 535 B.C.[935]

Circa **400 B.C.** Greeks drew away from the centre of lower Rhône valley to the Massaliote colony of Theline.[936] The city had a mixed population of Greeks and Celts.[937] In the mid-first century B.C. Julius Caesar rapidly built 12 warships in Arelate to fight Massalia during the Roman Civil War. The town of Arelate was awarded a 'Colona Romana' distinction in 46 B.C. when Caesar had given it most of Massalia's territory and settled his veteran troops there [938] under their general Tiberius Claudius Nero.[939] The troops were from the VI legion and the title given to the city was 'Colonia Julia Paterna Arelatensis Sextanorum'.[940] The port of Arles grew rich at the expense of Massalia particularly in the commercial traffic along its River Rhône.

Glanon (Latin *Glanum*, near St. Remy).[941] A Gallo-Greek city that had connections with Massalia as early as sixth century B.C. shown by pottery and coins found in a deep crevice in the rock.[942] Third century B.C. silver coins have been found with head of Persephone/bull and the city's name in Greek ΓΛΑΝΙΚΩΝ (of the Glanikans).[943] During second century B.C. the town grew and prospered. There was a serious destruction of the town in 120s B.C. and again in 90 B.C. by Romans as it had taken the side of the Salyes. During these thirty years the city saw Hellenistic Glanon reach its peak.[944] Following a period of abandonment after 90s B.C. the town probably became under Massaliote control as there developed a Greek town with Agora (Market), a bouleuterion (Council House), and peristyle houses. The Sanctuary area was dedicated to the native god Glan. There is a flight of steps, of the Nymphaeum leading down to an underground spring 'most likely Hellenistic in date'. To the south of the spring is a temple dedicated to Heracles. Across the other side is a smaller temple, according to an inscription, which is dedicated by Agrippa to Valetude (the goddess of health).[945]

Jovarnica or Gernica (Tarascon). Magi writes that this was established as a commercial colony of Massalia on the island in the middle of the River Rhône. Due to alluvial deposits the island joined up to the left bank and later the Romans founded a camp there called Tarusco.[946]

Livy mentions that some of the Volcae occupied the land east of the River Rhône. Rivet suggests that it was at Tarascon where Hannibal had crossed the River Rhône. This land may be the same that was handed over much later by Pompey the Great to the Massaliotes who may have controlled it from Avignon rather than Glanum.[947]

Mèze is a small port on a lagoon the Basin de Thau in the Languedoc region. The town's website explains Mèze or 'mansa, in the Phocaean language taken to mean 'A high place where smoke arises'. Like the small port of Marseillen nearby Mèze benefits from ships on the way to Sète. The description on their website claims it was founded by the Phocaeans around the same time as Massalia (Marseille) and Agathe Tyche (Agde) [948] though another website says it was founded by the Phoenicians in the eighth century B.C. then the Phocaeans took it over in the sixth century.[949]

Lattara (Lattes) is on the River Lez, 6 km south of Montpellier. Lattes were trading with the Etruscans in 550 B.C. By 500 B.C. the city main trade was with Massalia [950] though Etruscan merchants still seem to be present until c. 475 B.C. [951] Deep-sea traffic could unload here to smaller crafts. Wooden wharves served as the docks. As the site is not built over any future excavation may reveal who built the city. [952] There was found the worn remnant of a statue named the 'Warrior of Lattes' with lightly engraved body armour. Comparison with similar statues suggests the missing legs were in a kneeling position. The carving shows pleating of the kilt and suggests a Persian style archer. The disc plate body armour held in place by straps over the chest on the carving suggests a match to the Etruscan example as found at Elmea. (Connely, 1981).

The influence of Massalia in the Languedoc region appears in Lattes by the increase in grapevine cultivation in relation to traditional crops that were grown indicating a cultural change in the second half of the third century B.C. [953] Two coin hoards in pots mid-third century and end of third century B.C. with 993 and 2,000 Massaliote obols respectively were excavated. [954]

In the south of France the Greek cities of Olbia, Glanon and Sainte-Blaise fortunately became unoccupied up to the present day and have been good for excavation, as well as Emporion (Empúries) in Spain. [955]

Saint-Blaise. In this area there are names of cities to be identified. They are: Mastromela, Maritima Avaticorum, and Heraclea have been suggested for Saint-Blaise. [956] Pliny the Elder writes 'Some authorities state that at the mouth of the Rhône there was once a town called Heraclea' and also a Lake Mastromela. [957]

Saint-Blaise is between Martigues and Istres on the west side of the Étang de Berre founded c. 600 or a little earlier. With the arrival of the Greeks it seemed to be an Etruscan-Greek-Ligurian trading centre. By 520 B.C. based on pottery evidence there was more commercial contact with Massalia. Trade declined with Etruria after 474 B.C. (Battle of Cumae). There was high prosperity in the Hellenistic period declining in the first century and then the city was abandoned. [958]

The city walls have crenellations (merlons) with rounded tops, which is a feature of Carthaginian colonies e.g. Motya in Sicily. The workmanship seems Sicilian and perhaps that is the connection for this particular style? Two crenulations were also found in Glanum. [959] The large Hellenistic ramparts with rectangular towers date to 170–140 B.C. (Saint-Blaise V). Some of the blocks have mason's marks in archaic Greek letters. [960] Though the large stone blocks at Saint-Blaise have the Greek herringbone pattern like Massalia, Olbia and Glanum it would seem that the mixed style of the city wall in some way reflects the mixture of influences within the fine finish of the masonry in the Hellenistic period.

There are seven phases of occupation at Saint-Blaise and a destruction level coinciding with Roman armies campaigning in the area 125-123 B.C. at the request of Massalia. [961] This suggests Saint-Blaise had switched allegiances after the Hellenistic ramparts were built? Sling bullets (130-120 B.C.) and Roman Army stone catapult balls of different sizes were found here dating to between 150-120 B.C. [962] The city may have returned to Massalia's control/influence/network for the next period as it had a strategic position for carrying on trade up the Rhône valley. [963]

Also found there in a trench were thirty-nine large stone catapults-balls weighing between eight to forty pounds fired by Romans around the same time as Julius Caesar's siege at Massalia 49 B.C. [964] This may suggest that Julius Caesar's troops had under siege not only Massalia but also other Massaliote cities like Saint-Blaise and Olbia either at the same time or at some point during 49 B.C.

Martigues. The site of L'Ile on the islet in the channel connected the sea to the Étang de Berre received large amounts of Greek products from the Phocaeans to the natives. There are many storage containers thought to be for grain found here. [965]

Côte d'Azur

Athenopolis and Castrum Marselinum. There are other names given by Roman writers such as Pliny the Elder 'on the coast are Athenopolis of the Massilians' still belonging to Massalia, [966] while most of its empire had been confiscated by Julius Caesar, and 'Castrum Marselinum' the Massaliote Fort.[967] Without more archaeological evidence (a few Massaliote coins found on Cannes beach) it is a matter of conjecture to establish these as the locations of Saint-Tropez and Cannes respectively. [968]

The Antonine Itinerary, and the Chronicles of the Lérins (eighth century A.D.) both mention a 'Agathonis Portus' but with a lack of archaeological evidence on the land (though underwater evidence from shipwrecks shows Greek goods) Professor Hodge suggests the modern day port of Agay, as it has a sheltered harbour that would have been a welcome stopover between Antibes and Saint-Tropez on the rocky coast of the Esterel. [969]

The Lerins are two islands off Cannes and mentioned in Strabo [970] as 'Planisia and Lero, which have colonial settlements'. Hodge suggests a possible link to early Ionian influence with Lero in the Dodecanese. [971] Lero Island had a hero temple for Lero and a considerable naval station. A Greek and Latin inscription in honour of Pan was found on Saint Marguerite unfortunately it is now lost. Excavations at Fort Royal have revealed several buildings with wall paintings, mosaics, baths and fortifications dating to first century B.C. [972] The Athenaios inscription in Greek on an ivory cover is dated third to second century B.C. and mentions Leron and Lerine. [973]

Pliny writes after the Stoechades and next to them are 'Iturium, Phoenicia, Lero [Saint Margerit de Lérins] and opposite Antipolis, Lerina [Saint Honorat de Lérins]'. [974] Offshore islands were favoured by ancient Greeks for the first settlement before extending to the mainland.

The following two towns have a lack of archaeological evidence as yet though local tradition says they were founded by Greeks.

Citharista (La Ciotat). Mentioned in the Antonine Itinerary (A.D. 150) as a harbour Portus Citharista. [975] There have been suggestions that it may have been the port of Ceyreste a village in this mountainous region 3 km away. Noting similarities in the name Hodge points out this may be a *rhabillage* as Citharista = guitar-player is an unusual name for a town! He also mentions archaeological evidence in Ceyreste is fragmentary with a few ancient stone blocks scattered in the fields and some reused in stone walls. [976]

In modern time La Ciotat was the home of the French Lumiere brothers who made the first portable film camera, motion picture and cinema the Eden Theatre 1895. This cinema is being restored and is to be opened in 2013 by Hollywood film director Stephen Spielberg.[977]

Charsis (Cassis). Mentioned in the Antonine Itinerary and famous for its quality coral and limestone. At present we have only supposition that it was likely to have had a Greek presence before the Romans [978] as the ships of Massalia frequented the sea lanes of this coast for many centuries. Limestone slabs from here have been found at Massalia's main road (Bourse Centre) and laid during the late Roman period.

Other Cities in the Massaliote Chora (Territory)

There may be other Massaliote cities still to be discovered. Whether the following cities were Massaliote or just under their influence is not known as yet. They may have had mixed Gallo-Greek populations like Glanum, Avignon and Arles (Theline/Arelate).

Caenicenses between Massalia and Salon, (Est de l'Estang de Berre). A silver coin of the city shows on the obverse a head of a river-god Kaenos, the reverse has a lion with the inscription in Greek the name of the city ΚΑΙΝΙΚΗΤΩΝ (Kainiketon). See below endnote 979.

Samnagenses described by Pliny the Elder (*Natural Histories* 3.37) as the inhabitants of Sanga belonging to Narbonne. A bronze coin shows on the obverse a head of Apollo, and on the reverse a bull rushing and the city name in Greek ΣΑΜΝΑΓΗΤ (Samnagit). [979]

Another coin has inscribed on the obverse ACTICO with a head of Apollo facing right, and on the reverse a bull to the right and the city name in Greek ΣΑ [ΜΝΑ] ΓΗΤ. (Samnagit). The goddess Diana is represented on another coin with her head facing right wearing a diadem band and on the reverse inscribed in Greek ΣΑΜΝΑΓΗΤ (Samnagit). [980]

Enserune Phase II c. 425 B.C.–late third century B.C. Possibly a population of 10,000, Greek influence, east-west grid pattern of roads and new terraced houses covered earlier buildings in the south. Dolia replaced silos in the houses. A reservoir was created linking 45 silos on the south side with a capacity estimated at one million litres. [981]

Other Massaliote Cities

Ebel gives the following sources for:
Azania (Philo of Byblos)

Iberian Kyrene (Stephanus of Byzantium) or **Pyrene** (Avienus, *Ora Maritima*, 557)

Sekoanos (Stephanus of Byzantium). Ebel hints at Vix as the location for this city while Brunel suggested this refered to the River Seine.[982] Though going by the name could it be in the territory of the Sequani (Strabo IV.3.4) who came under Massaliote control? Ebel (1976) writes that there are more Massaliote cities listed by Stephanus but of which nothing else is known as yet. Stephanus (from Hecataeus) gives **Ampelus** a coastal city in Liguria that Pearson suggests as Massaliote.[983]

Troizen is recorded by Stephanus of Byzantium (639.9) as a city being in Italy and belonging to Massalia. This city/fortress may have been on the coast of Liguria past the frontier of the River Var and therefore Italy, as the new Roman frontier was placed there or the city may have been somewhere on the Italian peninsula καὶ ἑτέρα ἐν Ἰταλία Μασσαλιωτική. [984]

Massalia's Ally-The Albici

The Albici during the Roman Civil war 49 B.C. had aided Massalia in the siege and naval battles. Caesar's wrote of them, *Albicos, barbaros homines, qui in eorum fide antiquitus erant montesque supra Massiliam incolebant, ad se vocaverant*.[985] They were described as 'living in the mountains overhanging Massalia.'[986] Strabo writes that their territory included the plains as far as Luerion [Montagne du Luberon] and the Rhône.[987] They may have been centred at the hillforts of Perréal, and in the commune St. Saturnin about 6 km north of present day Apt.[988] The Romans built the town of Apt apparently to control the Albici.[989] A bronze urn was found here with hoard of Massaliote coins buried third to second century B.C. 13 drachms, 2 diobols, and 87 obols.[990]

Massalia's Political Constitution

A Greek View

Aristotle and Strabo wrote in detail on the Massalia (Marseille) constitution of government. Strabo wrote that 'of all the aristocracies, theirs is the best ordered'.[991] Massalia was ruled by an Assembly of 600, who hold the honour for life and called Timouchoi, and from them a 'cabinet' of 15 whom

> carry on the immediate business of the government . . . And in turn three, holding the chief power, preside over the fifteen . . . A Timouchi cannot become one of these three unless he has children or is a descendant of persons who have been citizens for three generations. Their laws are Ionic, and are published to the people.

The translation of Strabo's *Geography* by H. L. Jones, Loeb 1923 edition has

> 'And in turn three, holding the chief power, preside over the fifteen'

> πάλιν δὲ τῶν πεντεκαίδεκα προκάθηνται τρεῖς οἱπλεῖστον ἰσχύοντες

in the main text, but he adds an important footnote regarding the 'three, holding the chief power'. Jones writes, 'The later editors, by a slight emendation, add at this point 'and one over the three.''[992] This would indicate that Massalia had a chief magistrate that was a president, an Archon similar to that of Athens. The whole process of translation from an ancient language does seem tricky and is evident by several translations such as Homer's *Iliad* and *Odyssey* and Caesar's *Civil War* being published with a different emphasis on words that have more than one meaning and change by the context they are in. Jones does not say why the editors added this 'emendation.' Was it from a different manuscript of Strabo? If so he does not mention which version. Strabo's Greek text in Radt's translation does have a difference in the next line[993] but the line above about the chief power is the same as Jones's 1923 Loeb's edition of Strabo's Greek text.

However Professor Hodge has one reference[994] that suggests the Massaliotes had one person Apollonides in a position like a 'praetor' and Clerc suggests this was combining the offices as a Magistrate and Commander of the land and naval forces[995] in the siege by Julius Caesar 49 B.C. Apollonides would have overall command of the defence forces but also over the Government of Massalia. But this may have been a special office in time of war? Our very brief knowledge comes from a Roman source Cornutus Scholiast to Lucan[996] mentioned by Michel Clerc, archaeologist, historian and curator of the Museum at Marseille, that Apollonides commanded the land forces of Massalia:[997]

Massiliam autem aduersus Caesarem defensauit praetor Apollonides, urbi qui praefuit, classi autem Parmeno. [998]

Aristotle, *Politics*.

Aristotle's work *Constitution of Massalia* is now lost, but much was used in Strabo writings. There are still some comments by Aristotle on the government of Massalia in his book *Politics* that has survived:

V.6.2. Oligarchies 1305a37

> Sometimes an oligarchy can be undermined by people who, though wealthy themselves, are excluded from office. This happens when the holders of office are a very limited number, as for example at Massilia, at Istros, at Heraclea, and in other cities. Here those who had no share in office continued to cause disturbance till some share was finally given . . . The final result was that the oligarchy at Massilia was turned into something more of the nature of a 'constitutional government' [polity]. [999]

VI.7. 1321.26

> The multitude should be given a share in the governing class either in the way mentioned earlier [preceding section 1320] to those who own an assessed amount of property, or, as in Thebes, to those who have kept out of vulgar occupations, for a given period of time, or as in Massalia, to those who are judged to merit it, whether they came from inside or outside the governing class. [1000]

Aristotle tells us that the Phocaeans who founded Massalia were devoted to commerce. [1001] It would seem that their government was not based on hereditary power but on wealth that included merchants and therefore basically a Timocracy. [1002]

A Roman View

70–59 B.C. Cicero

The famous Roman orator Cicero in his speech *Pro Flacco*, 63–64, praises Massalia:

> And I do not omit you, Marseilles [Massalia], who knew Lucius Flaccus as a soldier and as a quaestor. I would be right in saying that in cultures and reliability this city is the superior not only of Greece but probably of the whole world. Although it is far from any area inhabited by Greeks and cut off from their culture and language, and although it is surrounded at the edge of the world by Gallic tribes and washed by the waves of their barbarism, it is so well governed by the prudence of its aristocracy that it is easier for everyone to praise its institutions than to copy them. [1003]

Cicero when talking about ideal forms of government praised Massalia and its system of government but still noticed that it was not a democracy 'the excellent Massilian government conducted by a few leading citizens'. [1004] Although a well-governed city it would appear the lower classes, the people, had no say in how things were run.

Cicero continues,

'even though the Massilians, now under our protection, are ruled by the greatest justice by a select number of their leading citizens, such a situation is nevertheless to some extent like slavery for a people.' [1005]

He warns of the dangers that certain systems can fall into and uses three examples of governing systems including Massalia of whom he had praised previously. In his opinion

'the governance of Massilia by a few of its leading citizens was close to the oligarchic conspiracy the Thirty who once ruled in Athens'. [1006]

Unfortunately the next leaf of his book is missing.

The Six Hundred

The Assembly/Senate of Massalia was known as the 'Six Hundred' as recorded by Valerius Maximus [1007] and Lucian. [1008] Strabo seems to imply that individually senators were called 'gerontes': [1009]

> Among Thesprotians and the Molossians old women are called "peliai" and old men "pelioi," as is also the case among the Macedonians; at any rate, these people call their dignitaries "peligones"(compare the "gerontes" among the Laconians and the Massaliotes). [1010]

Massalia's Explorers

Statues at the Bourse commemorate Massalia's two noted explorers Euthymenes and Pytheas in modern day Marseille (Massalia):

Euthymenes, who sailed south along the coast of Africa in the late c. sixth century to mid-fifth century B.C. as far as the River Senegal (though he mistook this for the Nile as he saw crocodiles in the river) [1011] and possibly as far as Ghana? [1012]

The theory of the extremes of the spring tides action, caused by the moon and sun in alignment with the earth, Aetios attributes to Pytheas of Massalia. While Pseudo-Galen *de Historia Philosophia* 88, puts it even earlier by crediting Euthymenes of Massalia with the idea of waxing and waning of the moon effecting daily tides.[1013] Aetios gave Pytheas as a source while Pseudo-Galen has the same wording but names Euthymenes as the source.[1014] Aetios wrote the *Placita* from which Roseman uses in translation number T26.[1015] Diels shows a source to *Placita* was a treatise *On the Rise of the Nile*; Hekataios also mentioned Euthymenes. A thirteenth century Latin epitome citing one theory used by Herodotus was from Euthymenes of Massalia. [1016]

Pytheas established within a few minutes of the correct figure the latitude of his home city Massalia at 43°3'25"N. 'With the semi-diameter of the sun added, the result is almost exactly the latitude for the Marseille observatory' [1017] at 43°17'N. [1018]

Pytheas investigated 'the Boiling Sea' of the volcanic Aeolian Islands near Sicily. He sailed into the North-West Atlantic and discovered Britain in the fourth century B.C.

Pytheas of Massalia named several islands. He was the first to give the name of Britain, recording the name of its people and circumnavigated the island. Pytheas calculated Britain's landmass to within 2.5 per cent accuracy: calculated the length of its coastline: described how the people lived: and found the origin of the valuable tin and amber trade. From Britain Pytheas went on to discover the island of Thule (Iceland): the frozen Congealed Sea and the Arctic Circle: saw a 22-hour day: and correctly calculated the position of the North Pole.

He developed theories of the tides being affected by the moon and that the earth was a sphere. Pytheas located Abalus, the Island near Denmark, and identified two Germanic tribes the *Guiones* and the *Teutoni* before returning to his starting point the city of Massalia (Marseille), a Greek colony on the Mediterranean coast of France. His accurate calculations were used to form the system of latitudes to map the earth by Dicaearchus, Eratosthenes, and Hipparkhos and still in use today 2,300 years later. He published his discoveries in a book *On the Ocean* though now lost there are fragments of his book quoted by eighteen ancient writers over eight and a half centuries (c. 300 B.C.–A.D. 550) [1019] together with the five measurements he took that proved he made the voyage.

Cleomedes 1st or 2nd century A.D. astronomer calls Pytheas a philosopher.[1020] In Greece the term philosopher (lover of wisdom)[1021] covered the subjects of science, astronomy, and natural history.

Battles

The position of Massalia was from time to time maintained by military engagements. We have only a few references surviving. Strabo says there were trophies of many naval victories in Massalia. [1022] The naval-station of Massalia was of considerable size. [1023]

'Later, however, their valour enabled them to take in some of the surrounding plains, thanks to the same military strength by which they founded their cities, I mean their stronghold-cities' (Strabo, IV.1.5).

The many wars the Greeks fought with the Ligurians and the Gauls 'made the valour of the Greeks celebrated among their neighbours' is recorded by Trogus in Justin's book. [1024] In the following we have references surviving for:

Navy

***Circa* 600–546 B.C.** Thucydides [1025] records a Phocaean victory against Carthage. [1026] Thucydides does not say where so we have no name of the battle only the victory.

***Circa* 540 B.C. Battle of Alalia.**[1027] Herodotus records that the Phocaean sixty ships 'were victorious' against the 120 ships of the combined fleets of Carthage and Tyrrhenians. He does not say how many the combined fleet lost only that the Phocaeans lost forty ships and the beaks of the remaining twenty were 'no longer serviceable'. This was a costly 'Cadmeian' or Pyrrhic victory. [1028]

260 B.C. Battle of Mylae. Thiel's hypothesis for the *socii navales* contingent was that Massalia and Italiote towns had provided thirty-five ships to reinforce their ally the Roman Fleet totalling together 143 ships and defeating the 130 ships of Carthage. [1029] This was Rome's first victory at sea with a fleet they built themselves probably with the help and training from their *socii navales* and allies.

217 B.C. Battle of the Ebro. Sosylus of Sparta recorded that Massalia's naval contingent together with Roman fleet defeats a Carthaginian fleet led by Hasdrubal (Hannibal's brother). Massalia's action defeated the Carthaginian's *diekplous* tactics. [1030]

49 B.C. Battle of the Frioul Islands outside of Massalia (Marseille) took place at the end of May. Massalia's Navy together with their local Celtic allies the Albici supplementing the crews was defeated by Decimus Brutus admiral for Julius Caesar during the Roman Civil War with Pompey the Great. [1031]

49 B.C. Battle of Tauroention (Le Brusc, Toulon) took place at the end of June. Massalia's Navy with Nasidius admiral for Pompey the Great were defeated by Decimus Brutus admiral for Julius Caesar during the Roman Civil War. [1032]

Liberati writes of several scenes portrayed on the Roman triumphal arch at Orange (Arausio) in France including a naval trophy commemorating Julius Caesar's victory at Massalia (Marseille). [1033]

Army

102 B.C. Battle of Aqua Sextae (Aix-in-Provence). Strabo records that the Marius Channel connecting to the River Rhône was cut by Marius and given by him to Massalia 'as a meed of their valour in the war against the Ambrones and Toygeni.' [1034] As this was an inland engagement the navy was not directly involved? Therefore we can surmise that Massalia, together with Marius and the Roman Army, fought against the Ambrones and Toygeni. Amongst the Roman allies *socii* were the Ingauni (Italian Ligurians).[1035] Local tradition places the battle-site at Mont Saint-Victoire. [1036]

49 B.C. The Greek Massaliote Army ably defended the city during the siege of Massalia by Julius Caesar April to September. Massalia's neighbouring Celtic allies the Albici took part in the naval Battle of the Frioul Islands and it is likely they fought in the city also. The city capitulated at the end of September. [1037]

Names of People from Massalia

From a city whose people we knew next to nothing of, archaeology and literary sources has been able to find some names and bring the past to life again.

Euthymenes, Pytheas. [1038]

Apollonides, Parmenon, and Hermon. [1039]

Nicostratus. [1040]

Zenothemis, Hegestratus. [1041]

Menecrates son of Charmolaus, Zenothemis, Cydimache. [1042]

Charmolean. [1043]

Ermokaikozanthos and Xanthermus. [1044]

Aristo. [1045]

Agroitos. [1046]

Crinas and Charmis. [1047]

Aristodemos son of Dionnis of Massalia. [1048]

Catus, Lycidas, Argus, Telo, and Gyareus. [1049]

Cynegirus. [1050]

Protis, Apellis, Aris, Alexis, Herylos, Hipponikos, Leukon, Lykaithos, Mikion, Oulis, Xeinandros Themis, Thespis, Prexis, Pythis. [1051]

Korinthos, Theumedon (second century A.D.). [1052]

Krates son of Apellas in memory of Syriske (funerary stone of the Hadrian period). [1053]

Herylos, Hipponikos, Leukon, Lykaithos, Mikion, Oulis, Xeinandros. [1054]

On the tomb of Glaucias 'eusevien' (ευσεβίην) and 'orfanie' (ὀρφανίη, orphan) were written in the Ionian dialect (second century A.D.) [1055] The inscription ends with a couplet '(envious fortune has done you wrong and) given tears to your mother in her old age, widowhood to your wife, as well as making an orphan of your poor child' (9-12). [1056]

Munna. [1057]

Poseidermos, Pythagoras, Xenocritos, Hephaistocles. [1058]

Zozimos (third century A.D.).[1059]

Athenades, son of Dioscourides, grammarian, in the Roman language. (third century A.D.) [1060]

Inscriptions Found

Over 200 Greek inscriptions from Gaul, Aquitania, Belgica and Corsica are also recorded in *Inscriptions Grecques de la France* (*IGF*).

Clerc gives one unusual inscription difficult to date and thought this was an epitaph of a courtesan.[1061] Decourt (*IGF*) concurs and suggests end of second century B.C. with a daughter, mother and grand-mother and translated as *À Mousè, fille d'Astykritè, sa fille Hymnis*.

       Μ Ο Υ Σ Η
       Α Σ Τ Υ Κ Ρ Ι
       ΤΗΣΥΜΝΙΣ
       ΗΘΥΓΑΤΗΡ

       Μούση Ἀστυκρίτης Ὑμνὶς ἡ θυγάτηρ.

At the sanctuary of Aristaios of l'Acapte, Giens peninsula near Olbia, Gaul (France).
Poulymachos, and popular Hellenistic names 'Demetrios, Dion, Dionysios' as well as those from the Phocaean cities of Massalia and Hyele (Elea-Velia) 'Apollonides, Hérylos, Hipponikos, Leukon, Lykaithos, Mikion, Oulis, Parmenon, and Xeinandros'.[1062]

Delphi
The Apellis inscription is dated to the second half of the sixth century B.C. fifty to sixty years after the foundation of Massalia.[1063] The inscription is in capitals and is also transcribed by Clerc in miniscule script with a partial letter restored.

       [Α]ΠΕΛΛΗ
       ΟΣΤΟΔΕ
       ΜΩΝΟΣΜ
       ΑΣΣΑΛΙ
       ΗΤΕΟ

       [Α]πέλλι
       ος τό Δή
       μωνος Μ
       ασσαλι
       ήτεο.

       Apellis son of Demon, Massalieteo.

In the Delphi list of honoured proxenes of Massalia:
Theodoros son of Heronax, Kleodamos son of Kaikos, Crinas son of Pythias and Pythias son of Crinas. [1064]

Clerc gives a transcription in miniscule script with the missing letters.
[Εμ Μασσαλίαι κοινᾶς Πυθία | Θεόδωρο]ς Ἡρών[ακτος], | Κλ[εόδ]ημος Καίκο[υ], | Πυθίας Κρινᾶ. [1065]

In the following Delphi inscription of Theorodokoi (receivers of the sacred envoys) in Massalia there is included the same names as above. [1066] For exact spacing see Clerc's photograph and *SIG,*3, N°. 585.

ΠΑΡΝΑΣΣΙΟΥΘΕΟΔΩΡΟΣΗΡΩΝΑΚΤΟ.ΚΛΕΟΔΑΜΟΣ
ΚΑΙΚΟΥΚΡΙΝΑΣΠΥΘΙΑΠΥΘΙΑΣΚΡΙΝΑΜΑ

Parnassiou Theodoros Eronakto. Kleodamos
Kaikou Krinas Pythia Pythias Krina Massaliotai.

Clerc gives all four lines of the above-mentioned capital letters in miniscule script. [1067]

Τοίδε Δελφῶν πρόζενοι _ _ _ Ἄρχοντος ὀρθαίου τοῦ Μαντία, βουλευόντων
τάν δευτέραν ἐζάμηνον Κλεοδάμου, Λύσωνος,
Παρνασσίου• Θεόδωρος Ἡρωνακτος, Κλεόδαμος
Καΐκου, Κρινᾶς Πυθία, Πυθίας Κρινᾶ, Μασσαλιῶται.

The Massaliote proxenes are mentioned during the archonate of Orthaios son of Mantias. Kleodamus, Lyson and Parnassos are magistrates in the year 196-195 B.C.

Athens

ΘΕΟΔΩΡΟΣ
ΛΕΩΜΑΧΟΥ
ΜΑΣΣΑΛΙΩΤΗΣ

Theodoros, son of Leomachos, Massaliotis. [1068]

ΑΚΡΟΠΟΛΙΣ
ΑΠΟΛΛΩΝΙΟΥ
ΜΑΣΣΑΛΙΗΤΙΣ

Acropolis, daughter of Apollonios, Massalietis. [1069]

ΚΛΕΟΠΑΤΡΑ
ΑΛΕΞΑΝΔΡΟΥ
ΜΑΣΣΑΛΙΗΤΙΣ

Cleopatra, daughter of Alexandros, Massalietis. [1070]

[Σ]ΦΑΙΡΟΣ
[Π]ΛΑΤΩΝΟΣ
[ΜΑ]ΣΣΑΛΙΩΤΗΣ

Sphairos, son of Platon, Massaliotis.[1071]

The ending of Massalia has either *ietis* or *iotis* while the next example has one *s* as Masa instead of two.

Melisos, son of Melisos, Masalio…[1072]

Delos

Leon son of Leon.[1073]

Philon son of Metrodoros.[1074]

Rhodes

ΕΠΑΦΡΟΔΕΙΤΟΥ
ΜΑΣΣΑΛΙΟΤΑ

son of Epaphrodites, Massalio(*sic*)ta.[1075]

Soteridas, Thales son of Poseidermos.[1076]

Tharros (east coast of Sardinia)

ΕΥΞΕ
ΝΕΑΝΑ
ΞΙΛΕΟ
ΜΑΣΣΑΛ
ΗΤΗ

Euxene daughter of Anaxilas of Massalia.
(Fourth to third century B.C.)[1077]

Lilybaeum (Punic Sicily)
Poseidermos, son of Pythagoras.[1078]

Syracuse (Greek Sicily)

ΞΕΝΟΚΡΙΤΟΣ
ΗΦΑΙΣΤοΚΛΕοΥ
[Μ]ΑΣΣΑΛΙΩΤΗΣ

Xenocritos, son of Hephaistocles, Massaliotis.
(Third century B.C.) [1079]

Greek Sicily

Found in a Jesuit collection of inscriptions in Palermo (ancient Panormus) in 1730.

ΚΛΕΑΓΟΡΑΣΜΑΣΣΑΛΙΩΤΗΣΑΦΡΟΔΙΤΗΙ

[Α]ΝΕΘΗΚΕ ΤΡΑΠΕΖΑΝ

Kleagoras Massaliotis Aphrodite,
[A]nethike Trapezan (ἀνέθηκε Τράπεζαν).

Dated to end of fifth century to beginning of the fourth century B.C.[1080] In the last word the letter Z (zeta) is written in the Ionian dialect script as Ɪ that has longer horizontals top and bottom than the letter I (iota). [1081]

Egypt

Kintos appears in the Greek mercenaries serving in Egypt

In the Valley of the Kings Luxor, Egypt inscribed on the wall at the tomb of 'Syringes' were visitors 'Poseidonax, son of Polyxenos of Massalia' and also 'Dionysius of Massalia'. [1082]

Rome

ΝΥΜΦΩΝΙΡΙΝΑ

ΜΑΣΣΑΛΙΩΤΑ

ΧΑΙΡΕ

Nymphon Irina, Massaliota, welcome. [1083]

ΝΟCΜΑC
CΑΛΙΗΤΑ
ΧΑΙΡΕ

... νος Μασσαλιῆτα χαῖρε [1084]

This double epitaph in Latin script is of a family that had settled in Rome and who named their daughter after the city of their origin Massalia.

    PHAEDER   MASSALIS
    ZENOTHEMIDS·F   PHAEDRI
    MASSALITANVS   ZENOTHEMIDOS
    VIX · A · LXXV   FILI·FILIA·V·A·VX

Phaeder, son of Zenothemis of Massalia, died seventy-five years old.

Massalis, daughter of Phaeder, son of Zenothemis, died fifteen years old. [1085]

Massalia's Fish

Though the land around Massalia was good for growing grapevines and olives it was 'on account of its ruggedness, too poor for grain' [1086] that would have to be imported or bought from the Celts further inland where the soil was better. Fishing in the Mediterranean would have been a welcome supplement and perhaps a staple to the diet of the Massaliotes.

    Mullets in Greek had several names. The larger of medium age are *platistakoi*; the smaller are *agnotidia*. Also known as *bacchus* and *oniskos* as well as *chellaries*. Aristophanes mentions them in *The Merchantmen*, 'Macrel, swordfish, lebiae, mullets, sea-perch, roe tunny'.[1087] Strabo also refers to 'dug mullets' as one of two marvels by the Massaliote seashore.[1088]

    We learn from Aelian and Oppian that the Massaliotes and Celts caught the tuna 'tunny'.[1089] Aelian further describes they did this by hook made of iron of great size and stout in contrast to the Ligurians, Italians and Sicilians who used nets.[1090] Tunny fish come from the Atlantic in shoals on the way to their spawning grounds in the Euxine (Black Sea)[1091] and were best fished in the Western Mediterranean. Ancient Massalia (Marseille) and its colony Antipolis (Antibes) were famous for these fish.[1092]

    Walking along present day Massalia's Lacydon Harbour (Vieux-Port) in the morning there were stalls on the quayside with freshly caught fish for sale including Mullets (Merlans du Marinee) Tuna, and two swordfish. The first swordfish I ever saw for real. They were cut into portions with a hacksaw. Smaller fish were kept just alive in shallow trays filled with water. Gutted fish and those not sold or kept were thrown into the harbour where the seagulls were well fed.

'The holy city of Massalia'

Oppian describes fishing around 'the holy city of Massalia'. The epithet 'holy' Mair translated and suggested this to refer to Massalia as the great outpost of Hellenic culture in the West.[1093] However, Massalia the city was made into a divinity by its mother-city Phocaea for saving them from Roman destruction following their siding against Rome during the Aristonicus revolt in 129 B.C. A temple to the goddess Massalia was built in Phocaea and the title of a priest and priestess to Massalia ΙΕΡΕΑ ΤΗΣ ΜΑΣΣΑΛΙΑΣ and ΙΕΡΕΙΑΝ ΤΗΣ ΜΑΣΣΑΛΙΑΣ are inscribed on the Phocaean stones in Oxford's Ashmolean Museum in Britain.[1094] See Chapter 15 for transcription.

Oppian wrote that the swordfish around Massalia were very big, in fact

> The fisherman fashion boats in the likeness of the Swordfishes themselves, with fishlike body and swords, and steer to meet the fish. The swordfish shrinks not from the chase, believing that what he sees are not benched ships but other Swordfishes, the same race as himself, until the men encircle him on every side. Afterwards he perceives his folly when pierced by the three-pronged spear . . . the valiant fish with his sword pierces in his turn right through the belly of the ship; and the fishers with blows of brazen axe swiftly strike all his sword from his jaws, and it remains fast in the ship's wound like a rivet, while fish orphaned of his strength, is hauled in.[1095]

Fishermen in the Tyrrhenian Sea also used the same method.[1096] Oppian continues that the 'greatly stupid Swordfish . . . perishes by his own folly' when encircled by a net 'forgetteth what manner of weapon is set in his jaws and is afraid of the plaited snare and shrinks back again' until 'they hale him forth upon the beach, where with downward sweeping blow of many spears men crush his head and he perishes by a foolish doom.'[1097]

The Massaliotes worshipped Apollo Dephinian[1098] and therefore appreciated dolphins as most Greeks did. The hunting of Dolphins Oppian considered immoral. The hunter was the same as a polluter of an altar. He polluted all those who 'shared the same roof with him'. Dolphins were useful to fisherman as when they hunted they drove fish into tight shoals and forced them towards fisherman's nets:

> The dolphins draw near and ask the guerdon of their friendship, even their allotted portion of the spoil. And the fishers deny them not, but gladly give them a share of their successful fishing; for if a man sin against them in his arrogance, no more are the Dolphins his helpers in fishing'.[1099]

Oppian continues that though Dolphins

> have a heart so much at one with men, the overweening Thracians and those who dwell in the city of Byzas [Byzantium] hunt them with iron-hearted devices—surely wicked men and sinful! who would not spare their children or their fathers and would lightly slay their brothers born.[1100]

Homeric Texts from Massalia

Further to being described as a 'great outpost of Hellenic culture in the West' and in line with being known for its many schools there were several undated Homeric texts known as politikai or 'city editions' including one from Massalia (Marseille) referred to as *ekdóseis* 'editions'. Aristarchus of Samothrace (Head of the Great Library at Alexandria after 180 B.C.) classified them as *khariéstatai* 'most-elegant' and he included these editions with the texts 'edited' by previous scholars in his own book on Homer that survived into the twelfth century A.D. Byzantine manuscripts *Commentary on Homer*, both *The Iliad* and *The Odyssey*, written by Eustathios, bishop of Thessaloniki, and in the 'Scholia A to *Iliad* 3.10 (Venetus)'.[1101]

Aelian when talking of Homer's *Odyssey* 19.518-523 discusses the sound of the nightingale and gives 'his own scholarly interpretation of the Homeric variant *poludeukia*'. His source is clear, 'I hear tell from Charmis of Massalia', Χάρμιδος ἀκούω τοῦ Μασσαλιώτου λέγοντος.[1102]

Mosquitoes

Though the Mediterranean is very beautiful in the day unfortunately Mother Nature unleashes fiendish insects [1103] that emerge around sunset such as mosquitoes. Pausanias records 'Mosquitoes in endless quantities bred in the marsh, till they compelled the poor people of Myus to leave the place'.[1104] Looking at the Ionian women's costume it seems much longer than is required.[1105] The Ionian costume came into fashion in the first half of the sixth century until the Persian Wars 490-479 B.C. Due to a reaction against everything eastern in Greece the old Hellenic fashion was revived called 'Dorian' as it was still preserved by the Spartans. However, the 'Ionian' dress still was worn in some parts. It would seem Massalia was one place where the Ionian style persisted as recorded in the first century B.C. by Cicero [1106] and later by Strabo,[1107] Livy,[1108] and first century A.D. by Silius Italicus.[1109]

Though there is still much controversy in interpreting the details from the sculptures there are some that mention 'over folds' of the peploi at the waist.[1110] If this is so then quite a bit of the material needs to be pulled up and overhangs from the girdle to avoid tripping over it? The costume seems cumbersome but when it comes to sunset the excess material can be drawn upwards over the head, shoulders and arms to protect against mosquito bites? Particularly if you do not have the excess material for a shawl as depicted in other sculptures. Originally there were several marshes on the landward side by the Horn of Lacydon that protected the city of Massalia from attack by humans but it was a place ideal for mosquitoes to breed.

Greeks in the medieval period [1111] and of modern times used garlic quite a lot in their food and the anise seed spirit drink of Ouzo to give some protection though not foolproof against mosquitoes. One can surmise that the ancient Greeks with the same food available would have had a similar diet. On receiving a mosquito bite garlic is used by slicing a clove and rubbing the open end onto the bite as a natural anti-septic and repeated for a few days until the bite is 'dead'. Modern Greeks also make a garlic salad called 'skordolia' from crushed garlic, bread, olive oil, and either lemon or vinegar all mashed together looking like porridge. Once eaten the garlic permeates the blood and skin and is believed to repel insects: and as anyone has experienced being next to someone who has eaten garlic, you are also repelled somewhat.

According to the Travel Health Tips card, that accompanied my impregnated 'pop-up' mosquito net by Worldwidenets, states categorically that 'Buzzers, Vitamin B and Garlick DO NOT work'. However without access to the effectiveness of modern day chemical and other mosquito repellents the Greeks believed, and many still do, that garlic gave protection. This believed 'protection' extends to other blood sucking creatures like vampires, as is evident in Balkan folklore. Garlic's use is well recorded across the ancient world right up to modern times. [1112]

Though it may seem incredible garlic is also known as an aphrodisiac! [1113] However, in the spirit of romance one can say if you have also eaten garlic you are not repelled by the smell of another who has.

The Greeks and Romans also used to suck anise seeds, which increases desire as it produces a strong estrogenic compound (female hormone) inducing a similar effect as testosterone. [1114] It is interesting to note that in modern day France that around Provence and Marseille they developed their own anise seed flavoured spirit called Pastis [1115] and the Greeks have long had their own version called Ouzo and Tsipouro in Greece.

It may be worth considering that a reason for Greek colonisation, overseas settlements, and relocation of people may owe its increase in population to the aphrodisiac effect of the humble garlic used as a protection against mosquitoes! But we would still not have a clincher for finding the elusive cause as we have the argument why were the Greeks more prolific than other Mediterranean peoples with the same ingredient in their diet? Depending on the answer we may have a causal factor or a contributory one.

Summary

We have been able to see Massalia (Marseille) had a long history from its foundation in 600 B.C. Archaeological evidence of an Ionian trading post at Gravisca c. 600-480 B.C. [1116] at the port of Tarquinii in Italy gives substance to Justin's story from Trogus of the Phocaeans in the vicinity making an alliance with the Romans in the reign of King Tarquin on their way to found Massalia. Livy says the Phocaeans arrived in Gaul during the reign of Rome's king Lucius Tarquinius Priscus (616–578 B.C.) and settled where they landed. Massalia not only established itself at the natural Harbour of Lacydon (Vieux-Port, Marseille) but also consolidated its position with a well-fortified city that expanded as the population increased. The Massaliotes were able to gain their control over the surrounding areas with treaties, naval and military battles. They created their own empire and trading network from Spain to Monaco; up the Rhône valley to Avignon and beyond to Mount Laissos; and it would seem their influence also reached the fortress construction of Heuneburg south-west of Munich.

Massalia's empire was different to the monolithic of the ancient world or of the nineteenth century being a scattered group of cities isolated on land but connected by sea, rivers and trade, somewhat like the 'Athenian Empire' in distance and typical of the Greek city-states innovative social and political experiments; though much more a merchant empire with a flexible system of direct rule and autonomy, as suggested by Emporion and Rhodus's own coin minting: while gregarious with the native populations wherever possible. Napoleon described Britain as a 'nation of Shopkeepers'. He subsequently clarified that he meant unlike its main rivals Britain's commerce was the source of its power and not the extent of its populations or land.[1117] Massalia's 'shops' were its many cities selling and trading. Plutarch tells us that Massalia was founded by 'merchants', Aristotle states for 'commerce', Pausanias confirms it 'reached great prosperity', and Ammianus Marcellinus records 'they established no small number of towns, as their strength and resources increased'.

From the first settlements set up from their mother-city Phocaea that of: Lampsakos (Lapseki, Dardanelles, Turkey), Amisos (Samsun, Black Sea), Naukratis (in Egypt combined venture with eleven other East Greek cities), Elea (Castellammare di Brucia, Italy): Heracles Monoikos (Monaco): in France Massalia (Marseille), Theline (Arelate, Arles), and in Spain Leuka Akra (Alicante); Alonis (Benidorm) and other names are known in the literary record [1118] but await either confirmation or discovery by archaeology.

Antipolis (Antibes) was founded by Phocaea or Massalia. The Massaliotes combined with Phocaea to found Alalia (Aléria in Corsica). With an expanding population and an influx of refugees due to invasions in Ionia, Massalia formed its own cities in France i.e. Olbia (by Saint Pierre L'Almanarre) and still existing today are Agathe Tyche (Agde), Nikaia (Nice), Tauroention (Le Brusc): in Spain, Emporion (Sant Marti d'Empuries), and Rhodus (Roses). Mixed populations seem to have existed at Aouenion (Avignon), Theline (Arles), Glanon and Saint-Blaise: Emporion and Santa Pola, Spain: and there were trading posts in indigenous towns and cities. Even though Massalia became established in its own right the people kept their Phocaean identity, Ionian laws and customs: links to the Games and Festivals in Greece: at Delphi with their statues, Treasury, and in the lists of proxenes and also Theorodokoi (receivers of sacred envoys).

The Greeks at Massalia introduced the cultivation methods of grapevines and olive trees spreading out, acquiring the surrounding territory and also in their colonies/settlements. Their lasting legacy is crucial to the economy of France and Spain today as enormous producers of wine, olives and olive oil.

Though we have stone inscriptions from Massalia no documents have been uncovered. However, scholars agree on a written Massaliote navigation manual periplus of the sixth century B.C. on the Western Mediterranean and Atlantic as a source used by other ancient scholars. More tangible is the city edition of Homeric texts from Massalia referred to as *ekdóseis* 'editions', which Aristarchus of Samothrace classified as *khariéstatai* 'most-elegant' and included them in his own book on Homer in the second century B.C. This survived into the twelfth century A.D. Byzantine manuscripts *Commentary on Homer*, both *The Iliad* and *The Odyssey*, written by Eustathios, bishop of Thessaloniki, and in the 'Scholia A to *Iliad* 3.10 (Venetus)'.

Aristotle described Massalia's government as going through some turmoil in its oligarchy phase becoming a 'constitutional government' and developed into what Strabo considered 'of all the aristocracies, theirs is the best ordered'.[1119] Cicero thought Massalia was 'so well governed by the prudence of its aristocracy' while noting it was not a democracy for the lower classes without a vote, it was for the people 'to some extent like slavery'.[1120] The government was basically a Timocracy, power based on wealth, which was administered by a council of the Six Hundred, with a 'cabinet' of fifteen above them, and three in the top position of decision. We know from Pausanias that Massalia was a prosperous city and this wealth must have filtered down so that most of the ordinary people had a living that was adequate, as we do not seem to have the wider discontent that led to democracy as in some other Greek city-states. Apollonides was put in charge of the government, military and naval forces of Massalia during the Roman civil war between Caesar and Pompey (see Chapter 13).

Celts went to the schools of Massalia and it would seem 'the Holy city of Massalia' deified by its mother-city Phocaea was also this outpost and bastion of Greek culture in the Western Mediterranean responsible for the knowledge the Celts had of spoken and written Greek that Caesar records of the Druids and also the Helvetii. Evidence of stone inscriptions in Gallo-Greek script are dated from the third century B.C. and ending around the mid-first century A.D. The schools of Massalia became famous and Strabo reports prominent Romans went there to study if they did not want to go to Athens for education. Several Romans spent their exile in this cultured city.

Phocaean contacts outside the Middle Sea (Mediterranean) with the Atlantic area of Spain at Tartessos are recorded by Herodotus as the first Greeks to make 'long voyages'. These journeys were not made with merchant boats but in penteconter warships. Evidence consists of high amounts of Greek pottery imports and the discoveries in the sea of three bronze Corinthian helmets from seventh and sixth century B.C. between Huelva and Cadiz. Massalia's cultivation of the olive and grape extended to the coastal areas of Catalonia and Murcia in Spain where they developed a Greek-Iberian script in the fourth century B.C., coin production, and taught Spaniards the worship of Ephesian Artemis in the Greek ritual.

From 540 B.C. Massalia's own mint produced silver and bronze coins that were the main currency in the Rhône Valley. Coin hoards third to second century B.C. were also found beyond in Bourges 60 km NE of Lyon and at Jersey, Channel Islands. Their designs were imitated on Celtic coins as far away as North Italy and in Britain. Massalia late third to early second century B.C. bronze coins have been found in Kent, Britain and were models for British Celtic potin coins of the second to first century B.C.

Euthymenes of Massalia sailed into the Atlantic and explored the west coast of Africa sometime between the sixth century B.C. to mid-fifth century B.C. Massalia broke the Carthaginian monopoly on tin with its discovery of Britain by the astronomer and explorer Pytheas of Massalia in the 320s B.C. who went on to find: the source of valuable amber: the frozen Congealed Sea: and established the position of the North Pole. His accurate calculations are still used today in Latitudes. Pytheas gave Britain its name, measured and circumnavigated the island, and made the earliest recorded description of Britain and the Britons. How this happened and the background to why Massalia was founded we will see in the following chapters.

Chapter 3

The Greek Phocaeans, Founders of Massalia (Marseille in France)

Here is a mystery to solve. There are many ancient books that are lost in the passing of time. Some may have gone forever, but others are waiting to be discovered by archaeologists or others by chance. We know some of these lost books existed because they were used and quoted by other ancient writers whose books have survived. By looking through many books, small pieces of information are gathered to make a picture of what happened. This is true of a Greek explorer and scientist who discovered Britain and the Arctic Circle, and who wrote a book of his exploration of the unknown North Atlantic called *On the Ocean* in the 320s B.C. Pytheas came from Massalia (Marseille) a Greek colony/settlement on the French coast.

In ancient Greece there were many mountains and only a small amount of land for growing food. There have been many theories why Greeks went to other lands to form cities to live in; wanting your own piece of land or overpopulation: food shortage, climate change, poor harvest, wanderlust or adventure,[1121] the grass is always greener on the other side, a cantankerous desire to run things your own way, which one can say is a characteristic of the different Greek city-states that some were prepared to fight and die more for these differences than for what they had in common with language, religion and culture.[1122] Whatever the reason some decided to go on their ships and travel overseas to either set up a trading post (*Emporion*) or find an empty piece of land they could settle on and start a new life. The Greeks called this an *Apoikia* (home from home).

During the eighth to sixth century B.C. many Greek colonies, cities and settlements were founded from the Black Sea to Spain in the Western Mediterranean. Never far from the sea or navigable rivers the ancient Greeks built cities and traded with the local people and other cities. It is not certain if their arrival was done peacefully or in conflict as the situations the Greeks met were different in each area i.e. Black Sea people were nomadic/semi-nomadic whereas Magna Graecia (in South Italy) had settled agriculturalists.[1123]

Strabo writes that Massalia did acquire their 'surrounding plains' through conquest.[1124] Justin records they made colonies in the territory they captured and Ammianus Marcellinus states they increased with a number of towns.[1125] In Sicily the Greeks generally got on with the locals Sicels but there is evidence of conflict with the native Sicans.[1126] The Greeks named the island Sikelia. Thucydides (VI.3.5) mentions the Chalcidians from Euboea driving out the Sicels at Naxos and Leontinii as well as several conflicts and displacements between Greek cities in Sicily and in South Italy (Magna Graecia)[1127] e.g. Kroton destroyed Sybaris in 510 B.C.[1128] or against other nations if their own trading interests were threatened. Though the colonies were politically independent they usually kept a loyalty and links to their homeland where they came from.[1129]

Figure 83. Kylix depicting a 'round-built merchant-ship' being attacked by a penteconter war-ship, 8 inches diameter and 3.5 inches high. This drinking cup was an Attic made black figure ware 520–500 B.C. and found in a tomb in Vulci, Italy.

Herodotus an ancient Greek historian known as 'the father of history' wrote,

> Now the Phocaeans were the first of the Greeks who performed long voyages, and it was they who made the Greeks acquainted with the Adriatic and with Tyrrhenia, with Iberia, and the city of Tartessus [in Atlantic Spain].[1130] The vessels that they used in their voyages were not the round-built merchant-ship, but the long penteconter [50-oared warship].[1131]

When the Phocaeans arrived at Tartessus (at the mouth of the Guadalquivir river in Atlantic Spain), the King Argathonius took such a liking to the Phocaeans that he begged them to quit Ionia and settle anywhere in his kingdom. Not being able to persuade them

> and hearing that the Mede was growing great in their neighbourhood, he gave them money to build a wall about their town, and certainly he must have given it with a bountiful hand, for the town is many furlongs in circuit, and the wall is built entirely of great blocks of stone skilfully fitted together. The wall, then, was built by his aid.[1132]

The Greeks from Phocaea in their 'swift ships' founded several cities on the Mediterranean coast of France. One of these settlements was founded in 600 B.C. and the Greek Phocaeans named their new city Massalia, which is known today in French as Marseille. For many centuries it was the largest city in France until the population of Paris became larger. Today Marseille (Massalia) is the second-largest city in size and third in population after Lyon.[1133]

Strabo on the other hand mentions the efforts from the island of Rhodes,

> It is also related of the Rhodians that they have been prosperous by sea, not merely since the time when they founded the present city, but that even many years before the establishment of the Olympian Games [776 B.C.] they used to sail far away from their homeland to insure the safety of their people. Since that time, also, they have sailed as far as Iberia, and there they founded Rhodes, of which the Massaliotes later took possession.[1134]

However the earliest evidence of the Greek foundation is fourth century B.C. and so far it seems that Rhodus was founded by Massalia.[1135]

Cunliffe suggests the protected area of the Greek city of Massalia (Marseille) of 50 ha had a population 30,000 to 40,000[1136] while Domínguez citing Bats estimates about 20,000.[1137] Massalia had a sheltered big natural harbour and deep water, ideal for the Greek ships. The city became prosperous[1138] trading with the local people and the other cities in Italy, Sicily, North Africa, Greece and the Greeks of Ionia in Asia Minor and the Black Sea.

In Ionia there was the Greek city of Phokaia (Phocaea) originally founded c. ninth century B.C. by Aeolians.[1139] The following Ionian settlers of Phocaea were from Phocis (Phokis near Parnassos Greece).[1140] The name of Phocaea was also that of the seals Φωκη[1141] that live on an island in the harbour.[1142] On its first electrum coins they used the image of a seal as a pun on their name.[1143] The letter Θ (Φ) appears below the seal.[1144] Their first coins were of Electrum an amalgam of gold and silver during the seventh century B.C. Phocaean pre-eminence, as a main port of trade seems to increase after the destruction of Smyrna by the Lydians. During the Milesian War 623–612 B.C Miletus stopped issuing stater coins. Phocaean staters were 256-248 g and darker due to more gold content than those of Miletus and Sardis, which was 219-215 g. The extension of Phocaean electrum staters seems to coincide within a period of naval supremacy c. 602-560 B.C. Eusebius records they were the leading Thalassocracy, 'who ruled the sea' for forty-four years.[1145]

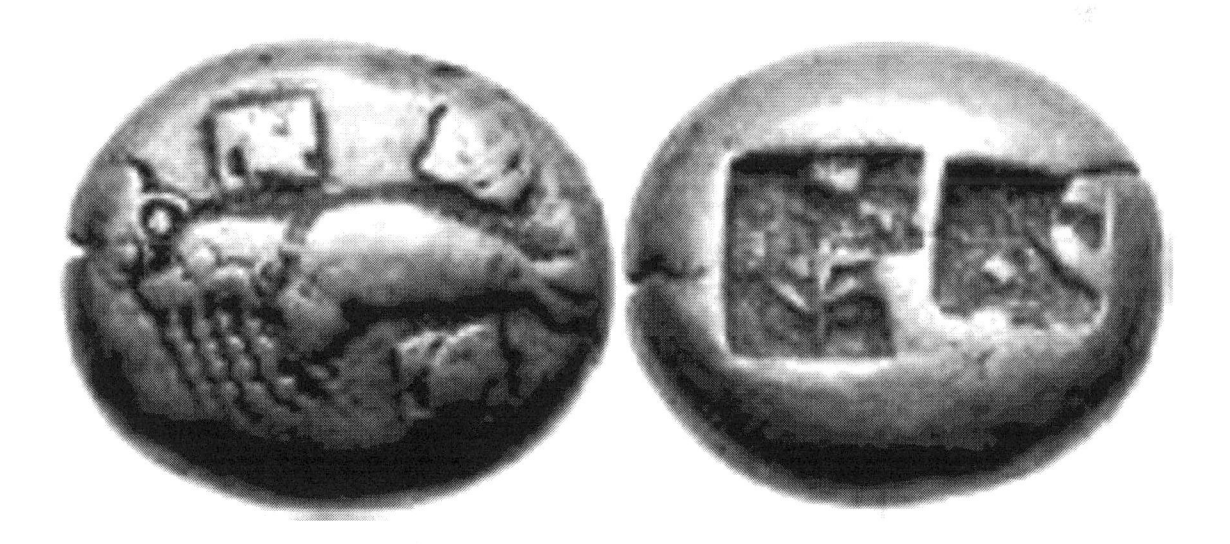

Figure 84. Phocaean coin seventh century B.C stater made of Electrum (amalgam of gold and silver). Obverse: seal (pun on the name of Phokaia Φωκη = seal) swimming facing left, and catching an octopus. Around the seal are two rectangles above and another object below/reverse: incuse with an emblem/map of Phokaia?

Throughout the fifth and most of the fourth century B.C. Electrum hectae minted at Mytilene and Phocaea were the chief currency of the west coast of Asia Minor At the last part of the fifth century Mytilene had a monetary convention with Phocaea in standardising the 'weight and fineness' of their coins and to take it each in turn for one year to issue these coins and deciding by lot that Mytilene began first.[1146] During this period the weight of one Mytilene stater was found to be 238.4 grs: Lampsacus (a Phocaean colony) 237 grs: and Phocaean hectae 39.4 grs.[1147] Phocaean staters and hectae were widely circulated in Greece and mentioned in Attic inscriptions.[1148]

Phocaeans also built their own trade network by founding several cities including:

- 🏛 Naukratis in Egypt (a joint venture with eleven other East Greek cities [1149] c. late seventh century B.C.).[1150]
- 🏛 Lampsacus (Lapseki) on the Dardanelles in Asia Minor 654 B.C. [1151]
- 🏛 Amisos (Samsun) on the Black Sea c. 600 B.C. [1152]
- 🏛 Massalia (Marseille) in France 600 B.C. [1153]
- 🏛 Antipolis (Antibes) in France sixth century B.C. (either by Phocaea direct or Massalia). [1154]
- 🏛 Alalia (Aléria) in Corsica c. 560s B.C. (Phocaea together with Massalia). [1155]
- 🏛 Hyele, (Elea, Velia) in Magna Graecia, South Italy 540 B.C. [1156]

An alliance between the Phokaians (Phocaeans) and Greek city of Rhegium [1157] facilitated passage through the Straits of Messina and the southern Tyrrhenian Sea (controlled by the Greek Chalcidians). The alliance remained solid and was not disturbed by Greek inter-state rivalries as found elsewhere. Perhaps it was kept solid in this area due to the threat of the Tyrrhenians and Carthaginians? [1158] Also the foundation and running of Naukratis showed remarkable cooperation while being surrounded by Egyptians.

This epigram was found on a tombstone:

> Phocaea, glorious city, these were the last words Theano spoke
> as she descended into the vast night:
> "Alas unhappy that I am, Apellichus!
> What sea, my husband, art thou crossing in thy swift ship?
> But by me death stands close, and would I could die holding thy
> dear hand in mine". [1159]

The first excavations of the city took place in 1914–20 by French archaeologist Felix Sartiaux,[1160] followed in the 1950s by Turkish archaeologists Akurgal and since the 1990s by Professor Özyğit. The city walls of Phokaia (Phocaea) in the archaic period are estimated over 5 km long. Present opinion is that the temple area of Phokaia was part of the peninsular and not a separate island.[1161] The main part of the city was on the mainland while the important buildings and temples were on the peninsula.[1162] On the mainland excavations at the hill of the Maltepe Tumulus have revealed the later ancient city walls dating to 590–580 B.C. In this first quarter of the sixth century B.C. Phokaia was surrounded 'by a great fortification wall some 7 to 8 km in length'.[1163] The length of these walls shows that at this period Phokaia was one of the largest cities in the world.[1164] The Maltepe Tumulus excavations by Professor Ö. Özyğit revealed walls that were sloped 30° for around eight courses from the base shown in the photograph but in the section drawing made shows twelve courses.[1165] The wall was made of finely trimmed ashlar masonry of tufa stone and above the slope the wall continued vertically to probably 15 metres height in total.

Professor Hodge makes the point that this wall 'ranks with the finest Greek work'.[1166] He distinguishes these are not the seventh to sixth century B.C. structures that Arganthonius paid for but are the later city walls mentioned and probably seen by Herodotus.[1167] You can see in the photograph 'great blocks of stone skilfully fitted together'.[1168] Next to the wall excavated at Maltepe was a four-metre space where the city gate had been. Wooden beams of the five metre towers on both sides had been charred by fire. Persian arrows and spearheads, a stone catapult ball, and broken amphorae indicated the period when the city was attacked by Harpagus and the Persians 546 B.C.[1169]

Figure 85. The ancient city walls of Phokaia (Phocaea) 590–580 B.C.

At Değirmenli Hill a development of apartment blocks was due to begin in 1991. Quick action by archaeologists Professor Özyğit and his colleagues commenced excavations. Fortunately they uncovered something before being stopped by the landowners. They had revealed a Greek amphitheatre dating to 340–330 B.C. and made of the local tufa stone. The dating was from a Phokaian coin found from beneath the seats, ceramic finds, and 'style of the analemma wall and the profiles of the seats'. This important discovery is the 'most ancient theatre' found in Anatolia.[1170] The analemma unearthed was 4.5 m in height. An inscription on the steps 'Fuyte Oyta' may suggest the ancient Greeks were seated in their distinct neighbourhoods?[1171] By the first century A.D. this theatre was used as a ceramic rubbish dump and then a cemetery in the following century. As a theatre was an important part of ancient Greek city life, with no T.V. or cinema this was the centre for entertainment with tragedies and comedies and as a regular social place to be seen, it is probable that it had been replaced by another elsewhere in the city, which is still to be found.

The find of a seventh century B.C. Megaron (main hall or the central room of a palace or house) near the ceramic rubbish dump also indicated that Phokaia was a large settlement in the archaic period.[1172] Between the ancient theatre and the peninsula mosaic floors have been found particularly one dating late fourth to early fifth century A. D. and now at the Archaeological Museum of Izmir.

Phokaia was famous for its purple dye that was an expensive luxury product.[1173] By the fifth century B.C. the city-state was a member of the Delian League paying two talents. During the Peloponnesian War Phokaia rebelled and left the League in 412 B.C.[1174] After an unsuccessful siege the Spartan general Agesilaus withdraws then returns and captures Phokaia 396-394 B.C., as their allies had gone home. [1175] At the end of the Corinthian War under the Peace of Antalcidas (the King's Peace) 387 B.C. Phokaia and the rest of Ionia came under the control of Persia.

Approaching the city from the sea you have on the right (south) the bigger harbour the Phokaians called Naustathmos and to the left the smaller harbour called Lampter. The headland between the two harbours has an acropolis where their Temple of Athena built in the first quarter of the sixth century B.C. [1176] stood on the level area next to it. Since Hodge wrote of the excavated sixth century B.C. column drums and a disc acroterion [1177] the acropolis has been cleared of the building that was there allowing access for archaeological excavations. Many more column drums have been found of substantial size, capitals and other large marble carved pieces. Some stele was found in the town. An 'upper part of a large quadrangular base with mouldings' with a Greek inscription was a stone base of an honorary statue for Lucius Vibius Eumenes, first century B.C. to second century A.D. (see Figures 86 and 87). 'H 1.02; w. 0.73; th. 0.61; letter height 0,015 to 0,045 m'.[1178]

```
         ΑΓΑΘΗΙ ΤΥΧΗ

         ΛΟΥΚΙ°ΝΟΥΙΒΙ°Ν
            ΕΥΜΕΝΗ
          ΦΙΛΟΣΟΦΟΝ
          . . ΡΑΤΗΓΟΝ
          . . . . . ΡΧΟΝ
          . . . . . . ΧΟΝ
```

When first recorded in 1971 there were ten lines visible as translated below. Lines 6 and 7 are now partial while lines 8, 9 and 10 are now missing completely. [1179] Other missing letters are in brackets and the translation is given below:

Good Luck	Ἀγαθῆ Τύχη[ι]
Lucius Vibius	Λούκιον Οὐίβιον
Eumenes	Εὐμένη
philosopher	φιλόσοφον
stratigon	στρατηγόν
[boul]archon	βούλαρχον
[eirina]rchon	εἰρήναρχον
efibarchon	ἐφήβαρχον
gimnasiarchon	γυμνασίαρχον
[agora]nomon	[ἀγορα]νόμον - - -

Figure 86. Broken stone base of an honorary statue standing upside down with Greek inscription for Lucius Vibius Eumenes, c. first century B.C. to second century A.D. Phokaia (Phocaea, Foça), photographed June 2011.

Figure 87. Close up of a partial Greek inscription for Lucius Vibius Eumenes, c. first century B.C. to second century A.D. Phokaia (Phocaea, Foça), photographed June 2011.

In addition to using the emblem of a seal on their coins McIerney mentions they had in one of their temples waterspouts in the image of 'seals' heads'.[1180] The Temple of Athena was destroyed during the Persian invasions [1181] and restored by the end of the sixth century B.C. After the temple was destroyed again much of the marble remains were burnt to make lime! There was a lime pit found on the western side edge of the level area.[1182] During the first phase of building the temple (early sixth century B.C.) it was made out of tufa stone in the Ionic order but during the Roman period it was made of marble and in the Corinthian order. A wall at the base on the side of the acropolis was made of finely trimmed stone blocks very similar to those of the city wall of the archaic period.[1183] Excavations were still in progress 2011. There were rectangles and steps cut into the rock of the acropolis leading down to and out of what seems to be a small pool which could be for ritual cleaning before going into the temple? Though some may belong to the cellars of houses that were built over it centuries later? The temple itself must have been an impressive sight not only in its location but also size justifying its fame. Xenophon wrote that the temple 'was struck by lightning and set on fire' in 408 B.C.[1184] Pausanias mentions the temple had been 'damaged by fire' but in spite of this still described it as 'a wonder'.[1185] Phocaean horses and griffin protomes 600-590 B.C. carved from tufa stone were found in 2005 with cella blocks in the earthquake destruction level of the temple in the second century AD.[1186]

Figure 88. Phokaia: Temple of Athena western podium walls, first quarter sixth century B.C.

Figure 89. The walls at the side of the acropolis of Phokaia: the finely made stone blocks are similar as the city wall.

Figure 90. Phokaia: a finely carved stone.

Figure 91. City wall of ancient Phokaia (Phocaea, Foça) beneath the acropolis facing the sea, below right are niches for the goddess Cybele.

Below the formal temple facing the sea there were carved into the rock cliff five niches dating to 580s B.C. with statues and reliefs of the Asiatic goddess Cybele. In this 'open air' temple votive pools were also carved into the rock and niches for sailors to place lanterns. Other sites dedicated to Cybele were found at Yeldeğirmeni Hill and on Incir Island. Interestingly worship of these goddesses Athena and Cybele existed side by side. [1187] Livy mentions during the war against Antiochus 129 B.C. two Galli (priests of Cybele) went out from Phocaea to ask Seleucus to take 'no extreme measures against the city'. [1188] A statue of Cybele was discovered in the Phocaean city of Massalia (Marseille) dating to the sixth century B.C. [1189] Phocaea's city walls on the rock cliff peninsula facing the sea clearly show four periods of history with the original mortar free ancient Greek large cut stone defences, then stones with lime mortar during the Roman period. The Genoese and Ottoman periods had lime, sand, brick pieces and tie powder to bind their smaller stone constructions. In some parts of the later wall you can see reused stone from the earlier periods such as a lion head carving (on its side) at the base of the wall below the acropolis, carved platform stones, columns and column bases.

There are seven islands at the entrance to Phocaea. They were made of different volcanic rock and particularly spectacular is Siren's Island where around 350–400 Monk seals live [1190] and added to the name of the city in Greek (Phocaea) and also Turkish (Foça) = Seal. I hired a small fishing boat that took me through smaller channels between the rocks. One of the rocks there was about 10 feet high and twenty feet long, very smooth and actually looked like a seal! Unfortunately we did not see any of the elusive and timid live seals. The seal also appears on Phocaea's ancient Greek coins as a pun on the name. These strange rocks and the seal's cry could have been the basis for the bewitchment of the Siren's songs that was the cause of shipwrecks as mentioned by Homer in *The Odyssey*. [1191] Scholars have suggested several locations for Siren's Island between Sicily and the Tyrrhenian Sea. Perhaps here is another possible location to consider? [1192]

Looking up at the night sky in June 2011 one can see the star constellation of the Plough (Big Dipper) with its open end facing and parallel to the coast of the little harbour and pointing out to sea. If one kept to the left of the Plough presumably one would be able to steer clear of the harbour and islands at night and into the open sea? The ancient Greek Phocaeans show once again naval skills to navigate their own harbour. According to Herodotus they evacuated the city by night leaving an empty town to the Persian besiegers 546 B.C. [1193] Today the Turkish fisherman of Foça go out and fish at night and with their considerable local knowledge and skill avoiding the rocks. However, to ensure the safety of locals and visitors on the sea the Turkish authorities maintain a lighthouse on the headland of the big harbour.

Due to Phocaea being hemmed in by hills the land only goes back for little more than a mile on the level for which to grow any food, a hardy landscape for the Phocaeans. When you can pass over the hills some 3 km the land levels and the soil is poor at first but olive trees are growing there. Beyond is a Persian monumental tomb 7 km away that from the style Professor Özyğit suggests may have been built by order of Cyrus in 546 B.C. possibly for King Abradatus of Susa; who according to Xenophon had died at the Battle of Sardis; and his wife Pantheia who killed herself on hearing the news. [1194] Here the land is fertile as there are growing olives, cotton, corn and some wheat. If the Phocaeans had controlled inland they would have been able to supplement their diet of the ample fish, which they could catch or use fish products to trade. Otherwise they relied on cereals and other food imports via the sea. To understand how these small Greek city-states could survive one only has to look at Monaco in the present time. Monaco a small independent European state hemmed in by mountains and with little spare arable land maintained itself in poverty. Only since the introduction of the railway in 1868 and the casino of Monte Carlo did it begin the transformation into a wealthy state with the recent high-rise apartments, villas and port for the yachts of millionaires. Incidentally Monaco was also the Phocaean colony of Heracles Monoikos from which we get the name Monaco. Their present main harbour is called Port Hercule (Hercules).

Vitruvius the Roman architect and engineer wrote that those great Greek artists like Myron, Poycletus, Phidias, Lysippus and others were famed for their art by making works 'for great states and kings or citizens of rank'. But others who made 'no less perfectly finished works for citizens of low station, are unremembered' like 'Teleas of Athens, Chion of Corinth, Myager the Phocaean, Praxas of Ephesus, Boedas of Byzantium, and many others'. [1195]

Pausanias mentions an epic poem the Minyad (late sixth century B.C. now lost) written by Prodicus of Phocaea and adds 'if indeed his'. [1196]

According to Pliny, Telephanes of Phocaea noted sculptor worked for the Achaemenid court in Persia and the stylistic similarities suggest the Persepolis bull is also his work. [1197]

The Greek architect Theodorus of Phokaia published a book on the Tholos building at Delphi around 380–370 B.C. [1198] and it is most likely to have been designed by him. The circular building had twenty Doric columns on the outside a ten Corinthian columns on the inside and was beautifully adorned. [1199] The Tholos is next to an earlier Phokaian building the Treasury of Massalia built around 540-530 B.C.

Telecles of Phocaea became Head of the Academy in Athens and was buried in Athens during the archonship of Nikosthenes (167/6 B.C.) [1200]

Phocaea was one of the very first states to use coins; an event with far reaching consequences that changed the world. From Phocaea the use of coins spread to the other Greek cities. Coins were originally made of Electrum (amalgam of gold and silver) [1201] and its attributed invention in Lydia during the seventh century B.C. [1202] Between 560–547 B.C. Lydia changed to make separate gold and silver coins. However, the spread of silver coins from Lydia and Ionia to other parts of Asia Minor 'was essentially a Greek phenomenon'. [1203] The surviving finds of Greek coins across the Mediterranean and Black Sea reflects just how far Greek settlements had spread their influence. Neighbouring tribes also imitated Greek coin design. The Ionian city-state of Phocaea was able to find a supply of silver.

The Phocaeans were the first Greeks 'who performed long voyages' in the 'long Penteconter', [1204] a 50-oared warship. With 50 oars they didn't need to rely just on sails and could row across currents and the wind. They could sail beyond the sight of land and also from the 'Middle Sea' (Messigion, Mediterranean) into the Atlantic past the Pillars of Hercules (Gibraltar) to Tartessus in Spain to get silver. [1205]

Greeks, Phoenicians and Carthage

Long before the Ionians Greeks, it was Minoans from the island of Crete first c. 2600 B.C. followed by the Mycenaean Greeks who had explored the Mediterranean between 1400–1200 B.C. and archaeological evidence of their trade is found in Sicily and Italy. Such as a sixteenth-century B.C. cup at Monte Sallia near Cosimo found in a tomb and a bone sword in another tomb nearby.[1206] The archaeological finds of Egyptian faience beads and Baltic amber is evidence of the distance of trade in the Bronze Age.[1207] There was a Mycenaean bronze dagger found at Pelynt in Cornwall.[1208] On a monolith at Stonehenge was a carving thought to be a Mycenaean dagger. Another Early Bronze Age dagger carving revealed in 2012 had 'few parallels in British or northern European' types.[1209]

Bronze Age Trade

Amongst revealing shipwrecks one off the south coast of Turkey in 1982 dating back to the fourteenth century B.C. was found at Ulu Burun near Kas. George F. Bass and Cemal Pulak of the Nautical Institute of Texas made ten years of excavations from 1984. The cargo showed just how international trade was. There was found in this one shipwreck ten tons of **copper** in the shape of 354 ox hide shape ingots and isotope analysis shows they were mined 'most certainly' in Cyprus.[1210] Further analysis revealed there was also a ton of **tin** in its raw form of 99.5 pure tin [1211] and other tin made objects though it is not clear where this tin was mined. The pottery found was Cannanite amphorae. Much held turpentine like resin from the Terebinth tree, olives, glass beads and an arsenical compound called orpiment. Similar jars have been found in Greece, Egypt and the Levantine coast. Exotic goods included lengths of wood like ebony, which grew in Africa in the south of Egypt. There was Baltic amber beads, from North Europe, possibly from the Mediterranean Ivory from Elephant and Hippopotamus tusks, and from either North Africa or Syria ostrich eggshells, bronze tools and weapons of Egyptian, Levantine and Mycenaean, spears and a ceremonial sceptre/mace from the Danube region of the Black Sea. Also found were several cylinder seals of Assyrian, Kassite and Syrian types, ingots of expensive glass and a chalice of gold.[1212]

There were finds of amber beads in Britain from the late N Bronze Age in Glentanar, Balmashanner and Adabrock in Scotland; in Angelsey Wales at Tŷ Mawr and Llangwyllog; in England at Heatherbury Burn Co. Durham, Feltwell Fen in Norfolk and Runnymede Bridge at Egham, Surrey. Finds were more common in Ireland.[1213] Taylor suggested amber used in Early Bronze Age Wessex Culture may have come from that washed up on Norfolk beaches and Wessex distribution along the ancient track Icknield Way to Norfolk could be a possible link.[1214]

Following the Mycenaean collapse and the Dark Ages in Greece it was the Phoenicians on the coast of Palestine, who filled the vacuum as traders around 1,000 B.C.[1215] In the Dark Ages there were no schools and the Greeks lost their knowledge of reading and writing. The memory of their earlier journeys elsewhere and in Sicily survived in folklore and repeated by storytellers from one generation to another 'in a most confused form in some myths, and especially in stories of Odysseus's wanderings'.[1216]

The ability of human memory with training could memorise large amounts of verse. In India there were professional storytellers that memorised. The 'works of poets in India were never for readers but always for the listener'.[1217] From the court the poems were taken over and spread by wandering singers.[1218] In ancient Greece Homer's epic poems like *The Iliad* would take two to three days to recite with special story-tellers who made it their profession to memorise large amount of verses. These professional reciters were called 'rhapsodes'.[1219]

After the Dark Ages Greek literature began to recover between ninth to eighth century B.C. [1220] They developed another alphabet based on the Phoenician characters [1221] made up of consonants, but with the improvement of adding short vowels [1222] making it very similar to our own a, e, i, o, u. [1223] Much knowledge could now be written down, like Hesiod and Homer's poems, and distributed far beyond local areas and the generations of oral memory. [1224] At festivals in Athens mid-sixth century B.C. there were competitions for reciting Homer as well as team and athletic events. [1225]

As soon as school children learnt basic reading and writing that could take four years, they began memorising the poetry of Homer, Hesiod, and in Athens Solon as well. Schoolmasters drew lessons from Homer's poems as the Greeks thought they had a wide range of knowledge that a man could use in life. [1226] Strabo wrote of Homer that he not only was 'the founder of the science of geography' but also 'surpassed all men . . . in his acquaintance with all that pertain to public life'. [1227]

Greeks ships began exploring the West again but it seems without the direct memory of former Minoan or Mycenaean routes as the break had been so long. [1228] By the eighth century B.C. Greek settlements had secured the route for valuable tin and amber over North Italy at Cumae and Pithekoussai. Only the Spanish route by sea lay open and the Phoenicians started to acquire this for themselves by founding trading posts from Carthage (in North Africa) to Spain, [1229] around the same time that that the Greeks began to spread creating settlements overseas. [1230] The Greeks used the star constellation of the Great Bear (Big Dipper) for navigation and the Phoenicians used the Little Bear (Cynosura). [1231] Parrhasian Helice: the constellation of the Great Bear, also called Helike from the Greek word meaning 'to turn' because it turns around the Pole. Parrhasian was from a legend set in Arcadia where Jupiter turns the girl Callisto into a bear. The stars that make up the 'paws' of the Great Bear could always be seen at night moving along the horizon in Greece. The Arctic Circle in Greek means the circle of the Bear. These denote stars that can be seen always circling the pole in contrast to further away from the pole where the stars rise and set at night. [1232]

Some ancient Greek historians had believed that the Phoenicians had been first to explore because they had thought that Homer's poems were also historically accurate. In Homer's epic poems the Phoenicians sail the Aegean and Sicilian Seas. Therefore in Strabo's opinion 'The Phoenicians, I say were the informants of Homer; and these people occupied the best of Iberia and Lybia before the age of Homer and continued to be the masters of those regions until the Romans broke up their empire'. Strabo in Book III.5.11 repeats the same idea 'Now in former times it was the Phoenicians alone who carried on this commerce (that is from Gades), [in Spain], for they kept the voyage hidden from everyone else'. [1233]

Since Boardman (1999) wrote that archaeological evidence does confirm it was the Greeks who first explored, particular in Sicily, there has been some radio carbon dating of material from the Phoenician trading posts that suggest they were ahead of the Greeks in Spain by around fifty years in actually making their own facilities on land rather than calling in at native settlements and trading. These Phoenician trading posts covered an area between two to ten hectares and are very small compared to Greek settlements such as Himera in Sicily with eighty hectares. East of the Straits of Gibraltar for 100 km along the coast there are ten Phoenician settlements approximately one every 10 km including Cerro de Villar. The location and architecture suggest they stored goods there to speculate and profit from 'price fluctuations and differences' in Mediterranean markets [1234] i.e. releasing goods when prices were higher.

Herodotus by contrast being 300 years before Strabo and nearer in time to the events recorded that it was the Greeks who were first to explore. He wrote,

'The sea frequented by the Greeks, that beyond the Pillars of Hercules, which is called the Atlantic, and also the Erythraean, are all one and the same Sea'. [1235]

When Alexander the Great's admiral Nearchus was sailing along the coast 300 stades from Carmania in the Erythraean Sea, he stopped at the island of Organa and moored at Oaracta. He was shown the tomb of the first chief of the territory whose name 'was Erythres, and hence came the name of the sea' [1236]

Herodotus also mentions that when Colaeus from Samos first sailed to Tartessus, on the Atlantic side of Spain, between 640–638 B.C. it was 'in those days a virgin port unfrequented by the merchants'. [1237] Knowledge of Tartessos and its silver is mentioned by the early sixth century B.C. Greek poet Stesichoros:

> Nearly opposite to famed Erytheia,
> In a hollow of the rock,
> Beside the boundless silver-rooted springs
> Of the river Tartessos. [1238]

Euthymenes of Massalia (Marseille) explored the coast of West Africa sometime during the late sixth century to mid-fifth century B.C. He reached as far as the River Senegal. [1239] Pseudo-Galen credits Euthymenes with the theory of the spring tides being connected when the earth, moon and sun is in alignment, while Aetios gives the credit to the astronomer and explorer in the fourth century B.C. Pytheas of Massalia. [1240]

The Phoenicians also had great skill as traders and sailors. Further south on the Mediterranean coast of Africa, Carthage was founded c. 814 B.C. by Phoenicians from Tyre [1241] and it grew into a great city. Herodotus shows Phoenician achievements in a story of the Pharaoh Necho II (609–593 B.C.) who ordered a flotilla of Phoenician ships from the Arabian Gulf to find the southern ocean. The Phoenicians circumnavigated Africa, passing the Pillars of Hercules into the Mediterranean and the journey had taken three years.

Barely nineteen years passed and power swiftly changed hands. In 574 B.C. King Nebuchadnezzar of Babylonia captured the city of Tyre, and subsequently the other coastal cities of Phoenicia. Carthage, now without its parent city and Phoenician control, [1242] became independent and quickly made an empire of its own and assuming leadership of the other Phoenician colonies in the West. They were now the main commercial rivals to the Greek city of Massalia (Marseille) in the Western Mediterranean as well as the Greek cities in Sicily and conflicts followed.

Phoenician Tablet

In 1844 by the sanctuary of the New Cathedral near to the quay in Massalia (Marseille) a workman repairing a wall of a nearby house discovered curious writing on a stone. This stone was found to be two large pieces of a tablet. The left piece was chipped along the lower half. Examination of a piece of the tablet with one from Carthage then in the Louvre museum showed the Massilia tablet made from the same type of rock found around Carthage. The writing in Phoenician contained instructions for sacrifice and the proper dues to be paid to a priest. Nathan Davis in Carthage discovered a similar tablet in 1858. [1243] The sacrificial tariffs referred to the Temple of Baal at Carthage. [1244]

How this tablet came to be at Massalia and under what conditions? One can speculate that the Phoenicians also came to Massalia and built a temple/shrine there? Perhaps the Greeks allowed a temple there for Phoenician merchant sailors to worship their own Gods? Greek religion was open to foreign gods and examples are given in fifth century Athens where another two gods were introduced i.e. Sabazius from Phrygia and Bendis from Thrace. [1245] Maybe it was a cargo in transport that never reached its destination or was it captured in one of the naval battles between Massalia and Carthage or piracy? An estimated date was given between fifth and fourth century B.C. [1246]

Also in Massalia a sixth century B.C. statue of the Asiatic goddess Cybele [1247] was found in les fouilles de la Place Villeneuve-Bargemon. Cybele was also worshipped in their mother-city of Phocaea. [1248]

However from all the foundation stories the immediate area of Massalia was empty when the Phocaean Greeks settled there. The nearest settlement was in the first quarter of the sixth century B.C. the Oppidum at Baou de Saint-Marcel on a plateau 167 metres du plateau de Beaumont-Saint-Julien and they penetrated the area up to 7 km from Massalia. Pottery fragments showed evidence of early commercial relations with Massalia sixth to fifth century B.C. The oppidum was abandoned due to recession leaving only a few people in the fourth century B.C. By 150 B.C. there was some renewal of defences in the traditional style mixed with that of Massalia i.e. stone blocks, until it was abandoned also in the second century B.C. [1249]

Later Carthage avoided coming under the Persian Empire because the Phoenicians, who were now the main part of the Persian Navy, refused Cambyses' order to sail against Carthage because 'they were bound to the Carthaginians by solemn oaths, and since besides it would be wicked in them to make war on their own children'. [1250] The Persians gave up plans to capture Carthage and continued conquering Egypt instead.

By mid-sixth century B.C. Carthage sent ships to occupy the island of Pityusa (Ibiza) and blocked the Greeks from travelling the North-West Mediterranean route to Atlantic Spain by sea. The Carthaginian Navy controlled much of the Western Mediterranean from North Africa to Iberia (Spain) and occupied the Straits of Gibraltar. Tartessos was destroyed c. 500 B.C. by the Carthaginians never to recover, which left the Massalia Greeks to control the Mediterranean coasts of Gaul (France) and the north-eastern Mediterranean part of Spain. [1251] Their knowledge of the furthest west may have begun to fade [1252] on an experiential everyday level but the Massaliote periplus must have kept some knowledge available for the next few centuries to those who read it though it may now be from a library private or public in Massalia and perhaps oral tradition?

Valuable Tin and Amber

According to Strabo the Carthaginians only let their own ships through the Pillars of Hercules (Gibraltar), and what they knew of the Atlantic they kept secret to protect their trade.[1253] Yet the Greeks knew by what the Carthaginians were selling that they had got the supply of the tin and amber trade. These were very valuable to Mediterranean cultures. Tin was the essential ingredient with copper that made bronze, and amber was made into jewellery. Where in the Atlantic did they come from? No Greek knew for sure as the world beyond the Mediterranean coast was a mystery and controlled by barbarian tribes. Herodotus recording what he knew of the extreme west of Europe wrote,

> nor do I not know of any islands called the Cassiterides (Tin Islands), whence the tin comes which we use... though I have taken vast pains, I have never been able to get an assurance from an eye-witness that there is any sea on the further side of Europe. Nevertheless, tin and amber do certainly come to us from the ends of the earth.[1254]

There were no maps beyond the Mediterranean to guide. There were only myths and also stories like *The Odyssey* written by Homer whose hero seemed to have sailed outside the Mediterranean Sea.[1255] If so, how did Homer know so much about the Atlantic? Regarding Homer's poem *The Odyssey*, ancient writers like Crates and Strabo had thought the poem contained geographic facts and that Homer was aware of tides 'Oceanus that floweth ever back upon himself'. Also the Charybdis 'thrice a day she spouts it forth, and thrice a day she sucks it down'. Strabo explains,

> For even if it be twice and not thrice—it may be that Homer really strayed from the fact on this point, or else that there is a corruption in the text—the principle of his assertion remains the same. And even the phrase "gently-flowing" contains a reference to the flood-tide.[1256]

Strabo locates the Charybdis and Sylla between the Straits of Messina despite Homer's description that the Straits were narrow enough for an arrow to be fired across.[1257] Gilbert Pillot also explored, quite literally, this Atlantic theory and Homer's geographical truths. Using Greek astronomy and their zodiac he attempted to calculate and follow the route. From Homer's description of the caves, 'polished' sheer rock, and position he suggested that the Whirlpool of Charybdis was the whirlpool of the Corryvreckan Passage in Scotland where 'thrice a day' three tides do cover a period of eighteen hours and twenty minutes corresponding to the 'long days' and short nights of the June Solstice and thereby verifying parts of Homer's description.[1258] Is it narrow enough for an arrow to be fired across as Homer mentions? Though Hyde's examination of various theories concluded that stories of earlier adventures in the Black Sea were transferred to the Greek exploration of the Western Mediterranean had 'much to recommend it'.[1259] Perhaps Homer was mentioning a memory that had survived from Mycenaean or earlier times? Strabo thought Homer 'rendered his fiction not implausible' particularly to the Atlantic as the scene for many of Odysseus's wanderings.[1260] This seems to be common knowledge amongst ordinary Greeks I talked to last summer in Greece whereas we have been only aware of the Straits of Messina.

From the sixth century B.C. around the Greek city of Massalia (Marseille) and the entire lands north, the Greeks called Keltike[1261] and the tribes Celts (Κελτοί, Keltoi).[1262] By the fourth century B.C. Pseudo-Skylax had listed the three greatest rivers of Europe as 'the Tanais [Don], the Istros [Danube], and the Rhodanos [Rhône]'.[1263] Beyond this nothing else was known for sure. Northern Europe was a very mysterious place.

Figure 92. Map of the known world in fourth century B.C. reconstructed from details in the fragments of the geography *Ges Peridos* by Hecataeus of Miletus. Some versions include the Tin Islands in the North Atlantic estimated somewhere off the European Atlantic coast.

Chapter 4

Pytheas of Massalia the Astronomer and Explorer

> Beyond Gadeira towards the western darkness
> There is no passage;
> Turn back the ships sail's again to the mainland of Europe,
> (Pindar, *Nemean,* IV. 68–71). [1264]

Among Greek ideas and philosophy was that the encircling ocean beyond the north of France must be frozen and lifeless. The Massaliotes began to doubt this by the knowledge they had gained from overland trade passing from one trader to another with goods from the Baltic Sea. Stefansson, the Polar Explorer, suggests that this 'may have been the moving cause that sent Pytheas north' [1265] to explore and know for sure. Though Strabo wrote that Pytheas of Massalia spoke about

'the Ocean coastlines in this area, using as a pretext his research into celestial phenomena and mathematics'. [1266]

Perhaps Pytheas was using the pretext as a cover story to hide another mission. Be that of trade or to combine the two. If it were only trade Pytheas would not have gone so far north as he did stopping when he found the origin of tin and amber? If you follow Stefansson's suggested anti-clockwise route around Britain Pytheas could have stopped instead of continuing to the Arctic.[1267] Because Pytheas would have found tin and amber before travelling further north. But in Cunliffe's suggested clockwise route north [1268] Pytheas would have discovered amber only on his way back. Aristotle tells us that Massalia was founded on commerce [1269] and Pausanias records that it was very prosperous. [1270] However curiosity was one thing that drove the Greeks to explore the world of ideas and also the physical world.

Pseudo-Scylax, fourth century B.C., recorded in his periplus, section 'Pillars of Herakles to Antion', that past the 'Pillars of Herakles in Europe are many trading-towns of the Karchedonioi (*Carthaginians*), and mud and flood-tides and shoals'. He also mentions the Hellenic city of Massalia and its colonies Emporion in Spain and Olbia and Antion (Antipolis, Antibes) in France. Massalia, Olbia and Antion have harbours.[1271]

There were several military conflicts between Carthage and the Greek cities in Sicily for control of the island. One that lasted between 338–318 B.C. could have left the Straits of Gibraltar unguarded, as Carthage [1272] needed its entire navy to fight elsewhere. Did Carthage block the Straits of Gibraltar to Greeks, as early on Phoenician and Greek settlements i.e. Sicily were located close to each other and lived in peace. But as Carthage expanded they took control of Phoenician settlements in Sicily and Sardinia.[1273] Possibly from this point healthy commercial rivalry changed as the Carthaginians assumed leadership of the Phoenician settlements in Spain? We do have evidence of many Phoenician settlements in Spain (Iberia) [1274] and though they may have at first lived in peace with the Greeks their presence was later possibly a deterrent either militarily or commercially in that they had established the lion's share of the business and trade so it was not possible for the Greeks to make any further journeys into the Atlantic via Gibraltar? Profits there were to be made but access to suppliers were taken by Carthaginian domination of the area and such a monopoly would certainly seem like 'blocking' or exclusion from the Straits to the Greeks albeit a commercial one and not military? The fact is we have references to Greeks in the Atlantic then an absence of it. Considering the adventurous nature of the Greeks, their curiosity, acumen and an overwhelming desire in trading what could account for an absence of journeys? Was it only that Carthage destroyed Tartessos c. 500 B.C. and the Phocaeans main contact of commerce gone? The treaty of 306 B.C. between Carthage and Rome and their allies' states the latter's western limit was agreed at Mastia. An earlier treaty 348 B.C. between Carthage and Rome also set the latter's limit at Mastia (Cartagena?).[1275] However with the entrance to the Atlantic now open 338-318 B.C. the Greeks at Massalia took their chance to find out where the tin and amber came from and try to secure a supply for themselves independent of Carthaginian traders.

When Rome took over Naples in 326 B.C. Campanian pottery ware begins to be found in Massalia. Rivet suggests that Massalia may have developed a trade route for tin and amber from the north-west around this time.[1276]

From all the people of Massalia, Pytheas was best qualified to be the explorer. He was a scientist and astronomer. He had already explored and studied 'the boiling sea'. This place was near the Aeolian Islands north of Sicily:

> These things Pytheas recounts in *Circuits of the Earth*, saying also that the sea boils. These are the names of the seven Aiolian Islands: Strongyle, Euonymos, Lipara, Hiera, Didyme, Erikode, Phoinikodes.[1277]

When the hot larva came up from the volcano it poured into the sea making the water 'boil'.

Massalia-First Measurement

Pytheas had gained a reputation for accuracy in fixing the latitude position of his city of Massalia for their ships. He could take measurements as he explored north and later someone could make a sailors guide (periplus). There was already a periplus from Massalia dating c. 500 B.C. describing the navigational route from Massalia to the tin region of Cape Finisterra N.W. Spain.[1278] A periplus (Greek *periplous*) was a navigation manual written in rhyme. Three Periploi have survived; the fourth century B.C. Periplus of Scylax on the Mediterranean shores; Periplus of Arrian-shores of the Black Sea (Euxine); Periplus of Erythraean Sea written around c. A.D. 89 covered the Red Sea, east coast of Africa up to Zanzibar. The Greeks loved didactic poetry and could use any subject from romance to geography in a rhyming meter[1279] All the great works of Hipparchus the mathematical astronomer are lost except one. In it he is pointing out some mistakes by the poem of Aratus on the universe.[1280] Aratus's poem was very popular and the most widely read in the ancient world after Homer's *The Iliad* and *The Odyssey*. 'Xenophanes, Parmenides and Empedocles wrote in verse' while the 'Milesians Anaximander and Anaximenes, the Ephesian Heraclitus and most of the later pre-Socratics chose prose as their medium'.[1281] Putting words into rhyme makes it much easier to remember long and maybe complicated subjects for others to use and follow later. Pytheas could have known some of the language of the surrounding Celts who lived in Massalia. Later Varro (first century B.C.) recorded that Massalia was a tri-lingual city that spoke Greek, Latin and Gallic (Celtic).[1282] Many different tribes of Celts occupied most of the lands north of Massalia.

Pytheas left Massalia (Marseille) during 320s B.C. [1283] on his voyage of discovery and he used a Gnomon (surveyor's staff) to take accurate measurements. The gnomon staffs were used in measuring, houses, city walls, buildings, and temples. Pytheas had held his staff upright on the ground on the longest day of the year at midday (summer solstice) to measure the staff's shadow from the light of the sun, [1284] having fixed the latitude for Massalia (43°N) he could take measurements along his journey using the gnomon, together with star positions. [1285]

The route he took may have been through the Pillars of Hercules (Gibraltar) [1286] or along the great rivers of Gaul (France) with local trading boats, changing several times until he reached the Atlantic Ocean via Bordeaux or Nantes. [1287] Perhaps he went by sea via Gibraltar first and returned by river to find more than one route in case the Carthaginian Navy came back and dominate the Straits of Gibraltar again (which they did).

Passing into the Atlantic, Pytheas would have seen a big difference in the many fish, as Strabo describes, with 'narwhales, whalebone whales, and spouting-whales; when these spout, the distant observer seems to see a cloud-like pillar. And further the conger-eels become monsters, far exceeding in size those of Our Sea'. [1288] They weighed more than eighty pounds and 'fat tunny-fish' gathered outside the Pillars feeding on acorns found on 'stunted oaks that grow at the bottom of the sea'. [1289] What with tides that could go out and return up to a fifteen metres high[1290] unlike the Mediterranean where tides are so small as to not be noticed, Pytheas had now entered a different world.

Pytheas discovered that Spain had a very long coastline sticking out into the Atlantic and gave 'the distance from Gadeira to the Sacred Promontory, [which Eratosthenes says] lies five days sail away'. The Sacred Promontory is identified as Cape St. Vincent. [1291] He realised that Spain stuck out into the Atlantic like a big square in shape. When at the top he could tell by the position of the stars, that they were almost the same as the stars over Massalia. Pytheas must be almost level with Massalia. Therefore Eratosthenes and his source Pytheas were able to work out that from the Mediterranean to the Atlantic,

'The northern sections of Iberia [Spain] offer easier passage [for those travelling] to Keltike [on foot] than those who sail over the Ocean'. [1292]

The distance is around 300 miles instead of the sea route of 1,700 miles. It is possible he got this information from other sailors but Pytheas said that after he returned from the north

'he traversed all the ocean-coast of Europe from Gaderia [Cadiz in Spain] as far as Tanais' [River Don in Russia]. [1293]

This would keep it as a part of the first journey. If it was Tanais could this refer to another separate journey? Tanais is the River Don in Russia and was thought by ancient Greeks to mark the furthest end of Europe and where Asia began. [1294] Roseman suggested that the reading should have been that he travelled 'from Gaderia to the limits of the cosmos', and it was a mistake by Timaeus or Polybius that wrote in Tanais [1295] as it could also be used metaphorically to mean a far off distant place. The phrase 'Limits of the cosmos' appears a few lines later in Strabo Book II. 4.1–2.

Also Lucan the Roman poet wrote in his book *Civil War*, 'where Tanais falls from the Riphaean heights and confers upon his banks the names of different worlds, and as the common boundary of Asia and Europe, divides the neighbouring parts of the middle of the earth'. [1296]

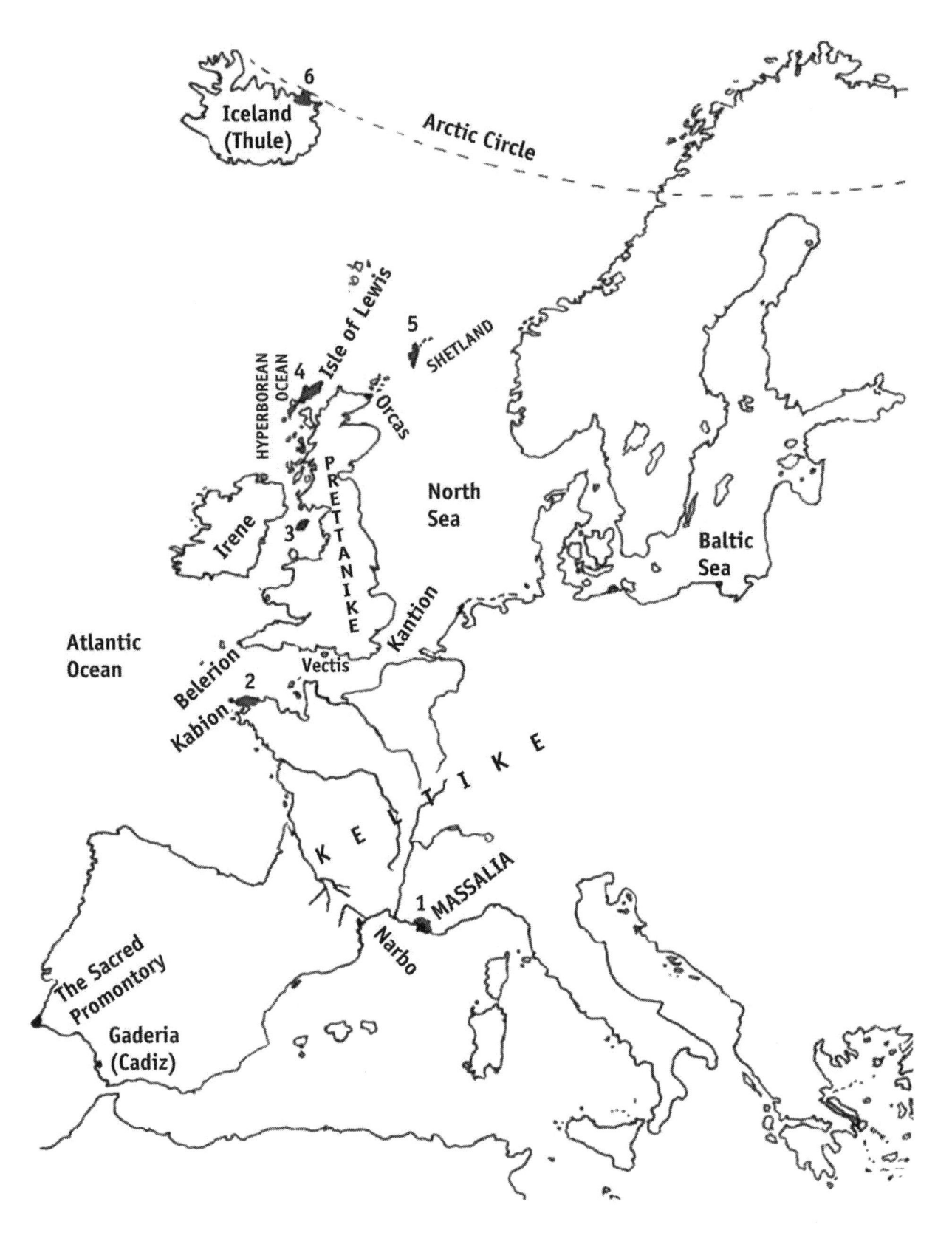

Figure 93. Pytheas of Massalia's voyage of discovery c. 320s B.C. Various routes are available, up the River Rhône, or Narbo along the river to Bordeaux on the Atlantic coast, or through the Straits of Gibraltar (The Pillars of Hercules) to where he took measurements and observations:

1 = Massalia (Marseille), 2 = Tregor, Brittany, 3 = Isle of Man, 4 = Isle of Lewis, 5 = Shetland, 6 = Thoule (Iceland).

The Tregor-Second Measurement

When Pytheas reached Brittany (Armorica) in North-West France he named the important passage for sailing around the south-western point. He called the promontories of the Oistimoi as Kabaion, which is thought to be the present day Pointe du Raz and the island of Sein.[1297] There were various promontories and islands and Pytheas says that three days voyage was the furthest Ouexisame (Ushant).[1298] Ouexisame (Ile d'Ouessant) is in a dangerous sea of reefs and storms. A Breton proverb is 'He who sees Belle-Ile sees an island; he who sees Groix sees joy; he who sees Ushant sees blood'.[1299] Pytheas describes the western edge of Europe as a 'Kyrtoma' (hump) 'not less than 3,000 stades long'.[1300] The 'Kyrtoma' was north of Iberia and part of Keltike. Somewhere between Baie de Morlaix and the Baie de St-Brieuc, he took his second measurement[1301] to see how far north he had travelled 9 cubits (48°N). The shadow cast from the sun shining on his surveyors staff was much longer the further north he was from Massalia.

One coin, a gold stater, was found here at Lampaul-Ploudalmezeau in North-West Finistere washed ashore in some deep-water seaweed.[1302] The coin was made in the Greek city of Cyrene (in Libya) 322-315 B.C.[1303] It would be amazing if Pytheas had dropped the coin, but we do not know. What we do know is that someone dropped the coin no earlier than 322 B.C., which is around the time when Pytheas made his voyage. Some Greek key patterns were also found here carved on stone stelae, which are from a century earlier.[1304] A silver drachma with a head of Artemis and on the reverse a lion, above it the name ΜΑΣΣΑΛΙΗΙΤΩΝ (MASSALITON) originating from Massalia second century B.C. was found at Chateau de Lesmel, Plouguerneau, north Finistere, Brittany by a farm worker; a bronze Sestos coin second century B.C. was found 'near edge of the sea' at Jard, Vendee;[1305] a coin hoard of twenty-five Massaliote obols found on Jersey, Channel Islands.[1306]

Local boats that knew their own area would sail between Britain and Brittany with Tin, and traders would exchange their tin for something else. Some ancient Greeks historians had thought that the Phoenicians had been before them in exploration. There are stories in Cornwall that the Phoenician traders came to Britain for tin and established the route but this may be from the later popular romantic ideas of the nineteenth century A.D.[1307] However, we do know that trading in tin was frequent between ancient Cornwall and the Western Mediterranean and evidence of a pre-A.D. 43 olive stone found at Silchester.[1308] Two bronze cauldrons were found in 1792 at Broadwater Luxulya, at the headwater of the Par River and thought by archaeologists C. F. C. Hawkes and M. A. Smith to be from the type found at Massalia c. 600 B.C. Cauldron number 1 in-bending of the rim may be of the type found as a late feature of Greek and Etruscan smiths from 650 B.C.[1309] but later Burgess stated that the British cauldrons 'comfortably' pre-date Continental examples.[1310]

Pre-Roman coins are found mostly in South England from the first three centuries B.C. as those found in Broadgate, Exeter, 1810.[1311] The first British coinage find were several cast bronze of the late second century B.C. Earliest found were at Thurrock in Essex 'Thurrock potins'. Metal detector finds show Kent as the main area of circulation with coins reaching as far as the Isle of Wight, East Anglia and Lincolnshire. The early British potin coins weigh 3–4 grains and the designs are copies of Massalia coins: head of Apollo facing left/reverse: butting bull facing right, above letters MA (for Massalia). During the first century these were replaced by flatter and lighter potin coins.[1312] One coin found in Studdal, Kent in 2009 dated to the second century B.C. is classified as a 'Celtic cast bronze coin of southern Gaul', obverse: head of laureate Apollo facing left/reverse: a butting bull facing right and letters above ΜΑΣΣΑΛ[Ι] for MASSAL[I] = Massalia, size 19 mm and possibly a prototype for British potin coins (cast bronze with a high tin content) see Figure 106, p. 555.[1313]

Celtic coin researcher David Holman has recorded among others two AE struck bronze coins from Massalia found in Kent, Britain. One is estimated to be between late third to early second century B.C. and found at Tilmanstone, obverse: head facing left/reverse: butting bull facing right, above Greek letters MA (worn coin possibly a Σ is faint?), diameter 15.8–18.2 mm (3.5–4.00 mm thick), weight 4.84 gm (worn), Die Axis 0°, CCI not yet, (another Massalia type found here CCI 05.0903). The other AE was found at Minster-in-Thanet, obverse: head facing left/reverse: bull facing right, above Greek letters MAΣ, exergual line below, off-centre, diameter 14.3-18.0 mm (4 mm thick), weight 4.7 gm (worn), Die Axis 180°, CCI 99.014.[1314] The heads though worn seem to be consistent with that of laureate Apollo see Figure 103 page 548. Van Arsdell reports that Massalia bronze coins were also found at Richborough and Canterbury, Kent.[1315]

Penhallurick mentions that there is a lack of coins in the south-west as the Dumnonii tribe insisted on barter and refused coins as late as third century A.D. However, a hoard of silver coins tetraobols was found in Paul, Penzance 1909. Celtic tribes from around the region of Milan and Ticino made them. The tetrabols were copies of Massaliote coins, obverse: the head of Artemis/reverse: a lion sometimes marked ΛΛΛΣΛΛ being a poor copy of MAΣΣA (Massa, short for Massalia). They were struck around 200 B.C. and in circulation for about 200 years.[1316] These are in The Royal Cornwall Museum in Truro, Britain.

Two Greek handled black glazed cups (bossae) together with a jug (oinochos)[1317] were found in an 'artificial cave at Teignmouth' and dated to fourth century B.C. Another find is a Greek anchor stock dredged up off Porth Felen at the tip of the Lyn peninsular in North Wales dated to late second or first century B.C.[1318]

Separate finds by a ploughman at Holne above the Dart near Buckfast revealed a worn silver coin of Alexander the Great and another of Aesillas, the Roman Quaestor in Macedonia in 90 B.C. In Exeter coins were found in 1931 from Velia (Hyele, Elea a Greek Phocaean colony) and Paestum. Archaeologist Aileen Fox writing in 1973 also mentions though the items are few there is a trickle of evidence, which needs consideration.[1319]

Would the Carthaginians, originally a Phoenician colony, have visited Britain? A Roman poem *Ora Maritima* was written by Avienus at the end of fourth century A.D. He used 11 different earlier sources[1320] mixed together that have Punic Himilco exploring the Atlantic for four months. Some parts are recognisably from Pytheas's descriptions of his own journey:[1321]

> The gulf Oestrymnian with its native folk;
> And widely scattered isles are stretched along,
> Rich with their lode of lead and metalled tin,
> Abundance is there here of proud-willed race
> Skilled and adroit, perpetually employed
> In trafficking on ships not built, but sewn,
> Cleaving the stormy strait afar, the surge
> Of monster-haunted Ocean. Not from pine
> Nor maple know these how to frame a keel,
> Nor yet from firwood do they curve a craft,
> But wondrous fit together skins and hides
> On which to cruise the vasty deep.
> (Avienus, *Ora Maritima*, lines 95–107)[1322]

Due to the condensing of several sources in the rest of the long poem including the Sargasso Sea and Canary Islands we are not sure what part of the voyage Himilco made around the sixth century B.C. but he may have visited as far as Spain or Brittany, and the Oestrymnid islands.[1323] Cunliffe deduces that Oestrymnis is a coastal region in Spain with Cape Finisterra as the high projecting headland. Overlooking the Bay of Corcubion and the Galician coast, the area is very rich in tin. Carpenter argues that Oestrymnis is known from Strabo's remarks [1324] on Pytheas in connection with Cape Kabion and from other sources to be North-West Brittany and the projecting headland as the Pointe du Raz. [1325] As to its location Avienus writes that from the gulf Oestrymnian it is two days to Ireland:

> Now from this place 'tis voyage of two suns
> Out to the "Holy Isle" (so named of yore).
> Wide on the water spreads this out its glebe
> Where folk Hiernan [Irish] dwell on it afar:
> There too, nearby, spreads out the Albions' isle [Britain].
> (Avienus, *Ora Maritima*, lines 108–112) [1326]

As the Carthaginians had access to the tin mines of North-West Spain it was not necessary for them to make a longer journey north. They could take advantage of well-established local traders (Oestrymnid) bringing the tin from Britain to Brittany and perhaps down to Spain: [1327]

> Tartessians to the Oestrymnid islands' bourn
> Once used to traffic. Folk from Carthage too
> Frequented once these waters, folk that dwelt
> And strove between the Pillars of Hercules
> (Avienus, *Ora Maritima*, lines 113–116) [1328]

However, it was different for Pytheas and the traders of Massalia. They had to know where the tin and amber came from itself in the hope of getting their own supply separate from the Carthaginians their rivals. [1329]

Chapter 5

Britain is Discovered and Named by Pytheas

From Brittany Pytheas sailed to Britain, which was thought of as one of the Kasserterides 'Tin Islands' where tin was found. In some later sources it was thought separate from the 'Tin Islands'.[1330] Kassiteros was the Greek word for Tin. Pytheas made his way to ancient Ictis. Ictis was described as an island just off the coast of Britain and connected to the mainland when the tide was low.[1331] When the tide rose Ictis became an island again, until the next tide. There was nothing like this in the Mediterranean. Ictis was the market place of the British tin trade.

Where Ictis was has been a mystery up till modern times. The tidal island of St. Michael's Mount in Cornwall was thought by some to be Ictis. Archaeologist Professor Barry Cunliffe considered Mount Batten in Devon's Plymouth Sound which 2,300 years ago might have had its joining strip to the land overlapped by waves at high-tide. He discovered there the remains of an ancient port-of-trade, evidence of objects and pottery from 900–100 B.C.[1332] including a trilobate arrowhead of Greco-Scythian type.[1333] Sixteen miles away archaeological divers in 1991 found an ancient shipwreck in Bigbury Bay with a cargo of knuckle size ingots of tin[1334] exactly the same shape as described by the ancient historian Diodorus Siculus.[1335]

In 1812 the 'St. Mances ingot' was dredged up at Carrick Roads, Falmouth. This ingot of tin was 72 kilograms (158 lbs.) and is known as an 'astragalus' in Greek. Though it is the shape of knuckle-bone some translators think that the Greek word Diodorus wrote 'ruthmon' does refers to the 'shape' and not the 'size' of tin ingots as in earlier translation by Oldfather.[1336] Gardiner suggests that the shape of the astragolos weighing approximately 80 kilograms would actually fit tied one to each side of a saddle on a packhorse and could carry a balanced total load of 160 kg.[1337]

At Ictis, a tidal island according to Diodorus Siculus, the ancient Britons would 'take the tin in large quantities over to the island on their wagons'.[1338] Pliny the Elder wrote that 'the island Ictis on which tin appears; the Britons sail to it in boats of hides sewn over with withies'.[1339]

The Needles are the last remnants of when the Isle of White was joined to the mainland at Dorset. This became an island due to rising sea levels, isostatic post-glacial rebound and erosion by the sea. Penhallurick examines the Isle of White named by Pytheas as Vectis Ούηκτίς as an area to find ancient Ictis because the name was similar. He also cites the Cormac's Glossary c. A.D. 900 as the name survives in Irish as Muir-n-Icht (Sea of Icht) for the English Channel.[1340] Though a causeway was 35.5 metres below low tide and suggested by geologist Reid to have submerged shortly before Caesar's invasion of Britain, Penhallurick thought rising sea levels had occurred much earlier.[1341] At the easternmost end was another island of Bembridge and Yaverland that only became joined to the Isle of Wight in Victorian times. Excavations by Time Team at Yaverland show evidence of a site from the Bronze Age to the Saxons in making bronze jewellery[1342] and therefore active at the time Pytheas named the island Vectis Ούηκτίς. Vectis could still fit in with Pliny's description of the Britons sailing to it there with tin, but does not with Diodorus who wrote they cross over in their wagons at low tide, unless there was still a causeway in the fourth century B.C. Could both versions be right in that there were several ports of trade i.e. Mount Batten, Ictis (St. Michael's Mount)/Vectis (Isle of Wight) or Yaverland?

Professor Cunliffe suggests Pliny's [1343] comment (using Timaeus as a source) that Ictis was 'six days inward from Britannia by boat' could have meant the continuing journey to an area between the rivers Loire and the Gironde or was added by error.[1344] Strabo mentions Corbilo an Emporion on the River Loire [1345] and the *Oxford Classical Dictionary* lists this as a place, which received tin from Britain in connection with the Veneti (a nation in Brittany with a large fleet).[1346] Whereas Diodorus's description was exact in that Ictis was joined to the mainland of Britain by a causeway that could be used at the ebb-tide.[1347]

Another route is suggested by Gardiner with boats carrying tin sailing eastwards then crossing over the shortest point to Normandy using the 180 metre high Cap de la Hague as a navigation point then along north-east coast of France to the River Seine then inwards until crossing overland by packhorse to the tributary of the River Sâone and down the River Rhône [1348] to Massalia. The historian Diodorus Siculus (writing between 60–30 B.C.) records that the journey from Belerion (Cornwall) across Gaul (France) to the Rhône estuary was 30 days.[1349]

Diodorus continues that the tin had already been made into ingots the size (or shape) of a knuckle-bone. This could then be melted down and mixed with copper to make the metal bronze. Between 5-15 per cent tin [1350] is added to make bronze. Bronze was very valuable and it was made into axes, knives, swords, armour, bridles for horses, statues, temple equipment, brooches, jewellery ornaments and coins. For 2,000 years bronze was the strongest metal and that period was called the Bronze Age until iron was discovered and eventually became known as the Iron Age.

Archaeologist Neil Oliver took part in a metal working demonstration using 90 per cent copper and 10 per cent tin to make a bronze sword poured the melted and molten liquid mixture into a rectangular mould. The mould was in two halves clamped together top and bottom and formed a block. The technique was that you could not release the sword from the mould too early otherwise it would snap. Nor could it be left too long otherwise it would stick to the mould. The top of the mould around the sword handle was detachable from the rest of the mould. Taking hold of the detachable section around the handle is quite a moment to have got the timing right as the smith drew the sword slowly upwards and out of the mould all in one piece only needing sharpening and a handle stock to finish. The visual effect was that it seemed like the sword was being drawn from a stone. Perhaps this is the basis for the 'sword in the stone' in the legend of King Arthur? A lingering memory from the different technique of making swords in the Bronze Age in contrast to the Iron Age where heated iron was beaten into the shape of a sword taking much time and work instead of just heated and poured? Tales of such a process would have seemed like magic in the Iron Age?[1351]

That the Britons made bronze themselves is evident from the many bronze objects found in graves. Tin was available to them from Cornwall and Devon and copper from the mines at Great Orme in Wales.[1352]

Pytheas Gives Britain its Name

Pytheas named the promontory of South-West Britain 'Belerion'. This is identified as the Penwith Peninsula of Land's End.[1353] Rivet says Land's End and mentions Diodorus has it as the Penwith Peninsula. Ptolemy also added on his map an alternative name of Antivestaeum as well Belerium. Belerion is older and the British native name.[1354] The best etymology suggests Belerion associated 'with the divine names Belenos, Belinos, which can be equated with Apollo', or with Antivestaeum associated with beacon'.[1355] Pytheas would have stayed in Cornwall to learn how the people found the tin in the mines, and how they extracted the tin from the rock. He would probably have noted the process in his book *On the Ocean* as part of his observations and discoveries but unfortunately this part has not survived. The small information we have from Pytheas was in the writings of Timaeus and a little from Diodorus.[1356] Buckley points out that the skills needed to produce pure tin metal are not easily acquired. 'Dressing the tin-bearing sand to produce black tin concentrate was a highly skilled operation'. This also needs accurate construction of furnaces and the ability to raise the temperature to 1,000 degrees centigrade.[1357]

In this unknown land Pytheas learned that the people were called *Pretani* [1358] and so he named the whole island *Prettanike* Πρεττανική after them. The use of the initial letter P to B seemed interchangeable for the next few centuries and the earliest written evidence after Pytheas of Massalia comes from the Greek historian Polybius τῶν Βρεταννικαὶ νῆσοι *Bretannic Islands*.[1359] Over 260 years later after Pytheas's discoveries the ancient Greek historian Diodorus Siculus writes the next earliest surviving description of Britain but he does not give Pytheas a reference. He uses Pytheas's word *Prettanike* to call Britain.[1360] The earliest reference in Latin literature is by the Roman poets Lucretius 94–55 B.C. who writes *Brittanni*, and Catullus 84–54 B.C. who records it as *Britannia* and *Britanni* [1361] possibly getting this spelling from Polybius. When the Romans invaded Britain 55 and 54 B.C. Julius Caesar recorded the name in his book *Gallic Wars* as *Britannia* [1362] and the people *Britanni*.[1363] Pytheas was the first person to give the name of Britain and measure its land mass and coast: record the name of the people, their lives and how they lived in this mysterious island of megaliths and stone circles. This is our earliest glimpse from literary evidence 265 years before the Romans invaded.

The *Pretani* is thought to mean 'painted ones', 'figured folk' or 'tattooed ones' due to their use of blue coloured patterns, and also tattoos to decorate their bodies. We are not sure what these people actually called themselves. Possibly *Pretani*, *Pritani* or *Priteni* was what the Celtic people called them [1364] or perhaps as a nickname? In Welsh and Gaelic this remained as *Prydain* (Britain) or the older form *Prydein*.[1365] Though the Romans used the letter B for *Britanni* they still used the letter P for *Priteni* (the Picts) to call the people living beyond the Antonine Wall [1366] that separated North Britain from the rest of the island before finally setting the Roman frontier further back at Hadrian's Wall.[1367] The Irish used the oldest form of Celtic, pronounced Qu instead of P, and *Quriteni* as the name of the Britons.[1368] Though the spelling looks different there is a similarity in the sound of the names *Prydein*, *Prydyn*, *Pretani* and *Quriteni*.

Pytheas may have picked up the name in Brittany (Amorica) when they described the people in the island opposite them with the name of the original race *Pretani* and not the Celtic invaders. The *Pretani* had a different name for the whole island and called it Albion. Albion stayed the native name as well as 'Prettanike' which eventually took over as the main name for the British Isles. Pliny the Elder recorded,

"'Albion' was its own name when all [the islands] were called "the Britannias;"'

Albion ipsi nomen fuit, cum Britanniae vocarentur omnes de quibus mox paulo dicemus.[1369]

Seventy years after Pliny the Elder, Ptolemy published his eight volumes of *Geography* including a map of Britain c. A.D. 140–150 using earlier sources.[1370] He shows the sea called Prettanic Ocean ΩΚΕΑΝΟΣ ΠΡΕΤΤΑΝΙΚΟΣ between France and Britain but he names Britain as Albion ΑΛΟΥΙΩΝ while in his *Almagest* Ptolemy calls Britain Μεγάλη Βρεττανία (Great Britain).[1371]

According to Watson Albion remains the name of Scotland in the Gaelic language.[1372] The name Albion is still used in England and you can find it in the name of some pubs and also English football teams e.g. 'West Bromwich Albion' and 'Brighton & Hove Albion' and in many other English organisations.

Isle of Man–Third Measurement

Despite criticism by Polybius to Pytheas's statement that he had 'travelled over the whole of Britain that was accessible'[1373] Eratosthenes decided to trust in the reports that Pytheas covered 'such distances by ship and foot' particularly 'Brettanike and areas close to Gadeira and Iberia'.[1374] Cunliffe deduces that Pytheas was also interested in anthropology as well as geography[1375] as this makes a whole picture of exploration. He took many journeys inland exploring the country and taking measurements wherever he went.[1376]

After learning all he could about the origin of tin and how it was extracted from the rock, Cunliffe suggests Pytheas sailed up the coast past Wales to the Isle of Man[1377] (Monapia or Mona)[1378] where he took his third measurement of 6 cubits (54°14'N).[1379] Later Caesar used the name Mona and this was thought to have meant Isle of Man but by Pliny's time it is called Monapia and Mona was the Isle of Anglesey.[1380]

On Ptolemy's Map (A.D. 140–150) there is a distinction between both islands as the Isle of Man is called Monaoeda (Μονάοιδα) whereas Anglesey is called Mona (Μόνα νῆσος = Mona Insula).[1381]

IRELAND

We do not know if Pytheas visited Ireland (Irene) but he may have learned something of the country from Irish sailors he could have met in western ports for we have the names in Avienus's poem *Ora Maritima* as 'Holy Isle' where 'folk Hiernan dwell',[1382] Julius Caesar on invading Britain knew the location, distance to, and size of Ireland[1383] even though the Romans had never been there. Caesar wrote that he got the information from 'some writers'.[1384] Only one explorer had been so far north right down to the time of Julius Caesar and that as several writers had acknowledged was Pytheas of Massalia.

When Tacitus A.D. 56–115 wrote the book *Agricola*, Ireland was thought as being between Britannia and Spain.[1385]

Marcianus c. A.D. 400 writing 300 years later after Ptolemy records,

> The Prettanic island of Ivernia (Ireland) is bounded on the north by the Ocean which is called *Hyperboreus*; . . . on the east by that called *Ivernicus* . . . on the west by the Western' . . . and on the south by the Ocean called *Veguius* (. . . *Vergivius*).[1386]

SCOTLAND

This region was called Caledonia by the Romans [1387] after the leading tribe there, then lands of the Picts as we do not know what the Picts called their land at this time (may have still been Albion?) or themselves,[1388] and much later amalgamating with the Scots to become Scotland.

Marcianus continues,

> The Prettanic island of Albion is bounded on the north by the Ocean called *Duecolidonius* . . . on the east by the *Oceanus Germanicus* . . . on the west by the *Oceanus Ivernicus* . . . beyond which is the island Ivernia, but also the *Oceanus Vergivius* . . . and on the south the *Oceanus Prettanicus* and the aforementioned regions and people of Gaul.[1389]

Pytheas describes Britain as triangular in shape. Hipparchus kept the shape of Britain as an 'obtuse-angled triangle' and therefore triangular as Pytheas described it.[1390] But the later Ptolemy's map has Scotland going off at a right angle instead of straight up. Ptolemy it seems in regard to Britain 'makes no mention of the use of triangulation in relating one place to others; where astronomical observation is lacking what are to be used are distance and bearing'.[1391] Rivet and Smith's adjustments to Ptolemy's map, which has Cape Wrath ('turning point')[1392] missing, aligning Scotland from east to west back to its correct position of south to north using the mouth of the Ituna (Eden) as the pivot, identifies Dumna (ΔOYMNA) as the Isle of Lewis or the Long Island.[1393]

Isle of Lewis–Fourth Measurement

From the Isle of Man Pytheas continued up to the Isle of Lewis in Scotland in the Hyperborean Ocean [1394] where he took his fourth measurement 4 cubits (58°N).[1395] We have stories from an ancient historian Diodorus Siculus between 60–30 B.C. in his book called *Library* (originally 40 volumes). In the fragments that survive (Book II, 47) he writes about a land called Hyperborea (beyond the north wind) the birthplace of Leto the mother of Apollo, and its people called the Hyperboreans who had a Spherical Temple of Apollo; a festival every 19 years in Apollo's honour when 'the god descends to the island'; and where the people 'are most kindly disposed towards Greeks especially the Athenians and Delians inheriting this friendship from ancient times'.

The 'myths' also recount that certain of the Greeks the Athenians and Delians visited the Hyperboreans, 'where they left costly votive offering inscribed in Greek characters', and 'that, reciprocally, Abaris the Hyperborean once travelled to Greece to renew the friendship existing between the two peoples'. The 'islander's city is also dedicated to Apollo . . . Most of its inhabitants are cithara players' and sang daily in the temple with citharas. 'The moon appears to be but a short distance away from the earth and, like the earth, to have certain visible prominences upon it'.[1396]

Strabo records that except at Abydos Osiris it was usual for temples to have singers, pipe players, and cithara players 'in rites celebrated in honour of the other gods'.[1397]

Diodorus used as his sources Hecataeus of Abdera (who wrote in the fourth century B.C.) 'and certain others'.[1398] Hecataeus wrote a book called 'Concerning the Hyperboreans', which describes:

1. An extraordinary voyage
2. An island no smaller than Sicily (and had a triangular shape)
3. The island was situated beyond Transalpine Gaul in the ocean.

Hecateus of Abdera lived c. 315–285 B.C. and may have based the story on Pytheas's own account of his voyage of discovery that had reached Athens and was spread to the Hellenistic world at that time.[1399] Aelian mention swans, birds sacred to Apollo, appearing in a ceremony at the precinct, which may have a basis in reality as Whooper Swans do migrate from Iceland to their southern limit that includes the Butt of Lewis or North Cape of Dumna.[1400]

To some in the ancient world Hyperborea ('Hyper' beyond, 'Borea' the north wind) was thought of as a mythical land far north of Greece and above Scythia[1401] beyond the Rhipean Mountains (Alps).

Diodorus Siculus reports the account that 'At the time of this appearance of the god he both plays on the cithara and dances continuously the night through from the vernal equinox until the rising of the Pleiades'.[1402]

From the Spring Equinox 21 March to the 1 May (Beltane, when the rising Pleiades could be seen at dawn), the moon seems to skim the horizon.[1403] The moon skimming along the horizon effect is known as a 'lunar standstill'. This effect occurs around latitudes of 58° degrees in the Northern Hemisphere and the Isle of Lewis.[1404] Diodorus refers to the Hyperborean festival held every 19 years when 'the god descends to the island'.[1405] This is a poetic way of recording the cycle (18.61 years) governing the movement of the moon in these regions of the north. The Greeks called this cycle 'the year of Meton' after the fifth century B.C. astronomer Meton who noted that every nineteen years the moon occurs again on the same calendar date.[1406]

There is on the Isle of Lewis (58°N) a large and well preserved stone circle, similar to the Celtic cross pattern. The Callanish Stone Circle dates back to 2,800 years B.C. One of its cardinal points is aligned with the dawn rising of the Pleiades (the Seven Sisters).[1407] Could this have been the spherical 'temple' Diodorus described and perhaps the one Pytheas saw on this island, as it was there when he was?

An interesting observation on the Callanish Circle appears on the Pretanic World website:

> Every 18.61 years a major lunar standstill occurs and the circle is in alignment with the effect. The moon appears to pass within the stones at this time. If a person stands on a rocky hillock at the higher south end of the site, the moon is dramatically "reborn" with a person silhouetted within it. The standing stones are 13 feet high and cover 3 square miles . . . Local folklore says that on midsummer's morning "the shining one" (the god 'Lugh') walks between the stones.[1408]

When Diodorus Siculus mentions that, 'Hecataeus and others' write of an 'island no smaller than Sicily'[1409] do they mean Britain? Where they add the location 'in the regions beyond the Celts' if they mean only Gaul, the island is Britain. However, if Britain has a Celtic population 'the regions beyond the land of the Celts' for the Hyperboreans is further north and west? 'The Hyperboreans have a language, we are informed which is peculiar to them' in difference to who? Presumably the Celts as they had already occupied most of Britain and the west coast of Ireland at the time Pytheas of Massalia explored Britain in the fourth century B.C.

Diodorus continues,

> And the island is both fertile and productive of every crop, and since it has an unusually temperate climate it produces two harvest each year . . . Leto [mother of Apollo and Artemis] was born on this island . . . And there is also on the island both a magnificent sacred precinct of Apollo and a notable temple which is adorned with many votive offerings and is spherical in shape. Furthermore, a city is there which is sacred to this god, and the majority of its inhabitants are players on the cithara; and these continually play on this instrument in the temple and sing hymns of praise to the god, glorifying his deeds . . . And the kings of this city and supervisors of the sacred precinct are called Boreadae . . . the succession to these positions is always kept in their family.[1410]

By the map made by Ptolemy A.D. 140–150 he places the *Ocean Hyperboreus* in the north-west between Wales and the Isle of Lewis and the Hebridean Islands.[1411] Considering Avienus's poem *Ora Maritima* lines 130–136 it could be that the Hyperboreans are part of the descendants of the Neolithic population that built Britain's stone circles, wood henges, Ness of Brodgar, Stonehenge, Silbury Hill, Avebury, Shap, New Grange in Ireland and constructed many other monoliths.

In Ptolemy's map perhaps due to development and occupation by the Romans we can still see the names given by Pytheas of Massalia that of the promontories Belerion (ΒΟΛΕΡΙΟΝ) Orca (ΟΡΚΑΣ ΑΚΡΑ) and Kantium (KANTION AKPON) and with Roman alternatives Antivestaeum, Tarvedum, and Cantium respectively.[1412] KANTION (Kantion) may have come from a native name or possibly a description meaning 'corner land, land on the edge' and became used for all of Kent.[1413] The name also survives today in Canterbury the capital of Kent. The ocean surrounding Britain may have been called the Ocean Hyperboreus or as parts of it were renamed a memory of the name was kept in the North West? But if the oceans had different names at the time of Pytheas's exploration then where Ptolemy had placed the Ocean Hyperboreus in the north-west was correct. Though the Isle of Lewis is smaller than Sicily the astronomical description is in its favour. From Cornwall to the end of the Channel is the Prettanic Ocean, then the Germanic Ocean.[1414]

Hyperborean Ocean

Marcianus c. A.D. 400 writing 300 years later after Ptolemy records the Hyperborean Ocean still on the north side of the Irish coast but on the west side of Albion it is replaced by the Ivernian [Irish] Ocean. Where the Hyperborean and Ivernian Oceans meet he does not say but it could still include the Isle of Lewis and surrounding islands. Marcianus writes 'the *Prettanic* island of *Ivernia* is bounded on the north by the Ocean *Hyperboreus* . . . on the east by that called *Ivernicus* . . . on the west by the Western; and on the south by the Ocean called *Veguius*'. While 'the Prettanic island of Albion is bounded on the north by the Ocean called *Duecolidonius* . . . on the east by the *Oceanus Germanicus* . . . on the west by the *Oceanus Ivernicus*, beyond which is the island *Ivernia*, but also the *Oceanus Vergivius* . . . on the south the *Oceanus Prettanicus* and the aforementioned regions and people of Gaul'.[1415]

We can see how some names survive while others begin to shrink in area or get replaced like Herculis Promontorium later became Hartland Point in Devon.[1416]

Taking Diodorus's description literally this suggests just one island but this does not suggest an absence of smaller islands nearby.

Regarding the 'Notable temple' that was 'Spherical in shape'

Alternatively this description could mean Pytheas had taken his gnomon reading on the Isle of Lewis but that Britain was the 'island no smaller than Sicily' and that the spherical temple may have been Stonehenge and the lost city of Apollo at Vespasian's Camp/King's Barrow Ridge nearby as suggested by archaeologist Dennis Price.[1417] There may be other stone circles now no longer in existence e.g. Shap in Cumbria was of a vast size.[1418] Who knows what still may remain buried in our wonderful and mysterious land? Another possible henge has been discovered at Hollingbourne within a handful of Neolithic sites in South-East England that includes the Isle of Thanet and Ringlemere.[1419] Perhaps the 'notable temple' Diodorus mentions may have been made of wood like Durrington Walls wood henge? Jenks claims to have found a faint outline of a Cithara Player on the surface of a large rock at the western end of the Preseli Hills, Wales; where the blue stones for Stonehenge are thought to have been quarried. This is highlighted on his book cover.[1420] The original outer ring of Blue Stones at Stonehenge revealed burials dating from 3,000 to 2,800 B.C. and therefore an earlier construction than previously thought. Strontium isotope tests on animal bones found at Durrington Walls near Stonehenge revealed animals brought from all over Britain including the Orkneys for feasting of around 4,000 people at mid-winter.[1421] The recent 3-D laser scan of the Stonehenge sarsen stones for English Heritage revealed carvings of axeheads and daggers in the style between 1750-1500 B.C. The team confirmed the stones astrological alignment.

Dennis Price suggested that Pytheas in undertaking such an enterprise into the unknown would most likely have consulted an oracle and with Massalia's connection to Apollo at Delphi i.e. their treasury at Delphi.[1422] In consideration one could add the regular links from a colony to the Archegates (Divine Leader) kept up by their Sacred Envoys (Theoroi)[1423] it is a feasible theory. The naming of the promontory may have had religious thanks for reaching *Prettanike* (Britain) safely by first naming the promontory Belerion with its etymological connection as a divine name which can be equated to Apollo.[1424] Though Rivet and Smith thinks Belerion is a native British name.[1425] Therefore Pytheas would have recorded an existing name though a coincidence being equated with Apollo, which may have been interpreted as a fortuitous omen.[1426]

Orcas

Pytheas sailed on to the top of Britain and named it 'Orkas'.[1427] This comes from Diodorus Siculus probably using Timaeus as a source;[1428] Pytheas reported seeing great tidal surges up to 35 metres in height. Pliny the Elder writes,

'Pytheas of Massalia is the authority [that] above Britannia, tidal waters swell to a height of 80 cubits'.[1429]

Octogenis cubitis supra Britannium intumescere aestus Pytheas Massiliensis auctor est.

At Pentland Firth this actually happens in the restricted seas. In A.D. 1862 a tidal surge was reported passing over cliffs nearly seventy metres high on the island of Stroma. There was nothing like this in the Mediterranean. Aetios writing on what causes high and low tides says Pytheas formed the theory that tides were affected by phases of the moon. Pytheas may have been referring in particular to the spring tides when two planets, the sun and moon, are in line with the earth.[1430]

Diodorus Siculus wrote that Britain 'was thickly populated and extremely cold'.[1431] They built houses of timber and reeds, and used chariots in war. Their harvesting method was to cut off the heads of grain[1432] and store them in roofed buildings, selecting only the ripe heads and grind them for food. By leaving the stalks this provided ample grazing for cattle, then sheep would eat the remaining shorter stalks, leaving the pigs turning over the ground to eat what was left. All these animals would leave their manure to enrich the soil for the next year's crop.[1433]

Diodorus continues that Britain 'we are told, is inhabited by tribes which are autochthonous', modest and simple in contrast to shrewd and corrupt people found in other lands. Many kings and aristocrats, who mainly lived at peace with each other, ruled them. The cold climate to a person from the warm Mediterranean may have been felt more bitter then it was and 'Extremely cold'. Whereas to the natives the cold was quite tolerable as they were used to it: for it to be 'thickly populated': and the land fertile with enough food to feed the population.[1434]

Strabo[1435] reports that Pytheas described that the 'people near the 'chilly zone' were 'nourished by millet' (a similar type of weed was used then)[1436] 'and other herbs, fruit and roots. Among those who have a little grain and honey even the resulting drink holds high regard'. Types of beer like this was used among the Celts 'the wheat beer prepared with honey' called corma and 'drunk by the poorer classes' in Gaul.[1437] Referring to this 'beverage' of the Gauls, it was made from 'barley'[1438] and 'mead', 'what is called beer'.[1439]

There are many ancient writers who discuss the differences between wine and the barbarian's beer and mead. Aristotle declares 'that men who have been intoxicated with wine fall face foremost, whereas they who have drunk barley beer lie outstretched on their backs; for wine makes one top-heavy, but beer stupefies'.[1440] Though it seems Pytheas is talking of the north of Scotland the 'resulting drink' may be one that was made by the original non-Celtic people the Picts. Back home in Massalia they had a law that 'made women to drink only water', as only men drank wine. 'In Miletus, also, Theophrastus says that this is customary even today. Among the Rhodians neither a slave nor free-born woman could drink wine, neither could the young men of the free class up to thirty years of age'.[1441]

Pytheas continued describing that the *Pretani* threshed their grain not in the open air like they did in hot countries of the Mediterranean but in 'large houses' to protect the grain 'from lack of sun and the rain storms'.[1442] It seems clear in Strabo's quote that Pytheas describes two distinct areas 'people near the chilly zone' and Thoule.[1443] Though we have no evidence of Bee-keeping in ancient Iceland for honey or mead, recently hives have been established there, as the Gulf Stream is condusive but it is mainly wind and rain that are problematic for bees.[1444]

In the poem *Ora Maritima*, Avienus the Roman poet refers to a time when the Celts had already invaded Britain and he calls the pre-Celtic population of Europe generally as Ligurians. As Pytheas was the only one to have explored Britain until the time of Roman Agricola's wars in the North, Avienus is not referring to the conflict between the Celts of Britain and Romans but of a period before when the Celts invaded and fought the 'Ligurians' a general name to cover the native British non-Celtic populations from the Neolithic onwards: [1445]

> . . . From isles Oestrymnic, anyone should dare
> To drive his pinnace northward through the sea
> To where 'neath polar stars the heavens freeze,
> He'd come to land Ligurian, of dwellers void.
> Through Celtic violence and constant fights
> The fields have long stood empty. Thus expelled,
> (As others oft have fared) Ligurians moved
> To that far land which they now do possess
> Mid thorny thickets. . . .
> (Avienus, *Ora Maritma*, lines 130–136) [1446]

The Neolithic Britons had built the recently discovered Ness of Brodgar temple complex site on the Orkneys 5,000 years ago, [1447] Stonehenge, wood henges and stone circles. [1448] From the invasion by the Celts, the descendants of the Neolithic Britons retreated to the more harsh uplands of Scotland and held on there for several generations. In Ireland they went westwards into the interior of the land leaving the eastern seaboard to the Celts.[1449]

A genetic study by University College London of over 2,000 men showed ¾ of 'men tested in the south of England had the same Y-chromosome as early Britons and Celts'. This chromosome in males is not changed by intermarriage. Between 50% and 75% of men tested showed they were 'directly descended from early Britons'. The study showed the same proportion in Scotland while in the islands of Scotland and Ireland the trend was reversed from the eighth century A.D. with the majority of the population from Scandinavian descent, while in Wales it was just 10%. [1450] Therefore the population in the south may have been ruled but not supplanted by the Anglo-Saxons (from the mid-fourth century A.D.) even though their language eventually predominated. While many Britons moved to Brittany many more stayed in Briton adopting Anglo-Saxon language in England whereas the western areas i.e. Cornwall, Wales and in Scotland keeping their own Brythonic, Gaelic language. (See endnote 2368 for Brythonic survival around the Isle of Ely). By contrast the Norman conquest of England A.D. 1066, though a small ruling elite, 10,000 Norman French words were added, (of which 7,000 survived to the present) [1451] but did not replace the majority spoken language of Anglo-Saxon England.

Carpenter reckoned that Pytheas's journeys by sea were over 7,000 miles [1452] a remarkable fete. Back home news of what he saw on his voyage would be hard to believe. Yet where he journeyed next to the frozen Congealed Sea was going to make others, except for astronomers and scientists, dismiss his book as fantasy. Peoples' imagination was stretched too far and caused controversy over many centuries. What he described seemed unbelievable a place where there was no night only daylight. Yet the claim by Pytheas that he travelled to the 'limits of the cosmos' have since been proved true.

Chapter 6

Shetland Islands to the Frozen Sea

Shetland Islands-Fifth Measurement

Pytheas sailed on until he reached the Shetland Islands where he took his fifth measurement. Here the sun's shadow at the winter solstice was less than 3 cubits high (61°N). [1453] Professor Cunliffe perceives that the extreme north of Shetland Islands correspond within this measurement. He also suggests that Pytheas had either written down what the native Shetland sailors had experienced or that he went himself to the island of Thoule. [1454] Pytheas would have heard from the local sailors here that there was an island; he wrote as Thoule (Thule), which was six days sailing north of Britain [1455] and one extra day's sailing the frozen 'Congealed Sea' began. [1456]

Some scholars are hesitant to say Pytheas went beyond the Shetland Islands. But the ancient Greek astronomer Geminos of Rhodes in A.D. 50 quoted from Pytheas's book *On the Ocean*:

> VI.9. And it seems that Pytheas of Massalia reached these places. At any rate, he says in his treatise *On the Ocean* that "the barbarians showed us where the Sun goes to sleep; for around these places it happens that night becomes very short, 2 hours for some, 3 for others, so that, a little while after setting, the Sun rises straightaway." [1457]

Cunliffe wonders if Geminos is quoting the whole piece from Pytheas or just the one line about the barbarians and then adding his own explanation. Geminos, a thorough astronomer, follows this piece that further north a 24-hour day will occur and that at the pole there would be alternating six months of continued darkness and then daylight. [1458] Is Geminos making his own calculations in VI.9 or taking this from Pytheas as we remember that when Julius Caesar invaded Britain one of the things he had expected at the 'winter solstice' was thirty days of 'continual darkness' and had tried to test this by water clocks and inquiries. [1459] Caesar must have got this from Pytheas who had included the island of Thoule at 'the very last regions' and 'the limits of the cosmos', as the most northern part of all the islands of the Prettans (see Chapter 14). The expectation of thirty continual days of light at the summer solstice was put to the test on reaching Britain as one of the Prettanic islands without realising just how much further north this effect would occur. [1460] Such was the distance Pytheas had included within the 'islands of the Prettans'. Evans and Berggren's above-mentioned translation of Geminos have the whole three lines in quotation marks from Pytheas.

The ancient geographer Strabo [1461] quoting Polybius wrote that Pytheas in

> ... describing matters concerning Thoule and those places "in which neither was earth in existence [ὑπῆρχεν] by itself nor yet sea nor vapour, but instead a sort of mixture of these similar to a marine lung in which," he says, "the earth and sea and all things together are suspended [αἰωρεῖσθαι], and this [mixture] is as if it were a fetter of the whole existing in a form [ὑπάρχοντα] impassable by foot or ship". The thing like a lung he himself had seen, but other things he told from hearsay. [1462]

When Strabo reports of 'other things he told from hearsay' this may well be so and that as we are dealing with only a fragment of Pytheas's book *On the Ocean* these 'other things' maybe in the part of the book that is still lost and could refer to other details. What we can be sure of is the definite comment 'The thing like a lung he himself had seen' and also the associated icy conditions. [1463]

In the icy sea there is little movement, a slow rise and fall like the movement of a jellyfish (Marine Lung) or the rib-cage of a human. [1464] So slow it seems suspended αἰωρεῖσθαι [1465] just like pancake or pack ice, a slush that you find before solid ice and could also be surrounded in fog. Pytheas used the similar movement of a Marine Lung (πλεύμονι θαλαττίῳ) to describe the slow motion of the frozen (πεπηγυίας) sea and this 'he himself had seen'. [1466]

Pytheas having travelled so far, with a chance to see the opposite to the 'boiling sea' which he had studied and recorded, [1467] it would be hard to believe that he did not take the opportunity to go to the frozen Congealed Sea to verify and examine it. Just seven days journey to the edge of the inhabitable world. But for a brief mention of legendary Odysseus[1468] and more materially Greeks that 'frequented' the seas of the Atlantic [1469] who else from Pytheas's world would have been so far north before and took measurements? (See Table 1, Chapter 11, section Latitude, p. 223).

The Island of Thule

Later the Greeks and Romans called the end of the inhabitable world Ultima Thule [1470] and beyond this the climate was too cold for humans to live and grow food. Pomponius Mela a first century A.D. Roman geographical writer had not seen Thule. From what he heard he described Thule as 'the isle opposite to the Belgian shoreline'. More revealing is that

> Here the rising and setting of the sun are so distant that night is foreshortened. But the winter is as dark as the summer is light. The south light becomes obscure, and it radiates only a lucidity that seems a reflection. During the summer solstice, there appears to be no real night: the sun refulgence in its high orbit. [1471]

This detail places Thoule (Thule) much further north than the 'Belgium shoreline'. Orosius A.D. 415 describing *Britannia* and the *Orcades* states the island of *Thyle* 'is separated from the rest by an infinite distance, lying in the middle of the ocean towards the west-north-west'. [1472] Even today some are not sure where Thoule was. Roseman is hesitant regarding Bede's contexts but Cunliffe is definite that by the eighth century A.D. the Venerable Bede 'believed Thule to be Iceland'. [1473] By the ninth century A.D. Dicuil, an astronomer and geographer, wrote about the Christian monks he had spoken to that had stayed in Thule during A.D. 795. They 'always had alternate day and night after the solstice; but they found that one day's sail from it towards the north the sea was frozen.' [1474]

Roseman thinks Dicuil's identifies Thule as Iceland and his 'description of the summer solstice period in Iceland sounds very much like Pytheas's description'.[1475]

Dicuil an Irish monk and scholar had written in A.D. 825 *On Measuring the Earth*. In it he recounts his meeting with Irish monks who had been to Iceland from 1 February to 1 August. They reported that at the mid-summer solstice evening the 'sun hides itself as if behind a small hill'[1476] but there was still no darkness and there was still enough light 'to do whatever he wishes, actually pick the lice from his shirt as if it were by the light of the sun'. Also they 'always had alternate day and night after the solstice'. This proved to Dicuil that previous writers had been wrong to say that Thule had continuous days for six months. Roseman discounts 24-hour days lasting 6 months around Iceland as this only occurs very close the Pole itself. Lastly the monks 'had found that one day's sail from Thule towards the north the sea was frozen'.[1477] Pytheas is not quoted anywhere as giving Thoule (Thule) anything more than a small twilight.[1478] These descriptions make Thule most likely to be Iceland.

On Ptolemy's Map although Scotland goes off to the right[1479] Thule is north of the Orcades, and the middle of Thule is placed at 63°N. Iceland by today's measurements is placed 63°N to 66°N.[1480]

In the first or second century A.D.[1481] Cleomedes the astronomer wrote,

'Concerning the island of Thoule, in which men say Pytheas, the Massaliote philosopher, was actually present, the report is that the whole summer [circle] is above the earth, it also being the arctic for them'.[1482]

Roseman explains that Cleomedes goes on to discuss the summer tropic, which is the 'circle drawn through the sun's most northern point (our Tropic of Cancer)'.[1483] While Strabo also quoting Pytheas about the island of Thoule writes 'near which the summer tropic is the same as the arctic circle'.[1484] At 66°N the Arctic Circle just reaches the northernmost part of Iceland.[1485]

Some Norwegians (Nansen, F.) had believed that Pytheas discovered the frozen Congealed Sea somewhere beyond Bergen (61°N) in Norway and not Iceland. Professor Cunliffe says this cannot be reached from Norway in one days sail.[1486] While Mills mentions the prevailing winds and currents would likely have taken him to Norway and it was inhabited and that Iceland was not,[1487] Cunliffe suggests seasonal and therefore temporary visits to Iceland. The circumpolar traveller Vilhjalmur Stefansson pointed out that had Pytheas taken local sailors with him they would not have mistaken Norway as the island of Thule because they knew the route.[1488] But where was Thule? One possibility is that there was an island near Norway that has now disappeared.

Nevertheless it does seem that Iceland fits the position:
- in sailing times from the north of Britain;[1489]
- that it is habitable having only one month a year with frost in Reykjavik;[1490]
- in the north of Iceland you can see the midnight sun for several nights;[1491]
- one day sailing up from the east coast there is the frozen sea.[1492]

Nansen was able to identify the pack ice sludge[1493] (Congealed Sea and the Marine Lung)[1494] and Stefansson[1495] identified the places where you can see a 21 to 22-hour day ('where the Sun goes to sleep')[1496] in Iceland that Pytheas had described.[1497]

Thoule may have been occupied only in the summer months, which can imply that local Shetland sailors made the journey several times. This was technologically feasible with the boats they had.[1498] It appears that in later years Iceland was empty for many centuries. Three Roman coins of Aurelian, Probus and Diocletian have been found there but as Iceland does not appear occupied by Romans it may have been carried by other travellers who had Roman money [1499] perhaps Shetland sailors? Irish monks lived there from A.D. 795 and fled when Vikings arrived in 850 and 875.[1500]

Pytheas reported that in the summer months the length of daylight was much longer and would stay daylight for 19 hours for Shetland 61°N.[1501] In the north of Iceland the Sun does set only just below the horizon but there is still enough daylight to see. So although it is a 21–22 hour day it seemed like there was daylight for 24 hours, a 24-hour day with no night. Also due to being so far north the earth's curve is greater and light that normally travels in straight lines can be bent. This means that you can actually see objects up to 3° degrees below the horizon. To work out a 'terrestrial point at which a star is visible above the horizon, one subtracts its latitude from 90° degrees, and then subtracts 36' for atmospheric refraction at the horizon'. The star will be visible from locations north of this.'[1502] What could Pytheas have thought of seeing a 21 to 22-hour day?[1503] He was well beyond the edge of the known world.

Strabo wrote that the idea of the earth being 'sphere-shaped' [1504] came from 'the phenomena observed at sea and in the heavens'. There were many islands in Greece and many sailors. They could see the shore disappear the further away they sailed but if they climbed their mast they could still see the land for a little while longer until it completely disappeared.[1505] This gave the idea that the earth could not be flat. Why then doesn't the sea pour away and empty? 'Each body inclines toward its own centre of gravity'.[1506] There were also sundials where one could observe the revolution of the shadow going around that also suggested the earth must be spherical. Pytheas developed the idea that the earth must be spherical.[1507] He recorded the longer daylight hours in summer the further north he travelled and measured the longer shadow cast by his gnomon from the light of the sun.[1508] Couprie says that to use a gnomon for latitude reading only makes sense if you have knowledge that the earth is spherical.[1509]

The North Pole

Knowledge of the stars was so important to Greek sailors of Massalia to navigate the seas. Pytheas was an astronomer and used his knowledge to accurately calculate the position of the North Pole. Eudoxos the astronomer had thought 'There is a certain star remaining always at the same place; this star is the pole of the cosmos', and this was the theory at that time. This theory was corrected by Pytheas as he realised there was no star above the North Pole (in the fourth century B.C.) it was actually an empty space, but nearby in the sky are three stars. When added to the empty space they formed a distorted but recognisable rectangle.[1510]

As the earth spins around in space it does have a small tilt and wobbles, which also means the Pole changes position. Pytheas's theory was proved correct by Hipparchus, the ancient Greek mathematical astronomer who wrote,

> . . . since no single star lies at the pole, but an empty space [instead], near which lie three stars. The spot marking the pole, aided by these [stars] encloses a figure very nearly resembling a quadrilateral—exactly, in fact, as Pytheas the Massaliote says.[1511]

. . . ἐπὶ γὰρ τοῦ πόλου οὐδε εἰς ἀστήρ κεῖται , ἀλλὰ κενός ἐστι τόπος , ᾧ παράκεινται τρεῖς ἀστέρες , μεθ᾽ ὧν τὸ σημεῖον τὸ κατὰ τὸν πόλον τετράγωνον ἐγγιστα σχῆμα περίεχει , καθάπερ καὶ Πυθέας φησίν ὁ Μασσαλιώτης.

This recognition by Hipparchus, the mathematical astronomer was the highest endorsement of Pytheas's astronomical skill and achievement. Converting into latitude was not available at the time of Pytheas who relied on the accurate gnomon reading from the sun that could only be taken on land and also proves he went ashore to take them. Hipparchus was the first person to use trigonometry and was able to convert Pytheas's gnomon readings into latitudes. It was not necessary to wait for the day of the summer solstice to get a gnomon reading. Converting could also be done if the 'interval between the date of the reading and the date of the solstice was known'.[1512] However for the winter positions Hipparchus would need precise observations regarding the sun's height at winter solstice. Roseman says these could not be calculated from other information such as 'the sun's height at summer solstice'. Pytheas must have made these observations that Hipparchus was able to use to prove his own theories. Strabo quotes Hipparchus regarding the sun's height above the horizon at the winter solstice.[1513] Pytheas had to have been in these northernmost regions as his astronomical calculations include winter observations. Sun heights instead of gnomon readings are given only where 'the sun's disk is obscured by mist or fog'.[1514] Therefore enough light to see the position of the sun safely but not strong enough to cast a clear shadow.

Snow in Massalia on the Mediterranean coast is not unknown. In the winter of A.D. 1955–56 temperatures reached minus 13.3°C.[1515] Olives freeze at minus 6°C. and occurs approximately every ten years in Massalia and described as 'gel des olivers'.[1516] Pytheas would also have seen snow on the mountaintops near Massalia. Even so to someone from the warm blue Mediterranean it must have been so fantastic where the sea became cold and white, so too the sky, there was nothing else of another colour to see, no point of reference, white mists and fog, just like when it snows so hard you see nothing but white, a 'white out'. It must have seemed that Pytheas had sailed to the end of the world. Would he ever get back home? Had he gone too far? Was he even beyond the reach of the Gods? The thirst for knowledge driving him on and his curiosity of the unknown making him even more excited? The sheer excitement of discovery can make you only wish it to continue or did the cold and the long journeys make him want to return home? What would have gone through Pytheas's mind?

With the ice preventing any further sailing due north, he may have turned north-west to Greenland but we do not know. More surely we can say that at some point having experienced the frozen Congealed Sea Pytheas sailed back to Orcas and continued his circumnavigation of Britain.

Professor Roseman is definite that the evidence of calculations and observations gives reasonable certainty that Pytheas got as far north as 62°N, as over time the position of the pole shifted and 'the gain in visibility from temperature inversion' the area near Thoule possibly might have been observed further south than at 66°N.[1517] Professor Cunliffe is also definite from the evidence of calculations that Pytheas reached the north Shetlands Islands at 61°N and on observation probably Iceland (at 66°N).[1518] The comments about Pytheas's observations by Geminos of Rhodes regarding the 'where the Sun goes to sleep', and by Strabo that 'Pytheas says he had glimpsed all the northern portion of Europe as far as the limits of the cosmos', and of the 'Marine Lung', which Pytheas 'he himself had seen' (and therefore its associated icy conditions), locates him reaching the frozen Congealed Sea and the Arctic Circle. There were also Hipparchus's calculations on the furthest North that could only have come from observations of the winter solstice by Pytheas.[1519] Sun heights are given where the sun's disk was obscured by mists and fog or where there was pack ice sludge and no solid land to take a gnomon reading.

As Pytheas, an astronomer, has proved the rest of his journey correct by careful calculations and measurements, there is no reason to doubt his equally careful and accurate observations on reaching Thoule and the frozen 'Congealed Sea' a total of six days plus one respectively sailing north of Britain.[1520] In fact his accurate calculations are still used today in the parallels of Latitude in which we map the earth.

Chapter 7

Abalus the Amber Island

Returning from the North to Orcas Pytheas would have sailed down along the east coast of Britain continuing his calculations as to the length of the coastline.[1521] When Diodorus Siculus writes about the use of chariots by the Britons in warfare he seems to be using two sources, *Gallic Wars* by Julius Caesar and another that could only be Pytheas. Archaeologists have found in Yorkshire burials of British chiefs together with their chariots dating around the period of the voyage of Pytheas.[1522] While in the rest of the Britain, chariots were used but not buried in graves.

Pytheas reached South-East Britain and he named the promontory Κάντιον Kantion (The South Foreland, Kent). Akrotirion . . . Kantion (Promontorium . . . Cantium) and not the North Foreland on Thanet, which was still an island.[1523] This name, as well as Orcas and Belerion, still appeared on Ptolemy's map of Britain produced A.D. 140–150. Ptolemy has Britain bounded on the east by the Ocean *Germanicus*, on the south by the oceans '*Prettanicus* and that called *Vergiovius*, on the west by the *Western* (Δυτικός), on the north by the *Hyperboreus* and that called *Duecaledonius*'.[1524]

At some point Pytheas heard of the 'Amber Island' he called Abalus,[1525] where amber was washed up on the shore. Pliny the Elder describes that there were islands in the 'Northern Ocean' many of them with no name.[1526] He states that Pytheas named one and recorded two names of the peoples nearby:[1527]

> 35. . . . Pytheas [believed] there is an estuary of the ocean occupied by the Guiones (a Germanic people) named Metuonis, 6,000 stades in extent. From here, the island Abalus is a day's voyage away, where [amber] is carried down by the floods in spring and excreted by the Congealed Sea; the local inhabitants use it as wood for fire and sell it the neighbouring Teutoni. 36. Timaeus (566 F 75b: Jacoby) also believed him [i.e. Pytheas], but called the island Basilia . . .[1528]

Carpenter mentions that the Guiones are identified with the Goths who at this time were thought to be around the lower basin of the Vistula. The Vistula empties into the Gulf of Danzig the eastern shore of what is the Amber Coast. Roseman mentions the possibility that the Gutones (*Gutonibus*) were in the Jutland Peninsula.[1529] The distance, from the 'Danish passage into the Baltic along that sea's southern shore to Samland, is almost exactly the seven hundred miles that Pytheas reported'.[1530]

There are many more islands by Britain in Pliny's list. Some of them are named which in addition to the above may also originate from Pytheas:

> 40 There are then 40 Orcades, separated by moderate distance [between them]; 7 Haemodes, 30 Hebudes and between Hibernia and Britannica are Mona [Anglesey], Monapia [Isle of Man], Riginia, Vectis [Isle of Wight], Silumnus, Andros (Samnis and

Axanthos [being] below) and, opposite in the German Sea, the scattered Glaesiae, which the more recent Greeks have called "Electrides" because amber is brought forth there.[1531]

Not only had Pytheas been and recorded what he had seen there but also that knowledge, and it would seem contact, between the Greeks and this area was still maintained over many years e.g. there was the Greek anchor stock found off Porth Felen at the tip of the Lyn peninsular in North Wales dated to late second to first century B.C.,[1532] even to the other 'more recent Greeks' nearer to Pliny's time.

Pytheas had already discovered the origin of tin and the second reason why he came north on his voyage of exploration was to find the origin of valuable amber. No one today is sure where Abalus the amber island was and is still to be discovered. Pytheas's description to reach Abalus seems to be the coast along Holland up towards Denmark or if Carpenter is correct from Denmark along the southern coast of the Baltic Sea.

Pliny the Elder wrote that the 'more recent Greeks' called the scattered islands of Glaesiae, the 'Electrides because amber is brought forth there'. Even today in the Frisian island chain off Holland, amber can be found from time to time washed up on the shore. There are some theories that Pytheas may have sailed to the continent before reaching Kantion (Kent) either from East Anglia to Holland or from Orkney across the North Sea to the Skaggerrak reaching the east coast of Sweden near present day Gothenburg and then through the Baltic Sea to the mouth of the Oder River.[1533] Whichever route Pytheas took we can be sure that he was at least close to Denmark (Jutland).

The coastline has altered quite a lot over 2,000 years with islands changing shape and size and sometimes disappearing altogether. Some theories say the island of Heligoland was Abalus the amber island, and it was a much bigger island long ago. Hawkes identifies Abalus as Vendyssel.[1534] Amber from the western side of Denmark was readily available being washed up on the shore. It seems only when the climate worsened in the Iron Age that this changed erosion patterns, and the Baltic became the chief producing area. Supplies of Danish amber were not as available as before and perhaps this was another reason for Pytheas's journey, because Baltic amber was beginning to find its way overland through central Europe via Moravia and Slovenia to the Etruscans in Italy.[1535]

In the poem about Jason and the Golden Fleece there is mention of 'the sacred Isle of Amber, the innermost of all the Amber Islands at the mouth of the Eridanus' (River Po)[1536] by Liguria. The Ligurians were the periodic hostile neighbours of Massalia. Strabo records that the name Linguria means 'gems of red amber'.[1537] Their country has 'excessive quantities of amber'.[1538] Baltic amber is of a different colour such as honey/orange, brown and white.

In the region of Basilicata in South Italy amber had become a characteristic material of their artwork from the second millennium B.C. This reached a high point between the seventh and fourth century B.C. Grave goods show gold, silver and amber jewellery. Exceptional miniature art was created by the Greek cities of Metapontion, Taras, Syvaris and Etruscan cities of Campania (Capua, Pontecagnano).[1539] Funerary couches were made for the Etruscans inlaid with ivory and amber from the sixth century B.C. During the second half of the sixth century there was a boom in amber art in Italy. This coincides with the arrival in Italy of 'specialised engravers, sculptors and jewellers' from the Greek cities of Asia Minor, which had been invaded by Lydians and Persians.[1540] Several works of craftsmen are recognised that created masterpieces in amber for funerals. The amber jewellery found in the graves at Oenotria date from the seventh and sixth century B.C. The pre-Roman populations of Italy used amber to further expound its magical qualities by engraving winged female figures. Harpies, sphinxes, sirens and winged nymphs were also reflected on pottery and grave sculptures and relate to the 'abduction of the soul and the mortals' journey to the otherworld'.[1541]

The Etruscans in Italy were an important market for Massalia. As the interest for amber became less with the Etruscans and Greeks, luckily the market started to grow with the Romans as amber became a fashion with them. Pliny the Elder wrote,

> . . . at the present day we see the female peasantry in the countries that lie beyond the river wearing necklaces of amber, principally as an ornament, no doubt, but on account of its remedial virtues as well; for amber, it is generally believed, is good for affections of the tonsillary glands and fauces, the various kinds of water in the vicinity of the Alps being apt to produce disease in the human throat.[1542] . . . It is beneficial for infants also, attached to the body in the form of an amulet; and, according to Callistratus, it is good for any age, as a preventative of delirium and as a cure for stranguary, either taken in drink or attached as an amulet to the body.[1543]

Rome finally took control over the Etruscans by c. 280 B.C. and this made a much larger market for the Massalian traders who were exempt from Roman tax duties.[1544]

The Greeks cities around the Black Sea knew about Baltic amber [1545] and were using it from the seventh century B.C. They did not know where it came from, only that it was north beyond the land of the Scyths. This amber came from Samland by the Baltic Sea. There were three routes in use:

1. Samland via the Vistula and Dniester (Tyras) rivers to the Black Sea
2. Samland via the Bug and Hypanis rivers to the Black Sea.
3. Samland overland via Moravia to Adria on the Adriatic Sea

and Herodotus tells us that it was the Phocaeans who 'made the Greeks acquainted with the Adriatic'.[1546] The old Celtic track from the Adriatic to Moravia was later made into a better road by the Romans in the first century A.D. and was called the Amber Road.[1547]

Before the Dark Ages in Greece (1100–900 B.C.) an earlier presence of the amber trade (c. 1220 B.C.) was proved with the excavation of large quantities of amber necklaces found at Troy by Schliemann.[1548] Momigliano suggests the difference between the Black Sea colonies and Massalia was that the former explored and informed Herodotus while Massalia had not yet organised any deeper exploration of the interior of Gaul or passed on any knowledge of the Celts to other Greeks.[1549] Though a Greek presence is indicated at Mt. Laissos (Vix Krater): possibly Heuneburg (fortress construction) south-west of Munich: and Asperg (bronze scales) 15 km from Stuttgart.[1550]

Controversy existed as to the interpretation of the chest area depicted on later stone statues of Artemis as fertility symbols. Excavations at Ephesus in the late 1980s revealed a 'number of pendulous amber droplets, pierced for suspension as beads', where they had fallen during a flood in the eighth century B.C. The current theory is that they decorated the original *Xoanon* wooden cult statue of Artemis. Amber with its sun like brightness may have been connected to earlier Mycenaean solar cults and not fertility.[1551]

The ancient Greek name for amber was elektron. Amber comes from the resin that leaks out of certain species of coniferous and deciduous trees and became solid some 40 to 25 million years ago. Winter storms churn at the bottom of the sea and amber gets washed up on the seashore. Some amber contains perfectly preserved insects that got stuck in the resin. A philosopher, mathematician and scientist called Thales of Miletus 635–543 B.C. (one of the Seven Sages of Greece), is assumed to have conducted a repeatable experiment and noticed that if you rubbed elektron (amber) it could pull small shavings to itself like a magnet can attract iron filings. Thales had actually discovered 'static electricity' [1552] though we cannot tell what he thought it was as he may have presumed the movement was due to it having a soul in line with his theories? [1553] Diogenes Laertius reported that both Hippias and Aristotle mentioned the soul in Thales understanding of amber, but unfortunately no work by Aristotle on this still exists. Aristotle did write a book *On the Magnet* that has not survived. O'Grady suggests a connection of the liquid sap that forms amber resin with Thales's general theory of water, from which he speculated that water is the basis for all things, and his interest in the animated power of amber and magnets. Pliny the Elder records,

> . . . in Syria the women make the whirls of their spindles of this substance, and give it the name of "harpax," from the circumstances that it attracts leaves towards it, chaff, and the light fringe of tissues [1554] . . . When a vivifying heat has been imparted to it by rubbing it between the fingers, amber will attract chaff, dried leaves, and thin bark, just in the same way that the magnet attracts iron. Pieces of amber, steeped in oil, burn with a more brilliant and more lasting flame than pith of flax.[1555]

Two thousand years later the English scientist William Gilbert in A.D. 1600 gave the name 'electricity', taken from the action of elektron (amber), to his own discovery.[1556] In the ancient world elektron (amber) must have seemed to possess magical qualities i.e. the power to move/attract.

From Abalus, the Amber Island, Pytheas returned to Kantion (Kent). He continued passed the Isle of Wight which he named Οὑηκτίς Vectis and on to where he first came to Britain (Cornwall/Devon) at Belerion (Land's End). Pytheas was the first to circumnavigate Britain. He named the three points (promontories) of the British mainland Belerion, Orkas, and Kantion declaring correctly that Britain was an island and triangular in shape. From his measurements he calculated Britain's landmass to within 2.5 per cent accuracy. He also calculated Britain's coastline as 'more than 40,000 stades as perimeter' = 7,500 km (the modern perimeter was estimated at 7,580.02 km in Encyclopaedia Britannica, 1957).[1557] Pytheas's calculations show a relative value in spite of erosion and natural reformation further along the British coast [1558] the figure is very close to modern day calculations. Also it would seem while sea levels have been stable that the length of Britain's coast is more or less the same for 2,300 years even though some of the shape may have changed.[1559]

His calculations were done without the help of modern techniques and satellites. This was a remarkable fete by any standards.

Three hundred and fifty years later the Roman writer Pliny the Elder wrote that 'the perimeter of Britain as reported by Pytheas and Isodorus is 4,875 miles [1560] [7,221.83 km] [1561] our Roman armies not having extended our knowledge of the island any further than the neighbourhood of the Caledonian woodlands'.

Chapter 8

Pytheas Writes His Book *On the Ocean*

We are not sure which way Pytheas came back to his home city of Massalia (Marseille). Did he return through Gibraltar (Pillars of Hercules) or overland from Brittany sailing down the great rivers of France on local trading boats changing frequently along the Loire, Garonne, Aude or Rhône? What route do you think he took?

Strabo writing in the first century A.D. recorded routes from Massalia to Britain.[1562] There were two main routes one was up the River Rhône the other from Narbo:

> . . . the Rhodanus [River Rhône] is succeeded by the Arar, and by the Dubis (which empties into the Arar); then the traffic goes by land as far as the Sequana River; and thence it begins its voyage down to the ocean, and to the Lexobii and Caleti; and from these peoples it is less than a day's run to Britain.[1563]

Strabo explains that due to the swiftness of the Rhodanus in the upper reaches some of the traffic would go overland [1564] 'by wagons' [1565] particularly traffic meant for the Avernians and the Liger River [Loire]. Even though the Rhodanus came near to them 'the road is level and not long (about eight hundred stadia) is an inducement not to use the voyage upstream . . . The road is naturally succeeded by the Liger; and it flows from the Cemmenus Mountains to the ocean [Atlantic]'.[1566]

Strabo also discusses the route from Narbo, which after a short way inland by the River Atax, then between 700–800 stadia overland to the River Garunna that 'flows into the ocean,' [Atlantic].[1567]

Diodorus Siculus mentions 'Much Tin is also conveyed from the *Prettanic* island to Gaul, lying opposite, and is brought on horses by merchants through the interior of Gaul both to the Massaliotes and to the city named Narbo'.[1568]

Even ninety years after Julius Caesar's invasion of Britain the island still kept its aura of mystery. During the campaign by Plautius he found it difficult to persuade his army to advance beyond Gaul. 'For the soldiers were indignant at the thought of carrying on a campaign outside the limits of the known world'.[1569]

Plautius's army landed in Britain A.D. 43. He killed Togdumnus son of Cynobellinus, however, this only rallied Britain to avenge his death. Plautius could go no further only guarding what he had won and sent a message that was the signal for Emperor Claudius to send reinforcements. Claudius sailed:

down the river to Ostia, and from there followed the coast to Massilia; thence, advancing partly by land and partly by the rivers, he came to the ocean and crossed over to Britain, where he joined the legions that were waiting for him near the Thames.[1570]

Suetonius writes that Claudius was nearly wrecked twice by 'the boisterous wind called Circius, upon the coast of Liguria, and near the islands called Stoechades. Having travelled by land from Marseilles [Massilia] to Gessoriachum [Boulogne],[1571] he thence passed over to Britain.'[1572]

When Pytheas returned to Massalia he wrote all the experience of his voyage of discovery, including his measurements from gnomon ratios, sun and stars, in a book called *On the Ocean* Περὶ τοῦ Ὠκεανοῦ. Copies of his books would have been made and found their way to other Greek cities of the Mediterranean.[1573] In Athens there was a brisk trade in copying books to sell.[1574] Pytheas wrote all his findings but may have left out the details of the exact route from Massalia to Brittany, as he had to keep the trade route for tin and amber a secret. We will not know for sure until more of his book has been discovered. However, we do know from eighteen other ancient writers who used and quoted Pytheas that he wrote everything else he had seen.

The book *On the Ocean* must have seemed fantastic to some people in the non-scientific world. How is it possible for a sea to freeze? The sea is made of water and salt but if you put salt on ice it melts. A story of a 22-hour day where it was still light for the remaining two hours before the sun rose again was incredible. In the following centuries some of the greatest brains and scientists accepted Pytheas as an accurate astronomer. Such as fourth century B.C. contemporaries Dicaearchus of Messene, the geographer and astronomer, who had invented the first latitude from the Straits of Gibraltar to Rhodes, he was correct in thinking that the earth was a sphere; and Timaeus of Tauromenium (in Sicily), historian of the Western Greek states. Both were pupils at Aristotle's school in Athens the Lyceum and with access to its library.

Already amongst the Greeks in the fifth century B.C. they had shown the 'awareness of the surface extension of space, oriented according to the cardinal points and able to be represented or drawn with a truly geometrical accuracy'.[1575] By the second century B.C. there were great developments in astronomy and mathematics including the world's first computer known as 'The Antikythera Mechanism' that calculated planetary orbits.[1576] Eratosthenes of Cyrene, geographer and scholar, and Hipparchus of Nicaea, astronomer and mathematical geographer, developed the systems of parallels of latitudes the same we still use today over 2,000 years later. They also used Pytheas's sun heights, gnomon ratios and observations from the stars in forming this system. Hipparchus was the earliest known mathematician to use trigonometry. He converted Pytheas's calculations proving them to be correct; that Pytheas had made his voyage of discovery and had gone ashore to take them.[1577]

Pliny the Elder, the Roman historian, accepted and used Pytheas in three books of his thirty-seven volumes called *Natural Histories*. Posidonius of Apameia 135–50 B.C. was a Stoic philosopher and scholar much quoted by other writers such as Cicero, Livy, Seneca the Younger, Plutarch, Strabo, Cleomedes, and Diodorus Siculus. He also wrote about the position of people living in the far north 'people whose shadows go round' where the shadow from a gnomon will make a full circle in 24 hours.[1578]

Posidonius was second only in influence to Aristotle. Did Posidonius use information from Pytheas, as he never quoted Pytheas directly in the fragments that survive?[1579] Indeed Strabo is very definite and criticizes Posidonius for accepting the reports of Pytheas.[1580]

Strabo used Posidonius as one of his main sources for this part of Europe. Therefore he was somewhat undermined and defensive that so great an authority as Posidonius could reject reports that Strabo considered trustworthy yet accept others as true that Strabo thought were false such as Pytheas, Euhemeros and Antiphanes.[1581]

Posidonius (c. 135–50 B.C.) visited Gades in Atlantic Spain and studied the tides. He also believed the tides of the outer ocean were influenced by the moon and wrote a book like Pytheas called *On the Ocean*.[1582] Posidonius wrote many books but like Pytheas no whole book survived to the present time. We know some of what he wrote from the other ancient writer's books that have survived and had quoted Posidonius. When two titles are the same we can know the difference when the writers quote the author and also which book they were getting their information from. Pliny the Elder researched 2,000 books to write his *Natural Histories* and listed them.[1583] This is the system we use today in writing; to back up our story we mention our sources of information.

Chapter 9

Alexander the Great, Carthage and the Pillars of Hercules

This was an age not only of conquest but also exploration and discovery.[1584] Theories of our unknown world were now being tested with Alexander the Great in the East, his Cretan Admiral Nearchus [1585] in the Persian Gulf 326–324 B.C. and Pytheas of Massalia in the Atlantic Ocean.[1586] One can wonder if Alexander the Great had seen Pytheas's book or heard of this Greek explorer's story. After Alexander had been to India he had more conquests in mind like Arabia as well as two expeditions: to the Caspian Sea to investigate any connection to the open sea; and south along the Red Sea from Egypt to see if Libya (the name the Greeks gave to all Africa at that time) was surrounded by water and if humans could survive the intense heat of the equator.[1587] Later Eratosthenes made a map of the inhabited world (oikoumene) partly inspired by Alexander's exploration.[1588] Eratosthenes with the information he had illustrated the inhabited world (oikoumene) in the shape of a Macedonian Chlamys (cloak).

Alexander loved to explore and to do what no one else had done before. On his way back from India at the royal palace of Gedrosia Alexander wanted to 'sail from the Euphrates with a great fleet, circle the coast of Arabia and Africa, and enter the Mediterranean by the Pillars of Hercules'. He collected a number of vessels, mariners and pilots at Thapsacus for this purpose.[1589]

In the seventh century B.C. Callinos of Ephesus wrote 'It is men's destiny to have no way to escape death, even if their ancestors were immortal'.[1590] If in the fourth century B.C. Alexander had ever read this he certainly tried to do the opposite and gain immortality by surpassing his contemporaries and others in deeds and glory. Alexander was a complex person but he always had a basic motivating drive to his life. This was in trying to do better than his ancestors Achilles [1591] and Hercules (Heracles). Arrian, reports Alexander as saying, 'we have passed beyond Nysa and we have taken the rock of Aornos which Heracles himself could not take'.[1592]

The Greeks believed if someone could do more than others they would become a Hero (Eponymoi). A shrine would be made to the Hero and in being remembered a part of them would live forever. Alexander said, 'and sweet is the savour of a life of courage and of deathless renown beyond the grave'.[1593] Gold tablets found in the tombs at Derveni, Macedonia dating to the fourth century B.C. attest to the belief in the Dionysiac mysteries promising 'heroization and life after death'. The burial rituals were Homeric in character.[1594] Alexander tried to be ever the best. In urging his men to go further in India Alexander said,

> Are you not aware that if Heracles, my ancestor, had gone no further than Tiryns or Argos—or even than the Peloponnese or Thebes—he could never have won the glory which changed him from a man into a god, actual or apparent? [1595]

In the myths Hercules in his twelve labours had been to India and also to the West at the outer ocean (Atlantic). The Greeks thought that on reaching the Caspian Sea, and then India, they would find the great ocean that encircled the earth. Alexander said,

> Moreover I shall prove to you, my friends, that the Indian and Persian Gulfs and the Hyrcanian Sea are all three connected and continuous. Our ships will sail round from the Persian Gulf to Lybia as far as the Pillars of Hercules, whence all Libya to the eastward will soon be ours, and all Asia too, and to this empire there will be no boundaries but what God Himself has made for the whole world. [1596]

There were no accurate maps for these unknown lands. Alexander had tried to find the 'eastern ocean' that his teacher Aristotle thought could be in India. The knowledge they had of India may have come from its partial exploration by Skylax of Caryanda the previous century.[1597] After the battle with Porus and possibly thinking he was near the end of his eastern exploration [1598] he instructed Nearchus to build a great fleet to sail to explore the Nile and back to Alexandria.[1599] Before this was finished Alexander discovered that the River Indus was not the upper reaches of the River Nile.[1600] Alexander now realised that the earth was much bigger than the Greeks had thought and that the eastern ocean was much further away. Seeing the fleet being built the army must have gone through the emotions of pleasure and realisation they were preparing to return home. Going from one march to another was the monotonous duty a soldier expects. However to then change your mentality in actually believing you are going home, thankful to have survived and reaching the end of the fighting and danger. From belief to disappointment, the prospect of endless campaigns ahead must have had a detrimental effect on his army [1601] who refused to go any further.[1602]

Arrian the Roman historian writes that awaiting Alexander's return in Babylon (323 B.C.) 'Embassies came to meet him from the Greeks'. [1603] Also on his way back to Babylon

> ... he was met by representatives from Libya, who with congratulatory speeches offered him a crown in recognition of his sovereignty over Asia; Bruttian, Leucanian, and Tyrrhenian envoys also arrived on the same mission from Italy. It is said that Carthage, too, sent a delegation at that time, and others came from the Ethiopians and European Scythians—not to mention Celts and Iberians—all to ask for Alexander's friendship. [1604]

Who knows how far Alexander would have gone if he had not died young?

While Alexander was still a prince he was involved in a brawl with Attalus at the wedding of his father King Philip to a new queen. Alexander and his mother Queen Olympias left with bad feelings all round [1605] and went to her brother Alexander the Molossian, king of Epirus. Prince Alexander, leaving his mother Olympias there, went on to Illyria [1606] before being recalled to Macedonia through Demaratus's mediations.[1607] Not much is known of Prince Alexander while he was away in Epirus and Illyria. Did he make any plans of grand design with his uncle to conquer one side of the Mediterranean and the other himself? Later his uncle died fighting on campaign in South Italy.[1608]

Would Alexander the Great have turned west adding the Greeks cities of South Italy (Magna Graecia), Sicily, Massalia, plus Carthage and other foreign states to his new empire? Curtius writes that he certainly planned to go to the Pillars of Hercules that 'were rumoured to be at' Gades, then from Spain skirting around the Alps and Italy from which it 'was a short passage to Epirus' opposite in Greece.[1609] However, in following his heroes and ancestors he had gone beyond Achilles and Hercules in the East, and now planning to the West on reaching the Pillars of Hercules surely he would have gone into the Atlantic not only equalling but also going further than his ancestor Hercules had done? Arrian tells us Alexander saw no limits to his empire.[1610]

Strabo mentions that the city of Antium,[1611] although Roman subjects, joined together with the Etruscans committing acts of piracy and Alexander had complained to Rome, as later did Demetrius Poliorcetes.[1612] The Etruscans interference with Greek shipping led to Athens founding a colony in the Adriatic c. 325 B.C. Athens acted with the approval of Alexander the Great.[1613] Perhaps an embassy from Rome was about Alexander's complaint and/or some other matter?

Arrian mentions the historians Aristus and Asclepiades, who assert 'that even the Romans sent envoys' and 'Alexander prognosticated something of their future power' by their 'orderliness and diligence and freedom' and their constitution. Arrian says he recorded this, 'neither as true or untrue'. He only adds that; with the sources he had; Rome was a Republic and free; not in conflict with Alexander or needing his help; and their 'dislike of kings', and lets the reader make up their own mind whether they sent an embassy.[1614] Though Arrian records that not even Ptolemy mentions it this could be because Rome was not an important state at that time and was in a second war with the Samnites. Arrian does mentions that some writers thought that Rome's growing reputation was causing Alexander some concern.[1615] However, Cleitarchus writing one generation after Alexander, did record that there was included a Roman embassy present at Babylon. While other Italian embassies the Libyans, Bruttians, Lucanians and Etruscans had met with Alexander on his way back to Babylon.[1616] With all these embassies from the different states in Italy would it not have been good politics to send a representative even as a precaution to ensure ones neighbours was not obtaining an alliance or advantages that might be used against yourself?

Diodorus Siculus writing between 60-30 B.C. also records,

> Apart from the tribes and cities as well as the local rulers of Asia, many of their counterparts in Europe and Libya put in an appearance; from Libya, Carthaginians and Libyaphoenicians and all those who inhabit the coast as far as the Pillars of Heracles; from Europe, the Greek cities and the Macedonians also sent embassies, as well as the Illyrians and most of those who dwell about the Adriatic Sea, the Thracian peoples and even those of their neighbours the Gauls, whose people became known then first in the Greek world.[1617]

Two hundred years later Rome was a big power. Justin using Pompeius Trogus as a source wrote that,

> While he was on his way back to Babylonia from the remote shores of the Ocean, Alexander was brought word that his arrival in Babylonia was awaited by embassies from Carthage and other African states, and also by embassies from Spain, Sicily, Gaul, and Sardinia, as well as a few from Italy.[1618]

Rome or the other Italian states are not individually mentioned. Perhaps having been going to Greeks for favours did not fit Rome's new status as a great power much later.[1619] Gaul is mentioned here but we can only wonder who was represented? Later Livy refutes Parthian claims 'that the Roman people must have bowed down before the greatness of Alexander's name—though I do not think they had even heard of him'.[1620] Perhaps the Parthians (247 B.C.–A.D. 224), the later inheritors of a part of Alexander's Persian Empire, knew from their own sources that the Romans had sent an embassy to Alexander?

Why did Alexander choose to travel across Gedrosia, losing many men, in the gruelling Makran Desert? Perhaps he was punishing his men for their refusal to go any further into India wanting to return home to Macedonia? Though he thought his life would be short like Achilles and had no time to lose to achieve his immortality, he overcame this frustration and gave in to his army. Did he do this for the love he had of his army or that he knew fresh replacements troops were coming from Macedonia and the Persians he was having trained as the successors to his army would soon be ready? Alexander was many things, generous and ruthless but not a mean person.[1621] His motivations of excelling his ancestors, to become immortal using as a means to achieve this merit and glory from conquest and that of discovery by exploration Alexander was inspired by challenges and the unknown. Possibly as he was not able to reach the Great Ocean eastwards he tried at least to attain and explore its southern limit.[1622] As he had to go back perhaps the disappointment disappeared when he saw a new challenge and could not resist travelling over the desert, which no army had done before as well as it being the shortest way back to Babylon? Arrian says that Nearchus was sure that it was because 'no man had ever succeeded in bringing an army safely through' and this 'inspired him to go one better the Cyrus and Semiramis' and to 'keep contact with the fleet'.[1623] Strabo using Nearchus as a source adds Semiramis with twenty and Cyrus with just seven men had both survived crossing Gedrosia.[1624]

An unexpected mountain range forced Alexander inland separating himself from the fleet and food supplies and the fleet was deprived of the fresh water wells he dug in return.[1625] Alexander 'considered it would be a glorious achievement for him to lead a conquering army safe through the same nations and countries where Semiramis and Cyrus had suffered such disasters'.[1626] Justin wrote that Alexander took this route because

> So far the terror of his name pervaded the whole world that all nations were ready to fawn upon him as though he were destined to be their king. For this reason he was making all haste to Babylonia to preside over what seemed to be a world-wide assembly.[1627]

Mediterranean Campaign

For over a year it was known that Alexander the Great had grandiose plans of conquest in the Western Mediterranean.[1628] Alexander had appointed Harpalus, viceroy in command of Babylon. He abused his position believing Alexander would not come back from India. When Harpalus heard that Alexander was returning, he fled (in the winter of 325–324 B.C.) with five thousand talents stolen from Alexander's treasury and six thousand mercenary soldiers. With thirty ships he made for Athens and anchored near Sunium and 'put himself in their hands with his ships and his treasury'.[1629] Demosthenes the Athenian orator opposed any revolt, thinking the time was not right and they would not win. Harpalus was confined and Alexander's money taken to the Acropolis until they received instructions from Alexander.

The surrender of Harpalus was demanded by Antipater, Regent of Macedonia, Queen Olympias, and also by Alexander's commander of Southern Asia Minor Philoxenus.[1630] There was a rumour that Harpalus had been well received by the Athenians and it was believed that Alexander was thinking of a great expedition against Athens because of it.[1631] The arrival of Philoxenus caused alarm in Athens, which prompted Demosthenes to ask the people 'If, you cannot look a candle in the face, how will you face the sun when it appears?'

Harpalus had paid some of the Athenians for their support. Demosthenes among others was charged for receiving money, fined fifty talents and sent to prison until Alexander's money was paid back. The remaining 350 talents [1632] were to be kept on the Acropolis until Alexander asked for it. Demosthenes escaped and after Alexander died was recalled back to Athens around the time of the Lamian War.

According to Justin, Alexander was making preparations to 'conduct war in the West' with a 1,000 warships and making an expedition to destroy Athens. This was in response of the reaction to the letter by Alexander 'read out at the Olympic festival' in 324 B.C. to restore all exiles except condemned murderers. Many cities in Greece had openly said they would use military means to assert their independence. Justin mentions in particular the Athenians and the Aetolians had already started the war while Alexander was still alive [1633] though Plutarch and also current histories record that hostilities, the Lamian War 323-322 B.C., took place after Alexander had died. [1634]

Diodorus Siculus (XVIII. 4.2–6) mentions that when Alexander died in Babylon, the Regent Perdiccas found in the Royal archive Alexander's next projects. [1635] Those projects listed were:

Military
1. The provision of 1,000 warships above trireme class for a campaign against Carthage and inhabitants of the Western Mediterranean.
2. Construction of military roads across North Africa and establishment of appropriate harbours and arsenals.

Building
1. The completion of Hephastion's pyre, his best friend, who had died shortly before Alexander.
2. Six colossal temples to be built in Greece and Macedonia.
3. A tomb for his father Philip II of Macedon to rival the great pyramid of Gizeh.
4. Finally transplanting populations from Europe to Asia and vice-versa.

Perdiccas and a Macedonian assembly formally cancelled these plans saying they were excessively ambitious and impracticable.[1636] Perdiccas acted quickly as general Craterus, popular with the troops, was now on the coast of Cilicia with a 'great arsenal of naval and land forces unmatched in quality and quantity' sent 'in advance' by Alexander to prepare for Alexander's Mediterranean war [1637] as well as to replace Antipater acting as Regent in Macedonia.

Having accepted the moral force of the Macedonian assembly, with Alexander dead and his projects cancelled; fortunately the Lamian War against Athens drew Craterus west back to Greece. He took the great fleet with him, which Perdiccas had not anticipated, and joined up with Antipater.

Some have doubted Alexander's written will was genuine and only invented to glorify him.[1638] Firstly why would Perdiccas (Regent of the empire in Asia) and the Macedonian Council reveal details of Alexander's will only to vote against it? Such a move would have been very unpopular with the army in the aftermath and shock of Alexander's death and the subsequent reverence that prevails after the departed? Any grievances the soldiers had had would have been submerged in the loss of two of their kings in their own lifetime Philip and now his son Alexander. Approximately 4,033 soldiers had voluntarily reenlisted for the payment of three talents each at Persepolis in 330 B.C.[1639]

Remorse and perhaps some guilt that after thirteen years of continuous conquests it was the soldiers who refused to go any further forcing Alexander's return to Babylon where he now met an untimely and inglorious death not on campaign and glory as befits the immortality of the hero he and his father [1640] had always tried to pursue.[1641] Anson suggests it was because Perdiccas did not want the blame for cancelling the dead king's wishes that he convened the first formal decision-taking assembly of the Macedonian Army to deal with the contents of the will.[1642] If there was little remorse in the army who only wished to return to Macedonia the question arises how many did actually return and how many stayed on with the different armies of the successors and why?[1643] Secondly the declaration of war on Carthage was already made at the siege of Tyre earlier in his campaign. Alexander would not have forgotten this, which is reflected in his will.

Arrian records that 'Alexander, indeed, once he was embarked upon any of his enterprises, never found anything to stop him from carrying it through'.[1644] With Alexander's drive and ambition all these projects were possible.

Carthage had everything to fear from Alexander.[1645] Alexander as Captain General of Greece had conquered their Phoenician kinsman in Tyre, and Phoenicia was now supplying ships and crews for his navy.[1646] The reason why Carthage could send no military aid to Tyre when under siege by Alexander the Great was that they were in danger from attack by the Greek Syracusians from Sicily[1647] Carthage did send 30 ambassadors encouraging Tyre to resist Alexander [1648] and evacuated to Carthage those not of the age for fighting.[1649] Quintus Curtius Rufus records that at the end of the six-month siege of Tyre, Alexander spared the Carthaginian ambassadors he captured, 'but he subjoined a formal declaration of war (a war which the pressures of the moment postponed)'.[1650] Now Alexander was the Great King, if the Sicilians Greek cities or Massalia in Gaul with its colonies or the other Greek cities in Spain should asked for his aid to stop any more attacks from Carthage? The change in the balance of power was certainly affecting the different Mediterranean states.

Greece led by Alexander the Great was now an unstoppable growing force and super power. Even so there were enough immediate and pressing issues of trade and survival within the local Western Mediterranean political background that Pytheas of Massalia made his voyage of discovery into the Atlantic Ocean.

Why didn't the Greeks conquer Britain having discovered it? Firstly as Aristotle wrote the Greek Phocaeans who founded Massalia were devoted to commerce. It would seem that colonies and settlements usually stayed near the sea or rivers with an amount of land beyond the walled city to grow food. Nevertheless Strabo tells that the Greeks did push inland taking land from the earlier inhabitants in Italy so much so that they called the new territory Magna Graecia (Greater Hellas, Greater Greece).[1651] Greek cities in Sicily did fight for control of each other.

Except for mercenaries, like Xenophon and the ten thousand, or to found a colony/settlement, there were very few leaders who had the ambition to go far outside of their own kingdom [1652] like King Agesilaus of Sparta (to Phrygia in the Persian Empire); King Alexander I (the Molossian) of Epirus (Alexander the Great's uncle) who died on campaign in South Italy (Magna Graecia); King Pyrrhus of Epirus who fought the Romans in South Italy and the Carthaginians in Sicily; King Phillip II of Macedon as Captain General of Greece started the invasion of the Persian Empire; and his son Alexander the Great who also had the ambition to go beyond his own kingdom of Macedonia and as Captain General of Greece conquered the Persian Empire and added territories to it. Without him his 'successors' generals fought each other for a part of the empire Alexander the Great had made. He had built eighteen cities, named after him, and others to trade and bind the empire together. The 'successors' added little territory to the Empire themselves though Seleucus I Nicator founded thirty-eight cities, extended into India and nearly reunited Alexander's Empire.[1653] Alexander planned to transfer populations as his father had done in Macedonia. After him King Cassander did the same in founding Thessaloniki in 315 B.C.[1654] naming it after his wife who was Alexander's half-sister.

What the Massaliotes knew of Briton from their explorer Pytheas they did not wish to conquer but only trade. With a trade route into the Atlantic now set up again they achieved their goal of profit and wealth from tin and amber providing a good living for Massalia. This economic stability may be the reason why Massalia stayed a Timocracy,[1655] political power based on wealth, and avoided the unrest leading to Democracy by the time Aristotle (382–322 B.C.), Cicero (106–43 B.C.) and Strabo (64/63 B.C.–A.D. 24) wrote about them.

Chapter 10

Pytheas of Massalia: Overlooked and Revalue

Amongst Greeks it was the style of writers in ancient times that they criticised their predecessors and contemporaries. In causing controversy their own book would be more noticed. Although 'one-upmanship made a man's name' the personal abuse was terrible and driven on by a belief (genuine or misguided) that they were defending a principal.[1656] Pytheas remained respected in the ancient world of scientists and astronomers. In Massalia there was a permanent gnomon made of masonry that commemorated Pytheas's astronomical skills in setting the latitude of his city at 43°N.[1657]

> Stefansson explains that a large gnomon erected at Marseille 'was divided into 120 parts':
>
> On the day of the solstice the length of the shadow at noon was 'forty-two of the parts on the gnomon, less one fifth–that is forty-one and four fifths to 120, or 209 to 600. This proportion gave 70° degrees 47' minutes and 50" seconds for the altitude for the sun. The length of the longest day was fifteen hours fifteen minutes.
>
> Eratosthenes and Hipparchus (later) found the obliquity of the ecliptic to be 23° degrees 51' minutes 15" seconds, which they deducted from the altitude. The complement of the result was the latitude of the place less the semi diameter of the sun, namely, 43° degrees 3' minutes 25" seconds. With the semi diameter added, the result is almost exactly the latitude of the Marseille observatory.[1658]

A century and a half after Pytheas's book *On the Ocean* was published doubt was cast elsewhere on Pytheas's story first by a historian and 300 years later by a geographer, who as it turns out were not as unbiased as one might expect from our point of view.

Polybius

Rome conquered Macedonia in 168 B.C. at the Battle of Pydna led by Aemilius Paullus. Polybius, a Greek hostage, was placed with Paullus's family in Rome and became a close friend of his adopted son Scipio Aemilianus. Polybius was freed in 150 B.C. Scipio led the Roman Army that destroyed Carthage in 146 B.C. and Polybius, invited as an advisor, and went with him. Once Carthage was captured Polybius was given ships by Scipio to go into the Atlantic and saw himself as its first explorer.[1659]

Polybius eventually found out, probably researching for his book on history in the Great Library of Alexandria, 'at the time of Eurgetes Physcon, in whose reign Polybius came to Alexandreia' [1660] that Pytheas of Massalia had been to the Atlantic 150 years earlier. Perhaps Polybius found out in Massalia? Rivet is certain Polybius visited there on his way back from Spain due to 'some of his convictions about Hannibal's route' who had crossed the River Rhône and the Alps. Polybius re-entered Italy via the Alps [1661] perhaps visiting sites where events had taken place as he thought this was crucial for a good historian. [1662]

What would his reaction have been, disappointment, disbelief? After all the current view then, outside of scientists, was that frozen seas were much further south and therefore any further north was not habitable. There was room for controversy as no one else had reported going north to prove it in all that time since Pytheas. Therefore Polybius could argue that Pytheas must have made it up. Also anyone else who had agreed with Pytheas was wrong as well. Polybius brushes aside Timaeus who up until then was regarded as the greatest historian of the West. His criticism was that Timaeus had based all his research entirely on books, for visiting libraries instead of sites [1663] and to think that by 'mastery of material alone one can write well the history of subsequent events is absolutely foolish'.[1664] Polybius even criticised Homer's epic poem *The Odyssey* limiting it to the Mediterranean Sea only. His reaction was excessive and biased. Homer was considered a basis for all good geographers and there were many studies done on his poems.

Crates of Mallus, in Cilicia, lived during the second century B.C. He was a Greek grammarian and Stoic philosopher. He was reported to have been the first to represent the map of the world as a globe and thereby representing the shape of the world as round and not flat.[1665] He maintained that Homer the Poet had intended to express scientific or philosophical truths in the forms of poetry.[1666] Geminos of Rhodes, the astronomer, writing on 'Day and Night' in the North (VI. 10 –11), states,

> Also, Krates the grammarian says that Homer mentioned these places in the passage where Odysseus says:
>
> Telepylos of the Laestrygon, where a shepherd hails while driving in his flock
> and another answers while driving his out.
> There a sleepless man might earn double wages,
> one tending cattle, and the other pasturing white sheep:
> For the roads of night and day are close together. [1667]

Geminos continues,

> For indeed, since around these places the longest day is 23 equinoctial hours, the night lacks only one hour of being shortened to nothing, so that the setting [point] draws near the rising [point and is separated from it only] by a very short arc of the summer tropic that is cut beneath the horizon. So if, he says, someone were able to stay awake during such long days, he would earn double wages, "one tending cattle, the other pasturing white sheep." And then he brings up the cause, which is mathematical and in conformity with the theory of the sphere: "for the roads of night and day are close together," that is, that the setting [point] lies near the rising point.

Geminos acknowledges other information from Pytheas of Massalia's book *On the Ocean* [1668] and continues adding to the theory of the earth being a sphere.

Polybius argued that Pytheas was a 'poor man' a 'private individual' and could not therefore finance an expedition. However it is usually other richer people who finance expeditions, just as Polybius own expedition was under Scipio's patronage. Pliny wrote that 'Scipio Aemilianus, during his command in Africa placed a fleet of vessels at the service of the historian Polybius for the purpose of making a voyage of discovery in that part of the world'.[1669] In fact Polybius, who had a whole fleet given to him, denies Pytheas the possibility of even obtaining just one ship. So his argument does not work as the city council or merchants in Massalia would have financed the voyage of Pytheas.

Though Polybius is being generous and grateful to previous Greek explorers 'for having ascertained something on the subject and advanced our knowledge' he excuses their findings from not being able to get information 'owing to the difference of the language'. Polybius explains that if anyone had 'reached the extremity of the world' and 'if anyone did see for himself and observe the facts, it was even more difficult for him to be moderate in his statements'. Polybius seems reasonable not to find fault with previous writers 'for their omissions and mistakes, but should praise and admire them, considering the times they lived in, for having ascertained something on the subject and advanced our knowledge'. He continues that regions had become more accessible since Alexander the Great's time:

> I shall then ask those who are curious about such things to give their undivided attention to me, in view of the fact that I underwent the perils of journeys through Africa, Spain, and Gaul, and of voyages on the seas that lie on the farther side of these countries, mostly for this very purpose of correcting the errors of former writers and making those parts of the world also known to the Greeks.[1670]

Polybius does not extend this 'reasonable' praise and admiration of previous writers when it comes to Pytheas. On the one hand he excuses the mistakes of nearby exploration but on the other hand the furthest away the exploration he thinks the more exaggerated the report. Why? Pytheas claimed to have gone north and the furthest distance. This was far beyond where Polybius had travelled. Polybius did not go any further north than South Spain. Polybius in dismissing Pytheas altogether can therefore discard the rest of his voyage in the areas around Spain leaving Polybius as the only explorer. There is no mention at all of the recently defeated Carthaginians and their own earlier exploration[1671] of the South Atlantic along the coast of Africa, which Polybius also visited. In writing his *Histories* Polybius was making a new career and name for himself in the reality of Roman power now in control of Greece:

> . . . since our men of action in Greece are relieved from the ambitions of a military or political career and have therefore ample means for inquiry and study, we ought to be able to arrive at a better knowledge and something like the truth about lands which were formerly little known.[1672]

Polybius anticipates that some of his readers will ask why, as he writes about Spain and Gaul, does he leaves out details about the

'mouth of the Mediterranean at the Pillars of Hercules, or about the Outer Sea and its peculiarities, or British Isles and the method of obtaining tin, and the gold and silver mines in Spain itself'.[1673]

He writes because these matters 'authors dispute with each other at great length'.[1674] This does establish that even if not believed that there were stories (from Pytheas) of Britain and as a source of tin production even at the time of Polybius writing around 250 B.C. With no other explorers going north Polybius's dismissal of Pytheas's voyage of discovery kept up the controversy a further 100 years. As Plutarch mentions many people in Rome still thought the existence of Britain was a 'fable or lie' at the time when Julius Caesar invaded and proved it was a fact.[1675] Polybius wrote one of the best surviving historical accounts of the Roman Empire, and this stature also diverted scholars up to the modern time from considering properly the voyage of Pytheas and his great achievements. Whether Polybius had ulterior motives or genuinely believed the voyage fantasy we can only speculate. What is sure is the doubt he cast was mistaken.

Strabo

It is not clear whether Strabo actually had a copy of Pytheas's book as most of the sources he uses are from other writers.[1676] Strabo, an ancient Greek geographer,[1677] criticised Polybius's comments on Homer particularly in limiting Odysseus's journey to the Mediterranean only,[1678] but in regard to Pytheas followed Polybius's line and with personal abuse. Strabo on the one hand had thought the voyage of Pytheas of Massalia was fantasy but on the other hand added,

'One may, however suppose he [Pytheas] made use of the facts in observations of celestial phenomena and mathematical theory'.[1679]

πρὸς μεντοι τὰ οὐράνια καὶ τὴν μαθηματικὴν θεωρίαν ἱκανῶς δόξειε <ν ἄν> κεχρῆσθαι τοῖς πράγμασι.

Pytheas's reputation must have been strong in astronomy and he could not be entirely dismissed without Strabo and his Stoic views [1680] receiving criticism in return. Though Roseman thought Strabo had to acknowledge some of Pytheas's observations otherwise he would lose the system of parallels in dismissing him altogether. This could be avoided by just calling Pytheas a liar for the rest of his story.[1681]

Polybius and Strabo preferred 'descriptive geography' [1682] that was useful to generals, politicians and historians. This was a lucrative market of people who would buy their books. Both thought the 'mathematical geography' of Eratosthenes, Dicaearchus or Pytheas not useful to their style of geography. [1683] Strabo actually considered it was unnecessary to draw exact curves of a coast 'for this is a thing geography does not do' and to estimate 'the distance on a straight line' instead.[1684]

Thinking that a geographer should only be concerned with habitable zones [1685] Strabo showed much annoyance and irritation with Pytheas for writing so much on the supposed 'uninhabitable zones' that he now had to spend unnecessary time on examining himself. Strabo had a fixed viewpoint that the earth's surface was not habitable beyond 9,000 Stades north of the Massalia-Byzantium parallel line: [1686]

> It is not necessary for those concerned with geography to bother about places outside our own inhabited world, nor should the many and various differences in its measurements themselves be set out for the politician, like proofs—they are hard, dry things indeed.[1687]

His attack on Pytheas became very personal it was as if that as a philosopher he was letting the side down by his discoveries that were so different from Strabo's own ideas of geography. Therefore Pytheas's claims may bring on the profession a lowering of status for professionals like himself from serious geographers to that of 'fable-mongers'.[1688] Maybe that is why Strabo sought excessively to distance Pytheas as a reliable geographer and calling him a liar several times.

When Strabo is defending the poets against criticism from Eratosthenes he says,

> For even if the poets do speak thus, rather mythically, those, at least, who expound the poets should give ear to sound doctrine, namely, that by the "Hyperboreans" were meant merely the most northerly peoples. And as for limits, that of the northerly peoples is the north pole, while the southerly peoples is the equator.[1689]

Yet elsewhere Strabo places the northerly limit for habitable lands at Ireland.[1690]

Strabo is unduly critical when Pytheas says there are habitable zones further north. As many of the surviving quotes about Pytheas came from Strabo, the unfounded criticism made later historians cautious. Habitable regions so far north; 22-hour days; great tides and islands that joined the mainland becoming islands again everyday were fantasy for Strabo. Yet we know today these things to be true.

Caesar's invasions of Britain in 55 and 54 B.C. had proved that Britain existed for a fact and therefore proved Pytheas's voyage of discovery as true. Though Caesar's book had been written and published probably around 52–51 B.C.[1691] and Strabo, who lived between 64 B.C–A.D. 24, only acknowledges the existence of Britain and Ireland while still saying Pytheas's voyage was fantasy.

Strabo, in following a biased Polybius, was mistaken in not accepting Pytheas of Massalia as all the great ancient scientists had done. Fortunately Strabo was thorough enough to include Pytheas's calculations when quoting him. Strabo had the view that the limit of habitable regions was Ireland:

> . . . the remotest voyage to the north; I mean the voyage to Irene [Ireland], which island not only lies beyond Britain but is such a wretched place to live in on account of the cold that the regions on beyond are regarded as uninhabitable.[1692]

> {But from other [writers] I ascertain nothing: neither that there is any "Thoule Island," nor whether areas indeed are habitable as far as this point where the summer tropic becomes the arctic circle. I think this northern boundary of the habitable world is much further south, because current investigators speak of nothing beyond Irene, which lies to the north off Prettanikē, nearby–[it being a land of] humans who are utterly uncultivated and live with difficulty because of the cold, so that I think the boundary ought to be placed there.}[1693]

Stories that did not fit this viewpoint must be fantasy. Strabo even dismisses Herodotus as a 'fable-monger':[1694] disregards Hanno's voyage,[1695] and only accepts the Mediterranean and astronomical calculations of Pytheas's voyage as correct.[1696]

Plutarch tells us that even at the time of the invasion of Britain by Julius Caesar (55 and 54 B.C.) many writers did not believe the island of Britain existed thinking it a 'fable or a lie'.[1697] Though one would think that Caesar's invasion of Britain had proved Pytheas of Massalia's discovery of the British Isles an undeniable fact at last and therefore logically the rest of his voyage was likely to be true. Strabo concedes Britain exists and Eratosthenes calculations as correct by general agreement but save one regarding Pytheas and Thule. Strabo is stubborn on Pytheas's claims by saying that 'men who have seen Britain and Irene do not mention Thule, though they speak of other islands, small ones, about Britain.'[1698] In Ptolemy's Map the middle of Thule is placed at 63°N. (Iceland by today's measurements lies between 63°N and 66°N).[1699] Eratosthenes using Pytheas's calculations proves him to be correct in the discovery of Thule and the closeness in position of no other island but Iceland. This was a remarkable feat of exploration and mathematics by any standards.

That Strabo was stubborn to any ideas outside of his own views on geography[1700] is illustrated in his own words even if those ideas had come from the messenger of the Gods. In finding Pytheas's discoveries hard to believe Strabo writes,

'but Pytheas says that he personally visited the whole of the northern coast of Europe as far as the ends of the world, a thing we would not believe of Hermes himself if he told us so'.[1701]

The Roman Pliny the Elder had never seen Strabo's books[1702] and is a valuable independent source on Pytheas. Pliny, a prolific writer and researcher, used original sources from Timaeus to accept Pytheas's discoveries and examined them without bias along with astronomers and scientists Geminos, Eratosthenes, Hipparchus and many other ancient writers. Pliny the Elder was famous for never wasting a waking moment in the pursuit of knowledge and he used Pytheas in three books of his forty volumes called *Natural Histories*.

As to Roman skills Strabo wrote,

> Now although the Roman historians are the imitators of the Greeks, while the fondness for knowledge that they of themselves bring to their histories is inconsiderable; hence, whenever the Greeks leave gaps, all the filling in that is done by the other set of writers is inconsiderable—especially since most of the very famous names are Greek.[1703]

Book copyists eventually turned to other books more popular. Over the course of time Pytheas's book became forgotten until no copies survived. At the collapse of the West Roman Empire so many books were lost in the barbarian invasions.

Ironically some of his critic's books have survived and in trying to prove Pytheas wrong, they had quoted sections of his own book. Polybius and Strabo were biased and being some of the main sources, continued that doubt about Pytheas's story until recently. From these two and sixteen other ancient writers with references and direct quotes, we do have revealing fragments of Pytheas's book *On the Ocean* and fortunately with his measurements and calculations.

The Sources

Professor Roseman brought all the known Greek and Latin fragments together and examined all eighteen in her book.[1704] The writer's works were produced within these dates, and where known the date of birth and death are also given:

- Dikaiarkhos of Messene active in Athens between 326–296 B.C.
- Timaios (Timaeus) of Tauromenium active in Athens between 356–270 B.C.
- Eratosthenes of Kyrene c. 275–194 B.C.
- Hipparkhos of Nikaia active between c. 162–126 B.C.
- Polybius c. 200–c.118 B.C.
- Artemidoros of Ephesos at his peak c. 104–100 B.C.
- Xenophon of Lampsakos second to first century B.C. (Lampsakos like Massalia were both Phocaean cities).
- Strabo c. 64 B.C.– A.D. 24
- Isidoros of Charax, a generation before Pliny the Elder.
- Pliny the Elder (Caius Plinius Secundus) b. A.D. 23–79.
- Geminos of Rhodes A.D. 50.
- Aetios first century A.D.
- Kleomedes first or second century A.D.
- Apollonius second century B.C. (surviving text a redaction in fourth century A.D. by the Scholiast to Apollonius).[1705]
- Martianus Capella A.D. 410–439.
- Makrinos of Herakleia late fifth century A.D.
- Stephanos of Byzantium sixth century A.D.
- Kosmas Indicopleustes sixth century A.D.

Roseman's analysis together with a decade of archaeological discoveries by Professor Barry Cunliffe has revealed an exceptional story of exploration and discovery.[1706] In the test of time Pytheas has proved his two critics wrong and the many who had accepted his work as correct.

From the five measurements Pytheas took from gnomon ratios, Sun heights and calculations from the stars, modern technology can prove Pytheas did make his voyage of discovery into the North Atlantic and that he:

- discovered Britain (over 265 years before the Romans)
- named Britain–***Prettanike***
- recorded the name of the people–***Pretani***
- Circumnavigated Britain and named its three points ***Belerion***, (Land's End) ***Orkas*** (Dunnet Head) and ***Kantion*** (The South Foreland, Kent), and correctly described the island of Britain as triangular in shape.
- Named the Isle of White Οὐηκτίς ***Vectis***.
- Named ***Monapia or Mona*** (the Isle of Man) [1707] and other islands.
- Calculated Britain's landmass within 2.5 per cent accuracy.
- Calculated Britain's coastline in fourth century B.C. as 'more than 40,000 stades perimeter' = 7,500 km (the modern perimeter is estimated at 7,580 km in Encyclopaedia Britannica, 1957).[1708]
- discovered the origin of the tin trade (Cornwall and Devon)
- discovered the great tides

- Developed the theory of the moon affecting the spring tides.[1709]
- discovered Thule (Iceland)
- discovered the Frozen 'Congealed Sea' and the Arctic Circle
- calculated the position of the North Pole correcting Eudoxos's theory
- saw a 22-hour day
- Added to the theory that the earth must be spherical (due to the length in daylight hours the further north he went in summer).
- Located Abalus, the Amber Island, near Denmark, and the origin of the amber trade.
- Explored the Dutch and German coast and the seas around Denmark (and possibly the Baltic Sea).
- Identified a Germanic tribe the Guiones, and the Teutoni around Jutland.[1710]
- Named islands in the North Sea; the Bay of Biscay; and the Ostimioi headland of Brittany as Kabion.[1711]
- calculated Spain's coastline

His calculations were used by Dicaearchus, Eratosthenes and Hipparchus in forming the system of parallels of Latitude to map the earth–the same we still use today over 2,000 years later. Even by Roman times in the first century B.C. Seneca remarked that

> It has not yet been fifteen hundred years since Greece
> Numbered the stars
> And gave them names
> (Virgil, *Geography*, 1.137)

> And yet there are many nations today that know the sky only by its face and do not understand why the moon lacks fullness and why it is obscured in an eclipse. Among us, too, only recently did science produce definite knowledge in these matters.[1712]

With Pytheas's skills in mathematics and astronomy [1713] he has proved his fantastic journey was more than a story and was indeed a fact. His writings gave us our first glimpses of the ancient Britons (*Pretani*). Cary and Warmington's revaluation in terms of scientific discovery was that Pytheas's journey north 'was more fruitful than any proceeding the age of Henry of Portugal' [1714] (fifteenth century A.D.).

In Marseille, France archaeologists have cleared and shown part of the foundations of the first Greek city of Massalia.[1715] The Bourse (Chamber of Commerce) is a modern building built in classical style with Greek columns. On the top is a statue of Neptune and below him on the pediment are inscribed the names of the great explorers, from left to right Lapervue, Tasman, Gama, Colomb, Vespuce, Magellan, Cook, and Durville. Lower down on the left is a portico with a statue named Euthymenes in a tunic and a turtle at his right foot. Over on the right side is another portico and statue with the name of Pytheas. Pytheas dressed for the North with trousers, tunic and thick cloak holding a gnomon, and at his left foot is a seal, which can refer to the emblem of Massalia's mother-city Phocaea and also the Arctic. On the right there is a square block, above it two globes/spheres, and on top an astragolos of tin? Though we do not know what Euthymenes and Pytheas looked like the people of Marseille, the Marseillais, have justly given their local boys pride of place to commemorate the explorers and their great achievements. After 2,300 years Pytheas of Massalia can at last get his deserved recognition as one of the great explorers, astronomers and scientists in extending the knowledge of our world.

Chapter 11

The Return Journey to Massalia

Regarding the return journey of Pytheas nothing is known except Strabo's comment that after Pytheas returned from the North

'he traversed all the ocean-coast of Europe from Gadeira [Cadiz, Spain] to as far as Tanais' [River Don, Russia].[1716]

We know he returned to Massalia at some point and wrote about his discoveries in his book *On the Ocean* Περὶ τοῦ Ὠκεανοῦ. One day we may recover from archaeological discoveries or an old manuscript in a library some more fragments of Pytheas's story in someone else's writings or we may discover a complete copy of his book *On the Ocean*.[1717] Will that answer all our questions?

Perhaps we will find that while Pytheas accurately measured five points on his journey north, he may have omitted the exact route he took. For in the written fragments found so far there is no mention of the directions of the route, only the stages he reached. These stages are far enough apart, so even if we draw a line to join up these five points, it does not tell us the exact route. Thinking in the context of the time, the tin and amber trade being controlled by the Carthaginians, having now discovered its origins Pytheas would hardly have published his route so that any outside of Massalia could follow! Take five towns in Britain far apart and draw a line to join them up. You will find that the route for travelling can still vary. Only with more points closer together, like those in a child's drawing book, can you get an accurate picture or find the exact route.

Diodorus Siculus writing between 60-30 B.C is known to have used earlier books for his sources and used Timaeus who had quoted Pytheas. Diodorus wrote,

> On the island of Ictis the merchants buy the tin from the natives and carry it from there across the Strait of Galatia [the Channel] and finally, making their way on foot through Gaul [France] for some thirty days, they bring the goods on horseback to the mouth of the [river] Rhône.[1718]

The knowledge of the route meant prosperity for Massalia. Therefore Pytheas could safely keep the exact route unmentioned yet proving his voyage by publishing the sun heights, gnomon readings and position of the stars. These were changed into latitudes by three of the greatest scientific brains of the ancient Greek world Dicaearchus of Messene, Eratosthenes of Cyrene, and Hipparchus of Nicaea. It was a brilliant lesson on how to explore but still keep the exact route secret. So that even today we can imagine the different routes he could have taken to reach Brittany, Isle of Man, Isle of Lewis, Shetland Islands, island of Thoule, the Arctic Circle and the frozen Congealed Sea, Abalus the Amber Island, (some scholars include the Baltic Sea to Samland), Kent, the Isle of White, Belerion (Cornwall) and then returning to Massalia (Marseille) his city.

Pytheas's Crew

Geminos the astronomer quoting from Pytheas's book *On the Ocean* reported,

> And it seems that Pytheas of Massalia reached these places. At any rate, he says in his treatise *On the Ocean* that "the barbarians showed us where the Sun goes to sleep; for around these places it happens that the night becomes very short, 2 hours for some, 3 for others, so that, a little while after setting, the Sun rises straightaway." [1719]

Who is the 'us' in 'the barbarians showed us'? Pytheas and who? How many? This is the only time Pytheas mentions 'us'. We do not have any more information and can only wonder did he have his own ship and crew there? He may have had for part of the journey then went on with a companion or on his own? Geminos is quoting Pytheas, and it may be that Pytheas had local(s) or a guide taking him north? Could it be his crew or companions from Massalia or the local sailors from mainland Britain, the Orkneys or Shetland?

Ship

Archaeologist C.F.C. Hawkes suggested 'a penteconter sturdier than normal' (50-oared warship) for the journey. [1720]

There were only fifteen years between the superior penteconter at the Battle of Alalia c. 540 B.C. and the appearance of a Persian fleet of Phoenician triremes at 525 B.C. at the conquest of Egypt. The trireme with seventy-two oarsmen over three levels was the 'equal of the best penteconter, even the Phocaean ones'. [1721]

Though Roseman discusses a trireme, citing the sea trials of the Olympias (a reconstructed trireme) that it could break up in prolonged swell making it risky in the Atlantic. [1722] Would the reconstruction have all the techniques of the ancient Greeks e.g. 'Hypozotoma' used to provide war-ships with a means of increasing their compactness, 'a band consisting of 4 stout ropes laid horizontally around the hull below the water-line; in case of a dangerous voyage the number of these ropes might be increased.' [1723] Would not the Massaliotes have just sent the best boat they had available? The British Naval commander and Polar explorer Markham's view was that a Massaliote ship was far stronger and bigger than the little boat, the Santa Maria that Columbus successfully used to sail across the Atlantic when he discovered America in A.D. 1492. [1724]

Regarding merchant boats, they had more room but relied only on sail and could only anchor offshore if there was no dock. Perhaps Pytheas went part of the way escorted by a Massaliote warship or merchant ship to Agathe Tyche (Agde) or Hemeroskopeion (Massaliote colonies) or to make sure he got safely past the Pillars of Hercules, (in case there was any hostile Carthaginian ships or pirates), to Gadeira (Cadiz) for silver, amber or tin, which would make a profit and pay for the journey so far? Then transferring to local boats that were built for local conditions and with local sailors who knew the tides, shallows, sandbanks, to the next port of call where other ships could be found that continued north to the Bay of Biscay, Brittany and then onto the British Isles.

Local Boats

Over time local boats are developed in a variety of shapes to sail to local conditions. There would be little changed once a ship had reached its working perfection. The 'Celts developed a wide variety of inland ship types' to sail on rivers [1725] such as the wooden dugout boat made from an 800 year old oak tree excavated at Hasholme, North Humberside dated third century B.C. This was 13 metres long, 1.40 metres in the beam and capable of carrying a 5.6 ton load. [1726]

As well as this type, in Britain they developed a boat made of a frame of wickerwork and osiers and then covered them with sewn animal hides. These craft were the same as currachs still used in Western Ireland today. There are many references of larger currachs making ocean trips by monks. These ships had a large square sail with a mast in the middle, with rowing oars and could carry up to seventeen people. A discovery of the gold model boat at Broighter in Ireland buried between first century B.C. or A.D. gave good detail of nine rowing benches for the crew and rowlocks for the oars, a large steering oar at the stern, 'a mast in the centre with a yard arm to take a square rigged sail'.[1727]

Caesar writes in order to get across one river unseen at night he

> Ordered his men to make boats of a type with which his experience of Britain had made him familiar some years before. The keel and the main frames were made of light timber; the rest of the hull of the ship was woven from osier and covered with skins.[1728]

He took them by wagons to the river 22 miles away. During the night Caesar was able to transport his soldiers to seize the hill opposite and later sent across a whole legion over the river.[1729]

Lucan the Roman poet also mentions boats with this type of construction:

> white willow twigs are soaked in water and woven
> into little boats, and, covered in the slaughtered ox's hide,
> able to bear a passenger, dart across the swollen river.
> In this way the Venetian sails upon the Po's lagoons and Briton
> on the wide Ocean;[1730]

Pliny the Elder wrote,

'The island Ictis on which tin appears; the Britons sail to it in boats of hide sewn over with withies'.[1731]

Length of Voyage

The style of Pytheas's writing from the fragments left seem to show it contemporary with those of Aristotle, Eudoxos of Knidos, and Herakleides of Pontos. Professor Roseman acknowledges the evidence is only fragmentary for a possible date of 350 B.C. and suggests that a large gap of time passed before Pytheas's book *On the Ocean* was published and used in Athens the 320s B.C. The fact that Aristotle (384–322 B.C.) never discussed Pytheas ideas means he did not know of this book in his lifetime as he commented and analysed every idea and subject he knew of. [1732] His appetite for knowledge was insatiable and his analysis prolific. Equally it is possible that the voyage could have taken place in the 320s B.C. but a copy of the book was not available yet in Athens while Aristotle still lived.

The earliest known use of Pytheas's book was by two of Aristotle's pupils, from his school the Lyceum in Athens, *circa* 320s B.C. They were Dicaearchus of Messene,[1733] the geographer and astronomer who invented the first latitude from Straits of Gibraltar to Rhodes, and also thought the earth was a sphere; and Timaeus of Tauromenium (in Sicily), the historian of the Western Greeks states. Timaeus writings were popular in Athens and Alexandria (Egypt) and he quoted from Pytheas's book spreading the story of these remarkable Atlantic discoveries to the Hellenistic kingdoms.[1734] 'All the courts had libraries, even on the Black Sea' and demand was insatiable.[1735] Even 200 years later the Roman orator Cicero who studied Greek philosophy and Greek language held Timaeus's writings in much esteem.[1736] There was even a trade in second-hand books. Libanius records that his own library had been burgled and a treasured copy of Thucydides was retrieved from a stall in Antioch.[1737]

Pytheas could still have made the journey in the 320s B.C. and published his book not long after. As the exact route does not appear, only the five main stages of the journey are measured, would the Massaliotes have kept it a secret for many years to protect their trade interests? Perhaps the Massaliotes made an agreement with Pytheas that he could publish his scientific and geographic exploration if he left the exact route out? That would protect their newly found trade route after all those years of Carthaginian obstruction.

Could it be that only a handful of people at any one time may have known the route like keeping a secret within a guild–a trade secret? None fell to the temptation of bribery or to sell the route to others. Knowledge of the route was kept successfully hidden.[1738] Even 150 years later the Roman general Scipio Aemelianus found the Massaliotes completely unhelpful and very vague when questioned about Britain.[1739]

What we can say from the evidence available is that Pytheas's Atlantic voyage of discovery definitely took place, and most likely in the fourth century B.C. This may have been just possible between 380-350 B.C. and more probable in the 320s B.C. [1740]

Due to some of the measurements Pytheas took of sun heights above the horizon at the winter solstice [1741] together with tides and wind he may have spent between 2–4 years on his journey north. Strabo records,

> On the winter days there the sun ascends only six cubits, and only four cubits among the people who are distant from Massilia nine thousand one hundred stadia; and less than three cubits among the people who live on beyond. [1742]

Latitude

Latitude can also be found by sighting on the North Star, Polaris, and working out the angle it stands above a level horizon. Pytheas would need to have taken this observation on land. As this sighting can take place on any cloudless night of the year, Pytheas may have spent less time on his voyage as he could determine latitude from mathematical calculations and not wait for a summer solstice.[1743] Pytheas had to have been in these northernmost regions as his astronomical calculations include winter observations of the sun's height, which Hipparchus must have used to prove his theories. Sun heights instead of gnomon readings are given were 'the sun's disk is obscured by mist or fog'.[1744]

Hipparchus of Nicaea was the first known person to use trigonometry and he was able to convert the observations of Pytheas from the height of the sun into latitudes and degrees. Strabo preferred describing latitude in 'stades distances and length of longest day'.[1745]

Pytheas's measurements on his voyage of discovery were:[1746]

PLACE	HEIGHT of SUN and LATITUDE	STARTING POINT	SUMMER SOLSTICE DAYLIGHT HOURS
Marseille	43°N.	Marseille (Massalia)	15 ½ on the longest day
Tregor, Brittany	9 cubits = 48°N.	From Massalia 3,800 stades	16 on the longest day
Isle of Man	6 cubits = 54°N.	From Massalia 6,300 stades	17 on the longest day
Isle of Lewis	4 cubits = 58°N.		18 on the longest day
Shetland Islands	>3 cubits = 61°N.	From Massalia 9,100 stades	19 on the longest day
Thule	66°N.		21-22 on the longest day

Table 1. Pytheas of Massalia's measurements in the North Atlantic fourth century B.C. and converted into latitudes by the mathematical astronomer Hipparkhos of Nikaia (Hipparchus of Nicaea, Bithynia, now Iznik, in Turkey) second century B.C.[1747]

Massalia (Marseille), Pytheas's home city, is the starting point for measuring these distances to the North. Despite his accuracy in recording travelling north and south of the Equator (latitude), by contrast Pytheas had no scientific way of knowing how far east or west he was going, as longitude had not been invented yet. How far he had journeyed east or west was estimated by dead reckoning of distance travelled day by day just as other ships captains did on their voyages. A good captain could make quite accurate calculations in this way and the Phocaeans and Massaliotes were skilful sailors. Dionysius of Phocaea even though he had three ships was invited to lead and train the 353 Ionian ships brought together at Lade to fight the Persians during the Ionian Revolt[1748] because of their reputation and naval skills.

Longitude

With the loss of the West Roman Empire it was the Arabs who made improvements on the navigational astrolabe and kept knowledge of Greek astronomy, medicine and philosophy alive particularly under the eighth century A.D. Abbasid dynasty in Baghdad: [1749] and with their introduction of paper, less expensive than papyrus, increased the availability of the Greek texts they copied and translated in contrast to the Byzantines (East Roman Empire) who at this period had an aversion to their Hellenistic 'pagan' heritage. [1750] The problem of not knowing accurately your Longitude position continued and ships were occasionally lost without trace. This was particularly so in the open seas of the Atlantic. The fact that so many ships did make it to their destination was down to the skill of the captain taking star positions, calculations from the sun, and estimating speed by the amounts of knots in a cord passing the hand by a weight dragged behind the ship by the sea over the space of a minute. When clouds covered the sky and the sun or stars there was only knots to go by which was not enough.

The English king Charles II heard that the French were building an observatory to map the stars so the attempt to solve the 'Longitude Problem' could begin. This had great implications, as the French were rivals in trade, colonies and exploration. King Charles II commissioned Sir Christopher Wren to build an observatory at Greenwich headed by the astronomer Flamsted.

On 22 October 1707 four ships of the Royal Navy led by Admiral Sir Cloudisley Shovell struck the Gilstone Ledges of the Silly Isles. Approximately 2,000 men died with only three survivors. [1751] Without accurate navigational techniques sailing was a disaster waiting to happen in not knowing your longitude position. Even so it shocked the nation and petitions from captains, merchants and the public made the Government finally take action in 1714 to solve the 'Longitude Problem'. [1752]

Several designers including Frenchman Christian Huygens creator of the first pendulum clock tried and failed to construct an accurate portable clock for finding longitude at sea. Englishman Henry Sully made a series of devices but they did not perform well and it was generally thought the task was impossible. George Graham in 1729 made an accurate portable pocket watch but was this was still no good as a longitude timekeeper. The 'Longitude Problem' was not solved until 1772. [1753]

To get longitude you measure the height of the sun at noon but also you need a second reading from a clock to know what the time is back home. However at sea the motion would interfere with the pendulum of a clock and accuracy of east or west direction was still guesswork. An Act of Parliament set a prize of £20,000 to anyone who could solve this problem. [1754]

It was not until 1772 John Harrison made the first accurate clock, a Maritime Chronometer, so Longitude could be measured and together with latitude gave an accurate position as to where you are at sea. Harrison had made three versions each improving over nineteen years from spring action to a jewelled action clock. The clocks can be seen at the Greenwich Observatory in London where the meridian of 0° degrees is set at Greenwich Mean Time. An imaginary line was set running north to south and named as the world's 'Longitude Zero' by the International Meridian Conference in 1884. Latitude and longitude are measured in segments of a circle in degrees °, minutes ', and seconds ". [1755] Here in the Astronomy Centre, behind the Greenwich Observatory, you can see on display a map of the stars by Albrecht Durer c. A.D. 1500 'Prospectus Textius Globi Celestis' based on the map made by Hipparchus the mathematical astronomer in 140 B.C.

Chapter 12

Massalia Ally of Rome

Massalia's good relations with Rome enabled Rome to 'store its votive offerings at Delphi, Greece, in Massalia's Delphic Treasury. There was a tradition that these 'good relations went right back to the period of Rome's Etruscan monarchy in the sixth century B.C.'[1756]

This was a measure of the trust and good relations that allowed the Romans have an access to the highest level of their gods and greatest of the oracles. Strabo discussing the mythical founding of Rome mentions among others that there was a Greek connection because the 'hereditary sacrifices to Heracles is after the Greek ritual'.[1757] However this could have been copied later as many rituals were adopted from the Greek gods. There was early contact between traders from Greek colonies in Italy going back to before Rome's foundation.[1758]

As well as the famous story of Romulus and Remus, Strabo records another story 'older and fabulous' that Greeks led by Evander from Arcadia founded Rome. Heracles on one of his twelve labours was driving the cattle of Geryon and entertained by Evander who had learned from his mother Nicostrate 'skilled in the art of divination' that Hercules would become a god. Evander consecrated a precinct to Hercules and sacrificed to him in the Greek ritual, which was still done in Strabo's time. Strabo says it was for these reasons that

> . . . Colelius himself, the Roman historian, puts this down as proof that Rome was founded by the Greeks–the fact that at Rome the hereditary sacrifice to Heracles is after the Greek ritual. And the Romans honour also the mother of Evander, regarding her as one of the nymphs, although her name has been changed to Carmentis.[1759]

Diodorus Siculus reports that the Romans deposited their votive offering to the oracle at Delphi for victory and capture of Veii[1760] c. 406–396/5 B.C.[1761] Dates that were listed according to the Varronian chronology before 300 B.C. are not the same as our own.[1762] Having been stuck in a long campaign against Veii the Romans had consulted the oracle at Delphi on what they needed to do to win.[1763]

Roman contact with Greek divination increased at the end of the third century B.C. by their dealings with mainland Greece. Following a ten-year siege 406-396 B.C. the Romans captured the nearby Etruscan city of Veii. They sent a gold mixing bowl as one-tenth of the spoil,[1764] to be dedicated at the sanctuary of Apollo in Delphi as vowed by Dictator Camillus.[1765] Plutarch mentions that the envoys went on a 'ship of war in festal array'. The Lipareans who mistook them for Etruscan pirates subsequently captured them.[1766] By order of their magistrate they were released and escorted to Delphi and back to Rome by the Lipareans.[1767] Diodorus reports that the votive offering was 'dedicated in the Treasury of the Massalians',[1768] which is next to the Tholos.

Later during the Third Sacred War the Phocians borrowed from the temple treasures to pay their mercenaries [1769] and the bowl had been melted down, but the bronze base on which it stood survived long after in the Treasury of Massalia. [1770]

Strabo mentions another sign of friendship in having the same religious sacred image 'the "xoanon" of that Artemis which is on the Aventine Hill was constructed by the Romans on the same artistic design as the "xoanon" which the Massaliotes have.' [1771]

Diana was the Roman equivalent to Artemis. Servius Tullius, king of Rome from 578–535 B.C. founded the Temple of Diana on the Aventine Hill as a religious centre for the Latin League.[1772]

First Treaty between Rome and Carthage 509 B.C.

Polybius records that there was a treaty binding on Rome and its allies during 'the consulship of Lucius Junius Brutus and Marcus Horatius, the first Consuls after the expulsion of the kings, and founders of the Temple of Jupiter Capitolinus. This is twenty-eight years before the crossing of Xerxes to Greece'.[1773] Polybius writes of the terms in the treaty,

> There is to be friendship between the Romans and their allies and Carthaginians and their allies on these terms: **The Romans and their allies** not to sail with their long ships beyond the Fair Promontory [lying in front of Carthage to the north] unless forced by storm or by enemies: it is forbidden to anyone carried beyond it by force to buy or carry away anything beyond what is required for the repair of his ship, or for sacrifice, and he must depart within five days. [1774]

The Treaties were seen by Polybius preserved as bronze tablets beside the Temple of Jupiter Capitolinus in the Treasury of the Quaestors. These bronze tablets were written in ancient Roman language, which differed to the Roman of Polybius's time and only the 'most intelligent' could only partially make it out.[1775] Polybius thinks that Carthage didn't want the Romans to become acquainted with south of this western side in longships, 'with the district round Byssatis or that near the greater Syrtis, which they call Emporia, [1776] owing to their great fertility.' [1777]

Second Treaty c. 306 B.C.

> There is to be friendship on the following conditions between the **Romans and their allies** and the Carthaginians, Tyrians and the people of Utica and their respective allies. The Romans shall not maraud or trade or found a city on the further side of the Fair Promontory, Mastia, and Tarseum. [1778]

Treaty of 348 B.C.

Wallbank mentions another treaty between Rome and Carthage in 348 B.C. In this treaty Mastia (probably Cartagena) was set as the limit for Roman ships in the Western Mediterranean. [1779]

Writing later in the first century Strabo (c. 64 B.C. to c. A.D. 23) disputes with Eratosthenes (234 to 197 B.C.) earlier stories on 'parts of the West' for example that Carthaginians drowned foreign sailors who sail past 'Sardinia or to the Pillars [Gibraltar]'.[1780]

***Circa* 390 B.C.** [1781] The Massaliotes were returning from Delphi after giving thanks from being delivered from the Ligurians. They heard that Rome was under siege from the Gauls. Because of their early ties of friendship, *foedus aequo iure percussum,* [1782] the news was 'met with public mourning' in Massalia. Massalia collected gold and silver 'from public and private sources' to help 'make up the total weight demanded by the Gauls' to pay the ransom they were asking from the Romans to leave Rome. In gratitude Rome made a new treaty where Massalia would be 'exempted from taxation, granted seats amongst the senators for public shows and given a treaty putting them on equal footing with Romans.' [1783]

390–389 and 389–388 B.C.
Croton, Magna Graecia (in Southern Italy) Resists Dionysius of Sicily

> While Dionysius was fighting the campaign he was approached by legates from the Gauls who had burned Rome some months before [1784] . . . Dionysius was pleased with the embassy [Gauls]. He confirmed the alliance and, now that his strength was augmented with Gallic auxiliaries, recommenced the war as if beginning afresh. [1785]

Dionysius was recalled to Sicily to fight Hanno and the Carthaginians. Justin relates the following:

> . . . Suniatus, at that time the most powerful man in Carthage. Out of hatred for Hanno, [the Carthaginian general in Sicily] Suniatus had written a letter in Greek telling Dionysius, as if confiding in him, of the coming of the Carthaginian army and the inertia of its general. The letter was intercepted and Suniatus was condemned for treason; and a decree was passed in the senate forbidding any Carthaginian thereafter to study Greek literature or language, to ensure that no one be able to communicate with the enemy orally or in writing without an interpreter. [1786]

260 B.C. Battle of Mylae

Polybius does not mention Massliote or Italiote contingents. Thiel says 'their presence is no more than a hypothesis, but a reasonable one'.[1787] The totals both Tarn and Thiel agree of 120 new Roman ships (minus seventeen that Asina lost at the previous engagement) and the final totals of 143 ships including the *socii navales* contingents. But they disagree as to the totals of the extra ships. Thiel gives Massiliote and Italiote town's *socii navales* contingent of thirty-five ships, plus five Punic refitted ships.[1788] Polybius does mention 130 Punic vessels.[1789] The Romans first attempt to build a fleet of its own was now put to the test.[1790]

In the first engagement the Carthaginians lose thirty-one ships including a flagship 'a seven'. The Carthaginians had 130 ships including a 'seven' banked galley that had belonged to King Pyrrhus of Epirus.[1791] The Romans first used 'Ravens' gangplanks that could swivel and be lowered onto an enemy ship. A pike at the far end of the gangplank enabled the Romans to grapple the enemy ship from getting away and their soldiers could board and attack. The Carthaginians lost 50 ships and Hannibal barely escaped in a jolly-boat.[1792] The Carthaginians tried the *diekplous* tactic. The Romans used one third of the fleet in a second line of defence.

Prior to the Romans building a permanent fleet there was a Neapolitan alliance with Rome 327 B.C. Locri deserted twice to Pyrrhus and returned to the Roman alliance in 275 B.C. Tarentum and Velia (Hyele, Elea) were allied to Rome by 272 B.C. As naval allies (*socii navales*) these Greek southern Italian towns were exempt from military levy but required to provide ships from time to time. They must have provided the bulk of the sailors for the new fleet and undertook much of the construction.[1793]

Massalia and Carthage

After the First Punic War when the trade of Spain began to go southwards direct to Carthage instead of eastwards through Massalia, the people of Massalia lost a great part of their livelihood. They had every motive to stir up the Romans against Carthage.[1794]

231 B.C.

Anxious at the renewed power of Carthage in Spain, an embassy sent from Rome was satisfied with Hasdrubal's (Hannibal's uncle) reason for fighting the Iberians and that was to earn money to pay off the war indemnity to Rome from their previous war (First Punic War).[1795]

The Romans had a genuine fear of the Celts that was justified and more immediate. Rome, except for the small area of the Capitol, had once been occupied by the Celts and there were many Celts settled in the north of Italy. Polybius wrote in his *Histories* what he thought had motivated the Roman way of thinking at the time around 228 B.C.

Seeing the growing empire of Carthage in Spain, Rome could not go to war as the 'threat of Celtic invasion was hanging over them, the attack being indeed expected from day to day'.[1796] The Romans planned to

> smooth things down and conciliate Hasdrubal in the first place, and then to attack the Celts and decide the issue by arms, for they thought that as long as they had these Celts threatening their frontier, not only would they never be masters of Italy, but they would not even be safe in Rome itself.[1797]

Roman envoys were sent to Hasdrubal and a Treaty made. With nothing mentioned about the rest of Spain only not to cross the River Ebro in arms, 'they at once entered on the struggle against the Italian Celts.'[1798]

229 B.C. Siege of Helike, Spain

Ellis mentions that during the siege of Helike (modern Elche in Spain) a Greek colony the Carthaginian leader Hamilcar Barca drowned crossing a river[1799] while retreating in 229 B.C.[1800] An important statue Dama de Elche was found near here dated to between 450–350 B.C. showing some Greek influences on a remarkable Iberian statue.[1801]

Ellis does not mention which Greeks the colony belonged to but could this be part of 'the other Greeks' as mentioned by Appian. [1802] Santa Pola at 9 miles distance was possibly the port for Illici or Helike. Excavations show a Greek presence in the design (possibly Massalia/Emporion) and a city shared with the indigenous people [1803] (see section on Santa Pola in Chapter 2).

226 B.C. Treaty of the Ebro

The Treaty of the Ebro (in Spain) between Rome and the Carthaginian Hasdrubal the Fair in Spain[1804] was assumed by Rome to be binding on all Carthaginians. [1805] It is not known how Massalia saw the treaty but Massalia lost control of three of their Spanish colonies, Hemeroscopium, Alonis (Benidorm), Leuka Akra (Alicante) and the boundary for the Carthaginian Army was set at the River Ebro.[1806]

The Greek Massalian colonies of Emporion and Rhodus (Rhode) in Spain were not included in the treaty and free from Hasdrubal's control. [1807] Rhodus built a new city wall during the Second Punic War and Emporion expanded its southern wall in the first half of the second century B.C.[1808]

219–218 B.C.
Saguntum

According to Strabo Saguntum was a colony of Massalia in Spain.[1809] Wallbank mentions the possibility that commercial relations between Saguntum and Massalia were possibly responsible for a Roman Alliance.[1810]

Appian writes of 'the other Greeks' in Spain (Iberia) being anxious about Carthaginian expansion there:

> The Saguntines, a colony of the island of Zacynthus, who lived about midway between the Pyrenees and the river Ebro, and all the other Greeks who dwelt in the neighbourhood of Emporiae and in other parts of Spain, having apprehensions for their safety, sent ambassadors to Rome. [1811]

Rome then sent an embassy to Carthage and the Carthaginians came to an agreement not to cross the River Ebro under arms. In return the Romans would not wage war beyond the Ebro on those subjects of the Carthaginians 'and that the Saguntines and the other Greeks in Spain should remain free and autonomous. And these agreements were added to the treaties between Rome and Carthage'.[1812]

Richardson (2000) mentions that archaeology had shown Saguntum to be an Iberian town with no observable Greek settlement. Nevertheless Wallbank mentions that a Temple of Aphrodite, '15 by 12 metres lies on the cape of the original coastline, but now 2 km from the sea at a point some 9 km north of Saguntum; it was probably built by the Phocaeans'.[1813] Why build a temple there if it was not for the town's people to visit? Though the temple may not have been just for Greeks as Strabo writes that

'(they [Massaliotes] also taught the Iberians the sacred rights of the Ephesian Artemis, as practised in the fatherland, so that they sacrifice by the Greek ritual).' [1814]

Saguntum may have been like Arles and not under direct Massaliote control as it may have been in the past but nevertheless had kept up its trading contact with them. Perhaps like a commonwealth? After all politics is one thing but earning a living is another and business is business.

After an eight-month siege [1815] Saguntum was destroyed by Hannibal despite his treaty with Rome and kindled the Second Punic War between Carthage and Rome. (218 B.C.). [1816] The Saguntines had appealed to the Roman Senate and an embassy was sent to Hannibal warning him not to attack Saguntum or cross the boundary set at the River Ebro. Hannibal and his army crossed the River Ebro. He was confident of Roman inaction.[1817] The Romans sent no aid to Saguntum during the siege (as problems with Illyria had kept Rome busy).[1818] Appian records that some of the Roman senators had 'urged that they support the Saguntines allies; but others held back, arguing that they were not allies according to the treaty, but were autonomous and free, and that those under siege were still free. This was the opinion that prevailed'.[1819] Another Roman delegation was sent to Carthage whose council said the Treaty of the Ebro had been done with their general Hasdrubal and not with them i.e. not ratified by the people. This deprived Rome of a legal basis for a declaration of war. Rome resorted to using the backdated conquest of Saguntum as an excuse for war even though Carthage also proved that the existing peace treaty of 226 B.C. had not included Saguntum.[1820]

Livy, the Roman historian, wrote that beneath the city walls of Saguntum, Hannibal was wounded in the leg by a javelin.[1821] Much later in the siege Alco, a Saguntine, secretly slipped over to the Carthaginians on his own and discussed peace terms with Hannibal. On hearing Hannibal's terms he did not negotiate knowing the Saguntines would not accept and deserted to Hannibal. Alorus (a Spaniard) decided to negotiate for Hannibal with the Saguntines.[1822] The terms he relayed to them were:

- Saguntum should make full restitution to their neighbours the Turdetani;
- They should give up all their gold and silver;
- Quit the city taking only one suit of clothes each;
- To go where ever the Phoenicians decided.

Some of the senators withdrew and on their return brought back silver and gold putting it into a bonfire and threw themselves on it. The people became agitated due to the horror. Just then one of the towers of the city walls collapsed with a bang. Hannibal was told that there were no guards on the wall and decided to attack. Livy records that Hannibal had issued instructions that 'all grown inhabitants' be put to the sword.[1823] 'This was a barbarous order: how would it have been possible to show mercy to men who in desperation, either fought to the death or set fire to their own houses and burned themselves alive, together with their wives and children'?

According to Appian,

> The Saguntines, when they despaired of help from Rome, and when famine weighed heavily upon them, and Hannibal kept up the blockade without intermission (for he heard that the city was very prosperous and wealthy, and for this reason did not relax the siege), issued an edict to bring all the silver and gold, public and private, to the forum, where they melted it down with lead and brass, so that it should be useless to Hannibal.'[1824]

Appian does not mention a pyre and says, 'Then thinking that it was better to die fighting than starve to death, they made a sally by night upon the lines of the besiegers while they were asleep'. The Carthaginians were 'arming themselves with difficulty' but subsequently all the Sanguntines were slain. 'When the women witnessed the slaughter of their husbands from the walls, some of them threw themselves from the housetops, others hanged themselves, and others slew their children then themselves. When Hannibal had learned what had been done with the gold he was furious, and put all the surviving adults to death with torture'. [1825]

Valerius Maximus wrote that the people unable to resist Hannibal any further withdrew inside the walls of the city and

> they gathered into the Forum the possessions that each person loved the most, put firewood around them, and set them alight. Then, rather than betray their alliance with us [Romans], they threw themselves onto this funeral pyre of their state and their society. [1826]

Polybius describing the size of the Carthaginian Empire says 'They had also crossed the Straits at the Pillars of Hercules' and by the time of the Hannabalic War had 'made themselves masters of the whole of Spain as far as the promontory on the coast of the Mediterranean known as Emporiae, where the Pyrenees which separates the Celts from the Spaniards meet the sea'. [1827]

Hannibal
218 B.C.

Livy records that Roman envoys were sent to many Gallic chiefs to request them to refuse the Phoenicians [Carthaginians] to pass through their land. They were met with laughter and the retort that the Romans were being no friends to themselves and by injuring their compatriots living in North Italy. The envoys met with a similar reaction everywhere. Only at Massilia their ally they found a friendly reception. The Massaliotes in the meantime had 'made enquiries with full diligence' and learnt that Hannibal was much quicker off the mark and 'had been beforehand with the Romans in gaining the good will of the Gauls'. [1828]

Connelly mentions that Hannibal had planned to use the fabled route of Hercules 'Voie Herculéenne' to Italy along the coast but the Greek city of Massalia was in the way.[1829] They were a threat to his lines of supply and much stronger than Saguntum. A time consuming siege could bog down his campaign; Rome was sure to help its oldest and faithful ally and the element of surprise would be lost. It would seem that Hannibal had to avoid Massalia and so crossed the River Rhône at the lowest point at Tarascon. Once he had crossed he abandoned his original route and went north to the Alps and to distance himself from Scipio's army.[1830]

The Roman consul Publius Cornelius Scipio enrols a new legion and with 60 warships arrived at Massalia their ally. Publius with 60 ships anchored off the first mouth of the Rhône 'Known as the Massaliotic Mouth [1831] . . . hardly believing, even then that Hannibal was actually planning how to cross the Rhône'. Scipio sent out 'a chosen band of 300 cavalry, with Massaliote guides and Gallic auxiliaries, to make while he was waiting, a thorough reconnaissance' [1832] to find Hannibal's army, as most of the Roman soldiers were suffering from the effects of sea sickness and fever. Hannibal had also sent a reconnaissance party of 500 horsemen towards the Roman camp. They met the 300 cavalry and fought. Livy says the Romans won but lost 150 Romans and Gauls and the Numidians lost 200.[1833]

Hannibal was located four days north crossing the River Rhône. He purchased 'all the river canoes and boats, amounting to a considerable number since the people of the banks of the Rhône engaged in maritime traffic.'[1834] Livy continues that the Celtic Volcae Tectosages inhabited both sides of the Rhône,

> but doubting their ability to keep the Phoenicians from the western bank, they had brought nearly all their people over the Rhône, so as to have the river for a bulwark, and were holding the eastern bank with arms. The rest of the dwellers by the river, and such of the Volcae themselves as had clung to their homes, were enticed by Hannibal's gifts to assemble large boats from every quarter and to fashion new ones; and indeed they themselves were eager to have the army set across as soon as possible and to relieve their district of the burden of so huge a hoard of men. So they brought together, a vast number of boats, and canoes roughly fashioned for local traffic, and made new ones by hollowing out single trees.[1835]

Hannibal's army of Carthaginians and Celtic-Iberian allies attacked across the River Rhône and beat the Volcae. Hannibal then made his way to the Alps. The Roman consul Publius Cornelius Scipio reached Hannibal's empty camp and was amazed at the speed Hannibal had travelled. Scipio was three days behind and could not catch up. Without wasting any more time Scipio returned to his ships sending most of the army with his brother to Spain to attack Hannibal's base and supplies. He himself made off to Italy to take control of another Roman Army in the Po valley.[1836]

Massalia's intelligence reports on what was happening in Gaul were invaluable. Appian briefly records that Publius Scipio the Consul learns 'from Massilian merchants that Hannibal had crossed the Alps and entered Italy'.[1837]

Polybius writes that Hannibal 'hearing that Scipio had crossed the Po at first did not believe it as he had left him only a few days previously near the crossing of the Rhône and that the coasting voyage from Massalia to Etruria was long and difficult'.[1838]

Here Hannibal with his army and elephants defeated the Consul Publius Cornelius Scipio. Later Consul Publius Cornelius Scipio joined his brother Gnaeus Cornelius in Iberia with 20 warships and 8,000 men[1839] to liberate the Greek colonies from Carthaginian control, which they did as far as Saguntum.[1840]

218 B.C.

Consul Scipio lands at the Massaliote colony of Emporion (Emporiae) with two Legions.[1841] Emporiae a 'Greek city, for they are also sprung from Phocaea'.[1842] Peddie writes that Scipio's army consisted of 10,000 foot, 1,000 horses[1843] and a fleet of thirty-five (five-banker)[1844] 300 rowers, two men to each oar of ninety oars each side, escorted by four Massaliote triremes,[1845] while Polybius write of 8,000 men and thirty-five warships.[1846] In the following year Scipio's advanced from Emporion to Tarraco (Tarragon) by land and held an assembly of all the allies, and received embassies 'out of the entire province . . . There he ordered the ships to be beached, while he sent back four triremes of the Massilians which out of courtesy had escorted him from their home.'[1847] On the second day out of Tarraco he came to anchorage ten miles from the mouth of the River Ebro.

'Thence he dispatched two Massaliot scouting vessels, which reported the Punic fleet lying in the mouth of the river and their camp established on the bank.'[1848]

A Greek trireme consisted of a captain (trieraroe), who was usually a wealthy citizen, sometimes this could be shared if there was not enough money who volunteered for one year to keep the ship seaworthy and hire a crew. In fourth century Athens symmorai (syndicates or companies) were organised to share the responsibility and costs.[1849] In addition there were marines (epibatai) ten citizen hoplites, four archers, ship's officers (a helmsman and a lookout); a rowing master assisted by a pipe player (trieraules), a purser and a shipwright to make emergency repairs.[1850] The crew were on the three levels of '62 thranite, 54 zygian and 54 thalamian (31, 27 and 27 on each side) making a total of 170 oars' (one man to each oar). Troop carriers held up to forty hoplites soldiers.[1851] Each rower had an oar, a cushion and rollock thong.[1852]

Battle of the Ebro, Spain
217 B.C.

As well as Livy[1853] Polybius records[1854] that the two Massaliote scouting vessels reported that the Punic fleet were lying at the mouth of the river and the men camped on the bank. The Romans advanced to catch the Carthaginians off guard. They were spotted from one of the many watchtowers on the hill built as lookout for pirates. The watchtower signalled to Hasdrubal and the alarm was raised. However, there was much confusion as those on the beach did not respond at first not believing the Romans were so close. Hasdrubal sent messengers to alert the fleet but as they lower down on the beach did not see the Romans or hear the beat of their oars they still did not respond when suddenly Hasdrubal and the army arrived in haste. The ships were launched in such haste that the soldier's gear and the sailor's confusion interfered with each other's preparations. The Roman battle-line extended along the shore. Once the Carthaginian ships had been launched they made pretence of fighting and turned about and ran for it. They broke their prows on the beach and grounded keels on the shoals. The Romans captured two ships and sunk four. They pressed home their attack on the terror stricken fleet. They attached cables to the undamaged ships and towed them out to sea. The fight continued and of the forty Carthaginian ships twenty-five were captured. Livy comments 'Nor was this the most brilliant feature of the victory, but in the fact that the Romans in one easy battle had made themselves master of that coast'.

The glory goes to Rome in the surviving written record but as we explained in Chapter One how easy it is to overlook the allies' contribution. Fortunately we have another account of the battle from Sosylus of Sparta who was Hannibal's tutor.

Sosylus of Sparta[1855] wrote that the Carthaginians were at a double disadvantage because the Massaliotes knew the naval tactics of the Phoenicians i.e. the *diekplous*. These involved fleets facing each other in line abreast then quickly turn right or left into column sailing through the gaps in the enemy fleet, then turning sharply around and ramming. The Massaliotes had heard of a defensive manoeuvre practiced at Artimisium and copied it at the Battle of the Ebro:

> They gave orders that when [the commanders] drew up the first ships in line abreast to face the enemy they should leave over other ships to support them at appropriate intervals. As well as alternating with the ships of the first line, these will be in a favourable position to attack the ships of the enemy which were making the offensive move, themselves staying in the aforesaid position.[1856]

Sosylus attributes the victory of the Roman fleet to their allied Massaliote naval squadron in paralysing the Carthaginian manoeuvre of *diekplous* by forming a second line to receive such ships as got through.[1857] This victory prevented Hasdrubal from reinforcing his brother Hannibal on campaign in Italy with much needed soldiers and supplies and left him unsupported from Carthage also giving the Roman Navy control of the sea.[1858]

Between the two versions one can see Livy's enthusiasm giving all the credit to a Roman victory with the briefest of mention of their ally Massalia's contribution whereas Sosylus on the opposite side only gives the Massaliote ships the credit and the briefest mention to the Romans. Even allowing for bias more or less from one or the other we still have the details to give some account of what took place that day in 217 B.C.

The twenty ships sent from Rome later in the year,[1859] which still left the fleet at thirty-five[1860] probably replaced a Massaliote squadron of same size.[1861] Polybius writes that Scipio had 8,000 men and thirty-five warships which meant there must have been a lot of transport ships in support.[1862]

212 B.C.
Hasdrubal and Mago (Hannibal's brothers) retake their area in Spain defeating the Romans and the Scipio brothers are killed. Mago is left in charge of Saguntum,[1863] which must have been rebuilt or repaired.

210 B.C.
Scipio's son Scipio Africanus lands in Iberia (Spain) and in 209 B.C. captures New Carthage (Cartagena) and Mago, who surrenders.[1864]

208 B.C.
Rumours of Hasdrubal's army, now massing in Iberia (Spain), cause much anxiety in Rome. His movement across the northern foothills of the Pyrenees went unreported. Massalia again was first with the news and 'the Six Hundred' (their senate) sent envoys to Rome to say that Hasdrubal had crossed over into Gaul with an army and a large amount of gold to hire mercenaries. Rome returned the envoys to Massalia and sent with them an intelligence team to recruit friendly Gallic chiefs and build a network to supply information.[1865]

206 B.C.
The Massaliote colonies are freed from control by the Carthaginians as the Romans finally drive them out of the Spanish peninsular.[1866]

197 B.C.
Appian also records that from 197 B.C. Spaniards had attempted a revolution while Rome was occupied with Gauls on the Po and with Philip of Macedon. The Romans had sent to Spain generals Sempronius Tuditanus, Marcus Helvius and after Minucius.

197–6 B.C.
Battle of Cynoscephalae 197 B.C. was between Rome and Macedonia. Two towns then resisted Antiochus III in Asia Minor; they were Smyrna in Ionia and Lampsacus in Aeolia. During the winter of 197–6 B.C. both appealed to the Roman general Flamininus, and Lampsacus (a Phocaean founded city) sent envoys to their kinsmen in Massalia asking them to use their influence with Rome. Then together with the Massaliotes they went to the Senate in Rome appealing to their mythical relationship with the Romans and asking them to be included in the Roman treaty with Philip V of Macedonia.[1867]

What was this 'mythical relationship'? Was it the Trojan connection or something else? Would either have accounted for the bond between Rome and Massalia almost at its foundation?[1868] Austin in note 2 says it was a fictitious connection based on Lampsacus's membership of the states of the Troad where Troy was situated and therefore they claimed a connection as Rome was mythically descended from Trojans refugees. However we do know that Massalia and Rome kept a long lasting close and loyal friendship as declared in the Decree of Lampsacus 196–5 B.C.[1869] One that seemed to go beyond common interest perhaps mythical or possibly mystical? Who knows what an oracle or prophecy might have said? Cicero describes it was their geographical destiny to protect Romans (*Fonteius*, 45). Lucan in his epic poem *Pharsalia* writes of the Massaliote envoys speech to Julius Caesar regarding their long support of the Romans that includes,

> Sacred to us you are–oh, may no stain
> Of Latin blood our innocence profane![1870]

On a material level Massalia and Rome throughout their history had threats in common such as Teutons, Cimbri, Ligurians, Celts (Gauls), and Carthaginians.

196–5 B.C.
The 'Decree of Lampsacus in honour of an ambassador to Massalia and Rome' (196/5 B.C.).[1871]

195 B.C.
The revolt in Spain continued and Cato was sent there with a larger force. Livy records Marcus Porcius Cato (Cato the Elder) who 'forcibly dislodged a garrison of Spaniards that were in that fortress' after a revolt by Rhodus (Rhode) during a major rebellion in Spain.[1872] Cato arrived at the Massaliote colony of Emporion and the Spaniards assembled 40,000 against him. Before the fight he 'dismissed all the ships back to Massilia so the troops having no escape had to win.'[1873]

193 B.C.
L. Tarentius Massaliota was in the Roman embassy sent to Antiochus.[1874]

***Circa* 190 B.C.**
The Celtic Galatians were raiding Pergamum in Asia Minor and demanding tribute from the city of Lampsacus. Lampsacus like Massalia was a Phocaean city.[1875] Ambassadors led by Hegesias from Lampsacus were sent to Massalia asking them to influence the Celtic Tolostoagian of Galatia in Asia Minor not to join Antiochus III of Syria in fighting Rome. There is mention of a letter in the Decree of Lampsacus 196–5 B.C. but Austin points out there are no more details of content.[1876] Ellis writes of the Massaliote letter to the Celts emphasised the good relations the Celts living around Massalia had with themselves and Rome.[1877] The Tolostoagians ignored the letter sent by the Massaliote senate via the ambassadors from Lampsacus. The Celtic Galatians joined Antiochus III. A Roman Army under the brothers Lucius Cornelius Scipio and Publius Cornelius Scipio, (called Africanus), together with their new ally Eumenes II of Pergamum, defeated them.[1878] Ellis points out the kinship that was felt in spite of distance between the Celts in Gaul and those in Asia Minor. Clerc mentions the importance of the letter to Massalia and with their endorsements to the Roman Senate that subsequently marks the beginning of intervention in Asia Minor by Rome.[1879]

Second and First Century B.C.

189 B.C.
The ambassadors from Massalia 'reported Lucius Baebius, the Praetor, who was on his way to Spain, had been surrounded by the Ligures, that a large part of his retinue had been killed and himself wounded, that he with a few attendants but no lictors had taken refuge at Massalia and had died within three days'.[1880]

Vulso's inflammatory speech to his Roman troops about the 'degenerate' Gallograeci where even Massalia, like a paragon of virtue in the Roman mind, had been touched by Celtic barbarism (Livy 38.17), in contrast to the Rhodian's speech of Massalia as unsullied and resistant (Livy 37.21).

181 B.C.
Strabo tells us that around the coast of Massalia the seaboard was 'inhabited by the Massaliotes and Sallyes [1881] as far as the Ligures, to those parts that lie towards Italy and to the Varus River'.[1882]

Massalia asked Rome for help against Ligurian pirates.[1883]

The defence of the coast was organised by the Roman Duumvirs. Ten ships were assigned to each with the promontory of Minerva (Sorrento) as the joint. One defends the right sector as far as Massilia and the other the left as far as Barium (Bari).[1884]

One may wonder why the Massaliotes with their navy could not deal with this alone. The sea can be a big place and skilful sailors can elude pursuers being in the same area but just below the horizon. Tracking pirates can be a lengthy process. Therefore the more ships you can have on patrol the more likely you will eventually find the pirates and come to a confrontation. Livy tells us that in this period piracy had become endemic. The Romans had been fighting Ligurian pirates since 203 B.C. along the Riviera coast [1885] and the Ligurians were threatening to invade North Italy.[1886]

The Ligurians were defeated by L. Aemilius Paullus and restricted as to the size of ship they could use.[1887]

180 B.C.
Tribune to the soldiers Lucius Tarentius Massiliota came from Quintus Fulvius Flaccus in Nearer Spain and was presented to the Senate by Consul Aulus Postumius. The Tribune reported two victories and the submission of the Celti-Iberians.[1888] Previously in their positions as Aedile's Lucius and Gnaeus Balbius Tamphilus, who had been chosen Praetor, 'repeated the Plebeian Games three times entire'.[1889]

Aulus Postumius destroys 'the vineyards and burned the crops of the Ligurians of the mountains, until compelled by the disaster of war, they submitted and gave up their weapons'.[1890] Ligurian wine was usually 'mixed with pitch, and harsh'.[1891] According to Dioscurides (5.8) this wine was mixed one or two ounces of pitch to six gallons of new wine. A resinated wine (Retsina) is still used in Greece.[1892]

173 B.C.
A Roman Praetor Numerius Fabius Buteo travelling to Nearer Spain died at Massilia. Massaliote ambassadors took the news to Rome.[1893]

All the lands between the Roman possessions in Spain and that of Italy were occupied by Gaul and Liguria with fierce Celts and Ligurians. Rome's only friend and ally en route was the Greek city-state of Massalia and its colonies. There was a coastal track the 'Voie Héracléene' (Via Heraclensis) but not suitable for 'serious transport' until the time of Augustus.[1894]

167 B.C. The current view of the wholesale influence of when Greek culture came to Rome is after the Roman conquest of Epirus 167 B.C.[1895] where 150,000 Greeks were enslaved and brought to Italy. The influence of Greeks culture, ideas and religion was so great the Roman Horace wrote that 'Captured Greece overcame its fierce conqueror, and brought the arts to rustic Latium' *Graecia capta ferum uictorem cepit, et artes / intulit agresti Latio.*[1896]

But does this infer the start of contact? In Rome within fifty years of its legendary foundation 754-753 B.C. by Romulus there is evidence of Euboean and Corinthian pottery.[1897] There had been contact by trade[1898] particularly with Massalia their ally, and the Greek cities of South Italy where there were so many that the whole area were called Magna Graecia (Greater Greece). In 272 B.C. there was the capture of Tarentum[1899] that brought the Greek Lucius Livius Andronicus to Rome who stayed on after becoming free staging plays and translating Greek works into Latin.[1900] The Romans had enslaved the entire population of the Greek city of Acragus in Sicily 261 B.C.[1901] There was also the annexation of Sicily in 210 B.C. with all its Greek cities that had an influence of Greek thought, lifestyle and study of the arts. Many of the Roman elite had a Greek education before 167 B.C. The difference after 167 B.C. is that there were so many Greek slaves that the contact with Roman families that owned slaves would have been more widespread and could be experienced at all walks of life and be seen by ordinary Romans.

155–154 B.C.
Due to a large population the Celts and Ligurians could frequently mass over 100,000 fighting men. Besieging several cities at the same time necessitated the Massaliotes to ask their ally Rome for help.

Polybius records that 'Envoys arrived from the people of Massilia who had long suffered the incursions of the Ligurians, and were now entirely hemmed in, the cities of Antibes [Antipolis] and Nice [Nikaia, Nicaea] being besieged as well'.[1902]

An attack on Massalia in 155 B.C.[1903] by the Salluvii caused Rome to send a commission with Flaminus, Popillius Laenas and Lucius Pupius together with the Massaliotes.[1904] They wanted to see for themselves and to reason with the tribes. They were attacked at Oxybian, the coastal city of Aegitna.[1905] Flaminus landed first at and 'the Ligurians on hearing they came to order them to raise the siege prevented the others who were bringing their ship to anchor from disembarking'. The Ligurians ordered Flaminus to quit and started rifling his luggage. His slaves tried to prevent this and a fight broke out with two slaves struck down. Flaminus is wounded but with two other slaves gets to the other ship and makes it back to Massalia. His servant is sent to the Consul in Rome with the news.[1906]

Rome dispatched an army[1907] under Consul Quintus Opimius and defeated the Oxybil and the Deciates at the Battle of Aeginta 3 km north of Antipolis (Antibes). The inhabitants of Aegitna are sold into slavery by Opimius. 'The campaign, then, both began and ended rapidly'.[1908] Opimius sent those who had attacked the commission to Rome in chains. He 'added as much of the captured territory as he thought fit to give to Massalia' and compelled the Ligurians to give hostages to them for certain periods.[1909] Wallbank comments that the sole beneficiaries of the Roman action were Massalia as the Ligurians were cut off from the sea.[1910]

129 B.C.
Cicero writes of large Roman taxes on wines sold in Gaul in that

> We ourselves, indeed the most just of men who forbid the races beyond the Alps to plant olive or the vine, so that our own olive groves and vineyards may be the more valuable, are said to act with prudence in doing so, but not with justice; so that you can easily understand that wisdom and equity do not agree. [1911]

This speech by Cicero is odd as the Romans still did not have any interest in keeping a permanent presence in this area and it seems that this ban was primarily for the benefit of their ally Massalia who were given the territory and hostages after the campaign by Opimius and Flaminius in 154 B.C. Since 200 B.C. Roman exports of wine and pottery to Gaul had begun to dominate the markets, which affected Massalia's with a decline in their own trade. The ban would help Massalia maintain dominance in at least their local markets.[1912] Sage points out that after 125 B.C. amphorae remains shows a ten-fold increase in Italian wines to Gaul and by 100 B.C. replacing those of Massalia for export.[1913] Black-painted Campanian vessels were also found. An introduction in Massalia of flat-bottomed amphorae 'later first century' indicates Massalia's own wine trade increased.[1914]

129 B.C.
The city of Phocaea in Asia Minor sided with the revolt of Aristonicus against Rome. Blossius the Greek tutor of the Roman reformer Tiberius Gracchus joined Aristonicus after Gracchus had been killed in Rome.[1915] Aristonicus promised freedom in his own kingdom to any slave that would fight for him but was subsequently defeated by the Romans. Phocaea only avoided destruction from the Romans by asking their settlement of Massalia to use their position as Rome's oldest ally to influence the Roman Senate:[1916]

> The senate had given orders for the destruction of the city and the entire people of Phocaeans because they had borne arms against the Roman people both in this war and, earlier, in the war fought with Antiochus; and after Aristonicus had been taken prisoner, the people of Massilia, since the Phocaeans were their founders, sent a deputation to Rome to make an appeal on their behalf, and succeeded in gaining a pardon from the senate.[1917]

Phocaea had really pushed their luck twice and could expect no mercy the second time. This is another instance that shows the high regard that the Romans had for their loyal and faithful ally of Massalia and subsequently their influence that could alter Roman policy and a decision of the Roman Senate. Then as now it is not an easy thing to alter government policy and decisions once made. For a government to adopt a different course of action a considerable effort is needed to present a better case or substantial influence is required.

Why did Phocaea turn against the Romans during the war against Antiochus? Livy records that 'Livius was in command of the Roman fleet. He proceeded with fifty decked ships to Neapolis [Naples a Greek city in South Italy, Magna Graecia], where the open vessels which the cities on that coast were bound by treaty to furnish had received orders to assemble'. Collecting more ships that were bound by the same treaty 'six from Carthage, and ships by Regium and Locris and other cities', he performed a ceremony 'the lustration of the fleet and put out to sea'.[1918]

The Romans take on supplies at Phanae in the south of Chios then set sail to Phocaea. Eumenes joins the Roman fleet there and altogether have 105 decked ships and 50 open ones: [1919]

> Meantime a revolutionary movement was started in Phocaea by certain individuals who tried to enlist the sympathies of the populace on the side of Antiochus. They had various grievances; the presence of the ships in their winter quarters was a grievance; [1920] the tribute of 500 togas and 50 tunics was a grievance; the scarcity of corn was an additional and serious grievance. Owing to this scarcity the Roman force in occupation left the place, and now the party which were haranguing the plebs in favour of Antiochus were freed from all apprehensions. The senate and the aristocracy were for maintaining the alliance with Rome, but the revolutionaries had more influence with the masses. [1921]

Polybius records that the Phocaean magistrates were alarmed at the 'state of popular excitement' and sent envoys for and against to Seleucus not to enter the Phocaea 'as they were resolved to remain neutral and await the final decision of the quarrel, and then obey orders'. Among these ambassadors were 'partisans of Seleucus, Aristarchus, Cassander, and Rhodon; those on the contrary, who inclined to Rome were Hegias and Gelias'. Seleucus ignored the latter but when he heard of the dissension in Phocaea and lack of food he discontinued discussions and marched on the town. Two Galli (priests of the goddess Cybele) went out from the town 'with sacred images on their breasts, and besought them not to adopt any extreme measures against the city'... [1922]

> Seleucus captured through an act of treachery the city of Phocaea; one of its gates was opened to him by a soldier on guard. The alarm this created led Cyme and other cities on that coast to go over to him. [1923]

Livy describes that Phocaea was situated in the innermost part of the bay. It was oblong in shape; two and a half miles of walls enclosed the city, then narrows on either side like a wedge. The apex of the wedge is called Lamptera. There were two harbours. One faced north called Naustathmon and was the anchorage for larger ships and the other faced towards Lamptera. The city had a breadth of 1200 paces and the tongue of land stretches seawards. [1924]

When the Roman fleet returned into the harbours, the Praetor thought to talk to the magistrates and leading people of the city before laying siege. But he found they were 'bent on resistance'. He attacked Phocaea at two different points. The first had one quarter that contained few private buildings and 'considerable space being occupied by temples'. [1925] The walls battered here and in the other section were ruined. The Romans entered but were met with determined resistance as the Phocaeans put more belief in their force of arms then the walls. The Praetor retires 'unwilling to expose them heedless to an enemy maddened by despair'. [1926] The Phocaeans would not rest and used the time instead to repair and strengthen 'what had been laid in ruins'. [1927] Q. Antonius is sent by the Praetor to tell them that they were more anxious than they were not to destroy the city and they could surrender on the same terms they had obtained from C. Livius. The Phocaeans asked for a five-day truce and sent an envoy to Antiochus to see if any support was coming. Antiochus told them not to expect any. So the Phocaeans opened their gates to the Romans after stipulating they should not be treated as enemies.

The Praetor announced his wish that those surrendered should be spared. On marching into the city his troops protested regarding the Phocaeans as 'never having been loyal allies, but always bitter enemies, getting off with impunity' [1928] There was shouting and the men at the cry, as though the Praetor had given the signal ran off to sack the city. Aemilius tried to stop them saying only 'captured and not surrendered cities were sacked and even in the case of these the decision rested with the general and not the soldiers'... [1929]

> When he saw that passion and greed were too strong for his authority, he sent heralds through the city with orders to summon all free men into the forum where they would be safe from injury, and so far as his authority extended kept his word. He restored to them their city, their lands and their laws, and as winter was now approaching he selected the harbours of Phocaea for the winter quarters of his fleet. [1930]

129 B.C.

Livy records that after the final defeat of Antiochus there was a meeting at the Senate in Rome. After a speech by King Eumenes, the envoys from Rhodes gave a long speech as to the division of spoils and the freedom of Greek cities whether on the mainland or founded elsewhere. They gave Massalia as an example and in it also refer to the opinion the Romans held towards its ancient ally:

> The people of Massilia, whom, if inborn nature could be conquered, so to speak, by the temper of a land, so many untamed tribes around them would have long ago been barbarised, we hear are held in the same respect and deservedly paid the same honour by you as if they dwelt in the very navel of Greece. For they have kept not only the sound of their speech along with their dress and their outward appearance, but, before all, their manners and laws and character pure and free from the corruption of their neighbours. [1931]

125 B.C. Province–Provence

As a result of a Salluvii attack, Massalia appealed to Rome for aid in 125 B.C. that resulted in the formation of the 'Province' (Narbonensis). There was a military campaign led by the consul Marcus Fulvis Flaccus. Flaccus controversially wanted to enfranchise Italians with Roman citizenship [1932] but was sent off at short notice by the Senate (conveniently diverting a political crisis in Rome) to help Massalia against the Saluvii and Vocontii. [1933] The campaign was continued by Giaus Sextus Calvinus 123–122 B.C. that destroyed their chief town and founded, near the ruins, a new colony of Aquae Sextiae (Aix-en-Provence). Part of their territory they gave to Massalia. The Roman garrison at Aqua Sextus kept the barbarians back from the seaboard Massalia to Italy, 'only 12 stadia' where the coast had good harbours, 'and at the rugged parts, only eight'. [1934]

The original 'Province' did not include the independent Greek city-state of Massalia (Marseille) or its colonies, which was an ally of Rome. The name 'Province' still exists today as Provence that now includes Massalia (Marseille). Nice (Nikaia) became part of Provence and France in 1860. [1935]

c. 123–122 B.C.

There must have still been a threat from the Saluvii for the following campaign was taken to pacify the area. There were buried Massalia coin hoards of 316 AR obols in Aix and 1,434 AR obols in Entremont. [1936] The Romans under the consuls M. Fulvius Flaccus and again by C. Sextus Calvinus sacked the Saluvii stronghold the oppidum (hillfort) of Entremont. Teutomalios 'king' of the Salyens escaped to the Allobroges. [1937] The Allobroges are also attacked and their chieftain Bitius taken captive to Rome. [1938] The capital of the Allobroges was at Vienne (in Gaul) and later became the Colonia Julia Viennensium during the reign of Augustus. [1939] In 122 B.C. C. Sextus Calvinus founded Aquae Sextiae at the springs (now called Aix-en-Provence) 3 km from Entremont.

Though the Romans thought of themselves as civilised and that the Celts as barbarians,[1940] it is interesting to note differences of viewpoint. Despite the appalling barbaric custom of the Celts in keeping and displaying the heads of their slain enemies, such as the skull tower at the Saluvii hillfort (oppidum) of Entremont,[1941] the Celts thought the Romans were barbaric because they slaughtered their prisoners or sold them into slavery instead of ransoming hostages as the Celts did.[1942]

Aristo of Massalia

Though we do not know what service Aristo performed Lucius Sulla confers Roman citizenship on Aristo of Massilia as mentioned in Cicero's speech *Pro Balbo*.[1943]

102 B.C. Battle of Aquae Sextiae

Seeing the Rhodanus (River Rhône) was silting up, Gaius Marius, Roman Consul, had a new channel cut and presented it to Massalia 'as a meed of their valour in the war against the Ambrones and Toygeni'[1944] at Aquae Sextiae (Aix-en-Provence) in 102 B.C. This is a rare surviving acknowledgement by the Romans of their ally's efforts and is recorded by Strabo.[1945]

Apart from naval battles Strabo words would suggest Massalia's Army fighting with the Romans at a named battle in particular. The other references are in general. As the Battle of Aquae Sextiae was an inland engagement Massalia's Navy was not involved directly.

The channel was named the Marius Channel or Trench.[1946] According to Professor Hodge the canal Fossae Marianae entered the sea at Fos and probably into the River Rhône at Boucle de l'Escale 7 km in length.[1947] Marius had made the channel to better supply the fortified camp he had made by the River Rhône while awaiting the invasion.[1948]

Sertorius disguised himself as a Gaul and obtained valuable information for Marius. The Cimbri were to cross the East Alps and enter Italy by way of Noricum, the Teutones and Ambrones to approach from the west.[1949] Local tradition situates the battle beneath Mont St Victoire where Marius's Roman Army (and allies including Massalia) fought the Ambrones and Toygeni.[1950]

Plutarch reports that the Romans 'slew or took alive over 100,000 of them' though various accounts disagree.[1951] There were so many dead it was said that

> The people of Massilia fenced their vineyards round with the bones of the fallen, and that the soil, after the bodies had wasted away in it and the rains had fallen all winter upon it, grew so rich and became so full to its depths of the putrefied matter that sank into it, that it produced an exceedingly great harvest in after years, and confirmed the saying of Archilochus that "fields are fattened" by such a process.[1952]

The Massaliotes set up two towers as beacons at the entrance of the channel Marius had cut at the River Rhône, to guide ships and they made much wealth by exacting tolls on the river traffic. There they enclosed 'a piece of land which is made an island by the mouths of the river' and 'made a temple to Ephesian Artemis'.[1953] With the changing course of the river this may no longer be an island and somewhere now buried landlocked or underwater are the remains of a Greek Massaliote temple to be discovered? Rivet claims that the temple area is now under the modern port of Fos.[1954] There is ample underwater archaeology and aerial photographs showing the ancient settlement of Fos.[1955]

The Romans, before Marius became leader, had suffered four defeats by the Celts.[1956] The battle, which averted a fearful time, had such an impact it created a lasting legacy to the present day in that many families in Provence usually named one of their sons Marius originally in his honour.[1957]

Circa 110–90 B.C.
The periodic enemies of Massalia receive a devastating blow when the Saluvii strongholds of the Entremont agglomeration were violently destroyed for good by the Romans.[1958]

97-93 B.C.
P. Licinius Crassus, Governor of Spain.

Strabo relates a story that in former times the 'Phoenicians alone carried on this commerce (that is from Gades)' to the Casserterides, or 'Tin Islands'.[1959] A Roman ship–captain followed one Phoenician ship to discover the route but the Phoenician lured him into the shoals and they both were run aground. The Phoenician escaping on the wreckage received many times the value by the State of the cargo he had lost. However, the persistent Romans eventually 'learned all about the voyage'. Strabo relates that Publius Crassus visited the islands and 'laid abundant information before all who wished to traffic over this sea, albeit a wider sea that which separates Britain from the continent'.[1960] De Beer points to Publius Licinius Crassus (the younger) in Brittany 58-56 B.C.[1961]

85 B.C.
With the murder of the Roman consul Lucius Flaccus in Asia his son Lucius Valerius Flaccus fled and joined his uncle Gaius (consul in 93 B.C.) who was staying with their allies the independent Greek city-state of Massalia in Gaul. (This nephew was the same Flaccus who was defended later by Cicero in his speech *Pro Flacco* during 64–63 B.C.).

The Roman Senate authorised Gaius Valerius Flaccus *imperator* to make coins to cover his expenses towards the end of his command. G. Valerius Flaccus issued the Denarius coins in 82 B.C. from the Greek mint at Massalia commemorating his victories. The obverse has a winged bust of victory and a caduceus. The reverse has a legionary aquila with military standards on either side, with the letter H and P (for spearmen), with the abbreviation *ex s(enatus) c(onsulto)* 'by decree of the senate', and on the right his name is abbreviated as *C(aius) Val(erius) Fla(ccus)* with *imperat(or)*.[1962]

Figure 94. Massalia minted this coin for the imperator and Roman Consul Gaius Valerius Flaccus in 85 B.C.

Massalia a Place of Exile for Prominent Romans
82 B.C.–A.D. 28.

Lucius Cornelius Scipio Asiaticus died in exile in Massalia. He was a Marian [1963] and a Consul in 83 B.C. during the Roman Civil War of 83–82 B.C. He unsuccessfully opposed Sulla in Italy at Teanum on the Via Latina, north-west of Casinum; his army deserted.[1964] His daughter Cornelia and son-in-law Publius Sestio spent time with him in Massalia whereas Cicero wrote he 'languished an outcast in a foreign land, a victim of the storms of trouble at home' (civil war) until he died.

Caius Verres as Quaestor of Asia had plundered the Phocaean colony of Lampsacus.[1965] He became the Governor of Sicily 73–71 B.C. After he left Sicily plaintiffs from all the major cities there went to Rome to make complaints against Verres. He was prosecuted by Cicero for corruption in 70 B.C. and after the first speech Verres was persuaded by his advocate Hortensius to go into exile in Massalia in return for low damages to pay the Sicilians.[1966] There he remained for twenty-seven years with some of his plundered treasures. Cicero published his actions in the *Actio Secunda.* When Mark Antony asked Verres in 43 B.C. to return some Corinthian vases he refused. Mark Antony had Verres now seventy years old executed.[1967]

Cataline Conspiracy

In 63 B.C. Cicero was Consul and L. Sergius Cataline offered to go into voluntary exile to Massalia 'to spare his country the horrors of civil war.'[1968]

The choice of Massalia for exile was also a statement that he was not contemplating an immediate return to Rome as the coastal road via Aurelia Sciuri was difficult in winter and spring due to floods and that Massalia by sea was unpredictable and vulnerable to the weather.[1969]

Therefore he would not be in any position to directly influence events in Rome otherwise Cataline could have chosen Dyrrichum on the Illyrian coast instead.[1970]

Though Cicero complains about the violent methods of the Roman Dictator Sulla that 'an unrighteous victory disgraced a righteous cause',[1971] Cicero with a majority of the Senate had voted to have some of Cataline's co-conspirators executed. At the end of his year's Consulship he went to give account as was customary and became accused by the Tribune Metellus Celer that he had violated the Roman Constitution. Only the whole body of the people assembled in their Comitia could pronounce death on Roman citizens. Cicero declared 'he had saved the Republic and city from ruin' and the crowd present supported him.[1972] Five years later his enemy the Tribune P. Clodius Pulcher proposed a bill forbidding fire and water to any who had put a Roman citizen to death without a trail. Cicero knew he was vulnerable if the bill was passed.

He had sympathy from the people but this time was without vital support where it mattered. Cicero wisely withdrew quietly from Rome and went off to Greece 58 B.C. Once this was known a law was passed to banish him, making a public enemy anyone who should recall him, and his houses were plundered.[1973] Clodius confident in his own power began insulting even Pompey the Great who then resolved to get Cicero back. With the support of the new Tribune T. Annius Milo, the Senate passed a bill recalling Cicero.

The Republic was becoming unstable with the intense rivalry amongst the senator class for the top positions in the state. Political unrest was due to both Clodius and Milo who being violent men had led rival gangs in street fights in Rome. The rivalry continued several years to when Milo was a candidate for the Consulship and Clodius for the Praetorship.[1974] Daily street fights had made it impossible to hold the elections. In one fight the gangs met just outside of Rome and Clodius was killed by Milo in 52 B.C. The Senate took a new measure and made Pompey sole consul to stop the street fighting. Milo was put on trial and Cicero defended Milo but was intimidated. As Cicero started speaking there were yells from Clodius's supporters, which the presence of soldiers did not stop. Plutarch mentions that on seeing so many 'weapons glistening all round the Forum, he [Cicero] was so confounded that he could scarce begin his oration. For he shook and his tongue faltered, though Milo attended the trail with great courage'.[1975]

Having lost the case Milo was sentenced to exile and he chose Massalia. He left within a few days and his property sold for one twenty-fourth of its value due to 'large debts'.[1976] He took with him many slaves.[1977] Milo perhaps chose Massalia in Gaul, as there were many Roman exiles in Epirus and enemies of his.[1978]

Milo's Mullets
Cicero sent the speech he had meant to speak at the trail to Milo now in Massalia. Upon reading it Milo replied,

'I am glad it was not delivered, for I should then have been acquitted, and never known the delicate flavour of these Massillon Mullets'.[1979]

Considering how close he had been to being elected Consul, the top job in Rome, and having got rid of his enemy Clodius, to suddenly now be in exile one could view Milo's comments not that of a lucky chap on holiday, but maybe taking a philosophical view of his situation or perhaps he was being sarcastic even though the Massillon Mullets were extremely good. Dio Cassius writes of Milo:

For he should not be eating such mullets in Massalia (where he had been passing his exile), if any such defence had been made. This he wrote, not because he was pleased with his condition—indeed he made many efforts to secure his return—but as a joke on Cicero, because the orator, after saying nothing useful at the time of the defence, had later composed and sent to him these fruitless words, as if they could then be of service to him.[1980]

When Julius Caesar was Dictator for eleven days before becoming Consul again during the Civil War he allowed all exiles to return except Milo.[1981] Though Caesar does not mention Milo in his book he would still have been at Massalia when Caesar was there to accept the city's surrender in 49 B.C. during the civil war and it seems probable that they would have met and more likely interviewed/assessed him? Whatever they may have said determined Caesar's actions in leaving Milo there in exile (no doubt to continue his 'appreciation' of Massalia's Mullets)! He was 'known to be a man of wicked daring' as was evident on his return to South Italy to join Caelius in the freebooter rising against Caesar in 48 B.C. where he was killed.[1982]

Later Clodius's widow Fulvia married Mark Antony. Fulvia was a most powerful force in Rome able to raise armies in defending Mark Antony's interests against Octavian.[1983] Her image also appears on coins 42 B.C.[1984] Fulvia exacted a revenge on Cicero when he was killed under the orders of proscription from Mark Antony and the Triumvirate in 43 B.C. When Cicero's head was delivered to Mark Antony his wife Fulvia pulled out her large hair pin and stabbed Cicero's tongue;[1985] the tongue that had supported Milo's candidature for consul and defended the murderer of her former husband.

Cicero

As well as five speeches already mentioned further evidence of Rome's admiration of Massalia their ally was given by Cicero.

Fonteius was accused by the Volcae and Indutiomarus a chieftain of the Allobroges[1986] of corrupt practices when Fonteius was Praetor in Gaul c. 75 to 73 B.C. Cicero in his defence speech of Fonteius calls on witnesses from Massilia, Narbo and Roman residents from the province:

> There is also the city of Massilia, to which I have already alluded, inhabited by brave and faithful allies, who have found in the resources and rewards of the Roman people a recompense for the dangers they have run in our Gallic wars.[1987]

Cicero continues,

> And what of the community of Massilia? While he [Marcus Fonteius] was with them they conferred upon him the highest distinctions they had to bestow; and now from their distant abode, they beg and implore you that their sense of honour, their commendation, their influence may appear to have been not without weight in determining your attitude.[1988]

56 B.C.
Rowers, seamen and pilots were transported from Massalia to the mouth of the Loire where Julius Caesar was building a fleet to attack the Veneti (in Brittany). After their submission in 57 B.C. the Veneti had risen up against officers of the Roman VII (seventh) Legion left to watch them. The Veneti were a maritime power with a fleet of 220. They traded along the coast of Gaul, Britain and Ireland. Much of their wealth originated from trading tin from the mines in Cornwall. It was the rumour that Caesar was going to invade Britain that made them fight to protect their trading interests.[1989]

A.D. 2
Augustus's adopted grandson Lucius Caesar consul designate died at Massalia. A bronze letter inscription [1990] dated to A.D. 4–5 [1991] dedicated to him and his brother Gaius was found in Nimes. Nimes was trading with Massalia from the fifth century B.C. and became a Roman colony under Julius Caesar, its coins being inscribed COL(onia) NEM(ausus). [1992] Maurel suggests a localised obol Massalia design 120–49 B.C. head (but with letter behind neck) /wheel, MA, at 0.45 g.[1993]

A.D. 25
Volcacius Moschus was in exile in Massalia and he became naturalized there and left all his property to it as if it was his own country. Massalia petitioned Rome and it was granted due to a precedent of an earlier exile, Publius Rutilius Rufus, who had become a citizen of Smyrna.[1994] Moschus was originally a citizen of Pergamum and had been accused of poisoning.[1995] He started a famous school of rhetoric in Massalia that was known as the School of Moschus the Apollodorean of Massalia.[1996]

Lucius Antonius had been as a boy dismissed 'to Massalia, where the name of exile could be veiled under the pretext of study' by his great-uncle Emperor Augustus. The emperor had executed Lucius's father for adultery with Julia who was the emperor's daughter. Lucius died in Massalia but the Senate decreed his remains were to be 'placed in the tomb of the Octavii'.[1997]

Petronius Arbiter (A.D. 27–66)
Petronius was a Roman writer and satirist. He is attributed to have written the Satyricon and there is some speculation from Sidonius Apollinaris in *Carmen* XXIII. 145. 155 that might imply that he lived and wrote in Massalia:[1998]

> Why should I hymn you, tuneful Latin writers, thou of Arpinum, thou of Patavium, thou of Mantua. And thou, Arbiter, who in the gardens of the men of Massalia findest a home on the hallowed tree-trunk as the peer of Hellespontine Priapus?[1999]

From the reconstructed fragments Servius cites Petronius [2000] for the 'Scapegoat' ritual from Massalia. Some scholars speculate that the leading character Encolpius had offered him as a 'scapegoat' and was ritually expelled.[2001] The cult of Priapus started in another Phocaean colony of Lampsakos in the Hellespont (Dardanelles) where a donkey was sacrificed.[2002]

A.D. 54–58
Seneca the Roman philosopher wrote an essay to Emperor Nero (A.D. 54–68) titled *On Mercy*. In it he used the example of Tarius who suspected his son was involved in a plot to kill him. Augustus Caesar came to his house and sat next to Tarius and they listened to the trail. The son was found guilty. Tarius won the admiration of everyone satisfying himself with exile of his son to Massilia. Tarius had condemned his son but could not hate him. This was generous as the punishment for

parricide was death by drowning in a sack with a snake inside. Tarius still 'furnished him with the same liberal allowance' that he had before his guilt. 'A luxurious exile' it was for his son in Massilia. 'In a community where a villain never lacks a defender no one doubted that the accused man had been justly condemned'.[2003]

Tacitus (A.D. 56–117)

Tacitus mentions Faustus Cornelius Sulla Felix who was falsely accused of plotting against Nero.[2004] Even though there was no evidence he was exiled to Massalia.[2005] Tigellinius intrigues had Cornelius Sulla assassinated there.[2006]

Crinas and Charmis Famous Doctors of Massalia

First Century A.D.
When in Rome be a Greek!

The Roman Pliny the Elder was comparing good doctors in Rome with those of the past and present 'It was not medicine that our forefathers condemned, but the medical profession, chiefly because they refused to pay fees to profiteers in order to save their lives'.[2007] Pliny complained of the enormous fees charged by the doctors. The emperors paid 250,000 sesterces annually to their doctors like Cassius, Calpetanus, Arrunuius and Rubrias. The doctors were invariably Greek and in this case one could change the old phrase to When in Rome be a Greek! During the time of Emperor Nero, Thessalus 'swept away all received doctrines, and preached against physicians of every age with a rabid frenzy'.[2008]

A.D. 100–200.
The average age of life expectancy was 20–30 years for women and a little higher for men,[2009] illnesses could be sudden and death followed.

No one wants to be ill and the instinct for survival left people in need vulnerable to anyone who claimed to offer a cure. The mainstream medical profession did not like alternative medicines or any claim to cures that may either be false or would interfere with its own profits, which has been the case up to modern times.[2010]

The leading doctors in Ancient Rome were given the adulation of celebrities and like leading surgeons in the U.S.A. today with enormous fees. Cosmetic surgeons attain much money and celebrity status in the U.S.A.[2011] Each Physician in Ancient Rome proclaimed his method best and others worthless and it seems they were taken up with different diets and exercise fads just like the last 30 years here in Britain.

Ancient Massalia benefited from this trend when Crinas of Massalia paid for the building of its walls from his medical profits [2012] during the reign of Nero.[2013] Emperor Nero (A.D. 54–68) may have had an interest in Massalia not only as a lover of Greek culture (Apollonius went so far as to declare he had set Greece 'free'), [2014] but also as the descendant of Cnaeus Domitius Ahenobarbus, who had helped Massalia against the Allobroges and the Arvernes.[2015] Also Lucius Domitius Ahenobarbus (Nero's grandfather) when Governor of Gaul had persuaded Massalia to join Pompey and the Roman government's side against Julius Caesar and fought with them in the Civil War during 49 B.C.

Pliny the Elder continues as for Thessalus on his

> monument on the Appian Way he described himself as *iatronices*, "the conqueror of physicians". . . No actor, no driver of a three-horse chariot, was attended by greater crowds than he [Thessalius] as he walked abroad in public, when Crinas of Massilia united medicine with another art, and being of a rather careful and superstitious nature, and regulated the diet of patients by the motions of the stars according to the almanacs of the astronomers, keeping watch for the proper times, and outstripped Thessalius in influence. Recently he left ten millions, and the sum he spent upon building the walls of his native city and other fortifications was almost as much.
>
> These men were ruling our destinies when suddenly the state was invaded by Charmis, also from Massilia, who condemned not only previous physicians but also hot baths, persuading people to bathe in cold water even during the winter frosts. His patients he plunged into tanks, and we used to see old men, consulars, actually stiff with cold in order to show off. Of this we have today a confirmation even in the writings of Annaeus Seneca [*Epistles* VI. 1, 3 and XII. 1, 5]. There is no doubt that all these, in their hunt for popularity by means of some novelty, did not hesitate to buy it with our lives. Hence those wretched, quarrelsome consultations at the bedside of the patient, no consultant agreeing with another lest he should appear to acknowledge a superior. [2016]

Pliny continues quoting a 'gloomy inscription on monuments: "It was the crowd of physicians that killed me"'.[2017] He goes on to say on the fads and fashions of medicine that 'anyone among them who acquires power of speaking at once assumes the supreme command over our life and slaughter'.[2018] 'Medicine changes every day' . . . 'being swept along on the puffs of the clever brains of Greeks'.[2019] Thousands of people live without doctors as the 'Roman people have done for six hundred years'.[2020] Pliny acknowledges the Roman's ability to adopt other skills from foreign cultures and it was 'Medicine alone of the Greek arts' very few had tried 'in spite of its great profits'.[2021] Pliny cites the famous doctor from Massilia,

> It is well known that Charmis aforesaid exchanged one sick provincial for 200,000 sesterces by a bargain with Alcon the wound-surgeon; that Charmis was condemned and fined by the Emperor Claudius the sum of 1,000,000 sesterces, yet as an exile in Gaul and on his return from banishment he amassed a like sum within a few years. [2022]

Scholars often argue what led to the decline of the Roman Empire. Was it too much wealth from their conquests, moral corruption, senatorial rivalry, ambitious generals, even Christianity? However no one thing could have done it alone and it seems a combination of all of them. Pliny the Elder blames the ruin on 'the Manners of the Empire' [2023] in agreement with Cato the Elder's ideas of Greek literature and their Medical Profession: [2024]

> It is certainly true that our degeneracy, due to medicine more than to anything else, proves daily that Cato was a genuine prophet and oracle when he stated that it is enough to dip into the works of Greek brains without making a close study of them. Thus much must be said in defence of that Senate and those 600 years of the Roman State, against a profession where the treacherous conditions allow good men to give authority to the worst, and at the same time against the stupid convictions of certain people who consider nothing beneficial unless it is costly.[2025]

One can see even in modern times how some ancient attitudes persists and how little seems to have changed with some human beings since then and now particularly in regard to valuing something only if it is expensive.

Summary

We can see that from other surviving written sources that Massalia had a connection with Rome almost at the time of its foundation on the coast of France in c. 600 B.C. Some scholars will only go as far as the fourth century B.C. regarding anything earlier as being invented or myth. However this 'early' connection was used by another Phocaean colony of Lampsakos (Lampsacus) in wanting to be included in a treaty. They asked Massalia to intervene on their behalf due to the good relations they had with Rome. When the mother-city of Phocaea had fought against the Rome twice they asked Massalia to make an appeal to their Roman ally and were granted a pardon from the senate not to have the city and people destroyed as punishment.

As to the mythical relationship claimed between Rome and Massalia was it the Trojan connection or some prophecy binding them together? Cicero says it was their destiny to protect Romans. Justin and Lucan record Massalia had supported Rome in all her wars. Rome placed its votive offerings in the treasury of the Massaliotes at Delphi in Greece. Rome was once occupied and besieged by the Celts in 390 B.C. it was a real fear of Celts and further invasions that frequently dominated the Roman mind. [2026] There must have been some awe and admiration of how Massalia had been able to keep its empire intact and prosper while surrounded on land by the formidable warrior Celtic and Ligurian tribes for many centuries. The same awe and wonder that Livy records to Massalia's colony of Emporion 'by what cause they were preserved' though 'deficient of strength' but with 'regular discipline' were thriving amongst the 'fierce and warlike' Spanish. [2027] Massalia was a suitably comfortable city in which prominent Romans spent their exile as well as its famous schools, which 'notable' Romans used for their education if they did not want to go to Athens. [2028]

As for Massalia and Rome's earliest contacts while scholars have doubted Justin's account by assuming the later treaty ties of the third century B.C. were also projected back to the era of the foundation of Massalia, Thiel clarifies that at least ties of friendship were early going back several centuries before the Punic Wars. [2029] Justin (from Trogus) mentions the treaty between Rome and Massalia for the help given by Massalia to end the siege of Rome by the Gauls in the 390 B.C. However since the doubts there has been archaeological discoveries of an Ionian trading post at Gravisca from 600-480 B.C., the Etruscan port of Tarquinia, that does give substance to Justin's story (from Trogus) of the Phocaeans being in the vicinity–visiting the 'mouth of the Tiber' and making an alliance with the Romans in the time of King Tarquin (Priscus) on their way to found Massalia–and according to Livy the *Massilienses* arrived in Gaul during the reign of L.Tarquinius Priscus, king of Rome (616–578 B.C.) and settled where they landed.

Having established themselves Massalia increased with colonies successfully for several centuries. By the second century B.C the enormous strength and mass of the Celts and Ligurians put pressure on Massalia and they increasingly asked their Roman ally for help. The Romans supported their Massaliotes allies as an independent city-state in a strategic position in the 'front line' that blocked part of the coastal route to Italy. The Celts would have to cross the Alps to join up with the large numbers of Celts already living in North Italy. Roman support of Massalia partly helped keep the Celts from the 'throat of Italy'. Celtic territories the Romans captured they gave to Massalia to administer, tax, and control. The joint action of Massalia and Marius turned the tide of four Roman defeats by the Celts with victory at the Battle of Aqua Sextae. The increasing pressure of the Celts necessitated the Romans to form the Province (Narbonensis) next to their ally the independent city-state of Massalia. This was done with Roman senatorial opposition in 118 B.C.[2030] Could this be because they did not want permanent involvement outside of Italy or was it their connection with Massalia? The Province with its port of Narbo would compete with Massalia's trade but it helped pay for the Romans to be there.

While we have a reasonable hypothesis from Thiel that the Greek cities of Naples (Neapolis) and Massalia's naval contingents as well as ships from the other Italiote towns joined the Roman fleet at the Battle of Mylae in 260 B.C., more certainly there is written evidence from Sosylos of Sparta of the crucial part Massalia's navy played allied to the Roman fleet at the Battle of the Ebro 217 B.C. This had enormous repercussions in supplies and men not reaching Hannibal fighting the Romans in Italy. Surely this was one of the crucial parts of the war as Hannibal fought on for sixteen years but with more men and supplies at his time may have been a turning point that could have brought the war to an early conclusion as he received no supplies from Carthage?

Hannibal wanted to take the fabled route of Hercules along the coast to invade Italy but there was in the way Massalia, a well-fortified city with an army and navy. A prolonged siege would bring Rome to help its ally and the element of surprise would be gone. This may be why Hannibal took his army and elephants over the formidable barrier of the Alps instead? Intelligence reports from Massalia proved accurate and vital to their ally Rome regarding Hannibal and advance warning of another army his brother Hasdrubal was preparing for invasion: who took the same route over the Alps into Italy.

Prior to the mass influx of Greek slaves from Epirus in 167 B.C. to Rome there was previous contact with Greeks: merchants by land and sea where some Romans would make trade with the Greek cities in Italy: the capture of Tarentum: and annexation of Sicily. There were so many Greek cities in South Italy it was called Magna Graecia (Greater Greece). Priestesses of Diana came from the Phocaean colony of Elea (Hyele) and also the Greek city of Naples (Neapolis) to serve in the temple in Rome. In addition we know of Senatorial/government contact with ambassadors and envoys of Massalia. Also the military contacts with the Roman Army and Navy they made fighting alongside each other and relating their exploits back home becoming part of the folklore. This increasing bond was given a treaty after 390 B.C. in gratitude for the help Massalia gave to Rome in helping raise and paying the ransom to the Celtic besiegers. Rome granted Massalians tax exemptions and privileges to their senators at the games in Rome. The Romans benefited from Massalia with trade that included wine and amber.

Amongst all the Greek doctors like Galen that dominated the medical profession in Rome two of the most famous, Charmis and Crinas, were from Massalia who earned great fortunes from the Romans. Charmis was fined a quarter of a million sesterces by Emperor Claudius and temporarily banished before amassing another fortune in Rome on his return. Crinas became a multi-millionaire and financed the rebuilding of Massalia's city walls and other fortifications during the reign of Nero. Massalia maintained its good relations and independent status with Rome long after losing most of its empire when the city capitulated to Julius Caesar during the civil war. How this happened is covered in the following chapters.

Chapter 13

Massalia Capitulates 49 B.C.

During the Roman civil war Massalia had supported Pompey the Great against Julius Caesar. The Massaliotes had received a message from Pompey not to forget the favours he had done them as well as Caesar. On this the Massaliotes 'closed their Gates against Caesar and invited over to them the Albici, who had formerly been in alliance with them, and who inhabited the mountains that overhung Massalia'. [2031] Caesar sent for fifteen of the principal persons of Massalia and used several arguments to persuade them to change. Their reply was revealing for the position of a loyal ally for whom to support when civil war breaks out. Reporting to their countrymen the deputies carried the reply,

> That they understood that the Roman people was divided into two factions: that they had neither judgement nor abilities to decide which had the juster cause; but that the heads of these factions were Cnieus Pompey and Caius Caesar, the two patrons of the state: the former of whom had granted to their state the lands of the Volcae Arecomici, and Helvii;[2032]
>
> while the other, having conquered the Sallyes, had attached this people to their state and boosted their revenues. Therefore, since the benefits the Massaliots had received were equal, their duty was to render equal goodwill to each, help neither against the other, and not receive either within the city or its harbours.[2033]

Dio Cassius the Roman historian writes 'Now the Massaliots, alone of the people living in Gaul, did not cooperate with Caesar, and did not receive him into the city, but gave a noteworthy answer'. He records the events in a similar order to Suetonius except adding that Massalia would receive both if approached in a friendly manner, 'without their arms, but if it were a question of making war, neither of them'.[2034]

Consistent with these views Lucan also writes the reply of the Greeks in his poem *Pharsalia*:

> And now, if you seek triumphs from an unknown sphere,
> our hands are ready, pledged to foreign battles.
> But if in discord you plan deadly battle-lines
> and ill-omened conflicts, to your civil war we give
> our tears and our withdrawal. Let sacred wounds be handled
> by no alien hand.[2035]

Figure 95. Captains by artist Andreas Müller in Braun and Schneider, *Historic Costumes in Pictures*, Plate 3 Ancient Greece: series 1861-90 and reissued by Dover Publications, 1975.

A virtue that was very important to the Romans was *fides* (trust, reliance, faith). Lucan's main theme in his epic civil war poem *Pharsalia* shows it was only Massilia that retains its political *fides* to the end unlike others who crumbled.[2036]

'Now the Greek city gained this eternal glory' (Lucan, III. 388–393)

Pompey the Great and most of the Roman Senate had abandoned Italy and made for Greece in which to organise the war against Caesar. His plan was a naval blockade of Italy and to trap Caesar between two great armies namely the seven legions in Spain under three Legates and the forces he was assembling from the Romans and allies in the eastern part of the empire.[2037] Caesar's claim was that he was defending the sacred office of the Tribunes, (Marc Antony and Quintius Cassius), whose power had now been reduced by Pompey and the Senate, and therefore he was upholding the constitution. The Thirteenth Legion 'shouted they were ready to defend their general and the tribunes from harm'.[2038]

Though Pompey was now with the Senate he had been accused in the past, by Cato the Younger, of 'promoting anarchy to achieve monarchy'.[2039] When the Roman Senate had voted a public thanksgiving of twenty days for Caesar during his Fourth Campaign and first invasion of Britain, Cato the Younger declared that Caesar ought to be given up to the Usipetes and Tenchtheri to atone for his treachery in seizing the sacred persons of their ambassadors.[2040] L. Domitius Ahenobarbus was Caesar's enemy and he also called for Caesar's prosecution for his consulship, 'which was supposed to be contrary both to the omens and the laws'. When Domitius was consul he had tried to deprive Caesar of the army.[2041] In spite of the unprecedented honours the threat of prosecution when Caesar had finished his commission and became a private citizen, and no longer covered by immunity, was one of the main causes in his refusing to give up the army and march on Rome. On the 7 January 49 B.C. the Roman senate had ordered Caesar to hand over his ten legions to a new Governor.[2042]

'By intrigue and cabal' Domitius was appointed Caesar's successor and at the beginning of the Civil War he had been captured at Corsinium by Caesar and dismissed.[2043] Once he was free L. Domitius Ahenobarbus as Caesar's successor, the Governor of Gaul, had requisitioned seven ships from 'private owners' at Igilium and Cosa [2044] on the Etrurian coast.[2045] The crews for the ships were 'manned with slaves, freedman, and tenant-farmers of his own'.[2046] He sailed straight to Massalia and arrived as the legal Governor of Gaul appointed by the Senate and by that position a representative of the officially elected Roman government. Just ahead of Domitius a Massaliote delegation of young nobles had arrived back from Rome having been instructed by Pompey as he was leaving Rome to remember the earlier favours he had done to Massalia and not to be swayed by the recent favours they had received from Caesar. 'The people of Massalia accepted these instructions and closed their gates to Caesar': imported all the corn from the surrounding countryside and their forts: opened the armouries: 'repairing the walls, the fleet, and the gates'.[2047]

Caesar summons 'the Fifteen' (cabinet) from Massalia urging 'the Massaliotes to follow the lead of the whole of Italy, rather than humour the wishes of a single man'. After the delegation reported back to Massalia what he said they returned and informed Caesar they made a decision on 'Public Authority' basically to favour neither Pompey or Caesar as they owed much to both equally for the favours done to their city-state and would therefore remain neutral.[2048] Caesar writes that negotiations were still proceeding when Domitius sailed into the harbour and 'being placed in charge; he was granted supreme military command.'[2049]

Siege by Julius Caesar

Suetonius writes that Pompey the Great had consulted his friends 'in what manner he should treat neutrals that regarded indifferently both sides of the contest, he [L. Domitius Ahenobarbus] was the only one who proposed that they should be reckoned as enemies and proceeded against accordingly'.[2050] Unfortunately for Massalia, who wanted to remain neutral, it was Domitius who arrived as Governor of Gaul and with his extreme views. One may hazard a guess that he had given Massalia no choice of staying neutral. If you are not with us, you are against us? They were either Caesar's or Pompey's enemies? Massalia's ruling aristocrats had been conservative in their outlook and siding with the lawful government of Rome would presumably have come more naturally to them when the time came to make a decision?

Domitius ordered the Massaliotes to collect all the boats and grain in the area to be ready in case of a siege. Lucan the Roman poet wrote:

> Now the Greek city gained this eternal glory,
> well deserving mention, that, not compelled or prostrated
> by sheer terror, it checked the headlong rush of war
> raging through the world and when Caesar seized all else at once
> it alone took time to be defeated. What an achievement, to
> detain the Fates. [2051]

Though Massalia had tried persuasion and neutrality Lucan recalls their long alliance with Rome, in their reply to Caesar, 'That Massalia has always shared your people's fates in foreign wars is attested by every age included in the Latin annals'.[2052] The Greek warriors ended their speech on a resolute note 'this people is not afraid to endure for the sake of freedom the ordeal of Saguntum besieged by Punic warfare'.[2053]

This provoked Caesar into sending three legions against Massalia.[2054] Carter suggests it was the VI, X, and XIV under Trebonius's command. Later one if not three was replaced by the VII, XII, and XIII, as the XIV went off to Ilerda to join Fabius's three legions.[2055] Cassius Dio wrote that 'For Caesar had persisted in his attempt for some time to capture them easily, and regarding it as absurd that after vanquishing Rome without a battle he was not received by the Massaliotes'.[2056] He had twelve ships built at Arelate (Arles) in thirty days under the command of Decimus Brutus.[2057] Brutus's flagship during his campaign against Massalia was a 'six' with towers and doubled-manned three-oared system '360 oarsmen to man the twelve oar files (30 in number) and entailed 180 oars'.[2058] Once the twelve ships had arrived Caesar 'put Decimus Brutus in command of them and left his deputy Gaius Trebonius to take charge of the assault on the city'.[2059] Caesar himself made for Spain.[2060]

Rowland writes that Massalia possessed a staff of trained engineers/architects and was 'one of the leading cities in siege craft' [2061] being well stocked in armaments.[2062] Massalia was under siege from April to September 49 B.C. and Caesar victorious took control of the city. This was the city's first defeat in 551 years since it was founded. Earlier the arrival at Massalia of a few ships from Pompey the Great had given much 'hope and enthusiasm' [2063] after a defeat at sea.

Naval Battles

Clerc questions Massalia's admiral Parmeno's strategy or lack of it? Caesar hurriedly had twelve warships built at Arelate (Arles) in thirty days. These ships had to sail down the River Rhône or along the Marius Channel to Fos to enter the Mediterranean. Clerc said it was 'absolutely incomprehensible' [2064] as to why the fleet of Massalia under Parmeno did not go on the attack and blockade Caesar's ships from reaching the Mediterranean. What were the factors in the context of the time? Was Parmeno hampered by the Roman Governor Domitius? Did Domitius or Parmeno know Caesar was building ships? Was there overconfidence? Was Massalia's fleet so run down they needed the time to bring their ships up to scratch? Yet in the thirty days Caesar built twelve new warships Massalia seemingly did not have access to obtaining new timbers and probably used what was available in the city? Perhaps they were able to get some timber elsewhere by sea while their city was blockaded by Caesar's legions on land until they were also blockaded by sea when Brutus arrived with Caesar's twelve warships. It is possible that Caesar had detachments covering strategic parts of the coast preventing Massalia from landing and foraging. The Romans also attacked Massalia's colonies of Olbia and St. Blaise that year. [2065] Once Brutus had arrived and started his naval blockade Parmeno went on the attack by the Frioul Islands outside Massalia.

The Battle of Frioul

Though the Massaliotes and their allies the Albici fought with valour Parmeno lost nine out of seventeen warships at the Battle of Frioul. While the Greeks fought skilfully giving the Romans the run around, Brutus worked out a tactic to his own advantage, which was to use his ships like dry land, a platform on which to fight. Lucan writes:

> Then Brutus says to his helmsman sitting in the ensign-bearing
> stern: "Why do you let the battle-lines range across the deep
> and compete with them in manoeuvres on the sea? Now join battle
> and present our vessels' sides to the Phocaean prows."
> He obeyed and offered his boats sidelong to the enemy.
> Then every ship which attacked Brutus' timbers
> stuck captive to the one hit, defeated by its own impact,
> while others are held fast by grappling-irons and smooth chains
> or tangled by their own oars: the sea is hidden and war stands still. [2066]

Caesar tells us that the Romans defeated the naval skills and speed of the Massaliotes by the use of grappling hooks to bring the ships together, boarding and close quarter hand to hand fighting. [2067] Lucan describes the siege of Massalia: this one of the two Massaliotes' naval battles: and the graphic fates of their sailors Catus, Lycidas, Tyrrhenus, Argus, Telo, and Gyareus. [2068] Suetonius mentions briefly a sea fight at Massalia with a Roman Acilius rivalling the feat of the Greek hero Cynegirus. [2069]

Massalia rebuilt its fleet after the naval Battle of Frioul. Caesar mentions that the authorities had 'repaired old ships' brought out of the ship sheds to bring up to 'its previous size'. They added fishing boats, which 'they had decked to keep the oarsmen safe from the impact of missiles. All these they manned with archers and artillery'.[2070] Pompey sent Nasidius with a fleet of sixteen ships, amongst them a few warships, from Dyrrachium (plus one Nasidius took from his surprise landing at Messana on the way), to help Lucius Domitius and the Massaliotes'.[2071]

The Battle of Tauroention

Nasidius sent one ship secretly to Domitius and the Massaliotes to inform them of his arrival and together with his fleet to try for another battle against Brutus's fleet. Caesar comments,

> . . . they embarked with no less courage and confidence then they had before their previous battle, spurred on by the tears and entreaties of the older men, the women, and the girls, who all begged them to help the city in its hour of crisis. It is a common failing of human nature to be more confident in strange and unprecedented circumstances, as happened on that occasion; for Nasidius' arrival had filled Massilia with hope and enthusiasm.[2072]

Waiting for a favourable wind Domitius's ships and the Massaliote fleet sailed out 'and reached Nasidius at Tauroeis, (Tauroention, Le Brusc, near Toulon) which was a fortified outpost of Massilia'. There 'they got their ships ready and for a second time prepared themselves mentally for battle and discussed their plans [2073] . . . All these they manned with archers and artillery' and by fitting catapults in the battle with Decimus Brutus.[2074] Brutus hurried to the same spot with an increased number of ships, Brutus's 12 ships plus the six captured from Massalia previously which he had repaired.[2075] Caesar writes 'At the same time a great hail of missiles thrown from the smaller boats caused many injuries to our men who were unprepared, encumbered, and taken by surprise'.[2076]

'From Trebonius' Camp and every piece of high ground it was easy to look over the city'.[2077] The population in Massalia were observed that those in the temples were prostrate and others on the battlements with uplifted hands, praying to heaven to grant them victory. Those on the ships were from their 'best known families, together with their most distinguished citizens in every period of life, all of whom had received a personal summons and earnest appeal for service'.[2078]

Caesar notes the skill of the Massaliote captains. When a Roman ship grappled and held a Massaliote ship, all the other Massaliote ships came to its assistance. Their allies the Albici fought courageously in the hand-to-hand fighting and the hail of missiles from the Massaliote ships caused many injuries to Brutus's ships. By contrast Caesar had little good to say about Massalia's Roman ally Nasidius and his ships, they 'were useless'.[2079]

On the left the squadron Nasidius withdrew out of the action intact, leaving the Massaliotes' squadron. Massalia's Navy was defeated a second time.[2080] Caesar thought little of the efforts of Nasidius for he writes

> Nasidius' ships, however, were useless and quickly withdrew from the fighting; no sight of native land, no exhortations of families and friends forced them to risk their lives. And so none of them were lost; from the Massiliot fleet five were sunk, four captured, and one escaped with Nasidius' squadron; these latter all sailed off to Nearer Spain.[2081]

One of the surviving ships went back to Massalia to relay the news of the defeat. 'A wail of lamentation ensued, that one might have thought the town had at that very moment been carried by assault'.[2082]

In spite of this the Massaliotes continued their efforts with dogged determination in the defence of their city. In his book *Civil War*, Caesar wrote that he thought Massalia's confidence had been 'too great' and Pompey's ships had not proved useful in the battle.

Following the victory Brutus did not force an entry into the harbour with his ships. His forces were not enough once they would have landed and could be repelled. He remained content to continue to blockade the port.[2083] While the city continued to live and fight their store of food and armaments would be reduced daily.

Massalia's Commanders 49 B.C.

As no documents survive from Massalia itself we fortunately have a reference in Roman sources that the Massaliote land forces were commanded by Apollonides and the navy by Parmenon, [2084] and his replacement Hermon. Professor Hodge [2085] has this reference from Cornutus Scholiast to Lucan. [2086]

This reference mentioned that the Massaliotes had one person Apollonides[2087] as a 'praetor'. Praetor is translated for stratigos στρατηγός (army leader, general).[2088] Clerc suggests this was combining the offices of a Magistrate and Commander of the land and naval forces in the siege against Julius Caesar 49 B.C.,

Le général qui commanda les forces de terre fut Apollonidès, qui n'était autre que le Président de la Commission des Trois, et par conséquent du Consiel des Six-Cents, et le commandant de la flotte fut Parménon.[2089]

'The general in command of the land forces was Apollonides, and also the President of the Commission of the Three, and consequently Consul of the Six Hundred, and Commander of the fleet of Parmenon'.

Apollonides would have overall command of the defence forces but also over the Government of Massalia.[2090] The translation of Strabo does not mention any person in the government of Massalia higher than the Three except in the footnote of H. L. Jones.[2091] The same edition is on the Perseus website but without Jones's footnote. I did see at the Museum of History in Marseille illustrated on display boards the political structure of ancient Greek Massalia based on Strabo's description. At the top they write after the 600 senators and above them the council of 15, *'L'un des Trois. Devient le premir magistrat de la cité pendant un an, et donne son nom à l'anneé en cours.* It would seem that above the Three there could have been a premier/supreme commander though this may have been a position enacted only in times of war? Our very brief knowledge comes from a Roman source Cornutus Scholiast to Lucan, III. 375 and 524 from the tenth century A.D. manuscript *Commenta Bernensia* (in Bern, Switzerland):

Massiliam autem aduersus Caesarem defensauit praetor Apollonides, urbi qui praefuit, classi autem Parmeno.[2092]

After Massalia's first naval defeat by Decimus Brutus at the Battle of the Frioul Islands Parmeno is replaced by Hermon in command of Massalia's Navy at the Battle of Tauroention (Le Brusc):

dux Gr[a]ecorum Parmeno nauali bello aduersus Brutum fuit prima pugna, sed sequenti, id est hac qua aput Tauronescum dimicatum est, Hermon ei substitutus est, quia Parmeno prius [rem] male gessisset. Hac pugna a Dirracio Lucius Nasidius, auxilo [missus] Massiliensibus, uictus Hispaniam petit. [2093]

Massalia's Fleet

How large was the fleet of Massalia? Why at the time of Caesar's and Pompey's civil war were Massalia's fleet so run down and a force was hurriedly patched together from a variety of old ship from their ship sheds? No matter how wealthy a city-state the cost of financing and maintaining ships, the wages of the crew, armaments, keeping the ships in a seaworthy condition are always under pressure in times of peace. The need for a fleet seems an unnecessary expense when there is no immediate threat anymore. Rather like the dominance of the British Navy in first half of the 1900s. Britain ruled the waves. Having won the First World War, of course not alone 'it goes without saying' but in consideration of the point made in Chapter 1 one should 'say it' otherwise a bias or false impression occurs from one's own point of view that certainly was not meant. So more accurately-Britain together with its Empire, Dominions and Allies that included France and its Empire, Russia, Serbia, Montenegro, Japan, Italy, Greece, the U.S.A. (1917-18) and 28 other countries, won the First World War 1914–18. This became known as 'the war to end all wars' where it was thought afterwards that due to the incredible loss of human life no one would be as stupid as to go to war again. However when one society becomes enlightened another is in a primitive and threatening state before it too hopefully develops better human relations. It is an unfortunate blight on humanity that all do not achieve an enlightened view at the same time. Then another generation seemingly having learnt nothing from the past starts the cycle again. In this view of history human progress is painfully slow and held back by temporary regressions.

The Allies mood to make Germany pay reparations for the war had repercussions. In a defeated country, Germany, with a humiliating peace treaty, economic disasters and runaway inflation fuelled resentment and revenge. Whereas in the country of the non-occupied victor Britain, anti-militarist movements were active such as The No More War Movement and the Peace Pledge Union. This saw the running down of its own armed forces i.e. The London Naval Treaty [2094] to the point when Britain found another war approaching they were not militarily ready to meet it and in 1935 increased spending on defence to counter the German threat of rearmament.[2095] The similarity to Massalia would be that the threat to its security was thought no longer there.[2096] Therefore no need for the expense to maintain a fleet of warships and that the fleet of Massalia became run down.

Strabo writes, 'And in their citadel are set up great quantities of the first fruits of their victories, which they captured by defeating in naval battles those who from time to time unjustly disputed their claim to mastery of the sea.' Many centuries later with the Roman dominance of Gaul, Massalia was free to pursue arts and develop training schools in the art of speaking and philosophy. In Strabo's time Massalia was still skilled in making navigational instruments and ships equipment.[2097]

As the Celts in the interior of Gaul had been conquered by Roman expansion [2098] particularly by Pompey the Great and Julius Caesar the threat of the Celts on land and also pirates at sea vanished and with it the need for a big navy by Massalia. This climate of peace lasted until 49 B.C. when Pompey and Caesar opposed each other and a Roman civil war began. Massalia's naval force was not only unready but had to be patched together from even old ships. Being blockaded on land they had no access to the forest for timber. A total of seventeen ships were hurriedly made ready once Massalia had changed from being neutral into joining Pompey's side when Domitius, the Roman Governor, sailed into Massalia while talks were going on with Caesar and would also have put pressure on them to make a choice.[2099]

As Pompey actually had 500 ships [2100] against the two fleets Caesar had built in the Adriatic and Tyrrhenian Sea [2101] it could seem to a city-state that lived traded and supplied itself mainly by the sea that on balance Pompey had the advantage. Pompey could control the Mediterranean and supplies to Massalia if they were blockaded on the landward side by Caesar's legions. The sudden arrival in Massalia of Domitius's ships with Domitius the legal Roman Governor of Gaul [2102] replacing Caesar [2103] would have made a great impact, a physical link to Pompey and his naval control of the Mediterranean; as well as Domitius's intolerant views on 'neutrals'; [2104] that must have influenced the decision of Massalia's government.

Pompey never used his navy to its potential [2105] only once sending, under Nasidius, sixteen ships from Dyrrachium to help Massalia. Pompey's strategy was to use his great fleet to stop corn ships from reaching Italy and to patrol the East Mediterranean protecting supplies to his own forces.[2106] Nasidius instructed the Massaliote Navy to meet him at Tauroention. On engaging the twelve ships Caesar had hurriedly made at Arelate (Arles) Nasidius withdrew and left the Massaliotes to it. This defeat at the Battle of Tauroention (Le Brusc) had won for Caesar control of the sea around Massalia. However devastating this was Massalia put renewed determination in defending the city by land with Apollonides in command.[2107]

Their city had never been defeated in all its 550 years and Pompey's navy still had overwhelming superiority in numbers. In hindsight Pompey could have broken the siege and relieved Massalia but never did. The fact that the city of Massalia held out for six months must have astonished everyone considering the speed in which Caesar had conquered in more complicated campaigns like the siege at Alesia in seven weeks. Lucan wrote of Massalia:

> Fearless of Caesar and his arms they stood,
> Nor drove before the headlong, rushing flood;
> And while he swept whole nations in a day,
> Massilia bade th' impatient victor stay,
> And clogged his rapid conquest with delay.[2108]

Caesar had left his legate Gaius Trebonius in charge of the siege [2109] and went to Spain to remove the threat of Pompey' Legions at his back.[2110] Caesar had said, 'he was going against an army without a captain, and would return thence against a captain without an army'.[2111] Marcus Varro in Further Spain had made no move against Caesar (being on good terms with him and Pompey) but hearing of Caesar being held up at Massalia; and that Petreius's army had joined Africanus's army; and Caesar's problem of food supplies at Ilerda, he made a levy to bring his two legions up to strength. Varro 'also requisitioned a quantity of grain to send to Massalia and also to Africanus and Petreius'. He had 'ten warships' built at Gades and many more at Hispalis.[2112] Varro surrendered to Caesar when one of his legions went over to Caesar's side.[2113]

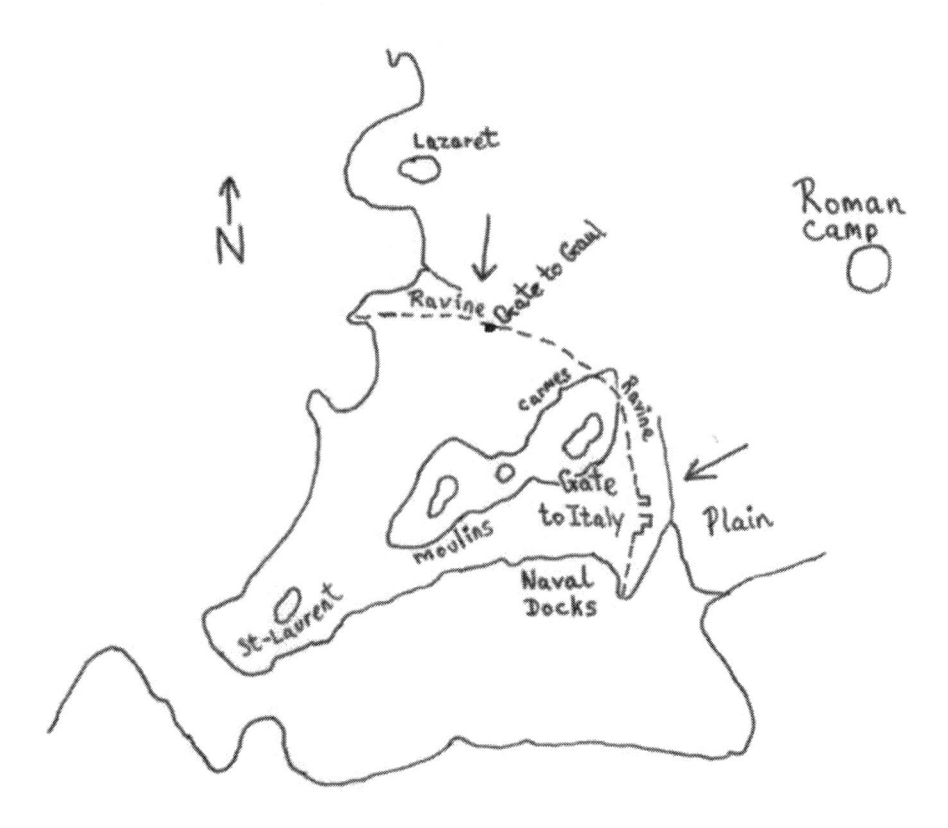

Figure 96. The siege of Massalia 49 B.C. Massalia was protected by the sea, marshes, ravines, high walls and towers. Arrows indicate the two main areas of attack by Julius Caesar and his Legate Trebonius in addition the Romans tunnelled thirty mines to the city walls.

Caesar's camp at the siege of Massalia was across the marsh at the site of the present railway station Gare St. Charles. This hill was higher than those in Massalia and had a commanding view into the city. The citadel of Massalia was on the hill at the Butte des Moulins.[2114]

The peculiarities of Massalia's terrain allowed the Massaliotes to dig down behind their own walls to a greater depth than the town-ditch and 'the miners [Romans] emerged into the open'. The Massaliotes ingeniously were able to flood Roman tunnels trying to undermine the walls from a specially constructed reservoir.[2115]

Massalia's artillery was formidable and its arsenal well stocked Caesar writes 'so great was the store of every sort of military equipment long held in the town, and so great the mass of artillery, that no siege screens of woven osier could possibly resist them'.[2116] No light shields could stand up to the artillery and the Massaliotes used palintone engines for shooting large bolts with devastating force. The added cross-fire must have been devastating:[2117]

'Twelve-foot shafts, sheathed with metal points and fired from the large catapults, would drive into the earth after passing through four layers of hurdles'.[2118]

Asseres enim pedum XII cuspidibus praefixi atque hi maximis ballistis missi per IV ordines cratium in terra defiebantur.[2119]

Evidence of the siege was found at Massalia at the Plaine du Port [2120] with stone balls fired at the city wall by the Romans and sling bullets. Lucan records that the Massaliote Tyrrhenus lost his sight when hit on the temple by a sling bullet when he looked up not wishing to miss any of the engagement but probably was exposed when aiming a ballista.[2121]

Caesar's Legate Trebonius built 'a siege ramp, siege sheds, and towers against the town in two places'.[2122] Trebonius decided to attack Massalia from the following two places. One near the port 'Plaine du Port' by the Gate to Italy, and the other near to the Gate to Gaul and Spain on the north side of the city by the Fabourg suburb.[2123] The citadel itself was difficult to attack due to a deep valley/ravine in front of it. The siege ramp Trebonius had constructed was 80 feet high.[2124] Julius Caesar wrote that on the arrival of a siege tower at the city wall,

> Panic stricken by this sudden reverse the defenders used crowbars to bring up the largest pieces of stone they could, and tipped these forward off the wall on to the gallery. The strength of the timber stood up to the impact, and everything that fell on the pitched roof of the gallery slid off. Seeing this, the defenders changed their plan. They set light to barrels full of pitch and pine-shavings and rolled these from the wall on to the gallery. The barrels spun along it and rolled off, and when they reached the ground they were pushed away from the sides of the structure with forks and poles.[2125]

Vitruvius (Marcus Vitruvius Pollio) was a Roman architect and engineer of the first century B.C. He uses in his book the example of Massalia to show that it is the clever architects who win the battles and not just the machines of war. The books were written to Julius Caesar to persuade him to give Vitruvius a position of employment. From the details given by Vitruvius he may have been at the siege himself and points out to Caesar just how well the Massaliotes nearly defeated all the Roman efforts. He shows it was a much more close-run thing than Caesar actually records in his own book *Civil War*. Vitruvius describes the siege of Massalia in his *Ten Books on Architecture*:

> The Romans were pushing forward more than thirty mines, the people of Massilia, distrusting the entire moat in front of their wall, lowered it by digging it deeper. Thus all the mines found their outlet in the moat. In places where the moat could not be dug they constructed, within the walls, a basin of enormous length and breadth, like a fish pond, in front of the place where the mines were being pushed, and filled it from wells and from the port. And so, when the passages of the mine were suddenly opened, the immense mass of water let in undermined the supports, and all who were within were overpowered by the mass of water, and the caving in of the mine.[2126]

> Again, when a rampart was being prepared against a wall in front of them, and the place was heaped up with felled trees and works placed there, by shooting at it with the ballistae red-hot iron bolts they set the whole work on fire. And when a ram-tortoise had approached to batter down the wall, they let down a noose, and when they caught the ram with it, winding it over by a drum turning a capstan, having raised the head of a ram, they did not allow the wall to be touched and finally they destroy the entire machine by glowing fire-darts and blows of the ballistae. Thus by such victory, not by machines but in opposition to the principle of machines, has the freedom of states been preserved by the cunning of architects.[2127]

Figure 97. Siege of Massalia 49 B.C. Roman strategies and Greek counter measures from Vitruvius's descriptions.

The Massaliotes' artillery had been formidable at the beginning of the siege but once the Romans got close to the city wall the front of the catapults could not be lowered down enough [2128] to be as effective 'due to the shortness of the range'.[2129] Lucan describes the predicament in his epic poem *Pharsalia*:

> But greater was the force of Greek weapons against the Roman
> bodies, because the lance was thrown not by arms
> alone but shot by the taut whirl of the ballista;
> it comes to rest only after passing through more than one body;
> it opens up a path through armour and through bones and speeds
>   away,
> leaving death behind: after dealing wounds the weapon still
>   moves onwards.

> But whenever a stone is shot by the thong's
> enormous force, like the rock severed
> from the mountain-top by age assisted by the winds' blast,
> it crushes everything in its path, not merely killing
> the pounded bodies but pulverizing entire limbs and blood alike.
> But when courage approaches the enemy walls, shielded
> by the dense-packed tortoise—the front line carrying
> overlapping shields, with shield-boss held out to protect the helmet—
> then missiles which, when shot from distant point, had damaged them before
> now fall behind them. And for the Greeks it is no easy task
> to steer the throw or alter the range of the machine
> made to hurl its weapons far;[2130]

Julius Caesar relates the events of undermining the city wall using a gallery:

> Meanwhile under the gallery the soldiers were levering away the lowest stones which formed the foundations of the enemy tower. Our side protected the gallery by firing javelins and artillery bolts from the brick tower, so that the enemy were driven from their wall and towers and given no real chance of defending the wall. By now a good number of stones had been removed from under the adjacent tower, and when suddenly a part of it collapsed and the rest of it in consequence was on the point of doing so, the enemy, terrified by the thought of a sack of their city, all poured out of the gate, unarmed and with the sacred ribbons of suppliants tied around their foreheads, stretching out their hands for mercy to the officers and army.[2131]

Caesar's officers received envoys from Massalia asking for a truce:

> They saw that their city was taken, that Caesars' siege works were complete, their own tower undermined, and that they were therefore ceasing their defence. [They said] nothing could happen to hinder Caesar from destroying the city utterly when he arrived, if they did not do exactly what he ordered. They explained that if their tower should collapse completely the [Roman] soldiers would not be able to be held back from bursting into the city in the hope of booty and destroying it. This and much more of the same type-given that they were educated men—was uttered with great pathos and lamentation.[2132]

The Roman Officers grant a truce [2133] while awaiting the arrival of Caesar [2134] and the Greeks use the time to make an attack and aided by the wind destroy with fire the siege works.[2135] Dio writes that it was the Romans who had broken the truce. Massalia 'sent out Domitius out of the harbour secretly and caused such injuries to these soldiers, who attacked them in the night in the midst of a truce'.[2136] Probably the thought of a settlement after a long siege with no booty had prompted the Romans soldiers into breaking the truce? After nearly six months of siege risking danger and one's comrades being injured or killed the thought of a settlement with no rewards must have angered the ordinary Roman soldiers.[2137] Caesar 'had sent the most strict instructions to Trebonius not to let the city be taken by force'. He records that the soldiers at the time of the first truce were threatening to kill all the adults, 'and were with difficulty restrained from bursting into the city, being much annoyed because it was apparently Trebonius's fault that they were not masters of the town'.[2138]

Though losing months of work in just a few hours the Romans got over this setback. 'Trebonius began to take his losses in hand and make them good',[2139] his soldiers proved resilient and resourceful. As all the wood surrounding Massalia 'far and wide' had been use up by the Romans they decided to build another ramp 'of a new and unprecedented sort' by laying two brick walls bricks six feet thick instead.[2140] The roof was covered in timber, 'wicker hurdles and coated with clay'.[2141] They also started to build an effective wall and towers that protected their men. The Massaliotes who had been living off 'old millet and rotting barley'[2142] with 'food running critically low'[2143] realised that their city wall could eventually be enclosed by the Roman's bastioned wall 'on the landward side'.[2144] This Roman wall would be higher and therefore their own would be no longer defendable. At a distance Massalia's artillery had been formidable and effective for six months. Now the Romans had got close up to the city-walls the Greeks 'realized that owing to the shortness of the range their own artillery, on which they rested their hopes, had become useless'.[2145] The grain Varro had requisitioned in Spain to send by ships to Massalia[2146] never arrived and neither supplies or soldiers from Pompey. Now the Massaliotes were 'without hope of assistance from provinces or armies which they had learnt had come under Caesar's control'.[2147] Therefore 'It was these considerations which induced them to fall back once more upon the previous terms of capitulation'.[2148]

Domitius the Governor heard of the decision to surrender a few days earlier. Caesar had pardoned many enemies who surrendered to him including Domitius before at Corsinium. Yet so implacable was Domitius to Caesar that he did not surrender himself and so escaped by sailing in 'wild weather' while two accompanying ships turned back to port when confronted by the ships of Decimus Brutus.[2149] He eventually joined Pompey at Pharsalia where they fought their final battle against Caesar. Domitius was slain in the battle.[2150]

'The Massaliotes, as instructed, brought their weapons and artillery out of the town, took their ships out of the port and the ship-sheds, and handed over the money in their treasury'.[2151] Dio says that when Caesar arrived 'he at that time deprived them of their arms, ships and money, and takes of everything except the name of freedom'. To offset this misfortune Phocaea, their mother-city, was made free by Pompey'[2152] and the Roman senate now at Thessaloniki.[2153] Caesar spared the city of Massalia leaving 'two legions there as a garrison and sent the others to Italy, while he himself set off for Rome'.[2154]

Julius Caesar also had good news when he had come to Massalia after conquering Spain regarding the Consular elections. Though a Praetor could not call an election for a Consul he could propose a law for the appointment of a Dictator and this was done by M. Aemilius Lepidus.[2155] This meant that Caesar could now act legally according to Roman law. When Caesar reached Rome he used his position as Dictator to call Consular elections. He resigned as Dictator after eleven days and was elected Consul for 48 B.C. together with P. Serilius Isauricus.[2156]

Appian does not mention the siege in *The Civil Wars* probably because Massalia was an independent city but he does mention the city in location to Caesar being there.[2157] Appian records that Caesar left for Italy 'About the time Antonius was defeated in Illyria by Octavius who was Pompeius's commander operating against Dolabella', part of Caesar's army in Placentia had mutinied 'on hearing this Caesar hastened away urgently from Massilia to Placentia'.[2158] 'Caesar went onto Rome after quelling the mutiny of Placentia, where a terrified people elected him Dictator without any decree of the senate or nomination of a magistrate'.[2159] Usually this was proposed by a consul.[2160] Earlier that year in a letter dated 25 March 49 B.C. Cicero thought it was illegal for a Praetor to hold consular elections or to nominate a Dictator, 'But if Sulla could arrange for a Dictator to be nominated by an Interrex, and a Master of the Horse, why not Caesar?'[2161]

From Caesar's point of view, Massalia had gone back on a promise of neutrality[2162] and attacked during a truce[2163] though Dio did record the truce was 'broken by the Romans'.[2164] Caesar says he was lenient when the city capitulated 'preserving the city more out of respect for its fame and antiquity than on account of any favours it had done to him'.[2165]

49 B.C.
- Julius Caesar had led three legions to start the siege of Massalia in April.
- The naval Battle of Frioul (Gaul) took place at the end of May.
- The naval Battle of Tauroention (Tauroentum, Gaul) took place at the end of June.
- The siege of Massalia ended with its capitulation at the end of September.[2166]

At Massalia's colony at Olbia there is a destruction level dated to the mid-first century B.C. and Professor Hodge surmises this may have coincided with the siege of Massalia by Julius Caesar in 49 B.C. There is a superimposed stratum of Roman occupation with hypocaust and Roman Bath.[2167] At St. Blaise thirty-nine large stone catapults-balls weighing between eight to forty pounds have been found in a trench that were fired by Romans around the same time as Julius Caesar's siege at Massalia 49 B.C.[2168] This may suggest that Julius Caesar's troops had under siege not only Massalia but also other Massaliote cities like St. Blaise and Olbia either at the same time or at some point during 49 B.C.

In April 49 B.C. Julius Caesar had rapidly built 12 warships at Arelate[2169] (Arles), Theline) in thirty days to fight Massalia during the Roman civil war. The town of Arelate was awarded a 'Colona Romana' distinction in 46 B.C. when Caesar gave it most of Massalia's territory and settled his veteran troops there.[2170] Arelate had been politically and economically dependent on Massalia. By supporting Caesar and the winning side Arelate now became a rich city 'the Rome of the Gauls' at the expense of Massalia by its geographical position, with roads link from Italy to Spain; a port on the River Rhône; and surrounded by fertile land, which provided military supplies.

Massalia's territory was given away in two pieces. The military city of Frejus (Forum Julii) received the lands to the east, and all the lands to the River Rhône went to Arelate (Arles), the civilian port founded by Caesar in 46 B.C. for his veteran soldiers. Caesar called Arelate 'Colonia Julia Paterna Arelatensis Sextanorum' and here he stationed the VI Legion. Only colonies founded by Caesar himself had the right to use the title.[2171] However, mindful of Massalia past friendship and help to Rome, Caesar left Massalia itself independent as a *civitas foederata*.[2172] Massalia was allowed to keep Nikaia (Nice), Olbia, the Stoechades Islands and Athenopolis from its former empire.[2173]

During Caesar's brief eleven days as Dictator before becoming Consul he appointed Decimus Brutus as Governor of the newly acquired Gaul.[2174] Decimus had been the admiral of the Roman fleet at the siege of Massalia by Caesar in 49 B.C. Trebonius as Caesar's Legate in charge of the army at the siege then served as a *praetor urbenis* in 48 B.C. also by favour of Caesar. Later Caesar and Trebonius were dead within a year of each other. Caesar had destroyed the barbarous ancient sacred grove outside Massalia ('mine is the guilt') where the Gauls groaned at its loss but Lucan has the watching Massaliotes jubilant expecting swift divine aid ('For who would think that gods are injured without revenge?'), which did not come to help them.[2175]

Julius Caesar's moneyer during the dictatorship was L. HOSTILIVS SASERNA. He was in the office of Triumvir Monetale (IIIVIR).[2176] HOSTILIVS issued coins in 48 B.C. from the mint in Rome. One coin is thought to commemorate Caesar's victory over Massalia the year before in Gaul.[2177] This now very rare silver Denarius coin shows on the obverse a longhaired woman's head possibly a captive or representing Gallia facing right, with a Carnyx (Celtic trumpet with a dragons head)[2178] behind. On the reverse is the goddess of Massalia Ephesian Artemis facing standing, with a leaping stag and it seems held by the antlers at the head or right hand on the stag's head, and holding an upright spear in the left hand, with the words L. HOSTILIVS vertically downwards on right, and SASERNA upwards on the left. Weight 3.66 gm.

Figure 98. Silver Denarius coin issued in Rome by Julius Caesar's moneyer L. Hostilius Saserna in 48 B.C. thought to commemorate Julius Caesar's victory in Gaul and Massalia 49 B.C.

Massalia Attempts to Reclaim its Territories

After Julius Caesar's assassination in March 44 B.C. events were becoming precarious as revealed by Cicero in a letter to Atticus on 26 April 44 B.C.:

> if there is going to be a civil war—and that there must be, if Sextus stays under arms, as I know for certain he will—I don't know what we are to do. For now there will be no chance of sitting on the fence, as there was in Caesar's war. For, if this gang of ruffians thinks anyone was rejoiced at the death of Caesar—and we all of us showed our joy quiet openly—they will count him an enemy; and that looks like a considerable massacre. Our alternative is to take refuge in Sextus' camp, or join ourselves to Brutus if we can.[2179]

Atticus wrote to his friend Cicero and asked him to restore Massilia's rights. However Mark Antony and his supporters were a power in the Senate. Cicero writes back to Atticus 27 April 44 B.C.:

> But here you are wanting to get back their rights for your neighbours the Massilians, as though we had recovered the republic. Perhaps they might be restored by arms—but how strong our arms are I do not know—by influence they certainly cannot.[2180]

After Trebonius had been killed by Dollabella in Smyrna 43 B.C the Senate declared Dollabella an 'Enemy to the Roman people'.[2181] Mark Antony wrote a letter with several complaints to the consul Hirtius and propraetor Caesar (Octavian), which included,

'You have taken away the veterans' colonies, though planted by law and by decree of the Senate. You are promising to restore to the Massilians what has been taken from them by the laws of war'.[2182]

Cicero comments in his *Philippic* against Mark Antony,

> Yet consider whether it is not you that have ruined these veterans who have been ruined, and planted them in a position from which they themselves already feel they will never escape. "You are promising to restore to the Massilians what has been taken away from them by the laws of war". I do not agree as to the laws of war—the argument is more easy than necessary; but notice this point, Conscript Fathers, what a born enemy to this State Antonius is; who so bitterly hates that community which he knows has been always most friendly to this State.[2183]

Cicero in speaking to restore Pompeius's dignity and his fortune to his son Pompeius Sextus said,

> in spite of our confirmation and ratification of the acts of Caesar, the son of Cnaeus Pompeius should be able to recover his dignity and the fortune of his father . . . illustrious envoys Lucius Paulus, Quintus Thermus, and Caius Fannius, whose unremitting and steadfast good will towards the State, you have realised, announce that they turned aside to Massilia in order to meet Pompeius, and recognised that he was most ready to go to Mutina with his forces, but feared to offend the veterans [of Caesar].[2184]

The veterans of the VI Legion that Caesar had settled at Arles (Arelate) were recalled, up to four years under the terms of their discharge in times of emergencies, by the summer of 44 B.C. They re-joined their legion now part of Lepidus's army encamped by the River Var.[2185]

After Caesar's assassination the Senate recalled Pompeius Sextus from Spain and he stayed in Massalia 44–43 B.C. keeping an eye on political developments in Rome while at a safe distance.[2186] If Lepidus's legions moved against him he could make a quick exit by sea.

Would the supporters of Pompey, Mark Antony or Octavian gain control of the Senate? Appian wrote that Mark Antony made a surprise proposal to recall Pompeius Sextus from Spain 'and that he should be paid 50 millions of Attic drachmas out of the public treasury for his father's confiscated property'.[2187] The Senate approved Pompeius Sextus command of the sea 'with charge of all Roman Ships, wherever situated, which were needed for immediate service'.[2188] Mark Antony was a masterful politician. He already had Amatius put to death by his authority as Consul without trail for making 'perpetual terror' on Caesar's murderers with several fleeing Rome. In doing so Mark Antony temporarily turned the people against himself; but gained the 'delight' of the Senate as the action clearly was to protect Gaius Cassius Longinus and Marcus Junius Brutus. Mark Antony broke up the following protest by Amatius's supporters and had several killed.[2189] He won much praise by the Senate and Cicero by this popular move where particularly the Pompeians, Appian records, readily believed 'the Republic would at last be restored' and 'their party successful'.[2190]

Clerc writes that Sextus in Massalia made Apollonides the overall Greek Commander of Massalia during the siege by Julius Caesar in 49 B.C. a Roman citizen.[2191] The Massalia mint was still active and issued coins for Sextus with his father Pompey the Great on the obverse and the reverse shows a galley with the word NASIDIVS. Nasidius was the admiral in charge of the Roman fleet helping Massalia during the Civil War against Julius Caesar's admiral Decimus Brutus at the naval Battle of Tauroention.

Figure 99. Made and issued from Massalia's mint 44–43 B.C. by Pompey's son Pompeius Sextus. Silver Denarius, obverse: Pompey the Great facing right, Trident, Dolphin, inscription Neptune/reverse: a crewed ship, oars and full sail, facing right, inscription NASIDIVS, 6 rayed star. Weight 3.73 g, 6 h.

Coins could also be used as blatant propaganda. Marcus J. Brutus had coins issued obverse: portraying his head, and around BRVT IMP L PLAET CEST and on the reverse a pileus between two daggers with letters below EID MAR (Ides of March) justifying his murder of Caesar as saving the Republic from a tyrant. Pompeius Sextus issuing a coin with his father's image and his admiral Nasidius would not have endeared himself to Mark Antony, Octavian or the supporters of Caesar.

To get all Caesar's decrees posthumously passed in the Senate Mark Antony had to agree to a decree allowing no prosecution of Caesar's murderers. With the leaders of the colonists also present in the Senate they asked for 'another act special to themselves'. This was also passed 'to secure them in possession of their colonies'.[2192] Cassius and Marcus Brutus were still in Rome as city

Praetors before taking up their Governorships of Syria and Macedonia respectively. They also 'conciliated the colonists by varying degrees, and among others by enabling them to sell their allotments, the law hitherto forbidding the alienation of the land till the end of twenty years'.[2193]

Appian records that Sextus still did not return to Rome but 'taking what ships he found in the harbours, and joining them with those he had brought from Spain, he put to sea'.[2194] This may suggest that Massalia also had ships again after their confiscation by Caesar following his siege in 49 B.C. Sextus spent part of 43 B.C. refurbishing his fleet in Massalia.[2195] Massalia now full of ships, a hive of industry and fully employed in building and supplies. However the wheel of fortune turned again when Mark Antony, Octavian (Caesar) and Lepidus formed the Triumvirate and took absolute power with a proscription (death list).[2196] Sextus sailed to Sicily and gained possession of the island in 42 B.C.[2197] and cut off corn supplies to Rome inducing famine.[2198] Following a temporary peace [2199] Sextus won naval battles against Octavian and exchanged the purple cloak of a Roman commander to that of blue 'to signify he was the adopted son of Neptune'.[2200] Finally Octavian beat Sextus at sea and Sextus died later while fighting against Mark Antony's forces on land in Bithynia (in North-West Asia Minor).[2201]

Roman Monarchy

The conflict of attitudes that fuelled the Roman civil wars was the strong underlying belief and tradition against one man ruling, a monarch, and the vying amongst the senatorial class for the limited top positions in the state. Justin records that

> Such was the principle of hatred towards all monarchs that they had established, evidently because they themselves had had kings who were such that even their names made them blush: shepherds from amongst the Aborigines, soothsayers from the Sabines, exiles from Corinth, slaves from Etruria, captured or bred at home, or—the most distinguished name of them all—the Superbi.[2202]

Many kings of Rome had been outsiders and not from the patrician class.[2203] Cornell points out that when the Republic was formed its first act was to make people swear never to allow a man to be a king in Rome and legislated against anyone seeking to become a king in the future.[2204] More than anything else it was the thought that one of their own should be higher than themselves by championing the needs of the lower classes and getting their political support. King Ancus Marcius had been a patron of the Plebs and King Lucius Tarquinius Priscus canvassed the people and his reforms angered the aristocrats.[2205]

Remarkably in the Republic those from the ruling class that made particular efforts to help the poorer classes were then accused of monarchism (*Regnum*) such as Sp. Cassius, Sp. Maelius, M. Manilus Capitolinus and T. Gracchi.[2206] It seems to have gone hand in hand that amongst those who hated kingship also feared the lower classes might have an increase in power in Rome because of it. Sharing power met with resistance as it did in not giving Roman citizenship to their Italian allies resulting in the Social Wars 90–89 B.C.

Massalia Survives as an Independent City-State

With Lepidus deprived of his province in Gaul and Spain [2207] and later deposed of his command; [2208] the loss of influence in the Senate of the Pompeians; Massalia having taken the losing side of the Republic and Pompey's cause had little chance of getting their empire back with Octavian and Mark Antony in power. [2209] Whichever side was in power neither risked offending the veterans Julius Caesar had planted in Arelate (Arles) or the Roman colony of Fréjus (Forum Julius) who both benefited from the surrounding lands given to them by the division of the Greek Empire of Massalia (Marseille).

Caesar also added a Roman colony to the mixed population of Iberians and Massaliotes in the Massaliote colony of Emporion (Ampurias, Spain) [2210] and a Roman colony had also been settled at the Phocaean colony of Lampsacus in Asia Minor. [2211]

Though it is thought that Massalia's commercial importance declined archaeological evidence suggests the opposite. There were major new port installations built late first century B.C. (in use until the third century A.D.), [2212] and in the city using building stone from Cap Couronne. [2213]

One funeral inscription dated to end of the first to beginning of second century A.D. [2214] shows the Roman system of three names *tria nomina* with family name preceded by Roman or name of ancient benefactor to the family. Clerc suggests that the name Titus Pompeius Apollonides found on a funerary stone might possibly be from the family of Apollonides who had been the overall Commander of Massalia in 49 B.C. siege against Julius Caesar. [2215] The Greek inscription was found at the necropolis of Carénage outside ancient Massalia. [2216]

ΤΙΤΟΣ • ΠΟΜΓΗΪΟΣ
ΑΠΟΛΛΩΝΙΔΗΣ
ΤΙΤΩΦΛΑΟΥΪΩΙ
ΝΕΙΚΟΣΤΡΑΤΩΙ
ΤΩΙΚΑΘΗΓΗΤΗΙ
ΜΝΗΜΗΣ • ΧΑΡΙΝ

Titus Pompeius Apollonides, (erected this gravestone) to Titus Flavius Nicostratus, (his) teacher, as a memorial. [2217]

With the consolidation of Mark Antony and the triumvirate upholding dead Caesar's decrees passed in the Senate regarding the settlement of the veterans, (Caesar's veterans were at Arles), all hope was gone for Massalia in getting their territories back, which had been given to those two cities of Frejus and Arles. This marked the end of an era but to be exact only a part of an era. Massalia was still independent but the 'Greek Empire of Marseille' (Massalia) had come to an end though it was allowed to keep and control Nikaia (Nice), Olbia, the Stoechades Islands and Athenopolis. [2218]

However, in trade Massalia's markets were still there, meeting supply and demand in which Massalia was very successful for 550 years. With that experience, contacts in trade, and allowing for costs for hiring other ships until you had your own again Massalia was still in business. That trade continued is archaeologically evident with renewed port installations in the late first century B.C. in use up to third century A.D. Roman traders were also in Massalia and it was now a Roman world and a global market but Massalia maintained its political and commercial independence *civitas foederata* as a Greek city within it: [2219]

'On the coast is Marseilles, founded by the Greeks of Phocaea and now a confederate city'.[2220]

at in ora Massilia Graecorum Phocaeensium foederata.

Leading families adopted the custom of giving themselves three names in the Roman style. As evident on funerary inscriptions found in Massalia starting with the benefactor of the family and ending with the family name. Trade went on and so did Massalia still trading with its other ex-colonies, not in political or military control but still as the independent Greek city-state of Massalia.[2221]

Though its city's treasury had been emptied into Julius Caesar's funds for bribery, triumphs, great civic works and military pay, it would seem that Massalia's citizens own private money had been left alone. Sextus refurbished his fleet there boosting Massalia's economy. Having survived an 'asset stripping' and now without the expense to keep a Greek Army or a Navy, a leaner Massalia could survive economically independent in a Roman world of trade and commerce not only as a cultural university city. Strabo in the first century A.D. reports that they 'were skilled in the making of navigational instruments and ships equipment'.[2222] This shows that maritime skills were present and active in an independent Massalia during the following era of the Roman peace-Pax Romana.

Massalia maintained its reputation for Greek culture and learning. Among other schools it was also the home of Agroitas. Here is a story related by Seneca the Elder:

> Agroitas of Marseille [Massalia] produced a much more forceful epigram than the other Greeks declaimers, who brawled in this *controversia* as though they were rivals in love. Now Agroitas had an unpolished technique (which showed he had not frequented the Greeks) and employed vigorous epigrams (which showed he had frequented the Romans). This was the epigram which won applause: "This is where we are at discord in our debauchery: you are debauched and enjoy it; I am debauched and do not." [2223]

There was also the School of Moschus the Apollodorean of Massalia.[2224] In Strabo's time Massalia 'attracted the most notable of the Romans, if eager for knowledge, to go to school there instead of making their foreign sojourn at Athens'.[2225] Among them was Agricola who studied philosophy and later became a Consul of Rome and Governor of Britain. Tacitus (c. A.D. 55–117) the Roman historian gave a good view of Massalia in his book called *Agricola* about his father-in-law:

> He was shielded from the snares of sinners not merely by his own good and upright nature but because from the outset of his childhood the home and guide of his studies was Massilia, a blend and happy combination of Greek refinement and provincial simplicity.

> I remember how he used himself to tell that in early life he was inclined to drink more deeply of philosophy than is permitted to a Roman and a Senator, had not his mother's discretion imposed a check upon his enkindled and glowing imagination.[2226]

There were two good reasons why Massalia had kept its own distinct culture. One was policy and the other geography. Morris points out that the Romans actively retained the Greek identity of Massalia, as a continuing, civilising buffer against the 'barbarians' of Gaul.[2227] Justin writes of the civilizing influence of Greek Massalia on its surrounding neighbours.[2228] While Bats thought the Greeks affected small and different parts of the populations yet they nevertheless 'prepared the ground for the subsequent acculturation by the Romans'.[2229]

Geographically Massalia was also able to maintain its own culture and character as it was not on the main road of the Via Domitia,[2230] only being reached by a spur off the road from Aix-en-Provence, or even the later Via Julia. The main routes went inland through Arelate (Arles) or Tarascon.[2231] Previously there was a rough track near Massalia known as the Via Heraclensis (used by Herakles [Hercules] in his Labours) but unsuitable for 'serious transport' until the Roman Emperor Augustus had constructed the Via Julia c. 13 B.C. further north.[2232]

Incidentally Morel mentions 'a Marseillan fact' in the *Geryoneis* as Hercules was saved by an attack of the Ligurians when Zeus made it rain pebbles that correspond to La Crau, a plain covered with pebbles close to Marseilles, east of the Rhône delta[2233] and west of the Camargue.[2234] Pliny the Elder also mentions a tradition of Hercules fighting battles in this area of the 'Stony Plains'.[2235]

Chapter 14

Julius Caesar, Britain and Pytheas of Massalia

The historian G. M. Trevelyan does mention in his book the *History of England* that 'Pytheas of Massalia the Greek traveller recorded his visit to the Prettanic Isle in the days of Alexander the Great.' [2236] Also there is an entry in Gardiner and Neil, *The History Today Companion of British History*,[2237] 'c. 310 B.C. **Pytheas of Massalia**: Earliest written evidence of Britain, France and Spain. Seems to have also discovered the Arctic'; and Winston S. Churchill wrote, 'Pytheas of Marseilles—surely one of the greatest explorers in history'. . . [2238]

Yet for many years most British history books only began with Julius Caesar's invasion of Britain taken from his own book *Gallic Wars*. This was a complete book and therefore a literary source that scholars could always refer to. Scholars have known about pre-Roman contacts between Greeks and Britain, but as these were mainly dismissive from Polybius and Strabo, they always stayed with Caesar as a starting point. This has inadvertently left a void in our history of pre-Roman Britain, a land of mysterious islands with stone circles and monoliths. At my own school nothing before Caesar was considered. On being told there was nothing here before the Romans a pupil in class asked the question, 'What about Stonehenge sir?' There was a silence. Plainly this was a fact against the usual line we were being taught. The history teacher then acknowledged Stonehenge only as a 'mysterious puzzle we knew little about so let us return to something we do know–the Romans'!

Tacitus in promoting his father-in-law Agricola's conquest of most of Britain wrote of Caesar as only 'The discoverer, not the conqueror of the island, he did no more than show it to prosperity'.[2239] Not quite 'the discoverer' even, but he certainly confirmed that Britain existed by his two invasions though if we are to believe Strabo the Romans already knew something of Britain.

Before Caesar, as Strabo tells us, Britain was safe from Roman invasion. Strabo explains that the 'Romans scorned to do so', because the *Pretani* (Britons) were no threat 'they were not strong enough to cross over and attack us'; there was no advantage in taking and holding their island; not profitable enough to maintain the expense of an occupying army to collect tribute as 'more revenue is derived from the duty on their commerce'.[2240] Does Strabo mean their 'commerce' coming to Rome or Narbo or from Britain to the coasts of Gaul? If the former then it implies a lot of commercial traffic, if the latter how, if the existence of Britain was thought of as a myth and the Romans still in southern Gaul, could they impose 'duty on their commerce'? Is Strabo using hindsight and referring to the opinion of those in the senate who were opposed to Caesar? Other writers such as Plutarch,[2241] Dio Cassius, and Appian verify that the existence of Britain was doubted and the island 'still unknown to the men of Rome' at the time of Caesar.[2242]

Caesar invaded Britain without the permission of the Roman Senate. He did this late in the campaigning season and does not state why he invaded. Some scholars suggest that this was because he did not achieve his objectives and therefore does not mention any in his book *Gallic War*. This book was published in three months and written mainly to answer his critics in the Roman Senate. Due to the lateness of the campaigning season perhaps he did achieve short-term objectives that were for propaganda and to test out the resistance of the *Britanni* (Britons). He says himself he questioned traders who went to Britain but knew nothing more than the coast.[2243]

In Britain Caesar found little to enrich his troops as Plutarch mentions that the Britons 'hardily brought up, and poor, there was nothing to be gotten. Whereupon his war has not such success as he looked for'.[2244] Caesar 'made requisition of hostages, and determined what tribute Britain should pay yearly to Rome'. He ordered the British Chief Cassivellaunus not to attack the Trinobantes or Mandubracius and left to winter in Gaul.[2245]

As a pretext he may have invaded *Prettanike* (Britain) to destroy the influence of Druids. In Gaul the Celts sent their Druids to be trained in *Prettanike* (Britain)[2246] and their influence for revolt was great. Suetonius records the then current comment that Caesar went to Britain 'in the hope of finding pearls' as it was rumoured that all colours and particularly white were found in the British seas and later he dedicated a cuirass made of British pearls at the temple of Venus Genetrix.[2247] But it may have been in attacking the fabled mysterious island of *Prettanike* (Britain)[2248] that ambitious Caesar was adding to his popularity and reputation amongst the Roman people as a conqueror to match the many victories, including the naval reputation, of his son-in-law Pompey the Great.[2249] Lucan portrays the rivalry and a Pompey not impressed with Caesar's adventure by 'calling some pools of uncertain depth "Ocean", seeking out the Britons and then turning his back on them in terror'.[2250] Though Caesar's first 'expedition' (Dio, XXXIX.53) embarked for Britain at night in August he also withdrew at night in September 55 B.C., was this for 'fair weather' or extrication?

Plutarch wrote that Caesar was the first to sail the western ocean with an army

> to make war in that so great and famous island, (which many ancient writers would not believe that it was so indeed, and did make them vary about it, saying that it was but a fable and a lie): and was the first that enlarged the Roman empire, beyond the earth inhabitable.[2251]

This shows in Rome (first-century B.C.) that the controversy like Polybius stated against Pytheas of Massalia, particularly about 'habitable zones' was still current. Plutarch also used Strabo as a source and we can see their influence by the use of 'fable', 'lie', 'habitable' zones, in relation to Britain and the North Atlantic.

The controversy added to the aura of a mysterious island,[2252] but as Caesar's conquests in Gaul drew him nearer *Prettanike* (Britain) he knew it was not a 'fable or lie' he could actually see it and this would be a fabulous piece of publicity to actually go there while in Rome many still did not believe Britain existed. Caesar would be doing the impossible entering the lands of Myths and conquering even there, surpassing all the victories his rival Pompey the Great had ever made.[2253]

Whatever the controversy, the story of a large island in the North Atlantic, from Pytheas of Massalia's voyage of discovery, was still alive. No one since Pytheas of Massalia had reported going there. This gave doubts to those in general except scientists and astronomers like Eratosthenes of Cyrene and Hipparchus of Nicaea, who had proved Pytheas's calculations on his voyage as correct.[2254] The equivalent in our age is like some scientific or astronomical facts and theories known to scientists but the general public still holds its own beliefs. It does take a concerted effort of education to spread knowledge that is a fact in science to the non-scientific world. Many people might be aware of the name Einstein but few can actually explain his theories?

In Caesar's account he tells that when in Gaul, the Gauls were not helpful to give him any information about Britain. Nevertheless Caesar was well informed about the size of Britain and Ireland from another source. Caesar writes about Britain that he got his information from 'de quibus insulis **non nulli scripserunt** [some writers]'.[2255]

The following are two translations of the same text about Britain. The first by H. J. Edwards,

> Here in mid-channel is an island called Man; in addition, several small islands are supposed to lie close to land, as touching which some have written that in midwinter night there lasts for thirty whole days. We could discover nothing about this by inquiries; but, by exact water measurements, we observed that the nights were shorter than on the Continent.[2256]

The second by C. Hammond,

> . . . midway lies an island called Mona [Isle of Man]. There are thought to be several smaller islands besides lying nearby, and several writers have recorded that over the winter solstice there is continual darkness there for thirty days. We were unable to find out the truth of this by inquiries, except that by accurate measurements with a water clock we observed that the nights were shorter than in mainland Gaul.[2257]

Here we have reference to 'some writers', 'some have written', and 'several writers' respectively. Why should Julius Caesar expect thirty days of continual darkness? Perhaps the thirty days was a copyist's error over time before it came down to Caesar or something else from parts of Pytheas's book? The longest day in southern England is seventeen hours.[2258] Strabo also states,

'However, the Massaliote Pytheas says that the very last regions are those around Thoule, the most northern of the Prettans, near which the summer tropic circle is the same as the arctic circle'.[2259]

Roseman estimates this to be 'somewhat south of 66°N' and Iceland actually covers between Latitudes 66°N and 63°N. In 2009 the shortest day in Ísafjördur was 2 hours 44 minutes and this made the longest night as 21 hours and 16 minutes.[2260] Therefore the shortest day at Rifstangi Iceland's most northerly point would be less.

Thoule would probably have been unknown to southern Britons of whom Caesar and his staff had made unsuccessful 'inquiries'. It is possible that a secretary filled in this part and other 'geographical digressions' for Caesar, as he was not interested in geography and this inclusion was for the readers who did not know anything definite about *Prettanike* (Britain).[2261] Caesar quotes 'Eratosthenes and certain Greeks' regarding reports of the Hercynian Forest elsewhere in his book *Bello Gallico* (Gallic Wars).[2262]

Caesar states correctly that:
- Britain was triangular in shape[2263] though he never circumnavigated it to know this.[2264]
- He also talks about the size and location of Ireland,[2265] and Mona for the Isle of Man,[2266] lands he never saw.
- While he was in Britain investigated the report that the length of night at midwinter solstice could last thirty days.[2267]

It would seem that the information Caesar had at that time was from Pytheas of Massalia's account repeated by 'several writers' as Pytheas had included the most northern region of his journey, the island of Thoule (Iceland), as part of all the British islands.[2268]

This was still the opinion by A.D. 200 when Solinus recorded

> There are many other islands around *Brittania*, of which the most distant is *Thyle*, where at the summer solstice, when the sun is passing through the sign of Cancer, there is no night, and likewise at the winter solstice no day.[2269]

Despite the passing of centuries the story of Pytheas was still current through the writings of Timaeus that were held in high regard in Rome by Cicero (a contemporary of Caesar).[2270] Many of the elite in Rome had a Greek education and could read and write in Greek.[2271] Therefore it is likely some read Timaeus's book: those of 'Eratosthenes and certain Greeks' including Polybius: and if available possibly *On the Ocean* itself. Though Caesar does not name the 'some writers' and 'certain Greeks' in *Gallic Wars* there was only one person in the previous 265 years who had claimed to have discovered, named and written about Britain and that was, as other writers quoted, the Greek astronomer, scientist and explorer Pytheas of Massalia.[2272]

Caesar also uses Pytheas's names:
- *Kantion* for Kent (Latin *Cantium*) [2273] and again when he talks about the British chief in Kent 'Cassivellaunus ad Cantium'. [2274]
- *Mona*,[2275] possibly mistaken for the Isle of Man [2276] (later Pliny records it as the name for Anglesey and *Monapia* as the Isle of Man). [2277]
- For the people *Pretani* (Latin *Britanni*) and for the country *Prettanike* (Latin *Britannia*).[2278]

Due to the work of modern scholars who have brought together in one book all the known fragments of Pytheas's book *On the Ocean* from references and quotes by eighteen ancient writers,[2279] and a recent decade of archaeological evidence,[2280] we are able to extend our knowledge of Britain by a further 265 years before the Roman invasion.

Though we do have stone inscriptions, no documents from ancient Marseille (Massalia) have been found as yet. The surviving references sometimes just a line, is spread over a wide range of ancient writers in Greek and Latin. Yet by persistent research enough references were found to make this book focussing our attention on the western settlements and colonies, revealing their achievements as the *Greek Empire of Marseille: Discoverers of Britain, Saviour of Rome*.

Chapter 15

Continuity within Change

Having gone so far in research on ancient Massalia the question now arises what happened to the Greeks and their city?

Since the siege and defeat of Massalia in 49 B.C. the period becomes known as the Roman era. One may get the impression of a Roman dominated city but this would be misleading due to the independence of Massalia's government and their political control of Nice, Olbia, the Stoechades Islands and Athenopolis from its former empire. How much territory beyond the cities was kept is not fully known and the only evidence found so far was a boundary stone that included the name Massiliensium. This divided its territory from that of Vintium (Vence) 14 km from Nikaea (Nice). Though found at the Cathedral of Vence it is not sure if the boundary stone stood there originally.[2281] There are inscriptions on the two columns:

First

        CVRANTE AC
        IVL • HONORATO
        P •P • PRAESID ALP

Second

        MASSILIEN
        SIVM

        DEDICANTE
        PROC • AVG• EX
        MARITIMAR VA *sic*

That some Romans came to live individually in Massalia is evidenced by their tombstones: a large Roman bathhouse A.D. 25–50 found in the port area at Place Villeneuve-Bargemon:[2282] and the Roman Docks section of the harbour.[2283] However, it was still a majority Greek population ruled by their own government, the Six Hundred, Council of Fifteen and the Three at the top,[2284] and possibly one over the three.[2285] It would seem from Procopius that this lasted until the city was taken over by the Franks in A.D. 536 [2286] or from Agathias's comments possibly by the late sixth century A.D.[2287]

Continuing Greek Presence in the City of Massalia

Strabo (64 B.C.–A.D. 24) recorded that Massalia maintained its independence under Rome:

> Both Caesar and the commanders who succeeded him, mindful of their former friendship, acted in moderation with reference to the wrongs done in the war, and preserved to the city the autonomy which it had had from the beginning; so that neither Massilia nor its subjects are subject to the praetors who are sent to the province. [2288]

As the Romans left them politically and militarily alone as a confederate city *civitas foederata* [2289] and due to being off the main road system of the Roman Empire [2290] then it is quite feasible that the Greek population would have continued living in their city where they had their property, family, friends, and place of business. Just as they did in the East Roman Empire [2291] and later under the Ottoman Empire in Alexandria: Constantinople and particularly in Asia Minor,[2292] Smyrna and Phocaea;[2293] along the coast right up to Pontos and Trebizond on the Black Sea; and also deep inland in Cappadocia.[2294] At the present time there are still nine Greek-speaking towns surviving in Apulia in South-East Italy [2295] and also seven Greek-speaking villages near Reggio di Calabria in South-West Italy. [2296]

In spite of being deprived of their navy initially by Caesar in September 49 B.C. they still had their long established commercial contacts and knew how to get goods transported anywhere in the Mediterranean and would by necessity hire ships of other nationalities for the meantime. Amphorae found dating 1st century B.C. to 1st century A.D. contained cores of peaches and olives, grape pips, branches of fennel and palm leaves.[2297] Redevelopment of the docks in Massalia 1st century B.C. to 3rd century A.D. confirms commercial activity.[2298]

Second Century A.D.

Phocaean Stone Inscription

An inscription on two stone tablets from Phocaea [2299] shows first a decree from Phocaea in honour of the citizens Demetrius Gallus, son of Demetrius, who serving the municipality of Prytane, stephanephore and Priest of Massalia, three times. The second decree is a tribute to Massalia the city, and also in honour of the woman, Flavia Ammion surnamed Ariston, daughter of Moschus and wife to Flavius Hermocrates, serving the arch-priestess at the Temple of Ephesus in Asia Minor, the Prytane, stephanephore two times, Priestess of Massalia and Agonothete (Presenter of the Games). The inscription finishes with contemplating the worth of valour, decency and purity of life:

```
ΟΔ . . . . .
ΔΗΜΗΤΡΙΟΝΔΗΜΗΤΡΙΟΥΓΑΛΛΟΝΤΟΝΠΡΥΤΑΝ . .
ΚΑΙΣΤΕΦΑΝΗΦΟΡΟΝΚΑΙΙΕΡΕΑΤΗΣΜΑΣΣΑΛΙΑΣΤΓ
ΗΡΩΑΠ . . ΜΕΛΗΘΕΝΤΟΣΤΗΣΓΥΜΝΑΣΙΑΡΧΙ
ΑΣ . . . . . . . . . ΝΤΕΙΜΩΝΛΟΥΚΙΟΥΑΥΙΔΙΟΥ.
Λ . . . . . . . . . . ΡΓΙΛ . . . . . . ΥΡΑΣΓΟΣΝΕΟΥ    [2300]
```

CIG (*Corpus Inscriptionum Graecarum*) has transcribed the inscription above into miniscule script and with some of the missing letters in brackets as follows:

Ὁ δ[ῆμος] Δημήτριον Δημητρίου Γάλλον τὸν πρύταν[ιν]
καὶ στεφανηφόρον καὶ ἱερέα τῆς Μασσαλίας τὸ γ̄ , ἥρωα ,
[ἐπι]μεληθέντος τῆς γυμνασιαρχίας [καὶ τῶν . . . ω]ν τειμῶν
Λουκίου Λὑιδίου - - - [λειτου]ργί[α]? - - - - νέου.

The rest of the inscription continues and is as followed with a transcription into miniscule script with missing letters in brackets:

ΗΤΕΥΘΑΔΕΩΝΦΥΛΗ
ΦΛΑΟΥΙΑΝΜΟΣΧΟΝΘΥΓΑΤΕΡΑΑΜΜΙΟΝ
ΤΗΝΚΑΛΟΥΜΕΝΗΝΑΡΙΣΤΙΟΝΑΡΧΙΕΡΕΙΑΝ
ΑΣΙΑΣΝΑΟΥΤΟΥΕΝΕΦΕΣΩΠΡΥΤΑΝΙΝΣΤΕΦΑΝΗΦΟΡΟΝ
ΔΙΣΚΑΙΙΕΡΕΙΑΝΤΗΣΜΑΣΣΑΛΙΑΣΑΓΩΝΟΘΕΤΙΝΤΗΝ
ΦΛΑΟΥΙΟΥΕΡΜΟΚΡΑΤΟΥΓΥΝΑΙΚΑΑΡΕΤΗΣΕΝΕΚΕΝ
ΚΑΙΤΗΣΠΕΡΙΤΟΝΒΙΟΝΚΟΣΜΩΤΗΤΟΣΤΕΚΑΙΑΓΝΕΙΑΣ [2301]

Ἡ Τευθαδέων
φυλὴ Φλαουΐαν , Μόσχο[υ] θυγατέρα , Ἄμιον ,
τὴν καλουμένην Ἀρίστιον , ἀρχιέρειαν
Ἀσίας ναοῦ τοῦ ἐν Ἐφεσῷ , πρύτανιν , στεφανηφόρον
δίς , καὶ ἱέρειαν τῆς Μασσαλίας , ἀγωνοθέτιν , τὴν
Φλαουΐου Ἑρμοκράτου γυναῖκα , ἀρετῆς ἕνεκεν
καὶ τῆς περὶ τὸν βίον κοσμ[ιό]τητός τε καὶ ἁγνείας.

The two stones were in the Ashmolean Museum Oxford when Clerc (1929) published a photograph of them in his book and they are still there.[2302] Clerc, archaeologist, scholar and curator at the Museum of Marseille, proposed something left in the inscriptions that suggested maybe the name Aristion, Aristarche or Aristarkeion, which would relate to the first and oldest cult of Massalia[2303] as recorded by Strabo. [2304]

In another inscription from Phocaea Clerc mentions 'king of Ionia' a unique title and purely an honorary one (or a descendant) to Titus Flavius Calvisianus Hermokrates, son of Stratonicus, of the tribe Quirina, of the ancient Ionian kings of Phocaea from the Council and the People of the Ionians. The Council existed up until the third century. He was a *Praefectus fabrum* twice at Rome, prefect of a cohort of auxiliaries and a military Tribune. A further inscription from Phocaea has Ciaus Flavius Julius Domitianus, son of Stratonicus, of the tribe Quirina, Hermocrates (it would seem the brother of Hermocrates). In Rome twice *Praefectus fabrum*, and a military Tribune, in Phocaea a stephanephore, High Priest of the temple of Ephesus, Priest of Massalia two times, and after Agonothete (Presenter of the Games) and king of the Ionians.[2305]

The Phocaeans (Phokaians) were originally settlers from Phocis in Greece. In one story reported by Pausanias of their arrival in Ionia 'their land they took from the Cymaeans, not by war but by agreement'. When the Phocaeans applied to join the Ionian confederacy they were not admitted until 'they accepted kings of the race of the Kodridai'.[2306] 'They accepted Deoetes, Periclus and Abartus from Erythrae and Teos'.[2307]

Clerc points out that the Romans allocated citizens into tribes. Greeks from Massalia who became Roman citizens were allocated into the 'tribe Quirina'. This would seem to have been because of their origin from the city of Phocaea being in Asia Minor and were therefore enrolled with new Roman citizens of Asia Minor and Syria. Whereas the surrounding cities that neighboured Massalia in Gaul Narbonnaise were allocated into the tribe Voltina.[2308]

In 129 B.C. Phocaea sided with the revolt of Aristonicus against Rome who was defeated. Phocaea only avoided destruction from the Romans by asking their compatriot but independent city Massalia to use its influence with their Roman ally in the Senate. Clerc suggests a possible connection with this saving from disaster and a new temple in Phocaea to 'the goddess Massalia'[2309] having deified the city.

Evidence showing the continuous presence of Greeks in Massalia can be found from funerary stones with inscriptions. An epitaph of the second century A.D. shows Ionian form and inscribed:[2310]

ΚΟΡΥΝΘΩΙ
ΘΕΥΜΕΔΟΝ
ΤΟΣΑΠΕΛΕΥ
ΘΕΡΩΙ

Κορύνθωι θευμέδοντος ἀπελευθέρωι.

An inscription was found of the cult of Zeus Patroos from an altar or base of a dedication set up by Lyketos Pythokritou between first or second century A.D.[2311]

Other inscriptions include a second century A.D. tomb of Glaucias includes the words 'eusevien' (εὐσεβίην) and 'orfanie' (ὀρφανίη orphan) in the Ionian dialect:[2312] 'Krates son of Apellas in memory of Syriske' from the time of Hadrian was found in the Sainte-Barbe necropolis:[2313] and later in the third century A.D. a funeral bust of Zozimos found in the Rue de Minimes.[2314] A marble inscription 'Athenades, son of Dioscourides grammarian in the Roman language' was found lors du percemont du basin de Carénage in 1833 dated to the third century A.D.[2315]

In addition other names found include Apollonides, Herylos, Hipponikos, Leukon, Lykaithos, Mikion, Oulis, Parmenon, Xeinandros.[2316] There are carved sarcophagi, other epitaphs in Greek and Latin and some stones dedicated to cults.[2317]

Knight (2001) reports that in the light of 'recent excavations' well-established large Roman houses throughout the city were abandoned during the third century A.D., which coincides with the 'urban recession seen in Aix-en-Provence, Vienne and elsewhere . . . Large parts of the upper city lay abandoned in late Roman times, and were not reoccupied until the twelfth or thirteenth century'. However, the lower city between the fifth and seventh centuries flourished with simple houses of beaten earth floors. There were craftsmen, 'iron workers, glassblowers, saltmakers, and workers in bone, leather and wood'.[2318] Local trade dating 2nd half of II–beginning of III century is shown by an amphorette H. 25.3 cm; D. 2.1 cm with an inscription in black capitals, from the region Cavares destination Massalia for Rubrius, 1500 *modii* of barley, *Massil(iam)* or *Massil(iensi) Rubrio / (...) sino, hord(ei) Cavar(um), / sicci, mundi / (...) i, m(odii) mille (et quingenti)*: estimated as a 7.4 ton cargo to have travelled on a small river boat down the Rhône.[2319] African Red Slip pottery remains in the Horn of the harbour dominate. African fine ware reached a peak the sixth century A.D. and less so into the seventh century. A wide range of common ware from all over the Mediterranean was present showing an active port.[2320] Around c. A.D. 600 the suburb outside the city gate at the Bourse excavation kept expanding. By the early seventh century the suburb extended over the Horn of the harbour, which had been in filled after several attempts to revive it did not succeed due to silting.[2321]

Change from Greek to Roman Administration?

Clerc suggests the possibility that from the time of Apollonides tomb description that the custom of adopting the Roman three name systems increased amongst the richer families in Massalia in the second century A.D. and by the end of the third century A.D. was a defining moment from Greek Massalia to Roman administration of Massilia. We do have a second century A.D. inscription from Nice to Macrinus.

Nicaea under the Supervision of Massalia:

> To Gaius Memmius Macrinus, quaestor and duovir at Massilia;
> quinquennial duovir and prefect representing the quinquennial duovir;
> agonothete; superintendent of the people of Nicaea; from his friends.[2322]

Nicaea (Nikaia, Nice) was a colony of Massalia[2323] and had remained under Massaliote control after losing most of its empire in 49 B.C. Macrinus held these regular municipal posts at Massalia, 'which enjoyed privileged treaty rights with Rome'.[2324]

The title 'agonothete' is Greek and means 'Presenter of the Games'. This title is rare in the West and is due to the influence of Massilia. The other title 'Superintendent' of the Nicaeans is also Greek and Levick points out that this is translated as 'bishop' in English.

The offices held by Macrinus included the financial post of the Quaestorship; the supreme magistracy; and the duovirate. Levick explains that the Duovirate was modelled on the Roman Consuls two-man system. The quinquennial duovirate ran every five years and kept the current list of citizens (like the Roman censors) and the current roll of councillors. Macrinus could also act on behalf of an absentee holder of this honourable position.

Though the inscription from Nice is estimated to the second century A.D.[2325] Macrinus's position poses a problem in that he has official Roman posts at Massalia yet the Massaliotes still have their own government as usual. It would seem from Procopius[2326] and Agathias that this lasted until the city was taken over by the Franks during the sixth century A.D.[2327]

Clerc noted such is the 'miserable state of our knowledge' that there is only the Macrinus inscription found to mention a Roman post at Massalia during the second century A.D. In the absence of any other documents Clerc surmises from the epitaph inscriptions and suggests that the posts of the Roman quaestor, duovir and quinquennial duovir replaced Massalia's government of the fifteen and the supreme three magistrates. Clerc suggests that the senators of the Hellenic city of Massalia the 'Six Hundred' was reduced as a body of up to one hundred but still aristocratic in essence as it was from the Order of Decurions. The nomination of the Decurions was one of the most important functions of the Duumviri. The position was for life but we do not know if the ordinary people were allowed to stand for these positions as from the time of its foundation Massalia had always been ruled by a restricted few that grew into a successfully run Timocracy.[2328] Strabo writing in the first century B.C. recorded that the Greek city of Massalia's government 'of all the aristocracies, theirs is the best ordered'.[2329] Cicero noted though not a democracy he praised how the Greek city was 'so well governed by the prudence of its aristocracy'.[2330]

Another inscription at the end of the second century A.D. found at the cemetery of Lazaret in bad condition shows a presence of an 'honorary Ducurion' in Massalia by the name of Cornelius, *decurionatus ornamentis honoratus.*[2331]

Rivet mentions two more *eqites* Porcius Aelianus, and T. Porcius Cornelianus who became governor of the *Alpes Maritimae* around A.D. 200.[2332] Clerc mentions the Porcius Aelianus inscription describing him as a knight and prophet,[2333] and a ΙΕΡΕΙ ΛΕΥΚΟΘΕΑΣ [2334] priest of Leucothea.[2335] An inscription on Cornelianus's statue base writes that he was an equestrian and a priest of Leucothea at Massalia, which can indicate the cult still active there in the third century A.D.[2336]

Clerc also points to evidence from a Latin inscriptions on the funerary stone of Cn. Valerius Pompeius Valerianus from the second century A.D., dedicated by the centonarii from Massalia, which approximately translated contains the following: Gnaeus Valerius, son of Gnaeus, of the Tribe Quirina, Pompeius Valerianus, Knight of the sacred Emperors Antonino and Vero Augustes: Augure of life, Gave to the city 100,000 sesterces: Agonothete [Presenter of the Games] in honour of (?): prophet, its benefactor: the 'centonarii corporati Massiliensis' dedicates this to its patron.[2337]

'Corparati' can also mean public body or Trade-Guild. There is also mention of another 'corporati' of carpenters, for the erection of a statue found in poor condition and now lost but fortunately recorded. This mentions a 'pontife and flamine' of Riez, owner of the dendrophores there, by the 'dendrophores of Massalia' and the sum of 12,000 sesterces.[2338] Missing letters are shown in italics:

. . . .
. . . . *ponti*F• FLAMI*ni* . . .
. . . . . . COL • RE*i*S APO*l*
lin*ARi* pATR• *dEndrophor*ORVM
bEne DE SE M*erenti* . . . . .
*de*NDROPH*ori* MASS*L*ienses
*cui*VS STATVAE *im*PENDIvm. . . . .
RE*mis.* ET *ob* DED*i*CATION• HS XII
n(omine) SPO*rt*VLARVM CORPORATIS DEDI*t*

Clerc further concludes that Massalia in the second century A.D. as having entered the Roman framework of tribes and designated as part of the Quirina tribe. Two more inscriptions occur with the three names that includes a Roman benefactor and Greek personal name. The first has a dedication to Apollo by L. Aelius Nymphicus, *Sevir Augustalis corporatus*, and the second a funerary inscription Quintus Gallius Euphemus, *Sevir Augustalis corporatus.*[2339]

However, Lucian writing in the second century A.D. shows in his story of Zenothemis of Massalia that Massalia's own traditional government of the 600 was still active. Lucian died in A.D. 180. [2340] Could Massalia's traditional system of government have co-existed alongside the Roman officials or was it later in the century or the third century that a transfer of governmental power to the Roman system occurred?

When Agathias is marking the change over to the Franks of the independence of Massilia could he mean a Roman governed independent city of Greeks and Romans, rather than a Greek governed city of Greeks and Romans? From Agathias's comment it would seem that Massalia 'a Greek city' had still maintained its 'ancestral constitution' until the Franks took over the city in the sixth century A.D. 'having abandoned its ancestral constitution and embraced the ways of its conquerors'.[2341]

One should note that in A.D. 212 Emperor Caracalla made all free men in the empire Roman citizens regardless of ethnicity. Also Alexander Severus emperor A.D. 222–235 allowed Roman citizens to make their last will and testaments in Greek and not just in Latin as before. [2342]

Had there been economic or political pressure to change? Was it voluntary that the conservative Massaliote Greeks decided to change their ancient and traditional Timocratic government and adopt the Roman system? Were there political and financial advantages for doing so rather like Britain voluntarily joining the larger economic and trading entity the EC, and Greece who on joining readily also gave up their ancient currency the drachma in favour of the Euro? [2343]

We have seen that Massalia's coin production from its own mint continued after 49 B.C., as to how long there seems to be a lack of evidence and information for this period. Brenot gives to the end of the first century B.C. but with a question mark. Barruol points to the Romanization of the area and its use of Roman money becoming the main currency and supplanting local coins. Whereas local religions continued in the usual Roman pattern of identifying their own gods with that of the indigenous people as is evident at Glanum.[2344] There are more Greek inscriptions found from the Roman period then before that shows a flourishing continuity within change.[2345]

Third Century A.D.

The Mists of Time

There is very little information on the actual population of Massalia in late antiquity. What happened to the Greeks? The following is an outline of what happened to their city so that you may draw your own inferences.

A.D. 273 The Catholic Encyclopaedia of 1911 mentions the sarcophagi in the Christian Museum at Marseille (Massalia). The earliest Christian sarcophagi in Massalia date from A.D. 273 and the epitaph of Volusianus and Fortunatus is the oldest Christian inscriptions [2346] while Bizot et al has a question mark as to whether it was Christian or pagan.[2347] They died violently either by accident or torture.[2348]

Mary Magdalene

According to the Greek Church Mary Magdalene retired to Ephesus with the Virgin Mary. She died there and her relics were taken to Constantinople in A.D. 886. There is a French tradition that Mary, Lazarus and others came to Massalia and converted Provence. They also say she retired to a hill at La Sainte-Baume and stayed for thirty years. Her body was removed to Aix. In 745 in fear of the Saracens attacks the relics were removed to Vézelay. The relics disappeared and were found centuries later back at Sainte-Baume in 1279 when Charles II, king of Naples was erecting a convent for Dominicans there. The head of Saint Mary now lies in the grotto at Sainte-Baum.[2349] Local tradition maintained that the actual stone Mary is reputed to have used to sleep on was 'observed as constantly to be dry, whereas all other parts of the cave, they say, is moist, water always distilling from the roof'.[2350]

A.D. 290. Saint Victor was a Roman Officer in Massalia (Marseille) and publicly denounced idol worship. He was taken before Emperor Maximian (286–305) during the last Christian persecution;[2351] beaten and thrown into prison; where he converted three Roman soldiers Longius, Alexander and Felician. All were executed and were later made saints. In the fourth century Saint John Cassian built a monastery over the cave where the bodies had been buried.

Fourth Century A.D.

A.D. 306. Constantine was hailed as Augustus by his Roman troops in York when his father died. He then took over the Roman Army in Britain.

Circa **A.D. 305–6.** The Roman Army in Britain declared Constantine anti-emperor to Maxentius. Constantine constructs a fleet in Arles and Massalia and gains control of the Tyrrhenian Sea.[2352]

A.D. 308. Emperor Maximianus Herculius claimed Constantine's title of Augustus. Constantine now in Germany brought his Legions to Gaul. Maximianus fled to Massalia and was besieged there by Constantine in A.D. 309.[2353] The first attack gave Constantine control of the port, 'but the assault on the ramparts of the city failed, because, we are told, the ladders had been made too short for the height of the walls' and to give time for the besieged to take up his offer of a pardon.[2354]

The garrison surrendered and Maximianus resigned to be a private citizen. Maximianus was later caught trying to assassinate Constantine and eventually took his own life at Massalia in A.D. 310 though in some histories he is killed.[2355] His body was rediscovered in the mid-eleventh century in a 'lead lined coffin fresh and entire'.[2356] Constantine went on to fight Maximianus's son Maxentius at Rome and eventually became sole emperor reuniting the political control of the Roman Empire A.D. 324.[2357]

Eumenes writes of this siege at Massalia[2358] and what is evident from the accounts is that Massalia was 'protected by a solid wall with many towers'[2359] and they were intact. We know from Pliny the Elder that Crinas of Massalia who became a very wealthy multi-millionaire in Rome as a doctor, had paid almost ten million sesterces for the rebuilding of the walls of Massalia and other fortifications[2360] during the reign of Nero A.D. 54–68.[2361]

Another point in the continuation of the Greeks in Massalia is Eumenes comment *Quippe olim Graecos Italosque illuc convenas.*[2362]

Strabo had recorded 'Massilia to the precinct of Aphrodite (Headland of the Pyrenees) was called the Galatic Gulf and also the Gulf of Massilia'.[2363] A map drawn by a monk from Colmar in A.D. 1265 was discovered in 1494 by Konrad Meissel and given to the antiquarian of Augsburg Konrad Peutinger. The map contains older names of cities from other maps from different times as it has the locations of cities no longer in existence like Pompeii A.D. 79 and Herculanum. Jerusalem is called by its name of A.D. 132 Aelia Capitolina.[2364] In the Peutinger Map it records *Massilia Graecorum* and the surrounding territory and a port named *de Gretia* and the gulf, the *mare graecum*.[2365] Had not the Greek influence lasted the name would eventually change as at present from the *Mare Graecum* to the Golfe du Lion. This change may have occurred during the fourth century A.D. as the historian Ammianus Marcellinus of that period describes the River Rhône, 'still navigable by large vessels from the point joined by the River Saône, flowing into the Gallic Sea at the Gulf of Lion'.[2366] However, one should note that names could survive even though the originating influence may have gone. At the present time we still have surviving the Ligurian Sea near Genoa and the Tyrrhenian Sea between Italy and Sardinia. Place-names are a useful indicator for the archaeologist and historian for example where was the road next to the River Thames in the original first Saxon city of Lundenwic (London)?[2367] The Saxons called this the 'Strand', which still survives today as The Strand proceeding straight along to the Aldwych (Saxon for 'old town').[2368]

While Ammianus Marcellinus records a different name for the *Mare Graecum* this could intimate that the Greeks were no longer dominant there. While at the same time he still records that the nearby mountains around Avenche were called the Grecian Alps.[2369] Ammianus Marcellinus recording the cities of the Galli, 'The Grecian and Pennine Alps, have besides other towns of no less note, Avenche.' Regarding the province of Vienne (in Gaul) he writes that

> The Viennese exults in the magnificence of many cities, the chief of which are Vienne itself, and Arles and Valence; to which may be added Marseilles [Massilia], by the alliance with and power of which we read that Rome itself was more than once supported in moments of danger.[2370]

As late as the fourth century A.D. the stories of Massalia's (Marseille) military and political help to Rome were still known.

By the time of Theodosius's son Honorius, the Emperor of the West Roman Empire A.D. 395-423, Massalia is listed as the third city in the province of Viennoise with the centre at Vienne (in Gaul).[2371]

Massalia's Renewed Energy

Massalia had renewed energy due to its Christianity and its Greek heritage was reflected in 'the names of its buildings, officials, and individuals.'[2372]

A.D. 314. There was the Council of Arles, attended by the first recorded bishop of Massalia[2373] Oresius[2374] together with his lector Nazareus.[2375] Three British bishops attended therefore evidence of Christianity in Britain before Saint Augustine.[2376] Constantine the Great convened the council.

The church at Nice (Nikaia) also sent representatives to the Council of Arles and were recorded as delegates from *Portus Nicaensium.*[2377]

Proculus (A.D. 381–428)

During the fifth century A.D. Proculus (A.D. 381–428) [2378] bishop of Massalia was in conflict with the bishop of Arles over treating ascetics as heretics. He uses client-bishops and former followers of Martin (called a semi-Pelasgian) for support.[2379] *Circa* A.D. 400 the Council of Turin decided in favour of Narbon against Massalia but allowed Proculus to keep his metropolitan rights until he died.[2380] Proculus had a reputation outside of Provence as a Holy Man.

Fifth Century A.D.

A.D. 413. The Visigoth king Athaulf fails to storm Massalia [2381] being resisted by the Roman General Bonifatius.[2382] Athaulf was asked 'at the urging especially of Constantius' to return Placidia[2383] in exchange for grain, 'The Barbarian pretended to agree and advanced to the city named Marseilles, which he hoped to capture by treachery. There he was wounded . . . and retired to his own tent'.[2384] Athaulf captures Narbonne later that year.[2385]

***Circa* A.D. 416.** John Cassian of Marseille. Saint John Cassian founded two monasteries in Massalia and wrote around A.D. 420–429 two influential documents the 'Institutes' and the 'Conferences'.[2386] His works were recommended by Benedict, and influenced western monastic orders.

Haldon writes of Cassian as a Greek who had lived in the deserts of Egypt and went to Massalia (Marseille).[2387] While Brown says he was a Latin-speaking monk from the Dobrudja (Roumania) who had lived in Egypt and arrived at Massalia in A.D. 415.[2388] While Gennadius wrote that he was a 'Scythian by race'.[2389]

Cassian was proud that with his codex one could live in a cell anywhere and live as if he were still in Egypt. As the West Roman Empire diminished Cassian showed the Christian networks could still be linked from 'East and West and between Roman and Barbarian Europe'.[2390]

An attempt to reconcile the positions of Pelagians and Augustine 'by pious monks' from Massalia was led by Cassian around A.D. 428 who explained their opinion on Nature and Grace. This was called Semi-pelagianism by the rest of the church. Though philosophically false it was not regarded as heretical. There was much disturbance in Massalia's churches and layman Hilary begged Augustine and the Pope St. Celestine to suppress this doctrine. [2391] Because of the Massilians Augustine wrote two books against the arguments of the Semi-pelagians *De Praedestinatione sanctorum* and *De dono perseverantia.*[2392]

Victorianus a rhetorician

Victorianus a rhetorician from Massalia wrote to his son Etherius a commentary *On Genesis* in four books of verse. Gennadius recorded that Victorianus was 'busied in secular literature' and not trained in Divine scripture 'though the words savour piety they are of slight weight'. Victorianus died during the reign of Theodosius and Valentinianus.[2393]

Presbyters of Massalia

Salvian settled in Massalia and wrote his treatise on *The Government of God* [2394] between A.D. 439 and 451.[2395] Salvian, a priest of Massalia, was born of a noble family. He wrote bitterly against the corruption and arrogance of officials. 'Not a few Romans' he said, 'preferred to live poor but free in the land of the barbarian rather than slaves in their own'.[2396]

Salvianus was a presbyter of Marseilles (Massalia) 'a master among bishops'. He also wrote:
- four books *On the Excellence of Virginity*
- three books *Against Avarice*
- five books *On the Present Judgement*
- one book *On Punishment according to Desert*
- one book on *Commentary* on the latter part of the book of Ecclesiastes
- one book of *Epistles*
- one book of verse 'after the Greek fashion, a sort of Hexameron, covering the period from the beginning of Genesis to the Creation of man'
- several homilies *On the Sacraments* [2397]

Musaeus was a presbyter at Marseille (Massalia) during the time of Saint Venerius the bishop. Musaeus was instructed by him to select passages for the clergy to read on feast days which was of great value to the church. He also addressed a sizeable volume, a *Sacramentary*, to Saint Eusthasius the bishop and successor to Venerius. Musaeus died in the reign of Leo and Majorianus.[2398]

> I GENNADIUS, a presbyter of Marseilles [Massalia], have written eight books *Against all Heresies*, five books *Against Nestorius*, ten books *Against Eutyches*, three books *Against Pelagius*, also treatises *On the Millenium* and *On the Apocalypse of Saint John*, also an epistle *On my Creed*, sent to the blessed Gelasius, bishop of Rome.[2399]

St. Honoratus started a monastery on one of the Lerin Islands (near Cannes) in the first quarter of the fifth century A.D. that became an intellectual centre and the heart of Christian religious life in Gaul. Among many who studied there were St Hilary, St. Valerianus, St. Vincent of Lerins, the polemist Salvian, and St. Eucherius.

In A.D. 524 Queen Radegund adopted Salvian's rules from his treatise for the convent of the Holy Cross at Poitiers.[2400]

In the seventh century A.D. Benedict Biscop was a monk at Lerins for two years and went on to found Monkwearmouth and Jarrow in Northumbria, Britain.[2401]

Visigoths

A.D. 413 Saint Jerome describes the Visigoths led by King Athaulf and their raid on southern Gaul. They were defeated at Massalia defended by the Roman general John Boniface.[2402] Athaulf married Princess Placidia the sister of Emperor Honorius and changed from a destroyer to a restorer of the Roman Empire.[2403] In 418 'Constantius settles Visigoths under Wallia in Aquitane' with their capital at Toulouse.[2404]

Philostorgius a Byzantine chronicler in the early fifth century A.D. interpreted the marriage of Athaulf and Placida as union of iron and clay. Sulpicius Severus (late third century A.D.) interpretation of the Old Testament prophet Daniel 2.31 vision of the 'great statue' was with the head representing the Chaldean Empire, the chest and arms of silver as the Persian Empire, the bronze belly as the empire of Alexander the Great, and the iron legs as the Roman Empire (West and East). The feet of iron and clay Severus saw as relevant to the time he was living in,[2405] as a mixture of Roman and Barbarian rulers.

Provence was raided by the Visigoths in A.D. 413, 426, 430 and 452. Theodoric II became king of the Visigoths in 451.

Roman Emperor Majorian reconquers Gaul A.D. 458-459 forcing Theodoric II and the Visigoths away from Arles returning them to federate status and defeats the Burgundians at Lyon. He gives Sidonius Apollinaris the title of *comespectablis* (Respectable) outranking the other aristocrats in Gaul. Majorian turned out to be one of the last effective West Roman emperors as the following became limited by internal squabbling amongst their barbarian generals.[2406]

Euric killed his brother Theodoric II, king of the Goths in Toulouse A.D. 467.[2407] Euric, now king of the Visigoths finally conquered Provence in A.D. 470. By 473 Euric captured Arles and Massalia but ceded them back to Rome in exchange for the remainder of the Auvergne. Within a year Euric regained Arles and the Visigoths occupied the part of Provence between the rivers Durance and Rhône.[2408]

A.D. 461. Mansuetus bishop of the Britons *episcopus Britannorum* (in Brittany) and Toul (in East France) attended the first Council of Tours. By 469 divisions amongst the Romans are shown by Arvandus Prefect of Lyon in his letter to Euric not to make alliance with 'the Greek emperor' Anthemius (appointed western emperor by his eastern counterpart Leo I) and to 'attack the Britons situated on the far side of the Loire'. A 12,000 strong army of Britons led by Riothamus a 'supreme king' (part of Anthemius's coalition to defend Aquitania Prima) invades and is defeated by Euric at Bourg-de-Déols in Berry. They obtained refuge with Anthemius's ally the Burgundians. These Britons came either from their recent settlements in Brittany (Amorica) or direct from Britain. There is conjecture that Riothamus may be a historical basis for the legendary King Arthur and Floyde also presents an older Avallon–with healing springs–still existing in Burgundy.[2409]

Last Roman Emperor of the West

By A.D. 475 Sidonius Apollinaris mentions that Zeno 'who now made the decisions regarding all the surviving Roman Empire from Constantinople conceded our whole area to him [Euric, king of the Visigoths]'.[2410]

Zeno was the emperor of the East Roman Empire ruling from Constantinople A.D. 474–5, then ousted (in which Odoacer's brother Armatus was involved) and returned 476–491 When the last emperor of the West Roman Empire Romulus Augustulus abdicated in A.D. 476 his final act was to send a senatorial embassy to Zeno to 'propose that no second emperor was now required in the West but that Odoacer should be given the rank *patricius* to wield authority on the Romans behalf.'[2411] Odoacer was the leader of the Germanic *foederati* living in Italy, (king of Hérules, and later king of Italy A.D. 476–493).

Zeno proposed Julius Nepos, who had been appointed Augustus by Leo in 474, and was Emperor of the West A.D. 474–475 until deposed by Romulus Augustulus (475–476), should be recognized as emperor with Odoacer as his *patricius*. Odoacer agreed and issued coins with Nepos's image and name. Nepos remained in Dalmatia as a bishop and was still legally the Emperor of the West until he was murdered in 480 and the lawful title ended. Though Odoacer brought ten years of stability in Italy, Gaul was left to itself. Between the regions controlled by the Merovingian Franks, Visigoths and Burgundians there were two main Roman enclaves around Soissons and Arles.[2412]

Paulinus Pellaeus wrote that the Visigoths were protectors of further depredation in southern Gaul. While he was in difficult times in Massalia he had news that a Goth wanted to buy for a fair price some parts of his wife's property long abandoned in their retreat southwards.[2413]

Eustachius Bishop of Massalia

He gave Amantius a position as Reader. Amantius got himself married under false pretences having the support of many including the Count of Massalia. After he had financially picked clean his wife's family he absconded from Clermont to Auvergne. Amantius is recorded in a letter by Sidonius who pleads with Eustachius's successor Graecus, bishop of Massalia, for his protégé from Auvergne. Sidonius ends in recommending Amantius to the new bishop, as his story was 'as good in its way as any out of Attic comedy or Milesian tale'.[2414]

***Circa* A.D. 475.** Epiphanius of Pavia, a North Italian bishop drew up a treaty with Euric, king of the Visigoths. Four Gallic bishops from the south were to receive the treaty; Basilius of Aix, who asked Sidonius to insert a clause into the treaty safeguarding consecrations; the metropolitan Leontius of Arles; Faustus of Riez; and **Graecus of Massalia** who had received Sidonius's formal protest against the treaty in A.D. 475.[2415]

Sidonius Apollinaris was from a noble family and a writer. His grandfather and father had been Prefects of the Pretorium of the Gauls. His father-in-law was Avitus who was proclaimed emperor in A.D. 455 Sidonius became Prefect of Rome A.D. 468. On his return to Gaul he was reluctant to be made bishop of the Averni (at Clermont) and he had been chosen as the only one capable of maintaining Roman power against Euric, king of the Visigoths. Together with general Ecdicius, his brother-in-law [2416] they resisted Euric until Clermont fell abandoned by Rome A.D. 474.[2417]

Euric annexed the city of Clermont and Sidonius Apollinaris was exiled to the fortress of Liviana. Sidonius Apollinaris asked Bishop Graecus of Massalia to use church funds in ransoming captives a priority. The church asked for nothing in return except prayer.[2418]

The rulers had changed from Rome to the Visigoths but the rest of the population carried on. The existing aristocrats in Gaul formed literary circles in Massalia, Arles, Narbonne, Bordeaux and Lyon. This gave another opportunity to socialise and to 'demonstrate their unity of spirit'. Sidonius says of one such meeting: 'O the feasts, stories and books, the laughter, seriousness and jests, the gatherings and comradeship, one and the same . . . Secular and ecclesiastical aristocrats participated equally' and there was no restriction of literary subjects. Sidonius in a letter to a relative mentions the strong bond these circles had and in literature 'we blame and we praise the same thing, and any sort of discourse pleases or displeases us equally'.[2419]

Near the end of Sidonius's life Euric starts a violent persecution of the Catholics. Sidonius wrote in a letter to Basilius, bishop of Aix, that 'I must confess that, formidable as the mighty Goths may be, I dread him less as the assailant of our walls than as the subverter of our Christian laws'.[2420] A different view is given by the Catholic Encyclopaedia that the image by Gregory of Tours of 'bloodthirsty persecutions' between Euric and his Catholic subjects was 'exaggerated'. Euric only took action against individual bishops and clergy that promoted religious quarrels and dissension in his kingdom. Other than that he 'was in general just towards his Catholics subjects'. Catholics that had fled Africa 'found an asylum among the Visigoths' and his first minister Leo was a Catholic.[2421]

Euric died in c. A.D. 484.[2422] The Burgundians appeared in Provence and it was divided. They controlled the north above the River Durance while to the south by the Visigoths. The Franks took North Provence in A.D. 543 and South Provence in 536 from the Ostrogoths in return for neutrality while the Goths struggled against the Roman Emperor Justinian's attempt to re-conquer the West Roman Empire.[2423] The Visigoths diplomacy after Athaulf, Theodoric the Great [2424] and Theodoric II began to alienate the Gallo-Roman population by their violence and Arianism.[2425] Arianism was Christian but came to be considered heretical by the Catholics.

During the A.D. 470's the aristocrat Eugenia of Massalia fed the hungry. Firminus and Gregoria of Arles spent their wealth on the poor. By the 490's Eugenia took part in the redemption of captives.[2426]

The *Comites Gothorum* were legal officers and the *comes* commanded Goth garrisons in cities like Massilia.[2427] Cassiodorus explained that governors of Provinces after a year in office and the Councillors of the Praefect could reach the rank of Comes. He himself had been a Quaestor as secretary to the monarch under the Ostrogoths.[2428]

Agathe Tyche (Agde)

Towards the end of the fifth century Sever, a Syrian prince, arrives at a small hermitage on the banks of the River Hérault greeted by Bishop Béticus of Agde. Sever gives the riches loaded in his ship to the bishop to rebuild the town and he is lodged in a small cell next to the church of Saint Andrew in Agde. As more disciples join Sever founds a monastery at Agde. Shortly after a final invasion of the Alamans in A.D. 500 Sever dies and is buried in the church he founded.[2429]

Sixth Century A.D.

Caesarius Bishop of Arles A.D. 502–542

St. Caesarius formed the first rules on monastic life and became the bishop of Arles.

A woman in Massalia badly dislocated her foot and could barely stand only 'with the support of her slaves'. Bishop Caesarius visits Massalia and the woman receives prayers and blessing but she did not mention her affliction. She asked his permission to go to his horse 'touching the injured spot with the cloth that was covering the saddle. Immediately she recovered her health'.

A house in Massalia next to the women's monastery caught fire. The women were not allowed to leave the monastery and feared that the fire would kill them. Caesarius ran out in the middle of the night to the wall where the fire was approaching. 'Throwing himself forward in prayer he gave them orders and shouted from the wall, "Do not fear, blessed women". Soon, burning with the flame of his own virtue he sent the fire away'.[2430]

Caesarius recalled his sister Caesaria from a monastery in Massalia where she was learning to become a teacher.[2431] He also raised one hundred pounds of gold to pay a ransom for captives in Gaul.[2432]

A.D. 506. The Council of Agde (*Concilium Agathense*)
Agde (Agathe Tyche–Good Fortune) was the second Greek city founded in France after Marseille (Massalia).

The Council of Agde (*Concilium Agathense*) was held in A.D. 506 with thirty-five bishops under Caesarius of Arles with the permission of the Visigoth king Alaric II (A.D. 485–507).[2433] The Council decreed forty-seven canons (laws of the church) that were an insight into the moral conditions of the clergy and laity in southern France at the beginning of the transition of Graeco-Roman social order to the barbarian conquerors.[2434]

Amongst its canons No. 7 and 29 was the confirmation of any slave of the church freed by a bishop would stay free by the bishop's successors.[2435]

According to local tradition Saint Venuste or Venustus was the first bishop of Agde who was martyred by the invasion of the barbarian Chrocus in A.D. 407 or 408. The first historically known bishop of Agde was Sophronius who assisted at the Council of Agde in A.D. 506.[2436]

Early Christians did not celebrate Christmas and the Roman Catholic Church did not begin its 'Feast of the Nativity' until A.D. 336.[2437] The Council of Agde A.D. 506 decreed Christians should take communion on Easter, Pentecost and Christmas Day.[2438]

What happened to the Greek population? We can only speculate that with the changes in the surrounding populations after the Roman period that intermarriage and immigration slowly began absorbing them? Were they also subject to plagues that attacked the region from the sixth century A.D. like Massalia? The first recorded plague in Gaul was in the year A.D. 543.[2439]

A.D. 507. The Ostrogoths were in power at Massalia.[2440]

A.D. 508. Theodoric rescues Arles from siege. He promptly re-establishes the Praetorian Prefecture that the Visigoths had abolished.[2441]

During the reign of Emperor Justinian (A.D. 527–568) the cult of Theotokos (a title of the Virgin Mary) spread rapidly in Italy. A new church of Saint Mariain Cosmedin was built in the Greek quarter of Rome ('ecclesia Graecorum').[2442]

A.D. 533. The Council of Massalia (Marseille) was presided over by Caesarius bishop of Arles.[2443] The Council decided that it was contrary to the canons for a bishop to sell property without the leave of the provincial council.[2444]

A.D. 550. The fortress city of Avignon continued with aspects of its Roman culture. An abbot from Paris called Dumnole refused to become bishop of Avignon, as he 'feared sophistic senators and philosophical magistrates'.[2445]

A.D. 555. Provence was divided between two brothers. Guntrum took the most part and Arles. Sigibert received Massalia and parts of Aix and Avignon. He establishes his own Governor at Massalia that became a separate regional capital.[2446]

By the sixth century A.D. the Franks are in control of Provence with the authorisation of the Roman Emperor Justinian in Constantinople.[2447]

Clovis I, the first Christian king of the Salian Franks [2448] was anointed in Reims A.D. 496 using olive oil from Saint-Rémy de Provence, which became a tradition for anointing all future kings of France.[2449] Clovis adopted the Catholic version of Christianity which at that time was one church from the East Roman Empire at Constantinople to what had been the West Roman Empire of Italy, France, Spain and Britain.

Provence divided and reunited at times with Merovingian kings at Arles and Massalia. The kings left intact the Roman political organisation as modified by the Burgundians and Ostrogoths.[2450]

Greek Language in Massalia

Massalia's population continued as Christian under the Visigoth and then the Ostrogoths in A.D. 507 who eventually ceded the city to the Franks in A.D. 536. There must have been enough of a Greek and Roman Christian population to have convened a Christian council in A.D. 533 the Council of Massalia (Marseille) with sixteen bishops of Provence [2451] presided over by St. Caesarius of Arles.[2452]

During this period what language was Massalia's Christian service conducted in, Greek or Latin? Presumably as the New Testament was first written in Greek Massalia would have continued using the language they also spoke? In the second century A.D. the churches at Lyon and Vienne commissioned the lives of the martyrs written in Greek: of 48 Christians martyred in Lyon A.D. 177 half were of Greek origin. [2453] 'Asian Greeks' were also mentioned by Toynbee as being a community in Lyon in the reign of Marcus Aurelius second century A. D. [2454] In its heyday Lyon had 50,000–80,000 population and '30 per cent of them had Greek names'. [2455] Lyon and Arles are connected by the River Rhône and once part of ancient Massalia's trade route.

Until the third century A.D. eastern influences dominated the Roman Church and the liturgy was in Greek.[2456] Miller writes that Greek was 'the (almost) universal language of both people and the Church, and Latin, as the inherited official language of government—but used only in its internal communications' during the period of Theodosius II in the first half of the fifth century A.D. in the Roman Empire.[2457]

In the sixth century A.D. 'Caesar bishop of Arles, wrote hymns in Greek for his people'.[2458] Lindsay comments that only after the founding of Byzantium did the see of Rome become decisively Latin. The African church was close to the Orthodox Church in the apostolic idea of self-governing churches only acknowledging the rule of the General Council. The Vandals conquered Carthage and North Africa and the African Church lost any influence they may have had. The Roman Church 'political rise was helped by the general chaos of seventh century Gaul: when the Church was reformed, the Papacy was able to impose its forms and attitudes'. 'Charles [Charlemagne] visited Pope Hadrian in Rome in A.D. 787 and chose to support the Roman mode of singing rather than the Gallic and asked the Pope to send Roman singers north with him'.[2459] Dunn clarifies 'the Gallic rites, those western Liturgies distinct from Roman, Hispanic, Celtic and possibly the Milanese in its early stages'.[2460] The Gallican *Ordines Baptismi* used by the Visigothic Church was in uncouth Latin achieved by word for word translation from Greek i.e. ante for anti.[2461]

A remnant of the Greek Liturgy 'Kyria Eleison' is still in use today in the Roman Catholic Latin Mass as given during Pope Benedict's visit to the Roman Catholic Cathedral in London 18 September 2010.

Iconoclasm: Destruction of Religious Icons

Loseby mentions Massalia's Greek orientation in the sixth century apparent by Serenus bishop of Massalia (A.D. 596–601) reaction to icons [2462] (in common with the Eastern Church and Byzantium) whereas this important religious struggle was otherwise 'alien to the Western Church'.[2463] Duprat also mentions that Bishop Serenius was an iconoclast. The heresy of iconoclasts (against the use of images in religious worship) had no success. [2464]

Pope Gregory I wrote two letters to the bishop of Massalia about his actions on icons. One contains,

> In that thou forbadest them to be adored, we altogether praise thee; but we blame thee for having broken them . . . to adore a picture is one thing *(picturam adorarae)*, but to learn through the story of the picture what is to be adored, is another. [2465]

The other letter explains,

> For what writing presents to the readers, the picture presents to the unlearned, who behold; for in it even those who are ignorant see what they should follow; in it the unlettered read. Thus is a picture, especially to the barbarians, instead of reading. [2466]

Duprat points out that Serenius's attack of iconoclasm in Massalia was long before the Byzantine Emperor Leo III started the iconoclast upheaval [2467] over 100 years later from A.D. 726 in the East Roman Empire (Byzantine). One chronicler referred to Emperor Leo as 'the Saracen-minded' due to the Saracen objections to images altogether.[2468]

Lindsay writes that the Gallic Church was closer in the iconoclastic position than to the Papal. Byzantine emperor Constantine V made efforts to win Gallic support.[2469] The Papacy intrigues with the Frankish king Pepin III who imposed his will on the Church Council held at Gentilly in A.D. 767. [2470]

***Circa* A.D. 575.** Langobard (Lombard) invasion of Gaul by their three dukes Amo, Zaban and Rodanus. Duke Amo

> subdued the province of Arelate (Arles) and the cities which lie around and coming up to Stony Field itself, which lies by the city of Massilia (Marseilles), he laid waste everything he could find, and laying siege to Aquae (Aix) he received twenty-two pounds of silver and departed from that place.

A general of the Franks 'Mummulus the patrician, he came with a strong band' and pursued the Langobards who retreated to their country never to return. [2471]

A.D. 581. King Chilperic forces King Guntrum to give to Childebert the Austrasian portion of Massalia and install their count and bishop. Chilperic forces Guntrum to give up the Burgundian portion of Massalia by A.D. 584 to the Austrasians. [2472]

Legates of King Chilperic returned from Constantinople but would not land at Massalia due to the arguments between the kings and made for Agde. They were 'driven by the wind and dashed upon the land and broken into fragments'. Several items were recovered and taken to the king but much was kept by the people of Agde. [2473]

A.D. 582. Gundovald the Pretender, illegitimate son of King Clothar I, came from Constantinople where he had taken refuge for several years, and landed at Massalia having been invited by Count Guntram Boso and was received by Theodore bishop of Massalia. After Gundovald leaves Massalia,[2474] Guntram Boso changes sides and arrests Bishop Theodore on the charge of

'having introduced a foreigner into Gaul, with the intention of subjecting a Frankish kingdom to Imperial rule'.[2475]

Gundovald flees to an island. Later King Guntrum (Guntram) of Burgundy accuses the bishop for his part in arranging the assassination of his brother Chilperic.[2476] As King Chilperic died in A.D. 584 and also his young son, Gundovald returns again and is proclaimed king but is eventually betrayed and killed by Boso.[2477] Was Bishop Theodore among others [2478] trying to bring Massalia in closer contact with Constantinople and perhaps under the rule of the East Roman (Byzantine) Empire? [2479] Though no Roman military or naval support was given to Gundovald he certainly brought a large treasure of gold and silver with him and therefore speculation that Emperor Maurice gave him finances though more likely it was his predecessor Tiberius II. [2480] According to Gregory of Tours (VI.42), 'Childebert had received 50,000 pieces of gold from Emperor Maurice to rid Italy of the Lombards'. But the Byzantine chronicler Menander mentions a sum of 30,000 gold coins was sent by Tiberius II to Childebert to buy their help (A.D. 577). King Guntram (c. 532–592) did not share the widespread desire of the Franks to attack the Lombards [2481] and may be the underlying politics of why Gundovald was invited to Gaul to claim a throne.[2482] Goffart says Boso's charge gave rise to a long-discredited claim that Gundovald 'represented an imperial attempt to recover Gaul'.[2483] Even though the Byzantines had South Spain c. 552–c. 624 and the Balearic Islands c. 552–late eighth century A.D. the motive seems to be more that they wanted to activate the only effective force able to combat the Lombards in the north threatening Italy and the Byzantine possessions there.

Throughout this period of invasions Massalia still had a direct main highway to Rome and Constantinople via its own ships. The East Roman Empire (Byzantine) was able to reunite some parts of the West that had access from the sea such as Corsica, Sardinia, Sicily, South Italy (Calabria and Apulia), Naples, Rome, Ravenna and Venice (c. A.D. 717). The emperor in Constantinople controlled the Roman (Byzantine) Navy. Whether the emperors ever sent the navy to Massalia we do not know. But merchant trade would have kept financial, cultural and religious contact with these centres. Duprat mentions Byzantine ships frequenting the port of Arles on the River Rhône c. A.D. 921.[2484]

East Roman Empire-Byzantine

The term 'Byzantine' was invented in the sixteenth century by Heironymus Wolf in his *Corpus Historiae Byzantinae* published in 1557 to distinguish the later reduced empire to the lands under Greek control from the earlier larger Roman Empire. By adopting this term 'Byzantine' it inadvertently overlooks the continuity and direct inheritance that was the East Roman Empire despite all attempts by the Pope to transfer the title of Emperor of the Romans to the Franks in the West from A.D. 800 and refer to the emperor at Constantinople instead as Emperor of the Greeks and their lands as the Greek Empire. This invented term 'Byzantine' would have been unknown to the Greeks [2485] as up to the time the Ottoman Turks captured Constantinople in A.D. 1453 they 'saw themselves not as a racial unit but the heirs of Greece and Rome' [2486] as Romans,[2487] and many Greeks continued to do so down to the twentieth century.[2488] This was still a Greek identity though not thinking of themselves as ethnic Romans but as inheritors of the Roman status as citizens and continuing the Roman Empire they grew into and ran. In this they had a dual image of themselves as Romans and Hellenes.[2489] Something like being English, Scottish or Welsh etc., yet also British.[2490]

When the Ottoman Sultan Mehmed II captured Constantinople in 1453 he claimed the title Emperor of the Romans. He attempted to reunite the Roman Empire by invading Italy capturing Otranto (ancient Hydrus) in 1480 and aiming for Rome itself.[2491] Mehmed died in 1481 and Pope Sixtus IV organised a force to defeat and expel the Ottomans from Italy in the same year. The Pope had intended his fleet to sail on to capture Valona. He also wrote to the bishop of Evora to help Andreas Palaeologus (who legitimately inherited the title Emperor of Constantinople) to cross the sea and regain his territory the Despotate of Morea (in Greece).[2492] The Ottomans continued to call Greece *Rumeli* (the land of the Romans) as illustrated in the map of 1801.[2493]

Gregory of Tours describes a scene, after one of many conflicts between Bishop Theodore with the secular power, of his restoration to Massalia (Marseille) to the ringing of bells, cheering crowds and waving of flags.[2494]

Pope Gregory the Great wrote to Theodore urging him only to use persuasion to convert Jews in A.D. 591. Theodore was later made a saint.[2495]

The Greek names of the bishops' of Massalia still occur from Graecus A.D. 475 and over a century later with the above-mentioned Theodore A.D. 582. This would seem to point to a Greek congregation and population continuing in Massalia large enough to warrant having its own bishop? From A.D. 566–594 Theodore was bishop of Massalia [2496] (though the Catholic Encyclopaedia says 566–591). There is also the Governor of Provence Nicetius with a Greek name.

A.D. 587. Gregory of Tours recorded that 'In the twelfth year of King Childebert's reign Nicetius of Clermont-Ferrand was made governor of the province of Massalia and of other towns in those parts which belonged to the King'.[2497]

However, it would seem from Procopius that there were still a majority of Catholics to prefer the Franks to rule and with the approval of Emperor Justinian. Justinian spent most of his reign trying to reunite various parts of the previous western half of the Roman Empire to the eastern half with the capital at Constantinople. Under the Franks the political circumstances proved favourable and Massalia grew rapidly and retrieved its importance in the Mediterranean world.[2498]

Procopius points to this period under the Franks (A.D. 536) as when the Greek city of Massalia lost its political independence. While Loseby writes Agathias lamented this taking place in the late sixth century A.D. but 'As Arles declined it was Marseille that was the active port in the Merovingian economy during the late sixth century period'.[2499]

Agathias wrote of Massalia as

> Once a Greek city it has now become barbarian in character, having abandoned its ancestral constitution and embraced the ways of its conquerors. But even now it does not seem to fall short at all of the dignity of its ancient inhabitants.[2500]

Agathias uses the present tense that can indicate the change was very recent or current. He says the administration and character has changed. Agathias implies that the population were still there as it was they who 'embraced the ways of its conquerors'. Whereas if the conquerors had also replaced the Greek population the Franks would have carried on in their own usual way and there would be nothing new to embrace. It was a change of regime not population and the new admixture was almost as good as the previous constitution of the Greek run city. This would seem to suggest that the city though probably coming closer into the Roman Empire around the second or third century A.D. still maintained the form of its traditional constitution. Agathias goes on to say that the Franks only difference is their 'uncouth style of dress and peculiar language' and in all else i.e. system of government 'modelled more or less on the Roman pattern'; that they were 'Christians and adhere to the strictest orthodoxy' and 'for a barbarian people, strike me as extremely well-bred and civilised'.[2501]

From this point the city presumably begins to change from Greek to French as the predominant language though Greek as well as Latin was kept amongst the Greek and Roman inhabitants. What would have happened to the Greek population? Would the Franks slowly have absorbed them? Other Greek cities outside of Greece like Alexandria in Egypt [2502] still kept their own language, culture and religion [2503] as they did in Constantinople, Smyrna, Trebizon; and other Greek cities in Asia Minor under the later Ottoman Empire; [2504] and to the present day in the Calabria and Apulia regions in South Italy.[2505] With the conversion to Christianity by the Franks [2506] particularly as Roman Catholics the church services in Massalia would presumably be conducted in Latin? Such religious changes usually occur with upheaval unless the balance of population had altered enough? Perhaps there was co-existence with the remaining Greeks having their own church(es) to worship in their own language?[2507]

Merchants from Alexandria specialised in the Gallic Trade (Γαλλοδρομοι) in the seventh century and at the other end of the route at Massalia there were 'in the late sixth century regular imports of Papyrus', oil from Africa, wines from Central Italy and Gaza. Greek merchants were also landing in Spanish ports and travelling up the Emerita.[2508]

However one must take into consideration that Massalia (Marseille) suffered several plagues. Gregory of Tours wrote that c. A.D. 588 a ship from Spain brought the pestilence.[2509] At first only the families that had received goods got ill and all eight members of one family died. After a while the disease spread to the rest of the city. Bishop Theodore had been away to see King Childebert 'for he had some complaint or other against the patrician Nicetius'. He returned and stayed in Saint Victor's church praying for the city in the midst of a plague. King Guntrum called the people to church and advised them to eat nothing but barley bread and water.[2510] The first wave of the plague burned itself out after two months. Many people came back to Massalia only to catch a second wave where many died. Gregory recorded that 'On several occasions later on Massalia suffered from an epidemic of this sort'.[2511]

We do not know how many died in A.D. 588. There were further plagues up to 1361 that took a toll on the population. At the time of The Black Death A.D. 1348 Massalia had a population of 25,000 of which 15,000 died from the pestilence (épidémie du peste). The population recovered to 90,000 by A.D. 1720 and the Plague that struck Massalia then killed 50,000 over a period of two years.[2512]

It seems that around a third to just over half of the population died from the disease each time. One can assume that with a population devastation that the remnant survives and grows again.[2513] If that remnant was Greek then it follows the Greek speaking population grew again. But if the growth were due to Franks being drawn into the city then the population's majority would have been predominantly Franks. With the addition of the Franks and loss to the population by several plagues the Greek population would not have disappeared entirely but would have reduced into a minority amongst the Franks. However it may be that when a minority diminishes to an unsustainable level then intermarriage with the majority population would naturally absorb them?

Duprat gave this list of Patricians of Provence at Arles:[2514]

Secundinius, av. 540
Parthenius, 542–44
Aurelianus?
Placidus, 556–57
Agricola, av. 561

Duprat continues with the following list of Governors of the Austrasienne at Marseille:

Hecca 561
Bodegiséle, rector, av. 572
Jovin, préfect, vers, 573 av
Albin, préfect, vers, 573 av, 581
Dynamius, rector, 581–87
Nicecius, rector, 587.

Dynamius was replaced by Liudegisei in 585 and Nicetius 587 but was reinstated by King Childebert in November 587.[2515] Duprat also mentions that Dynamius and Aurelia establish a monastery for women in Marseille but little is known about it.[2516] Bachrach also mentions that 'Duke Gundulf had humbled the prefect Dynamius and forced him to swear support for Bishop Theodore';[2517] and at the time of Gundovald, described as 'Duke Dynamius'.[2518]

By the end of the sixth century A.D. Massalia became the leading port in the region again. (Since losing most of its ancient empire after 49 B.C. Massalia had lost its position to Arles. Arles had been given Massalia's western territory up to the River Rhône by Julius Caesar). Now Massalia was producing the 'quasi-imperial and royal coins' and Arles became a subsidiary mint.[2519] As Arles is a river port, a short journey from the sea, it would seem that Massalians position and being a sea port[2520] with a great natural harbour would always have some advantage that would be in its commercial favour to have survived a 90 per cent loss of its empire.

Seventh Century A.D.

Coins

Jones writes the following on the currency of the period,

> The western barbarian kingdoms accepted imperial solidi, and most minted their own coins on the same standard. Only the gold coins of the Merovingians were lighter and not acceptable in Italy. Pope Gregory the Great (c. 540–604) asked the agent of the Gallic estates of the Roman Church not to remit his rents in local solidi, but to buy clothes and slaves and despatch them to Rome.[2521]

Along with Massalia and Arles there were mints at Uzes and Viviers. All four mints in the sixth century A.D. produced coins in the names of the Roman emperors from Justin II (578) down to Heraclius (610-640). It is thought that Byzantine coins arriving at ports in Provence were melted down and reminted. The series ends with these four mints replacing Heraclius's name with that of the Frankish king Chlothar II. The Frankish coinages from c. 575 to c. 620 were poor imitations of imperial types.[2522]

Coins minted at Massalia included an issue of a gold trine for King Childeric II born c. A.D. 653–died 675. The obverse has the letters [CHILDER]–ICTS RX, bust diademed, facing right, globe and cross, and on the reverse CIVI[TAS] MASILIE, a cross and globe in the centre, on either side of the cross an M and an A. Diameter 15.5 mm, weight 0.84 g. These currencies were the last with the name of a Merovingian king. Several of the ancient Greek coins of Massalia had an MA on the reverse.[2523]

On the CGB coin website they mention that after Childeric's assassination there followed five patricians/aristocrats leading the city, who issued Denier (penny) coins in their own names Antedates, Enmities, Antenor, Merinos and Abbot.[2524]

Duprat gave the following list of patricians and prefects at Marseille:[2525]

Dupuis 593
('Unite our In division à Marseille')
Siagrius, préfect, 613–629
Désiderius, préfect, 629–30
Hector, patrician, v. 675
Bonitus, préfect, 681–91 [2526]
Antenor or Antherius, patrician v. 714 [2527]
Metranus, patrician, (no date given)
Abbo, patrician, v. 726–35

A.D. 608. The last Imperial monument Columna Phocaea was erected in the Forum at Rome. Smaragdus Exarch of Ravenna ordered an inscription and gilded statue on top of a white marble column in gratitude to the help given him by Phoca the emperor in Constantinople.[2528] Phoca gave Pope Boniface IV the Pantheon in Rome to use as a church and also won praise from Pope Gregory I.[2529] The Byzantine emperors though living in Constantinople were still sovereigns over Rome and gave their support to the Pope.

The Byzantines (East Roman Empire) continued to be active when they could in the West. Plans to move the capital from Constantinople to Sicily by Emperor Heraclius were carried out by his grandson Constans II in A.D. 662 to Syracuse. Sicily and Calabria was still predominantly Greek speaking.[2530]

Emperor Constans II visited Rome for twelve days in A.D. 663 where he received all honours from the papacy and stripped many of the monuments of bronze.[2531] His lack of success against the Lombards and heavy taxation made him unpopular in Italy and he was murdered in his bath at Syracuse in A.D. 668.

Taranto in Italy [2532] was part of the Byzantine (East Roman) Empire A.D. 540 to 662 until conquered by the Lombards, led by Romuald I Duchy of Benevento. In the eighth century Taranto was captured by Saracens and held for forty years until re-conquered by the Byzantines in A.D. 880.[2533] Attacked again by Saracens in 922, again in 927 with the city destroyed and the survivors enslaved and taken to Africa. Seeing the strategic importance of Taranto the Byzantine Emperor Nicephorus II Phoca rebuilt Taranto in A.D. 967. In the eleventh century there was a struggle for possession between the Byzantines and the Normans who then ruled Taranto for the following four centuries.[2534]

A.D. 649. A Synod was called to condemn monotheletism. The emperor in Constantinople Constans II disagreed and sent Olympios Exarch of Ravenna to Rome to arrest Pope Martin. Seeing the strength of feeling in Rome against Constantinople Olympios exploits dissensions and attempts to detach Italy from the empire and rule it himself. He died in 652 and the rebellion collapses. The new Exarch in 653 arrests Pope Martin and later Maximos the Confessor a leading theologian [2535] and sent them from Rome to Constantinople where the Pope stood trial for treason for supporting the previous Exarch Olympias and though this was a death penalty the Pope was banished instead. Maximos was charged with supporting the rebel Exarch of North Africa Gregory and exiled.[2536]

A.D. 685–731. The Popes in Rome were of different nationalities and the Liber Pontificalis adds the nationality of Syrus after the name of five Popes, another is Phrygia, and two Greeks, 'while the Greek Zacchary held the seat A.D. 741–753'.[2537]

By the seventh century Frankish Burgundian families had established themselves by marriages with the local elite of Massalia and Arles.[2538]

A.D. 680. King Thierry III of Austrasia made Bonitus governor of Marseille and Provence. He became bishop of Auvergne succeeding his brother St. Avitus II in A.D. 689 and became a saint himself.[2539]

Eighth Century A.D.

A.D. 714. There began Arab incursions in Gaul. When pushed back from Aquitane they settled in Septimania [2540] and one of their generals Zama took Agde in 725. Though seizing Narbonne they allow the Visigoth government to remain and the Gothic Duke Ansemard continues to govern Béziers, Nimes and Agde. After the victory of Charles Martel in 737 against the Arab invaders Agde (Agathe Tyche) along with Béziers and Maguelonne are in ruins. King Pepin the Short finally completes the Franks control by taking Narbonne in 759. [2541]

A.D. 750. There was a revival of the mint at Massalia (Marseille),[2542] but during the early part of the reign of Charles the Bald (before A.D. 900) around the time of the Viking attacks Massalia (Marseille) ceased to coin money. [2543]

A.D. 790. Charlemagne the Great gave property and privileges to the abbey Saint Victor of Marseille.[2544]

The loss of Byzantine territory in Italy of Ravenna to the Lombards was a turning point in the history of Europe. The Byzantines under constant threat by the Arabs in the east could not spare an army to recapture Ravenna. Pope Stephen II fearing the Lombards, with no military help from the East Romans (Byzantines) dismissing their last minute diplomatic attempt 'to hold him back' went and formed an alliance with the Germanic Carolingians (kingdom of the Franks). Over the years they defeated the Lombards and gave land that had previously belonged to the Byzantines to the Pope. Pro-Byzantine factions ousted the Pope from Rome. The Carolingians support and reinstatement of Pope Leo III led him to crown their king Charlemagne, Emperor of the Romans in A.D. 800. [2545]

Ninth Century A.D.

In 800 Charlemagne built a fleet on the Gallic Sea, 'which was then infested with pirates, and set guards in different places'. [2546]

Einhard, a historian and servant of Charlemagne,[2547] wrote that

> The Constantinopolitan Emperors, Nicephorus, Michael, and Leo, of their own accord, also sought his [Charlemagne] friendship and alliance, and sent to him several embassies, and since by assuming the Imperial title he had laid himself open to the grave suspicion of wishing to deprive them of Empire, he made with them the most binding treaty possible, that there might be no occasion of offence between them. But the Romans and Greeks always viewed with distrust the power of the Franks; hence arose the Greek proverb "Have a Frank for a friend but not for a neighbour". [2548]

A.D. 822. Though the overland trade route to North-West Italy was important Louis the Pious gave the bishop of Marseille the 'teloneum' on salt and on ships, which arrived from Italy.[2549]

Depopulation

Duprat writes that following the plagues of the sixth and seventh century and after the wars with Charles Martel in the eighth century the population of Marseille had diminished. Therefore they did not have the manpower to successfully defend 'the great and ancient walls of Crinas'. This was why the raids by Saracens (838 AD) and Greeks (848 AD) were successful against Marseille.[2550]

A.D. 838. Due to attacks by Saracen pirates in Provence Charlemagne, king of the Franks acts to expel them. Not long after he died Saracens land in Massalia devastating the town, plundering and taking slaves.[2551] Saracens killed thirty-nine nuns and St Eusebia the Abbess of the monastery Cassian founded for nuns.[2552] The *Annals of St-Bertin* written between A.D. 830–882 records,

> Meanwhile fleets of Saracen pirates attacked Marseilles in Provence, carried off all the nuns, of whom there was a large number living there, as well as all the males, both clergy and laymen, laid waste the town [*urbs*] and took away with them *en masse* the treasures of Christ's churches.[2553]

A.D. 829–839. Civil wars in France followed by a division of the Frankish kingdom had led to destabilisation. Pepin II of Aquitaine asked the Vikings for assistance against his uncles Louis the German and Charles the Bald.[2554] Now familiar with Provence and its divisions the Vikings returned again later plundering for their own interests.

A.D. 842. Though information on Provence at this period is scarce A.D. 842 saw Massalia and Arles attacked by Moslems.[2555]

A.D. 845 saw Fulcrad, Duke of Provence, at Arles lead a rebellion against Emperor Lothair I, further destabilising the region from Frankish control. Though put down quickly Lothair gave an amnesty and confirmed the leaders in their positions. A charter of 845 mentions Massalia ruled by Count Aldebert.[2556] Duke Fulcrad seems to have been a pivitol figure heralding the end of the Carolingian Empire and the unity of the Frankish kingdoms. Duprat mentions more of him in his encyclopaedia.[2557]

Attack by Greeks on Massalia A.D. 848

Provence saw acts of piracy by the Vikings during the reign of Charles the Bald;[2558] on Massalia by the Saracens A.D. 838 and Arles 842[2559] and a Greek attack on Massalia in A.D. 848.[2560]

There is little known about the Greek attack on Massalia (A.D. 848) as to where they came from. Unfortunately Duprat does not give an individual reference for this and includes it under the description of piratical attacks. The following reference may have been the one Duprat used? If so he had written all there was on the Greek attack and it is only two lines. In the *Annals of St. Bertin* written by Fulco 830–843, Prudentius 843–861 and Hincma 861–882[2561] in the period which it covered A.D. 830-882 it is recorded for the year 848 that

'Greek Pirates ravaged Marseilles in Provence. No one offered any resistance and the pirates left unscathed.'[2562]

It is odd that there was no resistance offered. Was it simply lack of manpower? Was this purely piracy or under Imperial machinations from Constantinople, Byzantine Empire? The empire was under a 2-year old infant Emperor Michael III and was run by his mother Theodora the Armenian A.D. 842–855 as Regent. The Byzantine Navy had become run down after A.D. 711. With the end of iconoclasm the Byzantine Navy was revived and reorganised by Theodora and Michael III and continued by Basil I. [2563]

Duprat mentions the Byzantines frequenting the port of Arles c. A.D. 921. [2564] Baratier relates that in A.D. 941 Hugh of Provence, king of Italy made an alliance with the Emperor of the East Roman Empire (Byzantine) at Constantinople who sent him a navy with 'Greek Fire' to liberate 'Fraxinetum' from the Saracens. [2565]

An eleventh century Charter of St. Victor de Marseille describes 'Fraxinetum' as the area between Fréjus and Saint Tropez, while texts in the tenth century describe the territory of Mount Maure and its fortress by the sea and forest and also described in chronicles as l'oppidum, castrum or villa. [2566] The present La Garde Freinet marks the spot and the Massif des Maures (plateau of the Moors) takes its name from the Saracens of Fraxinet.

A.D. 848. Count Apollonius wins approval from King Charles the Bald to build a new church at Agde (Agathe Tyche) dedicated to Saint-Etienne. [2567]

Spolia

Spolia is Latin for Spoils and is used as a modern art-historical term Spoliation to means the re-use of earlier building material or decorative sculpture on new monuments. Originally in Latin it meant booty, plunder. [2568]

Marseille has been described by a paraphrase from Joseph Méry 1860, who actually said,

When Marseille did not rid herself of an ornament, she was divested of it by someone else. Ancient city that has nothing ancient, beautiful city that has nothing of beauty, she has made a two-thousand year voyage through history, and she has arrived like the ship *Argo*, having conserved only her name. [2569]

This was certainly true in 1860 when compared to the antique splendours of Arles. All was changed by the dynamiting of Marseille next to the port in 1944 and subsequently several Greek and Roman artefacts began to be uncovered. Prior to this material got reused or disappeared, which could account for the lack nearer to the surface as one might expect.

Verzone gives this reference from the *Henrici miracula S. Germani*. There was 'a reconstruction of the Church of St. Germain (at Auxerre) in the mid-ninth century'. 'Since there was a shortage of marble in the province' some brothers undertook a perilous expedition through 'the great gorges of the Rhône', journeying to Arles and Marseilles. There

with boldness and cunning they obtained a great abundance of precious marble by means of money as well as permission, and loading their ships with the booty they achieved a memorable triumph: this was brought about by divine favour, overcoming fear of the threatening waves of the infidel peoples. [2570]

Verzone sums up that,

> the employment of the meagre amount of marble thus recovered, lacking uniformity of colour or dimension, conditioned the forms of proto-Carolingian and Carolingian architecture. The use of these materials precluded the achievement of classical proportion and imposed the adoption of a decorative technique suited to the use of spoils.[2571]

The lack of antiquities when compared to Arles may indicate that the brothers 'great abundance' was taken far more from Massalia (Marseille).

Divided City

Massalia was divided between Segebert of Austrasia and Gontran of Burgundy and with different masters until Boson became King of Burgundy-Provence in A.D. 879.[2572]

A.D. 856. Following Charlemagne's death (814) Marseille is included in the division of territories to his descendants. Marseille belonging to the kingdom of Provence went to Emperor Lothair's younger son Charles.[2573]

A.D. 879. Under Boson's control Marseille made up part of the kingdom of Provence or Bourgogne Cis-jurane.[2574]

A.D. 897. Boson, the first Viscount of Agde also becomes Viscount of Béziers by marriage linking the towns for the next two centuries.[2575]

Tenth Century A.D.

A.D. 923. Massalia's canon artillery had to take refuge in the castle of Fos to escape Saracen attack.[2576]

A.D. 930. Massalia in the kingdom of Provence or Bourgogne Cis-jurane is joined to Bourgogne-Transjurane by Rudolph III the last king of an independent Burgundy.[2577]

Middle Ages

Eleventh Century A.D. Greeks at Marseille and Arles

Duprat mentions briefly the Greek monks of Marseille and a tribute by the abbot of Montmajour on the Greeks of Arles:

Au XI° siècle on voit des moines grecs à Marseille et un tribuit est persçu par l'abbé de Montmajour sur les Grecs d'Arles.[2578]

'In the eleventh century there were Greek monks in Marseilles, and a tribute [= tax] was collected by the abbot of Montmajour from the Greeks in Arles'.[2579]

The presence of Greeks in these cities is significant for continuity within change but somewhat tantalizing as this is the only information we have from Duprat.

St. Tzarn, Abbot of St. Victor, Marseille (d. A.D. 1041) urged on Raymond Berenger I the Old, Count of Barcelona to intervene and free the monks of Lerins from the Moors.[2580]

A.D. 965–1073. James tells us that in this period there was some secular control over the bishops by the Viscounts of Massalia.[2581]

A.D. 1032. Marseille was claimed by the German emperor Conrad Salic and Provence became a remote dependency of the Holy Roman Empire.[2582]

Between **A.D. 1000 and 1050** the Abbey of Saint Victor, which had been devastated by the Saracens was rebuilt by 'the efforts of Abbott St. Wilfred'. After 1050 the Abbey had a high reputation and appeals were sent there to renew 'decadent' monasteries' in the south. The Abbey kept contacts with Spain and Sardinia and owned property in Syria.[2583]

The bishop, who only acknowledged the authority of the emperor, controlled the Episcopal part of the town as Massalia became territorially divided between three allegiances:[2584]

- The **Episcopal town** included the Harbour of La Joliet, the fisherman's district, the three citadels of Château Babon, Roquebarbe, and the bishop's palace.
- The **abbatial town** was dependent on the Abbey of Saint Victor. This included of a few market towns and châteaux south of the harbour.
- The **lower town** was under the viscounts (and also became a republic between 1214-1246) when Charles of Anjou subjugated the whole of Massalia in 1246.[2585] Charles became the Count of Provence through marriage.[2586]

A.D. 1081. Byzantine Emperor Alexius I Comnenus sends money to Henry IV (German king 1056–1105 and Holy Roman emperor 1084–1105), for an alliance against Guiscard and his Normans. Alexius evacuates his soldiers from most of Anatolia to make an army to fight Guiscard. The Byzantine Army is routed by the Normans at the Battle of Dyrrachium. The Turks move into the vacuum left in Anatolia. The 'Emir' Tzachas seizes Smyrna and begins a naval domination of the area.[2587]

A.D. 1088. 'Emir' Tzachas of Smyrna (also known as Chaka Bey) seizes Phocaea and Clazomenae and his fleet takes Chios.[2588] In the winter of 1090 Tzachas's fleet blockades Constantinople coordinating with an attack on land by the Pechenegs. By February 1091 Tzachas is unable to defeat the Byzantine fleet and retires to the Aegean and captures the island of Lesbos.[2589] In 1092 the lands and islands he captured are retaken by John Dukas and return to Byzantine control. Emperor Alexius sends John Dukas and Caspax with a fleet to besiege Tzachas now in Smyrna. With his captured wife, or daughter (Kilij Arslan's wife) as an incentive he surrenders and is 'allowed to leave unmolested' on 1 July 1097.[2590] The Byzantine revival ended the brief occupation by the Seljuks around Smyrna and it was over a century before the Seljuk Turks as the Sultanate of Iconium or Rum were on the Aegean coast of Anatolia again taking the southern part, while the northern was split between the Byzantine Empire of Nicaea and the Latin Empire.[2591]

Twelfth Century A.D.

Provence Revives
Provence reached a high point of courtly civilisation in the days of Eleanor of Aquitaine 1122–1204. Professor Heer refers to the sculptures of the twelfth and thirteenth century that they 'speak the same language and bear the same imprint of pure classical form, in the classical setting of cypress and bay, olives and broom'. In similarity 'Only Greece and Greek Sicily have ruins which can compare with the gold-yellow, honey coloured stones of Provence'.[2592]

Jewish Minority in Massalia
In the second half of the twelfth century Massalia was a centre for Jewish studies and called by Benjamin of Tudela 'the city of geonim and sages'[2593]

Agde
A.D. 1173. A royal decree by King Louis VII (the Young) fixing the privileges of the bishop allows Agde's city centre fortifications to be restored and the wall was extended to include the new part of the town.[2594] Most of the city walls were demolished from 1848 following instruction by the town council.[2595]

A.D. 1187. The last secular Viscount of Agde Bernard Anton becomes Canon to the church of Saint-Etienne of Agde giving up all his personal possession in the diocese. Bishop Raymond of Montpeyroux takes possession and allows all future Counts of Agde to be the bishop there.[2596]

A.D. 1188. One of the oldest hospitals in France was established at Massalia.[2597]

Crusades

A.D. 1189 Third Crusade

Richard Coeur de Lion, king of England leased galleys from Massalia (Marseille) for the Third Crusade.[2598]

A.D. 1199 Fourth Crusade

Knights were instructed to meet at Venice to take ship to the Holy Lands. But many knights made their way to the nearest ports to sail from like Marseille. This left a serious shortfall of Knights at Venice to pay for the passage and meet the cost of the Venetian fleet already hired. The Venetians wanting their payment of 85,000 silver marks and half of any captured lands [2599] agreed to supply the fleet if the Crusaders would capture the city of Zara for them on the way as well. The Pope excommunicated the crusaders for this A.D. 1202. [2600] The Venetians manipulated events to their financial advantage culminating with the crusaders attacking, capturing, slaughtering and pillaging the Christian city of Constantinople in 1204 that they had gone to help.

A fleet from Flanders under Jean de Nestles, Governor of Bruge, arrived at Marseille and wintered in that port. Though they were to meet others at Methone they broke their word and set sail direct to Syria.[2601]

The Latins ruled Constantinople for 57 years until the Greeks from the Nicaean Empire (1204-61) [2602] took it back again to continue a weakened Byzantine Empire from their ancient city and capital.[2603] Crusades were used by Rome on other Christians such as the Cathars in France 1208-1255. Keen mentions another crusade of 1282, sanctioned by Pope Martin against Constantinople. This had descended into internal fighting with Charles of Anjou and Philip of France attacking instead fellow Christians of Sicily who had revolted against the French and joined with King Peter of Aragon. The rebellion had been skilfully planned and paid for by the Byzantine emperor in Constantinople Michael Palaeologus.[2604] This plan diverted and thwarted the campaign aimed at Constantinople. Pope Martin supported Charles and called for a crusade against King Peter both kingdoms were Christian and Roman Catholics. [2605]

'True to the Greek genius of its Fathers, the Eastern Church did not recognise any war as "holy"; a Christian should fight with the "weapons of Christ", his only battles should be spiritual'.[2606] The poets of Southern France came to describe the Crusaders as 'fools, criminals and madmen'. The Cathars professed a religious pacifism echoing Greek Fathers of the Church 'a Christian was not allowed to take part in wars of any kind'.[2607] Before A.D. 313 soldiers in the Roman Army who wanted to become Christians were forbidden to take life 'whether under orders or not'. [2608] There seemed to be a compromise when Christianity found itself no longer persecuted by the Romans and became the leading religion of their empire by the end of the fourth century A.D. They now had to deal with how to defend its people from foreigners who used force to steal: possessions, money, and land: kidnap and kill.

Thirteenth Century A.D.

A.D. 1202–1204. The Children's Crusade were composed of one group from Germany and the other from France and driven by the belief they were protected by God and would liberate Jerusalem. The 30,000 French 'children' led by a 12-year old shepherd boy Stephen of Cloyes made their way from Vendome to Marseille (Massalia). They prayed and expected the sea to part for them as it did for Moses and the Israelites. The sea did not.[2609] Undeterred they boarded seven ships at Massalia for the Holy Land. They disappeared and rumours circulated of an attack by pirates with two boats sunk and the others captured with the children being sold into slavery in Algiers and Egypt. No one knows for sure what happened to them. Heer mentions they fell into the hands of crooks at Marseille (Massalia) and were sold as slaves in Alexandria.[2610]

The German children led by Nicholas set off. On reaching Italy many of the girls were taken advantage of and coerced into disreputable establishments or as maidservants.[2611] The Pope told them they were too young and to go home. Most did but some continued their journey.[2612] Professor Heer mentions that the bishop of Brindisi tried to stop them from crossing the sea and Pope Innocent released the girls from their vows and the boys when they came of age. The boys who got to the East were sold as slaves. 'A remnant returned, ill-used and disillusioned'.[2613]

The Flag of Massalia

The present flag of Marseille is a blue cross on a white background, but for official occasions the French Tricolor is used. The municipal flag dates back to the thirteenth century A.D. Louis de Bresc quoting a rule of the time in Latin,

Quod quaelibet navis hominum Massilie portet et portare tenenture in nave vexillum communis Massilie cum crusce extensum in altum. [2614] Interestingly the name of the city *Massilie* is still near to its ancient form in Latin *Massilia* and Greek *Massalia*.

Municipal Republic

From the beginning of the thirteenth century Marseille saw a social change by freeing themselves from feudal submission to their Viscount and Counts of Provence by forming a municipal republic headed by the chief magistrate called a podestat.[2615]

A.D. 1214–1229. Pierre de Montlaur bishop of Marseille founded the first chapel at Notre dame-de-la-Garde on the hill opposite the ancient city of Marseille.[2616]

A.D. 1246. Charles of Anjou through his wife Beatrice, the younger daughter of Raymond Berenger IV of Provence and Forcalquier, acquired the county of Provence and with it the thriving port of Massalia (Marseille).[2617] As Count of Provence he took away many of the privileges of the Municipal Republic.[2618] Marseille, Arles and Avignon was still technically imperial cities of the Holy Roman Empire that were separate from the county and they enjoyed privileges. Charles was heavy handed on the cities that generally had a lot of independence and there was resistance by the nobles to Charles. He was committed to join his brother Louis IX for the Seventh Crusade. Resistance to Charles grew while he was away and were only settled on his return when Barral of Baux, Viscount of Marseille sued for peace in 1251.[2619] Ambitions by the kings of Anjou later ruined Massalia due to the burden put on them financially and militarily in wars of re-conquest in Italy.[2620]

A.D. 1257 The city regulations of Massalia did not distinguish between Christians or Jews and referred to all its inhabitants as *cives Massiliae* (citizens of Marseilles) though whether they had equal rights is not sure.[2621] After an unsuccessful rebellion in 1262 against the Count of Provence

Jewish families became the property of the Count having to pay all their taxes to him. However for this they were in his protection. In 1276 the Count made efforts to restrict money being extorted from them by the Holy Office that claimed Jews were wearing smaller badges than allowed by the Church after the Latern Council of 1215.[2622]

Note the closeness of the name *Massilae* to the original in Latin *Massilia* and the Greek *Massalia*.

A.D. 1275. The Byzantine Emperor Michael VIII grants Phocaea as a fief to the Genoese brothers Benedict and Manuel Zaccaria.[2623]

A.D. 1286. In the second ancient Greek city in France, Agathe Tyche (Agde), the survival of Greeks into late antiquity may have been possible. If some had survived the plagues that devastated Provence from the sixth century A.D. and Saracen attacks, the town of Agde suffered genocide after Philip the Hardy annexed Septimania creating Occitania. His subsequent campaign against Pierre II of Aragon was a disaster. This brought in return the Arogonese admiral Roger de Loria to raid Agde's coast.[2624] Agde was then burnt and pillaged sparing only women and children, all other people between fifteen and sixty years old were executed.[2625] The depopulated town recovered in the following century only to be hit by the Black Death in 1348 and four more plagues thereafter.

Fourteenth Century A.D.

A.D. 1361. On the 2 August William de Grimoard was made Abbot of St. Victor of Marseille and the following year became Pope Urban V. He increased the diocese with Episcopal jurisdiction and visited Massalia (Marseille) in 1365 consecrating the high altar, and held a consistory there in 1367.[2626]

A.D. 1361–1366. Cardinal William Sudre, bishop of Marseille, afterwards bishop of Ostia, commissioned in 1368 by Pope Urban V to crown the empress, wife of Charles IV, and in 1369 to receive the profession of faith of Johannes Palaeologus, Emperor of Constantinople.[2627]

A.D. 1366–1368. Philippe de Cabassole as bishop of Marseille gave his protection to Petrach the great humanist and poet during the Renaissance. Philippe was the author of a *Life of St. Mary Magdalen*; protector of St. Delphine; governor under Urban V of the Comtat Venaissin, 1367–69. He died in 1372 while legate of Gregory XI at Rome.[2628]

A.D. 1371–1401. Marseille today has fabulous varieties of soap ranging from honey, lavender of Provence to fragrant thyme for skin complaints like eczema on sale in shops and on stalls by the quayside. The soap industry is one of the main sources of revenue for Marseille. The origin of this industry is thought to be from a Jewish settler between 1371–1401 Crescas David sometimes nicknamed Sabonerius and his son Solomon David.[2629]

A.D. 1378. Venice takes Phocaea (in Asia Minor) from the Genoese.[2630]

Constantinople

By the end of the thirteenth century and during the fourteenth century Marseille (Massalia) like several other southern French and Italian cities, had colonies in Constantinople for trade activities.[2631] By the fourteenth century Constantinople was the busiest port in the East. However, competition was high. Nicephorus Gregoras wrote, 'The Latins have taken possession not only of all the wealth of the Byzantines, and almost all the revenues from the sea, but also all the resources that replenish the sovereign's treasury'.[2632]

Fifteenth Century A.D.

Some stories say that the fortune telling cards Tarot of Marseille was introduced towards the end of the fifteenth century from Italy then after some time was re-introduced back to Italy from Marseille. Other theories is that they were indigenous to Marseille, belonging to local cults and going back to first century A.D. and according to Camoin, a descendent of the oldest card printing family in Marseille,[2633] may have been the originator of all other Tarot cards in Europe.[2634]

A.D. 1423. Alphonse V of Aragon attacked Massalia devastating the town over three days. Massalia's great defensive chain used to block the entrance to the port was taken to where it can be seen today in the Cathedral at Valencia in Spain.[2635]

Massalia yet again showed its ability to rise above misfortune this time with the influence of the merchant Forbin brothers [2636] and in eight years was strong enough to repel another army sent from Aragon.[2637]

A.D. 1434. 'Bon Roi Rene' (Good King Rene) was crowned King Rene of Anjou, remaining popular in the people's memory. Based in Arles he visited Massalia several times encouraging business and exports with financial autonomy.[2638] As none of Rene's sons survived him he gave his states to his nephew Charles III in 1480.[2639]

A.D. 1467–1468. Sant Marti d'Empuries (the ancient Greek founded paleopolis of Emporion) in Spain was under siege and bombardment with damage to the town wall during a civil war between King John II of Aragon and the Generalitat de Catalunya. The Duke de Lorena commanded the king's forces. Seven large stone balls from the bombardment were excavated from a well. [2640]

A.D. 1481. Charles III of Maine was the twenty-third Count of Provence. He reigned over Provence for one year and died. With the King of Aragon and other princes wanting to possess Provence Charles had ceded Provence to his cousin King Louis XI of France in 1481 [2641] in his will. [2642] Louis was officially recognised by the Assembly of the States of Provence as the Count of Provence in 1482.[2643] In 1486 Provence was annexed to France under Charles VIII. [2644] Even under Charles VIII the title was king of France 'and count of Provence and of Forcalquier', and 'Provence always preserved a separate administrative organization'. [2645]

In December 1481 Louis XI called for two learned delegates from each town to meet one of his financial agents and 'Captain and grand patron of the galleys of France' Michael Gaillart to make a plan to develop 'famous Marseilles'. 'By means of great liberties and franchises' to 'Christian and Infidel' and come to 'Marseille and there to discharge their goods and merchandise'. Louis planned to distribute goods not only to France but exporting to England and 'other countries of the West'.[2646]

However it was not until 1487 that Provence was formally incorporated into the kingdom of France under Charles VIII. Provence still kept an independence 'as the king had to promise to maintain *les franchises, statuts, prérogatives, us et coutumes* of Provence, which was united to France not as *un accessoire à un principal,* but as *un principal à un autre principal* (peer to peer)'.[2647] Charles VIII was king of France 1470-1498. [2648]

Jewish Community at Massalia

Throughout the fourteenth century Jews in Massalia were under the protection of the Municipal Council and given equal rights and same trades as Christians. They also had the protection of the Count of Provence. During the fifteenth century there were thirty-four Jewish Physicians in Massalia and Bonnel de Lattès became the personal physician to Pope Alexander VI.[2649] In 1484 lawless bands took over the cities in Provence attacking and pillaging Jews. In 1485 there was also a massacre and pillaging of Jews in Massalia. Demands to expel the rest were resisted by Charles VIII only allowing them to depart voluntary and unmolested. Under Louis XII Jewish people were expelled by 1501.[2650]

Sixteenth Century A.D.

1524 August. Massalia (Marseille) successfully resisted a siege by Charles de Bourbon who was carving up François I kingdom. By 7 July Charles took Antibes, Grasse, Frejus and Aix in quick succession. Marseille manned by 3,000–4,000 held off Charles. Their citizens repaired the city walls as fast as Charles's artillery damaged them. There was a breach on the 22–23 September but Charles left on the 26 after a storm and the news of François had camped nearby. [2651]

A.D. 1536. A French fleet of twelve ships under Admiral Baron de Saint-Blancard and seven ships of the Ottoman fleet of Barbarossa were in alliance. This was because of an on-going dispute of power between the French king François I against the Habsburg Holy Roman Emperor Charles V. The French and Turkish fleets wintered together in Marseille. Between 1542–46 King François I and Suleiman I the Sultan of the Ottomans were fighting Charles V and Henry VIII of England. Suleiman made 110 galleys available to François. François and Ottoman forces led by Barbarossa joined at Marseille in 1543 and then laid siege and captured the city of Nice, [2652] which belonged to Savoy.

François offered the city of Toulon for the Ottoman fleet to winter and evacuated the population to avoid any friction. The cathedral becomes a temporary mosque for the Ottoman Army of 30,000.[2653] A French artillery unit was attached to the Ottoman Army in their attack on Hungary 1543.

The French kings Louis XII and Louis XIII both extended the quayside into the Harbour of Lacydon (Vieux-Port) at Massalia.[2654]

Figure 100. Engraving Marseille 1575, Braun and Hogenberg, *Civitas Orbis Terrarum*, vol. II–12 in 1575 edition of *Munster's Cosmographia*. The city wall extends beyond the Horn of Lacydon, which had been filled in during the seventh century A.D.

Name of Massalia Becomes Gallicized

It would seem that from maps of the town that the present spelling of Marseille is used from the sixteenth century. From the original Greek name *Massalia* it had continued under the Latin as *Massilia* then to *Marsilia* and finally Gallicized into Marseille.[2655]

Map of A.D. 1575

Taking advantage of the winds at Marseille on the hill at Moulins (windmills) stood twelve windmills these were reduced to two by the nineteenth century A.D. then replaced by machine pumps that drew up the water for the city.[2656] Were there windmills in ancient Massalia? We do not know. You can see they had them in the 1575 map by Braun and Hogenberg,[2657] which also shows the Horn of Lacydon harbour (now the Bourse), has been filled in and built over. The fortified city wall extended in front of the Bourse and continues along the bottom of the harbour to the other side of Lacydon. The two hills on Le Pharo side of Massalia have buildings. One is a church presumably the Chapel-de-la Garde. At the entrance to the harbour opposite Fort St-Jean is another fort where a retractable chain was connected to block the entrance into the harbour. Here it seems there are two extended bridges one from each side, with a building on the end of each and a space between to let ships in and out. There are two sets of windmills. At end of the nine on top right is the 'Tour de Horolog' clock tower and perhaps on the site of the masonry gnomon erected by the ancient Greek city to commemorate Pytheas of Massalia fixing their latitude at 43°N?

Seventeenth Century A.D.

At the beginning of the seventeenth century Marseille had a population of 50,000, which increased to 65,000 by 1666.[2658] Though the port executed few administrative functions the reason for this increase of population was of trade.[2659]

Malta Appoints a Consul for the Greeks

A.D. 1616–1635. During the seventeenth century the island of Malta became an important centre for the ransoming of Christian and Muslim slaves. Port records for 1616-1635 show that out of the ninety-five commercial ships that visited the grand harbour sixty-seven were from Marseille.

Many of the other ships were Greek particularly from Zachynthos, Rhodes and Chios. In 1623 Malta appointed a consul 'pro natione Graeca' Joseph Moniglia to facilitate the amount of Greek visitors. The consul was on a similar level as those for Britain and France but more remarkable as the Greeks did not have an independent country and only represented themselves as merchants.[2660]

A.D. 1639–1640
The Oratorian Eustace Gault was bishop of Marseille and his brother Jean-Baptiste Gault (1642–43) was famed for his charity to the galley slaves.[2661]

A.D. 1660 After two years King Louis XIV of France and Count of Provence had further rebellions brewing in 1660. There were troubles in Saintogne and Marseille had different factions causing unrest. The situation prompted Louis to head off a general rebellion. Louis with his court and army went into Provence. He entered Marseille by a breach in the wall on 2 March. Louis disarmed Marseille and razed its walls to the ground and had a new citadel built. Marseille lost its independent status and their magistrates were no longer allowed to call themselves Consuls.[2662] However, Arnoul Intendant of the Galleys (1665-1674)[2663] in a letter to Colbert from Marseille 4 December 1668 still uses the term Consuls.[2664]

Louis XIV also had the forts of St. Jean and St. Nicholas built at the entrance of the harbour and established an arsenal and fleet at the Old Port itself.[2665] Louis in his 'Memoirs for the instruction of the Dauphin' (1661) wrote that 'I ordered the continuation of the fortifications at the castle of Bordeaux and the citadel of Marseille, not only to remind these towns of their duty, but also to set an example to others'.[2666]

Louis XIV, Colbert and later Signally Secretary of State for the Navy, wanted a two level navy of 'wealthy' ships of the line and frigates at Brest, Toulon and Rochefort, and a 'poor' navy of galleys, set up in Marseille in 1665.[2667] Galleys were easily maintained and inexpensive due to the slaves and convicts used to man the oars.[2668]

By March 1669 King Louis XIV made an edict for a full free port of Marseille [2669] and some Jewish settlers also returned.[2670]

Arnoul describes the selfish actions of the 'Consuls of Marseille' in diverting water from an enterprising bourgeois and lesser merchant Monsieur Benat. His improvements to the city's sewage disposal were earning the king 100,000 livres.[2671] The aggressive trading policy of Louis offended the somewhat easy going merchants of Marseille.[2672]

In another letter to Colbert (15 January 1667) Arnoul writes,

> . . . The citizens of Marseille . . . must see the error of their ways, and must devote themselves to becoming efficient traders and reliable merchants if they can, without hunting so keenly for titles of chivalry and nobility which bring ruin upon them no sooner then they have amassed a little wealth. Because they are easy-going and idle, great talkers and spreaders of gossip, they like nothing better than to walk about on the quay with their swords at their sides, wearing pistols and a dagger . . . One thing which feeds their arrogance is the privilege of the citizens entailing that all other subjects of the King are treated in this city as if they were foreigners, namely that an outsider can acquire the rights of citizenship only by marrying a daughter of a Marseillais family. This has frightened the merchants away, or at least does not attract them to live here . . . [2673]

The Port of Marseille Attracted Several British Travellers in the Seventeenth Century

The easy-going attitude of the Marseillais was one that seemed characteristic of working to live and not living to work. There is only so much money one can earn and then knowing how to spend it, how to live from the earnings one has made instead of a relentless pursuit of money for its own sake and forgetting what money is for and forgetting to live life. The Marseillais attitude was frustrating for Louis's officials like Arnoul but it comes from a confidence and financial security from the abundant amount of trade that flowed through Marseille. It is an enviable position to have plentiful opportunities to be able to take it or leave it. The volume of the port's trade impressed the Englishman Burnet visiting Marseille:

> The Freedoms of this place, tho it is now at the mercy of the Citadel, are such, and its scituation draweth so much Trade to it, that there one seeth another appearance of wealth than I found in any Town in France . . . [2674]

William Bromley also observed in *Remarks in the grande tour of France and Italy. Lately by a Person of Quality*, published in London, 1692:

> The Exchange is new built, not large, but very neat, where the Merchants meet: the Trading is chiefly countenanced by the English and Dutch, those of any condition among the French, disdaining the Profession, and others dealing only in little pedling matters. The Native Tradesmen of Marseilles are particularly observed never to be very rich, and seldom to have regard to posterity; but delight to live well, and enjoy themselves, in so much that no one that can afford it, will be without his Country as well as City House.[2675]

Sir Philip Skippon visiting in 1665 wrote briefly on the city but his companion John Ray was more impressed to write,

> Marseille, an ancient City not great but well built with tall stone-houses for the most part, and very populous. We were told that the number of souls was about 120,000. The streets are narrow as in most of the ancient Towns in this Countrey, to keep off the scorching beams of the Sun in Summer time. The haven is the most secure and commodius that I have seen: the entrance into it is so straight and narrow that a man may easily cast a stone across it, but the haven within large enough to contain 500 vessels or more; of an oval figure. On one side of this haven the Town is built which compasses it more than half round, having before it a handsome kay well paved, which serves the Citizens for a walk or Promenade. This haven is not capable of ships of above 600 tun.[2676]

John Locke in Travels to France 1675–79 wrote,

> The key is handsome & long & full of people walking, espetially in the evenings, when the best company, men & women, meet & walk, which is not soe safe in other streets nor sweet, for the houses being fild most of them with several familys living one over an other, have no houses of offices, but instead of that all is don in pots & thrown out of the windows, which makes the streets very ill scented always & very inconvenient anights.[2677]

John Evelyn, Diarist and Author

Several travellers to Marseille commented on the situation of the galley-slaves. Not all were convicted criminals and included Huguenots (French Protestants) and prisoners of war particularly Turks. Slaves were allowed to earn money and John Evelyn noted:

> some have after many Yeares of cruel Servitude been able to purchase their liberty . . . There is nothing more strange then the infinite number of slaves, working in the Streets, & carrying burthens with their confus'd noises, & gingling of their huge Chaynes'.[2678]

Later travellers like Ellis Veryard observed,

> The Slaves have little Shops or wooden Boxes all along the Key where they work at their respective Trades, and all sell their Goods, whilst the Gallies continue in the Port; but they are fastned to a Block with a Chain of eight or ten Foot long, which keeps them from budging thence, till the Officer comes at Night to loose and conduct them to their Vessels. Such of them as have no Trades learn to knit Stockings, and to serve as Porters in the City, but are chain'd two and two together, having a Guard always following them, who share in what they get'.[2679]

Siegnally the Secretary of State for the Navy wrote to Dellafonte and d'Ortières the Galley Controllers in 1684 'Most of the convicts cannot eat the amount of bread given to them, and keep it to sell, and by the time they return they have enough of it to sell in Marseille'.[2680]

During the reign of Charles I the Angevin, chancery registers record ordering the construction of galleys conforming to the Red Galleys of Provence, which was considered a fine design.[2681] Galleys were a relatively cheap form of sea power.[2682]

Crews for the galleys were made up of three types:

1. Slaves (Turk's though this included many from North Africa)
2. Volunteers or 'bonevoglies'.
3. Condemned men and convicts.[2683]

The standard Galley had 260 oarsmen for the Réale or Patronne (squadron flagship). The king of France bought his slaves at market at Livorno, Malta, Alicante, Majorca, or Culiari where the slave trade prospered until the end of the eighteenth century.[2684] France under Francois I, Henry II, and Louis XIII drew heavily from the prisons. Under Louis XIV the state was not happy with the idea of rebuilding their fleets to use as a means of punishment again. Louis XIV built an impressive naval base at Marseille that was operational in peace or war, 'a city of galleys' whose penal population during 1690-1700 was about a fifth of the town's population. Ten thousand convicts and two thousand slaves kept in port and immediately available out of a town with fifty thousand to sixty thousand inhabitants.[2685] One third of the convicts usually died in the chiourme hospitals in homeports during the off-season. The death rate was the same if a year in port inactive or whether they rowed.[2686]

America and Marseille

A.D. 1685–1698. The native Iroquois Confederation had been an obstacle for establishing a profitable colony in North America for the French. For fifty years the Iroquois intercepted beaver pelts convoys of the French from the interior and sold them to the Dutch merchants in their colony of New Netherland. (Dutch merchants maintained contacts with the Iroquois after the final takeover of their colony by the English in 1674 who renamed it New York). After an attack by 1,500 French soldiers in 1666 the Iroquois stayed at peace up to 1680.[2687]

Jacques-René de Brisay de Denonville, Marquis de Denonville replaced Joseph Antoine de LaBarre as Governor of New France the colony in North America. Though England and France were at peace Denonville sent 105 men north of Montreal capturing English fur trading posts on James Bay.[2688] Denonville then set out himself with a strong force. Though there are discrepancies as to following numbers in some websites here is the entry in Webster's Online Dictionary. Denonville tricked fifty hereditary sachems (chiefs) of the Iroquois to a meeting at Fort Frontenac under a flag of truce and had them chained and sent to Marseille (Massalia) to be galley slaves.[2689]

The Canadian Biography online only mentions 36 of 58 prisoners sent to France to be oarsman in the galleys, and as prisoners of war, to be well treated and returned when a peace was established with the Iroquois. The Minister had ordered Denonville to send prisoners to France for the galleys. Denonville complied while protesting with this error of judgement.[2690]

Fenton mentions some Iroquois were rounded up and a 'troublesome Cayaga Chief and his followers' were captured and despatched by Denonville to hard labour on the Mediterranean prison galleys.[2691]

Denonville attacked the lands of the Seneca infuriating the Iroquois. He drew up detailed plans for an extensive conquest and sent them with Louis-Hector de Callière Governor of Montreal to France for approval requesting more troops to carry it out. Denonville proposed an attack on New York and to use Manhattan Island as a base for the French Navy to devastate the seaboard of New England down to Boston. His plan was that with New York devastated the French would have better success against the flank of the Iroquois rather than fruitless chasing in the forests and the Iroquois would have to sue for peace.[2692] In the meantime there was disease and exhaustion in the French colony. Denonville sought to buy time by having a peace treaty with the Five Nations (of Indians) to be ratified the following year.[2693] Before the treaty was ratified, unknown to Denonville, France and England were now at war. But the Iroquois heard this from the English at Albany and thinking they would get the support of England made a surprise attack on New France. The Iroquois harassed Montreal for many months then burnt down the adjacent town of Lachine.[2694] Frontenac replaced Denonville as Governor in 1689 and seeing the problem made efforts to find the Iroquois chiefs that had been sent to Marseille (Massalia) as galley slaves. He located 13 surviving and they returned with him to New France in America that October 1689.[2695]

Fenton mentions near the end of 1689 'two of the thirteen who had been carried to France' were to attend a grand council. The Iroquois were still angry that a number of their war chiefs were still captive in France or had died there.[2696] On 22 January 1690 three of the four messengers sent to a meeting of 80 sachems had been prisoners in France. The messengers gave Frontenac's message, 'He had returned as Governor, and had brought back a Cayuga sachem, Tawerahet, and twelve prisoners'. Tawerahet's message was also conveyed of the 'miseries' their countrymen had experienced in captivity and to 'hearken to *Yonodio*, if you desire to live'.[2697]

A.D. 1700. Master Fillol, chief navigator for the French Royal Fleet and cartographer sets up the School of Hydrography in the art of navigation at Agde (Agathe Tyche) training captains until 1914.[2698]

A.D. 1705. The French temporarily capture Nice (Nikaia) from the Duke of Savoy. The following year King Louis XIV ordered the dismantling of the citadel and ramparts on the promontory to stop it being of strategic value any more. The city was awarded back to Savoy in 1713 in the Treaty of Utrecht.

The city became a favourite place for wealthy Britons to winter from 1730 and eventually a promenade was built for them still called Promenade des Anglais. Queen Victoria regularly stayed in Cimiez in the 1890s,[2699] and there is a statue of her there.[2700]

A.D. 1788–1790 Jewish Political Freedom
Jews living in Marseille were recognised with rights and privileges by the Parliament of Aix-en-Provence in 1788. In January 1790 the community (numbering around 200) were granted full emancipation by the French Revolution two years before the rest of France.[2701]

A.D. 1792 La Marseillaise

Marseille voted to join the French Revolution and sent a company of 500 soldiers Fédéres to put down a Royalist insurrection in Arles. [2702] Roget d'Lisle wrote a song in Strasbourg on 25 April 1792 called 'War Song of the Army of the Rhine'. François Mireur sang this at a banquet [2703] it was then sung by the Marseillais (the people from Marseille). These soldiers from Marseille (Massalia) had made the song popular by the time they had reached Paris. The Chronique de Paris wrote that they

> sing this song with the greatest fervour. The passage where, waving their hats and brandishing their swords, they all sing together "aux armes, citoyens" is truly thrilling. They often sing at the Palais Royal sometimes inside the Theatre between two plays. [2704]

The song became known as 'from the people of Marseille' La Marseillaise. The Fédéres of Marseille were regarded as patriotic heroes but in the opinion of General Thiébault 'an infernal gang of assassins'. [2705] The song La Marseillais became enshrined as the national anthem of the French Republic. Later it was banned by different French governments and then reinstated.

Roses (Rosas) in Spain had continued to be an important fortress. A medal was issued 'Cruz de la Distincion de Rosas' [2706] for its defence during the Napoleonic wars. The stubborn Spanish defence was aided by British naval Captain Lord Thomas Cochrane.[2707] The fortress of Roses (encompassing the original fourth century B.C. Greek city Rhodus a colony of Massalia) became obsolete after the completion of the world's largest fortress San Fernando (Sant Ferran) at Figueras, and eventually became abandoned by the end of the nineteenth century while the town grew outside the fortress walls.[2708]

A.D. 1815. Antibes, the ancient Greek city of Antipolis on the coast of France, was covered by the tide of history. Emperor Napoleon Bonaparte after his abdication in 1814 had not received his agreed allowance: nor his wife and son: and the disenchantment with the restored Bourbon monarchy in France all contributed to his decision to leave his small empire of the island of Elba. With a detachment of his 'old guard' they landed at Golfe-Juan, France on the 1 March but failed to win over the nearby garrison at Antibes where his messengers were arrested. [2709] Napoleon then avoided royalist Provence and the easier Marseille-Lyon route marching instead via Cannes and Grenoble to Paris where he resumed control on the 20 March from King Louis XVIII who had fled. In his fateful '100 Days' Napoleon then defeated the Prussians at Ligny but two days later was defeated himself by Wellington's Anglo-Allied Army and the Prussians at Waterloo on 18 June.

Greeks at Marseille (Massalia) in the Nineteenth Century A.D.

Through all these centuries and an absence of details we now find mentioned again Greeks and Greek ships at Massalia (Marseille). The Greeks were determined not to let war interfere with commerce. Greek ships at Massalia often slipped through the French blockade during the Napoleonic Wars carrying grain from the Black Sea markets. [2710] The Greek shipping of the Diaspora developed a 'tradition' of ignoring blockades right up to the twentieth century. [2711]

Since its foundation Massalia, had the independent spirit of the Phocaean Greeks ingrained by necessity from its isolation and distance from other Greek city-states. A spirit it seems that continued to permeate the city's inhabitants through the ages.

This long tradition was evident again during the French Revolution 'as the early Federalist concepts were washed away in the blood of the Reign of Terror, however the city revolted against the ruling National Convention. Quickly mastered by force of arms, it was officially designated as 'the city without a name' [2712] *Sans Nom*. [2713] *Marseille est à jamais incurable*, said Fréron and together with Barras, Saliceti and Ricord decreed that the city should be called provisionally 'Sans Nom' (5 January 1794). By the 23 January the Committee of Public Safety advised the name of Marseille should be kept 'for it recalled the past services of that city to the Revolution'. [2714] Throughout August 1793 Marseille as a whole was on trial for federalism. [2715] 'When commerce was almost destroyed by the maritime blockade of the Continent against Napoleon, Marseille became bitterly anti-Bonarpartist and hailed the Bourbon restoration. Later under Napoleon III Marseille remained stubbornly Republican'. [2716]

The French revolutionary spirit and ideals spread across Europe [2717] by Napoleon remained long after his defeat causing revolutions. Following the French Revolution the fleets of Venice, Malta and France were excluded from the sea of the Levant. The Greeks were able to fill the vacuum and within thirty years Greek owned shipping increased from 400 in 1786 to 800 ships by 1813. Their main trade was grain. [2718] Consequently Greek ship owners expanded their maritime network to all Mediterranean ports. During the Greek War of Independence (1821–29) a new wave of prosperous Greek merchant families from Chios, Smyrna, and Constantinople move westwards and established themselves in Trieste, Livorno, Amsterdam, Marseilles and London. In these cities they already had family and business connections. [2719]

Who were these family connections that were already there and when did these people arrive? In regard to Marseille (Massalia) could it be possible that they were descended from the ancient Phocaean Greek population? Greek populations had survived in cities they had founded such as Alexandria, and also the many original Greek cities of Asia Minor that were later captured under the Ottoman Empire, which continued until the expulsion of 1.1 million Greek Orthodox in 1923 [2720] ending the 'Great Idea'. [2721] Incidentally for the Phocaeans it was to be only the third time they left their city due to invading armies. This was in 545 B.C. from Harpagus and the Persians, with over half the Phocaeans returning to their city shortly afterwards; and from the Turks in June 1914 almost all left and most returned 1 January 1920, then following the defeat of the Greek Army in Asia Minor they fled in August 1922 ending their presence in Phocaea for over 2,500 years. [2722]

In a recent genetic study published in the scientific journal *Molecular Biology and Evolution* co-authored by Jacques Chiaroni Director of the French Establishment of Blood (EFS) at Marseille samples were taken from fifty-one males in Provence and 323 in Corsica. The study found that in Provence 'In their blood, 4% of the men carry the Y-chromosome of a typical marker of the ancient Phocaeans'. The marker E-V13 was present in the samples with 4% of Provence, and 4.6% of East Corsica (in which Aleria was originally the Phocaean colony of Alalia) and 1.6% of West Corsica.[2723] This marker was compared to eighty-nine Greek males whose grandparents came from Phocaea and Smyrna areas in Ionia with 19% and 12% respectively showing E-V13. The results suggested this was a revealing marker showing input of a dominant male elite and it was estimated that their genetic input into the Provence area of the Iron Age would have been 10% compared to the Celts and Ligurians.[2724] The report's conclusion was that given the process of vine growing and wine culture attributed to Massalia the E-V13 marker may be useful indicator in tracing Greek impact socially and demographically in other parts of France and Spain and elsewhere in the Mediterranean.

The main trade from this new wave of merchants to Marseille in the nineteenth century was exporting from the Ottoman Empire. This included bulk cargoes of grain, wool, cotton, linseed and tallow from the East and in return from the West manufactured goods of thread and textiles. [2725]

Ironically the ancient Greek Chians from the island of Chios had refused refuge of permanent settlement to the Phocaean Greeks fleeing from the Persians. [2726] Some of the Phocaeans in 545 B.C. then came to join their already established settlement at Massalia. During the nineteenth century A.D. the Chians fleeing the Ottomans were now seeking refuge and came to Massalia (Marseille) and settled.

The Chian merchants in Massalia (Marseille) increased their network, related by marriages, through sixty families. The main network ran from Britain to the Black Sea 'with a chain of branch offices at Marseilles, Trieste, Livorno; cotton markets of Alexandria and Cairo; maritime centre in the Aegean archipelago, Syra; and in the two financial markets of the East Mediterranean, Constantinople and Smyrna'. [2727]

From 1816 Pierre-Emmanuel Schilizzi of 'Schilizzi & Cie' [2728] trading company originally from the Greek island of Chios, is present in Marseille. A school run by the *Pensionnat Massol père* in 1823 had 18 of its first 24 pupils from Greece. Many were refugees fleeing the massacres in Chios of 1822 and being sold into slavery during the Greek War of Independence from the Ottoman Empire. Amongst those Greeks who established businesses in Marseille from 1825 were members of the Ralli, Mavrogodato, Vlasto, Argenti, Rodocanachi and Sechiari trading families. [2729] The mainly Chian trading families also established their shipping businesses in London and Liverpool where the stability of the British Empire proved a prosperous market. [2730] The huge variety of goods now in Britain was more than the tin and amber that their ancient Greek forerunners had traded in.

In 1830 the Protocol of London declares the new Greek kingdom independent. A group of twenty-four predominantly Chians [2731] form a church in the house and offices of the Ionides family at Finsbury Park during 1837–49.[2732] The leader of the Chians Peter Ralli (nicknamed Zeus) becomes the first Greek Consul in London 1835. In 1879 the St. Sophia Cathedral was designed by George Oldrid Scott and built in Westminster where the interior decorations was paid for by the émigré families from Chios such as Ralli, Vlasto,[2733] Agelasto, Mavrocordato, Schilizzi, Ionides,[2734] Argenti, Zafiri and others.[2735]

The thoughts and experiences of massacres were hard lessons on the Greeks who made sure the goods they traded included something that could help protect them. 'Although Marseille traders began to speculate in other commodities, they still concentrated particularly on the grain trade, having immense influence in time of political and economic crises.'[2736]

By 1834 the Greek Orthodox community in Massalia (Marseille) had established a church and rebuilt it in 1844. There is an inscription in stone to the founders and later contributors like the Zafiri family in the entrance hall.[2737] The Eglise de la Dormition de la Vierge is the oldest Orthodox Church in West Europe. The first Archimandrite was Arsène Yannucos, a reservists Chaplin in the Bonapartist Army living in Paris.[2738]

From 1817 the British and Greeks controlled the trade to and from the Levant. The Greeks with a base at Marseille increased the prosperity of the city. The population almost doubled within 50 years from 106,000 in 1816, 132,000 in 1831, and by 1851 to 195,000.[2739]

The *ZZ Company* (Zafiriopoulo and Zafiri) was founded in 1852 in Marseille first as wheat importers from Odessa and after 1900 turning to industry and finance contributing greatly to the rise of Marseille. Echinard spoke of one hundred Greek businesses there in 1863. Greek maritime contacts in the nineteenth century were verified by an inspector of the Banque de France in 1860 when he observed 'The main headquarters of their businesses are found at the east and west of the Mediterranean, in Constantinople and Marseille'.[2740]

By the end of the nineteenth century profits diminished in the Mediterranean, Black Sea and the Levant markets with imports of wheat from the USA, Russian expansionism, and the collapsing Ottoman Empire. In 1890 the Zafiri family transferred all their assets from Constantinople to Marseille and London. They kept up their contacts in Constantinople by marrying into the Zafiropoulo family there, becoming successful bankers and also trading in grain and flour from the Black Sea.[2741]

The national drink of Greece is called Ouzo. It has its origins at least to the Byzantine era. There are stories that it was made from the waste products of wine by monks in Mount Athos and then spread to Greece. It was called Tsipoura or Rakija and still is in many parts. How Tsipoura got the name Ouzo was possibly in the nineteenth century, as Tirnavos in Thessaly, North Greece exported the finest quality silks[2742] and Tsipouro to Massalia in France. In 1800 the first shipment of Tsipouro was sent to Massalia. For trade purposes the shipping label was written in Italian as the cargo was transhipped at Genoa and the Italian customs offices wrote on the containers 'USO a Marsilla', meaning for Use in Marseille. The name became a slang expression that meant anything that was of top quality 'USO Massalia'. A Turkish physician named Anastas Bey visiting Tornados asked to try the local anise based drink tsipouro and declared it 'USO Marsilla'. The praise for the drink caught on and it became known as Ouzo. (Uso = 'fine quality').[2743]

Continuity of Name

The ancient Greek name of Massalia is the same in Modern Greek today. From the Latin version Massilia is written in Italian today as Marsiglia[2744] (see Figure 101). But in the pronunciation the 'g' is phonetically spoken as 'Massilia'. In the local Occitan language of Provence it is pronounced Marsejo or Marsijo.

It is remarkable that in over 2,600 years the name Marseille is so close to the original. The ancient Greek original name for France was Keltike after the Celts. Within a few centuries the ancient Greeks started using the term Gallia (Gaul) for France. This is still the same today in Modern Greek and calling the French language Gallica. Britain is still called Megali Bretannia Μεγαλι Βρεταννια and also Agglia Αγγλία in acknowledgement of a new dominant invader led by the Angles and Saxons (Anglo-Saxons) in England, with separate names for Scotland and Wales.

On the rare occasion one gets to hear an Anglo-Saxon poem/language it is hard to recognise the words in modern English. Once watching an England soccer football match on TV, over an hour had passed and the atmosphere at Wembley Stadium became tired and somewhat spaced out. The chanting changed as 60,000 English fans stretched out the name Eeeeeeeeen-ger-land, Eeeeeeeeen-ger-land. It was an uncanny experience and for the first time to hear modern English sounding like real Anglo-Saxon, a mainline back to its roots through the collective subconscious.

Figure 101. Both spellings of Marseille in Greek and Italian, Massalia and Marsiglia, appear on the Greek label of Formil washing machine liquid detergent with the 'aroma from the soap of Massalias' SAVONNERIE MARSELLA €3.99 Euros, Lidls, Thessaloniki, Greece, 7 September 2010.

Twenty-Fifth Centenary of the Founding of Massalia (Marseille)

Penteconter Ship Returns

A.D. 1899 was designated as the twenty-fifth centenary from the foundation of Marseille in 600 B.C. [2745] There were celebrations from the 14 to 22 October that included a replica Greek penteconter sailing into the Harbour of Lacydon (Vieux-Port) on the 15 October re-enacting the first Greek Phocaean sailors arrival in 600 B.C. [2746] This must have been a tremendous sight as many of the ships in the harbour sailed out to meet the penteconter and escorted it to the docks. On this day Dr Georgiades, 'mandaté par sa municipalité' gave a speech:

> *Le dèmos des Phocéens au dèmos des Massaliotes, salut, (...) Notre Ionie a ressenti une joie inexprimable de patriotisme et de fierté. Les ombres de nos ancêtres ont dû tressaillir de ce pieux témoignage de reconnaissance des Massaliotes envers les illustres fondateurs de cette grande cité méridionale'.*[2747]

The people of Phocaea to the people of Massalia, hello (…) Our Ionia felt an inexprimable joy of patriotism and pride. The shades of our ancestors are thrilled of this testimony of recognition of Massaliotes towards the famous founders of this large southernmost city.

There was also the speech by the Greek archimandrite of the Orthodox Church of Marseille Grégoire Zigavinos 'on the influence of the Hellenic spirit in the West'. [2748]

From those celebrations there is in Marseille (Massalia) a large bronze plaque taken from fort Saint-Jean [2749] and set into the eastern quayside promenade in 1954, [2750] it has at the bottom an image of a Greek coin with a head facing left and in Greek ΛΑΚΥΔΩΝ (Lacydon); above it an inscription in French. The translation in English is:

> Here
> c. 600 B.C.
> landed Greek sailors from Phocaea,
> a Greek city of Asia Minor.
> They founded Marseille,
> and from there Civilisation spread through the West'. [2751]

Figure 102. Legend of the foundation of Marseille with King Nannus, Glyptis and Protis beautifully decorated in 1899 with tiles, columns and pan-Athena in a small café 'En Suisse. Le Palais du Roi', Rue des Feuillants corner of Rue Canébiere, Marseille.

From the high point of the celebrations the following twentieth century saw the city's image suffer between the two world wars with gun running to the Spanish Civil War, drug-related violence, Corsican and other mafia activities and these minorities tarnished the rest of the city's image. A few incidents kept that reputation going such as the assassination of the king of Yugoslavia and the French Foreign Minister in 1934. Paul Carbone a gangster and Fascist supporter gained notoriety during the 1930s until the French Resistance eventually killed him in 1944. [2752] Hitler had called Marseille a nest of spies. [2753]

Several films and novels capitalised and perpetuated this criminal image. Yet in spite of this image the city 'had shown it capable of prospering' in adversity.[2754] The French also see the other side of Marseille famous for its humour, 'exaggeration and telling what the locals call tall stories-*la galéjade*'.[2755] At the present time OM (*Olympique de Marseille*) is one of the most successful football clubs in France. [2756] Its most famous player Didiere Drogba was transferred to Chelsea FC for £24 million in 2005, scoring 157 goals in 241 matches, winning English Premiership titles: the F.A. Cup: the double in 2009-10: the League Cup and scored the winning goal in the UEFA Champions League cup in 2012. Though he only spent a short time with OM Drogba's image is still used to represent Marseille, which was seen on posters in Paris (2010). Zidane Zidane born in Marseille became a famous and talented player in German football clubs and the French national soccer team.

During the eighteenth century half the city's population were immigrants mostly from Italy and also Greece, Spain, Berbers and the Levant. An increase of Greeks and Italians immigration continued into the nineteenth century. In the following century up to the Second World War nearly 40% of the population was Italian. The census of 2008 records a population of 859,453.[2757] Though the census does not record religion only an estimate can be given, which is approximately 600,000 Roman Catholics, between 150,000 to 200,000 Muslims, 80,000 Armenian Orthodox Christians, 80,000 Jews, 20,000 Protestants, 10,000 East Orthodox Christians (Greeks, which can also include the Balkans and Russians), and 3,000 Buddhists.[2758] During the urban riots affecting several cities in France 2005, Marseille was not one of them. Though they had similar problems of run down large estates there was not the sense of alienation. People in Marseille seem to have a strong sense of identity being Marseillais first no matter what ethnic group they come from.[2759]

Summary

Strabo recorded that Celts were being educated in Massalia before the Romans conquered the surrounding areas.[2760] From Justin (43. 4.1) we learn that Gaul (France) particularly in the south and the Rhône valley had become civilised economically and culturally from the influence of ancient Greek Massalia (Marseille). Having faced and survived many difficulties over the centuries Marseille has in 2009 been through a process of competition and selection. Marseille's credentials won the chance to make a new cultural contribution to France and across Europe. Marseille designated as the European Capital of Culture 2013 had been allocated 90 million Euros to spend on a series of cultural events in celebration.[2761]

Throughout its history Marseille (Massalia) with its changing admix of population, a common element of the Marseillais is evident and that is an independent spirit and resilience throughout its many downturns in fortune. The Greeks maintained an incredible continuity in Massalia for over 1,000 years. The independent Greek city-state of Massalia lasted for over 700 years: a further 300 years as part of the Roman Empire: and for an unclear period under the Franks from the sixth century A.D. Scant information briefly mentions Greek monks at Massalia and the tax on Greeks in Arles in the eleventh century A.D.

The discoveries and contacts ancient Massalia made in exploration and naming of Britain by Pytheas was renewed again by other Greek settlers of the nineteenth century also in maritime trade and commerce who joined Greeks already there in Marseille. Whether these Marseillais were of direct descent to their ancient Greek ancestors would be tenuous due to the population devastation by several plagues. Nevertheless Greek populations did tenaciously survive in the cities they had founded i.e. in Asia Minor they continued to thrive until 1.1 million were expelled in the exchange of 1923. Nine Greek-speaking towns and seven villages still survive in the south of Italy (Magna Graecia) today.

A recent genetic study found 4% of the fifty-one male samples from sites near Neolithic villages in Provence had the marker E-V13 also occurring in the sample taken in Greece of eighty-nine Greek males whose grandparents had come from the areas around Phocaea and Smyrna in Ionia.[2762] This study did reveal a genetic continuity within change as confirmed in the sample taken in Corsica. A new influx of Greeks to Marseille in the nineteenth century and their maritime trading contacts with Great Britain was a remarkable full circle of over 2,300 years.

APPENDIX

Massalia and Agricola the Roman Governor of Britain

Cnaeus Iulius Agricola (A.D. 37–93) was sent to school to study philosophy at Massalia as a youth. His father was Julius Graecinus, of senatorial rank, and his mother Julia Procilla. Later Agricola was elected consul of Rome in A.D. 77 and then given Britain as his province. He became the Roman Governor of Britain from A.D. 78–84 and launched seven campaigns conquering nearly all of North Britain up to the Grampian Hills. His fleet sailed to the Shetland Islands 'sighting' Thoule and on returning to Trutulens (Sandwich) they claimed to be the first Romans to circumnavigate Britain according to the book called *Agricola* written by his son-in-law the historian Tacitus.[2763]

The Massaliotes were not helpful in giving any information on Britain as Scipio Aemilianus had found. Maybe Agricola, as a youth would hear sea stories and tales by other children or adults? Perhaps he gained access to Massaliote books and in this way he knew more of Britain and the island of Thoule than other Romans? As Governor of Britain he sent a Roman fleet with marines as far as the Shetlands Islands. Was he following Pytheas's route, for his fleet reported 'sighting' Thoule? They certainly knew the name. The Romans may even have mistaken Thoule as one of the Orkneys or Shetland Islands and not Iceland, as they did not mention seeing the frozen sea and encountered instead the North Atlantic Drift Current.[2764] Perhaps they were only interested to find inhabitable lands to exploit. On 'sighting' Thoule they returned to Shetland.

We can only guess what information about Britain Agricola had picked up in Massalia if at all. However he did not continue his conquests, being recalled to Rome by the Emperor Domitian jealous of his successes in Britain.[2765] Pliny the Elder records that from Thoule one more days sailing the frozen 'Congealed Sea' began.[2766] This should place Thoule well beyond the Orkneys or Shetlands and therefore not visible to Agricola's fleet.

Island of Thoule (Iceland)

For a few days a year the midnight sun is visible in the north of Iceland.[2767] Pytheas wrote that Thule was six days sailing north of Britain.[2768] Pliny adds that one more days sailing the frozen Congealed Sea begins.[2769] The very north of Iceland is placed at 66°N.[2770] One day's sail from there the frozen Congealed Sea is found.

Kleomedes first or second century A.D. refers to Pytheas,

> Concerning the island of Thoule, in which men say Pytheas, the Massaliote philosopher, was actually present, the report is that the whole summer [circle] is above the earth, it also being the arctic for them.[2771]

Kosmas Indicopleustes sixth century A.D. recorded,

> Pytheas the Massaliote says in *On the Ocean* that when he was present in the most northerly places, the barbarians living there used to point out the sun's bed because there, the sun always remained with them throughout the nights. [2772]

Though Diodorus Siculus records the names of the promontories of Britain, Orcas is the northern tip of Scotland. The archaeologist C. F. C. Hawkes (1975) suggests that Pytheas completed his coastal journey by going to the Orkneys first at Hoy Sound and missing Cape Wrath, and first heard of Thoule in North Uistlanding at Dunnet Head (Orcas).[2773] Therefore one day's sail from here to the north-west corner of the Orkneys. Roseman argues that the island of Thoule was not thought of as big until Solinus wrote around A.D. 250 In a quote from Carpenter's book *Beyond the Pillars of Hercules* Solinus writes that 'From the Orkneys as far as Thule is a sea voyage of five days and nights. From the headland of Caledonia it is a two-day voyage for those seeking Thule.' [2774] The statement if correct may be solved with a suggestion by Hawkes (1975) that the Hebrides may be 'Berrice'. This is an island Pliny the Elder states, 'From which one sails to Tyle [Thoule]. Off Tyle by one days voyage is the 'Congealed Sea, which some call the Cronian.' [2775] Apollonius of Rhodes wrote *The Voyage of Argo: The Argonautica*. In it he mentions the return journey 'Tell me now, Muses, how *Argo* travelled far beyond the Cronian Sea'. In Rieu's glossary Cronian was also an ancient name for the Adriatic. [2776]

Solinus may mean it is two days sailing from the headland of Caledonia to Berrice (the port of embarkation) for those seeking Tyle? He does not mention Pytheas by name. What was Solinus source and was it a correct copy? However, he does write

> There are many other islands around *Brittania*, of which the most distant is *Thyle*, where at the summer solstice, when the sun is passing through the sign of Cancer, there is no night, and likewise at the winter solstice no day. We hear that beyond *Thyle* the sea is sluggish and frozen. [2777]

Ultima Thule became a remote place the Romans thought of as the end of the world. Thoule does not seem to have been reached again by anyone from the Mediterranean world for centuries. Orosius c. A.D. 415 writes that after Britain where

> it faces an unbounded ocean, it has the Orcades islands, of which 20 are uninhabited and 13 inhabited. Then there is the island of Thyle (variants Tyle, Tylae, Thulae, Thola, Tholae), which is separated from the rest by an infinite distance, lying in the middle of the ocean towards the west-north-west; it is held to be scarcely known to few people. [2778]

Procopius c. A.D. 500–565 records that the Eruli being defeated in battle by the Langobardi (A.D. 512) some settled in Illyria while the rest passed through the Slavs and then the Dani to the ocean and took ship to Thule. There were thirteen nations there each with a king and the Eruli settled alongside the Gaulti who were the most numerous. This land was large and '10 times greater than Brettania'. Around the summer solstice the sun never sets for forty days and six months later at the winter solstice the sun never rises for forty days 'but perpetual night envelops it'. He inquired from those he met from there how they can reckon the length of days without the sun. [2779] But later he admits he does not know the exact location of Thule 'so far as men know, lies in the furthest part of the ocean towards the north'.[2780]

Casserterides–the Tin Islands

By the time of Strabo 64 B.C.–A.D. 24 and using Posidonius as his source he writes about mining in Turdetania, 'and through it flows the Beatis River'.[2781] The River Beatis is thought to be the Guadalquivir in Iberia maybe between Cape St. Vincent and the Pillars of Hercules:[2782]

> Tin, however is not found there on the surface of the ground, he says, as the historians continually repeat, but it is dug up; and it is produced both in the country of the barbarians who live beyond Lusitania, and in the Casserterides Islands; and tin is brought to Massalia from the British Islands also.[2783]

Though there was some distinction between the Casserterides Islands and the British islands with Strabo saying 'the Casserterides are ten in number, and they lie near each other in the high sea to the north of the port of the Artabrians'.[2784] They have 'mines of tin and lead, with people living a mostly nomadic life and 'give these metals in exchange for pottery, salt and copper utensils'.[2785]

Diodorus Siculus also distinguishes between the Tin Islands and the 'Prettanic Island'. Both provided the metal but of the Tin Islands he says,

> For above the country of the Luistani there are many mines of tin, and on the islets which lie near Iberia in the ocean, and because of this are named *Cattiterides* (Καττιτερίδας, acc.). Much tin is also conveyed from the *Prettanic* island to Gaul, lying opposite, and is brought on horses by merchants through the interior of Gaul both to the Massaliotes and to the city named Narbo.[2786]

Pliny the Elder when he writes of the 'Tin Island' means Cornwall ('The Stannaries').[2787] The location of the Tin Islands still seemed much in question then as in modern times.[2788] Gavin de Beer identifies them as islands that once existed at the estuary of the Loire, Brittany, before it silted up in late Roman times and 'now represented by the lower reaches of the River Brivé and the marches of Brière'. Now all joined together by silt a number of Bronze Age foundries that used tin and lead have been discovered here.[2789]

Founding a Greek Colony

A Greek colony was called an Apoikia (a settlement far from home) whereas Phoenician settlements were not intended as permanent and were started as trading posts. The Greeks had some trading posts these were 'Emporia'. Due to Greek laws on the death of a father his land was usually divided equally between his sons. Such inheritance was called *kleros* or lot.[2790] This could lead to the situation where there was not enough land to support themselves and a family. Therefore the main reason for a Greek colony was a permanent settlement for land. There is currently the theory that colonies were started for other reasons as archaeological evidence shows that the land in Greece produced enough food.[2791] This may be so but there is still the desire of wanting to run things your own way if not at home than somewhere else.

Osborne suggests that early settlements of the eighth and seventh century B.C. were a result of private enterprise.[2792] Though going by the amount of Greeks who work abroad today [2793] they have something in common with their ancestors, the hope of more opportunities, a better life, and space to live. They have a tradition of someone from the family going abroad to work *Xeniteia*,[2794] as do the people from their immediate neighbouring Balkan countries. This gives some truth to their humorous question, 'Name the three biggest Greek cities today?' *Reply*: Athens, Thessaloniki and Patras? No! *Answer*: Athens, Melbourne [2795] and Chicago! [2796]

There were some Greek settlements that started out as trading posts and developed into cities like Naukratis in Egypt; Pitecusae on the island of Ischia (for the iron and copper trade from North Italy) that later founded Cumae on the coast of Italy: Massalia, near the mouth of the River Rhône (tin and amber route), and its colony of Emporion (Market) in Spain. [2797]

Strabo writes,

> Now the earlier Kings of the Aegyptians, being content with what they had and not wanting foreign imports at all, and being prejudiced against all who sailed the seas, and particularly against the Greeks, (for owing to scarcity of land of their own the Greeks were ravagers and coveters of that of others) [2798]

and granted them a place Rhacotis (which later became part of Alexandria). The Pharaoh Amasis did grant several privileges to Greeks including founding a city at Naukratis that was a joint venture between twelve East Greek cities (including Phocaea). [2799] However the archaeological finds of late seventh century B.C. suggests an earlier date than Herodotus. [2800]

The founding of a Greek colony was usually a public enterprise directed by the mother-city. [2801] However, Osborne suggests a different view of a society, used to travelling and seeking opportunities abroad before the sixth century B.C. [2802] This view can also find support in the foundation stories of Massalia as Simos and Protis persuade others to join them and there is no mention of the city-state government of Phocaea organising the expedition. Though if the state did organise such ventures it could go without saying, as it was so obvious at the time? D'Agostino explains Thucydides (I.5) meaning of 'piracy' led by a high social class and considered honourable, and the new economic opportunities that led aristocrats searching for political roles that they were denied back home. [2803]

On the display boards at the exploration section of the Maritime Museum in Greenwich, London, U.K. there is quote from Thomas Jefferson in A.D. 1814 'Merchants have no country'. Thomas Jefferson was the third President of the U.S.A. 1802–09. The phrase is taken from: 'Merchants have no country. The mere spot they stand on does not constitute so strong an attachment as that from which they draw their gains'.[2804] Also how governments are compromised by commerce and manufacturing see his speech numbered ME: 12:376. On the one hand it is not entirely accurate as we have seen with the Greeks they still keep an attachment to their homeland and those who do well abroad do something material for their original village or town by building a public hall or hospital or for Greek culture such as the Onassis Foundation etc. Yet on the other hand we see some British bankers defending a reckless risk taking and bonus culture though they only have kept their jobs due to the British government rescue and bailout of these banks with 1.5 trillion pounds [2805] of taxpayers money during the credit crunch of 2008/09 and then threatening the government that they will leave 'decamp' and set up elsewhere in another country [2806] if the government brings in any legislation to curb their excesses and the government would lose whatever they already get in tax. This may explain Gordon Brown and the previous Labour government's anger but inaction on this one point. People who work well should be rewarded. Bankers should get their rewards while at the same time as paying back to the government the taxpayer's money that was loaned to them to save their jobs. Certainly this is a case for 'Quid pro quo'? [2807]

The Greeks understood this truth and believed they were descended from the autochthones, sprung from the soil, rocks and trees, and their existence was owed to the homeland even if far away in their settlements overseas as well as the attachment and bond they formed to where they were now living.[2808] One can also point to many Americans with their continuing cultural connection to Britain [2809] and also Canadians, Australians, New Zealanders etc. support when dire danger arose.

The Oikistes, founding leader, became the traditional hero of the new colony, and was usually provided by the mother-city. The Oikistes would then have a cult in his honour. These cults were faithfully observed by the new colony. Fortunately for history the colonies always remembered the age of their foundation, the origin of the colony and the original leader [2810] in which worship of the Oikistes kept those memories alive. Aristotle wrote in *The Constitution of Massalia* 'And there is a clan in Massalia to this day descended from the woman and called Protiades for Protis was the son of Euxenus and Aristoxene'. [2811]

However, there is some current thinking that some of these foundation legends were invented in the fourth century B.C. where most of our information comes from. [2812] This still does not take away that some of the stories may well be true [2813] sustained by the rigid conservatism of folklore and oral tradition. Just like children once told a story they take delight in the story being repeated ad infinitum and are disturbed and quickly correct the adult to any changes or getting any part wrong. The story has to be told as it was first told. With adults subject to wars this would depend on who was left alive and how much they knew of the story. [2814]

If there were not enough settlers to go the Oikistes would invite settlers from other cities to make up the numbers. Two things was needed in establishing a Greek colony and was the duty of the Oikistes; he took some Sacred Fire that burnt in the town hall (prytaneion) from the mother-city [2815] to keep burning in the new settlement and also earth to be scattered on the new site.[2816]

To ensure they had the blessing of the gods and to be directed to a good place an Oracle had to be consulted before leaving. The Oracles of Delphi and Dodona both in Greece, and Didyma in Asia Minor were popular amongst many others. The God that gave the prophecy was the divine leader (Archegates) for the colony and would be worshipped to protect the new colony. Sacred envoys (*Theoroi*) were appointed to keep up contacts with the oracle and *Theorodokoi* looked after a sacred envoy sent to their own city (see Chapter 2, Inscriptions found, Delphi). In a new colony a temple to the god was amongst the first buildings to be established. Land in the new colony was divided up by surveyors and divided into plots (Kleroi) and drawn by lots. From the beginning the colonist was given a private holding.[2817] Archilochos gambled away his expected plot of land while still on board ship.[2818] Return to the mother-city could be permitted so long as they left an adult male from their family to protect the welfare of the colony.[2819]

Oracles

A statement from an oracle can have more than one meaning. Therefore it is the interpretation that is crucial. For example during the Persian invasion of Greece the oracle at Delphi had proclaimed that a 'wooden wall' would save Athens. Some Athenians stayed to defend the city and built a wooden wall as there used to be one. Themistocles and rest of the Athenians left the city believing that the 'wooden wall' meant their warships, being made of wood, was like a wall. The Persians burnt the wooden wall and captured Athens.[2820] Later at Salamis the Athenian warships and Greek allies beat the Persian Navy. Without his navy to supply the huge Persian Army with food, King Xerxes had to return home for the land of Greece was Greece's best defender, as it could not support a large invading army.[2821] The Athenians were able to reclaim their city and so the 'wooden wall' (ships) had saved Athens though it had been captured and burnt in the short-term.

This is part of the two prophecies given by Aristonice, the Pythoness, at the oracle of Delphi and you can find the rest in Herodotus, *Histories,* Bk.7, 140 &141:

> Then far-seeing Zeus grants this to the prayers of Athene:
> Safe shall the wooden wall continue for thee and thy children.
> Wait not the tramp of the horse, nor the footmen mightily moving
> Over the land, but turn your back to the foe, and retire ye.
> Yet shall a day arrive when ye shall meet him in battle.
> Holy Salamis, thou shalt destroy the offspring of women,
> When men scatter the seed, or when they gather the harvest.

Themistocles had made the right interpretation of the oracle.

Sometimes the Oracle was more confounding as Herodotus mentions an instance when bribery influenced predictions to suit the bribers.[2822]

Alexander the Great tried to get a prophecy from the oracle of Delphi before his Persian expedition. On it being closed due to an inauspicious day when no prophecy can be given, he grabbed hold of the Pythoness and dragged her to the shrine. On the way the Pythoness exclaimed at Alexander's persistence 'you are invincible my son!' Alexander stopped. He 'declared that he wanted no other prophecy, but had obtained from her the oracle he was seeking'. He could justly claim the Pythoness had said it even though she was not in the shrine.[2823]

By contrast his uncle King Alexander I of Epirus (the Molossian) was invited by the Greek city of Tarentum (Taras) in Italy to lead them in a war against the Messapians and Leucanians. A Leucanian killed him about 330 B.C.[2824] Alexander the Molossian was killed near the fortress of Pandosia above Consentia, the metropolis of the Brettii. There were two places called Pandosia. Strabo tells us what happened:

> He, too, was deceived by the oracle of Dodona, which bade him be on his guard against Acheron and Pandosia; for places which bore these names were pointed out to him in Thesprotia [in Greece], but he came to his end here in Brettium [in Italy].[2825] Now the fortress has three summits, and the River Acheron flows past it. And there was another oracle that helped to deceive him: "Three-hilled Pandosia, much people shalt thou kill one day"; for he thought that the oracle clearly meant the destruction of the enemy, not of his own people.[2826]

Alexander I (the Molossian) of Epirus was made king of Epirus by King Philip II of Macedon c. 342 B.C.

Diogenes the Cynic Philosopher

Diogenes had misunderstood an oracle of Delphi. The Pythia told him 'to alter the currency'.[2827] He dutifully obeyed and back home in Sinope he issued false coins but on being discovered he was driven into exile.[2828] A Greek identified himself with his city-state[2829] to be exiled from it and become a stateless person was the greatest loss.[2830] Was the Pythia wrong? The word 'currency' could also mean 'custom'. Then he followed this meaning by 'flouting all conventional restraints' in not performing the usual customs of Greece.[2831]

Professor Seltman proved there was a basis for fact in that Diogenes's father Hicesias, a banker, was actually in charge of the mint in Sinope and forced to deal with counterfeit coins from their neighbouring Persian Satrap. Surviving specimens of coin shows he had defaced them to put them out of currency. Symbolically Diogenes used what had happened to his family to 'deface the currency of Greek culture'.[2832]

Plutarch uses this analogy of currency with Alexander the Great saying 'Because of me even those faraway sages shall come to know of Diogenes, and he of them. And I also, like Diogenes, must alter the standard of coinage and stamp foreign states with the impress of Greek government.'[2833]

Distances

Stade = 185.4 meters (200 feet), with different variants of the Stade *stadion* existing + -30 m.[2834] 12 Stades = 1½ miles. The exact value of a stade is not known and ranges between 10 stades to the modern mile. A Stade was the length of the footrace of 600 feet at Olympia, which then came to mean the place where the footrace was run. The Stade from which we get the word stadium became used as a term of measure[2835] being a familiar term as we would to describe a distance e.g. it was the length of 50 football pitches etc.

Pytheas of Massalia gave distances in 'days of elapsed sailing times and not in measured stades.'[2836] Elapsed sailing times would take into account tides, currents and winds.

Pseudo-Skylax gave distances and Antion (Antipolis, Antibes) is given as the end of the first section of coast he describes from the Pillars of Hercules. He includes as a 'Hellenic city, Massalia with a harbour' and its colonies 'Olbia and Antion with a harbour'. Also mentioned is Massalia's colony in Spain Emporion. Rhodus and Agathe Tyche in Gaul are not mentioned. He gives the distance for the 'coastal voyage of Iberia: seven days and nights': the coastal voyage from the 'Rhodanos river as far as Antion is of days, *two*, and nights, *two*'.[2837] Furthermore he gives the sailing time for the whole length of Europe from the Pillars of Herakles to Tanais 'in place of the 500 stades *a day of a man sailing*-the coastal voyage of Europe becomes' 153 days.[2838]

Pomponius Mela wrote that a Stade was ⅛ of a Roman Mile. One Roman mile was 2000 paces counted off by a Roman Legion over level terrain.[2839]

For most people Strabo records there was 8 stades to a Roman mile. Polybius in his measurements adds two plethra making 8 ½ stades to a Roman mile. Therefore 40,000 stades equals 4,800 Roman miles.[2840]

Strabo gives the following distances: [2841]

- Temple of Pyrenaean Aphrodite to Narbo 63 Roman Miles.
- Narbo to Nemausus (Nimes) 88 Roman miles.
- Nemausus (Nimes) via Ugernum and Taruso to Sextian (Aqua Sextiae) near Massalia 53 Roman miles.
- Sextian to Antipolis (Antibes) and Varus River 73 Roman miles.

From Polybius we have,

> From the Ebro to Emporium it is about one thousand six hundred stades. From Emporium to Narbo it is about six hundred stades, and from Narbo to the Passage of the Rhône about sixteen hundred, this part of the road having now been carefully measured by the Romans and marked with milestones at every eighth stade. [2842]

Sailing Times

From Carthage on the African coast to Syracuse in Sicily the crossing is 260 nautical miles, two and a half days at 4.5 knots overall speed. Carthage to Gibraltar is 820 nautical miles; seven days at 4.9 knots speed overall. [2843]

Sailing times in the ancient world depend on the wind for sailing ships with only sail. Those with oars had greater control of direction. However, these ships were subject to seasonal winds as Strabo illustrates:

> Posidonius tells us that in his journey back from Spain he observed the singular phenomenon that in this sea, as far as the Gulf of Sardinia, the east winds blows continuously. On this account he strove in vain for the better part of three whole months to reach Italy, being driven by the wind to the Balearic Islands and Sardinia and the opposite shore of Africa.

Sailing under the island of Crete St. Paul reports a tempestuous wind that came up from the south-east called the Euroclydon. [2844]

Some voyages could be quick:

> Balibus went from Messina to Alexandria in six days. Valerius Maximus sailed from Peutoli to Alexandria *lenissimo flatu* in nine days, and the voyage from Gades to Ostia [port of Rome] took only seven days, in case the wind was favourable; that from Gades to Gallia Narbonensis (perhaps to Massalia), three days. [2845]

Pliny the Elder mentions sailing times under favourable winds Ostia to Provincia Narbonensis [Narbo] three days (345 nautical miles, overall speed 4.8 knots; Ostia to Gibraltar seven days (935 nautical miles, overall speed 5.6 knots). [2846]

Sulpicius Severus (*Dail,* 1.1.) mentions a prosperous trip he had from Alexandria to Narbo. He reached Massilia in thirty days (1500 nautical miles, overall speed 2.1 knots). Casson mentions that Severus was fortunate in making good time considering the usual unfavourable winds. Goitein in the eleventh century A.D. records a similar journey in distance Alexandria to Almeria that took 65 days.[2847] Sulpicius's journey from Narbo through the Gulf of Lion to the port of Africa (possibly Utica) 500 nautical miles, average 4.1 knots speed took five days. The course was south-east but as the prevailing winds were south-west this would have involved tacking (zigzag).[2848]

From Rome to Massalia over open water is estimated at four and a half to six days. Polybius (5.109–10) mentions Pisa to Massilia via the Ligurian coast was four and a half days (240 nautical miles, overall speed 2.2 knots). The northerly and north-westerly winds in this area would not be favourable for the first and last leg of the journey.[2849]

According to Xenophon it was a long day's voyage under oar for a trireme from Byzantium to Heraclea, 129 nm (236 km) along the Black Sea.[2850]

Early Explorers of the Atlantic

640–638 B.C. Colaeus of Samos

Colaeus was in a merchant vessel going to Egypt and blown off course in a storm beyond Gibraltar to Tartessos around the Mouth of River Baetis on the Atlantic coast of Spain. The Romans called the Guadalquiver the River Baetis but it had a different name before this.[2851] There were silver mines in the region, copper, with tin from South-West Britain. Archaeological evidence of Greek ceramics is found around the mouth of the Baetis from eighth century B.C.[2852] In 648 B.C. there was a dedication of Tartession bronze at Olympia, which showed contacts already being established.

Herodotus records that the voyage of Colaeus made enormous profits and

> From the tenth part of their gains, amounting to six talents, the Samians made a brazen vessel, in shape like an Argive wine-bowl, adorned with the heads of griffins standing out in high relief. This bowl, supported by three kneeling, colossal figures in bronze, of the height of seven cubits, was placed as an offering in the temple of Hera at Samos.[2853]

Evidence of Greeks in the Atlantic has been found with Greek Corinthian helmets: 650–625 B.C. dredged up from the Guadalette River, Cadiz, Spain in 1938:[2854] late 6th century B.C. found in the sea 50 miles away next to the Guadalquivir estuary near modern day Huelva:[2855] another in the Ria Huelva second half of 6th century B.C.

Midacritus (possibly from Phocaea)[2856] passed through the Straits of Gibraltar to get tin and according to Pliny the Elder[2857] he was 'the first to import lead from the Tin Land'. Pliny does not say when or how he travelled or who he was. Did he mean white lead that was a Latin variant name for tin?

The people from the isle of Samos did not follow up Colaeus's success.[2858] However, the skilful sailors of Phocaea did. With the route now firmly established it might have been this success that prompted the Phocaeans to form settlements/colonies at Massalia (Marseille, France) 600 B.C.,

Alalia (Aleria, Corsica) 565 B.C., Emporion (Ampuries, Spain) c. 600/575 B.C., Agathe Tyche (Agde, France) c. 580 B.C., and also in the sixth century B.C. Antipolis (Antibes, France) and Nikaia (Nice, France) to protect their new trade route. Just as other Greeks did 'In accordance with their practice elsewhere, they safeguarded their trade by founding colonies'.[2859]

Euthymenes of Massalia. Greek explorer, who in the late-sixth century to mid-fifth century B.C. travelled along the west coast of Africa as far as the River Senegal, and possibly as far as Ghana.[2860]

Hanno of Carthage. *Circa* end of the fifth century B.C. explored the west coast of Africa possibly as far as Sierra Leone and maybe beyond to Cameroun.[2861]

Himilco of Carthage, end of fifth century B.C. The Roman poet Avienus in the late fourth century A.D. described Himilco's journey in the poem *Ora Maritima*. As Avienus used eleven different sources and stories condensed into one explorer, we don't know which part Himilco actually did. In a four-month voyage he possibly explored the Sargasso Sea, Canary Islands and Cape Finisterra in Galicia, Spain. Details of places further north are so similar as to be the actual description of Pytheas's own voyage in the northern parts.[2862] Sources seem to include a Massaliote Periplus *circa* late sixth century B.C.;[2863] writings by Scymnos c. 110 B.C.; and another source was agreed as an older work of prose of Ephorus in the fourth century B.C. referring to a time older than the blocking of the Straits of Gibraltar to Greek ships c. 500 B.C. Ephorus died around 330 B.C. and not aware of Pytheas voyage.[2864]

The ancient Greeks regarded 'discoverers' as the first person to show it to their nation.[2865] In the modern time the word 'Discoverer' implies the first person to find. If we take the discovery of Australia for example the Dutch discovered the west coast in 1606 calling it New Holland. The Englishman William Dampier discovered the north-west coast in 1686 and the west coast in 1699. Captain James Cook discovered the east coast in 1770.[2866] It may be worthwhile to remember that when we say that Captain James Cook discovered Australia in 1770 and made maps this land was not empty of people. In fact Aborigines who had lived in the sub-continent of Australia for over 40,000 years populated this land. As they did not write we do not have the name of their own first discoverer of Australia. Oral memory has passed down the generations and preserved Aborigine folklore, myths and legends. But Captain Cook was amongst the first Europeans to find Australia and therefore discovered and made it known to the rest of the world.

Likewise Captain Columbus discovered America in 1492 while searching for a route to India though there is evidence that the Vikings may have been first in c. A.D. 1000 calling it Vinland.[2867] The land was not empty and therefore discovered by the natives, if they were not indigenous, but we do not have any name of their discoverer. However, Columbus is credited as the first European to have discovered the continent and made America known to the world.

When Pytheas of Massalia came to Britain it was not an empty land. He found it populated. We do not have the name of the first native person to have discovered it. However, Pytheas was the first known person from the Mediterranean to come to Britain and record his discoveries. Pytheas circumnavigated, measured and calculated the land mass and coastline. He also recorded the name of the people the *Pretani*. Following the usual convention he named the island after the people, and rightfully has the credit of being the first to do so. The island became known as *Prettanike* (Britain) and also *Bretannikai nisoi* Βρεταννικαὶ νήσοι (British islands).[2868]

However the native people, the *Pretani* (Britons), had their own name for the island and called it Albion. Later the Romans in their own language of Latin wrote *Prettanike* as Britannia and the *Pretani* as Britanni. We have the following recorded by the Roman writer Pliny the Elder:

'"Albion" was its own name when all [the islands] were called "the Britannias;"'[2869]

Albion ipsi nomen fuit, cum Britanniae vocarentur omnes de quibus mox paulo dicemus.

Pliny also writes,

'Across from this location Britannia Island (famed in Greek and in our own records)'.[2870]

Ex adverso huius situs Britannia insula, clara Graecis nostrisque monimentis.

Pillars of Hercules (Herakles)

Pindar the Greek poet wrote,

> If water is best, and gold the most revered of possessions,
> now Theron in his turn, by his deeds of merit,
> has travelled from his home to the world's limits
> and lays hold of the pillars of Heracles.
> Further than this neither simpletons or wise should go.
> I shall not venture there; I should be a fool to try. [2871]

The Pillars were thought to be the Straits of Gibraltar with Calpe (Rock of Gibraltar) and Abilyx (opposite on the African coast). Though there were some stories that the pillars were two bronze pillars eight cubits high in the temple of Heracles in Gades (Gaderia, Cadiz in Spain). Strabo [2872] argues that the pillars had inscriptions as to the expenses incurred in the construction of the temple and nothing about Hercules; it could not be there as Calpe and Abilyx (Ximiera) or the 'two isles near each mountain' one is 'called Hera's island' (not found today) actually 'denote the end and beginnings of regions' and the position of Gades does not. However, we do see that according to Appian that Fabius Maximus Aemilianus son of Aemilius Paulus was sent to Spain to levy an army and 'made a voyage through the Straits to Gades in order to sacrifice to Hercules'.[2873]

Early contact between the Greeks and Phoenicians identified Hercules with the Semitic god Ba'al Melqart. (There was a temple of Heracles in Tyre and Alexander the Great being refused entry to make sacrifice there laid siege to this Phoenician city). Gades was in the region controlled by Carthage. This would seem to emphasise the Melqart side of the story. [2874] But Lampriere writes in his *A Classical Dictionary* that Hercules was surnamed Gaditanus and the inhabitants of Gades were called Gaditani. His temple there was engraved with excellent workmanship of his twelve labours.[2875] There may have been actual pillars erected at Calpe as was done several times elsewhere and when in the course of time disappear just the name continued for example the Altars of the Philani (Strabo, III.5), 'The Altars of the Philaenus' [2876] originally the boundary between Carthage and Cyrene.[2877]

The Seven Sages of Greece

As well as Thales of Miletus these other six men were given the title Sage for their great knowledge; Bias of Priene, Chilon of Sparta, Ceobulus of Lindos, Periander of Corinth, Pittacus of Mitylene and Solon of Athens.

Diogenes Laertius writes that amongst the ancient Greeks

> There was a difference of opinion with respect to their number . . . Hermippus, in his *Treatise on the Wise Men* says that there were altogether seventeen . . . These seventeen were Solon, Thales, Pittacus, Bias, Chilon, Myson, Cleobulus, Periander, Anacharsis, Acusilaus, Epimenides, Leophantus, Pherecydes, Aristodemus, Pythagoras, Lasus the son of Charmantides, or Sisymbrinus, or as Aristoxenus calls him the son of Chabrinus, a citizen of Hermione, and Anaxagoras.

Hippobotus in his *Description of the Philosophers* added Myson and Orpheus to the following, 'Linus, Solon, Periander, Anacharsis, Cleobulus, Thales, Bias, Pittacus, Epicharmus, and Pythagoras'.[2878]

The Great Library of Alexandria and Pergamum Library

The Great Library at Alexandria in Egypt was based on Aristotle's Lyceum in Athens and Plato's Academy. It was Aristotle's pupil Demetrius who advised Greek king Ptolemy I of Egypt in setting up the library in Alexandria around 295 B.C.

Eratosthenes of Cyrene c. 274–194 B.C. was the Head of the Great Library of Alexandria and a polymath. He was the first man to calculate the circumference of the earth.[2879] Eratosthenes used Pytheas of Massalia's observations and calculations in developing the system of latitudes that we still use today.

The Great Library was said to have a half a million books. Books were in scrolls and kept in rolls. Any books found on ships docking at Alexandria had to be copied for the Great Library and stamped 'from the ships'.[2880] The library at Pergamum was started around 210 B.C. by Attalus I, and said to have had 200,000 books.[2881]

Rivalry between the two libraries increased and later Ptolemy V refused any exports of papyrus to Pergamum to write on. However, Eumenes II of Pergamum decided to use 'cured sheepskins' as the Ionians had done.[2882] This was parchment and called 'Pergamene paper'. As the skins were thicker than papyrus they could not be rolled as a scroll could. But they could be sewn and made into pages. This made it easier to read and gave us the form of the books we use today.[2883]

The Great Library was damaged in a fire caused by Julius Caesar's soldiers. Plutarch tells us that this was made up later with Mark Antony giving the entire book collection from the royal libraries of Pergamum, over 200,000 volumes, as a gift to Queen Cleopatra.[2884] Another fire destroyed the Great Library in A.D. 265 and its smaller Library at the Serapeum was destroyed in A.D. 391[2885] by the Christian Bishop Theophilus by command of Emperor Theodosius for the overthrow of pagan temples. Though Hyde mentions that according to Arab sources the 'treasures of this Library lasted until A.D. 651 when they were destroyed by the order of 'Amir, lieutenant of the caliph Omar and conqueror of Egypt.' [2886] Some scholars doubt this story and think it was Bishop Theophilus. There were also other periods of destruction i.e. between the occupation of Emperor Aurelian and the forces of Queen Zenobia of Palmyra A.D. 270-271. Aurelian burnt down the Brucheion (Royal Quarter) in which the Great library was situated. [2887] It is thought that a number of books were looted during Theophilus's action: and also believed that the Arabs translated several books before burning the originals: and that a number of other books made their way to monasteries in Italy still there today. [2888] However there is no archaeological evidence, no papyri nor even a burnt (carbonised) one, for a date of destruction. There is only a reference of a carbonised papyrus found by an engineer in the nineteenth century who unfortunately dumped it at Kom el-Dikka. The humid conditions in Alexandria make it unlikely to find any but in contrast outside of the city many hundreds of other papyri have been found preserved by the dry conditions of the desert. [2889]

With the introduction of lowercase miniscule Greek in the ninth century A. D. and joined up writing many original parchment books in uncial text (the uppercase of entirely capital letters) were re-used by Byzantines as parchment was expensive. The parchment had a thin layer with the text taken off with a razor! Patriarch Photius (c. A.D. 810–893) wrote the *Biblioteca* or *Myriobiblon* (possibly when in exile at Baghdad) a review of over 280 original ancient Greek books and only this survives today for many of these lost books. Fortunately X-Ray technology on one of the re-used books has been able to detect a faint trace of the original writing underneath the present text. There was an exciting discovery of the 'Archimedes Palimpsest' that includes underneath the later writing some ancient texts of Archimedes and Hyperides being revealed by the Stanford Synchrotron Radiation Laboratory. [2890]

There were other smaller libraries and private collections across the Hellenistic and later Roman world [2891] that may have had Pytheas of Massalia's book *On the Ocean*. As these libraries disappeared many books may have been buried or were copied by Arabs in Baghdad [2892] and also by monks and scholars in the East Roman (Byzantine) Empire. With its capital at Constantinople (Istanbul) the East Roman Empire lasted a thousand years more than the West Roman Empire until captured by the Ottoman Turks in A.D. 1493 [2893] Somewhere between the empire and India and beyond in China, maybe translated in a Moslem, Hindu or Buddhist manuscript or even in the West, under the Kremlin (Princess Sophia Paleologue's lost library) [2894] or from the Renaissance in monasteries and libraries perhaps there are later copies of Greek or Latin books from the ancient world waiting to be found.

Chronology and Biography

Minoan c. 2,200–1400 B.C. A civilization from Crete, who wrote in the Linear A script [2895] and a leading sea power in the Aegean, before being taken over by the Mycenaean Greeks.

Mycenaean c. 1400–1200 B.C. This period saw the development of trade in the Mediterranean under the Mycenaeans from mainland Greece. The Mycenaeans wrote in Linear B script. According to Homer's epic poem *The Iliad* the Mycenaean's led the Greeks in the ten-year Trojan War.

Dark Ages in Greece c. 1100–900 B.C.

Circa **1050–950 B.C.** Aeolians, Ionians, and Dorians from Greece colonised the coast of Asia Minor.

Homer c. eighth century B.C. Greek poet. He wrote epic poems notably *The Iliad*, and *The Odyssey* and considered to be the founder of the science of geography. [2896] There were many studies done on *The Odyssey* and whether part of Odysseus's travels took place in the Atlantic. His poems were taught in ancient Greek schools as they were considered to contain knowledge and morals that one could use in life.

The Oracle at Delphi had lapsed from giving prophesy in verse and during the second century A.D. the Roman Emperor Hadrian started the hexameter responses again when he asked the question of where Homer came from and who were his parents? The Pythia's replied,

> Do you ask me of the unknown family and native land of that ambrosial siren? By dwelling he belongs to Ithaca, and Telemachus was his father, and Epicaste, the daughter of Nestor, his mother, who bore him very omniscient among men. [2897]

Scholars have still preferred Chios, Ios, or Smyrna [2898] as the possible birthplaces of Homer.

Regarding *The Iliad* there were other versions like Palinode by Stesichorus [2899] that said Helen and Paris were not at Troy when attacked by the Greeks and in Egypt at the house of Proteus. [2900]

Arcintos of Miletus c. eighth century B.C. Greek poet who wrote the epic poems Aethiopis, and Iliu Persis or Sack of Troy.

City of Miletus (on the coast of Asia Minor)
During 770–570 B.C. the Greek city of Miletus established at least 80 colonies/settlements on the Black Sea coast and Mediterranean. Miletus was a centre of ideas using Egyptian geometry, Sumerian algebra and Assyrian astronomy. [2901] According to Pliny the Elder Miletos Μίλητος (Latin *Miletus*) sent out more than ninety colonies. [2902]

Thales of Miletus, c. 620s B.C.–c. 546 B.C. Greek, Sage and scientist. He showed it was possible to calculate the height of an object by measuring its shadow and comparing it with the shadow cast of a measuring stick. He made formulas of basic rules and proved it works in all cases. These, the mathematicians could call proofs. He is credited with six geometric propositions. Thales successfully predicted the eclipse of 28 May 585 B.C. [2903] and impressed his compatriots by predicting a bumper crop of olives. [2904] To prove his point he bought up all the olive presses in advance hiring them out at harvest time making a lot of money thereby showing another practical use for astronomy.

He was known as one of the Seven Sages of Greece. Unfortunately he died of sunstroke while watching the games at Miletus or Olympia as the spectators had to be bare headed to watch all athletic games. [2905] Sadly this is a case where an inflexible tradition prevailed over common sense.

Thales, Anaximander and Anaximenes started the process of looking at the world and explaining it not from mythological origins (mythos) but from theoretical thinking (logos), away from superstition to fact. [2906] Thales is assumed to have made the experiment with amber (elektron) and actually discovered 'static electricity'. [2907] Though we do not know exactly what he thought it was in line with his current theory of the soul and animated objects. [2908] Students of Thales included, Euclid, Pythagoras, and Eudemus. [2909]

Diogenes Laertius records this was put on Thales tomb,

> You see this tomb is small–but recollect,
> The fame of Thales reaches to the skies.

and he follows with an epigram of his own,

> O mighty sun our wisest Thales sat
> Spectator of the games, when you did seize upon him;
> But you were right to take him near yourself,
> Now that his aged sight could hardly reach to heaven. [2910]

Anaximander of Miletus. Born c. 610 B.C. Greek, pupil of Thales and a Philosopher. He was the first Greek to publish a map of the known world. (The Babylonian's had illustrated their known world on a clay map height: 12.200 cm x width: 8.200 cm, 700–500 B.C.). [2911] He is credited with introducing the gnomon (measuring staff) to the Greek world from Babylon. A gnomon's shadow from the sun at noon established a north-south line, or meridian (merides = noon). [2912] Gregory suggests he was probably the first to solve the problem of the equinoxes and the middle point position during the solstices and therefore improving on the Babylonian invention. [2913]

His two famous pupils were Anaximenes of Miletus 585–525 B.C. and Pythagoras of Samos c. 582-507 B.C.

Hecataeus of Miletus c. 546–c. 480 B.C. Greek, Geographer, Historian, Mythologist. He wrote *Ges Peridos* (in 2 volumes) containing a periplus on Europe and one on Asia. A first century A.D. copy of the Periplus of Asia still survives. Amongst fragments are details of an improved map of the world based on Anaximander's map. [2914] Apparently the map does not survive and all present maps are reconstructions based on the details found from the fragments and other authors. [2915] That is why some maps include the Tin Islands and other details while others reconstructions do not. Though only fragments remain it was thought to have been a prototype of many later periploi or coastal surveys. He covered the area between Tartessos in Spain to the Black Sea to Tanais (River Don), the Persian Gulf, Egypt and the edge of the Sahara, and was the first Greek to mention India, the Indus, and the Gandarae (in the middle of the Punjab): [2916]

Hecataeus tried to dissuade the Ionians from revolt against Persia (500 B.C.), and in 494, when they were obliged to sue for terms; he was one of the ambassadors to the Persian satrap, whom he persuaded to restore the constitution of the Ionic cities. [2917]

Aristagoras, Tyrant of Miletus, went to Sparta to see King Cleomenes to request their support in the Ionian Revolt. He 'produced a bronze tablet, whereupon the whole circuit of the earth was engraved, with all its seas and rivers'. [2918] He may have had the up to date map of Hecataeus *pinax*. [2919]

Euthymenes of Massalia (in Gaul, France). *Circa* mid-sixth century B.C. Greek explorer of the coast of West Africa sometime during the late sixth century to mid-fifth century B.C. He reached as far as the River Senegal. A modern statue of him is displayed at the Bourse in Marseille (Massalia) in commemoration of his achievements along with Pytheas of Massslia and the names of other great explorers. [2920] Pseudo-Galen credits Euthymenes with the theory of the spring tides being connected by the alignment of the earth, moon and sun while Aetios gives Pytheas of Massalia the credit. [2921]

Stesichorus of Himera (in Sicily) c. 632/629–c. 556/553 B.C. Greek, Lyric Poet. Possibly his name was Teisias but was called by the name of his profession 'instructor of choruses' Stesichorus. [2922] He was an outstanding poet that established the Greeks from the Western Mediterranean colonies amongst the great poets of mainland Greece. He gives one of the earliest references to Tartessos and its silver.

Xenophanes of Colophon c. 570–c. 475 B.C. Greek Philosopher, Poet, and Theologian. From 25 years old he travelled. Xenophanes possibly went to Cyrnus (Corsica) arriving with the Phocaeans who had fled the Persian invasion of Ionia 546 B.C. In surviving fragments he also writes of the Phocaean settlement of Elea in Italy c. 540 B.C. and was probably the source for Herodotus. [2923]

Pindar c. 518–438 B.C. Greek. He was a lyric poet writing the Epincian Odes and choral songs praising the victories in the Games at Olympia, Delphi, Nemea and Corinth, and covers the spectrum of Greek moral order. [2924] He records Greek attitudes and ideas on North Europe of his time.

Skylax of Caryanda, Greek from Caria. During 519 to 512 B.C. he was sent by Darius I of Persia to explore the Indus River. Starting from Caspatyrus in Pactyica, [2925] East Afghanistan, [2926] he reached then sailed across the Indian Ocean to the Red Sea and to the Isthmus of Heroonopolis (Suez) reporting back to Darius. The journey took two and a half years. [2927] He is attributed with writing a life of *Heraclides of Mylasa* (a contemporary from Caria) c. 480 B.C (mentioned in Herodotus 5.121).

The *Periplus of Pseudo-Skylax* was written later during the fourth century B.C. possibly as a reconnaissance of the coasts of the Persian Empire for King Philip II of Macedon [2928] and probably based on the previous exploration of Sklyax of the sixth–fifth century B.C. The periplus attributed to Skylax according to Shipley was not by him but an unknown author of the fourth century B.C. [2929] Skylax may have been the first westerner to explore a part of India though Hecataeus of Miletus was the first to write about it. [2930] Their partial information of India may have contributed to Alexander the Great's expedition in underestimating the unknown distance to find the Eastern Ocean. [2931]

Thucydides, Greek. Born c. 460–454 and died in 399 B.C. He commanded an Athenian trireme defending Amphipolis against Sparta, and wrote the *'History of the Peloponnesian War'* (between Athens and Sparta) an invaluable source book. He mentions briefly a naval battle between Massalia and Carthage.

Herodotus of Halicarnassus c. 480–425 B.C. A Greek historian known as 'the father of history' he wrote an invaluable source book called the *Histories*. He was a founding father of the town of Thurii in South Italy (Magna Graecia). Herodotus wrote of the Phocaeans trade with Tartessos; fleeing Ionia from the Persian invasion; and their colonies at Corsica, Elea and Massalia.

Antiochus of Syracuse, fifth century B.C. A Greek who wrote a highly praised history of Sicily and Italy from earliest period to 444 B.C.[2932] Thucydides, Dionysius of Halicarnassus, Strabo and [2933] Pausanias also uses him as a source. [2934] Only fragments of his original works exist. He gives one of the earliest references to Massalia.

Eudoxus of Cnidus, c. 408–c. 355 B.C. [2935] A leading Greek mathematician and astronomer of his day.[2936] The theory made by Eudoxus regarding the position of the North Pole was corrected by Pytheas of Massalia during his voyage into the North Atlantic and confirmed later by Hipparkhos of Nikaia (Hipparchus of Nicaea) the mathematical astronomer. [2937] This confirmation by Hipparkhos verified the great skill Pytheas of Massalia had as an accurate astronomer and mathematician.

Pytheas of Massalia, (Marseille in Gaul, France). A fourth century B.C. Greek explorer, scientist, astronomer and philosopher who fixed the latitude of his home city of Massalia (Marseille on the French coast) at 43°3'25"N. (With the semi-diameter of the sun added this makes the present 43°17'N almost exactly as the present Marseille observatory). [2938]

He studied the 'Boiling Sea' of the volcanic Aeolian Islands near Sicily. Pytheas discovered Britain, named it Britain and recorded the name of its people, circumnavigated and declared Britain triangular in shape, calculated Britain's coastline as 40,000 stades = 7,500 km, estimated its landmass with 2.5 per cent accuracy. Discovered and named several islands around Britain and in the North Atlantic including Thule (Iceland), and Abalus the Amber Island, saw the frozen Congealed Sea and Arctic Circle, calculated the position of the North Pole. His observations added to theory that the earth was a sphere and the tides were affected by the moon and may have been referring to spring tides when the earth, moon and sun are in alignment. He wrote a book of his discoveries called *On the Ocean* presently lost, but several fragments with quotes found in other books by eighteen ancient authors do survive; including the five measurements he took from gnomon readings, sun heights and positions of the stars that prove he made the journey into the North Atlantic. Dicaearchus, Eratosthenes and Hipparchus used his calculations in forming the system of parallels of latitude to map the earth, the same we still use today.

A modern statue of Pytheas is displayed at the Bourse in Marseille (Massalia) in commemoration of his achievements along with Euthymenes of Massalia and the names of the other great explorers.

Aristotle 382–322 B.C. Born in Stagira, Macedonia. A Greek, philosopher and polymath, pupil of Isocrates and Plato, tutor to Alexander the Great; founded the Lyceum in Athens, and the Peripatetic school of philosophy.

He wrote many books and these on:
- science–*The History of Animals, On the Parts of Animals*
- physical and astronomical conceptions–*De Caelo, Physica, Meteorologica*, (these ideas held sway for 2,000 years until being mostly superseded with new discoveries)
- nature of existence–*The Metaphysics*
- literary criticism–*The Rhetoric, The Poetics*
- logic–*Organon*
- morals and conduct–*The Nicomachaen Ethics*
- scientific psychology–*De Anima, Parva Naturalia*
- an examination of 158 political systems–*Politics*
- *On the Magnet*–now lost
- *Constitution of Massalia* now lost but used by Strabo [2939] and parts quoted by Athenaeus in his book *Deipnosophistai*.

Demosthenes c. 384/383 B.C.–322 B.C. Greek. A famous Athenian orator whose many speeches survived including the *Olynthiacs*, and the *Philippic* trying to halt the growing power of King Philip II of Macedon. He was later exiled and then recalled after the death of Alexander the Great. In *Private Orations* there is a court case between him and Massaliote Zenothemis who laid claim to his cargo of grain that Demosthenes had bought from Sicily and transported on a Massaliote ship with a crew from Massalia.[2940]

Isocrates c. 436–338 B.C. A Greek whose Literary School rivalled Plato's Academy. Aristotle first studied there before going to Plato's Academy. Isocrates taught political science and oratory but never spoke in the Assembly or courts due to a weak voice. He wrote pamphlets on issues of the day instead. His school obtained a Pan-Hellenic reputation with pupils from all over the world. He wisely saw that the Greek city-states were wasting their strength by warring against each other. He wrote an open letter in 346 B.C. to King Philip II of Macedon as a man who could bring the city-states together for a common purpose and annexing part, if not all, of the Persian Empire, where they could settle the excess of mercenaries and population. [2941] King Philip eventually became Captain General of Greece and started the invasion but was murdered. The invasion of the Persian Empire was continued and completed by his son Alexander the Great. Isocrates briefly compares Athens to Massalia.

Aristoxenus of Tarentum. Born c. 364 B.C.[2942] a Greek Peripatetic philosopher and a pupil of Aristotle. Aristoxenus produced 453 books. He wrote on Ethics, Philosophy, and Music. His reference to Massalia comes from a surviving fragment of his *Histories*.

Dicaearchus of Messene, active in Athens between 326–296 B.C. A Greek geographer, astronomer and a pupil at the Lyceum in Athens who wrote *Circuit of the Earth* mapping the known world based on a parallel running through Rhodes. [2943] While doubting Pytheas's discoveries that land could be inhabited so far north he accepted Pytheas of Massalia's calculations as accurate from a respected fellow astronomer and was one of the first to use them.

Timaeus of Tauromenium (in Sicily), Greek. He was active in Athens between 330–280 B.C., a notable historian of the Western Greek states and a pupil at the Lyceum Athens. Timaeus in 261 B.C. used the dates of the Olympic Games to place other facts and events of the past as a steady base of event chronology. [2944] Timaeus's dating system lasted into the sixth-century A.D. when Dionysius Exiguus a Scythian monk or abbot adopted the system we use today. [2945]

Timaeus was one of the first to write about Pytheas of Massalia's discoveries. This spread the story to Alexandria where Timaeus's writings were also fashionable. His writings were still held in regard 200 years later by Roman orator Cicero (106–43 B.C.) and would have been amongst books read by the Roman elite who had a Greek education including Julius Caesar. Pliny the Elder used Timaeus's references to Pytheas in his books *Natural Histories*.

Theophrastus. c. 372/372–c. 287/286 B.C.[2946] Greek botanist who took over running the Lyceum after Aristotle.

Hecataeus of Abdera, c. latter fourth century B.C. Greek historian accompanied Ptolemy I Soter on an expedition to Syria. He wrote the *Aegyptiaca* and *Concerning the Hyperboreans* that Diodorus Siculus used as a source for his own book. Hecataeus may have based his account of the Hyperboreans from the book by Pytheas of Massalia *On the Ocean*.

Cleitarchos of Alexandria, c. 315–300 B.C. Greek historian. He wrote an account of Alexander the Great.

Eratosthenes of Cyrene. c. 274–194 B.C. He was the Head of the Great Library of Alexandria, polymath; astronomer, geographer, chronographer, geometer, grammarian, poet, and historian of comedy. As he did so many things he was called 'pentathlos', and also 'beta' as he ranked second to the others. This may have been in the vein of 'Jack of all trades master of none' or a little jealousy as he was so good at all he applied himself to. He was actually the best brain of his time and the founder of astronomical geography. [2947]

Eratosthenes wrote the 'Geographica' in three volumes. He was the first man to calculate the circumference of the earth. He based his calculations on the earth being a perfect sphere when in fact it is a spheroid being compressed at the Poles. [2948] Vitruvius the Roman architect and engineer wrote in the first century B.C.,

> Remembering, however, that Eratosthenes of Cyrene, employing mathematical theories and geometrical methods, discovered from the course of the sun, the shadows cast by an equinoctial gnomon, and the inclination of the heaven that the circumference of the earth is two hundred and fifty-two thousand stadia. [2949]

Eratosthenes calculated the circumference of the earth at 25,000 miles (the circumference through the poles is 24,860 miles). His linear measurements were in Stades. The value of a stade is not known exactly but ranges between 10 stades to a modern mile. Therefore 5,000 stades divided by 10 was approximately 500 modern miles. [2950] He improved the idea of latitude to define your position on the earth originally used by Dicaearchus and included Pytheas of Massalia calculations.

Apollonius of Rhodes, born c. 295 and died after 247 B.C. He was a Greek poet who wrote the epic poem the *Argonautika* about Jason and the Golden Fleece. Surviving copies are a redaction made by unknown grammarian known only as the Scholiast to Apollonius around fourth century A.D. who compiling three contemporary commentators quotes Pytheas of Massalia's book together with his comments on the volcanic Aeolian Islands and the boiling sea.

Sosylus of Lacaedomaia (also known as Sosylus of Sparta). *Circa* third century B.C. Greek. He was tutor to Hannibal. He wrote an account of Hannibal's life and of the naval Battle of the Ebro 217 B.C. 'Together with Silenus of Caleacte accompanied Hannibal "quandiu fortuna passa est", and taught him Greek', (Nepos, *Hann*. 13.3) according to Diodorus (xxvi.4) he wrote about Hannibal Τα Περι Αννιβαν in seven books. A Wurzburg papyrus (FGH 176, F I) contains part of an account of a naval battle at the mouth of the Ebro (95–99n,) by Sosylus. [2951] Here Massalia's naval tactics was crucial to the Roman victory over the Carthaginian Navy led by Hasdrubal. Hasdrubal was Hannibal's brother and this vital victory prevented him sending supplies and men to Hannibal in Italy and gave Rome control of the coast around the Ebro.

Hipparkhos of Nikaia, (Hipparchus of Nicaea), in Bithynia (now Iznik in Turkey) c. late second century B.C. Greek. As a mathematical astronomer he calculated the distance of the earth to the moon at about 250,000 miles. He was remarkably close with 11,000 miles difference as the moon is 238,857 miles from earth. Only one of his many books survives, Hipparchus, *Commentaries on the Phaenomena of Aratus and Eudoxus*.

Hipparkhos invented the astrolabe, which was divided into 360 degrees and a rotating arm fixed at the centre. This made it possible while at sea, unlike a gnomon, of measuring latitude 'by observing the angle of the Pole Star'. [2952] He extended the system of latitudes from Eratosthenes and Dikaiarkhos (Dicaearchus). Hipparkhos was first to use trigonometry and convert Pytheas's calculations into Latitude proving he was correct and in those locations to have taken the measurements.

Polybios, (Polybius) 200–118 B.C. Greek Historian, who wrote best surviving account of the rise of Roman Empire in 40 volumes called *Histories*. He explored the western coasts of Africa and Spain with a fleet of ships in 146 B.C. given to him by his Roman friend Scipio Aemilianus (conqueror of Carthage). Polybios quoted Pytheas of Massalia's book *On the Ocean* attempting to dismiss those discoveries by promoting his own as the Atlantic's first explorer though Pytheas had preceded him by 150 years, which other writers like the astronomers Hipparkhos and Eratosthenes acknowledged. While Pytheas had used a P Prettanike Πρεττανική for Britain, Polybios was the earliest known to spell Britain with the initial letter B Βρεταννικαὶ νῆσοι Bretannic Islands. As his books on Roman history was more likely to have been read in Rome the Romans probably followed his spelling.

Poseidonius of Apameia, (Posidonius of Apamea) c. 135–c. 50 B.C. Greek polymath and stoic philosopher, second only to Aristotle in influence. His books were quoted by other ancient writers, such as Cicero, Livy, Plutarch, Strabo, Cleomedes, Seneca the Younger, and Diodorus Siculus. He was a Prytaneis (president), for six months of Rhodes, and ambassador to Rome 87–86 B.C. [2953] Cicero, and Pompey the Great visited him in Rhodes. Pompey as a mark of respect lowered the Fascia in front of Poseidonius's house. Poseidonius also studied the tides at Gades on the Atlantic coast of Spain and thought the moon influenced them. Strabo in his writings reproached Poseidonius for using the reports of Pytheas of Massalia. [2954]

Crattes of Mallus, a Greek grammarian, second century B.C. also known as Crattes 'Homericos' for his attention to the Homeric Poems. He was a stoic philosopher and leader of the literary school and head of the library at Pergamum. He was principally opposed to Aristarchus leader of the Alexandrian school. Crattes was the ambassador of Attalus II, king of Pergamum to Rome in 170 B.C. While in Rome he broke his leg and during this extended stay started giving lectures that first stimulated the Romans to the study of grammar and criticism. [2955] He was said to have made one of the earliest globes bearing a map of the earth c. 150 B.C. A coin issued by the Roman patrician Lucius Aemilius Buca in 44 B.C. shows a picture derived from the Globe of Crattes on the obverse with the earth divided into four parts by crossed oceans. [2956]

Aristarchus of Samothrace, Head of the Library in Alexandria after 180 B.C. There were several undated Homeric texts known as *politikai* or 'city editions' including one from Massalia referred to as *ekdóseis* 'editions'. Aristarchus of Samothrace classified them as 'khariéstatai most-elegant' and he included them with those texts 'edited' by previous scholars. Aristarchus produced two recensions on the texts and commentaries on these editions. Parts of these texts by Aristarchus survived to the twelfth century A.D. in the 'Commentary on Homer', both *The Iliad* and *The Odyssey,* written by Eustathios, bishop of Thessaloniki and the 'Scholia A of the Venetian codex of Homer's *Iliad'.*

Diodorus Siculus, date of birth and death not established but writing between 60–30 B.C.[2957] A Greek Historian, who wrote the *Library of History*, though no direct quotes of Pytheas of Massalia, his descriptions of British Isles and North Atlantic come from him via Timaeus of Tauromenium who was one of the first to use Pytheas of Massalia. Other sources he used were the later fourth century B.C. Hecataeus of Abdera, particularly on the Hyperboreans and also Posidonius who according to Strabo did use Pytheas of Massalia as he reproaches him for doing so.

Cicero, 106–43 B.C. the famous Roman orator, whose literary output was also prolific. He was an essayist, politician, Consul and Governor. Cicero wrote the *Defence Speeches, the Nature of the Gods, On Obligations, The Republic* and *The Laws* amongst many other surviving publications.

A pupil of Posidonius and fluent in Greek, he was reported to be the first Roman to give Latin names to Greek philosophical words [2958] and studied with Greek philosophers in Athens, Asia and Rhodes.[2959] Cicero appreciated the writings of Timaeus, which included Pytheas of Massalia's discoveries. The knowledge of Pytheas was still known in Rome contemporary with Caesar. Cicero mentions Massalia in six different speeches and states that without Massalia's help Rome's generals would never have triumphed over the Gallic tribes beyond Transalpine Gaul.

Julius Caesar, 100 B.C.–44 B.C. Consul of Rome. As Governor he discovered his military genius and enlarged the Roman Empire. Rivalry with Pompey caused a civil war and made the action 'crossing the Rubicon' a point of no return in our language. In honour of his many military victories he was made Dictator for life.

As Pontifex Maximus he reformed the calendar with the help of Sosigenes. He gained this knowledge from the Egyptians while in Egypt restoring Cleopatra to the throne. The intercalary months were in disorder as 'the Romans reckoned the year by the moon. Caesar changed it to the Sun's course as the Egyptians reckoned it'.[2960] He used the 365 and ¼ days from their religious and scientific calendar and not the incomplete vulgar or common year that the ordinary Egyptians used.[2961] Julius Caesar changed the beginning of the year from 1 March to 1 of January because that was the time for 'changing the supreme magistrate'. Later, after he was assassinated, the month of July was named after him.

Caesar wrote several books including [2962] *Civil War* that was fought against Pompey the Great, which includes the siege and capture of Massalia in 49 B.C. and *Gallic Wars* an account that includes both of his invasions of Britain in 55 and 54 B.C. Julius Caesar divided up the territories of Massalia between Arles and Frejus leaving Massalia as an independent city in control of Nice, Olbia, the Stoechades Islands and Athenopolis from its former empire. He uses Pytheas of Massalia's names for the Isle of Man (*Mona*), Kent (Latin *Cantium*, Greek *Kantion*), Britain (Latin *Britannia*, Greek *Prettanike* and also probably via Polybius *Bretannic islands* Βρεταννικαὶ νῆσοι)[2963] and Britons (Latin *Britanni*, Greek *Pretani*).

Marcus Terentius Varro 116–27 B.C. Roman scholar, satirist and polymath also known as Varro Reatinus to distinguish him from his younger contemporary Varro Atacinus who was also a Roman scholar and writer. Marcus Terentius Varro wrote an estimated 75 works in 600 volumes on all aspects of learning. Carried out public and roles and was legate for Pompey in Spain and fought at Pharsalus in the Civil War. Varro was pardoned by Caesar who then made him the director of the proposed public library. When Caesar was assassinated, Varro was on Mark Antony's list of enemies of the state and saved by intervention of Octavian. Varro spent the rest of his years reading and writing in seclusion.[2964] Varro made the comment of Massalia as a tri-lingual city.

Vitruvius. 116–27 B.C. A Roman architect and engineer: in his *Ten Books on Architecture* he describes the siege of Massalia in 49 B.C. (by Julius Caesar) and because of the details he gives may have been at the siege himself.

Timagenes of Alexandria. First century B.C. Greek historian who wrote a *Universal History* and *The History of the Gauls* now lost but used as a source by Ammianus Marcellinus.

Isidorus of Charax, c. first century B.C. Greek, geographer. A surviving book is called *Parthian Stations*.[2965] Pliny the Elder quotes Isidorus together with Pytheas of Massalia about the circumference of Britain.[2966]

Strabo, Geographer and Historian 64 B.C.–A.D. 24, Greek. He wrote a *History* now lost and *Geography* with seventeen books surviving. *Geography* became out of circulation until rediscovered six centuries later. In trying to dismiss Pytheas's discoveries on the 'inhabitable zones' as fantasy he quoted and discussed sections from Pytheas of Massalia book *On the Ocean* that included the measurements and calculations Pytheas had taken on his voyage.

Trogus Pompeius Latin historian writing in 10 B.C whose work the *Historiae Phillippicae* the original now lost is largely excerpted and surviving in the works of Justin in the second or third century A.D. His work contains information of Massalia from its earliest foundation onwards. Trogus Pompeius's forefathers were of Vocontian origin (Celtic) in Gallia Narbonensis and neighbours of Massalia. His grandfather received Roman citizenship from Pompey the Great in the war against Sertorius, his uncle was a cavalry squadron leader with Pompey against Mithridates VI. Trogus Pompeius's father served under Gaius Caesar and was responsible for his diplomatic missions, correspondence and seal.

Valerius Maximus. A Roman writer who flourished c. A.D. 30 and wrote the *Nine Books of Memorable Deeds and Sayings* for use by schools of rhetoric in which he describes some of the customs of Massalia.

Pliny the Elder, A.D. 23–79. He was a Roman Governor of Spain and Commander of the fleet. He died when investigating the volcanic eruption of Mt. Vesuvius. He was well known for not wasting a waking moment in the pursuit of knowledge. A prolific writer of over 160 books, and forty volumes called *Natural Histories* that included discussion and quotes on the discoveries of Pytheas of Massalia in three of the volumes. Pliny names his sources in considerable detail in Book I and Strabo did not appear.[2967] Pliny is an invaluable independent source regarding Pytheas of Massalia.[2968]

Silius Italicus, A.D. 26-102 was Roman consul in A.D. 68 and a poet who wrote the longest surviving poem in Latin literature the *Punica* on the Second Punic War. He writes a brief description of the people of Massalia

Geminos of Rhodes, c. A.D. 50. A Greek astronomer who quoted and used Pytheas of Massalia's calculations in his own book *Introduction to Celestial Phenomena*.

Lucan, A.D. 39–65 Roman. A prolific poet only the epic *Pharsalia* survives. The poem is about the Roman civil war between Pompey the Great and Julius Caesar. Lucan describes the war and reveals its horrors and foolishness of all wars. He describes in Book III. 298–762 the siege and in detail one of the two naval battles of Massalia when allied to Pompey. The conflict ended in Massalia's first defeat in 551 years.

Livy, 59 B.C.–A.D. 17. A Roman historian who wrote the *History of Rome* consisting of 142 books of which only thirty-five survive. He includes the [2969] first arrival of the Phocaeans and foundation of Massalia during the reign of King Tarquinius Priscus 616–578 B.C. when Rome was still under the Etruscan monarchy.

Tacitus, c. A.D. 55–120. Roman historian wrote *The Histories, The Annals, Germania*, and *Agricola* (who was his father-in-law). He mentions Massalia as the place where Agricola studied philosophy.

Appian, c. A.D. 95–165. A Greek from Alexandria. He moved to Rome where he became a barrister and later a Procurator. He wrote his *Roman Histories* in twenty-four volumes and nine books survive complete with fragments of the others. Most valuable are Books 13–17 which describe the Civil Wars between 146–70 B.C. Appian mentions 'the other Greeks' living in Spain.

Plutarch of Chaeronea, c. A.D. 46–120. Greek Historian, biographer and essayist. He wrote *The Lives of the Noble Grecians and Romans*. The translation by Thomas North was one of the best English proses of the sixteenth century and was used by Shakespeare as a main source for his plays Julius Caesar, Coriolanus, and Antony & Cleopatra. Plutarch (Julius Caesar, 63, p. 524) uses Strabo in his information. Plutarch shows us at the time of Julius Caesar's invasion of Britain that many ancient writers still did not believe Britain existed, thinking it was a 'fable or lie'. The words 'fable or lie' are the same Strabo uses when talking of Pytheas of Massalia's voyage of exploration.

Pomponius Mela first century A.D. Roman geographical writer. He mentions a description of the island of Thoule with very long days and short nights at the summer solstice.

Suetonius first century A.D. Roman Biographer. *Lives of the Caesars* was one of his major works and the novelistic interpretation of Suetonius by Robert Graves was the basis of the classic B.B.C. TV Roman serial 'I, Claudius' (and subsequently become the basis of the worldwide hit American TV series 'Dynasty' starring British actress Joan Collins).[2970]

Pausanias, Flourished c. A.D. 143–175. A Greek geographer who wrote the valuable travel guide *Description of Greece* and records Massalia's prosperity and bronze statues at Delphi.

Athenaeus c. A.D. 160–230 was a Greek from Naucratis, Egypt who lived in Rome. He wrote *Deipnosophistai* (Professors at the Dinner Table); seven of the fifteen books survive. They are important for he quoted many other ancient writers whose works have not survived including Aristotle's 'Constitution of Massalia'.

Cassius Dio, born between A.D. 155 and 164. A Roman Historian also called Cassius Dio Cocceianus (or in Greek 'Dion o Kassios'). He wrote a Roman history in 80 volumes many survived intact and as fragments. His volumes are published as *Dio's Roman History*. Cassius Dio was also a Senator, Governor of Smyrna, and a Consul of Rome.

Lucian of Samosata. c. A.D. 125–c. 180. A Syrian who wrote in Greek and became a well-travelled Rhetorician with several of his books surviving: including *Toxaris or Friendship* that has the story of Zenothemis of Massalia. [2971]

Oppian (of Corycus or Anazarba in Cilicia). Possibly a Greek writing in the second century A.D. He dedicated his poem the *Halieutica* (app. 3,500 lines) to Marcus Aurelius, Roman emperor A.D. 161-180 and his son Commodius. He used similes within the art of fishing to explain absolute power. [2972] In the *Halieutica* Oppian mentions 'the Holy city of Massilia'.

Aelian c. A.D. 175–c. 235. A Roman writer fluent in Greek who wrote *De natura animalium* 'On the Characteristics of Animals' in seventeen books, *Various Histories* and twenty epistles and some fragments of other works survive. In *De natura animalium* he mentions Homer's text of *The Odyssey* and his source is Charmis of Massalia.[2973] Aelian gives a reference to the swans appearing at the Hyperborean temple. [2974]

Justin, second or third century A.D. Roman historian, whose book *Historiae Philippicae* largely excerpted from the lost work of Trogus Pompeius a Latin historian writing in 10 B.C. Trogus Pompeius's forefathers were of Vocontian origin (Celtic) in Gallia Narbonensis and neighbours of Massalia.

Solinus, was a Roman encyclopaedic geographer c*irca* A.D. 250 who wrote about the sailing distances from Caledonia and Orkney to Thule (Gaius Julius Solinus, *Collectanea Rerum Memorabilium* (ed.). Th. Mommsen, 2d, ed., Berlin, 1958).

Ammianus Marcellinus, c. A.D. 330–d. 395. A Greek from a noble family in Antioch, served in the Roman Army. Around 390 he wrote the *Res Gestae* a Latin history in thirty-one books from Nerva to Valens (96 B.C.–A.D. 378) with eighteen books surviving.[2975] He used as a source Timagenes of Alexandria first century B.C.[2976] a Greek historian who wrote a *Universal History* and *The History of the Gauls* that acknowledged Massalia's help to Rome several times in moments of danger.

Postumous Rufus Festus Avienus was a Roman geographer and poet who flourished in the fourth century A.D. and became the Roman Proconsul of Africa A.D. 366. Avienus wrote *Ora Maritima*, condensing 11 earlier sources but naming only one explorer Himilicar. Parts of the poem are clearly that of Pytheas of Massalia's own northern voyage of exploration. His sources seem to include a Massaliote periplus late sixth century B.C. Bosch-Gimpera also mentions a lost periplus by Charon of Lampsakos (Lampsakos was also a Phocaean colony/settlement like Massalia), [2977] writings by Scymnos c. 110 B.C. and another source was agreed as an older work of prose of Ephorus in the fourth century B.C. referring to a time older than the blocking of the Straits of Gibraltar to Greek ships c. 500 B.C. Ephorus died around 330 B.C. and not aware of Pytheas voyage. [2978]

Procopius of Caesarea, A.D. 500–c. 565 was a Byzantine scholar who accompanied Belisarius on his campaign. Procopius wrote *Histories of the Wars* in 8 volumes covering the Persian wars of the Emperors Justinus and Justinian, the Vandals wars, and Gothic wars against the Ostrogoths in Sicily including information of events people and places. He mentions the change of control of Massalia to the Franks c. A.D. 536.

Agathias of Myrina, c. A.D. 536–582/594. Greek poet and historian. He wrote *On the Reign of Justinian* and is a main source for the period A.D. 552–558. He covered the struggles of the Byzantine Army against the Goths, Vandals, Franks and Persians. He mentions the change in control of Massalia to the Franks in the late sixth century A.D.

Isidore of Seville, c. A.D. 560–636. Latin scholar and Polymath. Montalebert considered him as the last scholar of the ancient world. He was 'A vastly influential conduit for classical antiquity into the medieval world'.[2979] He was archbishop of Seville for over thirty years and his brother Leander had converted the Visigoth king from the Arianism version of Christianity to the Catholic version and both brothers were later made Saints. Isidore wrote several works including *The Etymologies (or Origins)* from which we find the reference from Varro of the first century B.C. regarding Massalia as a tri-lingual city.

A few suggested questions for discussion and essay topics.

Without Massalia's military, naval and financial help at crucial times would Rome have survived to become a world power?

Why was there Senatorial opposition to establishing the first Roman colony and port outside of Italy 118 B.C. at Narbo in Gaul? What were the arguments for and against?

What routes were available from the Mediterranean to get tin from Britain? What sources are there to prove this?

Discuss the impact of the Greek city-state of Massalia (Marseille) on Gaul (France) and Iberia (Spain).

Discuss the strategic importance of Massalia (Marseille) in the Roman civil war between Pompey the Great and Julius Caesar and what measures were taken by them?

How did the Greek city-state of Massalia (Marseille) lose its empire? What stopped them from getting back their 'rights'?

Discuss coin production in the Greek city-state of Massalia (Marseille) and what were its effects?

Cicero praises Massilia (Massalia) 'surrounded at the edge of the world by Gallic tribes'. Discuss the images he and others record of Massilia.

Why would Pytheas of Massalia's discovery of 'inhabited zones' much further south than was believed cause controversy?

What do we know of the measurements and observations Pytheas of Massalia took on his voyage of discovery into the Atlantic?

Why did Julius Caesar on his invasion of Britain expect thirty days of continual darkness at the winter solstice and how did he investigate this?

Discuss Phocaean and Massalia's colonies/settlements in the Western Mediterranean and why were they established?

How did the Celts, Helvetii and Druids know and write in Greek letters? How did the Gallo-Greek and Iberian-Greek scripts come into use?

For grants to promote the study of Classics in UK schools
see the website <http://www.classicsforall.org.uk//>

Volunteering for an archaeological dig
< http://www.archaeologyuk.org/getinvolved/volunteer>
< http://www.archaeolink.com/archaeology_volunteer_opportunit.htm

NOTES

[1] Sir Clements Markham, naval officer, polar explorer, president of the Royal Geographical Society in his article 'Pytheas the Discoverer of Britain', Geographical Journal, June 1893, in V. Stefansson, *Great Adventures and Explorations*, Robert Hale Ltd., 1947, p. 4.

[2] Only the first five volumes survive covering 220–145 B.C. Book I & II are preludes to the main history that begins from Book III. Polybius gives good explanatory notes.

[3] *Polybius, The Histories*, vol. 2. Bk. III. 95. 4-96.3, trans. W. R. Paton, Heinemann, 1922, p. 235.

[4] *Justin: Epitome of the Philippic History of Pompeius Trogus*, 43.3.4, trans. J. C. Yardley, Scholars Press Atlanta, GA, 1994, p. 266.

[5] Lucan, *Civil War*, III, 307–309, trans. S. H. Braund, Oxford, 1992, p. 50.

[6] Polybius, *The Histories*. vol. 2. Bk. III 95. 4–96.3, trans. W. R. Paton, Heinemann, 1922, p. 235.

[7] Strabo, *Geography*, 4.1.5.

[8] R. Latouche, *Caesar to Charlemagne: the beginnings of France*, trans. J. Nicholson, Barnes & Noble, 1968, p. 93; Ammianus Marcellinus, XV.11. Ammianus Marcellinus used as a source Timagenes of Alexandria. J. F. Lazenby, *Hannibal's War: a military history of the Second Punic War*, University of Oklahoma Press, 1998, p. 40; G. Vermes, F. Millar and M. Black, *The History of the Jewish People in the age of Jesus Christ*, vol. 1. T&T Clark, 1973, p. 23; 'Timagenes of Alexandria, who according to Suidas, was brought to Rome as a prisoner of war by Pompey. He wrote a *History of Alexander* and *The History of the Gauls, Cf.* Hor, *Epist.* I.19.15; Quint., I.10.10; X.1.75'. *The Roman History of Ammianus Marcellinus*, vol. 1. XV.9. Loeb, 1935, p. 177 n. 62, ['Penelope. University of Chicago', digital library] <http://penelope.uchicago.edu/Thayer/E/Roman/Texts/Ammian/15*.html>, viewed 20 February 2012.

[9] Cicero, *Philippic*, VIII. vi. 18–19, trans. W. Ker, Loeb, 1926, p. 381; Caesar, *BG*. II.22.

[10] S. McGee, 'Objective Burma', ['Turner Classic Movies'] <http://www.tcm.turner.com/this-month/article/25882|0/Objective-Burma-.html>, viewed on 6 January 2009.

[11] United States General Joseph Stilwell was Chief in Staff to General Chiang Kai-shek Chinese Nationalist Army, fluent in Chinese, and as Commander of the 'China, Burma, India Theatre', to train and coordinate the Chinese divisions in India and China against the Japanese. In 1943 he was Deputy Supreme Allied Commander under the British Vice Admiral Lord Louis Mountbatten. American forces included the air force, (C. V. Glines, 'Flying the Hump', *Air Force Magazine*, Vol. 74. No.3. (March 1991), <http://www.airforce-magazine.com/MagazineArchive/Pages/1991/March%201991/0391hump.aspx>, viewed on 9 January 2012,) and 'Merrill's Marauders' that captured Myitkyina with losses of 2,200 men, together with Chinese troops (casualties 4,200), and Kachin Guerrillas. (D. W. Hogan, India-Burma. *The U.S. Army Campaigns of World War II*, ['U.S. Army Centre for Military History'] <http://www.ibiblio.org/hyperwar/USA/USA-C-India/index.html>, viewed on 9 January 2012). General Stilwell opened the Burma Road and supplies to China. Early in his career his caustic criticisms earned him the nickname 'Vinegar Joe' yet later was also known as 'Uncle Joe' due to his lack of formality with the soldiers. During the war he was a demanding and unsympathetic commander to his own troops in the debilitating environment of jungle fighting. Internal politics of his support to both Nationalist and Communist Chinese forces had the Nationalist leader Chiang Kai-shek demand his recall to the U.S.A. Stilwell was abrasive, as he tried to combat the misuse of American aid to Chiang. Also abrasive to the 'Limeys' in particular the British high command, which he regarded as pompous and stuffy (possibly echoing the republican resolve to the similar attitudes of the government's British aristocrats that resulted in the rebellion from Britain and the American War of Independence 1775-82). However as 'abrasive' as his reputation was he made efforts to cooperate. C. F. Romanus and R. Sunderland, *Stilwell's Command Problems*, R. Greenfield, (general editor), United States Army in World War II, China-Burma-India Theatre, Centre of Military History Publications, 1987, p. 169-170, ['Sribd'] <http://www.scribd.com/doc/48337542/Stillwell-s-Command-Problems>, viewed 4 June 2012.

'Stick-in-the mud' attitudes were expressed by David Low's fictitious comic strip character Colonel Blimp that was made into the endearing film of 1943 directed by Michael Powell and Emeric Pressburger 'The Life and Death of Colonel Blimp' starring Robert Livesey, Deborah Kerr and Anton Walbrook. During release of British government papers at the Public Record Office in the 1970s it was revealed that Winston Churchill had tried to have the film banned, thinking it satirised the British military establishment, until persuaded otherwise. He was trying to engender a 'total war' spirit as opposed to a defeatist attitude of not being honourable to fight if it was not played by the rules as the Nazis were using any method to win. C. Howse, 'An enduring vision of a life worth dying for', *Daily Telegraph*, 04 August 2005, <http://www.telegraph.co.uk/comment/personal-view/3618812/An-enduring-vision-of-a-life-worth-dying-for.html>, viewed on 9 January 2012; R. Chapman, 'The Life of Colonel Blimp Reconsidered', The Powell & Pressberger Pages, <http://www.powell-pressburger.org/Reviews/43_Blimp/Blimp02.html#Note_8>, viewed on 9 January 2012; Anna, 'Colonel Blimp vs Winston Churchill and the MoI', *The Crowd Roars*, [web blog], May 12, 2007, <http://silentfilmlegend.blogspot.com/2007/05/colonel-blimp-vs-winston-churchill-and.html>, viewed on 9 January 2012.

[12] S. McGee, 'Objective Burma', 1945, Director Raoul Walsh, Warner Brothers, ['Turner Classic Movies Film Article'] <http://www.tcm.turner.com/this-month/article/25882|0/Objective-Burma-.html>, viewed on 6 January 2009.

[13] As China had now become Communist and forced out pro-democracy forces Fuller an anti-communist did not wish to give them any credit. General Stilwell, the only American to command a Chinese Army, is still regarded as a hero in China. D. Barnett, 'War Movie Mondays: Merrill's Marauders', ['The Flick Cast'] Aug 30 2010, <http://theflickcast.com/2010/08/30/war-movie-mondays-merrills-marauders/>, viewed on 12 January 2012; *Movie Review, 'Merrill's Marauders'*, New York Times, published June 14, 1962, <http://movies.nytimes.com/movie/review?res=9900E7DF163DE63BBC4C52DFB0668389679EDE>, viewed on 12 January 2012.

[14] *Press Document*, ['Juno Beach Centre'] <http://www.junobeach.org/Centre/pdf/jB.C._press_document_2010.pdf>, viewed on 9 November 2010.

[15] *Index*, ['Juno Beach Centre'] <http://www.junobeach.org/centre/index.html>, viewed on 9 November 2010.

[16] *D-Day and the Battle of Normandy: Your Questions Answered*, ['D-Day Museum Portsmouth'] <http://www.ddaymuseum.co.uk/faq.htm>, viewed on 9 November 2010.

[17] *Press Document*, ['Juno Beach Centre'] <http://www.junobeach.org/Centre/pdf/jB.C._press_document_2010.pdf>, viewed on 9 November 2010.

[18] They include 88 Canadian, 7 USA, 141 Poles, and others. The RAF museum gives 98, 11, 146 respectively and mention of 16 nationalities that took part. Both lists agree on 13 Free French pilots. There was also 10 Irish, 126 New Zealanders, 33 Australians, 25 South Africans, 3 Rhodesians, 1 Jamaican, 1 Barbadian, (*A History of the Battle of Britain: Battle of the nations*, ['RAF Museum'] <http://www.rafmuseum.org.uk/online-exhibitions/battle-of-britain-history/battle-of-the-nations.cfm>, viewed on 23 February 2011), and 2,353 British. Air Chief Marshal Keith Park of the RAF 'the Defender of London' was also from New Zealand. (*Profile: Sir Keith Park*, ['B.B.C. News'] <http://news.bbc.co.uk/1/hi/uk/7837196.stm>, viewed on 10 August 2011).

[19] A. Allen, *Movie Reviews: The Battle of Britain*, ['History On Film'] <http://www.historyonfilm.com/reviews/battle-of-britain.htm.>, viewed on 14 December 2010.

[20] *Ibid.*

[21] T. Dirks, *Yankee Doodle Dandy* (1942), ['Filmsite'] <http://www.filmsite.org/yank.html>, viewed on 21 December 2010.

[22] Currently the tune has the words changed for the adverts of 'Go.compare' motor insurance in the UK and has been a most popular advert for the last two years on British commercial television. This shows the power of a good tune 90 years after it was first written.

[23] H. V. Kaltenborn, 'Why Does Hitler Hang On?' in *The Rotarian*, Rotary International, vol. 66, no. 2. (February 1945): 8-15, here p. 8. <http://www.rotary.org/en/mediaandnews/therotarian/archives/Pages/ridefault.aspx>, viewed on 6

January 2012. There was also a belief in the secret weapons the Nazi's were developing and also a mistaken belief that America and Britain would join Hitler and attack Stalin and his Communist Russia.

[24] Sir Norman Angell, 'Germany–Our Problem' in *The Rotarian,* Rotary International, vol. 65, no. 5, (November, 1944):11-13, here p. 11. <http://www.rotary.org/en/mediaandnews/therotarian/archives/Pages/ridefault.aspx>, viewed on 6 January 2012.

[25] S. C. Smith, *Reassessing Suez 1956: new perspectives on the crisis and its aftermath,* Ashgate Publishing Ltd., 2008, p. 215, and also Vietnam.

[26] K. S. Bright, director, *Ross's Wedding Part 2,* Warner Home Video, Season 4, 24, 1998, [videocassette]. America's French heritage and language of 1763 and subsequently the Louisiana purchase in 1803, represented in the French sounding name of the Friend's character Phoebe Buffay?

[27] L. Jordan, *A Brief Outline on the History of New Netherland,* ['University of Notre Dame'] <http://www.coins.nd.edu/ColCoin/ColCoinIntros/NNHistory.html>, viewed on 13 October 2010. Britain captured the city of New Amsterdam in 1664 during the Second Anglo-Dutch War becoming New York named after Charles II's brother James, Duke of York. The colony was retaken by the Dutch during the Third Anglo-Dutch War in 1673 renaming it New Orange, and finally becoming a British possession in A.D. 1674.

[28] M. Adkin, *The Waterloo Companion: The Complete Guide to History's Most Famous Battle,* Arum Press Ltd., 2008, p. 37.

[29] A. Barbero, *The Battle: A New History of the Battle of Waterloo,* Walker & Co, 2006, p. 60, and note 9.

[30] *Ibid*, p. 76.

[31] C. Summerville, *Who Was Who at Waterloo: A Biography of the Battle,* Longman, 2007, p. 37–40.

[32] *Ibid*, p. 55–58.

[33] A. Barbero, *The Battle: A History of the Battle of Waterloo,* Atlantic Books, 2006, p. 78–79.

[34] *Ibid*, p. 361–362.

[35] *Ibid*, p. 368.

[36] *Ibid*, p. 375–376.

[37] *Ibid*, p. 75– 76.

[38] M. Adkin, *The Waterloo Companion: The Complete Guide to History's Most Famous Land Battle,* Arum Press Ltd., 2008, p. 51.

Some histories have recorded 123,000–124,000 but Adkin explains the discrepancy on p. 51 by deducting 17,500 casualties from the Ligny and Quatre Bras battles in defeating the Prussians on 16 June. 'There were also prisoners and deserters'. A. Barbero, *The Battle: A History of the Battle of Waterloo,* Atlantic Books, 2006, p. 76.

[39] J. Black, *The Battle of Waterloo: A New History,* Icon Books, 2010, p. 88.

Grouchy's 30,000 French took Wavre defended by Blücher's rearguard the III Prussian Corps of 17,000 under Thielmann on the morning of the 19 June. Grouchy had not heard of Napoleon's defeat the night before at Waterloo and his own victory was short lived when he received the news. From preparing to march on Brussels Grouchy realised he would be trapped between two armies. He skilfully withdrew his force via the fortress town of Namur to Laon by 26 June and increased the army there to 60,000 French. J. Black, *The Battle of Waterloo: A New History*, Icon Books, 2010, p. 160.

[40] M. Adkin, *The Waterloo Companion: The Complete Guide to History's Most Famous Land Battle,* Arum Press Ltd., 2008, p. 37.

[41] *Ibid*, p. 66.

[42] T. E. Gregory, *A History of Byzantium,* Wiley-Blackwell, 2010, p. 403–404; S. Runciman, *The Fall of Constantinople 1453*, Cambridge, 1969, p. 184.

After the fall of Constantinople in 1453 and the death of the Emperor Constantine XI Palaeologus, his younger bother Thomas ruled independently in Morea Greece until attacked by the Ottoman Turks in 1460. He, his wife and children escaped to Italy. After Thomas died, his son Andreas needing money sold his title Emperor of Constantinople to Charles VIII of France in 1494 on condition he would invade Greece and get Morea back for him. (K. K. Setton, *The Papacy and the Levant 12041571*, vol. 2. The American Philosophical Society, 1997, p. 463.) The condition was not fulfilled and Andreas kept the title. Andreas died broke in 1502 having sold the title again to Ferdinand II of Aragon and Isabella I of Castile who never paid him. J. J. Norwich, *Byzantium: The Decline and Fall,* Penguin, 1996, p. 446.

[43] P. Levi, 'Greek Dramas', ch. 7 in J. Boardman, J. Griffin and O. Murray (eds.), *Greece and the Hellenistic World*, Oxford University Press, 2001, p. 183; A. Stewart, *Classical Greece and the Birth of Western Art,* Cambridge, 2008, p. 160.

[44] A. Chugg, 'The Death of Alexander the Great', in *Minerva: The International Review of Ancient Art & Archaeology,* vol. 15, number 5, (September/October 2004), p. 45.

[45] G. Phillips, *Alexander the Great Murder in Babylon,* Virgin Books, 2008, p. 231–237 and p. 248; *Justin: Epitome of the Philippic History of Pompeius Trogus,* 13.10-14.9, trans. J. C. Yardley, Scholars Press Atlanta, GA, 1994, p. 120-121.

[46] Of the three main suspected causes for the early death of Alexander the Great one is written by Plutarch, citing Aristobulus as his source, as excessive alcohol 'There he drank all that night and the next day. Till at last he found a fever coming upon him'. *Plutarch's Lives, Alexander,* trans. J. Langhorne and W. Langhorne, Sir John Lubbock's Hundred Books, Routledge, 1930, p. 488.

Also when Callanus had died at Gedrosia, Alexander held a banquet for a large number of his friends and officers, and he offered a prize for the man who could drink the most wine. 'Promachus drank four measures of wine [about fourteen quarts] and 'carried off the crown, which was worth a talent, but survived it only three days'. Chares tells us forty-one others 'drank to such a degree' also died, 'the weather coming upon them extremely cold during their intoxication'. *Plutarch's Lives, Alexander,* trans. J. Langhorne and W. Langhorne, Sir John Lubbock's Hundred Books, Routledge, 1930, p. 486.

Alexander's best friend Hephestion had died when breaking the diet prescribed to him 'he ate a roasted fowl, and drank a flagon of wine made as cold as possible' which aggravated his fever. *Plutarch's Lives, Alexander,* trans. J. Langhorne and W. Langhorne, Sir John Lubbock's Hundred Books, Routledge, 1930, p. 487.

[47] Dr W. Smith, *A Smaller History of Rome*, John Murray, 1884, p. 47.

[48] *Justin: Epitome of the Philippic History of Pompeius Trogus*, 37. 1-2, trans. J. C. Yardley, Scholars Press Atlanta, 1994, p. 233.

[49] *The History of Rome by Titus Livius*, War Against Antiochus, vol. V. XXXVI, trans. Canon Roberts, Dent, 1924–31, LIV, p. 240.

[50] Letter to King Pyrrhus quoted from Aulis Gellius, 'Attic Nights', 3.8 in P. Matyszak, *Classical Compendium*, Thames & Hudson, 2009, p. 28; for full text see Gellius, A. Cornelius. *Noctes Atticae (Attic Nights)*, 3.8. Loeb, 1923, revised 1946, ['Penelope', University of Chicago digital library]
<http://penelope.uchicago.edu/Thayer/E/Roman/Texts/Gellius/3*.html#ref33>, viewed on 20 February 2011.

[51] Cicero, *De Officiis*, Bk. II. 8, trans. W. Miller, Loeb, 1913, p.195; ['Penelope, University of Chicago' digital library] <http://penelope.uchicago.edu/Thayer/E/Roman/Texts/Cicero/de_Officiis/2A*.html> viewed 10 February 2012.

[52] *The Histories of Polybius*, vol.1, Bk.I. 83.3, trans. W. R. Paton, Heinemann, 1922, p. 247.

[53] F. W. Wallbank, *A Historical Commentary on Polybius*, vol. 1. Bk. I.6.6, Oxford, 1957, p. 51–52; and also *The Histories of Polybius*, trans. W. R. Paton, Heinemann, 1922, p. 21-25.

[54] *Caesar's Civil War,* Bk. 1. Ch. XXXIV, trans. W. A. M'Devitte, G. Bell & Sons, 1928, p. 65.

[55] J. B. Bury and R. Meiggs, *A History of Greece,* Macmillan, 1979, p. 293–310.

[56] On 21 May 2009 the British government of Prime Minister Gordon Brown and the Labour Party had its first defeat in Parliament 267 to 246 votes over unpopular moves against the Gurkhas equal right of residence in the UK. The motion was led by the Liberal Democrats and had been taken to the public by actress Joanna Lumley whose father a British Officer had served with the Gurkhas. The Gurkhas Justice campaign she ran gathered over 400,000 signatures. Though it has been 60 years since World War 2 yet such is their legend that has been passed down, the people and over half the MP's did not forget even if the Government did. Their legend preceded them to great advantage during the Falklands War in 1982. (B. Farwell, *The Gurkhas*, Penguin, 1985, p. 292). The 2nd Battalion Gurkhas were also given the Freedom of Folkstone on 16 June 2009.

[57] C. Kelly, *The Roman Empire,* Oxford University Press, 2006, p. 14; A coin was issued in 46 B.C. to commemorate Caesar's fourfold triumph. Obverse: veiled beardless head facing right, letters C.CAESAR COS. TER. Reverse: Lituus, ewer and axe, below letters A. HIRTIVS P R. Aureus, 8.07 gm (124.6 grains). B.M.C. I., p. 525, No. 4050. This was not the usual silver of the triumvirs of the mint but a special gold issue to be given out at his triumphs. G. F. Hill, *Historical Roman Coins: from the earliest times to the reign of Augustus*, Constable & Co. Ltd, 1909, p. 107–109. ['Archive'] <http://www.archive.org/stream/historicalromanc00hilluoft/historicalromanc00hilluoft_djvu.txt> viewed on 20 May 2012. The book has been reissued by Argonaut in 1966 and by Read Books Design in 2010.

[58] M. Wyke, *Caesar,* Granta Books, 2007, p. 128.

[59] Appian, *The Civil Wars*, 2.102, trans. John Carter, Penguin Books, 1996, p. 123.

[60] M. Wyke, *Caesar,* Granta Books, 2007, p. 128, Dio. 43.24.

[61] Appian, *The Civil Wars*, 2.101, trans. John Carter, Penguin Books, 1996, p. 123.

[62] M. Tullius Cicero, *Orations, the fourteen orations against Marcus Antonius (Philippics)*, VIII. 18–19, trans. C. D. Yonge, George Bell & Son, 1903, <http://www.perseus.tufts.edu/hopper/text?doc=Perseus%3Atext%3A1999.02.0021%3Aspeech%3D8%3Asection%3D18> viewed 28 December 2012.

[63] Cicero, *De Officiis,* Bk. II. 8. 28–29, trans. W. Miller, Loeb, 1975, p.197.

[64] M. Tullius. Cicero, *Orations, the fourteen orations against Marcus Antonius (Philippics),* II.94, trans. C. D. Yonge, George Bell & Son, 1903, ['Perseus, Tufts university' digital library], <http://www.perseus.tufts.edu/hopper/text?doc=Perseus%3Atext%3A1999.02.0021%3Aspeech%3D2%3Asection%3D94>, 4 June 2012.

[65] M. Grant, *Julius Caesar*, Phoenix, 2005, p. 170.

[66] *Ibid*, p. 171.

[67] Cicero, *Pro Milone, On Behalf of Fonteius*, 45, trans. H. Watts, Heinemann, 1972, p. 355.

[68] J. Leach, *Pompey the Great*, Croom Helm, 1978, p. 45.

[69] *Caesar's Civil War*, Bk.1, Chp. XXXV, trans. W. M. M'Devitte, G. Bell & Sons, 1928, p. 265.

[70] F. Millar, *The Roman Republic in Political Thought,* Brandeis University Press/University Press of New England, 2002, p. 25–26.

[71] W. Smith, *A Dictionary of Greek and Roman Antiquities,* John Murray, London, 1875, Third Period-Polybius, 4, p. 496 and 10, p. 498, ['Penelope' University of Chicago]

<http://penelope.uchicago.edu/Thayer/E/Roman/Texts/secondary/SMIGRA*/Exercitus.html>, viewed on 14 January 2011.

[72] F. Millar, *The Roman Republic in Political Thought*, Brandeis University Press/University Press of New England, 2002, p. 160.

[73] Dr B. Nagle, 'An Allied view of the Social War' in *American Journal of Archaeology*, Vol. 77. No. 4. (Oct, 1973): 376-378, here p. 377, ['JSTOR' archive journal] <http://www.jstor.org/pss/503306>, viewed on 20 February 2012. Some authors have this date as 91-87 B.C.

[74] C. Ebel, *Transalpine Gaul: the emergence of a Roman province*, Brill, 1976, p. 9-10.

[75] *Justin: Epitome of the Philippic History of Pompeius Trogus*, 43.5.9, trans. J. C. Yardley, Scholars Press Atlanta, GA, 1994, p. 269 & p. 28. 2.3–4. p. 200; There are errors in the Varronian chronology. Lendering is 'almost certain' that the real date would seem to be 387/386 B.C. See J. Lendering, *Varronian Chronology*, revised 6 November 2010, ['Livius.org'] <http://www.livius.org/cg-cm/chronology/varro.html>, viewed on 26 October 2011.

[76] Strabo, *Geography*, Bk. V. 2.3.

[77] *Ibid.*
> …achievements of the Caeretani: they defeated in war those Galatae who captured Rome, having attacked them when they were in the country of the Sabini on their way back, and also took away as booty from the Galatae, against their will, what the Romans had willingly given them; in addition to this, they saved all who fled to them for refuge from Rome, and the immortal fire, and the priestesses of Vesta. The Romans it is true, on account of the bad managers which the city had at that time, do not seem to have remembered the favour the Caeretani with sufficient gratitude, for, although they gave them the right of citizenship, they did not enroll them among the citizens, and even used to relegate all others who had no share in the equal right to the "Tablets of the Caeretani". Among the Greeks, however, this city was in good repute for both bravery and for righteousness; for it not only abstained from all piracy, but also set up at Pytho [Delphi] what is called "the treasury of the Agyllaei"; for what is now Caerea was formerly called Agylla, and is said to have been founded by Pelasgi who came from Thessaly.

Strabo further records that Agylla was captured by the Tyrrheni (Etruscans) who changed the name to Caerea.

[78] Dr W. Smith, *A Smaller History of Rome*, John Murray, 1884, p. 47.

[79] Polybius, *The Histories*, vol 1. II. 18.3–4, trans. W. R, Paton, Loeb, 1922, p. 285.

[80] *Justin: Epitome of the Philippic History of Pompeius Trogus*, trans. J. C. Yardley, Scholars Press Atlanta, GA, 1994, 43.5.9. p. 269 and 28. 2.3–4. p. 200–201.

[81] J. C. H. Williams, *Beyond the Rubicon: Romans and Gauls in Republican Italy*, Oxford, 2001, p. 143 and p. 150.

[82] M. Grant, *Roman Myths*, Weidenfield & Nicholson, 1971, p. 210; J. C. H. Williams, *Beyond the Rubicon: Romans and Gauls in Republican Italy*, Oxford, 2001, p. 146-147.

[83] Strabo, *Geography*, Bk. V. 2.3.

[84] *Plutarch Lives, Camillus*, trans. Langhorne, J. & Langhorne, W. Sir John Lubbock's Hundred Books, Routledge, 1930, p. 108, footnote.

[85] Suetonius, *The Twelve Caesars*, Tiberius 3.2, trans. R. Graves, Penguin, 2007, p. 106.

[86] J. C. H. Williams, *Beyond the Rubicon: Romans and Gauls in Republican Italy*, Oxford, 2001, p. 170 and p. 148-149.

[87] Dr W. Smith, *A Smaller History of Rome*, John Murray, 1884, p. 48.

[88] *The Histories of Polybius*, vol.1, Book.1, 6. 3-4, trans. W. R. Paton, Harvard University Press, 2010, p. 17.

[89] *Justin: Epitome of the Philippic History of Pompeius Trogus,* 38.4.8, trans. J. C. Yardley, Scholars Press Atlanta, GA, 1994, p. 239.

[90] *Justin: Epitome of the Philippic History of Pompeius Trogus,* 28.2.4–5, trans. J. C. Yardley, Scholars Press Atlanta, GA, 1994, p. 201.

[91] Caesar, *BG.* II.22.

[92] There are some Roman references that say even Capitoline Hill was taken by the Celts. Williams examines the different stories and analyses how the present version became dominant, see J. C. H. Williams, *Beyond the Rubicon: Romans and Gauls in Republican Italy*, Oxford, 2001, p. 142-157.

[93] Valerius mentions that as before when 'married ladies jewelry' had contributed to the tithe promised by Camillus to Apollo at Delphi for the capture of Veii, 'married ladies jewelry' had paid the 1,000 pounds of gold, 'which was owed to the Gauls in exchange for lifting the siege of the Capitol'. Valerius Maximus, *Memorable Deeds and Sayings: A Thousand and One Tales From Ancient Rome,* V.6.8., trans. Henry John Walker, Hackett Publishing Company Inc., 2004, p. 187.

[94] F. W. Wallbank, *A Historical Commentary on Polybius,* vol 1, Bk. III. 20.5. Oxford, 1970, p. 333; R. Gardiner, (ed.), *The Age of the Galley,* Conway Maritime Press, 1995, p. 60–61 n. 30, *F Gr Hist* 176 F 1. Hasdrubal Barca with his land forces nearby was powerless to stop his navy under Himilco being destroyed. Ten years later Hasdrubal Barca went over the Alps with an army and into Italy in 207 B.C. The letters he then sent to Hannibal revealing his plans to join forces with him were intercepted by the Romans and by a forced march they were able to surprise and defeat him at the Battle of Metaurus where he was killed. Livy, *The History of Rome,* vol. 4. XLIII-XLVIII, trans. Rev. Canon Roberts, Dent, 1924–31, p. 124-132.

[95] *Livy*, vol. 5, XXII. XIX. 2–8, trans. B.O. Foster, William Heinemann, 1929, p. 263–267.

[96] *Appian's Roman History*, 7.16, trans. Horace White. ['Livius.org']
<http://www.livius.org/ap-ark/appian/appian_hannibal_04.html>, viewed on 26 October 2011. Peddie gives a quote from Polybius with an implication Carthage sent help but none of the ancient annalists record its arrival. J. Peddie, *Hannibal's War*, Sutton, 2003, p. 86–88.

[97] J. E. Mansion, *Harrap's New Shorter French and Engish Dictionary*, Harrap, 1976, M:12.

[98] Institute national de statistique et de études économiques, *Resultats du recensement de la population 2006*, ['INSEE'], <http://www.recensement-2006.insee.fr/chiffresCles.action?codeMessage=5&zoneSearchField=MARSEILLE&codeZone=003-AU1999&idTheme=3&rechercher=Rechercher>, viewed 20 June 2012.

[99] Herodotus, *Histories,* trans. G. Rawlinson, Wordsworth Editions Ltd., 1996, p. 111, note 157; *Appian Wars of the Romans in Iberia,* trans. J. S. Richardson, Aris and Phillips Ltd., 2000, 2.(5).

[100] Strabo, *Geography*, III.4. 2.

[101] R. Carpenter, *The Greeks in Spain,* Bryn Mawr College, Longman, Greene & Co., 1925, p. 179; Aubet raises some doubts on Strabo's report and with a concentration of Phoenician archaeology suggests that Mainike might have been Phoenician. M. E. Aubet, 'Mainake: the Legend and New Archaeological Evidence', in B. Cunliffe and R. Osborne, (eds.), *Mediterranean Urbanisation 800–600 B.C.*, The British Academy, (Oxford University Press 2007):187–202, here p. 192-193 and 200.

[102] J. Boardman, *The Greeks Overseas,* Thames & Hudson, 1999, Ch. 5, p 162.

[103] J-P. Morel, 'Phocaean Colonisation' in G. R. Tsetskhladze (ed.), *Greek Colonisation: An Account of Greek Colonies and Other Settlements Overseas,* vol.1, (Leiden, 2006): 358–428, here p. 365.

[104] A. L. F. Rivet, *Gallia Narbonensis,* Batsford, 1988, p. 10–11.

[105] R. Carpenter, *The Greeks in Spain,* Bryn Mawr College, Longman, Greene & Co., 1925, p. 35.

[106] A. L. F. Rivet, *Gallia Narbonensis,* Batsford, 1988, p. 10–11.

[107] J. Knight, *Roman France: an archaeological field guide*, Tempus Publishing, 2001, p. 163.

[108] A. Blakeway, 'Prolegma to the Study of Greek Commerce with Italy, Sicily and France in the Eighth and Seventh Centuries B.C.' in *The Annual of British School of Athens*, vol. 33 (1932/1933): 170–208, here p. 199 and Plate 33. No. 85 & 86, ['JSTOR' journal archive] <http://www.jstor.org/stable/30096951>, viewed on 1 December 2009.

[109] Thucydides, *The History of the Peloponnesian War*, Book 1.13. 6.

[110] T. J. Dunbabin, *The Western Greeks: The History of Sicily and South Italy from the Foundation of the Greek Colonies to 480 B.C.*, Oxford University Press Monograph Reprints, 1998, p. 343 n. 3. Over half of the Phocaeans had returned to Phocaea shortly after the evacuation.

[111] O. Murray, *Early Greece*, Fontana, 1993, p. 112.

[112] J-P. Wilson, 'The nature of Greek overseas settlements in the archaic period: emporion or apoikia?' in L. Mitchell and P.J. Rhodes (eds.), *The Development of the Polis in Archaic Greece,* (London, 1997): 199-207.

[113] I. Malkin, 'Exploring the validity of the concept of a "foundation": a visit to Megera Hyblaia' in Gorman, V. B., and Robinson, E. W. (eds.), *Oikistes: studies in constitutions, colonies and military power in the ancient world: offered in honour of A. J. Graham*, (Leiden, 2002): 195–225, here p. 211.

[114] Plutarch, *The Rise and Fall of Athens*, 2.2, trans. I. Scott-Kilvert, Penguin Books, 1967.

[115] Athenaeus, *Deipnosophists*, vol. 6. XIII, 576, trans. C. B. Gulick, Loeb, William Heinemann, 1937, p. 109–111.

[116] *Justin: Epitome of the Philippic History of Pompeius Trogus,* 43. 3.11–12, trans. J. C. Yardley, Scholars Press Atlanta, 1994, p. 267.

[117] B. Cunliffe, *The Extraordinary Voyage of Pytheas the Greek: The man who discovered Britain,* Penguin Books, 2002, p. 21; R. Syme, 'The Date of Justin and the Discovery of Trogus', *Historia Zeitschrift fur Alte Geschichte*, (vol. 37, No. 3 (3rd Qtr., 1988): 358-371, here p. 362, [JSTOR' journal archive] <http:www.jstor.org/stable/4436062>, viewed 28 March 2011.

[118] *Justin: Epitome of the Philippic History of Pompeius Trogus,* 43.3.5, trans. J. C. Yardley, Scholars Press Atlanta, GA, 1994, p. 266.

[119] *Ibid,* 43.3.4, p. 266.

[120] J. H. Thiel, *A History of Roman Sea-Power Before the Second Punic War*, North Holland Publishing Co., Amsterdam, 1954, p. 86 n. 73.

[121] O. Murray, *Early Greece*, Fontana, 1993, p. 147, Dionysius of Halicarnassus, *Roman Antiquities*, 3.46.

[122] J. Heurgon, *Daily Life of the Etruscans*, Phoenix Press, 2002, p. 80.

[123] Lacus Curtius, *Strabo's Geography*, V.2.2. Loeb, 1922.

[124] O. Murray, *Early Greece*, Fontana, 1993, p. 147, Dionysius of Halicarnassus, *Roman Antiquities*, 3.46.

[125] R. Osborne, *Greece in the Making 1200–479 B.C.* Routledge, 2008, p. 125

[126] *Ibid*, p. 127, Tacitus, *Annuals*, 11.14.

[127] Strabo, *Geography,* V.2.2.

[128] *Ibid,* VIII.6.20.

[129] Dr W. Smith, *A Smaller History of Rome*, John Murray, 1884, p. 16.

[130] J. Heurgon. *Daily Life of the Etruscans*, trans. G. Baillet, Phoenix Press, 2002, p. 81, Livy, I. 34. 4.

[131] *Livy*, vol. I. Bk. I. xxiv. 4–9, trans. B.O. Foster, Heinemann, 1925, p. 125.

[132] Strabo, *Geography*, V.2.2.

[133] T. J. Cornell, *The Beginning of Rome: Italy and Rome from the Bronze Age to the Punic Wars (c. 1000–264 B.C.)*, Routledge, 1995, p. 142.

[134] Lacus Curtius, *Strabo's Geography*, V.2.2. Loeb, 1922, p. 393 n. 72. <http://penelope.uchicago.edu/Thayer/E/Roman/Texts/Strabo/5B*.html>, viewed on 14 January 2012.

[135] Strabo, *Geography*, V.2.2. and VIII.6.20.

[136] *Livy*, vol. I. Bk. I. xxiv. 4–9, trans. B. O. Foster, Heinemann, 1925, p. 127.

[137] *Ibid*, p. 129.

[138] T. J. Cornell, *The Beginning of Rome: Italy and Rome from the Bronze Age to the Punic Wars (c. 1000–264 B.C.)*, Routledge, 1995, p. 148.

[139] Strabo, *Geography*, V.2.2.

[140] *Ibid*.

[141] *Ibid*.

[142] *Ibid*, VIII.6.20

[143] *Ibid*.

[144] P. Orrieux and P. Schmitt Pantel, *A History of Greece*, Blackwell, 1999, p. 67.

[145] Strabo, *Geography*, VIII.6.20.

[146] A. Hermary, A. Hesnard, and H. Tréziny, *Marseille Grecque: La cite phocéenne (600–49 av. J-C)*, Editions Errance, 1999, p. 9 and p. 12.

[147] T. J. Cornell, *The Beginning of Rome: Italy and Rome from the Bronze Age to the Punic Wars (c. 1000–264 B.C.)*, Routledge, 1995, p. 122.

[148] *Ibid*, p. 120.

[149] B. D'Agostino, 'The First Greeks in Italy' in G. R. Tsetskhladze (ed.), *Greek Colonisation: An Account of Greek Colonies and Other Settlements Overseas*, vol. 1 (Leiden, 2006): 201–237, here p. 203.

[150] T. J. Cornell, *The Beginning of Rome: Italy and Rome from the Bronze Age to the Punic Wars (c. 1000–264 B.C.)*, Routledge, 1995, p. 124.

[151] E. Shuey, 'Underwater Survey and Excavations at Gravisca, The Port of Tarquinia', *Papers from the British School of Rome*, (vol. 49. 1981):17–45, here p. 17. n. 4, ['JSTOR' journal archive] <http://www.jstor.org/pss/40310871>, viewed on 17 January 2012. The site was discovered and excavated by Professor Mario Torelli, University of Perugia. See M. Torelli, 'Il Santuario Greco di Gravisca', *La Prarola del Passato* 177 (1977): 398-458, which has photographs and illustrations of the artefacts found. For an article in English see M. Torelli, 'Greek Artisans and Etruria: A problem concerning the relationship between two cultures', *Archaeological News* 5, Dept. of Classics, Florida State University, (1976): 134–8. There is a recent archaeological book in Italian by S. Fortunelli, *Gravisca: Scavi nel santuario Greco*, Edipuglia Bari, 2007.

[152] J-P. Morel, 'Phocaean Colonisation' in G. R. Tsetskhladze (ed.), *Greek Colonisation: An Account of Greek Colonies and Other Settlements Overseas,* vol.1, (Leiden, 2006): 358–428, here p. 372.

[153] M. Torelli, 'Greek Artisans and Etruria: A problem concerning the relationship between two cultures', *Archaeological News* 5, Dept. of Classics, Florida State University, (1976): 134–8, here p. 135.

[154] A. Johnston, *The Emergence of Greece,* Elsevier-Phaidon, 1976, p. 41.

[155] J-P. Morel, 'Phocaean Colonisation' in G. R. Tsetskhladze (ed.), *Greek Colonisation: An Account of Greek Colonies and Other Settlements Overseas,* vol.1, (Leiden, 2006): 358–428, here p. 372.

[156] M. Torelli, 'Greek Artisans and Etruria: A problem concerning the relationship between two cultures', *Archaeological News* 5, Dept. of Classics, Florida State University, (1976):134–8, here p.136.

[157] *Justin: Epitome of the Philippic History of Pompeius Trogus,* 43.3–7, trans. J. C. Yardley, Scholars Press Atlanta, 1994, p. 266.

[158] *Ibid,* 43.3.8–13, p. 267.

[159] This festival has a written reference in third century in Rome but its origin was thought much earlier from the Greeks and also from Italy. How much it was different to the original we do not know but this is the Roman version.

To the same circle as Ceres and Tellus belongs Flora. Original significance as goddess of flowering plants, her festival the Floralia, has unmistakable connexions with the cult of the dead, in this it reminds us of the Athenian Anthesteria, which bore the name of the flowering of the plants and yet were at the same time a festival for the dead. At the Floralia courtesans appeared in public. They carried out sham fights, a characteristic trait for the cult of feminine deities, and above all, stripped themselves and gave vent to all manner of indecent gestures and speeches. (F. Altheim, *A History of Roman Religion,* Metheun & Co, 1938, p. 122).

[160] *Justin: Epitome of the Philippic History of Pompeius Trogus,* 43.4.3–12, trans. J. C. Yardley, Scholars Press Atlanta, 1994, p. 268.

[161] *Ibid,* 43.5.1. p. 268.

[162] Lucan, *Civil War,* Bk. 3. 307–309, trans. Susan. H. Braund, Oxford World's Classics, 1999, p. 50.

[163] *Plutarch, The Rise and Fall of Athens: Nine Greek Lives,* Solon, trans. I. Scott-Kilvert, Penguin Books, 1967, p. 44–45 n. 4, Hesiod, *Work and Days*, 311.

[164] F. Meijer, *A History of Seafaring in the Classical World,* Croom Helm, 1986, p. 79. See also '11.24 The Thirty Attack Wealthy Metics, Lysias XII Against Eratosthenes, 4–20', Chapter 11, Labour, Slaves, Serfs and Citizens, in M. Dillon, and L. Garland, *Ancient Greece; social and historical documents from archaic times to the death of Socrates*, 2nd edition, (Routledge, 1994): 360-39; Metics featured in the Panathenaia Parthenon North Frieze V.13. British Museum.

[165] Robin Osborne, lecture 'Settlement and productivity in the Greek landscape', Ancient History Seminar, Institute of Classical Studies, Senate House University of London, 13 October 2011, questions and answer section.

[166] Livy, *The Early History of Rome,* V.34, trans. Aubrey De Selincourt, Penguin Classics, 2005, p. 410.

[167] *The Roman History of Ammianus Marcellinus,* XV.9. vol. 1. Loeb, 1935, p. 177, ['Penelope. University of Chicago', digital library] <http://penelope.uchicago.edu/Thayer/E/Roman/Texts/Ammian/15*.html>, viewed 20 February 2012. (XV.9, p. 177 n. 62. Ammianus Marcellinus used as his source Timagenes of Alexandria who wrote *The History of the Gauls* in the first century B.C).

[168] Strabo, *Geography,* Book IV.1.4.

[169] *Justin: Epitome of the Philippic History of Pompeius Trogus,* 43.5.3, trans. J. C. Yardley, Scholars Press Atlanta, 1994, p. 268.

[170] I saw this at the Musée d'Histoire de Marseille, 23 July 2009 on the Museum Display Boards.

[171] Though the Ligurians are recorded as having boats, their later piratical activities had become enough of a threat for Massalia to ask for Roman help against them in 182 B.C. F. W. Wallbank, *A Historical Commentary on Polybius.* vol. 3. XXXIII.8.1, Oxford, 1979, p. 550.

[172] B. Cunliffe, *The Extraordinary Voyage of Pytheas the Greek: The man who discovered Britain,* Penguin Books, 2002, p. 7.

[173] Strabo, *Geography,* Book IV. Chapter 1.4.

[174] D. Theodorescu and H. Treziny, 'Le chapiteau ionique archaïque de Marseille' in A. Hemary and H. Tréziny (eds.), *Les Cultes des citiés phocéennnes*, (Centre Camille Jullian, 2000): 135-146; A. Trevor. Hodge, *Ancient Greek France,* University of Pennsylvania Press, 1999, p. 249 n. 42.

[175] C. Seltman, *The Twelve Olympians and Their Guests,* Max Parrish & Co., 1956, p. 129.

[176] A. Trevor. Hodge, *Ancient Greek France*, University of Pennsylvania Press, 1999, p. 9.

[177] C. A. Barton, *Timaeus of Tauromenium and Hellenistic Historiography*, Cambridge, 2013, p. 134 n. 93.

[178] Pausanias, X.4.1.

[179] A. Trevor. Hodge, *Ancient Greek France*, University of Pennsylvania Press, 1999, p. 79–80.

[180] In Clerc's photograph the stone ends in the middle of the second last letter O. M. Clerc, *Massalia: Histoire de Marseille dans L'Antiquité des Origins a la Fin de l'empire Romain d'occident*, vol. 2, Librarie A. Tacussel, 1929, p. 279. There is an inscription for Massilia, *IG*, 2466, vol. XIV, G. Kaibel and A. Lebegue (eds.), Berolini, 1890, p. 650, and recorded as ΟΣΤΑΔΙC and the reference given is REN, 'Renier bull du comité de la langue, de l'histoire et des arts de la France, vol. IV (1860) p. 171 ab Dassio Massiensi acceptam'; *IGF* 7, p.13.

[181] A. Trevor. Hodge, *Ancient Greek France*, University of Pennsylvania Press, 1999, p.79 n. 39.

[182] M. Clerc, *Massalia: Histoire de Marseille dans L'Antiquité des Origins a la Fin de l'empire Romain d'occident*, vol. 2, Librarie A. Tacussel, 1929, p. 279.

[183] A. Hermary, A. Hesnard, and H. Tréziny, *Marseille Grecque: La cite phocéenne (600–49 av. J-C)*, Editions Errance, 1999, p. 76–77.

[184] *Ibid*, p. 74.

[185] A. Trevor. Hodge, *Ancient Greek France*, University of Pennsylvania Press, 1999, p. 79.

[186] J. Bromwich, *The Roman Remains of Southern France: a guidebook*, Routledge, 1993, p. 171.

[187] *Ibid*, p.73 n. 20; M. Clerc, *Massalia: Histoire de Marseille dans L'Antiquité des Origins a la Fin de l'empire Romain d'occident*, Librarie A. Tacussel, vol. 2, 1929, p. 276; M. Moliner, et al, *La nécropolie de Sainte-Barbe à Marseille,* (IVe s. av. J-C.–IIe s. ap. J-C.), Édisud, 2003, p. 240, Fig. 213.

[188] M. Clerc, *Massalia: Histoire de Marseille dans L'Antiquité des Origins a la Fin de l'empire Romain d'occident*, Librarie A. Tacussel, vol. 2, 1929, p. 278–279.

[189] A. Hermary, A. Hesnard, and H. Tréziny, *Marseille Grecque: La cite phocéenne (600–49 av. J-C)*, Editions Errance, 1999, p. 81.

[190] B. Bizot, et al. *Marseille Antique: guide archéologiques de la France*, Editions du Patrimonie, Centre des monuments nationaux, 2007, p. 80.

[191] P. Gallini, 'Des tombs grecques à Marseille' *La Provence*, 4 June 2012, <http://www.laprovence.com/article/a-la-une/des-tombes-grecques-a-marseille>; *Ancient Greek tombs discovered in Marseilles*, 8 June 2012, ['Archaeology News Network'] <http://archaeologynewsnetwork.blogspot.gr/2012/06/ancient-greek-tombs-discovered-in.html#.T_f0KJFRGuK>, viewed 7 July 2012.

[192] A. L. F. Rivet, *Gallia Narbonensis*, Batsford, 1988, p. 16.

[193] C. Seltman, *The Twelve Olympians and Their Guests*, Max Parrish & Co, 1956, p. 132.

[194] W. Scheidel, I. Morris, and R. P. Saller, *Cambridge Economic History of the Greco-Roman World,* Cambridge, 2007, p. 270.

[195] J. Boardman, *The Greeks Overseas,* Thames & Hudson, 1999, p. 163.

[196] M. Grant, *The Rise of the Greeks,* Ch. 6, Phoenix Press, 2005, p. 250.

[197] B. Cunliffe, *The Extraordinary Voyage of Pytheas the Greek: The man who discovered Britain,* Penguin Books, 2002, p. 21; At the Temple of Apollo were carved 3 maxims and the letter E, 'Know thyself', 'Nothing in excess' and 'Make a pledge and mischief is nigh'.

[198] C. Mee and A. Spawforth, *Greece an Oxford Archaeological Guide,* Oxford, 2001, p. 311 and Fig. 130.

[199] C. M. Emlyn-Jones, *The Ionians and Hellenism: A Study of the Cultural Achievements of the Early Greek Inhabitants of Asia Minor*, Routledge & Kegan Paul,1980, p. 55.

[200] D. S. Robertson, *Greek and Roman Architecture*, Cambridge, 1969, p. 100–101.

[201] *Archaeological Museum of Delphi*, Room 9, [Greek Hotels'] <http://www.greekhotel.com/sterea/fokida/delphi/photos/archaeological-museum-images-9.htm>, viewed on 7 November 2011.

[202] An alternative tradition mentions c. 545 as the foundation for Massalia but archaeology does bear out 600 B.C. The date of 545 may refer to a second wave of colonist refugees from the Persian invasion while the majority fled to their other colony of Alalia in Corsica. M. Grant, *The Rise of the Greeks,* Phoenix Press, 2005, Ch.6. p. 249; Herodotus, *Histories*, Book I. 166, trans. G. Rawlinson, Wordsworth Editions Ltd, 1996, p. 75.

[203] Herodotus, *Histories*, Book I. 170, trans. G. Rawlinson, Wordsworth Editions Ltd, 1996, p.77.

[204] *Ibid*, Book I. 162, p. 73.

[205] *Ibid*, Book I. 164, p. 74–75. Cawkwell mentions that a pentoconter had two officers and fifty oarsmen. Herodotus allows eighty men in all. However if used as a transport of 100 men per ship and we have the Phocaeans able to cram in their families and weighty personal possessions on board. G. Cawkwell, *Cyrene to Charonea*, Oxford, 2011, p. 13 n. 9, Herodotus, *Histories*, VII. 184.3 and p. 13 n. 10, Herodotus, *Histories*, I. 164.3.

[206] Strabo, *Geography,* Bk.VI, Ch.1.1. ['Penelope, University of Chicago' digital library] <http://penelope.uchicago.edu/Thayer/E/Roman/Texts/Strabo/6A*.html>, viewed on 10 October 2011.

[207] Sir Karl. Popper, *The World of Parmenides: Essays on the Presocratic Enlightenment*, Routledge, 2007, Essay 2,7.

[208] Herodotus, *Histories*, Bk.1. 164, trans. G. Rawlinson, Wordsworth Editions Ltd, 1996, p. 74.

[209] *Ibid,* and Bk.1.168 & 169, p. 75. The city of Teos did the same as the Phocaeans in 'forsaking their fatherland' on being besieged by Harpagus abandoned their city sailed to Thrace and founded Abdera.

[210] Strabo, *Geography,* Bk. VI.1.1.

[211] Aristoxenus of Tarentum (Fragment 23), fourth century B.C. A. Hermary, A. Hesnard, and H. Treziny, *Marseille Grecque: La cite phocéenne (600–49 av. J-C),* Editions Errance, 1999, p. 167.

[212] Aristoxenus, Histories, Fragment. Gr. 2.279.23. vol. 2, Anacreon, trans. J. M. Edmunds, *Lyra Graeca*, Heinemann, 1979, p. 121; see also another translation *Xenophanes of Colophon, Fragments: A Text and Translation with a Commentary* by J. H. Lesher, University of Toronto, 2001, p. 200.

[213] Herodotus, *Histories*, Book I. 165, trans. G. Rawlinson, Wordsworth Editions Ltd, 1996, p.74-75.

[214] *Ibid*, Book I. 166, p. 75.

[215] *Ibid*, Book I. 164, p. 74–75.

[216] *Ibid*, Book I. 166–167, p. 75-76.

[217] The Greeks called the Etruscans after Tyrrhenus, the son of Ayts, 'who sent forth colonists hither from Lydia' at a 'time of famine and dearth of crops'. The Romans called them Etrusci and Tusci. (Strabo, *Geography*, V.2.2) and the name survives as the region of Tuscany.

[218] J. Boardman, *The Greeks Overseas*, Thames & Hudson, 1999, Ch. 5, p. 228.

[219] From Strabo, *Geography*, VI.1.1.

[220] J-P. Morel, 'Phocaean Colonisation' in G. R. Tsetskhladze (ed.), *Greek Colonisation: An Account of Greek Colonies and Other Settlements Overseas*, vol.1 (Leiden, 2006) 358–428, here p. 369–370.

[221] Aristoxenus of Tarantum (Fragment 23), fourth century B.C. A. Hermary, A. Hesnard and H. Treziny, *Marseille Grecque: La cite phocéenne (600–49 av. J-C)*, Editions Errance, 1999, p. 167.

[222] Strabo, *Geography*, VI.1.1.

[223] Herodotus, *Histories*, Book I. 166, trans. G. Rawlinson, Wordsworth Editions Ltd, 1996, p. 75.

Though the Greek language survived in Calabria to the twentieth century it has declined since then due to compulsory schooling in Italian, military service and depopulation. At the present time there are surviving seven villages in the Calabria region that still speak Greek. *Greek (Grigo) in Italy*, ['Institut de Sociolingüistica Catalana'] <http://www.uoc.edu/euromosaic/web/document/grec/an/i1/i1.html>, viewed on 19 May 2011.

On the Ionic coast of Calabria the language is called 'Grecanico' and in Apulia 'Griko'. Francesca Labonia, University of Salenti, Italy, personal interview with the author at the British Epigraphic Society Conference, Senate House, University of London, 19 November 2011.

G. Rohlfs, 'Greek Remnants in Southern Italy' in *The Classical Journal*, vol. 62, no. 4 (Jan., 1967): 164-169, The Classical Association of the Middle West and South. ['JSTOR' journal archive] <http://www.jstor.org/stable/3295569>, viewed on 30 December 2010;

M. Lahanas, *Names of the Greeks*, <http://www.mlahanas.de/Greeks/LX/NamesOfTheGreeks.html>, viewed on 30 December 2010.

[224] T. J. Dunbabin, *The Western Greeks: The History of Sicily and South Italy from the Foundation of the Greek Colonies to 480 B.C.*, Oxford University Press Monograph Reprints, 1998, p. 346.

The city of Zancle needed to secure the straits opposite them and appealed to their mother-city. Rhegium was one of the earliest Greek colonies led mainly by people from Chalcis with Messenians to be established on southern mainland Italy. Founded in the mid-seventh century B.C. south of Cumae to secure the Straight of Zancle (opposite the Greek city of Zancle in Sicily). M. Grant, *The Rise of the Greeks*, Phoenix Press, 2005, Ch. 4, p. 116.

Rhegium was destroyed by Locrians and Syracuse in 387 B.C. Later it was rebuilt under the Pax Romana. A. G. Woodhead, *The Greeks of the West*, Thames & Hudson, 1962, p. 57–58.

[225] Herodotus, *Histories*, Book 1, 167, trans. Wordsworth Editions Ltd, 1996, p. 76 & p. 112 n. 164.

[226] Strabo, *Geography,* VI.1.1.

[227] M. Grant, *The Rise of the Greeks*, Phoenix Press, 2005, p. 350 n. 59.

[228] Strabo, *Geography*, VI.1.1.

[229] Philostratus, *The Life of Apollonius of Tyana,* vol. 2. Bk. VII. 2, trans. C. P. Jones, Harvard University Press, 2005, p. 211 n.1.

[230] Pausanias, *Description of Greece,* X.8.6-7. ['Perseus, Tufts University' digital library] <http://www.perseus.tufts.edu/hopper/text?doc=Perseus%3Atext%3A1999.01.0160%3Abook%3D10%3Achapter%3D8%3Asection%3D6>, viewed on 22 October 2011.

[231] *Pausanias,* X.18.7, ['Theoi' E-Texts library] <http://www.theoi.com/Text/Pausanias10B.html>, viewed 11 February 2012; Incidentally Phocaea was founded by settlers from Phocis (Phokis). J. McInerney, *The Folds of Parnassos: Land and Ethnicity in Ancient Phokis,* University of Texas Press, 1999, p. 157-162.

[232] R. Flaceliere, *Daily Life in Greece at the Time of Pericles*, trans. P. Green, Phoenix, 2002, p. 100.

[233] R. Osborne, *Classical Greece 500–323 B.C.* Oxford University Press, 2000, p. 168.

[234] P. Kyriakou, *A Commentary on Euripides' Iphigenia in Tauris*, UaLG80. Walter de Grutyer, 2006, p. 362.

[235] M. Grant, *The Rise of the Greeks*, Phoenix Press, 2005, Ch. 6, p. 249.

[236] M. Bats, 'The Greeks in Gaul and Corsica: the rhythm of the Greek emporion' in P. Carratelli (ed.), *The Western Greeks: Classical Civilization in the Western Mediterranean,* (London, 1996): 577–584, here p. 582.

[237] J. Bromwich, *The Roman Remains of Southern France: a guidebook*, Routledge, 1993, p. 172.

[238] Strabo, *Geography,* XIII.1.41.

[239] *Justin: Epitome of the Philippic History of Pompeius Trogus*, 43.5.5–7, trans. J. C. Yardley, Scholars Press Atlanta, 1994, p. 268.

[240] B. Bizot, et al. *Marseille Antique: guide archéologiques de la France*, Editions du Patrimonie, Centre des monuments nationaux, 2007, p. 33.

[241] On the Pharo side of Lacydon a city built there could be protected on two sides by the sea. A wall across facing the landward side would have had to be long and possibly there were not enough people to defend it? Also it had a large hill that would make an acropolis. This hill was later called Chapel de la Garde from when a Guard was posted there on the heights. This was replaced in 1864 by the present church Notre Dame-de-la-Garde with a bright golden coloured statue of the Virgin Mary at the top, called by the local Marseillais La Bonne-Mére. G. Magi, *Provence*, Bonechi, 2001, p. 70.

[242] *Notre-Dame-de-laGarde*, <http://www.marseille-tourisme.com/en/discover-marseille/city-of-art/notre-dame-de-la-garde/>, viewed on 1 November 2011.

[243] *Justin: Epitome of the Philippic History of Pompeius Trogus*, 43.3–7, trans. J. C. Yardley, Scholars Press Atlanta, 1994, p. 266.

[244] *Ibid,* 43.3.5, p. 266.

[245] A. Trevor. Hodge, *Ancient Greek France*, University of Pennsylvania Press, 1999, p. 12.

[246] M. Grant, *The Rise of the Greeks*, Phoenix Press, 2005, p. 249.

[247] From Strabo, *Geography,* VI.1.1.

[248] A. Hermary, A. Hesnard, and H. Treziny, *Marseille Grecque: La cité phocéenne (600–49 av. J-C)*, Editions Errance, 1999, p. 167, Aristoxenus of Tarentum (Fragment 23), fourth century B.C.

[249] M. Bats, 'The Greeks in Gaul and Corsica: the rhythm of the Greek emporion' in P. Carratelli (ed.), *The Western Greeks: Classical Civilization in the Western Mediterranean*, (London, 1996): 577–584, here p. 582.

[250] M. H. Morgan, *Vitruvius: The Ten Books on Architecture*, Bk. 2, Ch. I. 5, Dover Publication, 1960, p. 40.

[251] J-P. Morel, 'Phocaean Colonisation' in G. R. Tsetskhladze (ed.), *Greek Colonisation: An Account of Greek Colonies and Other Settlements Overseas*, vol.1, (Leiden, 2006): 358–428, here p. 376.

[252] J. Bromwich, *The Roman Remains of Southern France: a guidebook*, Routledge, 1993, p. 174.

[253] A. Trevor. Hodge, *Ancient Greek France*, University of Pennsylvania Press, 1999, p. 82.

[254] Braun and Hogenberg, *Civitates Orbis Terrarum*, II–12, published 1575.

[255] G. Barclay, *Pliny's Natural Histories*, Wernernian Club,1847–48, Bk. 2, LXXVI. p. 118. The Greeks regarded the discoverer as the first to show it to their nation.

[256] A. Trevor. Hodge, *Ancient Greek France*, University of Pennsylvania Press, 1999, p. 79.

[257] S. Crane, 'Digging up the Present in Marseille's Old Port: Toward an Archaeology of Reconstruction' in *Journal of the Society of Architectural Historians*, vol. 63, no. 3 (Sep., 2004): 296–319. ['JSTOR' journal archive] <http://www.jstor.org/stable/4127973>, viewed on 8 October 2010.

[258] A. L. F. Rivet, *Gallia Narbonensis*, Batsford, 1988, p. 220.

[259] S. Crane, 'Digging up the Present in Marseille's Old Port: Toward an Archaeology of Reconstruction' in *Journal of the Society of Architectural Historians*, vol. 63, no. 3 (Sep., 2004): 296–319, here p. 306, ['JSTOR' journal archive] <http://www.jstor.org/stable/4127973>, viewed on 8 October 2010.

[260] J-M. Gassend, *Les Vestiges de la Bourse*, Les Editions de la Nerthe, 1997, p. 8.

[261] *Ibid*, p. 22.

[262] J. Knight, *Roman France: an archaeological field guide*, Tempus Publishing, 2001, p. 164.

[263] A. Trevor. Hodge, *Ancient Greek France*, University of Pennsylvania Press, 1999, p. 246 n. 19.

[264] M. Bats, 'The Greeks in Gaul and Corsica: the rhythm of the Greek emporion' in P. Carratelli (ed.), *The Western Greeks: Classical Civilization in the Western Mediterranean*, (London, 1996): 577–584, here p. 581.

[265] Le Musée d'Histoire de Marseille, ['Culture.marseille.fr'] <http://www.marseille.fr/siteculture/les-lieux-culturels-municipaux/musees/le-musee-dhistoire-de-marseille>, viewed 4 June 2012.

[266] J-P. Morel, 'Phocaean Colonisation' in G. R. Tsetskhladze (ed.), *Greek Colonisation: An Account of Greek Colonies and Other Settlements Overseas*, vol.1, (Leiden, 2006): 358–428, here p. 380.

[267] Athenaeus, *Deipnosophists*, vol. 6. XIII, 576, trans. C. B. Gulick, Loeb, William Heinemann, 1937, p. 109–111.

[268] Strabo, *Geography*, V.3.8.

[269] J-P, Morel, 'Phocaean Colonisation' in G. R. Tsetskhladze (ed.), *Greek Colonisation: An Account of Greek Colonies and Other Settlements Overseas*, vol.1, (Leiden, 2006): 358–428, here p. 381 & p. 405. The Phocaeans had the same aims and eye for 'beauty' etc., as the other Greeks when they chose Emporion (Sant Marti d'Empúries), Rhodus (Roses) and Agathe Tyche (Agde) to settle.

[270] *Justin: Epitome of the Philippic History of Pompeius Trogus*, 43.4.1–2, trans. J. C. Yardley, Scholars Press Atlanta, 1994, p. 267.

[271] L. Foxhall, *Olive Cultivation in Ancient Greece: Seeking the Ancient Economy,* Oxford, 2007, p. 112.

[272] J-P. Morel, 'Phocaean Colonisation' in G. R. Tsetskhladze (ed.), *Greek Colonisation: An Account of Greek Colonies and Other Settlements Overseas,* vol.1, (Leiden, 2006): 358–428, here p. 382. n. 101.

[273] *Ibid,* p. 385.

[274] M. I. Rostovtzeff, *Social and Economic History of the Hellenistic World,* vol. 1, Oxford, 1941, p. 396.

[275] J-P. Morel, 'Phocaean Colonisation' in G. R. Tsetskhladze (ed.), *Greek Colonisation: An Account of Greek Colonies and Other Settlements Overseas,* vol.1, (Leiden, 2006): 358–428, here p. 382.

[276] N. Chadwick, *The Celts,* Pelican Books, 1970, p. 35.

[277] Athenaeus, *Deipnosophists,* vol. 1. I. 27, trans. C. B. Gulick, Loeb, William Heinemann, 1927, p. 119.

[278] *Ibid,* vol. 5. XI.501, p. 241.

[279] S. Gori and M. C. Bettini, 'Gli Etruschi da Genova ad Ampurias, Att del XXIV Convegno di Studi Etruschi ed Italici, Marseille,-Lattes, 26 settembre–1 octtobre 2002'. Two volumes. Pisa: Istituti Editoriiali e Poligrafici Internazionali, 2006. ISBN 88-8147-428-X, in *Bryn Mawr Classical Review* 2008.5.09, p. 4–5, reviewed by Jean MacIntosh Turfa, University of Pennsylvania Museum. <http://bmcr.brynmawr.edu/2008/2008-05-09.html>, viewed on 5 March 2011.

[280] Strabo, *Geography*, IV.1.5.

[281] A. Trevor. Hodge, *Ancient Greek France*, University of Pennsylvania Press, 1999, p. 122 n. 41.

[282] M. Thompson, O. Morkholm, and C. M. Kraay, *An Inventory of Greek Coin Hoards*, The American Numismatic Society, New York, 1973, p. 361-3.

[283] W. Scheidel, I. Morris, and R. P. Saller, *Cambridge Economic History of the Greco-Roman World,* Cambridge, 2007, p. 259.

[284] Plutarch, *The Parallel Lives*, Life of Marius, 21, vol. IX, Loeb, 1920, ['Penelope, University of Chicago' digital library] <http://penelope.uchicago.edu/Thayer/E/Roman/Texts/Plutarch/Lives/Marius*.html>, viewed on 29 October 2011.

[285] D. Garcia, 'Le casque corinthien des Baux-de-Provence' in S. Bouffir and A. Hemary (eds.) *L'occident grec, de Marseille à Mégara Hyblaea*, (Centre Camille Jullian, 2013): 85-90. Helmet found in 1813.

[286] Empire, ['The Free Dictionary] <http://www.thefreedictionary.com/Empire> viewed 20 May 2012.

[287] T. R. Martin, *An Overview of Classical Greek History from Mycenae to Alexander,* Athenian Empire in the Golden Age, TRM OV 9, ['Perseus' Tufts university digital library] <http://www.perseus.tufts.edu/hopper/text?doc=Perseus%3Atext%3A1999.04.0009%3Achapter%3D9> viewed 21 May 2012.

[288] Pausanias, X.4.1.

[289] Strabo, *Geography*, IV.1.9. Antipolis founded sixth century B.C. had a suit against Massalia and became an Italiote city and 'free from their orders'; 'Nicaea remains subject to the Massaliotes and belongs to the Province' Strabo, *Geography,* IV.1.9; Nicaea (Nice) remained under the supervision of Massalia. B. Levick, *The Government of the Roman Empire: A Sourcebook*, Croom Helm, 1985, Ch. 2, p. 24 –25, ILS 6761; Nicaea, Narbonensis; Pliny, *NH,* III.5.

[290] Empire,['The Free Dictionary] <http://www.thefreedictionary.com/Empire> viewed 20 May 2012

[291] J-P. Morel, 'Phocaean Colonisation' in G. R. Tsetskhladze (ed.), *Greek Colonisation: An Account of Greek Colonies and Other Settlements Overseas,* vol.1, (Leiden, 2006): 358–428, here p. 381. Morel mentions it is not always easy to distinguish between Massaliote amphorae with 'Corinthian B' and 'Ionian-Massaliot' which can be sometimes Italian or Sicilian. (Morel, p. 382).

[292] W. Scheidel, I. Morris, and R. P. Saller, *Cambridge Economic History of the Greco-Roman World,* Cambridge, 2007, p. 264.

[293] Gori, S and Bettini, M. C. 'Gli Etruschi da Genova ad Ampurias, Att del XXIV Convegno di Studi Etruschi ed Italici, Marseille,–Lattes, 26 settembre–1 octtobre 2002'. Two volumes. Pisa: Istituti Editoriiali e Poligrafici Internazionali, 2006. ISBN 88–8147–428–X, in *Bryn Mawr Classical Review* 2008.5.09, p. 4–5, reviewed by Jean MacIntosh Turfa, University of Pennsylvania Museum. <http://bmcr.brynmawr.edu/2008/2008-05-09.html>, viewed on 5 March 2011.

[294] M. Bats, 'The Greeks in Gaul and Corsica: the rhythm of the Greek emporion' in P. Carratelli (ed.), *The Western Greeks: Classical Civilization in the Western Mediterranean,* (London, 1996): 577–584, here p. 581.

[295] Michael M. Sage, *Roman Conquest: Gaul*, Pen & Sword Books, 2011, p. 18.

[296] W. Scheidel, I. Morris, and R. P. Saller, *Cambridge Economic History of the Greco-Roman World,* Cambridge, 2007, p. 267–8.

[297] E. Chazelles, 'Les Pinardiers de l'antiquité', *Marseille antique,* (July 10, 2009) p. 17, <http://issuu.com/klode/docs/marseille_antique>, viewed on 17 August 2011; DRASSM–*Departement Recherches Archéologiques Subaquatique Sous-Marines,* <http://www.culture.gouv.fr/fr/archeosm/archeosom/drasm.htm> viewed 17 August 2011.

[298] S. Crane, 'Digging up the Present in Marseille's Old Port: Toward an Archaeology of Reconstruction' in *Journal of the Society of Architectural Historians,* vol. 63, no. 3 (Sep., 2004): 296–319, here p. 307, ['JSTOR' journal archive] <http://www.jstor.org/stable/4127973>, viewed on 8 October 2010.

[299] J. Bromwich, *The Roman Remains of Southern France: a guide book*, Routledge, 1993, p. 171

[300] D. R. Shackleton Bailey, *Martial's Epigrams,* vol. 2. X, 36, Harvard, 1993, p. 359.

[301] MMSH–Maison Méditerranéenne des Sciences d'Homme. Emma Chazelles, 'Les Pinardiers de l'antiquité', *Marseille antique,* (July 10, 2009) p. 16-17, <http://issuu.com/klode/docs/marseille_antique>, viewed on 2009.

[302] E. Chazelles, 'Les Pinardiers de l'antiquité', *Marseille antique,* (July 10, 2009) p. 17, <http://issuu.com/klode/docs/marseille_antique>;<www.cabotages.fr-Edition2009-cabotages.Coastwise-25>, viewed on 2009.

[303] W. Scheidel, I. Morris, and R. P. Saller, *Cambridge Economic History of the Greco-Roman World,* Cambridge, 2007, p. 265.

[304] R. Stilwell, et al. (eds.), *The Princeton Encyclopaedia of Classical Sites,* Princeton University press, 1976, ['Perseus Project, Tufts University' digital library] <http://www.perseus.tufts.edu/hopper/text?doc=Perseus:text:1999.04.0006:entry=carpentorate&highlight=massalia>, viewed on 12 October 2011.

[305] J-P. Morel, 'Phocaean Colonisation' in G. R. Tsetskhladze (ed.), *Greek Colonisation: An Account of Greek Colonies and Other Settlements Overseas,* vol.1, (Leiden, 2006): 358–428, here p. 382. n. 97.

[306] W. Scheidel, I. Morris, and R. P. Saller, *Cambridge Economic History of the Greco-Roman World,* Cambridge, 2007, p. 265.

[307] S. Haynes. *Etruscan Civilization*, Paul Getty Trust, 2004, p. 266.

[308] British Museum reception, personal interview with the author of *Etruscan Civilization* Sybil Haynes on 13 February 2009.

[309] O. Murray, *Early Greece*, Fontana, 1993, p. 227.

[310] Nos Collections, *Les Vases en Bronze des Banquets Funéraries*, <http://www.musee-vix.fr/fr/index.php?page=38>, viewed on 11 November 2010.

[311] 1,466 bottles at today's standard bottle size containing 75cl (details from wine department Sainsbury's Supermarket, 11 November 2010).

[312] S. Piggott, G. Daniels, and C. McBurney, (eds.), *France Before the Romans*, Thames & Hudson, 1973, p. 172, Fig. 65.

[313] J. Knight, *Roman France: An Archaeological Field Guide,* Tempus Publishing Ltd., 2001, p. 134.

[314] S. Piggott, G. Daniels, and C. McBurney, (eds.), *France Before the Romans*, Thames & Hudson, 1973, p. 172, Fig. 68.

[315] J. Boardman, *The Greeks Overseas,* Thames & Hudson, 1999, Ch. 5. p. 221.

[316] J. Knight, *Roman France: An Archaeological Field Guide,* Tempus Publishing Ltd., 2001, p. 134.

[317] J. Boardman, *The Greeks Overseas*, Thames & Hudson, 1999, Ch. 5, p. 221; Trésor de Vix, *Âge de Fer,* ['Musée du Pays Châtillonais' Nos collections] <http://www.musee-vix.fr/fr/>, viewed on 11 November 2010.

[318] J-P. Morel, 'Phocaean Colonisation' in G. R. Tsetskhladze (ed.), *Greek Colonisation: An Account of Greek Colonies and Other Settlements Overseas,* vol.1, (Leiden, 2006): 358–428, here p. 384. The finds were on a road leading towards the Loire estuary via the River Cher. Nearby sites show the greatest concentration of Etruscan finds in Gaul.

[319] J. Knight, *Roman France: an archaeological field guide,* Tempus Publishing, 2001, p. 188.

[320] J. Boardman, *The Greeks Overseas*, Thames & Hudson, 1999, Ch. 5, p. 223.

[321] J. McIntosh, *Handbook of Life in Prehistoric Europe,* Oxford, 2006. p. 128.

[322] R. Gardiner, *The Earliest Ships*, Conway Maritime Press, 2004, p. 54–55.

[323] J. Boardman, *The Greeks Overseas*, Thames & Hudson, 1999, Ch. 5, p. 223.

[324] M. Nelson, *The Barbarians Beverage: A History of Beer in Ancient Europe, Routledge,* 2005, p. 51.

[325] J. Boardman, *The Greeks Overseas*, Thames & Hudson, 1999, Ch. 5, p. 223.

[326] R. Gardiner, *The Earliest Ships*, Conway Maritime Press, 1996, p. 54.

[327] J. Boardman, *The Greeks Overseas*, Thames & Hudson, 1999, Ch. 5, p. 224.

[328] J-P. Morel, 'Phocaean Colonisation' in G. R. Tsetskhladze (ed.), *Greek Colonisation: An Account of Greek Colonies and Other Settlements Overseas,* vol.1, (Leiden, 2006): 358–428, here p. 398. Bats also notes the increase in Massalia amphorae and Attic red-figure ware at Lyon-Vaise, and Bragny (junction of rivers Saône and Doubs). M.Bats, 'The Greeks in Gaul and Corsica: the rhythm of the Greek emporion' in P. Carratelli (ed.), *The Western Greeks: Classical Civilization in the Western Mediterranean,* (London, 1996): 577–584, here p. 580.

[329] B. B. Shefton, 'Massalia and colonization in the North-Western Mediterranean' in G. R. Tsetskhadze and F. de Angis (eds.), *The Archaeology of Greek Colonization* (Oxford, 1994): 61–86, here p. 69.

[330] J. Boardman, *The Greeks Overseas*, Thames & Hudson, 1999, Ch. 5, p. 224.

[331] *Ibid*, p. 226-227. During a visit there (1986) to see the Moreška, when Korčula was still part of Yugoslavia, we saw the name on the label of the local wine was called Grk (Greek). This red wine had a good taste with a meal and no headache afterwards.

[332] R. Osborne, 'Early Greek Colonization? The nature of Greek settlement in the West', in N. Fisher and H. van Wees (eds.), *Archaic Greeece: new approaches and new evidence,* (London, 1998): 251–269, here p. 253.

[333] J. Boardman, *The Greeks Overseas*, Thames & Hudson, 1999, Ch. 5, p. 227.

[334] *Ibid*, p. 228.

[335] *The Geography of Strabo*, V.1.7. Loeb, 1923, ['Penelope, University of Chicago' digital library],<http://penelope.uchicago.edu/Thayer/E/Roman/Texts/Strabo/5A*.html >, viewed on 11 February 2012.

[336] K. Lomas, 'Beyond Magna Graecia: Greeks and Non-Greeks in France, Spain and Italy' in K. Kinzl, (ed.), *A Companion to the Classical Greek World*, (Wiley-Blackwell, 2006):174-198, here p. 182.

[337] Athenaeus, *Deipnosophists,* vol. 4. X. 429, trans. C. B. Gulick, Loeb, William Heinemann, 1930, p. 443; Ebel says this may have been directed to the Celtic women who the Massaliotes had married. C. Ebel, *Transalpine Gaul: the emergence of a Roman province*, Brill, 1976, p. 30; and Dunbabin mentions Miletos part Carian and Greek where women were also forced to drink water by law. T. J. Dunbabin, *The Western Greeks: The History of Sicily and South Italy from the Foundation of the Greek Colonies to 480 B.C.,* Oxford University Press Monograph Reprints, 1998, p. 186.

[338] Cicero, *Pro Flacco,* 63–64.

[339] *Livy*, vol.10. XXXVII. 21–23, trans. E. T. Sage, Loeb Classical Library, 1935, p. 459; Strabo, *Geography,* IV.1.5; Valerius Maximus, *Memorable Deeds and Sayings: A Thousand and One Tales from Ancient Rome,* II.6.7-9.

[340] A. Momigliano, *Alien Wisdom: The Limits of Hellenization,* 1990, Cambridge University Press, 1975, p. 56, (from Silius Italicus, *Punica,* 15.169–72) in contrast to Consul C.M.Vulso 189 B.C. inflammatory and inaccurate speech of 'degenerate' Galatians where Celtic 'barbarism' had even touched that paragon of virtue Massalia (Livy, 38.17.11).

[341] E. Stefani, *Magic of Amber: amulets and jewellery from Magna Graecia and Macedonia*, University Studio Press, 2009, p 18-19; J-P. Morel, 'Phocaean Colonisation' in G. R. Tsetskhladze (ed.), *Greek Colonisation: An Account of Greek Colonies and Other Settlements Overseas,* vol.1, (Leiden, 2006): 358–428, here p. 372.

[342] A. J. Domínguez, 'Spain and France (including Corsica)' in H. H. Hanson and T. H. Nielsen, *An Inventory of Archaic and Classical Poleis*, (Oxford, 2004):157–171, here p. 163. ['Scribd'] <http://www.scribd.com/doc/82942410/An-Inventory-of-Archaic-and-Classical-Poleis-Ed-by-M-H-Hansen-Th-H-Nielsen#outer_page_174> viewed 3 April 2012.

[343] Aristoxenus, *Histories*, Fragment. Gr. 2.279.23. vol. 2, Anacreon, trans. J. M. Edmunds, *Lyra Graeca*, Heinemann, 1979, p. 121.

[344] *Ibid*.

[345] M. Grant, *The Rise of the Greeks*, Phoenix Press, 2005, Ch.6. p. 249; Herodotus, *Histories*, I.165–166, trans. G. Rawlinson, Wordsworth Editions Ltd., 1996, p. 74–75.

[346] A. R. Burn, 'Persia and the Greeks' in *The Median and Achaemenian Periods*, The Cambridge History of Iran, vol. 2. ch. 6. 1985, <http://histories.cambridge.org/extract?id=chol9780521200912_CHOL9780521200912A007>, viewed on 11 September 2011.

[347] Herodotus, *Histories*, I. 141, trans. G. Rawlinson, Wordsworth Editions Ltd, 1996, p. 65–66.

[348] *Ibid*, I. 141, p. 66.

[349] *Ibid*, I. 152, p. 69.

[350] *Ibid.*

[351] A. R. Burn, 'Persia and the Greeks' in *The Median and Achaemenian Periods*, The Cambridge History of Iran, vol. 2. ch. 6. 1985, <http://histories.cambridge.org/extract?id=chol9780521200912_CHOL9780521200912A007>, viewed on 11 September 2011.

[352] Herodotus, *Histories*, I. 152, trans. G. Rawlinson, Wordsworth Editions Ltd, 1996, p. 70.

[353] M. Grant, *The Rise of the Greeks*, Phoenix Press, 2005, Ch.6. p. 249.

[354] Herodotus, *Histories*, Book I. 165, trans. G. Rawlinson, Wordsworth Editions Ltd, 1996, p. 74.

[355] *Ibid*, Book I. 165, p. 75.

[356] *Ibid*, Book I. 167, p. 76.

[357] *Ibid*, Book I. 166, p. 75.

[358] J-P. Morel, 'Phocaean Colonisation' in G. R. Tsetskhladze (ed.), *Greek Colonisation: An Account of Greek Colonies and Other Settlements Overseas,* vol.1, (Leiden, 2006): 358–428, here p. 392.

Toynbee mentions that Asian Greeks had a community in Lyon during the reign of Emperor Marcus Aurelius A.D.161–180 which may indicate a continuous presence as with the other Greeks in France and Spain. A. Toynbee, *The Greeks and their Heritage,* Oxford, 1981, p. 195.

[359] *Gauls and Greeks, Relations with Greek Marseilles*, ['The Gauls in Provence, the oppidum of Entremont'] <http://www.entremont.culture.gouv.fr/en/index2.html.>, viewed 26 February 2012.

[360] A. Trevor. Hodge, *Ancient Greek France*, University of Pennsylvania Press, 1999, p. 160 n. 56, R. Amy, *Princeton Encyclopaedia of Classical Sites (PECS)*, 87.

[361] Bridges mentions that early versions of the Jason and the Argonauts suggest they sailed west and founded Theline. V. Bridges, 'Paganism in Provence: How the Mother-Goddess Became the Mother of God', *Journal of the Western Mystery Tradition*, No. 6. vol.1, Vernal Equinox 2004, <http://www.jwmt.org/v1n6/provence.html#13>, viewed on 2 September 2011.

[362] M. Heijmans, J-M. Roquette and C. Sintès, *Arles Antique: guide archéologiques de la France,* Editions Patrimone, Paris, 2006, p. 24.

[363] A. L. F. Rivet, *Gallia Narbonensis,* Batsford, 1988, p. 12 n. 27; Rufus Festus Avienus, *Ora Maritma, Lines 681-683,* <http://www.thelatinlibrary.com/avienus.ora.html> viewed 30 December 2012.

[364] J-P. Morel, 'Phocaean Colonisation', in G. R. Tsetskhladze (ed.), *Greek Colonisation: An Account of Greek Colonies and Other Settlements Overseas,* vol.1, (Leiden, 2006): 358–428, here p. 385.

[365] A. Furtwängler. 'Le trésor d'Auriol et les types monétaires phocéens' in A. Hemary and H. Tréziny (eds.), *Les Cultes des citiés phocéennes,* (Centre Camille Jullian, 2000):175-181and I. Picard p. 166-174.

[366] I. Carradice, *Greek Coins*, British Museum Press, 1995, p. 39 & p. 74.

[367] Herodotus, *Histories*, Book 6. 8, trans. G. Rawlinson, Wordsworth Editions Ltd, 1996, p. 451.

[368] S. Hornblower and A. Spawforth, *The Oxford Classical Dictionary*, Oxford, 2003, p. 764.

[369] Herodotus, *Histories*, Book 6. 8, trans. G. Rawlinson, Wordsworth Editions Ltd, 1996, p. 451.

[370] *Ibid,* Book 6. 12. p. 452; R. Gardiner, (ed.), *The Age of the Galley*, Conway Maritime Press, 1995, p. 48.

[371] Herodotus, *Histories*, Book 6. 17 and Book 6. 13-14, trans. G. Rawlinson, Wordsworth Editions Ltd, 1996, p. 453-4.

[372] *Diodorus of Sicily*, vol. 4. XI. 2. 2-5, trans. C. H. Oldfather, Loeb, 1966, p. 125.

[373] *Diodorus of Sicily*, vol. 5. XIII. 100. 1-7, trans. C. H. Oldfather, Heinemann, 1950, p. 407.

[374] A. de Jong, A. *Traditions of the Magi: Zoroastrianism in Greek and Latin Literature*, Brill, 1997, p. 278.

[375] Xenophon, *Anabasis*, Of Cyrus, Book 1, Chapter 10, trans. E. Spelman, 1830, H. Colburn and R. Bentley, p. 45 n. 2. <http://books.google.co.uk/books?id=zQl8i4ljaKgC&pg=PA45&lpg=PA45&dq=Xenophon+Phocaean+woman&source=bl&ots=26e6x8s42K&sig=giFmBrN0XTFs69eia-ebq-6HPac&hl=en&sa=X&ei=0SBnT8Irp6zRBbKj8aUI&ved=0CFQQ6AEwCQ#v=onepage&q&f=false> viewed 19 March 2012; Plutarch, *Artaxerxes*, 26.3–27.3; Plutarch, *Pericles*, 24.11; Athenaeus, *Deipnosophistae*, 13.27. 576D; Aelian, *Historical Miscellany*, 12.1.

[376] J. Knight, *Roman France: an archaeological field guide*, Tempus Publishing, 2001, p. 188.

[377] S. Piggott, G. Daniels, and C. McBurney, (eds.), *France Before the Romans*, Thames & Hudson, 1973, p. 175, Fig. 78; D. Darde and V. Lassalle, *Nimes Antique: Guides archéologiques de la France*, Imprimerie Nationale Editions 1993, p. 13.

[378] J-P. Morel, 'Phocaean Colonisation' in G. R. Tsetskhladze (ed.), *Greek Colonisation: An Account of Greek Colonies and Other Settlements Overseas*, vol.1, (Leiden, 2006): 358–428, here p. 398.

[379] M. Thompson, O. Morkholm, and C. M. Kraay, *An Inventory of Greek Coin Hoards*, The American Numismatic Society, New York, 1973, p. 361.

[380] A. Trevor. Hodge, *Ancient Greek France*, University of Pennsylvania Press, 1999, p. 160 n. 57, Pierre Rouillard, *Études Massaliètes*, 3, 183.

[381] N. Chadwick, *The Celts*, Pelican Books, 1970, p. 56.

[382] Strabo, Geography, Book II.5.28.

[383] Strabo, *Geography*, Vol. 2. 4.6.2, trans. H. L. Jones, Loeb, 1923, p. 267.

[384] *Justin: Epitome of the Philippic History of Pompeius Trogus,* 43.5.5–7, trans. J-C. Yardley, Scholars Press Atlanta, 1994, p. 269.

[385] Strabo, *Geography*, XIII.1.41. *The Geography of Strabo,* (ed.), H. L. Jones, Heinemann, 1924, ['Perseus, Tufts University' digital library] <http://www.perseus.tufts.edu/hopper/text?doc=Perseus%3Atext%3A1999.01.0198%3Abook%3D13%3Achapter%3D1%3Asection%3D41>, viewed on 21 October 2011.

[386] *Justin: Epitome of the Philippic History of Pompeius Trogus*, 43.5.8–10, trans. J. C. Yardley, Scholars Press Atlanta, 1994, p. 269.

[387] *Ibid*, 28. 2.3–3.7, p. 200–201, and 38.48. p. 239.

[388] *Ibid,* 43.5.8–10. p. 269.

[389] *Ibid*; King Artaxerxes who sent a Persian Embassy to Greece (392/1 B.C.) but peace was made later in 387/6 B.C. (Justin, 6.6.1) the Varronian date for the Gallic sack of Rome; 'This year was noteworthy…because it was at this time the city of Rome was captured by the Gauls'. *Justin: Epitome of the Philippic History of Pompeius Trogus*, 6. 6. 5, trans. J. C. Yardley, Scholars Press Atlanta, 1994, p. 71 n.7 and p. 72.

[390] *Ibid*, 38.4.8. p. 239.

[391] *Ibid,* 28.2.4–5. p. 201.

[392] F. Meijer, *A History of Seafaring in the Classical World*, Croom Helm, 1986, p. 79.

[393] Robin Osborne, 'Settlement and productivity in the Greek landscape', Ancient History Seminar, Institute of Classical Studies, Senate House, University of London, 13 October 2011, questions and answers section. He was of the opinion that there was nothing stopping Athenians to acquire wealth by trading and as Metics were not allowed to own land there would naturally be many Metics involved with trade as an occupation.

[394] J-P. Wilson, 'The nature of Greek overseas settlements in the archaic period: emporion or apoikia?', in L. Mitchell and P. J. Rhodes (eds.), *The Development of the Polis in Archaic Greece*, (London, 1997): 199-207, here p. 203 n. 26 [Xen] *Ath. Pol.* 1.10.

[395] *Ibid*, here p. 200–201 n. 9. [Arist.] *Ath. Pol.* 51.4.

[396] F. Meijer, *A History of Seafaring in the Classical World*, Croom Helm, 1986, p. 79.

[397] J-P. Wilson, 'The nature of Greek overseas settlements in the archaic period: emporion or apoikia?' in L. Mitchell and P.J. Rhodes (eds.), *The Development of the Polis in Archaic Greece*, (London, 1997): 199-207, p. 203.

[398] '11.24 The Thirty Attack Wealthy Metics, Lysias XII Against Eratosthenes, 4–20', Chapter 11, Labour, Slaves, Serfs and Citizens, in M. Dillon and L. Garland, *Ancient Greece: social and historical documents from archaic times to the death of Socrates,* (Routledge, 1994): 360–392.

[399] T. J. Dunbabin, *The Western Greeks: The History of Sicily and South Italy from the Foundation of the Greek Colonies to 480 B.C*, Oxford University Press Monograph Reprints, 1998, p. 216.

[400] Demosthenes, IV, *Private Orations*, XXVII–XL, trans. A. T. Murray, Heinemann, 1965, p. 183–191.

[401] *Ibid*.

[402] *Ibid*.

[403] Demosthenes, *Against Boeotus* 2. 40.36. n. 3, ['Perseus, Tufts University' digital library] <http://www.perseus.tufts.edu/hopper/text?doc=Perseus%3Atext%3A1999.01.0076%3Aspeech%3D40%3Asection%3D 36 > viewed 24 October 2011, and Cyzicus staters Demosthenes, *Against Phormio*, 34.23. n.1 http://www.perseus.tufts.edu/hopper/text?doc=Perseus%3Atext%3A1999.01.0076%3Aspeech%3D34%3Asection%3D2 3

[404] Demosthenes, *Against Phormio*, 34.23 n.1. ['Perseus, Tufts University' digital library] <http://www.perseus.tufts.edu/hopper/text?doc=Perseus%3Atext%3A1999.01.0076%3Aspeech%3D34%3Asection%3D 23> viewed 12 March 2012.

[405] Isocrates, vol.1. *Archidamus*, 83–84, trans. G. Norlin, Heinemann, 1928, p. 397.

[406] A. Trevor. Hodge, *Ancient Greek France*, University of Pennsylvania Press, 1999, p. 265 n. 15, (M. Clerc, *Massalia. Histoire de Marseille dans l'antiquité des origins à la fin de l'Empire romain d'Occident (476 ap. J.-C.),* TOME 1, Des origins jusqu 'au IIIme siècle av. J.-C. Marseille, Librairie A. Tacussel, 1927, p. 403); and Professor Hodge's email clarification of references to me September 2008; see also Anaximader's gnomon in Sparta. D. L. Couprie, *Heaven and Earth in Ancient Greek Cosmology: From Thales to Heraclides Ponticus*, Springer, 2011, p. 34.

[407] P. Valavanis, *Games and Sanctuaries in Ancient Greece,* trans. Dr David Hardy, Kapon Editions, 2004, p. 190.

[408] A. Giovanni, 'The Pan Hellenic Festivals' in *Images and Ideologies: Self-definition in the Hellenic World*, (eds.), A. Bulloch, et al, University of California Press, 1993, p.280 n. 65, A. Plasscart, 'Inscriptiones de Delphes la liste des Théodoriques', *B.C.H* 45 (1921), 1–85.

[409] P. Valavanis, *Games and Sanctuaries in Ancient Greece,* trans. Dr David Hardy, Kapon Editions, 2004, p. 190.

[410] *Ibid*, p. 191.

[411] Philostratus, *The Life of Apollonius of Tyana,* vol.III, Letters, 24, trans. C. P. Jones, Harvard University Press, 2005, p. 25. n. 24.

[412] Dio Chrysostom, *Discourses,* Book 1, 1–11, trans. J. W. Cohoon, Loeb, 2002, p. 377.

[413] P. Green, *Alexander the Great*, Weidenfield & Nicolson, 1970, p. 75

[414] *The Parallel Lives by Plutarch*, vol. VII, The Life of Alexander, 14, (Part 1 of 7), Loeb 1917. ['Penelope, University of Chicago' digital library] <http://penelope.uchicago.edu/Thayer/E/Roman/Texts/Plutarch/Lives/Alexander*/3.html>, viewed 17 June 2012; Plutarch, *De Fortuna Alexandri*, Loeb, 1926, Second Oration, Vol. IV, 332 A, B, & C. p. 413, ['Penelope, University of Chicago' digital library], viewed on 15 April 2011, <http://penelope.uchicago.edu/Thayer/E/Roman/Texts/Plutarch/Moralia/Fortuna_Alexandri*/1.html>, viewed on 15 April 2011,

[415] *Diogenes the Cynic: Sayings and Anecdotes with Other Popular Moralists*, (649. Diogenes 33, to Panomachos), trans. R. Hard, Oxford, 2012, p. 165.

[416] Philostratus, *The Life Of Apollonius of Tyana*, vol. 2. Bk.VII, 2.3, trans. C. P. Jones, Harvard University Press, 2005, p. 213.

[417] Dio Chrysostom, *Discourses* 1–11, trans. J. W. Cohoon, Loeb, 2002, p. 405.

[418] *Ibid*, p. 415.

[419] *Ibid*, p. 409.

[420] S. Goldhill, *Being Greek under Rome: cultural identity, the second sophist and the development of empire,* Cambridge, 2001, p. 310.

[421] P. Valavanis, *Games and Sanctuaries in Ancient Greece,* trans. Dr David Hardy, Kapon Editions, 2004 p. 254.

[422] C. F. C. Hawkes, *Pytheas: Europe and the Greek Explorers,* (Eighth J. L. Myers Memorial Lecture), Oxford, 1975, ASIN: B0007AMH16.

[423] W. M. M' Devitte, *Civil War*, I.34. G. Bell & Sons, 1933, p. 265.

[424] Strabo, *Geography*, IV.1.3.

[425] *Ibid*, IV.1.5.

[426] Athenaeus, *Deipnosophists,* vol. 5. XII, 523, trans. C. B. Gulick, Loeb, 1937, p. 359.

[427] *Ibid*, p. 359, note (a) Plutarch, Proverb. Alex., 60.

[428] A. Momigliano, *Alien Wisdom: The Limits of Hellenization,* 1990, Cambridge University Press, 1975, p. 56, (from Silius Italicus, *Punica,* 15.169–72).

[429] Strabo, *Geography,* Book IV, Ch. I, 5.

[430] K. Lomas, 'Beyond Magna Graecia: Greeks and Non-Greeks in France, Spain and Italy' in K. Kinzl, (ed.), *A Companion to the Classical Greek World*, (Wiley-Blackwell, 2006):174–198, p. 183.

[431] J-P. Morel, 'Phocaean Colonisation' in G. R. Tsetskhladze (ed.), *Greek Colonisation: An Account of Greek Colonies and Other Settlements Overseas,* vol.1, (Leiden, 2006): 358–428, here p. 378.

[432] *Ibid*.

[433] K. Lomas, 'Beyond Magna Graecia: Greeks and Non-Greeks in France, Spain and Italy' in K. Kinzl, (ed.), *A Companion to the Classical Greek World*, (Wiley-Blackwell, 2006):174–198, here p. 183.

[434] P. Gallini, 'Des tombs grecques à Marseille' *La Provence*, 4 June 2012, <http://www.laprovence.com/article/a-la-une/des-tombes-grecques-a-marseille>; *Ancient Greek tombs discovered in Marseilles*, 8 June 2012, ['Archaeology News Network'] <http://archaeologynewsnetwork.blogspot.gr/2012/06/ancient-greek-tombs-discovered-in.html#.T_f0KJFRGuK>, viewed 7 July 2012.

[435] J-P. Morel, 'Phocaean Colonisation' in G. R. Tsetskhladze (ed.), *Greek Colonisation: An Account of Greek Colonies and Other Settlements Overseas,* vol.1, (Leiden, 2006): 358–428, here p. 378.

[436] W. Burkert, *Greek Religion: Archaic and Classical*, II. 4–5, Blackwell, 1987, p. 83.

[437] D. D. Hughes, *Human Sacrifice in Ancient Greece,* Routledge, 1991, p. 156–159, Abdera and Massilia, Serv. Verg, *Aen,* 3.57=Petron, fr.1; Lactantius Placidus, Comm. in *Statius, Thebais*, 10.793.

Servius Petronius wrote on the custom:

> *Nam Massilienses quotiens pestilentia laborabant, unus se ex pauperibus offerebat alendus anno integro publicis sumptibus et puriorbus cibis. hic postea ornatus verbenis et vestibus sacris circumducebatur per totam civitatem cum execrationibus, ut in ipsum reciderent mala totius civitatis, et sic proiiciebatur (praecipitabatur, Stephanus): hoc autem in Petronio lectum est.*

L. R. Farnell, *The Cults of the Greek States,* Digitally Printed Version, Cambridge University Press, 2010, p. 419 n. 245; Serv. on Verg., in James Hastings, *Encyclopaedia of Religion and Ethics (1908)* v. 21, Kessinger, 2003, p. 220; see also John Cuthbert Lawson, *Modern Greek Folklore and Ancient Greek Religion: A Study in Survival* (1909), Kessinger, 2003, p. 357–358.

[438] In the Christian religion Jesus of Nazareth was the ultimate sacrifice taking on all the evils of the world and freeing all people from any further sacrifices of animals or human beings, conquering death itself and establishing a new level of human consciousness and way of life. A contemporary of Jesus the Pythagorean philosopher Apollonius of Tyana wrote against blood sacrifices and said the Gods require wisdom to please them instead. Philostratus, *The Life Of Apollonius of Tyana,* trans. C. P. Jones, Harvard University Press, 2005, vol. III, Letters, 26 & 27, p. 27 n. 30.

[439] P. Parker, 'Greek Religion', in J. Boardman, J. Griffin, and O. Murray, (eds.), *Greece and the Hellenistic World,* Oxford University Press, 2001, pp. 306–329, here p.317.

[440] Witnessed by Mrs. Argiro Gunstone who also had suffered the flu there and saw the parade come from Metropole and go past Tsimiski to the cinema Ellisa near the White Tower. Personal interview with the author January 2011.

[441] Pliny, *Natural Histories,* Book XXIX. V. 6–9, trans. H. J. Jones, William Heinemann, 1963, p. 187.

[442] M. Clerc, *Massalia: Histoire de Marseille dans L'Antiquité des Origins a la Fin de l'empire Romain d'occident,* Librarie A. Tacussel, vol. 2, 1929, p. 303, *CIL*, XII,725.

[443] *Ibid, CIL*, XII, 3343; H. N. Parker, 'Greece, Rome and the Byzantine Empire' in L. R. Furst, (ed.), *Women Healers and Physicians: Climbing a Long Hill,* , University of Kentucky, 1997, p. 135.

[444] *Ibid, CIL,* XII, 4487, and 4489.

[445] *Ibid, CIL,* XII, 1804.

[446] Pliny, *Natural Histories*, vol. 8. Book XXIX. V. 9–11, trans. H. J. Jones, William Heinemann, 1963, p. 189.

[447] *Ibid*, vol.8. Book XXIX, viii.19–23. p. 197.

[448] Clerc translates this as 'Euxéne fille d'Anaxilaos de Marseille'. M. Clerc, *Massalia. Histoire de Marseille dans l'antiquité des origins à la fin de l'Empire romain d'Occident* (476 ap. J.-C.), TOME 1, Des origins jusqu 'au IIIme siècle av. J.-C., Marseille, Librairie A. Tacussel, 1927, p. 320, *IG*, 610, vol. XIV; Hermary et. al. gives Aristodikos, son of Anaxilas and Euxenos of Massalia. A. Hermary, A. Hesnard, and H. Tréziny, *Marseille Grecque: La cite phocéenne (600–49 av. J-C),* Editions Errance, 1999, p. 92.

[449] A. Hermary, A. Hesnard, and H. Tréziny, *Marseille Grecque: La cite phocéenne (600–49 av. J-C)*, Editions Errance, 1999, p. 92.

[450] M. Clerc, *Massalia: Histoire de Marseille dans L'Antiquité des Origins a la Fin de l'empire Romain d'occident*, vol. 2, Librarie A. Tacussel, 1929, p. 303.

[451] A. Hermary, A. Hesnard, and H. Tréziny, *Marseille Grecque: La cite phocéenne (600–49 av. J-C)*, Editions Errance, 1999, p. 92; *CIA*, III, 2, 2568.

[452] M. Clerc, *Massalia: Histoire de Marseille dans L'Antiquité des Origins a la Fin de l'empire Romain d'occident*, vol. 2, Librarie A. Tacussel, 1929, p. 304, *CIA*, III, 2, 2570. Whereas some of these *CIA* numbers were superseded into the book *IG* (*Inscriptiones Graecae*) with the same numbers this one did not.

[453] A. Hermary, A. Hesnard, and H. Tréziny, *Marseille Grecque: La cite phocéenne (600–49 av. J-C)*, Editions Errance, 1999, p. 92, *IG*, III, 2570. *Inscriptiones Graecae*, Attic Inscriptions of the Roman Period, Inscriptiones Aetatis Romanae, TITVLI SEPVCRALES, G. Dittenberger (ed.), Berolini, 1878, p 157.

[454] M. Clerc, *Massalia: Histoire de Marseille dans L'Antiquité des Origins a la Fin de l'empire Romain d'occident*, vol. 2, Librarie A. Tacussel, 1929, p. 304 n. 3.

[455] *Ibid*, *IG*, III, 2567

[456] A. Hermary, A. Hesnard, and H. Tréziny, *Marseille Grecque: La cite phocéenne (600–49 av. J-C)*, Editions Errance, 1999, p. 92; M. Clerc, *Massalia: Histoire de Marseille dans L'Antiquité des Origins a la Fin de l'empire Romain d'occident*, vol. 2, Librarie A. Tacussel, 1929, p. 304. IG, III, 2569.

[457] J. Longrigg, 'Anatomy in Alexandria in the Third Century B.C.', *The British Journal for the History of Science*, Vol. 24, No. 4 (Dec., 1988): 455–488, Published by: Cambridge University Press on behalf of the British Society for the History of Science, ['JSTOR' journal archive] <http://www.jstor.org/stable/4026964>, viewed on 16 February 2010.

[458] L. B. Urdahl, *Foreigners in Athens: A study of grave monuments*, (4563, 1924), The University of Chicago, 1959, p.137, Telecles tombstone ref: (IG II 2 12764).

[459] M. Clerc, *Massalia. Histoire de Marseille dans l'antiquité des origins à la fin de l'Empire romain d'Occident (476 ap. J.-C.)*, TOME 1, Des origins jusqu 'au IIIme siècle av. J.-C. Marseille, Librairie A. Tacussel, 1927, p. 30, IG, XI 687.

[460] A. Hermary, A. Hesnard, and H. Tréziny, *Marseille Grecque: La cite phocéenne (600–49 av. J-C)*, Editions Errance, 1999, p. 92.

[461] *Ibid*.

[462] M. Clerc, *Massalia. Histoire de Marseille dans l'antiquité des origins à la fin de l'Empire romain d'Occident (476 ap. J.-C.)*, TOME 1, Des origins jusqu 'au IIIme siècle av. J.-C. Marseille, Librairie A. Tacussel, 1927, p. 292, Fig. 71, BCH (Bulletin de corresponance hellénique), VII, 1883, p. 191 and BCH, 1921, XLV, p. 23.

[463] A. Hermary, A. Hesnard, and H. Tréziny, *Marseille Grecque: La cite phocéenne (600–49 av. J-C)*, Editions Errance, 1999, p. 93.

[464] G. Woolf, *Becoming Roman: the origins of provincial civilization in Gaul*, Cambridge University Press, 1998, p. 92.

[465] F. W. Wallbank, A Historical Commentary on Polybius, vol. 2. XVIII, 47.1. Oxford, 1967, p. 614.

[466] P. B. Ellis, *The Celtic Empire: The First Millennium of Celtic History*, Constable, 1999, p. 100.

[467] R. Penhallurick, *Tin in Antiquity*, Institute of Metals, 1986, p.140, ref. D.F. Allen.

[468] *Livy*, Bk. XXI. XIX, II, xx 8, trans. B. O. Foster, Heinemann, 1929, p. 58–59.

[469] P. de Jersey, *Celtic Coinage in Britain*, Shire, 2001, p. 20.

[470] *Livy*, vol.10. XXXVII. 21–23, trans. E. T. Sage, Loeb Classical Library, 1935, p. 459.

[471] T. E. Page, *Martial's Epigrams,* vol. 2. Bk. XIII, cxxiii. Loeb, 1961, p. 435.

[472] *Ibid,* vol. 2. Bk. XIII, cxxiii, p. 434. n. 3.

[473] D. R. Shackleton Bailey, *Martial's Epigrams,* vol. 2. X, 36, Harvard, 1993, p. 359.

[474] *Ibid*, p. 359, Note c. Pliny, *Natural Histories*, 14.68.

[475] D. R. Shackleton Bailey, *Martial's Epigrams,* vol. 3. XIII. 123, Harvard, 1993, p. 271.

[476] Athenaeus, *Deipnosophists*, vol. 5. XII. 523, trans. C. B. Gulick, Loeb, William Heinemann, 1927.

[477] J. M. Edmonds, *Daphne & Chloe, Parthenius,* VIII, Heinemann, 1916, p. 279–283.

[478] *Ibid*.

[479] *Ibid*, p. 279 n. 3.

[480] Strabo, *Geography,* III. 4. 17.

[481] M. H. Morgan, *Vitruvius: The Ten Books on Architecture,* Bk. 2, Ch. I. 5, Dover Publication, 1960, p. 40.

[482] For comparison of Gallo-Greek and Greek-Iberian scripts see M. Dietler, 'The Iron Age in Mediterranean France: Colonial Encounters and Transformations'. *Journal of World Prehistory*, Vol. 11. No. 3. (1997): 269-358, here p. 305-307.
<http://chicago.academia.edu/MichaelDietler/Papers/218412/The_Iron_Age_In_Mediterranean_France_Colonial_Encounters_Entanglements_and_Transformations>, viewed 6 February 2012.

[483] G. Woolf, *Becoming Roman: the origins of provincial civilization in Gaul,* Cambridge University Press, 1998, p. 92.

[484] Strabo, *Geography*, vol.2. IV. I. 5, trans. H. L. Jones. Loeb, 1969, p. 179.

[485] Caesar, *The Gallic War*, I.29, trans. H. J. Edwards, Dover, 2006, p. 14.

[486] *Ibid*, II.28. p. 41.

[487] *Ibid*, VI.14. p. 103.

[488] W. M. Lindsay, *Isidore of Seville: The Etymologies (or Origins)*, vol.15. I. 63, Oxford University Press, 1911, ['Penelope, University of Chicago' digital library]
<htpp://Penelope.uchicago.edu/Thayer/E/Roman/Texts/isidore/home.html>, viewed on 26 December 2010.

[489] Strabo, *Geography,* vol. 2. IV.1.14, trans. H. L. Jones, Loeb, 1969, p. 211–213.

[490] S. Radt, *Strabon's Geographika,* Band I, Prolegma, Buch I–IV: Text und Ubersetzung, Vandenhoeck & Ruprecht, 2002, p. 240.

[491] Strabo, *Geography*, vol. 2. IV. 1.5, trans. H. L. Jones. Loeb, 1969, p. 179.

[492] Strabo, *Geography,* vol. 2. IV. 1.5.

[493] A. Bowman and G. Woolf (eds.), *Literacy and Power in the Ancient World*, Cambridge, 1996, p. 88-89.

[494] *Ibid*, p. 96.

[495] C. Ebel, *Transalpine Gaul: the emergence of a Roman province*, Brill, 1976, p. 31.

[496] Caesar, The Gallic War, I.29, trans. H. J. Edwards, Dover, 2006, p. 14.

[497] *Ibid*, VI.14. p. 103.

[498] *Justin: Epitome of the Philippic History of Pompeius Trogus,* 43.4.1, trans. J. C. Yardley, Scholars Press Atlanta, 1994, p. 267.

[499] Juvenal, *Satires*, Satire 15, An Egyptian Atrocity, trans. G. G. Ramsey, 1918, <http://www.tertullian.org/fathers/juvenal_satires_15.htm#13> viewed 21 February 2013.

[500] *Justin: Epitome of the Philippic History of Pompeius Trogus,* 43.3.13, trans. J. C. Yardley, Scholars Press Atlanta, 1994, p. 267.

[501] M. Crawford and D. Whitehead, *Archaic and Classical Greece; A selection of ancient sources in translation*, Cambridge, 1983, p. xvii.

[502] J. C. Koch, *Celtic Culture: A Historical Encyclopaedia,* vol. 1, AB.C. CLIO, 2006, p. 462.

[503] R. A. G. Carson, *Coins,* Hutchinson of London, 1963, p. 69.

[504] J. C. Koch, *Celtic Culture: A Historical Encyclopaedia,* vol.1, AB.C. CLIO, 2006, p. 462.

[505] Spain is Culture, *Treasure from the Neapolis, Ampurias,* ['Ministerio de Culture' National Art Museum of Catalonia, MNAC] <http://www.spainisculture.com/en/obras_de_excelencia/tesoro_neapolis_ampurias.html>, viewed on 7 December 2011.

[506] *Collection: IX British Museum Part II,* Mint: Emporion, ['The Fitzwilliam Museum'] <http://www.sylloge-nummorum-graecorum.org/>, viewed on 23 November 2010.

[507] X. Aquilué, P. Castanyer, M. Santos, and J. Tremoleda, *Empúries. Guidebooks to the Museu d'Arqueologia de Catalunya,* English language edition, Museu d'Arqueologia de Catalunya, 2008, p. 43-44.

[508] A. Trevor. Hodge, *Ancient Greek France*, University of Pennsylvania Press, 1999, p.163 & p. 276 n. 67; J. C. Koch, *Celtic Culture: A Historical Encyclopaedia,* vol.1, AB.C. CLIO, 2006, p. 462.

[509] R. A. G. Carson, *Coins,* Hutchinson of London, 1963, p. 72.

[510] Strabo, *Geography*, IV.3.8.

[511] Generalitat de Catalunya, *Phoenicians and Greeks in Catalonia: 7th century B.C.–6th century B.C.* <http://www20.gencat.cat/portal/site/culturacatalana/menuitem.be2B.C.
4cc4c5aec88f94a9710b0c0e1a0/?vgnextoid=d07cef2126896210VgnVCM1000000b0c1e0aRCRD&vgnextchannel=d07cef2126896210VgnVCM1000000b0c1e0aRCRD&vgnextfmt=detall2&contentid=810c110e279d7210VgnVCM1000008d0c1e0aRCRD&newLang=en_GB>, viewed on 22 July 2011.

[512] J-P. Morel, 'Phocaean Colonisation' in G. R. Tsetskhladze (ed.), *Greek Colonisation: An Account of Greek Colonies and Other Settlements Overseas,* vol.1, (Leiden, 2006): 358–428, here p. 385-6; see also A. Furtwängler, *Le trésor d'Auriol et le types monétaires phocéens*, <http://1.static.e-corpus.org/download/notice_file/522045/Etudes%20Massalietes%206%20-%20pp.175-181.pdf> accessed 10 December 2012, also available from Cambridge Journals online.

[513] C. Seltman, *Greek Coins*, Metheun, 2nd edition 1955, p.80, (Pl.IX, 12).

[514] T. Everson, *Warfare in Ancient Greece*, Sutton, 2004, p. 135–136.

[515] Org.numismatique, *Gaul Obole phocaeque la tete casque* (450–400 av. Chr.). <http://www.muenzauktion.com/crinon/item.php5?id=2822&lang=&psid=592bd763ea12c81ab39188fdc8df27e3>, viewed on 15 November 2010.

[516] M. Clerc, *Massalia: Histoire de Marseille dans l'antiquité des origins à la fin de l'Empire romain d'Occident (476 ap. J.-C.)*, TOME 1, Des origins jusqu 'au IIIme siècle av. J.-C. Marseille, Librairie A. Tacussel, 1927, p. 360.

[517] *Marseille (après 400 av. J-C.), obole au Lacydon et à la légende. R! R!* Réf: 83195, ['Poinsignon Numismatique'] <http://www.poinsignon-numismatique.com/photo_grande.asp?langue=fr&categorie=8&rubrique=MO&periode=3823&catalogue=83195&archive=>viewed on 3 April 2012.

[518] Jean-Claude Richard et Jean-Albert Chevillon, *Du Lacydon á Massalia, les émissions grecques en Gaule du Vème siècle av. J.-C.* pp. 295–302, here p. 296, <http://www.mcu.es/museos/docs/MC/ActasNumis/Du_Lacydon_Massalia.pdf>, viewed on 21 February 2011.

[519] The first were copies of the style of engraver Euainetos's beautiful coins in Syracuse <http://www.acsearch.info/search.html?search=similar%3A172152#8>, viewed 28 January 2013.

[520] A. Trevor. Hodge, *Ancient Greek France*, University of Pennsylvania Press, 1999, p. 126.

[521] R. A. G. Carson, *Coins,* Hutchinson of London, 1963, p. 69.

[522] *Ibid.*

[523] I. Carradice, *Greek Coins,* British Museum Press, 1995, p. 72.

[524] C. Seltman, *Greek Coins,* Methuen & Co. Ltd, 1960, p. 196.

[525] P. Jersey, *Celtic Coinage in Britain,* Shire, 2001, p. 20.

[526] *Ancient Coinage of Gaul, Massalia,* Re. DLT_1673, ['Wildwinds'] <http://www.wildwinds.com/coins/greece/gaul/massalia/i.html>, viewed on 17 February 2012.

[527] *Massalia, Gaul, 149-40 B.C.*, Re. GB80741, ['Forum Ancient Coins'] <http://www.forumancientcoins.com/catalog/roman-and-greek-coins.asp?zpg=14611>, viewed 17 February 2012.

[528] W. Scheidel, I. Morris, and R. P. Saller, *Cambridge Economic History of the Greco-Roman World*, Cambridge, 2007, p. 271.

[529] *Massalia Coins after 49 B.C.* ['ACSEARCH'] <http://www.acsearch.info/search.html?search=similar%3A439534&view_mode=1#0>; 214: Lot 14, from the J. P. Righetti Collection 7529, GAUL, Massalia. After 49 B.C. ['CNG'], <http://cngcoins.com/Coin.aspx?CoinID=145117>, viewed on 14 September 2011. G. Maurel, *Le Corpus des monnaies de Marseille et Provence*, Omni, 2013, p. 144–150.

[530] F. Kemmers, 'The coin finds from the Augustan legionary fortress at Nijmagen (The Netherlands): coin circulation in the lower Rhine area before Drusus's campaigns' in C. Alfaro, C. Marcos and P. Otero (eds.), *XIIIth Congreso Internacional de Numismática*, Madrid 2003, Actas-Proceedings-Actes, pp. 987-990, <www.mcu.es/museos/docs/MC/ActasNumis/The_coin_finds.pdf>, viewed on 20 June 2010.

[531] G. Barruol, 'La Massalie dans la Provincia' in *Voyage en Massalie: 100 ans d'archéologie en Gaule du sud,* Catalogue de l'exposition, (Musées de Marseille/Édisud, 1990): 242–243.

[532] M. Bats, *Olbia de Provence (Hyères, Var) a l'epoque romaine (1ers. av. J-C.–VIIe s. ap J-C),* Edisud, 2006, p. 409–415.

[533] H. Cleere, *Southern France: An Oxford Archaeological Guide*, Oxford, 2001, p.138; Strabo, *Geography,* IV.1.5; Pliny the Elder, *Natural Histories*, vol. 2, III, 34, trans. H. Rackham, Heinemann, 1947, p. 29; Caesar, *Civil War*, II.22.

[534] C. Brenot, 'Marseille et les réseaux phocéens. Remarques sur le témoignage des monnaise', ATTI DEL 'XI CONVEGNO DEL CENTRO INTERNAZIONALE DI STUDI NUMISMATICI-NAPOLI 25-27 OTTOBRE 1996, in *La monetazione dei Focei in Occidente, Instituto Italiano di Numismatica Roma*, (2002): 113-137, here p. 122.

[535] See also A. Furtwängler, 'Monnaies grecques en Gaule: Nouvelle trouvailles (6-5ème s. av. J.-C.), ATTI DEL 'XI CONVEGNO DEL CENTRO INTERNAZIONALE DI STUDI NUMISMATICI-NAPOLI 25-27 OTTOBRE 1996, TAV. XI, 2, in *La monetazione dei Focei in Occidente*, Instituto Italiano di Numismatica Roma, (2002): 93-111, here p. 102.

[536] See also C. Brenot, 'Marseille et les réseaux phocéens. Remarques sur le témoignage des monnaise', ATTI DEL 'XI CONVEGNO DEL CENTRO INTERNAZIONALE DI STUDI NUMISMATICI-NAPOLI 25-27 OTTOBRE 1996, TAV. XV, 14, in *La monetazione dei Focei in Occidente*, Instituto Italiano di Numismatica Roma, (2002): 113-137, here p. 117.

[537] *Valerius Maximus, Memorable Deeds and Sayings: A Thousand and One Tales from Ancient Rome*, II.6.9, trans. Henry John Walker, Hackett Publishing Company Inc., 2004, p. 59.

[538] *Ibid*, II.6.7. p. 58.

[539] *Ibid*.

[540] For a new interpretation on Greek slavery see K. Vlassopoulos, 'Greek Slavery: From Domination to Property and Back Again' in *Journal of Hellenic Studies*, 131 (2011):115-130, here p. 116–117.

[541] W. E. Klingshirn, *Caesarius of Arles: Life, Testament, Letters,* Bk. 2. 25. Liverpool University Press, 1994, p. 55–56.

[542] R. Gardiner, *The Age of the Galley*, Conway Maritime Press, 1995, p. 111.

[543] M. Clerc, *Massalia: Histoire de Marseille dans L'Antiquité des Origins a la Fin de l'empire Romain d'occident*, Librarie A. Tacussel, vol. 2, 1929, p. 303, *CIL*, XII, 3349.

[544] *Ibid*, p. 303 n.1.

[545] C. H. Benedict, 'The Romans in Southern Gaul' in *The American Journal of Philology*, vol. 63, no.1 (1942): 38–50, here p. 50, ['JSTOR' journal archive] <http://www.jstor.org/stable/291079>.

[546] *The Library of History of Diodorus Siculus*, vol. 3. V. 26. Loeb, 1939, ['University of Chicago' digital library] <http://penelope.uchicago.edu/Thayer/E/Roman/Texts/Diodorus_Siculus/5B*.html > viewed 27 January 2012.

[547] F. Beauvais, 'American Indians and Alcohol' in *Alcohol Health and Research World*, Vol. 2, No. 4.(1998):253-259. < http://pubs.niaaa.nih.gov/publications/arh22-4/253.pdf> viewed 10 February 2013.

[548] W. Scheidel, *The Roman Slave Supply*, [Princeton/Stanford Working Papers in Classics] (May 2007): 1-22, here p.13. <http://www.princeton.edu/~pswpc/pdfs/scheidel/050704.pdf > viewed on 10 November 2011.

[549] *Livy*, Bk. XXI. XIX, II, xx 8, trans. B.O. Foster, William Heinemann, 1929, p. 58–59.

[550] T. Rihill, 'War, Slavery and Settlement in Early Greece' in J. Rich and G. Shipley, (eds.), *War and Society in the Greek World*, London, 1993, p. 77–107, here p. 102. n.1.

[551] K. Arafat and C. Morgan, 'Athens, Etruria and the Heuneburg: mutual misconceptions in the study of Greek-barbarian relations' in I. Morris, (ed.), *Classical Greece: Ancient histories and modern archaeologies,* (Cambridge University Press 1994): 108–134, here Ch. 7, p. 127, p. 129–130.

[552] *Livy*, Vol. IX. Bk. XXXIV. VIII. 4–IX.4. IX. E. T. Sage, Loeb Classical Library, 1935, p. 441–443.

[553] P. B. Ellis, *The Celtic Empire: The First Millennium of Celtic History,* Constable, 1999, p. 100.

[554] J. M. Riddle, (ed.), *Tiberius Gracchus: Destroyer or Reformer of the Republic*, D. C. Heath & Co, 1970, p. 87.

[555] T. Urbainczyk, *Slave Revolts in Antiquity*, University of California Press, 2008, p. 124 n. 23.

[556] N. S. Gill, *Slave Revolts or Servile Wars in Italy: The Sicilian Slave Wars and Spartacus*, <http://ancienthistory.about.com/cs/slavesandslavery/a/slavewars.htm>, viewed on 20 January 2010.

[557] Strabo, *Geography*, IV.1.5.

[558] Strabo, *Geography*, XIV.2.5. H. C. Hamilton and W. Falconer, (eds.), *The Geography of Strabo: Literally translated, with notes, in three volumes*, George Bell & Sons, 1903, ['Perseus, Tufts University' digital Library] <http://www.perseus.tufts.edu/hopper/text?doc=Perseus%3Atext%3A1999.01.0198%3Abook%3D14%3Achapter%3D2%3Asection%3D5>, viewed on 19 May 2009.

[559] H. L. Jones, *Strabo Geography*, vol.5. XII. 8.11. Loeb, 1928, p. 501 n. 2. 'Apparently a soil containing lime carbonate'. ['Perseus. Tufts University' digital library] <http://www.perseus.tufts.edu/hopper/text?doc=Perseus%3Atext%3A1999.01.0198%3Abook%3D12%3Achapter%3D8%3Asection%3D11>, viewed 6 February 2012.

[560] Lucian, *Toxaris or Friendship*, vol. 5, 24-26, trans. A. M. Harmon, William Heinemann, 1955, p. 143-149.

[561] J-P. Morel, 'Phocaean Colonisation' in G. R. Tsetskhladze (ed.), *Greek Colonisation: An Account of Greek Colonies and Other Settlements Overseas*, vol.1, (Leiden, 2006): 358–428, here p. 392.

[562] F. W. Wallbank, *A Historical Commentary on Polybius*, vol. 1. III.17.1, Oxford, 1970, p. 328.

[563] Isidore of Seville, *The Etymologies (or Origins)*, vol.15. 1. 68. ['Penelope, University of Chicago' digital library] <htpp://Penelope.uchicago.edu/Thayer/E/Roman/Texts/isidore/home.html>, viewed on 23 August 2011.

[564] A. J. Domínguez, 'Hellenization in Iberia: The Reception of the Greek Products and influences by Iberians' in G. R. Tsetskhladze, (ed.), *Ancient Greeks West and East*, (Brill, 1999): 301–330, here p. 310.

[565] R. Carpenter, *Beyond the Pillars of Hercules: The classical world seen through the eyes of its discoverers*, Tandem Press (UK), 1973, Ch 2, p. 64; P. Bosch-Gimpera, 'The Phokaians in the Far West: A Historical Reconstruction', *The Classical Quarterly*, vol. 38, no. 1/2 (Jan.–Apr., 1944): 53–59, here p. 53 n. 2, Peman, C. *Archivo Esp. de Archueologia*, 1941, p. 407, Schulten (Forschungen u. Fortschritte, 1929) and on the later Peman, C. *Archivo Esp. de Archueologia*, 1941, Schulten (*Investigación y Progreso, 1931)*, ['JSTOR' journal archive] <www.jstor.org/stable/636879>, viewed on 20 August 2010.

[566] *Greek Corinthian Helmet*, ['MVESO Arqueológico de Jerez'] <http://www.jerez.es/nc/en/the_collection/selection_of_pieces/?tx_photoblog_pi1[showUid]=840>, viewed on 20 August 2010.

[567] R. Carpenter, *Beyond the Pillars of Hercules: The classical world seen through the eyes of is discoverers*, Tandem Press (UK), 1973, Ch 2, p. 64; P. Bosch-Gimpera, 'The Phokaians in the Far West: A Historical Reconstruction', *The Classical Quarterly*, vol. 38, no. 1/2 (Jan.–Apr., 1944): 53–59, here p. 53 n. 2, Peman, C. *Archivo Esp. de Archueologia*, 1941, p. 407, Schulten (Forschungen u. Fortschritte, 1929) and on the later Greek helmet of Huelva, Schulten (*Investigación y Progreso*, 1931), ['JSTOR' journal archive] <www.jstor.org/stable/636879>, viewed on 20 August 2010.

[568] Museo Arqueológico Nacional, <http://man.mcu.es/>, viewed on 19 August 2011; D, Garcia, p. 88 <https://www.academia.edu/4457711/Le_casque_corinthien_des_Baux-de-Provence> viewed 25.11.2013.

[569] T. Braun, 'Hecataeus' Knowledge of the Western Mediterranean' in K.Lomas, (ed.), *Greek Identity in the Western Mediterranean: papers in honour of Brian Shefton*, (Brill 2004): 287-348, here p. 308 n.40, Schulten, *Tartessos, arquelogia protohistorica del bajo Guadalquivir* (Madrid 1945).

[570] A. Johnston, *The Emergence of Greece*, Elsevier-Phaidon, 1976, p. 39.

[571] R. Carpenter, *The Greeks in Spain,* Bryn Mawr College, Longman, Greene & Co., 1925, p. 179.

[572] B. B. Shefton, 'Massalia and colonization in the North Western Mediterranean' in G. R. Tsetskhladze and F. de Angis (eds.), *The Archaeology of Greek Colonization* (Oxford, 1994): 61–86, here p. 72 n. 69 & 70.

[573] F. Quesada-Sanz, 'From Quantity to Quality: wealth, status and prestige in the Iberian Iron Age' in D. Bailey (ed.). *The Archaeology of Value,* BAR IS 730. (1998), Oxford, pp. 70-96, here p.88.

[574] A. M. Puig and A. Martin, (Coordinadores), *La colònia grega de Rhode (Roses, Alt Empordà)*, Serie Monongrafica 23, Museu d'Arqueologia de Catalunya Girona. 2006, p. 612 and p. 619.

[575] X. Aquilué, P. Castanyer, M. Santos, and J. Tremoleda, *Empúries. Guidebooks to the Museu d'Arqueologia de Catalunya,* English language edition, Museu d'Arqueologia de Catalunya, 2008, p. 17-18, p. 91 and p. 106.

[576] B. Tang, *Delos, Carthage, Ampurias: the housing of three Mediterranean trading centres,* L'Erma di Bretschneider Rome, 2005, p. 113.

[577] X. Aquilué, P. Castanyer, M. Santos, and J. Tremoleda, *Empúries. Guidebooks to the Museu d'Arqueologia de Catalunya,* English language edition, Museu d'Arqueologia de Catalunya, 2008, p. 90–91.

[578] *Ibid*, p. 106.

[579] R. Carpenter, *The Greeks in Spain,* Bryn Mawr College, Longman, Greene & Co., 1925, p.180.

[580] A. J. Domínguez, 'Hellenization in Iberia: The Reception of the Greek Products and influences by Iberians' in G. R. Tsetskhladze (ed.), *Ancient Greeks West and East,* (Brill, 1999): 301–330, here p. 305.

[581] Museo Arqeológico Nacional, <http://man.mcu.es/>, viewed on 11 August 2011. Though most of the museum was closed for refurbishment (July 2011) fortunately this statue and others were available to see in the one gallery that was open to the public.

[582] R. Olmos and T. Tortosa, 'Appendix: The Case of the Lady of Elche: a Review Article' in G. R. Tsetskhladze (ed.), *Ancient Greeks West and East,* (Brill, 1999): 352–360, here p. 354; P. Rouillard, 'Greeks in the Iberian Peninsula', in M. Dietler, and C. Lopez-Ruiz, (eds.), *Colonial Encounters in Ancient Iberia: Phoenicians, Greek, and Indigenous Relations,* (University of Chicago Press, 2009): 131–154, here p. 143.

[583] S. Aguilar, 'Dama de Elche: Embodying Greek-Iberian interaction' in G. R. Tsetskhladze (ed.), *Ancient Greeks West and East,* (Brill, 1999): 331–351, p. 349; A.J. Domínguez, 'Hellenization in Iberia: The Reception of the Greek Products and influences by Iberians'' in G. R. Tsetskhladze (ed.), *Ancient Greeks West and East,* (Brill, 1999): 301–330, here p. 307.

[584] J. de Hoz, 'The Greek Man in the Iberian Street' in K. Lomas (ed.), *Greek Identity in the Western Mediterranean,* Papers in Honour of Brian Shefton, (Brill, 2004):411-428, here p. 424.

[585] J-P. Morel, 'Phocaean Colonisation' in G. R. Tsetskhladze (ed.), *Greek Colonisation: An Account of Greek Colonies and Other Settlements Overseas,* vol.1, (Leiden, 2006): 358–428, here p. 372; Shipwrecks see S. Mark. *Homeric Seafaring,* Texas A&M University Press, 2005, p. 41-45.

[586] E. Shuey, 'Underwater Survey and Excavations at Gravisca, The Port of Tarquinia' *Papers from the British School of Rome,* (vol. 49. 1981):17-45, here p. 17. n. 4, ['JSTOR' journal archive] <http://www.jstor.org/pss/40310871>, viewed on 17 January 2012. The site was discovered and excavated by Professor MarioTorelli, University of Perugia, Italy. See also M. Torelli, 'Il Santuario Greco di Gravisca', *La Prarola del Passato* 177 (1977): 398-458. For an article in English see M. Torelli, 'Greek Artisans and Etruria: A problem concerning the relationship between two cultures', *Archaeological News* 5, Dept. of Classics, Florida State University, (1976): 134–8.

[587] M. Torelli, 'Greek Artisans and Etruria: A problem concerning the relationship between two cultures', *Archaeological News* 5, Dept. of Classics, Florida State University, (1976): 134–8, here p. 135.

[588] A. Johnston, *The Emergence of Greece,* Elsevier-Phaidon, 1976, p. 41.

[589] J-P. Morel, 'Phocaean Colonisation' in G. R. Tsetskhladze (ed.), *Greek Colonisation: An Account of Greek Colonies and Other Settlements Overseas,* vol.1, (Leiden, 2006): 358–428, here p. 372.

[590] 'exiles from Corinth'. *Justin: Epitome of the Philippic History of Pompeius Trogus,* 38.5–6.7, trans. J. C. Yardley, Scholars Press Atlanta, 1994, p. 241.

[591] Strabo, *Geography,* VIII.6.20.

[592] J-P. Morel, 'Phocaean Colonisation' in G. R. Tsetskhladze (ed.), *Greek Colonisation: An Account of Greek Colonies and Other Settlements Overseas,* vol.1, (Leiden, 2006): 358–428, here p. 389.

[593] *Ibid,* here p. 392.

[594] Strabo, *Geography,* vol. 3. IV.1.6.

[595] J-P. Morel, 'Phocaean Colonisation' in G. R. Tsetskhladze (ed.), *Greek Colonisation: An Account of Greek Colonies and Other Settlements Overseas,* vol.1, (Leiden, 2006): 358–428, here p. 392.

[596] Strabo, *Geography,* vol. 2. IV.1.14, trans. H. L. Jones, Loeb, 1969, p. 211–213.

[597] This section of the Greek text in the Loeb 1923 edition is the same as that in Radt's 2002 edition. Radt, S. *Strabon's Geographika,* Band I, Prolegma, Buch I–IV: Text und Ubersetzung, Vandenhoeck & Ruprecht, 2002, p. 240. Some differences occur either by different manuscripts and/or the translations of them.

[598] M. Clavel, *Bèziers et son Territoire dans L'Antique,* La Belle Lettres, Annales Littéraires de l'Université de Besançon, 1970, p. 180–1.

[599] *Ibid (*Clavel p. 180–1); Stele inscription *IG* XIV 2516, *IGF* 131, p. 174.

[600] Strabo, *Geography,* vol. 3. IV.I.3. and IV.1.6.

[601] M. Grant, *The Rise of the Greeks,* Phoenix Press, 2005, Ch.6. p. 249; Herodotus, Histories, I.165–166, trans. G. Rawlinson, Wordsworth Editions Ltd., 1996, p. 74–75.

[602] A. J. Domínguez, 'Spain and France (including Corsica)' in H. H. Hanson and T. H. Nielsen, *An Inventory of Archaic and Classical Poleis,* (Oxford, 2004):157–171, here p. 163. ['Scribd'] <http://www.scribd.com/doc/82942410/An-Inventory-of-Archaic-and-Classical-Poleis-Ed-by-M-H-Hansen-Th-H-Nielsen#outer_page_174> viewed 3 April 2012.

[603] Herodotus, *Histories,* I.167, trans. G. Rawlinson, Wordsworth Editions Ltd., 1996. p. 76.

[604] A. J. Domínguez, 'Spain and France (including Corsica)' in H. H. Hanson and T. H. Nielsen, *An Inventory of Archaic and Classical Poleis,* (Oxford, 2004):157–171, here p. 163. ['Scribd'] <http://www.scribd.com/doc/82942410/An-Inventory-of-Archaic-and-Classical-Poleis-Ed-by-M-H-Hansen-Th-H-Nielsen#outer_page_174> viewed 3 April 2012

[605] Philippe Laure, 'On a retrouvé les fils des Protis. Une etude sur le sang désigne les descendants direct des Phocéens', *La Provence,* Vendredi 22 Avril 2011, 22042011 Journal La Provence, p. 3.
<http://www.scribd.com/doc/53641055/Journal-La-Provence-22042011>, viewed 10 February 2012.

Samples taken from 51 people from villages near Neolithic sites in Provence were compared to 368 from Provence with French surnames. J. Charoni, et al., *The coming of the Greeks to Provence and Corsica: Y-chromosome models of archaic Greek colonization of the western Mediterranean,* p. 7. BMC Evolutionary Biology, published 14 March 2011, ['BioMed Central'] <http://www.biomedcentral.com/1471-2148/11/69> viewed 3 April 2012.

[606] T. J. Dunbabin, *The Western Greeks: The History of Sicily and South Italy from the Foundation of the Greek Colonies to 480 B.C,* Oxford University Press Monograph Reprints, 1998, p. 342 n. 4, Diodorus, V.13.

[607] *Diodorus of Sicily,* vol. 3, Bk.V, 13.3-14.I, trans. C. H. Oldfather, Heinemann, 1952, p. 133 n. 1.

[608] D. Abram, *Rough Guide to Corsica*, Rough Guides: Map edition, 2005, p. 151 gives a Phoenician origin.

[609] T. J. Dunbabin, *The Western Greeks: The History of Sicily and South Italy from the Foundation of the Greek Colonies to 480 B.C*, Oxford University Press Monograph Reprints, 1998, p. 342 n. 4, Diodorus, V.13.

[610] See Rawlinson's explanatory note. Herodotus, *Histories*, V. 125, trans. G. Rawlinson, Wordsworth Editions Ltd., 1996, p. 439 n.155.

[611] T. J. Dunbabin, *The Western Greeks: The History of Sicily and South Italy from the Foundation of the Greek Colonies to 480 B.C*, Oxford University Press Monograph Reprints, 1998, p. 342 n. 2, Pausanias, x. 17.1; Solinus, iv.1.

[612] *Ibid*, p. 342, n 3; Pausanias, x. 17. 5; Diodorus. iv. 29.

[613] Herodotus, *Histories*, I.170, trans. G. Rawlinson, Wordsworth Editions Ltd., 1996. p. 76 n. 168.

[614] *Ibid*.

[615] *Ibid*, V. 126. p. 439.

[616] T. J. Dunbabin, *The Western Greeks: The History of Sicily and South Italy from the Foundation of the Greek Colonies to 480 B.C*, Oxford University Press Monograph Reprints, 1998, ch 11, p. 346.

[617] J. A. Allen, 'Magna Graecia' in N. G. Wilson, (ed.), *Encyclopaedia of Ancient Greece*, (Routledge, 2006): 442-444, here p. 443.

[618] J-P. Morel, 'Phocaean Colonisation' in G. R. Tsetskhladze (ed.), *Greek Colonisation: An Account of Greek Colonies and Other Settlements Overseas*, vol.1, (Leiden, 2006): 358–428, here p. 406.

[619] Strabo, *Geography*, VI.1.1.

[620] J. Matthews, *Heyele/Elea/Velia*, Around Naples Encyclopedia, ['University of Maryland University College' Italian Studies], entry July 2009, <http://ac-support.europe.umuc.edu/~jmatthew/naples/Velia.html>, viewed on 7 January 2012.

[621] M. Grant, *The Rise of the Greeks*, Phoenix Press, 1962, p. 350 n. 59.

[622] Strabo, *Geography*, VI.1.1.

[623] J-P. Morel, 'Phocaean Colonisation' in G. R. Tsetskhladze (ed.), *Greek Colonisation: An Account of Greek Colonies and Other Settlements Overseas*, vol.1, (Leiden, 2006): 358–428, here p. 415.

[624] J. Matthews, *Heyele/Elea/Velia*, Around Naples Encyclopedia, ['University of Maryland University College' Italian Studies], entry July 2009, <http://ac-support.europe.umuc.edu/~jmatthew/naples/Velia.html>, viewed on 7 January 2012.

[625] *Ibid*.

[626] F. W. Wallbank, *A Historical Commentary on Polybius*, vol.1. 1.20.14. Oxford, 1957, p. 75.

[627] J-P. Morel, 'Phocaean Colonisation' in G. R. Tsetskhladze (ed.), *Greek Colonisation: An Account of Greek Colonies and Other Settlements Overseas*, vol.1, (Leiden, 2006): 358–428, here p. 415.

[628] *Ibid*, p. 406-407.

[629] *Ibid*, here p. 415.

[630] K. Lomas, *Rome and the Western Greeks 350 BC–AD 200: Conquest and Acculturation in Southern Italy*, Taylor & Francis e-Library, 2005, p. 151–152.

[631] Strabo, *Geography,* IV, 1, 5.

[632] R. A. G. Carson, *Coins,* Hutchinson of London, 1963, p. 69.

[633] R. Buxó, 'Botanical and Archaeological Dimensions' in M. Dietler, and C. Lopez-Ruiz, (eds.), *Colonial Encounters in Ancient Iberia: Phoenicians, Greek, and Indigenous Relations,* (University of Chicago Press, 2009): 155-168, here p. 160-161.

[634] L-F. Gantes, 'Marseilleveyre' in *Voyage en Massalie: 100 ans d'archéologie en Gaule du sud,* Catalogue de l'exposition, (Musées de Marseille/Édisud, 1990): 156-161.

[635] *Provence Chapter 4,* ['Discover France'] <http://www.discoverfrance.net/France/Provinces/Provence-4.shtml>, viewed on 21 December 2011; *Athena Review,* Vol.1. No.4. <http://www.athenapub.com/rhone1.htm>, viewed on 21 December 2011.

[636] M. Heijmans, J-M. Roquette and C. Sintès, *Arles Antique: guide archéologiques de la France,* Editions Patrimone, Paris 2006. p. 24.

[637] A. Trevor. Hodge, *Ancient Greek France*, University of Pennsylvania Press, 1999, p. 160.

[638] *Ibid,* p. 160 n. 56, R. Amy, *Princeton Encyclopaedia of Classical Sites (PECS)*, 87.

[639] A. Trevor. Hodge, *Ancient Greek France*, University of Pennsylvania Press, 1999, p. 82.

[640] H. Cleere, *Southern France: An Oxford Archaeological Guide*, Oxford, 2001, p. 118.

[641] *Ibid*, p. 125.

[642] A. Trevor. Hodge, *Ancient Greek France*, University of Pennsylvania Press, 1999, p. 161.

[643] M. Clerc, *Massalia: Histoire de Marseille dans l'antiquité des origins à la fin de l'Empire romain d'Occident (476 ap. J.-C.),* TOME 1, Des origins jusqu 'au IIIme siècle av. J.-C. Marseille, Librairie A. Tacussel, 1927, p. 337.

[644] M. Thompson, O. Morkholm, and C. M. Kraay, *An Inventory of Greek Coin Hoards*, The American Numismatic Society, New York, 1973, p. 361. Now in Avignon, Calvert Museum.

[645] J. Bromwich, *The Roman Remains of Southern France: a guidebook*, Routledge, 1993, p. 153.

[646] A. L. F. Rivet, Gallia Narbonensis, Batsford, 1988, p. 268, Livy, XXI. 26.6; Caesar's Civil War, Bk. 1, Chp. XXXV, trans. W. A. M'Devitte, G. Bell & Sons, 1928, p. 265.

[647] A. Trevor. Hodge, *Ancient Greek France*, University of Pennsylvania Press, 1999, p. 161.

[648] M. Christol and M. Heijmans, 'Les colonies latines de Narbonnaise: un nouveu document d'Arles mentionnant la colonia Iulia Augusta Avennio', *Gallia*, vol. 49, (1992): 37-44, here p. 37. *CIL* 12. 1120. <http://www.persee.fr/web/revues/home/prescript/article/galia_0016-4119_1992_num_49_1_2927>, 20 June 2012.

[649] H. Cleere, *Southern France: An Oxford Archaeological Guide*, Oxford, 2001, p. 124.

[650] A. L. F. Rivet, *Gallia Narbonensis,* Batsford, 1988, p. 42 n. 29.

[651] A. Trevor. Hodge, *Ancient Greek France*, University of Pennsylvania Press, 1999, p. 161.

[652] *Ibid*, p. 182.

[653] Strabo, *Geography,* vol. 2. IV. 6. 3. Loeb 1923, p. 267-269 n. 177. ['Penelope, University of Chicago' digital library] <http://penelope.uchicago.edu/Thayer/E/Roman/Texts/Strabo/4F*.html>, viewed on 2 February 2007.

[654] R. Latouche, *Caesar to Charlemagne: the beginnings of France*, trans. J. Nicholson, Barnes & Noble, 1968, p. 96, Ammianus Marcellinus (3:pp.75–6).

[655] *Ibid*, p. 95.

[656] Strabo, *Geography*, vol. 2. IV.6.3.

[657] M. Thompson, O. Morkholm, and C. M. Kraay, *An Inventory of Greek Coin Hoards*, The American Numismatic Society, New York, 1973, p. 360.

[658] 'Monaco on the Mediterranean' in *The Illustrated Magazine of Art*, Vol. 3, No. 13 (1854): 49-51, ['JSTOR' journal archive] <http:www.jstor.org/stable/20538205>, viewed on 19 July 2011.

[659] Strabo, *Geography*, vol. 2. VI. 1.1.

[660] Lacus Curtius, *Strabo's, Geography*, III.4.2. n. 85 gives the present city of Almunecar for ancient Maenaca. *The Geography of Strabo*, Loeb, 1923, ['Penelope, University of Chicago', digital library] <http://penelope.uchicago.edu/Thayer/E/Roman/Texts/Strabo/3D*.html>, viewed on 8 January 2007.

Marion suggested Almunecar but there does not seem to be any evidence found since to say the Greeks took over here from the Phoenicians. Prof. A. F. Marion and M. G. Vasseur, *Annals of Musée D'Histoire Naturelle de Marseille foundateur*, TOME XII, Marseille, 1914, p. 35. It was an old idea that Maenace was either Almunecar or Cerro del Mar. J. Boardman et al., *The Cambridge Ancient History*, vol. 3. Part 2. Cambridge, 2003, p. 525.

For analysis of the different theories and the suggestion that Cerro del Villar is Mainake and was therefore a Phoenician city see M. E. Aubet, 'Mainake: the Legend and New Archaeological Evidence', in B. Cunliffe and R. Osborne, (eds.), *Mediterranean Urbanisation 800–600 B.C.*, The British Academy, (Oxford University Press 2007): 187–202, here p. 198. Among many candidates for the location Aubet suggests Cerro del Villar is Mainake and that the island and archaeology shows it was abandoned between 600-570 B.C. See M. E. Aubet, 'Mainake: the Legend and New Archaeological Evidence', in B. Cunliffe and R. Osborne, (eds.), *Mediterranean Urbanisation 800–600 B.C.*, The British Academy, (Oxford University Press 2007): 187–202, here p. 200.

[661] Strabo, *Geography*, III. 4.2.

[662] M. E. Aubet, 'Mainake: the Legend and New Archaeological Evidence', in B. Cunliffe and R. Osborne, (eds.), *Mediterranean Urbanisation 800–600 B.C.*, The British Academy, (Oxford University Press 2007):187–202, here p. 192-193. Aubet argues that Strabo never went to Spain and used sources (unfortunately now lost) of Poseidonius and Artemedoros of Ephesus, both had lived in Gades around 100 B.C. There might be a possibility Strabo used Pseudo-Skymnos's description who in turn had used Ephorus from the fourth century B.C. The possibility she raises is the Greeks much earlier had recorded the names of Phoenician or indigenous settlements on navigation charts. Names were recorded into the nearest sounding Greek and this passed down. Later on in sounding Greek it was thought of as a Greek settlement. There is in Aubet's argument a concentration of Phoenician finds in the areas of Mainake and Hemeroscopium and also in areas of the further supposed three cities given by Strabo as Greek, there is a lack of Greek archaeology.

[663] R. Carpenter, *The Greeks in Spain*, Bryn Mawr College, Longman, Greene & Co., 1925, p. 30 and p. 179.

[664] M. E. Aubet, 'Mainake: the Legend and New Archaeological Evidence', in B. Cunliffe and R. Osborne, (eds.), Aubet, 'Mainake: the Legend and New Archaeological Evidence' *Mediterranean Urbanisation 800–600 B.C.*, The British Academy, (Oxford University Press 2007): 187–202, here p. 200.

[665] R. Carpenter, *The Greeks in Spain*, Bryn Mawr College, Longman, Greene & Co., 1925, p. 31.

[666] M. E. in B. Cunliffe and R. Osborne, (eds.), *Mediterranean Urbanisation 800–600 B.C.*, The British Academy, (Oxford University Press 2007):187–202, here p. 188.

[667] R. Carpenter, *The Greeks in Spain*, Bryn Mawr College, Longman, Greene & Co., 1925, p. 35.

[668] A. E. Astin. *The Cambridge Ancient History: Rome and the Mediterranean to 133 B.C.*, 2nd edition, vol. 8, Cambridge, 2003, p. 20.

[669] R. Carpenter, *The Greeks in Spain,* Bryn Mawr College, Longman, Greene & Co., 1925, p. 35. For recent scientific examinations to pinpoint the site of Tartessos at Doñana National Park Andalusia see Zacher, E. M. 'The Recent "Discovery" of the Legendary Atlantis, Truth or Fiction?' *The Epoch Times*, April 17, 2011, <http://www.theepochtimes.com/n2/science/the-recent-discovery-of-the-legendary-atlantis-truth-or-fiction-54862.html>, viewed on 15 December 2011.

[670] M. E. Aubet, 'Mainake: the Legend and New Archaeological Evidence', in B. Cunliffe and R. Osborne, (eds.), *Mediterranean Urbanisation 800–600 B.C.*, The British Academy, (Oxford University Press 2007):187–202, here p. 188.

[671] J-A. Chevillon, *Emporion,* The Greco-Iber, <http://numis-ext-occ.monsite-orange.fr/>, viewed on 1 January 2009.

[672] J. C. Koch, *Celtic Culture: A Historical Encyclopaedia,* AB.C. CLIO, 2006, vol.1, p. 462; R.A.G. Carson, *Coins,* Hutchinson of London, 1963, p. 69.

[673] A. J. Domínguez, 'Spain and France (including Corsica)' in H. H. Hanson and T. H. Nielsen, *An Inventory of Archaic and Classical Poleis,* (Oxford, 2004):157–171, here p. 165.

[674] Prof. A. F. Marion and M. G. Vasseur, *Annals of Musée D'Histoire Naturelle de Marseille foundateur,* TOM XII, Marseille, 1914, p. 35, footnote Strabo, III.4.2: Clerc mentions 3 ports Mainake, d'Abdera and Hermeroskopeion. M. Clerc, *Massalia. Histoire de Marseille dans l'antiquité des origins à la fin de l'Empire romain d'Occident (476 ap. J.-C.),* TOME 1, Des origins jusqu 'au IIIme siècle av. J.-C. Marseille, Librairie A. Tacussel, 1927, p. 121.

[675] Strabo, *Geography,* III, 4.3.

[676] M. E. Aubet, 'On the Organization of the Phoenician Colonial System in Iberia' in C. Riva and N. C. Vella, (eds.), *Debating Orientalizing: Multidisciplinary Approaches to Change in the Mediterranean,* (Equinox, 2006): 94-109, here p. 105.

[677] T. Braun, 'Hecataeus' Knowledge of the Western Mediterranean' in K. Lomas (ed.), *Greek Identity in the Western Mediterranean,* Papers in Honour of Brian Shefton, (Brill, 2004): 287-348, here p. 309.

[678] J. Boardman et al., *The Cambridge Ancient History,* vol. 3. Part 2. Cambridge, 2003, p. 525.

[679] P. Bosch-Gimpera, 'The Phokaians in the Far West: A Historical Reconstruction', *The Classical Quarterly,* vol. 38, no. 1/2 (Jan.–Apr., 1944,): 53–59, here p. 58 n. 4 (Arabic Al-lacant=Alicante), ['JSTOR' journal archive] <www.jstor.org/stable/636879>, viewed on 20 August 2010.

[680] A. E. Astin. *The Cambridge Ancient History: Rome and the Mediterranean to 133 B.C.*, 2nd edition, vol. 8, Cambridge, 2003, p. 20.

[681] F. Quesada-Sanz, 'From Quantity to Quality: wealth, status and prestige in the Iberian Iron Age' in D. Bailey (ed.). *The Archaeology of Value,* BAR IS 730. (1998), Oxford, pp. 70-96, here p. 87.

[682] P. Rouillard, 'Greeks in the Iberian Peninsula', in M. Dietler, and C. Lopez-Ruiz, (eds.), *Colonial Encounters in Ancient Iberia: Phoenicians, Greek, and Indigenous Relations,* (University of Chicago Press, 2009): 131–154, here p. 141.

[683] For fuller discussion see A. Badie, et al, *Le site antique de la Picola à Santa Pola (Alicante, Espagne),* Éditions des Recherche sur le civilisations, Casa del Velazquez, 2000. <http://www.casadevelazquez.org/publications/librairie-en-ligne/livre/le-site-antique-de-la-picola-a-santa-pola-alicante-espagne/>, viewed on 1 October 2011.

[684] P. Rouillard, 'Greeks in the Iberian Peninsula', in M. Dietler, and C. Lopez-Ruiz, (eds.), *Colonial Encounters in Ancient Iberia: Phoenicians, Greek, and Indigenous Relations,* (University of Chicago Press, 2009): 131–154, here p. 141.

[685] Zacher, E. M. 'The Recent "Discovery" of the Legendary Atlantis, Truth or Fiction?' *The Epoch Times*, April 17, 2011, <http://www.theepochtimes.com/n2/science/the-recent-discovery-of-the-legendary-atlantis-truth-or-fiction-54862.html>, viewed on 15 December 2011; <http://www.elitevillas.net/places.htm>, viewed on 12 December 2011.

[686] Alquileres Guzmán, *History of Altea,* <http://www.villasguzman.com/gb/holiday-rentals/spain/costa-blanca/alicante/altea_location_3.aspx>, viewed on 4 October 2011.

[687] 'The other Greeks' in Spain see *Appian Wars of the Romans in Iberia,*7.25, trans. J. S. Richardson, Aris & Phillips Ltd., 2000.

[688] R. Carpenter, *The Greeks in Spain,* Bryn Mawr College, Longman, Greene & Co., 1925, p. 179

[689] *Ibid*, p. 50; Cunliffe has c.500 B.C. B. Cunliffe, *The Extraordinary Voyage of Pytheas the Greek: The man who discovered Britain,* Penguin Books, 2002, p. 42, p. 45-48; A. L. F. Rivet and C. Smith, *The Place-Names of Roman Britain,* B. T. Batsford Ltd, 1982, p. 39.

[690] *Ibid* (Carpenter), p. 52; Rufus Festus Avienus, *Ora Maritma,* <http://www.thelatinlibrary.com/avienus.ora.html> viewed 30 December 2012.

[691] R. Carpenter, *The Greeks in Spain,* Bryn Mawr College, Longman, Greene & Co., 1925, p. 25 and p. 28.

[692] F. W. Wallbank, *A Historical Commentary on Polybius,* vol.1. I. 10.5, Oxford, 1957, p. 59.

[693] R. Carpenter, *The Greeks in Spain,* Bryn Mawr College, Longman, Greene & Co., 1925, p. 96.

[694] T. Braun, 'Hecataeus' Knowledge of the Western Mediterranean' in K. Lomas (ed.), *Greek Identity in the Western Mediterranean*, Papers in Honour of Brian Shefton, (Brill, 2004): 287-348, here p. 309.

[695] R. Carpenter, *The Greeks in Spain,* Bryn Mawr College, Longman, Greene & Co., 1925, p. 53;Rufus Festus Avienus, *Ora Maritima,* <http://www.thelatinlibrary.com/avienus.ora.html> viewed 30 December 2012.

[696] Callipolis, [' l'Enciclopèdia'] <http://www.grec.net/cgibin/hecangcl.pgm?&USUARI=&SESSIO=&NDCHEC=0013625&PGMORI=E>, viewed 11 February 2012.

[697] A. Trevor. Hodge, *Ancient Greek France*, University of Pennsylvania Press, 1999, p. 158 n. 51, Skymnos 208; Mela 5, 3, 2; Ptolemy 2.

[698] *Ibid*, p. 160 n. 53.

[699] Strabo, *Geography,* IV.1.6.

[700] A. Nickels, 'Les Sondages de la rue Perben à Agde (Hérault)' in P. Arcelin, M. Bats, D. Garcia, G. Marchand, and M. Schwaller, (eds.), *Sur les pas des Grecs en Occident',* Hommage de André Nickels, Collection Etudes Massaliètes, 4, (1995): 59-98.

[701] A. Nickels and G. Marchand 'Recherches stratigraphiques ponctuelles a proximité des ramparts antiques d'Agde' in *Revue Archéologique de Narbonnaise*, vol. 9. (1976): 45-62, here p. 62. <http://www.persee.fr/web/revues/home/prescript/article/ran_0557-7705_1976_num_9_1_986>, viewed 25 February 2012.

[702] 'Musée de L'Éphèbe' at Le Cap d'Agde, France visited 30 March 2011.

[703] O. Bérard-Azzouz, *Musée de L'Éphèbe: archéologie sous-marine,* Agde, 2008, p. 15.

[704] A. Morea, *La Perle Noire de la Méditerranée,* Éditions Milan, 1999, p. 54.

[705] A. Trevor Hodge, *Ancient Greek France*, University of Pennsylvania Press, 1999, p. 159.

[706] C. Ebel, *Transalpine Gaul: the emergence of a Roman province*, Brill, 1976, p. 31.

[707] *IG*, vol. XIV, 2514 XII; *IGF* 128, p. 171.

[708] Agathe (Agde); O. Bérard, A. Nickels, and M. Schwaller, 'Agde' in *Voyage en Massalie: 100 ans d'archéologie en Gaule du sud,* Catalogue de l'exposition, (Musées de Marseille/Édisud, 1990): 182-189, here p. 183; *IGF* 130, *IGF* 129.

[709] W. Scheidel, I. Morris, and R. P. Saller, *Cambridge Economic History of the Greco-Roman World*, Cambridge, 2007, p. 260.

[710] A. L. F. Rivet, *Gallia Narbonensis,* Batsford, 1988, p.150, Clavel-Léveque, M. (1984), (Table Ronde de Besançon, Mai 1980).

[711] A. Trevor Hodge, *Ancient Greek France*, University of Pennsylvania Press, 1999, p. 160

[712] J. L. Reille, (2001)–"L'importation des meules domestiques dans la fortresse grecque d'Olbia (Hyères, Var) entre le IIe s. av. n. è. et le Haut Empire", *Documents d'archéologie méridionale*, n° 24, p. 207-211, viewed on 21 May 2011, <http://dam.revues.org/docannexe1161.html>; Olbia/Pomponiana, <http://www.arbre-celtique.com/encyclopedie/olbia-pomponiana-saint-pierre-de-l-almanarre-hyeres-5576.htm>, viewed on 21 May 2011.

[713] W. Scheidel, I. Morris, and R. P. Saller, *Cambridge Economic History of the Greco-Roman World,* Cambridge, 2007, p. 260.

[714] A. Trevor. Hodge, *Ancient Greek France,* University of Pennsylvania Press, 1999, p. 159.

[715] J-P. Morel, 'Phocaean Colonisation' in G. R. Tsetskhladze (ed.), *Greek Colonisation: An Account of Greek Colonies and Other Settlements Overseas,* vol.1, (Leiden, 2006): 358–428, here p. 390.

[716] B. B. Shefton, 'Massalia and Colonization' in Gocha R. Tsetskhladze and Franco De Angeis, (eds.), *The Archaeology of Greek Colonization,* (Oxford University School of Archaeology, 1994): 61–86, here p. 63.

[717] Of several reports published the following is available on the internet. A. Nickels and G. Marchand 'Recherches stratigraphiques ponctuelles a proximité des ramparts antiques d'Agde' in *Revue Archéologique de Narbonnaise*, vol. 9. (1976): 45-62. <http://www.persee.fr/web/revues/home/prescript/article/ran_0557-7705_1976_num_9_1_986>, viewed 25 February 2012.

[718] A. Morea, *La Perle Noire de la Méditerranée,* Éditions Milan, 1999, p. 61.

[719] O. Bérard, A. Nickels, and M. Schwaller, 'Agde' in *Voyage en Massalie: 100 ans d'archéologie en Gaule du sud,* Catalogue de l'exposition, (Musées de Marseille/Édisud, 1990): 182-189, here p. 183.

[720] *Agde, Place François-Conesa*, ['Adlfi Archéologie de la France'] <http://www.adlfi.fr/SiteAdfi/document?base=base_notices&id=N2004-LA-0164>, viewed 25 February 2012.

[721] A. Trevor. Hodge, *Ancient Greek France*, University of Pennsylvania Press, 1999, p. 159.

[722] B. Cunliffe, *The Extraordinary Voyage of Pytheas the Greek: The man who discovered Britain,* Penguin Books, 2002, p. 58.

[723] *Travel in Gallia Narbonensis,* School District of Clermont-Ferrand, <www.musagora.education.fr/voyages/provence-en/agde-en.htm>, viewed on 2 April 2011.

[724] M. Thompson, O. Morkholm, and C. M. Kraay, *An Inventory of Greek Coin Hoards*, The American Numismatic Society, New York, 1973, p. 361.

[725] O. Bérard-Azzouz, *Musée de L'Éphèbe: archéologie sous-marine,* Agde, 2008, p. 134.

[726] J. Lendering, *Diadem,* ['Livius.org'] <http://www.livius.org/di-dn/diadem/diadem.html>, viewed on 20 August 2011.

[727] The bust of Seleucus is on display at the Museo Archaeologica Nazionale, Napoli Italy. J. Lendering, *Diadem,* ['Livius.org'] <http://www.livius.org/di-dn/diadem/diadem.html>, viewed on 5 April 2011.

[728] O. Bérard-Azzouz, *Musée de L'Éphèbe: archéologie sous-marine,* Agde, 2008, p. 134.

[729] *Ibid.*

[730] Pliny, *Natural Histories,* 34. 63.

[731] O. Bérard-Azzouz, *Musée de L'Éphèbe: archéologie sous-marine,* Agde, 2008, p. 136.

[732] A. Stewart, *Classical Greece and the Birth of Western Art,* Cambridge, 2008, p. 268.

[733] O. Bérard-Azzouz, *Musée de L'Éphèbe: archéologie sous-marine,* Agde, 2008, p. 108.

[734] *Ibid,* p. 130.

[735] *Ibid,* p. 96–100.

[736] *Ibid,* p. 106.

[737] *Ibid,* p. 146.

[738] *Ibid,* p. 152.

[739] *Ibid,* p. 142.

[740] *Ibid,* p. 26.

[741] Landuedoc-Rouchillon, Province France, *Agde,* ['Greek Travel Pages'] Princeton Encyclopaedia of Classical Sites, 1976, cited from the Perseus Project February 2006, <http://www.gtp.gr/LocInfo.asp?infoid=49&code=EFRZLR&PrimeCode=EFRZLR&Level=4&PrimeLevel=4&IncludeWide=0&LocId=14429>, viewed on 4 April 2011.

[742] A. J. Domínguez, 'Spain and France (including Corsica)' in H. H. Hanson and T. H. Nielsen, *An Inventory of Archaic and Classical Poleis,* (Oxford, 2004):157–171, here p.159.

[743] A. Guillon, *Complexe Volcanique du mont Saint-Loup,* 2001, <http://membres.multimania.fr/volcanogeol/agde/AgdeV2_2.htm>, viewed on 4 April 2011.

[744] Languedoc-Rouchillon, Province France, *Agde,* ['Greek Travel Pages'] Princeton Encyclopaedia of Classical Sites, 1976, cited from the Perseus Project February 2006, 2011. <http://www.gtp.gr/LocInfo.asp?infoid=49&code=EFRZLR&PrimeCode=EFRZLR&Level=4&PrimeLevel=4&IncludeWide=0&LocId=14429>, viewed on 4 April 2011.

[745] New Advent, *Council of Agde,* ['Catholic Encyclopaedia'] <http://www.newadvent.org/cathen/01206b.htm>, viewed on 2 April 2011.

[746] Book Chapter One, P.1-7, here p. 3 n. 4 <http://www.marseillanhistorique.info/pdf%20files/book%20Chapter%20One.pdf> viewed 20 March 2012.

[747] Strabo, *Geography,* III.4.8.

[748] *Ibid.*

[749] *Ibid,* III.4.9.

[750] *Ibid.*

[751] B. Tang, *Delos, Carthage, Ampurias: the housing of three Mediterranean trading centres*, L'Erma di Bretschneider Rome, 2005, p. 108.

[752] P. Rouillard, 'Greeks in the Iberian Peninsula', in M. Dietler and C. Lopez-Ruiz, (eds.), *Colonial Encounters in Ancient Iberia: Phoenicians, Greek, and Indigenous Relations,* (University of Chicago Press, 2009): 131–154, here p. 141.

[753] *Ibid.*

[754] B. Tang, *Delos, Carthage, Ampurias: the housing of three Mediterranean trading centres*, L'Erma di Bretschneider Rome, 2005, p. 108.

[755] M. Santos, (ed.), *Sant Marti d'Emprúies: Una illo en el temps,* Museo d'Arqueologia de Catalunya-Empúries, ISBN 84-393-4543-7, p. 36.

[756] Archaeologists Elisa Hernández and Director Marta Santos Retolaza leading the training excavation, personal interview with the author on site at Emporion, Spain on 14 July 2011. <http://www.mac.cat/eng/Activities>.

[757] Catalogued as Emporion, AE denomination, c. 150–100 B.C. Obverse: helmeted head of Athena facing right/reverse: flying Pegasus to the right, above wreath on left, below letters UNTIKESEN that may refer to the indigenous tribe (Strabo writes Indicetans) that shared the city with the Greeks. Weight 19.98. SNG Vol. VI 2 Fitzwilliam Museum. <www.sylloge-nummorum-graecorum.org>, viewed on 20 November 2010; The 'X4 coin hoard' buried 200 B.C. at Cuidad Real-Cuenca included 95 AR from Emporion and another coin burial 230-220 B.C. at Ullastret consisted of 54 AR Emporion. O. Hoover, A. Meadows and U. Wartenberg, *Coin Hoards: Greek Hoards*, Vol. X, The American Numismatic Society, 2010, p. 70.

[758] K. Lomas, 'Beyond Magna Graecia: Greeks and Non-Greeks in France, Spain and Italy' in K. Kinzl, (ed.), *A Companion to the Classical Greek World*, (Wiley-Blackwell, 2006):174–198., here p. 186.

[759] A. J. Domínguez, 'Spain and France (including Corsica)' in H. H. Hanson and T. H. Nielsen, *An Inventory of Archaic and Classical Poleis*, (Oxford, 2004):157–171, here p. 165.

[760] Spain is Culture, *Treasure from the Neapolis, Ampurias,* ['Ministerio de Culture' National Art Museum of Catalonia, MNAC] <http://www.spainisculture.com/en/obras_de_excelencia/tesoro_neapolis_ampurias.html>, viewed on 7 December 2011.

[761] I. Carradice, *Greek Coins*, British Museum Press,1995, p.74, Fig. 48, a; Collection: IX British Museum Part II, mint Emporion,
<http://www.sylloge-nummorum-graecorum.org/>, viewed on 23 November 2010.

[762] X. Aquilué, P. Castanyer, M. Santos, and J. Tremoleda, *Empúries. Guidebooks to the Museu d'Arqueologia de Catalunya,* English language edition, Museu d'Arqueologia de Catalunya, 2008, p. 43-44.

[763] By permission of CNG coins <http://www.acsearch.info/record.html?id=38567> viewed on 20 November 2010. See also M. Campo, 'Las emisiones de Emporion y su difusión en el entorno iberico', ATTI DEL 'XI CONVEGNO DEL CENTRO INTERNAZIONALE DI STUDI NUMISMATICI-NAPOLI 25-27 OTTOBRE 1996, TAV. XVI, 3, in *La monetazione dei Focei in Occidente*, Instituto Italiano di Numismatica Roma, (2002): 139–166, here p. 142.

[764] J. Sanmartí, 'Colonial Relations and Social Change in Iberia' in M. Dietler, and C. Lopez-Ruiz, (eds.), *Colonial Encounters in Ancient Iberia: Phoenicians, Greek, and Indigenous Relations,* (University of Chicago Press, 2009): 49–90, here p. 67–68.

[765] R. Buxó, 'Botanical and Archaeological Dimensions' in M. Dietler, and C. Lopez-Ruiz, (eds.), *Colonial Encounters in Ancient Iberia: Phoenicians, Greek, and Indigenous Relations,* (University of Chicago Press, 2009): 155–168, here p. 160; Silius Italicus, *Punica,*15.175–77.

[766] F. Quesada-Sanz, 'From Quantity to Quality: wealth, status and prestige in the Iberian Iron Age' in D. Bailey (ed.). *The Archaeology of Value*, BAR IS 730. (1998), Oxford, pp. 70-96, here p.89.

[767] R. Buxó, 'Botanical and Archaeological Dimensions' in M. Dietler, and C. Lopez-Ruiz, (eds.), *Colonial Encounters in Ancient Iberia: Phoenicians, Greek, and Indigenous Relations,* (University of Chicago Press, 2009): 155–168, here p. 160-161.

[768] *Livy,* vol. 9. Bk. XXXIV. VIII. 4–IX.4. IX, trans. E. T. Sage, Loeb Classical Library, 1935, p. 441–443.

[769] K. Lomas, 'Beyond Magna Graecia: Greeks and Non-Greeks in France, Spain and Italy' in K. Kinzl, (ed.), *A Companion to the Classical Greek World*, (Wiley-Blackwell, 2006):174-198, here p. 185-186.

[770] M. Clerc, *Massalia: Histoire de Marseille dans l'antiquité des origins à la fin de l'Empire romain d'Occident (476 ap. J.-C.)*, TOME 1, Des origins jusqu 'au IIIme siècle av. J.-C. Marseille, Librairie A. Tacussel, 1927, p. 277 n. 1, Fig. 69, *Revue des etudes grecques*, REG. 1909, XXII, p. 332; *L'Epigrafia Grega a Catalunya*, 2002, p. 109.

[771] J. B. Curbera, 'The Greek Curse Tablets of Emporion', *Zeitschrift für Papyrologie und Epigraphik*, Bd. 117, (1997): 90–94, here p. 90. Available from <http://www.jstor.org/stable/20190008>, viewed on 16 January 2011.

[772] E. Eidinow, *Oracles, Curses and Risk Among the Ancient Greeks,* Oxford, 2007, p. 434, and methods p. 140–141.

[773] J. B. Curbera, 'The Greek Curse Tablets of Emporion', *Zeitschrift für Papyrologie und Epigraphik*, Bd. 117 (1997):90-94, here p. 92–4, ['JSTOR' journal archive] <http://www.jstor.org/stable/20190008>, viewed on 16 January 2011.

[774] *Ibid*, here p. 92 n. 4, J. Coupry and M. Giffault, "La clientèle d'un sanctuaire d' Aristée aux îles d'Hyère (I er siècle avant J.C.)", PP 37 (1982).

[775] R. Jones and J. Buxeda i Garrigós, 'The Identity of Early Greek Pottery in Italy and Spain: An Archeometric Perspective' in K. Lomas (eds.), *Greek Identity in the Western Mediterranean,* Brill, 2003, p. 106.

[776] X. Aquilué, P. Castanyer, M. Santos, and J. Tremoleda, *Empúries. Guidebooks to the Museu d'Arqueologia de Catalunya*, Museu d'Arqueologia de Catalunya, English language 2nd edition, 2008. p. 34.

[777] *Ibid*, p. 60 and p. 32. Asclepius left hand leaning on a staff with patera in right hand.

[778] B. Tang, *Delos, Carthage, Ampurias: the housing of three Mediterranean trading centres*, L'Erma di Bretschneider Rome, 2005, p. 110.

[779] *Ibid*, p. 108.

[780] X. Aquilué, P. Castanyer, M. Santos, and J. Tremoleda, *Empúries. Guidebooks to the Museu d'Arqueologia de Catalunya*, Museu d'Arqueologia de Catalunya, English language 2nd edition, 2008, p. 58.

[781] J-P. Morel, 'Phocaean Colonisation' in G. R. Tsetskhladze (ed.), *Greek Colonisation: An Account of Greek Colonies and Other Settlements Overseas,* vol.1, (Leiden, 2006): 358–428, here p. 401.

[782] *Appian Wars of the Romans in Iberia,* 7.25, trans. J. S. Richardson, Aris & Phillips Ltd., 2000; *Appian's Roman History,* vol. 1. Bk. 7. 2, trans. H. White, Heinemann, 1912, p. 307.

[783] *Appian's Roman History,* Bk. IV, Ch.VIII, 40, trans. H. White, Heinemann, 1912, p. 201.

[784] *Livy*, Vol. IX. Bk. XXXIV. VIII. 4–IX.4. IX, trans. E. T. Sage, Loeb Classical Library, 1935, p. 441-443.

[785] A. W. Lawrence, *Greek Arms and Fortifications,* Oxford, 1979, p. 176 n. 3.

[786] D. Baatz, 'Recent Finds of Ancient Artillery', *Britannia*, vol. 9. (1978): 1–17, here p.1, Society for the Promotion of Roman Studies, ['JSTOR' journal archive] <http://jstor.org/stable/525936>, viewed on 16 January 2011.

[787] B. Tang, *Delos, Carthage, Ampurias: the housing of three Mediterranean trading centres*, L'Erma di Bretschneider Rome, 2005, p. 110.

[788] X. Aquilué, P. Castanyer, M. Santos, and J. Tremoleda, *Empúries. Guidebooks to the Museu d'Arqueologia de Catalunya*, Museu d'Arqueologia de Catalunya, English language 2nd edition, 2008, p. 49.

[789] *Ibid*, p. 63–65.

Curnow mentions there was also an oracle here. T. Curnow, *The Oracles of the Ancient World*, Duckworth, 2004, p. 116.

[790] M. Amalgro, *Ampurias, Guide to the Excavations and Museum*, Barcelona, 1968, Plate VI; X. Aquilué and J. Monturiol, (eds.), *1908-2008: 100 anys d'excavacions arqueologiques a Empuries*, Museu d'Arqueologia de Catalunya-Empuries, 2008, p. 29.

[791] X. Aquilué, P. Castanyer, M. Santos, and J. Tremoleda, *Empúries. Guidebooks to the Museu d'Arqueologia de Catalunya*, Museu d'Arqueologia de Catalunya, English language 2nd edition, 2008, p. 56.

[792] A. Nesteroff, (ed.), *Istanbul*, Everyman, 2001, p. 76.

[793] X. Aquilué, P. Castanyer, M. Santos, and J. Tremoleda, *Empúries. Guidebooks to the Museu d'Arqueologia de Catalunya*, Museu d'Arqueologia de Catalunya, English language 2nd edition, 2008, p. 69.

[794] *Ibid*, p. 69–70.

[795] J. Lendering, *Emporiae (Ampurias)*, ['Livius.org'] <http://www.livius.org/ei-er/emporiae/emporiae.html>, viewed on 1 August 2011.

[796] X. Aquilué, P. Castanyer, M. Santos, and J. Tremoleda, *Empúries. Guidebooks to the Museu d'Arqueologia de Catalunya*, Museu d'Arqueologia de Catalunya, English language 2nd edition, 2008, p. 67.

[797] *Ibid*, p. 74.

[798] X. Aquilué, P. Castanyer, M. Santos, and J. Tremoleda, *Empúries. Guidebooks to the Museu d'Arqueologia de Catalunya*, Museu d'Arqueologia de Catalunya, English language 2nd edition, 2008, p. 75.

[799] B. Tang, *Delos, Carthage, Ampurias: the housing of three Mediterranean trading centres*, L'Erma di Bretschneider Rome, 2005, p. 110–1.

[800] T. E. Page, *Appian's Roman History*, vol. 5. Bk. V, ch. XIV, 137, Heinemann, 1913, p. 605.

[801] M. Clerc, *Massalia: Histoire de Marseille dans L'Antiquité des Origins a la Fin de l'empire Romain d'occident*, vol. 2, Librarie A. Tacussel, 1929, p. 247 n.1. Livy, XXXIV, 9.

[802] J. Briscoe, *A Commentary on Livy*, Bk. XXXIV–XXXVII, Oxford, 1981, Bk. XXXIV, 9.3, p. 68, (*Fuentes escritas*, 58).

[803] Strabo, *Geography*, III.4.8.

[804] X. Aquilué, P. Castanyer, M. Santos, and J. Tremoleda, *Empúries. Guidebooks to the Museu d'Arqueologia de Catalunya*, Museu d'Arqueologia de Catalunya, English language 2nd edition, 2008, p. 90.

[805] *Ibid*, p. 88; Coins have Roman letters EMPOR but still use Greek images obverse: head of Athena/reverse: flying Pegasus, see <http://www.acsearch.info/search.html?search=similar%3A224271> viewed 9 December 2012.

[806] B. Tang, *Delos, Carthage, Ampurias: the housing of three Mediterranean trading centres*, L'Erma di Bretschneider Rome, 2005, p. 113.

[807] Pliny the Elder, *Natural Histories*, vol.2, III. 3.22, trans. H. Rackham, Heinemann, 1947, p. 21.

[808] X. Aquilué, P. Castanyer, M. Santos, and J. Tremoleda, *Empúries. Guidebooks to the Museu d'Arqueologia de Catalunya,* English language edition, Museu d'Arqueologia de Catalunya, 2008, p. 91.

[809] Marta Santos Director of Excavations at Empúries, personal interview with the author on site, 14 July 2011.

[810] X. Aquilué, P. Castanyer, M. Santos, and J. Tremoleda, *Empúries. Guidebooks to the Museu d'Arqueologia de Catalunya,* Museu d'Arqueologia de Catalunya, English language 2nd edition, 2008, p. 106-109.

[811] *Ibid*, p. 106. and p. 110.

[812] *Ibid*, p. 110-111 and p. 115.

[813] *Ibid*, p. 116–115.

[814] *Ibid*, p. 116–117.

[815] Strabo, *Geography*, Book III.4.8.

[816] Pliny the Elder, *Natural Histories*, vol.2, III, 33, trans. H. Rackham, Heinemann, 1947, p. 27.

[817] T. J. Dunbabin, *The Western Greeks: The History of Sicily and South Italy from the Foundation of the Greek Colonies to 480 B.C*, Oxford University Press Monograph Reprints, 1998, p. 340 n. 4, Strabo, *Geography,* VI.5.4 and XIV.2.10.

[818] T. J. Dunbabin, *The Western Greeks: The History of Sicily and South Italy from the Foundation of the Greek Colonies to 480 B.C*, Oxford University Press Monograph Reprints, 1998, p. 340 and p. 237.

[819] Pithekoussai 775 B.C. settlers moved from the island to the mainland and founded Cumae c. 750, (O. Murray, *Early Greece,* Fontana, 1993, p. 74). Pithekoussai has been regarded different to a settlement (apoikia) as a trading-post (emporion) even though it had between 5,000–10,000 people. (R. Osborne, *Greece in the Making, 1200–479 B.C.* Routledge, 2008, p. 114 & p.119). Can Pithekousssai be some sort of substantial centre due to its trading position a place to make your fortune where either wages were high or where the buying and selling goods on had good profits and this attracted many particularly in the eighth and seventh century B.C. in search of high earnings to take back home? Attracting people like a gold rush city springing up in the Canadian Yukon and the American 'Wild West' but with more emphasis on several products such as valuable tin, amber, and a fine ware pottery distribution centre. Pottery finds confirm variety from Euboean, Proto-Corinthian, East Greek, Italy, Carthage, the Levant, 'Phoenician' Rhodes, and the Iberian Peninsula. (R. Osborne, 'Early Greek Colonization? The nature of Greek settlement in the West*'*, in N. Fisher and H. van Wees (eds.), *Archaic Greece; new approaches and new evidence,* (London, 1998): 251–269, here p. 258–259*)*

When does an emporion become an Apoikia? When enough women of one's own race and culture join to make it a permanent settlement? Was there inter-marriage? Polybius mentions amongst the Carthaginian soldiers at the end of the Punic War were offspring from Greeks and Barbarians. 'Some of these troops were Iberians, some Celts, some Ligurians and some from the Balearic Islands; there was a good many Greek half-breeds, mostly deserters and slaves, but the largest portion consisted of Libyans'. *Polybius*, vol.1. I. 1.67.6, trans. W. R. Paton, Heinemann, 1922, p. 183. Livy also mentions the Gallograeci who were formidable warriors and from the inter-marriage of Greeks and the Galatian Celts that lived in Asia Minor during the war against Antiochus 189 B.C. (J. Briscoe, *A Commentary on Livy,* Books 38–40, 38.17.9, Oxford, 2008, p. 79). Either way the first Olympiad at 776 B.C. would predate both the Pithekoussai trading post and the permanent settlement of Cumae (A. Trevor. Hodge, *Ancient Greek France*, University of Pennsylvania Press, 1999, p. 163 &, p. 292).

How did the ancient Greek see other races? On the one hand there was elitism born from the knowledge that their own small city-states had produced a very high standard of culture, inventions (including the world's first computer i.e. Antikythera Mechanism*) and knowledge, in comparison to their contemporaries, spreading out across the known world, but as proved in Massalia (France) and Emporion (Spain) they also had a gregarious nature and mostly kept good relations with the native populations proving themselves adaptable, while maintaining their own culture. One should be wary of looking at the past with the changeable trends of your own present day.

*The Antikythera Mechanism was a small portable box containing a set of geared wheels that computed the movement of the planets, predicting solar and lunar eclipses and the dates of the four Pan-Hellenic games, Olympic, Nemean, Pythian and Isthmian. Due to the name of Isthmian being prominent the mechanism was considered to have been made by Corinthians either in Greece or its colony of Syracuse in Sicily. M. Wright, 'The Antikythera Mechanism', in *Interdisciplinary Science Reviews,* vol. 37, No. 1. (2007): 27-43, here p. 41.
<http://fsoso.free.fr/antikythera/DOCS/TheAntikytheraMechanismReconsidered.pdf>, viewed on 13 May 2012; *The Antikythera Mechanism Research Project* <http://www.antikythera-mechanism.gr/> viewed on 13 May 2012.

[820] Generalitat de Catalunya, *Phoenicians and Greeks in Catalonia: 7th Century B.C.– 6th Century B.C.*
<http://www20.gencat.cat/portal/site/culturacatalana/menuitem.be2B.C.
4cc4c5aec88f94a9710b0c0e1a0/?vgnextoid=d07cef2126896210VgnVCM1000000b0c1e0aRCRD&vgnextchannel=d07
cef2126896210VgnVCM1000000b0c1e0aRCRD&vgnextfmt=detall2&contentid=810c110e279d7210VgnVCM1000008
d0c1e0aRCRD&newLang=en_GB >, viewed on 22 July 2011.

[821] Archaeologist Maria Anne Puig Griessenberger, Projecte Museològic, Museu De La Cuitadela Roses, leading the excavations, personal interview with the author on site, 26 July 2011.

[822] B. Tang, *Delos, Carthage, Ampurias: the housing of three Mediterranean trading centres,* L'Erma di Bretschneider Rome, 2005, p. 155.

[823] J. S. Richardson. *Hispaniae: Spain and Development of Roman Imperialism 218–82 B.C.* Cambridge University Press, 2004, p. 3.

[824] C. Díaz, H. Palou, and A. M. Puig, *La Ciudadela de Roses*, Ayuntamiento de Roses Fundació Roses Història i Natura, 2003, p. 19.

[825] X. Aquilué, P. Castanyer, M. Santos, and J. Tremoleda, *Empúries. Guidebooks to the Museu d'Arqueologia de Catalunya*, Museu d'Arqueologia de Catalunya, English language 2nd edition, 2008, p. 49 and p. 51.

[826] A. M. Puig and A. Martin, (Coordinadores), *La colònia grega de Rhode (Roses, Alt Empordà)*, Serie Monongrafica 23, Museu d'Arqueologia de Catalunya Girona. 2006, p. 140.

[827] L. Buscato i Samoza, *La Colònia Grega de Rhode,* Brau, 1999, p. 135–166.

[828] A. Trevor. Hodge, *Ancient Greek France,* University of Pennsylvania Press, 1999, p. 163 and p. 276 n. 67; J. C. Koch, *Celtic Culture: A Historical Encyclopaedia,* AB.C. CLIO, 2006, vol.1, p. 462.

[829] R. A. G. Carson, *Coins,* Hutchinson of London, 1963, p. 69.

[830] Archaeologist Maria Anne Puig Griessenberger, Projecte Museològic, Museu De La Cuitadela Roses leading the excavations, personal interview with the author on site, 26 July 2011; A.M. Puig and A. Martin, (Coordinadores), *La colònia grega de Rhode (Roses, Alt Empordà)*, Serie Monongrafica 23, Museu d'Arqueologia de Catalunya Girona. 2006, p. 619.

[831] *Roman History (incomplete) Titus Livius,* Livy, 10. XXXIV. 8. <http://thriceholy.net/Texts/Livy10.html>, viewed on 29 July 2011.

[832] A.M. Puig and A. Martin, A. (Coordinadores), *La colònia grega de Rhode (Roses, Alt Empordà)*, Serie Monongrafica 23, Museu d'Arqueologia de Catalunya Girona. 2006, p. 593–596.

[833] Castillo de San Fernando, <http://www.castellsantferran.org/>, viewed on 4 August 2011.

[834] Pliny the Elder, *Natural Histories*, vol.2, III, 30, trans. H. Rackham, Heinemann, 1947, p. 27.

[835] Archaeologists Marta Santos Retolaza and Elisa Hernández, Empuries Archaelogical excavation team, personal interview with author on site 14 July 2011 and confirmed to me by email 25 January 2012.

[836] J. S. Richardson. J. S. *Hispaniae: Spain and Development of Roman Imperialism 218–82 B.C.* Cambridge University Press, 2004, p. 3; F. W. Wallbank, *A Historical Commentary on Polybius,* vol.1, III.13.1–2, 1970, p. 316.

[837] A. E. Astin. *The Cambridge Ancient History: Rome and the Mediterranean to 133 B.C.*, 2nd edition, vol. 8, Cambridge, 2003, p. 24.

[838] A. Trevor. Hodge, Ancient Greek France, University of Pennsylvania Press, 1999, p. 173 n. 8.

[839] Artemision/Dianum (Dénia), <www.arbre-celtique.com/encyclopedie/artemision-dianum-denia-5585.htm>, viewed on 3 October 2010.

[840] Strabo, *Geography*, III. 4.6.

[841] P. Bosch-Gimpera, 'The Phokaians in the Far West: A Historical Reconstruction', *The Classical Quarterly*, vol. 38, no. 1/2 (Jan.–Apr., 1944): 53–59, here p. 58 n. 4 (Arabic Al-lacant=Alicante), ['JSTOR' journal archive] <www.jstor.org/stable/636879>, viewed on 20 August 2010.

[842] R. Gardiner, (ed.), *The Age of the Galley*, Conway Maritime Press, 1995, p. 60–61.

[843] P. A. Sabin, Hans Van Wees, and M. Whitby, (eds.), *The Cambridge History of Greek and Roman Warfare, vol. 1: Greece, the Hellenistic World, the Rise of Rome*, Cambridge, 2007, p. 232; Momigliano conjectures Sosylus may have used directly or indirectly Skylax to get his information on the naval battle. A. Momigliano, *The Development of Greek Biography*, First Harvard University Press paperback edition, 1993, p. 29. (FgrHist, 176F1); J. F. Lazenby, *The Peleponessian War: A military study*, Routledge, 2004, p. 231.

[844] *Ibid*; F. W. Wallbank, *A Historical Commentary on Polybius*, vol. I, Bk. III. 20.5. Oxford, 1957, p. 333.

[845] Appian, *Wars of the Romans in Iberia*, 7.25, trans. J. S. Richardson, Aris & Phillips Ltd., 2000; *Appian's Roman History*, vol.1, Ch. 1, 2, trans. H. White, Heinemann, 1912, p. 307.

[846] J-P. Morel, 'Phocaean Colonisation' in G. R. Tsetskhladze (ed.), *Greek Colonisation: An Account of Greek Colonies and Other Settlements Overseas*, vol.1, (Leiden, 2006): 358–428, p. 329.

[847] Strabo, *Geography*, III. 4.6.

[848] R. Carpenter, *Beyond the Pillars of Hercules: The classical world seen through the eyes of its discoverers*, Tandem Press (UK) 1973, p. 48.

[849] Strabo, *Geography*, III. 4.6.

[850] R. Carpenter, *The Greeks in Spain*, Bryn Mawr College, Longman, Greene & Co., 1925, p. 179.

[851] A. J. Domínguez, 'Spain and France (including Corsica)' in H. H. Hanson and T. H. Nielsen, *An Inventory of Archaic and Classical Poleis*, (Oxford, 2004):157–171, here p. 162.

[852] Strabo, *Geography*, III. 4.6.

[853] *Ibid*.

[854] Appian, *Wars of the Romans in Iberia*, 7.25, trans. J. S. Richardson, Aris & Phillips Ltd., 2000.

[855] W. M. Lindsay, *Isidore of Seville: The Etymologies (or Origins)*, vol.15. 1. 68, Oxford University Press, 1911, ['Penelope, University of Chicago' digital library] <htpp://Penelope.uchicago.edu/Thayer/E/Roman/Texts/isidore/home.html>, viewed on 26 December 2010.

[856] F. W. Wallbank, *A Historical Commentary on Polybius*, vol. 1. III.17.1, Oxford, 1970, p. 328.

[857] F. W. Wallbank, *A Historical Commentary on Polybius*, vol.1. III.15, Oxford, 1957, p. 320, (Schulten, Phil, Woch., 1927, col.1582–Schulten, A. Numantia, die Ergebmisse der Aausgra' bugen, 1905–12, 4 vols. Munich, 1914–31).

[858] Strabo, *Geography*, Book III.4.6.

[859] Appian, *Wars of the Romans in Iberia*, 7.25, trans. J. S. Richardson, Aris & Phillips Ltd., 2000; *Appian's Roman History*. vol.1. Ch. 1, 2, trans. H. White, Heinemann, 1912, p. 307.

[860] A. Trevor. Hodge, *Ancient Greek France*, University of Pennsylvania Press, 1999, p. 135, p. 296 n. 4; M. E. Aubet, 'Mainake: the Legend and New Archaeological Evidence', in B. Cunliffe and R. Osborne, (eds.), *Mediterranean Urbanisation 800–600 B.C.*, The British Academy, (Oxford University Press 2007): 187–202, here p. 193.

[861] Strabo, *Geography*, Book IV. 1.9.

[862] Seventeen warships plus fishing boats that had been decked to protect the oarsmen from missiles. All were 'manned with archers and equipped with artillery'. Caesar, *The Civil War*, Bk. II.4 and Bk. I.56 trans. J. Carter, Oxford, 1998, p. 51–52, and p. 32.

[863] *Ibid*, Bk. II.4 and Bk. I.36 trans. J. Carter, Oxford, 1998, p. 51–52, and p. 23.

[864] A. Trevor. Hodge, *Ancient Greek France*, University of Pennsylvania Press, 1999, p. 172 n. 4. (B.C. 2.4)

[865] A. J. Domínguez, 'Spain and France (including Corsica)' in H. H. Hanson and T. H. Nielsen, *An Inventory of Archaic and Classical Poleis*, (Oxford, 2004):157–171, here p. 160–161.

[866] M. Thompson, O. Morkholm, and C. M. Kraay, *An Inventory of Greek Coin Hoards*, The American Numismatic Society, New York, 1973, p. 363.

[867] F. Brien-Poitevin, 'Tauroeis' in *Voyage en Massalie: 100 ans d'archéologie en Gaule du sud*, Catalogue de l'exposition, (Musées de Marseille/Édisud, 1990): 202-205.

[868] A. Trevor. Hodge, *Ancient Greek France*, University of Pennsylvania Press, 1999, p. 175–176; *IGF* 64, p. 75.

[869] *Ibid*.

[870] M. Bats, 'Olbia' in *Voyage en Massalie: 100 ans d'archéologie en Gaule du sud*, Catalogue de l'exposition, (Musées de Marseille/Édisud, 1990): 206-213, here p. 213, Exhibit No. 23.

[871] *Ibid*, Exhibit No. 25.

[872] On site archaeological information sheet provided at Olbia July 2011; *IGF* 66, p. 76, *IGF* 67, p. 77.

[873] M. Bats, 'The Greeks in Gaul and Corsica: the rhythm of the Greek emporion' in P. Carratelli (ed.), *The Western Greeks: Classical Civilization in the Western Mediterranean*, (London, 1996): 577–584, here p. 582.

[874] Cultural Visits in Hyères Les Palmiers : Monuments and Sites, *Olbia Archaeological Site*, <http://www.hyeres-tourisme.com/en/decouverte_lieux_culturels.asp>, viewed on 11 July 2011.

[875] J.-L. Reille, (2001)–"L'importation des meules domestiques dans la fortresse grecque d'Olbia (Hyères, Var) entre le IIe s. av. n. è. et le Haut Empire", *Documents d'archéologie méridionale*, n° 24, p. 207-211, <http://dam.revues.org/docannexe1161.html>, viewed on 21 May 2011; Olbia/Pomponiana, <http://www.arbre-celtique.com/encyclopedie/olbia-pomponiana-saint-pierre-de-l-almanarre-hyeres-5576.htm>, viewed on 21 May 2011.

[876] M. Bats, *Olbia de Provence (Hyères, Var) a l'epoque romaine (1ers. av. J-C.–VIIe s. ap J-C)*, Edisud, 2006, p. 409–415.

[877] *Ibid*.

[878] A. Trevor. Hodge, *Ancient Greek France*, University of Pennsylvania Press, 1999, p. 177 n. 17.

[879] H. Hermary, A. Hesnard, and H. Tréziny, *Marseille Grecque: La cite phocéenne (600–49 av. J-C)*, Editions Errance, 1999, p. 93; *IGF* 68, p. 78.

[880] J. B. Curbera, 'The Greek Curse Tablets of Emporion', *Zeitschrift für Papyrologie und Epigraphik*, Bd. 117 (1997): 93–4, here p. 92 n. 4, J. Coupry and M. Giffault, "La clientèle d'un sanctuaire d' Aristée aux îles d'Hyère (I er siècle avant J.C.)", PP 37 (1982). ['JSTOR' journal archive] <http://www.jstor.org/stable/20190008>, viewed on 16 January 2011.

[881] A. Trevor. Hodge, *Ancient Greek France*, University of Pennsylvania Press, 1999, p. 182.

[882] *Ibid*, p. 184.

[883] M. Bats, 'Antibes' in *Voyage en Massalie: 100 ans d'archéologie en Gaule du sud*, Catalogue de l'exposition, (Musées de Marseille/Édisud, 1990): 220–221.

[884] M. Bats, *Olbia de Provence (Hyères, Var) a l'epoque romaine (1ers. av. J-C.–VIIe s. ap J-C)*, Edisud, 2006, p. 409–415.

[885] M. Clerc, *Massalia: Histoire de Marseille dans L'Antiquité des Origins a la Fin de l'empire Romain d'occident*, vol. 2, Librarie A. Tacussel, 1929, p. 247; G. Maurel, *Le Corpus des monnaies de Marseille et Provence*, Omni, 2013, p.164.

[886] *Appian's Roman History,* vol. 2, trans. H. White, Heinemann, 1913, p. 143.

[887] D. R. Shackleton Bailey, *Martial's Epigrams,* vol 1.IV. Harvard, 1993, p. 359 n.d.

[888] J. Knight, *Roman France: An Archaeological Field Guide,* Tempus Publishing Ltd., 2001, p. 210.

[889] *Pliny Natural Histories,* Vol.8, XLIII. 94. & XLIV. 97. fp. 237–9, trans. W. H. S. Jones, Heinemann, 1962.

[890] D. R. Shackleton Bailey, *Martial's Epigrams,* vol 1. Bk. IV, Harvard, 1993, p. 359 n.d.

[891] *Pliny Natural Histories,* vol. VIII, XXXI, XLII. 97, trans. W. H. S. Jones, Heinemann, 1962, p. 239.

[892] A. Trevor. Hodge, *Ancient Greek France*, University of Pennsylvania Press, 1999, p. 186 n. 37.

[893] *Ibid.*

[894] *Ibid*, p. 186.

[895] IG 2424, *Inscriptionum Graecarum*, vol. XIV. Inscriptiones Galliae, I. ANTIPOLIS (Antibes), G. Kaibel, (ed.), Berolini, 1890, p. 641.The Π is actually writen in the Ionic Π .

[896] J. Bromwich, *The Roman Remains of Southern France: a guidebook*, Routledge, 1993, p. 251.

[897] CIG 6776, *Corpus Inscriptionum Grecarum*, vol. 3, Pars XXXIV, Inscriptiones Gallarium, Section 1, Pars Prima, Inscriptiones Galliae Narbonensis et Aquitanicae, A. Boeckhio, Berolini, 1853, p. 1034.

[898] A. L. F. Rivet, *Gallia Narbonensis,* Batsford, 1988, p. 239.

[899] J. Knight, *Roman France: An Archaeological Field Guide,* Tempus Publishing Ltd., 2001, p. 210.

[900] A. L. F. Rivet, *Gallia Narbonensis,* Batsford, 1988, p. 239–240.

[901] A. Trevor. Hodge, *Ancient Greek France*, University of Pennsylvania Press, 1999, p. 186 n. 36.

[902] M. Bats, 'Antibes' in *Voyage en Massalie: 100 ans d'archéologie en Gaule du sud,* Catalogue de l'exposition, (Musées de Marseille/Édisud, 1990): 220–221. The anse is being excavated in 2013 see Artdaily.org 21 May 2013.

[903] *Universite de Nice Sophia Antipolis*, <http://portail.unice.fr/jahia/Jahia/>, viewed on 9 December 2011.

[904] Strabo, *Geography*, IV.1.9.

[905] Pliny the Elder, *Natural Histories*, vol.2, III, 35, trans. H. Rackham, Heinemann, 1947, p. 29.

[906] A. L. F. Rivet, *Gallia Narbonensis*, Batsford, 1988, p. 239.

[907] M. Bats and D. Mouchot, 'Nice' in *Voyage en Massalie: 100 ans d'archéologie en Gaule du sud*, Catalogue de l'exposition, (Musées de Marseille/Édisud, 1990): 222–225.

[908] Strabo, *Geography*, IV. 1.9.

[909] B. Levick, *The Government of the Roman Empire: A Sourcebook*, Croom Helm, 1985, Ch. 2, p. 24–25, ILS 6761; Nicaea, Narbonensis. Also in *CIL*, 5.7914.

[910] S. P. Aloupes, *He Archaia Massalia kai ho Politismos tes,* Eleuthere Skepsis, 1996, p. 72; Strabo, IV.6.2.

[911] A. Trevor. Hodge, *Ancient Greek France*, University of Pennsylvania Press, 1999, p. 188, p. 269 n. 4, and p. 135.

[912] *Ibid*, p. 190.

[913] M. Clerc, *Massalia: Histoire de Marseille dans L'Antiquité des Origins a la Fin de l'empire Romain d'occident*, Librarie A. Tacussel, 1929, vol. 2, p. 270 n. 5, Tacitus, *Histories*, III, 43 (ed Budé); Strabo, *Geography*, IV.1.9–10.

[914] M. Bats and D. Mouchot 'Nice', in *Voyage en Massalie: 100 ans d'archéologie en Gaule du sud*, Catalogue de l'exposition, (Musées de Marseille/Édisud, 1990): 222–225, see no. 4 & no. 11 in catalogue section p. 224–225; M. Bats, 'The Greeks in Gaul and Corsica: the rhythm of the Greek emporion' in P. Carratelli (ed.), *The Western Greeks: Classical Civilization in the Western Mediterranean,* (London, 1996): 577–584, here p. 581.

[915] A. Trevor. Hodge, *Ancient Greek France*, University of Pennsylvania Press, 1999, p. 190.

[916] A. L. F. Rivet, *Gallia Narbonensis*, Batsford, 1988, p. 222.

[917] A. Trevor. Hodge, *Ancient Greek France,* University of Pennsylvania Press, 1999, p. 186, Mela (2.77) and p. 88.

[918] A. L. F. Rivet, *Gallia Narbonensis*, Batsford, 1988, p.150, Clavel-Léveque, M. (1984), (Table Ronde de Besançon, Mai 1980).

[919] J-P. Morel, 'Phocaean Colonisation' in G. R. Tsetskhladze (ed.), *Greek Colonisation: An Account of Greek Colonies and Other Settlements Overseas,* vol.1. (Leiden, 2006): 358–428, here p. 401.

[920] *Kérylos Greek Villa*: French Riviera, <http://www.villa-kerylos.com/en/kerylos/>, viewed on 16 October 2011.

[921] J. Bromwich, *The Roman Remains of Southern France: a guidebook*, Routledge, 1993, p. 277.

[922] Strabo, *Geography,* IV.1.5.

[923] R. Buxó, 'Botanical and Archaeological Dimensions' in M. Dietler, and C. Lopez-Ruiz, (eds.), *Colonial Encounters in Ancient Iberia: Phoenicians, Greek, and Indigenous Relations,* (University of Chicago Press, 2009): 155-168, here p. 160-161.

[924] Strabo, *Geography,* IV. 1.10; Pliny 3.1; Pomponius Mela, 2.7.

[925] M. Clerc, *Massalia: Histoire de Marseille dans L'Antiquité des Origins a la Fin de l'empire Romain d'occident*, vol. 2. Librarie A. Tacussel, 1929, p. 270 n. 5, Tacitus, *Histories*, III, 43 (ed Budé).

[926] Tacitus *The Histories,* Bk. 3. 43, trans. K. Wellesley, Penguin. 1964, p. 171.

[927] Apollonius of Rhodes, *The Voyage of Argo: The Argonautica,* trans. E. V. Rieu, Penguin, 1959, p. 162.

[928] A. Trevor. Hodge, *Ancient Greek France*, University of Pennsylvania Press, 1999, p. 53.

[929] Porquerolles (Les isles d' Hyères), ['Provence hideaway'] <http://www.provence-hideaway.com/251.html > viewed 26 April 2012.

[930] A. L. F. Rivet, *Gallia Narbonensis,* Batsford, 1988, p. 223, Pliny, *Natural Histories*, III. 79.

[931] J-P. Morel, 'Phocaean Colonisation' in G. R. Tsetskhladze (ed.), *Greek Colonisation: An Account of Greek Colonies and Other Settlements Overseas,* vol.1, (Leiden, 2006): 358–428, here p. 391.

[932] J. Boardman, *The Greeks Overseas*, Thames & Hudson, 1999, Ch. 5, p. 224.

[933] A. G. Woodhead, *The Greeks in the West*, Thames and Hudson, 1962, p. 68.

[934] J-P. Morel, 'Phocaean Colonisation' in G. R. Tsetskhladze (ed.), *Greek Colonisation: An Account of Greek Colonies and Other Settlements Overseas,* vol.1, (Leiden, 2006): 358–428, here p. 392.

[935] A. Trevor. Hodge, *Ancient Greek France,* University of Pennsylvania Press, 1999, p. 160 n.56, R. Amy, *Princeton Encyclopaedia of Classical Sites (PECS)*, 87.

[936] Les Grands Sites Archéologique, *Les Gaulois en Provence: L'oppidum d'Entremont,* <http://www.grands-sites-archeologiques.culture.fr/catalogue.php?id=18>, viewed on 21 August 2011.

[937] A. Trevor. Hodge, *Ancient Greek France,* University of Pennsylvania Press, 1999, p. 160 n. 57, Pierre Rouillard, *Études Massaliètes,* 3, 183.

[938] Julius Caesar, *Civil War,* 1.36; H. Cleere, *Southern France: An Oxford Archaeological Guide,* Oxford, 2001, p. 111.

[939] J. Knight, *Roman France: an archaeological field guide*, Tempus, 2001, p. 156.

[940] G. Magi, *Provence,* Bonechi, 2001, p. 81.

[941] A. G. Woodhead, *The Greeks in the West*, Thames and Hudson, 1962, p. 68.

[942] H. Cleere, *Southern France: An Oxford Archaeological Guide*, Oxford, 2001, p. 159.

[943] A. Trevor. Hodge, *Ancient Greek France,* University of Pennsylvania Press, 1999, p. 151; 34.26 grs silver coins 3rd century BC <http://www.snible.org/coins/hn/gallia.html> viewed on 20 August 2011.

[944] J. Bromwich, *The Roman Remains of Southern France: a guidebook*, Routledge, 1993, p. 204.

[945] H. Cleere, *Southern France: An Oxford Archaeological Guide*, Oxford, 2001, p. 159.

[946] G. Magi, *Provence,* Bonechi, 2001, p.128.

[947] A. L. F. Rivet, *Gallia Narbonensis,* Batsford, 1988, p.268, Livy, XXI. 26.6; *Caesar's Civil War,* Bk. 1, Chp. XXXV, trans. W. A. M'Devitte, G. Bell & Sons, 1928, p. 265.

[948] <http://www.cabotages.fr/cabotages-coastwise/Languedoc-Roussillon_english/Hérault-english/meze-english/eggs-shellfish-barrels-and-regattas.html>, viewed 19 December 2010; Issuu, June 12, 2009, Klode, 28, *Thau,* <http://issuu.com/klode/docs/thau>, viewed on 21 August 2011.

[949] Vaucluse Visites Virtuelle, *Meze, Hérault, Languedoc–Roussillon,* <http://www.vaucluse-visites-virtuelles.com/glvirtualbluepopouts/meyronne-english.html>, viewed on 19 December 2010.

[950] A. Trevor. Hodge, *Ancient Greek France,* University of Pennsylvania Press, 1999, p. 150.

[951] M. Dietler and M. Py, 'The Warrior of Lattes: an Iron Age statue discovered in Mediterranean France', *Antiquity* 77 (2003), pp. 789–795.

952 A. Trevor. Hodge, *Ancient Greek France,* University of Pennsylvania Press, 1999, p.151.

953 R. Buxó, 'Botanical and Archaeological Dimensions' in M. Dietler, and C. Lopez-Ruiz, (eds.), *Colonial Encounters in Ancient Iberia: Phoenicians, Greek, and Indigenous Relations,* (University of Chicago Press, 2009): 155-168, here p. 160.

954 M. Thompson, O. Morkholm, and C. M. Kraay, *An Inventory of Greek Coin Hoards*, The American Numismatic Society, New York, 1973, p. 360.

955 A. Trevor. Hodge, *Ancient Greek France,* University of Pennsylvania Press, 1999, p. 144.

956 *Ibid*, p. 143. n. 18

957 Pliny the Elder, *Natural Histories*, vol.2, III, 34, trans. H. Rackham,Heinemann, 1947, p. 29.

958 A. Trevor. Hodge, *Ancient Greek France,* University of Pennsylvania Press, 1999, p. 143 n. 20 (Bouloumie, 1992).

959 *Ibid*, p. 144. n. 23.

960 J. Knight, *Roman France: An Archaeological Field Guide,* Tempus Publishing Ltd., 2001, p. 166.

961 J. Bromwich, *The Roman Remains of Southern France: a guidebook*, Routledge,1996, p. 197.

962 B. Bouloumié and P. Arcelin, 'Saint-Blaise' in *Voyage en Massalie: 100 ans d'archéologie en Gaule du sud,* Catalogue de l'exposition, (Musées de Marseille/Édisud, 1990): 32–41, here p. 35.

963 A. Trevor. Hodge, *Ancient Greek France,* University of Pennsylvania, 1999, p. 144.

964 P. MacKendrick, *Roman France,* G. Bell & Sons, 1971, p. 11.

965 J-P. Morel, 'Phocaean Colonisation' in G. R. Tsetskhladze (ed.), *Greek Colonisation: An Account of Greek Colonies and Other Settlements Overseas*, vol.1, (Leiden, 2006): 358–428, here p. 396.

966 Pliny, *Natural Histories,* vol. 2, trans. H. Rackham, Heinemann, 1942, p. 29; A. Trevor. Hodge, *Ancient Greek France,* University of Pennsylvania, 1999, p. 179 n. 21.; Mela, 2.5.77; Varro, *De lingua latina* 8.18.35. Pliny, *NH,* III.5.

967 A. Trevor. Hodge, *Ancient Greek France,* University of Pennsylvania, 1999, p. 182 n. 26.

968 *Ibid*, p. 179–182. A few Massaliote coins have been found on the beach at Cannes.

969 *Ibid*, p. 180.

970 Strabo, *Geography,* IV.1.10.

971 *Ibid*, vol. 10. V.12–13.

972 A. Trevor. Hodge, *Ancient Greek France,* University of Pennsylvania, 1999, p. 179–182.

973 *IGF* 86, p. 108.

974 Pliny, *Natural Histories*, vol. 2. Bk. III. v.77–vi. 80, trans. H. Rackham, Heinemann, 1962, p. 59, ref 4. 25. 5; 5.36, 2.

975 Greek 5th century B.C. lion face coins found here, A. Furtwängler,'Monnaies grecques en Gaule: Nouvelle trouvailles (6-5ème s. av. J.-C.), ATTI DEL 'XI CONVEGNO DEL CENTRO INTERNAZIONALE DI STUDI NUMISMATICI-NAPOLI 25-27 OTTOBRE 1996, TAV. XI, 1 & XIII, 2 in *La monetazione dei Focei in Occidente*, Instituto Italiano di Numismatica Roma, (2002): 93-111, here p. 101.

976 A. Trevor. Hodge, *Ancient Greek France,* University of Pennsylvania, 1999, p. 171 n. 2 & n. 3.

[977] M. Portillo, 'Great Railway Journeys', BBC 2 [TV broadcast] 8 November 2012.

[978] A. Trevor. Hodge, *Ancient Greek France,* University of Pennsylvania, 1999, p. 171.

[979] Blanchet, A. *Traité des monnaies gauloises,* Paris, 1905, p. 239, ['Gallia'] <www.snible.org/coins/hn/gallia/html>, viewed on 20 August 2011.

[980] L. de La Saussaye, *Numismatique de la Gaule narbonnaise,* BLUIS Beaureaide la Revue nusimatique, 1842, V. Samngenses, pl. XIII, p. 99.

[981] J. Bromwich, *The Roman Remains of Southern France: a guidebook*, Routledge, 1993, p. 72.

[982] C. Ebel, *Transalpine Gaul: the making of a Roman province,* Brill, 1976, p. 32–34.

[983] L. Pearson, *Early Ionian Historians*, Oxford, 1939, p. 38, Stephanus (F. 58).

[984] A. J. Domínguez, 'Spain and France (including Corsica)' in H. H. Hanson and T. H. Neilsen, *An Inventory of Archaic and Classical Poleis*, (Oxford, 2004):157–171, here p. 161. Eust. *Il,* 1.442, source was Stephanus of Byzantium.

[985] *Caii Julii Caesaris Commentarii de belo civili*, I. 34, trans J. C. Held, Sulzbach, 1822, p. 45, <http://books.google.co.uk/books?id=_jogAAAAMAAJ&pg=PA45&lpg=PA45&dq=%E2%80%98barbaros+hominess,+Massilian&source=bl&ots=XrtM-w_FlR&sig=_o7JU0P2JQlWE87mmKhiYpKbAa4&hl=en&sa=X&ei=Np3ET-CSDsKQ8QOux8iFCw&ved=0CDgQ6AEwAQ#v=onepage&q=%E2%80%98barbaros%20hominess%2C%20Massilian&f=false>, viewed 29 May 2012.

[986] *Civil War*, Book I. Chp. 34, trans. W. A. M' Devitte, G. Bell & Sons, 1928, p. 265.

[987] A. L. F. Rivet, *Gallia Narbonensis,* Batsford, 1988, p. 256 n. 2, Strabo, *Geography*, IV.6.3–4.

[988] *Ibid*, p. 256.

[989] *Ibid*, p. 75.

[990] M. Thompson, O. Morkholm, and C. M. Kraay, *An Inventory of Greek Coin Hoards*, The American Numismatic Society, New York, 1973, p. 361.

[991] Strabo, *Geography,* vol. 2. IV.1.5.

[992] H. L. Jones, *Strabo Geography,* vol. 2. IV.1.5. Loeb, 1923, p. 175. n. 3. The editors of this edition were E. Capps. PH,D. LL.D., T. E. Page. LITT.D., W.H.D. Kouse. LITT.D.

[993] S. Radt, *Strabon's Geographika,* Band I, Prolegma, Buch I–IV: Text und Ubersetzung, Vandenhoeck & Ruprecht, 2002, p. 240.

[994] A. Trevor. Hodge, *Ancient Greek France,* University of Pennsylvania, 1999, p. 104 n. 34.

[995] M. Clerc, *Massalia: Histoire de Marseille dans L'Antiquité des Origins a la Fin de l'empire Romain d'occident*, vol. 2, Librarie A. Tacussel, 1929, p. 78, & n. 2.

[996] A. Trevor. Hodge, *Ancient Greek France,* University of Pennsylvania, 1999, p. 103–104 & p. 255 n. 34.

[997] M. Clerc, *Massalia: Histoire de Marseille dans L'Antiquité des Origins a la Fin de l'empire Romain d'occident*, 1927–9, vol. 2, Lafitte, reprint 1971, p. 78 n. 2 & p. 123 n. 1; Cornutus also mentions Massalia no. 301, 453, 497, 516.

[998] M. Clerc, *Massalia: Histoire de Marseille dans L'Antiquité des Origins a la Fin de l'empire Romain d'occident*, vol. 2, Librarie A. Tacussel, 1929, p. 78 n. 2 (*RA*, 1891, XVIII, II, p. 322); Fröhner gives the reference M. H. Usener, *Scholia*

in Lucani bellum civile; commenta Bernensia, 1869, (Leipzig, chez Teubneri) which is now available to download online at <http://archive.org/details/scholiainlucani00usengoog>, viewed 5 June 2012.

[999] Aristotle, *Politics*, trans. E. Barker, Oxford, 1995, p. 192.

[1000] Aristotle, *Politics,* Book VI, ch.7, 1321–26-31, trans. C. D. C. Reeve, Hackett Publishing Co., 1998, p. 186.

[1001] Athenaeus, *Deipnosophists*, vol. 6. XIII, 576, trans. C. B. Gulick, Loeb, William Heinemann, 1937, p. 109–111.

[1002] A. Trevor. Hodge, *Ancient Greek France,* University of Pennsylvania, 1999, p.111.

[1003] Cicero, *The Speeches: In Catilinam I–IV. Pro Murena. Pro Sulla. Pro Flacco*, trans. C. MacDonald, Heinemann, 1977, p. 511. *Pro Flacco* 63–64.

[1004] C. W. Keyes, *Cicero De Re Publica,* 1.27, Heinemann, 1927, p. 69.

[1005] *Ibid.*

[1006] James. E. G. Zetzel, (ed.), *Cicero, On the Commonwealth and On the Laws,* I.43–44, Cambridge, 1999, p. 19–20.

[1007] Valerius Maximus, *Memorable Deeds and Sayings: A Thousand and One Tales From Ancient Rome*, Book II.6.7, trans. H. J. Walker, Hackett Publishing Company Inc., 2004, p. 58.

[1008] Lucian, *Toxaris or Friendship*, vol. 5, trans. A. M. Harmon, William Heinemann, 1936, p. 143–199.

[1009] Lacus Curtius, *The Geography of Strabo*, vol. 3. Book VII. Fragments, 2. ['Penelope, University of Chicago', digital library] <http://penelope.uchicago.edu/Thayer/E/Roman/Texts/Strabo/7Fragments*.html>, viewed on 26 October 2011.

[1010] *The Geography of Strabo*, vol. 3. Book VII. Fragments, 2. ['Penelope, University of Chicago', digital library] <http://penelope.uchicago.edu/Thayer/E/Roman/Texts/Strabo/7Fragments*.html>, viewed on 26 October 2011. Thayers note 476: 'The senators at Sparta were called "gerontes" literally "old men", "senators"'.

[1011] R. Carpenter, *Beyond the Pillars of Hercules*: *The classical world seen through the eyes of is discoverers*, Tandem (UK), 1973, p. 101; D. W. Roller, *Through the Pillars of Herakles:Greco-Roman Exploration of the Atlantic*, Routledge, 2006, p. 15-19.

[1012] B. Cunliffe, *The Extraordinary Voyage of Pytheas the Greek: The man who discovered Britain,* Penguin Books, 2002, p. 1.

[1013] C. H. Roseman, *Pytheas of Massalia: Text, Translation and Commentary,* Ares Publishing, 1994, p. 103. Aitios, was copied into Stobaeus (*Eclogae*, 1.38.3); Pseudo-Plutarch (*Epitome*, 3.17.2).

[1014] *Ibid*, p. 81 and p. 103.

[1015] *Ibid,* p. 13.

[1016] J. Burnet, *Early Greek Philosophers*, Kessinger, 2003, p. 39 n 23 & 24 *Dox*, pp. 226-229, 'The Latin epitome will be found in Val. Rose's edition of the Aristotlean Fragments'. Hekataios, fr. 278 (Müller, *F.H.G.* vol. i. p.19).

[1017] V. Stefansson, *Great Adventurers and Explorations: from the earliest times to the present, as told by the explorers themselves,* Robert Hale Ltd., 1947, p. 12; C.R. Markham, 'Pytheas, the Discoverer of Britain', p. 512, *The Geographical Journal*, Blackwell Publishers on behalf of The Royal Geographical Society (with The Institute of British Geographers) Vol.1, No. 6 (June, 1893): 504–524, here p. 512, ['JSTOR' journal archive] <http://www.jstor.org/stable/1773964>, viewed on 21 August 2011.

[1018] M. Cary and E. H. Warmington, *The Ancient Explorers*, Methuen, 1929, p. 33 n. 28.

[1019] C. H. Roseman, *Pytheas of Massalia: Text, Translation and Commentary,* Ares Publishing, 1994, p. 2 & p. 7.

[1020] *Ibid*, p. 104–109, Kleomedes, *Meteora*, 1.4, 208-210 (Todd, p. 25).

[1021] J. Warren, 'Diogenes Laertius, biographer of philosophy' in Konig, J., and Whitmarsh, T. *Ordering Knowledge in the Roman Empire,* Cambridge University Press, 2007, p. 143 n. 40, (Diogenes Laertius 1.12).

[1022] Strabo, *Geography,* IV. 1. 5. 27.

[1023] *Ibid*, IV. 1. 10.

[1024] *Justin: Epitome of the Philippic History of Pompeius Trogus*, 43.5.1, trans. J. C. Yardley, Scholars Press Atlanta, 1994, p. 268.

[1025] Thucydides, Book I.13. 6.

[1026] Thucydides writes that the Phocaeans founded Massalia after a naval victory over the Carthaginians though he may have been referring to the reinforcement of Massalia from those of the Phocaeans who left Ionia from the Persian invasion in 546 B.C. rather than submit to their rule. T. J. Dunbabin, *The Western Greeks*: *The History of Sicily and South Italy from the Foundation of the Greek Colonies to 480 B.C*, Oxford University Press Monograph Reprints, 1998 p. 343 n. 3.

[1027] Herodotus, *Histories,* Book I. 166, trans. G. Rawlinson, Wordsworth Editions Ltd., 1996, p. 75.

[1028] M. Grant, *The Rise of the Greeks,* Phoenix Press, 1987, Ch.6. p. 249; Herodotus, *Histories,* Book I. 166, trans. G. Rawlinson, Wordsworth Editions Ltd., 1996, p. 75.

[1029] J. H. Thiel, *A History of Roman Sea-Power Before the Second Punic War,* North Holland Publishing Co., Amsterdam, 1954, p. 86 n.73 and 77.

[1030] F. W. Wallbank, *A Historical Commentary on Polybius,* vol. 1. Bk. III. 20.5. Oxford, 1957, p. 333; R. Gardiner, (ed.), *The Age of the Galley,* Conway Maritime Press, 1995, p. 60–61 n. 30, *F Gr Hist* 176 F 1. Also known as Sosylus the Lacedaemon.

[1031] M. Clerc, *Massalia: Histoire de Marseille dans L'Antiquité des Origins a la Fin de l'empire Romain d'occident*, vol. 2. Librarie A. Tacussel, 1929, p. 155.

[1032] *Ibid*; Caesar, *The Civil War*, Book II. 3, trans. J. Carter, Oxford, 1998, p. 51.

[1033] A. M. Liberati and F. Bourbon, *Splendours of the Roman World,* Thames & Hudson, 1996, p. 218.

[1034] Strabo, *Geography,* Book IV.1.8.

[1035] Hall mentions the Ingauni as a *socii* contingent of Italian Ligurians in Marius's Roman Army whose soldiers 'were the first to turn the tide of victory in favour of Rome'. W. H. (Bullock) Hall. *The Romans on the Riviera and the Rhone: a sketch on the conquest of Liguria and the Roman Province*, Chp. VII, 105/248, Macmillan, London, 1898, p. 76, reprinted by Ares Publishers, Chicago, 1974, ['Open Library']
<http://openlibrary.org/books/OL5069373M/The_Romans_on_the_Riviera_and_the_Rhone>, viewed on 19 December 2011.

[1036] G. Magi, *Provence,* Bonechi, 2001, p. 175; W. H. (Bullock) Hall. *The Romans on the Riviera and the Rhone: a sketch on the conquest of Liguria and the Roman Province*, Ch.XII. Macmillan, 1898, p. 112 and p. 115-116, reprinted by Ares Publishers, Chicago, 1974, ['Open Library']
<http://openlibrary.org/books/OL5069373M/The_Romans_on_the_Riviera_and_the_Rhone>, viewed on 19 December 2011.

[1037] Caesar, *The Civil War*, Bk. II. 1–16, Bk. II. 22, trans. J. Carter, Oxford, 1998. p. 50–58, p. 62.

[1038] B. Cunliffe, *The Extraordinary Voyage of Pytheas the Greek: The man who discovered Britain,* Penguin Books, 2002, p. 1.

[1039] A. Trevor. Hodge, *Ancient Greek France,* University of Pennsylvania, 1999, p. 104 n. 34. Reference comes from Clerc (see Hodge's bibliography), (Clerc) 2.78 n. 2 & 2. 123 n. 1, M. Clerc, *Massalia,* (2 vols.), Marseille, 1927–9, reprint Lafitte, Marseille, 1971.

[1040] M. Clerc, *Massalia: Histoire de Marseille dans L'Antiquité des Origins a la Fin de l'empire Romain d'occident,* vol. 2, Librarie A. Tacussel, 1929, p. 324 & Fig. 23.

[1041] Demosthenes, IV, *Private Orations,* XXVII–XL, trans. A. T. Murray, 1965, p. 183–191.

[1042] Lucian, *Toxaris or Friendship,* vol. 5, trans. A. M. Harmon, William Heinemann, 1936, p. 143–199.

[1043] Strabo, *Geography,* Bk. III. 4. 17.

[1044] J. B. Curbera, 'The Greek Curse Tablets of Emporion', *Zeitschrift für Papyrologie und Epigraphik,* Bd. 117 (1997): 90–94, here p. 92, ['JSTOR' journal archive] <http://www.jstor.org/stable/20190008>, viewed on 16 January 2011.

[1045] R. Gardiner, Cicero, XIII, *Pro Balbo,* xxi. 49–xxii, 50; *Cicero Letters to Atticus III,* XIV. 14, Loeb, 1961, p. 695.

[1046] The Elder Seneca, *Controversiae,* vol.1. 2.6.12, trans. M. Winterbottom, William Heinemann Ltd., 1974, p. 361.

[1047] Pliny, *Natural Histories,* trans H. J. Jones, Heinemann, 1963, Book XXIX. V. 6–9, p.187; Also a Charmis of Massalia as a source for Aelian writing on Homeric texts. G. Nagy, *Poetry as Performance: Poetry and Beyond,* Cambridge, 1996, p. 32-34, Aelian, *De natura animalium,* 5.38

[1048] A. Trevor. Hodge, *Ancient Greek France,* University of Pennsylvania Press, 1999, p. 177.

[1049] Lucan, *The Civil War,* III, 870–1100, trans. N. Rowe, Everyman, 1998, p. 82–88.

[1050] Seutonius, *The Lives of the Caesars,* The Deified Julius, vol. 1. LXVIII.4, trans. J. C. Rolfe, Heinemann, 1979, p. 91.

[1051] H. Hermary, A. Hesnard, and H. Tréziny, *Marseille Grecque: La cite phocéenne (600–49 av. J-C),* Editions Errance, 1999, p. 93.

[1052] M. Clerc, *Massalia: Histoire de Marseille dans L'Antiquité des Origins a la Fin de l'empire Romain d'occident,* vol. 2. Librarie A. Tacussel, 1929, p. 348.

[1053] Exhibits I saw at the Musée d'Histoire de Marseille July 2009 found in the Sainte-Barbe necropolis. Also in B. Bizot, et al. *Marseille Antique: guides archéologiques de la France,* Editions du Patrimonie, Centre des monuments nationaux, 2007, p. 84.

[1054] A. Hermary, A. Hesnard, and H. Tréziny, *Marseille Grecque: La cite phocéenne (600–49 av.J-C,* Editions Errance, 1999, p. 93.

[1055] M. Clerc, *Massalia: Histoire de Marseille dans L'Antiquité des Origins a la Fin de l'empire Romain d'occident,* vol. 2, Librarie A. Tacussel, 1929, p. 377 n. 3; *IGS,* 2437.

[1056] G. H. R. Horsley, *New Documents Illustrating Early Christianity: A Review of the Greek Inscriptions and Papyrii published in 1979,* vol. 4. Macquarie University, 1987, p. 163.

[1057] J. Liversidge, *Everyday Life in the Roman Empire,* Batsford, 1976, p. 142; D. R. Shackleton Bailey, *Martial's Epigrams,* vol 2. Bk. X, 36, Harvard, 1993, p. 359.

[1058] A. Hermary, A. Hesnard, and H. Tréziny, *Marseille Grecque: La cite phocéenne (600–49 av. J-C),* Editions Errance, 1999, p. 92.

[1059] Exhibit of a funeral bust I saw at the Musée d'Histoire de Marseille July 2009 that was found in the Rue de Minimes; See also Latin inscription M. Clerc, *Massalia: Histoire de Marseille dans L'Antiquité des Origins a la Fin de l'empire Romain d'occident,* vol. 2. Librarie A. Tacussel, 1929, vol. 2. 1929, p.345-346, *CIL,* vol. XII, 468.

¹⁰⁶⁰ M. Clerc, *Massalia: Histoire de Marseille dans L'Antiquité des Origins a la Fin de l'empire Romain d'occident*, vol. 2. Librarie A. Tacussel, 1929, p. 322, *IG*, 2434. vol. XIV.

¹⁰⁶¹ M. Clerc, *Massalia: Histoire de Marseille dans L'Antiquité des Origins a la Fin de l'empire Romain d'occident*, vol. 2. Librarie A. Tacussel, 1929, p. 339, Fig. 24, *IGS*, XIV, 2452; *IGF* 16, p. 27.

¹⁰⁶² A. Hermary, A. Hesnard, and H. Tréziny, *Marseille Grecque: La cite phocéenne (600–49 av. J-C)*, Editions Errance, 1999, p. 93.

¹⁰⁶³ M. Clerc, *Massalia. Histoire de Marseille dans l'antiquité des origins à la fin de l'Empire romain d'Occident (476 ap. J.-C.)*, TOME 1, Des origins jusqu 'au IIIme siècle av. J.-C. Marseille, Librairie A. Tacussel, 1927, p. 184 n. 3, p. 185, Fig. 28. p. 184 n. 1 *Review des Universites du midi*, RUM, III, 1897, p. 129; J-P. Morel, 'Phocaean Colonisation' in G. R. Tsetskhladze (ed.), *Greek Colonisation: An Account of Greek Colonies and Other Settlements Overseas*, vol.1, (Leiden, 2006): 358–428, here p. 381.

¹⁰⁶⁴ A. Hermary, A. Hesnard, and H. Tréziny, *Marseille Grecque: La cite phocéenne (600–49 av. J-C)*, Editions Errance, 1999, p. 92.

¹⁰⁶⁵ M. Clerc, *Massalia. Histoire de Marseille dans l'antiquité des origins à la fin de l'Empire romain d'Occident (476 ap. J.-C.)*, TOME 1, Des origins jusqu 'au IIIme siècle av. J.-C. Marseille, Librairie A. Tacussel, 1927, p. 292, Fig. 71, *BCH (Bulletin de corresponance hellénique)*, VII, 1883, p. 191 and *BCH*, 1921, XLV, p. 23.

¹⁰⁶⁶ *Ibid*, p. 293. Fig. 72 for Clerc's photograph of the full four line inscription with the Theorodokoi of Massalia. Note the right horizontal of the letter Π was shorter at the bottom i.e. ⊓ . The end of the third word first line (either Σ or Ξ) was unclear so I have put a full stop to indicate a letter should be there following Parsinou and Shipley's guide. See <http://www.heacademy.ac.uk/assets/hca/classics/featureResources/practicalAdvice/languageTeaching/Beginners/hellenizein_GS_final_with_ISBN_added_09122.pdf.> viewed on 25 March 2012.

¹⁰⁶⁷ M. Clerc, *Massalia. Histoire de Marseille dans l'antiquité des origins à la fin de l'Empire romain d'Occident (476 ap. J.-C.)*, TOME 1, Des origins jusqu 'au IIIme siècle av. J.-C. Marseille, Librairie A. Tacussel, 1927, p. 291 n. 3, Dittenberger, *Sylloge Inscriptioneum Graecorum*, 3, N°. 585; Wescher et Foucart, Ins. Inéd. De Delphes, N°. 18, lig. 8-11.

¹⁰⁶⁸ M. Clerc, *Massalia: Histoire de Marseille dans L'Antiquité des Origins a la Fin de l'empire Romain d'occident*, vol. 2. Librarie A. Tacussel, 1929, p. 304, CIA, III, 2, 2568, *Corpus Inscriptionum Atticarum*, Berlin, (reissued as *Inscriptiones Graecae* 1-3), *IG*, III, 2568, *Inscriptiones Graecae*, Attic Inscriptions of the Roman Period, Inscriptiones Atticae Aetatis Romanae, vol. III, 1, 2 and 3, Pars Decima, TITVLI SEPVLCRALES, G. Dittenberger, (ed.), Berolini, 1878, p. 157.

¹⁰⁶⁹ *Ibid*, *IG*, III, 2567, *Inscriptiones Graecae*, Attic Inscriptions of the Roman Period, Inscriptiones Atticae Aetatis Romanae, Pars Decima, TITVLI SEPVLCRALES, G. Dittenberger, (ed.), Berolini, 1878, p. 157.

¹⁰⁷⁰ *Ibid*, *IG*, III, 2569, p. 157.

¹⁰⁷¹ *Ibid*, *IG*, III, 2570, p. 157.

¹⁰⁷² A. Hermary, A. Hesnard, and H. Tréziny, *Marseille Grecque: La cite phocéenne (600–49 av. J-C)*, Editions Errance, 1999, p. 92; M. Clerc, *Massalia: Histoire de Marseille dans L'Antiquité des Origins a la Fin de l'empire Romain d'occident*, vol. 2, Librarie A. Tacussel, 1929, vol. 2 p. 304 n. 2. Fig. 19. There may be more letters to complete the name of Massalia but I have put what could be seen in the photograph. Clerc writes that this inscription was in the Museum of Athens.

¹⁰⁷³ M. Clerc, *Massalia. Histoire de Marseille dans l'antiquité des origins à la fin de l'Empire romain d'Occident (476 ap. J.-C.)*, TOME 1, Des origins jusqu 'au IIIme siècle av. J.-C. Marseille, Librairie A. Tacussel, 1927, p. 30, IG, XI 687.

¹⁰⁷⁴ A. Hermary, A. Hesnard, and H. Tréziny, *Marseille Grecque: La cite phocéenne (600–49 av. J-C)*, Editions Errance, 1999, p. 92.

[1075] M. Clerc, *Massalia: Histoire de Marseille dans L'Antiquité des Origins a la Fin de l'empire Romain d'occident*, vol. 2. Librarie A. Tacussel, 1929, p. 305 n.1, *IG*, XII, 444.

[1076] A. Hermary, A. Hesnard, and H. Tréziny, *Marseille Grecque: La cite phocéenne (600–49 av. J-C)*, Editions Errance, 1999, p. 92.

[1077] I have written what is in the inscription for IG, 610, vol. XIV. Clerc translates this as 'Euxéne fille d'Anaxilaos de Marseille'. M. Clerc, *Massalia. Histoire de Marseille dans l'antiquité des origins à la fin de l'Empire romain d'Occident* (476 ap. J.-C.), TOME 1, Des origins jusqu 'au IIIme siècle av. J.-C., Marseille, Librairie A. Tacussel, 1927, p. 320, *IG*, 610, vol. XIV; Hermary et. al. gives 'Aristodikos fils d'Anaxilas et Euxénos le Massaliète, également fils d'un Anaxilas et donc probablement frère du précédent'. A. Hermary, A. Hesnard, and H. Tréziny, *Marseille Grecque: La cite phocéenne (600–49 av. J-C)*, Editions Errance, 1999, p. 92.

[1078] A. Hermary, A. Hesnard, and H. Tréziny, *Marseille Grecque: La cite phocéenne (600–49 av. J-C)*, Editions Errance, 1999, p. 92.

[1079] M. Clerc, *Massalia. Histoire de Marseille dans l'antiquité des origins à la fin de l'Empire romain d'Occident* (476 ap. J.-C.), TOME 1, Des origins jusqu 'au IIIme siècle av. J.-C., Marseille, Librairie A. Tacussel, 1927, p. 318-319, Figure 84.

[1080] *Ibid*, p. 319 n. 2, *IG*, 295, vol. XIV.

[1081] E. Parsinou, G. Shipley, and A. Salt, *Hellenizein: A Flexible Structure for Teaching Greek to Archaeologists and Ancient Historians*, The Subject Centre for History, Classics and Archaeology, The Higher Education Academy, 2004 (with corrections 2008), University of Leicester, ISBN 0 74929 6550, <http://www.heacademy.ac.uk/assets/hca/classics/featureResources/practicalAdvice/languageTeaching/Beginners/hellenizein_GS_final_with_ISBN_added_09122.pdf> viewed on 23 March 2012.

[1082] M. Clerc, *Massalia: Histoire de Marseille dans L'Antiquité des Origins a la Fin de l'empire Romain d'occident*, vol. 2. Librarie A. Tacussel, 1929, p. 303.

[1083] M. Clerc, *Massalia: Histoire de Marseille dans L'Antiquité des Origins a la Fin de l'empire Romain d'occident*, vol. 2. Librarie A. Tacussel, 1929, p. 305, *IG*, XIV, 1884, p. 466. The letter Σ is replaced by C twice in the second line.

[1084] M. Clerc, *Massalia: Histoire de Marseille dans L'Antiquité des Origins a la Fin de l'empire Romain d'occident*, vol. 2. Librarie A. Tacussel, 1929, p 305 n. 3, *IG* 2178, XIV, p. 525.

[1085] *Ibid*, p. 305, *CIL*, VI, 3, 24057.

[1086] Strabo, *Geography*, IV.1.5.

[1087] Athenaeus, *Deipnosophistae*, vol. 2. Bk.III.118, trans. C. B. Gulick, Loeb, William Heinemann, 1928, p. 53.

[1088] Strabo, *Geography*, IV.1.7.

[1089] Oppian, *Halieutica*, 3. 625, trans. A. W. Mair, Heinemann, 1928, p. 399.

[1090] Aelian, *Characteristics of Animals*, vol. 3. 13.16, trans. A. F. Schofield, Loeb, 1959.

[1091] Oppian, *Halieutica*, 3. 620. n.d. trans. A. W. Mair, Heinemann, 1928, p. 397. Present day Blue Fin tuna have been over fished and are at dangerously low levels. There needs to be a ban of fishing until stocks have recovered. M. Hickman, 'Europe unites in attempt to protect Blue Fin Tuna', Wednesday 9 September 2009, Independent, <http://www.independent.co.uk/news/world/europe/europe-unites-in-attempt-to-protect-bluefin-tuna-1783864.html>, viewed on 21 August 2011.

[1092] A. Trevor. Hodge, *Ancient Greek France*, University of Pennsylvania, 1999, p. 56 n. 37.

[1093] Oppian, *Halieutica*, trans. A. W. Mair, III.544. Heinemann, 1928, p. 391 n. C.

[1094] M. Clerc, *Massalia: Histoire de Marseille dans L'Antiquité des Origins a la Fin de l'empire Romain d'occident*, vol. 2. Librarie A. Tacussel, 1929, p. 262, (*CIG*, II, XIV, Inscriptiones Lydiae, 3413 and 3415) and p. 265. The city of Rome was also personified into a deity Roma and worshipped in the Greek east with temples and cults. See commemorative coin A.D. 330–333 Thessaloniki mint.
<http://www.vcoins.com/romaeaeternaenumismatics/store/viewItem.asp?idProduct=170>, viewed on 23 November 2011.

[1095] Oppian, *Halieutica*, III. 544–575, trans. A. W. Mair, Heinemann, 1928, p. 393.

[1096] *Ibid*, III.544, p. 391.

[1097] *Ibid*, III. 544–575, p. 393.

[1098] B. Cunliffe, *The Extraordinary Voyage of Pytheas the Greek: The man who discovered Britain*, Penguin Books, 2002, p. 7.

[1099] Oppian, *Halieutica*, V. 411–600, trans. A. W. Mair, Heinemann, 1928, p. 493–507.

[1100] *Ibid*, V. 520–525, p. 503.

[1101] G. Nagy, *Poetry as Performance: Homer and Beyond*, Cambridge University Press, 1996, p. 116 n. 46, Scholia A to *Iliad* 3.10 (Venetus); M. Clerc, *Massalia. Histoire de Marseille dans l'antiquité des origins à la fin de l'Empire romain d'Occident (476 ap. J.-C.)*, TOME 1, Des origins jusqu'au IIIme siècle av. J.-C. Marseille, Librairie A. Tacussel, 1927, p. 459.

For information on getting all the Homeric texts together: C. Blackwell and T. R Martin, 'Technology, Collaboration and Undergraduate Research', paragraphs 40-48, *Digital Humanities Quarterly*, ['DHQ']
<http://www.digitalhumanities.org/dhq/vol/003/1/000024/000024.html> viewed 29 March 2012; *The Homer Multitext*, Homer Multitext: Scholia Inventory, C. Dué and M. Ebbott, (eds.), ['The Centre for Hellenic Studies']
<http://pinakes.hpcc.uh.edu/scholinv/> viewed 29 March 2012.

[1102] G. Nagy, *Poetry as Performance: Poetry and Beyond*, Cambridge, 1996, p. 32-34, Aelian, *De natura animalium*, 5.38

[1103] Unfortunately we have the small and vicious Midge in Britain as well as mosquitoes in the countryside.

[1104] Pausanias, *Description of Greece*, Book VII. Achaia. 5.
<http://www.archive.org/stream/pausaniasdescrip02pausuoft/pausaniasdescrip02pausuoft_djvu.txt>, viewed on 22 October 2011.

[1105] M. Johnson, E. Abrahams and Lady. M. M. Evans, *Ancient Greek Dress*, Argonaut, 1964, p. 50, Fig. xxxvii & p. 29.

[1106] Cicero, *Pro Flacco*, 63–64.

[1107] Strabo, *Geography*, IV.1.4-5.

[1108] Titus Livius, *The History of Rome*, vol. 5. LIV, Final Defeat of Antiochus, trans. Rev. Canon Roberts, Dent, 1924–31, p. 241–243.

[1109] A. Momigliano, *Alien Wisdom: The Limits of Hellenization*, 1990, Cambridge University Press, 1975, p. 56, (from Silius Italicus, *Punica*, 15.169–72).

[1110] M. Miller, *Athens and Persia in the 5th Century*, Cambridge, 2004, p. 174.

[1111] J. Herrin, *Byzantium: The Surprising Life of a Medieval Empire*, Penguin, 2008, p. 211.

[1112] E. S. Platt, *Garlick, Onions and other Alliums*, Stackpole, 2003, p. 29–41.

[1113] Lee Ann Obringer, *How Aphrodisiacs Work*, <http://science.howstuffworks.com/aphrodisiac3.htm>, viewed on 21 August 2011; K. Lasinski, *The History of Garlick: Nature's Ancient Superfood,* June 28, 2005, <http://www.googobits.com/articles/1167-the-history-of-garlic-natures-ancient-superfood.html>, viewed on 21 August 2011; Even in modern times some Greek women on hearing something shocking or outrageous pull their blouse outwards and spit on their chest rapidly 3 times for protection saying at the same time 'Ptu, Ptu, Ptu, Skordo' (translated as Ptu Ptu Ptu, Garlick!).

[1114] Lee Ann Obringer, *How Aphrodisiacs Work*, <http://science.howstuffworks.com/aphrodisiac3.htm>, viewed on 21 August 2011.

[1115] J. T. Ehler, *Pastis: the French national, versatile and much-loved drink,* <http://www.foodreference.com/html/artpastis.html>, viewed on 29 October 2010.

[1116] E. Shuey, 'Underwater Survey and Excavations at Gravisca, The Port of Tarquinia' *Papers from the British School of Rome*, (vol. 49. 1981):17-45, here p. 17. n. 4, ['JSTOR' journal archive] <http://www.jstor.org/pss/40310871>, viewed on 17 January 2012. The site was discovered and excavated by Professor Mario Torelli, University of Perugia. See also M. Torelli, 'Il Santuario Greco di Gravisca', *La Prarola del Passato* 177 (1977): 398-458. For an article in English see M. Torelli, 'Greek Artisans and Etruria: A problem concerning the relationship between two cultures', *Archaeological News* 5, Dept. of Classics, Florida State University, (1976): 134–8.

[1117] Definitions, <http://www.definitions.net/definition/nation%20of%20shopkeepers> viewed 30 January 2014.

[1118] C. Ebel, *Transalpine Gaul: the making of a Roman province,* Brill, 1976, p. 33. Ebel (1976) says there are more Massaliote cities listed by Stephanus of Byzantium but of which nothing else is known as yet.

[1119] Strabo, *Geography*, IV. 1. 5.

[1120] Cicero, *Pro Flacco,* 63-64.

[1121] R. Osborne, 'Early Greek Colonization? The nature of Greek settlement in the West' in N. Fisher and H. van Wees (eds.), *Archaic Greece; new approaches and new evidence,* (London, 1998): 251–269, here p. 251.

[1122] The main political view of the Greek states was expressed by Demosthenes 'it is a noble thing for Greeks to contend one with another for supremacy'. *The Oration of Demosthenes Upon the Crown*, trans. Henry Lord Brougham, Sir John Lubbock's Hundred Books, Routledge & Sons Ltd., 1930, p. 161. This view had plagued Greece with constant wars with city-states fighting each other. Isocrates saw a way to put an end to these wars. The Greek states, which all had so much in common, should be drawn together under one leader for a special purpose. He had suggested the tyrant Jason of Pherae, Thessaly but he was assassinated. Isocrates wrote an open letter to King Philip II of Macedon as a Greek who had the brains, the power and the gold to draw the states together, while still maintaining their independence, to solve the excess of population by annexing part if not all of the Persian Empire. J. B. Bury and R. Meiggs, *A History of Greece,* Macmillan, 1979, p. 431–432.

[1123] P. Attema, 'Conflict or Coexistence? Remarks on Indigenous Settlement and Colonization in the Foothills and Hinterland of the Sibaritde (Northern Calabria, Italy)' in P. G. Bilde and J. H. Petersen (eds.), *Meeting of Cultures in the Black Sea Region,* (University of Aarhus, 2008) :67-99, here p. 68-69 <http://www.pontos.dk/publications/books/bss-8-files/bss-8-04-attema>, viewed 12 February 2012.

[1124] Strabo, *Geography,* IV.1.5.

[1125] *Justin: Epitome of the Philippic History of Pompeius Trogus,* 43.3.13, trans. J. C. Yardley, Scholars Press Atlanta, 1994, p. 267; *The Roman History of Ammianus Marcellinus*, XV.9. vol. 1. Loeb, 1935, p. 177, ['Penelope. University of Chicago', digital library] <http://penelope.uchicago.edu/Thayer/E/Roman/Texts/Ammian/15*.html>, viewed 20 February 2012. (XV.9, p. 177 n. 62

[1126] J. Boardman, *The Greeks Overseas,* Thames & Hudson, 1999, Ch. 5, p 190.

[1127] *Ibid*, p 162; Franco De Angelis, 'The Foundation of Selinous: overpopulation or opportunities?' in R. Gocha, G. R. Tsetskhladze, and F. De Angelis, (eds.), *The Archaeology of Greek Colonization,* (Oxford University School of Archaeology, 1994): 87-110, here p. 104.

[1128] P. Attema, 'Conflict or Coexistence? Remarks on Indigenous Settlement and Colonization in the Foothills and Hinterland of the Sibaritde (Northern Calabria, Italy)' in P. G. Bilde and J. H. Petersen (eds.), *Meeting of Cultures in the Black Sea Region,* (University of Aarhus, 2008) :67-99, here p. 69 <http://www.pontos.dk/publications/books/bss-8-files/bss-8-04-attema>, viewed 12 February 2012.

[1129] One exception to this was Corfu, a colony of Corinth, who asserted her independence by a successful sea-battle against the mother-city in the mid-seventh century B.C. J. B. Bury and R. Meiggs, *A History of Greece,* Macmillan, 1979, p. 106.

[1130] Herodotus, *Histories,* trans. G. Rawlinson, Wordsworth Editions Ltd., 1996, p. 111 n. 157 (Tarsus, Tartessos, Tarshish are variants of the same word); Carpenter suggests that the name Tarshish was also a type of ship developed in the Greek trading town of Tarsus in Cilicia that carried metallic ore or bulk metal which the Phoenicians used. Therefore King Solomon was referring to this type of ship and not the city in Spain. R. Carpenter, *Beyond the Pillars of Hercules: The classical world seen through the eyes of is discoverers,* Tandem, 1975, p. 60, (Book of Kings, X.22).

[1131] Herodotus, *Histories,* Bk.I.163, trans. G. Rawlinson, Wordsworth Editions Ltd., 1996, p. 74; see Gardiner regarding theories of size and development. R. Gardiner, (ed.), *The Age of the Galley,* Conway Maritime Press, 1995, p. 44–48.

[1132] *Ibid.*

[1133] *Resultats du recensement de la population 2006,* ['INSEE'], <http://www.recensement-2006.insee.fr/chiffresCles.action?codeMessage=5&zoneSearchField=MARSEILLE&codeZone=003-AU1999&idTheme=3&rechercher=Rechercher>, viewed 20 June 2012.

[1134] *The Geography of Strabo,* 14. 2. 10, trans. (ed.), H. L. Jones, Heinemann, 1924, ['Perseus, Tufts University' digital library]<http://www.perseus.tufts.edu/hopper/text?doc=Perseus%3Atext%3A1999.01.0198%3Abook%3D14%3Achapter%3D2%3Asection%3D10>, viewed 31 January 2012.

[1135] Generalitat de Catalunya, *Phoenicians and Greeks in Catalonia: 7th Century B.C.–6th Century B.C.* <http://www20.gencat.cat/portal/site/culturacatalana/menuitem.be2B.C.4cc4c5aec88f94a9710b0c0e1a0/?vgnextoid=d07cef2126896210VgnVCM1000000b0c1e0aRCRD&vgnextchannel=d07cef2126896210VgnVCM1000000b0c1e0aRCRD&vgnextfmt=detall2&contentid=810c110e279d7210VgnVCM1000008d0c1e0aRCRD&newLang=en_GB>, viewed on 22 July 2011.

[1136] B. Cunliffe, *The Extraordinary Voyage of Pytheas the Greek: The man who discovered Britain,* Penguin Books, 2002, p. 23.

[1137] A. J. Domínguez, 'Spain and France (including Corsica)' in H. H. Hanson and T. H. Nielsen, *An Inventory of Archaic and Classical Poleis,* (Oxford, 2004):157–171, here p. 166.

[1138] Pausanias, *Description of Greece,* X.8.6, trans. W. H. S. Jones, and H. A. Ormerod, 4 vols. Heinemann, 1918. ['Perseus, Tufts University', digital library] <http://www.perseus.tufts.edu/hopper/text?doc=Perseus%3Atext%3A1999.01.0160%3Abook%3D10%3Achapter%3D8%3Asection%3D6>, viewed 15 January 2012

[1139] J. McInerney, *The Folds of Parnassos: Land and Ethnicity in Ancient Phokis,* University of Texas Press, 1999, p. 158.

[1140] *Ibid*, p. 157-162; Pausanias, *Description of Greece,* VII.3.10. ['Perseus, Tufts University', digital library] <http://www.perseus.tufts.edu/hopper/text?doc=Perseus%3Atext%3A1999.01.0160%3Abook%3D7%3Achapter%3D3%3Asection%3D10> viewed on 9 January 2012. All three foundation stories mention Phocis and two definitely link the Phocaeans with Phocis as their origin. One version says they received the land in Ionia as a reward for fighting for Ouatias against his brother Menes who was the local tyrant at Cymae (*Kyme*). In the other they received the land peacefully by agreement with the Cymaeans.

[1141] I. Carridice, *Greek Coins,* British Museum Press, 1995, p. 22.

[1142] W. M. Johnson, and D. L. Lavigne, 'Monk Seals in Antiquity, The Mediterranean Monk Seal (Monachus monachus)' in *Ancient History and Literature,* Mededelingen No. 35, The Netherlands Commission for International Nature Protection, (Leiden 1999): 1-101, PDF edition 2008, here p. 14. <http://www.monachus-guardian.org/library/mededelingen35_2008a.pdf>, viewed on 18 September 2011.

[1143] C. Seltman, *Greek Coins,* Methuen & Co, 1960, p. 30. Griffins were also portrayed on 1/6 and 1/24th value staters <http://www.nomosag.com/default.aspx?page=ucDetails&auctionid=3&id=129> viewed 6 November 2013. Other puns of city names on coins were Melos (Melon) apple, Rhodes (Rhodon) rose, and Zancle (Zanklon) sickle.

[1144] Barclay Vincent Head and Reginald Stuart Poole, *Catalogue of Greek Coins of Ionia*, British Museum Department of Coins, 1892, p. xxi. ['Archive'] <http://www.archive.org/stream/cataloguegreekc05medagoog#page/n25/mode/2up>, viewed 15 January 2012.

[1145] *Ibid,* p. xx-xxi; Eusebius, *Chronicles,* 225. <http://www.attalus.org/translate/eusebius2.html#225> viewed 5 January 2013. The *Chronicle* was written c. 325.

[1146] *Ibid, Catalogue of Greek Coins of Ionia,* p. xx-xxii.

[1147] *Ibid*, p. xxx.

[1148] *Ibid*, p. xxii, *Thucydides*, IV. 52; *Demosthenes*, XI, 36. 'Staters and Hecatae of Phocaea are mentioned in several Attic inscriptions from 429 B.C. to 397'. T. J. Figueira, *The Power of Money: Coinage and Politics in the Athenian Empire*, University of Pennsylvania Press, 1998, p. 274.

[1149] A. Villing and A. Mollër, *Naukratis: Greek Diversity in Egypt*, The British Museum, 2006, p. 2; Herodotus, *Histories,* 2.178–9.

[1150] J. Boardman, *The Greeks Overseas: Their Early Colonies and Trade,* Thames & Hudson, 1999, p. 121.

[1151] C. Orieux and P. Schmitt-Pantel, *A History of Ancient Greece,* Blackwell, 1999, p. 43; Phocaeans led by Phoxus invited by King Mandron of the Bebrycians (Pituoessans) to settle in his kingdom. Winning many victories together a plot was made by the Berbycians to get rid of the Phocaeans while King Mandron was away. The plot was revealed to the Phocaeans by his daughter Lampsace and the Phocaeans laid a trap and took control of the city. Lampsace died of an illness and the Phocaeans named the city in her honour, made her a goddess and performed an annual sacrifice. Polyaenus: *Stratagems,* Book 8, Chapter 37. ['Attalus'] <http://www.attalus.org/translate/polyaenus8B.html> viewed 19 March 2012; In Plutarch their leader is called Phobus. 'Plutarch, Mulerium virtutes, Example 18. Of Lampsace', *Plutarch's Morals*, W. W. Goodwin, (ed.) Little, Brown & Co., Cambridge, 1874, ['Perseus, Tufts, University of Texas' digital library] <http://www.perseus.tufts.edu/hopper/text?doc=Perseus%3Atext%3A2008.01.0208%3Achapter%3D18> viewed 19 March 2012.

[1152] Amisos (Samsun) founded c. 600 B.C. by Ionian settlers. Strabo (XII.3.4.) has it founded by Miletus, but Ps.-Skymnos (1016–1917) by Phokaians. L. Summerer, *Indigenous Responses to Encounters with the Greeks in Northern Anatolia:The Reception of Architechtural Terracottas in the Iron age Settlements of the Halys Basin,* pp. 263–286, here p. 264 n. 12,<http://www.pontos.dk/publications/books/BSS%208>, viewed on 10 September 2011. For fuller discussion see L. Summerer, 'Amisos, Eine griechishe Polis im Land der Leukosyrer' in D. Kacharava, M. Faudot, and E. Geny (eds.), *Pont Euxin et Polis. Polis Hellnis et Polis Barbaron. Actes du Xe Symposium de Vani, 23–26 September 2002.* Franc-Comtoises, 129–165.

[1153] I. Carradice, *Greek Coins,* British Museum Press, 1995, p. 29 and p. 39. Velia (Elea) in Magna Graecia (southern Italy) started issuing coins before 500 B.C. and Massalia in Gaul issued coins c. 500 B.C.

[1154] A. Trevor. Hodge, *Ancient Greek France*, University of Pennsylvania Press, 1999, p. 182.

[1155] Herodotus, *Histories*, I.165, trans. G. Rawlinson, Wordsworth Editions Ltd., 1996, p. 75.

[1156] *Cilento and Vallo di Diano National Park with the Archaeological sites of Paestrum and Velia, and the Certosa di Padula,* ['UNESCO'] <http://whc.unesco.org/en/list/842>, viewed on 21 August 2011.

The Tourist Information Office leaflet at Foça is well informed with archaeological details also gives Methymna (Molyvos on the island of Lesvos) in the list of Phocaea's colonies. Grant mentioned that traditionally Phocaea was founded by Ionian settlers who were 'Phocians from near Parnassus, brought from Attica under the leadership of two Athenians, Philogenes and Damon'. M. Grant, *The Rise of the Greeks*, Phoenix, 2005, p. 175; see Pausanias, *Description of Greece*, VII.3.10 <http://www.archive.org/stream/pausaniasdescrip02pausuoft/pausaniasdescrip02pausuoft_djvu.txt>, viewed on 9 January 2012. He further mention Methymna was settled from Erythrae, Phocis and Scyros (Grant, 2005, p. 178). Perhaps it is the Phocis link in suggesting Methmyna was a Phocaean colony? There is archaeological evidence of an early 7th or possibly 8th century B.C. settlement at Dambia in the north-west of Methymna but no mention of who the people were. R. Stilwell, et al (eds.), *Lesvos*, (Princeton Encyclopaedia of Classical Sites, Princeton University Press, 1976), ['Perseus, Tufts University' digital library] <http://www.perseus.tufts.edu/hopper/text?doc=Perseus:text:1999.04.0006:id=lesbos>, viewed on 10 October 2011. For a history of Methymna see, S. Salaville, 'Methymna', *The Catholic Encyclopaedia*, vol.10. New York: Robert Appleton Company, 1911, <http://www.newadvent.org/cathen/10243b.htm>, viewed on 10 September 2011); 'Methymna', [Enotes] <http://www.enotes.com/topic/Mithymna>, viewed on 10 September 2010.

For examination of three foundation stories of Phocaea see J. McInerney, *The Folds of Parnassos: Land and Ethnicity in Ancient Phokis*, University of Texas Press, 1999, p. 157-162. Archaeologically from Protogeometric pottery finds the date for the foundation of a settlement at Phocaea is likely to have been c. ninth century B.C. This settlement was originally Aiolian before becoming Ionian in a peaceful transition. (McInerney, p. 158).

[1157] T. J. Dunbabin, *The Western Greeks: The History of Sicily and South Italy from the Foundation of the Greek Colonies to 480 B.C*, Oxford University Press Monograph Reprints, 1998, ch. 11, p. 346.

[1158] J-P. Morel, 'Phocaean Colonisation', in G. R. Tsetskhladze (ed.), *Greek Colonisation: An Account of Greek Colonies and Other Settlements Overseas,* vol.1, (Leiden, 2006): 358–428, here p. 373–374 and p. 408.

[1159] *The Greek Anthology,* Sepulchral Epigrams, No. 375–Demagetus, trans. W. R. Paton, William Heinemann, 1917, p. 391.

[1160] *Phokaia 1913-1920,* ['Imerisia Online'] <http://www.imerisia.gr/article.asp?catid=13774&subid=2&pubid=4031188>, viewed on 27 November 2011; *Livre Phocee Kallimage,* ['Scribd'] <http://www.scribd.com/doc/8636978/Livre-Phocee-Kallimages>, viewed on 15 June 2012.

[1161] Ö. Özyğit, 'Recent Work at Phokaia in the Light of Akurgal's Excavations', in *Anadolu/Anatolia* 25, (2003): 109–127, here p. 118, <http://dergiler.ankara.edu.tr/dergiler/14/715/9072.pdf>, viewed on 10 October 2011.

[1162] *Ibid,* here p. 116.

[1163] *Ibid,* here p. 119.

[1164] *Ibid,* here p. 116.

[1165] Ö. Özyğit, '1994 Yili Phokaia Kazi Çalişmalari' KAZI SONUÇLARI TOPLANTISI, 17 Kazi II, KÜLTÜR BANKANLIGI YAYINLARI/1811, (Ankara 1996):1–26, here p. 16.

[1166] A. Trevor. Hodge, *Ancient Greek France,* University of Pennsylvania, 1999, p. 13.

[1167] *Ibid.*

[1168] Herodotus, *Histories,* I. 163, trans. G. Rawlinson, Wordsworth Editions Ltd., 1996, p. 74.

[1169] Ö. Özyğit, 'Recent Work at Phokaia in the Light of Akurgal's Excavations', in *Anadolu/Anatolia* 25, (2003): 109–127, here p. 116, <http://dergiler.ankara.edu.tr/dergiler/14/715/9072.pdf>, viewed on 10 October 2011.

[1170] *Ibid,* here p. 118. Özyğit suggests there were similarities of these seat profiles with the Erythrai theatre that was possibly built in the last quarter of the fourth century B.C.

[1171] *Historical and Natural Assets in Foça, (Phocaea),* Tourist Information Leaflet/Map 2011.

[1172] Ö. Özyğit, 'Recent Work at Phokaia in the Light of Akurgal's Excavations', in *Anadolu/Anatolia* 25, (2003): 109–127, here p. 116, <http://dergiler.ankara.edu.tr/dergiler/14/715/9072.pdf>, viewed on 10 October 2011.

[1173] Ovid, *Metamorphosis*, VI.1, trans. Brookes More, ['Theoi E-texts'] <http://www.theoi.com/Text/OvidMetamorphoses6.html >, viewed on 3 July 2012; George, *The Temple of the Goddess Athena at Phocaea*, ['The Museum of the Goddess Athena'] <http://www.goddess-athena.org/Museum/Temples/Phocaea/index.htm> viewed 26 November 2011.

Purple dye came from the hypobranchial glands of the Murex Truncalis and the Murex Brandaris snails (the latter producing a heavy dark tint), together with the dye of a non-murex snail produced the royal purple. Approximately 60,000 snails were needed to produce one pound of dye. Including the techniques and time needed in production that is why purple dye was a very expensive luxury item. All Tyrian purple dyes were colourfast. To avoid discolour the best dyers would process in lead or tin pans. M. A. Edey, *The Sea Traders*, Time Life Books, 1974, p. 61; see also C. Çakilar and R. Becks, '*Murex' Dye Production at Troia: Assessment of Archomalacological Data from New and Old Excavations*, ['si.academia.com']:87–103, here p. 90, <http://si.academia.edu/CananCakirlar/Papers/453623/MUREX_DYE_PRODUCTION_AT_TROIA>, viewed on 27 November 2011.

[1174] R. Stilwell, et al (eds.), *Phokaia*, Princeton Encyclopaedia of Classical Sites, Princeton University Press, 1976, ['Perseus, Tufts University' digital library] <http://www.perseus.tufts.edu/hopper/text?doc=Perseus%3Atext%3A1999.04.0006%3Aid%3Dphokaia&redirect=true>, viewed on 10 October 2011.

[1175] Julius Sextus Frontinus,*Stategems*, 3. 11.2; Polyaenus, *Strategems*, 2.1.6.

[1176] Ö. Özyğit, 'Recent Work at Phokaia in the Light of Akurgal's Excavations', in *Anadolu/Anatolia* 25, (2003): 109–127, here p. 117, <http://dergiler.ankara.edu.tr/dergiler/14/715/9072.pdf>, viewed on 10 October 2011.

[1177] A. Trevor. Hodge, *Ancient Greek France,* University of Pennsylvania, 1999, p. 9 n. 15.

[1178] C. Tanriver, 'Some New Texts Recording Occupations', in *Epigraphica Anatolica*, (Heft 18, 1991):79-90, here p. 81, Epigraphica Anatolica 17-20, 1991-92, Dr R. Halbelt, GMBH, Bonn. The text was first mentioned by Bull. ép. 1971, 553. The lower part of the stone was missing when photographed for Jean and Louis Robert. Since then another piece recording three lines has disappeared as in my photograph.

[1179] *Supplementum Epigraphicum Graecum*, vol. XLI, 1044, Aiolis, (eds.), H. W. Pleket and R. S. Stroud, J. C. Gieben, Amsterdam, 1991, p. 363.

[1180] J. McInerney, *The Folds of Parnassos: Land and Ethnicity in Ancient Phokis*, University of Texas Press, 1999, p. 103. n. 51.

[1181] Pausanias, *Description of Greece,* II. 31–6., and VI. 5.4., trans. W. H. S. Jones, and H. A. Ormerod, in 4 vols., Heinemann, 1918. ['Perseus Project, Tufts University' digital library] <http://www.perseus.tufts.edu/hopper/text?doc=Perseus%3Atext%3A1999.01.0160%3Abook%3D2%3Achapter%3D31%3Asection%3D6>, viewed on 12 October 2011.

[1182] Ö. Özyğit, 'Recent Work at Phokaia in the Light of Akurgal's Excavations', in *Anadolu/Anatolia* 25, (2003): 109–127, here p. 111, <http://dergiler.ankara.edu.tr/dergiler/14/715/9072.pdf>, viewed on 10 October 2011.

[1183] *Ibid*, here p. 117.

[1184] Xenophon, *Hellenica,* I.3.1, in seven volumes, 1 and 2, Carleton L. Brownson, Harvard University Press, Cambridge, MA, Heinemann, London, vol. 1: 1918, vol. 2: 1921, ['Perseus Project, Tufts University' digital library] <http://www.perseus.tufts.edu/hopper/text?doc=Perseus%3Atext%3A1999.01.0206%3Abook%3D1%3Achapter%3D3%3Asection%3D1>, viewed on 23 November 2011.

[1185] Pausanias, *Description of Greece,* VI. 5.4, trans. W. H. S. Jones, and H. A. Ormerod, in 4 vols. Heinemann, 1918. ['Perseus Project, Tufts University' digital library]

<http://www.perseus.tufts.edu/hopper/text?doc=Perseus%3Atext%3A1999.01.0160%3Abook%3D7%3Achapter%3D5%3Asection%3D4 >, viewed on 12 October 2011.

[1186] Ö. Özyğit, 'Phocaean Horse and Griffon Protomes' in S. Bouffir and A. Hemary (eds.) *L'occident grec, de Marseille à Mégara Hyblaea*, (Centre Camille Jullian, 2013): 5-26.

[1187] Ö. Özyğit, 'Recent Work at Phokaia in the Light of Akurgal's Excavations', in *Anadolu/Anatolia* 25, (2003): 109–127, here p. 118, <http://dergiler.ankara.edu.tr/dergiler/14/715/9072.pdf>, viewed on 10 October 2011.

[1188] E. S. Shuckburgh, *The Histories of Polybius*, vol. 2. XXI. 6. Macmillan, 1884, p. 265; F. W. Wallbank, *A Historical Commentary on Polybius*, vol. 3. XXI. 6.1–6, Oxford, 1979, p. 96. Wallbank gives his reference as Livy, XXXVII. 9. 5–8.

[1189] Found in les fouilles de la Place Villeneuve-Bargemon, Marseille. On display at the Musée d'Histoire Marseille, July 2009. Around 50 seated Cybele discovered in Marseille made of local limestone and shaped as miniature temples.

[1190] *All about Foça*, ['Izmie.cx'] <http://www.izmir.cx/html/foca.htm>, viewed on 22 June 2011; W. M. Johnson, 'Mediterranean Monk Seal (*Monachus monachus*)' <http://www.monachus-guardian.org/factfiles/medit01.htm>, viewed on 13 January 2012; W. M. Johnson, and D. L. Lavigne, 'Monk Seals in Antiquity, The Mediterranean Monk Seal (Monachus monachus)' in *Ancient History and Literature,* Mededelingen No. 35, The Netherlands Commission for International Nature Protection, (Leiden 1999): 1-101, PDF edition 2008, here p. 14. <http://www.monachus-guardian.org/library/mededelingen35_2008a.pdf>, viewed on 18 September 2011.

[1191] Homer, *The Odyssey,* Book XII. <http://ancienthistory.about.com/od/trojanwarinlit/a/OdysseyXII.htm>, viewed on 11 October 2011.

[1192] The first major Geek city south of Phokaia was Smyrna. According to Pseudo-Skylax description of the cities 'Smyrna, in which Homer was; Phokaia with a harbour and the Hermos river'. G. Shipley, *Pseudo-Skylax: The Circumnavigation of the Inhabited World-Text, Translation and Commentary*, 98.2, Bristol Phoenix Press, 2011, p. 75. The Oracle at Delphi named Ithaca as Homer's birthplace in response to Emperor Hadrian's question. H. W. Parke and D. E. W. Wormell, *The Delphic Oracle*, Blackwell, 1956, vol.1, p. 285.

[1193] Herodotus, *Histories*, Book I. 164, trans. G. Rawlinson, Wordsworth Editions Ltd, 1996, p. 74.

[1194] Built shortly before Phokaia was besieged that year. Ö. Özyğit, 'Recent Work at Phokaia in the Light of Akurgal's Excavations', in *Anadolu/Anatolia* 25, (2003): 109–127, here p. 119, <http://dergiler.ankara.edu.tr/dergiler/14/715/9072.pdf>, viewed on 10 October 2011.

[1195] Vitruvius, *The Ten Books on Architecture,* Bk. 3, Introduction. 2, trans. M.H. Morgan, Dover Publication, 1960, p. 70.

[1196] Pausanias, Description of Greece, IV.33.7, trans. W. H. S. Jones, and H. A. Ormerod, 4 vols. Heinemann, 1918. ['Perseus, Tufts University', digital library] <http://www.perseus.tufts.edu/hopper/text?doc=Perseus:text:1999.01.0160:book=4:chapter=33&highlight=phocaea#note-link4 >, viewed 15 January 2012.

[1197] Trudy S. Kawami, 'Greek Art and Persian Taste: Some Animal Sculptures from Persepolis', *American Journal of Archaeology,* vol. 90. No. 3, (July 1986): 259–267, here p. 259 and p. 264. n. 59, Pliny *N.H.* 24.68, ['JSTOR' journal archive] <http://www.jstor.org/pss/505686>, viewed on 22 June 2011.

[1198] Vitruvius, *Ten Books on Architecture,* trans. I. D. Rowland, Cambridge, 1999, p. 266, Silenius, Theodorus and p. 86, Bk. VII, 12. Though in Morgan's translation he write Theodorus of Phocis, (Bk. VII, 12. p. 198.), this may be a printing error as the Latin text is 'Theodorus Phocaeus de tholo qui est Delphis', see Lacus Curtius, *Marcus Vitruvius Pollio: de Architectura*, Liber VII. 12. ['Perseus, Tufts University' digital library] <http://penelope.uchicago.edu/Thayer/L/Roman/Texts/Vitruvius/7*.html>, viewed on 10 October 2011; E. VerMeulen, 'Delphi, The Tholos of Athena Pronaia', Coastal Carolina University, <http://www.coastal.edu/ashes2art/delphi2/marmaria/tholos_temple.html> viewed on 31 December 2012; Phocaea was founded by settlers from Phocis. J. McInerney, *The Folds of Parnassos: Land and Ethnicity in Ancient Phokis*, University of Texas Press, 1999, p. 157-162.

[1199] P. Valavanis, *Games and Sanctuaries in Ancient Greece,* trans. Dr David Hardy, Kapon Editions, 2004, p. 232.

[1200] L. B. Urdahl, *Foreigners in Athens: A study of grave monuments,* (4563, 1924), The University of Chicago, 1959, p. 137, Telecles tombstone ref: (IG II 2 12764).

[1201] *The Geography of Strabo,* Loeb, 1923, Thayer's note 41, Strabo, 3.2.8, ['Penelope, University of Chicago' digital library] <http://penelope.uchicago.edu/Thayer/E/Roman/Texts/Strabo/3B*.html>, viewed on 24 August 2011.

[1202] *The Origins of Coinage*, [The British Museum] <http://www.britishmuseum.org/explore/themes/money/the_origins_of_coinage.aspx>, viewed on 21 November 2010.

[1203] I. Carradice, *Greek Coins*, British Museum Press, 1995, p. 24.

[1204] Herodotus, *Histories*, I. 163, trans. G. Rawlinson, Wordsworth Editions Ltd., 1996, p. 74.

[1205] Ibid, p. 111 n. 157; *Appian, Wars of the Romans in Iberia*, 2.(5). translated from the Greek by J. S. Richardson, Aris & Phillips Ltd., 2000.

[1206] A. G. Woodhead, *The Greeks in the West,* Thames and Hudson, 1962, p. 21.

[1207] C. McEvedy, *The Penguin Atlas of Ancient History*, Penguin Books, 1979, p. 34.

[1208] A. G. Woodhead, *The Greeks in the West,* Thames and Hudson, 1966, p. 66; M. Morgan, Documentation Officer, The Royal Cornwall Museum, Truro, email to me 23 April 2013, 'Fragment of short bronze sword/dagger, which shows striking parallels with daggers or short swords made c. 1300-1230 BC Mycenean IIIb.'

[1209] *Ibid*, Plate 2, p. 177, refs. J. F. S. Stone, *Wessex Before the Celts,* p. 97–9 and R. J. Atkinson, *Stonehenge*, p. 30–1 & plate XII; A recent scan by a 3-D laser of the 83 surviving stones has been issued by English Heritage on 8 October 2012. The survey also revealed 72 previously unknown Early Bronze Age carvings each cut to a depth of 1-3 mm into 5 of the stones: 71 carvings of Early Bronze Age unhafted metal axe-heads: another dagger (NW face stone 53). In total 118 (inc. 3 daggers) carvings have been revealed of types between 1750-1500 B.C. Examination of the earlier dagger of 1953 thought it started as an axe head carving but was changed to a dagger by adding a hilt and pommel and lengthening the point is now revealed as two axe heads. Pick dressing of certain stones indicates mid-winter sunset and viewed from the North-East to be most significant to the Stonehenge builders. <http://www.englishheritage.org.uk/about/news/stonehenge-solstitial-function/> viewed 11 March 2013; J.P. Reedman, English Heritage guide at Stonehenge mentioned the daggers may be of snowhills Iberian type (21 April 2013). Seven sites in Britain with these rock carvings <http://www.archaeologyuk.org/ba/ba73/feat1.shtml> viewed 21 April 2013.

[1210] C. Renfrew and P. G. Bahn, *Archaeology: Theories, Methods and Practice*, Thames and Hudson Ltd., 2008, p. 380.

[1211] J-Y. Blot, *Underwater Archaeology: Exploring the World beneath the sea*, Thames and Hudson, 1995, p. 139.

[1212] C. Renfrew and P. G. Bahn, *Archaeology: Theories, Methods and Practice*, Thames and Hudson Ltd., 2008, p. 381.

[1213] S. M. Pearce, 'Amber Beads from the late bronze-age hoard from Glentanar, Aberdeenshire', in *Proceedings of the Society of Antiquaries Scotland*, Archaeology Data Service, University of York, vol. 108 (1976–7): 124–129, <http://ads.ahds.ac.uk/catalogue/adsdata/arch-352-1/dissemination/pdf/vol_108/108_124_129.pdf>, viewed on 19 October 2011.

[1214] J. J. Taylor, *Bronze Age Goldwork of the British Isles*, Cambridge, 1980, p. 45–6.

[1215] M. Grant, *The Rise of the Greeks*, Phoenix, 2005, p. 294.

[1216] J. Boardman, *The Greeks Overseas,* Ch. 5, Thames & Hudson, 1999, p. 164.

[1217] Maurice. Wintemitz, Monz. Wintemitz, and V. Srinivasa Sarma, *A History of Indian Literature*, vol.1. Motila Banarsidass Publishers, 2003, p. 29, p. 32, p. 92, and p. 476–478. The Ramayana has three versions with 12,000 core verses and in total around 24,000 each. A. W. P. Guruge, *The Society of the Ramayana*, Abhinav Publications, New

Delhi, 1991, p. 31 and p. 305. The final version of the Mahabarata went from its origin of the Jaya at 8,800 verses to the Bharata of 24,000, and finally recited by Ugrasravas as the Mahabharata with 100,000 verses. S. Kak, 'The Mahabharata and the Sindhu-Sarasvati Tradition', <http://www.ece.lsu.edu/kak/MahabharataII.pdf>, viewed on 22 October 2010.

[1218] *Ibid*, Maurice Wintemitz, Monz. Wintemitz, and V. Srinivasa Sarma, p. 294–5.

[1219] C. Orieux and P. Schmitt-Pantel, *A History of Ancient Greece,* Blackwell, 1999, p. 28.

[1220] P. Parker, 'Greek Religion', ch. 11, in J. Boardman, J. Griffin, and O. Murray, (eds.), *Greece and the Hellenistic World,* Oxford University Press, 2001, p. 310.

[1221] Herodotus, *Histories*, V.58, trans. G. Rawlinson, Wordsworth Classics, p. 411.

[1222] O. Orrieux and P. Schmitt Pantel, *A History of Ancient Greece*, Blackwell, 1999, p. 26.

[1223] M. Roberts, *The Ancient World,* Macmillan Education Ltd, 1979, p. 111; *Compendium of Ancient Greek Phonology*, 63-75, here p. 64, Arts & Sciences, ['Washington University in St. Louis'] <http://www.artsci.wustl.edu/~cwconrad/docs/CompPhon.pdf>, viewed 2.June 2012.

[1224] P. Parker, 'Greek Religion', ch. 11, in J. Boardman, J. Griffin, and O. Murray, (eds.), *Greece and the Hellenistic World,* Oxford University Press, 2001, p. 310.

[1225] R. Osborne, *Classical Greece 500–323 B.C.,* Oxford University Press, 2000, p. 16.

[1226] R. Flaceliere, *Daily Life in Greece At the Time of Pericles,* Phoenix, 2002, p. 97.

[1227] Strabo, *Geography,* Book. 1, Ch. 1. 2.

[1228] J. Boardman, *The Greeks Overseas*, Thames & Hudson, 1999, p. 164.

[1229] *Ibid*, p. 210.

[1230] *Ibid*, p. 38.

[1231] See note 218–219 in Book 3, p. 253 Lucan, *Civil War*, trans. Susan. H. Braund, Oxford World's Classics, 1999, a reference to Ovid. Fast.3. 107–8; Reference to Ovid, Fast. 2. 153–92 Note. 237 Bk. 2, in *Lucan Civil War*, p. 240; See also Arrian, *Life of Alexander the Great,* trans. Aubrey de Sélincourt, Penguin Classics, 1958, p. 219.

[1232] C. H. Roseman, *Pytheas of Massalia: On the Ocean: Text, Translation and Commentary,* Ares Publishers, 1994, p. 57.

[1233] Strabo, *Geography,* Book III. 2.14.

[1234] M. E. Aubet, 'On the Organization of the Phoenician Colonial System in Iberia' in C. Riva and N. C. Vella, (eds.), *Debating Orientalizing: Multidisciplinary Approaches to Change in the Mediterranean,* (Equinox, 2006): 94-109, here p. 95 and p. 105.

[1235] The Erythraean Sea that the ancient Greeks described was the present day Red Sea, which also included the Indian Ocean and the Persian Gulf. The Atlantic and Erythraean Seas were all part of the circular ocean which was believed to flow around the earth. Diodorus Siculus, *Library of History,* Bk. I, Appendix B, trans. E. Murphy, Transaction Publishers, 1989, p. 94; Herodotus, *Histories*, I. 203, trans. G. Rawlinson, Wordsworth Editions Ltd., 1996, p. 91.

[1236] Arrian, *History of Alexander and Indica,* vol. 2. VIII. 37. 3–4, trans. E. Iliff. Robson, Heinemann, 1966, p. 415–416.

[1237] Herodotus, *Histories*, IV. 152, trans. G. Rawlinson, Wordsworth Editions Ltd., 1996, p. 358.

[1238] R. Carpenter, *Beyond the Pillars of Hercules: The classical world seen through the eyes of its discoverers,* Ch. 2, Tandem, 1973, p. 59.

[1239] B. Cunliffe, *The Extraordinary Voyage of Pytheas the Greek: The man who discovered Britain,* Penguin Books, 2002, p. 1 and p. 47.

[1240] C. H. Roseman, *Pytheas of Massalia: Text, Translation and Commentary,* Ares Publishing, 1994, p. 81.

[1241] The founders of Carthage were Phoenicians but as to who we have only the legends. *Dido and the Founding of Carthage,* ['Ancient Numismatic Mythology']
<http://numismaticmythology.com/DidoandtheBuildingofCarthage.aspx>; S. G. Khaleph, *Elissar, Dido, Queen of Carthage and her City,* <http://phoenicia.org/elissardidobio.html>, viewed on 14 December 2011.

[1242] Herodotus, *Histories,* III. 19, trans. G. Rawlinson, Wordsworth Editions Ltd., 1996, p. 233.

[1243] J. Middleton. MacDonald, *Massilia Carthago: Sacrifice Tablets of the Worship of Baal,* D. Nutt, 1897, reprint Kessinger, 2003. p. 3–5. Also available online ['Archive.org']
<http://www.archive.org/stream/massiliacarthago00macdrich#page/4/mode/2up>, viewed on 19 September 2011.

[1244] D. Harden, *The Phoenicians,* Thames & Hudson, 1963, p. 105.

[1245] P. Parker, 'Greek Religion', ch. 11, in J. Boardman, J. Griffin, and O. Murray, (eds.), *Greece and the Hellenistic World,* Oxford University Press, 2001, p. 311.

[1246] M. Clerc, *Massalia. Histoire de Marseille dans l'antiquité des origins à la fin de l'Empire romain d'Occident* (476 ap. J.-C.), TOME 1, Des origins jusqu 'au IIIme siècle av. J.-C., Marseille, Librairie A. Tacussel, 1927, p. 335.

[1247] 'Petit Chapellis/Naos dediée à Cybele, divinite asiatique Calacaire VI e seicle B.C.' Description by the statue in the Musée d'Histoire de Marseille (July 2009). Around 50 found in Marseille made of local limestone.

[1248] Ö. Özyğit, 'Recent Work at Phokaia in the Light of Akurgal's Excavations', in *Anadolu/Anatolia* 25, (2003): 109–127, here p. 118, <http://dergiler.ankara.edu.tr/dergiler/14/715/9072.pdf>, viewed on 10 October 2011.

[1249] Information was from the Display Boards in Musée d'Histoire, Marseille, July 2009; also in G. Rayssiguier and C. Guichard, 'Baou de Saint-Marcel' in *Voyage en Massalie: 100 ans d'archéologie en Gaule du sud,* Catalogue de l'exposition, (Musées de Marseille/Édisud, 1990): 46-53, here p. 47.

[1250] Herodotus, *Histories,* trans. G. Rawlinson, Bk. III.19. Wordsworth Editions Ltd., 1996, p. 233.

[1251] T. J. Dunbabin, *The Western Greeks: The History of Sicily and South Italy from the Foundation of the Greek Colonies to 480 B.C,* Oxford University Press Monograph Reprints, 1998, p. 344.

[1252] A. G. Woodhead, *The Greeks of the West,* 1962, p. 68; H-G. Nasselrath, '"Where the Lord of the Sea Grants Passage to the Sailors through the Deep-Blue Mere No More:" The Greeks and the Western Seas' in *Greece and Rome,* Second Series, vol. 52. no. 2 (Oct 2005): 153-171, here p. 159. ['JSTOR' archive journal] <www.jstor.org/stable/3567866> viewed 6 April 2012.

[1253] Strabo, *Geography,* III. 5.11.

[1254] Herodotus, *Histories,* Bk. III. 115, trans. G. Rawlinson, Wordsworth Editions Ltd., 1996, p. 274.

[1255] Solinus writing in A.D. 200 states 'In this fastness [Britannia] an altar inscribed with Greek letters proves that Ulysses was driven to *Calidonia.*' A. L. F. Rivet and C. Smith, *The Place-Names of Roman Britain,* B. T. Batsford Ltd, 1982, p. 85, Solinus, *Collectanea Rerum Memorabilium,* 22, 1–12.

[1256] Strabo, Geography, I. 1.7; *Geminos's, Introduction to the Phenomena: a translation and study of a Hellenistic survey of astronomy,* c. 6. On day and Night, trans. by J. Evans and J. L. Berggren, Princeton University Press, 2006, p. 163 n. 4.

[1257] R. Bittlestone, *Odysseus Unbound,* Cambridge, 2005, p. 49.

[1258] G. Pillot, *The Secret Code of the Odyssey: Did the Greeks Sail the Atlantic?*, English translation by Francis Albert, Abelard-Schuman Ltd, 1972, p. 64 & p. 101. The roar of the maelstrom can be heard up to 16 km away.

[1259] W. W. Hyde, *Ancient Greek Mariners*, Oxford, 1947, p. 93; Also Homer's River Phasis possibly connected the Black Sea to the Caspian Sea when sea levels were much higher during Neolithic period, D. Adams, Episode 1of 6, Exploration of an Ancient Sea, *Alexander's Lost World*, Yesterday Channel 19 [UKTV broadcast] 9.00 p.m. 21 May 2013 <http://www.alexanderslostworld.com/>; Route from India via River Bactrus tributary of the river Oxus (Amu Darya) to the Caspian Sea. O. Lordkipandze, *Phasis: The River and City in Cholcis*, Steiner, 2000, p. 28-30.

[1260] Strabo, *Geography*, III.4.4; Geminos's, *Introduction to the Phenomena: a translation and study of a Hellenistic survey of astronomy*, c. 6. On day and Night (VI 9–VI 22), trans. by J. Evans and J. L. Berggren, Princeton University Press, 2006, p. 163–165.

[1261] *Dionysius of Halicarnassus*, vol.7, Excerpts, Bk. XIV, 1, 3–2, 1, trans. E. Cary, Loeb, 1950, p. 261. Dionysius thought the origin of the name was from when Greeks first landed in the Gallic Gulf from a violent wind, Kelsike–to put ashore.

[1262] The Greeks also called the Celts Galatae and later the term Gaul for France was used. In Ptolemy's map of Britain he uses both terms in one name to describe that opposite southern Britain as Keltogallatia Belgiki. A. L. F. Rivet and C. Smith, *The Place-Names of Roman Britain*, B. T. Batsford Ltd, 1982, p 107.

[1263] G. Shipley, *Pseudo-Skylax: The Circumnavigation of the Inhabited World-Text, Translation and Commentary*, 69, Bristol Phoenix Press, 2011, p. 72.

[1264] Pindar, *Odes*, Nemean 4. 68-71, trans. D Svarlien, 1990, ['Perseus,Tufts University' digital library] <http://www.perseus.tufts.edu/hopper/text;jsessionid=A829C9C15DC11C290074E002D22F0954?doc=Perseus%3Atext%3A1999.01.0162%3Abook%3DN.%3Apoem%3D4> viewed 31 January 2012.

[1265] V. Stefansson, *Ultima Thule*, George Harrap & Co., 1942, p. 14-17.

[1266] Strabo, *Geography*, VII. 3.1.

[1267] V. Stefansson *Ultima Thule*, George Harrap & Co., 1942, p. 18 and p. 61.

[1268] B. Cunliffe, *The Extraordinary Voyage of Pytheas the Greek: The man who discovered Britain*, Penguin Books, 2002, p. 99.

[1269] From Athenaeus, *Deipnosophists*, vol. 6. XIII, 576.

[1270] Pausanias, *Description of Greece*, X.8.6, trans. W. H. S. Jones, and H. A. Ormerod, 4 vols. Heinemann, 1918, ['Perseus, Tufts University', digital library] <http://www.perseus.tufts.edu/hopper/text?doc=Perseus%3Atext%3A1999.01.0160%3Abook%3D7%3Achapter%3D3%3Asection%3D10>, viewed 15 January 2012.

[1271] G. Shipley, *Pseudo-Skylax: The Circumnavigation of the Inhabited World-Text, Translation and Commentary*, 1-4, Bristol Phoenix Press, 2011, p. 54–55.

[1272] B. Cunliffe, *The Extraordinary Voyage of Pytheas the Greek: The man who discovered Britain*, Penguin Books, 2002, p. 56.

[1273] W. Ameling, 'The Rise of Carthage to 246 B.C.' in D. Hoyos, (ed.), *A Companion to the Punic Wars*, Wiley-Blackwell, 2011, p. 43.

[1274] M. E. Aubet, 'On the Organization of the Phoenician Colonial System in Iberia' in C. Riva and N. C. Vella, (eds.), *Debating Orientalizing: Multidisciplinary Approaches to Change in the Mediterranean*, (Equinox, 2006): 94-109, here p. 95 and p. 105.

[1275] Polybius, *The Histories*, vol. 2. Bk. III, 23.2-3, trans. W. R. Paton, Heinemann, 1922, p. 57; Treaty 348 B.C. F. W. Wallbank, *A Historical Commentary on Polybius*, vol. 1. Book I. 10.5. Oxford, 1957, p. 59.

[1276] A. L. F. Rivet, *Gallia Narbonensis*, Batsford, 1988, p. 17

[1277] C. H. Roseman, *Pytheas of Massalia: On the Ocean: Text, Translation and Commentary,* Ares Publishers, 1994, p. 113, Scholiast to Apollonius of Rhodes, Argonautika, 4.761–5a (Wendel, p. 291).

[1278] B. Cunliffe, *The Extraordinary Voyage of Pytheas the Greek: The man who discovered Britain,* Penguin Books, 2002, p. 44–46; G. Aujac, 'Chapter 9. The Growth of Empirical Cartography in Hellenistic Greece' in J. B. Hartley and J. Woodward (eds.). *The History of Cartography* Vol. 1. University of Chicago Press, (1987): 148-160, here p. 150, <http://www.press.uchicago.edu/books/HOC/HOC_V1/HOC_VOLUME1_chapter9.pdf> viewed 07 February 2013.

[1279] Geoffrey. J. Martin, *All Possible Worlds: A History of Geographical Ideas*, Oxford, 2005, p. 36.

[1280] J. B. Harley, and D. Woodward, *The History of Cartography: Cartography in prehistoric, ancient, and Medieval Europe and the Mediterranean,* University of Chicago Press, 1987, p. 164. Hipparchus wrote 'My concern is rather to prevent you and others who are eager to learn to give consent to things which are incompatible with the phenomena and with investigations about the universe. Indeed, this has befallen to many for good reasons. For the charm of poetry, lends a certain persuasiveness to what Aratus says'. (Hipparchus, *Commentaries on the Phaenomena of Aratus and Eudoxus,* 1.2. 5–7).

[1281] G. E. R. Lloyd, *Early Greek Science: Thales to Aristotle,* W. W. Norton & C. 1970, p. 37 n. 2; A. Bartley, 'What's Fishing Like?: The Rhetoric of Similes in Oppian's "Halieutica"', *Classics Ireland*, vol.12. (2005): 1–17, here p. 11 n. 15, Classical Association of Ireland, ['JSTOR' journal archive] <http://www.jstor.org/stable25528414>, viewed on 16 January 2011, A. N. Bartley, *Stories from the Mountains, Stories from the Sea: The Digressions and Similes of Oppian's Halieutica and the Cynergetia,* Vandenhoeck & Ruphrect, (Gottingen 2003): 29–45. ['JSTOR' journal archive], <http://www.jstor.org>, viewed on 16 January 2011.

[1282] W. M. Lindsay, *Isidore of Seville: The Etymologies (or Origins),* vol.15. 1. 63. Oxford University Press, 1911, re. Varro first century B.C. who mentions Massalia was tri-lingual Greek, Latin and Gallic; *Isidore of Seville: The Etymologies (or Origins)*, ['Penelope, University of Chicago' digital library] <htpp://Penelope.uchicago.edu/Thayer/E/Roman/Texts/isidore/home.html>, viewed on 23 August 2011.

[1283] B. Cunliffe, *The Extraordinary Voyage of Pytheas the Greek: The man who discovered Britain,* Penguin Books, 2002, p. 57.

[1284] 'A gnomon was divided into 120 parts. On the day of the solstice the length of the shadow at noon was 41 of the parts of the gnomon, less 1/5th, that is 41 & 4/5th to 120 or 209 to 600. Proportion gave 70° degrees 47 minutes and 50 seconds for the altitude for the sun 'the length of the day was 15 hours and 15 minutes. Eratosthenes and Hipparkhos (later) found obliquity of the ecliptic to be 23° degrees 51' minutes 15" seconds which they deducted from the altitude. The compliment of the result was the latitude of the place less the semi diameter of the sun, namely 43° degrees 3' minutes 25" seconds. With the semi-diameter added, the result is almost exactly the latitude for the Marseille observatory'. V. Stefansson, *Great Adventurers and Explorations: from the earliest times to the present, as told by the explorers themselves,* Robert Hale 1947, p. 12; See also G. Aujac, 'Chapter 9. The Growth of Empirical Cartography in Hellenistic Greece' in J. B. Hartley and J. Woodward (eds.). *The History of Cartography* Vol. 1. University of Chicago Press, (1987): 148-160, here p. 150-152, Fig. 9.1, Pytheas's Observation of the Latitude of Marseille, <http://www.press.uchicago.edu/books/HOC/HOC_V1/HOC_VOLUME1_chapter9.pdf> viewed 07 February 2013.

[1285] D. L. Couprie, *Heaven and Earth in Ancient Greek Cosmology: From Thales to Heraclides Ponticus*, Springer, 2011, p. 33.

[1286] R. Carpenter, *Beyond the Pillars of Hercules: The classical world seen through the eyes of its discoverers,* Tandem Press (UK), 1973, p. 156.

[1287] B. Cunliffe, *The Extraordinary Voyage of Pytheas the Greek: The man who discovered Britain,* Penguin Books, 2002, p. 58; Strabo, *Geography,* IV. 1.14.

[1288] *The Geography of Strabo*, vol. 2. III. 2. 7. Loeb, 1923, ['Penelope. University of Chicago' digital library] <http://penelope.uchicago.edu/Thayer/E/Roman/Texts/Strabo/3B*.html>, viewed on 24 August 2011.

[1289] *Ibid,* Thayer suggests Strabo meant the *Quercus coccifera*, Thayer's note 36,

[1290] B. Cunliffe, *The Extraordinary Voyage of Pytheas the Greek: The man who discovered Britain,* Penguin Books, 2002, p. 102.

[1291] Strabo lists Eratosthenes description of the Iberian coast 'which he had made in reliance upon Pytheas'. C. H. Roseman, *Pytheas of Massalia: On the Ocean: Text, Translation and Commentary,* Ares Publishers, 1994, p. 60. Strabo, *Geography,* III.2.11. The Sacred Promontory is Cape St. Vincent.

[1292] *Ibid*; R. Carpenter, p.195.

[1293] Strabo, *Geography*, vol. 2. IV.1-2, C. H. Roseman, *Pytheas of Massalia: On the Ocean: Text, Translation and Commentary,* Ares Publishers, 1994, p. 48; Carpenter thought that Tanais might be a mistake and the River Thames (Tamesis) or the Isle of Thanet (Tanat?) was meant. R. Carpenter, *Beyond the Pillars of Hercules: The classical world seen through the eyes of its discoverers,* Tandem Press (UK), 1973, Ch 5, p. 189.

[1294] G. Shipley, *Pseudo-Skylax: The Circumnavigation of the Inhabited World-Text, Translation and Commentary,* 69-70, Bristol Phoenix Press, 2011, p. 72

[1295] C. H. Roseman, *Pytheas of Massalia: On the Ocean: Text, Translation and Commentary,* Ares Publishers, 1994, p. 50.

[1296] *Lucan: Civil War*, Bk. 3. 272–276, trans. Susan H. Braund, Oxford World Classics, 1999, p. 49; Strabo, Geography, Book II.4.1–2.

[1297] B. Cunliffe, *The Extraordinary Voyage of Pytheas the Greek: The man who discovered Britain,* Penguin Books, 2002, p. 61; M. Renouard, *Wonderful Finistère,* trans. A. Moyon, Éditions Ouest-France, 1988, p. 92. Battered dramatically by the waves there is a deep depression called 'Hell of Plogoff' and reputed as 'where the souls of the departed can be heard moaning'. Local tradition says Baie des Trépassés (Bay of the Dead) was where the souls departed for the hereafter and 'the mortal remains of dead Druids were taken from here' to the island of Sein for burial.

[1298] C. H. Roseman, *Pytheas of Massalia: On the Ocean: Text, Translation and Commentary,* Ares Publishers, 1994, p. 123, Strabo, *Geography,* I. 4.5.

[1299] Ushant (Ouessant in French, and Enez-Eussa in Breton from the Gallic 'Uxisana' meaning 'the highest'). M. Renouard, *Wonderful Finistère,* trans. A. Moyon, Éditions Ouest-France, 1988, p. 74.

[1300] See appendix for distance conversion.

[1301] B. Cunliffe, *The Extraordinary Voyage of Pytheas the Greek: The man who discovered Britain,* Penguin Books, 2002, p. 64–65.

[1302] R. Penhallurick, *Tin in Antiquity: Its Mining and Trade Throughout the Ancient World with Particular Reference to Cornwall,* Institute of Metals, 1986, p.139, Ref. Bosquet, J. 'Une monnaie d'or de Cyrene sur la cote nord l'Amorique', *Annales de Bretagne,* 1961, 68. 25–39; P. R. Giot, J. Briand, and L. Page, 'Prehistoire de la Bretagne', Rennes, 1979, 253.

[1303] B. Cunliffe, *The Extraordinary Voyage of Pytheas the Greek: The man who discovered Britain,* Penguin Books, 2002, p. 72; Penhallurick, R. *Tin in Antiquity: Its Mining and Trade Throughout the Ancient World with Particular Reference to Cornwall,* Institute of Metals, 1986, p. 139, Ref. Bosquet, J. 'Une monnaie d'or de Cyrene sur la cote nord de l'Amorique', *Annales de Bretagne,* 1961, 68. 25–39, Goit et al, 1979, 253.

[1304] *Ibid,* B. Cunliffe, 2002, p. 68.

[1305] R. Penhallurick, *Tin in Antiquity: Its Mining and Trade Throughout the Ancient World with Particular Reference to Cornwall,* Institute of Metals, 1986, p. 139, ref: Bosquet, J. 'Deux monnaies greques: Massalia, Sestos', *Annales de Bretagne,* 1968, vol. 75, pp. 277–9, <http://www.persee.fr/web/revues/home/prescript/article/abpo_0003-391x_1968_num_75_1_246>

[1306] *Ibid*, p. 140 ref. M. Cary, 'The Greeks and Ancient Trade with the Atlantic', *J. Hellenic Studies*, 1924, 44, 166–79. Discovered 1875, MA 'au type de la roué, très usées' no details of obverse but MA with wheel design could also be from 4th–1st century B.C. In Dr P. de Jersey's email to me 20 June 2013, though no images were available for the coins, suggests here possibly 3rd or 2nd century B.C. date. He mentions the hoard examined amongst 700 various silver coins buried c. 30-20s B.C., there may have been more coins, and gives this reference A. de Barthélemy, 'Etude sur les monnaies gauloises découvertes à Jersey en 1875', *Revue Numismatique* series 3, vol. 2 (1884), pp. 177–202, here p.184 <http://www.medievalcoinage.com/pdfbooks/00-Zeitschrift/Revue_Numismatique_Troisieme_Tome02.pdf>

[1307] R. Penhallurick, *Tin in Antiquity: Its Mining and Trade Throughout the Ancient World with Particular Reference to Cornwall*, Institute of Metals, 1986, p. 123. Stories of Cornish tin being used in some of the fittings in Solomon's Temple, transported there via Phoenician ships. In May 1863 the Journal of the Royal Institution of Cornwall published that the story of Phoenician contact with Britain had no basis in fact. Penhallurick (1986) puts forward the argument that there is no evidence for direct trade between Cornwall and the Phoenician ports of Tyre and Sidon in the two centuries before Christ, but there was an abundance of trade between Cornwall and the western Mediterranean and this was run by Greek traders from Massalia (Marseille). The Massaliotes then distributed goods throughout the Mediterranean.

[1308] A. Buckley, *The Story of Tin Mining in Cornwall*, Cornwall Editions Ltd, 2005, p. 17; *Current Archaeology* (250) reports pre-43AD olive stone, celery and corriander seeds were found in the bottom of a late Iron Age well at Silchester. <http://www.archaeology.co.uk/articles/news/iron-age-olives-and-pampered-pets.htm> viewed 27 February 2013.

[1309] C. F. C. Hawkes and M. A. Smith, 'On some buckets and cauldrons of the Bronze and Early Iron Ages', *Ant. J.* 1957, 37, 131–98; R. Penhallurick, *Tin in Antiquity*, Institute of Metals, 1986, p. 200.

[1310] R. Penhallurick, *Tin in Antiquity*, Institute of Metals, 1986, p. 199–200.

[1311] *Ibid*, p. 139 (Ref. Fox, A. *South-West England 3500 B.C–AD 600*, David & Charles, 1973, p.135) though Fox thought the Broadgate coins a bit suspect.

[1312] P. de Jersey, *Celtic Coinage in Britain*, Shire, 2001, p. 20-21.

[1313] <http://www.ukdfd.co.uk/ukdfddata/showrecords.php?product=20157&cat=52> viewed 29 November 2013.

[1314] David Holman's email and photographs to me 15.12.2013. Copper from S.W. Britain 'apparently' found in some bronze coins from Massalia M. Fox, 'Tale of the Thurrock Potins', ANA 3134438, *The Numismatist*, Sept. 2013 [Academia], p.40 <https://www.academia.edu/5043356/The_Tale_of_the_Thurrock_Potins> viewed on 16.12.13.

[1315] R. D. Van Arsdell, 'Earliest British Coinages' [Celtic Coinage of Britain] <http://vanarsdellcelticcoinageofbritain.com/history/earliest_british_coinages_1.html> viewed 31.12.2013.

[1316] R. Penhallurick, *Tin in Antiquity*, Institute of Metals, 1986, p. 140, Solinus,; p. 140, Ref. Allen, D.F. 'The Paul (Penzance) hoard of imitation Massaliote Drachmas', *Numismatic Collectanea Rerum Memorabilium Chronicle*, 7th ser. No.1, 1961, 91–106.

[1317] Lin Watson, Deputy Curator, Teignmouth & Shalson Museum informed me by email 18 November 2010 that these items are now in the Torquay Museum.

[1318] R. Penhallurick, *Tin in Antiquity*, Institute of Metals, 1986, p. 140 n. 14. A. Fox, (ed.), *South-West England 3500 B.C.–A.D. 600*, David & Charles, 1973, p. 135.

[1319] A. Fox, *South-West England 3500 B.C.–AD 600*, David & Charles, 1973, p. 135.

[1320] B. Cunliffe, *The Extraordinary Voyage of Pytheas the Greek: The man who discovered Britain*, Penguin Books, 2002, p. 42.

[1321] Avienus also used a periplus from Massalia dating c. sixth century B.C. see A. L. F. Rivet and C. Smith, *The Place-Names of Roman Britain*, B. T. Batsford Ltd, 1982, p. 39; B. Cunliffe, *The Extraordinary Voyage of Pytheas the Greek: The man who discovered Britain*, Penguin Books, 2002 p. 45–46.

[1322] R. Carpenter, *Beyond the Pillars of Hercules: The classical world seen through the eyes of its discoverers*, Tandem Press (UK), 1973, VI, p. 203.

[1323] B. Cunliffe, *The Extraordinary Voyage of Pytheas the Greek: The man who discovered Britain*, Penguin Books, 2002, p. 45–46.

[1324] Strabo, *Geography*, I.4.5 see Roseman (1994) p. 38–39 and 1.4.5 fragment *see* Roseman (1994) p. 123-4.

[1325] R. Carpenter, *Beyond the Pillars of Hercules: The classical world seen through the eyes of its discoverers*, Tandem Press (UK), 1973, p. 202 and p. 205.

[1326] *Ibid*, p. 203.

[1327] By Julius Caesar's time the trade was handled by the Veneti of Brittany. Caesar, *The Gallic War*, III. 8, trans. H. J. Edwards, Dover Publications, 2006, p. 47.

[1328] R. Carpenter, *Beyond the Pillars of Hercules: The classical world seen through the eyes of its discoverers*, Tandem Press (UK), 1973, p. 203.

[1329] B. Cunliffe, *The Extraordinary Voyage of Pytheas the Greek: The man who discovered Britain*, Penguin Books, 2002, p. 54.

[1330] Strabo, *Geography*, Book III. 2.9. & Book II, V. 15.

[1331] Diodorus Siculus, *Histories*, V.22, *The Library of History of Diodorus Siculus,* vol. 3. Loeb, 1939. ['Penelope, University of Chicago' digital library] <http://penelope.uchicago.edu/Thayer/E/Roman/Texts/Diodorus_Siculus/5B*.html#ref19> viewed 30 March 2012.

[1332] B. Cunliffe, *The Extraordinary Voyage of Pytheas the Greek: The man who discovered Britain*, Penguin Books, 2002, p. 78–79.

[1333] B. Cunliffe, *Greeks, Romans and Barbarians: Spheres of Interaction,* Guild Publishing, 1988, p. 26.

[1334] B. Cunliffe, *The Extraordinary Voyage of Pytheas the Greek: The man who discovered Britain*, Penguin Books, 2002, p. 91.

[1335] Diodorus Siculus, *Histories*, V.22, *The Library of History of Diodorus Siculus,* vol. 3. Loeb, 1939. ['Penelope, University of Chicago' digital library] <http://penelope.uchicago.edu/Thayer/E/Roman/Texts/Diodorus_Siculus/5B*.html#ref19> viewed 30 March 2012.

[1336] A. Buckley, *The Story of Tin Mining in Cornwall,* Cornwall Editions Ltd, 2005, p. 14.

[1337] R. Gardiner, *The Earliest Ships*, Conway Maritime Press, 1996, p. 54.

[1338] Diodorus Siculus, *Histories*, V.22, *The Library of History of Diodorus Siculus,* vol. 3. Loeb, 1939. ['Penelope, University of Chicago' digital library] <http://penelope.uchicago.edu/Thayer/E/Roman/Texts/Diodorus_Siculus/5B*.html#ref19> viewed 30 March 2012.

[1339] Pliny the Elder, *Natural Histories*, IV.104.

[1340] R. Penhallurick, *Tin in Antiquity*, Institute of Metals, 1986, p. 146; A. L. F. Rivet and C. Smith, *The Place-Names of Roman Britain,* B. T. Batsford Ltd, 1982, p. 488-489. Ptolemy II, 3, 14: Οὐηκτίς (Vectis). On Ptolemy's map only Οὐηκτίς Vectis appears in the English Channel roughly in line with the Isle of Wight but mid-way between Britain and France. The Irish *Muir n-Icht* for the English Channel may have been derived from a learned tradition as the other names of the seas around Britain seem to be from Graeco-Latin and not British ones, possibly Icht came from Pliny (*M)Ictim*.

[1341] Ibid, p.145 Ref. C. Reid, 'The Island of Ictis' (Reid 1905) *Archaeologia*, 1906, 59, 281–8, & Reid, C. 'Submerged Forests', 1913, CUP; M. Neville, *Stone Age village found under sea,* September 30, 2009, ['County Press online', Isle of Wight] http://www.iwcp.co.uk/news/news/stone-age-village-found-under-sea-28794.aspx, viewed on 5 July 2012.

[1342] Time Team 2002, Channel 4 TV, *Yaverland, Isle of Wight,* 24 March, <http://www.channel4.com/history/microsites/T/timeteam/yaver_dig.html>, viewed on 23 October 2010.

[1343] Pliny the Elder, *Nat. Hist.* IV. 104.

[1344] 'Six days inwards from Britannia' could be, if not a mistake, sailing up the Channel along English coast north-east and crossing over to France then down the River Seine, River Loire, and River Rhône to Massalia? This could fit with the 6 days inward as written by Pliny the Elder, *Nat. Hist,* IV.104.

[1345] Strabo, *Geography*, IV. 2.1.

[1346] S. Hornblower and A. Spawforth, *The Oxford Classical Dictionary*, 3rd edition, Oxford, 2003, p. 388.

[1347] B. Cunliffe, *The Extraordinary Voyage of Pytheas the Greek: The man who discovered Britain,* Penguin Books, 2002, p. 76–77, Dio. Sic. *Histories,* V. 1–4.

[1348] R. Gardiner, *The Earliest Ships*, Conway Maritime Press, 1996, p. 53–54.

[1349] Diodorus Siculus, *Histories*, V.22, *The Library of History of Diodorus Siculus,* vol. 3. Loeb, 1939. ['Penelope, University of Chicago' digital library] <http://penelope.uchicago.edu/Thayer/E/Roman/Texts/Diodorus_Siculus/5B*.html#ref19> viewed 30 March 2012.

[1350] Chapter 4 The Bronze Age, < http://mygeologypage.ucdavis.edu/cowen/~GEL115/115CH4.html>.

[1351] 'Coast', episode *Land's End to Porthcawl*, Series 4, televised on B.B.C. TV. 2 July 2009, <http://www.bbc.co.uk/programmes/b00lyljl> & <http://www.open2.net/coast/s4_e3.html>, viewed on 23 October 2010; also demonstrated re. Francis Pryor, Time Team, Freeview Channel 47, [TV Broadcast] 18 March 2013, 8.00 pm. Regarding other legends e.g. The Legend of the Golden Fleece, has a basis in fact where to this day in Kolchis (now the Republic of Georgia) by the Black Sea the smallest of gold pieces and mainly dust travel along rivers and steams which is too fine to pan. Tim Sevrin noticed that some Georgians would spread out the fleece of a sheep in a riverbed and leave it there for a long period. The hairs of a fleece would trap the gold dust until enough was gathered to make the venture worthwhile. (T. Severin, *The Jason Voyage: A Quest for the Golden Fleece*, Simone & Schuster, 1986). Folklore tales and legends no matter how fantastic always have some kernel of truth practical, spiritual or historical. From Homer's *Iliad*, the city of Troy was long thought to have been a myth until discovered by Schliemann 1871–3. From Homer's *Odyssey*, Odysseus's original island of Ithaca (not the present one) was found joined to the western side of Cephalonia by Bittlestone. The channel (that made it an island) as mentioned by Strabo, had since been completely filled in by landslips from Cephalonia due to several devastating earthquakes, which had led to the abandonment of the island. R. Bittlestone, *Odysseus Unbound,* Cambridge, 2005, p. 360–425.

[1352] N. Oliver, Episode 1 of 4, The Age of Iron, *A History of Ancient Britain*, BBC 2, Series Producer Cameron Balbime, [TV broadcast] October 2011, <http://www.bbc.co.uk/programmes/b0108tsq>, viewed on 19 October 2011; Bronze goods made in Britain and the Continent dated to 750–600 B.C. found in the Llyn Fawr hoard in Glamorgan Wales, <http://www.museumwales.ac.uk/en/2351/>, viewed on 19 October 2011;The bronze Battersea Shield dated between 350–50 B.C. <http://www.britishmuseum.org/explore/galleries/europe/room_50_britain_and_europe.aspx.>, viewed on 19 October 2011. As well as having their own supply there were still imports as is evident from the Salcombe shipwreck c. 900 B.C. that had 259 copper ingots and 27 Tin ingots and were thought to have been collected from different parts of Europe. Jasper Copping, 'Bronze Age shipwreck found off the Devon coast', *The Telegraph*, 13 February 2010, <http://www.telegraph.co.uk/earth/environment/archaeology/7228108/Bronze-Age-shipwreck-found-off-Devon-coast.html>, *viewed on* 19 October 2011.

[1353] B. Cunliffe, *The Extraordinary Voyage of Pytheas the Greek: The man who discovered Britain,* Penguin Books, 2002, p. 76.

[1354] A. L. F. Rivet and C. Smith, *The Place-Names of Roman Britain,* B. T. Batsford Ltd., 1982, p. 253.

[1355] *Ibid*, p. 266.

[1356] C. H. Roseman, *Pytheas of Massalia: On the Ocean: Text, Translation and Commentary,* Ares Publishers, 1994, p. 20.

[1357] A. Buckley, *The Story of Tin Mining in Cornwall*, Cornwall Editions Ltd, 2005, p. 17.

[1358] B. Cunliffe, *The Extraordinary Voyage of Pytheas the Greek: The man who discovered Britain,* Penguin Books, 2002, p. 94.

[1359] A. L. F. Rivet and C. Smith, *The Place-Names of Roman Britain,* B. T. Batsford Ltd., 1982, p. 282; Use of P and B see Roseman (1994), p. 45 & p. 55, also Cunliffe (2002) p. 94.

[1360] B. Cunliffe, *The Extraordinary Voyage of Pytheas the Greek: The man who discovered Britain,* Penguin Books, 2002, p. 73 and p. 94.

[1361] A. L. F. Rivet and C. Smith, *The Place-Names of Roman Britain,* B. T. Batsford Ltd., 1982, p. 40 and p. 282.

[1362] *Ibid*, p. 282; R. C. Carrington, *Caesar's Invasions of Britain*, Alpha Classics, G. Bell & Sons, 1952, XXXII. (v.13), p. 44, and '**Britannia, -ae** (*f.*): Britain', Index of Proper Names, p. 89; Caesar, *The Gallic Wars*, Book IV. 27-28, trans. H. J. Edwards, Loeb, 1966, p. 216-217.

[1363] *Ibid*, p. 280; R. C. Carrington, *Caesar's Invasions of Britain*, Alpha Classics, G. Bell & Sons, 1952, XXXIII. (v.14), p. 45, and '**Brittani, -orum** (*m.*) **: Britons**', Index of Proper Names, p. 89; Caesar, *The Gallic Wars*, Book V.11, trans. H. J. Edwards, Loeb, 1966, p. 248-249.

[1364] B. Cunliffe, *The Extraordinary Voyage of Pytheas the Greek: The man who discovered Britain,* Penguin Books, 2002, p. 95; William. J. Watson, *The History of Celtic Place Names in Scotland,* Williams Blackwood & Sons Ltd, Edinburgh & London, 1926, p. 13. This is an easy assumption to make for example Germany, one may hear the name Germans, assuming that is the real name one would then name the country Germany after them, while the natives own name for the country was Deutschland.

[1365] William. J. Watson, *The History of Celtic Place Names in Scotland,* Williams Blackwood & Sons Ltd, Edinburgh & London, 1926, p. 13.

[1366] B. Cunliffe, *The Extraordinary Voyage of Pytheas the Greek: The man who discovered Britain,* Penguin Books, 2002, p. 95.

[1367] In A.D. 210. D. Shotter, *The Roman Frontier in Britain: Hadrian's Wall, The Antonine Wall and Roman Policy in the North*, Carnegie Publishing, 1996, p. 106.

[1368] B. Cunliffe, *The Extraordinary Voyage of Pytheas the Greek: The man who discovered Britain,* Penguin Books, 2002, p. 95

[1369] Pliny the Elder, *Nat. Hist.*, IV.102. C. H. Roseman, *Pytheas of Massalia: On the Ocean: Text, Translation and Commentary,* Ares Publishers, 1994, p. 87-88.

[1370] A. L. F. Rivet and C. Smith, *The Place-Names of Roman Britain,* B. T. Batsford Ltd, 1982, p. 103.

[1371] *Ibid*, p. 115.

[1372] William. J. Watson, *The History of Celtic Place Names in Scotland,* Williams Blackwood & Sons Ltd, Edinburgh & London, 1926, p. 14.

[1373] Strabo, *The Geography of Strabo,* vol.1. II.4.1-2. Loeb, 1917, ['Penelope, University of Chicago' digital library] <http://penelope.uchicago.edu/Thayer/E/Roman/Texts/Strabo/2D*.html>, viewed on 8 January 2007.

[1374] Strabo, *Geography*, II 4.1-2, C. H. Roseman, *Pytheas of Massalia: On the Ocean: Text, Translation and Commentary,* Ares Publishers, 1994, p. 48–52.

[1375] B. Cunliffe, *The Extraordinary Voyage of Pytheas the Greek: The man who discovered Britain,* Penguin Books, 2002, p. 98–99.

[1376] *Ibid, Geography,* II.4.1.

[1377] B. Cunliffe, *The Extraordinary Voyage of Pytheas the Greek: The man who discovered Britain,* Penguin Books, 2002, p. 99.

[1378] A. L. F. Rivet and C. Smith, *The Place-Names of Roman Britain,* B. T. Batsford Ltd., 1982, p. 419–420 and p. 410–411.

[1379] B. Cunliffe, *The Extraordinary Voyage of Pytheas the Greek: The man who discovered Britain,* Penguin Books, 2002, p. 99 & p. 124.

[1380] The location of Mona according to Pliny the Elder was from 'Camalodunum the British tribal capital about 200 miles' [Roman miles]. (*Natural Histories,* 2.186–187). Camalodunum is thought to be Colchester. C. H. Roseman, *Pytheas of Massalia: Text, Translation and Commentary,* Ares Publishing, 1994, p. 79; A. L. F. Rivet and C. Smith, *The Place-Names of Roman Britain,* B. T. Batsford Ltd, 1982, p. 295. There was a second Camulodunum probably the Roman fort at Slack in Yorkshire: presumably the name was transferred from a native hillfort, either Almondbury, or Old Lindley Moor.

[1381] A. L. F. Rivet and C. Smith, *The Place-Names of Roman Britain,* B. T. Batsford Ltd., 1982, p. 113, p. 410, p. 419.

[1382] R. Carpenter, *Beyond the Pillars of Hercules: The classical world seen through the eyes of its discoverers,* Tandem Press (UK), 1973, Ch.6, p. 203; Strabo, *Geography,* 1.4.3 & 4.5.4. and as 'Irene' Ιριν Ireland) by Diodorus Siculus, *Histories,* V.32.3. in A. L. F. Rivet and C. Smith, *The Place-Names of Roman Britain,* B. T. Batsford Ltd., 1982, p. 63.

[1383] Julius Caesar, *The Gallic Wars,* V.13, trans. H. J. Edwards, Dover, 2006, p. 78.

[1384] R. C. Carrington, *Caesar's Invasions of Britain,* Alpha Classics, G. Bell & Sons, 1952, XXXII. (v.13), p. 44, Notes XXXII. (v.13.12), p. 81.

[1385] A. L. F. Rivet and C. Smith, *The Place-Names of Roman Britain,* B. T. Batsford Ltd., 1982, p. 93, Tacitus, *Agricola,* 23–26.

[1386] A. L. F. Rivet and C. Smith, *The Place-Names of Roman Britain,* B. T. Batsford Ltd., 1982, p. 73.

[1387] Ancient writers recorded the Caledonii as the inhabitants 'north of the Forth-Clyde isthmus while Xiphilnius (=Cassius Dio) referred to a specific confederation of tribes occupying North Scotland as opposed to the *Maeatae* (q. v.) who occupied the south'. A. L. F. Rivet and C. Smith, *The Place-Names of Roman Britain,* B. T. Batsford Ltd., 1982, p. 291.

[1388] A. L. F. Rivet and C. Smith, *The Place-Names of Roman Britain,* B. T. Batsford Ltd., 1982, p. 439.

[1389] *Ibid,* p. 74.

[1390] *Ibid,* p. 110. see maps based on Tierney's arguments.

[1391] *Ibid,* p. 106.

[1392] *Ibid,* p. 112. Cape Wrath from Old Norse language *hvarf* meaning turning point.

[1393] *Ibid,* p. 113–114 & p. 342.

[1394] *Ibid,* p. 74.

[1395] B. Cunliffe, *The Extraordinary Voyage of Pytheas the Greek: The man who discovered Britain,* Penguin Books, 2002, p. 100.

[1396] *Diodorus Siculus,* Bk. 2.47, trans. E. Murphy, Transaction, 1989, p. 61 & footnote 146.

[1397] Strabo, *Geography,* XVII. 1.44.

[1398] *Diodorus of Sicily,* Bk. 2. 47, trans. C. H. Oldfather, Loeb, 1933, p. 37–41.

[1399] C. F. C. Hawkes, *Pytheas: Europe and the Greek Explorers,* (Eighth J. L. Myers Memorial Lecture), ASIN: B0007AMH16, Oxford, 1975, p. 38. Hawkes thinks Hecataeus wrote a parody of Pytheas's story. Does this make Diodorus who does say accounts by "Hecataeus and certain others" make the Hyperborea story not a real place? Yet even if a parody, the description of the moon near the horizon gives the northern latitudes where the Isle of Lewis fits: plus the 19-year cycle of the moon completing a Metonic cycle. C. F. C. Hawkes, *Pytheas: Europe and the Greek Explorers,* (Eighth J. L. Myers Memorial Lecture), ASIN: B0007AMH16, *Oxford,* 1975 p. 48.

[1400] Aelian using Hecataeus of Abdera for his source says the Rhipaion Mountains swans appear after a ritual conducted by the three priests, the sons of Boreas (North wind) and Khoine (snow). The swans circle then land in the precinct. They join in the chant of the singers and harpers in tune. (Aelian, *On Animals,* 11.1). The swans, birds that are sacred to Apollo, circling around the Hyperborean temple have some base in reality as Whooper Swans do migrate from Iceland to their southern limit to winter which is the 'Butt of Lewis, or North Cape of Dumna' (C. F. C. Hawkes, *Pytheas: Europe and the Greek Explorers,* Eighth J. L. Myers Memorial Lecture), Oxford, 1975, p. 34 & p. 38) though the current RSPB map shows they also include part of England in the present day. This is possibly due to climate changes over 2,300 years? RSPB, *Whooper Swan,* <http://www.rspb.org.uk/wildlife/birdguide/name/w/whooperswan>, viewed on 23 October 2010.

[1401] Herodotus, *Histories,* Book 4, 33, trans. G. Rawlinson, Wordsworth Editions Ltd., 1996, p. 316.

[1402] *The Library of History of Diodorus Siculus,* II. 47, vol. 2. Loeb, 1935, ['Penelope, University of Chicago' digital library] <http://penelope.uchicago.edu/Thayer/E/Roman/Texts/Diodorus_Siculus/2B*.html>, viewed on 19 September 2011.

[1403] B. Cunliffe, *The Extraordinary Voyage of Pytheas the Greek: The man who discovered Britain,* Penguin Books, 2002, p. 173; A. Burl, *From Carnac to Callanish,* Shire, 1993.

[1404] B. Cunliffe, *The Extraordinary Voyage of Pytheas the Greek: The man who discovered Britain,* Penguin Books, 2002, p. 173. You can also see recordings of this on You Tube.

[1405] Lacus Curtius, *The Library of History of Diodorus Siculus,* vol. 2. II. 47, Loeb, 1935, ['Penelope, University of Chicago' digital library] <http://penelope.uchicago.edu/Thayer/E/Roman/Texts/Diodorus_Siculus/2B*.html>, viewed on 19 September 2011.

[1406] *Ibid,* note 37. Meton an astronomer, mathematician, geometer and engineer introduced this cycle to Athens 432 B.C.

[1407] B. Cunliffe, *The Extraordinary Voyage of Pytheas the Greek: The man who discovered Britain,* Penguin Books, 2002, p. 173.

[1408] Pretanic World, *Sacred Sites,* <www.Pretanicworld.com/Sacred_Sites.html>, viewed on 23 August 2011.

[1409] *Diodorus of Sicily,* Bk.2 46. 47, trans. C. H. Oldfather, Loeb, 1933, p. 37–41.

[1410] *The Library of History of Diodorus Siculus,* vol. 2. II. 47. Loeb, 1935, ['Penelope, University of Chicago' digital library] <http://penelope.uchicago.edu/Thayer/E/Roman/Texts/Diodorus_Siculus/2B*.html>, viewed on 19 September 2011.

[1411] A. L. F. Rivet and C. Smith, *The Place-Names of Roman Britain,* B. T. Batsford Ltd, 1982, p. 107.

[1412] *Ibid,* p. 252, p. 133, p. 469 and p. 300.

[1413] *Ibid,* p. 300; In Anglo-Saxon Kent is *Cantware* and Cantebury is *Cantwaraburh.* Lyn Blackmore, Museum of London Archaeology, Second London Anglo-Saxon Symposium, Senate House, University of London, 13 March 2013.

[1414] *Ibid*, p. 107.

[1415] *Ibid*, p. 74-74, Marcianus, *Periplus Maris Exteri* II, 41–45.

[1416] A. L. F. Rivet and C. Smith, *The Place-Names of Roman Britain*, B. T. Batsford Ltd, 1982, p. 135 & p. 373.

[1417] C. Hooper, *Lost city found at Stonehenge*, <http://www.archaeology.ws/2007-9-4.htm>, viewed on 23 August 2011.

[1418] N. McDonald, Lake District: A Megalithic Journey, Megalithic Publishing, 2011, p. 50–60.

[1419] 'Unpicking Hollingbourne's Henge' *Current Archaeology*, Issue 272, vol. XXIII, No. 8, November 2012, p. 6.

[1420] H. Jenks, *The Bones of Stonehenge*, Comments section, October 2, 2008, 'Pytheas of Massalia and the Lost City of Apollo-Part III', by Dennis, September 25, 2007, <http://www.eternalidol.com/?p=366>, viewed on 15 September 2011.

[1421] M. Parker Pearson, 'Secrets of the Stonehenge Skeletons', Channel 4, 8.00 pm [TV broadcast] 10 March 2013. Annual feasts suddenly end after 45years and after 2,500 B.C. Durrington also eased in activity.

[1422] D. Price, *'Pytheas of Massalia and the lost City of Apollo Part 3'*, <www.eternalidol.com> viewed on 15 September 2011.

[1423] P. Bradley, *Ancient Greece: Using Evidence,* p. 28, Edward Arnold (Australia) Pty Ltd, 1988.

[1424] A. L. F. Rivet and C. Smith, *The Place-Names of Roman Britain,* B. T. Batsford Ltd, 1982, p. 266.

[1425] *Ibid*, p. 253.

[1426] Time Team programme on Channel 4 [TV broadcast] 1 June 2009 gave the results of six years of excavation led by archaeologist Dr Mike Parker-Pearson, University of Sheffield. Excavations proved that Woodhenge at Durrington Walls two miles away and Stonehenge were built at the same time and each with its own causeway that went down to the River Avon, which linked the two sites. Durrington Walls wooden henge symbolised the perishable life and there was evidence of extensive feasting somewhat like a wake. There was conjecture that it was families carrying the cremated ashes of their loved ones may have cast the ashes into the River Avon. Then people processed along the river to Stonehenge and the afterlife. Stonehenge represented the permanence of the afterlife for the ancestors. The older Cursus split the two areas. The team explained the existence of the original outer ring of Blue Stones in the Aubrey holes before being moved to the centre of Stonehenge. Excavations found a natural feature on the causeway between two ridges had been cut into the limestone by weather erosion. These straight lines of the final section of the causeway actually are in line with Midsummer Sunrise and Parker-Pearson suggests that maybe this was the reason why Stonehenge was placed there at the head of a natural phenomenon. Time Team Specials, *The Secrets of Stonehenge*, <http://www.channel4.com/programmes/time-team-specials/episode-guide/series-1/episode-2>, viewed on 1 June 2009.

[1427] This may have been a 'term of convenience to describe that part of Britain nearest to the *Orcades* islands'. A. L. F. Rivet and C. Smith, *The Place-Names of Roman Britain,* B. T. Batsford Ltd., 1982, p. 434 and p. 115

[1428] C. H. Roseman, *Pytheas of Massalia: On the Ocean: Text, Translation and Commentary,* Ares Publishers, 1994, p. 20.

Hawkes suggests Dunnet Head in the Orkneys for Orcas. C. F. C. Hawkes, *Pytheas: Europe and the Greek Explorers,* (Eighth J. L. Myers Memorial Lecture), ASIN: B0007AMH16, Oxford, p. 34.

[1429] C. H. Roseman, *Pytheas of Massalia: On the Ocean: Text, Translation and Commentary,* Ares Publishers, 1994, p. 80, Pliny the Elder, *Natural Histories*, 2.217.

[1430] C. H. Roseman, *Pytheas of Massalia: On the Ocean: Text, Translation and Commentary,* Ares Publishers, 1994, p. 103.

[1431] Lacus Curtius, *The Library of History of Diodorus Siculus*, vol. 3. V. 21. Loeb, 1939, p. 155, ['Penelope, University of Chicago' digital library] <http://penelope.uchicago.edu/Thayer/E/Roman/Texts/Diodorus_Siculus/5B*.html#ref14>, viewed on 11 October 2011.

[1432] B. Cunliffe, *The Extraordinary Voyage of Pytheas the Greek: The man who discovered Britain*, Penguin Books, 2002, p. 108.

[1433] *Ibid*, p. 109.

[1434] Lacus Curtius, *The Library of History of Diodorus Siculus*, vol. 3. V. 21.3. Loeb, 1939, p. 155, ['Penelope, University of Chicago' digital library] <http://penelope.uchicago.edu/Thayer/E/Roman/Texts/Diodorus_Siculus/5B*.html#ref14>, viewed on 11 October 2011.

[1435] Strabo, *Geography*, IV.5.5.

[1436] B. Cunliffe, *The Extraordinary Voyage of Pytheas the Greek: The man who discovered Britain*, Penguin Books, 2002, p. 110.

[1437] Strabo, *Geography*, IV. 5.5. Thayer's note 167, Athenaeus IV.36. ['Penelope, University of Chicago' digital library], <http://penelope.uchicago.edu/Thayer/E/Roman/Texts/Strabo/4E*.html#ref139> viewed 20 October 2011.

[1438] *The Library of History of Diodorus Siculus*, vol. 3. V.26, Loeb, 1939, p. 167, ['Penelope, University of Chicago' digital library] <http://penelope.uchicago.edu/Thayer/E/Roman/Texts/Diodorus_Siculus/5B*.html> viewed 17 October 2011.

[1439] The Ethiopians also made a drink from 'millet and barley' Strabo, *Geography*, XVII. 2.2.

[1440] Athenaeus, *Deipnosophists*, vol. 1. I.34, trans. C. B. Gulick, Loeb, William Heinemann, 1927, p. 149.

[1441] Athenaeus, *Deipnosophists*, vol. 4. X. 429, trans. C. B. Gulick, Loeb, William Heinemann, 1928, p. 443.

Most societies seem to have found some way to make a kind of alcoholic drink with varying strengths and effects. There seems some desire in human beings to have out of the body experiences or at least some different experience from their everyday activity. However it is a weakness in some human beings, in not knowing when to stop and sometimes incurring ill health, drug dependency and fatal consequences. In Britain statistics for only specific conditions of alcohol-related death have doubled since 1993 at 1,771 to 3,884 in 2005. For women this has gone up from 1,049 to 1,873 during the same years. Charities like Alcohol Concern estimate the real, including all non-specific alcohol-related deaths, is around 60 Britons dieing each day from drinking to excess, and that is nearly 22,000 each year! (Metro newspaper, 25 May 25 2007, p.7)

On today's wine bottles in the UK there is on Sainsbury's supermarket label the Government's recommended limit from its own Medical Health Officer 'Do not regularly exceed 1.4 units'. This limit is '3-4 units for men and 2-3 units for women' (whose body mass is much less then men). A unit is a normal size wine glass of 1.4 units. One bottle is 8.3 units. In modern Greece there is a phrase for pleasurable drinking without the problems 'an metrio kai aristo' one measure is excellent and enough.

Each society made rules for drinking to prevent the bad effects of excessive drinking. In present day Britain the older generation knows the code 'You are not a man if you can not hold your liquor' but unfortunately a fashion of being so drunk, being ''legless', vomiting, and making a complete fool of oneself has somehow become the thing to be. Athenaeus had recommended it was best to throw up and vomit before going to bed. (vol. 5. XI. 484).

Due to the debilitating effects on the Celts Julius Caesar recorded that the Nervii actually banned all alcohol in its territory. Caesar, *BG*, 2. 15.4; A. Trevor. Hodge, (1999) p. 212–214.

Of the three main suspects for the early death of Alexander the Great one is written by Plutarch citing Aristobulus as his source, excessive alcohol drinking all night and the following day which then aggravated a fever. (*Plutarch's Lives, Alexander*, J. Langhorne and W. Langhorne, Sir John Lubbock's Hundred Books, Routledge, 1930, p. 488). See also the deaths of Promachus and forty-one others from a drinking party at Gedrosia (*ibid*, p. 486).

Football and Natural 'Highs'.
However as in the past those who are lucky come back to their senses and adopt a different code of behaviour and keep away from artificial 'highs' for something real. An example for people is that football is a 'natural high', but gets corrupted at the legal age to drink at 18 years old by the pressure of other adults. In wanting to have a 'good time' with 'artificial highs' they take you away from 'real highs' and eventually from the pure 'real high' of the game that you love.

The effects of too much alcohol can shorten the playing career of a soccer footballer, which is already short at around 30 years of age. Whereas a player that has very little alcohol can play at the top for many more years on a natural high like Sir Stanley Mathews, one of the greatest ever professional football players who retired at 50 years of age. Stanley was the first footballer to be knighted. From the age of 30 Stanley didn't want to give up football and started taking care of his body with a healthier diet. He would also fast one day a week to get rid of impurities.

In hindsight he regretted retiring at 50 because he was still fit at 52! Not in the public eye after retiring and with two generations on nearly 40 years had passed. Who would remember him? But it was incredible to see so many people of all ages line the streets for his funeral. It brought a lump to your throat to see a legend still has the power to reach beyond the boundaries of time. (See article by Brian Pugh on
<www.coventryweb.co.uk/editorials/writers/StanleyMathews.html> (viewed 2008). I was lucky to see him play for Stoke City FC 1962–63 season against Charlton Athletic in the then Second Division and it was the first time I ever a saw a living legend—it was magic—and the memory of it still is! Democritus of Abdera was asked how to live a long life replied 'by wetting his inside with honey, his outside with oil'. (Athenaeus, *Deipnosophists*, vol. II. 47).

At the Dionysian Anthesteria festival in Athens the wife of a king (Basilinia) is given to the god as wife and the union was at the Boukolion (marketplace). The festival was much concerned with wine-drinking but was overshadowed due to the tale told there of the death of a father (Icarius) and a maiden sacrifice. (W. Burkert, *Greek Religion*, Blackwell, 1985, p. 109 & p. 164). Icarius, a peasant in Attica was shown the art of planting vines and pressing wine by the god Dionysos. He gave some wine to his neighbours who, in feeling the strange effect of wine for the first time, thought they were being poisoned so they slew Icarius. However in the morning the peasants awoke having slept well, they realised their mistake and buried Ikaros and ran away. His daughter, 'Eirgone was led to the burial' by their faithful dog Maera. After a funeral lament Erigone called down curses then hanged herself a soon after Athenian girls began hanging themselves. 'Finally an oracle bid the Athenians to honour Icarius, Erigone, and the dog every year and to appease Erigone with an annual "swinging" festival' (Aiora). (Jon. D. Mikalson, *Ancient Greek Religion*, Blackwell, 2005, p. 60–61).

[1442] Strabo, *Geography*, IV. 5.5.

[1443] C. H. Roseman, *Pytheas of Massalia: On the Ocean: Text, Translation and Commentary,* Ares Publishers, 1994, p. 134–135.

[1444] <http://www.apiservices.com/articles/us/iceland.htm>,<http://www.eastridinghoney.co.uk/Iceland%202007.html> viewed 17 February 2013.

[1445] R. Carpenter, *Beyond the Pillars of Hercules: The classical world seen through the eyes of its discoverers,* Tandem Press (UK), 1973, p. 208-209.

[1446] *Ibid*, p. 203; and <http://www.thelatinlibrary.com/avienus.ora.html> viewed 30 December 2012.

[1447] A History of Ancient Britain: Orkney's Stone Age Temple, presenter Neil Oliver, Series Editor Cameron Balbimie, BBC 2 [TV broadcast] 1 January 2012, <http://www.bbc.co.uk/programmes/b01971gm>. Excavations of a multiple stone supposed temple site built over 5,000 years ago. The site so far excavated show over 12 stone buildings. R. Mckie, 'Neolithic Discovery: why Orkney is the centre of Britain' *The Observer*, 6 October 2012, <http://www.guardian.co.uk/science/2012/oct/06/orkney-temple-centre-ancient-britain >, viewed on 10 March 2013.

Entrances, exits and positions for fires plus the winding layouts suggest processional movement. Surrounded by an estimated ten foot wall situated between the nearby Ring of Brodgar stone circle and the standing stones of Stenness. While a possible relationship to these was mentioned (*The Ness of Brodgar Excavations*, <http://www.orkneyjar.com/archaeology/nessofbrodgar/excavation-background-2/maeshowe-alignments/>, viewed on 6 January 2012) perhaps a wider relationship to the total landscape should be considered i.e. the hills and mountains on the horizon for the daytime and of course the night sky. The alignment at Maes Howe passage is lit up by the setting sun twenty days before and after the winter solstice and due to the hills on the horizon, Ward Hill and Brunt Hill, actually lights up the passage twice in the same day (C. Knight and R. Lomas, *Uriel's Machine: The Ancient Origins of Science*,

Arrow Books, 2000, p. 205-206). This must have been a special occurrence to the beliefs of Neolithic people to enable the construction of this whereas other sites had one solstice appearance at summer and winter to calculate.

[1448] *Ibid*, p. 209.

[1449] R. Carpenter, *Beyond the Pillars of Hercules: The classical world seen through the eyes of its discoverers,* Tandem Press (UK), 1973, p. 209.

Later as most of Europe became dominated by the Celts it was called after them Keltike. The name Ligurian survived for one of the non-Celtic tribes that lived independently in the Maritime Alps down to the Mediterranean coast (Liguria) between North Italy and Massalia. Today the sea there is still called the Ligurian Sea. These Ligurians lived next to the Salyes. They were both in conflict with Massalia periodically over several centuries.

[1450] News, 'Celts Rule OK!', *Practical Archaeology*, Issue No.5 (Winter 2001/2): p. 9. The Kent Archaeological Field School. DNA swabs were taken at 30 locations around Britain and 400 swabs taken from Norway and Denmark. Tests revealed '60% of men on Orkney were descended from Vikings' who invaded from the 8th century A.D. The study led by Prof. David Goldstein was commissioned by BBC 2 for their 'Blood of the Vikings' TV series. While several Britons migrated to Brittany 5th –6th century A. D., (C. Waldman and C. Mason, *Encyclopaedia of European Peoples*, Facts on File, 2006, p.76) it is now evident that more had remained in England becoming part of the Anglo-Saxon kingdoms.

[1451] <http://www.scribd.com/doc/114485337/French-Words-in-English> viewed 6 July 2013.

[1452] R. Carpenter, *Beyond the Pillars of Hercules: The classical world seen through the eyes of its discoverers,* Tandem Press (UK), 1973, p. 189.

[1453] Strabo, *Geography*, II.1.8.

[1454] B. Cunliffe, *The Extraordinary Voyage of Pytheas the Greek: The man who discovered Britain*, Penguin Books, 2002, p. 131. Out Stack north of Unst is given as Shetland's most northerly point at Latitude 60° 51' 45" and within the 'less than 3 cubits high' of Pytheas' measurement.

[1455] Pliny the Elder, *Natural Histories,* 2, 187; Strabo, *Geography*, I.4.2.

[1456] C. H. Roseman, *Pytheas of Massalia: On the Ocean: Text, Translation and Commentary,* Ares Publishers, 1994, p. 92, Pliny the Elder, *Natural Histories*, IV.104.

[1457] Geminos, *Introduction to the Phenomena: a translation and study of a Hellenistic survey of astronomy,* VI. 9, trans. J. Evans and J. Lennart Berggren, Princeton University Press, 2006. p. 162.

[1458] B. Cunliffe, *The Extraordinary Voyage of Pytheas the Greek: The man who discovered Britain*, Penguin Books, 2002, p. 127.

[1459] Caesar, *The Gallic War*, V.13, trans. C. Hammond, Oxford World Classics, 1996, p. 96, and Explanatory Notes 5.13, p. 232.

[1460] C. H. Roseman, *Pytheas of Massalia: Text, Translation and Commentary,* Ares Publishing, 1994, p. 131-133 n. 21, Strabo, *Geography*, 2.5.7.The Fragments, and p. 45.

[1461] 'Strabo, Geography, The Fragments 2.4.1' in C. H. Roseman, *Pytheas of Massalia: On the Ocean: Text, Translation and Commentary,* Ares Publishers, 1994, p. 125.

[1462] *Ibid*.

[1463] *Ibid*.

[1464] C. H. Roseman, *Pytheas of Massalia: On the Ocean: Text, Translation and Commentary,* Ares Publishers, 1994, p. 130.

[1465] 'Strabo, *Geography*, The Fragments 2.4.1' in C. H. Roseman, *Pytheas of Massalia: On the Ocean: Text, Translation and Commentary,* Ares Publishers, 1994, p. 125.

[1466] *Ibid*, p. 125 and p. 121

[1467] B. Cunliffe, *The Extraordinary Voyage of Pytheas the Greek: The man who discovered Britain,* Penguin Books, 2002, p. 153; C. H. Roseman, *Pytheas of Massalia: On the Ocean: Text, Translation and Commentary,* Ares Publishers, 1994, p. 113–116 Scholiast to Apollonios Rhodios, *Argonautika,* 4.761-5a (Wendel, p. 291).

[1468] Perhaps Odysseus given the astronomical description according to Pillot placing part of his journey between latitude 60° to 65° degrees North? (G. Pillot, *The Secret Code of the Odyssey: Did the Greeks Sail the Atlantic?,* English translation by Francis Albert, Abelard-Schuman Ltd, 1972, p. 21-22) while Vinci places it along the Norwegian coast. F. Vinci, *The Baltic Origins of Homer's Epic Tales: The Odyssey and the Migration of Myth,* Inner Traditions Bear & Co., 2006, p. 17-18.

[1469] Herodotus, *Histories,* Bk. I. 203.

[1470] Antonius Diogenes wrote a 'fabulous tale of romance and adventure' called *The Wonders beyond Thule* (second century AD?) Philostratus, *The Life Of Apollonius of Tyana,* trans. C.P. Jones. Harvard University Press, 2005, Vol. III, Eusebius Reply to Hierocles, 17 n. 31, p. 191; For the text see Photius Biblioteca, 'Codices 166–185 [Extracts]', 166. <http://www.tertullian.org/fathers/photius_copyright/photius_04bibliotheca.htm>, viewed on 24 August 2011.

[1471] Pomponius Mela, *Geography,* Bk. III, trans. P. Berry, The Edwin Mellen Press 1977, p. 14; 'Thyle, famous in the poems of the Greeks and our own writers, is situated opposite the shores of the Belgae'. Rivet & Smith (1982), p. 76.

[1472] A. L. F. Rivet and C. Smith, *The Place-Names of Roman Britain,* B. T. Batsford Ltd, 1982, p. 77, Orosius, *Historiae adversum Paganos* 1, 2, 75–82; <http://cartographic-images.net/210_The_Cottoniana_or_Anglo-Saxon_Map.html>.

[1473] C. H. Roseman, *Pytheas of Massalia: On the Ocean: Text, Translation and Commentary,* Ares Publishers, 1994, p. 157; B. Cunliffe, *The Extraordinary Voyage of Pytheas the Greek: The man who discovered Britain,* Penguin Books, 2002, p. 116.

[1474] B. Cunliffe, *The Extraordinary Voyage of Pytheas the Greek: The man who discovered Britain,* Penguin Books, 2002, p. 116–117, Dicuil, *Demensura Orbis Terrae.*

[1475] C. H. Roseman, *Pytheas of Massalia: On the Ocean: Text, Translation and Commentary,* Ares Publishers, 1994, p.157.

[1476] *Ibid*, p. 93. An optical illusion caused by atmospheric refraction.

[1477] B. Cunliffe, *The Extraordinary Voyage of Pytheas the Greek: The man who discovered Britain,* Penguin Books, p.116–117, 2002, Dicuil, *Demensura Orbis Terrae.*

[1478] C. H. Roseman, *Pytheas of Massalia: On the Ocean: Text, Translation and Commentary,* Ares Publishers, 1994, p.93.

[1479] See corrected map regarding Scotland in A. L. F. Rivet and C. Smith, *The Place-Names of Roman Britain,* B. T. Batsford Ltd, 1982, p. 111-114.

[1480] V. Stefansson, *Ultima Thule,* George Harrap & Co., p.61, p. 194, p. 68.

[1481] B. Cunliffe, *The Extraordinary Voyage of Pytheas the Greek: The man who discovered Britain,* Penguin Books, p.128.

[1482] C. H. Roseman, *Pytheas of Massalia: On the Ocean: Text, Translation and Commentary,* Ares Publishers, 1994, p.104–109, Kleomedes, *Meteora,* 1.4, 208-210 (Todd, p. 25).

[1483] *Ibid*, p. 105.

[1484] C. H. Roseman, *Pytheas of Massalia: On the Ocean: Text, Translation and Commentary,* Ares Publishers, 1994, p. 132-134, Strabo, *Geography,* Fragments, II. 5.7-8.

[1485] B. Cunliffe, *The Extraordinary Voyage of Pytheas the Greek: The man who discovered Britain,* Penguin Books, p. 130.

[1486] *Ibid.*

It is suggested that Nansen did not allow for oars in Greek ships of 300 B.C. and so concluded Thule must be Norway. V. Stefansson *Ultima Thule,* George Harrap & Co. 1942, p. 61.

[1487] W. J. Mills, *Exploring Polar Frontiers: A Historical Encyclopaedia,* vol. 1, ABC-CLIO, 2003, p. 537.

[1488] V. Stefansson, *Ultima Thule,* George Harrap & Co., 1942, p. 61. Stefansson also thought Pytheas's Journey took an anti-clockwise direction around Britain finding Abalus first before Thule.

[1489] Six days sailing: Day 5 and Day 6 would be so far north in summer and have very long days to give the extra hours of travelling needed with sail and oar. V. Stefansson *Ultima Thule,* George Harrap & Co., 1942, p. 61.

[1490] V. Stefansson, *Ultima Thule,* George Harrap & Co. 1942, p. 46.

[1491] *Ibid*, p. 66 & p. 77.

The Arctic Circle just reaches the northernmost part of Iceland at Rifstangi 66°N 32'. B. Cunliffe, *The Extraordinary Voyage of Pytheas the Greek: The man who discovered Britain,* Penguin Books, p. 124.

[1492] V. Stefansson, *Ultima Thule,* George Harrap & Co., 1942, p. 77.

[1493] R. Carpenter, *Beyond the Pillars of Hercules: The classical world seen through the eyes of its discoverers,* Tandem Press (UK), 1973, p. 179.

[1494] Strabo, *Geography,* II.4.1.

[1495] B. Cunliffe, *The Extraordinary Voyage of Pytheas the Greek: The man who discovered Britain,* Penguin Books, 2002, p. 124.

[1496] Geminos, *Introduction to Celestial Phenomena,* 6.9; C. H. Roseman, *Pytheas of Massalia: On the Ocean: Text, Translation and Commentary,* Ares Publishers, 1994, p. 139–140, her translation is 'where the sun lies down'.

[1497] V. Stefansson, *Ultima Thule,* George Harrap & Co., 1942, p. 77. In Norway the midnight sun can be seen for several weeks.

[1498] B. Cunliffe, *The Extraordinary Voyage of Pytheas the Greek: The man who discovered Britain,* Penguin Books, 2002, p. 104–105, p.119 and p. 132–133.

[1499] A. L. F. Rivet and C. Smith, *The Place-Names of Roman Britain,* B. T. Batsford Ltd, 1982, p. 43.

[1500] V. Stefansson, *Ultima Thule,* George Harrap & Co Ltd., 1942, p. 46.

[1501] B. Cunliffe, *The Extraordinary Voyage of Pytheas the Greek: The man who discovered Britain,* Penguin Books, 2002, p. 124.

[1502] C. H. Roseman, *Pytheas of Massalia: On the Ocean: Text, Translation and Commentary,* Ares Publishers, 1994, p.107 n. 113.

[1503] V. Stefansson, *Ultima Thule,* George Harrap & Co., 1942, p. 66; *Geminos of Rhodes, Introduction to the Phenomena* c. 6. On day and Night (VI 9–VI 22), trans. J. Evans and J. Lennart. Berggren, Princeton University Press, 2006, p. 163–165.

[1504] Strabo, *Geography,* I. 1.20 and II. 2.1. Lacus Curtius Strabo's Geography, ['Penelope, University of Chicago' digital library],<http://penelope.uchicago.edu/Thayer/E/Roman/Texts/Strabo/1A*.html>, viewed on 8 January 2007.

[1505] *Ibid,* I.1. 20.

[1506] *Ibid.*

[1507] C. H. Roseman, *Pytheas of Massalia: On the Ocean: Text, Translation and Commentary*, Ares Publishers, 1994, p.34.

[1508] *Ibid*, p. 57.

[1509] D. L. Couprie, *Heaven and Earth in Ancient Greek Cosmology: From Thales to Heraclides Ponticus*, Springer, 2011, p. 33.

[1510] C. H. Roseman, *Pytheas of Massalia: On the Ocean: Text, Translation and Commentary*, Ares Publishers, 1994, p.117–119, Fig. 7. re. Hipparchus of Nicaea, *Commentary on the Phenomena of Aratos and Eudoxos*, 1.4.1 (Mantinus).

[1511] *Ibid*, p. 117.

[1512] B. Cunliffe, *The Extraordinary Voyage of Pytheas the Greek: The man who discovered Britain,* Penguin Books, 2002, p. 64.

[1513] C. H. Roseman, *Pytheas of Massalia: Text, Translation and Commentary,* Ares Publishing, 1994, p. 4, Strabo, *Geography*, II.1.18.

[1514] C. H. Roseman, *Pytheas of Massalia: Text, Translation and Commentary,* Ares Publishing, 1994, p. 4.

[1515] *So Where is Marseille?*, viewed on 24 August 2011. <www.marseille-sur-web.fr/anglais/hisgeo.htm>.

[1516] A. Trevor. Hodge, *Ancient Greek France,* University of Pennsylvania, 1999, p. 51.

[1517] C. H. Roseman, *Pytheas of Massalia: On the Ocean: Text, Translation and Commentary*, Ares Publishers,1994, p.156 and p.107.

[1518] B. Cunliffe, *The Extraordinary Voyage of Pytheas the Greek: The man who discovered Britain,* Penguin Books, 2002, p. 131–3.

[1519] C. H. Roseman, *Pytheas of Massalia: Text, Translation and Commentary,* Ares Publishing, 1994, p. 4. Strabo, *Geography*, II.1.18.

[1520] Pliny the Elder, *Natural Histories,* II.187 & IV.104; Strabo, *Geography*, I.4.2.

[1521] B. Cunliffe, *The Extraordinary Voyage of Pytheas the Greek: The man who discovered Britain,* Penguin Books, 2002, p. 112.

[1522] *Ibid*, p. 111-112.

[1523] A. L. F. Rivet and C. Smith, *The Place-Names of Roman Britain,* B. T. Batsford Ltd, 1982, p. 300 & p. 136. Diodorus Siculus V. 21, akrotirion…Kantion, Ptolemy II. 3, 3 and II, 3, 4: Kantion akron=Cantium Promontorium.

[1524] *Ibid*, p. 146, (re. From the Summary (Ptolemy, *Geography* V, III, 3, 1–11 in Nobbes's numeration).

[1525] C. H. Roseman, *Pytheas of Massalia: On the Ocean: Text, Translation and Commentary*, Ares Publishers, 1994, p.86 and p. 95, Pliny, *Natural Histories,* XXXVII.35.

[1526] *Ibid,* p. 83, Pliny the Elder, *Natural Histories,* IV. 95.

[1527] *Ibid,* p. 95, Pliny the Elder, *Natural Histories*, XXXVII.35.

[1528] Pliny the Elder, *Natural Histories*, Book 37.35–36, C. H. Roseman, *Pytheas of Massalia: On the Ocean: Text, Translation and Commentary*, Ares Publishers, 1994, p. 95, and regarding Timaeus' use of information from Pytheas p.7–8; B. Cunliffe, *The Extraordinary Voyage of Pytheas the Greek: The man who discovered Britain,* Penguin Books, 2002, p. 164.

[1529] C. H. Roseman, *Pytheas of Massalia: On the Ocean: Text, Translation and Commentary*, Ares Publishers, 1994, p. 96.

[1530] R. Carpenter, *Beyond the Pillars of Hercules: The classical world seen through the eyes of its discoverers,* Tandem Press (UK), 1973, p. 185–6.

[1531] C. H. Roseman, *Pytheas of Massalia: On the Ocean: Text, Translation and Commentary*, Ares Publishers, 1994, p. 89–90 n. 93, Pliny the Elder, *Natural Histories,* IV.103.

[1532] R. Penhallurick, *Tin in Antiquity*, Institute of Metals, 1986, p. 140.

[1533] V. Stefansson, *Ultima Thule,* George Harrap & Co., 1942, p. 18.

[1534] C. H. Roseman, *Pytheas of Massalia: On the Ocean: Text, Translation and Commentary*, Ares Publishers, 1994, p.97 n. 109.

[1535] B. Cunliffe, *The Extraordinary Voyage of Pytheas the Greek: The man who discovered Britain,* Penguin Books, 2002, p. 142.

[1536] Apollonius of Rhodes, *The Voyage of Argo: the Argonautica*, trans. E.V. Vieu, Penguin, 1959, p. 161.

[1537] Strabo, *Geography,* vol. 2. IV.6.2, trans. H. L. Jones, Loeb, 1923, p. 267 n. 5. & p. 259 n. 1.

[1538] Strabo, *Geography,* vol. 2. IV.6.3, trans. H. L. Jones, Loeb, 1923, p. 267.

[1539] E. Stefani, *Magic of Amber: amulets and jewellery from Magna Graecia and Macedonia*, University Studio Press, 2009, p. 19–24.

[1540] *Ibid*, p.18–19.

[1541] *Ibid*. p. 23–24.

[1542] Pliny the Elder, *The Natural Histories*, 37.11. J. Bostock, and H. T. Riley, (eds.), Taylor & Francis, 1855, ['Perseus, Tufts University' digital library] <http://www.perseus.tufts.edu/hopper/text?doc=Perseus%3Atext%3A1999.02.0137%3Abook%3D37%3Achapter%3D11>, viewed on 29 October 2009; A. Spekke, *The Ancient Amber Routes and Geographical Discovery of the Eastern Baltic*, M. Goppars Publishers, Stockholm, 1957, p. 38 and p. 5.

[1543] Pliny the Elder, *The Natural Histories*, 37.12. J. Bostock, and H. T. Riley, (eds.), Taylor & Francis 1855, ['Perseus, Tufts University' digital library] <http://www.perseus.tufts.edu/hopper/text?doc=Perseus%3Atext%3A1999.02.0137%3Abook%3D37%3Achapter%3D12 >, viewed on 29 October 2009; Sweet fragrance of amber for Roman ladies J. Riddle, 'Pomum ambracae:Amber and Ambergis in Plague Remedies', *Sulhoffs Archiv fur Geschichte der Medzin un der Naturwissenschaften* Bd.48, H.2 (JUNI 1964):111-122.['JSTOR' archive journal] <www.jstor.org/stable/20775083> viewed 5 March 2013, Juvenal, *Sat.*VI, 573, IX. 50-53, Martial, *Epi.*V. 37.9-14, III. 65.4-6.XI.8.6.

[1544] *Justin: Epitome of the Philippic History of Pompeius Trogus*, 43.10, trans. J. C. Yardley, Scholars Press Atlanta, 1994, p. 269.

[1545] C. F. C. Hawkes, *Pytheas: Europe and the Greek Explorers,* (Eighth J. L. Myers Memorial Lecture), ASIN: B0007AMH16, Oxford, 1975, p. 5.

[1546] Herodotus, *Histories,* trans. G. Rawlinson, Wordsworth Editions Ltd., 1996, Book I. 163.

In the poem Argonautica, Apollonius writes that the Argo sailed homeward bound to 'the sacred Isle of Amber, the innermost of all the Amber Islands at the mouth of the Eridanus'. *The Voyage of Argo: the Argonautica,* trans. E. V. Rieu, Penguin, 1959, p. 161.

[1547] 'Amber Road', <http://iguide.travel/Amber_Road>, viewed on 25 August 2011.

[1548] A. Spekke, *The Ancient Amber Routes and Geographical Discovery of the Eastern Baltic,* M. Goppars Publishers, Stockholm, 1957, p. 5.

[1549] A. Momigliano, *Alien Wisdom: The Limits of Hellenization,* Cambridge University Press, 1990, p. 57; Strabo conjectures on the Celts. Strabo, *Geography,* vol. 2. IV.1.14.

[1550] J. Boardman, *The Greeks Overseas: Their Early Colonies and Trade,* Thames & Hudson, 1999, Ch. 5, p. 223; R. Gardiner, *The Earliest Ships*, 2004, p. 54–55. Also Strabo, (IV.1.14) speculates on knowledge of the Celts.

[1551] A. M. Greaves, *The Land of Ionia: Society and Economy in the Archaic Period*, Blackwell, 2010. p. 228.

[1552] S. H. Voldman, *ESD: physics and devices*, John Wiley & Sons Ltd, 2004, p. 1–2.

[1553] J. Barnes, *The Pre-Socratic Philosophers,* vol.1, Routledge & Kegan Paul, 1979, p. 6–7

The Venerable Bede writing in the seventh century A.D. also mentions Amber's attracting abilities when rubbed in comparison to Jet. 'The Ecclesiastical History of the English People', 6.1. in R. Anderson, and D. A. Bellenger, (eds.), *Medieval Worlds: A Sourcebook,* (Routledge, 2003), p. 139.

[1554] Pliny the Elder, *The Natural Histories*, XXXVII.11. J. Bostock, and H. T. Riley, (eds.), Taylor & Francis, 1855, ['Perseus, Tufts University' digital library], <http://www.perseus.tufts.edu/hopper/text?doc=Perseus%3Atext%3A1999.02.0137%3Abook%3D37%3Achapter%3D11>, viewed on 29 October 2009; P. F. O'Grady, *Thales of Miletus*, Ashgate, 2002, p. 113–114, & p. 240–242.

[1555] *The Natural Histories*, Pliny the Elder, 37.12; J. Bostock, and H. T. Riley, (eds.), Taylor & Francis, 1855, ['Perseus, Tufts University' digital library] <http://www.perseus.tufts.edu/hopper/text?doc=Perseus%3Atext%3A1999.02.0137%3Abook%3D37%3Achapter%3D12>, viewed on 29 October 2009.

[1556] W. Gilbert, *'De Magneto Magneticisque Corporibus'*, published in Britain A.D. 1600.

[1557] C. H. Roseman, *Pytheas of Massalia, On the Ocean, Text, Translation and Commentary*, Ares Publishing, 1994, p. 89.

[1558] Erosion from the chalk cliffs of Suffolk was washed down to Romney Bay creating a barrier of shingle that allowed the Romney Marshes to form. B. W. Cunliffe, 'The Evolution of Romney Marsh: a Preliminary Statement, Archaeology and Coastal Change', *The Society of Antiquaries of London*, Occasional Paper (New Series) I, 1980, 37–55, here p. 39.

[1559] Though with Global warming sea levels will rise again as the Polar Ice caps melt much more. In 2007 the North-West Passage had become clear of ice in summer and just navigable. *Warming 'opens Northwest passage'*, <http://news.bB.C.co.uk/1/hi/6995999.stm>, viewed on 7 March 2011.

[1560] B. Cunliffe, *The Extraordinary Voyage of Pytheas the Greek: The man who discovered Britain,* Penguin Books, 2002, p. 93, (Pliny, *Nat. Hist*. IV.102)

See Isidorus of Charax c.first century B.C. geographer, *Parthian Stations by Isidore of Charax,* 33, translation from Greek by W. H. Schoff, p. 6 of 27, <http://www.parthia.com/doc/parthian_stations.htm>, viewed on 3 July 2009.

In A.D. 551 Jordanes (Iordanes) a beaureaucrat in the East Roman Empire wrote a history of the Goths and records from 'Greek and Latin authors' that Britain is shaped like 'a triangle pointing between the north and the west…Its breadth is said to be over two thousand three hundred and ten stadia, and its length not more than seven thousand one hundred and thirty-two stadia'. Jordanes, *The Origin and Deeds of the Goths*, trans. C. C. Mierow, Dodo Press, 2007, p. 3.

[1561] C. H. Roseman, *Pytheas of Massalia, On the Ocean, Text, Translation and Commentary*, Ares Publishing, 1994, p. 89.

[1562] Strabo, *Geography*, IV.1.14.

[1563] Lacus Curtius, *The Geography of Strabo*, IV.1.14. n. 63, 'The former lived south, and the latter north, of the mouth of the Sequana'. ['Penelope, University of Chicago', digital library] <http://penelope.uchicago.edu/Thayer/E/Roman/Texts/Strabo/4A*.html>, viewed on 8 January 2007.

[1564] Strabo, *Geography*, IV.1.14. n. 64. Possibly at Lyon.

[1565] Strabo, *Geography*, IV.1.14.

[1566] *Ibid*.

[1567] *Ibid*.

[1568] A. L. F. Rivet and C. Smith, *The Place-Names of Roman Britain*, B. T. Batsford Ltd, 1982, p. 63, Diodorus Siculus, Histories, V.38. 4–5.

[1569] *Dio's Roman History*, vol. 7. Bk. LX.19, trans. E. Carey, Heinemann, 1924, p. 415–416.

[1570] *Ibid*, LX.21. p. 421.

[1571] 'Gesoriacum Bononia', R. Stilwell, et al (eds.), *The Princeton Encyclopaedia of Classical Sites*, ['Perseus, Tufts University' digital library], <http://www.perseus.tufts.edu/hopper/text?doc=Perseus%3Atext%3A1999.04.0006%3Aalphabetic+letter%3DG%3Aentry+group%3D2%3Aentry%3Dgesoriacum-bononia>, viewed on 2 July 2012.

[1572] T. Griffith, (ed.), *Suetonius, Lives of the Twelve Caesars*, Claudius, 17, Wordsworth Editions Ltd., 1999, p. 221.

[1573] Strabo, *Geography*, XIII.1.54. line 245.

[1574] B. Cunliffe, *The Extraordinary Voyage of Pytheas the Greek: The man who discovered Britain*, Penguin Books, 2002, p. 155.

[1575] C. Nicolet, *Space, Geography, and Politics in the Early Roman Empire*, University of Michigan, 1991, p. 71.

[1576] The Antikythera Mechanism was a small portable box containing a set of geared wheels that computed the movement of the planets, predicting solar and lunar eclipses and the dates of the four Pan-Hellenic games, Olympic, Nemean, Pythian and Isthmian. Due to the name of Isthmian being prominent the mechanism was considered to have been made by Corinthians either in Greece or its colony of Syracuse in Sicily. M. Wright, 'The Antikythera Mechanism', in *Interdisciplinary Science Reviews*, vol. 37, No. 1. (2007): 27-43, here p. 41. <http://fsoso.free.fr/antikythera/DOCS/TheAntikytheraMechanismReconsidered.pdf>, viewed on 13 May 2012; *The Antikythera Mechanism Research Project* <http://www.antikythera-mechanism.gr/> viewed on 13 May 2012.

[1577] B. Cunliffe, *The Extraordinary Voyage of Pytheas the Greek: The man who discovered Britain*, Penguin Books, 2002, p. 64.

[1578] C. H. Roseman, *Pytheas of Massalia, On the Ocean, Text, Translation and Commentary*, Ares Publishing, 1994, p.56, Strabo, Geography, II.5.43.

[1579] C. H. Roseman, *Pytheas of Massalia, On the Ocean, Text, Translation and Commentary*, Ares Publishing, 1994, p.18.

[1580] *Ibid*, p. 46, Strabo, *Geography*, II.3.5.

[1581] *Ibid*.

[1582] C. H. Roseman, *Pytheas of Massalia, On the Ocean, Text, Translation and Commentary,* Ares Publishing, 1994, p. 18.

[1583] Geoffrey. J. Martin, *All Possible Worlds: A History of Geographical Ideas*, John Wiley & Sons, 1993, p. 37.

[1584] 'Eratosthenes has himself told what great advances in the knowledge of the inhabited world has been made not only by those who came after Alexander but by those of Alexander's own time'. (Strabo, *Geography,* I.3.3).

[1585] M. B. Hatzopoulos, *Philip of Macedon*, Heinemann, 1981, p. 154.

[1586] C. Nicolet, *Space, Geography, and Politics in the Early Roman Empire,* University of Michigan, 1991, p. 60–61.

[1587] Alexander the Great's tutor Aristotle thought that beyond Libya it would be hotter at the equator and life impossible. The Eukmene, temperate zone–(liveable) was in between the torrid zone and the frozen zone. He thought there was also a southern temperate zone but doubted it, as people would be 'upside-down'. Geoffrey. J. Martin, *All Possible Worlds: A History of Geographical Ideas*, John Wiley& Sons, 1993, p. 28.

Crates also showed in his Globe the world divided in four parts and one part in the south he called the Antipodes. C. Nicolet, *Space, Geography, and Politics in the Early Roman Empire,* University of Michigan, 1991, p. 63 & Fig. 25.

Captain Cook found the Australian continent south coast in 1700 yet it is still a current idea when as children in Britain we first see a globe of the earth and think of how people can live 'upside down' in Australia and not fall off the earth, until we learn about gravity. Any trip to Australia from Britain is still called colloquially 'going down under'.

[1588] J. B. Harley, and D. Woodward, *The History of Cartography: Cartography in prehistoric, ancient, and Medieval Europe and the Mediterranean*, University of Chicago Press, 1987, p. 150 n. 10.

[1589] Plutarch's Lives, *Alexander*, trans. J. Langhorne and W. Langhorne, Sir John Lubbock's Hundred Books, Routledge, 1930, p. 486.

[1590] Display boards in the Archaeological Museum, Thessaloniki, Greece August 2008.

[1591] Arrian, *History of Alexander and Indica,* vol. 2. VII. 14. 3-7, trans. E. Iliff. Robson, Heinemann, 1966, p. 251.

[1592] Arrian, *The Life of Alexander the Great*, V. 26-27, trans. Aubrey de Sélincourt, Penguin, 1958, p. 189.

[1593] *Ibid*, p. 188.

[1594] A. Stewart, *Classical Greece and the Birth of Western Art*, Cambridge, 2008, p. 277.

[1595] Arrian, *The Life of Alexander the Great*, V. 26-27, trans. Aubrey de Sélincourt, Penguin, 1958, p. 188-189.

[1596] *Ibid*, V.25-26, p. 188.

[1597] J. Elaye and J. Sapin, *Beyond the River: New Perspectives on Transeuphratene,* Sheffield Academic Press, 1991, p.98. The *Periplus of Pseudo-Skylax* is thought to have been a reconnaissance of the coasts of the Persian Empire carried out for Philip II of Macedon and therefore compiled from the exploration by Skylax the previous century.

[1598] Arrian, *History of Alexander and Indica,* vol. 2. V. 26. 1-4, trans. E. Iliff. Robson, Heinemann, 1966, p. 87.

[1599] K. Geus, 'Space and Geography', in A. Erskine (ed.), *A Companion to the Hellenistic World,* Blackwell, 2003, p. 240. (Strabo, 15.1.25; cf. Diod. 17.89. 4–5; Curt. 9.1. 3–4).

[1600] K. Geus, 'Space and Geography', in A. Erskine (ed.), *A Companion to the Hellenistic World,* Blackwell, 2003, p. 240.

[1601] Arrian, *The Life of Alexander the Great*, Bk. V.25, trans. Aubrey de Sélincourt, Penguin, 1958, p.187.

[1602] A Macedonian Assembly of the Army had not only the power to appoint a king but also to dismiss as happened with Amyntas III in 375 B.C. and acclaimed his guardian Philip II as king. N. G. L. Hammond, 'The Continuity of Macedonian Institutions and the Macedonian Kingdoms of the Hellenistic Era', *Historia: Zeitschrift für Alte Geschiichte*, vol. 49, no. 2. (2nd Qtr., 2000): 141–160, here p. 143, ['JSTOR' journal archive] <http://www.jstor.org/stable/4436574>, viewed on 28 March 2011.

[1603] In Anabasis Arrian states' history does not record for what purpose each embassy came' but says they 'were from the Greeks'. Arrian, *History of Alexander and Indica*, vol. 2. VII. 19, trans. E. Iliff Robson, Heinemann, 1966, p. 267.

[1604] Arrian, *Life of Alexander the Great*, VII, 15.4–6, trans. Aubrey De Sélincourt, Penguin Books,1958, p. 241.

[1605] M. B. Haztopoulos, (ed.), *Philip of Macedon*, Heinemann, 1981, p. 168.

[1606] Plutarch, *Lives of the Noble Grecians and Romans*, trans. T. North, Alexander the Great, 9, Wordsworth Editions Ltd, 1998, p. 393.

[1607] *Plutarch's Lives,* Alexander, trans. J. Langhorne and W. Langhorne, Sir John Lubbock's Hundred Books, Routledge, 1930, p. 462.

King Philip had arranged a marriage between Alexander's full sister Cleopatra and the King of Epirus (prince Alexander's uncle). King Philip was murdered during these wedding festivities and prince Alexander became King Alexander III of Macedon and later known as Alexander the Great. M. B. Haztopoulos, (ed.), *Philip of Macedon*, Heinemann, 1981, p. 168.

[1608] King Alexander I of Epirus (the Molossian) was invited by the Greek city of Tarentum in Italy to lead them in a war against the Messapians and Leucanians. He was killed by a Leucanian about 330 B.C. (Strabo, *Geography*, VI. 3.4.) Alexander I (the Molossian) of Epirus was made King of Epirus by King Philip II of Macedon c. 342 B.C. (Strabo, *Geography*, VI. 1.5.).

[1609] Quintus Curtius Rufus, *History of Alexander*, Bk. 10.1.17. Penguin, 2001, p. 239; see Appendix at the end of this book, section Pillars of Hercules for its location. Re. Strabo, *Geography,* Book III.5.5–6.

[1610] Arrian, *The Life of Alexander the Great*, V. 25-26, trans. Aubrey de Sélincourt, Penguin, 1958, p. 188; Arrian, *History of Alexander and Indica,* vol. 2. VII. 1. 4-2. 1., trans. E. Iliff. Robson, Heinemann, 1966, p. 207.

[1611] Strabo, *Geography,* V. 3.5. 232.

[1612] A. B. Bosworth, *From Arrian to Alexander*, Clarendon, 1988, p. 84–85.

[1613] *Ibid*, p. 185, (Will, W. Munich 1983. 112).

[1614] Arrian, *History of Alexander and Indica*, vol. 2. VII. 15. 5-16. 2., trans. E. I. Robson, Heinemann, 1966, p. 257.

[1615] Arrian, *Life of Alexander the Great*, Bk. VII.1, trans. Aubrey de Sélincourt, Penguin, 1958, p. 225.

[1616] A. B. Bosworth, *From Arrian to Alexander,* Clarendon, 1988, p. 91; Pliny, *Natural Histories,* vol. 2. Bk. III, V. 56–59, trans. H. Rackham, Heinemann, 1962, p. 45. Pliny says Rome was only mentioned by Greeks first by Theopompus as Rome taken by the Gauls; by Clitarchus when the Roman's sent an embassy to Alexander the Great; and also by Theophrastus in the 440th year of the city and gave the measurement of the island of Circello.

[1617] *Diodorus of Sicily,* Bk. 17.113, trans. C. H. Oldfather, Heinemann, 1989, ['Perseus, Tufts University' digital library] <http://www.perseus.tufts.edu/hopper/text?doc=Perseus%3Atext%3A1999.01.0084%3Abook%3D17%3Achapter%3D113#note-link3>, viewed 3 February 2012; Justin, 12.13.1–2; Arrian 7. 15.4–6 embassies from the west; 19.1–2 embassies from the Greeks.

[1618] Pompeius Trogus wrote in the first century B.C. *Justin: Epitome of the Philippic History of Pompeius Trogus*, vol.1, Book XII.13, Scholars Press Atlanta, GA, 1994, p. 119; Alexander the Great, trans. J. C. Yardley, Clarendon, 1997, p. 66.

[1619] Cineas speaks of the Roman boast that Alexander would not have been invincible if he had come into Italy, being killed in battle or driven out. Plutarch, *Selected Lives, The Lives of the Noble Grecians and Romans*, Pyrrhus, 18, trans. T. North, Wordsworth Editions, 1998, p. 210.

Livy speculated that Rome and Carthage had at that time a 'long-standing treaty' and allied together would have resisted Alexander. Also Rome fought 24 years at sea in the First Punic War and he doubted whether Alexander would have lived long enough to see a war through. But of course that would depend on being able to avoid a complete defeat while he lived. Still this shows Roman faith in their abilities to sustain a long struggle. Titus Livius, *The History of Rome*, vol. 2, trans. Rev. Canon Roberts, Dent, 1924–31, p. 184.

[1620] Titus Livius, *The History of Rome*, vol. 2, trans. Rev. Canon Roberts, Dent, 1924–31, p. 182.

[1621] Arrian, *History of Alexander and Indica*, vol. 2. VII. 27. 3-28. 3, trans. E. I. Robson, Heinemann, 1966, p. 297, VII. 4. 7-5. 3. p. 217-219, and VII. 9. 8-10. 2, p. 233.

[1622] K. Geus, 'Space and Geography', in A. Erskine (ed.), *A Companion to the Hellenistic World*, Blackwell, 2003, p. 240.

[1623] Arrian, *Life of Alexander the Great*, trans. Aubrey de Sélincourt, Penguin Classics, 1958, p. 216. Strabo using Nearchus as a source adds Semiramis with 20 and Cyrus with just 7 men had both survived crossing Gedrosia. Strabo, *Geography*, XV.2.5.

[1624] Strabo, *Geography*, XV.1.5.

[1625] L. Foreman, *Alexander: The Conqueror*, Da Capo Press, 2004, p. 188.

[1626] Strabo, *Geography*, XV.1.5.

[1627] *Justin: Epitome of the Philippic History of Pompeius Trogus*, vol.1, Book XII.13, Scholars Press, Atlanta GA, 1994, p. 119-120.

[1628] A. B. Bosworth, *From Arrian to Alexander*, Clarendon, 1988, p. 91; Coenus speaking for the army now in India wanting to go home mentions the possible future campaigns including Carthage. Arrian, *Life of Alexander the Great*, V.27, trans. Aubrey de Sélincourt, Penguin Classics, 1958, p. 190.

[1629] Plutarch, Demosthenes, 25. Plutarch, *Plutarch's Lives*, trans. B.Perrin, Heinemann, 1919. ['Perseus, Tufts university', digital library]
<http://www.perseus.tufts.edu/hopper/text?doc=Perseus%3Atext%3A2008.01.0039%3Achapter%3D27> viewed 3 February 2012.

[1630] A.W. Pickard-Cambridge, *Demosthenes*, G.P. Putnam's Sons, 1914, p. 452.

[1631] *Ibid*, p. 453 n.1. Pickard-Cambridge writes that the 'rumour is alluded to in the fragments of a satiric play named *Agen*, performed before Alexander, probably at Susa, early March 324', see Athenaeus, *Deipnosophists*, XIII.586, trans. C. B. Gulick, Heinemann, 1950, p. 163; Quintus Curtius Rufus, *The History of Alexander*, Bk. 10.2, trans. J. Yardley, Penguin, 1984, p. 241.

[1632] *Ibid*.

[1633] *Justin: Epitome of the Philippic History of Pompeius Trogus*, 13. 5.1-10, trans. J. C. Yardley, Scholars Press Atlanta, 1994, p. 127 n. 8. Plut. *Phocion* 23ff.; Plut. *Demosthenes* 27ff.; *AO* 406ff. (the years 323/2 and 321/0).

[1634] Lamian War, ['Encyclopaedia Britannica' eb.com] <http://www.britannica.com/EBchecked/topic/328715/Lamian-War> viewed 2 February 2012; Plutarch, Demosthenes, 27. Plutarch, *Plutarch's Lives*, trans. B. Perrin, Heinemann, 1919. ['Perseus, Tufts university', digital library]
<http://www.perseus.tufts.edu/hopper/text?doc=Perseus%3Atext%3A2008.01.0039%3Achapter%3D27> viewed 3 February 2012; Also Phocion tried to stop Harpalus's bribery of Athenians and when Antipater demanded his surrender Harpalus fled to Crete where he was assassinated. Plutarch, Phocion, 21.3-22.2. Plutarch, *Plutarch's Lives*, trans. B. Perrin, Heinemann, 1919. ['Perseus, Tufts university', digital library]

<http://www.perseus.tufts.edu/hopper/text?doc=Perseus%3Atext%3A2008.01.0039%3Achapter%3D27> viewed 3 February 2012; Curtius says he was sent away by an 'assembly of the people'. Quintus Curtius Rufus, *The History of Alexander*, Bk. 10.2, trans. J. Yardley, Penguin, 1984, p. 241; C. W. Blackwell, 'Athens and Macedonia in the Absence of Alexander,' in C.W. Blackwell, (ed.), *Demos: Classical Athenian Democracy*, (R. Scaife, (ed.), The Stoa: a consortium for electronic publication in the humanities, edition of July 1, 2005) [www.stoa.org].
<http://www.stoa.org/projects/demos/article_alexander?page=4&greekEncoding=>, viewed 3 February 2012.

[1635] A. B. Bosworth, *From Arrian to Alexander*, Clarendon, 1988, p. 185.

[1636] *Ibid.*

Perdiccas may have acted quickly because Craterus was with 10,000 veterans returning to Macedonia to replace the regent Antipater and building a fleet of 100 triremes on the coast of Cilicia on Alexander's orders 'in advance'. A. B. Bosworth, *From Arrian to Alexander*. Clarendon Press, 1988, p. 209–210.

[1637] A. B. Bosworth, *From Arrian to Alexander*. Clarendon Press, 1988, p. 210–211. Bosworth's note 98, Craterus was taking 10,000 veterans back to Macedonia to replace the Regent Antipater who was to go Alexander with replacement troops. Diodorus Siculus wrote that Craterus was sent 'in advance'. ετυχε προεσταλμενος εις Κιλικιαν (4.1) ουτος γαρ προεσταλμενος εις Κιλικιαν (12.1) Bosworth's note 99: A favourite verb of Diodorus used some 20 times to refer to an individual or group sent as a forerunner of a greater enterprise and 3 times for the Macedonian advance force sent to Asia Minor in 336 B.C. (xvi. 91.2, 93.9; xvii. 2.4). Bosworth continues that Craterus' apparent delay in Cilicia was not suspicious but the fulfilment of Alexander's orders for Alexander's next project of Mediterranean war.

[1638] J. B. Harley and D. Woodward, *The History of Cartography: Cartography in prehistoric, ancient, and Medieval Europe and the Mediterranean*, University of Chicago Press, 1987, p. 151 n. 24.

[1639] L. Foreman, *Alexander: The Conqueror*, Da Capo Press, 2004, p. 157.

[1640] *Ibid*, p. 57.

[1641] Demosthenes, *Speeches,* 18.67, ['Perseus, Tufts University' digital library]
<http://perseus.uchicago.edu/perseus-cgi/citequery3.pl?dbname=GreekTexts&query=Dem.%2018.67&getid=1>, viewed on 16 March 2011.

[1642] E. M. Anson, 'The Evolution of the Macedonian Assembly (330–315 B.C.)'. *Historia: Zeitschrift für Alte Geschiichte.* Vol. 40, No. 2 (1991): 230–247, here p. 238. Franz Steiner Verlag, ['JSTOR' journal archive] <http://www.jstor.org/stable/4436191>, viewed on 24 April 2011.

[1643] N. G. L. Hammond, 'Literary Evidence for Macedonian Speech'. *Historia: Zeitschrift für Alte Geschichte.* Vol. 43, No. 2, (2nd Qtr. 1994): 131–142, here p. 136 & p. 138, (Curt. 8.5.7), ['JSTOR' journal archive] <http://www.jstor.org/stable4436322>, viewed on 28 March 2011.

[1644] Arrian, *The Life of Alexander the Great*, Book 7.15, trans. Aubrey de Sélincourt, Penguin, 1984. p.241

[1645] Quintus Curtis Rufus, *History of Alexander*, Book 10.1.17, trans. J. Yardley, Penguin, 2001, p. 239.

[1646] Arrian, *History of Alexander and Indica*, vol. 2. VII. 7.19. 3-5, trans. E. I. Robson, Heinemann, 1966, p. 269.

[1647] Quintus Curtis Rufus, *History of Alexander*, Book 4.3.19, trans. J. Yardley, Penguin, 1984, p. 58.

[1648] *Ibid.*

[1649] *Justin: Epitome of the Philippic History of Pompeius Trogus,* 11.10.14, trans. J. C. Yardley, Scholars Press Atlanta, 1994, p. 103.

[1650] Quintus Curtius Rufus, *The History of Alexander*, Bk. 4. 4.18–19, trans. J. Yardley, Penguin, 2001, p. 61.

[1651] Lacus Curtius, Strabo, *Geography,* VI. 2. ['Penelope, University of Chicago' digital library']
<http://penelope.uchicago.edu/Thayer/E/Roman/Texts/Strabo/6A*.html>, viewed on 10 October 2011.

[1652] Thucydides, *History of the Peloponnesian War,* I.15. ['Perseus, Tufts University', digital library] <http://www.perseus.tufts.edu/hopper/text?doc=Perseus%3Atext%3A1999.01.0247%3Abook%3D1%3Achapter%3D15 >, viewed on 25 October 2011.

[1653] G. W. Bromiley, *The International Standard Bible Encyclopaedia*, vol. IV, W. M. Eerdman Publishing Co., 1988, p. 385; Rickard, J. (4 July 2007), *Seleucus I Nicator (358–280)*, <http://www.historyofwar.org/articles/people_seleucus_I_nicator.html>, viewed on 20 September 2011.

[1654] Strabo, *Geography,* VII. Fr. 21 & 24. ['Perseus, Tufts University' digital library] <http://www.perseus.tufts.edu/hopper/text?doc=Perseus%3Atext%3A1999.01.0198%3Abook%3D7%3Achapter%3Dfragments%3Asection%3D21>, viewed on 22 March 2011.

[1655] A. Trevor. Hodge, *Ancient Greek France,* University of Pennsylvania Press, 1999, p. 111.

[1656] R. L. Fox, 'Hellenistic Culture and Literature', ch. 14, in J. Boardman, J. Griffin, and O. Murray, (eds.), *Greece and the Hellenistic World,* Oxford University Press, 2001, p. 404.

[1657] M. Clerc, *Massalia. Histoire de Marseille dans l'antiquité des origines à la fin de l'Empire romain d'Occident (476 ap. J.-C.)*, TOME 1, Des origins jusqu 'au IIIme siècle av. J.-C. Marseille, Librairie A. Tacussel, 1927, p. 403 "une véritable célébrité s'etait attachée au gnomon qu'il avait fait construire, á Marseille, afin de déterminer la latitude exacte de celle ville" from A. Trevor. Hodge, Ancient Greek France. p. 265 n. 15; C. R. Markham, 'Pytheas, the Discoverer of Britain', Geographical Journal, Blackwell Publishers on behalf of *The Royal Geographical Society* (with The Institute of British Geographers) vol.1. no. 6 (Jun., 1893): 504–524, here p. 512, ['JSTOR' journal archive] <http://www.jstor.org/stable/1773964>, viewed on 25 August 2011;

There were other large permanent sundials set up like the one by Augustus Caesar at Campus Martius based on that invented by Aristarchos of Samos. P. Rahak and J. G. Younger, *Imperium and Cosmos Augustus and the Northern Campus Martius*, The University of Wisconsin Press, 2006, p. 63–64.

[1658] V. Stefansson *Great Adventurers and Explorations: from the earliest times to the present, as told by the explorers themselves,* Robert Hale Ltd., 1947, p. 12; C. R. Markham, 'Pytheas, the Discoverer of Britain', *The Geographical Journal*, Blackwell Publishers on behalf of The Royal Geographical Society (with The Institute of British Geographers) vol.1, no. 6 (Jun., 1893):504–524, here p. 512, ['JSTOR' journal archive] <http://www.jstor.org/stable/1773964>, viewed on 25 August 2011.

[1659] Pliny, *Natural Histories*, Book V.I.8–1, trans. H. Rackham, Loeb, William Heinemann, 1942, p. 225.

[1660] Strabo, *Geography,* XVII.1.12.

[1661] A. L. F. Rivet, *Gallia Narbonensis,* Batsford, 1988, p. 33 n. 33; F. W. Wallbank, *A Historical Commentary on Polybius*, vol. I. (revised edition) 1970, p. 4 n. 10, III.48.12. p. 383. Probably in 151 B.C. as he had gone to Spain with Scipio who was Legatus to the Consul. Though Wallbank thinks Polybius had made a mistake thinking the Alps began a little to the north of Massalia. Wallbank thought the route was through Liguria and over the Apenines by passes north of Genoa. (Wallbank, vol. 1. II.32.1 p. 207).

[1662] C. Porter, *A Guide to Greek Thought*, Belknap Press of Harvard University, 2003, p. 194–195.

[1663] Polybius, XII.14.27.

[1664] C. Porter, *A Guide to Greek Thought*, Belknap Press of Harvard University, 2003, p. 194–195.

[1665] J. B. Harley and D. Woodward, *The History of Cartography: Cartography in prehistoric, ancient, and Medieval Europe and the Mediterranean,* University of Chicago Press, 1987, p.164; C. Nicolet, *Space, Geography, and Politics in the Early Roman Empire*, University of Michigan, 1991, p. 63 & Fig. 25, Map of Crates globe from K. Miller.

[1666] Strabo, *Geography,* III.4.4.

[1667] Geminos's, *Introduction to the Phenomena: a translation and study of a Hellenistic survey of astronomy*, On Day and Night (VI 9–VI 22), trans. J. Evans and J. L. Berggren, Princeton University Press, 2006, p. 163, Homer, Odyssey, X, 82–86; Sir Thomas, L. Heath, *Greek Astronomy*, Geminos of Rhodes, Dover, 1991, p. 132–133.

[1668] Geminos's, *Introduction to the Phenomena: a translation and study of a Hellenistic survey of astronomy*, On Day and Night (VI 9–VI 22), trans. J. Evans and J. L. Berggren, Princeton University Press, 2006, p. 162-4.

[1669] Pliny the Elder, *Natural Histories,* vol. 2. Book V.I.8–1, trans. H. Rackham, Loeb, William Heinemann, 1962, p. 225.

[1670] Polybius, *The Histories,* vol. 2. Bk. 3. 58.8–59.7., trans. W. R. Paton, Loeb, 1980, p. 141.

[1671] Pliny the Elder, *Natural Histories*, 2. 169. Polybius does mention Hamilco and Hanno. Arrian mentions Hanno. Arrian, *History of Alexander and Indica,* vol. 2. VIII. (Indica) 43. 5-13, trans. E. Iliff. Robson, Heinemann, 1966, p. 433.

[1672] Polybius, *The Histories*, vol. 2. Bk. 3. 58.8–59.7, trans. W. R. Paton, Loeb, 1980, p. 141.

[1673] *Ibid*, vol. 2. Bk. 3. 56.6–57.7, p. 137.

[1674] *Ibid*.

[1675] *Plutarch's Lives,* Julius Caesar, trans. J. Langhorne and W. Langhorne, Sir John Lubbock's Hundred Books, Routledge, 1930, p. 497.

[1676] B. Cunliffe, *The Extraordinary Voyage of Pytheas the Greek: The man who discovered Britain,* Penguin Books, 2002, p. 167.

[1677] Strabo is known as a geographer but could equally have been known as a historian as he had written before *Historical Sketches* in forty-seven books which does not survive (*The Geography of Strabo*, Loeb, 1917, p. xxix, ['Penelope, University of Chicago' digital Library] <http://penelope.uchicago.edu/Thayer/E/Roman/Texts/Strabo/Introduction*.html>, viewed 6 June 2012) only in quotations from Strabo, Josephus and other ancient authors. *From Hyrcanus to Salome*, Gnaeus Pompey and the End of Jewish Independence (67-51 B.C), 1, Last modified 03/23/12, ['Crandall University' Canada] <http://www.abu.nb.ca/courses/ntintro/intest/Hist5.htm>, viewed 6 June 2012.

[1678] C. H. Roseman, *Pytheas of Massalia: On the Ocean: Text, Translation and Commentary,* Ares Publishers, 1994, p. 51; Strabo, *Geography*, I.2.18.

[1679] Strabo, *Geography,* IV. 5.5.

[1680] *The Geography of Strabo*, Loeb, 1917, p. xviii, ['Penelope, University of Chicago' digital Library] <http://penelope.uchicago.edu/Thayer/E/Roman/Texts/Strabo/Introduction*.html>, viewed 6 June 2012.

[1681] C. H. Roseman, *Pytheas of Massalia: On the Ocean: Text, Translation and Commentary,* Ares Publishers, 1994, p. 72-73.

[1682] *Ibid*, p. 47.

[1683] *Ibid*.

[1684] Strabo, *Geography*, IV.2. 4.

[1685] *Ibid*, II. 5.34. ['Penelope, University of Chicago' digital library] <http://penelope.uchicago.edu/Thayer/E/Roman/Texts/Strabo/2E2*.html>, viewed on 17 October 2011.

[1686] C. H. Roseman, *Pytheas of Massalia: On the Ocean: Text, Translation and Commentary,* Ares Publishers, 1994, p. 35.

[1687] *Ibid*, Strabo, *Geography*, II.5.34.

[1688] J. O. Thomson, *History of Ancient Geography*, Cambridge, 1948, p. 321–322; Geoffrey. J. Martin, *All Possible Worlds: A History of Geographical Ideas*, John Wiley & Sons, 1993, p. 36.

[1689] Strabo, *Geography*, I.3.22.

[1690] *Ibid*, II.1.13.

[1691] Caesar, *The Gallic War*, trans. H. J. Edwards, Dover Publications, 2006, p. xi–xii. With the surrender of Vercingetorix in 52 B.C. the wars in Gaul were virtually over and Caesar decided to compile from his various notebooks of the campaigns of Britain and Gaul into one volume. R. C. Carrington, *Caesar's Invasions of Britain*, Alpha Classics, G. Bell & Sons, 1952, p. 11-12, (*Gallic War*, Book IV, ch. 20–Book V, ch. 24).

[1692] Strabo, *Geography*, II.1.13. <http://penelope.uchicago.edu/Thayer/E/Roman/Texts/Strabo/2A1*.html> 8 Nov, 2013.

[1693] C. H. Roseman, *Pytheas of Massalia: On the Ocean: Text, Translation and Commentary*, Ares Publishers, 1994, p. 132, Strabo, Geography, II.5.8.

[1694] J. O. Thomson, *History of Ancient Geography*, Cambridge, 1948, p. 321–322; Geoffrey. J. Martin, *All Possible Worlds: A History of Geographical Ideas*, John Wiley & Sons, 1993, p. 36.

[1695] Arrian, *History of Alexander and Indica,* vol. 2, VIII, (Indica) 43. 5–13, trans. E. Iliff. Robson, Heinemann, 1966, p. 433; M. Mund-Dopchie, 'Hanno' in V. Brown (ed.), *Catalogus Translationum Et Commentariorum: Medieval and Rennaisance Latin Translations and Commentaries, Annotated Lists and Guides*, Vol.3, The Catholic University Press of America, (2003):49-56.

[1696] Geoffrey. J. Martin, *All Possible Worlds: A History of Geographical Ideas*, Oxford, 2005, p. 36. Even with all the great discoveries the ancient Greeks had made, with the ideas of Thales, Plato, Aristotle, Pythagoras and all the philosophers scientists and astronomers, it is remarkable that much of the population still held on to their religion, myths and superstitions. Alexander the Great, a pupil of Aristotle, was very much up with the latest developments and thinking but also lived his life with the ancient Myths as real i.e. Herakles. It seems even today that it is the technology that changes and used readily, but that human beings change very little in taking on new ideas, like climate change and global warming, making slow progress, though progress it does make particularly among the young.

[1697] Plutarch, *Selected Lives,* Julius Caesar, 63, Wordsworth Editions Ltd., 1998, p. 488.

[1698] Strabo, *Geography*, I.4.3. n. 192 "Eratosthenes own figure of 700 stadia to the degree, we get 12,950 stadia; since he calculates the distance at 11,500, we might conclude that he puts Thule at 62° 55'. The southern coast of Iceland extends to 63° 25'." Lacus Curtius, Strabo's Geography, Bk. I. 4, page 4 of 4, *The Geography of Strabo*, vol.1. Loeb Classical Library Edition, 1923, ['Penelope, University of Chicago' digital library] <http://penelope.uchicago.edu/Thayer/E/Roman/Texts/Strabo/1D*.html>, viewed on 25 August 2011.

[1699] V. Stefansson *Ultima Thule*, George Harrap & Co., p. 61, 194, p. 68.

[1700] C. H. Roseman, *Pytheas of Massalia: On the Ocean: Text, Translation and Commentary,* Ares Publishers, 1994, p. 35.

[1701] Strabo (id.II.4.1–3, C104), on Pytheas in *Polybius*, vol. 6, Bk. XXXIV. 5. 9, trans. W. R. Paton, Heinemann, 1980, p. 307; C. H. Roseman, *Pytheas of Massalia: On the Ocean, Text, Translation and Commentary,* Ares Publishing, 1994, p. 48-49., Strabo, *Geography*, 2.4.1-2.

[1702] Pliny the Elder researched 2,000 books to write his *Natural Histories*. He published his sources and Strabo is not among them. A copy of Strabo's, *Geography*, was found six centuries later A.D. and became known. Geoffrey. J. Martin, *All Possible Worlds: A History of Geographical Ideas*, John Wiley & Sons, 1993, p. 37.

[1703] Strabo, *Geography,* III. 4.19.

[1704] C. H. Roseman, *Pytheas of Massalia: On the Ocean, Text, Translation and Commentary,* Ares Publishing, 1994, p. 7–9.

[1705] *Ibid*, p. 15-16.

[1706] A realisation of what Pytheas had achieved started again modern time with Sir Clements Markham, naval officer, polar explorer, president of the Royal Geographical Society in his article 'Pytheas the Discoverer of Britain', Geographical Journal, June 1893, in V. Stefansson, *Great Adventures and Explorations*, Robert Hale Ltd., 1947, p. 4; C. R. Markham, 'Pytheas, the Discoverer of Britain', *The Geographical Journal*, Blackwell Publishers on behalf of The Royal Geographical Society (with The Institute of British Geographers) vol.1, no. 6 (Jun., 1893):504–524, here p. 512, ['JSTOR' journal archive] <http://www.jstor.org/stable/1773964>, viewed on 25 August 2011.

[1707] Caesar was thought to have referred to Mona as the Isle of Man but by Pliny's time (Pliny, *N.H.* 4.103) was recorded as Monapia (Roseman, 1994, p. 77–79 & p. 89) and the Isle of Anglesey was called Mona (Rivet and Smith, p. 410–11 & p. 419–420) both or either are likely to have come from Pytheas.

[1708] B. Cunliffe, *The Extraordinary Voyage of Pytheas the Greek: The man who discovered Britain*, Penguin Books, 2002, p. 96–97.

[1709] C. H. Roseman, *Pytheas of Massalia, On the Ocean, Text, Translation and Commentary*, Ares Publishing, 1994, p. 103; B. Cunliffe, *The Extraordinary Voyage of Pytheas the Greek: The man who discovered Britain*, Penguin Books, 2002, Ch. 5.p. 109.

[1710] B. Cunliffe, *The Extraordinary Voyage of Pytheas the Greek: The man who discovered Britain*, Penguin Books, 2002, p.147.

[1711] Strabo, *Geography*, I.4.5 & IV.4.1; C. H. Roseman, *Pytheas of Massalia, On the Ocean, Text, Translation and Commentary*, Ares Publishing, 1994, p. 38–39, p. 67–68, p. 123–124.

[1712] Seneca, *Natural Quaestiones*, Vol. 2. VII. 25, 2–5, trans. T. H. Corcoran, Loeb, 1962, p. 279.

[1713] C. H. Roseman, *Pytheas of Massalia, On the Ocean, Text, Translation and Commentary*, Ares Publishing, 1994, p.117, Hipparkhos of Nikaia, *Commentary on the "Phenomena" of Aratos and* Eudoxos, 1.4.1, (Manitius);Strabo, *Geography*, IV. 5.5; B. Cunliffe, *The Extraordinary Voyage of Pytheas the Greek: The man who discovered Britain*, Penguin Books, 2002, p. 62-64.

[1714] M. Cary and E. H. Warmington, *The Ancient Explorers*, Methuen, 1929, p. 33.

[1715] B. Cunliffe, *The Extraordinary Voyage of Pytheas the Greek: The man who discovered Britain*, Penguin Books, 2002, p. 1–2.

[1716] Strabo, *Geography*, II. 4.1–2 n. 33.

[1717] From the ninth century A.D. some book parchments were skimmed by the Byzantines and reused. There was an exciting discovery of the 'Archimedes Palimpsest' that includes underneath the later writing some ancient texts of Archimedes and Hyperides being revealed by the Stanford Synchrotron Radiation Laboratory. Mary. K. Miller, 'Reading Between the Lines', Smithsonian Magazine March 2007, <http://www.smithsonianmag.com/science-nature/archimedes.html>, viewed on 12 February 2011.

[1718] Diodorus Siculus, *Histories*, V.22.4.

[1719] Geminos's, *Introduction to the Phenomena: a translation and study of a Hellenistic survey of astronomy*, VI. 9, trans. J. Evans, and J. Lennart. Berggren, Princeton University Press, 2006, p. 162.

[1720] C. F. C. Hawkes, *Pytheas: Europe and the Greek Explorers*, Oxford, 1975, p. 44.

[1721] R. Gardiner, (ed.), *The Age of the Galley*, Conway Maritime Press, 1995, p. 48.

[1722] C. H. Roseman. *Pytheas of Massalia, On the Ocean, Text, Translation and Commentary*, Ares Publishing, 1994, p. 149.

[1723] E. Guhl and W. Koner, *The Greeks; Their Life and Customs*, Senate, 1994, p. 256; see also the method used in R. Gardiner, (ed.), *The Age of the Galley*, Conway Maritime Press, 1995, p. 64.

[1724] R. Carpenter, *Beyond the Pillars of Hercules: The classical world seen through the eyes of is discoverers*, Tandem Press (UK), 1973, p. 152.

[1725] R. Gardiner, *The Earliest Ships: The Evolution of Boats into Ships*, Conway Maritime Press, 1996, p. 55.

[1726] *Ibid*; D. Alberge, 'Bronze age man's lunch' *The Observer*. 6 Bronze Age dugout boats found in Cambridgeshire. <http://www.guardian.co.uk/science/2011/dec/04/bronze-age-archaeology-fenland> viewed 7 March 2013.

[1727] B. Cunliffe, *The Extraordinary Voyage of Pytheas the Greek: The man who discovered Britain*, Penguin Books, 2002, p. 103–105.

[1728] Caesar, *The Civil War*, I.54, trans. J. Carter, Oxford World's Classics, 1998, p. 32.

[1729] *Ibid.*

[1730] Lucan, *Civil War*, IV.131–135, trans. Susan. H. Braund, Oxford World's Classics, 1999, p. 66.

[1731] C. H. Roseman, *Pytheas of Massalia, On the Ocean, Text, Translation and Commentary*, Ares Publishing, 1994, p. 91–92, Pliny the Elder, *Natural Histories*, IV. 104.

[1732] Due to the insatiable demand for books several texts were faked including attributing works to Aristotle. R. L. Fox, 'Hellenistic Culture and Literature', ch. 14 in J. Boardman, J. Griffin, O. Murray, *Greece and the Hellenistic World*, Oxford University Press, 2001, p. 392.

The mention of Albion and Irene in the treatise De Mundo has no claim to be written by Aristotle according to Wilhelm Capelle (Neue Jahrbucher, xv (1905) pp. 529–68) who traced most of its doctrines to Posidonius and founded on two popular treatises, Meteorogiki Stoechesis and the Peri Kosmon. 'In this sea are situated two very large islands, the so called British Isles, Albion and Irene which are greater than any which we have mentioned and lie beyond the land of the Celts'. A possible date is between the second half the first century A.D. and the first half of the second century A.D. Capelle thought that the dedication to Alexander is intended to Tiberius Claudius Alexander, the nephew of Philo Judaeus and Procurator of Judea, and Procurator of Egypt in A.D. 67. 'De Mundo', trans. E. S. Forrester, Clarendon Press, 1914, p. 392–393, in *Works of Aristotle in English*, vol. III, Clarendon Press, Oxford, 1931.

[1733] B. Cunliffe, *The Extraordinary Voyage of Pytheas the Greek: The man who discovered Britain*, Penguin Books, 2002. p. 154–155.

[1734] C. H. Roseman, *Pytheas of Massalia, On the Ocean, Text, Translation and Commentary*, Ares Publishing, 1994, p. 7–8; B. Cunliffe, *The Extraordinary Voyage of Pytheas the Greek: The man who discovered Britain*, Penguin Books, 2002, p. 154–155.

[1735] R. L. Fox, 'Hellenistic Culture and Literature', ch. 14, in J. Boardman, J. Griffin, O. Murray, *Greece and the Hellenistic World*, Oxford University Press, 2001. p. 392.

Just as the Imperial powers of the nineteenth century sought to have a great museum with artefacts from the ancient world, the Hellenistic kingdoms had to have libraries not only as a practical store of knowledge but equally the tremendous prestige and a mark of their cultural appreciation of civilization.

[1736] C. H. Roseman, *Pytheas of Massalia, On the Ocean, Text, Translation and Commentary*, Ares Publishing, 1994, p. 8.

[1737] J. Liversidge, *Everyday Life in the Roman Empire*, Batsford, 1976, p. 80.

[1738] Keeping secrets amongst groups and cults were rife e.g. despite many initiates we still know little about the Eleusinian Mysteries. Hippasus discovered the value of irrational number and wanted to make it known whereas the Pythagorean sect he belonged to wanted to keep it secret. Some say it was they who killed him for sharing his discovery.

Hippasus of Metapontium, <http://www.britannica.com/EB.C.hecked/topic/266577/Hippasus-of-Metapontum>, viewed on 26 August 2011.

[1739] C. H. Roseman, *Pytheas of Massalia, On the Ocean, Text, Translation and Commentary*, Ares Publishing, 1994, p. 65–66, (Strabo, IV.2.1.). Julius Caesar in first century B.C. met with same lack of information when questioning Gauls. (*Gallic Wars*, IV. 20–21) C. H. Roseman, *Pytheas of Massalia, On the Ocean, Text, Translation and Commentary*, Ares Publishing, 1994, p. 66.

[1740] G. Shipley, *Pseudo-Skylax: The Circumnavigation of the Inhabited World-Text, Translation and Commentary*, 2-4, Bristol Phoenix Press, 2011, p. 17.

[1741] C. H. Roseman, *Pytheas of Massalia, On the Ocean, Text, Translation and Commentary*, Ares Publishing, 1994, p. 4.

[1742] Lacus Curtius, *Strabo's Geography,* II.1.18 ['Penelope, University of Chicago' digital library] <http://penelope.uchicago.edu/Thayer/E/Roman/Texts/Strabo/2A1*.html>, viewed on 8 January 2007; C. H. Roseman. *Pytheas of Massalia, On the Ocean, Text, Translation and Commentary*, Ares Publishing, 1994, p. 42–45.

[1743] R. Carpenter, *Beyond the Pillars of Hercules: The classical world seen through the eyes of its discoverers*, Tandem Press (UK), 1973, p. 191.

[1744] C. H. Roseman, *Pytheas of Massalia, On the Ocean, Text, Translation and Commentary*, Ares Publishing, 1994, p. 4 and p. 42, p. 43 n. 29, and p.-44, Strabo, *Geography*, II.1.18.

[1745] B. Cunliffe, *The Extraordinary Voyage of Pytheas the Greek: The man who discovered Britain,* Penguin Books, 2002, p. 123–124.

[1746] *Ibid.*

[1747] *Ibid*, p. 124.

[1748] Herodotus, *Histories,* VI.11–12. trans G. Rawlinson, Wordsworth Classics, 1996, p. 452

[1749] D. Gutas, *Greek Thought, Arab Culture: The Graeco-Arabic movement in Baghdad and early 'Abbasid Society* (2nd–$4^{th}/8^{th}$–10th), (Arab Thought and Culture), Routledge, 1998, p. 1.

[1750] *Ibid*, p. 13. The Abbasids learned how to make paper from Chinese artisans they had captured at the Battle of Talas River A.D. 751. K. Szczepanski, *Invention of Paper,* ['About.com'] <http://asianhistory.about.com/od/chineseinventions/p/Invention-of-Paper.htm>, viewed on 28 June 2012.

[1751] D. Sobel, *Longitude,* Fourth Estate Publishers, 1998, p. 12.

[1752] *Ibid*, p. 16.

[1753] See the displays at the Royal Observatory, Greenwich, London, U.K.

[1754] *Ibid.*

[1755] See Royal Observatory, Greenwich, London, U.K.; also Dr D. P. Stern, *Latitude and Longitude*, [From Stargazers to Starships], last updated 9–17–2004, <http://www-istp.gsfc.nasa.gov/stargaze/Slatlong.htm>, viewed on 20 October 2011.

[1756] M. Grant, *The Rise of the Greeks*, Ch. 6, Phoenix, 2005, p. 251.

[1757] Strabo, *Geography,* V.3.3.

[1758] S. Perowne, *Roman Mythology*, Hamlyn, 1969, p.14, & p. 48.

[1759] Strabo, *Geography,* V. 3.3.

[1760] *Diodorus of Sicily,* XIV. 92. 3-93. 5, trans. C. H. Oldfather, Heinemann, 1954, p. 259.

[1761] A. Momigliano, *Alien Wisdom: The Limits of Hellenization*, 1990, Cambridge University Press, 1990, (Dio.14.93.4; App. Ital. 8.11).

[1762] J. Lendering, *Varronian Chronology*, revised 6 November 2010, ['Livius.org'] <http://www.livius.org/cg-cm/chronology/varro.html>, viewed 26 October 2011; J. Lendering, *Marcus Furius Camillus* (3), ['Livius.org'] <http://www.livius.org/fo-fz/furius/camillus2.html#Veii>, viewed on 26 October 2011.

[1763] J. Lendering, *Marcus Furius Camillus* (3), ['Livius.org'] <http://www.livius.org/fo-fz/furius/camillus2.html#Veii>, viewed 26 October 2011. Veii was under siege for ten years.

[1764] *Diodorus of Sicily,* XIV. 92. 3-93. 5, trans. C. H. Oldfather, Heinemann, 1954, p. 259.

[1765] Cicero, *Pro Balbo,* XIII. viii. 21–ix, 23, trans. R. Gardiner, Loeb, 1961, p. 651, Note c.

[1766] Plutarch, *Camillus,* 8, trans. B. Perrin, Loeb, 1914, p. 115.

[1767] J. H. Thiel, *A History of Roman Sea-Power Before the Second Punic War,* North Holland Publishing Co., Amsterdam, 1954, p. 6-7.

[1768] *Diodorus of Sicily,* XIV. 92. 3-93. 5, trans. C. H. Oldfather, Heinemann, 1954, p. 259.

[1769] M. B. Hatzopoulos, (ed.), *Philip of Macedon*, Heinemann, 1981, p. 86.

[1770] H. W. Parke, *Greek Oracles,* Hutchinson & Co Ltd, 1972, Ch.12, p. 130.

[1771] Strabo, *Geography,* IV.1.5.

[1772] S. Goldhill, 'Artemis and Cultural Identity in Empire Culture: how to think about polytheism, now?' in D. Konstan and S. Saïd, *Greeks on Greekness: Viewing the Past Under the Roman Empire*, Cambridge Classical Journal Proceedings of the Cambridge Philosophical Society, Supplementary Volume 29, 2006, p. 141.

[1773] Polybius, *The Histories*, vol. 2. Bk. III, 22.3, trans. W. R. Paton, Heinemann, 1922, p. 55.

[1774] *Ibid.*

[1775] *Ibid*, vol. 2. III. 26.1.

[1776] I. Scott-Kilvert, *Polybius The Rise of the Roman Empire*, Penguin, Books, 1981, Bk. III. 23, p. 200 n. 4, Lesser Syrtes in the Gulf of Gabes south of Carthage; 'Emporia, it forms the shore of the lesser Syrtis', Roman History, Titus Livius, *Livy,* 10. XXXIV.62, <http://thriceholy.net/Texts/Livy10.html>, viewed on 28 August 2011.

[1777] Polybius, *The Histories,* vol. 2. Bk. III, 23.2-3, trans. W. R. Paton, Heinemann, 1922, p. 57.

[1778] *Ibid*, p. 57.

[1779] F. W. Wallbank, *A Historical Commentary on Polybius,* vol. 1. Book I. 10.5. Oxford, 1957, p. 59.

[1780] Strabo, *Geography,* XVII.1.19.

[1781] Lendering is 'almost certain' that the real date would seem to be 387/386 B.C. see J. Lendering, *Varronian Chronology*, revised 6 November 2010, ['Livius.org'] <http://www.livius.org/cg-cm/chronology/varro.html> viewed on26 October 2011.

[1782] A. L. F. Rivet, *Gallia Narbonensis,* Batsford, 1988, p. 11, n 21, Justin XLIII, 4, 7–5.10.

[1783] *Justin: Epitome of the Philippic History of Pompeius Trogus*, 43.5.8–10, trans. J. C. Yardley, Scholars Press Atlanta, 1994, p. 269. Caerea had the reputation amongst the Greeks as a brave and righteous city. The Caeretani 'defeated those Galatae who had captured Rome' (390 B.C.), attacking them on the way back taking as their booty 'what the Romans had willingly given them'. They saved all those who fled from Rome for refuge; the immortal fire; and the priestesses of Vesta. The Romans gave the Caeretani the right of citizenship but did not enrol them among the citizens, relegating them with the others who had no share in equal rights to the 'Tablets of the Caeretani.' (Strabo, Book V.2.3). Any Roman citizens being disenfranchised by the Censor were enrolled in the "Tabulae Caeritum." (Strabo, Book V.2.3. Thayer's Note 79). Caerea was formerly called Agylla and founded by the Pelasgi from Thessaly in Greece. Strabo, Book V.2.3. ['Penelope, University of Chicago' digital library] <http://penelope.uchicago.edu/Thayer/E/Roman/Texts/Strabo/3B*.html>, viewed on 25 August 2011.

[1784] *Justin: Epitome of the Philippic History of Pompeius Trogus*, 20.5.6, trans. J. C. Yardley, Scholars Press Atlanta, GA, 1994, p. 167.

[1785] *Ibid*, 20.4.6, p. 167.

[1786] *Ibid*, 20.5 12–13, p. 168.

[1787] J. H. Thiel, *A History of Roman Sea-Power Before the Second Punic War*, North Holland Publishing Co., Amsterdam, 1954, p. 86 n.73.

[1788] *Ibid*, p. 86 n.77.

[1789] F. W. Wallbank, *A Historical Commentary on Polybius*, Oxford, 1957, vol.1. 1.23. 2–10 p. 79, (Thiel, *Hist*, 84–86).

[1790] F. Meijer, *A History of Seafaring in the Classical World*, Croom Helm, 1986, p. 155.

[1791] Polybius, *The Histories*, Bk.1, 21, trans. W. R. Paton, Loeb, 1922, p. 63.

[1792] *Ibid*, Bk.1, 23, p. 65.

[1793] F. W. Wallbank, *A Historical Commentary on Polybius*, vol.1. 1.20.14. Oxford, 1957, p. 75.

[1794] Sir Isaac F. R. Cowell, *Cicero and the Roman Republic*, Pitman & Sons Ltd, 1948, p. 26.

[1795] H. H. Scullard, *A History of the Roman World 753–146 B.C.* Routledge, 1991, p.196. Polybius records the terms of peace of the First Punic War were: 20,000 Euboean talents. This was reduced to half by the 10 commissioners sent to Carthage then they added 1,000 talents to the indemnity and evacuation of all the islands between Sicily and Italy. (Polybius, *Histories,* vol.1, Bk.1. 63, 3).

[1796] Polybius, *The Histories,* vol. 1, Bk.2. 13.5–7, trans. W. R. Paton, Heinemann, 1922, p. 271–273.

[1797] *Ibid*.

[1798] *Ibid*.

[1799] P. B. Ellis, *The Celtic Empire: The First Millennium of Celtic History,* Constable, 1990, p. 47.

[1800] J. Lendering, *Hamilcar Barca*, ['Livius.Org'], revised 17 July 2010, <http://www.livius.org/ha-hd/hamilcar/hamilcar2.html> viewed on 25 August 2011.

[1801] R. Olmos and T. Tortosa, 'Appendix: The Case of the Lady of Elche: a Review Article', in *Ancient Greeks West and East,* G. R. Tsetskhladze (ed.), (Brill, 1999): 352–360 p. 354.

[1802] *Appian Wars of the Romans in Iberia,* 7.25. translated from the Greek by J. S. Richardson, Aris & Phillips Ltd., 2000; *Appian's Roman History*. vol.1. Ch. 1.2, trans. H. White, Heinemann, 1912, p. 307.

[1803] P. Rouillard, 'Greeks in the Iberian Peninsula', in M. Dietler, and C. Lopez-Ruiz, (eds.), *Colonial Encounters in Ancient Iberia: Phoenicians, Greek, and Indigenous Relations,* (University of Chicago Press, 2009): 131–154, here p.

141; For fuller discussion see A. Badie, et al, *Le site antique de la Picola à Santa Pola (Alicante, Espagne)*, Éditions des Recherche sur le civilisations, Casa del Velaquez, 2000. <http://www.casadevelazquez.org/publications/librairie-en-ligne/livre/le-site-antique-de-la-picola-a-santa-pola-alicante-espagne/>, viewed on 1 October 2011.

[1804] Polybius, *The Histories,* vol. 2, Bk. III. 27. 9-10., trans. W. R. Paton, Heinemann, 1922, p. 65.

[1805] K. Bringmann, *The History of the Roman Republic*, Polity Press, 2006, p. 75–76.

[1806] J. S. Richardson. *Hispaniae: Spain and Development of Roman Imperialism 218–82 B.C.* Cambridge University Press, 2004, p. 3; F. W. Wallbank, *A Historical Commentary on Polybius,* vol.1. III.13.1–2, p. 316.

[1807] J. S. Richardson. *Hispaniae: Spain and Development of Roman Imperialism 218–82 B.C.* Cambridge University Press, 2004, p. 3.

[1808] X. Aquilué, P. Castanyer, M. Santos, and J. Tremoleda, *Empúries. Guidebooks to the Museu d'Arqueologia de Catalunya*, Museu d'Arqueologia de Catalunya, English language 2nd edition, 2008, p. 49; C. Díaz, H. Palou, and A. M. Puig, *La Ciudadela de Roses*, Ayuntamiento de Roses Fundació Roses Història i Natura, 2003, p. 19.

[1809] Strabo, *Geography*, Book III. Chapter 4. 6.

[1810] F. W. Wallbank, *A Historical Commentary on Polybius*, Oxford, 1957, vol.1. Bk. III. 15. p. 320, (Schulten, Phil, Woch., 1927, col.1582–A. Schulten, Numantia, die Ergebmisse der Aausgra' bugen, 1905–12, 4 vols. Munich, 1914–31).

[1811] *Appian's Roman History*, The Wars in Spain, II.7, trans. H. White, Heinemann, 1964, p. 149.

[1812] *Ibid*, II.7. p. 151.

[1813] F. W. Wallbank, *A Historical Commentary on Polybius*, vol.1. Bk. 3. 97.6. Oxford, 1957, p. 432.

[1814] Strabo, *Geography,* IV.1.5.

[1815] P. B. Ellis, *The Celtic Empire: The First Millennium of Celtic History,* Constable, 1990, p. 47.

[1816] Strabo, *Geography*, Book III.4.6.

[1817] K. Bringmann, *History of the Roman Republic,* Polity Press, 2006, p. 76.

[1818] H. H. Scullard, *A History of the Roman World 753–146 B.C.* Routledge, 1991, p. 198.

[1819] *Appian Wars of the Romans in Iberia,* 11.43. translated from the Greek by Richardson, J.S. Aris & Phillips Ltd., 2000, p. 23.

[1820] K. Bringmann, *The History of the Roman Republic*, Polity Press, 2006, p. 75–76.

[1821] *Livy,* Vol. 5, XXI. VII.3, trans. B.O. Foster, William Heinemann, 1929, p. 21.

[1822] Titus Livius Livy, *The War With* Hannibal, XXI. 12, trans. Aubrey de Sélincourt, Penguin, 1972, p. 36.

[1823] *Livy,* vol. 5. XXI. XIII–XIV.4, trans. B.O. Foster, William Heinemann, 1929, p. 41.

[1824] *Appian's Roman History*, The Wars in Spain, II. 12, trans. H. White, Heinemann, 1964, p. 157.

[1825] *Ibid.*

[1826] Valerius Maximus, *Memorable Deeds and Sayings: A Thousand and One Tales From Ancient Rome*, Foreign Stories, V.6. ext. 1, trans. Henry John Walker, Hackett Publishing Company Inc., 2004, p. 223.

[1827] I. Scott-Kilvert, *Polybius The Rise of the Roman Empire*, Penguin Books, 1981, p. 212.

[1828] *Livy*, Bk. XXI. XIX, II, xx 8, trans. B.O. Foster, William Heinemann, 1929, p. 58–59.

[1829] P. Connelly, *Hannibal and the Enemies of Rome,* Macdonald Educational, 1978, p. 46.

[1830] *Ibid.*

[1831] Polybius, *The Histories,* vol. 2. Bk. 3, 40. 14–41.8, trans. W. R. Paton, Loeb, 1980, p. 97.

[1832] *Livy,* vol. 5. Bk. XXI.XXVI 3–7, trans. E. T. Sage, Loeb Classical Library, William Heinemann, 1935, p. 75; Polybius, *The Histories,* vol. 2. Bk. 3, 41.8–42.7, trans. W. R. Paton, Loeb, 1980, p. 99.

[1833] *Livy,* vol. 5. Bk. XXI. XXVIII, 7–XXIX.3, trans. B.O. Foster, William Heinemann, 1929, p. 83–85.

[1834] A. Spekke, *The Amber Routes and Geographical Discoveries of the Eastern Baltic,* M. Goppars Stockholm, 1956, ref. Polybius III. 4. 2, Loeb Classical Library.

[1835] *Livy,* vol. 5. Bk. XXI. XXVII.3-6, trans. B.O. Foster, William Heinemann, 1929, p. 75–77.

[1836] H. H. Scullard. *A History of the Roman World 753–146 B.C.* Routledge, 1991, p. 213.

[1837] *Appian's Roman History,* Bk. IV, Ch. III, 14, trans. H. White, Heinemann, 1912, p. 161.

[1838] W. R. Paton, *Polybius The Histories*, vol. 2, Bk. III, 61.2. Loeb, 1922, p. 145.

[1839] H. H. Scullard. *A History of the Roman World 753–146 B.C.* Routledge, 1991, p. 213.

[1840] P. B. Ellis, *The Celtic Empire: The First Millennium of Celtic History,* Constable, 1990, p. 48.

[1841] J. Peddie, *Hannibal's War*, Sutton Publishing, 2005, p. 163.

[1842] *Livy,* vol. VII. Bk. XXVI. XIX. 7–13, trans. F. G. Moore, Heinemann, 1943, p. 75–77.

[1843] J. Peddie, *Hannibal's War*, Sutton Publishing, 2005, p. 163.

[1844] *Livy.* vol. VII. Bk. XXVI. XIX. 7–13, trans. F. G. Moore, Heinemann, 1943, p. 75–77.

[1845] J. Peddie, *Hannibal's War*, Sutton Publishing, 2005, p. 163.

[1846] F. W. Wallbank, *A Historical Commentary on Polybius*, vol.1. Bk. 3. 95.5. Oxford, 1957, p. 431, (Thiel, 1.54).

[1847] *Livy.* vol. 7. Bk. XXVI. XIX. 7–13, trans. F. G. Moore, Heinemann, 1943, p. 75–77.

[1848] *Livy,* vol. 5. Bk. XXII. XIX. 2–8, trans. B. O. Foster, William Heinemann, 1929, p. 263-237.

[1849] R. Flaceliere. *Daily Life in Greece At the Time of Pericles*, trans. P. Green, Phoenix, 2002, p. 265–267.

[1850] R. Osborne. *Classical Greece 500–323 B.C.* Oxford University Press, 2000, p. 91.

[1851] R. Gardiner, (ed.), *The Age of the Galley*, Conway Maritime Press, 1995, p. 63–64.

[1852] Thucydides, *History of the Peloponnesian Wars,* 2.93.

[1853] *Livy*, vol. 5, XXII. XIX. 2–8, trans. B.O. Foster, William Heinemann, 1929, p. 263–267.

[1854] W. R. Paton, *Polybius, The Histories*, vol. 2. Bk. III. 88. 2–89. Heinemann, 1980, p. 217.

[1855] Also known as Sosylus the Lacedaemon. F. W. Wallbank, *A Historical Commentary on Polybius*, vol.1, Bk. III. 20.5. Oxford, 1957, p. 333.

[1856] R. Gardiner, (ed.), *The Age of the Galley*, Conway Maritime Press, 1995, p. 60–61 n. 30, *F Gr Hist* 176 F 1. Hemeroscopium was also called Dianium, the Roman equivalent of Artemisium. Strabo, *Geography,* III. 4.6.

[1857] F. W. Wallbank, *A Historical Commentary on Polybius*, vol.1. III. 95.7. Oxford, 1957, p. 431.

[1858] H. H. Scullard. *A History of the Roman World 753–146 B.C.* Routledge, 1991, p. 213.

[1859] F. W. Wallbank, *A Historical Commentary on Polybius*, vol.1. Bk. III. 97.1–2. Oxford, 1957, p. 431.

[1860] *Ibid,* vol.1. Bk. III. 95.5. (x. 17.13). Oxford, 1957, p. 431.

[1861] F. W. Wallbank, *A Historical Commentary on Polybius*, vol.1. Bk. III. 95.5. Oxford, 1957, p. 431, (cf. Thiel, 40–42, J. H. Thiel, *Studies on the History of Roman Sea-Power in Republican Times*, Amsterdam, 1946 also Thiel, *A History of Roman Sea-Power before the Second Punic War,* North Holland Publishing Co., Amsterdam, 1954.

[1862] F. W. Wallbank, *A Historical Commentary on Polybius*, vol.1. Bk. III. 97.2. Oxford, 1957, p. 431, (Thiel, 1.54).

[1863] P. B. Ellis, *The Celtic Empire: The First Millennium of Celtic History,* Constable, 1990, p. 49.

[1864] *Ibid.*

[1865] J. Peddie. *Hannibal's War*, Sutton, 1997, p. 171–172.

[1866] P. B. Ellis, *The Celtic Empire: The First Millennium of Celtic History,* Constable, 1990. p. 49.

[1867] F. W. Wallbank, *A Historical Commentary on Polybius*, vol. 2. XVIII. 47.1. Oxford, 1967, p. 614.

[1868] *Justin: Epitome of the Philippic History of Pompeius Trogus*, 43. 3.4, trans. J. C. Yardley, Scholars Press Atlanta, 1994. p. 266.

[1869] M. M. Austin, *The Hellenistic World from Alexander to the Roman Conquest: A Selection of Ancient Sources in Translation*, Cambridge University Press, 2003, p. 258–260, *Syll* 3. 591; M. Holleaux, *Etudes*, V. 1957, 141–55; P. Frisch, *Die Inschriften von Lampsacos* (Bonn, 1978), no. 4.

[1870] Lucan, *Pharsalia*, III.470, trans. N. Rowe, Everyman, 1998, p. 72

[1871] M. M. Austin, *The Hellenistic World from Alexander to the Roman Conquest: A Selection of Ancient Sources in Translation*, Cambridge University Press, 2003, p. 258–260, *Syll* 3. 591; M. Holleaux, *Etudes*, V. 1957, 141–55; P. Frisch, *Die Inschriften von Lampsacos* (Bonn, 1978), no. 4.

[1872] *Roman History (incomplete) Titus Livius,* Livy, 10. XXXIV. 8, <http://thriceholy.net/Texts/Livy10.html> viewed on 29 July 2011.

[1873] H. White, *Appian's Roman History,* The Wars in Spain, Ch.VIII, 40. Heinemann, 1964, p. 201.

[1874] F. W. Wallbank, *A Historical Commentary on Polybius,* vol. 2. XVIII. 50.2. Oxford, 1967, p. 621. Going only by the surname he may have been from Massalia. He appears in 180 B.C. as a Roman Tribune and was previously an Aedile.

[1875] F. W. Wallbank, *A Historical Commentary on Polybius,* vol. 2. XVIII, 47. 1. Oxford, 1967, p. 614.

[1876] M. M. Austin, *The Hellenistic World from Alexander to the Roman Conquest: A Selection of Ancient Sources in Translation*, Cambridge University Press, 2003, p. 258–260, *Syll* 3. 591, M. Holleaux, Syll³ 591; *Etudes*, V. 1957, 141–55; I Lampsakos No. 4; BD 35; P. Frisch, *Die Inschriften von Lampsacos* (Bonn, 1978), no. 4.

[1877] Clerc discusses the possibilities. M. Clerc, *Massalia. Histoire de Marseille dans l'antiquité des origins à la fin de l'Empire romain d'Occident (476 ap. J.-C.),* TOME 1, Des origins jusqu 'au IIIme siècle av. J.-C. Marseille, Librairie A. Tacussel, 1927, p. 298.

[1878] P. B. Ellis, *The Celtic Empire: The First Millennium of Celtic History,* Constable, 1999, p. 100.

[1879] M. Clerc, *Massalia. Histoire de Marseille dans l'antiquité des origins à la fin de l'Empire romain d'Occident* (476 ap. J.-C.), TOME 1, Des origins jusqu 'au IIIme siècle av. J.-C., Marseille, Librairie A. Tacussel, 1927, p. 299, REA (Revue des Etudes Ancienne), XVII, 1916, p. 1-11 for discussion and examination by M. Holleaux of the text from the Decree of the Council and People of Lampsacus inscription.

[1880] *Livy*, vol.10. XXXVII, LVII, trans. T. Sage, Heinemann, 1935, p. 467.

[1881] 'Salyens, (*Giog. Anc.*) en latin *Salyes*, ou *Sallyes, Salyi, Salvii, Saluvii'*, various spellings of the same name. D. Diderot et J. Le Rond d'Alember, *Encyclopédie ou Dictionnaire raissoné des Sciences, des Arts et des Metiers*, A. Neufchastel, 1765, p. 590. <http://books.google.co.uk/books?id=Rd8jqiMG6y0C&pg=PA590&lpg=PA590&dq=Salyes,+Sallyes,+Salyi,&source=bl&ots=WDIP1QR3xZ&sig=9RU4SxmoQgJkzXqzUqbW1FMAeZE&hl=en&ei=1adYTraAJsLG8QPO6LmhDA&sa=X&oi=book_result&ct=result&resnum=9&ved=0CFMQ6AEwCA#v=onepage&q=Salyes%2C%20Sallyes%2C%20Salyi%2C&f=false>, viewed on 27 August 2011.

[1882] Strabo, *Geography*, IV.1.3.

[1883] F. W. Wallbank, *A Historical Commentary on Polybius,* vol.3. XXXIII.8.1. Oxford, 1979. p. 550.

[1884] *Livy*, vol. 12, trans. E. T. Sage, Loeb, 1928, p. 61; Gaius Matienus commanded the section from Massilia to the Bay of Naples. Michael M. Sage, *Roman Conquests: Gaul*, Pen & Sword Books Ltd, 2011, p. xxi.

[1885] F. W. Wallbank, *A Historical Commentary on Polybius,* vol.3. XXXIII.8.2, Oxford, 1979, p. 550.

[1886] K. Lomas, *Roman Italy, 338 BC-AD 200: A sourcebook,* Routledge, 2004, p. 61.

[1887] F. W. Wallbank, *A Historical Commentary on Polybius,* vol. 3. XXXIII.8.1, Oxford, 1979, p. 550.

[1888] *Livy,* vol. 12, trans. E. T. Sage, Loeb, 1928, p. 107. I mention Lucius Tarentius Massiliota only for the similarity of the surname to Massilia (Latin) and Massaliote (Greek).

[1889] *Livy*, vol. 9. XXXI, XLIX. 12–L8, trans. E. T. Sage, Loeb, 1935, p. 147.

[1890] *Livy,* vol. 12. XL. XLI. 4-8, trans. E. T. Sage and A. C. Schlesinger, Loeb, 1928, p. 129.

[1891] H. L. Jones, *Strabo Geography,* vol. 2, IV.6.2. Loeb, 1923, p. 267.

[1892] *Ibid*, p. 267 n. 2; Pliny, *Natural Histories,* vol. 4, Bk. XIV. XXIV. 1231–XXV, trans. H. Rackham, Heinemann, 1945, p. 267-9.

[1893] Livy, Vol. XII. Book XLII.iv. I-V.2. trans. E. Sage and A. C. Schlesinger, Heinemann, 1948, p. 301-2.

[1894] A. Trevor. Hodge, *Ancient Greek France,* University of Pennsylvania, 1999, p. 159 & p. 36; P. Connelly, *Hannibal and the Enemies of Rome,* Macdonald Educational, 1978, p. 46.

[1895] W. Scheidel, *The Roman Slave Supply*, [Princeton/Stanford Working Papers in Classics] (May 2007): 1-22, here p.7. <http://www.princeton.edu/~pswpc/pdfs/scheidel/050704.pdf > viewed on 10 November 2011.

[1896] Horace, *Epistles,* 2.1.156-157, <http://www.thelatinlibrary.com/horace/epist2.shtml> viewed 24 April 2013.

[1897] J. Boardman, *The Greeks Overseas,* Thames & Hudson, 1999, p 192.

[1898] R. M. Errington, 'Overview', *The Cambridge Ancient History*, vol. 8. Rome and the Mediterranean to 133 B.C., Chapter 4: Greece and Rome to 205 B.C., 1989, ['Cambridge Histories Online'] <http://histories.cambridge.org/extract?id=chol9780521234481_CHOL9780521234481A005> viewed 26 April 2012.

[1899] W. C. Morey, *Outlines of Roman History*, Chp. XII, American Book Company (1901), <http://www.forumromanum.org/history/morey12.html> viewed 27 January 2012.

[1900] Lucius Livius Andronicus, ['Encyclopaedia Britannica' eb.com] <http://www.britannica.com/EBchecked/topic/344903/Lucius-Livius-Andronicus> viewed 27 January 2012.

[1901] W. Scheidel, *The Roman Slave Supply*, [Princeton/Stanford Working Papers in Classics] (May 2007): 1-22, here p.7. <http://www.princeton.edu/~pswpc/pdfs/scheidel/050704.pdf > viewed on 10 November 2011.

[1902] W. R. Paton, *Polybius The Histories*, vol. 4. XXXIII, 6. 8–83, Loeb, 1922, p. 271

[1903] E. S. Shuckburgh, *The Histories of Polybius*, vol. 2. XXXIII. 7. Macmillan, 1884, p. 472.

[1904] W. R. Paton, *Polybius The Histories*, vol. 6. XXXIII, 10.1–11, Loeb, 1922, p. 275.

[1905] *Ibid*, vol. 6. XXXIII.10, p. 275.

[1906] *Ibid*, vol. 6. XXXIII, 10.1–11, p. 275.

[1907] F. W. Wallbank, *A Historical Commentary on Polybius*, vol. 3. XXXIII. 8.3. Oxford, 1979, p. 551–552.

[1908] W. R. Paton, *Polybius The Histories*, vol. 6. XXXIII. 10.1–11, Loeb, 1922, p. 275–7.

[1909] F. W. Wallbank, *A Historical Commentary on Polybius*, vol. 3. XXXIII.9.12. Oxford, 1979, p. 533.

[1910] F. W. Wallbank, *A Historical Commentary on Polybius*, vol. 3. XXXIII. 10. 1.12. Oxford, 1979, p. 532-533; Hall wrote the Massaliotes were to undertake construction of a coastal road with the obligation that the Romans could use it. W. H. (Bullock) Hall. *The Romans on the Riviera and the Rhone: a sketch on the conquest of Liguria and the Roman Province*, Chp. IX. Macmillan, 1898, p. 99–100, reprinted by Ares Publishers, Chicago, 1974, ['Open Library'] <http://openlibrary.org/books/OL5069373M/The_Romans_on_the_Riviera_and_the_Rhone>, viewed on 19 December 2011.

[1911] Cicero, *De Res Publica*, 3. IX.15, trans. C. W. Keynes, Harvard, 1944, p. 197.

[1912] Michael. M. Sage, *Roman Conquests: Gaul*, Pen & Sword Books, 2011, p. xxx.

[1913] *Ibid*, p. 18.

[1914] M. Bats, 'The Greeks in Gaul and Corsica: the rhythm of the Greek emporion' in P. Carratelli (ed.), *The Western Greeks: Classical Civilization in the Western Mediterranean*, (London, 1996): 577–584, here p. 581.

[1915] J. M. Riddle, (ed.), *Tiberius Gracchus: Destroyer or Reformer of the Roman Republic*, Heath & Co, 1970, p. 87.

[1916] M. Clerc, *Massalia: Histoire de Marseille dans L'Antiquité des Origins a la Fin de l'empire Romain d'occident*, vol. 2, Librarie A. Tacussel, 1929, p. 265.

[1917] *Justin: Epitome of the Philippic History of Pompeius Trogus*, Bk. 37.1.1, trans. J. C. Yardley, Scholars Press Atlanta, GA, 1994, p. 232-233.

[1918] *The History of Rome by Titus Livius*, vol. 5. XXXVI, War Against Antiochus, XLII, trans. Canon Roberts, Dent, 1924–31, p. 184.

[1919] *Ibid*, vol. 5, XXXVI, War Against Antiochus, XLIII, p. 185-186.

[1920] Livy mentions the fleet moved on but left 4 Quinquremes at Phocae. *The History of Rome by Titus Livius*, vol. 5, XXXVI, Final Defeat of Antiochus, XLV, trans. Canon Roberts, Dent, 1924–31, p. 187.

[1921] *The History of Rome by Titus Livius*, vol. 5, XXXVI, War Against Antiochus, IX, trans. Canon Roberts, Dent, 1924–31, p. 195-196.

[1922] E. S. Shuckburgh, *The Histories of Polybius*, vol. 2. XXI. 6. Macmillan, 1884, p. 265; F. W. Wallbank, *A Historical Commentary on Polybius*, vol. 3. XXI. 6.1–6, Oxford, 1979, p. 96. Wallbank gives his reference as Livy, XXXVII. 9. 5–8.

[1923] *The History of Rome by Titus Livius*, vol.5, XXXVII, War Against Antiochus, XI, trans. Canon Roberts, Dent, 1924–31, p. 199.

[1924] *Ibid*, vol. 5. XXXVII, War Against Antiochus, XXXI, p. 217.

[1925] *Ibid*, Final Defeat of Antiochus, XXXII, p. 218.

[1926] *Ibid.*

[1927] *Ibid.*

[1928] *Ibid.*

[1929] *Ibid.*

[1930] *Ibid.* Final Defeat of Antiochus, XXXII, p. 219.

[1931] *Livy*, vol.10. XXXVII. 21–23, trans. E. T. Sage, Loeb Classical Library, 1935, p. 459.

[1932] R. Seager, *Pompey the Great,* Blackwell, 2003, p. 5.

[1933] F. W. Wallbank, *A Historical Commentary on Polybius,* vol. 3. XXXIII. 9. 8. Oxford, 1979, p. 552.

[1934] Strabo, *Geography*, IV. 1. 5 and IV. 6. 3.

[1935] N. Williams and C. Le Nevez, *Provence and the Cote d'Azur,* Lonely Planet Publications, 2010, p. 26.

[1936] M. Thompson, O. Morkholm, and C. M. Kraay, *An Inventory of Greek Coin Hoards*, The American Numismatic Society, New York, 1973, p. 362-3.

[1937] S. Piggott, *The Druids*, Pelican, 1975, p. 40; Les Grands Sites Archéologiques, *Les Gaulois en Provence: L'oppidum d'Entremont*, Gauls and Greeks, The Gallic populations of Provence, <http://www.grands-sites-archeologiques.culture.fr/catalogue.php?id=18>, viewed on 27 August 2011.

[1938] P. B. Ellis, *The Celtic Empire: The First Millennium of Celtic History,* Constable, 1990.

[1939] J. Knight, *Roman France: an archaeological field guide,* Tempus Publishing, 2001, p. 172.

[1940] C. MacDonald, *Cicero Pro Flacco,* 63–64, William Heinemann Publishers, 1977, p. 511; A. Momigliano, *Alien Wisdom: The Limits of Hellenization*, 1990, Cambridge University Press, 1975, p. 56, (from Silius Italicus, *Pun* 15.169–72).

[1941] J. Knight, *Roman France: an archaeological field guide*, Tempus Publishing, 2001, p. 163.

[1942] P. B. Ellis, *The Celtic Empire: The First Millennium of Celtic History,* Constable, 1990, p. 135.

While on a mission to civilise the world such as banning human sacrifice in the Roman Empire 97 B.C. (T. R. Glover, *The Conflict of Religions in the Roman Empire*, Metheuen, 1919, p. 26 n.1 Pliny, *N.H.* XXX, 12. 13,) the Romans still continued staging Public Games with Gladiators fighting to the death.

[1943] R. Gardiner, *Cicero, XIII, Pro Balbo*, xxi. 49–xxii, 50. Cicero Letters to Atticus III, XIV. 14. Loeb, 1961, p. 695.

[1944] Strabo, *Geography,* IV.1.8.

[1945] Hall mentions the Ingauni as a *Socii* contingent of Italian Ligurians in Marius's Roman Army whose soldiers 'were the first to turn the tide of victory' in favour of Rome'. W. H. (Bullock) Hall. *The Romans on the Riviera and the Rhone: a sketch on the conquest of Liguria and the Roman Province*, Chp. VII, 105/248, Macmillan, London, 1898, p. 76, reprinted by Ares Publishers, Chicago, 1974, ['Open Library'] <http://openlibrary.org/books/OL5069373M/The_Romans_on_the_Riviera_and_the_Rhone>, viewed on 19 December 2011.

[1946] Plutarch, *Lives of the Noble Grecians and Romans,* Life of Marius 15, trans. T. North, Wordsworth Editions Ltd., 1998, p. 251.

[1947] A. Trevor. Hodge, *Ancient Greek France,* University of Pennsylvania, 1999, p. 148.

[1948] A. L. F. Rivet, *Gallia Narbonensis,* Batsford, 1988, p. 46 n. 67, near the confluence of the Isère according to Orosius, V, 16. 9.

[1949] A. L. F. Rivet, *Gallia Narbonensis,* Batsford, 1988, p. 46 n. 69.

[1950] G. Magi, *Provence,* Bonechi, 2001. p. 175; W. H. (Bullock) Hall. *The Romans on the Riviera and the Rhone: a sketch on the conquest of Liguria and the Roman Province*, Chp.XII. Macmillan, 1898, p. 112 and p. 115-116, reprinted by Ares Publishers, Chicago, 1974, ['Open Library'] <http://openlibrary.org/books/OL5069373M/The_Romans_on_the_Riviera_and_the_Rhone>, viewed on 19 December 2011.

[1951] *Plutarch's Lives*, Caius Marius, vol. IX, trans. B. Perrin, Loeb, 1920, p. 521.

[1952] Plutarch, *The Parallel Lives*, Life of Marius, 21, vol. IX, Loeb, 1920, ['Penelope, University of Chicago' digital library] <http://penelope.uchicago.edu/Thayer/E/Roman/Texts/Plutarch/Lives/Marius*.html>, viewed on 29 October 2011.

[1953] Strabo, *Geography,* Book IV, 1.8.

[1954] A. L. F. Rivet, *Gallia Narbonensis,* Batsford, 1988, p. 203.

[1955] S. T. Loseby, 'Marseille: A Late Antique Success Story?' in *Journal for Roman Studies*, vol. 82, (1992):165–185, here p. 181 n. 128, Society for the Promotion of Roman Studies, ['JSTOR' journal archive] <http://www.jstor.org/stable/301290>, viewed on 11 November 2010.

[1956] *Cicero, De Provinciis Consularibis*, trans. R. Gardiner, Heinemann, 1970, Bk. XIII, 32–33, note b, p. 579.

[1957] G Magi, *Provence,* Bonechi, 2001, p. 12; W. H. (Bullock) Hall. *The Romans on the Riviera and the Rhone: a sketch on the conquest of Liguria and the Roman Province*, Chp. XI, Macmillan, 1898, p. 118, reprinted by Ares Publishers, Chicago, 1974, ['Open Library'] <http://openlibrary.org/books/OL5069373M/The_Romans_on_the_Riviera_and_the_Rhone>, viewed on 19 December 2011.

[1958] Les Grands Sites Archéologiques, *Les Gaulois en Provence: L'oppidum d'Entremont*, Chronology, Research and Interpretations, <http://www.grands-sites-archeologiques.culture.fr/catalogue.php?id=18>, viewed on 27 August 2011.

[1959] Strabo, *Geography,* III.5.11.

[1960] *Ibid.*

[1961] During the *Gallic War*, III.7-8. Beer locates the Cassiterides at the River Brivé in the Loire estuary. G. de Beer, 'Iktin', *The Geographical Journal*, Vol. 126, No. 2, (June 1960): 160-167, here p. 167, ['JSTOR' journal archive] <http://www.jstor.org/stable/1793956>, viewed on 5 July 2012

[1962] L. Kelpie, *The Making of the Roman Empire: from Republic to Empire*, University of Oklahoma Press, 1998, p. 224.

[1963] Cicero, *The Speeches, Pro Sesto and In Vatinum,* VII, trans. R. Gardiner, Heinemann, 1958, p. 322.

[1964] Cicero, *The Speeches, Pro Sesto*, iii, 6–7, trans. R. Gardiner, Heinemann, 1958, p. 41, notes c and d.

[1965] S. Hornblower and A. Spawforth, *The Oxford Classical Dictionary*, Oxford, 2003, p. 813. Lampsacus was famous for its wine paying a high rate of twelve talents to the Delian League in the fourth century B.C. and had continued as a prosperous city.

[1966] E. Badian, *Gaius Verres*, ['Encyclopaedia Britannica' eb.com] <http://www.britannica.com/EBchecked/topic/626413/Gaius-Verres>, viewed on 4 November 2011.

[1967] D. O. Linder, *The Trail of Caius Verres: An Account*, ['umkc.edu'] <http://law2.umkc.edu/faculty/projects/ftrials/verres/verresaccount.html>, viewed on 4 November 2011.

[1968] *Cicero in Catilinam*, I–IV, trans. C. MacDonald, Heinemann, 1977, p. 19.

[1969] Strabo, *Geography*, V.187.

[1970] G. P. Kelly, *A History of Exile in the Roman Republic*, Cambridge, 2006, p. 109 n. 50.

[1971] Cicero, *De Officiis*, Bk. 2, viii, 28, trans. W. Miller, Loeb, 1975, p. 197.

[1972] Dr W. Smith, *A Smaller History of Rome*, John Murray, 1884, p. 222.

[1973] *Ibid*, p. 227.

[1974] Cicero, *Pro Milone*, Appendix, trans. N. H. Watts, Heinemann, 1931, appendix from the Commentary of Quintus Asconius Pedianus, p. 124.

[1975] *Ibid*, p. 134, note a.

[1976] *Ibid*, Appendix, p. 136.

[1977] G. P. Kelly, *A History of Exile in the Roman Republic*, Cambridge, 2006, p. 134.

[1978] *Ibid*, p. 126.

[1979] Cicero, *Pro Milone*, trans. N. H. Watts, Heinemann, 1972, p. 5; Dr W. Smith, *A Smaller History of Rome*, John Murray, 1884, p. 238.

[1980] *Dio's Roman History*, vol. 3. XL, trans. E. Carey, Heinemann, 1914, p. 489.

[1981] H. White, *Appian's Roman History*, vol. 3. II. 48, Heinemann, 1913, p. 317; J. Carter, *Appian The Civil Wars*, Book II, 48, Penguin, 1996, p. 94.

[1982] Cicero, *Pro Milone*, Appendix from the Commentary of Quintus Asconius Podianus, trans. N. H. Watts, Heinemann, 1931, p. 135.

[1983] *Cassius Dio*, vol. 5. Book XLVIII. 4–15, Loeb, 1917, p. 227–251, ['Penelope, University of Chicago' digital library] <http://penelope.uchicago.edu/Thayer/E/Roman/Texts/Cassius_Dio/48*.html>, viewed on 20 February 2011.

[1984] *Fulvia*, ['Coinarchive.com'] <http://www.coinarchives.com/a/results.php?results=100&search=Fulvia%20#fulvia1>, viewed on 21 September 2011.

[1985] Dr W. Smith, *A Smaller History of Rome*, John Murray, 1884, p. 257. Cassius Dio, *Roman History*, vol.5.47.8.

[1986] Cicero, *Pro Milone, On Behalf of Fonteius*, 26-28, trans. N. H. Watts, Heinemann, 1931, p. 333–335.

[1987] *Ibid*, 13-14, p. 319.

[1988] *Ibid*, 14-15, p. 321.

[1989] P. B. Ellis, *The Celtic Empire: The First Millennium of Celtic History*, Constable, 1990, p.135–136.

[1990] J. Knight, *Roman France: an archaeological field guide*, Tempus Publishing, 2001, p. 188.

[1991] A. L. F. Rivet, *Gallia Narbonensis*, Batsford, 1988, p. 79.

[1992] J. Knight, *Roman France: an archaeological field guide*, Tempus Publishing, 2001, p. 188.

[1993] G. Maurel, *Le Corpus des monnaies de Marseille et Provence*, Omni, 2013, p. 79–80.

[1994] M. Grant, *Tactius The Histories*, IV, 40–44. Penguin, 1996, p. 179.

[1995] M. Clerc, *Massalia: Histoire de Marseille dans L'Antiquité des Origins a la Fin de l'empire Romain d'occident*, vol. 2, Librarie A. Tacussel, 1929, p. 316–317.

[1996] The Elder Seneca, *Controversiae*, vol.1. 2.5.13, trans. M. Winterbottom, William Heinemann Ltd., 1974, p. 333.

[1997] Tacitus, *Annals*, IV.44, Loeb, 1931, ['Penelope, University of Chicago' digital library] <http://penelope.uchicago.edu/Thayer/E/Roman/Texts/Tacitus/Annals/4C*.html#ref41> viewed on 15 March 2012.

[1998] Reference.com, *Petronius*, <www.reference.com/browse/wiki/Petronius>, viewed on 28 August 2011.

[1999] *Petronius, Seneca, Apocolocyntosis*, Fragment 1. IV, trans. Heseltine, M., and Rouse, W. H. Loeb, 1913, p. 327.

[2000] Serv. on Verg., in J. Hastings, *Encyclopaedia of Religion and Ethics*, (1908), v. 21, Kessinger, 2003, p. 220.

[2001] E. Courtney, *A Companion to Petronius*. Oxford University Press, 2001, 44–45.

[2002] T. Hard, *The Routledge Handbook of Greek Mythology*, Routledge, 2004, p. 222.

[2003] Seneca, *Moral Essays*, vol.1. XIV. 3–XV.4, trans. J. Basmore, Harvard University Press, 1994, p. 401.

[2004] M. Clerc, *Massalia: Histoire de Marseille dans L'Antiquité des Origins a la Fin de l'empire Romain d'occident*, vol. 2, Librarie A. Tacussel, 1929, p. 282.

[2005] *Tacitus, Annals of Imperial Rome*, XIII. 47, trans. M. Grant, Penguin, 1996, p. 307.

[2006] *Ibid*, XIV. 56–57, p. 340.

[2007] Pliny, *Natural Histories*, Book XXIX. V. 6–9, trans. W. H S. Jones, William Heinemann, 1963, p. 187.

[2008] *Ibid*.

[2009] L. Gigante, *Death and Disease in Ancient Rome*, <http://www.innominatesociety.com/Articles/Death%20and%20Disease%20in%20Ancient%20Rome.htm>, viewed on 20 October 2010; Life Expectancy, *Old age: Physiological effects*, ['Brittanica.com'] <http://www.britannica.com/EB.C.hecked/topic/340119/life-expectancy>, viewed on 22 December 2010.

[2010] It is relatively recently that some acceptance by mainstream (allopathic) medicine has been acknowledged to alternatives like Homeopathy (mainly used by the British Royal Family), P. Morrell, *A History of Homeopathy in Britain*, <http://www.homeopathyhome.com/reference/articles/ukhomhistory.shtml>, viewed on 22 December 2010;

Acupuncture, *NHS to give back pain acupuncture*, page last updated 6 May 2009, <http://news.bB.C.co.uk/1/hi/health/8068427.stm>, viewed on 22 December 2010,; NHS Choices, *Acupuncture Evidence*, <http://www.nhs.uk/Conditions/Acupuncture/Pages/Evidence.aspx>, viewed on 22 December 2010.

Chinese Medicine, <http://www.nhsdirectory.org/default.aspx?page=TCM&t=y>, viewed on 22 December 2010; *About TCM*, <http://www.atcm.co.uk/>, viewed on 28 August 2011.

Herbal, Auryvedic (Indian) still exists though Osteopathy is still outside the mainstream approval whose doctors have no cure for back problems only prescribing 'rest'. Big business is also involved with drug companies and their profits have been a strong consideration in not recognising other forms of medicine and any possible cures. H. R. Larsen, *Alternative Medicines: Why so popular?* <http://www.yourhealthbase.com/alternative_medicine.html>, viewed on 22 December 2010.

[2011] L. Samuel, *Rich: The Rise and Fall of American Wealth Culture,* Amacom, 2009, p. 157–158.

[2012] In the siege of A.D. 308 by Constantine against Maximian we learn from the writers like Eumenes *Panegyric of Constantine* 19, that the walls and towers were intact and therefore rebuilt and or added to. M. Clerc, *Massalia: Histoire de Marseille dans L'Antiquité des Origins a la Fin de l'empire Romain d'occident*, vol. 2. Librarie A. Tacussel, 1929, p. 266 n. 1.

[2013] P. MacKendrick, *Roman France,* G. Bell & Sons, 1971, p. 250.

[2014] Philostratus, *The Life Of Apollonius of Tyana,* trans. C. P. Jones. Harvard University Press, 2005, vol. 3, Letters, 42h. p. 35 & vol. 2. Bk. V, 41 n. 57, p. 86–87.

[2015] M. Clerc, *Massalia: Histoire de Marseille dans L'Antiquité des Origins a la Fin de l'empire Romain d'occident*, vol. 2, Librarie A. Tacussel, 1929, p. 257 n. 5; T. Griffith, *Suetonius, Lives of the Twelve Caesars,* Nero, 2, Wordsworth Editions Ltd., 1999, p. 242.

Cnaeus Domitius Ahenobarbus (consul 96 B.C.), his son Lucius Domitius Ahenobarbus (consul 54 B.C.), his son Cnaeus Domitius Ahenobarbus, (consul 32 B.C.) and his son Lucius Domitius Ahenobarbus became Emperor Nero (A.D. 54–68).

[2016] Pliny, *Natural Histories*, vol. 8. Book XXIX. V. 9–11, trans. W. H S. Jones, Heinemann, 1963, p. 189.

[2017] *Ibid.*

[2018] *Ibid*, Book XXIX. V. II–VII, p. 191.

[2019] *Ibid*, Book XXIX. V. 9–11, p. 189.

[2020] *Ibid*, Book XXIX. V. II-VII. 14, p. 191.

[2021] *Ibid*, Book XXIX. VII. 14–VIII. 17, p. 193.

[2022] *Ibid*, Book XXIX, VIII.19–27, p. 197.

[2023] *Ibid*, Book XXIX. VIII. 23–26, p. 199.

[2024] *Ibid*, Book XXIX. VII. 14–VIII.17, p. 193.

[2025] *Ibid*, Book XXIX. VIII. 26–IX. 29, p. 201.

[2026] Rome sacrificed 2 Greeks and 2 Gauls one of each sex in the Forum Boarium due to a Sibyline prophecy. Such was Roman fear that even priests who were normally exempt to take up arms had to if the enemy were Gauls. *Plutarch's Lives*, Marcellus, trans. J. Langhorne and W. Langhorne, Sir John Lubbock's Hundred Books, Routledge, 1930, p. 216; M. Beard, J. A. North, and F. R. S. Price, *Religions of Rome: Volume1, a history*, Cambridge, 2004, p. 80–82.

[2027] Roman History (incomplete) *Titus Livius'*, Livy, 10. XXXIV. 9,<http://thriceholy.net/Texts/Livy10.html> viewed on 29 July 2011.

[2028] Strabo, *Geography*, IV. 1. 5.

[2029] The island of Rhodes, a great naval power, assisted Rome in the Second Macedonian War and the Syrian War without any formal treaty between them. J. H. Thiel, *A History of Roman Sea-Power Before the Second Punic War*, North Holland Publishing Co., Amsterdam, 1954, p. 86 n. 73.

[2030] Narbonne was the first permanent colony outside of Italy and the single Roman port in Gaul. C. H. Benedict, 'The Romans in Southern Gaul', p. 50, *The American Journal of Philology*, vol. 63, no.1 (1942): 38–50, John Hopkins University Press, ['JSTOR' journal archive] <http://www.jstor.org/stable/291079> viewed on 17 November 2009.

[2031] *Caesar's Civil War*, Chp. Bk. 1, Chp. XXXIV, trans. W.M. M'Devitte, G. Bell & Sons, 1928, p. 265.

[2032] *Ibid*, Bk. 1, Chp. XXXV, p. 265.

[2033] Caesar *The Civil War*, Bk. I.35, trans. J. Carter, Oxford's World Classics, 1998, p. 23.

[2034] *Dio's Roman History*, vol.4. Bk. XLI, trans. E. Carey, Heinemann, 1916, p. 37.

[2035] Lucan, *Civil War*, Bk. 3, 310–314, trans. Susan. H. Braund, Oxford World's Classics, 1999, p. 50.

[2036] R. J. Rowland, Jnr., 'The Significance of Massilia in Lucan', *Hermes*, vol. 97, no. 2 (1969): 204–208, here p. 205, ['JSTOR' journal archive] <http://www.jstor.org/stable/4475586> viewed on 17 November 2009.

[2037] J. Leach, *Pompey the Great*, Croom Helm, 1978, p. 184.

[2038] Caesar, *The Civil War*, Bk. I.7, trans. J. Carter, Oxford's World Classics, 1998, p. 7.

[2039] E. Rawson, *Cicero: a portrait*, Allen Lane, 1975, p. 137.

[2040] Dr W. Smith, *A Smaller History of Rome*, John Murray, 1884, p. 232 –234; T. Griffith, *Suetonius, Lives of the Twelve Caesars*, Julius Caesar, 24, Wordsworth Editions Ltd., 1999, p. 18.

[2041] T. Griffith, *Suetonius, Lives of the Twelve Caesars*, Julius Caesar, 24, Wordsworth Editions Ltd., 1999, p. 18, and Nero, 2, p. 242.

[2042] J. Lendering, *Gaius Julius Caesar*, Part Six, Civil Wars (51–47), ['Livius.Org'] <www.livius.org/caa-can/caesar/06.html>, viewed on 26 September 2010.

[2043] T. Griffith, *Suetonius, Lives of the Twelve Caesars*, Julius Caesar, 34, Wordsworth Editions Ltd., 1999, p. 24; Domitius wants death but Caesar uses a pardon as a policy so that 'Magnus, all the Senate is–to be forgiven'. Domitius could not bear to owe anything to Caesar? Lucan, *Civil War*, II, 510-520. trans. S. H. Braund, Oxford, 1992, p. 35.

[2044] Caesar, *The Civil War*, Bk. I, 34. trans. J. Carter, Oxford's World Classics, 1998, p. 22.

[2045] J. Leach, *Pompey the Great*, Croom Helm, 1978, p. 184.

[2046] Caesar, *The Civil War*, Bk. I. 34. trans. J. Carter, Oxford's World Classics, 1998, p. 22.

[2047] *Ibid; The Works of Julius Caesar*, trans. W. S. McDevitte and W. S. Bohn,1869, <http://www.sacred-texts.com/cla/jcsr/civ1.htm> viewed 22 April 2013.

[2048] Caesar, *The Civil War*, Bk. I. 35. trans. J. Carter, Oxford's World Classics, 1998, p. 23.

[2049] *Ibid*, Bk. I. 36, p. 23.

[2050] T. Griffith, *Suetonius, Lives of the Twelve Caesars*, Nero, 2, Wordsworth Editions Ltd., 1999, p. 242.

[2051] *Lucan: Civil War*, Bk. III. 388–393, trans. Susan H. Braund, Oxford World's Classics, 1999, p. 53.

[2052] *Ibid*, Bk. III. 307–309, p. 50.

[2053] *Ibid,* Bk. III. 349–350, p. 51. In Book III. 298–762 Lucan describes the siege and in graphic detail one of the two naval battles of Massalia allied to Pompey, which ended in defeat by Caesar's ships. Strabo (III.4.6) mentions that Saguntum was a Massaliote city though by origin founded by Zakynthos.

[2054] Caesar had ten legions. The sixteenth legion crossed the Rubicon with him in Italy leaving nine legions in Gaul numbered between one and fifteen. Legions 1 to 4 and 9 are not accounted for in the list given on the Livius.com website and the three legions Caesar had at Massalia may have been from these? J. Lendering, *Gaius Julius Caesar,* Part six, ['Livius.com'] <www.livius.org/caa-can/caesar/06.html> viewed on 26 September 2010.

[2055] Caesar, *The Civil War,* Bk. I. 36, trans. J. Carter, Oxford's World Classics, 1998, p. 279 n. 1.36.

[2056] *Dio's Roman History,* vol.4, Book XLI.19, trans. E. Cary, Loeb Classical Library, William Heinemann, 1916, p. 37.

[2057] *Caesar's Civil War,* Bk. I, Chp. XXXV, trans. W. A. M'Devitte, G. Bell & Sons, 1928, p. 265.

[2058] R. Gardiner, (ed.), *The Age of the Galley,* Conway Maritime Press, 1995, p.70.

[2059] Caesar, *The Civil War,* Bk. I, 36. trans. J. Carter, Oxford's World Classics, 1998, p. 23.

[2060] *Ibid,* Bk. I, 39 & 41, p. 24–5.

[2061] I. D. Rowland, *Vitruvius Ten Books on Architecture,* Cambridge, 1999, p. 317, Commentary: Book 10, Massilia (10.16.11–12) (Figure 139).

[2062] Strabo, *Geography,* IV.1.5.

[2063] W. W. Bateson and C. Damon, *Caesar's Civil War,* Oxford, 2006, p. 127. (Caesar, *B.C.* 2.4.4).

[2064] M. Clerc, *Massalia: Histoire de Marseille dans L'Antiquité des Origins a la Fin de l'empire Romain d'occident,* vol. 2, Librarie A. Tacussel, 1929, p. 117.

[2065] P. MacKendrick, *Roman France,* G. Bell & Sons, 1971, p. 11.

[2066] Lucan, *Civil War,* Bk. III. 560–566, trans. Susan. H. Braund, Oxford World's Classics, 1999, p. 56.

[2067] *Caesar's Civil War,* Bk. 1, Chp. LVIII, trans. W. A. M'Devitte, G. Bell & Sons, 1928, p. 275.

[2068] Lucan, *Civil War,* Bk. III. 298-762, trans. Susan. H. Braund, Oxford World's Classics, 1999.

[2069] Suetonius, *The Lives of the Caesars,* The Deified Julius, vol. 1. LXVIII.4, trans. J. C. Rolfe, Heinemann, 1979, p. 91.

[2070] Caesar, *The Civil War,* Bk. II.3-4, trans. J. Carter, Oxford, 1998, p. 51.

[2071] *Ibid,* p. 51.

[2072] Caesar, *The Civil War,* Bk. II. 4, trans. J. Carter, Oxford, 1998, p. 51.

[2073] *Ibid,* p. 51–52.

[2074] *Ibid,* p. 51.

[2075] *Caesar's Civil War with Pompeius,* Bk. II.5–7, trans. F. P. Long, Oxford, 1906, p. 95.

[2076] Caesar, *The Civil War,* Bk. II.5, trans. J. Carter, Oxford, 1998, p. 53.

[2077] *Ibid,* p. 52.

[2078] Caesar's *Civil War with Pompeius,* Bk. II. 5, trans. F. P. Long, Oxford, 1906, p. 76.

[2079] Caesar, *The Civil War*, Bk. II.7, trans. J. Carter, Oxford, 1998, p. 53.

[2080] *Caesar's Civil War with Pompeius,* Bk. II.5–7, trans F. P. Long, Oxford, 1906, p. 76–78.

[2081] Caesar, *The Civil War*, Bk. II. 7, trans. J. Carter, Oxford, 1998, p. 53.

[2082] F. P. Long, *Caesar's Civil War with Pompeius,* Bk. II. 7, trans. F. P. Long, Oxford, 1906, p. 78.

[2083] M. Clerc, *Massalia: Histoire de Marseille dans L'Antiquité des Origins a la Fin de l'empire Romain d'occident*, vol. 2, Librarie A. Tacussel, 1929, p. 179.

[2084] A. Trevor. Hodge, *Ancient Greek France,* University of Pennsylvania, 1999, p. 104.

[2085] *Ibid*, p. 104 n. 34, M. Clerc, *Massalia*, 2 vols. (Marseille, 1927–9; reprint Lafitte, Marseille, 1971) 2, p. 78 n. 2 & 2, p. 123 n. 1.

[2086] A. Trevor. Hodge, *Ancient Greek France*, University of Pennsylvania, 1999, p. 103–104, p. 255 n. 34 and n. 36. Lucius Anneas Cornutus from Leptis and in Rome during the reign of Emperor Nero. M. Fröhner, 'Scolies latines relative a l'histoire et a la topographie de Marseille', *Revue Archéologique*, XVIII, II, (1891): 321-332, here p. 325.

Lucan's epic poem *Pharsalia* (*Di Bello Civili,* The Civil War) was written in ten books (all survive and the tenth was unfinished). The later books became more pro-republican and anti-imperial. Nero and Lucan, at first friends had a falling out and Lucan was forbidden to publish his poems. Lucan continued writing insulting poem about Nero, which he ignored. Unfortunately for Lucan he joined the Piso conspiracy A.D. 65 and on being discovered Nero forced Lucan to commit suicide at the age of 25.

[2087] *Ibid*, p. 106.

[2088] M. Fröhner, 'Scolies latines relative a l'histoire et a la topographie de Marseille', *Revue Archéologique*, XVIII, II, (1891): 321-332, here p. 325-326, Scholiast to Lucan III.524.

[2089] M. Clerc, *Massalia: Histoire de Marseille dans L'Antiquité des Origins a la Fin de l'empire Romain d'occident*, vol. 2. 1929, p. 78, & n. 2.

[2090] *Strabo Geography,* Vol. 2, IV.1.5, trans. H. L. Jones, Loeb, 1923, p. 175 n. 3.

[2091] *Ibid.*

[2092] M. Clerc, *Massalia: Histoire de Marseille dans L'Antiquité des Origins a la Fin de l'empire Romain d'occident*, vol. 2, Librarie A. Tacussel, 1929, p. 78 n. 2; (*Revue Archéologique*, 1891, XVIII, II, p. 322). Praetor is translated for stratigos στρατηγός=army leader, general.

[2093] *Ibid*, p. 123 n. 1, (*Revue Archéologique*, 1891, XVIII, II, p. 325-326), Scholiast to Lucan III.524. Fröhner gives the reference M. H. Usener, *Scholia in Lucani bellum civile; commenta Bernensia*, 1869, (Leipzig, chez Teubneri) which is now available to download online at <http://archive.org/details/scholiainlucani00usengoog>, viewed 5 June 2012.

[2094] D. Mercer, *Chronicle of the Twentieth Century*, 21 April 1932, Longman, 1998, p. 392.

[2095] *Ibid*, p. 450.

[2096] Strabo, *Geography,* IV. 1.5.28.

[2097] *Ibid.*

[2098] *Ibid.*

[2099] A. Trevor. Hodge, *Ancient Greek France*, University of Pennsylvania, 1999, p. 103 n. 33. Caes. *B.C.* 1. 34–6, 56–8; 2,1–16. Lucan, *Pharsalia*, 3, 30–374, Vell.Pat. 2 50. Dio Cass. 41.19. Rivet, 65–66.

[2100] A. Trevor. Hodge, *Ancient Greek France*, University of Pennsylvania, 1999, p. 255 n. 37; M. Clerc, *Massalia: Histoire de Marseille dans L'Antiquité des Origins a la Fin de l'empire Romain d'occident*, vol. 2. Librarie A. Tacussel, 1929, p. 127. n. 1, Plutarch, Pompey, 64.

[2101] H. White, *Appian's Roman History*, vol. 3. Bk. II. 41, Heinemann, 1913, p. 305. Julius Caesar appointed Hortensius and Dollabella admirals while both fleets were under construction.

[2102] A. Trevor. Hodge, *Ancient Greek France*, University of Pennsylvania, 1999, p. 103.

[2103] H. White, *Appian's Roman History,* vol. 3. Bk. II, ch. 11, Heinemann, 1913, p. 379.

[2104] T. Griffith, *Suetonius, Lives of the Twelve Caesars,* Nero, 2, Wordsworth Editions Ltd., 1999, p. 242.

[2105] H. White, *Appian's Roman History*, vol. 3. Bk. I, ch. 10, Heinemann, 1913, p. 359.

[2106] J. Leach, *Pompey the Great,* Croom Helm, 1978, p. 188.

[2107] M. Clerc, *Massalia: Histoire de Marseille dans L'Antiquité des Origins a la Fin de l'empire Romain d'occident*, vol. 2, Librarie A. Tacussel, 1929, p.78 n.2;(RA, 1891, XVIII, II, p. 322).

[2108] Lucan, *The Civil War*, Book 3, 575–580, trans. N. Rowe, Everyman, 1998, p. 75.

[2109] Caesar, *The Civil War*, Bk. I.36, trans. J. Carter, Oxford, 1998, p. 23.

[2110] R. Seagar, *Pompey: A Political Biography*, University of California Press, 1979, p. 178.

[2111] T. Griffith, *Suetonius, Lives of the Twelve Caesars*, Julius Caesar, 34, Wordsworth Editions Ltd., 1999, p. 24.

[2112] Caesar, *The Civil War*, Bk. II.17–18, trans. J. Carter, Oxford, 1998, p. 59.

[2113] *Ibid*, p. 61.

[2114] M. Clerc, *Massalia: Histoire de Marseille dans L'Antiquité des Origins a la Fin de l'empire Romain d'occident*, vol. 2, Librarie A. Tacussel, 1929, p. 209.

[2115] A. W. Lawrence, *Greek Arms and Fortifications,* Oxford, 1979, p. 93–95.

[2116] Caesar, *The Civil War*, Bk. II.1, trans. J. Carter, Oxford, 1998, p. 50.

[2117] A. W. Lawrence, *Greek Arms and Fortifications,* Oxford, 1979, p. 95, (Lucan, III.685–695): for a diagram showing effective cross-fire ranges of catapults from the city wall towers see Lawrence p. 155, Diagram 1. Coverage illustrated is based on 9 catapults per tower and 3 either side on the city wall. Therefore six towers 100 yards apart=54 catapults for that section. The cross-fire was formidable.

[2118] Caesar, *The Civil War,* Bk. 2.2.2, trans. J. Carter, Oxford, 1998, p. 50.

[2119] A. W. Lawrence, *Greek Arms and Fortifications,* Oxford, 1979, p. 95, Caesar, *B.C.* 2.2.2.

[2120] A. Hermary, A. Hesnard, and H. Tréziny, *Marseille Grecque: La cite phocéenne (600–49 av. J-C),* Editions Errance, 1999, p. 152.

[2121] A. W. Lawrence, *Greek Arms and Fortifications,* Oxford, 1979, p. 93–95; 'Roman lead sling bullets found at the siege of Perusia 41/40 B.C. were marked with thunderbolt motifs, some with names of centurions and legions, others with obscene insults of its intended target such as the intimate parts of Mark Antony's wife Fulvia'. D. B. Campbell, *Siege Warfare in the Roman World* 146 BC–AD 378, Osprey Publishing, 2005, p. 29.

[2122] Caesar, *The Civil War*, Bk. II. 1, trans. J. Carter, Oxford, 1998, p. 50.

[2123] A. Hermary, A. Hesnard, and H. Tréziny, *Marseille Grecque: La cite phocéenne (600–49 av. J-C),* Editions Errance, 1999, p. 152.

[2124] Caesar, *The Civil War*, Bk. II.1, trans. J. Carter, Oxford, 1998, p. 50.

[2125] *Ibid*, Bk. II.11, p. 55–56.

[2126] *Vitruvius: The Ten Books on Architecture,* Bk. X. Ch. VI. 11, trans. M. H. Morgan, Dover Publication, 1960, p. 318.

[2127] *Ibid*, Bk. X, Ch. VI. 12, p. 318.

[2128] E. W. Marsden, *Greek and Roman Artillery: Historical Development,* Oxford, 1969, p. 113 n. 2, Caesar, *Civil War*, 16.3.

[2129] Caesar, *The Civil War*, Bk. II.16. trans J. Carter, Oxford, 1998, p. 58.

[2130] Lucan, *Civil War*, Bk. 3. 463–480, trans. Susan. H. Braund, Oxford World's Classics, 1999, p. 54.

[2131] Caesar, *The Civil War*, Bk. II.11. trans J. Carter, Oxford, 1998, p. 56.

[2132] W. W. Bateson and C. Damon, *Caesar's Civil War*, 2.12. 3–4, Oxford, 2006, p. 159.

[2133] Caesar, *The Civil War*, Bk. II.13. trans J. Carter, Oxford, 1998, p. 56.

[2134] *Ibid*.

[2135] *Ibid*, Bk. II.14, p. 57.

[2136] *Dio's Roman History*, vol.6, Bk. XLI, trans. E. Carey, Heinemann, 1916, p. 47.

[2137] Caesar, *The Civil War*, Bk. II.13. trans J. Carter, Oxford, 1998, p. 57.

[2138] *Ibid*. Bk. II.13. p. 57.

[2139] *Ibid*, Bk. II.15. p. 57.

[2140] *Ibid*, Bk. II.15. p. 58.

[2141] *Ibid*.

[2142] *Ibid*, Bk.II. 22, p. 62.

[2143] *Ibid*.

[2144] *Ibid*, Bk. II. 16, p. 58.

[2145] *Ibid*.

[2146] *Ibid*, Bk. II. 18, p. 59.

[2147] *Ibid*, Bk. II. 22, p. 62.

[2148] F. P. Long, *Caesar's Civil War with Pompeius,* Bk. II. 14, trans. F. P. Long, Oxford, 1906, p. 76.

[2149] Caesar, *The Civil War*, Bk.II, 22 trans J. Carter, Oxford's World Classics, 1998, p. 62.

[2150] T. Griffith, *Suetonius, Lives of the Twelve Caesars,* Nero, 2, Wordsworth Editions Ltd., 1999, p. 242.

[2151] Caesar, *The Civil War*, Bk. II. 22, trans. J. Carter, Oxford's World Classics, 1998, p. 62–63.

[2152] *Dio's Roman History*, vol. 4, Book XLI.19, trans. E. Cary, William Heinemann, Loeb Classical Library, 1916, p. 47.

[2153] M. Clerc, *Massalia: Histoire de Marseille dans L'Antiquité des Origines a la Fin de l'empire Romain d'occident*, vol. 2, Librarie A. Tacussel, 1927, p. 127 n. 4, Lucan V.53, cf Dion, XLI, 25.

[2154] Caesar, *The Civil War*, Bk. II. 22, trans. J. Carter, Oxford's World Classics, 1998, p. 63.

[2155] *Ibid*, p. 62.

[2156] R. Seagar, *Pompey: A Political Biography*, University of California Press, 1979, p. 178.

[2157] Appian, *The Civil Wars*, Book II. 48, trans. J. Carter, Penguin, 1996, p. 372 n. 103.

[2158] *Ibid*, Book II, 47, p. 93–94.

[2159] *Ibid*, Book II. 48, p. 94.

[2160] *Ibid*, Book II. 48, p. 372 n. 101.

[2161] Cicero, *Letters to Atticus*, vol. 3. 183 (IX.15), trans. D. R. Shackleton Bailey, Harvard University Press, 1999, p. 87.

[2162] Caesar, *The Civil War*, Bk. I.35–36, trans. J. Carter, Oxford's World Classics, 1998, 23.

[2163] *Ibid*, Bk. II. 14, p. 57.

[2164] *Dio's Roman History*, vol.6. Bk. XLI, trans. E. Carey, Heinemann, 1916, p. 37.

[2165] W. W. Bateson and C. Damon, Caesars' Civil War, Oxford, 2006, p. 128, Caesar, *BG*. II.22.

[2166] M. Clerc, *Massalia: Histoire de Marseille dans L'Antiquité des Origines a la Fin de l'empire Romain d'occident*, vol. 2, Librarie A. Tacussel, 1927, p. 155.

[2167] A. Trevor. Hodge, *Ancient Greek France*, University of Pennsylvania Press, 1999, p. 175–176.

[2168] P. MacKendrick, *Roman France*, G. Bell & Sons, 1971, p. 11.

[2169] Caesar, *The Civil War*, Bk. I. 36, trans. J Carter, Oxford's World Classics, 1998, p. 23.

[2170] H. Cleere, *Southern France: An Oxford Archaeological Guide*, Oxford, 2001, p. 111, Caesar, *Civil War* 1.36.

[2171] G. Magi, *Provence*, Casa Editrice Bonechi, 2001, p. 81.

[2172] H. Cleere, *Southern France: An Oxford Archaeological Guide*, Oxford, 2001, p.138.

[2173] A. Hermary, A. Hesnard, A., and H. Tréziny, *Marseille Grecque: La cite phocéenne (600–49 av. J-C)*, Editions Errance, 1999, p. 155 n. 35 Tacitus, *Histories*, 3.43; M. Bats, 'The Greeks in Gaul and Corsica: the rhythm of the Greek emporion' in P. Carratelli (ed.), *The Western Greeks: Classical Civilization in the Western Mediterranean*, (London, 1996): 577–584, here p. 581; Pliny, *NH*, III.5.

[2174] *Appian's Roman History*, vol. 3. Bk. II. 48, trans. H. White, Heinemann, 1913, p. 317.

[2175] Trebonius published a collection of his friend Cicero's witty sayings and puns in 47 B.C. He became *pro-praetor* of Spain 47-46 B.C. Caesar rewarded his loyalty with a Consulship 45 B.C. and promise of being the Governor of Asia. Trebonius then joined the conspiracy to murder Caesar in 44 B.C. and detained Mark Antony at the door of the Senate on the day. Trebonius left Rome to become Governor of Asia and was murdered in Smyrna 43 B.C. on the orders of Dollabella becoming the first of Caesar's murderers to die. M. Bunson, *A Dictionary of the Roman Empire*, Oxford, 1990, p. 426; 'Appian, The Civil Wars', III.26, *The Histories of Appian*, Loeb, 1913, p. 567, ['Penelope' University of Chicago digital library] <http://penelope.uchicago.edu/Thayer/E/Roman/Texts/Appian/Civil_Wars/3*.html> viewed 14

May 2012, Cassius Dio, vol.5.46.49; Sacred grove outside Massalia, Lucan, *Civil War*, III.445, trans. S. H. Braund, Oxford, 1992, p. 53. See also A. Augoustakis, 'Cutting Down the Grove in Lucan, Valerius Maximus and Dio Cassius', *The Classical Quarterly*, vol. 56, No. 2 (Dec, 2006):634-638 <www.jstor.org/stable/4493456>.

[2176] The Coinage of Julius Caesar, *Catalogue*, ['Macquarie University']
<www.humanities.mq.edu.au?acans/Caesar/Catalogue.htm>, viewed on 29 August 2011.

[2177] *The Numismatics of Celtic Warriors*, (HCRI 19), D. R. Sear, *The History of Coinage of the Roman Imperators 49–27 B.C.* Spink, London, 1998, ISBN 090 0760 5982. <http://www.kernunnos.com/culture/warriors/>, viewed on 29 August 2011.

[2178] J. Leversidge, *Everyday Life in the Roman Empire*, Batsford, 1976, p. 90.

[2179] *Cicero Letters to Atticus,* vol. 3, XIV. 13, trans. E. O. Winstedt, Heinemann, 1961, p. 243.

[2180] *Ibid,* vol. 3, XIV. 14, p. 258–259; Possibly Massilians ambassadors were neighbours of Atticus in Rome. W. Guthrie, *Cicero's Epistles to Atticus: With Notes, Historical, Explanatory, and Critical*, vol. 3, London, 1806, p.225 n.1.

[2181] P. Bayle, A. Tricaud, and A. Gaudin, *The Dictionary Historical and Critical of Mr. Peter Bayle,* vol. 2, London, 1735, p. 680.
<http://books.google.co.uk/books?id=QE8hAQAAMAAJ&pg=PA680&lpg=PA680&dq=Trebonius+killed+by+Dolabella+when?&source=bl&ots=Q3CLxtx4ir&sig=dv3B7gbm2ptW6i7GqOoJWBTaT-I&hl=en&sa=X&ei=8167T_auH8fD8QOt79nRCg&ved=0CFgQ6AEwBg#v=onepage&q=Trebonius%20killed%20by%20Dolabella%20when%3F&f=false> viewed on 22 May 2012; 43 B.C. Olympiad 184.2, ['Attalus'] <http://www.attalus.org/bc1/year43.html#7> viewed on 22 May 2012.

[2182] J. Ussher, *The Annals of the World,* Master Books, 2003, p. 676;Cicero, *Philippics*: 3-9, Edited with Introduction, Translation and Commentary,Vol. 2, Commentary, by G. Manuwald, Walter de Gruyter, 2007, p. 906-7.

[2183] *Cicero Philippic,* XIII. xv. 30–32, trans. W. Ker, Loeb, 1926, p. 583.

[2184] *Ibid,* XIII. v. 12–vi, 14, p. 559.

[2185] S. Dando-Collins, *Cleopatra's Kidnappers: How Caesar's Sixth Legion Gave Egypt to Rome and Rome to Caesar,* John Wiley & Sons, 2005, p. 222-241.

[2186] *Appian's Roman History,* IV, 11, 84, trans. H. White, Heinemann, 1913, p. 281.

[2187] *Appian's Roman History*, III, 4. trans. H. White, Heinemann, 1964, p. 523.

[2188] *Ibid*, III, 4. p. 523.

[2189] *Ibid*, III, 3. p. 521-523.

[2190] *Ibid*, III, 4. p. 525. ['Penelope, University of Chicago' digital library]
<http://penelope.uchicago.edu/Thayer/E/Roman/Texts/Appian/Civil_Wars/3*.html>, viewed 27 May 2012.

[2191] M. Clerc, *Massalia: Histoire de Marseille dans L'Antiquité des Origins a la Fin de l'empire Romain d'occident*, vol. 2, Librarie A. Tacussel, 1929, p. 246 n.1.

[2192] Appian The Civil Wars, II, 135, *The Histories of Appian*, Loeb, 1913, p. 477, ['Penelope, University of Chicago' digital library] <http://penelope.uchicago.edu/Thayer/E/Roman/Texts/Appian/Civil_Wars/2*.html >, viewed 7 February 2012.

[2193] *Appian The Civil Wars*, III, 1. 2, ['Perseus, University of Chicago' digital library]
<http://perseus.uchicago.edu/perseus-cgi/citequery3.pl?dbname=GreekTexts&query=App.%20BC%203.1&getid=1 >, viewed 7 February 2012.

[2194] *Appian The Civil Wars,* IV, 11, 84, H. White (ed.),Macmillan & Co., 1899, ['Perseus' Tufts university digital library], <http://www.perseus.tufts.edu/hopper/text?doc=Perseus%3Atext%3A1999.01.0232%3Abook%3D4%3Achapter%3D11%3Asection%3D84> viewed 21 May 2012.

[2195] A. L. F. Rivet, *Gallia Narbonensis,* Batsford, 1988, p.75 n. 37.

[2196] *Appian's Roman History,* IV, ch. XI, 84, trans. H. White, Heinemann, 1913, p. 299.

[2197] *Ibid,* IV, ch. XII, 95, p. 281.

[2198] *Ibid,* V, ch. VIII, 67, p. 491.

[2199] *Ibid,* V, ch. VIII, 72, p. 500–511.

[2200] *Ibid,* V, ch. XI, 100, p. 547.

[2201] *Ibid,* V, ch. XIV, 140 & 144, p. 609–615.

[2202] *Justin: Epitome of the Philippic History of Pompeius Trogus,* 38.6.7, trans. J. C. Yardley, Scholars Press Atlanta, GA, 1994, p. 241.

[2203] T. J. Cornell, *The Beginning of Rome: Italy and Rome from the Bronze Age to the Punic Wars (c. 1000–264 B.C.),* Routledge, 1995, p. 148.

[2204] *Ibid,* p. 150.

[2205] *Ibid,* p. 148.

[2206] *Ibid,* p. 150.

[2207] *Appian's Roman History,* V. ch. 1, 3, trans. H. White, Heinemann, 1913, p. 381.

[2208] *Ibid,* Bk. V. ch. XIII, 126, p. 587.

[2209] M. Clerc, *Massalia: Histoire de Marseille dans L'Antiquité des Origins a la Fin de l'empire Romain d'occident*, vol. 2. Librarie A. Tacussel, 1929, p. 246 n. 1.

The city of Thessaloniki had also supported Pompey and the losing side. Subsequently they took extraordinary steps to gain favour with Octavian Caesar (Augustus) by dismantling a large sixth-century temple of Aphrodite at Aeneia on the Thermaic gulf: re-erecting it in Thessaloniki: and dedicated to Octavian. Aeneia was said to have been founded by Aeneas from Troy, *(Ancient coins of Macedonia,* <http://www.snible.org/coins/hn/macedon.html>, viewed on 28 August 2010), and Julius Caesar had claimed descent from Aphrodite. Part of the temple and statues can be seen in the Archaeological Museum Thessaloniki Greece.

[2210] M. Clerc, *Massalia: Histoire de Marseille dans L'Antiquité des Origins a la Fin de l'empire Romain d'occident*, vol. 2. Librarie A. Tacussel, 1929, p. 247 n.1. Livy, XXXIV, 9.

[2211] *Appian's Roman History,* Bk. V, ch. XIV, 137, trans. H. White, Heinemann, 1913, p. 605.

[2212] H. Cleere, *Southern France: An Oxford Archaeological Guide,* Oxford, 2001, p. 138.

[2213] *Ibid,* p. 125.

[2214] M. Clerc, *Massalia: Histoire de Marseille dans L'Antiquité des Origins a la Fin de l'empire Romain d'occident*, Librarie A. Tacussel, vol. 2, 1929, p. 78. *IGIS,* vol. XIV, 2454; CF, n° 105; *IGF* 17, p. 28.

[2215] *Ibid,* Clerc, 1929, p.78.

[2216] *Ibid*, p. 324, *IG* 2454, *Inscriptiones Graecia*, vol. XIV. Appendix, Inscriptiones Galliae, III, Massalia, 2454. Berolini, 1890, p. 647. See *IG*, XIV, 2454 for exact spacing of inscription letters; the Π and H in Pompeius are joined together.

[2217] G. H. R. Horsley, *New Documents Illustrating Early Christianity: A Review of the Greek Inscriptions and Papyrii published in 1979*, vol. 4, Macquarie University, 1987, p. 156.

[2218] M. Clerc, *Massalia: Histoire de Marseille dans L'Antiquité des Origins a la Fin de l'empire Romain d'occident*, vol. 2. Librarie A. Tacussel, 1929, p. 247; M. Bats, 'The Greeks in Gaul and Corsica: the rhythm of the Greek emporion' in P. Carratelli (ed.), *The Western Greeks: Classical Civilization in the Western Mediterranean*, (London, 1996): 577–584, here p. 581; Pliny, *NH*, III.5.

[2219] H. Cleere, *Southern France: An Oxford Archaeological Guide*, Oxford, 2001, p. 138.

[2220] Pliny the Elder, *Natural Histories*, vol.2, III, 34, trans. H. Rackham, Heinemann, 1947, p. 29.

[2221] W. E. Klingshirn, *Caesarius of Arles, The Making of a Christian Community in Late Antique Gaul*, Cambridge University Press, 1994, p. 37.

[2222] Strabo, *Geography*, IV. 1.5.27-28.

[2223] The Elder Seneca, *Controversiae*, vol.1. 2.6.12, trans. M. Winterbottom, William Heinemann Ltd., 1974, p. 361.

[2224] *Ibid*, vol.1. 2.5.13, p. 333.

[2225] Strabo, *Geography*, IV.1. 5.

[2226] Tacitus, *Agricola*, IV, trans. M. Hutton, Heinemann, 1980, p. 33.

[2227] S. P. Morris, 'Greeks and Barbarians–Linking with a wider world', in S. Alcock, and R. Osborne, (eds.), *Classical Archaeology*, Blackwell, 2007, p. 391.

[2228] *Justin: Epitome of the Philippic History of Pompeius Trogus*, 43.4.1, trans. J. C. Yardley, Scholars Press Atlanta, GA, 1994, 267.

[2229] M. Bats, 'The Greeks in Gaul and Corsica: the rhythm of the Greek emporion', P. Carratelli (ed.), *The Western Greeks: classical civilization in the Western Mediterranean* (London, 1996): 577–584, here p. 583.

[2230] A. Trevor. Hodge, *Ancient Greek France*, University of Pennsylvania, 1999, p. 160.

[2231] *Ibid*, p. 220.

[2232] *Ibid*, p. 36.

[2233] J-P. Morel, 'Phocaean Colonisation' in G. R. Tsetskhladze (ed.), *Greek Colonisation: An Account of Greek Colonies and Other Settlements Overseas*, vol.1, (Leiden, 2006): 358–428, here p. 380, (Aeschylus *apud*, Strabo 4.1.7).

[2234] A. Trevor. Hodge, *Ancient Greek France*, University of Pennsylvania, 1999, p. 46.

[2235] Pliny the Elder, *Natural Histories*, vol.2, III, 34, trans. H. Rackham, Heinemann, 1947, p. 29.

[2236] G. M. Trevelyan, *History of England*, Longman Green & Co., 1947, p. 10.

[2237] J. Gardiner and N. Wenborn, (eds.), *The History Today Companion to British History*, Collins & Brown, 1995, p. 629.

[2238] W. S. Churchill, *A History of the English-Speaking Peoples*, Vol. 1, Bk. 1, Britannia, Rosetta Books, 1956.

[2239] Tacitus, *Agricola*, XIII. Also 'untouched, intact', Horace, *Epode*, VII.7 '*Intactus aut Britannus ut descenderet Sacra catenatus via;*' Dio Cassius, XXXIX.53, Caesar 'magnified' greatly what was actually an 'expedition'.

[2240] Strabo, *Geography,* Book II, 5.8.

[2241] Plutarch, *The Lives of the Noble Grecians and Romans*, Julius Caesar, 23, trans. T. North, Wordsworth Editions Ltd., 1998, p. 488.

[2242] Appian's *History of Rome: The Gallic Wars*, trans. H. White, ['Livius'] <http://www.livius.org/ap-ark/appian/appian_gallic_1.html> viewed 22 May 2012; also 'the formerly unknown had become certain and the previously unheard-of accessible' Dio Cassius, *Roman History*, XXXIX. 53.

[2243] Caesar, *The Gallic War*, Bk. IV. 20-21, trans. H. J. Edwards, Dover Publications, 2006, p. 64.

[2244] Plutarch, *The Lives of the Noble Grecians and Romans*, trans. T. North. Wordsworth Editions Ltd., 1998, p. 489.

[2245] Caesar, *The Gallic War*, Book V. 22, trans. H. J. Edwards, Dover Publications, 2006, p. 81.

[2246] *Ibid*, Bk. VI. 13, p. 103.

[2247] Suetonius, *Lives of the Twelve Caesars,* Caius Julius Caesar, 47, trans. H. M. Bird, Wordsworth Editions, 1997, p. 32 & 34. Pearls must have been highly valued as Suetonius writes that Caesar above all loved Servilia, mother of Marcus Brutus, and when he was in his first consulship he bought her a pearl for six million sesterces; Cuirass of pearls see Pliny, *N.H.* IX.57., and M.B. Flory, 'Pearls for Venus' *Historia: Zeitschrift für Alte Geschichte*, Bd.37.H.4 (4th Qtr., 1988):498-504 ['JSTOR' journal archive] <www.jstor.org/stable/4436082> viewed 28 March 2013.

[2248] Plutarch, *The Lives of the Noble Grecians and Romans*, trans. T. North, Wordsworth Editions Ltd., 1998, p. 488.

[2249] Cicero, *Pro Caelio,* XIII, trans. R. Gardiner, Heinemann, 1970, p. 381; R. Gardiner, (ed.), *The Age of the Galley,* Conway Maritime Press, 1995, p. 67; Plutarch, *The Lives of the Noble Grecians and Romans*, Julius Caesar, 28, trans. T. North, Wordsworth Editions Ltd., 1998, p. 493.

[2250] *Plutarch Caesar: Translated with Introduction and Commentary* by C. Pelling, Oxford, 2011, 23.2-23.3, p.256, Lucan, *Civil War*, 2.571-2; Caesar, *BG*, IV.36 'weighed anchor a little after midnight'.

[2251] Plutarch, *The Lives of the Noble Grecians and Romans*, Julius Caesar, 23, trans. T. North, Wordsworth Editions Ltd., 1998, p. 488.

[2252] *Appian's Roman History,* vol.1. Bk. IV, 55, trans. H. White, Heinemann, 1913, p. 105.

[2253] Plutarch, The *Lives of the Noble Grecians and Romans*, Julius Caesar, 28, trans. T. North, Wordsworth Editions Ltd., 1998, p. 493.

[2254] B. Cunliffe, *The Extraordinary Voyage of Pytheas the Greek: The man who discovered Britain,* Penguin Books, 2002, p.159–160.

[2255] R. C. Carrington, *Caesar's Invasion of Britain, Gallic Wars*, chapter XXXII. (v.13.12), Alpha Classics, G. Bell & Sons Ltd., 1952, p. 44 and Notes. XXXII.(v.13.12) p. 81. Caesar's comments in his book *Gallic Wars* that: *In hoc medio cursu est insula quae appellatur Mona: complures praeterea minores subiectae insulae existimantur, de quibus insulis non nulli scipserunt dies continuos XXX sub bruma esse noctem. Nos nihil de eo percontationibus reperiebamus nisi certis ex aqua mensuris breviores esse quam in continenti noctes videbamus.*

[2256] Caesar, *The Gallic War,* V.13, trans. H. J. Edwards, Dover Publications, 2006, p. 77–78

[2257] Caesar, *The Gallic War*, V.13, trans. C. Hammond, Oxford World Classics, 1996, p. 96, and Explanatory Notes 5.13, p. 232.

[2258] C. H. Roseman, *Pytheas of Massalia: Text, Translation and Commentary,* Ares Publishing, 1994, p. 76–77.

[2259] *Ibid*, p. 131 n. 21, Strabo, *Geography*, 2.5.8. The Fragments, The Prettans included Ireland, Britain and all the outlying islands p.132 n.21; habitable regions and Strabo's fixed views see p. 45 and p. 52.

[2260] The shortest day at the winter solstice in Iceland in the north-west fjords of Ísafjördur is 2 hours and 44 minutes. Sun rises at 12.09 and sets 14.53. Morganbludid, Iceland Review, 'Winter Solstice Celebrated in Iceland Today', *Daily News* article 21 December 2009, <http://icelandreview.com/icelandreview/daily_news/?ew_0_a_id=355697>, viewed on 30 August 2011.

Rifstangi in the north-east is Iceland's most northerly point and therefore the day would be even less than at Ísafjördur whose were the only tables available.

[2261] R. C. Carrington, *Caesar's Invasion of Britain, Gallic Wars*, Alpha Classics, G. Bell & Sons Ltd., 1952, p. 13.

[2262] Caesar, *The Gallic War*, IV. 24, trans. H. J. Edwards, Dover Publications, 2006, p. 107.

[2263] *Ibid*, V.13, p. 77.

[2264] Over a century later Agricola's (A.D.78–84) fleet 'ascertained Britain is an island'. Tacitus, *Agricola*, Bk.1.10. ['Internet Sacred Texts Archive'] <http://www.sacred-texts.com/cla/tac/ag01010.htm>, viewed on 5 September 2011.

[2265] Caesar, *The Gallic War*, V.13, trans. H. J. Edwards, Dover Publications, 2006, p. 78.

[2266] C. H. Roseman, *Pytheas of Massalia: Text, Translation and Commentary*, Ares Publishing, 1994, p. 90 n. 95.

[2267] Caesar, *The Gallic War*, V.13, trans. H. J. Edwards, Dover Publications, 2006, p. 78.

[2268] Though the sun does set around the summer solstice in Iceland except for the northernmost part of the island of Rifstangi, the amount of ambient light is so much as to allow by law that lighthouse beacons are turned off for three months each year. B. Cunliffe, *The Extraordinary Voyage of Pytheas the Greek: The man who discovered Britain*, Penguin Books, 2002, p. 124–125.

[2269] A. L. F. Rivet and C. Smith, *The Place-Names of Roman Britain*, B. T. Batsford Ltd, 1982, p. 85, Solinus, Collectanea Rerum Memorabilium, 22, 1–12.

[2270] C. H. Roseman, *Pytheas of Massalia: Text, Translation and Commentary*, Ares Publishing, 1994, p. 8.

[2271] Caesar, *The Gallic War*, Book V. 48, trans. H. J. Edwards, Dover Publications, 2006, p. 92.

[2272] The basis for Strabo's and Polybius's dismissive argument was that no one else had been north since Pytheas of Massalia to corroborate his discoveries.

[2273] R. C. Carrington, *Caesar's Invasion of Britain, Gallic Wars*, Alpha Classics, G. Bell & Sons Ltd., 1952, XXXIII (v.14.2), p. 45.

[2274] *Ibid*, XLI. (v. 22.1–2), p. 51.

[2275] *Ibid*, XXXII. (v. 13.10) p. 44 and Notes XXXII. (v. 13.10) p. 81.

[2276] *Ibid*, 'Britannia' XXXII (v.13) p. 44, and Notes XXXII. (v. 13.10) p. 81.

[2277] The location of Mona according to Pliny the Elder was to "Camalodunum the British tribal capital about 200 miles" [Roman miles]. Pliny, *Natural Histories*, 2.186–187, For Mona and Monapia, Pliny, *N.H.* 4.102; C. H. Roseman, *Pytheas of Massalia: Text, Translation and Commentary*, Ares Publishing, 1994, p. 90 and note 95; A. L. F. Rivet and C. Smith, *The Place-Names of Roman Britain*, B. T. Batsford Ltd, 1982, p.410–11 and p. 419–420.

[2278] R. C. Carrington, *Caesar's Invasion of Britain, Gallic Wars*, XXXIII. (v.14.6), p. 45, XL. (v.21.7). p. 50, XXXII. (v.13.12)., p. 45, and p. 81, Alpha Classics, G. Bell & Sons Ltd., 1952; R. G. Collingwood, and J. N. L. Myers, *Roman Britain and English Settlements*, Oxford, 1937, p. 31.

Another theory current in the twentieth century was expressed by Collingwood who had conjectured the possibility that Caesar knew of the Belgae side of the channel (Caesar, *The Gallic War*, trans. H. J. Edwards, Loeb, 1966, p. 251) a tribe called the *Britanni* and that the Belgae had invaded part of Britain he presumed opposite in Kent. Caesar possibly hearing the similarity of the names might have called the rest of the island *Britannia* thinking to correct previous writers that had used the name *Pretani* since the fourth century B.C. from Pytheas's exploration of Britain. Therefore perhaps Caesar changed the existing Latinised form of *Pretani* and *Pretania* to *Britanni* and *Britannia* respectively? (Collingwood & Myers, 1937, p. 31). Though Rivet and Smith mention that Catullus the Roman poet 84-54 B.C. was already using B instead of P for *Britannia* **before** Caesar's invasion of Britain. Polybius a Greek was also using B for Brettanic Islands **a 100 years earlier than Caesar**. (A. L. F. Rivet and C. Smith, *The Place-Names of Roman Britain*, B. T. Batsford Ltd., 1982, p. 40 and p. 282). Professor B. Cunliffe has proved since the Belgae actually had their territory elsewhere in Britain based around the 'Solent, and the Test and Itchen valleys'. Later Winchester (*Venta Belagarum*) became the Roman administrative centre there. (B. Cunliffe, *Greeks, Romans and Barbarians: Spheres of Interaction*, Guild, 1988, p. 148).

[2279] C. H. Roseman, *Pytheas of Massalia: Text, Translation and Commentary*, Ares Publishing, 1994, p. 7–17.

There are also in German two small books of the ancient references: H. J. Mette, *Pytheas von Massalia*, Walter de Gruyter & Co., Berlin, 1952; D. Stichtenoth, *Pytheas von Marseille*; *Über das Weltmeer*, Herman Böhlaus Nachfolger, Wiemar, 1959.

[2280] B. Cunliffe, *The Extraordinary Voyage of Pytheas the Greek: The man who discovered Britain*, Penguin Books, 2002.

[2281] A. L. F. Rivet, *Gallia Narbonensis*, Batsford, 1988, p. 222 n. 25, *CIL*. XII. 7, p.3. The cathedral stands on the site of the Temple of Mars in Vintium (Vence). Apparently on the northern side of the previous cemetery is a grey basalt column given by people from Massalia in A.D. 230 with an inscription on the base.
<http://www.flickr.com/photos/martin-m-miles/5571990931/>, viewed on 21 December 2011: For a photograph of the 2 columns and 2 inscriptions, dedication by Julius Honoratus, procurator, governor of the Province of Alpes Maritime see M. Clerc, *Massalia: Histoire de Marseille dans L'Antiquité des Origins a la Fin de l'empire Romain d'occident*, vol. 2. Librarie A. Tacussel, 1929, p. 273, n.1, Fig. 10. O. Hirschfeld, *CIL* XII, 7, Alpes Maritmae VINTIVM, p.3.

[2282] J. Knight, *Roman France: an archaeological field guide*, Tempus Publishing, 2001, p. 164.

[2283] *Musée des Docks Romains*, ['Culture.marseille.fr']
<http://www.marseille.fr/siteculture/les-lieux-culturels-municipaux/musees/le-musée-des-docks-romains>, viewed on 18 November 2011.

[2284] Strabo, *Geography*, IV, I, 5.

[2285] *Strabo Geography*, vol. 2. IV.1.5, trans. H. L. Jones, Loeb, 1923, p. 175. n. 3. The editors of this edition were E. Capps. PH,D., LL.D, T. E. Page. LITT.D, W.H.D. Kouse. LITT.D.

[2286] M. Clerc, *Massalia: Histoire de Marseille dans L'Antiquité des Origins a la Fin de l'empire Romain d'occident*, vol. 2. Librarie A. Tacussel, 1929, p.293, p. 296 n. 1 & n. 2.

[2287] S. T. Loseby, 'Marseille: A Late Antique Success Story?', p. 183, *Journal for Roman Studies*, vol. 82, (1992):165–185, here p. 183. Society for the Promotion of Roman Studies, ['JSTOR' journal archive]
<http://www.jstor.org/stable/301290>, viewed on 11 October 2010.

[2288] Strabo, *Geography*, IV.1.5.

[2289] H. Cleere, *Southern France: An Oxford Archaeological Guide*, Oxford, 2001, p. 138.

[2290] Once the Romans had established their own settlements in Gaul they preferred going inland from their city of Frejus (Forum Julii) to Aix as to continue on the coastal road the Massaliotes built was double the distance. W. H. (Bullock) Hall. *The Romans on the Riviera and the Rhone: a sketch on the conquest of Liguria and the Roman Province*, Chp. IX. p. 99, and XIX, p. 184-185, Macmillan, 1898, reprinted by Ares Publishers, Chicago, 1974, ['Open Library']
<http://openlibrary.org/books/OL5069373M/The_Romans_on_the_Riviera_and_the_Rhone>, viewed on 19 December 2011.

[2291] G. Woolf, 'Becoming Roman, Staying Greek: culture, identity and the civilising process in the Roman east' in *Proceedings of the Cambridge Philosophical Society*, 40 (1994):116–43.

[2292] In Constantinople (Istanbul) despite the Treaty between Greece and Turkey in 1923 (after the Ionian War 1919–1922) to respect each others minorities living in Thrace, the Turks had periodically squeezed the original Greek population down to around 3,000, there were riots directed against the Greek minority in Istanbul in 1955. (R. Clogg, *A Concise History of Greece*, Cambridge University Press, 1997, p. 101, p. 150, p. 208).

Istanbul is where the Patriarch (Pope) head of the Eastern Catholic Orthodox church still has his seat. Though present day relations between Greece and Turkey has undergone a positive transformation having improved greatly since the Turkish earthquake of 1999 and the assistance Greece gave them, the Turkish government still require candidates for the Patriarch to be working in Turkey and Turkish citizens.

[2293] The mainly Greek population 1.1 million were expelled from Asia Minor under the terms of the 'Convention Concerning the Exchange of Greek and Turkish Populations 1923' which had begun before the Treaty of Lausanne was signed also the same year. The Convention identified persons only by religion and not ethnicity or language i.e. Greek Orthodox or Moslem. *Permanent Court of International Justice*, File F. c. XI° °Docket VI. I., Advisory opinion No. 10°, 21 February 1925. 'Exchange of Greek and Turkish Populations (Lausanne Convention VI, January 30th, 1923, Article 2)' <http://www.worldcourts.com/pcij/eng/decisions/1925.02.21_greek_turkish.htm>, viewed on 29 November 2011. The Greek Prime Minister Eleftheros Venizelos had actually suggested an exchange on a smaller scale at the beginning of World War I. R. Clogg, A *Concise History of Greece,* Cambridge University Press, 1997, 101.

Regarding the 1.1 million Greeks according to the Pontos World website most had already fled before the Convention. After the Convention, 189,916 Greeks and 355,635 Moslems were exchanged during the period 1923-26. A. Tsifildis, *Exchange of Populations Between Greece and Turkey*, <http://pontosworld.com/index.php?option=com_content&task=view&id=1140&Itemid=90>, viewed on 29 November 2011.

Greek Moslems from Crete were transferred to the west coast of Turkey where the previous Greek Orthodox had been living before the 'Exchange'. The only exemptions of any Exchange were western Thrace, Istanbul, Imvros and Tenedos. Some 380,000 Moslems were expelled from other Greek territory to Turkey. R. Clogg, *A Concise History of Greece,* Cambridge University Press, 1997, p. 101.

Phokaia and New Phokaia are listed in the Greek cities in the area north of Smyrni. The Greek Army had occupied the Metropolitanate of Ephesus, Ionia in April 1919 until their defeat in August 1922. Following the defeat all Orthodox Christians here were evacuated to Greece. D. Kiminas, *The Ecumenical Patriarchate: A History of it's Metropolitanates with Annotated Hierarch Catalogs*, Wildeside Press, 2009, p. 85. There had been atrocities committed by both sides during the conflict. R. Clogg, A *Concise History of Greece,* Cambridge University Press, 1997, p. 94 and p. 97.

French archaeologists Félix Sartiaux and Monsieur Manciet were excavating in Phocaea when the Turkish *chettes* (irregular forces) arrived. They reported some of the population were massacred and the rest brutally expelled. G. Milton, *Paradise Lost*, Sceptre, 2009, p. 50. Felix saved some of the Phocaeans by placing the French flag on four of the houses to be under the protection of France. F. Sartiaux, *Phoccee 1913-1920: Le temoignage de Felix Sartiaux,* <http://www.scribd.com/doc/8636978/Livre-Phocee-Kallimages>, viewed 13 June 2012. Felix was an eye-witness to the other massacre in Phocaea in June 1914. *Greek Genocide 1914-23,* <http://www.greek-genocide.org/asia_minor.html>, viewed 13 June 2012. This attack was described by George Horton, the American Consul at Izmir (1911-1917 and 1919-1922), in his book *Blight of Asia,* published in 1926, and reprinted by Sterndale Classics, Taderon Press, 2008.

The population of old Phokaia was 9,000 Greeks and 3,000 Turks. Further down the coast was New Phokaia with a population of 6,500 Greeks and 1,000 Turks. Hatzalexandrou Patroklos, *H Idiateri Patrida Mou,*<http://www.peri-grafis.com/ergo.php?id=1125>, viewed on 27 November 2011. Some of the original Greek houses in old Phokaia remained derelict until recently and due to the architectural character those surviving have been undergoing restoration. <http://www.fotothing.com/sscelebi/photo/1d589a1c11c345a979683bf9c010d088/>, viewed on 27 November 2011; <http://www.kucukvebutikoteller.com/eng/griffon-butik-hotel>, viewed on 27 November 2011.

See also Matt Barrett, *Venizelos and the Asia Minor Catastrophe,* ['Matt Barrett's Travel Guides']
<http://www.ahistoryofgreece.com/venizelos.htm>, viewed on 26 October 2011; Yaprak Gursoy, *The Effects of the Population Exchange on the Political Regimes of Greece and Turkey in the 1930s*,

<http://findarticles.com/p/articles/mi_7063/is_2_42/ai_n31184449/?tag=content;col1>, viewed on 26 October 2011; Rosamie Moore, *Fochies (Eski Foca)*, <http://romeartlover.tripod.com/Foca.html>, viewed on 28 October 2011.

[2294] R. Clogg, A *Concise History of Greece,* Cambridge University Press, 1997, p. 96 and p. 49; J. Herrin, *Byzantium: The Surviving Life of a Medieval Empire*, Penguin, 2008, p. 274.

[2295] G. Rohlfs, 'Greek Remnants in Southern Italy' in *The Classical Journal*, vol. 62, no. 4 (Jan., 1967): 164-169, The Classical Association of the Middle West and South, viewed on 30 December 2010, <http://www.jstor.org/stable/3295569>; *Names of the Greeks*, <http://www.mlahanas.de/Greeks/LX/NamesOfTheGreeks.htm>, viewed on 30 December 2010;

Italian Language School, *Salentinian Greece: in Salento, Southern Italy,* Greek-Salentinian Language and traditions–History and Language of Terra d'Otranto, <http://www.ilsonline.it/salentiniangreece/>.

Rohlfs (p. 165–166) examined the dialects and found them to be directly from Magna Graecia period and not from the later influx of Byzantine Greeks when Leo VI enfranchised 3,000 slaves of Danielis of Patras after death establishing them to Apulia to cultivate the land as serfs. Between the eighth and tenth centuries there were 200 Greek monasteries erected in southern Italy subject to the Patriarch of Constantinople. A. Louth, *Greek East and Latin West: the Church, AD 681–1071*, St. Vladimir's Seminary Press, 2007, p. 38–39.

I was fortunate to see on TV when in Greece a folk dance group from Salento Italy. The programme features Ellenophones–Greek speaking folk culture. They sang and spoke in their dialect which was in clear understandable Greek. The dances I saw were in couples and tarantellas. *Το αλάτι της γης,* Channel ET1, [TV broadcast] 16 September 2012.

[2296] Institut de Sociolingüística Catalana, *Greek (Griko) in Italy,* <http://www.uoc.edu/euromosaic/web/document/grec/an/i1/i1.html>, viewed on 30 December 2010.

[2297] J. Santrot, *Le Trésor de Garonne:IIe siècle après Jesus Christ,* [catalogue de l'exposition] 'Des monnaies dans la "grave"', Musées departmentaux de Loire-Atlantique, 1987, p. 67. Also found was an amphorae of *garum* and sardines 1st century A.D.

[2298] H. Cleere, *Southern France: An Oxford Archaeological Guide*, Oxford, p 118, 2001.

[2299] M. Clerc, *Massalia: Histoire de Marseille dans L'Antiquité des Origins a la Fin de l'empire Romain d'occident*, vol. 2. Librarie A. Tacussel, 1929, p. 262.

[2300] M. Clerc, *Massalia: Histoire de Marseille dans L'Antiquité des Origins a la Fin de l'empire Romain d'occident*, vol. 2. Librarie A. Tacussel, 1929, p. 263, *CIG*, II, XIV, Inscriptiones Lydiae, 3413. A. Boeckhuis, Berlini, 1843, p. 798. See *CIG* for exact spacing of letters.

[2301] *Ibid*, *CIG*, II, XIV, Inscriptiones Lydiae, 3415. A. Boeckhuis, Berlini, 1843, p. 798. See *CIG* for exact spacing of letters.

[2302] M. Clerc, *Massalia: Histoire de Marseille dans L'Antiquité des Origins a la Fin de l'empire Romain d'occident*, vol. 2. Librarie A. Tacussel, 1929, p. 262, *Inscriptiones Greacia*. 3413 & 3415. Susan Walker, Keeper of Antiquities, Ashmolean Museum, emailed me 1November 2010, to say they are still there and in store while the museum was undergoing refurbishment.

[2303] M. Clerc, *Massalia: Histoire de Marseille dans L'Antiquité des Origins a la Fin de l'empire Romain d'occident*, vol. 2. Librarie A. Tacussel, 1929, p. 262 n.3.

[2304] Strabo, *Geography*, Book IV. Chapter 1.4.

[2305] M. Clerc, *Massalia: Histoire de Marseille dans L'Antiquité des Origins a la Fin de l'empire Romain d'occident*, vol. 2. Librarie A. Tacussel, 1929, p. 263-264.

[2306] J. McInerney, *The Folds of Parnassos: Land and Ethnicity in Ancient Phokis*, University of Texas Press, 1999, p. 161. n. 25. Pausanias 7.3.10.

[2307] Pausanias, *Description of Greece*, VII.3.10, trans. W. H. S. Jones, and H. A. Ormerod, 4 vols. Heinemann, 1918. ['Perseus, Tufts University', digital library] <http://www.perseus.tufts.edu/hopper/text?doc=Perseus%3Atext%3A1999.01.0160%3Abook%3D7%3Achapter%3D3%3Asection%3D10>, viewed 15 January 2012.

[2308] M. Clerc, *Massalia: Histoire de Marseille dans L'Antiquité des Origins a la Fin de l'empire Romain d'occident*, vol. 2. Librarie A. Tacussel, 1929, p. 293.

[2309] *Ibid*, p. 265. Cities could be personified into deities. The personification of the city of Rome that is the deified form of the Roman state, as the deity Roma 'was chiefly worshipped in the cities in the Greek east as early as the second century B.C.' In ancient Thessaloniki Roma worship is referred to in an inscription of the first century A.D. connected with the community of Romans who had settled in the city during the Hadrian period A.D. 117–138. Part of the temple and the statue of Roma are on display in the Archaeological Museum at Thessaloniki Greece 2010.

See commemorative coin A.D. 330–333 Thessaloniki mint, <http://www.vcoins.com/romaeaeternaenumismatics/store/viewItem.asp?idProduct=170>, viewed on 23 November 2011.

[2310] M. Clerc, *Massalia: Histoire de Marseille dans L'Antiquité des Origins a la Fin de l'empire Romain d'occident*, vol. 2. Librarie A. Tacussel, 1929, p. 348, Inscriptiones Graecia, vol. XIV, Appendix Inscriptiones Galliae, 2446.

[2311] K. Lomas, 'Hellenism, Romanization and Cultural Identity in Massalia', in K. Lomas (ed.), *Greek Identity in the Western Mediterranean: Papers in Honour of Professor Brian Shefton*, Brill, 2003, p. 484 n. 34, P. Ghiron-Bistagne, 'Un autel Massiliotte de Zeus Patroos' in Bats, M. *Marseille Greque et la Gaule*, 152–4.

[2312] M. Clerc, *Massalia: Histoire de Marseille dans L'Antiquité des Origins a la Fin de l'empire Romain d'occident*, vol. 2. Librarie A. Tacussel, 1929, p. 377 n. 3; *IG*, 2437.

[2313] Exhibits I saw in the Musée d'Histoire de Marseille, July 2009; B. Bizot, et al. *Marseille Antique: guides archéologiques de la France*, Editions du Patrimonie, Centre des monuments nationaux, 2007, p. 84.

[2314] Exhibits I saw in the Musée d'Histoire de Marseille, July 2009.

[2315] M. Clerc, *Massalia: Histoire de Marseille dans L'Antiquité des Origins a la Fin de l'empire Romain d'occident*, vol. 2. Librarie A. Tacussel, 1929, p. 322, *IG*, 2434. In this inscription the Greek Σ is replaced by a C. In ΓΡΑΜΜΑΤΙΚΟC the middle of both M's go right to the bottom looking more like a U with tails front and back: a C replaces the Σ. In the last line there is the usual Greek shaped M in ΡΩΜΑΙΚΟC. See *IG* 2434 for exact copy.

[2316] A. Hermary, A. Hesnard, and H. Tréziny, *Marseille Grecque: La cite phocéenne (600–49 av.J-C*, Editions Errance, 1999, p. 93.

[2317] M. Clerc, *Massalia: Histoire de Marseille dans L'Antiquité des Origins a la Fin de l'empire Romain d'occident*, vol. 2. Librarie A. Tacussel, 1929, p. 348–381.

[2318] J. Knight, *Roman France: an archaeological field guide,* Tempus Publishing, 2001, p. 164–165.

[2319] J. Santrot, *Le Trésor de Garonne:IIe siècle après Jesus Christ,* [catalogue de l'exposition] 'Des monnaies dans la "grave"', Musées departmentaux de Loire-Atlantique, 1987, p. 70.

[2320] S. T. Loseby, 'Marseille: A Late Antique Success Story?', *Journal for Roman Studies,* vol. 82, (1992): 165–185, here p. 171–172, Society for the Promotion of Roman Studies, ['JSTOR' journal archive] <http://www.jstor.org/stable/301290>, viewed on 17 November 2009.

[2321] *Ibid*, here p. 168–171.

[2322] B. Levick, *The Government of the Roman Empire: A Sourcebook*, Croom Helm, 1985, Ch. 2, p. 24–25, ILS 6761; Nicaea, Narbonensis. Levick's selection covers a period 30 B.C. to A.D. 284.

[2323] Strabo, *Geography,* IV.1.9.

[2324] B. Levick, *The Government of the Roman Empire: A Sourcebook*, Croom Helm, 1985, Ch. 2, p. 24–25, ILS 6761; Nicaea, Narbonensis.

[2325] K. Lomas, 'Hellenism, Romanization and Cultural Identity in Massalia', in K. Lomas (ed.), *Greek Identity in the Western Mediterranean: Papers in Honour of Professor Brian Shefton*, Brill, 2003, p. 481 n. 22, *CIL,* 5.7914.

[2326] M. Clerc, *Massalia: Histoire de Marseille dans L'Antiquité des Origins a la Fin de l'empire Romain d'occident*, vol. 2. Librarie A. Tacussel, 1929, p.293, p. 296 n. 1 & n. 2.

[2327] Agathias, *The Histories,* Bk.I. 2. 1, trans. J. D. Frendo, (Corpus fontium historiae Byzantinae; vol. 2 A: Ser. Berlinensis). Elnheitssacht: Historiaa (engl.), Walter de Gruyter Co, 1975, p. 10.

[2328] M. Clerc, *Massalia: Histoire de Marseille dans L'Antiquité des Origins a la Fin de l'empire Romain d'occident*, vol. 2, Librarie A. Tacussel, 1929, p. 296.

[2329] Strabo, *Geography,* IV, 1, 5.

[2330] Cicero, *Pro Flacco,* 63–64.

[2331] M. Clerc, *Massalia: Histoire de Marseille dans L'Antiquité des Origins a la Fin de l'empire Romain d'occident*, vol. 2, Librarie A. Tacussel, 1929, p. 296. CIL, XII, 407, O. Hirschfield, (ed.), Berolini,1887; CF, 169.

[2332] A. L. F. Rivet, *Gallia Narbonensis,* Batsford, 1988, p. 219–220.

[2333] M. Clerc, *Massalia: Histoire de Marseille dans L'Antiquité des Origins a la Fin de l'empire Romain d'occident*, vol. 2, Librarie A. Tacussel, 1929, p. 293 n.1, *CIG,* XIV, 2433, and p. 375.

[2334] *CIG,* XIV, 2433; *IGF* 8, p. 14-16.

[2335] J-P. Morel, 'Phocaean Colonisation' in G. R. Tsetskhladze (ed.), *Greek Colonisation: An Account of Greek Colonies and Other Settlements Overseas,* vol.1, (Leiden, 2006): 358–428, here p. 380, re. M. Clerc, *Massalia,* (2 vols.) (Marseille 1927–29; reprint Lafitte, Marseille, 1971), vol. 2. p. 375.

[2336] K. Lomas, 'Hellenism, Romanization and Cultural Identity in Massalia', in K. Lomas (ed.), *Greek Identity in the Western Mediterranean: Papers in Honour of Professor Brian Shefton*, (Brill, 2003): 475-498, here p. 484.

[2337] M. Clerc, *Massalia: Histoire de Marseille dans L'Antiquité des Origins a la Fin de l'empire Romain d'occident*, vol. 2, Librarie A. Tacussel, 1929, p. 294–295 and p. 297, *CIL,* XII, 410, (ed.) O. Hirschfield, Berolini, 1887, p. 58.

[2338] *Ibid*, p. 297–298, *CIL,* XII, 411. (ed.) O. Hirschfield, Berolini, 1887, p. 58.

[2339] M. Clerc, *Massalia: Histoire de Marseille dans L'Antiquité des Origins a la Fin de l'empire Romain d'occident*, vol. 2, Librarie A. Tacussel, 1929, p. 298; *CIL,* XII, 400, 409.

[2340] Lucian, *Toxaris or Friendship*, vol. 5, 24-26, trans. A. M. Harmon, William Heinemann, 1955, p. 143-149.

[2341] Agathias, *The Histories*, Bk.I. 2. 1, trans. J. D. Frendo, (Corpus fontium historiae Byzantinae; vol. 2 A: Ser. Berlinensis). Elnheitssacht: Historiaa (engl.), Walter de Gruyter Co., 1975, p. 10.

[2342] M. I. Rostovtzeff, *The Social and Economic History of the Roman Empire*, vol. 2, Chapter IX, Clarendon, 1963, p. 605 n. 37.

[2343] Though as subsequent events led to the debt crisis in 2011, for Greece it was because the Euro was too expensive. Fully embracing the European ideal Greece would have been better off by staying out of the Euro as Britain had done. All prices were rounded up on conversion and Greek wages and pensions could not keep up with the increased cost of living thereafter whereas it had managed before with their drachma currency. During the 1980s several South American countries economies could not grow due to overwhelming debt and debilitating interest repayments. After much public pressure on the western banks they wrote off the debts. Ever since the South American countries recovered and began to grow. A possible solution for the present crisis is for the main core EU countries that invented the Euro and can afford it should have the Euro. This would make it stronger. While the other EU members e.g. Spain and Italy should have their own national currency but only at the same time **wiping off all debt and interest repayments** allowing those countries' economies free to grow again? It was events in faraway Greece and the wider implications on the Euro that focussed the main British political parties to form a coalition government speedily in 6 days after an inconclusive election result 6 May 2010, to keep the Euro zone markets stable.

Austerity measures forced on Greece in return for an EC financial bailout is causing large unemployment 26% in 2013 and set to last at least a decade. This seems a short-sighted policy as there are less people available paying tax and the government has even less funds to pay back debts with business and the economy shrinking. Young Greeks will have to emigrate to find work elsewhere. There has been an increase of suicides in Greece (3,000 January to June 2012) that have no money to pay bills. Many Greeks have cancelled their electricity this winter yet many modern flats and houses like ours do not have fireplaces and chimneys, and it is a dangerous situation when law abiding people cannot pay bills or the new taxes the Greek government have passed because of the bailout. Pensions have been drastically cut and another tax on the square metre size of their property imposed with no extra income to pay for it. This has forced Greece into two general elections so far in 2012. Cyprus heavily affected by a Greek austerity economy needed an EC bailout in March 2013 given on draconian and uncreative conditions. Some creative thinking is necessary to solve these problems as was done for South America. Greece has suffered many problems in her history but of all the ancient nations they have survived into modern times whereas others have disappeared. Rome is called the 'eternal city' but a water melon seller in Greece told me 'the Greek people are eternal'.

[2344] G. Barruol, 'La Massalie dans la Provincia' in *Voyage en Massalie: 100 ans d'archéologie en Gaule du sud*, Catalogue de l'exposition, (Musées de Marseille/Édisud, 1990): 242-243.

[2345] M. Bats, 'The Greeks in Gaul and Corsica: the rhythm of the Greek emporion' in P. Carratelli (ed.), *The Western Greeks: Classical Civilization in the Western Mediterranean*, (London, 1996): 577–584, here p. 581.

[2346] 'Diocese of Marseilles', *The Original Catholic Encyclopaedia,* Encyclopaedia Press, 1913, vol. 1. p. 2 of 8, <http://oce.catholic.com/index.php?title=Diocese_of_Marseilles>, viewed on 15 September 2009.

[2347] B. Bizot, et al. *Marseille Antique: guides archéologiques de la France*, Editions du Patrimonie, Centre des monuments nationaux, 2007, p. 89.

[2348] M. Clerc, *Massalia: Histoire de Marseille dans L'Antiquité des Origins a la Fin de l'empire Romain d'occident*, vol. 2, Librarie A. Tacussel, 1929, p. 406.

[2349] H. Pope, 'St. Mary Magdalen', *The Catholic Encyclopaedia,* vol. 9, New York: Robert Appleton Co., 1910, <www.newadvent.org/cathen/09761a.htm>, viewed on 15 September 2009.

[2350] J. Lough, *France Observed in the Seventeenth Century by British Travellers*, Oriel Press, 1984, p. 227–228.

[2351] M. Hassett, 'John Cassian', *The Catholic Encyclopaedia,* vol. 3, New York: Robert Appleton Co., 1908, <http://www.newadvent.org/cathen/03404a.htm>, viewed on 3 December 2010.

[2352] F. Meijer, *A History of Seafaring in the Classical World*, Croom Helm, 1986, p. 232.

[2353] B. Bizot, et al. *Marseille Antique: guide archéologiques de la Fra*nce, Editions du Patrimonie, Centre des monuments nationaux, 2007, p. 38.

[2354] N. Samuel, C. Lieu, and D. Montserrat, *From Constantine to Julian*, Routledge, 1996, p. 70–72; 'The Anonymous Panegyric on Constantine' (310), Pass. Lat. VII. (6), trans. M. Vemes, in Samuel N. C. Lieu, and Dominic Montserrat, *From Constantine to Julian,* Routledge, 1996, p. 88. A miscalculation of ladders too short also happened to the Macedonian King Philip V when attacking Larissa. P. Matyszak, *Classical Compendium*, Thames & Hudson, 2009, p. 25.

[2355] Constantine I, [The 1911 Classical Encyclopaedia], <http:www.1911Encyclopaedia.org/Constantine_I> viewed on 29 September 2009.

[2356] F. A. Wright, *Lempriere's Classical Dictionary*, Routledge & Keegan Paul, 1951, p. 361–362.

[2357] D. Jacobs, *Constantinople and the Byzantine Empire*, Cassel, 1969, p. 46.

[2358] M. Clerc, *Massalia: Histoire de Marseille dans L'Antiquité des Origins a la Fin de l'empire Romain d'occident*, vol. 2, Librarie A. Tacussel, 1929, p. 266 n. 1, Eumene, *Panégyric de Constantine*, 19; Aurelius Victor, *Epitome* 38; Eutrope, x, p. 582; Orose, vii, 27; Lactance, *De mort.* persac., 29.

[2359] 'The Anonymous Panegyric on Constantine' (310), Pass. Lat. VII (6) trans. Mark Vemes, in Samuel N.C. Lieu., and Dominic Montserrat, *From Constantine to Julian,* Routledge, 1996, p. 88.

[2360] Pliny, *Natural Histories*, Book XXIX. V. 9–11, trans. W. H. S. Jones, William Heinemann, 1963, p.189.

[2361] M. Clerc, *Massalia: Histoire de Marseille dans L'Antiquité des Origins a la Fin de l'empire Romain d'occident*, vol. 2, Librarie A. Tacussel, 1929, p. 267.

[2362] *Ibid*, p. 267 n. 1; A. J. Valpy, 'Eumenii Panegyicus' in *Scriptores latini, jussu christianissimi Regis ad usnum serenissimi Delphini*, CAP. XIX. 1828, p. 1369. <http://books.google.co.uk/books?id=K8YjAQAAIAAJ&pg=PA1369&lpg=PA1369&dq=Quippe+olim+Graecos+Italosque+illuc+convenas%E2%80%99&source=bl&ots=FkbzulFdSJ&sig=S8l8fnwnn9kyuWobRj-E3vaGN2I&hl=en&ei=CzO9TuzHAYar8AOtl6WrBA&sa=X&oi=book_result&ct=result&resnum=2&ved=0CCYQ6AEwAQ#v=onepage&q=Quippe%20olim%20Graecos%20Italosque%20illuc%20convenas%E2%80%99&f=false>, viewed on 11 November 2011.

[2363] Strabo, *Geography,* IV. 1.

[2364] C. Nüssli, *The Complete Tabula Peutingeriana–a Roman Road Map compared with a modern map*, <http://www.euratlas.net/cartogra/peutinger>, viewed on 1 September 2011.

[2365] M. Clerc, *Massalia: Histoire de Marseille dans L'Antiquité des Origins a la Fin de l'empire Romain d'occident*, vol. 2, Librarie A. Tacussel, 1929, p. 267.

[2366] R. Latouche, *Caesar to Charlemagne: the beginnings of France*, trans. J. Nicholson, Barnes & Noble, 1968, p. 94.

[2367] The Saxon's preferred site for their city was around Convent Garden due to the long beach by The Strand where they could beach their ships and have their beach market easily unlike abandoned Roman London between St Paul's and the Tower of London where the Roman Wall went right down close to the riverbank. The Saxons only moved into the derelict Roman city (calling it Ludenburh) 200 years later by the orders of Alfred the Great because the Roman Walls were mainly intact and gave protection against Viking attacks. *Ludenvwic,* <http://www.kcl.ac.uk/somersethouse/index.php?id=9>, viewed on 21 October 2011.

[2368] Regarding the Anglo-Saxon conquest of England there was a survival of the Brythonic speaking native people for a while in the isolated and marshy terrain of the Isle of Ely near Cambridge. Brythonic survival in the name of a two or three pronged long spear for fishing named Gleave is evident and in village names. Also the names of three clan village units/hamlets beginning with Tydd 'the same as Fen kinship' according to author, archaeologist and Fenland researcher Dr Tim Reynolds, archaeological tour of Ely, March 17, 2012, Birkbeck Archaeological Society.

[2369] They were described as the Grecian or Raetian Alps. Justin (XX.5.9) records that 'The Etruscans for their part, after losing their ancestral homes, seized the Alps under the leadership of Raetus and founded the Raetian people, so named after their leader'.

[2370] R. Latouche, *Caesar to Charlemagne: the beginnings of France*, trans. J. Nicholson, Barnes & Noble, 1968, p. 93; Ammianus Marcellinus, XV.11.

[2371] M. Clerc, *Massalia; Histoire de Marseille dans L'Antiquité des Origins a la Fin de l'empire Romain d'occident*, vol. 2, Librarie A. Tacussel, 1929, p. 267.

[2372] S. T. Loseby, 'Marseille: A Late Antique Success Story?', *Journal for Roman Studies*, vol. 82, (1992):165-185, here p. 180 n. 129, & n. 128, Society for the Promotion of Roman Studies, ['JSTOR' journal archive] <http://www.jstor.org/stable/301290>, viewed on 17 November 2009.

[2373] B. Bizot, et al. *Marseille Antique: guides archéologiques de la France*, Editions du Patrimonie, Centre des monuments nationaux, 2007, p. 122.

[2374] 'Diocese of Marseilles', *The Original Catholic Encyclopaedia,* Encyclopaedia Press, 1913, vol. 1. p. 2 of 8, <http://oce.catholic.com/index.php?title=Diocese_of_Marseilles>, viewed on 15 September 2009.

[2375] A. L. F. Rivet, *Gallia Narbonensis*, Batsford, 1988, p. 220.

[2376] Eborius bishop of York, Restitutus, bishop of London 'civitate Londinensi', Adelfius bishop of 'civitae Colonia Londinensium' (possibly Caerleon-on-Usk), Sacredos, priest and Arminius, deacon. A. W. Haddan and W. Stubbs, *Councils and Ecclesiastical Documents Relating to Great Britain and Ireland*, Vol.1, Oxford,1869, p. 7.

[2377] A. Arnaud, 'Les temps préhistoriques et protohistoriques', in A. Ruggiero (ed.), *Nouvelle histoire de Nice*, Edition Privat, 2006, p. 24.

[2378] 'Diocese of Marseille', *The Original Catholic Encyclopaedia*, Encyclopaedia Press, 1913, vol.1. p. 2 of 8, <http://oce.catholic.com/index.php?title=Diocese_of_Marseilles>, viewed on 15 September 2009.

[2379] J. Harries, *Sidonius Apollinaris and the Fall of Rome AD 407–485,* Oxford University Press, 1999. p. 119.

[2380] 'Diocese of Marseille', *The Original Catholic* Encyclopaedia, Encyclopaedia Press, 1913, vol.1. p. 2 of 8, <http://oce.catholic.com/index.php?title=Diocese_of_Marseilles>, viewed on 15 September 2009.

[2381] T. Venning, (ed.), *A Chronology of the Byzantine Empire,* Palgrave Macmillan, 2006, Part 2, p. 47.

[2382] A. M. Jimenez Garnica, 'Settlement of the Visigoths in the Fifth Century' in P. J. Heather, (ed.), *The Visigoths. From Migration Period to the Seventh Century*, (Boydell Press, 1999): 93-128, here p. 95.

[2383] Aelia Galla Placidia grand-daughter to Emperor Theodosius I (379-395), half-sister to Emperor Honorius (393-423) and married to Athaulf in 414-416. R. W. Mathisen, *Galla Placidia*, University of South Carolina, ['De Imperatoribus Romanis, Online Encyclopaedia of Roman Emperors'] updated 1 June 1999, <http://www.roman-emperors.org/galla.htm>, viewed on 12 January 2012.

[2384] H. Sivan, *Galla Placidia: The Last Roman Empress*, Oxford, 2011, p. 24-25 n. 64 and n. 66, Olympiodorus Fr. 22.1-22.4.

[2385] T. Venning, *Chronology of the Byzantine Empire*, Palgrave, 2006, Part 2, p. 47.

[2386] M. Hassett, 'John Cassian', *The Catholic Encyclopaedia,* vol. 3, New York: Robert Appleton Co., 1908, <http://www.newadvent.org/cathen/03404a.htm>, viewed on 4 December 2010.

[2387] J. F. Haldon, *Byzantium in the Seventh Century*, Cambridge, 1990, p. 189.

[2388] P. Brown, *The Rise of Western Christendom*, Blackwell, 2006, p. 111.

[2389] K. Knight (ed.), *Gennadius,* Supplement to De Viris Illustribis, Chapter 62, ['New Advent'] <http://www.newadvent.org/fathers/2719.htm>, viewed on 1 September 2011.

[2390] P. Brown, *The Rise of Western Christendom*, Blackwell, 2006, p. 111.

[2391] G. Goyau, 'Marseilles (Massilia)', Abbey of St. Victor, in *The Catholic Encyclopaedia,* vol. 9. New York, Robert Appleton Company, 1910, <http://www.newadvent.org/cathen/09715b.htm>, viewed on 11 June 2012.

[2392] J. Pohle, 'Actual Grace', Semipelagianism, in *The Catholic Encyclopaedia*, vol. 6. New York: Robert Appleton Company, 1909, <http://www.newadvent.org/cathen/06689x.htm>, viewed on 3 December 2010.

[2393] K. Knight (ed.), *Gennadius,* Supplement to De Viris Illustribis, Chapter 61, ['New Advent'] <http://www.newadvent.org/fathers/2719.htm>, viewed on 15 December 2010.

[2394] Salvian, *On the Government of God*, trans. E. M. Stanford, Columbua University Press, 1930, <http://www.tertullian.org/fathers/salvian_gov_00_intro.htm>, viewed on 11 March 2012.

[2395] R. Latouche, *Caesar to Charlemagne: the beginnings of France,* trans. J. Nicholson, Barnes & Noble, 1968, p. 194.

[2396] P. Verzone, *From Theodoric to Charlemagne,* Methuen & Co. Ltd., 1968, p. 16–17.

[2397] K. Knight (ed.), *Gennadius,* Supplement to De Viris Illustribis, Chapter 68, ['New Advent'] <http://www.newadvent.org/fathers/2719.htm>, viewed on 1 September 2011.

[2398] *Ibid,* Chapter 80.

[2399] *Ibid*, Chapter 99.

[2400] R. Latouche, *Caesar to Charlemagne: the beginnings of France,* translated by Nicholson, J. Barnes & Noble, 1968, p. 287-288.

[2401] J. Knight, *Roman France: an archaeological field guide*, Tempus Publishing, 2001, p. 211.

[2402] T. Jaques, *Dictionary of Battles and Sieges,* Greenwood Press, 2007, p. 642.

[2403] R. Latouche, *Caesar to Charlemagne: the beginnings of France,* trans. J. Nicholson, Barnes & Noble, 1968, p. 164.

[2404] T. Venning, *Chronology of the Byzantine Empire*, Palgrave, 2006, Part 2, p. 49.

[2405] R. W. Mathisen, *Roman Aristocrats in Barbarian Gaul: strategies for survival in an age of transition*, University of Texas, 1993, p. 46-46.

[2406] R. W. Mathisen, 'Julius Valerius Maiorianus'['De Imperatoribus Romanis'] < http://www.roman-emperors.org/major.htm> updated 7 February 1998, viewed 28 December 2012.

[2407] A. C. Murray, *From Roman to Merovingian Gaul*, Broadview, 2000, p. 101.

[2408] W. E. Klingshirn, *Caesarius of Arles: The Making of a Christian Community in Late Antique Gaul,* Cambridge University Press, 1994, p. 70 n. 270, 271, 272.

[2409] T. M. Charles-Edwards, *Wales and the Britons 350-1064*, Oxford, 2013, p. 58-59, Sidonius, *Letters*, vol.1, VII; J. Harries, *Sidonius Apollinaris and the Fall of Rome AD 407-485*, Oxford, 2002, p. 160-2; P. L. Kessler, 'Riothamus', <http://www.historyfiles.co.uk/FeaturesBritain/BritishRiothamus.htm> viewed on 17 March 2013; M. Floyde, *King Arthur's French Odyssey*, <http://www.burgundytoday.com/grapevine/good-read.htm> viewed on 17 March 2013.

[2410] A. L. F. Rivet, *Gallia Narbonensis,* Batsford, 1988, p. 108 n. 78.

[2411] S. Mitchell, *A History of the Later Roman Empire: The Transformation of the Ancient World*, Wiley-Blackwell, 2006, p. 119.

[2412] *Ibid.*

[2413] T. S. Burns, *A History of the Ostrogoths,* Indiana University Press, 1984, p.125, 58. Paulinus Pellaeus, Eucharisticus 575–80 (Loeb edition, in vol. 2 of Ausonius Opuscula, (ed.), H. G. White).

[2414] *R. Latouche, Caesar to Charlemagne: the beginnings of France, trans. J. Nicholson, Barnes & Noble, 1968, p. 190).*

[2415] J. Harries, *Sidonius Apollonaris and the Fall of Rome AD 407–485,* Oxford University Press, 1999, p. 237.

[2416] J. D. Harries, 'Apollinaris Biography–Carm, Carmina, Epistulae, Misssae', <http://biography.jrank.org/pages/5345/Sidonius-Apollinaris.html>, viewed on 9 December 2010.

[2417] P. Lejay, 'Sidonius Apollinarius', *The Catholic Encyclopaedia*, vol.13. New York: Robert Appleton Company, 1912, <http://www.newadvent.org/cathen/13778a.htm>, viewed on 17 December 2010.

[2418] J. Harries, *Sidonius Apollinaris and the Fall of Rome AD 407–485*, Oxford University Press, 1999. p. 217.

[2419] R. W. Mathisen, *Roman Aristocrats in Barbarian Gaul: strategies for survival in an age of transition*, University of Texas, 1993, p. 111.

[2420] R. Latouche, *Caesar to Charlemagne: the beginnings of France,* trans. J. Nicholson, Barnes & Noble, 1968, p. 192.

[2421] K. Löffler, 'Visigoths', *The Catholic Encyclopaedia,* vol. 15. New York: Robert Appleton Company, 1912, <http://www.newadvent.org/cathen/15476b.htm>, viewed on 15 December 2010.

[2422] Clerc estimates between A.D. 484 and 485. M. Clerc, *Massalia: Histoire de Marseille dans L'Antiquité des Origins a la Fin de l'empire Romain d'occident*, vol. 2, Librarie A. Tacussel, 1929, p. 268.

[2423] P. Geary, *Phantoms of Remembrance: Memory and Oblivion of the end of the first millennium*, Princeton Paperbacks, 1994, p. 32.

[2424] T. S. Burns, *A History of the Ostrogoths*, Indiana University Press, 1984, p. 216.

[2425] R. Latouche, *Caesar to Charlemagne: the beginnings of France,* trans. J. Nicholson, Barnes & Noble, 1968, p. 166.

[2426] R. W. Mathisen, *Roman Aristocrats in Barbarian Gaul: strategies for survival in an age of transition*, University of Texas, 1993, p. 111, *CIL*. 12.481.

[2427] T. S. Burns, *A History of the Ostrogoths*, Indiana University Press, 1984, p. 176.

[2428] *Ibid*, p. 170.

[2429] A. Morea, *La Perle Noire de la Méditerranée,* Éditions Milan, 1999, p. 55.

[2430] W. E. Klingshirn, *Caesarius of Arles: Life, Testament, Letters*, Liverpool University Press, 1994, p. 55–56.

[2431] *Ibid*, p. 26–27.

[2432] P. Brown, *The Rise of Western Christendom*, Blackwell, 2006, p. 116.

[2433] The People's Chronology, *6th Century A.D.*, ['eNotes'] <http://www.enotes.com/peoples-chronology/year-6th-century>, viewed on 4 April 2011.

[2434] T. Sahan, 'Council of Agde', *The Catholic Encyclopaedia,* vol. 1. New York: Robert Appleton Company, 1907, <http://www.newadvent.org/cathen/01206b.htm>, viewed on 2 April 2011.

[2435] J. D. Mansi, (ed.), *Sacrorum Conciliorum Nova et Amplissima Collectio*, (Paris: H. Welter, 1901), vol. 8, pp. 325, 329; reprinted in Roy C. Cave & Herbert H. Coulson, (eds.), *A Source Book for Medieval Economic History*, (Milwaukee: The Bruce Publishing Co., 1936; reprint ed., New York: Biblo & Tannen, 1965), pp. 280–281, <http://www.fordham.edu/halsall/source/506agdechurchslaves.html>, viewed on 4 April 2011.

[2436] G. Goyau, 'Montpellier', *The Catholic Encyclopaedia',* vol. 10. New York: Robert Appleton Company, 1911, <http://www.newadvent.org/cathen/10545a.htm>, viewed on 2 April 2011

For a catalogue and biography of the bishops of Agde see J-J. Balthazar Jordan, *Histoire de la Ville d'Agde*, Montpellier 1824, *Lafitte* Reprints, 1996, p. 341-390.

[2437] K. Cappocia, *Christmas Traditions*, A Brief Study of the Origins of Modern Christmas Celebrations, <http://www.biblebb.com/files/christmas00.htm>, viewed on 4 April 2011.

[2438] God's Guarantees for Giving! *Council of Agde,* <http://godsguarantees.com/council-of-agde/#0>, viewed on 4 April 2011.

[2439] R. Collins, 'Plague (La Peste)', *History of Provence and France,* <http://www.beyond.fr/history/plague.html>, viewed on 14 April 2011; Christine A. Smith, 'Plagues from Athens to Justinian (mid–6th century)', *Plague in the Ancient World: A Study from Thucidydes to Justinian,* [University of Wisconsin-Marathon County] <http://marathon.uwc.edu/academics/departments/political_science/IGS_AIDSinAFRICA/Justinianplague.htm#45>; Loyola University, *The Student Historical Journal 1966-7,* <http://www.loyno.edu/~history/journal/1996-7/1996-7.htm>, viewed on 4 April 2011.

A plague at Agde is also mentioned by Nostradamus but we do not know which year he was alluding to. N. Halley, *The Complete Prophecies of Nostradamus,* Wordsworth Edition Ltd., 1999, p. 206, (8/21–early 2000s); for a different interpretation see *Century VIII, Quatrain 21,* <http://www.reocities.com/hightechjim/CenturyVIII.htm>, viewed on 2 April 2011.

[2440] B. Bizot, et al. *Marseille Antique: guides archéologiques de la France,* Editions du Patrimonie, Centre des monuments nationaux, 2007, p. 122.

[2441] W. E. Klingshirn, *Caesarius of Arles: The Making of a Christian Community in Late Antique Gaul,* Cambridge University Press, 1994, p. xiii.

[2442] P. Verzone, *From Theodoric to Charlemagne,* Methuen & Co. Ltd., 1968, p. 72.

[2443] B. Bizot, et al. *Marseille Antique: guide archéologiques de la France,* Editions du Patrimonie, Centre des monuments nationaux, 2007, p. 122.

[2444] A. H. M. Jones, *The Later Roman Empire 284–602,* vol. II. XXII, Basil Blackwell, 1973, p. 898.

[2445] *The History of Avignon,* ['Avignon-et-Provence.com'] <http://www.avignon-et-provence.com/avignon-tourism/avignon-history/haut-moyen-age.htm#.T-gXqpFRGuI>, viewed 25 June 2012.

[2446] W. E. Klingshirn, *Caesarius of Arles,: The Making of a Christian Community in Late Antique Gaul,* Cambridge University Press, 1994, p. 267.

[2447] M. Clerc, *Massalia: Histoire de Marseille dans L'Antiquité des Origins a la Fin de l'empire Romain d'occident,* Librarie A. Tacussel, 1929, vol. 2, p. 268-269 n. 1, Procopius (500–565 AD), *Histoires,* II, iii, 33 n. 2, Agathias, *Histories,* I, 2.

[2448] R. Latouche, *Caesar to Charlemagne: the beginnings of France,* trans. J. Nicholson, Barnes & Noble, 1968, p. 211 and p. 229.

[2449] *Moulin du Calanquet Saint-Rémy de Provence,* A Family Story, <http://www.moulinducalanquet.fr/olive-oil/historique/historique-history-geschichte.html>, viewed on 2 September 2011.

[2450] P. Geary, *Phantoms of Remembrance: Memory and Oblivion of the end of the first millennium,* Princeton Paperbacks, 1994, p. 32.

[2451] 'Diocese of Marseilles', *The Original Catholic Encyclopaedia,* Encyclopaedia Press, 1913, vol. 1. p. 2 of 8, <http://oce.catholic.com/index.php?title=Diocese_of_Marseilles>, viewed on 15 September 2009.

[2452] B. Bizot, et al. *Marseille Antique: guide archéologiques de la France,* Editions du Patrimonie, Centre des monuments nationaux, 2007, p. 122.

[2453] J. Liversidge, *Everyday Life in the Roman Empire,* Batsford, 1976, p.78; Martyrs in A.D. 177 the other half were Gallo-Romans <http://www.newadvent.org/cathen/09472a.htm> viewed on 15 January 2014.

[2454] A. Toynbee, *The Greeks and their Heritage,* Oxford, 1981, p. 195.

[2455] P. MacKendrick, *Roman France*, G. Bell & Sons, 1971, p. 72; Many fragments of Massaliote amphorae from 540 B.C. in Vaise quarter of Lyon. J-P. Morel, 'Phocaean Colonisation' in G. R. Tsetskhladze (ed.), *Greek Colonisation: An Account of Greek Colonies and Other Settlements Overseas,* vol.1, (Leiden, 2006): 358–428, here p. 392.

[2456] J. Lindsay, *Byzantium into Europe,* The Bodley Head, 1952, p. 393.

[2457] F. Miller, *A Greek Roman Empire: Power and Belief under Theodosius II (408–450),* University of California Press, 2007, p. 157 and p. 22, p. 97.

[2458] J. Lindsay, *Byzantium into Europe,* The Bodley Head, 1952, p. 393.

[2459] *Ibid*, p. 218, and p. 219 n. 2.

[2460] E. C. Dunn, *The Gallican Saint's Life and the Late Roman Dramatic Tradition*, The Catholic University of America Press, 1989, p. 36.

[2461] J. Lindsay, *Byzantium into Europe*, The Bodley Head, 1952, p. 396.

[2462] G. Goyau, 'Marseilles (Massilia)', Bishops of Marseilles, in *The Catholic Encyclopaedia,* vol. 9. New York, Robert Appleton Company, 1910,<http://www.newadvent.org/cathen/09715b.htm>, viewed 11 June 2012.

[2463] S. T. Loseby, 'Marseille: A Late Antique Success Story?', *Journal for Roman Studies*, vol. 82, (1992): 165–185, here p. 180 n. 121 (Gregory I, Reg. IX. 208; XI, 10; R. Markus, 'The cult of icons in the sixth–century Gaul', *JTS* 29 (1978), 151–7), ['JSTOR' journal archive] <http://www.jstor.org/stable/301290>, viewed on 17 November 2009.

[2464] E. Duprat, *Bouches du Rhône: Encyclopédie départementale*, vol. 2. Marseille, 1923, p. 102.

[2465] A. A. Vasilev, *History of the Byzantine Empire 324–1453*, The University of Wisconsin Press, 1952, p. 255.

[2466] J. F. Haldon, *Byzantium in the Seventh Century*, Cambridge, 1990, p. 406.

[2467] E. Duprat, *Bouches du Rhône: Encyclopédie départementale*, Vol. 2. Marseille, 1923, p.102.

[2468] A. A. Vasilev, *History of the Byzantine Empire 324–1453*, The University of Wisconsin Press, 1952, p. 616; There was a submarine eruption of the volcano at Thera in A.D. 726 Leo maintained this was 'Divine wrath at the worship of icons as idolatry'. He ordered a picture of Christ to be taken down from the Palace gateway and the soldiers who did it were 'lynched by a mob'. Leading rioters were later mutilated and Leo started banning worship of Saints. 'Patriarch Germanus does not react'. T. Venning, (ed.), *A Chronology of the Byzantine Empire*, Palgrave Macmillan, 2006, p. 199.

[2469] M. McCormick, 'Byzantium and the West: 700–900', in R. McKitterick, (ed.), *New Cambridge Medieval History II,* 1995, pp. 349–380, here p. 365.

[2470] J. Lindsay, *Byzantium into Europe*, The Bodley Head, 1952, p. 87.

[2471] Written by Paul the Deacon in the late eighth-century A.D. Langobards are also known as Lombards. Paul the Deacon, *History of the Langobards*, VIII. 3, trans. W. D. Foulke, University of Pennsylvania, 1907, <http://www.thule-italia.org/Nordica/Paul%20the%20Deacon%20-%20History%20of%20the%20Lombards%20%281907%29%20%5BEN%5D.pdf >, viewed 24 June 2012; Paul the Deacon, *History of the Lombards*, VIII. 3, trans W. D. Foulke, University of Pennsylvania, 2003, p. 100 n. 1. and p. 102 n. 1.

[2472] M. Deanesly, *A History of Early Medieval Europe, 467-911*, Methuen, 1956, p. 267. Austrasia was the eastern part of the Frankish kingdom sixth to eighth century that included eastern France, western Germany and the Netherlands.

[2473] Gregory of Tours, *History of the Franks*, VI. 2.<http://www.fordham.edu/halsall/basis/gregory-hist.asp#book6>, viewed 17 June 2012.

[2474] Boso and Gundovald arrived together from Constantinople at Marseille. B. S. Bachrach, *The Anatomy of a Little War: A Diplomatic and Military History of the Gundovald Affair (568-586),* Westview Press, 1994, p. 52, p. 59, p. 64.

[2475] *Gregory of Tours History of the Franks*, VI.24, trans. L. Thorpe, Penguin, 1983, p. 35 n. 45: According to Gregory of Tours, Boso is also charged by the king. B. S. Bachrach, *The Anatomy of a Little War: A Diplomatic and Military History of the Gundovald Affair (568-586)*, Westview Press, 1994, p. 64.

Possibly Boso changed sides as there was now a direct heir as Fredegund had given birth to Chilperic's son before Gundovald had arrived at Marseille. W. F. Goffart, 'Byzantine policy in the West Under Tiberius II and Maurice: The Pretenders Hermenegild and Gundovald (579-585)', *Traditio*, vol. 13 (1957): 73-118, here p. 103, ['JSTOR' archive journal] <www.jstor.org/stable/27830344>, viewed on 12 June 2012.

[2476] S. T. Loseby, 'Marseille: A Late Antique Success Story?' *Journal for Roman Studies*, Vol. 82, (1992): 165–185, here, p. 182 n. 134, Gregory of Tours, *Hist.* VIII.5, Society for the Promotion of Roman Studies, ['JSTOR' journal archive] <http://www.jstor.org/stable/301290>, viewed on 11 November 2010; B. S. Bachrach, *The Anatomy of a Little War: A Diplomatic and Military History of the Gundovald Affair (568-586)*, Westview Press, 1994, p. 89.

[2477] Gregory of Tours, *History of the Franks*, VII.10 and VII. 38, Medieval Sourcebook, Gregory of Tours (539-594), History of the Franks: Books I-X ['Fordham University'] <http://www.fordham.edu/halsall/basis/gregory-hist.asp>viewed 12 June 2012.

[2478] W. F. Goffart, 'Byzantine policy in the West Under Tiberius II and Maurice: The Pretenders Hermenegild and Gundovald (579-585)', *Traditio*, vol. 13 (1957):73-118, here p. 94-96, ['JSTOR' archive journal] <www.jstor.org/stable/27830344>, viewed 12 June 2012.

[2479] B. S. Bachrach, *The Anatomy of a Little War: A Diplomatic and Military History of the Gundovald Affair (568-586)*, Westview Press, 1994, p. 68.

[2480] W. F. Goffart, 'Byzantine policy in the West Under Tiberius II and Maurice: The Pretenders Hermenegild and Gundovald (579-585)', *Traditio*, vol. 13 (1957): 73-118, here p. 101-102, ['JSTOR' archive journal] <www.jstor.org/stable/27830344>, viewed 12 June 2012.

[2481] E. James, *The Franks*, Blackwell, 1988, p.99-100.

[2482] B. S. Bachrach, *The Anatomy of a Little War: A Diplomatic and Military History of the Gundovald Affair (568-586)*, Westview Press, 1994, p. 69 and p 95.

[2483] W. F. Goffart, 'Byzantine policy in the West Under Tiberius II and Maurice: The Pretenders Hermenegild and Gundovald (579-585)', *Traditio*, vol. 13 (1957): 73-118, here p. 103 n. 133., ['JSTOR' archive journal] <www.jstor.org/stable/27830344>, viewed 12 June 2012,

[2484] E. Duprat, *Bouches du Rhône: Encyclopédie départementale*, vol. 2. Marseille, 1923, p. 184.

[2485] Though there are references to the term being used by some in Constantinople when they referred with pride to their city by using their ancient first name of Byzantion, which is not to be confused with the empire. N. Siniossoglou and Judith Herrin, One day workshop, Questions and Answers section, 'An Immortal Debate: Philosophy and Ideology between Late Byzantium and Modern Greece', Kings College London, 9 June 2012.

[2486] S. Runciman, *The Fall of Constantinople 1453*, Cambridge, 1969, p. 189.

[2487] 'The Roman idea that citizenship transcended mere ethnic origins'. R. Collins, *Charlemagne*, University of Toronto, 1998, p. 151.

[2488] A. Kaldellis, *Hellenism in Byzantium: Transformation of the Greek identity and the reception of the classical tradition (Greek Culture in the Roman World)*, Cambridge, 2008, p. 42–45, p. 63, p. 81, p. 111–112, p. 345.

[2489] A. Kaldellis, One day workshop, Questions and Answers section, 'An Immortal Debate: Philosophy and Ideology between Late Byzantium and Modern Greece', Kings College London, 9 June 2012.

[2490] The English thought being British and English was the same. It is only in recent years because of Scottish Devolution and a Welsh Assembly that the English were forced to establish an identity as British into a dual identity as

English and British. A view of identity was illustrated in a scene from the film 'The Man Who Never Was', 1956, Directed by Ronald Neame, Twentieth Century Fox.

[2491] *Mehmed II*, <http://www.mlahanas.de/Ottoman/MehmedII.html>, viewed on 14 February 2011.

[2492] K. M. Setton, *The Papacy and the Levant 1204–1571*, The Fifteenth Century, vol. II. The American Philosophical Society, 1997, p. 371–373.

[2493] W. Miller, *The Ottoman Empire 1801–1913*, Cambridge, 1913.
<http://en.wikipedia.org/wiki/File:Rumelia_map.jpg>, viewed on 14 February 2011.

[2494] S. T. Loseby, 'Marseille: A Late Antique Success Story?', *Journal for Roman Studies*, vol. 82, (1992): 165–185, here p. 182 n. 134, Society for the Promotion of Roman Studies, ['JSTOR' journal archive]
<http://www.jstor.org/stable/301290>, viewed on 11 November 2010.

[2495] G. Goyau, 'Marseilles (Massilia)', *The Catholic Encyclopaedia,* vol. 9. New York: Robert Appleton Company, 1910, <www.newadvent.org>, viewed on 17 October 2010.

[2496] *Gregory of Tours, History of the Franks*, IX. 22. trans L. Thorpe, Penguin, 1983, p. 442.

[2497] *Ibid,* VIII. 43. p. 474.

[2498] M. Clerc, *Massalia: Histoire de Marseille dans L'Antiquité des Origins a la Fin de l'empire Romain d'occident*, vol. 2, Librarie A. Tacussel, 1929, p. 269.

[2499] S. T. Loseby, 'Marseille: A Late Antique Success Story?', *Journal for Roman Studies*, vol. 82, (1992): 165–185, here p. 183, Society for the Promotion of Roman Studies, ['JSTOR' journal archive]
<http://www.jstor.org/stable/301290>, viewed on 11 October 2010.

[2500] Agathias, *The Histories*, Bk.I. 2. 1, trans. J. D. Frendo, (Corpus fontium historiae Byzantinae; vol. 2 A: Ser. Berlinensis). Elnheitssacht: Historiaa (engl.), Walter de Gruyter Co., 1975, p. 10.

[2501] *Ibid*.

[2502] Alexandria was surrendered to the Arabs in A.D. 641. Amr found the inhabitants ready to resist except for the Copts who preferred peace. He 'reduced the city by sword and plundered all that was in it, sparing its inhabitants'..."The Greeks wrote to Constantine, son of Herculius, who was their king at that time" relating that Moslems in the city were few 'and how humiliating the Greek's condition was, and how they had to pay a poll tax. Constantine sent Manuwil and three hundred ships full of fighters'. They captured Alexandria but it was recaptured by Amr who 'killed the fathers and carried away the children as captives. Some of its Greek inhabitants left to join the Greeks somewhere else; and Allah's enemy, Manuwil, was killed'. J. S. Arkenberg, 'Al-Baladhuri: The Conquest of Alexandria'. *Medieval Sourcebook: Account of the Arab Conquest of Egypt 642*, <http://fordham.edu/halsall/source/642Egypt-conq2.html>, viewed on 13 August 2010.

P. Charanis, 'On the Question of Hellenization of Sicily and Southern Italy During the Middle Ages', *The American Historical Review*, Vol. 52, No. 1 (Oct., 1946):74-86, here p. 79-80. ['JSTOR' archive journal]
www.jstor.org/stable/1845070, viewed 24 May 2012.

[2503] Alexandria in Egypt continued with a Greek population, which was added to particularly when Greece became independent 1828 and after the exchange of populations between Greece and Turkey in 1923. There were dozens of Greek churches, a number of Greek schools, a Greek college 'Salvagio', and the most modern hospital in the Middle East the 'Theohari Kotsika'. Before 1940 Greeks in Alexandria numbered a quarter of a million. They lived in every part of Alexandria and the district of Mazarita was 90% Greek. Twenty minutes from here was the 'Athletiki Enosis Ellinon Alexandrias' with a stadium and sports facilities. There were Greek communities in more than twenty cities and many Egyptians learned Greek to secure employment in a Greek company. As a student Gamal Abdel Nasser, the future President of Egypt, learned the language and worked in a Greek pharmacy. After the revolution of 1952 and nationalization of 1956 there were fewer than 70,000 Greeks left in Egypt and many were repatriated to Greece or emigrated to Canada, and Australia. Robert Menzies the Australian Prime Minister visited President Nasser offering to mediate while two large liners were anchored outside Alexandria Harbour. Many hundreds of Greek families were evacuated during the night to start a new life, mostly in Melbourne. Today many of the Greek churches in Alexandria only open on Saints days, while the schools and the Theohari Kotsika hospital have been donated to the Egyptian government. There are still a few hundred Greeks living in many parts of Egypt and many of the girls have married Egyptians. Email to me 12 June 2012 from Mr. Constantine Louis, a Greek born and brought up in Alexandria, and now a teacher in London, U.K.

See also 'The Hellenic Community of Alexandria, Egypt', <http://www.greece.org/alexandria/eka2/eka1.htm>, viewed on13 June 2012: 'The Hellenic Literary and Historical Archive', <http://www.elia.org.gr/pages.fds?pagecode=02.02&langid=2>, viewed on 13 June 2012; 'The Greeks of Egypt' [NOCTOC] <http://noctoc-noctoc.blogspot.co.uk/2007/06/greeks-of-egypt.html>, viewed on 13 June 2012.

It would seem when an ethnic population becomes low in numbers that they become eventually absorbed by intermarriage. It is possible that over the years the same happened to Massalia with the visible signs of the language and culture disappearing but as the recent genetic studies have revealed the DNA continued and survives in 4% of the sample taken in Provence.

[2504] R. Clogg, *A Concise History of Greece*, Cambridge University Press, 1997, p. 49; Turkish Official Statistics for 1910: Constantinople, Turks 450,000, Greeks 260,000: Province of Aidin (Smyrna) Turks 974,225, Greeks 629,002. D. Pentzoupoulos, *The Balkan Exchange of Minorities and its Impact on Greece*, C. Hurst & Co., 2002, p. 29-30.

[2505] G. Rohlfs, 'Greek Remnants in Southern Italy', in *The Classical Journal*, vol. 62, No. 4 (Jan., 1967): 164–169, The Classical Association of the Middle West and South, ['JSTOR' journal archive] <http://www.jstor.org/stable/3295569>, viewed on 30 December 2010.

Sicily was predominantly Greek speaking in the seventh century A.D. and continued to be so until Italian immigration from the mainland during the Norman Kingdom of Sicily (10-11th century A.D.). See P. Charanis, 'On the Question of Hellenization of Sicily and Southern Italy During the Middle Ages', *The American Historical Review*, Vol. 52, No. 1 (Oct., 1946):74-86, here p. 83-84. ['JSTOR' archive journal] www.jstor.org/stable/1845070, viewed 24 May 2012.

[2506] Clovis I converted in A.D. 496 and his wife Clotilda was already a Catholic when he married her around 492/493. *The Chronicle of St. Denis*, I.18-19, 23, <http://history-world.org/conversion%20of%20clovis.htm>, viewed on 11 June 2012; G. Kurth, 'Clovis', in *The Catholic Encyclopaedia*, Vol. 4. New York, Robert Appleton Company, 1908, <http://www.newadvent.org/cathen/04070a.htm>, viewed on 11 June 2012.

[2507] J. Lindsay, *Byzantium into Europe*, The Bodley Head, 1952, p. 393; F. Miller, *A Greek Roman Empire: Power and Belief under Theodosius II (408–450)*, University of California Press, 2007, p. 157 and p. 22, p. 97.

[2508] A. H. M. Jones, *The Later Roman Empire 284–602*, vol. II. XXI, Basil Blackwell, 1973, p. 824.

[2509] L. Thorpe, *Gregory of Tours, History of the Franks*, IX.22, Penguin, 1983, p. 510–511.

[2510] G. C. Kohn, *Encyclopaedia of Plague and Pestilence*, 3rd edition, Facts on File Books, 2008, p. 129. See also M. Frassetto, *Encyclopaedia of Barbarian Europe: Society in Transformation*, ABC-CLIO, 2003, p. 195.

[2511] L. Thorpe, *Gregory of Tours, History of the Franks*, IX.22, Penguin, 1983, p. 510–511.

[2512] R. Collins, 'Plague (La Peste)', *History of Provence and France*, <http://www.beyond.fr/history/plague.html>, viewed on 14 April 2011; G. C. Kohn, *Encyclopaedia of Plague and Pestilence*, 3rd edition, Facts on File Books, 2008, p. 253-255.

[2513] As they did after several plagues in Constantinople including 541-542, 745*, 1334 and 1347. See Uli Schamiloglou, 'The Rise of the Ottoman Empire: The Black Death in Medieval Anatolia and its Impact on Turkish Civilization' in N. Yavari, L. G. Potter., and J-M. R. Oppenheim, (eds.), *Views from the Edge: Essays in Honour of R. W. Bulliet*, (Columbia University Press, 2004): 255-279, here p. 258-259.

[2514] E. Duprat, *Bouches du Rhône: Encyclopédie départementale*, vol. 2. Marseille, 1923, p. 149.

[2515] *Ibid*. Nicetius and Nicecius both spelling for the same person.

²⁵¹⁶ *Ibid*, p. 105.

²⁵¹⁷ B. S. Bachrach, *The Anatomy of a Little War: A Diplomatic and Military History of the Gundovald Affair (568-586)*, Westview Press, 1994, p. 61.

²⁵¹⁸ *Ibid*, p. 66 and p. 68.

²⁵¹⁹ S. T. Loseby, 'Marseille: A Late Antique Success Story?' *Journal for Roman Studies*, vol. 82, (1992): 165–185, here p. 180, Society for the Promotion of Roman Studies, ['JSTOR' journal archive] <http://www.jstor.org/stable/301290>, viewed on 17 November 2009.

²⁵²⁰ M. Euzennat, 'Ancient Marseille in the light of recent excavations', *American Journal of Archaeology* 84, No. 2. (Apr., 1980): 133–140, here p. 139–140, ['JSTOR' journal archive] <http://www.jstor.org.uk/stable/504261>, viewed on 17 November 2009.

²⁵²¹ A. H. M. Jones, *The Later Roman Empire 284–602*, vol. II. XXI, Basil Blackwell, 1973, p. 825.

²⁵²² E. James, *The Franks*, Blackwell, 1988, p. 195.

²⁵²³ Marseille-Massilia-Childéric II (662–675), N° v11_0586, <http://www.cgb.fr/monnaies/vso/v11/gb/monnaiesgb5d3c.html>, viewed on 24 September 2011.

²⁵²⁴ Re. 7736, <www.cgb.fr/monnaies/vso/v11/gb/monnaiesgb5d3c.html>; P. Grierson and M. Blackburn, *Medieval European Coinage: The Early Middle Ages (5th to 10th centuries)*, Cambridge 1986, p.144: P. Spufford, *Money and its use in Medieval Europe*, Cambridge, 1989, p. 27.

²⁵²⁵ E. Duprat, *Bouches du Rhône: Encyclopédie départementale*, vol. 2. Marseille, 1923, p. 149.

²⁵²⁶ James writes that Bonitus was appointed by Theodoric III before 680. E. James, *The Origins of France: From Clovis to the Capetians 500–1000*, Macmillan, 1989, p. 149.

²⁵²⁷ K. Uhalde, 'Quasi-Imperial Coinage of Merovingian Provence' in R. W. Mathisen and D Shauzer, (eds.), *Society and Culture in Late Antique Gaul,* Ashgate, 2001, p. 163.and p. 141-143

²⁵²⁸ L. Jnr. Richardson, *A New Topographical Dictionary of Rome*, John Hopkins University, 1992, p. 96.

²⁵²⁹ *Phocas*, <www.brittanica.com>, viewed on 13 August 2010.

²⁵³⁰ M. Whittow, *The Making of Orthodox Byzantium 600–1025*, Palgrave, 1996, p. 302; J. A. Palermo, 'The Latinity of Sicily', *Italica*, Vol. 30, No. 2, (Jun., 1953): 65-80, here p.70. ['JSTOR' archive journal] <www.jstor.org/stable/477471> viewed 24 May 2012; P. Charanis, 'On the Question of Hellenization of Sicily and Southern Italy During the Middle Ages', *The American Historical Review*, Vol. 52, No. 1 (Oct., 1946): 74-86, here p. 83-84. ['JSTOR' archive journal] www.jstor.org/stable/1845070, viewed 24 May 2012.

²⁵³¹ E. Duffy, *Saints and Sinners: A History of the Popes*, Yale University Press, 2002, p. 77.

²⁵³² Taranto was founded by the Spartans as Taras in 707 B.C. also called Tarentum. J. B. Bury and R. Meiggs, *A History of Greece*, Macmillan, 1979, p. 79.

²⁵³³ M. Whittow, *The Making of Orthodox Byzantium 600–1025*, Palgrave, 1996, p. 308.

²⁵³⁴ *Taranto, Region Puglia (Apulia), Italy*, <http://www.italyworldclub.com/puglia/taranto/taranto.htm>, viewed on 10 August 2010.

²⁵³⁵ A. Louth, 'Christology and Heresy' in L. James (ed.), *A Companion to Byzantium*, Wiley-Blackwell, (2010): 187–199, here p. 195.

²⁵³⁶ G. Ostrogorsky, *History of the Byzantine State,* Blackwell, 1980, p. 119–120.

[2537] J. Lindsay, *Byzantium into Europe*, The Bodley Head, 1952, p. 397.

[2538] P. Geary, *Phantoms of Remembrance: Memory and Oblivion of the end of the first millennium*, Princeton Paperbacks, 1994, p. 33.

[2539] A. Butler, *The Lives of the Primitive Fathers, Martyrs and other Principal Saints,* Jan. 15. S. Bonitus, B. S. ITA, V. A., vol.1, Edinburgh, 1798, p. 175.

[2540] The western region of the Roman province of Gallia Narbonensis in Gaul (France).

[2541] J-J. Balthazar Jordan, *Histoire de la Ville d'Agde*, Montpellier 1824, Lafitte Reprints, 1996, p. 22-24; A. Morea, *La Perle Noire de la Méditerranée,* Éditions Milan, 1999, p. 55.

[2542] A. R. Lewis, *The Development of Southern French and Catalan Society 718–1050,* University of Texas Press, Austin, 1965, p. 86.

[2543] *Ibid*, p. 173.

[2544] *Ibid*, p. 76 & p. 70 (ref. Cart. De Saint-Victor, No. 8).

[2545] M. Whittow, M. *The Making of Orthodox Byzantium 600–1025*, Palgrave, 1996, p. 304.

[2546] B.W. Scholtz, (ed.), *Carolingian Chronicles: Royal Frankish Annals and Nithard's Histories,* trans. B. Rogers, Ann Arbor, 1972, p. 77–83.

[2547] P. Schlager, *Einhard, The Catholic Encyclopedia*, vol. 5. New York, Robert Appleton Company, 1909, <http://www.newadvent.org/cathen/05366b.htm>, viewed on 29 October 2011.

[2548] 'Einhard: The Life of Charlemagne', Chapter 16, in N. F. Cantor, *The Medieval Reader*, Harper Collins, 1994, p. 100 ; To see full text, P. Halsall, 'Contents, 16, Foreign Relations', *Medieval Sourcebook: Einhard: The Life of Charlemagne,* <http://www.fordham.edu/halsall/basis/einhard.asp#Foreign%20Relations>, viewed on 26 January 2011.

[2549] A. R. Lewis, *The Development of Southern French and Catalan Society 718–1050,* University of Texas Press, Austin, 1965, p. 86.

[2550] E. Duprat, in P. Masson, (ed.), *Bouches du Rhône*, vol. XIV, Marseille, 1935. p. 72.

[2551] *Marseille*, <http://www.france-la-visite.com/english/heritage/marseille.html>, viewed on 1 September 2009.

[2552] 'Diocese of Marseilles', *The Original Catholic Encyclopaedia,* Encyclopaedia Press, 1913, vol.1. p. 2 of 8, <http://oce.catholic.com/index.php?title=Diocese_of_Marseilles>, viewed on 15 September 2009.

[2553] *The Annals of St. Bertin; Ninth Century Histories*, vol. 1, translated and annotated by J. L. Nelson, Manchester University Press, 1991, p. 39.

[2554] A. R. Lewis, *The Development of Southern French and Catalan Society 718–1050,* University of Texas Press, Austin, 1965, p. 173.

[2555] *Ibid*, p.101 note 40, E. Duprat, *Bouches du Rhône: Encyclopédie départementale*, vol. 2. Marseille, 1924, pp. 134–135, (not pp. 134–135 but actually pp. 34–35, and year 1923 in the copy I saw at the library BNF in Paris France).

[2556] A. R. Lewis, *The Development of Southern French and Catalan Society 718–1050,* University of Texas: Austin, 1965, p.102. n. 42, E. Duprat, *Bouches du Rhône: Encyclopédie départemental*e, vol. 2. Marseille, 1924, pp. 132–133 (Carte. de Saint-Victor).

[2557] E. Duprat, *Bouches du Rhône: Encyclopédie départementale*, vol. 2. Marseille, 1923, p. 34–37.

[2558] A. R. Lewis, *The Development of Southern French and Catalan Society 718–1050,* University of Texas Press, Austin, 1965, p. 173.

[2559] E. Duprat, *Bouches du Rhône: Encyclopédie départementale*, vol. 2. Marseille, 1923, p. 34.

[2560] *Ibid*, pp. 34–35. (Not available here so I checked this copy at the BNF, Paris). See also E. Duprat, in P. Masson, (ed.), Bouches du Rhône, vol. XIV, Marseille, 1935, p. 72. (There was a copy of this at the British Library in London.)

[2561] *The Annals of St. Bertin; Ninth Century Histories,* vol.1, translated and annotated by J. L. Nelson, Manchester University Press, 1991, p. 6–7.

[2562] *Ibid*, p. 66.

[2563] S. Runciman, *Byzantine Civilization,* Edward Arnold, 1943, p. 150–151.

[2564] E. Duprat, *Bouches du Rhône: Encyclopédie départementale*, Vol. 2. Marseille, 1923, p. 184.

[2565] E. Baratier, *Documents de l'Historie de Provence*, Univers de la France, 1971, p. 58–59, (Liutprand de Crémone, *Antapodosis*, livre I, Chap. 1–4, et livre V, chap. 9 et 16–17, Edit. J. Becker, 3 édit. Hanovre, 1915, Mon. Germ. Hist. in usum scholarum).

[2566] E. Baratier, *Documents de l'Histoire de Provence*, Univers de la France, 1971, p. 58–59.

[2567] A. Morea, *La Perle Noire de la Méditerranée*, Éditions Milan, 1999, p. 55; *Toulouse Nobility*, updated 10 February 2011, <http://fmg.ac/Projects/MedLands/TOULOUSE%20NOBILITY.htm#_Toc255726438>, viewed 11 June 2012.

[2568] *Spolia*, ['Museum of Learning'] <http://www.museumstuff.com/learn/topics/spolia>, viewed on 12 February 2011.

[2569] S. Crane, 'Digging up the Present in Marseille's Old Port: Toward an Archaeology of Reconstruction', *Journal of the Society of Architechtural Historians,* vol. 63, no. 3 (Sep., 2004), pp. 269–319, here p. 306 n. 46, ['JSTOR' journal archive] <http://www.jstor.org/stable/4127973> viewed on 8 October 2010).

[2570] P. Verzone, *From Theodoric to Charlemagne*, Methuen & Co. Ltd., 1968 p. 179–180, (*Henr. Mir. S.G.* ed. Duru, II, 162–4).

[2571] P. Verzone *From Theodoric to Charlemagne*, Methuen & Co. Ltd., 1968 p. 179–180.

[2572] G. Goyau, 'Marseilles (Massilia)', *The Catholic Encyclopaedia*, vol. 9. New York: Robert Apppleton Company, 1910, <http://www.newadvent.org/cathen/09715b.htm>, viewed on 3 September 2011; Geni, Boson d'Autun, Comte de Vienne, Dux de Provence, <http://www.geni.com/people/Boson-d-Autun/6000000008799837188>, viewed on 3 September 2011; R. Reuter, (ed.), The New Cambridge Medieval History: c. 900–c. 1024. vol. 3, Cambridge University Press, 1999, p. 330–333.

[2573] G. Long, *Penny Cyclopaedia of the Society for the Diffusion of Useful Knowledge*, vols. 13-14, Charles Knight & Co., London, 1839, p. 446.

[2574] *Ibid.*

[2575] A. Morea, *La Perle Noire de la Méditerranée*, Éditions Milan, 1999, p. 55; Boson son-in-law to Viscount Rainald who was called *fidelis* in 881 by King Carloman. A. R. Lewis, *The Development of Southern French and Catalan Society 718–1050,* The Governmental System of the Midi and Catalonia, (116), University of Texas Press, Austin, 1965, <http://libro.uca.edu/lewis/sfc7.htm#N_14_>, viewed 11 June 2012.

[2576] A. R. Lewis, *The Development of Southern French and Catalan Society 718–1050,* University of Texas Press, Austin, 1965, p. 60 n. 4 9, (Carte. de St Victor, No. 1.), and p. 222.

[2577] G. Long, *Penny Cyclopaedia of the Society for the Diffusion of Useful Knowledge*, vols. 13-14, Charles Knight & Co., London, 1839, p. 446.

[2578] E. Duprat, *Bouches du Rhône: Encyclopédie départementale,* vol. 2. Marseille, 1923, p. 184.

[2579] Translation by Dr J. Braybrook, Department of French Language, Birkbeck College, University of London, email to me 20 November 2010.

[2580] G. Goyau, 'Marseilles (Massilia)', Abbey of St. Victor, in *The Catholic Encyclopaedia,* vol. 9. New York, Robert Appleton Company, 1910,<http://www.newadvent.org/cathen/09715b.htm>, viewed 11 June 2012.

[2581] E. James, *The Origins of France: From Clovis to the Capetians 500–1000,* Macmillan, 1989, p. 65.

[2582] G. Long, *Penny Cyclopaedia of the Society for the Diffusion of Useful Knowledge,* vols. 13-14, Charles Knight & Co., London, 1839, p. 446.

[2583] 'Diocese of Marseilles', *The Original Catholic Encyclopaedia,* Encyclopaedia Press, 1913, vol. 1. p. 4 of 8, <http://oce.catholic.com/index.php?title=Diocese_of_Marseilles>, viewed on 15 September 2009.

[2584] G. Goyau, 'Marseilles (Massilia)', *The Catholic Encyclopaedia,* vol. 9. New York: Robert Apppleton Company, 1910, <http://www.newadvent.org/cathen/09715b.htm> viewed on 15 September 2009.

[2585] *Ibid,* <http://www.newadvent.org/cathen/09715b.htm>, viewed on 31 December 2010,

[2586] J. J. Norwich, *The Popes: A History,* Chatto & Windus, 2011, p. 185.

[2587] T. Venning, (ed.), *A Chronology of the Byzantine Empire,* Palgrave Macmillan, 2006, p. 413.

[2588] *Ibid,* p. 422.

[2589] *Ibid,* p. 424-435.

[2590] *Ibid,* p. 426 and p. 432.

[2591] Map including the Byzantine Empire after A.D. 1204 Conquest of Constantinople by the Latins of the Fourth Crusade. W. R. Shepherd, *Historical Atlas,* New York, Henry Holt and Company, 1911, 73. ['Shadowed Realm, Political Medieval Maps']
<http://www.shadowedrealm.com/maps/political/view/the_mediterranean_lands_after_1204>, viewed on 12 January 2012;

Map of Byzantine Empire at A.D. 1265. W. R. Shepherd, *Historical Atlas,* New York, Henry Holt and Company, 1911, 89. ['Shadowed Realm, Political Medieval Maps']
<http://www.shadowedrealm.com/maps/political/view/the_byzantine_empire_1265>, viewed on 12 January 2012.

[2592] *Ibid,* p. 125.

[2593] *Marseilles,* ['1906 Jewish Encyclopeadia'] <http://www.jewishencyclopedia.com/articles/10438-marseilles>, viewed 10 February 2012.

[2594] A. Morea, *La Perle Noire de la Méditerranée,* Éditions Milan, 1999, p. 55.

[2595] *Ibid,* p. 60.

[2596] *Ibid,* p. 55.

[2597] 'Diocese of Marseille', *The Original Catholic Encyclopaedia,* Encyclopaedia Press, 1913, vol. 1. p. 6 of 8, <http://oce.catholic.com/index.php?title=Diocese_of_Marseilles>, viewed on 15 September 2009.

[2598] R. Gardiner, *The Age of the Galley,* Conway Maritime Press, 1995, p. 110.

[2599] *History of the Byzantine Empire,* page 4 of 5, ['History World']
<http://www.historyworld.net/wrldhis/PlainTextHistories.asp?historyid=ac59>, viewed on 13 August 2010.

[2600] D. Jacobs, *Constantinople and the Byzantine Empire,* Cassell, 1971, p. 111.

[2601] *Joinville and Villehardouin Chronicles of the Crusades*, trans. Shaw, M. R. B., Penguin, 1963, p. 52. No. 25, <http://www.fordham.edu/halsall/basis/villehardouin.html>, viewed on 30 January 2011. Villehardouin writes [Modon] Methone in Roumania. (Methone is a port in South-East Greece). Roumania was still being used to describe the East Roman Empire in spite of papal efforts to call it the Empire of the Greeks since the coronation of Charlemagne in A.D. 800 as 'the great and peaceful emperor of the Romans'. S. Kreis, Lecture 20 Charlemagne and the Carolingian Renaissance, ['History Guide'] <http://www.historyguide.org/ancient/lecture20b.html>, viewed on 21 December 2011.

The crusaders being told they were now going via Egypt threatened to go no further as they were being diverted from their vows. Geoffrey de Villehardouin wrote that Baron Simon [IV] de Montfort 'made a private agreement with the King of Hungary their enemy and "went over to his side" with his brother and many others' including Abbot Guy of Vaux-de-Cernay who had forbidden any attack on Zara. (*Joinville and Villehardouin Chronicles of the Crusades*, trans. Shaw, M. R. B., Penguin, 1963, p. 54. No. 20-21 <http://www.fordham.edu/halsall/basis/villehardouin.html>, viewed on 31 January 2011).

[2602] D. Oblensky, *The Byzantine Commonwealth, Eastern Europe 500–1453*, Cardinal, 1974, p. 313.

[2603] J. Jacobs, *Constantinople and the Byzantine Empire*, Cassell, 1969, p. 117

[2604] M. Keen, *Medieval Europe*, Penguin, 1991, p.188–189.

[2605] G. Hindley, *The Crusades*, Constable & Robinson, 2004, p. 209; Cicero 70s B.C. re. misuse of religion 'What then, think you, is the honour, what the piety, of those who even think that the immortal gods can best be appeased by human crime and bloodshed?' Cicero, *Pro Milone, On Behalf of Fonteius*, 30-32, trans. N. H. Watts, Heinemann, 1972, p. 339

[2606] F. Heer, *The Medieval World: Europe 1100-1350*, Weidenfeld & Nicolson, 1961, p. 97.

[2607] *Ibid*, p. 109-110.

[2608] J. Haldon, *Warfare, State and Society in the Byzantine World 565-1204*, Routledge, 1999, p. 14 n. 2.

[2609] P. Halsall. 'The Children's Crusade', *The History Guide,* <http://www.historyguide.org/ancient/children.html>, viewed on 3 September 2011.

[2610] F. Heer, *The Medieval World: Europe 1100–1350*, Weidenfeld & Nicolson, 1961, p. 106.

[2611] *Ibid*.

[2612] P. Halsall. 'The Children's Crusade', *The History Guide,* <http://www.historyguide.org/ancient/children.html>, viewed on 3 September 2011.

[2613] F. Heer, *The Medieval World: Europe 1100–1350*, Weidenfeld & Nicolson, 1961, p. 106.

[2614] I. Sache and P. Vagnat, (1999), 'Early records of the flag', *Marseille*, 8 July 2004, source Louis de Bresc, *Amorial des Communes de Provence*, 1866, <http://www.crwflags.com/fotw/flags/fr-13-ms.html>, viewed on 1 September 2009.

[2615] G. Long, *Penny Cyclopaedia of the Society for the Diffusion of Useful Knowledge*, vols. 13-14, Charles Knight & Co., London, 1839, p. 446.

[2616] G. Goyau, 'Marseilles (Massilia)', *The Catholic Encyclopaedia,* vol. 9. New York: Robert Apppleton Company, 1910, <http://www.newadvent.org/cathen/09715b.htm>, viewed on 7 October 2010.

[2617] J. J. Norwich, *The Popes: A History*, Chatto & Windus, 2011, p. 185.

[2618] G. Long, *Penny Cyclopaedia of the Society for the Diffusion of Useful Knowledge*, vols. 13-14, Charles Knight & Co., London, 1839, p. 446.

[2619] N. Coulet, 'Enquets sur les droits et revenues de Charles Ier d'Anjou en Provence (1252 et 1278)', *Annales, Economies*, Societies, Civilisations, Vol. 26, No. 6, (1971):1315-1317.

<http://www.persee.fr/web/revues/home/prescript/article/ahess_0395-2649_1971_num_26_6_422414_t1_1315_0000_4>, viewed 25 June 2012.

[2620] *Ibid*; Marseille, <www.france-la-viste.com/english/heritage/marseille.html>, viewed on 3 September 2011.

[2621] *Marseilles*, ['1906 Jewish Encyclopedia'] <http://www.jewishencyclopedia.com/articles/10438-marseilles>, viewed 10 February 2012.

[2622] H. F. Ghiuzeli, Jewish *Community of Marseilles*, ['Beit Hatfutsot', The Museum of the Jewish People] <www.bh.org.il/database-article.aspx?48710>, viewed on 3 September 2011.

[2623] T. Venning, (ed.), *A Chronology of the Byzantine Empire*, Palgrave Macmillan, 2006, p. 612.

[2624] A. Morea, *La Perle Noire de la Méditerranée*, Éditions Milan, 1999, p. 55.

[2625] E. Delamont, 'III-Une irruption aragonaise en Languedoc (1286)', La croisade de 1285—se causes, ses resultants et ses suites, *Muntaner Chronicle*, p. 368–369, <http://www.mediterranees.net/histoire_roussillon/moyen_age/delamont3.html<, viewed 7 May 2011.

[2626] 'Diocese of Marseilles', *The Original Catholic Encyclopaedia*, Encyclopaedia Press, 1913, vol. 1. p. 4 of 8, <http://oce.catholic.com/index.php?title=Diocese_of_Marseilles>, viewed on 15 September 2009.

[2627] G. Goyau, 'Marseilles (Massilia)', *The Catholic Encyclopaedia*, vol. 9. New York: Robert Apppleton Company, 1910, <http://www.newadvent.org/cathen/09715b.htm>, viewed on 7 October 2010.

[2628] *Ibid*.

[2629] H. F. Ghiuzeli, *Jewish Community of Marseilles*, ['Beit Hatfutsot', The Museum of the Jewish People] <www.bh.org.il/database-article.aspx?48710>, viewed on 3 September 2011.

[2630] T. Venning, (ed.), *A Chronology of the Byzantine Empire*, Palgrave Macmillan, 2006, p. 684.

[2631] A. A. Vasilev, *History of the Byzantine Empire 324–1453*, The University of Wisconsin Press, 1952, p. 616.

[2632] C. Diehl, *Byzantium: Greatness and Decline*, trans. N. Walford, Rutgers University Press, 1957, p. 196.

[2633] *Pilgrim, Ancient wisdom for self-realisation*, ['Tarot of Marseilles'] <http://www.legends-and-myths.com/40_1.cfm?f=8-legends-myths-tarot-marseilles>, viewed on 5 April 2011.

[2634] P. Camoin, *The Origin and History of the Tarot de Marseille*, ['Camoin'] <http://en.camoin.com/tarot/MarseillesTarot-Origin-History-1.html>, viewed on 24 March 2011.

[2635] Valencia Cathedral, *The Holy Chalice Chapel*, <http://www.catedraldevalencia.es/en/el-santo-caliz_lacapilla.php>, viewed on 3 September 2011.

[2636] R. Collins, *Marseille*, Provence Beyond, <http://www.beyond.fr/villages/marseille-history-provence-france.html>, viewed on 3 September 2011.

[2637] Editions Montparnasse, 2000, *Marseille*, <www.france-la-viste.com/english/heritage/marseille.html>, viewed on 3 September 2011.

[2638] *Marseilles, from Rome to France, Marseille Part 1*, <http://www.sagaplanet.com>, viewed on 4 September 2009.

[2639] I. Sache, *Provence, Traditional province, France*, 2003, source Louis de Bresc, *Amorial des Communes de Provence*, 1886 [bjs94] <http://flagspot.net/flags/fr-prove.html>, viewed on 1 September 2009.

[2640] T. Carreras Rossell, *Intervencions arqueologiques a Sant Marti d'Empúries (1994-1996): De l'assentament precolonial a l'Empuries actual*, Monograpfies Emporitanes 9, Musee d'Arqueologiques de Catalunya Empuries, Girona, 1999, p. 430.

[2641] A. Vauchez, (ed.), *Encyclopaedia of the Middle Ages,* vol. 2. James Clarke & Co., 2000, p. 1195; I. Sache, 2003. source Louis de Bresc, *Amorial des Communes de Provence,* 1886, [bjs94] <http://flagspot.net/flags/fr-prove.html>, viewed on 1 September 2009.

[2642] *Provence,* ['The 1911 Classic Encyclopaedia'] <http://www.1911Encyclopaedia.org/Provence>, viewed on 29 September 2009.

[2643] Editions Montparnasse, 2000, *Marseille,* <http://www.france-la-visite.com/english/heritage/marseille.html>, viewed on 4 September 2011.

[2644] *Provence,* ['The 1911 Classic Encyclopaedia'] <http://www.1911Encyclopaedia.org/Provence>, viewed on 29 September 2009.

[2645] *Ibid.*

[2646] P. M. Kendal, *Louis XI,* Cardinal, 1974, p. 427.

[2647] I. Sache, 2003. 'The takeover by France 1481', *Provence, (Traditional province, France),* source Louis de Bresc, *Amorial des Communes de Provence,* 1886, [bjs94] <http://flagspot.net/flags/fr-prove.html>, viewed on 1 September 2009.

[2648] In A.D. 1491 Charles VIII acquires Brittany. To maintain Brittany's independence Anne, Duchess of Brittany was married by proxy to Maximillian I of Austria (also King of the Romans) in Rennes giving her the title Queen of the Romans in 1490. Maximillian's father was Frederick III Holy Roman Emperor. France saw this as a provocation and would now have Austrian controlled lands on two borders. Charles VIII already betrothed to Maximillian's daughter Margaret invaded Brittany besieging Rennes. Without help from Maximillian Anne annulled her marriage to him and Charles married Anne of Brittany at Langeais instead. This marriage was ratified by Pope Innocent VIII in 1492 (K. M. Setton, *The Papacy and the Levant 1204–1571,* vol. 2. The American Philosophical Society, 1997, p. 398 & p. 422).

Charles VIII and the title Emperor of Constantinople
When Constantinople fell to the Ottomans in 1453 and the Emperor Constantine XI Palaeologus was killed the title went to his brother Thomas Palaeologus the Despot of Morea in Greece. After a Turkish invasion in 1460 Thomas, his wife and children escaped to Italy with the holy relic the head of the apostle Saint Andrew and were given a pension by the Pope of 300 gold ducats a month (S. Runciman, *The Fall of Constantinople 1453,* Cambridge, 1969, p. 182). After Thomas died three of his four children were adopted by the Papacy. The Pope in 1472 arranged for Zoe (renamed Sophia) to marry the Grand Prince of Moscow, Ivan III and gave them a dowry of six thousand golden ducats. She brought as part of the dowry the emblem of the double-headed eagle together fostering the idea of Moscow as the 'Third Rome' (S. Runciman, 1969, p. 183), and a library of Greek books (A. Vinogradskaya, *The Mystery of the Byzantine Library,* <http://www.richarddoetsch.com/the_kremlin_and_its_secrets> viewed 17 January 2014). Andreas received a pension of fifty ducats a month. Later he persuaded Pope Sixtus IV to give him two million golden ducats for an expedition to Morea but he spent it on other things (S. Runciman, 1969, p. 184).

Now on hard times Andreas arranged a visit to Charles VIII king of France in 1491. The Cardinal of Gurk anticipating the reason for the visit now drew up a document unknown to Charles and presented the following terms to Andreas Palaeologos on 6 November 1494; to sell to Charles VIII the title of Emperor of Constantinople, and his rights in Trebizond and the Despotate of Serbia. For this Charles VIII would offer Andreas a command of 100 lances to be paid and maintained by Charles; a pension of 4,300 gold ducats (2,000 up front), and lands in either France or Italy to produce an income of 5,000 ducats per year. All this was on the condition that Charles VIII would employ his land and naval forces to recover the Despotate of Morea for Andreas for the feudal payment (pro perpetuo censu) of 'one white saddle horse (unis gradarius albus)', and to use all his influence to get the Papal pension of 1,800 ducats, which was in arrears since it was granted by Pope Sixtus IV 'de pecuniis Cruciatae' (K. M. Setton, p. 463). Andreas signed over the titles, except Morea and the cessation were considered valid unless Charles rejected the terms before 1 November 1495. The Pope was aware of the cessation of rights even if Charles did not. If the western emperor Maximillian protested at an Imperial rival in the West the Pope could say that the cardinal had acted on his own initiative. Maximillian I (Habsburg) of Austria, 1459–1519, (King of the Romans from 1486 and Holy Roman Emperor from 1493) liked to dream of being emperor in the east as well as the west. (K. M. Setton, 1997, p. 463 n. 51). The document was witnessed in the church of S. Peitro in Montorio 'where Blessed Peter, Prince of the Apostles, had received the crown of sacred martyrdom' (K. M. Setton, 1997, p. 463).

Charles VIII accepted the terms but would not be diverted from his attempt to acquire the Kingdom of Naples first and only after would he go east. News of Charles's visit to Italy escorted by a large fleet prompted Sultan Beyazid taking this legitimate transfer of the title and Charles VIII's ambition seriously. He had 120 ships made in a state of readiness; strengthened the defences at the Dardanelles, canons were mounted in a series of shore batteries; 3,000 Janissaries were sent to Gallipoli; he sent one son to the Negroponte and the another to Mytilene; in case Charles should go over to Rumeli (Greece) together with the rival Ottoman claimant prince Jem Sultan (K. M. Setton, 1997, p. 464 and n. 53) who had been in France 1482–1489 (K. M. Setton, 1997, p. 385). Charles VIII planned a general council of all Christendom for a crusade to destroy Ottoman power. False rumours circulated that Pope Alexander IV had invested Charles with the Kingdom of Naples and offered to crown him Emperor of Constantinople but Charles replied that he would prefer first to conquer the eastern empire 'et poi haver el titolo d'imperator' (K. M. Setton, 1997, p. 476 n. 101).

Andreas's younger brother Manuel went back to Constantinople in 1477. Sultan Mehmet gave him an estate and pension. He married and had two sons; one converted to Islam and became Mehmet Pasha an official at court (S. Runciman, 1969, p. 183). Andreas died broke in 1502 having sold the title again to Ferdinand II of Aragon and Isabella I of Castile but he never received any money from them (S. Runciman, 1969, p. 184). Andreas' widow begged the Pope for 104 ducats to pay for his funeral. Andreas's son Constantine commanded the Papal Guard for a time (S. Runciman, 1969, p. 184). Setton writes that the document Andreas had signed with the Cardinal of Gurk became invalid as the terms had not been fulfilled by Charles VIII. In Andreas's will dated 7 April 1502 he bequeathed 'his imperial rights to Ferdinand and Isabella of Spain' (K. M. Setton, 1997, p. 463 n. 46).

[2649] H. F. Ghiuzeli, *Jewish Community of Marseilles*, ['Beit Hatfutsot', The Museum of the Jewish People] <www.bh.org.il/database-article.aspx?48710>, viewed on 3 September 2011.

[2650] *Marseilles*, ['1906 Jewish Encyclopedia'] <http://www.jewishencyclopedia.com/articles/10438-marseilles>, viewed 10 February 2012.

[2651] J. Garrison, *A History of Sixteenth Century France 1483–1598*, Macmillan, 1995, p.145.

[2652] P. M. Holt, A. K. Lambton, and B. Lewis, *The Cambridge History of Islam*, Cambridge University Press, 1978, vol. 1, p. 328. In the embassy from Charles V to Henry VIII at Greenwich 1545 with Gerald was a Greek Nicander Nicius of Corfu (under the Venetian Republic) who wrote an account of his visit in classical Greek. D.E. Eichholz, 'A Greek Traveller in Tudor England', *Greece & Rome*, Vol. 16, No. 47 (Apr., 1947): 76-84 <www.jstor.org/stable/641783>.

[2653] *Ibid* (Holt, p 328).

[2654] Destination 360, *Vieux-Port Marseilles*, <http://www.destination360.com/europe/france/marseille/vieux-port>, viewed on 5 September 2011.

[2655] One engraving dated 1713 is titled MARSSILIA from a German book Savonarola Innocenzio Raffael, *Universus terrarumorbis scriptorium calamo delineatus,* and the description is in Latin. *Cartes & Documents*, [Lexilogos'] <http://www.imagesdupatrimoine.marseille.fr/detail.cfm?cfid=616130&cftoken=26327544&idmedia=0017821&w=2>; <http://www.lexilogos.com/marseille_carte.htm>, viewed on 6 December 2011.

[2656] Bruno Roberty (archaeologist, curator of the Museum of Marseille) compiled a map of the city from all the information c. A.D. 1423 Roberty left a mass of references in the departmental archives including the index to streets. Daniel. Lord. Smail, *Imaginary Cartographies: possession and identity in late medieval Marseille*, Cornwell University Press, 2000, p. 63. The 1950 reconstructed map of information for c. A.D. 1423 also shows the Horn of Lacydon filled in and built over. There are 10 windmills at Butte des Moulins.

[2657] Braun and Hogenberg, *Civitas Orbis Terrarum,* vol. II–12, 1575. Engraving Marseille 1575, Braun and Hogenberg, *Civitas Orbis Terrarum*, vol. II–12., admitted to Sebastian Munster and first published in the 1575 edition of Munster's *Cosmographia*. The National Library of Israel, Eran Laor Cartographic Collection, *Cities in the World*, ['Shapell Family Digitization Project and the Hebrew University of Jerusalem' Historic Cities Research Project, Department of Geography] <http://historic-cities.huji.ac.il/>, viewed on 30 October 2010.

[2658] E. Baratier, *Histoire de la Provence*, E. Privat, (ed.), Univers de la France, 1969, p. 276.

[2659] M. P. Holt, *Renaissance and Reformation France 1500–1648*, Oxford, 2002, p. 42.

[2660] M. Greene, *Catholic Pirates and Greek Merchants: A Maritime History of the Mediterranean*, Princeton University Press, 2010, p. 170–171.

[2661] G. Goyau, 'Marseilles (Massilia)', *The Catholic Encyclopaedia*, vol. 9. New York: Robert Appleton Company, 1910, <www.newadvent.org>, viewed on 17 October 2010.

[2662] G. R. R. Treasure, *The Making of Modern Europe 1648–1780*, Methuen, 1985, p. 246–8.

[2663] E. Duprat, in P. Masson, (ed.), *Bouches du Rhône*, vol. 14, Marseille, 1935. p. 119 n. 2.

[2664] R. Mettam, *Government and Society in Louis XIV's France*, MacMillan Press, 1977, p. 80.

[2665] G. R. R. Treasure, *The Making of Modern Europe 1648–1780*, Methuen, 1985, p. 246–8.

[2666] R. Mettam, *Government and Society in Louis XIV's France*, Macmillan Press, 1977, p. 6.

[2667] E. Baratier, in E. Privat, (ed.), *Histoire de la Provence*, Univers de la France, 1969, p. 189.

[2668] R. Gardiner, *The Age of the Galley*, Conway Maritime Press, 1995, p. 190.

[2669] F. Blanche, *Louis XIV*, Basil Blackwell Ltd., 1990, p. 148.

[2670] H. F. Ghiuzeli, *Jewish Community of Marseilles*, ['Beit Hatfutsot', The Museum of the Jewish People] <www.bh.org.il/database-article.aspx?48710>, viewed on 3 September 2011.

[2671] R. Mettam, *Government and Society in Louis XIV's France*, Macmillan Press, 1977, p. 80.

[2672] *Ibid*, p. 189.

[2673] *Ibid*, p. 188.

[2674] J. Lough, *France Observed in the Seventeenth Century by British Travellers*, Oriel Press, 1984, p. 63.

[2675] *Ibid*.

[2676] *Ibid*, p. 62.

[2677] *Ibid*.

[2678] *Ibid*, p. 110.

[2679] *Ibid*, p. 111.

[2680] E. Baratier, in E. Privat, (ed.), *Histoire de la Provence*, Univers de la France, 1969, p. 193.

[2681] R. Gardiner, *The Age of the Galley*, Conway Maritime Press, 1995, p. 111.

[2682] *Ibid*, p. 190.

[2683] *Ibid*, p. 111.

[2684] *Ibid*.

[2685] *Ibid*.

[2686] *Ibid*, p. 190.

[2687] P. S. Boyer, et al. *The Enduring Vision: A History of the American People*, Houghton Miflin, 2008, p. 81.

[2688] W. J. Eccles, *Brisay de Denonville:Jacques-René de, Marquis de Denonville*, [Dictionary of Canadian Biography Online']
<http://www.biographi.ca/009004-119.01-e.php?&id_nbr=673&interval=25&&PHPSESSID=8l2vojaefug5c5kr7863r2n1p0>, viewed on 31 December 2010.

[2689] Beaver Wars, *Definition Iroquois*, ['Webster's Online Dictionary']
<http://www.websters-online-dictionary.org/definitions/Iroquois>, viewed on 31 December 2010.

[2690] W. J. Eccles, *Brisay de Denonville: Jacques-René de, Marquis de Denonville*, [Dictionary of Canadian Biography Online']
<http://www.biographi.ca/009004-119.01-e.php?&id_nbr=673&interval=25&&PHPSESSID=8l2vojaefug5c5kr7863r2n1p0>, viewed on 31 December 2010.

[2691] W. N. Fenton, *The Great Law and the Longhouse: a political history of the Iroquois confederacy*, University of Oklahoma, 1998, p. 257.

[2692] W. J. Eccles, *Brisay de Denonville: Jacques-René de, Marquis de Denonville*, [Dictionary of Canadian Biography Online']
<http://www.biographi.ca/009004-119.01-e.php?&id_nbr=673&interval=25&&PHPSESSID=8l2vojaefug5c5kr7863r2n1p0>, viewed on 31 December 2010.

[2693] *Ibid.*

[2694] N. Dionne, 'Seigneur and Marquis de Denonville', *The Catholic Encyclopaedia*, vol. 9. New York: Robert Appleton Company, 1908, <http://www.newadvent.org/cathen/04732a.htm>, viewed on 31 December 2010.

[2695] Beaver Wars, *Definition Iroquois*, ['Webster's Online Dictionary']
<http://www.websters-online-dictionary.org/definitions/Iroquois>, viewed on 31 December 2010.

[2696] W. N. Fenton, *The Great Law and the Longhouse: a political history of the Iroquois confederacy*, University of Oklahoma, 1998, p. 315-316.

[2697] *Ibid*, p. 264.

[2698] A. Morea, *La Perle Noire de la Méditerranée*, Éditions Milan, 1999, p. 58.

[2699] M. Nelson and A. Briggs, *Queen Victoria and the Discovery of the Riviera,* Tauris Parke Paperbacks, 2007, p. 90.

[2700] *Ibid*, p. 120–121. Provence attracted many 19th & 20th century painters due to its particular blue light and climate.

[2701] H. F. Ghiuzeli, *Jewish Community of Marseilles*, ['Beit Hatfutsot', The Museum of the Jewish People] <www.bh.org.il/database-article.aspx?48710>, viewed on 3 September 2011.

[2702] C. Hibbert, *The French Revolution,* Penguin, 1980, p. 153–4.

[2703] *Marseille,* Part 2, <www.sagaplanet.com>, viewed on 4 September 2009.

[2704] C. Hibbert, *The French Revolution*, Penguin, 1980, p. 153–4.

[2705] *Ibid*, p. 153–4.

[2706] C. Díaz, H. Palou, and A. M. Puig, *La Ciudadela de Roses*, Ayuntamiento de Roses Fundació Roses Història i Natura, 2003, p. 84.

[2707] T. Jaques, *Dictionary of Battles and Sieges: A Guide to 8,500 Battles from Antiquity through the Twenty-first Century*, vol. 3, Greenwood Press, 2007, p. 864.

[2708] C. Díaz, H. Palou, and A. M. Puig, *La Ciudadela de Roses*, Ayuntamiento de Roses Fundació Roses Història i Natura, 2003, p. 86 and p. 91.

[2709] J. Anderson. Black, *The Life and Times of Napoleon Bonaparte*, Parragon, 1994, p. 46-47. <http://francemonthly.com/n/0508/index.php>,< http://www.amb-cotedazur.com/Museums/napoleon-museum.html> viewed 25 February 2014.

[2710] B. McCabe, G. Harlaftis, and I. P. Minoglou, *Diaspora Entrepreneurial Networks: four centuries of History*, Berg, 2005, p. 154.

[2711] *Ibid*, p.160 f–161.

[2712] Marseille, *Uneasy Union with France*, ['Encyclopaedia Britannica'] <http://www.britannica.com/EB.C.hecked/topic/366460/Marseille/12518/Uneasy-union-with-France>, viewed on 5 September 2011.

[2713] W. Scott, *Terror and Repression in Revolutionary Marseilles*, Macmillan Press, 1973, p. 136.

[2714] *Ibid*, p. 138.

[2715] *Ibid* p. 143.

[2716] Marseille, *Uneasy Union with France*, ['Encyclopaedia Britannica'] <http://www.britannica.com/EB.C.hecked/topic/366460/Marseille/12518/Uneasy-union-with-France>, viewed on 5 September 2011,

[2717] R. Clogg, *A Concise History of Greece*, Cambridge University Press, 1997, p. 29–30 and p. 224. An attempt at a coordinated revolt to take over the Ottoman Empire embracing all its inhabitants but with the republican institutions based on the French model was developed by the Greek Rigas Velestinlis and aborted when he was arrested and put to death with some of his conspirators by the Ottoman authorities in Belgrade 1798.

[2718] B. McCabe, G. Harlaftis, and I. P. Minoglou, *Diaspora Entrepreneurial Networks: four centuries of History*, Berg, 2005, p. 154.

[2719] *Ibid*, p. 154–156.

[2720] R. Clogg, *A Concise History of Greece*, Cambridge University Press, 1997, p. 101; Phokaia and New Phokaia are listed amongst the Greek cities in the area north of Smyrni. D. Kiminas, *The Ecumenical Patriarchate: A History of its Metropolitanates with Annotated Hierarch Catalogs*, Wildeside Press, 2009, p. 85

[2721] *Ibid*, p. 47–48. The 'Great Idea' (Megali Idea) was put forward by Ioannis Kolettis in 1844 to include all of the scattered Greek communities into one state with its capital at Constantinople where there was still a large Greek population. Only a third of the Greeks actually lived in the new independent Kingdom of Greece in mainland Greece. The 'Great Idea' became a driving force in Greek aspirations until the catastrophic results of the Greek-Turkish war by 1922. The enlargement of the state to the borders of a former time of greatness was a common aspiration of the Balkan states during the nineteenth century.

[2722] R. Clogg, *A Concise History of Greece*, Cambridge University Press, p. 98–99.

In 1914 The Phocaeans dispersed 6,000 to Mytilini, 1,600 to Pireus and Athens, 3,000 to Volos and Thessaloniki, 150 to Euboia, 150 to Heraklion Crete and elsewhere. On 1 January 1920 11,000 Phocaeans returned to Old Phocaea and New Phocaea in Ionia with 5,000 remaining in Greece. In August 1922 the 11,000 in Ionia fled for Greece, Mytilini and elsewhere. Felix Sartiaux, *Phokaia* 1913-20, ΡΙΖΑΡΕΙΟ/ΔΡΥΜΑ, KALLIMAGES, 2008, p. 301-2

See also <http://diaspora-grecque.com/modules/altern8news/print.php?storyid=2270>, viewed on 6 July 2012.

Greek Moslems from Crete were transferred to the west coast of Turkey where the previous Greek Orthodox had been living before the 'Exchange'. R. Clogg, *A Concise History of Greece,* Cambridge University Press, 1997, p. 101.

[2723] Philippe Laure, 'On a retrouvé les fils des Protis. Une etude sur le sang désigne les descendants direct des Phocéens', *La Provence*, Vendredi 22 Avril 2011, 22042011 Journal La Provence, p. 3.
<http://www.scribd.com/doc/53641055/Journal-La-Provence-22042011>, viewed 10 February 2012.

Samples taken from 51 people from villages near Neolithic sites in Provence were compared to 368 from Provence with French surnames. See published report J. Charoni, et al., *The coming of the Greeks to Provence and Corsica: Y-chromosome models of archaic Greek colonization of the western Mediterranean*, BMC, p.7. Evolutionary Biology, published 14 March 2011, ['BioMed Central'] <http://www.biomedcentral.com/1471-2148/11/69>, viewed 3 April 2012.

[2724] J. Charoni, et al., *The coming of the Greeks to Provence and Corsica: Y-chromosome models of archaic Greek colonization of the western Mediterranean*, BMC, p. 1. Evolutionary Biology, published 14 March 2011, ['BioMed Central'] <http://www.biomedcentral.com/1471-2148/11/69>, viewed 3 April 2012.

[2725] B. McCabe, G. Harlaftis, and I. P. Minoglou, *Diaspora Entrepreneurial Networks: four centuries of History*, Berg, 2005, p. 155.

[2726] Herodotus, *Histories*, Book I. 165, trans. G. Rawlinson, Wordsworth Editions Ltd, 1996, p. 74–75.

[2727] B. McCabe, G. Harlaftis, and I. P. Minoglou, *Diaspora Entrepreneurial Networks: four centuries of History*, Berg, 2005, p. 156.

[2728] In the following twentieth century the wealthy Helena Schilizzi was the second wife of the Prime Minister of Greece Eleftherios Venizelos. R. Clogg, *A Concise History of Greece*, Cambridge University Press, 1997, p. 111.

[2729] C. A. Long, *The Chios Diaspora 1822–1899*, <http//:www.christopherlong.co.uk/per/chiosdiaspora.html>, viewed on 5 September 2010. See *Grecs et Philhellenes A Marseille* by Pierre Echinard-Institue Historique de Provence, translated by CAL; in French from Chez l'Auteur, 1973., ASIN B003WRSK12.

[2730] T. Catsiyannis, Bishop of Militoupolis. *Pandias Stephen Rallis 1793–1865*, Ekdotike Hellados, 1986, p. 17 and p. 48.

[2731] C. A. Long, *The Chios Diaspora 1822–1899*, <http//:www.christopherlong.co.uk/per/chiosdiaspora.html>, viewed on 5 September 2010.

[2732] T. Catsiyannis, Bishop of Militoupolis. *Pandias Stephen Rallis 1793–1865*, Ekdotike Hellados, 1986, p. 68.

[2733] Alexis Vlasto, as well as being a historian at Cambridge was one of the British code-breakers at Bletchley Park that made a vital contribution for Britain in World War II. C. A. Long, *The Chios Diaspora 1822–1899*, <http//:www.christopherlong.co.uk/per/chiosdiaspora.html>, viewed on 5 September 2010.

[2734] Constantine Alexander Ionides (1833–1900) born in Manchester donated his huge art collection to the Victoria & Albert Museum when he died. His father's house in London later became the Greek Embassy. C. A. Long, *The Chios Diaspora 1822–1899*, <http//:www.christopherlong.co.uk/per/chiosdiaspora.html>, viewed on 5 September 2010.

[2735] C. A. Long, *The Chios Diaspora 1822–1899*, <http//:www.christopherlong.co.uk/per/chiosdiaspora.html>, viewed on 5 September 2010. Ref. Treasured Offerings, Byzantine and Christian Monuments, 2002.

The cathedral's beautiful interior featured briefly in the James Bond film Goldeneye (1995), and also Stardust (2007).

[2736] C. A. Long, *The Chios Diaspora 1822–1899*, <http//:www.christopherlong.co.uk/per/chiosdiaspora.html>, viewed on 5 September 2010. See *Grecs et Philhellenes à Marseille* by Pierre Echinard–Institue Historique de Provence, translated by CAL; in French from Chez l'Auteur, 1973. ASIN B003WRSK12.

[2737] C. A. Long, *The Chios Diaspora 1822–1899*, <http//:www.christopherlong.co.uk/per/chiosdiaspora.html>, viewed on 5 September 2010.

[2738] Emmanuel Laugier, *Places of Worship in Marseille—studies representativeness in the city*, <http://www.coe.int/t/dg4/cultureheritage/heritage/identities/edifreligieux_EN.pdf>, viewed on 30 January 2011.

[2739] G. Rambert, in *Bouches du Rhône*, (ed.), P. Masson, vol. 14, Marseille, 1935, p. 147.

[2740] E. Paris, *The Greeks of Marseille and Greek Nationalism*, 20 November 2000, viewed <http://barthes.ens.fr/clio/revues/AHI/articles/English/pari.html> on 5 September 2010.

[2741] C. A. Long, *The Chios Diaspora 1822–1899*, <http//:www.christopherlong.co.uk/per/chiosdiaspora.html>, viewed on 5 September 2010.

[2742] Spirits, Ouzo Plomari, *What is Ouzo?*, <http://www.avenuewine.com/singlemaltscotches/item.nhtml?profile=singlemaltscotches&UID=149>, viewed on 5 September 2011.

[2743] L. Taylor, TED Case Studies Number 723, 2004, *Ouzo, Trade and Culture*, <http://www1.american.edu/TED/ouzo.htm>, viewed on 5 September 2011.

[2744] *The Origin of the Name Marseille*, <http://www.massalia.net/eng_avant-propos2.html>, viewed on 5 September 2011.

[2745] A. Hermary, A. Hesnard, and H. Tréziny, *Marseille Grecque: La cite phocéenne (600–49 av. J-C)*, Editions Errance, 1999, p. 9 & p. 12.

[2746] *Ibid*, p. 12.

[2747] *Ibid*, p. 11.

[2748] E. Paris, *The Greeks of Marseille and Greek Nationalism*, (20 November 2000). <http://barthes.ens.fr/clio/revues/AHI/articles/English/pari.html>, viewed on 31 January 2011; M. Calapodis, *La Communauté grec à Marseille: Genèse d'un paragdime identitaire (1794-1914)*, L'Harmattan, 2010, p. 152.

[2749] A. Hermary, A. Hesnard, and H. Tréziny, *Marseille Grecque: La cite phocéenne (600–49 av. J-C)*, Editions Errance, 1999, p. 11.

[2750] S. Crane, 'Digging up the Present in Marseille's Old Port: Toward an Archaeology of Reconstruction' in *Journal of the Society of Architectural Historians,* vol. 63, no. 3 (Sep., 2004): 296–319, here p. 312, ['JSTOR' journal archive] <http://www.jstor.org/stable/4127973>, viewed on 8 October 2010.

[2751] *A. Trevor. Hodge,* Ancient Greek France, *University of Pennsylvania Press, 1999, p. 72, Fig. 48.*

[2752] M. Garrett, *Provence: a cultural history*, Oxford, 2006, p. 121.

[2753] A. L. F. Rivet, *Gallia Narbonensis,* Batsford, 1988, p. 220.

[2754] *Ibid.*

[2755] M. Garrett, *Provence: a cultural history*, Oxford, 2006, p. 122.

[2756] *Ibid.*

[2757] INSEE, *13 Bouches-du-Rhône*, Code commune 13055, ['Institute national de statistique et de études économiques'] <http://www.insee.fr/fr/ppp/bases-de-donnees/recensement/populations-legales/departement.asp?dep=13>, viewed on 5 September 2011.

[2758] N. Khouri-Dager, *Marseille-Esperence. All different, all Marseillais*, <http://www.diplomatie.gouv.fr/en/article_imprim.php3?id_article=6065>, viewed on 4 September 2009.

[2759] S. Poggioli, *Diverse Marseille Spared in French Riots*, ['NPR'] <http://www.npr.org/templates/story/story.php?storyId=5044219>, viewed on 5 September 2011; <www.Diplomatie.gouv.fr/en/france_159/label-France-2554/label-France-issues_2>, viewed on 4 September 2009.

[2760] Strabo, *Geography*, IV. 1.5; A. Bowman and G. Woolf (eds.), *Literacy and Power in the Ancient World*, Cambridge, 1996, p. 88-89.

[2761] C. Canetti, *Marseille, European Capital of Culture 2013*, ['France Diplomatie'], Source: Actualité en France n° 43, October 2008, <http://www.diplomatie.gouv.fr/en/france_159/geography_6812/regions-and-towns_6931/towns_6933/marseille-european-capital-of-culture-2013_12660.html>, viewed on 5 September 2011.

[2762] Philippe Laure, 'On a retrouvé les fils des Protis. Une etude sur le sang désigne les descendants direct des Phocéens', *La Provence*, Vendredi 22 Avril 2011, 22042011 Journal La Provence, p. 3. <http://www.scribd.com/doc/53641055/Journal-La-Provence-22042011>, viewed 10 February 2012.

J. Charoni, et al., *The coming of the Greeks to Provence and Corsica: Y-chromosome models of archaic Greek colonization of the western Mediterranean*, BMC Evolutionary Biology, published 14 March 2011, ['BioMed Central'] <http://www.biomedcentral.com/1471-2148/11/69>, viewed 3 April 2012.

[2763] Tacitus, *Agricola*, Bk.1. 38. <http://www.sacred-texts.com/cla/tac/ag01010.htm>, viewed on 5 September 2011; Agricola 10.4 see K. Clarke, 'An Island Nation: Re-reading Tacitus' *Agricola*' in R. Ash, (ed.). *Oxford Readings in Tacitus*, (Oxford, 2012):37-72, here p. 47-49; see also different interpretation of translation S. Wolfson, *Reassessment of Vocabulary and Sense*, <http://myweb.tiscali.co.uk/fartherlands/vocabulary.html> viewed 22 February 2013.

[2764] The sea was reported as 'sluggish and heavy' for rowing i.e. The North Atlantic Drift Current and not ice. *Agr.* 10.5. K. Clarke, 'An Island Nation: Re-reading Tacitus' *Agricola*' in R. Ash, (ed.). *Oxford Readings in Tacitus*, (Oxford, 2012):37-72, here p. 46. Solinus' account of Thyle is 'sluggish and frozen' see Rivet & Smith, 1982, p. 85.

[2765] Pytheas of Massalia wrote that Thoule was six days sailing north from Britain, Pliny the Elder, *Natural Histories*, 2. 187; Strabo, *Geography*, Bk. I.4.2.

[2766] Pliny the Elder, *Natural Histories*, IV.104.

[2767] V. Stefansson, *Ultima Thule*, George Harrap & Co, 1942, p. 77.

[2768] Pliny the Elder, *Natural Histories*, II. 187; Strabo, *Geography*, Bk.I. 4.2.

[2769] Pliny the Elder, *Natural Histories*, IV.104.

[2770] B. Cunliffe, *The Extraordinary Voyage of Pytheas the Greek: The man who discovered Britain*, Penguin Books, 2002, p. 128.

[2771] C. H. Roseman, *Pytheas of Massalia: Text, Translation and Commentary*, Ares Publishing, 1994, p. 104, (Kleomedes, *Meteora*,1.4, 208–210, from *Cleomedes, Calestia*, R. B. Todd, (ed.), Leipzig. 1990, Teubner, now thought to have been writing in the second century A.D. Kleomedes is drawing much of his work from Eratosthenes and Poseidonios (Roseman, p. 14).

[2772] C. H. Roseman, *Pytheas of Massalia: Text, Translation and Commentary*, Ares Publishing, 1994, p. 143, Kosmas Indicopleustes, *Christian Topography*, II.80. 6–9. Kosmas probably saw this quote in isolation for he used it against pagan ideas of a spherical earth. Had he seen more he would have realised Pytheas's description were for proving the earth was spherical. Inadvertently Kosmas had saved a valuable quote. (Roseman, 1944, p. 144–145).

[2773] C. F. C. Hawkes, *Pytheas: Europe and the Greek Explorers*, Oxford, (1975) p. 34.

[2774] R. Carpenter, *Beyond the Pillars of Hercules: The classical world seen through the eyes of its discoverers*, Tandem Press (UK), 1973, p. 175 n. 26, Gaius Julius Solinus, *Collectanae Rerum Memorabilium* (ed. Th. Mommsen, 2d, ed., Berlin, 1958) 28 (12) and 22 (17).

[2775] Pliny the Elder, *Natural History*, IV.104.

[2776] Apollonius of Rhodes, *The Voyage of Argo: The Argonautica*, trans. E. V. Rieu, Penguin, 1959, p. 162 & p. 164–165. Rieu in his glossary says Cronian was also an ancient name for the Adriatic p. 201.

[2777] A. L. F. Rivet and C. Smith, *The Place-Names of Roman Britain*, B. T. Batsford Ltd, 1982, p. 85, Solinus, *Collectanea Rerum Memorabilium*, 22, 1–12.

[2778] *Ibid*, p. 77, Orosius, *Historiae adversum Paganos* 1, 2, 75–82.

[2779] A. L. F. Rivet and C. Smith, *The Place-Names of Roman Britain*, B. T. Batsford Ltd, 1982, p. 82, Procopius, *De Bellis*, VI (=De Bello Gothico), 15, 1–26.

[2780] A. L. F. Rivet and C. Smith, *The Place-Names of Roman Britain*, B. T. Batsford Ltd, 1982, p. 83.

[2781] Strabo, *Geography*, Book III, 2.1.

[2782] M. Grant, *The Rise of the Greeks*, Phoenix, 2005, p. 150.

[2783] Strabo, *Geography*, Book III. 2.9. & Book II. 5. 15.

[2784] Lacus Curtius, *The Geography of Strabo*, vol. 2. III. 3.11.Loeb, 1923, ['Penelope, University of Chicago' digital library] <http://penelope.uchicago.edu/Thayer/E/Roman/Texts/Strabo/3E*.html>, viewed on 29 October 2011.

[2785] *Ibid*.

[2786] A. L. F. Rivet and C. Smith, *The Place-Names of Roman Britain*, B. T. Batsford Ltd, 1982, p. 63, Diodorus Siculus, *Histories*, V. 38. 4–5. C. H. Oldfather. (ed.), London and Cambridge, Mass., 1939.

A different spelling is given by Dionysius Periegetes (c. A.D. 125) as Cassiterides.

[2787] M. Grant, *The Rise of the Greeks*, Ch. 3, Phoenix, 2005 p. 176, Pliny the Elder, *Natural Histories*, VII, 197.

Pliny's mention of another people called Albiones living on the north coast of Spain which may have led to the confusion of position and location of Albion by the other writers. C. F. C. Hawkes, *Pytheas: Europe and the Greek Explorers,* a lecture delivered at New College, Oxford on 20th May, 1975 (The J. L. Myers memorial lecture), p. 22. ASIN: B0007AMH16.

[2788] H. F. Tozer, *History of Ancient Geography*, Biblo-Moser, 2nd edition, 1965, p. 37–38.

[2789] G. de Beer, 'Iktin', *The Geographical Journal*, Vol. 126, No. 2, (June 1960): 160-167, here p. 166–7, <http://www.jstor.org/stable/1793956>, viewed on 5 July 2012.

[2790] O. Murray, 'Life and Society in Classical Greece', ch. 9, in J. Boardman, J. Griffin, and O Murray, *Greece and the Hellenistic World*, Oxford University Press, 2001, p. 249; O. Murray, *Early Greece*, Fontana, 1993, p. 111.

[2791] L. Foxhall, 'Cultural Landscapes, and Identities in the Mediterranean World' in *Mediterranean Historical Review*, vol. 18, no. 2, (December 2003): 75–92.

[2792] R. Osborne, 'Early Greek Colonization? The nature of Greek settlement in the West' in N. Fisher and H. van Wees (eds.), *Archaic Greece; new approaches and new evidence,* (London, 1998): 251–269, here p. 268–269; R. Osborne, *Greece in the Making 1200–479 B.C.* Routledge, 2008, p. 129.

One can see a parallel for the Indian part of the later British Empire. This was private enterprise of the East India Company founded for trade. It was much later when the state intervened and brought it into the British Empire.

[2793] B. Softas-Nall, 'Reflections on Forty Years of Family Therapy: Research and Systemic Thinking in Greece, in K.S. Ng. (ed.), *Global Perspectives on Family Therapy: Practice, Development and Trends*, Brunner-Routledge, (2003):126–147, here p. 128.

[2794] R. Clogg, *A Concise History of Greece,* Cambridge University Press, 1997, p. 112–113, plate 35.

[2795] *Ibid*, p. 112, plate 35, & p. 149.

[2796] A. T. Kopan, *Greeks*, ['Encyclopaedia of Chicago'] <http://Encyclopaedia.chicagohistory.org/pages/548.html>, viewed on 26 January 2011.

[2797] P. Bradley, *Ancient Greece: Using Evidence*, Edward Arnold (Australia) Pty Ltd, 1988, p. 22.

[2798] Strabo, *Geography*, Bk. XVII.1.6.

[2799] A. Villing and A. Möllër, *Naukratis: Greek Diversity in Egypt*, The British Museum, 2006, p. 2; Herodotus, *Histories*, II.178–9.

[2800] J. Boardman, *The Greeks Overseas: Their Early Colonies and Trade*, Thames & Hudson, 1999, p. 121.

[2801] C. F.C. Hawkes, *Pytheas: Europe and the Greek Explorers,* a lecture delivered at New College, Oxford on 20th May, 1975 (The J. L. Myers memorial lecture), ASIN: B0007AMH16.

[2802] R. Osborne, 'Early Greek Colonization? The nature of Greek settlement in the West' in N. Fisher and H. van Wees (eds.), *Archaic Greece; new approaches and new evidence,* (London, 1998): 251–269, here p. 258; Osborne, R. *Greece in the Making 1200 – 479 B.C.* Routledge, 2008, p. 129.

[2803] B. D'Agostino, 'The First Greeks in Italy', in G. R. Tsetskhladze (ed.), *Greek Colonization: An account of Greek Colonization and Other Settlements Overseas*, vol.1, (Leiden, 2006): 201–237, here p. 218–219.

[2804] W. J. Federer, *America's God and Country: Encyclopaedia of quotations*, Amerisearch Inc., 2000, p. 329. Thomas Jefferson to Horatio G. Spafford, 1814, ME: 14–119 & ME 12.376 <http://etext.virginia.edu/jefferson/quotations/jeff1320.htm>, viewed on 7 October 2010

[2805] C. Cardingham, *Bank Bailout to add up to 1.5 Trillion to Public Debt*, published 19 February 2009, <http://www.money.co.uk/article/1002877-bank-bailout-to-add-up-to-1-5-trillion-to-public-debt.htm>, viewed on 5 December 2010.

[2806] Interview with banker seen on B.B.C. 1 TV '6.00 pm News', 21 September 2010.

[2807] Karl Marx made much of the workers owning the means of production. City bank workers certainly do not own the 'means' but they do share in the huge profits. It is with some irony that those from the heart of capitalism are defending a Marxist principle in redistributing wealth? The workers must have their share, especially that which they have made, and it is expected that seven billion pounds is to be given in bonuses amongst themselves. ('B.B.C. 1 TV News', 5 October 2010). However, the 'redistribution' is only for them. This money would start paying back what they owe the government at a time when the rest of the country is to endure cuts and job losses to pay the debt incurred in rescuing the banks. (Seager, A., and Treanor, A. 'Mervyn King Launches Blistering Attack on £1tn Banks Bailout', *The Guardian*, article date 21 October 2009 <http://www.guardian.co.uk/business/2009/oct/21/mervyn-king-attack-banks-bailout>, viewed on 5 December 2010).

When the 'credit crunch' came, which was caused by the bank's investments in dodgy U.S.A. primary mortgage loans, the bankers all excused their behaviour in countless interviews on TV and the press by saying nobody not even the government saw it was coming. Not true! An article/report was sent in May 2007 to all the main newspaper editors B.B.C. TV News and Radio and leaders of the three main political parties and the Chancellor of the Exchequer in Britain warning of an impending collapse in the economy. The article/report was titled 'The Archbishop says, Do not get a mortgage'. No one published it. No one wanted to hear bad news (only the Lib Dems, particularly Dr Vince Cable, to their credit, working along similar lines spoke out). The article was sent the week Gordon Brown became Prime Minister.

Six months later when Northern Rock nearly went bust Gordon Brown's (to his credit) tough and radical action averted a collapse that would have been greater than the South Sea Bubble or the Wall Street Crash. Blair and Brown's Britain was awash with money (unfortunately not for everyone as London became the second most expensive city in the world to live in and for many people all their wages went on rent) in an artificial rising house price boom. Buying to rent forced up rents and increased the cost of living while tenants were actually paying for their landlord's mortgage payments and a profit on top. How did this occur? Basic living bills were paid for by credit cards. One estate agent advertised in Metro newspaper new flats for sale. Appointments to view would be conducted every half hour with ten clients at the same time! This left no chance to bargain with the price. All clients were forced by peer group pressure if you delay someone else will buy it. Brown when Chancellor in the earlier part of the Labour government (that had continued John Major's Conservative budget) had declared it was an end of Tory 'boom and bust' economy but now it had happened to him. <wwww.guardian.co.uk/political2008/sep/11/gordonbrown.economy>, viewed on 29 September 2010)

The latest figures published shows one third of all new houses in London are bought by China. Due to the credit crunch the pound being lower made the exchange rate 50% cheaper for Chinese to buy property here. (Liam Bell Knight Frank Estate Agents B.B.C. TV News 29 September 2010). In the last decade we see the UK housing market, with low supply and high demand from the East Europeans and now the Chinese, continually rise becoming grossly overvalued and artificially high. This leaves no chance for a British single person or single breadwinner of a family on normal wages to buy a home in their own country. As the consumer does not act together houses are one instance where it cannot be left to 'market forces'. The consumer's only hope was to pray for a house market crash to bring house prices down. Unfortunately this can only happen in a recession. The Briton then has no job to buy at the lower price. Those with money and foreign buyers then buy up houses. When the Briton is working again the price of houses are beyond their wages to buy and rents are too high. Britons have political freedoms but a section have inadvertently become economic slaves. The government needs to take action in reducing house prices and rents as mentioned in my article/report. On 12 December 2011 BBC TV News reported that the Mayoral candidate for London 2012 Ken Livingstone was proposing a plan to get the government to enact a control on rents to one third of people's wages if he is elected. In the election manifestos of the other candidates in May, the Lib Dems and the Greens also committed themselves to combat high rent.

For British citizens to pay their tax abroad yet still expecting and using the facilities and infrastructure of Britain is unfair when the rest of the country has to pay tax to maintain the country you like being in. The tax free offshore accounts of businessmen, investors, formula one racing drivers, pop stars and entertainers, (who make millions from their record sales and tours here), should help the country as everyone else does. Their fans made them rich and the fans still pay taxes to maintain the country they like to visit. Other people still have businesses and property here. They can certainly afford something when even the unemployed who cannot on Jobseeker's Allowance have to pay tax? Many people on the dole are there through no fault of their own particular in times of recession and government spending cuts. There is always a minority that may be 'scroungers' who don't want to work. The usual joke is Jobseeker Allowance, good hours but lousy pay! One could make a case as to who are the 'scroungers'? Is it people with no money or opportunities living on JSA survival money and pay tax or is it those who have money and opportunities who use the facilities of Britain's roads, street lighting, hospitals, police and security yet by their offshore accounts do not pay any tax to help and are in a better financial position to afford that help to the country they use? They do nothing illegal and have taken proper advice from accountants, but is that fair? Every club has a membership fee to pay so you are entitled to use the facilities. Belonging to any country requires similar fees. Let all the (tax) exiles return and take their rightful place.

'One good turn deserves another', doing one a favour and that favour being returned is a basic action of human behaviour and certainly continues even in a competitive business world. One can say of the British banks (not Barclays who had wisely spread their investments took no money from the government bailout) their current attitude (a far cry from the traditional Victorian profit and philanthropy bankers) is at the least ungrateful and at the most unpatriotic, selfish and it would seem they have different priorities. However, Thomas Jefferson had a point that merchants can be governed by the fluidity of money wherever that is in a global marketplace. Ethics course for bankers are now proposed.

[2808] The aboriginal, the first inhabitants of the land. Herodotus, *Histories*, 8.73; *Illogical Geology*, ['Findstone.com'] <http://www.findstone.com/geo_illogic.htm>, viewed on 6 September 2011. Some ancient Athenians took to wearing golden grasshoppers in their hair as a badge of their antiquity as they believed grasshoppers were also 'sprung from the earth'. J. Robinson, *Archaeologica Graeca or the Antiquities of Greece,* Baldwin, Cradock and Joy, 1827, p.1 note c. Menand, *Rhetor.*, and p. 542, <http://books.google.co.uk/books?id=P-LQzMJWs0QC&pg=PA1&lpg=PA1&dq=Athenians+wore+golden+grasshoppers?&source=bl&ots=N_KxvAK7Me&sig=hxxXLSeIEVjNJQmqdKwUFmbKYxw&hl=en&sa=X&ei=Yy2uT8qvFM2p8AP8s-iKCQ&ved=0CDcQ6AEwAg#v=onepage&q=Athenians%20wore%20golden%20grasshoppers%3F&f=false> viewed 12 May 2012.

[2809] One notable contribution was made by Sam Wanamaker, American actor, director, film producer and the 'visionary who recreated Shakespeare's Globe' theatre at Southwark. <http://www.william-shakespeare.info/william-shakespeare-new-globe-theatre-history-timeline.htm, viewed 27 December 2012. Also £10,000 raised by private donations from

Americans, Commonwealth etc. to Philippa Langley, Richard III Society, when a funding grant failed for excavation of a car park over the site of Grey Friars by the University of Leicester team where it was thought the remains of Richard III, king of England lay after the Battle of Bosworth 1485. DNA taken from an excavated skeleton matched that of a Canadian Michael Ibsen and another who were descended 17 generations from Richard's sister Anne of York.

[2810] O. Murray, *Early Greece*, Fontana, 1993, p. 112.

[2811] Aristotle from Athenaeus, *Deipnosophists*, vol. 6. XIII, 576.

[2812] J-P. Wilson, 'The nature of Greek overseas settlements in the archaic period: emporion or apoikia?' in L. Mitchell and P.J. Rhodes (eds.), *The Development of the Polis in Archaic Greece*, (London, 1997): 199-207, here p. 9.

[2813] I. Malkin, 'Exploring the validity of the concept of a "foundation": a visit to Megera Hyblaia' in V. B. Gorman and E. W. Robinson (eds.), *Oikistes: studies in constitutions, colonies and military power in the ancient world: offered in honour of A. J. Graham*, (Leiden, 2002): 195–225, here p. 211.

[2814] This is different to Chinese Whispers, ('Longman Dictionary of Contemporary English', <http://www.ldoceonline.com/dictionary/Chinese-whispers>, viewed on 22 October 2010) where a message is passed around a classroom, passed on from one to another and comparing the message received at the end with that of the original at the beginning. With folklore we are talking of complete and larger stories and told over a period of time. Of course with folklore this does not stop embellishments and regional variations. Though there will be embellishment some elements of the story will be intact. One example is the Cinderella story very much a western fairytale? An ancient Greek origin is claimed of Rhodopis living in Naucratis Egypt. (Strabo, *Geography*, 17. 33). <http://penelope.uchicago.edu/Thayer/E/Roman/Texts/Strabo/17A3*.html#ref178>, viewed on 25 September 2011; see also Sherry Climo, *The Egyptian Cinderella*, Harper Collins, New York, 1989. Last edited: Jul 20, 2005–00:08, <http://www.ancientsites.com/aw/Article/461904>, viewed on 25 September 2011.

There is a Chinese version of this story recorded A.D. 850 Certain elements parallel the glass shoe that had to fit. A. Waley, 'The Chinese Cinderella Story', *Folklore,* vol. 58, no. 1 (Mar., 1947): 226–238, published by: Taylor & Francis, Ltd. on behalf of Folklore Enterprises, Ltd., ['JSTOR' journal archive] <http://www.jstor.org/stable/1256703>, viewed on 22 October 2010; R. D. Jameson, *If the Shoe Fits*, [#510] <http://www.artic.edu/webspaces/510ifttheshoefits/2criteria.html>, viewed on 22 October 2010.

Feet in some societies were synonymous with eroticism and fertility, as in China even in the early part of the last century binding feet was still practiced to keep the feet unnaturally small when growing into an adult. Though considered attractive to men it was detrimental to women. M. Vento, *One Thousand years of Chinese Footbinding: Its Origins, Popularity and Demise*, <http://academic.brooklyn.cuny.edu/core9/phalsall/studpages/vento.html>, viewed on 22 October 2010.

In Britain there is a wedding custom to tie boots and shoes to the rear bumper of the car that the newly wedded couple drives away in to their honeymoon. Most people do not know why this is done but by the rigid conservatism of folk tradition this 'symbol of fertility' survives. There is also a British colloquialism for an aging, unattractive/unpleasant lady 'an old boot'! Dictionary of Slang, O, *old boot,* <http://dictionaryofslang.co.uk/>, viewed on 22 October 2010.

[2815] H. B. Cotterill, *Ancient Greece*, revised by Geddes and Grosset 2004, p. 143.

[2816] P. Bradley, *Ancient Greece: Using Evidence*, Edward Arnold (Australia) Pty Ltd, 1988, p. 28.

[2817] *Ibid*, p. 28 and p. 29.

[2818] I. Malkin, 'Exploring the validity of the concept of a 'foundation': a visit to Megera Hyblaia' in V. B. Gorman and E. W. Robinson (eds.), *Oikistes: studies in constitutions, colonies and military power in the ancient world: offered in honour of A. J. Graham*, (Leiden, 2002): 195–225, here p. 215, (Archilocos, ap. Athenaeus, 167 d).

[2819] P. Bradley, *Ancient Greece: Using Evidence*, Edward Arnold (Australia) Pty Ltd, 1988, p. 29.

[2820] *Ancient Greek Battles*, <http://www.ancientgreekbattles.net/Pages/48030_AthXerxesEnters.htm>, viewed 11 June 2012.

[2821] Montenegro, a small Balkan kingdom, was able to defend an independence within the Ottoman Empire on many occasions for the same reason. C. Swallow, *The Sick Man of Europe: Ottoman Empire to Turkish Republic 1789–1923*, Ernest Benn Ltd., 1973, p. 5 and p. 57.

[2822] Herodotus, *Histories*, V.63, trans. G. Rawlinson, Wordsworth Classics, p. 412 and n. 85.

[2823] Plutarch, *The Age of Alexander*, Nine Greek Lives, Alexander, 14, trans. I. Scott-Kilvert, Penguin Books, 1980, x, p. 266.

[2824] Strabo, *Geography*, VI, Ch. 3. 4.

[2825] It is a common thing for colonists to name settlements after places they knew back home e.g. Yorktown, Virginia named after York in England in 1691, sometimes native names are kept like Chicago <http://www.chicagohistoryjournal.com/2008/03/how-chicago-got-its-name.html>, viewed on 23 November 2011.

[2826] Strabo, *Geography*, VI. Ch. 1, 5.

[2827] H. W. Parke and D. E. W. Wormell, *The Delphic Oracle,* vol. 1, Blackwell, 1956, p. 406.

[2828] *Diogenes the Cynic: Sayings and Anecdotes with Other Popular Moralists*, trans. R. Hard, Oxford, 2012, p. 6.

[2829] E. Hall, *Inventing the Barbarian,* Clarendon, 1989, p. 9.

[2830] Herodotus, *Histories*, Bk. VIII. 61, trans. G. Rawlinson, Wordsworth Classics, 1996, p. 635; Aristotle, *Politics,* Book I. 1253a3, ['Internet Encyclopaedia of Philosophy'] <http://www.iep.utm.edu/aris-pol/>, viewed on 23 November 2010.

[2831] H. W. Parke and D. E. W. Wormell, *The Delphic Oracle,* vol. 1, Blackwell, 1956, p. 406.

[2832] *Ibid*.

[2833] Plutarch, *De Fortuna Alexandri*, Loeb, 1926, Second Oration, vol. 4, 332C. ['Penelope, University of Chicago' digital library] <http://penelope.uchicago.edu/Thayer/E/Roman/Texts/Plutarch/Moralia/Fortuna_Alexandri*/1.html>, viewed on 15 April 2011.

[2834] M. Lahanas, *Measurements*, <http://www.mlahanas.de/Greeks/Measurements.htm>, viewed on 30 October 2010; Crawford and Whitehead also points to variants as the distance of a *stadion* 'normally covered by a single draught of a plough, contained 600 feet and was thus *of the order of* 200 metres'. *Archaic and Classical Greece*, Cambridge, 1983, p. xvii.

[2835] *Stadium,* ['Encyclopaedia Brittanica'] <http://www.britannica.com/EBchecked/topic/562319/stadium#ref100143> viewed 14 May 2012.

[2836] C. H. Roseman, *Pytheas of Massalia: Text, Translation and Commentary,* Ares Publishing, 1994, p. 3.

Strabo only took measurements of stades from sailing in Mediterranean conditions, which would give very different times to that of Pytheas who was dealing with Atlantic tides, winds and currents. Also he believed the geographer should not draw and measure every detail of a winding coastline and should just make straight lines. There were only two writers, Polybius and Strabo, whose criticisms have since been proved to be unfounded. Pytheas used observational science we now know from archaeology and satellite technology to be correct together with all the great Greek astronomers, geographers and Romans who had accepted his calculations.

[2837] G. Shipley, *Pseudo-Skylax: The Circumnavigation of the Inhabited World-Text, Translation and Commentary*, 69, Bristol Phoenix Press, 2011, p. 91–93.

[2838] *Ibid*, p.71-72.

[2839] Pomponius Mela, *Geography,* Bk. III, trans. P. Berry, The Edwin Mellen Press, 1977, p.14.

[2840] C. H. Roseman, *Pytheas of Massalia: Text, Translation and Commentary,* Ares Publishing, 1994, p. 126.

[2841] Strabo, *Geography,* IV. 1.3.

[2842] Polybius, *The Histories,* vol. 2. Bk. III. 40. 14–41.8, trans. W. R. Paton, Heinemann, 1980, p. 91.

[2843] L. Casson, *Ships and Seamanship in the Ancient World,* The John Hopkins University Press, 1995, p. 284.

[2844] R. Carpenter, *Beyond the Pillars of Hercules: The classical world seen through the eyes of its discoverers,* Tandem Press (UK), 1973, Ch. 2, p. 54.

[2845] E. Guhl and W. Koner, *The Greeks; Their Life and Customs.* Senate, 1994, p. 264.

[2846] L. Casson, 'Speed under Sail of Ancient Ships', *Transactions and Proceedings of the American Philological Association,* vol. 82 (1951): 136–148, here p. 139, The John Hopkins University Press, ['JSTOR' journal archive] <http://www.jstor.org/stable/283426>, viewed on 17 November 2009.

[2847] L. Casson, *Ships and Seamanship in the Ancient World,* The John Hopkins University Press, 1995, p. 289 n. 86.

[2848] *Ibid,* p. 286 n. 69, (Sulpicius Severus, *Dial.* 1.31) and n. 70.

[2849] L. Casson, 'Speed under Sail of Ancient Ships', *Transactions and Proceedings of the American Philological Association,* vol. 82 (1951): 136–148, here p. 147 n. 28, The John Hopkins University Press, ['JSTOR' journal archive] <http://www.jstor.org/stable/283426>, viewed on 17 November 2009.

[2850] R. Gardiner, *The Age of the Galley,* Conway Maritime Press, 1995, p. 57.

[2851] R. Carpenter, *Beyond the Pillars of Hercules: The classical world seen through the eyes of is discoverers,* Tandem Press (UK), 1973, p. 60.

[2852] M. Grant, *The Rise of the Greeks,* Phoenix 2005, p. 150.

[2853] Herodotus, *Histories,* Book IV. 152.

[2854] R. Carpenter, *Beyond the Pillars of Hercules: The classical world seen through the eyes of is discoverers,* Tandem Press (UK), 1973, Ch 2, p. 64; P. Bosch-Gimpera, 'The Phokaians in the Far West: A Historical Reconstruction', *The Classical Quarterly,* vol. 38, no. 1/2 (Jan.–Apr., 1944): 53–59, here p. 53 n. 2, Peman, C. *Archivo Esp. de Archueologia,* 1941, p. 407), Schulten (Forschungen u. Fortschritte, 1929), ['JSTOR' journal archive] <www.jstor.org/stable/636879>, viewed on 20 August 2010.

[2855] *Ibid,* and on the later Greek helmet of Huelva, I. Schulten, *Investigación y Progreso,* 1931.

[2856] M. Grant, *The Rise of the Greeks,* Phoenix, 2005, p. 176.

[2857] Pliny the Elder *Natural Histories,* VII, 197.

[2858] Herodotus, *Histories,* Bk. IV.152.

[2859] J. Boardman, *The Greeks Overseas,* Thames and Hudson, 1995, p. 216.

[2860] B. Cunliffe, *The Extraordinary Voyage of Pytheas the Greek: The man who discovered Britain,* Penguin Books, 2002, p. 1 and p. 47.

[2861] *Ibid,* p. 42: M. Mund-Dopchie, 'Hanno' in V. Brown (ed.), *Catalogus Translationum Et Commentariorum: Medieval and Rennaisance Latin Translations and Commentaries, Annotated Lists and Guides,* Vol.3, The Catholic University Press of America, (2003):49-56.

[2862] R. Carpenter, *Beyond the Pillars of Hercules: The classical world seen through the eyes of is discoverers,* Tandem Press (UK), 1973, p. 204.

[2863] B. Cunliffe, *The Extraordinary Voyage of Pytheas the Greek: The man who discovered Britain,* Penguin Books, 2002, p. 44-46; A. L. F. Rivet and C. Smith, *The Place-Names of Roman Britain,* B. T. Batsford Ltd, 1982, p. 39.

[2864] C. F. C. Hawkes, *Pytheas: Europe and the Greek Explorers,* a lecture delivered at New College, Oxford on 20th May, 1975 (The J. L. Myers memorial lecture), p. 19. ASIN: B0007AMH16.

[2865] *Pliny's Natural Histories*, Philemon Holland, printed by G. Barclay for the Wernernian Club, 1847–48, Bk. 2, LXXVI, p. 118, note; also Herodotus, *Histories*, V.58, trans. G. Rawlinson, Wordsworth Classics, p. 411, 'as justice required, after the name of those who were the first to introduce them into Greece'.

[2866] *Australia History Timeline*, <http://www.history-timelines.org.uk/places-timelines/05-australia-history-timeline.htm>, viewed on 5 September 2011.

[2867] M. Magnusson, *Vikings*, Book Club Associates, 1985, p. 220–247; Excavations in L'Anse aux Meadows, Newfoundland, Canada revealed a small Viking settlement that lasted three to ten years. Radio carbon dating on the artefacts found was between A. D. 990-1030. K. K. Hirst, *L'Anse aux Meadows, A Viking Colony in the New World*, ['About.com'] <http://archaeology.about.com/cs/explorers/a/anseauxmeadows.htm>, viewed on 22 June 2012.

[2868] A. L. F. Rivet and C. Smith, *The Place-Names of Roman Britain,* B. T. Batsford Ltd., 1982, p. 282; Use of P and B see Roseman (1994), p. 45 & p. 55, also Cunliffe (2002) p. 94.

[2869] C. H. Roseman, *Pytheas of Massalia: Text, Translation and Commentary*, Ares Publishing, 1994, p. 87, Pliny the Elder, *Natural Histories*, 4. 102. From Solinus we have a double t and single n and by 5th century AD widely used.

[2870] *Ibid.*

[2871] Pindar, *The Complete Odes*, Olympian III, 42–47, trans. A. Verity, Oxford, 2007, p. 12.

[2872] Strabo, *Geography,* Book III.5.5–6.

[2873] H. White, *Appian's Roman History,* Heinemann, vol.1, Bk.VI, Ch. XI, 65. 1912, p. 239.

[2874] C. Seltman. *The Twelve Olympians and Their Guests,* Max Parrish, & Co, 1956, p. 176–177.

[2875] J. Lempriere, *A Classical Dictionary*, new edition Wright, F.A., Routledge & Keegan Paul Ltd. Book 2.17, 1951, p. 78–79; Philostratus, *The Life Of Apollonius of Tyana*, vol. 2, Bk. V. 4–5 trans. C.P. Jones. Harvard University Press, 2005, p, 5–7.

[2876] Polybius, *The Histories,* vol. 2. Bk. 3, 40. 14–41.8 footnote, trans. W. R. Paton, Heinemann, 1922.

[2877] Valerius Maximus, *Memorable Deeds and Sayings: A Thousand and One Tales From Ancient Rome,* V. 6. ext. 4, trans. Henry John Walker, Hackett Publishing Company Inc., 2004, p. 188.

[2878] Diogenes Laertius, *Lives of the Philosophers: Thales*, trans. C. D. Yonge, London: H.G. Bohn, 1863, XIV, p. 7 of 9, <http://www.classicpersuasion.org/pw/diogenes/dlthales.htm>, viewed on 29 October 2010.

[2879] W. W. Hyde, *Ancient Greek Mariners*, Oxford, 1947, p. 14 n. 24.

[2880] R. L. Fox, 'Hellenistic Culture and Literature', ch. 14 in J. Boardman, J. Griffin, and O. Murray, *Greece and the Hellenistic World,* Oxford University Press, 2001, p. 392.

[2881] B. Cunliffe, *The Extraordinary Voyage of Pytheas the Greek: The man who discovered Britain*, Penguin Books, 2002, p. 157.

[2882] Herodotus, *Histories*, V.58, trans. G. Rawlinson, Wordsworth Classics, p. 411.

[2883] B. Cunliffe, *The Extraordinary Voyage of Pytheas the Greek: The man who discovered Britain*, Penguin Books, 2002, p. 158; The introduction of paper by the Arabs particularly the Abbasid dynasty in Baghdad mid-eighth century

A.D. (learned from captured Chinese prisoners) was far less expensive than papyrus and more easily available. D. Gutas, *Greek Thought, Arab Culture: The Graeco-Arabic movement in Baghdad and early 'Abbasid Society (2nd–4th/8th–10th) (Arab Thought and Culture),* Routledge, 1998, p. 13.

[2884] Plutarch, *The Lives of the Noble Grecians and Romans,* Marcus Antonius, verse 58, trans, T. North, Wordsworth Editions Ltd, 1998, p. 731.

[2885] B. Cunliffe, *The Extraordinary Voyage of Pytheas the Greek: The man who discovered Britain,* Penguin Books, 2002, p. 158.

[2886] W. W. Hyde. *Ancient Greek Mariners,* Oxford, 1947, p.191 n.7, see G. H. Bushnell, 'The Alexandrian Library,' *Antiquity* II (1928), 196.204.

[2887] B. Haughton, *What Happened to the Great Library?* Published 1 February 2011, [Ancient History Encyclopaedia'] <http://www.ancient.eu.com/article/207/>, viewed on 6 September 2011; V. A. M. Ashrof, *Who Destroyed Alexandria Library?* <http://www.milligazette.com/Archives/01122002/0112200252.htm>, viewed on 6 September 2011.

[2888] Email to me on 12 June 2012 from Mr. Constantine Louis, a Greek born and brought up in Alexandria from the 1940s and now a teacher in London, U.K.

[2889] J-Y. Empereur, 'The Death of the Library of Alexandria' in M. El-Abbadi and O. M. Fathalleah (eds.), *What Happened to the Ancient Library of Alexandria?,* (Brill, 2008): 75-88, here p. 76-77.

[2890] Mary. K. Miller, 'Reading Between the Lines', *Smithsonian Magazine* March 2007, <http://www.smithsonianmag.com/science-nature/archimedes.html>, viewed on 12 February 2011.

[2891] J. Leversidge, *Everyday Life in the Roman Empire,* Batsford, 1976, p. 80; F.M. Haikal, 'Private Collections and Temple Libraries in Ancient Egypt' in M. El-Abbadi and O. M. Fathalleah (eds.), *What Happened to the Ancient Library of Alexandria?,* (Brill, 2008): 39-54, here p. 50-51.

[2892] D. Gutas, *Greek Thought, Arab Culture: The Graeco-Arabic movement in Baghdad and early 'Abbasid Society (2nd–4th/8th–10th) (Arab Thought and Culture),* Routledge, 1998, p. 1.

[2893] *Ibid,* p. 174. The court of Sultan Mehmed II, the Conqueror (1451-81) at Constantinople had several Greek and Arabic manuscripts translated.

[2894] Sophia the niece of the last Byzantine emperor married Ivan III Grand Prince of Moscow in 1472. A. Vinogradskaya, *The Mystery of the Byzantine Library,* <http://www.richarddoetsch.com/the_kremlin_and_its_secrets> viewed 17 January 2014.

[2895] Lawrence Lo, *Linear A,* ['Ancient Scripts'] <http://www.ancientscripts.com/lineara.html>, viewed on 12 December 2011; K.K. Hirst, *Undeciphered Minoan Script Linear A,* ['About.com' Archaeology'] <http://archaeology.about.com/od/ancientwriting/ss/undeciphered_3.htm>, viewed on 12 December, 2011.

[2896] Strabo, *Geography,* Book. I. Ch. 1. 2.

[2897] H. W. Parke and D. E. W. Wormell, *The Delphic Oracle,* Blackwell, 1956, vol.1, p. 285.

[2898] *Pseudo-Skylax: The Circumnavigation of the Inhabited World-Text, Translation and Commentary,* 98.2, Bristol Phoenix Press, 2011, p. 75; Pausanias, *Descriptions of Greece,* 10.24.

[2899] E. Hall, *Inventing the Barbarian,* Clarendon Press, 1989, p. 112.

[2900] Philostratus, *The Life of Apollonius of Tyana,* trans. C. P. Jones. Harvard University Press, 2005, vol. 1. Bk. IV. 16.5, p. 353–354 n. 24.

[2901] Geoffrey, J. Martin, *All Possible Worlds: A History of Geographical Ideas,* Oxford, 2005, p.15; Strabo, XIV.1.6. (635); Anaximenes FGH 72 F26; Pliny, *Natural Histories,* V. 31. 112.

[2902] M. Dillon, and L. Garland, *Ancient Greece*, Routledge, 1994, p.11, 1.13, Pliny, *Natural Histories,* V. 31. 112; H. W. Hyde, *Ancient Greek Mariners*, Oxford, 1947, p. 100–102.

[2903] Internet Encyclopaedia of Philosophy, *Thales of Miletus* (c. 620 B.C.E–c. 545 B.C.E), 8.a. The Eclipse of Thales, <www.utm.edu/reseach/iep/t/thales.htm>, viewed on 6 September 2011; Herodotus, *Histories,* 1.74.

[2904] Philostratus, *The Life Of Apollonius of Tyana*, vol. 2. Bk. VIII, 26, trans. C. P. Jones. Harvard University Press, 2005, p. 355.

[2905] G. Vlachos, *Bizarre Events of the Ancient Olympic Games*, Epimelia S. A. Kallipoleos str.28 A, GR 10444, Athens. ISBN: 9789940349431; Diogenes Laertius, *Lives of the Philosophers: Thales*, trans. C. D. Yonge, XII, London: H.G. Bohn, 1863, p. 6 of 9, <http://www.classicpersuasion.org/pw/diogenes/dlthales.htm>, viewed on 29 October 2009.

[2906] A. Gregory, *Eureka! The Birth of Science*, Icon Books Ltd., 2001, p. 12–16.

[2907] S. H. Voldman, *ESD: physics and devices*, John Wiley & Sons Ltd, 2004, p. 1–2.

[2908] P. F. O'Grady, *Thales of Miletus*, Ashgate, 2002, p. 113–114, and p. 240–242.

[2909] S. H. Voldman, *ESD: physics and devices*, John Wiley & Sons Ltd, 2004, p. 1–2 n. 2. Philologus 1944; 96, 170–182.

[2910] Diogenes Laertius, *Lives of the Philosophers: Thales*, trans. C. D. Yonge, XII, London: H.G. Bohn, 1863, <http://www.classicpersuasion.org/pw/diogenes/dlthales.htm>, viewed 21 February 2012.

[2911] Explore Highlights, *Map of the World*, ME 92687, ['The British Museum'] <http://www.britishmuseum.org/explore/highlights/highlight_objects/me/m/map_of_the_world.aspx>, viewed on 29 October 2010.

[2912] Geoffrey. J. Martin, *All Possible Worlds: A History of Geographical Ideas*, John Wiley & Sons, 1993, p. 15: D. L. Couprie, *Heaven and Earth in Ancient Greek Cosmology: From Thales to Heraclides Ponticus*, Springer, 2011, p. 32-33.

[2913] A. Gregory, *Eureka! The Birth of Science*, Icon Books Ltd., 2001; other sources for Anaximander see G. S. Kirk, J. E. Raven, and M. Schofield, *The Pre-Socratic Philosophers: a critical history with a selection of texts,* Cambridge, 2003, p. 103.

[2914] J. Lendering, *Hecataeus of Miletus*, ['Livius.org'] <http://www.livius.org/he-hg/hecataeus/hecataeus.htm>, viewed on 7 September 2011; M. Allaby, *Earth Science: A Scientific History of the Solid Earth*, Facts of File, 2009, p. 22-23; Herodotus, *Histories,* IV.36, trans. G. Rawlinson, Wordsworth Classics, p. 317 n. 50. Rawlinson explains that Herodotus was finding fault most likely with Anaximander's map where the continents are drawn at equal sizes as Herodotus correctly believed they were different. The ides of a spherical earth had been around since the sixth century B.C. but it was not until the third century when Hellenistic astronomy proved this.

[2915] Three hundred and four of the surviving fragments come from Stephanus of Byzantium *Ethnika*, sixth century A.D. No one is sure as to what extent these reflect a copy of Hecataeus' original or an interpretation from the lexicographer. J. Wiesehöfer, *Hecataeus of Miletus*, ['Encyclopaedia Iranica'], last updated 15 December 2003, <http://www.iranicaonline.org/articles/hecataeus-of-miletus>, viewed on 13 January 2012; Braun mentions 295 out of a total of 345 fragments derive from Stephanus of Byzantium. T. Braun, 'Hecataeus' Knowledge of the Western Mediterranean' in K. Lomas (ed.), *Greek Identity in the Western Mediterranean*, Papers in Honour of Brian Shefton, (Brill, 2004): 287-348, here p. 290.

[2916] W. W. Hyde, *Ancient Greek Mariners*, Oxford, 1947, p. 112–115.

[2917] *Hecataeus of Miletus,* ['Encyclopaedia Britannica'] <http://www.britannica.com/EB.C.hecked/topic/259133/Hecataeus-of-Miletus>, viewed on 29 October 2010.

[2918] Herodotus, *Histories,* V.49, trans. G. Rawlinson, Wordsworth Classics, 1996, p. 406.

[2919] T. Braun, 'Hecataeus' Knowledge of the Western Mediterranean' in K. Lomas (ed.), *Greek Identity in the Western Mediterranean*, Papers in Honour of Brian Shefton, (Brill, 2004):287-348, here p. 288.

[2920] B. Cunliffe, *The Extraordinary Voyage of Pytheas the Greek: The man who discovered Britain,* Penguin Books, 2002, p. 1 and p. 47.

[2921] C. H. Roseman, *Pytheas of Massalia: Text, Translation and Commentary,* Ares Publishing, 1994, p. 81.

[2922] *Stesichorus*, ['Encyclopaedia Britannica'] <http://www.britannica.com/EB.C.hecked/topic/565868/Stesichorus>, viewed on 7 September 2011.

[2923] Sir Karl. Popper, *The World of Parmenides:Essays on the Presocratic Enlightenment*, Routledge, 2007, Essay 2,7.

[2924] *Pindar,* ['Encyclopaedia Britannica'] <http://www.britannica.com/EB.C.hecked/topic/460865/Pindar>, viewed on September 2011.

[2925] Herodotus, *Histories*, IV. 44, trans. G. Rawlinson, Wordsworth Classics, 1996, p. 320. n. 68. Rawlinson suggests the Cabul River may have been mistaken for the true Indus, which 'is west of south'.

[2926] *Skylax of Caryanda*, [Livius.org'] <http://www.livius.org/sao-sd/scylax/scylax.htm>, viewed on 15 December 2011.

[2927] *Skylax of Caryanda*, ['Encyclopaedia Britannica eb.com'] <http://www.britannica.com/EBchecked/topic/530323/Scylax-Of-Caryanda>, viewed on 15 December 2011.

[2928] J. Elaye and J. Sapin, *Beyond the River: New Perspectives on Transeuphratene,* Sheffield Academic Press, 1991, p. 98.

[2929] G. Shipley, *Pseudo-Skylax: The Circumnavigation of the Inhabited World-Text, Translation and Commentary*, Bristol Phoenix Press, 2011, p. 6.

[2930] W. W. Hyde, *Ancient Greek Mariners*, Oxford, 1947, p. 112–115.

[2931] Arrian, *History of Alexander and Indica,* vol. 2. V. 26. 1-4, trans. E. Iliff. Robson, Heinemann, 1966, p. 87.

[2932] J. Thomas, *The Universal Dictionary of Biography and Mythology*, vol.1, Cosimo, 2009, p. 137.

[2933] *Antiochus of Syracuse,* ['Online Encyclopaedia'] <http://Encyclopaedia.jrank.org/ANC_APO/ANTIOCHUS_OF_SYRACUSE.html>, viewed on 7 September 2011.

[2934] M. Hammond, *The Peloponnesian War*, Oxford, 2009, p. 534, notes to 3.88, Paus. 10.11.

[2935] J. J. O'Connor and E. F. Robertson, *Eudoxus of Cnidus,* ['School of Mathematics and Statistics', University of St. Andrews] <http://www-history.mcs.st-and.ac.uk/Biographies/Eudoxus.html>, viewed on 7 September 2011.

[2936] G. D. Allen, *Eudoxus of Cnidus*, article 10 February 1997, <http://www.math.tamu.edu/~dallen/history/eudoxus/eudoxus.html>, viewed on 7 September 2011.

[2937] C. H. Roseman, *Pytheas of Massalia: Text, Translation and Commentary,* Ares Publishing, 1994, 117.

[2938] V. Stefansson, *Great Adventurers and Explorations: from the earliest times to the present, as told by the explorers themselves,* Robert Hale Ltd., 1947, p. 12.

[2939] Strabo, *Geography,* vol. 2. IV. I. 5.

[2940] Demosthenes, IV, *Private Orations*, XXVII–XL, trans. A. T. Murray, 1965, p. 183–191.

[2941] B. Bury and R. Meiggs, *A History of Greece,* Macmillan, 1979, p. 431–432.

[2942] S. Gibson, *Aristoxenus of Tarentum and the Birth of Musicology*, Routledge, 2005, p. 3.

[2943] B. Cunliffe, *The Extraordinary Voyage of Pytheas the Greek: The man who discovered Britain,* Penguin Books, 2002, p. 154.

[2944] G. Vlachos, *Bizarre Events of the Ancient Olympic Games*, EPIMELIA S.A. Kallipoleos str.28 A, GR 10444, Athens. ISBN: 9789940349431.

[2945] W. W. Hyde, *Ancient Greek Mariners*, Oxford, 1947, p. 109.

[2946] M. Lahanas, *Theophrastus of Eresos: The Father of Botany and Ecology*, <http://www.mlahanas.de/Greeks/Theophrast.htm>, viewed on 7 September 2011.

[2947] W. W. Hyde, *Ancient Greek Mariners*, Oxford, 1947, p. 14 n. 23 and p. 109.

[2948] *Ibid*, p. 14 n. 24.

[2949] M. H. Morgan, *Vitruvius: The Ten Books on Architecture,* Bk. I. Ch. VI. 9. Dover Publication, 1960, p. 27.

[2950] Geoffrey. J. Martin, *All Possible Worlds: A History of Geographical Ideas*, Oxford, 2005, p. 32–33 and footnote.

[2951] F. W. Wallbank, *A Historical Commentary on Polybius*, vol. 2. Bk. III. 20.5. Oxford, 1967, p. 333.

[2952] Geoffrey. J. Martin, *All Possible Worlds: A History of Geographical Ideas*, Oxford, 2005, p. 36.

[2953] Poseidonius, *The Translation of the Fragments*, trans. I. G. Kidd, Cambridge University Press, 1999; see all refs. Attalus.org, *Poseidonius: fragments about history and geography*, <http://www.attalus.org/translate/poseidonius.html>, viewed on 7 September 2011; *Poseidonius*, <http://www.1911Encyclopaedia.org/Poseidonius>, viewed on 7 September 2011.

[2954] Strabo, *Geography*, Bk. 2.3.5.

[2955] *Suetonius on Grammarians,* 2, ['Penelope, University of Chicago' digital library] <http://penelope.uchicago.edu/Thayer/E/Roman/Texts/Suetonius/de_Grammaticis*.html>, viewed on 7 September 2011.

[2956] J. B. Harley, and D. Woodward, *The History of Cartography: Cartography in prehistoric, ancient, and Medieval Europe, and the Mediterranean*, University of Chicago Press, 1987, p. 164; C. Nicolet, *Space, Geography, and Politics in the Early Roman Empire*, University of Michigan, 1991, p. 63.

[2957] J. Lendering, Diodorus of Sicily, <http://www.livius.org/di-dn/diodorus/siculus.html> viewed 8 January 2013.

[2958] Plutarch, *The Lives of the Noble Grecians and Romans*, trans. T. North, Wordsworth Editions, 1998, p. 602.

[2959] *Ibid*, p. 566.

[2960] Appian's Roman History, *The Civil Wars*, vol. III, Bk. II, trans. H. White. Heinemann, 1913, p. 513.

[2961] *Sosigenes of Alexandria,* ['Encyclopaedia Britannica'] <http://www.britannica.com/EB.C.hecked/topic/555018/Sosigenes-of-Alexandria>, viewed on 7 September 2011.

[2962] T. Griffith, *Suetonius, Lives of the Twelve Caesars*, Julius Caesar, 56, Wordsworth Editions Ltd., 1999, p. 37–38.

[2963] A. L. F. Rivet and C. Smith, *The Place-Names of Roman Britain,* B. T. Batsford Ltd., 1982, p. 282; Use of P and B see Roseman (1994), p. 45 & p. 55, also Cunliffe (2002) p. 94. Polybius gives the earliest surviving text of the name with a B.

[2964] *Marcus Terentius Varro,* ['Encyclopaedia Britannica'] <http://www.britannica.com/EB.C.hecked/topic/623569/Marcus-Terentius-Varro>, viewed on 7 September 2011.

[2965] *Parthian Stations by Isidore of Charax*, trans. W. H. Schoff, 1914, last updated 21 January, 2011, E. C. D. Hopkins. <http://www.parthia.com/doc/parthian_stations.htm>, viewed on 7 September 2011.

[2966] C. H. Roseman, *Pytheas of Massalia: Text, Translation and Commentary,* Ares Publishing, 1994, p. 12.

[2967] Geoffrey. J. Martin, *All Possible Worlds: A History of Geographical Ideas*, John Wiley & Sons, 1993, p. 37.

[2968] *Ibid*, p. 11 and p. 76; B. Cunliffe, *The Extraordinary Voyage of Pytheas the Greek: The man who discovered Britain,* Penguin Books, 2002, p. 169.

[2969] A. L. F. Rivet, *Gallia Narbonensis,* Batsford, 1988, p. 268.

[2970] F. Sturges, 'The good, the bad and wildly bitchy', *The Independent*, 24 January 2011, <http://www.independent.co.uk/arts-entertainment/tv/features/the-good-the-bad-and-the-wildly-bitchy-2192378.html>, viewed on 7 September 2011.

[2971] Lucian, *Toxaris or Friendship,* vol. 5, 24-26, trans. A. M. Harmon, William Heinemann, 1955, p. 143-149.

[2972] A. Bartley, 'What's Fishing Like? The Rhetoric of Similes in Oppian's "Halieutica"' in *Classics Ireland,* vol. 12. (2005): 1–17, here p. 10, Classical Association of Ireland, ['JSTOR' journal archive] <http://www.jstor.org/stable25528414>, viewed on 16 January 2011.

[2973] G. Nagy, *Poetry as Performance: Poetry and Beyond,* Cambridge, 1996, p. 32-34, Aelian, *De natura animalium*, 5.38

[2974] Aaron J. Atsma, 'Hyperboreades', Aelian, *On Animals* 11.1, trans. Scholfield, Greek Natural History 2nd century A.D. ['Theoi'] <http://www.theoi.com/Gigante/GigantesHyperboreades.html>, viewed on 4 September 2012.

[2975] G. Kelly, *Ammianus Marcellinus*, ['Oxford Biographies Online'] <http://oxfordbibliographiesonline.com/view/document/obo-9780195389661/obo-9780195389661-0115.xml>, viewed on 13 January 2012.

[2976] A. D. Lee, *Information and Frontiers*: Roman Relations in Late Antiquity, Cambridge, 1993, p. 82.

[2977] P. Bosch-Gimpera, 'The Phokaians in the Far West: A Historical Reconstruction', *The Classical Quarterly*, vol. 38, No. 1/2 (Jan.–Apr., 1944): 53–59, here p. 57, ['JSTOR' journal archive] <www.jstor.org/stable/636879>, viewed on 20 August 2010.

[2978] C. F. C. Hawkes, *Pytheas: Europe and the Greek Explorers,* a lecture delivered at New College, Oxford on 20th May, 1975 (The J. L. Myers memorial lecture), p. 19. ASIN: B0007AMH16.

[2979] J. Henderson, 'The Creation of Isodore's Etymologies or Origins', in J. Konig, and T. Whitmarsh, *Ordering Knowledge in the Roman Empire*, Cambridge University Press, 2007. p. 151; <http://www.newadvent.org/cathen/08186a.htm> viewed 5 April 2013.

Bibliography

Abbreviations
BCH   Bulletin de correspondance hellénique
CIA   Corpus Inscriptionum Atticarum
CIG   Corpus Inscriptionum Graecarum.
CIL   Corpus Inscriptionum Latinarum
IG   Inscriptiones Graecae
IGF   Inscriptions Grecques de la France
ILS   Inscriptiones Latinae Selectae
RA   Revue Archéologique
REA   Revue des études anciennes
REG   Revue des études grecques.
SEG   Supplementum Epigraphicum Graecum

For itemised Greek inscriptions in Catalonia, Spain, 6th century B.C–10th century A.D. including photographs:
Canoś i Villena, I. *L'Epigrafia Grega a Catalunya*, HPS vol. 9, University of Debrecen, 2002.

Phocaea (the Latin form was originally in typography written with a diphthong ligature æ), **Phokaia** (Greek form).

These three books are recommended for information on Pytheas of Massalia:

Carpenter, R. *Beyond the Pillars of Hercules: The classical world seen through the eyes of its discoverers*, Delacourte Press (USA), 1966, Tandem Press (UK) 1973. Chapters 2, 5 and 6.
Rhys Carpenter, Professor at Brwyn Mawr College and at the American School for Classical Studies in Athens. He was also their Director 1927-32 overseeing the excavations of the Agora at Athens.

Cunliffe, B. *The Extraordinary Voyage of Pytheas the Greek: The man who discovered Britain*, Penguin Books, 2002.
Sir Barry W. Cunliffe, Emeretus Professor of European Archaeology at Oxford University.

Roseman, C. H. *Pytheas of Massalia: On the Ocean: Text, Translation and Commentary*, Ares Publishers, 1994.
Christina Horst Roseman, Emerita Professor of Classics and Art History at Seattle Pacific University.

Primary Sources
Aelian, *Characteristics of Animals*, vol. 3. 13.16, trans. A. F. Schofield, Loeb, 1959.

Agathias, *The Histories*, Bk.I. 2. 1, trans. J. D. Frendo, (Corpus fontium historiae Byzantinae; vol. 2 A: Ser. Berlinensis). Elnheitssacht: Historiaa (engl.), Walter de Gruyter Co., 1975.

Apollonius of Rhodes, The Voyage of Argo: The Argonautica, trans. E. V. Rieu, Penguin, 1959.

Appian, *The Civil Wars*, 2.102, trans. John Carter, Penguin Books, 1996.

Appian's Roman History, vol. 1. Ch. 1.2, trans. H. White, Heinemann, 1912.

Appian's Roman History, Bk. IV, ch. XI, 84, trans. H. White, Heinemann, 1913.

Appian Wars of the Romans in Iberia, trans. J. S. Richardson, Aris and Phillips Ltd., 2000.

Aristotle, *Politics*, trans. E. Barker, Oxford, 1995.

Aristotle, *Politics*, Book VI, ch.7, trans. C. D. C. Reeve, Hackett Publishing Co., 1998.

Aristotle, *Politics*, Book I, 1253a3, ['Internet Encyclopaedia of Philosophy'] <http://www.iep.utm.edu/aris-pol/>, viewed on 23 November 2010.

'Aristoxenus, Histories', Fragment. Gr. 2.279.23. vol. 2. Anacreon, trans. J. M. Edmunds, in *Lyra Graeca*, Heinemann, 1979.

Arrian, *The Life of Alexander the Great*, V.25, trans. Aubrey de Sélincourt, Penguin, 1958.

Arrian, *History of Alexander and Indica*, vol. 2, VII, 19, trans. E. Iliff. Robson, Heinemann, 1966.

Athenaeus, *Deipnosophists*, vol. 1. I. 27. trans. C.B. Gulick, Loeb, William Heinemann, 1927.

Caesar's Civil War, Bk.I. Ch. XXXV, trans. W. A. M'Devitte, G. Bell & Sons, 1928.

Caesar, *The Civil War,* trans. J. Carter, Oxford's World Classics, 1998.

Caesar's Civil War with Pompeius, trans. F. P. Long, Oxford, 1906.

Caii Julii Caesaris Commentarii de belo civili, I. 34, trans J. C. Held, Sulzbach, 1822, p. 45, <http://books.google.co.uk/books?id=_jogAAAAMAAJ&pg=PA45&lpg=PA45&dq=%E2%80%98barbaros+hominess,+Massilian&source=bl&ots=XrtM-w_FlR&sig=_o7JU0P2JQlWE87mmKhiYpKbAa4&hl=en&sa=X&ei=Np3ET-CSDsKQ8QOux8iFCw&ved=0CDgQ6AEwAQ#v=onepage&q=%E2%80%98barbaros%20hominess%2C%20Massilian&f=false>, viewed 29 May 2012.

Canoś i Villena, I. *L'Epigrafia Grega a Catalunya*, Hungarian Polis Studies (HPS) 9, University of Debrecen, 2002.

Cassius Dio, vol.5. Book XLVIII. 4-15, Loeb, 1917, p. 227-251, ['Penelope, University of Chicago' digital library] <http://penelope.uchicago.edu/Thayer/E/Roman/Texts/Cassius_Dio/48*.html>, viewed on 20 February 2011.

Cicero, *De Officiis*, Bk. II, V. iii, trans. W. Miller, Heinemann, 1975.

Cicero, *De Provinciis Consularibis*, trans. R. Gardiner, Heinemann, 1970.

Cicero, *De Res Publica,* 3.IX.15, trans. C.W. Keynes, Harvard, 1944.

Cicero, *Letters to Atticus,* vol. 3, XIV. 14, trans. E. O. Winstedt, Heinemann, 1961.

Cicero, *On the Commonwealth and On the Laws,* I. 43-44. Edited and translated by James. E. G. Zetzel, Cambridge, 1999.

Cicero, M. Tullius. *Orations, the fourteen orations against Marcus Antonius (Philippics)*, II.94, trans. C. D. Yonge, George Bell & Son, 1903, ['Perseus, Tufts university' digital library], <http://www.perseus.tufts.edu/hopper/text?doc=Perseus%3Atext%3A1999.02.0021%3Aspeech%3D2%3Asection%3D94>, 4 June 2012.

Cicero, *Philippic*, VIII. vi, 18-19, trans. W. Ker, Loeb, 1926.

Cicero, *Philippic*, II. 94, trans. D. R. Shackleton Bailey, University of Carolina Press, 1986.

Cicero, *Philippics*: 3-9, Edited with Introduction, Translation and Commentary, Vol. 2, Commentary, by G. Manuwald, Walter de Gruyter, 2007, p. 906-7.

Cicero, XIII, *Pro Balbo*, viii.21-ix, 23, trans. R. Gardiner, Loeb, 1961.

Cicero, *Pro Caelio*, XIII. trans. R. Gardiner, Heinemann, 1970.

Cicero, *Pro Milone*, On Behalf of Fonteius, 45, trans. N. H. Watts, Heinemann, 1972.

Cicero, *The Speeches: In Catilinam I-IV*: Pro Murena: Pro Sulla: Pro Flacco, trans. C. MacDonald, Heinemann, 1977.

Cicero, *The Speeches, Pro Sesto and In Vatinum*, VII, trans. R. Gardiner, Heinemann, 1958.

Corpus Inscriptionum Grecarum, vol. 3, Pars XXXIV, Inscriptiones Gallarium, Section 1, Pars Prima, Inscriptiones Galliae Narbonensis et Aquitanicae, A. Boeckhio, Berolini, 1853.

Corpus Inscriptionum Latinarum, vol. XII, (ed.), O. Hirschfield, Berolini, 1887.

Decourt, Jean-Claude. *Inscriptions Grecques de la France* (IGF), Maison de l'Orient et de la Méditerranée, 2004.

Demosthenes, *Against Boeotus*, 2. 40.36. ['Perseus, Tufts University' digital library] <http://www.perseus.tufts.edu/hopper/text?doc=Perseus:text:1999.01.0076:speech=40:section=36&highlight=apollonides>, viewed on 24 October 2011.

Demosthenes, *Against Phormio*, 32.23, ['Perseus, Tufts University' digital library] <http://www.perseus.tufts.edu/hopper/text?doc=Dem.%2034.23&lang=original>, viewed on 27 October 2011.

Demosthenes, *Speeches*, 18.67, ['Perseus, Tufts University' digital library] <http://perseus.uchicago.edu/perseus-cgi/citequery3.pl?dbname=GreekTexts&query=Dem.%2018.67&getid=1>, viewed on 16 March 2011.

Demosthenes, IV, *Private Orations*, XXVII-XL, trans. A. T. Murray, Heinemann, 1965.

'De Mundo', trans. E. S. Forrester. Clarendon Press, 1914, p. 392-393, in *Works of Aristotle in English*, vol. III, Clarendon Press, Oxford 1931.

Diodorus Siculus, *Library of History*, Bk. I. Appendix B, trans. E. Murphy, Transaction Publishers, 1989.

Diodorus of Sicily, Bk. 2. 46, 47, trans. C. H. Oldfather, Loeb, 1933.

Diodorus of Sicily, vol. 3. Bk. V. 13. 3-14. I, trans. C. H. Oldfather, Heinemann, 1952.

Dio Chrysostom, *Discourses*, Book I, 1-11, trans. J. W. Cohoon, Loeb, 2002.

Diogenes the Cynic: Sayings and Anecdotes with Other Popular Moralists, trans. R. Hard, Oxford, 2012.

Diogenes Laertius, Lives of the Philosophers: Thales, trans. C. D. Yonge, London: H.G. Bohn, 1863, XIV, p 7 of 9, <,http://www.classicpersuasion.org/pw/diogenes/dlthales.htm>, viewed on 29 October 2010.

Dio's Roman History, vol. 3. XL, trans. E. Carey, Heinemann, 1914.

Dio's Roman History, vol.6. XLI, trans. E. Carey, Heinemann, 1916.

Dio's Roman History, vol. 7. LX, trans. E. Carey, Heinemann, 1924.

Dionysius of Halicarnassus, Excerpts, vol.7, Bk.1, 3–2, 1, trans. E. Cary, Loeb, 1950.

Edmonds, J. M. *Daphne & Chloe*, Parthenius, VIII, Heinemann, 1916.

'Einhard: The Life of Charlemagne', Chapter 16, in *The Medieval Reader*, N. F. Cantor, Harper Collins, 1994.

Empereur, J-Y. 'The Death of the Library of Alexandria' in El-Abbadi, M., and Fathalleah, O. M. (eds.), *What Happened to the Ancient Library of Alexandria?* (Brill, 2008): 75-88.

Eusebius, *Chronicles*, 225. <http://www.attalus.org/translate/eusebius2.html#225> viewed 5 January 2013.

Fulvia, ['Coinarchive.com'] <http://www.coinarchives.com/a/results.php?results=100&search=Fulvia%20#fulvia1>, viewed on 21 September 2011.

Gellius, A. Cornelius. *Noctes Atticae (Attic Nights)*, 3.8. Loeb, 1923, revised 1946, ['Penelope' University of Chicago digital library] <http://penelope.uchicago.edu/Thayer/E/Roman/Texts/Gellius/3*.html#ref33>, viewed on 20 February 2011.

Geminos's, Introduction to the Phenomena: a translation and study of a Hellenistic survey of astronomy, On day and Night, trans. by J. Evans and J. L. Berggren, Princeton University Press, 2006.

Gregory of Tours, *History of the Franks*, trans. L. Thorpe, Penguin, 1983.

Griffith, T. (ed.), *Suetonius, Lives of the Twelve Caesars*, Claudius, 17, Wordsworth Editions Ltd., 1999.

Guthrie, W. *Cicero's Epistles to Atticus: With Notes, Historical, Explanatory, and Critical*, vol. 3, London, 1806.

Haikal, F. M. 'Private Collections and Temple Libraries in Ancient Egypt' in M. El-Abbadi, and O. M. Fathallah, (eds.), in *What Happened to the Ancient Library of Alexandria?* (Brill, 2008): 39-54.

Halsall, P. 'Contents, 16, Foreign Relations', *Medieval Sourcebook: Einhard: The Life of Charlemagne,* <http://www.fordham.edu/halsall/basis/einhard.asp#Foreign%20Relations>, viewed on 26 January 2011.

Herodotus, *Histories*, trans. G. Rawlinson, Wordsworth Editions Ltd., 1996.

Horace, *Epistles*, 2. 1. 156-157.

Inscriptiones Graecae, Attic Inscriptions of the Roman Period, Inscriptiones Atticae Aetatis Romanae, vol. III, 1, 2 and 3, Pars Decima, TITVLI SEPVLCRALES, G. Dittenberger, (ed.), Berolini, 1878.

Inscriptiones Graecia, vol. XIV, G. Kaibel, (ed.), Berolini, 1890.

Inscriptiones Latinae Selectae, H. Dessau, (ed.), Berlin, 1892-1916.

Isocrates, vol. 1, Archidamus, 83-84, trans. G. Norlin, Heinemann, 1928.

Isidore of Seville, *The Etymologies (or Origins)*, vol. 15. 1. 68. ['Penelope, University of Chicago' digital library] <htpp://Penelope.uchicago.edu/Thayer/E/Roman/Texts/isidore/home.html>, viewed on 23 August 2011.

James, E. *The Origins of France: From Clovis to the Capetians 500-1000*, Macmillan, 1989.

Joinville and Villehardouin Chronicles of the Crusades, trans. Shaw, M. R. B., Penguin, 1963, <http://www.fordham.edu/halsall/basis/villehardouin.html>, viewed on 30 January 2011.

Jones, W. H. S. *Pausanias*, IV.viii.7, Loeb, 1925.

Jordanes, *The Origin and Deeds of the Goths*, trans. C. C. Mierow, Dodo Press, 2007.

Justin's Epitome of the Philippic History of Pompeius Trogus, vol. 1, Book 11-12, 13, Alexander the Great, trans. J.C. Yardley, Clarendon, 1997.

Justin: Epitome of the Philippic History of Pompeius Trogus, trans. J. C. Yardley, Scholars Press Atlanta, GA, 1994.

Lacus Curtius, *Strabo's Geography*, V.2.2. Loeb, 1922, p. 393, n. 72. <http://penelope.uchicago.edu/Thayer/E/Roman/Texts/Strabo/5B*.html>, viewed on 14 January 2012.

Lacus Curtius, *The Library of History of Diodorus Siculus*, vol. 2. Loeb, 1935, ['Penelope, University of Chicago' digital library] <http://penelope.uchicago.edu/Thayer/E/Roman/Texts/Diodorus_Siculus/2B*.html>, viewed on 19 September 2011.

Levick, B. *The Government of the Roman Empire: A Sourcebook*, Croom Helm, 1985.

Livy, vol. I. Bk. I. xxiv-4-9, trans. B. O. Foster, Heinemann, 1925.

Livy, vol. VII. Bk. XXVI. XIX. 7–13, trans. F. G. Moore, Heinemann, 1943.

Livy, vol. IX. Bk. XXXIV. VIII. 4-IX.4. IX, trans. E. T. Sage, Loeb Classical Library, 1935.

Livy, vol. 12. XL. XLI. 4-8, trans. E. T. Sage and A. C. Schlesinger, Loeb, 1928.

Livy, *The Early History of Rome*, 5.34, trans. Aubrey De Selincourt, Penguin Classics, 2005.

Lucan, *The Civil War*, trans. Rowe, N. Everyman, 1998.

Lucan, *Civil War*, trans. Susan. H. Braund, Oxford World's Classics, 1999.

Lucian, *Toxaris or Friendship*, vol. 5, 24-27, trans. A. M. Harmon, William Heinemann, 1955.

Martial's Epigrams, vol. 2. Bk. X. 36, edited and translated by D. R. Shackleton Bailey, Harvard, 1993.

Oppian, *Halieutica*, 3. 625, trans. A. W. Mair, Heinemann, 1938.

Parthian Stations by Isidore of Charax, 33, translation from Greek by W. H. Schoff, p. 6 of 27, <http://www.parthia.com/doc/parthian_stations.htm>, viewed on 3 July 2009.

Parthian Stations by Isidore of Charax, trans. W. H. Schoff, 1914, last updated 21 January, 2011, E. C. D. Hopkins. <http://www.parthia.com/doc/parthian_stations.htm>, viewed on 7 September 2011.

Paul the Deacon, *History of the Lombards*, VIII. 3, trans W. D. Foulke, University of Pennsylvania, 2003.

Pausanias, *Description of Greece*, IV.viii.7, trans. W. H. S. Jones, Loeb, 1925.

Pausanias, *Description of Greece*, 7.3.10, trans. W. H. S. Jones, and H.A. Ormerod, 4 vols. Heinemann, 1918. ['Perseus, Tufts University', digital library] <http://www.perseus.tufts.edu/hopper/text?doc=Perseus%3Atext%3A1999.01.0160%3Abook%3D7%3Achapter%3D3%3Asection%3D10>, viewed 15 January 2012.

Petronius, Seneca, Apocolocyntosis, Fragment 1. IV, trans. M. Heseltine and W. H. Rouse, Loeb, 1913.

Philostratus, *The Life Of Apollonius of Tyana*, trans. C. P. Jones, Harvard University Press, 2005.

Pindar, *The Complete Odes*, trans. A. Verity, Oxford, 2007.

Pliny, *Natural Histories*, trans. W. H. S. Jones, Heinemann, 1962.

Pliny, *Natural Histories*, vol. 2, trans. H. Rackham, Heinemann, 1962.

Pliny's Natural Histories, by Philemon Holland, printed by G. Barclay for the Wernernian Club, 1847-48.

Plutarch, *De Fortuna Alexandri*, Loeb, 1926, Second Oration, Vol. IV, 332A, B, & C. ['Penelope, University of Chicago' digital library] <http://penelope.uchicago.edu/Thayer/E/Roman/Texts/Plutarch/Moralia/Fortuna_Alexandri*/1.html>, viewed on 15 April 2011.

Plutarch's Lives, trans. J. Langhorne and W. Langhorne, Sir John Lubbock's Hundred Books, Routledge, 1930.

Plutarch Caesar: Translated with Introduction and Commentary, C. Pelling, Oxford, 2011.

Plutarch, Camillus, 8, trans. B. Perrin, Loeb, 1914.

Plutarch, Lives of the Noble Grecians and Romans, trans. T. North, Alexander the Great, 9, Wordsworth Editions Ltd, 1998.

Plutarch's Lives, Caius Marius, vol. IX, trans. B. Perrin, Loeb, 1920.

Plutarch, Mulerium virtutes, Example 18. Of Lampsace, *Plutarch's Morals*, W. W. Goodwin, (ed.) Little, Brown & Co., Cambridge, 1874, ['Perseus, Tufts, University of Texas' digital library] <http://www.perseus.tufts.edu/hopper/text?doc=Perseus%3Atext%3A2008.01.0208%3Achapter%3D18> viewed 19 March 2012.

Plutarch, *The Parallel Lives*, Life of Marius, 21, vol. IX, Loeb, 1920, ['Penelope, University of Chicago' digital library] <http://penelope.uchicago.edu/Thayer/E/Roman/Texts/Plutarch/Lives/Marius*.html>, viewed on 29 October 2011.

Plutarch, *The Age of Alexander*, Nine Greek Lives, Alexander, 14, trans. I. Scott-Kilvert, Penguin Books, 1980.

Plutarch, *The Lives of the Noble Grecians and Romans*, Marcus Antonius, verse 58, trans, T. North, Wordsworth Editions Ltd, 1998.

Plutarch, *The Rise and Fall of Athens: Nine Greek Lives*, Solon, trans. I. Scott-Kilvert, Penguin Books, 1967.

Polyaenus: Stratagems, Book 8, Chapter 37. ['Attalus'] <http://www.attalus.org/translate/polyaenus8B.html> viewed 19 March 2012.

Polybius, *The Histories*, vol. 2. III, trans. W. R. Paton, Heinemann, 1922.

Pomponius Mela, *Geography*, Bk. III, trans. P. Berry, The Edwin Mellen Press 1977.

Poseidonius: fragments about history and geography, <http://www.attalus.org/translate/poseidonius.html>, viewed on 7 September 2011.

Posidonius, The Translation of the Fragments, trans. I G. Kidd, Cambridge University Press, 1999.

Posidonius, <http://www.1911encyclopaedia.org/Posidonius>, viewed on 7 September 2011.

Radt, S. *Strabon's Geographika*, Band I, Prolegma, Buch I-IV: Text und Ubersetzung, Vandenhoeck & Ruprecht, 2002.

Roman History, (incomplete), Titus Livius, Livy 10. XXXIV. 8, <http://thriceholy.net/Texts/Livy10.html>, viewed on 29 July 2011.

Roman History, Titus Livius, Livy 10. XXXIV.62. <http://thriceholy.net/Texts/Livy10.html>, viewed on 28 August 2011.

Salvian, *On the Government of God*, trans. E. M. Stanford, Columbia University Press, 1930, <http://www.tertullian.org/fathers/salvian_gov_00_intro.htm>, viewed 11 March 2012.

Seneca, *Moral Essays*, vol. I. XIV. 3-XV.4, trans. J. Basmore, Harvard University Press, 1994.

Seneca, *Natural Quaestiones*, vol. 2. VII. 25, 2–5, trans. T. H. Corcoran, Loeb, 1962.

Shackleton Bailey, D. R. *Martial's Epigrams*, vol. 1. IV, Harvard, 1993.

Shipley, G. *Pseudo-Skylax: The Circumnavigation of the Inhabited World-Text, Translation and Commentary*, Bristol Phoenix Press, 2011.

Strabo, *Geography*, vol. 2. IV.6.2, trans. H. L. Jones, Loeb, 1923.

Strabo, *Geography*, 15.1.7. Hamilton, H. C., and Falconer, W. (eds.), The Geography of Strabo: Literally translated with notes, in three volumes, George Bell & Sons, 1903, ['Perseus, Tufts University' digital Library] <www.perseus.tufts.edu>, viewed on 19 May 2009.

Suetonius on Grammarians, 2, ['Penelope, University of Chicago' digital library] <http://penelope.uchicago.edu/Thayer/E/Roman/Texts/Suetonius/de_Grammaticis*.html>, viewed on 7 September 2011.

Suetonius, *Lives of the Twelve Caesars*, Caius Julius Caesar, 47, trans. H. M. Bird, Wordsworth Editions, 1997.

Suetonius, *The Lives of the Caesars*, The Deified Julius, vol. 1. LXVIII.4, trans. J. C. Rolfe, Heinemann, 1979.

Suetonius, *The Twelve Caesars*, Tiberius 3.2, trans. R. Graves, Penguin, 2007.

Supplementum Epigraphicum Graecum, vol. XLI, 1044, Aiolis, (eds.), H. W. Pleket and R. S. Stroud, J. C. Gieben, Amsterdam, 1994.

Tacitus, *Agricola*, 4, trans. M. Hutton, Heinemann, 1970.

Tacitus, *Agricola*, Bk.I.10. <http://www.sacred-texts.com/cla/tac/ag01010.htm>, viewed on 5 September 2011.

Tacitus, *Annals of Imperial Rome*, trans. M. Grant, Penguin, 1996.

Tacitus, *The Histories*, trans. K. Wellesley, Penguin. 1964.

Tacitus, *The Histories*, trans. M. Grant, Penguin, 1996.

The Annals of St. Bertin; Ninth Century Histories, vol. 1, translated and annotated by J. L. Nelson, Manchester University Press, 1991.

'The Anonymous Panegyric on Constantine' (310), Pass. Lat. VII (6) trans. Mark Vemes, in S. N. C. Lieu, and D. Montserrat, *From Constantine to Julian*, Routledge, 1996.

The Elder Seneca, *Controversiae*, trans. M. Winterbottom, William Heinemann Ltd., 1974.

The Greek Anthology, Sepulchral Epigrams, No. 375–Demagetus, trans. W. R. Paton, William Heinemann, 1917.

The History of Rome by Titus Livius, War Against Antiochus, trans. Canon Roberts, Vol. V, XXXVI, Dent, 1924-31.

The Roman History of Ammianus Marcellinus, vol. 1. XV.9. Loeb, 1935, ['Penelope. University of Chicago', digital library] <http://penelope.uchicago.edu/Thayer/E/Roman/Texts/Ammian/15*.html>, viewed 20 February 2012.

'11.24 The Thirty Attack Wealthy Metics, Lysias XII Against Eratosthenes, 4–20', Chapter 11, Labour, Slaves, Serfs and Citizens, in Dillon, M., and Garland, L. *Ancient Greece; social and historical documents from archaic times to the death of Socrates*, 2nd edition, (Routledge, 1994): 360-392.

The Works of Julius Caesar, trans. W. S. McDevitte and W. S. Bohn, 1869, <http://www.sacred-texts.com/cla/jcsr/civ1.htm> viewed 22 April 2013.

Thucydides, *The History of the Peloponnesian War*, I.13. 6.

Titus Livius, *The History of Rome*, trans. Rev. Canon Roberts, Dent, 1924-31.

Titus Livius Livy, *The War With Hannibal*, XXI. 12, trans. Aubrey de Selincourt, Penguin, 1972.

Usener, H. *Scholia in Lucani Bellum Civile, Commenta Bernensia*, Teubneri, 1869, <http://archive.org/stream/scholiainlucani00usengoog#page/n6/mode/2up> viewed 22 April 2013.

Valerius Maximus, *Memorable Deeds and Sayings: A Thousand and One Tales From Ancient Rome*, trans. Henry John Walker, Hackett Publishing Company Inc., 2004.

Valpy, A. J. 'Eumenii Panegyicus' in *Scriptores latini, jussu christianissimi Regis ad usnum serenissimi Delphini*, CAP. XIX. 1828, p. 1369.
<http://books.google.co.uk/books?id=K8YjAQAAIAAJ&pg=PA1369&lpg=PA1369&dq=Quippe+olim+Graecos+Italosque+illuc+convenas%E2%80%99&source=bl&ots=FkbzulFdSJ&sig=S8l8fnwnn9kyuWobRj-E3vaGN2I&hl=en&ei=CzO9TuzHAYar8AOtl6WrBA&sa=X&oi=book_result&ct=result&resnum=2&ved=0CCYQ6AEwAQ#v=onepage&q=Quippe%20olim%20Graecos%20Italosque%20illuc%20convenas%E2%80%99&f=false>, viewed on 11 November 2011.

Vitruvius, *The Ten Books on Architecture*, Bk. 3, Introduction. 2, trans. M. H. Morgan, Dover Publication, 1960.

Vitruvius, *Ten Books on Architecture*, trans. I. D. Rowland, Cambridge, 1999.

Xenophanes of Colophon, Fragments: A Text and Translation with a Commentary by J. H. Lesher, University of Toronto, 2001.

Xenophon, *Anabasis*, Of Cyrus, Book 1, Chapter 10, trans. E. Spelman, 1830, H. Colburn and R. Bentley, p. 45 n. 2. <http://books.google.co.uk/books?id=zQl8i4ljaKgC&pg=PA45&lpg=PA45&dq=Xenophon+Phocaean+woman&source=bl&ots=26e6x8s42K&sig=giFmBrN0XTFs69eia-ebq-6HPac&hl=en&sa=X&ei=0SBnT8Irp6zRBbKj8aUI&ved=0CFQQ6AEwCQ#v=onepage&q&f=false> viewed 19 March 2012.

Map, Engraving Marseille 1575, Braun and Hogenberg, *Civitas Orbis Terrarum*, vol. II-12., admitted to Sebastian Munster and first published in the 1575 edition of Munster's Cosmographia. The National Library of Israel, Eran Laor Cartographic Collection, Cities in the World, ['Shapell Family Digitization Project and the Hebrew University of Jerusalem' Historic Cities Research Project, Department of Geography] <http://historic-cities.huji.ac.il/>, viewed on 30 October 2010.

Secondary Sources

A History of the Battle of Britain: Battle of the nations, ['RAF Museum'] <http://www.rafmuseum.org.uk/online-exhibitions/battle-of-britain-history/battle-of-the-nations.cfm>, viewed on 23 February 2011.

Adkin, M. *The Waterloo Companion: The Complete Guide to History's Most Famous Land Battle*, Arum Press Ltd., 2008.

Aguilar, S. 'Dama de Elche: Embodying Greek-Iberian interaction' in G. R. Tsetskhladze, (ed.), *Ancient Greeks West and East*, (Brill, 1999): 331–351, p. 349.

Allen, A. *Movie Reviews: The Battle of Britain*, ['History On Film'] <http://www.historyonfilm.com/reviews/battle-of-britain.htm>, viewed on 14 December 2010.

Allen, G. D. *Eudoxus of Cnidus*, article 10 February 1997, <http://www.math.tamu.edu/~dallen/history/eudoxus/eudoxus.html>, viewed on 7 September 2011.

Allen, J. A. 'Magna Graecia' in N. G. Wilson, (ed.), *Encyclopaedia of Ancient Greece*, (Routledge, 2006): 442-444.

Aloupes, S. P. *He Archaia Massalia kai ho Politismos tes*, Eleuthere Skepsis, 1996.

Altheim. F, *A History of Roman Religion*, Methuen & Co, 1938.

Amalgro, M. *Ampurias, Guide to the Excavations and Museum*, Barcelona, 1968.

Ameling, W. 'The Rise of Carthage to 246 B.C.' in D. Hoyos, (ed.), *A Companion to the Punic Wars*, Wiley-Blackwell, 2011.

Angelis, F. De. 'The Foundation of Selinous: overpopulation or opportunities?' in G. R. Tsetskhladze, and F. De Angelis, (eds.), *The Archaeology of Greek Colonization*, (Oxford University School of Archaeology, 1994): 87-110.

Angell, Sir Norman. 'Germany-Our Problem' in *The Rotarian*, Rotary International, vol. 65, no. 5. (November, 1944):11-13. <http://www.rotary.org/en/mediaandnews/therotarian/archives/Pages/ridefault.aspx>, viewed on 6 January 2009.

Anna, 'Colonel Blimp vs. Winston Churchill and the MoI', *The Crowd Roars*, [web blog], May 12, 2007, <http://silentfilmlegend.blogspot.com/2007/05/colonel-blimp-vs-winston-churchill-and.html>, viewed on 9 January 2012.

Anson, E. M. 'The Evolution of the Macedonian Assembly (330-315 B.C.)'. *Historia: Zeitschrift für Alte Geschiichte*. vol. 40, no. 2 (1991): 230-247. Franz Steiner Verlag, ['JSTOR' journal archive] <http://www.jstor.org/stable/4436191>, viewed on 24 April 2011.

Antiochus of Syracuse, ['Online Encyclopaedia'] <http://encyclopaedia.jrank.org/ANC_APO/ANTIOCHUS_OF_SYRACUSE.html>, viewed on 7 September 2011.

Aquilué, X., and Monturiol, J., (eds.), *1908-2008: 100 anys d'excavacions arqueologiques a Empúries*, Museu d'Arqueologia de Catalunya-Empúries, 2008.

Aquilué, X., Castanyer, P., Santos, M. and Tremoleda, J., *Empúries. Guidebooks to the Museu d'Arqueologia de Catalunya*, Museu d'Arqueologia de Catalunya, English language 2nd edition, 2008.

Arafat, K., and Morgan, C. 'Athens, Etruria and the Heuneburg: mutual misconceptions in the study of Greek-barbarian relations' in I. Morris, (ed.), *Classical Greece: Ancient histories and modern archaeologies,* (Cambridge University Press 1994):108-134.

Ancient Greek tombs discovered in Marseilles, 8 June 2012, ['Archaeology News Network'] <http://archaeologynewsnetwork.blogspot.gr/2012/06/ancient-greek-tombs-discovered-in.html#.T_f0KJFRGuK>, viewed 7 July 2012

Arkenberg, J. S. 'Al-Baladhuri: The Conquest of Alexandria', *Medieval Sourcebook: Account of the Arab Conquest of Egypt 642*, <http://fordham.edu/halsall/source/642Egypt-conq2.html>, viewed on 13 August 2010.

Arnaud, A. 'Les temps préhistoriques et protohistoriques', in A. Ruggiero (ed.), *Nouvelle histoire de Nice*, Edition Privat, 2006.

Artemision/Dianum (Dénia), <www.arbre-celtique.com/encyclopedie/artemision-dianum-denia-5585.htm>, viewed on 3 October 2010.

Ashrof, V. A. M. *Who Destroyed Alexandria Library?* <http://www.milligazette.com/Archives/01122002/0112200252.htm>, viewed on 6 September 2011.

Astin. A. E. *The Cambridge Ancient History: Rome and the Mediterranean to 133 B.C.,* 2nd edition, vol. 8, Cambridge, 2003.

Attema, P. 'Conflict or Coexistence? Remarks on Indigenous Settlement and Colonization in the Foothills and Hinterland of the Sibaritde (Northern Calabria, Italy)' in P. G. Bilde and J. H. Petersen (eds.), *Meeting of Cultures in the Black Sea Region,* (University of Aarhus, 2008):67-99. <http://www.pontos.dk/publications/books/bss-8-files/bss-8-04-attema>, viewed 12 February 2012.

Aubet, M. E. 'On the Organization of the Phoenician Colonial System in Iberia' in C. Riva and N. C. Vella, (eds.), *Debating Orientalization: Multidisciplinary Approaches to Change in the Mediterranean*, (Equinox, 2006): 94-109.

Aubet, M. E. 'Mainake: the Legend and New Archaeological Evidence' in B. Cunliffe and R. Osborne, (eds.), *Mediterranean Urbanisation 800–600 B.C.*, The British Academy, (Oxford University Press 2007):187-202.

Aujac, G. 'Chapter 9. The Growth of Empirical Cartography in Hellenistic Greece' in J. B. Hartley and J. Woodward (eds.). *The History of Cartography* Vol. 1. University of Chicago Press, (1987): 148-160, <http://www.press.uchicago.edu/books/HOC/HOC_V1/HOC_VOLUME1_chapter9.pdf> viewed 07 February 2013.

Austin, M. M. *The Hellenistic World from Alexander to the Roman Conquest: A Selection of Ancient Sources in Translation*, Cambridge University Press, 2003.

Baatz, D. 'Recent Finds of Ancient Artillery', Britannia, vol. 9. (1978): 1-17, *Society for the Promotion of Roman Studies*, ['JSTOR' journal archive] <http://jstor.org/stable/525936>, viewed on 16 January 2011.

Bachrach, B. S. *The Anatomy of a Little War: A Diplomatic and Military History of the Gundovald Affair (568-586)*, Westview Press, 1994.

Badie, A. et al, *Le site antique de la Picola à Santa Pola (Alicante, Espagne)*, Éditions des Recherche sur le civilisations, Casa del Velaquez, 2000. <http://www.casadevelazquez.org/publications/librairie-en-ligne/livre/le-site-antique-de-la-picola-a-santa-pola-alicante-espagne/>, viewed on 1 October 2011.

Balthazar Jordan, J-J. *Histoire de la Ville d'Agde*, Montpellier 1824, Lafitte Reprints, 1996.

Baratier, E. *Documents de l'Historie de Provence*, Univers de la France, 1971.

Barbero, A. *The Battle: A History of the Battle of Waterloo*, Atlantic Books, 2006.

Barclay, G. *Pliny's Natural Histories*, Bk. 2. LXXVI. Wernernian Club, 1847-48.

Barnett, D. 'War Movie Mondays: Merrill's Marauders', Aug 30 2010, <http://theflickcast.com/2010/08/30/war-movie-mondays-merrills-marauders/>, viewed on 12 January 2012.

Barrett, M. *Venizelos and the Asia Minor Catastrophe*, ['Matt Barrett's Travel Guides'] <http://www.ahistoryofgreece.com/venizelos.htm>, viewed on 26 October 2011.

Barruol, G. 'La Massalie dans la Provincia' in *Voyage en Massalie: 100 ans d'archéologie en Gaule du sud*, Catalogue de l'exposition, (Musées de Marseille/Édisud, 1990): 242–243.

Bartley, N. 'What's Fishing Like? The Rhetoric of Similes in Oppian's "Halieutica"' in *Classics Ireland*, vol. 12. (2005): 1-17, Classical Association of Ireland, ['JSTOR' journal archive] <http://www.jstor.org/stable25528414>, viewed on 16 January 2011.

Barton, C. A. *Timaeus of Tauromenium and Hellenistic Historiography*, Cambridge, 2013.

Bats, M. 'Antibes' in *Voyage en Massalie: 100 ans d'archéologie en Gaule du sud*, Catalogue de l'exposition, (Musées de Marseille/Édisud, 1990): 220–221.

Bats, M. 'Olbia' in *Voyage en Massalie: 100 ans d'archéologie en Gaule du sud*, Catalogue de l'exposition, (Musées de Marseille/Édisud, 1990): 206-213.

Bats, M. *Olbia de Provence (Hyères, Var) a l'epoque romaine (1ers. a v. J-C.-VIIe s. ap. J-C)*, Edisud, 2006.

Bats, M. 'The Greeks in Gaul and Corsica: the rhythm of the Greek emporion' in P. Carratelli (ed.), *The Western Greeks: Classical Civilization in the Western Mediterranean*, (London, 1996): 577-584.

Bats, M., and Mouchot, D., 'Nice', in *Voyage en Massalie: 100 ans d'archéologie en Gaule du sud, Catalogue de l'exposition*, (Musées de Marseille/Édisud, 1990): 222-225.

Bateson, W. W., and Damon, C., *Caesar's Civil War*, Oxford, 2006.

Beard, M. North, J. A., and Price, F. R. S., *Religions of Rome: Volume1, a history*, Cambridge, 2004.

Beaver Wars, *Definition Iroquois*, ['Webster's Online Dictionary'] <http://www.websters-online-dictionary.org/definitions/Iroquois>, viewed on 31 December 2010.

Beer, G. de. 'Iktin', *The Geographical Journal*, Vol. 126, No. 2, (June 1960): 160-167, here p. 166-7, <http://www.jstor.org/stable/1793956>, viewed on 5 July 2012.

Benedict, C. H. 'The Romans in Southern Gaul' in *The American Journal of Philology*, vol. 63, no.1 (1942): 38-50, John Hopkins University Press, ['JSTOR' journal archive] <http://www.jstor.org/stable/291079>, viewed on 17 November 2009.

Bérard-Azzouz, O. *Musée de L'Éphèbe: archéologie sous-marine*, Agde, 2008.

Bérard, O., Nickels, A. and Schwaller, M., 'Agde' in *Voyage en Massalie: 100 ans d'archéologie en Gaule du sud*, Catalogue de l'exposition, (Musées de Marseille/Édisud, 1990): 182-189.

Bittlestone, R. *Odysseus Unbound*, Cambridge, 2005.

Bizot, B. et al. *Marseille Antique: guide archéologiques de la France*, Editions du Patrimonie, Centre des monuments nationaux, 2007.

Black, J. Anderson. *The Life and Times of Napoleon Bonaparte*, Parragon, 1994.

Black, J. *The Battle of Waterloo: A New History*, Icon Books, 2010.

Blakeway, A. 'Prolegma to the Study of Greek Commerce with Italy, Sicily and France in the Eighth and Seventh Centuries B.C.' in *The Annual of British School of Athens*, vol. 33 (1932/1933):170-208, ['JSTOR' journal archive] <http://www.jstor.org/stable/30096951>, viewed on 1 December 2009.

Blackwell, C. W. 'Athens and Macedonia in the Absence of Alexander', in C. W. Blackwell, (ed.), *Demos: Classical Athenian Democracy*, (R. Scaife, ed., The Stoa: a consortium for electronic publication in the humanities [www.stoa.org]) edition of July 1, 2005. <http://www.stoa.org/projects/demos/article_alexander?page=4&greekEncoding=>, viewed on 3 February 2012.

Blackwell, C., and Martin, T. R., 'Technology, Collaboration and Undergraduate Research', paragraphs 40-48, *Digital Humanities Quarterly* ['DHQ'] <http://www.digitalhumanities.org/dhq/vol/003/1/000024/000024.html> viewed 29 March 2012.

Blanchet, A. *Traité des monnaies gauloises*, Paris, 1905, p. 240, ['Gallia' Snible] <www.snible.org/coins/hn/gallia/html>, viewed on 20 August 2011.

Blot, J-Y. *Underwater Archaeology: Exploring the World beneath the sea*, Thames and Hudson, 1995.

Boardman, J. *The Greeks Overseas*, Thames & Hudson, 1999.

Bosch-Gimpera, P. 'The Phokaians in the Far West: A Historical Reconstruction', *The Classical Quarterly*, vol. 38, no. 1/2 (Jan.–Apr., 1944): 53-5. ['JSTOR' journal archive] <www.jstor.org/stable/636879>, viewed on 20 August 2010.

Bosworth, A. B. *From Arrian to Alexander*, Clarendon, 1988.

Bouloumié, B., and Arcelin, P., 'Saint-Blaise' in *Voyage en Massalie: 100 ans d'archéologie en Gaule du sud*, Catalogue de l'exposition, (Musées de Marseille/Édisud, 1990): 32–41.

Bowman, A., and Woolf, G., (eds.), *Literacy and Power in the Ancient World*, Cambridge, 1996.

Boyer, P. S. et al. *The Enduring Vision: A History of the American People*, Houghton Miflin, 2008.

Bradley, P. *Ancient Greece: Using Evidence*, Edward Arnold (Australia) Pty Ltd, 1988.

Braun, T. 'Hecataeus' Knowledge of the Western Mediterranean' in K. Lomas (ed.), *Greek Identity in the Western Mediterranean, Papers in Honour of Brian Shefton*, (Brill, 2004):287-348.

Brenot, C. 'Marseille et les réseaux phocéens. Remarques sur le témoignage des monnaise', ATTI DEL 'XI CONVEGNO DEL CENTRO INTERNAZIONALE DI STUDI NUMISMATICI-NAPOLI 25-27 OTTOBRE 1996, TAV. XV, 14, in *La monetazione dei Focei in Occidente*, Instituto Italiano di Numismatica Roma, (2002): 113-137.

Bridges, V. 'Paganism in Provence: How the Mother-Goddess Became the Mother of God' in *Journal of the Western Mystery Tradition*, no. 6. vol. 1, Vernal Equinox 2004, <http://www.jwmt.org/v1n6/provence.html#13>, viewed on 2 September 2011.

Brien-Poitevin, F. 'Tauroeis' in *Voyage en Massalie: 100 ans d'archéologie en Gaule du sud*, Catalogue de l'exposition, (Musées de Marseille/Édisud, 1990): 202-205.

Bright, K. S. director, *Ross's Wedding Part 2*, Warner Home Video, Season 4, 24, 1998, [videocassette].

Bringman, K. *History of the Roman Republic*, Polity Press, 2006.

Briscoe, J. *A Commentary on Livy*, Oxford, 1981.

Bromiley, G. W. *The International Standard Bible Encyclopaedia*, vol. 4. W. M. Erdman Publishing Co., 1988.

Bromwich, J. *The Roman Remains of Southern France: a guide book*, Routledge, 1996.

Brown, P. *The Rise of Western Christendom*, Blackwell, 2006.

Buckley, A. *The Story of Tin Mining in Cornwall*, Cornwall Editions Ltd, 2005.

Budin, S. L. *The Ancient Greeks: an introduction*, Oxford, 2004.

Bunson, M. *A Dictionary of the Roman Empire*, Oxford, 1990.

Burkert. W, *Greek Religion: Archaic and Classical*, II. 4-5, Blackwell, 1987.

Burl, A. *From Carnac to Callanish*, Shire, 1993.

Burl, A. *Stonehenge: How did the stones get there?* ['Historytoday.com' History Bookshop] <http://www.historybookshop.com/articles/commentary/stonehenge-myth-ht.asp>, viewed on 17 October 2011.

Burn, A. R. 'Persia and the Greeks' in The Median and Achaemenian Periods, *The Cambridge History of Iran*, vol. 2. Ch. 6. 1985, <http://histories.cambridge.org/extract?id=chol9780521200912_CHOL9780521200912A007>, viewed on 11 September 2011.

Burns, T. S. *A History of the Ostrogoths*, Indiana University Press, 1984.

Bury, J. B., and Meiggs, R., *A History of Greece*, Macmillan, 1979.

Buscato i Samoza, L. *La Colònia Grega de Rhode*, Brau, 1999.

Buxó, R. 'Botanical and Archaeological Dimensions' in M. Dietler, and C. Lopez-Ruiz, (eds.), *Colonial Encounters in Ancient Iberia: Phoenicians, Greek, and Indigenous Relations*, (University of Chicago Press, 2009): 155-168.

Çakilar, C., and Becks, R., 'Murex' *Dye Production at Troia: Assessment of Archomalacological Data from New and Old Excavations*, ['si.academia.com']:87-103, <http://si.academia.edu/CananCakirlar/Papers/453623/MUREX_DYE_PRODUCTION_AT_TROIA>, viewed on 27 November 2011.

Calapodis, M. *La Communauté grec à Marseille: Genèse d'un paragdime identitaire (1794-1914)*, L'Harmattan, 2010.

Camoin, P. *The Origin and History of the Tarot de Marseille*, ['Camoin'] <http://en.camoin.com/tarot/MarseillesTarot-Origin-History-1.html>, viewed on 24 March 2011.

Campbell, D. B. *Siege Warfare in the Roman World 146 B.C.-A.D. 378*, Osprey Publishing, 2005.

Campo, M. 'Las emisiones de Emporion y su difusión en el entorno iberico', ATTI DEL 'XI CONVEGNO DEL CENTRO INTERNAZIONALE DI STUDI NUMISMATICI-NAPOLI 25-27 OTTOBRE 1996, TAV. XVI, 3, in *La monetazione dei Focei in Occidente*, Instituto Italiano di Numismatica Roma, (2002): 139-166.

Canetti, C. *Marseille, European Capital of Culture 2013*, ['France Diplomatie'], Source: Actualité en France n° 43, October 2008, <http://www.diplomatie.gouv.fr/en/france_159/geography_6812/regions-and-towns_6931/towns_6933/marseille-european-capital-of-culture-2013_12660.html>, viewed on 5 September 2011.

Cappocia, K. *Christmas Traditions, A Brief Study of the Origins of Modern Christmas Celebrations*, <http://www.biblebb.com/files/christmas00.htm>, viewed on 4 April 2011.

Cardingham, C. *Bank Bailout to add up to 1.5 Trillion to Public Debt*, published 19 February 2009, <http://www.money.co.uk/article/1002877-bank-bailout-to-add-up-to-1-5-trillion-to-public-debt.htm>, viewed on 5 December 2010.

Carradice, I. *Greek Coins*, British Museum Press, 1995.

Carson, R. A. G. *Coins*, Hutchinson of London, 1963.

Carpenter, R. *The Greeks in Spain*, Bryn Mawr College, Longman, Greene & Co., 1925.

Carreras Rossell, T. *Intervencions arqueologiques a Sant Marti d'Empúries (1994-1996): De l'assentament precolonial a l'Empúries actiual*, Monograpfies Emporitanes 9, Musee d'Arqueologiques de Catalunya Empúries, Girona, 1999.

Carrington, R. C. *Caesar's Invasion of Britain*, Gallic Wars, Alpha Classics, G. Bell & Sons Ltd., 1952.

Cary, M., and Warmington, E. H., *The Ancient Explorers*, Methuen, 1929.

Casson, L. 'Speed under Sail of Ancient Ships', Transactions and Proceedings of the *American Philological Association*, vol. 82 (1951): 136-148, The John Hopkins University Press, ['JSTOR' journal archive] <http://www.jstor.org/stable/283426>, viewed on 17 November 2009.

Casson, L. *Ships and Seamanship in the Ancient World*, The John Hopkins University Press, 1995.

Castillo de San Fernando, <http://www.castellsantferran.org/>, viewed on 4 August 2011.

Catsiyannis, T. Bishop of Militoupolis. *Pandias Stephen Rallis 1793-1865*, Ekdotike Hellados, 1986.

Chadwick, N. *The Celts*, Pelican Books, 1970.

Charanis, P. 'On the Question of Hellenization of Sicily and Southern Italy During the Middle Ages', *The American Historical Review*, Vol. 52, No. 1 (Oct., 1946):74-86, ['JSTOR' archive journal] www.jstor.org/stable/1845070, viewed 24 May 2012

Charoni, J. et al., The coming of the Greeks to Provence and Corsica: Y-chromosome models of archaic Greek colonization of the western Mediterranean, *BMC Evolutionary Biology*, published 14 March 2011, ['BioMed Central'] <http://www.biomedcentral.com/1471-2148/11/69> viewed 3 April 2012.

Chapman, R. 'The Life of Colonel Blimp Reconsidered', *The Powell & Pressberger Pages*, <http://www.powell-pressburger.org/Reviews/43_Blimp/Blimp02.html#Note_8>, viewed on 9 January 2012.

Cawkwell, G. *Cyrene to Charonea*, Oxford, 2011.

Charles-Edwards, T. M. *Wales and the Britons 350-1064*, Oxford, 2013.

Chazelles, E. 'Les Pinardiers de l'antiquité', *Marseille antique*, (July 10, 2009) p. 16-17, ['Issuu'] <http://issuu.com/klode/docs/marseille_antique.>, viewed on 17 August 2011.

Chevillon, J-A. *Emporion,* Les Greco-Iberes, <http://numis-ext-occ.monsite-orange.fr/>, viewed on 1 January 2009.

Chinese Medicine, <http://www.nhsdirectory.org/default.aspx?page=TCM&t=y>, viewed on 22 December 2010.

Christol, M and Heijmans, M. 'Les colonies latines de Narbonnaise: un nouveu document d'Arles mentionnant la colonia Iulia Augusta Avennio', *Gallia*, vol. 49, (1992): 37-44. <http://www.persee.fr/web/revues/home/prescript/article/galia_0016-4119_1992_num_49_1_2927>, 20 June 2012.

Chugg, A. 'The Death of Alexander the Great' in *Minerva: The International Review of Ancient Art & Archaeology*, (September/October 2004), vol. 15, Number 5.

Churchill, W. S. *A History of the English-Speaking Peoples*, Vol. 1, Bk. 1, Britannia, Rosetta Books, 1956.

Cilento and Vallo di Diano National Park with the Archaeological sites of Paestrum and Velia, and the Certosa di Padula, ['UNESCO'] <http://whc.unesco.org/en/list/842>, viewed on 21 August 2011.

Clarke, K. 'An Island Nation: Re-reading Tacitus' Agricola' in R. Ash, (ed.). *Oxford Readings in Tacitus*, (Oxford, 2012): 37-72.

Clavel, M. *Bèziers et son Territoire dans L'Antique*, La Belle Lettres, Annales Literaraires de l'université de Besançon, 1970.

Cleere, H. *Southern France: An Oxford Archaeological Guide*, Oxford, 2001.

Clerc, M. *Massalia: Histoire de Marseille dans l'antiquité des origins à la fin de l'Empire romain d'Occident (476 ap. J.-C.)*, TOME I, Des origins jusqu 'au IIIme siècle av. J.-C., Marseille, Librairie A. Tacussel, 1927.

Clerc, M. *Massalia: Histoire de Marseille dans L'Antiquité des Origins a la Fin de l'empire Romain d'occident*, TOME 2, Librarie A. Tacussel, 1929.

Clerc, M. *Massalia: Histoire de Marseille dans L'Antiquité des Origins a la Fin de l'empire Romain d'occident*, (Marseille, 1927-9, (2 vols.), Lafitte, reprint 1971.

Climo, S. *The Egyptian Cinderella*, Harper Collins, New York, 1989. Posted Dec 6 2004-21:09, last edited: Jul 20, 2005-00:08, <http://www.ancientsites.com/aw/Article/461904>, viewed on 25 September 2011.

Collection IX British Museum, <http://www.sylloge-nummorum-graecorum.org/>, viewed on 23 November 2010.

Collins, R. *Charlemagne*, University of Toronto, 1998.

Collins, R. Plague (La Peste), *History of Provence and France*, <http://www.beyond.fr/history/plague.html>, viewed on 14 April 2011.

Collins, R. *Marseille,* Provence Beyond, <http://www.beyond.fr/villages/marseille-history-provence-france.html>, viewed on 3 September 2011.

Compendium of Ancient Greek Phonology, 63-75, Arts & Sciences, ['Washington University in St. Louis'] <http://www.artsci.wustl.edu/~cwconrad/docs/CompPhon.pdf>, viewed 2.June 2012.

Connelly, P. *Hannibal and the Enemies of Rome*, Macdonald Educational, 1978.

Cornell, T. J. *The Beginning of Rome: Italy and Rome from the Bronze Age to the Punic Wars (c.1000-264 BC.)*, Routledge, 1995.

Copping, J. 'Bronze Age shipwreck found off the Devon coast', *The Telegraph*, 13 February 2010, <http://www.telegraph.co.uk/earth/environment/archaeology/7228108/Bronze-Age-shipwreck-found-off-Devon-coast.html >, viewed on 19 October 2011.

Constantine I, [The 1911 Classical Encyclopaedia] <http:www.1911encyclopaedia.org/Constantine_I>, viewed on 29 September 2009.

Cotterill, H. B. *Ancient Greece*, revised by Geddes and Grosset 2004.

Coulet, N. 'Enquets sur les droits et revenues de Charles Ier d'Anjou en Provence (1252 et 1278)', *Annales, Economies, Societies, Civilisations,* Vol. 26, No. 6, (1971):1315-1317. <http://www.persee.fr/web/revues/home/prescript/article/ahess_0395-2649_1971_num_26_6_422414_t1_1315_0000_4 >, viewed 25 June 2012.

Couprie, D. L. *Heaven and Earth in Ancient Greek Cosmology: From Thales to Heraclides Ponticus*, Springer, 2011.

Courtney, E. *A Companion to Petronius*, Oxford University Press, 2001.

Cowell, Isaac . F. R. Sir, *Cicero and the Roman Republic*, Pitman & Sons Ltd, 1948.

Crane, S. 'Digging up the Present in Marseille's Old Port: Toward an Archaeology of Reconstruction' in *Journal of the Society of Architectural Historians*, vol. 63. No. 3 (Sep., 2004): 296-319, ['JSTOR' journal archive] <http://www.jstor.org/stable/4127973>, viewed on 8 October 2010.

Crawford, M. and Whitehead, D. *Archaic and Classical Greece; A selection of ancient sources in translation*, Cambridge, 1983.

Cultural Visits in Hyeres Les Palmiers: Monuments and Sites, *Olbia Archaeological Site*, <http://www.hyeres-tourisme.com/en/decouverte_lieux_culturels.asp>, viewed on 11 July 2011.

Cunliffe, B. W. *Greeks, Romans and Barbarians: Spheres of Interaction*, Guild, 1988.

Cunliffe, B. W. 'The Evolution of Romney Marsh: a Preliminary Statement, Archaeology and Coastal Change', *The Society of Antiquaries of London*, Occasional Paper (New Series) I, 1980: 37-55.

Curbera, J. B. 'The Greek Curse Tablets of Emporion', *Zeitschrift für Papyrologie und Epigraphik*, Bd. 117, (1997): 90-94, ['JSTOR' journal archive] <http://www.jstor.org/stable/20190008>, viewed on 16 January 2011.

Curnow, T. *The Oracles of the Ancient World*, Duckworth, 2004.

D'Agostino, B. 'The First Greek in Italy' in G. R. Tsetskhladze (ed.), *Greek Colonization: An account of Greek Colonization and Other Settlements Overseas*, vol. 1, (Leiden, 2006): 201–237.

Dando-Collins, S. *Cleopatra's Kidnappers: How Caesar's Sixth Legion Gave Egypt to Rome and Rome to Caesar*, John Wiley & Sons, 2005.

Delamont, E. 'III-Une irruption aragonaise en Languedoc (1286)', La croisade de 1285- se causes, ses resultants et ses suites, *Muntaner Chronicle*, p. 368-369, <http://www.mediterranees.net/histoire_roussillon/moyen_age/delamont3.html>, viewed on 7 May 2011.

Darde, D., and Lassalle, V., *Nimes Antique: Guides archéologiques de la France*, Imprimerie Nationale Editions, 1993.

D-Day and the Battle of Normandy: Your Questions Answered, ['D-Day Museum Portsmouth'] <http://www.ddaymuseum.co.uk/faq.htm>, viewed on 9 November 2010.

Deanesly, M. *A History of Early Medieval Europe*, 467-911, Methuen, 1956.

Díaz, C., Palou, H. and Puig, A. M., *La Ciudadela de Roses*, Ayuntamiento de Roses Fundació Roses Història i Natura, 2003.

Dictionary of Slang, O, *old boot*, <http://dictionaryofslang.co.uk/>, viewed on 22 October 2010.

Diderot, D. et Le Rond d'Alember, J. *Encyclopédie ou Dictionnaire raissoné des Sciences, des Arts et des Metiers*, A. Neufchastel, 1765, p. 590, <http://books.google.co.uk/books?id=Rd8jqiMG6y0C&pg=PA590&lpg=PA590&dq=Salyes,+Sallyes,+Salyi,&source=bl&ots=WDIP1QR3xZ&sig=9RU4SxmoQgJkzXqzUqbW1FMAeZE&hl=en&ei=1adYTraAJsLG8QPO6LmhDA&sa=X&oi=book_result&ct=result&resnum=9&ved=0CFMQ6AEwCA#v=onepage&q=Salyes%2C%20Sallyes%2C%20Salyi%2C&f=false>, viewed on 27 August 2011.

Diehl, C. *Byzantium: Greatness and Decline*, trans. N. Walford, Rutgers University Press, 1957.

Dietler, M. 'The Iron Age in Mediterranean France: Colonial Encounters and Transformations', *Journal of World Prehistory*, Vol. 11, No. 3, (1997): 269-358, <http://chicago.academia.edu/MichaelDietler/Papers/218412/The_Iron_Age_In_Mediterranean_France_Colonial_Encounters_Entanglements_and_Transformations>, viewed 6 February 2012.

Dietler, M., and Lopez-Ruiz, C., (eds.), *Colonial Encounters in Ancient Iberia: Phoenicians, Greek, and Indigenous Relations*, University of Chicago Press, 2009.

Dietler, M., and Py, M., 'The Warrior of Lattes: an Iron Age statue discovered in Mediterranean France', *Antiquity* 77 (2003): 789-795.

'Diocese of Marseilles', *The Original Catholic Encyclopaedia*, Encyclopaedia Press, 1913, vol. 1. p. 2 of 8, <http://oce.catholic.com/index.php?title=Diocese_of_Marseilles>, viewed on 15 September 2009.

Dionne, N. 'Seigneur and Marquis de Denonville', *The Catholic Encyclopaedia*, vol. 9. New York: Robert Appleton Company, 1908, <http://www.newadvent.org/cathen/04732a.htm>, viewed on 31 December 2010.

Dirks, T. *Yankee Doodle Dandy* (1942), ['Filmsite'] <http://www.filmsite.org/yank.html>, viewed on 21 December 2010.

Domínguez, A. J. 'Hellenization in Iberia: The Reception of the Greek Products and influences by Iberians' in G. R. Tsetskhladze (ed.), *Ancient Greeks West and East*, Brill, 1999): 301-330.

Domínguez, A. J. 'Spain and France (including Corsica)' in H. H. Hanson, and T. H. Nielsen, *An Inventory of Archaic and Classical Poleis*, (Oxford, 2004): 157-171.

Duffy, E. *Saints and Sinners: A History of the Popes*, Yale University Press, 2002.

Dunbabin, T. J. *The Western Greeks: The History of Sicily and South Italy from the Foundation of the Greek Colonies to 480 B.C.*, Oxford University Press Monograph Reprints, 1998.

Dunn, E. C. *The Gallican Saint's Life and the Late Roman Dramatic Tradition*, The Catholic University of America Press, 1989.

Duprat, E. *Bouches du Rhône: Encyclopédie départementale*, vol. 2. Marseille, 1923.

Duprat, E. in P. Masson, (ed.), *Bouches du Rhône*, vol. XIV, Marseille, 1935, p. 72.

Ebel, C. *Transalpine Gaul: the making of a Roman province*, Brill, 1976.

Eccles, W. J. *Brisay de Denonville: Jacques-René de, Marquis de Denonville*, ['Dictionary of Canadian Biography Online'] <http://www.biographi.ca/009004-119.01-e.php?&id_nbr=673&interval=25&&PHPSESSID=8l2vojaefug5c5kr7863r2n1p0>, viewed on 31 December 2010.

Edey, M. A. *The Sea Traders*, Time Life Books, 1974.

Eidinow, E. *Oracles, Curses, and Risk Among the Ancient Greeks*, Oxford, 2007.

Editions Montparnasse, 2000, *Marseille*, <www.france-la-viste.com/english/heritage/marseille.html>, viewed on 3 September 2011.

Ehler, J. T. *Pastis: the French national, versatile and much-loved drink*, <http://www.foodreference.com/html/artpastis.html>, viewed on 29 October 2010.

Elaye, J., and Sapin, J., *Beyond the River: New Perspectives on Transeuphratene*, Sheffield Academic Press, 1991.

Ellis, P. B. *The Celtic Empire*, Constable, 1990.

Emlyn-Jones, C. M. *The Ionians and Hellenism: A Study of the Cultural Achievements of the Early Greek Inhabitants of Asia Minor*, Routledge & Kegan Paul, 1980.

Errington, R. M. 'Overview', *The Cambridge Ancient History*, vol. 8. Rome and the Mediterranean to 133 B.C., Chapter 4: Greece and Rome to 205 B.C., 1989, ['Cambridge Histories Online'] <http://histories.cambridge.org/extract?id=chol9780521234481_CHOL9780521234481A005> viewed 26 April 2012.

Euzennat, M. 'Ancient Marseille in the light of recent excavations' in *American Journal of Archaeology*, 84, no. 2. (Apr., 1980): 133-140, ['JSTOR' journal archive] <http://www.jstor.org.uk/stable/504261>, viewed on 17 November 2009.

Everson, T. *Warfare in Ancient Greece*, Sutton, 2004.

Explore Highlights, *Map of the World*, ME 92687, ['The British Museum'] <http://www.britishmuseum.org/explore/highlights/highlight_objects/me/m/map_of_the_world.aspx>, viewed on 29 October 2010.

Farnell, L. R. *The Cults of the Greek States*, Digitally Printed Version, Cambridge University Press, 2010.

Farwell, B. *The Gurkhas*, Penguin, 1985.

Federer, W. J. *America's God and country: Encyclopaedia of quotations*, Amerisearch Inc., 2000.

Fenton, W. N. *The Great Law and the Longhouse: a political history of the Iroquois confederacy*, University of Oklahoma, 1998.

T. J. Figueira, *The Power of Money: Coinage and Politics in the Athenian Empire*, University of Pennsylvania Press, 1998.

Flaceliere, R. *Daily Life in Greece at the Time of Pericles*, trans. P. Green, Phoenix, 2002.

Flory, M. B. 'Pearls for Venus' *Historia: Zeitschrift fur Alte Geschichte*, Bd.37.H.4 (4th Qtr., 1988):498-504 ['JSTOR' journal archive] <www.jstor.org/stable/4436082> viewed 28 March 2013.

Foreman, L. *Alexander: The Conqueror*, Da Capo Press, 2004.

Foster, B.O. *Livy*, Bk. XXI. XIX, II, xx 8, Heinemann, 1929.

Fox, R. L. 'Hellenistic Culture and Literature', ch. 14, in J. Boardman, J. Griffin, and O. Murray, (eds.), *Greece and the Hellenistic World*, Oxford University Press, 2001, p. 404.

Foxhall, L. 'Cultural Landscapes, and Identities in the Mediterranean World' in *Mediterranean Historical Review*, vol. 18, no.2, (December 2003): 75-92.

Foxhall, L. *Olive Cultivation in Ancient Greece: Seeking the Ancient Economy*, Oxford, 2007.

Fröhner, M. 'Scolies latines relative a l'histoire et a la topographie de Marseille' in *Revue Archéologique*, XVIII, II, (1891): 321-332.

Furtwängler, A. 'Monnaies grecques en Gaule: Nouvelle trouvailles (6-5ème s. av. J.-C.), ATTI DEL 'XI CONVEGNO DEL CENTRO INTERNAZIONALE DI STUDI NUMISMATICI-NAPOLI 25-27 OTTOBRE 1996, TAV. XI, 2, in *La monetazione dei Focei in Occidente*, Instituto Italiano di Numismatica Roma, (2002): 93-111.

Furtwängler. A, 'Le trésor d'Auriol et les types monétaires phocéens' in A. Hemary and H. Tréziny (eds.), *Les Cultes des cités phocéennes*, (Centre Camille Jullian, 2000):175-181.

Gallini, P. 'Des tombs grecques à Marseille' *La Provence*, 4 June 2012, <http://www.laprovence.com/article/a-la-une/des-tombes-grecques-a-marseille>; viewed 7 July 2012.

Gantes, L-F. 'Marseilleveyre' in *Voyage en Massalie: 100 ans d'archéologie en Gaule du sud,* Catalogue de l'exposition, (Musées de Marseille/Édisud, 1990): 156-161.

Garcia, D. 'Le casque corinthien des Baux-de-Provence' in S. Bouffir and A. Hemary (eds.) *L'occident grec, de Marseille à Mégara Hyblaea,* (Centre Camille Jullian, 2013): 85-90.

Gardiner, J., and Wenborn, N., (eds.), *The History Today Companion to British History,* Collins & Brown, 1995.

Gardiner, R. (ed.), *The Age of the Galley,* Conway Maritime Press, 1995.

Gardiner, R. *The Earliest Ships,* Conway Maritime Press, 1996.

Garrett, M. *Provence: a cultural history,* Oxford, 2006.

Garrison, J. *A History of Sixteenth Century France 1483-1598,* Macmillan, 1995.

Gassend, J-M. *Les Vestiges de la Bourse,* Les Editions de la Nerthe, 1997.

Gaul Obole phocaeque la tete casque (450-400). 450-400. v. Chr., ['ogn-numismatique'] <http://www.muenzauktion.com/crinon/item.php5?id=2822&lang=jp&psid=592bd763ea12c81ab39188fdc8df27e3>, viewed on 15 November 2010.

Geary, P. *Phantoms of Remembrance: Memory and Oblivion of the end of the first millennium,* Princeton Paperbacks, 1994.

Generalitat de Catalunya, *Phoenicians and Greeks in Catalonia: 7th century BC-6th century BC,* <http://www20.gencat.cat/portal/site/culturacatalana/menuitem.be2bc4cc4c5aec88f94a9710b0c0e1a0/?vgnextoid=d07cef2126896210VgnVCM1000000b0c1e0aRCRD&vgnextchannel=d07cef2126896210VgnVCM1000000b0c1e0aRCRD&vgnextfmt=detall2&contentid=810c110e279d7210VgnVCM1000008d0c1e0aRCRD&newLang=en_GB>, viewed on 22 July 2011.

Geni, *Boson d'Autun, Comte de Vienne, Dux de Provence,* <http://www.geni.com/people/Boson-d-Autun/6000000008799837188>, viewed on 3 September 2011.

George, R. *The Temple of the Goddess Athena at Phocaea,* ['The Museum of the Goddess Athena'] <http://www.goddess-athena.org/Museum/Temples/Phocaea/index.htm>, viewed on 26 November 2011.

Geus, K. 'Space and Geography' in A. Erskine (ed.), *A Companion to the Hellenistic World,* Blackwell, 2003.

Ghiuzeli, H. F. *Jewish Community of Marseilles,* ['Beit Hatfutsot', The Museum of the Jewish People], <www.bh.org.il/database-article.aspx?48710>, viewed on September 2011.

Gibson, S. *Aristoxenus of Tarentum and the Birth of Musicology,* Routledge, 2005.

Gigante, L. *Death and Disease in Ancient Rome,* <http://www.innominatesociety.com/Articles/Death%20and%20Disease%20in%20Ancient%20Rome.htm>, viewed on 20 October 2010.

Gill, N. S. *Slave Revolts or Servile Wars in Italy: The Sicilian Slave Wars and Spartacus,* <http://ancienthistory.about.com/cs/slavesandslavery/a/slavewars.htm>, viewed on 20 January 2010.

Giovanni, A. 'The Pan Hellenic Festivals' in *Images and Ideologie: Self-definition in the Hellenic World,* (eds.), Bulloch, A., et al, University of California Press, 1993, p.280, n. 65, A. Plasscart, 'Inscriptiones de Delphes la liste des Théodoriques.', BCH 45 (1921), 1-85.

Glines, C. V. 'Flying the Hump', *Air Force Magazine,* Vol. 74. No.3. (March 1991), <http://www.airforce-magazine.com/MagazineArchive/Pages/1991/March%201991/0391hump.aspx>, viewed on 9 January 2012.

Glover, T. R. *The Conflict of Religions in the Roman Empire*, Methuen, 1919.

God's Guarantees for Giving! *Council of Agde*, <http://godsguarantees.com/council-of-agde/#0>, viewed on 4 April 2011.

Goffart, W. F. 'Byzantine policy in the West Under Tiberius II and Maurice: The Pretenders Hermenegild and Gundovald (579-585)', *Traditio*, vol. 13 (1957):73-118, ['JSTOR' archive journal] <www.jstor.org/stable/27830344>, viewed 12 June 2012.

Goldhill, S. *Being Greek under Rome: cultural identity, the second sophist and the development of empire*, Cambridge, 2001.

Goldhill, S. 'Artemis and Cultural Identity in Empire Culture: how to think about polytheism, now?' in D. Konstan and S. Saïd, *Greeks on Greekness: Viewing the Past Under the Roman Empire*, Cambridge Classical Journal Proceedings of the Cambridge Philosophical Society, Supplementary Volume 29, 2006, p. 141.

Gori, S. and Bettini, M.C. 'Gli Etruschi da Genova ad Ampurias, Att del XXIV Convegno di Studi Etruschi ed Italici, Marseille,-Lattes, 26 settembre–1 octtobre 2002'. Two volumes. Pisa: Istituti Editoriiali e Poligrafici Internazionali, 2006. ISBN 88-8147-428-X, in *Bryn Mawr Classical Review* 2008.5.09, p. 4-5, reviewed by Jean MacIntosh Turfa, University of Pennsylvania Museum, <http://bmcr.brynmawr.edu/2008/2008-05-09.html>, viewed on 5 March 2011.

Goyau, G. 'Montpellier', *The Catholic Encyclopaedia*, vol. 10. New York: Robert Appleton Company, 1911, <http://www.newadvent.org/cathen/10545a.htm>, viewed on 2 April 2011.

Grant, M. *Julius Caesar*, Weidenfeld & Nicolson, 1969.

Grant, M. *Roman Myths*, Weidenfeld & Nicolson, 1971.

Grant, M. *The Rise of the Greeks*, Phoenix Press, 2005.

Greaves, A. M. *The Land of Ionia: Society and Economy in the Archaic Period*, Blackwell, 2010.

Gregory, A. *Eureka! The Birth of Science*, Icon Books Ltd., 2001.

Gregory, T. E. *A History of Byzantium*, Wiley-Blackwell, 2010.

Greek (Grigo) in Italy, ['Institut de Sociolingüistica Catalana']
<http://www.uoc.edu/euromosaic/web/document/grec/an/i1/i1.html>, viewed on 19 May 2011.

Greek Corinthian Helmet, ['MVESO Arqueológico de Jerez']
<http://www.jerez.es/nc/en/the_collection/selection_of_pieces/?tx_photoblog_pi1[showUid]=840>, viewed on 20 August 2010.

Greene, A. *Catholic Pirates and Greek Merchants: A Maritime History of the Mediterranean*, Princeton University Press, 2010.

Green, P. *Alexander the Great*, Weidenfeld & Nicolson, 1970.

Grierson P., and Blackburn, M., *Medieval European Coinage: The Early Middle Ages (5th to 10th centuries)*, Cambridge 1986, p. 144.

Guhl, E., and Koner, W., *The Greeks; Their Life and Customs*, Senate, 1994.

Guillon, A. *Complexe Volcanique du mont Saint-Loup*, 2001,
<http://membres.multimania.fr/volcanogeol/agde/AgdeV2_2.htm>, viewed on 4 April 2011.

Guruge, A. W. P. *The Society of the Ramayana*, Abhinav Publications, New Delhi, 1991.

Gutas, D. *Greek Thought, Arab Culture: The Graeco-Arabic movement in Baghdad and early 'Abbasid Society (2nd-4th/8th-10th)*, (Arab Thought and Culture), Routledge, 1998.

Guzmán, A. *History of Altea*, <http://www.villasguzman.com/gb/holiday-rentals/spain/costa-blanca/alicante/altea_location_3.aspx>, viewed on 4 October 2011.

Haddan. A. W. and Stubbs, W. *Councils and Ecclesiastical Documents Relating to Great Britain and Ireland*, Vol.1, Oxford,1869.< http://books.google.co.uk/books?id=knzbNgOreRwC&q=caerleon#v=snippet&q=caerleon&f=false> viewed 4 March 2013.

Haldon, J. F. *Byzantium in the Seventh Century*, Cambridge, 1990.

Haldon, J. *Warfare, State and Society in the Byzantine World 565–1204*, Routledge, 1999.

Hall, E. *Inventing the Barbarian*, Clarendon, 1989.

Hall. W. H. (Bullock), *The Romans on the Riviera and the Rhone: a sketch on the conquest of Liguria and the Roman Province*, Chp. XI, Macmillan, 1898, p. 118, reprinted by Ares Publishers, Chicago, 1974, ['Open Library'] <http://openlibrary.org/books/OL5069373M/The_Romans_on_the_Riviera_and_the_Rhone>, viewed on 19 December 2011.

Halley, N. *The Complete Prophecies of Nostradamus*, Wordsworth Edition Ltd., 1999.

Halsall. P. *The Children's Crusade*, ['The History Guide'] <http://www.historyguide.org/ancient/children.html>, viewed on 3 September 2011.

Halsall, P. (adapted from Thatcher), *Medieval source book: Urban II: Speech at Council of Clermont, 1095*, according to Fulcher of Chartres, <http://fordham.edu/halsall/source/urban2-fulcher.html>, viewed on 28 September 2010.

Hammond, M. *The Peloponnesian War*, Oxford, 2009.

Hammond, N. G. L. 'The Continuity of Macedonian Institutions and the Macedonian Kingdoms of the Hellenistic Era', *Historia: Zeitschrift für Alte Geschiichte*, vol. 49, no. 2. (2nd Qtr., 2000): 141-160, ['JSTOR' archive journal], <http://www.jstor.org/stable/4436574>, viewed on 28 March 2011.

Hard, T. *The Routledge Handbook of Greek Mythology*, Routledge, 2004.

Harden, D. *The Phoenicians*, Thames & Hudson, 1963.

Harley, J. B., and Woodward, D., *The History of Cartography: Cartography in Prehistoric, Ancient, and Medieval Europe and the Mediterranean*, University of Chicago Press, 1987.

Harries, J. *Sidonius Apollinaris and the Fall of Rome AD 407–485*, Oxford University Press, 1999.

Harries, J. D. *Apollinaris Biography–Carm, Carmina*, Epistulae, Misssae, <http://biography.jrank.org/pages/5345/Sidonius-Apollinaris.html>, viewed on 9 December 2010.

Hassett, M. 'John Cassian', *The Catholic Encyclopaedia*, Vol. 3, New York: Robert Appleton Co., 1908, <http://www.newadvent.org/cathen/03404a.htm>, viewed on 3 December 2010.

Hastings, J. *Encyclopaedia of Religion and Ethics*, Kessinger, 2003.

Hatzopoulos, M. B. (ed.), *Philip of Macedon*, Heinemann, 1981.

Haughton, B. *What Happened to the Great Library?* Published 1 February 2011, [Ancient History Encyclopaedia'] <http://www.ancient.eu.com/article/207/>, viewed on 6 September 2011.

Hawkes, C. F. C. *Pytheas: Europe and the Greek Explorers*, 1975 (Eighth J. L. Myers Memorial Lecture), Oxford, 1975, ASIN: B0007AMH16.

Hawkes, C. F. C., and Smith, M. A., 'On some buckets and cauldrons of the Bronze and Early Iron Ages', *Ant. J.* (1957, 37): 131-98.

Haynes, S. *Etruscan Civilization*, Paul Getty Trust, 2004.

Head, B. V., and Poole, R. S., *Catalogue of Greek Coins of Ionia*, British Museum Department of Coins, 1892.

Heath, Thomas L., Sir. *Greek Astronomy*, Geminos of Rhodes, Dover, 1991.

Hecataeus of Miletus, ['Encyclopaedia Britannica'] <http://www.britannica.com/EB.C.hecked/topic/259133/Hecataeus-of-Miletus>, viewed on 29 October 2010.

Heer, F. *The Medieval World: Europe 1100-1350*, Weidenfeld & Nicolson, 1961.

Heijmans, M. Roquette, J. M. and Sintès, C., *Arles Antique: guide archéologiques de la France,* Editions Patrimone, Paris, 2006.

Hermary, A., Hesnard, A. and Tréziny, H., *Marseille Grecque: La cite phocéenne (600-49 av. J-C)*, Editions Errance, 1999.

Henderson, J. 'The Creation of Isidore's Etymologies or Origins', in J. Konig, and T. Whitmarsh, *Ordering Knowledge in the Roman Empire*, Cambridge University Press, 2007.

Herrin, J. *Byzantium: The Surprising Life of a Medieval Empire*, Penguin, 2008.

Heurgon, J. *Daily Life of the Etruscans*, Phoenix Press, 2002.

Hibbert, C. *The French Revolution*, Penguin, 1980.

Hill, G. F. *Historical Roman Coins: from the earliest times to the reign of Augustus*, Constable & Co. Ltd, 1909.

Hindley, G. *The Crusades*, Constable & Robinson, 2004.

Hippasus of Metapontium, <http://www.britannica.com/EBchecked/topic/266577/Hippasus-of-Metapontum>, viewed on 26 August 2011.

History of the Byzantine Empire, ['History World'] <http://www.historyworld.net/wrldhis/PlainTextHistories.asp?historyid=ac59 >, viewed on 13 August 2010.

Hodge, A. Trevor. *Ancient Greek France*, University of Pennsylvania Press, 1999.

Hogan, D. W. India-Burma. *The U.S. Army Campaigns of World War II*, ['U.S. Army Centre for Military History'] <http://www.ibiblio.org/hyperwar/USA/USA-C-India/index.html>, viewed on 9 January 2012.

Holleaux, M. 'Etudes, V'. 1957, 141-55 in M. M. Austin, *The Hellenistic World from Alexander to the Roman Conquest: A Selection of Ancient Sources in Translation*, Cambridge University Press, 2006, p. 355-357.

Holt, M. P. *Renaissance and Reformation France 1500-1648*, Oxford, 2002.

Holt, P. M., Lambton, A. K. and Lewis, B., *The Cambridge History of Islam*, vol. 1, Cambridge University Press, 1978.

Hooper, C. *Lost city found at Stonehenge*, <http://www.archaeology.ws/2007-9-4.htm>, viewed on 23 August 2011.

Hornblower, S., and Spawforth, A., *The Oxford Classical Dictionary*, 3rd edition, Oxford, 2003.

Horsley, G. H. R. *New Documents Illustrating Early Christianity: A Review of the Greek Inscriptions and Papyrii published in 1979*, vol. 4, Macquarie University, 1987.

Hoz, J. de. 'The Greek Man in the Iberian Street' in K. Lomas (ed.), *Greek Identity in the Western Mediterranean, Papers in Honour of Brian Shefton*, (Brill, 2004):411-428.

Hughes, D. D. *Human Sacrifice in Ancient Greece*, Routledge, 1991.

Hyde, W. W. *Ancient Greek Mariners*, Oxford, 1947.

Illogical Geology, ['Findstone.com'] <http://www.findstone.com/geo_illogic.htm>, viewed on 6 September 2011.

Index, ['Juno Beach Centre'] <http://www.junobeach.org/centre/index.html>, viewed on 9 November 2010.

INSEE, *13 Bouches-du-Rhône*, Code commune 13055, ['Institute national de statistique et de études économiques'] <http://www.insee.fr/fr/ppp/bases-de-donnees/recensement/populations-legales/departement.asp?dep=13>, viewed on 5 September 2011.

Institut de Sociolingüística Catalana, *Greek (Griko) in Italy*, <http://www.uoc.edu/euromosaic/web/document/grec/an/i1/i1.html>, viewed on 30 December 2010.

Issuu, June 12, 2009, Klode, 28, *Thau*, <http://issuu.com/klode/docs/thau>, viewed on 21 August 2011.

Italian Language School, *Salentinian Greece: in Salento, Southern Italy,* Greek-Salentinian Language and traditions– History and Language of Terra d'Otranto, <http://www.ilsonline.it/salentiniangreece/>, viewed on 30 December 2010.

Jacobs, D. *Constantinople and the Byzantine Empire*, Cassel, 1969.

James, E. *The Origins of France: From Clovis to the Capetians 500-1000*, Macmillan, 1989.

James, E. *The Franks*, Blackwell, 1988.

Jameson, R. D. *If the Shoe Fits*, [#510] <http://www.artic.edu/webspaces/510iftheshoefits/2criteria.html>, viewed on 22 October 2010.

Jaques, T. *Dictionary of Battles and Sieges: A Guide to 8,500 Battles from Antiquity through the Twenty-first Century*, vol. 3, Greenwood Press, 2007.

Jersey, P. de. *Celtic Coinage in Britain*, Shire, 2001.

Jimenez Garnica, A. M. 'Settlement of the Visigoths in the Fifth Century' in P. J. Heather, (ed.), *The Visigoths. From Migration Period to the Seventh Century*, (Boydell Press, 1999): 93-128.

Johnson, M., Abrahams, E. and Evans, M. M. Lady., *Ancient Greek Dress*, Argonaut, 1964.

Johnson, W. M., and Lavigne, D. L., 'Monk Seals in Antiquity, The Mediterranean Monk Seal (Monachus monachus)' in *Ancient History and Literature,* Mededelingen No. 35, The Netherlands Commission for International Nature Protection, (Leiden 1999): 1-101, PDF edition 2008, <http://www.monachus-guardian.org/library/mededelingen35_2008a.pdf>, viewed on 18 September 2011.

Jones, A. H. M. *The Later Roman Empire 284-602,* vol. 2. XXII, Basil Blackwell, 1973.

Jones, R., and Buxeda i Garrigós, J., 'The Identity of Early Greek Pottery in Italy and Spain: An Archeometric Perspective' in K. Lomas (eds.), *Greek Identity in the Western Mediterranean,* Brill, 2003.

Jones, W. H. S. *Pliny, Natural Histories*, Book XXIX. V. 9-11, William Heinemann, 1963.

Jong, A. de. *Traditions of the Magi: Zoroastrianism in Greek and Latin Literature*, Brill, 1997.

Johnston, A. *The Emergence of Greece,* Elsevier-Phaidon, 1976.

Jordan, L. *A Brief Outline on the History of New Netherland,* ['University of Notre Dame'] <http://www.coins.nd.edu/ColCoin/ColCoinIntros/NNHistory.html>, viewed on 13 October 2010.

Kak, S. *The Mahabharata and the Sindhu-Sarasvati Tradition,* <http://www.ece.lsu.edu/kak/MahabharataII.pdf>, viewed on 22 October 2010.

Kaltenborn, H. V. 'Why Does Hitler Hang On?' in *The Rotarian,* Rotary International, vol. 66. no. 2, (February 1945): 8-15. <http://www.rotary.org/en/mediaandnews/therotarian/archives/Pages/ridefault.aspx>, viewed 6 January 2009.

Kaldellis, A. *Hellenism in Byzantium: Transformation of the Greek identity and the reception of the classical tradition (Greek Culture in the Roman World)*, Cambridge, 2008.

Kawami, Trudy. S. 'Greek Art and Persian Taste: Some Animal Sculptures from Persepolis', *American Journal of Archaeology,* vol. 90. no.3. (July 1986): 259-267. ['JSTOR' journal archive] <http://www.jstor.org/pss/505686>, viewed 22 June 2011.

Kelly, G. P. *A History of Exile in the Roman Republic,* Cambridge, 2006.

Kelly, C. *The Roman Empire,* Oxford University Press, 2006.

Kelly, G. *Ammianus Marcellinus,* ['Oxford Biographies Online'] <http://oxfordbibliographiesonline.com/view/document/obo-9780195389661/obo-9780195389661-0115.xml>, viewed 13 January 2012.

Kemmers, F. 'The coin finds from the Augustan legionary fortress at Nijmagen (The Netherlands): coin circulation in the lower Rhine area before Drusus's campaigns' in Alfaro, C. Marcos, C., and Otero, P. (eds.), *XIIIth Congreso Internacional de Numismática*, Madrid 2003, Actas-Proceedings-Actes, pp. 987-990, <www.mcu.es/museos/docs/MC/ActasNumis/The_coin_finds.pdf>, viewed on 20 June 2010.

Kendal, P. M. *Louis XI*, Cardinal, 1974.

Keppie, L. *The Making of the Roman Empire: from Republic to Empire*, University of Oklahoma Press, 1998.

Kessler, P. L. 'Riothamus', <http://www.historyfiles.co.uk/FeaturesBritain/BritishRiothamus.htm>, viewed 17 March 2013.

Khouri-Dager, N. *Marseille-Esperence. All different, all Marseillais,* <http://www.diplomatie.gouv.fr/en/article_imprim.php3?id_article=6065>, viewed on 4 September 2009.

Kiminas, D. *The Ecumenical Patriarchate: A History of Its Metropolitanates with Annotated Hierarch Catalogs*, Wildeside Press, 2009.

Kinzl, K. *A Companion to the Classical Greek World*, Wiley-Blackwell, 2006.

Klingshirn, W. E. *Caesarius of Arles: Life, Testament, Letters,* Bk. 2. 25, Liverpool University Press, 1994.

Knight, J. *Roman France: an archaeological field guide*, Tempus Publishing, 2001.

Knight, K. (ed.), *Gennadius,* Supplement to De Viris Illustribis, ['New Advent'] <http://www.newadvent.org/fathers/2719.htm>, viewed on 1 September 2011.

Koch, J. C. *Celtic Culture: A Historical Encyclopaedia,* vol.1, AB.C. CLIO, 2006.

Kohn, G. C. *Encyclopaedia of Plague and Pestilence*, 3rd edition, Facts of File Books, 2008.

Kopan, A. T. *Greeks,* ['Encyclopaedia of Chicago'] <http://encyclopaedia.chicagohistory.org/pages/548.html>, viewed on 26 January 2011.

Kreis, S. *Lecture 20 Charlemagne and the Carolingian Renaissance*, ['History Guide'] <http://www.historyguide.org/ancient/lecture20b.html>, viewed on 21 December 2011.

Kyriakou, P. *A Commentary on Euripides' Iphigenia in Tauris*, Walter de Grutyer, 2006.

Lahanas, M. *Measurements*, <http://www.mlahanas.de/Greeks/Measurements.htm>, viewed on 30 October 2010.

Lahanas, M. *Names of the Greeks,* <http://www.mlahanas.de/Greeks/LX/NamesOfTheGreeks.html>, viewed on 30 December 2010.

Lahanas, M. *Theophrastus of Eresos: The Father of Botany and Ecology*, <http://www.mlahanas.de/Greeks/Theophrast.htm>, viewed on 7 September 2011.

Landuedoc-Rouchillon, Province France, *Agde,* ['Greek Travel Pages'] Princeton Encyclopaedia of Classical Sites, 1976, cited from the Perseus Project February 2006, <http://www.gtp.gr/LocInfo.asp?infoid=49&code=EFRZLR&PrimeCode=EFRZLR&Level=4&PrimeLevel=4&IncludeWide=0&LocId=14429>, viewed on 4 April 2011.

La Saussaye, L. de. *Numismatique de la Gaule narbonnaise*, BLUIS Beaureaide la Revue nusimatique, 1842.

Lasinski, K. *The History of Garlick: Nature's Ancient Superfood*, June 28, 2005, <http://www.googobits.com/articles/1167-the-history-of-garlic-natures-ancient-superfood.html>, viewed on 21 August 2011.

Larsen, H. R. *Alternative Medicines: Why so popular?* <http://www.yourhealthbase.com/alternative_medicine.html>, viewed on 22 December 2010.

Latouche, R. *Caesar to Charlemagne: the beginnings of France*, trans. J. Nicholson, Barnes & Noble, 1968.

Laugier, E. *Places of Worship in Marseille-studies representativeness in the city*, <http://www.coe.int/t/dg4/cultureheritage/heritage/identities/edifreligieux_EN.pdf>, viewed on 30 January 2011.

Laure, P. 'On a retrouvé les fils des Protis. Une etude sur le sang désigne les descendants direct des Phocéens', La Provence, Vendredi 22 Avril 2011, 22042011 *Journal La Provence*, p. 3. <http://www.scribd.com/doc/53641055/Journal-La-Provence-22042011>, viewed 10 February 2012.

Lawrence, A. W. *Greek Arms and Fortifications*, Oxford, 1979.

Lawson, J. C. *Modern Greek Folklore and Ancient Greek Religion: A Study in Survival*, Kessinger, 2003.

Lazenby, J. F. *Hannibal's War: a military history of the Second Punic War*, University of Oklahoma Press, 1998.

Lazenby, J. F. *The Peleponessian War: A military study*, Routledge, 2004.

Leach, J. *Pompey the Great*, Croom Helm, 1978.

Lee, A. D. *Information and Frontiers: Roman Relations in Late Antiquity*, Cambridge, 1993.

Lejay, P. 'Sidonius Apollinarius', *The Catholic Encyclopaedia,* vol. 13. New York: Robert Appleton Company, 1912, <http://www.newadvent.org/cathen/13778a.htm>, viewed on 17 December 2010.

Lendering, J. *Diadem,* ['Livius.org'] <http://www.livius.org/di-dn/diadem/diadem.html>, viewed on 20 August 2011.

Lendering, J. *Emporiae (Ampurias)*, ['Livius.org'] <http://www.livius.org/ei-er/emporiae/emporiae.html>, viewed on 1 August 2011.

Lendering, J. *Gaius Julius Caesar*, Part Six, Civil Wars (51-47), ['Livius.org'] <www.livius.org/caa-can/caesar/06.html>, viewed on 26 September 2010.

Lendering, J. *Hamilcar Barca,* ['Livius.org'], revised 17 July 2010, <http://www.livius.org/ha-hd/hamilcar/hamilcar2.html>, viewed on 25 August 2011.

Lendering, J. *Hecataeus of Miletus*, ['Livius.org'] <http://www.livius.org/he-hg/hecataeus/hecataeus.htm>, viewed on 7 September 2011.

Lendering, J. *Marcus Furius Camillus* (3) ['Livius.org'] <http://www.livius.org/fo-fz/furius/camillus2.html#Veii>, viewed on 26 October 2011.

Lendering, J. *Varronian Chronology*, ['Livius.org'], revised 6 November 2010, <http://www.livius.org/cg-cm/chronology/varro.html>, viewed 26 October 2011.

Les Grands Sites Archéologique, *Les Gaulois en Provence: L'oppidum d'Entremont*, <http://www.grands-sites-archeologiques.culture.fr/catalogue.php?id=18>, viewed on 21 August 2011.

Levi, P. 'Greek Dramas', chapter 7 in J. Boardman, J. Griffin and O. Murray (eds.), *Greece and the Hellenistic World*, Oxford University Press, 2001.

Lewis, A. R. *The Development of Southern French and Catalan Society 718-1050*, University of Texas Press, Austin, 1965.

Liberati, A. M., and Bourbon, F. *Splendours of the Roman World*, Thames & Hudson, 1996

Lieu, Samuel. N. C., and Montserrat, D., *From Constantine to Julian*, Routledge, 1996.

Life Expectancy, *Old age: Physiological effects*, ['Brittanica.com'] <http://www.britannica.com/EB.C.hecked/topic/340119/life-expectancy>, viewed on 22 December 2010.

Linder, D. O. *The Trail of Caius Verres: An Account*, ['umkc.edu'] <http://law2.umkc.edu/faculty/projects/ftrials/verres/verresaccount.html>, viewed on 4 November 2011.

Lindsay, W. M. *Isidore of Seville: The Etymologies (or Origins)*, vol. 15. 1. 63, Oxford University Press, 1911, ['Penelope, University of Chicago' digital library] <htpp://Penelope.uchicago.edu/Thayer/E/Roman/Texts/isidore/home.html>, viewed 26 December 2010.

Liversidge, J. *Everyday Life in the Roman Empire*, Batsford, 1976.

Löffler, K. 'Visigoths', *The Catholic Encyclopaedia,* vol. 15. New York: Robert Appleton Company, 1912, <http://www.newadvent.org/cathen/15476b.htm>, viewed 15 December 2010.

Lomas, K. 'Beyond Magna Graecia: Greeks and Non-Greeks in France, Spain and Italy' in K. Kinzl, (ed.), *A Companion to the Classical Greek World*, (Wiley-Blackwell, 2006):174-198.

Lomas, K. 'Hellenism, Romanization and Cultural Identity in Massalia', in K. Lomas (ed.), *Greek Identity in the Western Mediterranean: Papers in Honour of Professor Brian Shefton*, Brill, 2003, 475-498, p. 484, n. 34, P. Ghiron-Bistagne, 'Un autel Massiliotte de Zeus Patroos' in Bats, M. Marseille Greque et la Gaule, 152-4.

Lomas, K. *Roman Italy, 338 BC-AD 200: A sourcebook*, Routledge, 2004.

Lomas, K. *Rome and the Western Greeks 350 BC-AD 200: Conquest and Acculturation in Southern Italy*, Taylor & Francis e-Library, 2005.

Long, C. A. *The Chios Diaspora 1822-1899*, <http//:www.christopherlong.co.uk/per/chiosdiaspora.html>, viewed on 5 September 2010.

Long, G. *Penny Cyclopaedia of the Society for the Diffusion of Useful Knowledge*, vols. 13-14, Charles Knight & Co., London, 1839.

Longrigg, L. 'Anatomy in Alexandria in the Third Century B.C.', *The British Journal for the History of Science*, Vol. 24, No. 4 (Dec., 1988): 455-488, Published by: Cambridge University Press on behalf of the British Society for the History of Science, <http://www.jstor.org/stable/4026964>, viewed on 16 February 2010.

Lordkipandze, O. *Phasis: The River and City in Cholcis*, Steiner, 2000.

Lough, J. *France Observed in the Seventeenth Century by British Travellers*, Oriel Press, 1984.

Louth, A. 'Christology and Heresy' in L. James (ed.), *A Companion to Byzantium*, Wiley-Blackwell, (2010): 187-199.

Louth, A. *Greek East and Latin West: the Church, AD 681-1071*, St. Vladimir's Seminary Press, 2007.

Markham, Clements, Sir. 'Pytheas the Discoverer of Britain', Geographical Journal, June 1893, in V. Stefansson, *Great Adventures and Explorations*, Robert Hale Ltd., 1947.

Markham, C. R. 'Pytheas, the Discoverer of Britain', Geographical Journal, Blackwell Publishers on behalf of *The Royal Geographical Society* (with The Institute of British Geographers) vol. 1, no. 6 (Jun., 1893): 504-524, ['JSTOR' journal archive] <http://www.jstor.org/stable/1773964>, viewed on 25 August 2011.

MacDonald, C. *Cicero Pro Flacco*, 63-64, William Heinemann Publishers, 1977.

MacDonald, J. Middleton. *Massilia Carthago: Sacrifice Tablets of the Worship of Baal*, D. Nutt, 1897, reprint Kessinger, 2003.

MacKendrick, P. *Roman France*, G. Bell & Sons, 1971.

Magi, G. *Provence*, Bonechi, 2001.

Magnusson, M. *Vikings*, Book Club Associates, 1985.

Malkin, I. 'Exploring the validity of the concept of a "foundation": a visit to Megera Hyblaia' in V. B. Gorman, and E. W. Robinson, (eds.) *Oikistes: studies in constitutions, colonies and military power in the ancient world: offered in honour of A. J. Graham*, (Leiden, 2002): 195-225.

Mansi, J. D. (ed.), *Sacrorum Conciliorum Nova et Amplissima Collectio*, (Paris: H. Welter, 1901), vol. VIII, pp. 325, 329; reprinted in Roy C. Cave & Herbert H. Coulson, (eds.), *A Source Book for Medieval Economic History*, (Milwaukee: The Bruce Publishing Co., 1936; reprint ed., New York: Biblo & Tannen, 1965), pp. 280-281, <http://www.fordham.edu/halsall/source/506agdechurchslaves.html>, viewed on 4 April 2011.

Mansion, J. E. *Harrap's New Shorter French and Engish Dictionary*, Harrap, 1976.

Marus Terentius Varro, ['Encyclopaedia Britannica'] <http://www.britannica.com/EB.C.hecked/topic/623569/Marcus-Terentius-Varro>, viewed on 7 September 2011.

Marion, A. F., and Vasseur, M. G. *Annals of Musée D'Histoire Naturelle de Marseille foundateur*, TOM XII, Marseille, 1914.

Marsden, E. W. *Greek and Roman Artillery: Historical Development*, Oxford, 1969.

Marseille, <http://www.france-la-visite.com/english/heritage/marseille.html>, viewed on 1 September 2009.

Marseille (après 400 av. J-C.), obole au Lacydon et à la légende. R! R! Ref: 83195, ['Poinsignon Numismatique'] <http://www.poinsignon-numismatique.com/monnaie.asp?langue=fr&rubrique=&categorie=&periode=&catalogue=83195>, viewed 15 November 2010.

Marseille, Part 1. Marseilles, from Rome to France, <http://www.sagaplanet.com>, viewed on 4 September 2009.

Marseille, Part 2, <www.sagaplanet.com>, viewed on 4 September 2009.

Marseilles, ['1906 Jewish Encyclopedia'] <http://www.jewishencyclopedia.com/articles/10438-marseilles>, viewed 10 February 2012.

Marseille, *Uneasy Union with France*, ['Encyclopaedia Britannica'] <http://www.britannica.com/EB.C.hecked/topic/366460/Marseille/12518/Uneasy-union-with-France>, viewed on 5 September 2011.

Martin, Geoffrey. J. *All Possible Worlds: A History of Geographical Ideas*, Oxford, 2005.

Martin, T. R. *An Overview of Classical Greek History from Mycenae to Alexander, Athenian Empire in the Golden Age*, TRM OV 9, ['Perseus' Tufts university digital library] <http://www.perseus.tufts.edu/hopper/text?doc=Perseus%3Atext%3A1999.04.0009%3Achapter%3D9> viewed 21 May 2012.

Masson, P. (ed.), *Bouches du Rhône*, Vol. XIV, Marseille, 1935.

Mathisen, R. W. *Roman Aristocrats in Barbarian Gaul: strategies for survival in an age of transition*, University of Texas, 1993.

Mathisen. R. W. 'Julius Valerius Maiorianus'['De Imperatoribus Romanis'] < http://www.roman-emperors.org/major.htm> updated 7 February 1998, viewed 28 December 2012.

Matthews, J. *Heyele/Elea/Velia*, Around Naples Encyclopedia, ['University of Maryland University College' Italian Studies], entry July 2009, <http://ac-support.europe.umuc.edu/~jmatthew/naples/Velia.html>, viewed 7 January 2012.

Matyszak, P. *Classical Compendium*, Thames & Hudson, 2009.

Maurel, G. *Le Corpus des monnaies de Marseille et Provence, Languedoc Oriental et Vallée du Rhône 525-25 avant notre ère*, Omni, 2013.

McCabe, B., Harlaftis, G. and Minoglou, I. P., *Diaspora Entrepreneurial Networks: four centuries of History*, Berg, 2005.

McCormick, M, 'Byzantium and the West: 700-900' in R. McKitterick, (ed.), *New Cambridge Medieval History II*, 1995, pp. 349-380.

McDonald, N. *Lake District, A Megalithic Journey*, Megalithic Publishing, 2011.

McEvedy, C. *The Penguin Atlas of Ancient History*, Penguin Books, 1979.

McGee, S. 'Objective Burma', Director Raoul Walsh, Warner Brothers ['Turner Classic Movies Film Article'] <http://www.tcm.turner.com/this-month/article/25882|0/Objective-Burma-.html>, viewed on 6 January 2009.

McIntosh, J. *Handbook of Life in Prehistoric Europe*, Oxford, 2006.

McInerney, J. *The Folds of Parnassos: Land and Ethnicity in Ancient Phokis*, University of Texas Press, 1999.

Mee, C., and Spawforth, A. *Greece an Oxford Archaeological Guide*, Oxford, 2001.

Meijer, F. *A History of Seafaring in the Classical World*, Croom Helm, 1986.

Mehmed II, <http://www.mlahanas.de/Ottoman/MehmedII.html>, viewed on 14 February 2011.

Mercer, D. *Chronicle of the Twentieth Century*, Longman, 1998.

Mettam, R. *Government and Society in Louis XIV's France*, Macmillan Press, 1977.

Mikalson, D. *Ancient Greek Religion*, Blackwell, 2005.

Millar, F. *The Roman Republic in Political Thought*, Brandeis University Press/University Press of New England, 2002.

Miller, F. *A Greek Roman Empire: Power and Belief under Theodosius II (408-450)*, University of California Press, 2007.

Miller, M. *Athens and Persia in the 5th Century*, Cambridge, 2004.

Miller, Mary. K. 'Reading Between the Lines', *Smithsonian Magazine* March 2007, <http://www.smithsonianmag.com/science-nature/archimedes.html>, viewed on 12 February 2011.

Miller, W. *The Ottoman Empire 1801-1913*, Cambridge, 1913. <http://en.wikipedia.org/wiki/File:Rumelia_map.jpg>, viewed on 14 February 2011.

Mills, W. J. *Exploring Polar Frontiers: A Historical Encyclopaedia*, vol. 1, ABC-CLIO, 2003.

Milton, G. *Paradise Lost*, Sceptre, 2009.

Mitchell, S. *A History of the Later Roman Empire: The Transformation of the Ancient World*, Wiley-Blackwell, 2006.

Moliner, M. et al, *La nécropolie de Sainte-Barbe à Marseille*, (IVe s. av. J-C.–IIe s. ap. J-C.), Édisud, 2003.

Momigliano, A. *Alien Wisdom: The Limits of Hellenization*, Cambridge University Press, 1990.

Momigliano, A. *The Development of Greek Biography*, First Harvard University Press paperback edition, 1993.

'Monaco on the Mediterranean' in *The Illustrated Magazine of Art*, Vol. 3, No. 13 (1854): 49-51. ['JSTOR' journal archive] <http:www.jstor.org/stable/20538205>, viewed 19 July 2011.

Moore, F. G. *Livy*, vol. VII. Bk. XXVI. XIX. 7-13, Heinemann, 1943.

Morea, A. *La Perle Noire de la Méditerranée*, Éditions Milan, 1999.

Morel, J-P. 'Phocaean Colonisation' in G. R. Tsetskhladze (ed.), *Greek Colonisation: An Account of Greek Colonisation and Other Settlements Overseas*, vol. 1, (Leiden, 2006): 358-428.

Morganbludid, Iceland Review, 'Winter Solstice Celebrated in Iceland Today', *Daily News* article 21 December 2009, <http://icelandreview.com/icelandreview/daily_news/?ew_0_a_id=355697>, viewed on 30 August 2011.

Morrell, P. *A History of Homeopathy in Britain*, <http://www.homeopathyhome.com/reference/articles/ukhomhistory.shtml>, viewed on 22 December 2010.

Morris, S. P. 'Greeks and Barbarians–Linking with a wider world' in S. Alcock, and R. Osborne. (eds.), *Classical Archaeology*, Blackwell, 2007.

Moulin du Calanquet Saint-Rémy de Provence, A Family Story, <http://www.moulinducalanquet.fr/olive-oil/historique/historique-history-geschichte.html>, viewed on 2 September 2011.

Movie Review, 'Merrill's Marauders', *New York Times*, published June 14, 1962, <http://movies.nytimes.com/movie/review?res=9900E7DF163DE63BBC4C52DFB0668389679EDE>, viewed 12 January 2012.

Mund-Dopchie, M. 'Hanno' in V. Brown (ed.), *Catalogus Translationum Et Commentariorum: Medieval and Rennaisance Latin Translations and Commentaries, Annotated Lists and Guides*, Vol.3, The Catholic University Press of America, (2003):49-56.

Murray, A. C. *From Roman to Merovingian Gaul*, Broadview, 2000.

Murray, O. *Early Greece*, Fontana, 1993.

Nagle, Dr B. 'An Allied view of the Social War', *American Journal of Archaeology*, Vol. 77. No. 4. (Oct, 1973): 376-378, ['JSTOR' archive journal] <http://www.jstor.org/pss/503306>, viewed on 20 February 2012.

Nagy, G. *Poetry as Performance: Homer and Beyond*, Cambridge University Press, 1996.

Nasselrath, H-G. '"Where the Lord of the Sea Grants Passage to the Sailors through the Deep-Blue Mere No More:" The Greeks and the Western Seas', *Greece and Rome*, Second Series, Vol. 52. No. 2 (Oct 2005): 153-171. ['JSTOR' archive journal] <www.jstor.org/stable/3567866> viewed 6 April 212.

Nelson, M. *The Barbarians Beverage: A History of Beer in Ancient Europe*, Routledge, 2005.

Nelson, M., and Briggs, A., *Queen Victoria and the Discovery of the Riviera*, Tauris Parke Paperbacks, 2007.

Nesteroff, N. (ed.), *Istanbul*, Everyman, 2001.

Neville, M. *Stone Age village found under sea*, September 30, 2009, ['County Press online', Isle of Wight] http://www.iwcp.co.uk/news/news/stone-age-village-found-under-sea-28794.aspx, viewed 5 July 2012.

News, 'Celts Rule OK!', *Practical Archaeology*, Issue No.5 (Winter 2001/2).

Nickels, A. 'Les Sondages de la rue Perben à Agde (Hérault)' in Arcelin, P. Bats, M., Garcia, D., Marchand, G. and M. Schwaller, M., (eds.), *Sur les pas des Grecs en Occident',* Hommage de André Nickels, Collection Etudes Massaliètes, 4, (1995): 59-98.

Nickels, A., and Marchand, G., 'Recherches stratigraphiques ponctuelles a proximité des ramparts antiques d'Agde' in *Revue Archéologique de Narbonnaise*, vol. 9. (1976): 409-428. <http://www.persee.fr/web/revues/home/prescript/article/ran_0557-7705_1976_num_9_1_986>, viewed 25 February 2012.

Nicolet, C. *Space, Geography, and Politics in the Early Roman Empire*, University of Michigan, 1991.

Norwich, J. J. *Byzantium: The Decline and Fall,* Penguin, 1996.

Norwich, J. J. *The Popes: A History*, Chatto & Windus, 2011.

Nos Collections, *Les Vases en Bronze des Banquets Funéraries*, <http://www.musee-vix.fr/fr/index.php?page=38>, viewed on 11 November 2010.

Nüssli, C. *The Complete Tabula Peutingeriana–a Roman Road Map compared with a modern map*, <http://www.euratlas.net/cartogra/peutinger>, viewed on 1 September 2011.

Oblensky, D. *The Byzantine Commonwealth, Eastern Europe* 500–1453, Cardinal, 1974.

Obringer, L. A. *How Aphrodisiacs Work,* <http://science.howstuffworks.com/aphrodisiac3.htm>, viewed on 21 August 2011.

O'Connor, J. J., and Robertson, E. F., *Eudoxus of Cnidus*, ['School of Mathematics and Statistics', University of St. Andrews] <http://www-history.mcs.st-and.ac.uk/Biographies/Eudoxus.html>, viewed on 7 September 2011.

Olbia/Pomponiana, <http://www.arbre-celtique.com/encyclopedie/olbia-pomponiana-saint-pierre-de-l-almanarre-hyeres-5576.htm>, viewed 21 May 2011.

Olmos, R., and Tortosa, T., 'Appendix: The Case of the Lady of Elche: a Review Article' in G. R. Tsetskhladze (ed.), *Ancient Greeks West and East,* (Brill, 1999): 352-360.

Oliver, N. Episode 1 of 4, The Age of Iron, *A History of Ancient Britain*, BBC 2, Series Producer Cameron Balbime, [TV broadcast] October 2011, <http://www.bbc.co.uk/programmes/b0108tsq>, viewed 19 October 2011.

Osborne, R. *Classical Greece 500-323 B.C.* Oxford University Press, 2000.

Osborne, R. *Greece in the Making 1200–479 B.C.*, Routledge, 2008.

Osborne, R. 'Early Greek Colonization? The nature of Greek settlement in the West' in N. Fisher and H. van Wees (eds.), *Archaic Greece: new approaches and new evidence* (London, 1998): 251-269.

Orrieux, P., and Schmitt Pantel, P, *A History of Ancient Greece,* Blackwell, 1999.

Ostrogorsky, G. *History of the Byzantine State,* Blackwell, 1980.

Özyğit, Ö. '1994 Yili Phokaia Kazi Çalişmalan', *KAZI SONUÇLARI TOPLANTISI*, 17 Kazi 2, KÜLTÜR BANKANLIGI YAYINLARI/1811, (Ankara 1996):1-26.

Özyğit, Ö. 'Phocaean Horse and Griffon Protomes' in S. Bouffir and A. Hemary (eds.) *L'occident grec, de Marseille à Mégara Hyblaea*, (Centre Camille Jullian, 2013): 5-26.

Özyğit, Ö. 'Recent Work at Phokaia in the Light of Akurgal's Excavations', in *Anadolu/Anatolia* 25, (2003): 109-127, <http://dergiler.ankara.edu.tr/dergiler/14/715/9072.pdf>, viewed on 10 October 2011.

Page, T. E. *Martial's Epigrams,* vol. 2. Bk. XIII, cxxiii. Loeb,1961.

Palermo, J. A. 'The Latinity of Sicily', *Italica*, Vol. 30, No. 2, (Jun., 1953): 65-80. ['JSTOR' archive journal] <www.jstor.org/stable/477471>, viewed 24 May 2012.

Paris, E. *The Greeks of Marseille and Greek Nationalism*, 20 November 2000, <http://barthes.ens.fr/clio/revues/AHI/articles/English/pari.html>, viewed on 5 September 2010.

Parke, H. W. *Greek Oracles,* Hutchinson & Co Ltd, 1972.

Parke, H. W., and Wormell, D. E. W., *The Delphic Oracle,* vol. 1, Blackwell, 1956.

Parker, H. N. 'Greece, Rome and the Byzantine Empire' in L. R. Furst, (ed.), *Women Healers and Physicians*: *Climbing a Long Hill,* , University of Kentucky, 1997.

Parker, P. 'Greek Religion', in Boardman, J., Griffin, J. and Murray, O., (eds.), *Greece and the Hellenistic World*, Oxford University Press, 2001.

Parker Pearson, M. 'Secrets of the Stonehenge Skeletons', Channel 4, 8.00 pm [TV broadcast] 10 March 2013.

Parsinou, E. Shipley, G., and Salt, A., *Hellenizein: A Flexible Structure for Teaching Greek to Archaeologists and Ancient Historians*, The Subject Centre for History, Classics and Archaeology, The Higher Education Academy, 2004 (with corrections 2008), University of Leicester, ISBN 0 74929 6550, <http://www.heacademy.ac.uk/assets/hca/classics/featureResources/practicalAdvice/languageTeaching/Beginners/hellenizein_GS_final_with_ISBN_added_09122.pdf> viewed on 23 March 2012.

Pearce, S. M. 'Amber Beads from the late bronze-age hoard from Glentanar, Aberdeenshire'*,* in *Proceedings of the Society of Antiquaries Scotland*, Archaeology Data Service, University of York, vol. 108 (1976-7):124-129, <http://ads.ahds.ac.uk/catalogue/adsdata/arch-352-1/dissemination/pdf/vol_108/108_124_129.pdf>, viewed on 19 October 2011,

Peddie, J. *Hannibal's War*, Sutton Publishing, 2005.

Penhallurick, R. *Tin in Antiquity: Its Mining and Trade Throughout the Ancient World with Particular Reference to Cornwall*, Institute of Metals, 1986.

Pentzoupoulos, D. *The Balkan Exchange of Minorities and its Impact on Greece*, C. Hurst & Co., 2002.

Perowne, S. *Roman Mythology*, Hamlyn, 1969.

Phillips, G. *Alexander the Great Murder in Babylon,* Virgin Books, 2008.

Picard, I. 'L'iconographie religieuse sur le monnaies au type d'Auriol' in A. Hemary and H. Tréziny (eds.), *Les Cultes des citiés phocéennes*, (Centre Camille Jullian, 2000): 165-174.

Pickard-Cambridge, A. W. *Demosthenes,* G. P. Putnam's Sons, 1914.

Piggott, S., Daniels, G. and McBurney, C., (eds.), *France Before the Romans*, Thames & Hudson, 1973.

Pilgrim, Ancient wisdom for self-realisation, ['Tarot of Marseilles']
<http://www.legends-and-myths.com/40_1.cfm?f=8-legends-myths-tarot-marseilles>, viewed on 5 April 2011.

Pindar, ['Encyclopaedia Britannica'] <http://www.britannica.com/EB.C.hecked/topic/460865/Pindar>, viewed on September 2011.

Pillot, G. *The Secret Code of the Odyssey: Did the Greeks Sail the Atlantic?* trans. Francis Albert, Abelard-Schuman Ltd, 1972.

Platt, E. S. *Garlick, Onions and other Alliums*, Stackpole, 2003.

Poggioli, S. *Diverse Marseille Spared in French Riots*, ['NPR']
<http://www.npr.org/templates/story/story.php?storyId=5044219>, viewed on 5 September 2011.

Pohle, J. 'Actual Grace', Semipelagianism, *The Catholic Encyclopaedia,* vol. 6. New York: Robert Appleton Company, 1909, <http://www.newadvent.org/cathen/06689x.htm>, viewed on 3 December 2010.

Porter, C. *A Guide to Greek Thought*, Belknap Press of Harvard University, 2003.

Pope, H. 'St. Mary Magdalen', *The Catholic Encyclopaedia,* vol. 9, New York: Robert Appleton Co., 1910, <www.newadvent.org/cathen/09761a.htm>, viewed on 15 September 2009.

Popper, Karl R, Sir. *The World of Parmenides:Essays on the Presocratic Enlightenment*, Routledge, 2007.

Press Document, ['Juno Beach Centre'] <http://www.junobeach.org/Centre/pdf/jbc_press_document_2010.pdf>, viewed on 9 November 2010.

Price, S. 'The History of the Hellenistic Period', Ch. 13., in J. Boardman, J. Griffin, and O. Murray, (eds.), *Greece and the Hellenistic World*, Oxford University Press, 2001.

Profile: Sir Keith Park, ['BBC News'] <http://news.bbc.co.uk/1/hi/uk/7837196.stm>, viewed on 10 August 2011.

Provence, ['The 1911 Classic Encyclopaedia'] <http://www.1911Encyclopaedia.org/Provence>, viewed on 29 September 2009.

Puig, A. M., and Martin, A., (Coordinadores), *La colònia grega de Rhode (Roses, Alt Empordà),* Serie Monongrafica 23, Museu d'Arqueológia de Catalunya Girona, 2006.

Quesada-Sanz, F. 'From Quantity to Quality: wealth, status and prestige in the Iberian Iron Age' in D. Bailey (ed.). *The Archaeology of Value*, BAR IS 730. (1998), Oxford, pp. 70-96.

Rayssiguier. G., and Guichard, C., 'Baou de Saint-Marcel' in *Voyage en Massalie: 100 ans d'archéologie en Gaule du sud*, Catalogue de l'exposition, (Musées de Marseille/Édisud, 1990):46-53.

Rawson, E. *Cicero: a portrait*, Allen Lane, 1975.

Rahak, P., and Younger, J. G., *Imperium and Cosmos Augustus and the Northern Campus Martius*, The University of Wisconsin Press, 2006.

Reille, J-L. (2001)–'L'importation des meules domestiques dans la fortresse grecque d'Olbia (Hyères, Var) entre le IIe s. av. n. è. et le Haut Empire', *Documents d'archéologie méridionale*, n° 24, p. 207-211, <http://dam.revues.org/docannexe1161.html>, viewed on 21 May 2011.

Renfrew, C., and Bahn, P. G., *Archaeology: Theories, Methods and Practice*, Thames and Hudson Ltd., 1996.

Renouard, M. *Wonderful Finistère*, trans. A. Moyon, Éditions Ouest-France, 1988.

Reuter, R. (ed.), *The New Cambridge Medieval History: c. 900-c. 1024.* Vol. III, Cambridge University Press, 1999.

Rickard, J. (4 July 2007), *Seleucus I Nicator (358-280)*, <http://www.historyofwar.org/articles/people_seleucus_I_nicator.html>, viewed on 20 September 2011.

Richard, J-C., and Chevillon, J-A. *Du Lacydon á Massalia, les émissions grecques en Gaule du Vème siècle av. J.-C.* pp. 295-302. <http://www.mcu.es/museos/docs/MC/ActasNumis/Du_Lacydon_Massalia.pdf>, viewed on 21 February 2011.

Richardson. J. S. *Hispaniae: Spain and Development of Roman Imperialism 218 - 82 B.C.* Cambridge University Press, 2004.

Richardson, L. Jnr., *A New Topographical Dictionary of Rome*, John Hopkins University Press, 1992.
Riddle, J. M. (ed.), *Tiberius Gracchus: Destroyer or Reformer of the Republic,* D.C. Heath & Co, 1970.

Rihill, T. 'War, Slavery and Settlement in Early Greece' in J. Rich, and G. Shipley, (eds.), *War and Society in the Greek World*, London, 1993, p. 77-107.

Rivet, A. L. F. *Gallia Narbonensis*, Batsford, 1988.

Rivet, A. L. F., and Smith, C., *The Place-Names of Roman Britain*, B. T. Batsford Ltd, 1982.

Roberts, M. *The Ancient World*, Macmillan Education Ltd, 1979.

Robertson, D. S. *Greek and Roman Architecture*, Cambridge, 1969.

Robinson, J. *Archaeologica Graeca or the Antiquities of Greece*, Baldwin, Cradock and Joy, 1827, 1 note c. <http://books.google.co.uk/books?id=P-LQzMJWs0QC&pg=PA1&lpg=PA1&dq=Athenians+wore+golden+grasshoppers?&source=bl&ots=N_KxvAK7Me&sig=hxxXLSeIEVjNJQmqdKwUFmbKYxw&hl=en&sa=X&ei=Yy2uT8qvFM2p8AP8s-iKCQ&ved=0CDcQ6AEwAg#v=onepage&q=Athenians%20wore%20golden%20grasshoppers%3F&f=false> viewed 12 May 2012.

Rohlfs, G. 'Greek Remnants in Southern Italy' in *The Classical Journal*, vol. 62, no. 4 (Jan., 1967): 164-169, The Classical Association of the Middle West and South, ['JSTOR' journal archive] <http://www.jstor.org/stable/3295569>, viewed on 30 December 2010.

Roller, D. W. *Through the Pillars of Herakles:Greco-Roman Exploration of the Atlantic*, Routledge, 2006.

Romanus, C. F., and Sunderland, R. *Stilwell's Command Problems*, R. Greenfield, (ed.), United States Army in World War II, China-Burma-India Theatre, Centre of Military History Publications, 1987, p. 169-170, ['Sribd'] <http://www.scribd.com/doc/48337542/Stillwell-s-Command-Problems>, viewed 4 June 2012.

Rostovtzeff, M. I., *Social and Economic History of the Hellenistic World*, vol.1, Oxford, 1941.

Rostovtzeff, M. I., *The Social and Economic History of the Roman Empire*, vol. 2, Chapter IX, Clarendon, 1963.

Rouillard, P. 'Greeks in the Iberian Peninsula', in M. Dietler, and C. Lopez-Ruiz, (eds.), *Colonial Encounters in Ancient Iberia: Phoenicians, Greek, and Indigenous Relations*, (University of Chicago Press, 2009): 131-154.

Rowland, Jnr. R. J., 'The Significance of Massilia in Lucan', *Hermes*, vol. 97, no. 2 (1969): 204-208. ['JSTOR' journal archive] <http://www.jstor.org/stable/4475586>, viewed on 17 November 2009.

Runciman, S. *The Fall of Constantinople 1453*, Cambridge, 1969.

Sabin, P. A. G. van Wees, Hans., and Whitby, M. (eds.), *The Cambridge History of Greek and Roman Warfare, vol. 1: Greece, the Hellenistic World, the Rise of Rome*, Cambridge, 2007, p. 232.

Sache I., and Vagnat, P. (199), *Early records of the flag, Marseille*, 8 July 2004, source Louis de Bresc, Amorial des Communes de Provence, 1866, <http://www.crwflags.com/fotw/flags/fr-13-ms.html>, viewed on 1 September 2009.

Sache, I, *Provence, Traditional province, France*, 2003, source Louis de Bresc, *Amorial des Communes de Provence*, 1886 [bjs94] <http://flagspot.net/flags/fr-prove.html>, viewed on 1 September 2009.

Sage, Michael M. *Roman Conquests: Gaul*, Pen & Sword Books Ltd, 2011.

Sahan, T. 'Council of Agde', *The Catholic Encyclopaedia*, vol. 1. New York: Robert Appleton Company, 1907, <http://www.newadvent.org/cathen/01206b.htm>, viewed 2 April 2011.

Samuel, L. *Rich: The Rise and Fall of American Wealth Culture*, Amacom, 2009.

Sanmartí, J. 'Colonial Relations and Social Change in Iberia' in M. Dietler and C. Lopez-Ruiz, (eds.), *Colonial Encounters in Ancient Iberia: Phoenicians, Greek, and Indigenous Relations*, (University of Chicago Press, 2009): 49-90.

Santrot, J. *Le Trésor de Garonne:IIe siècle après Jesus Christ*, [catalogue de l'exposition] 'Des monnaies dans la "grave"', Musées departmentaux de Loire-Atlantique, 1987.

Sartiaux, Felix. *PHOKAIA 1913-20*, ΡΙΖΑΡΕΙΟ/ΔΡΥΜΑ, KALLIMAGES, 2008.

Schamiloglou, U. 'The Rise of the Ottoman Empire: The Black Death in Medieval Anatolia and its Impact on Turkish Civilization' in N. Yavari, L. G. Potter., and J-M. R. Oppenheim, (eds.), *Views from the Edge: Essays in Honour of R. W. Bulliet*, (Columbia University Press, 2004): 255-279.

Scheidel, W., Morris, I. and Saller, R. P., *Cambridge Economic History of the Greco-Roman World*, Cambridge, 2007.

Scheidel, W. *The Roman Slave Supply*, [Princeton/Stanford Working Papers in Classics] (May 2007): 1-22, <http://www.princeton.edu/~pswpc/pdfs/scheidel/050704.pdf> viewed on 10 November 2011.

Scholtz, B. W. (ed.), *Carolingian Chronicles: Royal Frankish Annals and Nithard's Histories*, trans. B. Rogers, Ann Arbor, 1972.

Scott, W. *Terror and Repression in Revolutionary Marseilles*, Macmillan Press, 1973.

Scullard. H. H. *A History of the Roman World 753-146 B.C.*, Routledge 1991.

Seager, A., and Treanor, A. 'Mervyn King Launches Blistering Attack on £1tn Banks Bailout', *The Guardian*, article date 21 October 2009 <http://www.guardian.co.uk/business/2009/oct/21/mervyn-king-attack-banks-bailout>, viewed on 5 December 2010.

Seager, R. *Pompey the Great*, Blackwell, 2003.

Seltman, C. *Greek Coins*, Methuen & Co. Ltd, 1960.

Seltman, C. *The Twelve Olympians and Their Guests*, Max Parrish & Co., 1956.

Setton, K. M. *The Papacy and the Levant 1204–1571*, vol. 2, The American Philosophical Society, 1978, reprinted 1997.

Severin, T. *The Jason Voyage: A Quest for the Golden Fleece*, Simone & Schuster, 1986.

Shefton, B. B. 'Massalia and colonization in the North-Western Mediterranean' in G. R. Tsetskhladze and F. de Angis., (eds.), *The Archaeology of Greek Colonization* (Oxford, 1994): 61-86.

Shepherd, W. R. *Historical Atlas*, New York, Henry Holt and Company, 1911, ['Shadowed Realm, Political Medieval Maps'] <http://www.shadowedrealm.com/maps/political/view/the_byzantine_empire_1265>, viewed on 12 January 2012.

Shotter, D. *The Roman Frontier in Britain: Hadrian's Wall, The Antonine Wall and Roman Policy in the North*, Carnegie Publishing, 1996.

Shuckburgh, E. S. *The Histories of Polybius*, vol. 2. XXI. 6, Macmillan, 1884.

Shuey, E. 'Underwater Survey and Excavations at Gravisca, The Port of Tarquinia', *Papers from the British School of Rome*, (vol. 49. 1981):17-45, ['JSTOR' journal archive] <http://www.jstor.org/pss/40310871>, viewed on 17 January 2012.

Sivan, H. *Galla Placidia: The Last Roman Empress*, Oxford, 2011.

Smail, Daniel. Lord. *Imaginary Cartographies: possession and identity in late medieval Marseille*, Cornwell University Press, 2000.

Smith, Christine. A. 'Plagues from Athens to Justinian (mid-sixth century)', *Plague in the Ancient World: A Study from Thucydides to Justinian*, <http://marathon.uwc.edu/academics/departments/political_science/IGS_AIDSinAFRICA/Justinianplague.htm#45>, viewed on 4 April 2011.

Smith, S. C. *Reassessing Suez 1956: new perspectives on the crisis and its aftermath*, Ashgate Publishing Ltd., 2008.

Smith, Dr W. *A Smaller History of Rome*, John Murray, 1884.

Smith, W. *A Dictionary of Greek and Roman Antiquities*, John Murray, London, 1875.

Sosigenes of Alexandria, ['Encyclopaedia Britannica''] <http://www.britannica.com/EB.C.hecked/topic/555018/Sosigenes-of-Alexandria>, viewed on 7 September 2011.

Softas-Nall, B. 'Reflections on Forty Years of Family Thearapy: Research and Systemic Thinking in Greece, in K. S. Ng. (ed.), *Global Perspectives in Family Therapy: Practice, Development and Trends*, Brunner-Routledge, (2003):126-147.

Spain is Culture, *Treasure from the Neapolis, Ampurias*, [Ministerio de Culture] <http://www.spainisculture.com/en/obras_de_excelencia/tesoro_neapolis_ampurias.html>, viewed 7 December 2011.

Spekke, A. *The Ancient Amber Routes and Geographical Discovery of the Eastern Baltic*, M. Goppars Publishers, Stockholm, 1957.

Spufford, P. *Money and its use in Medieval Europe*, Cambridge, 1989.

Stefani, E. *Magic of Amber: amulets and jewellery from Magna Graecia and Macedonia*, University Studio Press, 2009.

Stefansson, V, *Great Adventurers and Explorations: from the earliest times to the present, as told by the explorers themselves*, Robert Hale Ltd., 1947.

Stefansson, V. *Ultima Thule*, George Harrap & Co., 1942.

Stern, Dr D. P. *Latitude and Longitude*, [From Stargazers to Starships], last updated 9-17-2004, <http://www-istp.gsfc.nasa.gov/stargaze/Slatlong.htm>, viewed on 20 October 2011.

Stesichorus, ['Encyclopaedia Britannica'] <http://www.britannica.com/EB.C.hecked/topic/565868/Stesichorus>, viewed on 7 September 2011.

Stewart, A. *Classical Greece and the Birth of Western Art*, Cambridge, 2008.

Stilwell, R. et al (eds.), *Princeton Encyclopaedia of Classical Sites*, (Princeton University Press, 1976), ['Perseus, Tufts University' digital library] <http://www.perseus.tufts.edu/hopper/text?doc=Perseus:text:1999.04.0006:id=lesbos>, viewed on 10 October 2011.

Sturges, F. 'The good, the bad and wildly bitchy', *The Independent*, 24 January 2011, <http://www.independent.co.uk/arts-entertainment/tv/features/the-good-the-bad-and-the-wildly-bitchy-2192378.html>, viewed on 7 September 2011.

Summerer, L. *Indigenous Responses to Encounters with the Greeks in Northern Anatolia: The Reception of Architectural Terracottas in the Iron age Settlements of the Halys Basin*, pp. 263-286, <http://www.pontos.dk/publications/books/bss-8-files/bss-8-14-summerer>, viewed on 10 September 2011.

Summers, D. *No Return to Boom and Bust: what Brown said when he was Chancellor*, published 11 September 2008. <http://www.guardian.co.uk/politics/2008/sep/11/gordonbrown.economy>, viewed on 29 September 2010.

Summerville, C. *Who Was Who at Waterloo: A Biography of the Battle*, Longman, 2007.

Swallow, C. *The Sick Man of Europe: Ottoman Empire to Turkish Republic 1789-1923*, Ernest Benn Ltd., 1973.

Syme, R. 'The Date of Justin and the Discovery of Trogus', *Historia Zeitschrift fur Alte Geschichte*, (vol. 37, No. 3 (3rd Qtr., 1988): 358-371, [JSTOR' journal archive] <http:www.jstor.org/stable/4436062>, viewed 28 March 2011.

Szczepanski, K. *Invention of Paper*, ['About.com'] <http://asianhistory.about.com/od/chineseinventions/p/Invention-of-Paper.htm>, viewed on 28 June 2012.

Tang, B. *Delos, Carthage, Ampurias: the housing of three Mediterranean trading centres*, L'Erma di Bretschneider Rome, 2005.

Taranto, Region Puglia (Apulia), Italy, <http://www.italyworldclub.com/puglia/taranto/taranto.htm>, viewed on 10 August 2010.

Tanriver, C. 'Some New Texts Recording Occupations' in *Epigraphica Anatolica*, (Heft 18, 1991):79-90, Epigraphica Anatolica 17-20, 1991-92, Dr R. Halbelt, GMBH, Bonn.

Taylor, J. J. *Bronze Age Goldwork of the British Isles*, Cambridge, 1980.

Taylor, L. TED Case Studies Number 723, 2004, *Ouzo, Trade and Culture*, <http://www1.american.edu/TED/ouzo.htm>, viewed on 5 September 2011.

The Coinage of Julius Caesar, *Catalogue*, ['Macquarie University'] <www.humanities.mq.edu.au?acans/Caesar/Catalogue.htm>, viewed on 29 August 2011.

The Homer Multitext, Homer Multitext: Scholia Inventory, C. Dué and M. Ebbott, (eds.), ['The Centre for Hellenic Studies'] <http://pinakes.hpcc.uh.edu/scholinv/> viewed 29 March 2012.

The Numismatics of Celtic Warriors, (HCRI 19), Sear, D. R. *The History of Coinage of the Roman Imperators 49-27 B.C.* Spink, London, 1998, <http://www.kernunnos.com/culture/warriors/>, viewed on 29 August 2011.

The origins of coinage, ['The British Museum'] <http://www.britishmuseum.org/explore/themes/money/the_origins_of_coinage.aspx>, viewed on 21 November 2010.

Theodorescu, D. and Treziny, H. 'Le chapiteau ionique archaïque de Marseille' in A. Hemary and H. Tréziny (eds.), *Les Cultes des citiés phocéennnes*, (Centre Camille Jullian, 2000): 135-146.

Thomas, J. *The Universal Dictionary of Biography and Mythology*, vol.1, Cosimo, 2009.

Thompson, M. Morkholm, O., and Kraay, C. M. *An Inventory of Greek Coin Hoards*, The American Numismatic Society, New York, 1973.

Thomson, J. O. *History of Ancient Geography*, Cambridge, 1948.

Time Team 2002, Channel 4 TV, *Yaverland, Isle of Wight,* 24 March. <http://www.channel4.com/history/microsites/T/timeteam/yaver_dig.html>, viewed on 23 October 2010.

Torelli, M. 'Greek Artisans and Etruria: A problem concerning the relationship between two cultures', *Archaeological News* 5, Dept. of Classics, Florida State University, (1976), 134–8.

Toynbee, A. *The Greeks and their Heritage,* Oxford, 1981.

Tozer, H. F. *History of Ancient Geography*, Biblo-Moser, 2nd edition, 1965.

Travel in Gallia Narbonensis, School District of Clermont-Ferrand, <www.musagora.education.fr/voyages/provence-en/agde-en.htm>, viewed 2 April 2011.

Treasure, G. R. R. *The Making of Modern Europe 1648-1780,* Methuen, 1985.

Trésor de Vix, *Âge de Fer,* ['Musée du Pays Châtillonais' Nos collections] <http://www.musee-vix.fr/fr/>, viewed on 11 November 2010.

Trevelyan, G. M. *History of England*, Longman Green & Co., 1947.

Uhalde, K. 'Quasi-Imperial Coinage of Merovingian Provence' in R. W. Mathisen and D Shauzer, (eds.), *Society and Culture in Late Antique Gaul,* Ashgate, 2001.

Urbainczyk, T. *Slave Revolts in Antiquity,* University of California Press, 2008.

Urdahl, L. B. *Foreigners in Athens: A study of grave monuments*, (4563, 1924), The University of Chicago, 1959.

Ussher, J. *The Annals of the World,* Master Books, 2003.

Valavanis, P. *Games and Sanctuaries in Ancient Greece,* trans. Dr David Hardy, Kapon Editions, 2004.

Valencia Cathedral, *The Holy Chalice Chapel*, <http://www.catedraldevalencia.es/en/el-santo-caliz_lacapilla.php>, viewed on 3 September 2011.

Vasilev, A. A. *History of the Byzantine Empire 324-1453*, The University of Wisconsin Press, 1952.

Vauchez, A. (ed.), *Encyclopaedia of the Middle Ages,* vol. 2, James Clarke & Co., 2000.

Venning, T. (ed.), *A Chronology of the Byzantine Empire*, Palgrave Macmillan, 2006.

Vento, M. *One Thousand Years of Chinese Footbinding: Its Origins, Popularity and Demise*, <http://academic.brooklyn.cuny.edu/core9/phalsall/studpages/vento.html>, viewed on 22 October 2010.

Vermes, G., Millar, F. and Black, M., *The History of the Jewish People in the age of Jesus Christ,* vol. 1. T&T Clark, 1973.

VerMeulen, E. 'Delphi, The Tholos of Athena Pronaia', Coastal Carolina University, <http://www.coastal.edu/ashes2art/delphi2/marmaria/tholos_temple.html> viewed on 31 December 2012

Vèrzone, P. *From Theodoric to Charlemagne,* Methuen & Co. Ltd., 1968.

Villing, A., and Mollër, A., *Naukratis: Greek Diversity in Egypt*, The British Museum, 2006.

Vinci, F. *The Baltic Origins of Homer's Epic Tales: The Odyssey and the Migration of Myth,* Inner Traditions Bear & Co., 2006.

Vinogradskaya, A. *The Mystery of the Byzantine Library,* <http://www.richarddoetsch.com/the_kremlin_and_its_secrets> viewed 17 January 2014.

Vlachos, G. *Bizarre Events of the Ancient Olympic Games,* Epimelia S. A. Kallipoleos str.28 A, GR 10444, Athens.

Vlassopoulos, K. 'Greek Slavery: From Domination to Property and Back Again' in *Journal of Hellenic Studies,* 131 (2011):115-130.

Voldman, S. H. *ESD: physics and devices,* John Wiley & Sons Ltd, 2004.

Waldman, C. and Mason, C. *Encyclopaedia of European Peoples,* Facts on File, 2006.

Waley, A. 'The Chinese Cinderella Story', *Folklore,* vol. 58, no. 1 (Mar., 1947): 226-238, published by: Taylor & Francis, Ltd., on behalf of Folklore Enterprises, Ltd., ['JSTOR' journal archive] <http://www.jstor.org/stable/1256703>, viewed on 22 October 2010.

Wallbank, F. W. *A Historical Commentary on Polybius,* (3 vols.), Oxford 1959-1979.

Watson, W. J. *The History of Celtic Place Names in Scotland,* Williams Blackwood & Sons Ltd, 1926.

Whittow, M. *The Making of Orthodox Byzantium 600-1025,* Palgrave, 1996.

Wilson, J-P. 'The nature of Greek overseas settlements in the archaic period: emporion or apoikia?' in L. Mitchell and P. J. Rhodes (eds.), *The development of the polis in archaic Greece,* (London, 1997): 199-207.

Williams, J. H. C. *Beyond the Rubicon: Romans and Gauls in Republican Italy,* Oxford, 2001.

Williams, N., and Le Nevez, C., *Provence and the Cote d'Azur,* Lonely Planet Publications, 2010.

Wintemitz, Maurice., Wintemitz, Monz. and Srinivasa Sarma, V., *A History of Indian Literature,* vol. 1. Motila Banarsidass Publishers, 2003.

Wiesehöfer, J. *Hecataeus of Miletus,* ['Encyclopaedia Iranica'], last updated 15 December 2003, <http://www.iranicaonline.org/articles/hecataeus-of-miletus>, viewed on 13 January 2012.

Wolfson, S. *Reassessment of Vocabulary and Sense,* <http://myweb.tiscali.co.uk/fartherlands/vocabulary.html> viewed 22 February 2013.

Woodhead, A. G. *The Greeks of the West,* Thames & Hudson, 1962.

Woolf, G. *Becoming Roman: the origins of provincial civilization in Gaul,* Cambridge University Press, 1998.

Woolf, G. 'Becoming Roman, Staying Greek: culture, identity and the civilising process in the Roman east' in *Proceedings of the Cambridge Philisophical Society,* 40 (1994): 116-43.

Wright, F. A. *Lempriere's Classical Dictionary,* Routledge & Keegan Paul, 1951.

Wyke, M. *Caesar,* Granta Books, 2007.

Zacher, E. M. 'The Recent "Discovery" of the Legendary Atlantis, Truth or Fiction?' *The Epoch Times,* April 17, 2011, <http://www.theepochtimes.com/n2/science/the-recent-discovery-of-the-legendary-atlantis-truth-or-fiction-54862.html>, viewed on 15 December 2011.

Figure 103. Left to right: first is estimated between late 3rd to early 2nd century B.C. Massalia AE struck bronze found in Kent, UK: at Tilmanstone, laureate Apollo/bull facing right, above Greek letters ΜΑ[Σ]: and Minster-in-Thanet, laureate Apollo/bull facing right, above Greek letters ΜΑΣ. Courtesy of David Holman.

Figure 104.
Greek Corinthian helmets 6th century B.C. dredged up from the: Guadalquivir estuary Huelva, Spain. Front and side view, Museo Arqueológico Nacional, Madrid, Spain <http://ceres.mcu.es/pages/Main>: and (below) from the Ria Huelva, Academia de la Historia-Collecion Madrid, copyright <www.superstock.co.uk>.

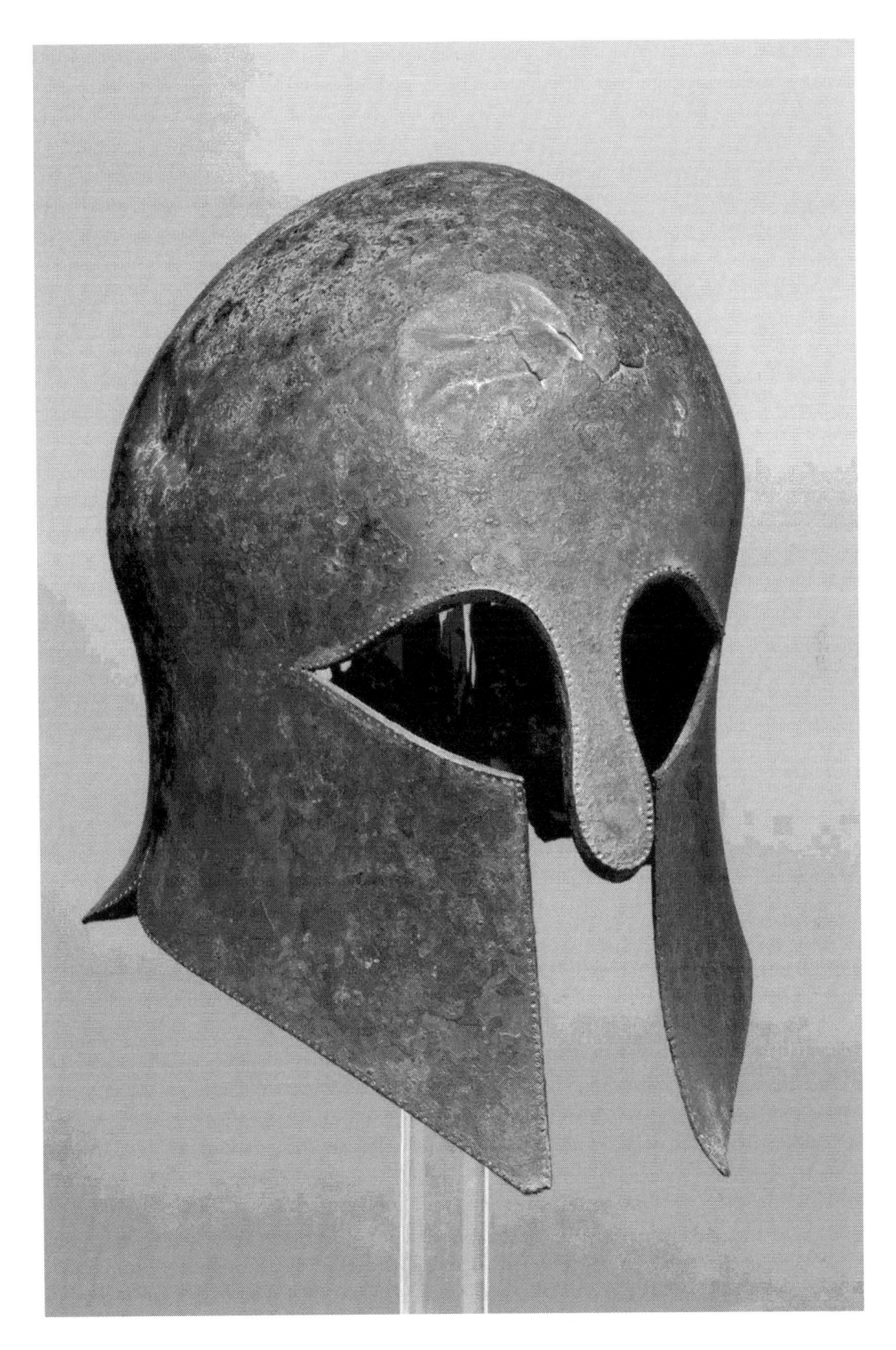

Figure 105.
Greek Corinthian bronze helmet 6th century B.C. found in a grave in Baux-de-Provence, France. By permission of: D. Garcia, 'Le casque corinthien des Baux-de-Provence' in S. Bouffir and A. Hemary (eds.) *L'occident grec, de Marseille à Mégara Hyblaea*, (Centre Camille Jullian, 2013): 85-90.

Index

Aelian: Fishing, 147; Homer, 149; Hyperboreans, 184

Africans: Phocaean coins, 47

Agde: (Agathe Tyche), 87; Arabs, 300; Boson, 303; city walls, 305; Council of, 291; Count Apollonius, 302; L'Éphèbe d'Agde, 88; plagues, 308; School of Hydrography, 316; Sever, 290

Agroitas: Massalia school, 271

Albici: ally of Massalia, 53, 137, 141, 251, 255, 256

Aléria: city, 79; foundation, 24, 151; Phocaean refugees, 29, 47

Alexander the Great, 331; bronze statue, 89; Chapter 9, 203; coin, 176; Daniel's prophecy, 288; Delphic oracle, 330; Polybius, 213; Pytheas, 273

Alexandria, 56, 149, 204, 212, 222, 278, 296, 307, 318, 319, 328, 332-333, 336-337, 344

Amber: Abulus the Amber Island, 195; Argo, 132; Baltic, 165; Britain, 165; Gaul, 36; Halstatt burial, 45; Herodotus, 169; Massalia, 81; Provence, 94; route, 171, 177; trade, 169; route, 166, 172; Thales, 198

Ammianus Marcellinus: Grecian Alps, 84; Massalia, 3, 18, 285; River Rhone, 285

Amphorae: Massalia, 38, 44, 47

Antibes, 79, 84, 124-129, 135, 147, 151, 171, 237, 310, 317, 331-332, 334

Antiochus of Syracuse, 25

Apollo: Agde emblema, 94; Avignon coins, 83; Britain, 181, 183, 186; British coins, 62, 175; Delphi, 26; Delphinian, 20, 24; Gravisca, 78; Massalia, 36; Massalia coins, 61; Massalia temple, 28; Olbia coins, 123; Roman dedication, 225; Samnagenses coins, 136

Apollonides, 257; commander of Massalia, 137, 257, 268; inscription, 270, 281

Apulia: Byzantines, 295; surviving Greek population, 278; ware, 126

Arctic Circle: circle of the Bear, 166; Iceland, 191; Pytheas, 193

Argathonius: king, 154

Aristotle: alcohol, 187; amber, 198; eastern ocean, 204; Isocrates, 51; Massalia, 329; Massalia's constitution, 137, 138; Parmenides, 26; Pytheas, 222

Aristoxenus of Tarentum: Massalia, 26, 29

Arles, 45, 47, 49, 82, 96, 133, 136, 150, 270, 272, 285, 288-290, 296-299, 301-304, 309, 317; Avignon inscription, 82; Bishop of Massalia, 286; Byzantine ships, 295; Caesarius, 96, 290, 291; Constantine, 284; Council of, 285; foundation, 82; Greek doctors, 55; Greek language, 292; Holy Roman Empire, 307; King Guntrum, 292; Literary circles, 289; Lombards, 294; Merovingian kings, 292; Roman enclave, 289; Saracens, 301; Siege of Massalia, 254, 255; Sixth Legion, 265, 267; Theline, 133; Theodoric, 291; Visigoths, 288, 289

Artemis: amber, 197; Aspasia, 49; Britain, 185; Caesar's victory coins, 266; Celtic coins, 176; Emporion temple, 97; Ephesian, 19, 21, 23; Hemeroscopium temple, 116; Massalia, 36; Massalia coins, 48, 61, 175; Massalia temple, 28, 241; Olbia temple, 119; Spain, 132, 229; Xoanon, 19, 226

Athenopolis, 135, 265, 270, 277

Atlantic, 1, 85, 164, 169, 172-173, 203-205, 209, 211-213, 217, 220, 222, 224, 274, 333, 417, 541; Alexander the Great, 205; Carthaginians, 169; Euthymenes, 152; Gades, 201; Greeks, 168, 190; Hercules, 204; Herodotus, 167; Himilco, 176; Massalia, 45, 151; Odysseus, 169; Pytheas, 140, 153, 208, 274; route, 88, 173, 199; Spain, 173; Tartessus, 154, 167

Avignon, 150; fortress city, 292; Greek coins, 83; Holy Roman Empire, 307; Massalia, 82, 133; Sigibert, 292

Battle of Aeginta, 237
Battle of Alalia, 24, 26, 47, 79, 141, 220
Battle of Aquae Sextiae, 37, 241
Battle of Frioul, 255
Battle of Lade, 48
Battle of Tauroention, 256, 258-259, 265, 268
Battle of the Ebro, 12, 116, 141, 233, 250; Massalia, 3
Belerion, 180-181, 185, 186, 195, 198, 217
Bourges, 37, 45, 49
Brittany, 44, 175-177, 179-181, 199-200, 218-220, 242, 246, 327
Brutus: Lucius Junius, 226; Massalia, 118, 141, 254-256, 264-265
Byzantine: Arles, 302; capital moved to Syracuse, 299; Charlemagne, 300; Childebert, 294; coins, 298; Gundovald, 294; identity, 295; Massalia iconoclast, 293; navy, 302; Normans, 299, 304; pope, 299; revival, 305; Taranto, 299

Calabria: Byzantines, 295; Italy, 299; Rhegium, 26; surviving Greek population, 278
Callanish, 184
Cape Kabion, 176
Carthage: Alexander the Great, 204-205, 207-208; bans study of Greek, 227; boundary with Cyrene, 335; destroyed, 211; foundation, 167; Greeks in Spain, 229; Hannibal, 250; independent, 167; Massalia, 228; occupies Ibiza, 168; Persian navy, 168; Roman treaty, 226, 238; Saguntum, 230; Sicily, 171; tablet, 168; Vandals, 293

Castrum Marselinum, 135
Charmis: doctor of Massilia, 248
Charmis of Massilia: scholar, 149
Chios, 25, 47, 49, 239, 305, 312, 318, 319
Cicero: Aristo of Massilia, 241; Cataline, 244; civil war, 266; Fulvia, 245; Massalia, 7, 235, 267; Massilia, 9, 10, 138, 151, 245, 267; Scipio Asiaticus, 243; Verres, 243; wine tax, 238
Claudius: emperor, 55, 199, 248, 250
Clodius, 244, 245
Coins: Antibes, 125; Avignon, 82; Britain, 175-6; Celtic, 57; Celts, 61, 176; Emporion, 100; Massalia hoards, 37, 47, 61, 88, 118, 123, 134, 137, 175, 240; Rhodus, 115
Cornutus Scholiast to Lucan: Massalia's commanders, 137, 257
Count of Provence: Charles III of Maine, 309; Charles of Anjou, 307; King Charles VIII of France, 309; King Louis XI of France, 309; King Louis XIV of France, 312
Crinas: doctor of Massilia, 247; Theorodokoi Delphi, 56, 144
Corinthian helmet: France, 37, 549; Spain, 75-6, 548

Demosthenes: Against Boeotus, 51; Against Zenothemis, 50; Harpalus, 206
Dicaearchus, 140, 200, 222
Diodorus Siculus: Alexander the Great, 205, 207; Britain, 186-187, 194; Hyperboreans, 184-185; Tin, 179, 199, 219, 327; Treasury of Massalia, 225,
Diogenes Laertius, 198, 336, 340
Diogenes of Sinope: philosopher, 52, 331
Dionysius Exiguus, 343
Dionysius of Massalia, 146
Dionysius of Phocaea, 48, 223
Dionysius, god of wine: Massalia, 36

Egypt, 9, 18, 71, 150, 156, 165, 168, 203, 220, 222, 286, 296, 307, 328, 333, 336-337, 525; Athens, 50; Massalia, 36, 56, 146
Elea, 26, 29, 36, 47, 79, 80-81, 84, 94, 124, 143, 150, 156, 176, 228, 250
Emporion, 42, 72, 77, 86, 94, 100, 110-112, 116, 129, 134, 151, 153, 171, 180, 229, 232, 235, 249, 270, 309, 328, 331, 334; agora, 100, 106; Appian, 106; arsenal, 106; coins, 61, 100; grain silos, 106; grapevines, 104; Greek curse tablets, 104; Julius Caesar, 77; lead letter, 104; Livy, 109; Rhodus, 112; three cities, 110; Treaty of the Ebro, 114
Entremont, 53, 240, 241, 242
Eratosthenes: latitude, 140; map, 203; Massalia, 211; mathematical geography, 214; Pytheas, 173, 182, 216
Etruscans, 15, 17-18, 25-26, 37, 42, 79, 134, 196, 197, 205

Eudoxos, 192, 218, 222
Euthymenes of Massalia, 47, 139, 167, 218, 341
Euxenus, 14, 329
Flaccus: Gaius Valerius, 242; Lucius, 138; Lucius Valerius, 242; Marcus Fulvius, 240; Quintus Fulvius, 236
Flavia Hedone: female doctor, 55
Frozen Sea, 191; Agricola, 325; Marine lung, 190
Fulvia: 245, 462 n. 2123

Galatae: Massalia, 59; Massalia schools, 59, 60; siege of Rome, 11
Gallo-Greek, 49, 56, 59-60, 81; city, 133
Geminos of Rhodes, 189, 193, 212, 217
Genetic Study, 80, 318, Britain, 188
Glanon, 133, 134
Gnomon, 173, 192, 193, 200; permanent Massalia, 51, 211
Gracchi: Tiberius, 269
Gravisca, 16, 17, 78, 150, 249
Greek-Iberian: script, 77, 81, 151

Hannibal: Battle of Mylae, 227; Massalia, 231; Saguntum, 230; Sosylus of Sparta, 234, 344
Harbour of Lacydon, 13, 14, 19, 27, 73
Hasdrubal: Battle of the Ebro, 233; Hannibal's brother, 12, 116, 141; Hannibal's uncle, 228; Treaty of the Ebro, 229
Hemeroscopian, 86
Hermon: admiral of Massalia, 142, 257, 258
Herodotus, 1, 13, 17, 25, 26, 47, 78-80, 141, 154, 157, 163, 167, 169, 197, 215, 328, 330, 370, 384, 446
Hipparchus: Aratus, 172; Britain, 183; latitude, 218; latitude table, 223; map, 224; Pytheas, 192, 193, 200
Homer: city editions Massalia, 166; Phoenicians, 166; Siren's Island, 163; sphere, 212; tides, 169
Horn of Lacydon, 27, 311; city walls, 35; size, 35
Hyperborean, 183-185

Iceland, 140, 184, 190-193, 216, 218, 275-276, 325
Ictis, 179-180, 219, 221, 422
Inscriptions, 126, 143; Agde, 88, 95; Antibes, 125; Athens, 56; Etruscan, 37; Emporion, 104; Gades, 335; Gallo-Greek, 60, 151; Massalia, 271, 280, 281; Olbia, 119; Phocaea, 279; Sicily, 146; Vence, 277
Ireland, 182, 188; amber, 165; Avienus, 176; Broighter, 221; currachs, 221; Julius Casaer, 275; Strabo, 215; Veneti, 246
Isle of Lewis, 183-186, 219
Isle of Man, 182, 195; Julius Caesar, 275

Julius Caesar: Antipolis, 129; Arelate, 133; Britain, 189; Caesarian, 94; Dictator, 264; Emporion, 110; Greek script, 59; Lucan, 235; Massalia, 10, 251-265; Massalia victory coin, 266; Milo, 245; Olbia, 119;

Saint-Blaise, 134; solstice, 275; Triumphs 46 B.C., 9; Veneti fleet, 246

Kalaris: Corsica, 80, 124
Kantion, 185, 196, 198, 217; Kent, 195, 276
King Arthur, 180, 288

L. Domitius Ahenobarbus: Governer of Gaul, 253
L'Éphèbe d'Agde, 88, 89, 94
Le Brusc, 118, 141, 151, 256, 258, 259; (Tauroention), 53
Ligurians, 17; Antibes, 129; Celtic invasion, 188; Hercules, 272; Ingauni, 141; Massalia, 49, 60, 237; Nice, 129; pirates, 236; Theline, 47; Tunny fish, 147; wine, 236
Livy: Alexander the Great, 205; Battle of the Ebro, 233; Emporion, 104, 106, 110; Hannibal, 230, 232; Massilia, 18, 57, 231, 240; Phocaea, 163, 238; ransom of gold, 11; Rhodus, 235; Volcae, 133, 232
Lucan, 3, 12, 17, 173, 221, 235, 249, 251, 253-255, 259, 261, 405, 445, 463; Massalia, 253, 254, 262
Lucian, 73, 139
Lyon, 288-289; coin, 124; Greeks, 47, 292; population, 154

Mainake, 13, 85-86, 94, 156, 386
Marine Lung, 190, 191, 193
Marius, 7, 141, 241-242, 250, 255
Mark Antony, 10, 94, 125, 243, 267, 268, 269, 270, 456; Great Library of Alexandria, 336; Massalia, 267, 270
Marseille. See Massalia
Massalia: agora, 22, 23; amphitheatre, 22; Apollonides, 270; battles, 140; Celts, 56, 60; coins, 62; colonies/settlements, 79; commanders, 257; Constantinople, 309; Council of, 291, 292; explorers, 139; fleet, 258; Greek docks, 72; Holy Roman Empire, 307; independent city, 265; influence in Rome, 238; Merovingian kings, 292; names and inscriptions, 141;name origin, 22; necropolis, 54, 71, 270, 280, 282; Opimus, 238; periplus, 87, 168, 172, 181, 334; political constitution, 137; pottery, 40; Roman docks, 40; Roman exiles, 243; siege by Julius Caesar, 251; sacred grove, 465; Sigibert, 292; slaves, 71; stadium, 22; temples, 20; territory, 37; Treasury Delphi, 24, 225; vinyards, 36
Martial, 57, 125
Meton, 184
Milo, 244, 245
Monaco: Heracles Monoikos, 84, 150, 163, 164
Moschus the Apollodorean: Massalia school, 271
Mount Batten, 179, 180

Nasidius: admiral, 118, 141, 256, 258, 259, 268

Nearchus, 167, 203, 204, 206
Nero: emperor, 246, 247, 250, 284; general Tiberius Claudius, 133
Nimes, 49, 89, 332:coins, 124, 246; doctor, 55; Gallo-Greek inscriptions, 60; Gaius and Lucius Caesar, 246; slave-dealer, 71; Visigoths, 300
North Pole, 192

Octavian Caesar (Augustus), 125, 245, 267, 269, 466 n 2218
Olbia, 62, 88, 118-124, 132, 134, 171, 265, 331; Sardinia, 237
Opimus: Battle of Aegitna, 80
Oppidum, 20, 82, 119, 124, 129, 168, 240, 241, 302
Orange: Triumphal arch, 141
Orkas, 186, 198, 217
Orkneys, 188, 220, 325, 326

Pech-Maho: Emporion contract, 42
Penteconter, 47, 154, 220, 322
Periplus, 87, 168, 171-2, 181, 340-1, 334, 349
Phocaea, 154-156, 163; city walls, 156; coins, 164; Myager sculptor, 164; Prodicus poet, 164; Roman pardon, 238; Telecles Head of the Academy Athens, 164; Telephanes sculptor, 164; Theodorus architect, 164
Phoenician, 165-168, 171, 242, 327, 335; navigation, 166
Pindar: Pillars of Hercules, 335; western ocean, 171
Plutarch, 11, 13-14, 18-19, 53, 200, 207, 214, 216, 225, 241, 244, 273-274, 331, 336, 355, 437, 455
Pompeius Trogus, 7
Pompey the Great: Clodius, 244; Massalia, 8, 10, 82
Posidonius, 58, 200, 327, 332, 345
Pretani: Julius Caesar, 274, 276; name, 181; Pytheas, 187, 334; Roman invasion, 273
Prettanike: Britain, 181, 186, 217
Priest of Massalia, 278, 279
Protis, 14, 17, 18, 19, 20, 56, 142, 328, 329
Pseudo-Scylax: Massalia, 171
Ptolemy, 94; geographer, 56, 94, 181, 182, 183, 185, 191, 195, 205, 216, 336, 418
Ptolemy Philadelphus, 56; Egypt, 36
Pytheas of Massalia, 139; Chapters 4-11 & 14, 140

Ransom of gold, 11
Rhodus: Spain, 61, 74, 77, 86, 94, 112, 114-116, 132, 151, 155, 229, 235, 317, 331; Treaty of the Ebro, 114
River Rhône, 27-28, 112, 133, 141, 241, 328

Saguntum, 74, 104, 117, 229; Hannibal, 230; Lucan, 254; Mago, 234
Saint Blaise, 29, 37
Saluvi, 53, 241, 242
Santa Pola, 86, 150, 229

Satyricon: Massalia, 246
Scotland: Albion, 182; amber, 165; Celtic invasion, 188; Homer, 169; Hyperborean Ocean, 183; Orcas, 326; Picts, 187; Ptolemy's map, 183
Seneca: 218, 248, 271; Massalia, 246
Sextus: Apollonides, 268; Cicero, 266; Massalia, 269; Massalia coins, 268; Massilia, 267
Sextus Calvinus: Aix-en-Provence, 240
Shetland, 189, 192, 219, 220, 325
Shipwrecks, 38, 94, 104, 135, 163, 165, 179
Sidonius Apollinaris, 246, 288, 289
Silius Italicus, 46
Solinus, 276, 326
Solstice, 169, 173, 189-191, 193, 211, 222, 223, 275, 276, 326
Sosylus of Sparta, 12, 116, 141, 233
Spherical Temple, 183, 186
St. Michael's Mount, 179, 180
Stoechades Islands, 129, 132, 265, 270, 277
Stonehenge, 165, 186, 188

Tacitus, 15, 132, 182, 247, 271, 273, 325, 425, 464

Tartessos, 77, 85, 94; Colaeus of Samos, 333; destroyed, 168; Phocaeans, 13, 25; Stesichoros, 167
Theline, 45, 47, 49, 82, 133, 136, 150, 265
Thessaloniki: Cassander, 209; Homer, 149, 151; Octavian, 466 n 2218; Roma worship, 473 n 2331; Pompey the Great, 264
Thule. *See* Iceland
Timaeus, 22, 173, 180, 181, 186, 195, 200, 212, 216, 217, 219, 222, 344; Cicero, 276
Tin: routes, 180, 199; St. Mances ingot, 179
Trebonius: Julius Caesar, 265; killed, 267; Massalia, 254, 261, 263, 264

Valerius Maximus: Massalia, 71; Saguntum, 231; seige of Rome, 358 n 92
Vikings, 192, 301, 334
Vitruvius: Siege of Massalia, 261
Vix: Krater, 42; princess, 42
Volcacius Moschus: Massalia, 246

Zenothemis, 56
Zenothemis of Massalia: Lucian, 73, 283; Phaeder, 147

About the Author.

Christopher Gunstone BA (Hons), ACIM is a historian, archaeologist, and writer. He read Independent Studies at Lancaster University, thesis Origins of the British: and read History and Archaeology at Birkbeck.

At fourteen years of age his first experience of excavation was as a volunteer at Reculver Iron Age/Roman fort and discovered a burial in the foundations! As a student at Lancaster he also worked as a museum assistant in charge of the Campbell Legend Exhibition on Lake Windermere. He has had articles published in the London Greek newspapers Eleftheria and Parikiaki, and appeared on TV and Radio. Recently he has been working in London as part of the Foreshore Recording and Observation Group, Thames Discovery Programme (TDP): TDP photographic exhibition at Discover Greenwich, ORNC: and visited several of the archaeological sites featured in this book.

ಌ ೲ

Postscript

Figure 106. As well as Celtic coins struck with a die others were cast into a mold. As time went on the latest coin would make a weaker impression lacking definition until just circles and lines were left. This good example was found in 2009 at Studdal, Kent, UK: cast bronze, 2nd century B.C., mint southern Gaul, obverse: head of laureate Apollo facing left/ reverse: butting bull facing right, above Greek letters ΜΑΣΣΑΛ[Ι] for Massalia, Marseille. This may have been a prototype for British potin coins c. second century to early first century B.C. Particular thanks to Rod Blunt, John Winter and the finder Mike Jameson.

<http://www.ukdfd.co.uk/ukdfddata/showrecords.php?product=20157&cat=52> viewed 29 November 2013.

Made in the USA
Charleston, SC
06 March 2014